Routines Common to Turbo C++ and ANSI C Library

The Waite Group's Turbo C++ *Bible*

Nabajyoti Barkakati

SAMS

A Division of Prentice Hall Computer Publishing

11711 North College, Carmel, Indiana 46032 USA

To Leha, Ivy, and Emily

FIRST EDITION
FOURTH PRINTING—1992

International Standard Book Number: 0-672-22742-8
Library of Congress Catalog Card Number: 90-61917

From The Waite Group, Inc.:
Development Editor: *Mitchell Waite*
Editorial Director, Revised Edition: *Scott Calamar*
Editorial Director, First Edition: *James Stockford*
Content Editor: *Harry Henderson*
Assistant Editor, Revised Edition: *Joel Fugazzotto*

From SAMS:
Acquisitions Editor: *James S. Hill*
Development Editor: *James Rounds*
Editor, Revised Edition: *Albright Communications, Incorporated*
Illustrator: *T. R. Emrick*
Cover Illustration: *Kevin Caddell*
Production: *Travia Davis, Susan Hill, Betty Kish, Bob LaRoche, Diana Moore, Dennis Sheehan*
Indexers: *Hilary Adams, Jill Bomaster, Joelynn Gifford*
Composition: *Shepard Poorman Communications Corp.*

Printed in the United States of America

Contents

Preface

A lot has happened in the short span of just over a year since *The Waite Group's Turbo C Bible* was published. The ANSI X3J11 committee has finalized the ANSI standard for C—now it has an official name: ANSI X3.159 1989. C++ is gaining prominence as a language of choice for many and everyone is talking about object-oriented programming (OOP). Of course, one reason for C++'s popularity is that it supports OOP. The other is that C++ is a superset of ANSI C. Borland has noticed the trend and it has upgraded Turbo C 2.0 to Turbo C++, which is a complete implementation of AT&T's C++ Release 2.0—the latest version of C++. With Turbo C++, you get all the features of ANSI C as well as C++ and you still get to use the large library of routines that has been a part of Turbo C.

The Waite Group's Turbo C Bible was written to address the need for a comprehensive reference guide for the huge Turbo C library, to succinctly explain the basic concepts and illustrate the use of each function with a short, complete example. Judging by the response of our readers, the book has been a helpful, ready-reference for Turbo C programmers.

Turbo C++ adds in the features of C++ to Turbo C, but it also retains Turbo C as is. The huge library is still available for use—both from C as well as C++. If anything, the library has grown in size—from 445 functions to over 460—partly to support the ANSI standard for C and partly to provide some more DOS-specific functions. Although Turbo C has come a long way since its version 1.0 days, even with improved reference manuals and extensive on-line help, there is still a need for an all-in-one, comprehensive reference guide. This is the reason for bringing out *The Waite Group's Turbo C++ Bible,* a revised and updated version of *The Waite Group's Turbo C Bible* that covers the latest features of Turbo C++.

The book's features now include the following:

- Three "quick start" tutorials: one on ANSI standard C, another on object-oriented programming and C++, and the third on using the Turbo C++ compiler from the interactive development environment and the command line.
- Tutorials on using every category function in the library.
- ANSI standard prototypes and complete examples for each function.
- A unique compatibility header for each function indicating whether it is available in earlier versions of Turbo C, the ANSI standard for C, UNIX System V, and Microsoft C versions 3.0, 4.0, 5.1, 6.0, and QuickC versions 1.0, 2.0, and 2.5. If a version of Microsoft C or QuickC has a similar function, a number will appear under its name in the compatibility box, and a note will appear in the Description section.
- "Jump tables" inside the front and back covers for quick access to the functions.

Your use of this book can grow along with your programming ability. If you are new to programming, you can use this book as a learning resource together with a good C primer such as those suggested in the Further Reading sections of Chapters 1 and 2. By reading the tutorials in order, you can ensure that you grasp all the key ideas of C, C++, and Object-Oriented Programming (OOP), move beyond the coverage of a "beginner" book, and get a feel for the practical considerations involved in each area of programming. As you start to write programs, you can refer to and study the various groups of functions in detail.

If you are an experienced programmer in languages other than C, this book can give you a fast start to learning C by providing a survey of C that is complete, yet concise and without excessive hand-holding. Since you already know what programs have to do, you can quickly find out how to do it with Turbo C++.

If you are an experienced C or C++ programmer, you can jump right to the Chapter 3, quickly master the compiler, and then survey the functional areas to find out, for example, how Turbo C++ deals with your interests. This book will also help you port your applications to Turbo C++ by helping you find equivalent functions (in Microsoft C and UNIX) fast.

I hope you will be pleased with the convenience and utility of this book. If you have questions or suggestions, or would like to contribute to a future revision, contact The Waite Group, 100 Shoreline Highway, Suite A-285, Mill Valley, CA 94941.

Acknowledgments

From the author
I am grateful to Mitchell Waite for his continued support and guidance during this project. I would like to thank Harry Henderson for his helpful suggestions and encouraging comments. Thanks to Scott Calamar for arranging the beta disks and for keeping the project on schedule. I am also thankful to the many readers who have written to me, expressing their positive opinion of the Turbo C Bible and occasionally pointing out errors in the book. Your comments are really helpful in correcting the errors that seem to creep into a book, no matter how hard we try.

Finally, I thank my wife Leha and my daughters, Ivy and Emily, for their love and support and for being so understanding as I go through these periods of hibernation with computers and books.

Nabajyoti Barkakati
April 25, 1990

From The Waite Group:
Naba Barkakati should be called the Isaac Asimov of computer book authors—in the short span of one year he has written six very important, very interesting, and very big books for us. To each of these books Naba has applied a degree of attention to detail that is rarely found in publishing today. While cataloging, comparing, and creating thoughtful examples for thousands of C functions, he maintained a degree of professionalism, warmth, and integrity that we will always recall fondly.

This particular book, *The Waite Group's Turbo C++ Bible* is Naba's fifth in the Bible series. As in his other volumes on Microsoft C and QuickC, Naba introduces you to the C language and all the basic functions in the C library and provides tutorials, insightful examples, and details for every function, while noting the differences between Turbo C++, Turbo C,

Microsoft C, UNIX C, and ANSI C implementations. This last task is truly outstanding when you consider there are about 450 Turbo C functions to cover. For each Turbo C++ function you will find the exact name of the same function in the other compiler libraries, as well as whether it is available in the Turbo C 1.0, 1.5, 2.0, and Turbo C++ versions. This not only allows you to write code that is portable across all compilers, but also reveals where these compilers deviate from the ANSI standard.

I would like to take the opportunity to thank Naba for his commitment to this project and for his diligence and sensitivity to the subject.

Thanks to Harry Henderson, editor of The Waite Group's UNIX and C series, for his meticulous editing, ideas for example programs, and sincere letters to the author. Thanks to Scott Calamar for keeping this book on track, and to Joel Fugazzotto and Ruth Myers for their help with the final package.

All the folks at Borland who have helped make this book possible, especially Nan Borreson, deserve a kind thanks. Nan provided constant beta updates of the Turbo C++ compiler and continuing support to our author. I would also like to thank Phil Kahn for having the vision that there could be an under-$100 C compiler that could outperform $500 C compilers, for having the wherewithal to make it a success, and for taking the pioneering initiative to add object-oriented power to the C compiler. It is because of his hammering away at the technical edge of language software that we are able to write this book in the first place.

Finally, I give my thanks to the people behind the scenes at SAMS, who took our manuscript and turned it into a marketable product that we are all proud of: to Jim Hill for his faith in the original idea of a user-friendly C reference book, to Jim Rounds for his good-natured assistance over the years, to Gregory Croy for casting off this manuscript, to Kevin Caddell for the book's great cover painting, to Glenn Santner for bringing our cover versions to fruition over the past many years, to Nancy Albright for her thorough editing of the manuscript and invaluable assistance in making the process run as smooth as possible, to Marj Hopper for her perpetually chipper coordination and dogged pursuit of the perfect compatibility box, and to all the people at SAMS who in one way or another were involved in making *The Waite Group's Turbo C++ Bible* a success.

Mitchell Waite

Introduction

Overall Organization

The book is organized into the following parts.

PART I: THE C LANGUAGE AND TURBO C++

This part is a refresher on C and the features of Turbo C suitable for beginning and intermediate C programmers. Chapter 1, "Overview of the C Language," provides a succinct discussion of the C programming language, including references to the proposed ANSI extensions. You can skip this section if you are already familiar with C. Chapter 2, "An Overview of C++ and Object-Oriented Programming," gives a quick introduction to object-oriented programming (OOP) and how C++ supports OOP. Other features of C++ are also covered here. Chapter 3, "Turbo C++ Features and Options," discusses keywords and features of C programming that are specific to Turbo C++. For example, this section describes the memory models offered by Turbo C++ and discusses keywords such as *interrupt* that are distinct to Turbo C++. We also detail the operation of the interactive environment, TC, and the command-line options for the command-oriented version of the compiler, TCC.

PART II: PROCESS CONTROL AND MEMORY MANAGEMENT

Part II begins the tutorials and reference pages on the functions in the Turbo C++ library. The common themes in this part are the management of processes, communication between functions, and memory management. This part includes the following categories of functions listed by chapters:

4. Process Control
5. Variable-Length Argument List
6. Memory Allocation and Management
7. Buffer Manipulation

PART III: DATA PROCESSING

This part covers the routines that process, convert, calculate, and handle data. Tasks such as mathematical computations, searching, and sorting are discussed here. This part includes these categories (by chapters):

8. Data Conversion Routines
9. Math Routines
10. Character Classification and Conversion
11. String Comparison and Manipulation
12. Searching and Sorting
13. Time Routines

PART IV: FILES AND I/O

Part IV focuses on routines that manipulate files and perform Input and Output (I/O) operations. The MS-DOS and BIOS interface routines are covered in Chapter 17, "System Calls." By chapters, these categories include the following:

14. File Manipulation
15. Directory Manipulation
16. Input and Output Routines
17. System Calls

PART V: GRAPHICS

The four chapters in this part describe the graphics routines that were introduced in Turbo C 1.5. Chapter 18, "Graphics Modes, Coordinates, and Attributes," includes all the preliminary information you need to get started with graphics programming using Turbo C++. Among the routines discussed are those that set colors, line styles, and fill masks, and those that enable you to determine the status of various parameters maintained internally by the graphics library. Chapter 19, "Drawing and Animation," covers the basic objects that you can draw using Turbo C++ graphics routines, including point, line, rectangle, ellipse, arc, and pie. We also show how to perform animation using the "image save and restore" feature available in the graphics library. Chapter 20, "Combining Graphics and Text," describes how you can output text in the graphics mode, including selection of different font types and sizes, and positioning and justification of the text being displayed. Chapter 21, "Text Mode Routines," is devoted to the output routines that work in text mode only. This chapter tells you how to control the appearance of text on the screen, and how to confine text to a window.

Chapter Organization

Beginning with Chapter 4, each chapter starts with a tutorial on the category of routines being discussed in that chapter. Each tutorial establishes the concepts necessary to understand and use that category of routines. In each category the routines are catalogued alphabetically and also grouped according to the tasks they perform. The tutorials show how the functions in a group are related, and detail their similarities and differences so you will know which of many similarly named functions is appropriate for a given situation. They show you how to use the functions to perform commonly needed programming tasks and, in most cases, offer suggestions for further reading.

The tutorial is followed by the reference entries, arranged alphabetically, for the functions in that category. The reference entries provide a structured guide to the purpose, syntax, and usage of the function, and contain an example call and example program using the function. Many useful tips and cautionary notes are also provided. Figure I-1 shows how each reference entry is presented.

Although this book is very useful for in-depth study, we realize that you probably will use it most frequently as a ready reference resource. For this purpose, "locator tables" inside the front and back covers allow you to find any function by name or by category. The reference entries also refer back to the appropriate tutorials for further details.

And in Conclusion . . .

Now that you know more about the *The Waite Group's Turbo C++ Bible*, it's time for you to jump right in and use the book to explore the capabilities of Turbo C++. You may be pleasantly surprised by how helpful the Turbo C++ library can be. I hope you will enjoy this book as much as I have enjoyed writing it!

About the Author

Nabajyoti Barkakati works as an electronics engineer for a well-known research laboratory. He began his programming career in 1975 and he has worked extensively with FORTRAN, C, and several assembly languages. He is the author of a number of other Waite Group books including *The Waite Group's Microsoft C Bible*, *The Waite Group's Microsoft Macro Assembler Bible*, and The Waite Group's essential guides to ANSI C, Microsoft C, and Turbo C. An avid programmer still, he is primarily interested in developing communications and graphics software on the IBM PC and Macintosh. He has a Ph.D. in electrical engineering from the University of Maryland at College Park.

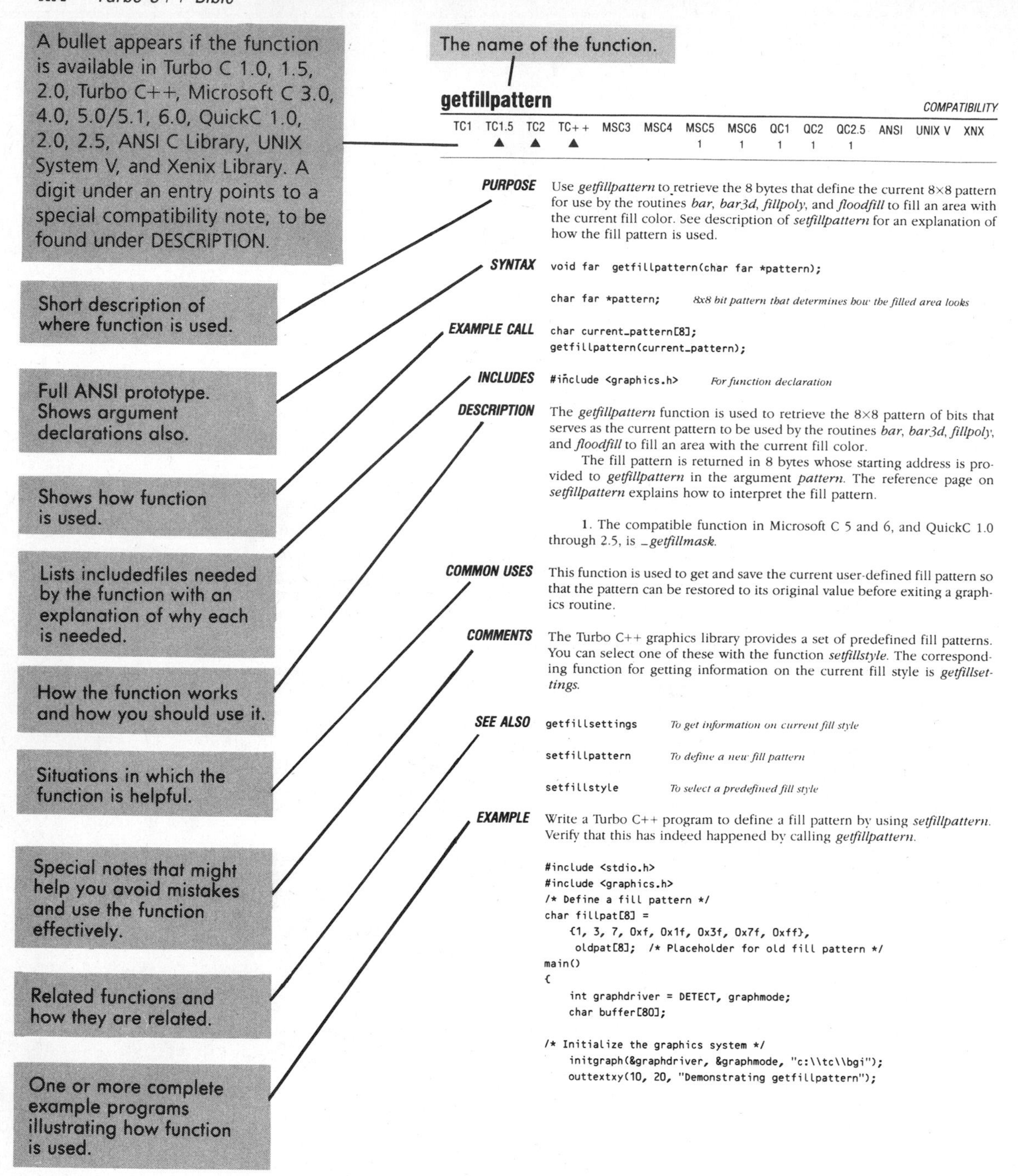
The name of the function.
A bullet appears if the function is available in Turbo C 1.0, 1.5, 2.0, Turbo C++, Microsoft C 3.0, 4.0, 5.0/5.1, 6.0, QuickC 1.0, 2.0, 2.5, ANSI C Library, UNIX System V, and Xenix Library. A digit under an entry points to a special compatibility note, to be found under DESCRIPTION.
Short description of where function is used.
Full ANSI prototype. Shows argument declarations also.
Shows how function is used.
Lists includedfiles needed by the function with an explanation of why each is needed.
How the function works and how you should use it.
Situations in which the function is helpful.
Special notes that might help you avoid mistakes and use the function effectively.
Related functions and how they are related.
One or more complete example programs illustrating how function is used.

getfillpattern *COMPATIBILITY*

TC1	TC1.5	TC2	TC++	MSC3	MSC4	MSC5	MSC6	QC1	QC2	QC2.5	ANSI	UNIX V	XNX
	▲	▲	▲			1	1	1	1	1			

PURPOSE Use *getfillpattern* to retrieve the 8 bytes that define the current 8×8 pattern for use by the routines *bar, bar3d, fillpoly,* and *floodfill* to fill an area with the current fill color. See description of *setfillpattern* for an explanation of how the fill pattern is used.

SYNTAX

```
void far  getfillpattern(char far *pattern);

char far *pattern;      8x8 bit pattern that determines how the filled area looks
```

EXAMPLE CALL

```
char current_pattern[8];
getfillpattern(current_pattern);
```

INCLUDES

```
#include <graphics.h>      For function declaration
```

DESCRIPTION The *getfillpattern* function is used to retrieve the 8×8 pattern of bits that serves as the current pattern to be used by the routines *bar, bar3d, fillpoly,* and *floodfill* to fill an area with the current fill color.

The fill pattern is returned in 8 bytes whose starting address is provided to *getfillpattern* in the argument *pattern*. The reference page on *setfillpattern* explains how to interpret the fill pattern.

1. The compatible function in Microsoft C 5 and 6, and QuickC 1.0 through 2.5, is *_getfillmask*.

COMMON USES This function is used to get and save the current user-defined fill pattern so that the pattern can be restored to its original value before exiting a graphics routine.

COMMENTS The Turbo C++ graphics library provides a set of predefined fill patterns. You can select one of these with the function *setfillstyle*. The corresponding function for getting information on the current fill style is *getfillsettings*.

SEE ALSO

getfillsettings	*To get information on current fill style*
setfillpattern	*To define a new fill pattern*
setfillstyle	*To select a predefined fill style*

EXAMPLE Write a Turbo C++ program to define a fill pattern by using *setfillpattern*. Verify that this has indeed happened by calling *getfillpattern*.

```
#include <stdio.h>
#include <graphics.h>
/* Define a fill pattern */
char fillpat[8] =
    {1, 3, 7, 0xf, 0x1f, 0x3f, 0x7f, 0xff},
     oldpat[8];  /* Placeholder for old fill pattern */
main()
{
    int graphdriver = DETECT, graphmode;
    char buffer[80];

/* Initialize the graphics system */
    initgraph(&graphdriver, &graphmode, "c:\\tc\\bgi");
    outtextxy(10, 20, "Demonstrating getfillpattern");
```

Figure I-1. *Layout of reference entries*

I The C Language and Turbo C++

- ▶ Overview of the C Language
- ▶ Overview of C++ and Object-Oriented Programming
- ▶ Turbo C++ Features and Options

Chapter 1 Overview of the C Language

Introduction

The composition of C—a sparse core with a large support library—makes it an ideal language for developing software on the IBM PC. The core offers a good selection of data types and control structures while all additional tasks, including input and output (I/O), graphics, math computations, and access to peripheral devices are relegated to a library of functions. This access to all parts of the system enables you to harness the system's full potential.

Many C compilers are available for use with PCs, but with such utilities as MAKE for automating recompilations and with the integrated program development environment with full-screen user interface, Turbo C offers one of the best environments for program development. The 2.0 version introduced in 1988 improved an already-good product. The library was enhanced with many more routines, most notably for graphics. The language implementation conforms to the ANSI standard for C and the library is also compatible with UNIX System V.

Turbo C++, introduced in 1990, retains all the features of Turbo C 2.0, adds several new library routines to enhance ANSI compatibility, and incorporates a complete implementation of the latest release of AT&T's C++ language. With Turbo C++, you have the best of both worlds: you can write standard C programs as well as programs that take advantage of the object-oriented programming (OOP) techniques that C++ supports. Chapter 2 gives you an overall view of OOP and how C++ supports OOP, and explains the features of C++ that differ from standard C.

This book is designed to help you use the Turbo C++ compiler to its fullest potential. We focus on the library because it is the library that gives a C compiler its personality. The concepts that unify each group of related functions are presented in a *tutorial* section followed by individual *reference* pages on each member function.

This chapter constitutes a refresher course on C, including a list of reading material on C and programming on the IBM PC. Chapter 3 summarizes features specific to Turbo C++ and describes the compiler and the linker that you use to build your programs. In the following discussion of the basic features of C, we will point out how the ANSI standard for C affects a particular feature. For your convenience, these notes are marked with the symbol: ANSI

Structure of a C Program

As shown in Figure 1-1, a file containing a C program consists of preprocessor directives, declarations of variables and functions, a *main* function, the body of the *main* function, and other functions. The body of each function, including *main*, contains expressions and statements.

The "preprocessor" is a facility unique to C. As its name implies, it processes the source file before the compilation begins. The preprocessor performs several important tasks such as incorporating the contents of another file into the C program (the *#include* directive) and replacing one string pattern in the program with another (the *#define* directive).

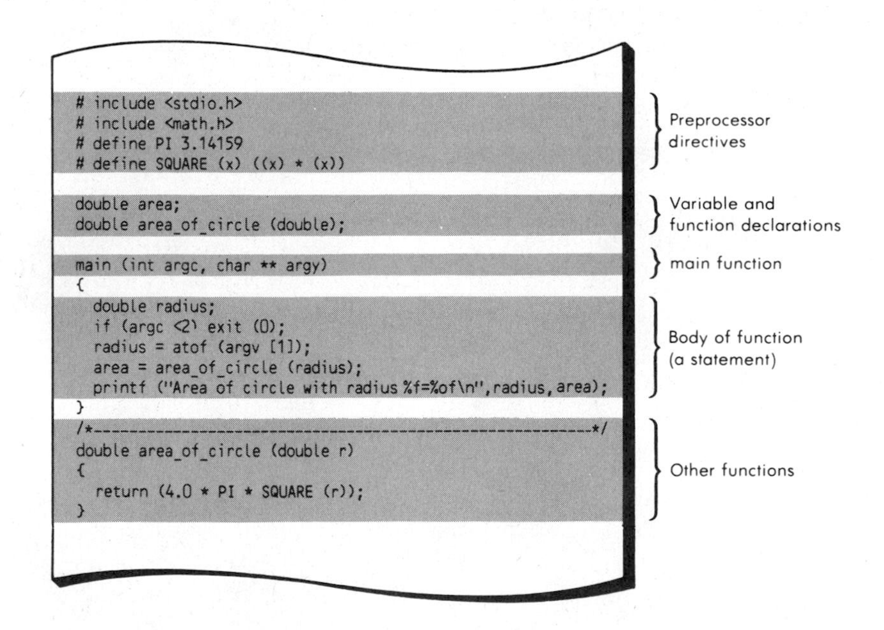

// include <stdio.h>
// include <math.h>
// define PI 3.14159
// define SQUARE (x) ((x) * (x))
double area;
double area_of_circle (double);
main (int argc, char ** argy)
{
double radius;
if (argc <2) exit (0);
radius = atof (argv [1]);
area = area_of_circle (radius);
printf ("Area of circle with radius %f=%of\n",radius, area);
}
/*---*/
double area_of_circle (double r)
{
return (4.0 * PI * SQUARE (r));
}
Preprocessor directives
Variable and function declarations
main function
Body of function (a statement)
Other functions

Figure 1-1. ***Structure of a C program***

"Declarations" state which variables and functions will be used in the program and what type of data will be used by each. Declarations outside the body of the functions are *global*, that is, they are available to any functions, including code in other source files. Variables and functions from other files used by functions in this file are also declared: these declarations are "external." Variables "local" to a function are declared within the body of the function. Declaring a variable also informs the compiler to allocate storage for that variable. Storage is not allocated, however, for variables referenced from other files.

The "body of a function" contains declarations that are local to that function and statements and expressions that implement the procedure being performed by that function. The "statements" control the flow of execution and use the values provided by expressions. An "expression" is a combination of operators, variables, and function calls that results in a single value. An expression is always part of a statement.

Preprocessor Directives

The preprocessor processes the source text of a program file and acts on commands, called "preprocessor directives," embedded in the text. These directives begin with the character #. The compiler automatically invokes the preprocessor before beginning compilation. The preprocessor provides three important services that enable users to make their programs modular, more easily readable, and easier to customize for different computer systems: including the contents of a file into their C program (file inclusion), replacing one string with another (token replacement and macro processing), and compiling selected portions of a program (conditional compilation).

FILE INCLUSION

The ability to include files provides for modularity. Declarations that are used repeatedly can be held in a file and included where needed using *#include*, which can be used in three formats:

```
#include <stdio.h>
#include "local.h"
#include "c:\test\specific.h"
```

The first and the most common format asks the preprocessor to read in the named file, in this case a standard C header file, *stdio.h*, from the default include directory. In Turbo C++, the default directory is specified either by the compiler option –I or from the *Options* menu in the interactive environment. The next two forms of the directive each specify the exact pathname of the file to be included. In the example, the preprocessor will first try to locate *local.h* in the directory in which the source code resides, whereas the search for *specific.h* occurs in the directory *test* of drive *c*.

Search Rules for Header Files

The preprocessor in Turbo C++ searches up to two sets of directories for a file to be included: the current working directory and the directories specified with the compiler option –I. The order in which these directories are searched depends on the format of the file name in the *#include* directive.

<filename> Search the directories specified with the –I compiler option.

"filename" First search the current working directory, then the directories given with the –I compiler option.

"c:\ . . . \filename" Look for the file in the specified directory only.

macroname The macro is first expanded. The expanded file name must match one of the three formats shown above. The search rules depend on the expanded form.

Token Replacement and Macro Processing

One common use of the preprocessor is to replace all occurrences of a "string" (or "token") with another, for example, to define a symbolic name for a numerical constant. This greatly improves the readability of the source code. The *#define* directive is used for this purpose. This directive can be used in two forms, one of which takes optional parameters. Here is an example:

```
#define PI        3.14159
#define SQUARE(x) ((x)*(x))
```

The first *#define* directive simply stipulates that the string *3.14159* be substituted at every occurrence of the string *PI* in the source file. The second line defines a macro with one parameter. A "macro" can have arguments or parameters just as a function does. In this case, if you use *SQUARE(2)* in your code, it becomes *((2)*(2))* after the preprocessor has performed the replacement. This macro is the equivalent of a function that squares its arguments. By the way, notice the number of parentheses in the definition of *SQUARE(x)*. They are absolutely necessary. To understand why, consider what happens when we define *SQUARE(x)* simply as *x*x*. Suppose you use the macro in the form *SQUARE(y+z)* to square the sum of two variables *y* and *z*. After the preprocessor makes the replacements, the macro reduces to *y+z*y+z* which is certainly not what you want. With the definition shown earlier, the macro would have generated *((y+z)*(y+z))* which gives the correct result. Use parentheses liberally when defining macros with arguments that could possibly be ambiguous.

ANSI

TOKEN PASTING AND STRING-IZING OPERATORS

The ANSI standard C includes two new preprocessor operators that are part of Turbo C++. The first one, called the "token-pasting" operator, enables you to join one token to another to create a third token. Here is an example:

```
#define TURBOC1 1
#define TURBOC2 2
#define version(x) TURBOC##x
```

When the preprocessor replaces *version(2)*, it first gets the string *TURBOC##2* which, upon interpretation of the token-pasting operator, reduces to the token *TURBOC 2*. The preprocessor finds that this token is defined to be *2* and uses it as the replacement for the macro *version(2)*.

The "string-izing" operator makes a string out of an operand with a # prefix. It does this by putting the operand in quotes. For example, if you defined and used a macro *value_now* as

```
#define value_now(x)  printf(#x" = %d\n", x)
    :
    :
value_now(counter);
```

the preprocessor generates the statement

```
printf("counter"" = %d\n", counter);
```

as the replacement. Since the ANSI standard also stipulates that adjacent strings will be concatenated, this becomes equivalent to

```
printf("counter = %d\n", counter);
```

which illustrates when the string-izing operator is useful.

Conditional Compilation

This feature lets you control which parts of a source file get compiled, under which conditions. This capability enables you to maintain a single set of source files that can be compiled with different compilers and in different environments. Other forms of customization are also possible; for example, you may decide to insert *printf* statements for debugging that are compiled only if a symbol named DEBUG is defined.

The directives *#if, #elif, #else* and *#endif* are the primary means of conditionally excluding portions of text from use by the compiler. The *#ifdef* and *#ifndef* directives, special cases of the *#if* directive, are used more widely than the other conditional directives. The typical use of these directives is of the form:

```
    :
    :
#ifdef DEBUG
    printf("Count = %d\n", count);
#endif
    :
    :
#if defined(MSC)
  #include <graph.h>
#elif defined(TURBOC)
  #include <graphics.h>
#endif
```

The first fragment shows the use of *#ifdef* to compile a *printf* statement only if the symbol DEBUG is defined. This can be done by using the /D option at compile time. The second fragment of code shows how you can include a different header file depending on which symbol, MSC or TURBOC, is defined.

Other Preprocessor Directives

There are several other preprocessor directives meant for miscellaneous tasks. For example, the *#undef* directive can be used to undo the current definition of a symbol. Using *#undef DEBUG* removes the definition of *DEBUG*, for instance.

The Turbo C compiler maintains two predefined preprocessor symbols, __FILE__ and __LINE__. The first refers to the current input file name and the latter refers to the current line number being processed by the compiler. You can use the *#line* directive to change their values. For example, *#line 20 "myprog.c"* causes the line number maintained by the compiler to be reset to 20 and the file name to be changed to *myprog.c*. This feature is useful when you write a translator that takes an input file in a *language* of your design (let us call it MY4GL, for "my 4th-generation language") and generates a C source file. When working with the source file, you can insert *#line* directives to refer to the file name of the MY4GL file and the line number that you are translating and use the __FILE__ and the __LINE__ symbols in reporting errors. That way, the printed error messages make sense because they refer to the line numbers in the original MY4GL file. Turbo C++ has further means to control compilation through predefined preprocessor symbols. (See our discussion in Chapter 3 and Table 3-4.)

The *#pragma* is another special-purpose directive that you can use to instruct the C compiler to turn on or off certain features. Pragmas vary from one compiler to another. Here is a list of pragmas supported by the Turbo C++ compiler.

#pragma inline Tells the compiler that there are in-line assembly language statements in the program. This causes the compiler to restart itself with the -B option (which is equivalent to this pragma).

#pragma warn + <xxx> or – <yyy> or . <zzz> Turns on or off generation of warning messages for a specific class of warning. The tokens <xxx>, <yyy>, and <zzz> are names of warnings as they appear in the -w compiler option (see Table 3-13 in Chapter 3). This pragma overrides the -w option. Here the warning <xxx> will be turned on, <yyy> turned off, and <zzz> restored to the value it had when the compilation started.

#pragma saveregs Generates code to save all CPU registers upon entering a function and restore them when exiting it. Place this directive immediately before the function to which it applies.

#pragma argsused Tells the compiler not to complain even if all parameters are not used in the function that follows.

#pragma exit <func> <priority> Sets up <func> as a function to be called just before the program exits by calling *_exit.* <func> should not take any arguments and should not return anything. The <priority> should be between 64 and 255 (the lower the value, the higher the priority). If unspecified, a priority of 100 is assumed. If several routines are specified with this pragma, those with higher priorities are called last.

#pragma option [options . . .] Here [options . . .] denotes one or more command-line options (see Table 3-12). You cannot use the following options with this pragma:

-B, -c, -d, -D, -I, -L, -l, -M, -o, -Q, -S, -U, -V, -Y

#pragma startup <func> <priority> Behaves just like #pragma exit, except <func> is called before the *main* function is called. The routines with higher priorities are called first.

Declarations in C

All variables and functions must be declared before use. The declaration of a variable specifies the "visibility" and the "lifetime" of the variable, its "type," and, where allowed, its initial value. The declaration of a function specifies its visibility as well as the type of value it returns.

DATA TYPES IN C

There are four basic data types in C: *char, int, float,* and *double*. The *char* and *int* are for storing characters and integers, and *float* and *double* are for floating-point numbers. The storage sizes for the floating-point types depend on the convention used to represent floating-point numbers in binary form. Turbo C++ uses the Institute of Electrical and Electronics Engineers (IEEE) format for floating-point numbers. A *char* takes a single byte while an *int* is the same size as a word on the underlying machine (for instance, 2 bytes on the IBM PC—and in Turbo C++—and 4 bytes on a DEC VAX). Here are some declarations using the basic types:

```
char   c;
int    count, i, j;
float  a, b;
double x, y, z;
```

The basic data types can be expanded into a much larger set with the use of the *long, short*, and *unsigned* qualifiers as prefixes. The *long* and the *short* qualifiers are size modifiers. For example, a *long int* is 4 bytes long in Turbo C++, capable of holding a much larger value than an *int*. In Chapter 3 (in Table 3-1) we list the sizes of data types in Turbo C++ and the range of values that each type can store. The *unsigned* qualifier is for *int* and *char* types only. Normally, each holds negative as well as positive values; this is the default *signed* form of these variable types. With the *unsigned* qualifier, you tell the compiler that the variable will hold positive values only, which allows the variable to hold maximum values twice as large as signed ones. Here is a fragment of C code showing the use of the qualifiers:

```
unsigned char  c;
short i, j, small_int;  /* Shorthand for "short int" */
long large_int;         /* Shorthand for "long int"  */
unsigned count;         /* Shorthand for "unsigned int" */
unsigned short ui, uj;
unsigned long  ul;

long double    xlarge;
```

Note that when the *long, short,* and *unsigned* qualifiers are used with *int* types, you can drop the *int* from the declaration. Also, among the floating-point types, only *double* takes the *long* qualifier.

NEW DATA TYPE: ENUM

The ANSI C standard introduces the type *enum*, which holds one integer value from a fixed set of named integer constants. An *enum* variable can be used anywhere an *int* type is used. The *enum* type can be used in such a situation as

```
enum boolean {false = 0, true = 1, no = 0, yes = 1, off = 0, on = 1};
enum boolean flag = off;
```

The example shows several properties of *enum*. The first line defines *boolean* to be an enumerated type. The list within the braces shows the constants that are valid values of a *enum boolean* variable. Each constant can be initialized to a value of your choice and several constants can use the same value. In our example, we have chosen the constants *false, no,* and *off* to be 0 and *true, yes,* and *on* to be 1. The second line shows the declaration of an enumerated variable of type *boolean*. Its name is *flag* and it is initially set to *off*. Note that *enum* does not introduce a new basic data type; it simply improves the readability of your programs.

The *long double* is another type of floating-point variable specified in the ANSI standard. Some older compilers recognize the type *long float*, which is no longer valid under the standard.

ARRAYS

An "array" is a convenient way to organize a large number of identical data items. You can declare arrays of any type of data item, including structures and types defined by the *typedef* statement. Arrays can be single- or multi-dimensional. For example,

```
char    str[81];
int     id[100];
double  x[40], a[5][10];
:
str[0] = 'A';     /* Set the first character in str to 'A'  */
id[99] = -1;      /* The last element in array id is -1     */
a[4][9] = x[1]; /* Copy an element of x into another in a */
```

declares a character string, *str*, capable of holding 81 characters, an array of 100 integers named *id*, an array of 40 double variables *x*, and a 5×10 two-dimensional array of doubles, *a*. Using the syntax of the last three lines any element in an array can be referenced. Notice that while the dimension of an array shows the actual number of items, the index goes up from 0. So an array with 100 elements can have indices ranging from 0 to 99. Also, strings in C are always terminated by a byte containing a 0 (a "null character" denoted by \0). Thus, in our example, *str* can only hold 80 characters because the last space will be occupied by a null. A two-dimensional array represents a "matrix," such as a spreadsheet. Think of a *[5][10]* as a spreadsheet with 5 rows and 10 columns, capable of holding up to 50 elements. Since memory is not laid out like a spreadsheet, the actual storage is done by laying out one row after another in memory. In the notation shown above, the second dimension denotes the number of columns, or the number of elements along a row. Because C stores a matrix by row, it always needs the second dimension in the declaration of a matrix.

POINTERS

A "pointer" is a variable that can hold the address of an object that can be either a variable or a function. If *px* is a pointer to an integer, you would declare and use it as

```
int *px, x;
:
px = &x;
```

The compiler will allocate storage space for an integer *x* and a *pointer to the integer px*. The number of bytes necessary to hold the address will depend on the machine's addressing scheme. Of course, you should not use *px* until it contains the address of a valid object. The last line shows *px* being initialized to the address of the integer variable *x* (The & operator extracts the address of *x*). Following this, you can refer to the value of *x* with **px* ("the contents of the object whose address is in *px* ").

Pointers are useful in many situations. Consider, for example, dynamic allocation of memory. In C you can request a chunk of memory—enough to hold, say, 100 integers. Once the memory is reserved, you get back the starting address of the block. Since this address is the only way to reach that memory block, you must store it in a variable capable of holding the address of an integer, so you need a pointer to an integer. If you used *px* for this purpose, how could you access the integers in that block of memory? You would treat it like an "array" of 100 integers with the name *px*. So the last element in the array is referenced as

```
px[99]
```

which is equivalent to

```
*(px+99)
```

Similarly, the compiler treats the name of an array as a pointer to the first element of the array (element 0). The difference between the name of an array and a pointer variable is that the first is a "constant" lacking explicit storage necessary to hold the address of the array's first element, whereas the latter is actually a "storage bin" capable of holding the address of any data of a specific type.

Neither an array nor a function can be returned by a function. To circumvent this, you can give the address of the array or the function that you want as the return value. (We will discuss *pointers to functions* in a later section.)

STRUCTURES AND UNIONS

When organizing any type of data, it is preferable to group items in a way that makes sense. For example, when storing the names and addresses of acquaintances, we treat the name and the address of each person as a single data record. In C you can organize your data in this manner with "structures." The definition of a structure to hold names, addresses, and some other information might look like this:

```
struct financial;
{
    double        annual_income;
    double        life_insurance;
    double        net_worth;
    unsigned char investment_strategy;
};

struct client_info
{
    char              name[80];
    char              company[80];
    char              mailstop[20];
    char              street[80];
    char              city[40];
    char              state[40];
    unsigned int      zipcode;
    struct financial  details;
};

struct client_info client[100];
```

This is the data base of an investment counselor. First we define a structure called *financial* that contains information about the client's financial situation. Each of the data fields in the *financial* structure, such as *annual_income* and *life_insurance*, is called a "member" of the structure. Next we define the structure *client_info* that contains the name and address of the client as well as the *financial* structure embedded in it. The last line declares a 100-element array called *client* in which each element is a structure of type *client_info*. (The fields of a structure are accessed by the "member selection" operator, which we will discuss later.)

"Unions" are declared like structures, but they are used when you want to view the same data item in different ways. The header file *dos.h* in the Turbo C library includes an example. Each of the 8086 registers AX, BX, CX, and DX is 16 bits in size, but each can also be thought of as two 8-bit registers; for example, the 16-bit AX comprises the 8-bit registers AH and AL. To use one storage area for these registers, but to refer to them in either manner, we first declare a structure, WORDREGS, containing the 16-bit registers:

```
struct WORDREGS
{
    unsigned int ax;
    unsigned int bx;
    unsigned int cx;
    unsigned int dx;
    unsigned int si;
    unsigned int di;
    unsigned int cflag;
    unsigned int flags;
};
```

Then we define another structure, BYTEREGS, using symbols for the 8-bit registers:

```
struct BYTEREGS
{
    unsigned char al, ah;
    unsigned char bl, bh;
    unsigned char cl, ch;
    unsigned char dl, dh;
};
```

Now a "union" of the two structures enables us to refer either to WORDREGS or BYTEREGS, accessing the registers as 16-bit or as 8-bit entities. The union that overlays the two structures is defined as

```
union REGS
{
    struct WORDREGS x;
    struct BYTEREGS h;
};
```

Now if we declare *union REGS reg1* in the program, we can access the AH register using the name *reg1.h.ah*, and a reference such as *reg1.x.ax* gets the 16-bit AX register.

NAMING YOUR OWN DATA TYPES

Using the *typedef* facility, you can define names for your own data types. Here are some examples:

```
typedef unsigned char byte;
typedef struct POINT
{
    short x;
    short y;
} POINT;

typedef POINT *P_POINT;  /* Defines P_POINT as pointer to POINT */

byte   flag;
POINT  a, b;
P_POINT p_a = &a;
```

We have defined *byte*, POINT, and P_POINT as synonyms for other data types. The last three lines show the use of the new data types. Note that we first defined POINT and then used it in the definition of P_POINT. In this way, you can use *typedef* to declare complex data types.

Visibility and Lifetime of Variables

The visibility or the "scope" of a variable tells you which source file (also called a "module") of your program can use the variable without declaring it. For example, all variables that are declared outside the body of functions are global in nature; any module can use them. On the other hand, declarations within the function's body define variables that are visible only inside that function. Take, for example, the code

```
:
int current_object_id;
:
:
main()
{
    int id;
    :
    :
    id = create_object();
    :
}
int create_object()
```

```
{
    int id;
    :
    :
    if(current_object_id == 0) ...
    :
    return(id);
}
```

The variable *current_object_id* is declared before any of the functions (including *main*), so it is visible in the entire source file. On the other hand, the variable *id* is local to *main( )* and to *create_object( )*. Each function has its own copy of *id*. Changes made to one copy do not affect any of the others.

The variable *current_object_id* is not only visible in its source file, it can even be referenced from any other file with the declaration

```
extern int current_object_id;
```

This is how global variables are used in C. Since the variable may be accessed at any time during the execution of the program, these variables are allocated storage for the life of the program and are said to have global "lifetimes."

The qualifier *static* also declares variables with global lifetimes, but it restricts the visibility of variables to a single source file. For example, you could define the variable *current_object_id* as

```
static int current_object_id = 0;
```

in a file and use it within the file without altering its globally visible counterpart with the same name. In other words, you have a separate storage location for the copy of *current_object_id* that is visible only in the file in which it is declared.

When a variable, such as *id* in our example, is defined within the body of a function, its storage remains allocated as long as that function is active. Such variables are said to have local lifetimes. You can also declare variables with local lifetimes by using the reserved words *auto* and *register*. Variables declared inside a function are by default of type *auto*. The *register* storage specifier is a hint to the compiler to place that variable in a register, if possible. You can use the *register* qualifier only for variables of type *int* or for pointers that can be stored in the same number of bytes as an *int*. Table 1-1 summarizes the information on the visibility and lifetime of declarations in C.

Table 1-1. *Scope and Lifetime of C Declarations*

Where Declared	Keyword	Visibility	Lifetime
Before all functions in a file (may be initialized here).	None	Entire file plus other files where variable is declared extern.	Until program ends (global).
Before all functions in a file (cannot be initialized here).	extern	Entire file plus other files where variable is declared.	Global.
Before all functions in a file.	static	Only in that file.	Global.
Inside a function.	None or auto	Only in that function.	Until function returns.
Inside a function.	register	Only in that function.	Until function returns.
Inside a function.	static	Only in that function.	Global.

NEW KEYWORDS: CONST *AND* VOLATILE

Two new keywords, *const* and *volatile*, are part of the ANSI standard C. You can use *const* as a modifier in a declaration to tell the compiler that the particular data object must not be modified by the program. This means the compiler must not generate code that might alter the contents of the location where that data item is stored. On the other hand, *volatile* specifies that the value of a variable may be changed by factors beyond the control of the program. You can use both keywords on a single data item to mean that while the item must not be modified by your program, it may be altered by some other process. The *const* and *volatile* keywords always modify the item immediately to their right. The information provided by *const* and *volatile* helps the compiler optimize the code it generates. For example, if you declare and initialize the variable *x* as

```
const int x = 1024;
```

the compiler need not generate code to load the value of *x* from memory. Instead it can use the value 1024 wherever *x* is used. However, if you add *volatile*:

```
volatile const int x = 1024;
```

the compiler cannot optimize away any reference to *x* because its contents might be changed by an external process. This can happen when you declare a pointer to an I/O port or video memory in order to access it from your program.

FUNCTION DECLARATIONS

A function declaration tells the compiler the type of value the function returns and the number and type of arguments it takes. Most of us are used to declaring functions only when they return something other than an *int*. For example, a typical declaration would be

```
char *locate_char();
```

This changes in ANSI standard C.

PROTOTYPES

The introduction of *function prototypes* is probably the most significant feature of ANSI C. It requires you to declare the formal parameters that a function takes as well as the return value. If our sample function *locate_char( )* takes a string and an integer as an argument, the ANSI-style prototype for this function is

```
char *locate_char(char *, int);
```

with the formal argument list shown with the type of each parameter only. You may include an identifier for each formal parameter, such as

```
char *locate_char(char *str, int c);
```

In this case, the prototype can look exactly like the first line in the definition of the function, except that in the prototype you terminate the line with a semicolon.

What is the purpose of the prototype? It is mainly there to help the compiler check function arguments and to let it generate code that uses a faster mechanism to return from functions. Since the prototype tells the compiler the exact number and type of arguments to expect, it can catch any mistakes you might make when calling a function, such as passing the wrong number of arguments (when the function takes a fixed number of arguments), or passing the wrong type of argument to a function.

Prototypes also allow the C compiler to use a calling convention different from the usual one used by C. (See the tutorial in Part IV for a discussion of the ordinary argument passing mechanism used by C.) The non-C convention, used by all other languages, involves placing the arguments on the stack in the order that they appear in the function call. In this case, the function knows the exact number of arguments placed on the stack and can clean up the stack with a single 8086 assembly language statement of the form *RET<n>* where *<n>* refers to the number of bytes to be discarded from the stack before returning. The usual C calling convention places arguments in the reverse order and does not require a fixed number of arguments in each call. Since the function does not know the number of arguments on the stack, only the calling program can clean up the stack by adjusting the stack pointer (SP). This is normally done with the assembly language instruction *ADD SP,<n>*. Not only is this instruction slower than *RET<n>* but it also makes the program larger because the *ADD SP,<n>* instruction appears wherever a function is called. By the way, Turbo C++ provides the nonstandard keyword *cdecl* which, when appearing in a function declaration, specifies that the C calling convention must be used for that function.

What do you do when a function does not return anything or when it does not accept any parameters? To answer this, we have to describe a new data type that is part of ANSI standard C.

ANSI

***THE TYPE* VOID**

The ANSI standard adds to C the type *void*, which is useful for declaring functions and for describing pointers that can point to any type of data. If a function does not return anything, say the *exit* function in the library, it can be declared as

```
void exit(int);
```

If a function does not accept formal parameters, its list of arguments can be represented by the word *void*:

```
int getchar(void);
```

The use of a pointer to a *void* as a data type is appropriate for functions that manipulate contiguous arrays of bytes ("buffers") in memory. For example, when you request a certain number of bytes from the memory allocation routine *malloc*, you can use these locations to store any data that fits the space. In this case, the address of the first location of the allocated block of memory is returned as a pointer to a variable of type *void* with

```
void *malloc(size_t size);
```

as the prototype. By the way, *size_t* is a new standard data type in ANSI C. Turbo C uses *typedef* to define *size_t* as an alias for *unsigned int.* Most library routines that require the size of a data item use the *size_t* type. The *sizeof* operator also returns a value of type *size_t* in ANSI C.

Expressions in C

An expression in C is a combination of variables, function calls, and operators with the result a single value. For example,

```
(strlen(my_string) * sizeof(char) + 1)
```

is an expression, which yields a value of type *size_t*, involving a function call, *strlen(my_string)*, and the operators *sizeof*, a multiplication (*) and an addition (+).

Since operators are at the heart of expressions, let us summarize the operators available in C. We do this in Table 1-2, where each operator is shown with an example and a short explanation of its usage.

Table 1-2. *Operators in C*

<table>
<tr><th>Operator</th><th>Name</th><th>Example</th><th>Explanation</th></tr>
<tr><td colspan="4">Arithmetic Operators</td></tr>
<tr><td>*</td><td>Multiplication</td><td>x*y</td><td>Multiply x and y.</td></tr>
<tr><td>/</td><td>Division</td><td>x/y</td><td>Divide x by y.</td></tr>
<tr><td>%</td><td>Modulo</td><td>x%y</td><td>Divide remainder of x by y.</td></tr>
<tr><td>+</td><td>Addition</td><td>x+y</td><td>Add x and y.</td></tr>
<tr><td>−</td><td>Subtraction</td><td>x−y</td><td>Subtract y from x.</td></tr>
<tr><td>++</td><td>Increment</td><td>x++</td><td>Increment x after use.</td></tr>
<tr><td>−−</td><td>Decrement</td><td>−−x</td><td>Decrement x before use.</td></tr>
<tr><td>−</td><td>Negation</td><td>−x</td><td>Negate the value of x.</td></tr>
<tr><td colspan="4">Relational and Logical Operators</td></tr>
<tr><td>></td><td>Greater than</td><td>x>y</td><td>1 if x exceeds y, else 0.</td></tr>
<tr><td>>=</td><td>Greater than or equal to</td><td>x>=y</td><td>1 if x is greater than or equal to y, else 0.</td></tr>
<tr><td><</td><td>Less than</td><td>x<y</td><td>1 if y exceeds x, else 0.</td></tr>
<tr><td><=</td><td>Less than or equal to</td><td>x<=y</td><td>1 if x is less than or equal to y, else 0.</td></tr>
<tr><td>==</td><td>Equal to</td><td>x==y</td><td>1 if x equals y, else 0.</td></tr>
<tr><td>!=</td><td>Not equal to</td><td>x!=y</td><td>1 if x and y unequal, else 0.</td></tr>
<tr><td>!</td><td>Logical NOT</td><td>!x</td><td>1 if x is 0, else 0.</td></tr>
<tr><td>&&</td><td>Logical AND</td><td>x&&y</td><td>0 if either x or y is 0.</td></tr>
<tr><td>||</td><td>Logical OR</td><td>x||y</td><td>0 if both x and y are 0.</td></tr>
<tr><td colspan="4">Assignment Operators</td></tr>
<tr><td>=</td><td>Assignment</td><td>x=y;</td><td>Put value of y into x.</td></tr>
<tr><td>0=</td><td>Compound assignment</td><td>x 0= y;</td><td>Equivalent to x = x 0 y; where 0 is one of the operators: + − * / % << >> & ^ |.</td></tr>
<tr><td colspan="4">Data Access and Size Operators</td></tr>
<tr><td>[ ]</td><td>Array element</td><td>x[0]</td><td>First element of array x.</td></tr>
<tr><td></td><td>Member selection</td><td>s.x</td><td>Member x in structure s.</td></tr>
</table>

Table 1-2. ***(cont.)***

Operator	Name	Example	Explanation
		Data Access and Size Operators	
→	Member selection	p→x	Member named x in a structure that p points to.
*	Indirection	*p	Contents of location whose address is in p.
&	Address of	&x	Address of x.
sizeof	Size in bytes	sizeof(x)	Size of x in bytes.
		Bitwise Operators	
~	Bitwise complement	~X	Flip 1 bits to 0 and 0 bits to 1.
&	Bitwise AND	x&y	Bitwise AND of x and y.
¦	Bitwise OR	x¦y	Bitwise OR of x and y.
^	Bitwise exclusive OR	x^y	Value with 1s at bits where corresponding bits of x and y differ.
<<	Left shift	x << 4	x shifted to the left by 4 bit positions.
>>	Right shift	x >> 4	x shifted to the right by 4 bit positions.
		Miscellaneous Operators	
( )	Function	malloc(10)	Call malloc with argument 10.
(type)	Type cast	(double)i	i converted to a double.
? :	Conditional	x1 ? x2 : x3	If x1 is not 0, x2 is evaluated, else x3 is evaluated.
,	Sequential evaluation	i++, j++	First increment i, then increment j.

Operator Precedence

Typically, you use several operands and operators in many statements of your program. For example, if you write

```
*ptr[2]
```

is the result the value to which ptr[2] points, or is it the third element from the location whose address is in *ptr*? To determine this, you need to know the order in which operators are applied. This is specified by operators' *precedence*, which is summarized in Table 1-3. Operators with highest precedence—those which are applied first—are shown first. The order in which operators at the same level get evaluated ("associativity") is also shown. If you consult the table, you will find that the [ ] operator has precedence over the * operator. So in our example, ptr[2] will be evaluated first and then the "indirection" operator applied, resulting in the value whose address is in ptr[2].

Table 1-3. ***Operator Precedence and Associativity in C***

Operator Type	Operators	Associativity
Expression	( ) [ ] . →	Left to right
Unary	- ~ ! * & ++ -- sizeof (type)	Right to left
Multiplicative	* / %	Left to right
Additive	+ -	Left to right
Shift	<< >>	Left to right
Relational (inequality)	< <= > >=	Left to right
Relational (equality)	== !=	Left to right
Bitwise AND	&	Left to right
Bitwise XOR	^	Left to right
Bitwise OR	¦	Left to right
Logical AND	&&	Left to right
Logical OR	¦¦	Left to right
Conditional	? :	Right to left
Assignment	= *= /= %= += -= <<= >>= &= ¦= ^=	Right to left
Sequential Evaluation	,	Left to right

Statements in C

Statements control the flow of execution of a C program. A statement consists of keywords, expressions, and other statements. Each statement ends with a semicolon. Here are some simple C statements:

```
;          /* a null statement */
x = y = 2;
x++;
if(y > 0) x /= y;
```

The body of a function that is enclosed in a pair of braces ({ . . . }) is considered a single statement. Known as "blocks," such compound statements can have local variable declarations and statements.

Here is a summary of C statements, in terms of keywords.

assignment statement Assigns a value of the expression on the right hand side to the variable on the left hand side of the equality (=).

Example:

```
pages = 800;
```

---

break; Ends the innermost do, for, switch, or while statement in which it appears.

Example:

```
while(i > 0)
{
    if(i < 10) break; /* Loop ends when i < 10
*/
}
```

---

continue; Begins the next iteration of the innermost do, for, or while statement in which it appears, skipping the loop body.

Example:

```
for (1=0; i < 100; i++)
{
    if(i == 50) continue; /* Loop skipped for
i=50 */
}
```

---

do-while loop Executes a block of statements until the expression in the while statement fails.

Example:

```
do   /* Copy y to x until i exceeds 10 */
{
    x[i] = y[i];
} while (++i < 10)
```

---

for loop For (*expr1*; *expr2*; *expr3*) <*statements*>
Evaluates *expr1* once. The <*statements*> are executed as long as *expr2* is true (nonzero). After each pass through the loop, *expr3* is evaluated. Loop stops when *expr2* becomes false (0).

Example:

```
for (i=0, sum=0; i < 11; i++) sum += i;
/* Computes sum of integers 0 through 10 */
```

---

goto statement Transfers control to statement designated LABEL.

Example:

```
if(i == 0) goto L1;
    a = x[i];
L1: x[i] = c;
```

---

if statement

If (*expr1*) *statement1* else *statement2*

Executes *statement1* if *expr1* is nonzero. Otherwise *expr2* is executed. The else clause is optional.

Example:

```
if (y !=0)
    x /= y;
else
    x = 0;
```

Null statement

Indicates, with a solitary semicolon, that nothing happens. Used, for example, when all processing is to be done in the loop expressions rather than the body of the loop.

Example:

```
for (i=0; str[i] != '\0'; i++)
    ;  /* Null statement */
```

---

return

Stops executing the current function and returns control to the calling function. A single value can be passed back.

Example:

```
return (answer);
```

---

switch

```
switch (expr)
{
    case value1: statement_block_1
    case value2: statement_block_2
    :
    :
    default: statement_default
}
```

If *expr* evaluates to *value1*, *statement_block_1* is executed. If it is equal to *value2*, *statement_2* is executed. If the value does not match any of the case statements, control passes to the block *statement_default*. Each statement block typically ends with a break statement.

Example:

```
switch (interrupt_id)
{
    case MDMSTATUS:   s_ms();
                      break;
    case TXREGEMPTY:  s_trmty();
                      break;
    case RXDATAREADY: s_rda();
                      break;
    case RLINESTATUS: s_rls();
                      break;
```

```
    default:
}
```

while loop	while *(expr) statement_block* The *statement_block* is executed repeatedly as long as *expr* evaluates to a nonzero value.

Example:	`while (i < 10)   /* Copy one string onto another */`
	`{`
	`   str1[i] = str2[i];`
	`   i++;`
	`}`

Function Definitions

The building blocks of C programs, *functions* are independent collections of declarations and statements you mix and match to create stand-alone applications in C. Each C program has at least one function: the *main* function. The library supplied with the Turbo C compiler consists mainly of functions (in addition to quite a few macros). For the most part, developing software in C is a matter of writing functions.

COMPLEX RETURN TYPES FOR FUNCTIONS

The definition of a C function starts with the type of value returned by the function; the function's name; and, in parentheses, the list of arguments the function accepts. For example, a function *getmax* that returns the larger of two *double* variables can be declared as

```
double getmax( double a, double b)
{
    if ( a >= b)
        return (a);
    else
        return (b);
}
```

If you wanted the definition of this function to be localized to the source file in which it appears, you could use the keyword *static* as a prefix on the line declaring *getmax*. Without *static*, the function would be visible outside the source file.

Sometimes you need to return more complicated data types from your function. Normally these would be pointers to one data type or another, but a structure might be returned too because the ANSI C standard allows this. When declaring complex return types, you can use the *typedef* statement to your advantage. Suppose you want to write a function that accepts a pointer to an array of three double variables and its return value is of the same type. In notation cryptic enough to confuse even an expert, the function that we call *process3double* can be declared as

```
double (*process3double(double (*)[3]))[3];          /* Prototype */
:
:
double (*process3double(double (*x)[3]))[3]          /* Definition */
{
    return (x);
}
```

On the other hand, with a judicious use of *typedef*s you can rewrite the example as

```
typedef double DBL3[3];    /* DBL3 will mean array of 3 doubles */
typedef DBL3   *PDBL3;     /* PDBL3 will mean pointer to DBL3   */
PDBL3          process3double(PDBL3);            /* Prototype */
:
:
PDBL3 process3double(PDBL3 x)                    /* Definition */
{
    return (x);
}
```

The first approach takes less space, but the second method is certainly more readable than the first.

POINTERS TO FUNCTIONS

A function cannot return an array or another function directly. Also, an array cannot have functions among its elements. This is not a problem because you can always use pointers to functions in places where functions themselves are not allowed. Declaring a pointer to a function is similar to declaring a pointer to a variable. For example, you can declare a pointer to a function that accepts two *int* arguments and returns an *int* as

```
int (*p_func)(int, int)
```

Once *p_func* is initialized to point to the appropriate function, its invocation will look like the declaration above:

```
z = (*p_func)(x, y);
```

Again, the *typedef* keyword can come to your rescue when you have to declare something complicated, say an array of 5 functions, each like the *process3double* function of our earlier example. Using *typedef*, the declaration will be as simple as

```
/* First define a synonym for a pointer to this function */
typedef PDBL3  (*P_F_PDBL3)(PDBL3);

/* Now declare the array of functions */
P_F_DBL3   funclist[5];

funclist[0] = process3double;
```

In this example, we even initialized the first element of the array *funclist* to the function *process3double*, which we defined in our previous example.

Further Reading

If you are beginning to learn C on an IBM PC, Lafore's book[1] is an ideal place to start. An alternative is the best-selling introduction to the C language by Waite, Prata, and Martin[2]; it is based on UNIX C. You can follow up with the more advanced guide by Prata[3].

Once you feel comfortable with C, there are several resources that can help you learn more about using C effectively on the IBM PC. The books by Hansen[4], Biggerstaff[5], Campbell[6], and Rochkind[7] develop libraries of functions that show you how to use the DOS and BIOS services for file input/output (I/O) and fast screen updates.

If you wish to program the serial communications port or the graphics cards directly, another Campbell book[8] has all you need to know to access the serial port and Johnson's book[9] shows examples of graphics programming for the EGA. The text by Lafore also shows how to program the graphics adapters.

On the MS-DOS front, Duncan[10] and The Waite Group[11] can advise you of the various services available. Another recent book by the Waite Group[12] is a collection of essays, each of which illustrates a specific aspect of the PC and MS-DOS. This can be a valuable source for ideas for your programs.

For information on the IBM PC and the PC-AT, the popular book by Norton[13] and the one by Smith[14] can provide all the information you need to get started.

1. Robert Lafore, The Waite Group, *Turbo C Programming for the IBM*, Howard W. Sams & Company, Indianapolis, IN, 1987, 608 pages.

2. Robert LaFore, The Waite Group, *C Programming Using Turbo C++*, SAMS, Carmel, IN, 1990, 645 pages.
3. Mitchell Waite and Stephen Prata, *The Waite Group's New C Primer Plus*, SAMS, Carmel, IN, 1990, 730 pages.
4. Augie Hansen, *Proficient C*, Microsoft Press, Redmond, WA, 1987, 492 pages.
5. Ted J. Biggerstaff, *Systems Software Tools*, Prentice-Hall, Englewood Cliffs, NJ, 1986, 317 pages.
6. Joe Campbell, *Crafting Tools for the IBM PCs*, Prentice-Hall, Englewood Cliffs, NJ, 1986, 434 pages.
7. Marc J. Rochkind, *Advanced C Programming for Displays*, Prentice-Hall, Englewood Cliffs, NJ, 1988, 331 pages.
8. Joe Campbell, *C Programmer's Guide to Serial Communications*, Howard W. Sams & Company, Indianapolis, IN, 1987, 655 pages.
9. Nelson Johnson, *Advanced Graphics in C*, Osborne McGraw-Hill, Berkeley, CA, 1987, 670 pages.
10. Ray Duncan, *Advanced MS-DOS*, Microsoft Press, Redmond, WA, 1986, 468 pages.
11. The Waite Group, *MS-DOS Developer's Guide*, Second Edition, Howard W. Sams & Company, Indianapolis, IN, 1989, 813 pages.
12. The Waite Group, Ed., *MS-DOS Papers*, Howard W. Sams & Company, Indianapolis, IN, 1988, 608 pages.
13. Peter Norton, *The Peter Norton Programmer's Guide to the IBM PC*, Microsoft Press, Redmond, WA, 1985, 426 pages.
14. James T. Smith, *The IBM PC AT Programmer's Guide*, Prentice-Hall, New York, NY, 1986, 277 pages.

Chapter 2 Overview of C++ and Object-Oriented Programming

In Chapter 1, we presented an overview of the C programming language. The elements of C discussed there are found in all versions of Turbo C up to 2.0 and in Turbo C++ as well. Now we have a whole new dimension to C—a superset called C++. This chapter summarizes and illustrates the features that make C++ interesting and useful. First, we give you an overview of *object-oriented programming* (OOP)—a specific programming style that C++ supports. Next, we describe the new capabilities that C++ brings to C and how they are useful for implementing object- oriented programming. Other features of C++, not directly tied to OOP, are also covered briefly. Several small examples illustrate the concept of object-oriented programming.

This chapter by no means provides a complete description of all the features of C++. As a reference guide, this book can only touch upon the most important and useful features. To learn more about C++ and OOP, you should consult one or more of the references listed at the end of this chapter.

What Is Object-Oriented Programming?

Even though the term *object-oriented programming* (OOP) is widely used, there is a distinct lack of concensus when it comes to defining it. Many people prefer to think of it loosely as a new way of modeling software based on real-world objects, and some like to use terms such as *abstract data types* (ADT) and talk about how an OOP involves using a collection of ADTs. We prefer to take the less rigorous approach and describe OOP as a new way of organizing your programs. It has nothing to do with any programming language, although a programming language that supports OOP makes it easier to implement the OOP techniques.

OOP is only a method of designing and implementing software. The use of OOP in itself does not impart anything to a finished software product that the user can see. However, you, the software's developer, may gain some advantages by using OOP methods, especially in large software projects. Because OOP allows you to remain close to the conceptual, higher-level model of the real-world problem you are trying to solve, you can manage the complexity better with it than with approaches that force you to map the problem to fit the features of the language. You can take advantage of the modularity of objects and implement the program in relatively independent units that are separately maintainable. You can also share code and data among objects through inheritance.

CONVENTIONAL PROCEDURE-ORIENTED PROGRAMMING

Before getting into OOP, let us take a quick look at conventional programming using languages such as C. For want of a better name, we use the term *procedure-oriented programming* to describe the conventional programming techniques.

In the procedure-oriented approach, you view a problem as a sequence of things to do. You write a number of functions (procedures) that let you complete the sequence of tasks. The data may be organized into structures, but your primary focus is always on the functions. As illustrated in Figure 2-1, a function transforms the data in some way. For example, you may have a function to add a set of numbers, another that computes the square root, and one that displays a string. You do not have to look far to find this type of organization—the C run-time library is implemented in this manner. Each function in the C library performs a well-defined operation on its input arguments and returns the transformed data as a return value, through a pointer to a storage location, or directly to a device such as the display screen.

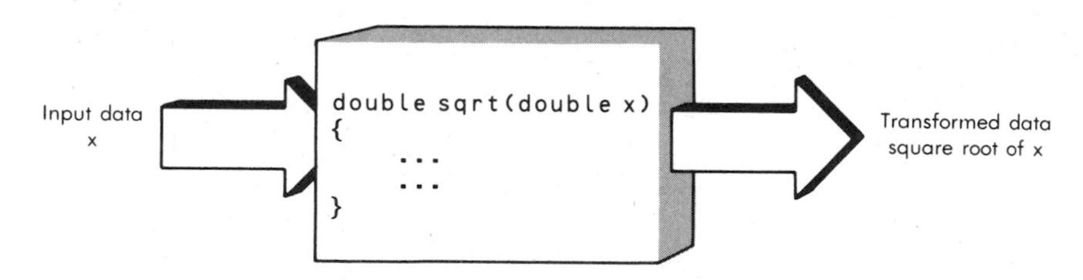

Figure 2-1. ***A function transforms data***

This is not to say that in procedure-oriented approach you do not care about data organization. In fact, you pay close attention to the data to be handled by an application and usually organize related pieces of data into one unit using C *structs*. Then, you write the functions that operate with these data structures. It is just that there are no close ties between the data and functions. OOP is different in how the data and functions are grouped together.

BASICS OF OOP

Unlike procedure-oriented programming, OOP treats data as primary and functions as secondary. You might say that instead of data being what the functions *use*, functions are what the data *does*. Instead of standing alone, functions are closely associated with the data. If the programming language supports OOP, there is usually a specific syntax that you can use to indicate this close relationship (for example, the *class* construct in C++).

Although experts do not agree on the definition of OOP, everyone's description of OOP can be distilled down to a few basic ideas: *data abstraction*, *inheritance*, and *polymorphism*. As we describe these, many of you will realize that you already know and use some of them because they make good sense. However, even though many of the parts that comprise OOP are old and familiar, their integration under the label of OOP is somewhat new to the programming community. Therefore, the topic merits some scrutiny.

DATA ABSTRACTION

As a C programmer, you are familiar with the file I/O routines in the C run-time library. These routines view the file as a stream of bytes and allow you to perform various operations on this stream. For example, you can open a file (*fopen*), close it (*fclose*), read a character from it (*getc*), write a character to it (*putc*), and so on. This abstract model of a file is implemented by defining a new data type, FILE, using C's *typedef* mechanism. (You will find the definition in the header file *stdio.h*.)

However, to use the FILE data type, you never have to see or worry about the C data structure that defines it. In fact, FILE's data structure can vary from one system to another. Yet, the C file I/O routines work in the same manner on all systems. This is what is known as information hiding or data hiding.

Data abstraction is the combination of defining a data type and data hiding. Thus, C's FILE data type is an example of data abstraction (see Figure 2-2).

Objects and Data Abstraction

You use the idea of data abstraction to create an *object* by defining a block of data together with the functions necessary to operate on that data. The data represents the information contained in the object and the functions model the behavior of the object—they define the operations that can be performed on that object. The data is not accessible to the outside world. The only way to do anything to an object is by calling one of the functions that implement the object's behavior.

Thus, the FILE data type in C together with the file I/O routines can be thought of as the definition of an object. You create a FILE object by

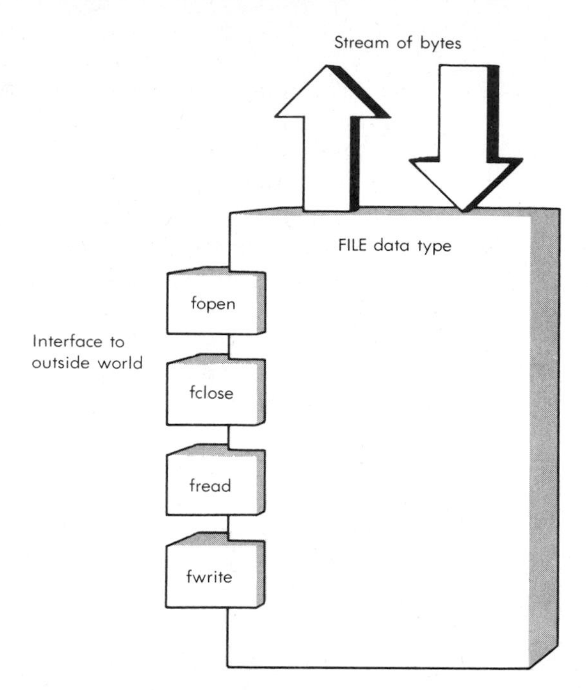

Figure 2-2. ***C's FILE data type is an example of data abstraction***

calling the *fopen* function, which returns a pointer to a FILE structure. You access the FILE object through this pointer. Every time you call *fopen*, you create a new FILE object. You can think of the FILE data type as a template that is used to generate new *instances* of FILEs when you call *fopen*. The term *object* refers to the instance.

Classes and Methods

In OOP terminology, the template defining an object's data type is usually called a *class*—the term may differ from one object-oriented programming language to another. Thus, each object is an instance of a class.

The functions that operate on an object have a special name—they are known as *methods* because that was the name used in the object-oriented language Smalltalk. The methods define the behavior of an object. In C++, methods are called *member functions* of the class. As you will see, they belong to the class just as surely as do the data members.

Smalltalk also lent another concept to OOP—that of *sending messages* to an object. This refers to the act of instructing an object to perform an operation by invoking one of the methods. In C++, this is done by calling the appropriate member function of the object.

INHERITANCE

A real-world object is often an extension of an existing object. For example, we often describe things using sentences such as: *Y is just like X, except that Y has . . . and Y does . . . .* When doing this, we are defining a new object by pointing out how the new object's characteristics and behavior differ from that of the old one.

OOP supports this notion of defining a new object in terms of an old one. The term *inheritance* is used for this concept because you can think of one object inheriting the properties from another, or, more correctly, a *class* inheriting the behavior from another class. Inheritance imposes a parent-child hierarchical relationship among classes where a child inherits from its parent. The parent class is often called the *super* class or *base* class (the latter in C++).

Multiple Inheritance

In real-world, an object can have behavior that may be attributed to more than one immediate ancestor. For instance, on the basis of eating habits, an animal may be classified as a carnivore, although other ways of classification place it in a specific family, such as the bear family. In the programmer's world, a full-screen text editor has two prominent facets: it can store an array of text which you can manipulate (insert a character, delete a character) and it can display a block of text on the screen. Thus, a text editor can be thought of as inheriting behavior from a *text buffer* class as well as from a *text screen* (which manages an 80-character by 25-line text display area) class.

These examples illustrate *multiple inheritance* the concept of a class inheriting from more than one super class. Many object-oriented programming languages do not allow multiple inheritance, but Turbo C++ does.

POLYMORPHISM

Polymorphism is the property that allows an operation to have different behavior in different objects. In other words, different objects react differently to the same message. For example, consider the operation of addition. For two numbers, addition generates the sum. What if the objects being added are character strings? Most likely, for strings, the addition will result in a concatenation of one string to the other.

Similarly, suppose a number of geometrical shapes all understand the message *draw*. Each object reacts to this message by displaying itself on a video display. Obviously, a rectangle object will draw itself differently from a circle object.

Polymorphism plays an important part in helping us simplify the syntax of performing the same operation on a collection of objects. For example, polymorphism allows you to draw all the geometrical shapes in an array with a loop that goes like this:

```
for each shape in the array of shapes
    send message draw to the shape
```

This is possible because regardless of the exact geometrical shape, each object understands the *draw* message and reacts to it in a way appropriate for that shape.

DEFINING OBJECTS IN C

We have said that OOP does not depend on any specific language. Let us give a concrete example using the common problem of drawing graphical shapes such as rectangles and circles.

To implement an object with inheritance, you can use the following simple data structure to represent the class:

```
typedef struct CLASS
{
    int          (*message_handler)();
    struct CLASS *base_class;
} CLASS;
```

Here, the *message_handler* member of the structure is a pointer to a function that processes messages sent to the object. Inheritance is implemented via *base_class*, which is a pointer to the class from which the current one inherits behavior. We send unprocessed messages to the super class and thereby inherit its behavior.

Because the *CLASS* structure has only one super class, there is no provision for multiple inheritance. If you want multiple inheritance, you have to allow for more than one super class, perhaps through an array in place of the *base_class* member in the *CLASS* structure.

The *CLASS* structure takes care of the methods of an object, but it has no room for the object's data. This is because each object has its own data. In other words, a single copy of the class structure can serve all the objects of that class, but each object must have room for its own data. We can handle this by defining another structure as follows:

```
typedef struct OBJECT
{
    void         *data;  /* This object's data */
    struct CLASS *class; /* Pointer to class   */
} OBJECT;
```

We call this structure *OBJECT* to signify that it represents an instance of an object. The file *oop.h*, shown in Listing 2-1, defines these data structures as well as the prototypes of the functions used in this example.

Listing 2-1. oop.h—*Header File for OOP in C*

```
/*  File:  oop.h
 *
 *  Header file with definitions for an example of
 *  object-oriented programming in C.
```

Listing 2-1. *(cont.)*

```
 *
 */

#if !defined(OOP_H)
#define OOP_H

#include <stdio.h>
#include <stdlib.h>    /* For mem. alloc routines       */
#include <stdarg.h>    /* For variable no. of arguments */
#include <graphics.h>  /* Turbo C graphics routines     */

typedef struct CLASS
{
    int          (*message_handler)();
    struct CLASS *base_class;
} CLASS;

typedef struct OBJECT
{
    void         *data;  /* This object's data */
    struct CLASS *class; /* Pointer to class   */
} OBJECT;

/* Define some messages */
#define  ALLOC_DATA  1
#define  POS_REPORT  2
#define  DRAW        3
#define  MOVE        4

/* Colors (should be in separate header file)  */
#define  FGCOLOR    WHITE
#define  BGCOLOR    BLACK

/* Functions to create various objects */

OBJECT *make_circle(int x, int y, int radius);
OBJECT *make_rectangle(int x, int y, int width, int height);

int send_message(CLASS *p_class, OBJECT *p_obj, int msgid, ...);
int class_message(CLASS *p_class, OBJECT *p_obj, int msgid,
                  va_list argp);
void *get_memory(size_t bytes);

#endif /* #if !defined(OOP_H) */
```

Graphical Objects

We implement two classes of graphical objects, circle and rectangle, using OOP techniques. As shown in Figure 2-3, each of these classes will inherit from a class that we call the generic graphics object. Listings 2-2, 2-3, and 2-4 show the implementation of the generic graphics object, the circle, and the rectangle, respectively.

Each file includes a *CLASS* structure initialized with the address of the routine that handles all messages. The *base_class* member of the class structure is also intialized. For each of the circle and rectangle classes, we provide a routine to create an instance. For example, to create a circle, you will call the function, *make_circle* with the coordinates of the center and the radius as arguments.eg

Each class defines its own data structure, a copy of which is allocated for each instance of the object. For example, the generic graphics objects store the position of the object in a *D_GROBJ* structure (Listing 2-2) which is defined as follows:

```
typedef struct D_GROBJ
{
    int x;    /* Position of the object */
    int y;
} D_GROBJ;
```

Rectangles, on the other hand, store their information (width and height) in the *D_RECT* structure (see Listing 2-4):

```
typedef struct D_RECT
{
    int width;
    int height;
} D_RECT;
```

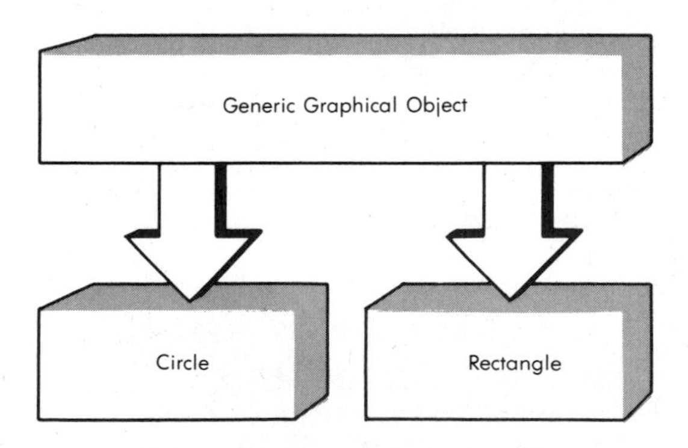

Figure 2-3. ***Class hierarchy for example of OOP in C***

The position of the rectangle is inherited from the generic graphics object. In other words, that data is managed by the generic object class (see Figure 2-3).

Listing 2-2. graphobj.c—*Implementation of a Generic Graphics Object*

```
/*  File:  graphobj.c
 *
 *  Implements the generic graphics object.
 *
 */
#include <oop.h>

typedef struct D_GROBJ
{
    int x;    /* Position of the object */
    int y;
} D_GROBJ;

static int   grobj_messages(OBJECT *p_obj, int msgid,
                             va_list argp);

CLASS graph_object =
{
/* Message handler */   grobj_messages,
/* Super class     */   NULL
};

/*-----------------------------------------------------------*/
/*  g r o b j _ m e s s a g e s
 *
 *  Process messages sent to this object
 */
static int grobj_messages(OBJECT *p_obj, int msgid,
                           va_list argp)
{
    int        status = 0, size, x, y;
    D_GROBJ   *p_data;

    p_data = (D_GROBJ *)p_obj->data;

/* Handle messages according to message id */
    switch(msgid)
    {
        case ALLOC_DATA:
```

Listing 2-2. *(cont.)*

```
/* Argument expected: int size */
            size =  va_arg(argp, int);
            size += sizeof(D_GROBJ);
/* Allocate the requested number of bytes */
            p_obj->data = get_memory(size);
/* Return offset for next one in the class hierarchy */
            status = sizeof(D_GROBJ);
        break;

        case POS_REPORT:
/* Arguments expected: int x, int y */
            p_data->x = va_arg(argp, int);
            p_data->y = va_arg(argp, int);
            status = 1;
        break;

        case MOVE:
/* Argument expected: int x, int y */
            x = va_arg(argp, int);
            y = va_arg(argp, int);
/* Crude way of doing it...draw at old location using
 * background color, then draw with foreground color
 * at the new location
 */
            send_message(p_obj->class, p_obj, DRAW,
                         BGCOLOR, p_data->x, p_data->y);
            send_message(p_obj->class, p_obj, DRAW,
                         FGCOLOR, x, y);
/* Save new position */
            p_data->x = x;
            p_data->y = y;
        break;

    }
    return(status);
}
```

Listing 2-3. circle.c—*Implementation of the Circle Object*

```
/*  File:  circle.c
 *
 *  Implements the "circle" class of objects.
 *
 */
```

Listing 2-3. ***(cont.)***

```
#include <oop.h>

typedef struct D_CIRCLE
{
    int radius;
} D_CIRCLE;

extern CLASS graph_object; /* The parent class */

static int   circle_offset;
static int   circle_messages(OBJECT *p_obj, int msgid,
                     va_list argp);

CLASS circle_obj =
{
/* Message handler */   circle_messages,
/* Super class     */   &graph_object
};

/*-------------------------------------------------------------*/
/*  m a k e _ c i r c l e
 *
 *  Create an instance of a circle and initialize it
 */
OBJECT *make_circle(int x, int y, int radius)
{
    OBJECT   *p_obj;
    D_CIRCLE *p_data;

    p_obj = (OBJECT *) get_memory(sizeof(OBJECT));
    p_obj->class = &circle_obj;
/* Send message to allocate room for data */
    send_message(p_obj->class, p_obj, ALLOC_DATA, 0);
    p_data = (D_CIRCLE *)((char *)p_obj->data + circle_offset);
    p_data->radius = radius;

/* Send position up the chain to generic graphics object */
    send_message(p_obj->class, p_obj, POS_REPORT, x, y);

/* Draw the circle */
    send_message(p_obj->class, p_obj, DRAW, FGCOLOR, x, y);
    return(p_obj);
}
```

Listing 2-3. *(cont.)*

```
/*-------------------------------------------------------------*/
/*  c i r c l e _ m e s s a g e s
 *
 *  Process messages sent to this object
 */
static int circle_messages(OBJECT *p_obj, int msgid, va_list argp)
{
    int         status = 0, size, color, x, y;
    D_CIRCLE    *p_data;

    p_data = (D_CIRCLE *)((char *)p_obj->data + circle_offset);

/* Handle messages according to message id */
    switch(msgid)
    {
        case ALLOC_DATA:
/* Argument expected: int size */
            size =  va_arg(argp, int);
            size += sizeof(D_CIRCLE);
            circle_offset =
                send_message(p_obj->class->base_class,
                             p_obj, ALLOC_DATA, size);
/* Return offset for next one in the class hierarchy */
            status = circle_offset + sizeof(D_CIRCLE);
        break;

        case DRAW:
/* Argument expected: int color, int x, int y */
            color = va_arg(argp, int);
            x = va_arg(argp, int);
            y = va_arg(argp, int);
            setcolor(color);
            circle(x, y, p_data->radius);
        break;

        case POS_REPORT:
            status = class_message(p_obj->class->base_class,
                         p_obj, POS_REPORT, argp);
        break;
    }
    return(status);
}
```

Listing 2-4. rect.c—*Implementation of the Rectangle Object*

```
/*  File:  rect.c
 *
 *  Implements the "rectangle" class of objects.
 *
 */
#include <oop.h>

typedef struct D_RECT
{
    int width;
    int height;
} D_RECT;

extern CLASS graph_object; /* The parent class */

static int rect_offset;
static int rect_messages(OBJECT *p_obj, int msgid,
                 va_list argp);

CLASS rectangle_obj =
{
/* Message handler */   rect_messages,
/* Super class     */   &graph_object
};

/*--------------------------------------------------------------*/
/*  m a k e _ r e c t a n g l e
 *
 *  Create an instance of a rectangle and initialize it
 */
OBJECT *make_rectangle(int x, int y, int width, int height)
{
    OBJECT   *p_obj;
    D_RECT *p_data;

    p_obj = (OBJECT *) get_memory(sizeof(OBJECT));
    p_obj->class = &rectangle_obj;
/* Send message to allocate room for data */
    send_message(p_obj->class, p_obj, ALLOC_DATA, 0);
    p_data = (D_RECT *)((char *)p_obj->data + rect_offset);
    p_data->width = width;
    p_data->height = height;
```

Listing 2-4. *(cont.)*

```
/* Send position up the chain to generic graphics object */
    send_message(p_obj->class->base_class, p_obj,
                 POS_REPORT, x, y);

/* Draw the rectangle */
    send_message(p_obj->class, p_obj, DRAW, FGCOLOR, x, y);
    return(p_obj);
}
/*-------------------------------------------------------------*/
/*  r e c t _ m e s s a g e s
 *
 *  Process messages sent to this object
 */
static int rect_messages(OBJECT *p_obj, int msgid, va_list argp)
{
    int         status = 0, size, color, x, y;
    D_RECT    *p_data;

    p_data = (D_RECT *)((char *)p_obj->data + rect_offset);

/* Handle messages according to message id */
    switch(msgid)
    {
        case ALLOC_DATA:
/* Argument expected: int size */
            size =  va_arg(argp, int);
            size += sizeof(D_RECT);
            rect_offset =
                send_message(p_obj->class->base_class,
                             p_obj, ALLOC_DATA, size);
/* Return offset for next one in the class hierarchy */
            status = rect_offset + sizeof(D_RECT);
        break;

        case DRAW:
/* Argument expected: int color, int x, int y */
            color = va_arg(argp, int);
            x = va_arg(argp, int);
            y = va_arg(argp, int);
            setcolor(color);
            rectangle(x, y, x+p_data->width, y+p_data->height);
        break;
```

Listing 2-4. *(cont.)*

```
        case POS_REPORT:
            status = class_message(p_obj->class->base_class,
                                        p_obj, POS_REPORT, argp);
        break;
    }
    return(status);
}
```

Handling Messages

As shown in Listings 2-2 through 2-4, messages for a class are handled by a central message-handling routine. Messages are identified by a number. In *oop.h* (Listing 2.1), we defined the possible message identifiers:

```
#define  ALLOC_DATA  1
#define  POS_REPORT  2
#define  DRAW        3
#define  MOVE        4
```

As the symbol implies, DRAW and MOVE are used to draw and move an object, respectively. The POS_REPORT message is sent by subclasses to report their initial position to the generic graphics object.

Data Inheritance

ALLOC_DATA is a message that helps us implement inheritance of data. When an object has to allocate data for itself, it does not do the allocation itself. Instead, the request is passed on to the super class using a ALLOC_DATA message. Each class in the hierarchy adjusts the number of bytes to be allocated. The final allocation is done by the root class (the class with no super class), which, in this example, is the generic graphical object shown in Listing 2-2. In that listing you can see the action taken by this routine to allocate the necessary memory.

This approach results in allocation of a single block of memory for all the classes in the chain of inheritance. For example, the data allocated for a rectangle will include a *D_GROBJ* structure followed by a *D_RECT* structure (see Figure 2-4). Each class can access the data, provided it knows the offset of the start of its data in this block of memory. This information is set up in the code that handles the *ALLOC_DATA* message (see Listings 2-2, 2-3, and 2-4).

Utility Routines

Because C does not support OOP directly, we had to implement our mechanism for invoking methods in a class. Listing 2-5 shows the file *ooputil.c* which contains a collection of utility routines developed for this example.

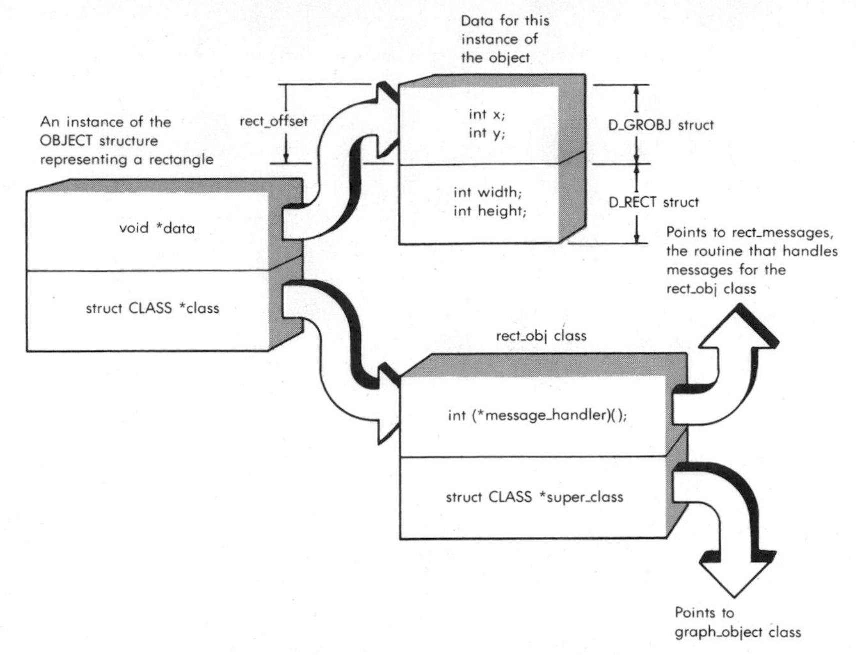

Figure 2-4. *Data inheritance in example of OOP in C*

Of particular note is the *send_message* function which is used to send a message to an object.

Listing 2-5. ooputil.c—*Utility Routines for OOP in C*

```
/*  File: ooputil.c
 *
 *  Utility routines for example of OOP in C.
 *
 */

#include <oop.h>
/*-------------------------------------------------------------*/
/*  s e n d _ m e s s a g e
 *
 *  Send a message to an object
 */
int send_message(CLASS *p_class, OBJECT *p_obj, int msgid, ...)
{
    int     status;
    va_list argp;
    va_start(argp, msgid);
```

Listing 2-5. ***(cont.)***

```
    status = class_message(p_class, p_obj, msgid, argp);
    va_end(argp);
    return(status);
}
/*-------------------------------------------------------------*/
/*  c l a s s _ m e s s a g e
 *
 *  Send a message to a class
 */
int class_message(CLASS *p_class, OBJECT *p_obj, int msgid,
                  va_list argp)
{
    int status;

    if(p_class == NULL) return 0;

    if(p_class->message_handler != NULL &&
      (status = (*p_class->message_handler)(p_obj,
                                 msgid, argp)) == 0)
    {
/* If message not handled, send it to the super class */
        status = class_message(p_base->base_class, p_obj,
                          msgid, argp);
    }
    return(status);
}
/*-------------------------------------------------------------*/
/*  g e t _ m e m o r y
 *
 *  Allocate memory, with error checking
 */
void *get_memory(size_t bytes)
{
    void *p;
    if((p = calloc(1, bytes)) == NULL)
    {
     fprintf(stderr, "Error allocating %d bytes of memory."
          "Exiting...", bytes);
        exit(1);
    }
    return(p);
}
```

Using the Objects

Once the structures and support routines are in place, it is simple to create and manipulate the graphical objects. For instance, to create a circle of radius 50 centered at (100,100), you call *make_circle* as follows:

```
OBJECT *c1;
c1 = make_circle(100, 100, 50);
```

You can move this circle to (200,200) by sending it a *MOVE* message:

```
send_message(c1->class, c1, MOVE, 200, 200);
```

The file *oopdemo.c* (Listing 2-6) shows a complete example of how you might use the circle and rectangle objects. It creates a circle and a rectangle and moves them around on the screen.

You can try out this example in Turbo C++—after all C++ supports all of C's features (you can use Turbo C 2.0 as well). Simply create a new project and add the following files to it:

```
oopdemo.c
ooputil.c
graphobj.c
circle.c
rect.c
```

After setting up the project, select *Build all* from the *Compile* menu. This will create the executable *oopdemo.exe* which you can run to see how the program works.

Listing 2-6. oopdemo.c—*An Example of OOP in C*

```
/*  File:  oopdemo.c
 *
 *  Demonstrate OOP in C using some graphical objects.
 *
 */

#include <oop.h>

void main(void)
{
    int     i, j, x, y;
    OBJECT *gr_objects[4];
    int     graphdriver = DETECT, graphmode, g_errorcode;
```

Listing 2-6. *(cont.)*

```
/* Detect adapter type and initialize graphics system
 * Assume that Turbo C's BGI drivers are in "d:\tc\bgi"
 */
    initgraph(&graphdriver, &graphmode, "d:\tc\bgi");
    if((g_errorcode = graphresult()) != grOk)
    {
        fprintf(stderr, "initgraph: %s\n",
                grapherrormsg(g_errorcode));
        exit(1);
    }
/* Set background and foreground colors */
    setbkcolor(BGCOLOR);
    setcolor(FGCOLOR);

/* Create some graphical objects */
    gr_objects[0] = make_circle(100, 100, 50);
    gr_objects[1] = make_rectangle(150, 150, 20, 20);

    x = 100;
    y = 100;
    for(j = 0; j < 100; j++)
    {
/* Move the objects around the screen */
     for(i = 0; i < 2; i++)
         send_message(gr_objects[i]->class,
                gr_objects[i], MOVE, x, y);
        x += 2;
    }

/* Wait until user presses a key */
    outtextxy(10, getmaxy()-50," Press any key to exit");

    getch();
    closegraph();
}
```

C++ and Object-Oriented Programming

Earlier, we had explained how C's FILE data type can serve as an example of an object. However, in C's implementation of FILE, the functions that operate on FILE and the FILE data structure are not tied together closely.

Also, the details of the FILE data type are not really hidden because C does not stop you from accessing the members of the FILE data type. It is essentially up to you, the programmer, to enforce data hiding and associate the functions (methods) with the FILE object.

With some careful design, you can tie down the data and functions together as an object, even in C. You have seen an example of this in Listings 2.1 through 2-6. While it is possible to apply OOP techniques in C, the lack of built-in support for OOP requires extra work to set up the mechanism for inheritance and polymorphism.

C++, on the other hand, was designed with OOP in mind. It includes the features that can ease the task of implementing objects. Let us take a look at these features and reimplement the example of graphical objects using C++.

CLASSES PROVIDE DATA ABSTRACTION AND INHERITANCE

In C++, objects are defined using the *class* construct which is similar to *struct* in C. For example, the circle object can be defined as follows:

```
class circle_object: public graph_object
{
    int  radius;
public:
    circle_object(int x, int y, int radius);
    void draw(int color, int x, int y);
};
```

First look at the lines inside the curly braces. The integer variable *radius* represents the data in the *circle_object* class. Immediately following the data are some function prototypes preceded by the keyword *public*. These are the member functions of this class and the *public* keyword specifies that they are visible to the other parts of the program. An instance of the *class* is declared and its member functions are accessed just like a C structure. For example, to call the *draw* function of a *circle_object* named *c1*, you would write

```
circle_object c1;
...
c1.draw(7, 100, 100);
```

The variable *radius*, which appears before *public*, is by default *private* and not accessible to any function other than those defined within this *class*.

Data Abstraction in C++ Class

When you define a *class*, you are defining a new, possibly complex, data type. You use the keyword *private* to hide the internal details of this data structure to the outside world. The only way the world can operate on the data is through the *public* member functions. Thus, the *class* mechanism allows you to implement data abstraction and promotes modularity.

Inheritance in C++ Classes

When declaring a class, you also indicate if it inherits from any other class. On the first line of the *class* declaration, you place a colon (:) followed by a list of base classes from which this class inherits. Since the *circle_object* inherits from *graph_object*, the first line of the *class* declaration indicates this with the statement:

```
class circle_object: public graph_object
{
 ...
}
```

Here, the *graph_object* class is the *base class* and *circle_object* is the *derived class*. The keyword *public* preceding *graph_object* signifies that any public members (both data and function) of *graph_object* will be accessible to the *circle_object* class.

Incidentally, we wanted to use the names *circle* and *rectangle* for the graphical objects, but Turbo C++'s graphics library includes routines with similar names. Since class names have to be unique, we picked *circle_object* and *rect_object* as our classes.

IMPLEMENTING THE GRAPHICAL OBJECTS IN C++

The first task in implementing the graphical objects in C++ is to define the classes. The file *oopcpp.h* (Listing 2-7) shows the class definitions.

Listing 2-7. oopcpp.h—*Classes of Graphical Objects in C++*

```
/*  File:  oopcpp.h
 *
 *  Header file with definitions for an example of
 *  object-oriented programming in C++.
 *
 */

#if !defined(OOPCPP_H)
#define OOPCPP_H

#include <stdio.h>
#include <stdlib.h>    /* Prototype of 'exit'          */
#include <conio.h>     /* Prototype of 'getch'         */
#include <graphics.h>  /* Turbo C graphics routines    */
```

Listing 2-7. ***(cont.)***

```
/* Colors */
#define  FGCOLOR    WHITE
#define  BGCOLOR    BLACK

/* Class definitions */
class graph_object
{
/* Data */
    int   x;
    int   y;
public:
/* Member functions */
    void          move(int x, int y);
    virtual void draw(int color, int x, int y) { }
};

/* Note: cannot use 'circle' and 'rectangle' as names
 *       because Turbo C includes routines with similar
 *       names in header file graphics.h
 */
class circle_object: public graph_object
{
    int  radius;
public:
    circle_object(int x, int y, int radius);
    void draw(int color, int x, int y);
};

class rect_object: public graph_object
{
    int   width;
    int   height;
public:
    rect_object(int x, int y, int width, int height);
    void  draw(int color, int x, int y);
};

#endif /* #if !defined(OOPCPP_H) */
```

The header file only shows the prototypes of the member functions. The functions are implemented in separate files.

Constructors and Destructors

Note that each of the classes—*circle_object* and *rect_object*—has a member function with the same name as that of the class. These routines are known as *constructors*.

The constructor, if defined, is called whenever an object of this class is created. It allows you to allocate extra memory (when creating an array, for example), if needed, and initialize the object's data. The constructor always has the same name as the class.

You can also define a *destructor*, if there is any need to clean up after an object is destroyed (for example, if you want to free memory allocated in the constructor). The destructor has the same name as the class except for a tilde (~) prefix. Thus, the destructor for the class *circle_object* would be *~circle_object*.

Circles, Rectangles, and Generic Graphical Objects

Listings 2-8, 2-9, and 2-10 show the implementations of the classes *graph_object*, *circle_object*, and *rect_object* respectively. This example is so small that we could have placed all the code in a single file, but we chose to illustrate how you might handle a more complex project using OOP techniques. As we have done for this example, you will first define the classes of objects for your problem. This part may be easier said than done because for many problems it is difficult to identify the classes and decide the hierarchy. Once the classes are defined, you can decide on the interface to the outside world—the member functions. Then you can implement the member functions of each class in its own file as we have done in Listings 2-8 through 2-10.

The definition of the member functions for each class looks like a standard C function except that a special notation is used to indicate the class to which that function belongs. For example, the *move* member function of the *graph_object* is declared as follows:

```
void graph_object::move(int newx, int newy)
{
      .
      .
      .
}
```

Listing 2-8. grobj.cpp—*The* graph_object *Class*

```
/*  File:  grobj.cpp
 *
 *  Implements the generic graphics object in C++.
 *
 */
```

Listing 2-8. *(cont.)*

```
#include <oopcpp.h>

/*-------------------------------------------------------------*/
/*  m o v e
 *
 *  Move graphical objects
 */
void graph_object::move(int newx, int newy)
{
/* Crude way of moving objects...draw at old location using
 * background color, then draw with foreground color
 * at the new location
 */

    draw(BGCOLOR, x, y);
    draw(FGCOLOR, newx, newy);

/* Save new position */
    x = newx;
    y = newy;
}
```

Listing 2-9. circle.cpp—*The* circle_object *Class*

```
/*  File:  circle.cpp
 *
 *  Implements the "circle" class in C++.
 */
#include <oopcpp.h>

/*-------------------------------------------------------------*/
/*  c i r c l e _ o b j e c t
 *
 *  Handles the creation of circles
 */
circle_object::circle_object(int x, int y, int r)
{
    radius = r;
    move(x, y);
}
/*-------------------------------------------------------------*/
/*  d r a w
 *
```

Listing 2-9. *(cont.)*

```
 *  Handles drawing of circles
 */
void circle_object::draw(int color, int x, int y)
{
    setcolor(color);
    circle(x, y, radius);
}
```

Listing 2-10. rect.cpp—*The* rect_object *Class*

```
/*  File:  rect.cpp
 *
 *  Implements the "rectangle" class in C++.
 */
#include <oopcpp.h>

/*-------------------------------------------------------------*/
/*  r e c t _ o b j e c t
 *
 *  Handles the creation of rectangles
 */
rect_object::rect_object(int x, int y, int w, int h)
{
    width = w;
    height = h;
    move(x, y);
}
/*-------------------------------------------------------------*/
/*  d r a w
 *
 *  Handles drawing of rectangles
 */
void rect_object::draw(int color, int x, int y)
{
    setcolor(color);
    rectangle(x, y, x+width, y+width);
}
```

Testing the Example of OOP in C++

After implementing the classes, all that remains is to test them in a sample program. Listing 2-11 shows a sample program that performs the same task as its C counterpart in Listing 2-6. You can test the program under Turbo C++ by setting up a project with the following files:

```
oopcpp.cpp
grobj.cpp
circle.cpp
rect.cpp
```

After setting up the project, select *Build all* from the *Compile* menu to build the executable *oopcpp.exe*. When you run *oopcpp*, you will see a circle and a rectangle moved around the screen a number of times.

Listing 2-11. oopcpp.cpp—*An Example of OOP in C++*

```
/* File: oopcpp.cpp
 *
 *  Demonstrate OOP in C++ using some graphical objects.
 *
 */

#include <oopcpp.h>

void main(void)
{
    int    i, j, x, y;
    graph_object *gr_objects[4];
    int    graphdriver = DETECT, graphmode, g_errorcode;

/* Detect adapter type and initialize graphics system
 * Assume that Turbo C's BGI drivers are in "d:\tc\bgi"
 */
    initgraph(&graphdriver, &graphmode, "d:\tc\bgi");
    if((g_errorcode = graphresult()) != grOk)
    {
        fprintf(stderr, "initgraph: %s\n",
                grapherrormsg(g_errorcode));
        exit(1);
    }
/* Set background and foreground colors */
    setbkcolor(BGCOLOR);
    setcolor(FGCOLOR);

/* Create some graphical objects */
    gr_objects[0] = new circle_object(100, 100, 50);
    gr_objects[1] = new rect_object(150, 150, 20, 20);

    x = 100;
    y = 100;
```

Listing 2-11. *(cont.)*

```
    for(j = 0; j < 100; j++)
    {
/* Move the objects around the screen */
     for(i = 0; i < 2; i++)
         gr_objects[i]->move(x, y);
        x += 2;
    }


/* Wait until user presses a key */
    outtextxy(10, getmaxy()-50," Press any key to exit");

    getch();

/* Clean up */
    delete gr_objects[0];
    delete gr_objects[1];

    closegraph();
}
```

Creating Objects on the Fly

In C, you use memory allocation routines such as *calloc* or *malloc* to dynamically create data structures. These functions return the address of the allocated memory (a *pointer*). When you no longer need a structure, you can reclaim the memory by calling *free* with the address of that structure as the argument. C++ introduces two new operators, *new* and *delete*, to create and destroy objects, respectively. Listing 2-11 illustrates how the *new* operator is used to create the graphical objects. Like *calloc* or *malloc*, *new* also returns a pointer to the object. At the end of the program, we have used *delete* to destory the objects.

Virtual Functions Support Polymorphism

We have not yet identified how C++ handles one important aspect of OOP—polymorphism. Let us look at how our example of OOP uses polymorphism.

Look at the declaration of the *graph_object* class in Listing 2-7. You will notice that the function *draw* is declared as follows:

```
virtual void draw(int color, int x, int y) { }
```

The keyword, *virtual*, precedes the function declaration and the function is defined to be an empty one that does nothing.

The virtual function is the key to polymorphism which, you will recall, allows different objects to react differently to the same operation (or, in the case of C++, the same function call). In the example, each of the classes *circle_object* and *rect_object* defines *draw* to suit its need. The following code fragment in Listing 2-11 illustrates how polymorphism is exploited:

```
    int     i, j, x, y;
    graph_object *gr_objects[2];
    .
    .
    .
/* Create two graphical objects */
    gr_objects[0] = new circle_object(100, 100, 50);
    gr_objects[1] = new rect_object(150, 150, 20, 20);

    x = 100;
    y = 100;
    for(j = 0; j < 100; j++)
    {
/* Move the objects on the screen */
      for(i = 0; i < 2; i++)
          gr_objects[i]->move(x, y);
        x += 2;
```

Notice that we create a circle and a rectangle and store their pointers in an array of generic graphical objects, *gr_objects*. In the *for* loops that follow, we move both objects by invoking the *draw* function through the pointer to the object. Because the *draw* function in the base class, *graph_object*, is declared to be *virtual*, the *draw* function that gets called at run-time is the one defined in the derived class. This is how the *virtual* keyword is interpreted in C++.

More on C++

So far, you have seen a small subset, albeit an important one, of the syntax of C++—the part that provides support for OOP. There are many more features of C++ which are not directly in support of OOP, but are nevertheless useful and important. First we will look at features of C++ that are different from ANSI standard C. At the end of this section, we discuss the cases where things that used to work one way in C either work differently or not at all in C++.

VERSIONS OF C++

C++ was developed in the early 1980s by Bjarne Stroustrup of AT&T Bell Laboratories. He created C++ while adding features to C to support efficient event-driven simulation programs. His inspiration came from the language Simula67 which supported the concept of a *class.* Many improvements were made to this initial language before it was commercially released for the first time in 1985. Since then, C++ has continued to evolve, with AT&T controlling the releases.

Initially, C++ programs were first translated into C, which were then compiled using a C compiler. By the time Release 1.2 of AT&T's C++ came out, C++ compilers were becoming available for PCs and workstations. AT&T released C++ 2.0 in 1989. Turbo C++ is a compiler for AT&T C++ 2.0.

COMMENTS IN C++

C++ recognizes the standard C comments which are delimited by the pair /* . . . */. It also supports a new syntax for comments. It takes as comment everything following a pair of slashes (//) up to the end of the line. Thus, the following are valid comments in C++:

```
/* Move the objects by drawing at the old location using the
 * background color, then drawing at the new location with
 * the foreground color.
 */
    draw(BGCOLOR, x, y);        // Draw at old location
    draw(FGCOLOR, newx, newy); // Now draw at new location
```

You can use the C-style comments for comments spanning multiple lines while the new format is ideal for single-line comments.

FUNCTIONS IN C++

Whether you use OOP or the traditional procedure-oriented approach, functions remain the workhorse of C++ programs, just as they are in C. There are several ways in which C++ has strived to make functions efficient and safe to use. The first change is the use of *prototypes* for functions. This is already a part of the ANSI standard for C, but C++ goes a step further by *requiring* a function to be defined (either through a prototype or an actual function definition) before it is used.

Default Arguments

Another improvement to functions in C++ is that you can specify the default values for the arguments when you provide a prototype for a function. For example, when defining the function *new_window* that sets up a rectangular region of the display (a window) and fills it with a background color, you can give default values for the window's location, size, and background color, as follows:

```
// Function prototype with default argument values

int new_window(int x = 0, int y = 0, int width = 40,
               int height = 10, int bgcolor = 0);
```

With this declaration, you can use any of the following calls to *new_window*:

```
int id;

// Equivalent to new_window(0, 0, 40, 10, 0);
id = new_window();

// Equivalent to new_window(12, 0, 40, 10, 0);
id = new_window(12);

// Equivalent to new_window(5, 4, 40, 10, 0);
id = new_window(5, 4);
```

From the example, you can see that it is impossible to give a nondefault argument for *height* without specifying the values for *x*, *y*, and *width* as well because *height* comes after them and the compiler can only match arguments by position. In other words, the first specified argument in a call to *new_window* always matches *x*, the second one matches *y*, and so on. Thus, only trailing arguments can be left unspecified.

Overloaded Function Names

Unlike C, C++ allows you to define several functions with the same name even though they differ in the type or number of arguments. For example, the following example shows two versions of a function named *show*, one for displaying an integer, the other for printing a string:

```
#include <stdio.h>

// Overloaded function "show"

void show(int);
void show(char *);

/*------------------------------------------*/
main()
{
    show("'show' is an overloaded function");
    show(10);
```

```
}
/*-------------------------------------------*/
void show(int x)
{
    printf("%d\n", x);
}
/*-------------------------------------------*/
void show(char *x)
{
    printf("%s\n", x);
}
```

When *show* is used in *main*, the compiler generates code to call the correct version by looking at the type and number of arguments.

In-Line Functions

In-line functions are like macros. The entire body of the function is placed at the point where the function is called. The in-line functions are provided to support efficient implementation of OOP techniques in C++. Since OOP approach requires extensive use of member functions (methods), the overhead of function calls can hurt the performance of a program. For smaller functions, you can use the *inline* qualifier to avoid the overhead of function call.

Although in-line functions behave like macros, there is a crucial difference. Unlike macros, the compiler treats in-line functions as true functions. For example, you define a macro named *mult* as follows:

```
#define mult(a,b) (a * b)
```

Suppose you use this macro:

```
x = mult(3+1,5);
```

The preprocessor will transform this into

```
x = (3+1*5);
```

This will evaluate to 8 instead of the result of multiplying (3+1) and 5, which should have been 20. Of course, you know that the solution is to use parentheses around the macro arguments, but in-line functions behave similarly with no possibility of this type of error. Also, in-line functions, being true functions, are type-checked during compilation.

Here is an example program with an in-line version of *mult*:

```
#include <stdio.h>
```

```
// Define in-line function

inline int mult(int a, int b)
{
    return(a * b);
}

main()
{
    printf("Product of 3 and 4 = %d\n", mult(3,4));
    printf("Product of 3, 4, 5 = %d\n",
        mult(3, mult(3+1,5)));
}
```

When you run this program, it correctly produces the following output:

```
Product of 3 and 4 = 12
Product of 3, 4, 5 = 60
```

You should use in-line functions in class definitions whenever the functions are small in size. You can find examples of in-line functions in the definition of the *complex* class which appears in the header file *complex.h*.

Friend Functions

The *friend* qualifier for a function also stems from a need to make OOP efficient in C++. The rules for data hiding in a class give access to private data only to member functions. Sometimes it may be necessary to allow a function outside the class to use data private to the class. In this case, that outside function is declared within the class with a *friend* qualifier. For example, suppose you wanted to define a nonmember addition routine for the *complex* class. Here is a small program that defines a complex class (not the same as the one in *complex.h*) and uses friend functions to add two complex numbers and display the results:

```
#include <stdio.h>

class complex
{
    float real;
    float imag;
public:
    friend complex sum(complex x, complex y);
    friend void show(complex);
```

```
    complex(){}
    complex(float a, float b) { real = a; imag = b;}
};

complex sum(complex x, complex y)
{
    complex z;
    z.real = x.real + y.real;
    z.imag = x.imag + y.imag;
    return(z);
}

void show(complex x)
{
    printf(" (%f + i %f)\n", x.real, x.imag);
}

main()
{
    complex x, y, z;
    x = complex(1., 2.);
    y = complex(4.,5.);

    printf("Sum of ");
    show(x);
    printf("and");
    show(y);

    z = sum(x,y);

    printf("=");
    show(z);
}
```

When executed, the program generates the result:

```
Sum of  (1.000000 + i 2.000000)
and (4.000000 + i 5.000000)
= (5.000000 + i 7.000000)
```

OVERLOADING OPERATORS

In addition to overloaded functions, C++ also allows you to define the meaning of common operators (such as +, -, *, /, +=, -=, *=, /=) for any class. Since a class is essentially a new data type, this is equivalent to allowing you to define operations on this data.

For example, instead of writing an addition function for complex variables, you can define the + operator to perform addition for the *complex* class of the previous example. Here is how the definition might look:

```
class complex
{
    float real;
    float imag;
public:    friend complex operator+(complex, complex);

    complex(){}
    complex(float a, float b) { real = a; imag = b;}
};

// Define + operator

complex operator+(complex x, complex y)
{
    complex z;
    z.real = x.real + y.real;
    z.imag = x.imag + y.imag;
    return(z);
}
```

Once this is done, you can use the operator to perform the addition of two complex numbers as follows:

```
    complex x, y, z;
    x = complex(1., 2.);
    y = complex(4.,5.);

    z = x+y;
```

Turbo C++ comes with a *complex* class that you can study to see how overloaded operators are defined. Look in the header file *complex.h* for the definition of this class.

DATA DECLARATIONS IN C++

In addition to the changes to functions and operators, C++ introduced the *class* data declaration which you have seen in our earlier discussions on OOP in C++.

Additionally, the meaning of C's *struct* construct has been enlarged. In C++, a *struct* is just like a *class*. You can have member functions in a *struct*. The difference between a *class* and a *struct* is that by default all members of a *struct* are public but *class* members are private. Of course, you can make *struct* members private by using the *private* keyword.

Variables Can Be Declared Anywhere

In C, you declare all variables at the beginning of a block. You cannot mix declarations with the statements of a program. C++ treats a declaration as a type of statement and allows you to place it anywhere. Thus, in C++, you can write code like this:

```
#include <stdio.h>
#include <string.h>
.
.
void process_string(char *str)
{
    if(str == NULL) printf("Null string in process_string\n");
    int length = strlen(str);
    .
    .
    for(int i = 0; i < length; i++)
    {
// process characters in the string...
    }
}
```

This feature of C++ is very handy because you can declare a variable when needed and initialize it immediately. Since the declaration is close to where the variable is actually used, the program is more readable.

Structure Names Are Stand-Alone

In C++, the name of a *struct* can be used as soon as its definition is started. For example, suppose you are defining a structure representing one element of a doubly-linked list. Here is what you can do in C++:

```
struct list
{
    list  *next;   // OK in C++
    list  *prev;   // OK in C++
    void  *data;
};

list *mylist;     // OK in C++
```

You will get errors when you try to compile this code in C. The closest you can come in C will be to use *typedef*, but, even with *typedef*, you cannot use the name of a *struct* inside its definition. Here is the C equivalent:

```
typedef struct list
{
```

```
    struct list *next; /* Need 'struct' in C */
    struct list *prev; /* Need 'struct' in C */
    void        *data;
} list;

list *mylist;     /* Ok to use after 'typedef' */
```

Reference Types

You know that C passes arguments by value. When you call a function with some arguments, the values of the arguments are copied in a special area of memory known as the stack. The function uses these copies for its operation. The following code illustrates the effect of *call by value*:

```
    void f(int a)
    {
        a *= 10;
    }
    .
    .
    int x = 10;

/* Call f */
    f(x);
/* x is still 10 */
```

The only way you can have a function change the value of a variable is by explicitly passing the address of the variable to the function. This method of calling is known as *call by reference* and in C, we can implement it as follows:

```
    void f(int *a)
    {
        *a *= 10;    /* Make the value 10 times */
    }
    .
    .
    .
    int x = 10;
/* Call f with address of x as argument */
    f(&x);
/* Now x is 100 */
```

Thus, you can have call by reference in C, but the syntax can be messy. In the function, you have to always dereference the argument by using the * operator.

C++ provides a way of passing arguments by reference. In fact, it introduces the concept of a *reference* which is the idea of defining an *alias* or alternative name for any instance of data. The syntax is to append an ampersand (&) to the name of the data type. Here is an example:

```
int x = 10;
int &rx = x;
```

From this point on, you can refer to *x* by *rx*. In fact, if you write:

```
rx += 5;
```

x will change to 15.

Using reference types, you can write a function to multiply a value by 10 in a much simpler manner:

```
    void f(int &x)
    {
        x *= 10;
    }
    .
    .
    int x = 10;
/* Call f, argument automatically passed by reference */
    f(x);
/* Now x is 100 */
```

This is a good use of the reference type. Notice how easy it is to write the function *f* which gets its argument by reference.

The call by reference mechanism is also useful in OOP because manipulating objects by reference instead of by value allows an efficient implementation of OOP. The reason is that call by reference saves the time needed to copy objects from and to the stack as required by the call by value approach.

DIFFERENCES BETWEEN C AND C++

Although we often blithely state that C++ is a superset of C, especially ANSI standard C, there are a small number of things in ANSI C that do not work quite the same way in C++. In the next sections we present a summary description of the differences.

New Reserved Keywords

Because of the new OOP features of C++, it requires a number of extra keywords. You have to watch out for any C programs that might use these reserved words:

```
asm        friend     private    this
catch      inline     protected  virtual
class      new        public
delete     operator   template
```

Function Prototypes

In C, if you use a function without declaring its prototype, the function is taken as one returning an integer. C++ strictly enforces the prototypes and generates an error if you use a function without declaring it. Thus, in C++, you will get an error from the following:

```
main()
{
    printf("Hi\n");  // OK in C, but not in C++

                     // Must have prototype before use
}
```

You also get an error from old-style C code where functions are declared only when they do not return an *int*. For example, many C programs use *malloc* as follows:

```
char *malloc();
double array;

array = (double *) malloc(512);
```

This code will generate an error in C++ because the latter interprets empty argument lists differently from ANSI C. ANSI standard C interprets the empty argument list in *malloc* to mean that it takes zero or more arguments, but C++ considers an empty argument list as being equivalent to the prototype:

```
char *malloc(void);
```

When C++ encounters the call, *malloc(512)*, it finds an argument where it expects none and this causes an error.

void Pointers

C allows any pointer to be assigned to a *void* * variable and a *void* * to be assigned to any pointer. C++ does not allow assignment of a *void* * variable to any other pointer without explicit casting. Here is an example:

```
void *p_void;
int  x = 10, *p_x;

p_void = &x;  /* Allowed in C and C++      */
p_x = p_void; /* OK in C, but not in C++   */
p_x = (int *)p_void; /* Allowed in C++     /
```

Initialization of Character Arrays

In C, if you want to initialize an array of three characters, you could do the following:

```
char cpp[3] = "C++"; // Allowed in C, but not in C++
```

The result will be the three characters *C*, +, and +. C++ does not allow this because the array does not have room for the terminating null character. To achieve the same result in C++, you have to write the initialization as

```
char cpp[3] = {'C', '+', '+'}; // Allowed in both C and C++
```

You can also avoid the error by omitting the size of the array:

```
char cpp[] = "C++"; // Allowed in both C and C++
```

sizeof a Character Constant

In C, *sizeof('a')* results in the number of bytes in an *int*, but C++ evaluates this to *sizeof(char)*.

Scope of enums

In ANSI C, the elements of an *enum* are known throughout the file. In C++, you can have local *enums* inside a *struct* or a *class*. For example, the following will work in C++, but not in ANSI C:

```
struct fsm
{
    enum state {init, escape, end};
    ...
}

int init(int);  // Allowed in C++, but not in ANSI C
```

A Restriction on goto

Suppose you have a block of code with some variables declared at the beginning of the block. In C, you can use *goto* to jump into the block, skipping over the declarations. C++ does not allow this. Here is an example:

```
goto StartWorking;    // OK in ANSI C, but not in C++
.
.
{
    int x = 4, y = 8;
    char buf[10];

StartWorking:
    ...
}
```

This code would be correct in C++ only if the *goto* jumps over the entire block containing the declarations.

Summary

Loosely speaking, object-oriented programming refers to a new way of organizing your programs into *objects* that encapsulate data with a set of well-defined operations and that share code with other objects in a predefined hierarchy by *inheritance*. Although OOP techniques can be implemented in any programming language (C being a good example), it is easier when the language has the features necessary to support objects. In C++, objects are defined by the *class* construct which is similar to C's *struct* but has many more features. In particular, using *class* you can define the operations on the object via member functions and operators. A C++ program manipulates objects by calling the member functions only. This enhances the modularity of programs because you are free to change the internal data of objects without affecting other parts of a program.

C++ is a superset of C designed to support object-oriented programming through its *class* data type, the concepts of overloading functions and operators, and *virtual* functions. Many features, such as function prototypes and the *void* keyword, that were originally introduced in C++ have been already incorporated into the ANSI standard C (known as ANSI X3.159 1989). The *class* type with overloaded functions and operators support data abstraction and inheritance. The *virtual* functions provide the mechanism for implementing polymorphism.

Although a C++ compiler accepts most ANSI C programs, there are certain constructs in ANSI C that behave differently in C++. You have to watch out for the new reserved words and for the strict enforcement of the function prototypes in C++.

Further Reading

As C++ and object-oriented programming gain popularity, the number of books and articles on these topics keeps growing steadily. Here is a short list of resources that will help you learn more about C++ and object-oriented programming.

For an official definition of C++, you would want a copy of Stroustrup's book[1]. For beginners, The Waite Group[2] has a suitable title. Another good text[3] is the book by Stanley Lippman, who helped implement AT&T's C++ translator. Lippman's book covers AT&T C++ Release 2.0.

Every book on C++ also tries to cover the topic of object-oriented programming. However, as you have seen in this chapter, the techniques of object-oriented programming stand apart from the language used to implement those techniques. Thus, you can learn about object-oriented programming from a variety of other sources.

Bertrand Meyer's book[4] has a good description of the object-oriented approach. This book's examples are in a language called Eiffel, which Meyer developed. Historically, Smalltalk is regarded as one of the early object-oriented languages. Goldberg's book[5] is a good source for this. Brad Cox[6] uses Objective-C as the basis of his book.

Stroustrup's article[7] describes object-oriented programming from the point of view of a C++ programmer. The recent book by Mullin[8] is also worth noting because it covers object-oriented techniques with one large example in C++.

1. Bjarne Stroustrup, *The C++ Programming Language*, Addison-Wesley, Reading, MA, 1986, 336 pages.
2. John Berry, *The Waite Group's C++ Programming*, Howard W. Sams & Company, Indianapolis, IN, 1988, 397 pages.
3. Stanley B. Lippman, *C++ Primer*, Addison-Wesley, Reading, MA, 1989, 474 pages.
4. Bertrand Meyer, *Object-Oriented Software Construction*, Prentice-Hall International (UK) Ltd., Hertfordshire, HP2 4RG Great Britain, 1988, 552 pages.
5. Adele Goldberg, *Smalltalk-80: The Interactive Programming Environment*, Addison-Wesley, Reading, MA, 1985.
6. Brad J. Cox, *Object-Oriented Programming: An Evolutionary Approach*, Addison-Wesley, Reading, MA, 1986, 287 pages.
7. Bjarne Stroustrup, What is object-oriented programming?, *IEEE Software*, May 1988, pp.10-20.
8. Mark Mullin, *Object-Oriented Program Design with Examples in C++*, Addison-Wesley, Reading, MA, 1989, 329 pages.

Chapter 3 Turbo C++ Features and Options

Implementation Notes

In this chapter we discuss some of the features of Turbo C++ related to the 8086 microprocessor, including storage size of variables in Turbo C++, the concept of "memory models" that arise in 8086 microprocessors, special purpose keywords, global variables, and certain preprocessor constants defined by Turbo C.

We will also describe Turbo C++'s remarkable interactive program development environment and show you how best to take advantage of it.

STORAGE SIZE OF DATA ITEMS

Table 3-1 shows the storage size of the basic data types in Turbo C++. The table also shows the range of values that each type of variable can hold.

MEMORY MODELS IN TURBO C++

The memory addressing scheme used by the 8086 microprocessor forces the concept of memory models onto any C compiler designed to generate code for 8086 machines. The 8086 microprocessor family uses 16-bit registers (the 80386 is a 32-bit processor). Since the processor has to manipulate memory addresses using registers, and 16 bits can only address 64 K of memory, a different scheme is used in the 8086 to address memory. The address of each byte in memory is considered to be composed of two parts: a "segment" address and an "offset" from the starting byte of the segment. Each segment and each offset is a 16-bit value which the microprocessor can manipulate using its 16-bit registers. The segment and the offset addresses are combined in a special way to generate the final "physical address" which is only 20 bits long, specifically, using the formula: Physical Address (20-bit) = Segment Address (16-bit) * 16 + Offset (16-bit).

Table 3-1. ***Data Types and Sizes in Turbo C++***

Type Name	Storage Size	Range of Values
char	1 byte	−128 to 127
int	2 bytes	−32768 to 32767
short	2 bytes	−32768 to 32767
long	4 bytes	−2,147,483,648 to 2,147,483,647
unsigned char	1 byte	0 to 255
unsigned	2 bytes	0 to 65,535
unsigned short	2 bytes	0 to 65,535
unsigned long	4 bytes	0 to 4,294,967,295
enum	2 bytes	0 to 65,535
float	4 bytes	Approximately 3.4E−38 to 3.4E+38 with 7 digit precision
double	8 bytes	Approximately 1.7E−308 to 1.7E+308 with 15 digit precision
long double	10 bytes	Approximately 3.4E−4932 to 1.1E+4932 with 19 digit precision

One advantage of this strategy is that if all of your data fits into a single 64-K segment, the 8086 can set up the segment address in a segment register (specifically, the register named DS) and refer to data items using only the 16-bit offset. This results in faster code because the code does not have to manipulate the segment portion of the address (this is the "small" memory model).

A C compiler for the 8086 machines has two choices: either it forces you to write programs that use only a single segment of data and code or it can provide you with options to mix and match different addressing schemes for data and code. The concept of memory models arises from the availability of these choices. A specific memory model in Turbo C++ refers to one of six ways of addressing code and data, shown in Table 3-2.

In addition to the six standard memory models, with the keywords *far*, *near*, and *huge*, you can mix data items with an addressing scheme different from the default allowed by the standard model. These keywords can qualify the address of a data item as well as of a function. Table 3-3 summarizes the meaning of each of these keywords.

The memory model concept is not a part of the C language. It is an artifact necessary to exploit the architecture of the 8086 microprocessor, so programs with the keywords *near*, *far*, and *huge* are not portable.

KEYWORDS SPECIFIC TO TURBO C++

In addition to the standard C keywords, Turbo C++ allows several extra keywords. We have already discussed some of the keywords—*near*, *far*, *huge*, and *interrupt*. A complete summary of the Turbo C++ specific keywords is given in Table 3-4.

Table 3-2. ***Memory Models in the Turbo C++ Compiler***

Memory Model	Meaning
Tiny	All code and data must reside within a single 64-K segment. Data and code addresses are 16-bit offsets. Compiler option: −mt
Small	All data and code addresses are 16-bit offsets. Program size limited to one segment of code and one segment of data. Compiler option: −ms NOTE: This is the default in Turbo C++.
Medium	All data addresses are 16-bit offsets, but code addresses use explicit segment and offset. A program can have a single segment of data, but many segments of code. Compiler option: −mm
Compact	All code addresses are offset only, but data addresses use segment as well as offset. Program can have multiple data segments, but only one code segment. Compiler option: −mc
Large	All data and code addresses include explicit segment and offset. Program size is limited only by available memory (which is limited by the 20-bit physical address), but a single data item cannot exceed a 64-K segment. Compiler option: −ml
Huge	Same as the large model, but address arithmetic is performed in such a way that an array can span multiple segments. Compiler option: −mh

Table 3-3. ***The* near, far, *and* huge *Keywords in Turbo C++***

Keyword	When Used with Data	When Used with Function
near	Data addresses are 16-bit offsets with respect to the segment address of a default data segment.	Function is assumed to be in the current code segment.
far	Full segment and offset addresses used. Data may be anywhere in memory.	Referenced using full segment and offset address.
huge	Full segment and offset addresses used. An array can be larger than a 64-K segment because 32-bit arithmetic is used on pointers.	Not applicable to functions.

Table 3-4. ***Summary of Turbo C++ Specific Keywords***

Keyword	Use
asm	Use to embed 8086 assembly language statements directly in a Turbo C++ program. The format is:

Table 3-4. ***(cont.)***

Keyword	Use
	asm <opcode> <operands> <; or newline> where <opcode> is a mnemonic code for an 8086 instruction (consult the *Turbo C++ User's Guide* for a list), and <operands> are the necessary operands for that opcode. Each line of assembly language statement must begin with the *asm* keyword. You can use semicolons to separate multiple statements on the same line. For example, you can write: asm pop ax; asm pop ds; When compiling programs with in-line assembly language statements, you have to use the -B compiler option or the *inline* pragma. Note that you will need an assembler during the compilation phase. Turbo C++ uses the Turbo Assembler by default; you can specify a different one with the -E option in the command-line compiler, TCC. Turbo C++ also allows you to embed 8086 machine instructions directly in the object code generated by the compiler. See the *__emit__* function in Chapter 17 for further details.
cdecl	Use to force the C argument passing convention for a function when the remainder of the program is being compiled with the -p option, which enables the Pascal convention.
far	Use to tell the compiler to use full segment:offset address for a pointer.
huge	Use to qualify a pointer so that the compiler maintains it in a normalized form. This ensures that pointer arithmetic will work properly even when the address differences exceed 64 K.
interrupt	Use to qualify a function as an interrupt handler. See text for further explanation.
near	Use in a large model program to force the use of offset addresses only for a pointer.
pascal	Use to generate code using the Pascal calling convention for a function (see Chapter 5 for an explanation of different calling conventions).
_cs	Declares a near pointer to be an offset from the CS segment register.
_ds	Declares a near pointer to be an offset from the DS segment register. For example, *int _ds *p_data;* declares *p _data* to be an offset from the DS register.
_es	Qualifies a near pointer to be an offset from the ES segment register.
_ss	Qualifies a near pointer to be an offset from the SS segment register.
_CS	Denotes the CS segment register.
_DS	Denotes the DS segment register.
_ES	Denotes the ES segment register.
_SS	Denotes the SS segment register.
_AH	Denotes the AH register.
_AL	Denotes the AL register.
_AX	Denotes the AX register.
_BH	Denotes the BH register.
_BL	Denotes the BL register.
_BX	Denotes the BX register.

Table 3-4. *(cont.)*

Keyword	Use
_CH	Denotes the CH register.
_CL	Denotes the CL register.
_CX	Denotes the CX register.
_DH	Denotes the DH register.
_DL	Denotes the DL register.
_DX	Denotes the DX register.
_BP	Denotes the BP register.
_DI	Denotes the DI register.
_SI	Denotes the SI register.
_SP	Denotes the SP register.
_export	Used for creating functions that will reside in OS/2's dynamic-link libraries. (See Gordon Letwin's *Inside OS/2*, Microsoft Press, 1988, for a discussion of dynamic-link libraries and other major features of OS/2.) Turbo C++ accepts this keyword, but does nothing with it because there is no need for it in MS-DOS programs.
_loadds	Causes the compiler to generate code to load the data segment register (DS) with a specific value upon entry to the function that is qualified by this keyword.
_saveregs	When prefixing a function declaration, this instructs the compiler to generate code to save all CPU registers upon entering the function and restore them when exiting it. The AX register is not restored if the function returns a value.

You can refer to registers directly by using the keywords shown in Table 3-4. You should, however, have a good understanding of the register usage in Turbo C before changing them in your program. These register "pseudo-variables" are very handy when writing interrupt handlers or TSR programs in Turbo C++.

THE INTERRUPT *ATTRIBUTE*

If you write C applications that require handling interrupts (for example, programming the serial communication ports for interrupt-driven I/O), you will find the *interrupt* keyword useful. This keyword serves as a qualifier for a function that you wish to install as the *interrupt handler* for a specific interrupt number. When the compiler translates a function with the *interrupt* attribute, it generates code to push the registers AX, BX, CX, DX, ES, DS, SI, DI, and BP (IP, CS, and the flags are pushed automatically when an interrupt handler is called). Then it sets up the DS register to point to the data segment of that function. After this initial sequence comes the code of the function. Finally, the compiler uses an IRET instruction instead of a normal RET to return from the function. A typical use of the *interrupt* attribute is

```
void interrupt int_handler (unsigned bp, unsigned di,
                            unsigned si, unsigned ds,
                            unsigned es, unsigned dx,
                            unsigned cx, unsigned bx,
                            unsigned ax, unsigned ip,
                            unsigned cs, unsigned flags)
{
/* Place code to handle interrupt referring to registers by
 * name when necessary.
 */
}
```

Within the interrupt handler, you can access the values of registers by referring to them by name. Other precautions that apply to assembly language interrupt handlers also apply to the C function. For example, you should not call a library routine that calls a DOS function, such as stream and low-level I/O routines. On the other hand, such routines as those in the string manipulation category are safe inside the *interrupt* function. See the reference entry for the *setvect* function (Chapter 17) for an example of an interrupt handler that uses the *interrupt* keyword.

PREDEFINED GLOBAL VARIABLES

Turbo C++ includes a number of predefined global variables and preprocessor constants. The global variables contain the DOS version number, last error number, pointer to the process environment block, and other useful information. We refer to these global variables as predefined variables. Table 3-5 summarizes the predefined global variables and their purpose.

Table 3-5. *Predefined Globals in Turbo C++*

Name	Declaration and Purpose
_8087	int _8087; This variable is set to 1 if the Turbo C start-up code detects the presence of a math coprocessor or if the *87* environment variable is set to *Y* (you can do this using the DOS command SET 87=Y). Otherwise, *_8087* is set to 0. Note: this variable is not set if your program does not have floating-point calculations. Declared in: dos.h
_argc	int _argc; This global variable contains the number of command-line arguments passed to the *main* function. Declared in: dos.h
_argv	char **_argv; This is the array of strings containing the command-line arguments that were passed to *main*.

Table 3-5. ***(cont.)***

Name	Declaration and Purpose
	Declared in: dos.h
daylight	int daylight; This variable is set to 1 if daylight saving time is specified. It is used when converting local time to Greenwich Mean Time (see Time functions for details). Declared in: time.h
directvideo	int directvideo; If this variable is 1, video output in text mode goes directly to the video memory (this is the default setting). When *directvideo* is 0, the ROM BIOS routines are used for text mode output. You should set *directvideo* to 0 if your display adapter is not completely compatible with the IBM adapters. Declared in: conio.h
_doserrno	int _doserrno; Contains the MS-DOS error code returned by the last MS-DOS system call. Declared in: dos.h and errno.h
environ	char *environ[ ]; This is an array of strings where the strings constitute the environment table of the process. Allows you to access the environment variables for use in your program. Declared in: dos.h
errno	int errno; Contains an error code corresponding to the last system call. Declared in: errno.h
_fmode	int _fmode; Contains the default file translation mode. The default value is 0 which means files are translated in the text mode (see File Manipulation routines for more details). Declared in: fcntl.h and stdlib.h
_heaplen	unsigned int _heaplen; The *_heaplen* variable specifies the size of *near heap* in tiny, small, and medium models. If *_heaplen* is set to 0, Turbo C allocates 64-K bytes for the data segment and the effective heap size is obtained by subtracting the size of global data and the stack size (see *_stklen* in this table). The default value of *_heaplen* is 0. Declared in: dos.h
_osmajor	unsigned char _osmajor; The major version number of MS-DOS. For example, if you have MS-DOS 3.10, _osmajor will be 3. Declared in: dos.h
_osminor	unsigned char _osminor; The minor version number of MS-DOS. For MS-DOS 3.10, _osminor will be 10. Declared in: dos.h

Table 3-5. *(cont.)*

Name	Declaration and Purpose
_psp	unsigned int _psp; This variable contains the segment address of the program segment prefix (PSP) of the current process. The PSP contains information about the process such as the command-line arguments, pointer to the environment block and the return address. The PSP begins at offset 0 of the segment address contained in _psp. Declared in: stdlib.h
_stklen	unsigned int _stklen; The *_stklen* variable specifies the stack size in all six memory models available in Turbo C. The default stack size is 4096 bytes; the minimum allowed is 256 bytes. Declared in: dos.h
sys_errlist	char *sys_errlist[ ]; This is an array of strings each of which corresponds to a system error message. Declared in: errno.h
sys_nerr	int sys_nerr; This is the total number of strings in the sys _errlist array. Declared in: errno.h
timezone	long timezone; The timezone variable contains the difference in seconds between Greenwich Mean Time and the local time (see Time functions for details). Declared in: time.h
_version	unsigned int _version; *_version* contains the MS-DOS version number. The major version number is in the low byte and the minor version number is in the high byte. For example, if you are using MS-DOS verison 3.10, *_version* will be 0A03 in hexadecimal format. Declared in: dos.h

PREDEFINED PREPROCESSOR CONSTANTS

Preprocessor constants are used extensively in the library routines to define values for specific parameters in a more readable fashion. A few of the preprocessor symbols are defined by the compiler itself. These predefined symbols, shown in Table 3-6, can help you write code that can be easily ported to other machines. For example, consider the fragment of code:

```
#ifdef __MSDOS__
   :
/*   MS-DOS specific code goes here */
   :
#endif
```

```
#ifdef vms
   :
/*   DEC VAX/VMS specific code goes here */
   :
#endif
```

Table 3-6. ***Predefined Preprocessor Symbols in Turbo C++***

Symbol	Purpose
__CDECL__	This symbol is set to 1 to indicate that the -p compiler option was not used. This means that C calling convention is being used (see Chapter 5 for a discussion of the convention C uses to pass arguments to a function).
__COMPACT__	This symbol is defined to be 1 when the compact memory model is in use. Otherwise, it is undefined.
__DATE__	This symbol is defined to be a string containing the date when the preprocessor began processing the file. An example: *Jun 10 1988*.
__FILE__	This is defined to be the name of the current source file being processed.
__HUGE__	This symbol is defined to be 1 when the huge memory model is in use. Otherwise, it is undefined.
__LARGE__	This symbol is defined to be 1 when the large memory model is in use. Otherwise, it is undefined.
__LINE__	The line number being processed (the first line is line number 1).
__MEDIUM__	This symbol is defined to be 1 when the medium memory model is in use. Otherwise, it is undefined.
__MSDOS__	This symbol indicates that the operating system is MSDOS. It is always defined as 1 in Turbo C++.
__OVERLAY__	This symbol is defined to be 1 when you compile with the -Y option, which enables support for overlays. It is undefined if overlay support is not used.
__PASCAL__	This symbol becomes defined when the -p option is used to enable the function calling convention of Pascal.
__SMALL__	This symbol is defined to be 1 when the small memory model is in use. Otherwise, it is undefined.
__STDC__	This symbol is defined as 1 when you compile with the -A flag which checks your source code for strict ANSI compatibility.
__TIME__	This is the time that the preprocessor began processing the current source file. The time is of the form: HH:MM:SS (for example, 15:32:10).
__TINY__	This symbol is defined to be 1 when the tiny memory model is in use. Otherwise, it is undefined.
__TURBOC__	This symbol is set to the current Turbo C version number in hexadecimal form. For example, in Turbo C 2.0, __TURBOC__ is defined to be 0200 in hexadecimal.

When this code is compiled with the Turbo C++ compiler, the symbol __MSDOS__ comes predefined, so only the first chunk of code appropriate for MS-DOS machines will be processed. On the other hand, on a DEC VAX/VMS system, the symbol *vms* is predefined. So on that system we get only the part that applies to DEC VMS systems. This is a typical use of the predefined preprocessor constants.

DISPLAYING DIAGNOSTIC MESSAGES

Turbo C++ also supports the ANSI-compatible preprocessor directive *#error*, which causes the compiler to display a diagnostic message during compilation. You can use the *#error* directive to remind the user to compile the program with a specific compiler option. The syntax of this directive is

```
#error <message string>
```

where the rest of the line following the word *#error* is considered to be the message string to be printed by *#error*. For example, suppose you know the source file contains nonstandard extensions to the C language. If compiled with the –A option enforcing strict ANSI compatibility, you could remind the user to drop that option (which enables the extensions) instead. Here's how:

```
#ifdef __STDC__
  #error Program uses nonstandard extensions. Recompile without  -A
#endif
```

Since the __STDC__ symbol becomes defined when the –A option is used, the error message will be printed only when you enforce strict ANSI compliance.

Turbo C++ Interactive Environment

Turbo C++ is attractive as a development tool because of its fast interactive environment. You can edit, compile, link, execute, and debug a program without leaving the Turbo C++ environment. If you normally use compilers and assemblers from the DOS command line, switching to the Turbo C++ environment will require some preparation, but the advantages are well worth it. Here we summarize the steps you will follow when developing C and C++ programs in the Turbo C++ environment. First let us take a look at the traditional command-line approach to building an executable program (an .EXE file).

COMMAND-LINE APPROACH TO BUILDING PROGRAMS

Traditionally, programming has involved the use of several tools, each invoked separately from the DOS command prompt. In this environment, which we will call the command-line environment, you start by typing a C program into a file using a text editor of your choice. The next step is to compile the source file and produce an object file (with an .OBJ extension). The last step is to link several .OBJ files to produce an MS-DOS .EXE file. This is the file that you can execute by giving its name at the DOS prompt.

The command-line environment relies on disk files for all of these steps. Temporary files are generated during compilation, and at each step a file is transformed into a different form and saved in a new file. This makes the edit-compile-link cycles slow, even with a hard disk in the system. Turbo C++ changes all this by integrating all the steps in program development into a single harmonious environment which is also faster because all work is done in-memory with little or no disk access. We will describe the Turbo C++ environment in the following section.

Note, however, that Turbo C++ also provides a command-line environment, called TCC, for compiling and linking programs. You rarely have to use the TCC command-line interface because the Turbo C++ interactive environment provides almost all the options that are available with TCC. You may have to use TCC, for example, if you want to see the assembly language code generated by TCC (–S option) when compiling a C program. You also need TCC to compile your program if it uses in-line (embedded) 8086 assembly language code.

GETTING STARTED WITH THE TURBO C++ ENVIRONMENT

Use the INSTALL program, provided by Borland, to install Turbo C++ on a hard disk. Programs are now so large that you cannot use Turbo C++ without a hard disk. After installing Turbo C++, you should customize the interactive environment, TC, by running the utility program TCINST which accepts your choices and modifies the executable file TCC.EXE accordingly. Using TCINST, you can specify the directories where the include files and library files are located. TCINST also allows you to change screen colors, set up Turbo C's on-screen appearance, and customize the editor command keys. The command-line version of Turbo C++, TCC, reads default options from an ASCII file named TURBOC.CFG. If you plan to use TCC often, you should also prepare this file at the same time, using the editor in Turbo C++'s interactive environment. For example, if you install Turbo C++ in the hard disk C using the default directory names provided by the INSTALL utility, the TURBOC.CFG file might contain

```
-v
-IC:\TC\INCLUDE
-LC:\TC\LIB
```

which tells TCC to generate information for source level debugging (–v), and look for include files and library files in the directories C:\TC\INCLUDE and C:\TC\LIB respectively.

After you have installed and customized Turbo C++, you can invoke the Turbo C++ interactive environment with a command line of the form

```
TC
```

Turbo C++ will automatically open a temporary file named NONAME00 in its edit window. In later sessions, Turbo C++ will use saved information to open the files you were editing when you last used the interactive environment.

GETTING HELP IN TURBO C++

The Turbo C++ interactive environment has an extensive help facility. On Turbo C++'s initial screen (see Figure 3-1), you will notice that the bottom left corner says *F1-Help*. This means that you can get help by pressing function key F1. If you press the F1 key you will get a help message which depends on your position on the screen when you asked for help. For example, if you were editing a file, the help message will summarize the editor commands. Pressing the F1 key while in *Help* brings up the help contents. Figure 3-2 shows the table of contents for help. You can step through the screens displayed during the previous invocation of *Help* by pressing *Alt-F1*. Press the *Esc* key to exit from Help.

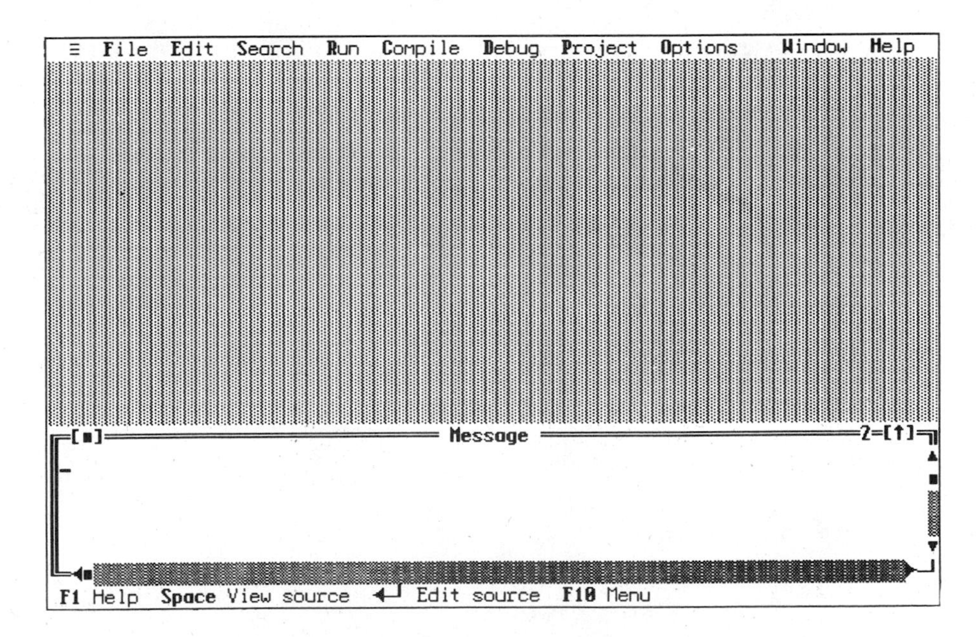

Figure 3-1. ***Turbo C++'s initial screen and menu bar***

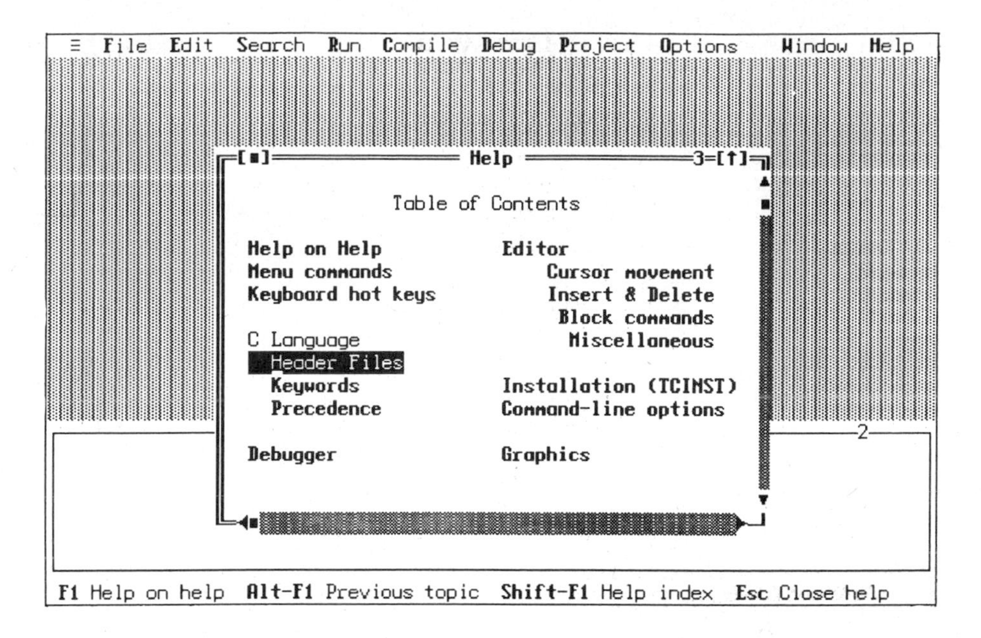

Figure 3-2. ***The help "Table of Contents" in Turbo C++***

If you want to find out information about the C language, you can select the *Keywords* item in the help index (Figure 3-2). In this case, you will see another screen with a list of the keywords to get more help. You can then get information on a particular C keyword by selecting that keyword. To select a keyword, use the mouse or the cursor movement keys to go from one selection to another, and press *Enter* to indicate your selection. You can also click the left mouse button twice to indicate a selection.

For help on run-time library routines, you should select the *Header files* item from the contents. This will take you to a display of the header files. You can look at the details of a function by first selecting a header file, then selecting the function within the header file. For example, to find the syntax of *calloc*, first select the header file *alloc.h*, then choose *calloc* from the next list. Figure 3-3 shows the final screen for *calloc*.

THE MENUS IN TURBO C++

You interact with Turbo C++ by selecting items from menus. Unlike Turbo C 2.0, Turbo C++ supports a mouse. Therefore, you can use the mouse as well as the keyborad to indicate menu selections. To use the mouse, you must have the mouse driver loaded. Figure 3-1 shows the initial screen in Turbo C++. Turbo C++ supports multiple, overlapping windows. Figure 3-1 shows a single "Message" window. When editing files (you can edit more than one at a time), the "Edit" windows appear above the Message window. However, you can move and resize these windows to suit your need. There is a main menu bar at the top of the screen showing the first

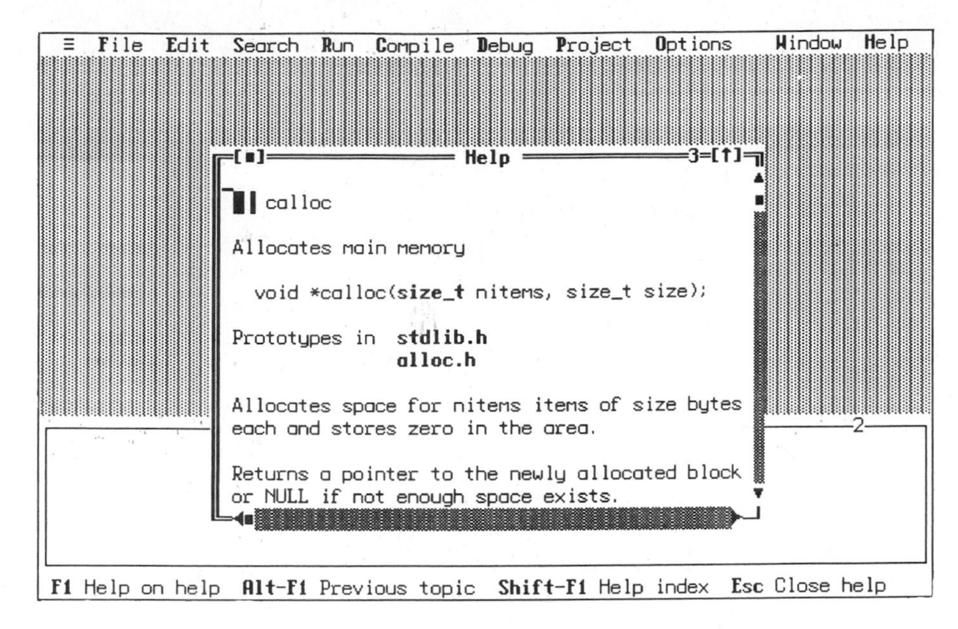
≡ File Edit Search Run Compile Debug Project Options Window Help
Help
calloc
Allocates main memory
void *calloc(size_t nitems, size_t size);
Prototypes in stdlib.h
alloc.h
Allocates space for nitems items of size bytes
each and stores zero in the area.
Returns a pointer to the newly allocated block
or NULL if not enough space exists.
F1 Help on help Alt-F1 Previous topic Shift-F1 Help index Esc Close help

Figure 3-3. ***Getting help on*** **calloc** ***in Turbo C++***

level of menus and a status line at the bottom of the screen showing the current meaning of certain function keys or the purpose of a menu item.

The main menu has eleven items: *System*, *File*, *Edit*, *Search*, *Run*, *Compile*, *Debug*, *Project*, *Options*, *Window*, and *Help*. Each item on the menu bar leads to a pull-down menu through which you can perform various tasks such as load a file, compile it, and run the linked executable. The choices available through the pull-down menus are summarized in Table 3-7.

Table 3-7. ***Summary of Pull-Down Menu Options***

Title	Summary
System	Get information about Turbo C++.
	Repaint screen.
	Access utilities such as grep.
	Jump to Turbo assembler.
	Jump to Turbo Debugger.
File	Create or open a source file for editing.
	Save a file on the disk.
	See a listing of the current directory.
	Change directory.
	Temporarily enter DOS.

Table 3-7. *(cont.)*

Title	Summary
	Quit the Turbo C++ session.
Edit	Edit a source file.
Search	Cut and paste lines.
	Clear a window.
	Search and replace strings.
	Look for a function.
Run	Compile, link, and run a program.
	Automatically invoke debugger if program was compiled with the Debug option.
Compile	Compile a file.
	Link object modules into an executable file.
Debug	Inspect variables.
	Set and clear breakpoints.
	Evaluate expressions and show call stack.
	Select variables to watch.
Project	Set up a project (list of modules that make up an executable program).
Options	Select compiler options.
	Select linker options.
	Specify location of include files and libraries.
Window	Move and resize window.
	Close window.
	Jump from one window to another.
	See a list of windows.
Help	Display table of contents for help.
	Show help index.
	Search for information on a topic.
	See previous topic.

Menu Selection with a Mouse

If you have a mouse installed on your system, you can use it to select menu items in Turbo C++. You will have to install the mouse driver as instructed by the manufacturer before you can use it.

When you start Turbo C++ (by typing *TC*) on a system with a mouse, you will see a *mouse cursor* in the shape of a block character. When you move the mouse around, the cursor will track the motion on the screen. All you need to do is move the cursor to a menu item of choice and click on the left button of the mouse. The pull-down menu will appear. Once again you can move down to the desired item on the pull-down menu and click. Turbo C++ will accept that item as your selection and act upon it.

The mouse is used in the same manner when Turbo C++ prompts you for selections or file names in dialog boxes. You simply position the mouse cursor on the box or area and click the left button. If the box denotes a choice, it takes effect immediately. If the box is meant for typing in a file name, you will see another cursor in that area waiting for you to type in the requested information.

Menu Selections from the Keyboard

Menu selection from the keyboard takes more steps than menu selection with a mouse.

You can select an item from the menu bar by pressing the *Alt* key and the first letter of the item's name. Thus, *Alt-f* (means press the *Alt* key and *f* simultaneously) will activate the *File* menu. Once the pull-down menu appears, you can move up and down using the arrow keys. As you do so, the selected item will appear highlighted. You can press the Enter key to select that item. If you change your mind about making a selection from that pull-down menu, you can use the right and left arrow keys to switch to other pull-down menus. If you don't want to make any selection, press the ESC key to get rid of the pull-down menu.

There is a faster way to select from a menu, however. Turbo C++ always highlights a single character in each menu item in the pull-down menu. You can indicate your choice by pressing that single key. For example, after you select the *File* menu with *Alt-f*, you will notice that the letter *Q* in the item *Quit* is underlined. At this point if you press *q* or *Q*, you will exit Turbo C++.

There are several function keys (*hot keys*) that let you perform specific tasks with a single keystroke. Turbo C++'s hot keys are summarized in Table 3-8.

Table 3-8. ***Summary of Turbo C++'s Hot Keys***

Keystroke	Function
F1	Provide context-sensitive help.
F2	Save the file being edited.
F3	Prompt for a file name and load it into the editor.
F4	Execute program, stopping at the line where the cursor lies.
F5	Toggle between zoomed and unzoomed states of the current window (when zoomed, the entire screen is used to display the window you are in).
F6	Switch to the other window (used to move back and forth between the *Edit* and the *Message* windows).
F7	Execute next statement, stepping into function calls.
F8	Execute next statement, stepping over function calls.
F9	Use MAKE to compile and link your project.
F10	Go to the main menu bar.

Table 3-8. ***(cont.)***

Keystroke	Function
Alt-Spacebar	Go to system menu.
Alt-0	Display a list of windows.
Alt-F1	Go to previous help screen.
Alt-F3	Close currently active window.
Alt-F4	Open an "inspector" window to examine and modify the value of a variable.
Alt-F5	Switch between a saved output screen and the Turbo C++'s interactive screen.
Alt-F7	Go to previous error.
Alt-F8	Go to next error.
Alt-F9	Compile the file currently in the editor.
Alt-C	Go to the *Compile* menu.
Alt-D	Go to the *Debug* menu.
Alt-E	Go to the editor.
Alt-F	Go to the *File* menu.
Alt-H	Go to the *Help* menu.
Alt-O	Go to the *Options* menu.
Alt-P	Go to the *Project* menu.
Alt-R	Run your program.
Alt-S	Go to the Search menu.
Alt-W	Go to the Window menu.
Alt-X	Quit Turbo C++ and return to DOS.
Ctrl-F2	Cancel current debugging session.
Ctrl-F3	Display the call stack.
Ctrl-F5	Change size or position of active window.
Ctrl-F7	Add a watch expression.
Ctrl-F8	Set or clear a breakpoint at the current line.
Ctrl-F9	Begin executing a program.
Ctrl-Break	Stop currently executing program and enter debugger.

Full Menus

Because there are a large number of menu options in the interactive environment, Turbo C++ allows you to manage the complexity by hiding some of these options. The first item in the *Options* menu is used to hide or show some of these less-used menu options. This item is a toggle—each time you select it, you reverse the previous selection. When this line says *Full menus On*, all menu items are accessible to you.

All figures in this chapter were created with the full menus on.

If you run TC and notice that certain menu items are not listed, you should immediately check the first item in the *Options* menu. If this item says *Full menus Off*, select it once to turn the full menus on. Note that when you run TC for the first time, the full menus are off.

EDITING A PROGRAM IN TURBO C++

The first step in creating a program is entering the text and editing it. The Turbo C++ environment provides an editor whose commands are modeled after the popular word processing program, WordStar. If you are familiar with WordStar, you will feel right at home in the Turbo C++ editor. If you don't know the Wordstar commands, learning just a few of them can get you started. As you go along, you can add more commands to your repertoire and before you realize it, you will be proficient with the Turbo C++ editor (and with WordStar as well). Here we will describe the basic editing steps to get you started.

When you start Turbo C++, you are automatically set up ready to type in text. If you want to edit an existing program, you must first open that file. You can do this by selecting the *Open . . .* option from the *File* menu (Figure 3-4). Turbo C++ will ask you for a file name. You can use wildcards: for example, if you enter **.CPP*, Turbo C will display a list of all the files with a *.CPP* extension and let you choose the file to be opened (Figure 3-5).

In the list of file names, you can select ..\ to move up to the parent directory, and if a directory name is displayed, selecting it will bring up a

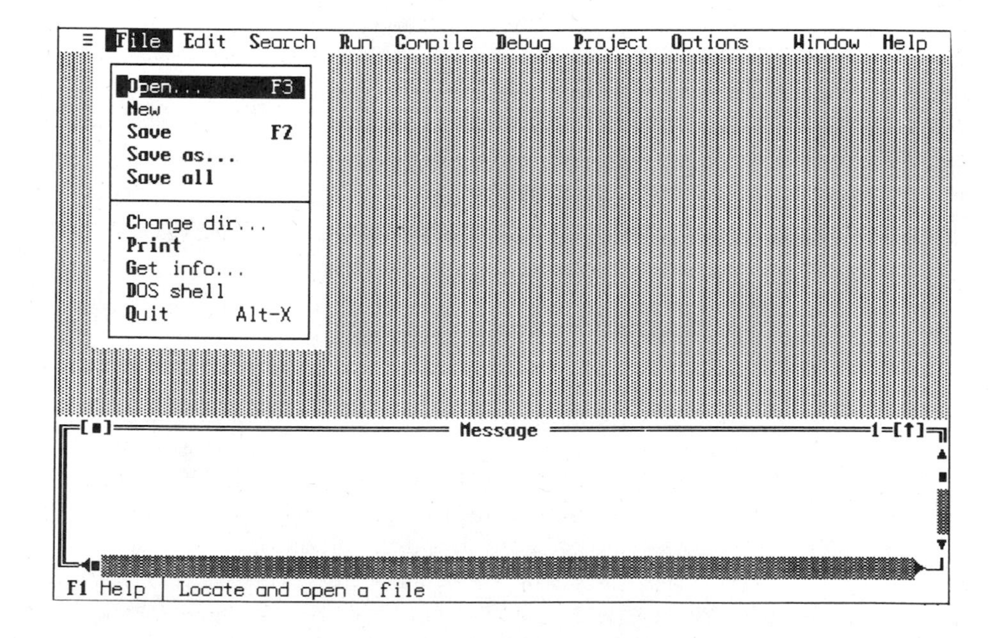

Figure 3-4. ***The* File *menu***

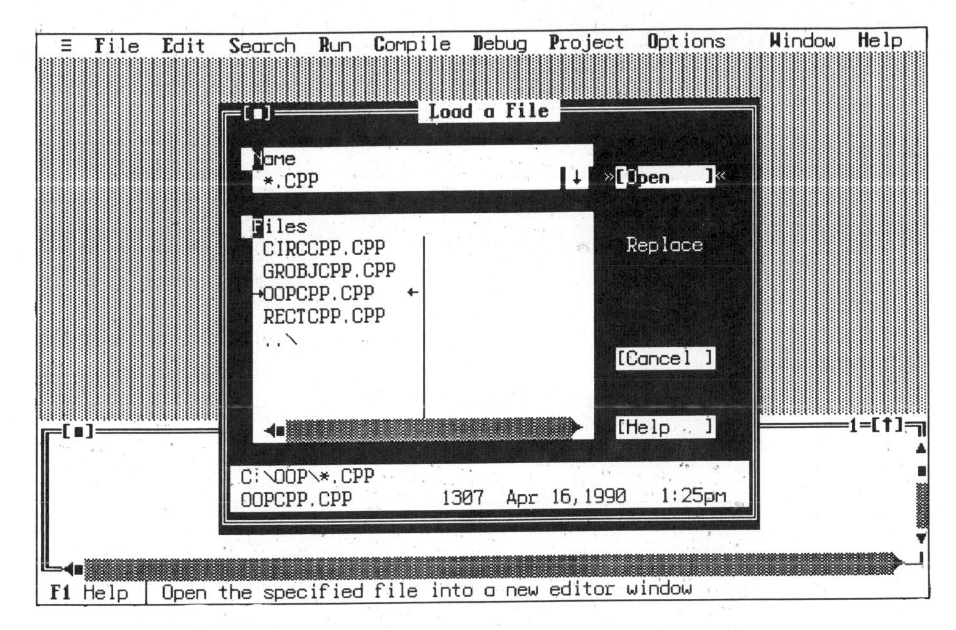

Figure 3-5. *Loading a file into the Turbo C++ environment*

list of the files in that directory. Thus, you can browse through your directories with the *Open* option from the *File* menu.

The Turbo C++ editor has two modes: "insert" and "overtype." In the insert mode, text that you type is inserted into the file, whereas in the overtype mode, each character you type replaces the character that used to be at that position in the file. Normally, you will work in the insert mode. You can toggle between the two modes by pressing Control-V or the *Ins* key (0 on the numeric keypad). The cursor will change shape to indicate the mode: in "insert" mode it is a blinking underline, in "overtype" mode, it changes to a block cursor.

Editing with the Mouse

The mouse makes editing very easy because you simply have to move the cursor to a point and click the left button. You can then begin typing new text there.

When editing multiple files, you can go from one window to another by clicking on the destination window. If that window is obscured, use *List . . .* option in the *Window* menu to get a list of windows. Then you can select the destination window from this list.

You can select a portion of text (for copying or deleting) by placing the mouse cursor at the starting point and dragging it up to the end of the selected text. The selected area will be displayed in reverse video. Once the text is selected, you can select the *Cut* option from the *Edit* menu. This removes the text to an internal buffer called the *Clipboard.* After cutting, the text is held in a buffer, so that the user can move to another place in the file and paste it using the *Paste* option from the *Edit* menu. You can use the *Copy* option to copy text from one location to another. The cut, paste, and copy operations work across multiple windows. Thus, using the interactive environment, you can easily move text from one file to another.

Editor Commands

Table 3-9 gives a summary of the basic editing functions and the keystrokes necessary to do each task.

When you are done editing a source file, you can save it to the disk by selecting the *Save* or the *Save as . . .* option in the *File* menu. The *Save* option saves the file you were editing under its current name. The *Save as . . .* option allows you to save the file under a new name. If you select the *Save as . . .* option, Turbo C++ will prompt you for the new file name.

Table 3-9. ***Basic Editing Functions***

Editing Task	Instructions	
Insert text.	Make sure you are in Insert mode. Now position cursor and type text.	
	Control-N inserts a blank line.	
Toggle mode.	Press the *Ins* key or *Control-V* to toggle between Insert and Overtype modes.	
Position cursor.	Use the arrow keys or the mouse to move around in text.	
	The PGUP and PGDN keys let you scroll text up and down, respectively. Here are a few more keystrokes for moving about:	
	Control-A	Previous word
	Control-F	Next word
	Control-E	Previous line
	Control-X	Next line
	HOME	Beginning of line
	END	End of line
	Control-Q R	Beginning of file
	Control-Q C	End of file
Select text.	Position cursor at the starting character.	
	Press *Control-K B* to mark the beginning of a block. Now move to the end of the block by using the cursor movement keys. Press *Control-K K* to mark the end of the block. The selected text will appear highlighted on the screen.	
Delete text.	The DEL key as well as *Control-G* deletes the character where the cursor is. *Control-Y* deletes the line where the cursor is, and *Control-K Y* deletes selected text.	
Search and replace.	Use *Control-Q F* to search for a string. The editor will appear to prompt you for the string to search. You can repeat the search for the same string by pressing *Control-L*.	

Table 3-9. ***(cont.)***

Editing Task	Instructions
	Use *Control-Q A* to change from one text string into another. You will be prompted for the original string and its replacement.
Copy and move.	You can copy a selected block of text by the *Control-K C* command while *Control-K V* moves the block. The block can be written to the disk with a *Control-K W* and read back by a *Control-K R*.
Undo changes.	You can undo changes to a line as long as the cursor has not moved from that line. Press *Control-Q L* to undo changes to a line.

COMPILING, LINKING, AND RUNNING A PROGRAM IN TURBO C++

Once the source text is ready, you have to compile and link it to build an executable. You can use the *Run* menu to perform these tasks in a single step or you can use the *Compile* menu for this purpose (Figure 3-6). The compiler options are set from the *Options* menu item on the main menu, and the source files that make up a program are specified in a project file.

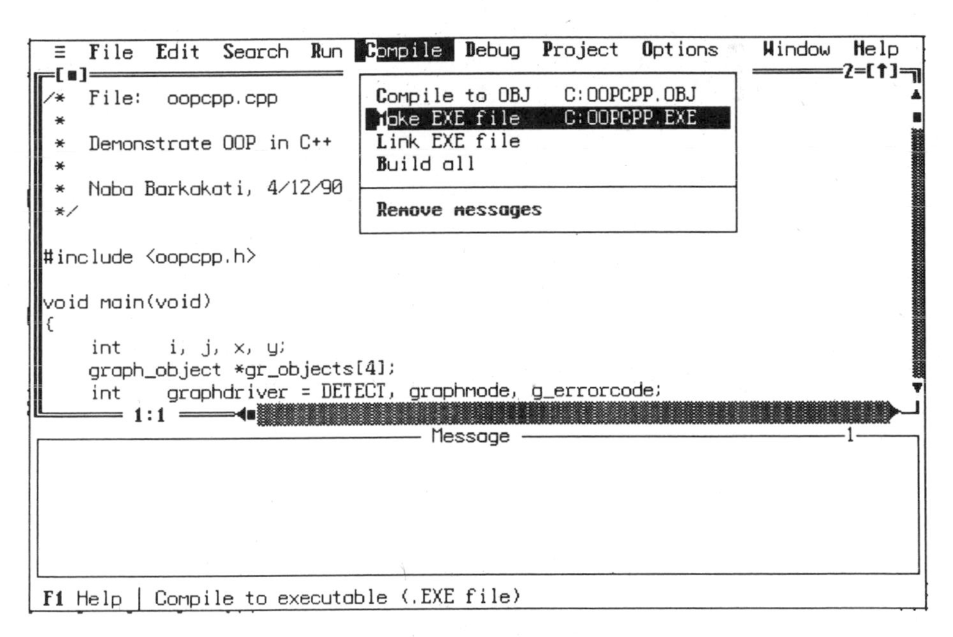

Figure 3-6. ***The* Compile *menu in Turbo C++***

Turbo C++ Project

When you have a single source file in an application you can build the *.EXE* file by using the *Alt-R* (Run) command or by using the *Make EXE file* option in the *Compile* menu. When your program consists of several source file modules, however, you have to create a Turbo C++ project. A *project* is a list of modules that make up your program. For example, if your application requires two files *myappl.c* and *myfuncs.c*, the project will contain

```
myappl
myfuncs
```

You can define the project from the *Project* menu (Figure 3-7). Figure 3-8 shows an examle of adding files to a project. You can save this project definition in a file named *myappl.prj*. From then on, you can create the *.EXE* file for your application by simply pressing the *F9* function key or by selecting the *Run* menu with an *Alt-R*. If you quit Turbo C++ and restart, you can load the project by going to the *Project* menu and selecting the *Open Project* menu option. When you select this option, Turbo C++ will prompt for the name of the project. Once this is done, you can again build your application with a single keystroke (*F9*).

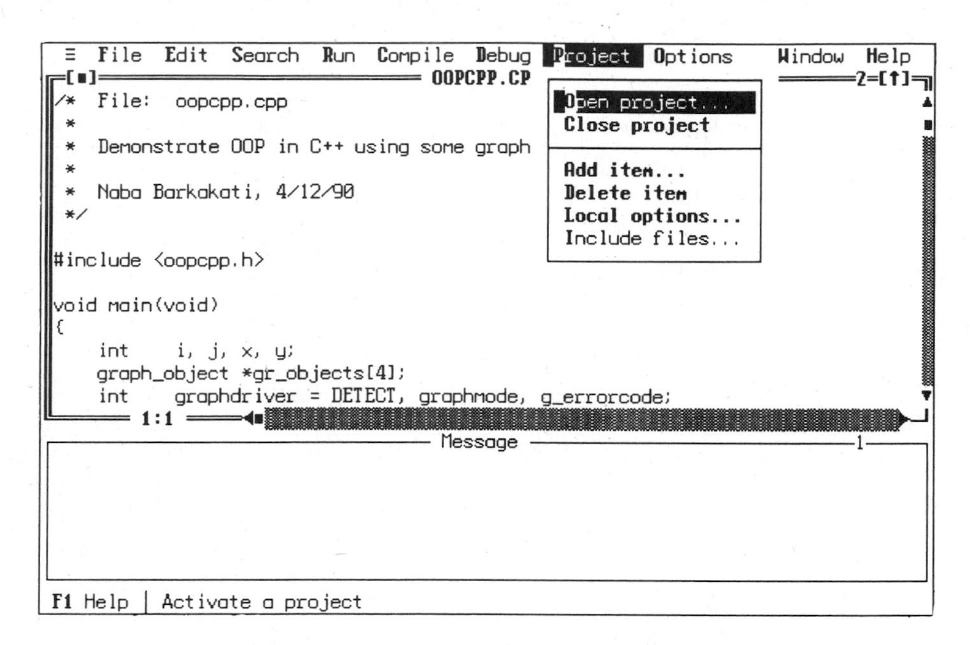

Figure 3-7. ***The* Project *menu in Turbo C++***

Setting the Compile and Link Options

You have to use the *Options* menu (Figure 3-9) to set the options for compiling and linking the current file. When you select the *Compiler* item in the *Options* menu, Turbo C++ presents you with the choices shown in Figure 3-9. Each of these options brings up other menus for specific compiler commands. Some of the items in the submenus are toggles that en-

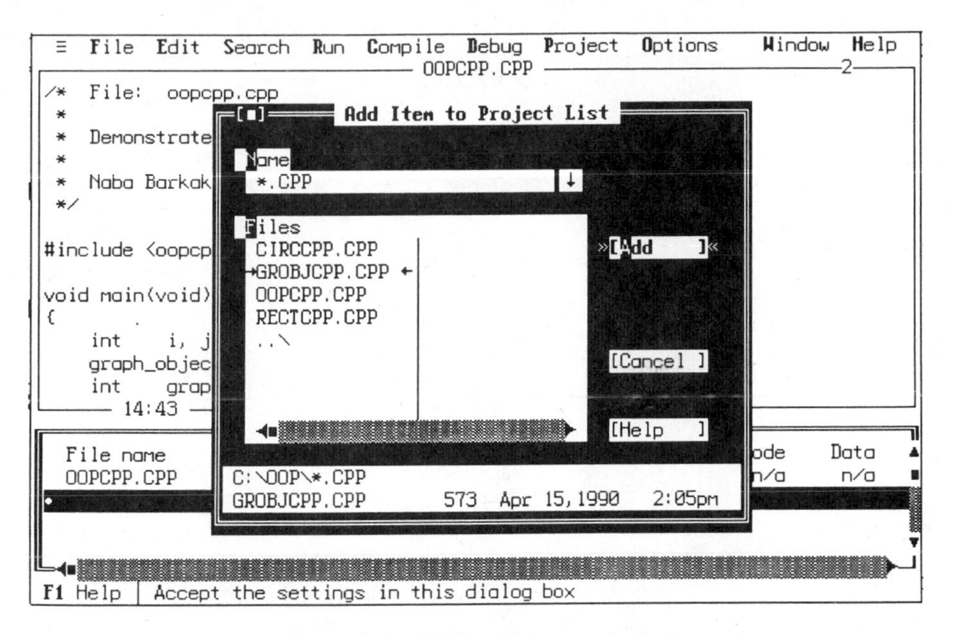

Figure 3-8. ***Adding files to a project***

able or disable a particular feature. The available compiler options are summarized in Table 3-10 along with their command-line equivalents.

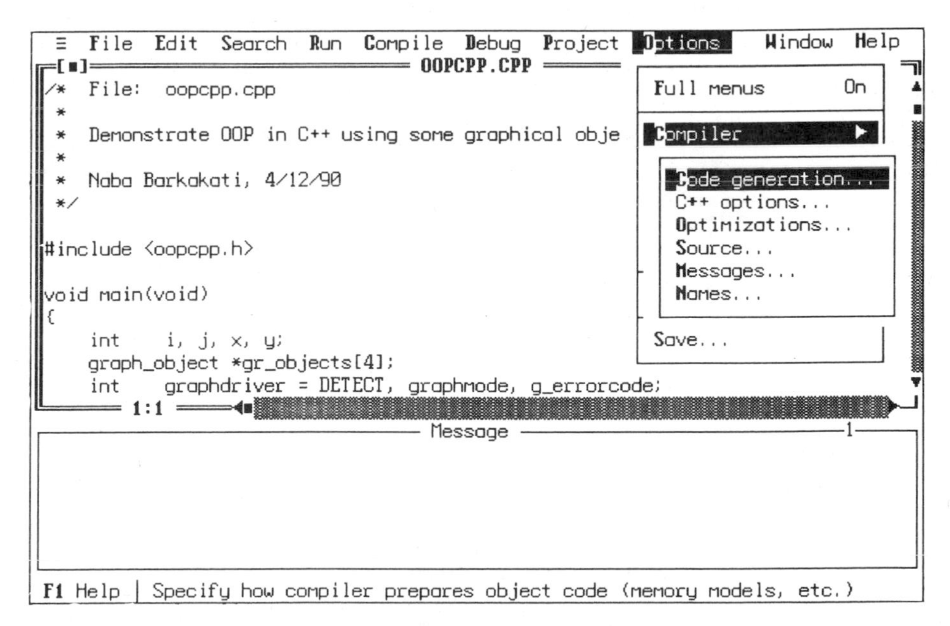

Figure 3-9. ***The* Options *menu in Turbo C++***

Table 3-10. ***Compiler Options in the Interactive Environment***

Option	Meaning
Code generation	This option controls the following features

Option	Command-line equivalent
Model (You can select one of six memory models, tiny, small, medium, compact, large, and huge, from this item)	-mX where X is model
Defines (This will prompt you for definitions of macros in your program)	-D<name>[=<string>]
Calling convention (C or Pascal)	-p- or -p
Instruction Set (8088/8086 or 80186 or 80286)	-1- or -1 or -2
Floating El point (none, emulation, or 8087, or 80287)	-f- or -f or -f87 or -f287
Default char type (signed or unsigned)	-K- or -K
Alignment (byte or word)	-a- or -a
Generate underbars (off or on) (when turned on all external names will be assumed to have a leading underscore)	-u- or -u
Merge duplicate strings (off or on)	-d- or -d
Test stack overflow (off or on)	-N- or -N
Overlay support (on or make this module an overlay)	-Y or -Yo
Treat enums as ints (off or on)	-b- or -b
Fast floating-point (off or on)	-ff- or-ff
Assume SS not equal to DS	-mX! where X is memory model
Line numbers (off or on) (embedded in object code)	-y- or -y
OBJ debug information (off or on) (embedded in object code)	-v- or -v

Option	Meaning
C++ options . . .	This option controls the code generation for C++ programs. The options are as follows:

Option	Command-line equivalent
C++ Virtual tables	None
Use C++ compiler (when file is .CPP or always)	-P forces a C++ compile
Out-of-line in-line functions (on or off)	-vi or -vi-

Table 3-10. *(cont.)*

Option	Meaning
Optimizations	This option controls the optimization strategy to be used by Turbo C++ during code generation. The options are as follows

Option	Command-line equivalent
Optimize for (size or speed)	-O or -G
Use register variables (on or off)	-r or -r-
Register optimization (on or off)	-Z or -Z-
Jump optimization (on or off)	-O or -O-

Option	Meaning
Source	This option specifies the characteristics of the source code. It has the following options

Option	Command-line equivalent
Identifier length (asks compiler to recognize only the first <number> characters of an identifier)	-i<number>
Nested comments (on or off)	-C or -C-
ANSI keywords only (on or off) (checks source for full ANSI compliance)	-A
Turbo C++	-A-
UNIX V	-AU
Kernighan and Ritchie	-AK

Option	Meaning
Messages . . .	This option specifies how Turbo C should deal with errors. The options are

Option	Command-line equivalent
Errors: stop after (how many errors can occur before compilation is stopped)	-j<number>
Warnings: stop after (how many warnings can occur before compilation is stopped)	-g<number>
Display warnings (on or off)	-w or -w-
Portability warnings (enable or disable specific warnings)	-wXXX to turn on -w-XXX to turn off (see Table 3-13)
ANSI violations (enable or disable specific warnings)	-wXXX to turn on -w-XXX to turn off (see Table 3-13)
C++ warning (enable or disable specific warnings)	-wXXX to turn on -w-XXX to turn off (see Table 3-13)

Table 3-10. ***(cont.)***

Option	Meaning	
	Option	**Command-line equivalent**
	Frequent errors (enable or disable specific warnings)	−wXXX to turn on −w−XXX to turn off (see Table 3-13)
Names	This option lets you change the default names of the code and data segments. Normally you do not need to change these names (see Table 3-14).	

After selecting the appropriate options, you can use the *Run* command (*Alt-R*) or select *Build all* under the *Compile* menu to prepare the executable file for your program.

DEBUGGING IN TURBO C++

Turbo C++ includes a source level debugger which is an integrated part of the Turbo C++ interactive environments, and its options are set by selecting the *Debugger* item from the *Options* menu (Figure 3-10). You have to select the *Source Debugging On* option when building the program before you can debug a program in Turbo C++. You can choose to watch the value of certain variables as the program executes or you can set "breakpoints"

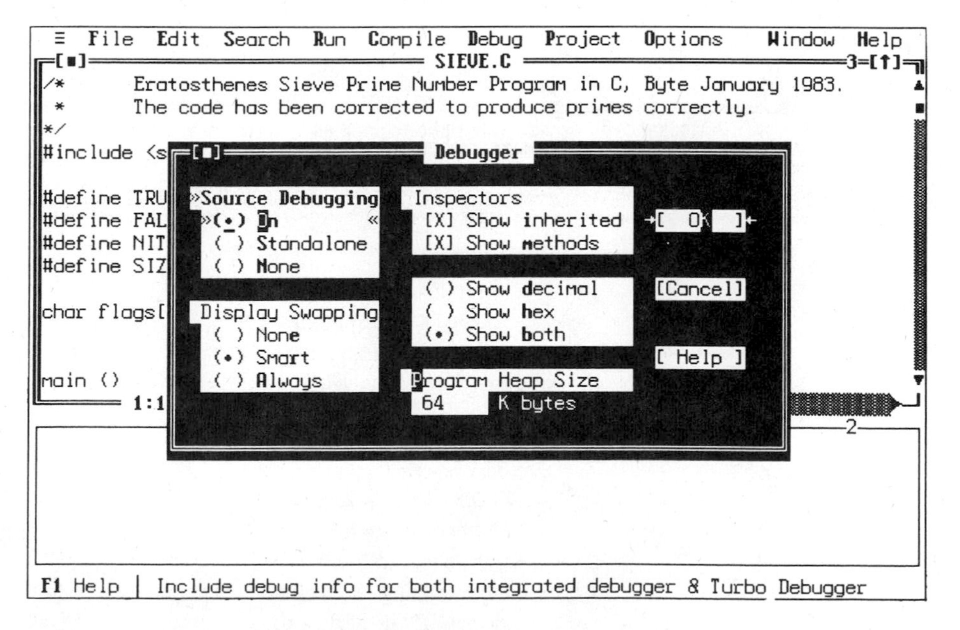

Figure 3-10. ***Setting debugger options***

at certain points in the source file so that the program will stop ("break") when it reaches that line. The debugger in the integrated environment is a subset of a stand-alone debugger also sold by Borland.

When you choose the *Add Watch* option from the *Debug* menu (Figure 3-11), you will be asked to enter an expression whose value you want to watch (Figure 3-12). This expression can be the name of a variable or an expression involving variables appearing in your program. The default expression is the word on which the cursor rests in the Edit window. You can set a breakpoint by first placing the text cursor on the line where the program should break, and then selecting the *Toggle breakpoint* item from the *Debug* menu. Pressing *Control-F8* will also set a breakpoint at the current line. Once these steps are complete, you can run the program by selecting *Run* option from the *Run* menu. Turbo C++ will display (at the bottom of the screen) the values of the expressions being watched whenever they change, and stop when execution reaches the line where you set the breakpoint. Figure 3-13 shows a sample screen display during debugging.

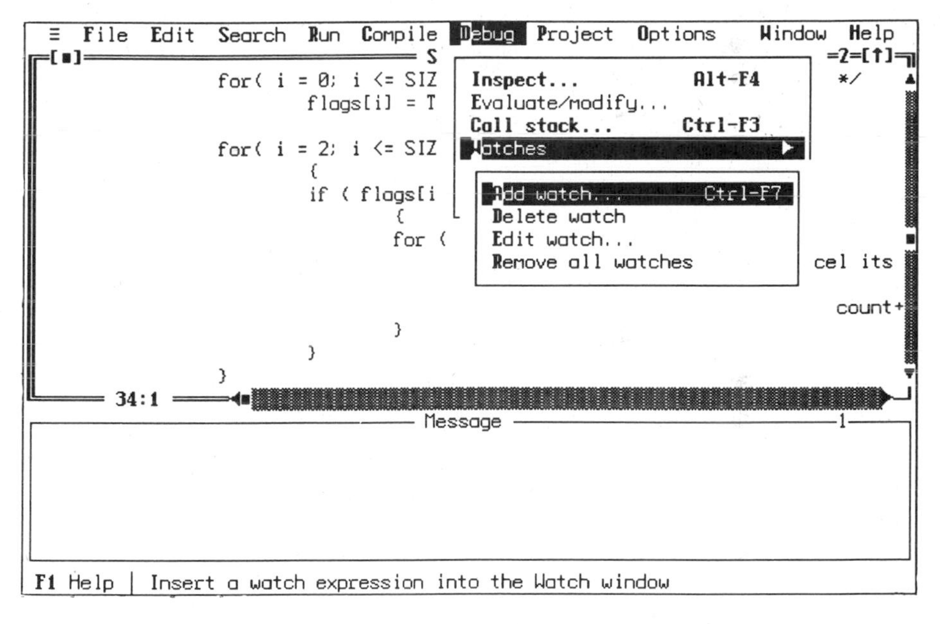

Figure 3-11. Add Watch *option in the* Debug *menu*

You can press function key F7 to execute the program one statement at a time, stepping into each function as it is called. Pressing F8 works similarly, but steps over function calls. Even if you forget to set breakpoints, you can stop a running program and enter the debugger by pressing *Ctrl-Break*.

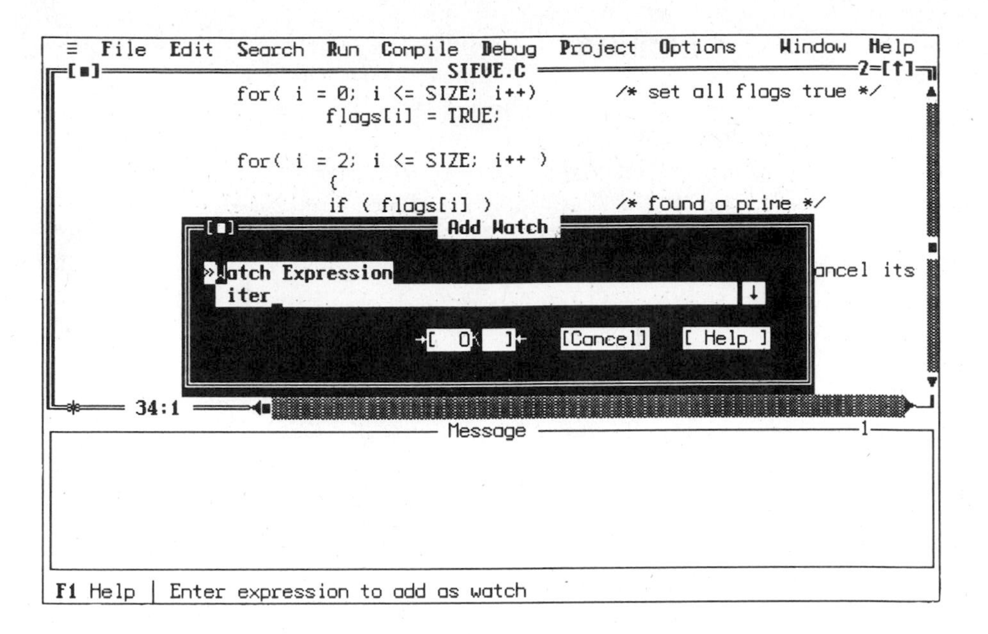

Figure 3-12. **Add Watch** ***dialog box in Turbo C++***

```
 ≡  File  Edit  Search  Run  Compile  Debug  Project  Options   Window  Help
 ─────────────────────────── SIEVE.C ──────────────────────────────────2─
                for( i = 0; i <= SIZE; i++)        /* set all flags true */
                        flags[i] = TRUE;

                for( i = 2; i <= SIZE; i++ )
                        {
                        if ( flags[i] )            /* found a prime */
                                {
                                for ( k = i + i; k <= SIZE; k += i )
                                        flags[k] = FALSE;       /* Cancel its

                                    count++;
                                }
                        }
                }
 ─*── 34:1 ──────────────────────────────────────────────────────────────
 ═[■]══════════════════════════ Watch ═══════════════════════════3═[↑]═
  iter: 1
  i: 73
  count: 20

 F1 Help  F7 Trace  F8 Step  ↵ Edit  Ins Add  Del Delete  F10 Menu
```

Figure 3-13. ***Watch expressions and breakpoint in Turbo C++***

Command-Line Version of Turbo C++

Sometimes a command-line oriented interface is more suitable for your work. For example, you may already have a favorite editor and may not wish to learn to use the editor in the Turbo C++ integrated environment. Another more serious reason may be that your program is too big to be compiled and linked in memory. Or, perhaps your program needs in-line assembly language code which is not allowed in Turbo C++'s interactive environment. In such cases, you can use TCC, the command-line version of the Turbo C++ compiler. Both the compiler and the linker may be accessed via this command-line oriented program named TCC.EXE, but the linker can also be invoked separately as TLINK. Object modules can be organized into libraries by the TLIB utility. The MAKE utility lets you automate the steps involved in creating a new executable: it helps you manage the *compile-link* cycle that you go through when developing a program. In this section, we will provide a quick summary of TCC and the linker to get you going.

TCC: COMPILING AND LINKING

The Turbo C++ compiler is accessed from the command line via the TCC command. You must use the command-line environment when your program needs a feature such as generating assembly language files or compiling in-line assembly language code.

TCC is your gateway to both the compiler and the linker. For a small program with a few modules, you can compile the files and link them into an executable using TCC as simply as

```
TCC test.c rest.c
```

where we assume the *main* function to be in the file TEST.C and some more functions in the file REST.C. TCC will create the object files TEST.OBJ and REST.OBJ, using the small memory model as the default, and invoke the linker to generate the executable TEST.EXE.

Using TCC without any options may be good enough for small test programs, but when you are developing a larger application, you will want to explicitly specify certain options such as the memory model, the type of math library you want to use, and whether or not you want the compiler to optimize your code. You have to specify these choices through command-line options to TCC. For example, we can compile the example program using the large model, generate code for the 8087 math coprocessor, and turn off the generation of stack-checking code by the command:

```
TCC -ml -f87 -N- TEST.C REST.C
```

As you can see from the example, each option begins with a minus sign (–). The next letter tells the compiler the type of the option and subsequent characters and digits specify your complete choice for that type. In the example, the *–ml* option specifies the large memory model, the *–f87* tells the compiler to embed 8087 code in the output, the *–N–* option tells the compiler to turn off stack checking logic it generates at the entry to each function. This last option illustrates another aspect of Turbo C's command-line options. A feature with an *on* or *off* value is turned off by placing a negative sign after the option. Thus, *–N* would enable stack checking while *–N–* would disable that feature.

Table 3-11 shows the options according to the purpose of each category. The complete list of options for TCC is quite extensive and is shown

Table 3-11. ***Option Categories for TCC***

Purpose of Option	Options
Selecting a memory model.	–mc –mh –ml –mm –ms –mt
Default: –ms	–mm! –ms! –mt!
Selecting a floating-point library. Default: –f	–f –f87 –ff –287
Controlling optimization. Default: –r	–G –O –r –Z –rd
Controlling the preprocessor.	–D<name>[=text] –U<name>
Generating code for specific processor and mixed language calls. Default: –1– –d– –p– –u –b	–1 –d –N –p –u –2 –b
Debugger support, error checking and language extensions.	–a –A –C –i<number> –K –y –v –AT –AU –AK
Creating listing, object and executable files.	–B –c –o<filename> –S –X
Specifying assembler to be used to assemble in-line assembly language statements.	–E<name>
Linking.	–e<filename> –M
Errors and warnings.	–g<number> –j<number> –w<XXX>
Naming code and data segments.	–zA<name> –zB <name> –zC<name> –zD<name> –zG<name> –zP<name> –zR<name> –zS<name> –zT<name> –z<letter>*
Passing options to assembler and linker.	–T –l
Compiling as a C++ program.	–P
Using expanded (EMS) or extended memory during compiling. Default: –Qe –Qx–	–Qe –Qx –Qx<number>
Controlling overlays.	–Y –Yo
Controlling in-line expansion in C++.	–Vi
Controling virtual tables in C++.	–V –Vs –V0 –V1

in Table 3-12. For example, all options relating to memory models are listed under the category named *memory model.* This should help you locate the options that are relevant to your specific need.

Some of the options are straightforward, but a few, like the segment naming options (the −*z* family), are difficult to use. To use them intelligently, you need to understand how names of segments affect the layout of code and data in memory. For most applications, you should not have to rename segments at all.

The best approach is to use a minimal set of simple options in the beginning and then as you learn more about the capabilities of the Turbo C++ compiler, you can add the more exotic ones to your repertoire. Table 3-12 gives a brief description of each compiler option. Turbo C++ has a large number of error reporting (−*w*) and segment naming options (−*z*). These are summarized in Tables 3-13 and 3-14, respectively.

Table 3-12. ***List of Options for TCC****

Option	Action by TCC
−1	Generate 80186/286 Instructions.
	Default setting: −1− (8088/8086 instructions).
−2	Generate 80286 protected mode instructions.
−A	Check code for full ANSI compliance.
	Otherwise, compiler allows the non-ANSI keywords (default).
	`asm cdecl far huge interrupt near pascal`
	`_cs _ds _es _ss _CS _DS _ES _SS _AH _AL _AX _BH _BL _BX`
	`_CH _CL _CX _DH _DL _DX _BP _DI _SI _SP`
−AT	Allow Turbo C++ keywords (same as −A−).
−AK	Allow Kernighan and Ritchie keywords only.
−AU	Allow UNIX System V keywords only.
−B	Compile via an intermediate assembly language step.
	Invoke assembler to process the in-line assembly code.
−C	Allow nested comments.
−D<name>	Define a macro.
−E<name>	Use alternate assembler to assemble in-line assembly language statements.
−G	Optimize code for speed.
−I<dirname>	Search the named directory for include files.
−K	Assume that *char* data type is unsigned (default is −K− meaning that *char* is signed).
−L<dirname>	Search the named directory for library files.
−M	Generate link map.
−N	Check for stack overflow at each function entry.
−O	Optimize for smaller code size by eliminating redundant jumps.
−P	Compile source file assuming it is a C++ program.

Table 3-12. (cont.)

Option	Action by TCC
−Qe	Use all available expanded memory (default).
−Qx	Use all available extended memory.
−Qx<number>	Use extended memory beyond <number>-K bytes.
−S	Generate assembly language output.
−T<string>	Pass the string as an option to the assembler.
−U<name>	Undefine a macro.
−V	Generate smart virtual tables.
−Vs	Generate local virtual tables.
−V0	Generate external virtual tables.
−V1	Allow virtual tables to be references by other modules.
−X	Do not generate autodependency output.
−Y	Enable overlay code generation.
−Yo	Make this file an overlay.
−Z	Optimize register usage.
−a	Use word-alignment for integer sized data items (default is −a− meaning use byte alignment).
−b	Assume thast enums are integers.
−c	Compile and generate object file only.
−d	Merge duplicate strings (default is −d − meaning do not merge).
−e<filename>	Use <filename> as the name of the executable file.
−f	Use the floating-point emulator (default).
−ff	Generate code for fast floating-point (default).
−f87	Generate code for 8087 coprocessor.
−f287	Generate code for 80287 coprocessor.
−f−	Assume no floating-point operations in this file.
−g<number>	Stop after <number> warnings.
−i<number>	Use maximum identifier length equal to <number>.
−j<number>	Stop after <number> errors.
−k	Generate a standard stack frame (default).
−l<option>	Pass options to the linker.
−mc	Use the compact memory model.
−mh	Use the huge memory model.
−ml	Use the large memory model.
−mm	Use the medium memory model.
−mm!	Use medium memory model but assume DS! = SS.
−ms	Use the small memory model (default).
−ms!	Use small memory model but assume DS! = SS.
−mt	Use the tiny memory model.
−mt!	Use tiny memory model but assume DS! = SS.
−n<dirname>	Save output files in directory named <dirname>.

Table 3-12. ***(cont.)***

Option	Action by TCC
–o<filename>	Save object code in file named <filename>.
–p	Generate code that uses the Pascal calling convention (default is –p– meaning calling convention is C).
–r	Use register variables (default).
–rd	Use register storage only for the variable declared with the register keyword.
–u	Assume that all external variable names begin with an underscore (default).
–v	Include information in the object code so that the program can be debugged by the Turbo C++ integrated or stand-alone debugger.
–vi	Enable in-line expansion in C++ programs.
–w	Enable all warnings.
–w<XXX>	Enable the warning named <XXX> (See Table 3-13).
–w–<XXX>	Disable the warning named <XXX>.
–y	Embed line number information in object code for use by a symbolic debugger.
–z<letter><name>	Class of options for renaming code and data segments (see Table 3-14).

*[. . .] denotes option items; < . . . > indicates required arguments.

Table 3-13. ***Error and Warning Reporting Options of TCC Compiler****

Option	Message Generated by TCC
	Category: ANSI Violation (all except –wbbf –weas –will –wpin ON by default)
–wbbf	Bit fields must be signed or unsigned int.
–wbei	Initialized with wrong type.
–wbfs	Bit field assumed signed int.
–wbig	Hexadecimal or octal constant too large.
–wdcl	Declaration with no identifier.
–wdpu	Declare <function> prior to use in prototype.
–wdup	Redefinition of <name> is not identical.
–weas	Integer assigned to enum.
–wext	<name> is both static and extern.
–will	Bad syntax in pragma.
–wpin	Brackets not closed in initialization.
–wret	Both return and return of a value are used.
–wstr	<name> not part of structure.
–wstu	Undefined structure <name>.
–wsus	Suspicious pointer conversion.

Table 3-13. *(cont.)*

Option	Message Generated by TCC
	Category: ANSI Violation (all except −wbbf −weas −will −wpin ON by default)
−wvoi	Void functions may not return a value.
−wzdi	Dividing by zero.
−wzst	Zero length structure.
	Category: Common Errors (all except −wrvl ON by default)
−waus	<name> is assigned a value that is never used.
−wdef	Possible use of <name> before definition.
−weff	Code has no effect.
−wpar	Parameter <name> is never used.
−wpia	Possible incorrect assignment.
−wrch	Unreachable code.
−wrvl	Function should return a value.
	Category: Less Common Errors (all OFF by default)
−wamb	Ambiguous operators need parentheses.
−wamp	Superfluous & with function or array.
−wnod	No declaration for function <name>.
−wpro	Call to function with no prototype.
−wstv	Structure passed by value.
−wuse	<name> declared but never used.
	Category: Portability Warnings (−wapt, −wcpt, −wrng, and −wrpt ON by default)
−wapt	Nonportable pointer assignment.
−wcln	Constant is long.
−wcpt	Nonportable pointer comparison.
−wrng	Constant out of range in comparison.
−wrpt	Nonportable return type conversion.
−wsig	Conversion may lose significant digits.
−wucp	Mixing pointers to signed and unsigned char.
	Category: C++ Warnings (all except −watt, −whid, −wncf, −wscp ON by default)
−watt	Assignment to *this* not allowed.
−wflo	Program might skip initialization.
−whid	One function is another virtual function.
−winl	Function not expanded in-line.
−wlin	Variable initialized with temporary value.
−wlvc	Temporary value passed to function.
−wncf	Nonconstant function called *const*.
−wnci	Uninitialized *const* member.

Table 3-13. ***(cont.)***

Option	Message Generated by TCC
Category: C++ Warnings (all except –watt, –whid, –wncf, –wscp ON by default)	
–wobi	Base initialization without a class name.
–wofp	Obsolete style for function definition.
–womf	Obsolete syntax.
–wovl	Use of *overload* unnecessary.
–wscp	Same identifier used for structure name and tag.

*< . . . > is replaced by actual name in error message.

Table 3-14. ***Segment Naming Options of the TCC Compiler***

Option	Action by TCC
–zA<name>	Change name of the code segment class to <name>. The default name is CODE.
–zB<name>	Change name of the uninitialized data segment class to <name>. The default name is BSS.
–zC<name>	Change name of the code segment to <name>. The default name is _TEXT, except in medium, large, and huge models, where it is <filename>_TEXT.
–zD<name>	Change the name of the uninitialized data segment to <name>. The default name is _BSS. Note: there is no such segment in the huge memory model.
-ZE<name>	Use <name> as the name of the segment where far data is stored. The default name is the name of the far data item with a _FAR as suffix.
-ZF<name>	Change the name of the class of far data to <name>. The default name is FAR_DATA.
–zG<name>	Change the name of the uninitialized data segment group to <name>. The default name is DGROUP. Note: there is no such segment in the huge memory model.
-ZH<name>	Place all far data into the group named <name>. The default is to not group far data.
–zP<name>	Use <name> as the name of the code segment group. Normally there is no code segment group.
–zR<name>	Change the name of the initialized data segment to <name>. The default name is _DATA except in the huge models, where the name is <filename>_DATA.
–zS<name>	Change the name of the initialized data segment group to <name>. The default name is DGROUP. Note: there is no such segment in the huge model.
–zT<name>	Change the name of the initialized data segment class to <name>. The default name is DATA.

*<name> denotes the actual name for the segment. If <name> is a *, the default segment name is used.

It is quite tedious to type in the options you choose to use with TCC to compile and link your program, especially since you would have to do it repeatedly as you develop your program. Besides, you can only enter a maximum of 128 characters on the command line which means that if you select a large number of options you will not be able to enter them on the command line to TCC even if you were willing to type them at the keyboard. Turbo C++ provides three ways to solve this problem.

You can define a configuration file named TURBOC.CFG with the options you plan to use. For example, if we placed the following line in TURBOC.CFG:

```
-mm -N- -f87 -IC:\TURBOC\INCLUDE -LC:\TURBOC\LIB
```

then invoking the compiler with a *TCC <filename>* will be equivalent to the command *TCC –mm –f87 –IC:\TURBOC\INCLUDE –LC:\TURBOC\LIB <filename>*. Thus, the named program will be compiled and linked using the medium model (–mm), without any stack checking calls (–N–), and using in-line 8087 instructions for floating-point operations. We have also specified that the include files and the object libraries are in the directories C:\TURBOC\INCLUDE and C:\TURBOC\LIB, respectively.

Another approach is to place the compile command in a DOS batch file that takes the file name as an argument and use the batch file to do the job. An example (using the same options as before) might be

```
echo off
if not "%1" == "" goto run
:usage
echo ! usage:  RUNTC filename
echo !
echo ! where    filename is the program you are testing
echo !          (do not include extension, .C assumed)
echo !
goto end
:run
if exist %1.c goto filefound
echo ! RUNTC: File %1.c not found. Exiting...
goto end
:filefound
echo ! Now starting TCC...
TCC -mm -N- -f87 -IC:\TURBOC\INCLUDE -LC:\TURBOC\LIB %1.c
:end
```

If this batch file is named RUNTC.BAT, you can compile and link a file TEST.C by the command *runtc test.* The batch file first checks if there is an argument present. If it finds the argument, it checks if the file named by the argument exists. If all goes well, RUNTC.BAT invokes TCC using the options of your choice.

These two approaches are fine when you have the entire program in a single file. If you are working on a larger project, it is best to use the Turbo C++ MAKE utility. MAKE is invoked by the command *MAKE –f<makefile>* where <makefile> is the name of a file that contains the commands for MAKE. For a program that consists of several files, you will set up the MAKE commands to generate the object codes and then separately invoke LINK to build the executable. Apart from automating the building of an executable, MAKE also makes sure that it compiles only those modules that have changed since the last compilation, thus saving considerable time. It does so by examining the time of last modification stamped on the files. A source file is compiled only if it was modified at a later time than the corresponding object file. Refer to the documentation on MAKE included in the *Turbo C++ User's Guide* that comes with the Turbo C++ compiler for full details. Here is a short sample <makefile>.

```
################################################################# #
#   Makefile for Turbo C++ MAKE
#   Comments start with '#'
#
#   Model set to small

MODEL=s

# Compiler flags -- generate object code only (-c option)

CFLAGS=-m$(MODEL) -N- -f87 -IC:\TURBOC\INCLUDE;. -c

TCC=TCC $(CFLAGS)

# Path for library files

LIB=C:\TURBOC\LIB

# General inference rules
# Rule to make .OBJ files from .C files

.C.OBJ:
      $(TCC) $*.C

# Rule to make the executable

OBJLIST=prog.obj file1.obj file2.obj
```

```
prog.exe:  $(OBJLIST)
        TLINK $(LIB)\c0$(MODEL) $(OBJLIST), $*,,\
             $(LIB)\fp87 $(LIB)\math$(MODEL) $(LIB)\c$(MODEL)

# Dependencies for the object files

prog.obj: prog.c local.h common.h

file1.obj: file1.c common.h

file2.obj: file2.c local.h
```

This MAKE file is for building a program named PROG.EXE which has three source files: PROG.C, FILE1.C, and FILE2.C. There are two include files LOCAL.H and COMMON.H. The MAKE commands consist of dependency rules showing, for each file, the other files that it depends on. The dependency list is followed by a line showing how to prepare that file. If a generic rule is defined (for example, "build an .OBJ file out of a .C by using TCC with the following options"), you do not have to explicitly state the command to build a file. In our sample make file, PROG.OBJ depends on the source files PROG.C, COMMON.H, and LOCAL.H and PROG.EXE depends on the object files PROG.OBJ, FILE1.OBJ, and FILE2.OBJ. The TLINK command to build the executable is explictly stated because we have not provided a rule to arrive at an executable from object modules.

TLINK: THE LINKER

Although TCC invokes the linker, you may sometimes want to invoke the linker alone, especially when no compilation is necessary. So you need to know the command-line options for the linker as well. Table 3-15 describes the linker options together with their meaning.

Table 3-15. ***List of Options for TLINK***

Option	Action by TLINK
/3	Enables 32-bit processing which is necessary when linking modules containing object code for the Intel 80386 microprocessor.
/c	Assumes that case of letters is significant in symbols. (By default, TLINK ignores case, regarding TURBO, Turbo, and turbo as the same.)
/d	Warns if it finds duplicate symbols in the libraries.
/e	Disables the use of extended dictionaries when searching a library for a module.
/i	Initializes and outputs all segments to the executable file.
/l	Includes source line numbers in the map file. (You must have used the –y option with TCC.)
/m	Produces map file with a list of public symbols.
/n	Does not search the default libraries indicated by the compiler in the object file.

Table 3-15. ***(cont.)***

Option	Action by TLINK
/o	Overlays all modules and libraries that follow this switch.
/s	Produces a detailed map of segments.
/t	Produces a .COM file instead of an .EXE file. The object modules should be compiled with the –mt compiler flag (tiny model).
/x	Does not create any map file at all.
/ye	Uses expanded memory for swapping.
/yx	Uses extended memory for swapping.
/v	Includes debugging information in the executable file so that the Turbo C debugger can be used to debug the resulting program.

Let's C . . .

This tutorial covered the basics of programming in Turbo C++. With the information we have provided in this chapter, you should now be familiar with the steps involved in using Turbo C to edit, compile, and link a C or C++ program.

This is, however, only the beginning. As you learn more about C, C++, and the Turbo C++ environment, you will, no doubt, want to build larger and more complicated programs. You can make your job easy by exploiting the large assortment of routines available in the Turbo C++ library. In the remainder of this book, we will show you how to use the library routines. We will provide detailed coverage of Turbo C++'s run-time library routines, complete with how and why they work, and present examples showing how to use each routine. As you go through the sections, you may find it instructive to compile and run some of the examples in Turbo C++. This will help you learn more about the untapped capabilities of the Turbo C++ library.

II Process Control and Memory Management

- Process Control
- Variable-Length Argument List
- Memory Allocation and Management
- Buffer Manipulation

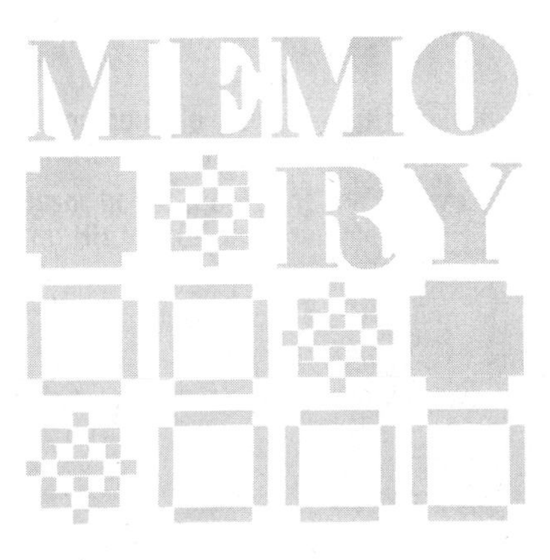

Chapter 4 Process Control

Introduction

One way to reduce software development time is to reuse existing code. You can use existing C routines by function calls from your C program. Turbo C++ even allows you to call routines written in other languages. But what if the existing code that suits your need is an "executable" (an MS-DOS .COM or .EXE) file? Here is an example.

Suppose you are developing an application that provides an electronic mail (e-mail) service. You want the user to enter and edit a message that your application will then send over the network to another computer. An editor is ideal for entering and editing text, and every PC has one. If you can invoke the editor from your application program while you have the text prepared and stored in a temporary file, you won't have to develop and debug an editor from scratch. Luckily, the Turbo C++ library provides the facilities that let you run another program from your program. This is called "executing a child" process, or "spawning" or "launching" a child. The Turbo C++ library contains a set of "process control" routines that help you launch a child process and control certain aspects of your own process. For our e-mail example, you could use the *spawnlp* function in the process control category to invoke an editor (you can ask the user to enter the name) in which the user can prepare the mail message. Use of the *spawn* functions is demonstrated in the reference pages.

Next we examine what MS-DOS processes are, how they are started and terminated, and how error conditions (exceptions) are handled by processes.

Concepts: Process, Environment, and Signals

A process is an executable program in memory and its associated *environment.* Anytime you run a program, you create a process. A program's environment is stored in the PSP and it includes all the information necessary to execute the program. This includes information about the locations of its code and data in memory and which files were opened in the program.

ENVIRONMENT OF A PROCESS

When you run MS-DOS on your PC, and see the familiar *A>* (or *C>*, if you have a hard disk) prompt, you are talking to a process that is running the DOS command processor COMMAND.COM. In this case, the environment includes the DOS variables of PATH, COMSPEC, and PROMPT. Specifically, the environment associated with a process in MS-DOS consists of an array of null-terminated strings, with each string defining a symbol in the format *VARIABLE=Value.* For example, the MS-DOS command interpreter, COMMAND.COM, is located by DOS using the definition of an environment variable named COMSPEC. You can see a list of the environment variables by typing SET at the DOS prompt. On my PC-AT, the result of typing SET is

```
C:\> set
COMSPEC=C:\COMMAND.COM
PATH=C:\;C:\DOS31;C:\BIN;C:\KERMIT;C:\TC\BIN
INCLUDE=c:\include
LIB=c:\lib
TMP=c:\tmp
PROMPT=$p$g
```

Each symbol to the left of the equal sign is an environment variable and the string to the right of the equal sign is its value. As shown in Figure 4-1, the environment strings are laid out one after another with a zero byte (a null character) separating one variable's definition from the next. The end of the environment is marked by two consecutive null characters.

You can also define environment variables with the DOS command SET. When defining in batch files, you embed the definition in a line. Typically you define the variables PATH and PROMPT in the AUTOEXEC.BAT file.

Passing Information via Environment Variables

The environment variables are used to pass information to processes. For example, when you type the program name, TCC, COMMAND.COM will look up the list of directories in the PATH environment variable and search in each directory for an executable file named TCC (TCC.COM, TCC.EXE, or TCC.BAT). Since TCC.EXE is the Turbo C++ compiler's command inter-

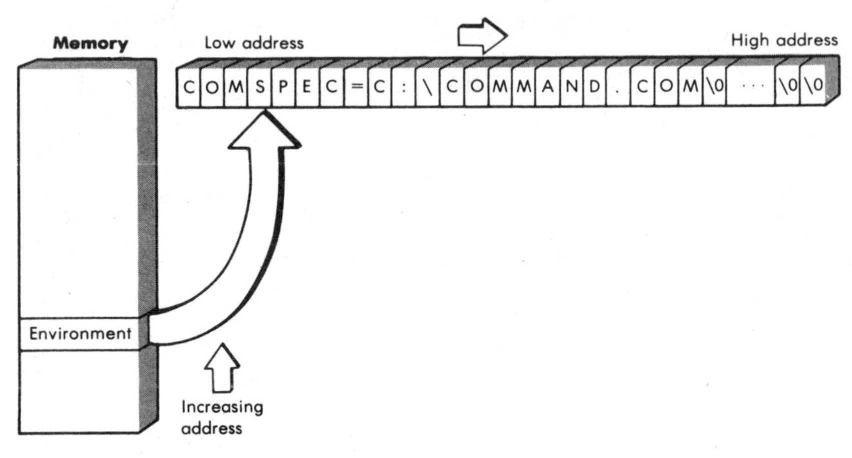

Figure 4-1. ***The MS-DOS environment***

face program, COMMAND.COM will find it in the directory C:\TC\BIN (where this program normally resides), load it into memory, and run it. When DOS runs a program, in this case, TCC.EXE, it passes a copy of the parent's environment to the child. Thus the environment variables that you saw when you typed SET will be available to the TCC.EXE.

Using the Environment in Your Programs

The capability of accessing environment variables can be exploited by your C programs as well. For example, if you are developing an e-mail application, you can decide that you will send a copy of a mail message to all addresses listed in an environment variable DISTLIST. You can get at this environment variable via the library routine *getenv*. There is another routine named *putenv* which lets you add new definitions to your environment table. Keep in mind, however, that these definitions will vanish the moment your program exits because your program's environment table is only a copy of the parent's environment. Changes made to this copy will not affect the parent's table. A little later, we will describe another way of accessing the environment of your process.

CHILD PROCESS

Suppose you wrote, compiled, and linked a small C program called TEST.EXE whose source file is

```
#include <stdio.h>
main(int argc, char **argv, char **envp)
{
    int i;
/* Print the command-line arguments */
    printf("Number of command-line arguments = %d\n", argc);
```

```
    for (i = 0; i < argc; i++)
    {
        printf("Argument %d = %s\n", i, argv[i]);
    }
/* Print the environment */
    printf("\nEnvironment contains:\n");
    for(i = 0; envp[i] != NULL; i++)
    {
        printf("%s\n", envp[i]);
    }
}
```

You run the program by typing *TEST One Two Three* at the DOS prompt. The *One Two Three* following the name of the program are called "command-line arguments." This mechanism is used to pass optional items to the program. As shown in Figure 4-2, COMMAND.COM will execute TEST.EXE as a child process. If the file TEST.EXE is in the directory C:\TEST, COMMAND.COM will find it, no matter what the current default directory is, as long as the environment variable PATH has C:\TEST in it. For example, you may define PATH as PATH=C:\DOS;C:\BIN;C:\TEST. The child process running TEST.EXE also receives a copy of all the DOS environment variables.

To the child process running TEST.EXE, COMMAND.COM is the parent. In this case, the parent waits until the child finishes its job. When TEST.EXE exits, the PC will run the parent process again and you will see the DOS prompt.

ACCESSING COMMAND-LINE ARGUMENTS AND ENVIRONMENT

Let's see how to access the command-line arguments and the environment in a Turbo C++ program (this is the second method of accessing the environment, the first is to use the function *getenv*). Note that in the example program, the *main* function has three arguments. The first argument is an integer, *argc*, containing the number of command-line arguments. In MS-DOS versions 3.0 and later, the first argument is always the full pathname of the program. So *argc* will be 4 in our example. The argument *argv* is a pointer to an array of C strings (see Figure 4-2), each containing one command-line argument. In our example, argv[0] will be C:\TEST \TEST.EXE, which is the full pathname of the executable file.

The environment is passed to a process in the same manner as the command-line arguments. Thus, *envp* is also a pointer to an array of null-terminated C strings, each containing one environment setting. A NULL entry signifies the end of the environment table.

EXIT CODES FOR PROCESSES

When a child process exits, it returns an integer value, called the "exit code," to its parent just as a function call would return a value. The exit code signifies whether the program executed successfully. An exit code

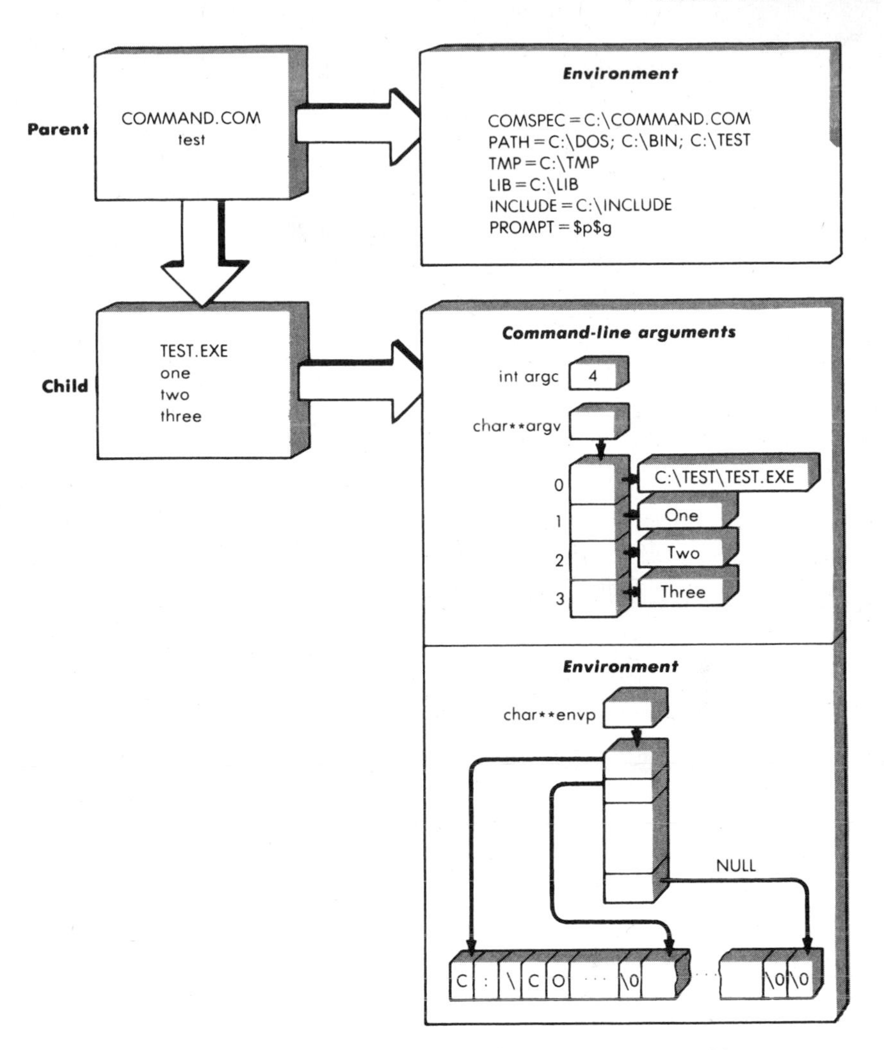

Figure 4-2. *Process running TEST.EXE under MS-DOS*

equal to zero normally means that the child process executed successfully. Nonzero exit codes indicate error. If you execute a program from a DOS batch file, the exit code from the program is available in a parameter named ERRORLEVEL. You could check for erroneous return from our example program by using the batch code fragment:

```
TEST One Two Three
if not ERRORLEVEL 0 echo TEST failed
```

SIGNALS

"Signals" are the operating system's way of interrupting a process when certain error conditions, also called "exceptions," occur. The signal mechanism is present in UNIX and is supported by most C libraries. Prior to version 2.0 Turbo C did not support UNIX and ANSI conformant signals. A software-only signalling mechanism was available via the *ssignal* and *gsignal* routines. Turbo C 2.0 and Turbo C++, however, provide full support for UNIX and ANSI conforming signals, and discontinue the *ssignal* and *gsignal* functions. Each recognized exception has a routine to handle the exception, and you can use the library routine *signal* to install your own routine to handle a particular signal. When a signal occurs, the appropriate handler is called. The *raise* function can be used to artificially generate a signal.

Constants are defined in the *signal.h* header for each signal that Turbo C++ can handle. Although there are six signals, as shown in Table 4-1, only three are relevant in MS-DOS systems: SIGABRT, SIGFPE, and SIGINT. Of these, the SIGINT signal is most often used. Generated when you hit a Control-C on the PC's keyboard, it normally terminates the process, but you can install your own handler for SIGINT to do something else. The example in the reference page on *signal* shows how this is done.

Table 4-1. ***List of Signals in Turbo C++***

Signal	Exception Condition	Default Action
SIGABRT	Abnormal termination of program.	Terminate program with exit code 3.
SIGFPE	Floating-point error, such as overflow, division by zero, etc.	Terminate program.
SIGILL	Illegal instruction. This exception is not generated by MS-DOS, but is included for ANSI compatibility.	Not applicable in MS-DOS.
SIGINT	Generated when user hits Control-C.	Generate software interrupt number 23h.
SIGSEGV	Illegal memory access. This exception is not generated under MS-DOS, but is included for ANSI compatibility.	Not applicable in MS-DOS.
SIGTERM	Termination request sent to the program. This is not generated in MS-DOS, but is included for ANSI compatibility.	Not applicable in MS-DOS.

NONLOCAL GOTOS *IN C:* LONGJMP *AND* SETJMP

Sometimes it is handy to be able to abort what you were doing and get back to where you started. For example, you may want to return to execute some code for error recovery no matter where an error is detected in your application. The *setjmp* and the *longjmp* functions provide the tools to accomplish this. The *setjmp* function saves the "state" or the "context" of the process and the *longjmp* uses the saved context to revert to a previous point in the program. What is the context of the process? In general, the context of a process refers to information that enables you to reconstruct exactly the way the process is at a particular point in its flow of execution. In C programs the relevant information includes quantities such as the address of the current instruction and of the registers SP, BP, SI, DI, DS, ES, and SS.

To understand the mechanics of *setjmp* and *longjmp*, look at the following code fragment:

```
#include <setjmp.h>
jmp_buf saved_context;

main()
{
    if (setjmp(saved_context) == 0)
    {
        do_something();
    }

    else
    {
/* This part executed when longjmp is called */
        handle_error();
    }
}

do_something()
{
    int something_wrong;
    :
    :
    if(something_wrong) longjmp(saved_context, 1);
}
```

Incidentally, the data type *jmp_buf* is defined in the header file *setjmp.h*. This is a system-dependent data type because different systems might require different amounts of information to capture the context of a process. In Turbo C++, *jmp_buf* is simply an array of ten 2-byte integers, as shown in Figure 4-3. Upon entry to *setjmp*, the stack contains the address of the buffer *saved_context* and the address of the *if* statement in the main function, to which *setjmp* will return. The *setjmp* function copies this return address (2 bytes of segment address and 2 bytes of offset) as well as the current values of the seven registers, SP, BP, SI, DI, DS, ES, and SS, and the processor flags into the buffer *saved_context*. Then *setjmp* returns with a zero. In this case, the *if* statement is satisfied and *do_something( )* is called.

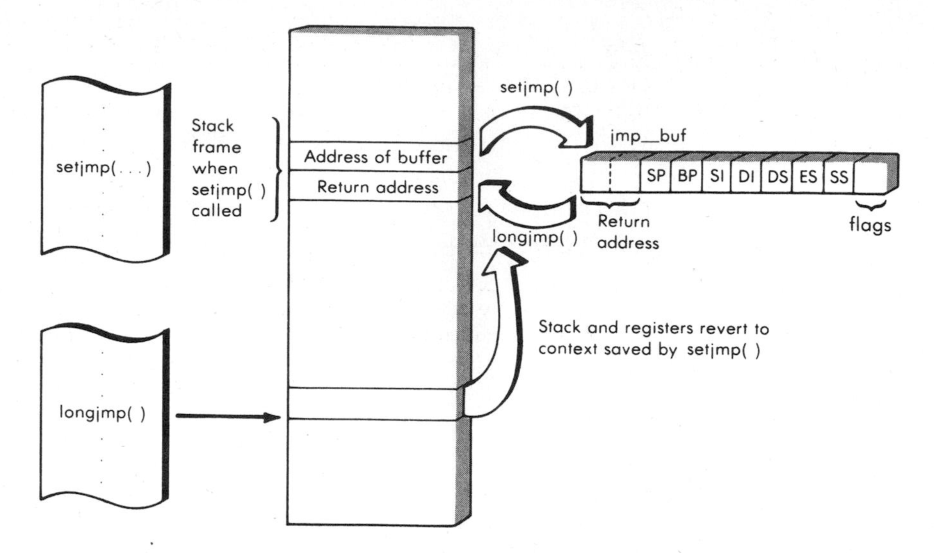

Figure 4-3. setjmp *and* longjmp *in action*

When something goes wrong in *do_something( )* (indicated by the flag *something_wrong*), we call *longjmp* with two arguments: the first is the buffer that contains the context to which we will return. When the stack reverts back to this saved state, and the return statement in *longjmp* is executed, it will be as if we were returning from the call to *setjmp*, which originally saved the buffer *saved_context*. The second argument to *longjmp* specifies the return value to be used during this return. It should be other than zero so that in the *if* statement we can tell whether the return is induced by a *longjmp*.

The *setjmp/longjmp* combination enables you to jump unconditionally from one C function to another without using the conventional return statements. Essentially, *setjmp* marks the destination of the jump and *longjmp* is a nonlocal *goto* that executes the jump.

LOCALE OF A PROGRAM

The term locale refers to the locality (a country) for which certain aspects of your program can be customized. ANSI standard C groups the country or locale-dependent aspects of a C program into six categories. Table 4-2 summarizes the locale categories defined in the header file *locale.h*. You can use the *setlocale* function to selectively set each category shown in Table 4-2 to conform to a selected locale. The locale named "C" indicates the minimal environment for C translation. Other locale names will be implementation-dependent.

You can obtain the numeric and currency formatting style for the current locale by calling the function *localeconv*. This formatting information, returned in a *lconv* structure (defined in *locale.h*), includes such details as the decimal point character, the currency symbol for the current

Table 4-2. ***Locale Categories***

Locale Category	Parts of Program Affected
LC_ALL	The entire program's locale-specific parts (all categories shown below).
LC_COLLATE	Behavior of the routines *strcoll* and *strxfrm* (see Chapter 11).
LC_CTYPE	Behavior of the character handling functions and multibyte functions.
LC_MONETARY	Monetary formatting information returned by the *localeconv* function.
LC_NUMERIC	Decimal point character for the formatted output routines (for example, *printf*) and the conversion functions (see Chapter 8), and the nonmonetary formatting information returned by the *localeconv* function.
LC_TIME	Behavior of the *strftime* function (see Chapter 13).

locale. The reference entry for the *localeconv* function shows the fields in the *lconv* structure.

The locale-specific functions and formatting information were not present in earlier versions of the Turbo C compiler. They were added in Turbo C++.

Notes on Process Control

The process control functions (see Table 4-3 for a complete catalog) can perform a variety of functions beyond the task of starting and stopping a process. Table 4-4 shows the process control routines listed by task. As you can see, many of the routines are for spawning or executing a child process.

Table 4-3. ***Catalog of Process Control Routines***

Routine	Description
abort	Raises the SIGABRT signal after printing a message to *stderr*. The normal handler for SIGABRT terminates the process without flushing file buffers.
assert	Prints a diagnostic message and aborts program, if a given logical expression is false.
atexit	Installs a routine to a stack of up to 32 routines that will be called in "last-in first-out" order when the process terminates.
execl	Executes a child process that overlays the parent in memory. Command-line arguments to the child are passed in a list terminated by a NULL and the child inherits the parent's environment.
execle	Executes a child process that overlays the parent in memory. Command-line arguments and a new environment are passed to the child in the form of a NULL-terminated list.

Table 4-3. ***(cont.)***

Routine	Description
execlp	Executes a child process that overlays the parent in memory. Command-line arguments to the child are passed in a NULL-terminated list and the PATH environment variable is used to locate the file to be executed as a child.
execlpe	Executes a child process that overlays the parent in memory. Command-line arguments and a new environment are passed to the child in a NULL-terminated list and the PATH environment variable is used to find the file which is executed as a child.
execv	Executes a child process that overlays the parent in memory. A pointer to a variable-length array of command-line arguments is passed to the child. The child also receives a copy of the parent's environment.
execve	Executes a child process that overlays the parent in memory. Command-line arguments and a new environment are passed in variable length arrays with NULLs indicating the end of each array.
execvp	Executes a child process that overlays the parent in memory. Command-line arguments are passed in a variable-length array that ends with a NULL. The child inherits a copy of the parent's environment and the PATH environment variable is used to locate the program executed as a child.
execvpe	Executes a child process that overlays the parent in memory. Command-line arguments for the child and a specified environment are passed via pointers to NULL-terminated variable-length arrays. The environment variable PATH specifies the directories in which the program to be executed as a child can reside.
exit	Calls the functions installed by *atexit* or *onexit*, flushes all buffers associated with files that are open for I/O, and terminates the process and returns to the parent.
_exit	Terminates the process and immediately returns to the parent without performing the services that *exit* provides.
getenv	Returns the definition of an environment variable from the environment of the process.
localeconv	Sets the componets of a *lconv* structure with information about numeric and monetary formatting appropriate for the current locale.
longjmp	Restores the context of a process thus affecting an unconditional jump to the place where *setjmp* was called to save that context.
perror	Prints an error message using your message and the system message corresponding to the value in the global variable *errno*.
putenv	Adds the definition of a new environment variable to the process environment table.
raise	Generates a signal (an exception).
setjmp	Saves the context of a process in a buffer that can be used by *longjmp* to jump back.
setlocale	Selects a locale for a specified portion of the program's locale-dependent aspects.
signal	Installs a function to handle a specific exception or signal.
spawnl	Executes a child process either by destroying the parent in memory or leaving

Table 4-3. *(cont.)*

Routine	Description
	it intact and returning to it when the child terminates. The command-line arguments to the child are passed in a NULL-terminated list and the child receives a copy of the parent's environment.
spawnle	Functions as *spawnl* does, but a new environment is passed in a list that ends with a NULL.
spawnlp	Functions as *spawnl* does and also searches all the directories named in the PATH environment variable to locate the program that is executed as a child.
spawnlpe	Behaves as *spawnle* does and also uses the setting of the PATH environment variable to locate the executable file to be run as a child.
spawnv	Executes a child process either by destroying the parent in memory or leaving it intact and returning to it when the child terminates. The command-line arguments to the child are passed as a pointer to a variable-length array whose last element is a NULL. The child receives a copy of the parent's environment.
spawnve	Functions as *spawnv* does, but a new environment is passed via a pointer to a variable-length array that ends with a NULL.
spawnvp	Functions as *spawnv* does and also searches all the directories named in the PATH environment variable to locate the program that is executed as a child.
spawnvpe	Behaves as *spawnve* does and also uses the setting of the PATH environment variable to locate the executable file to be run as a child.
system	Executes an MS-DOS system command.

Table 4-4. *Process Control Routines by Task*

Task	Name of Routines
Launch a child process that destroys the parent in memory.	execl, execle, execlp, execlpe, execv, execve, execvp, execvpe
Launch a child process that optionally overlays the parent in memory or returns to the parent when it exits.	spawnl, spawnle, spawnlp, spawnlpe, spawnv, spawnve, spawnvp, spawnvpe
Execute an MS-DOS command.	system
Terminate a process.	abort, _exit, exit
Handle errors.	assert, perror
Get and set environment.	getenv, putenv,
Install exception handler and generate an exception.	raise, signal
Nonlocal jump from one function to another.	longjmp, setjmp
Install routines to be called when the process terminates.	atexit
Control locale-specific numeric and currency formatting.	localeconv, setlocale

There are also routines that take care of error conditions and set up numeric and currency formats depending on the locale for which your program is customized. These routines are declared in the header files *locale.h*, *signal.h*, *setjmp.h*, and *stdlib.h*.

SPAWN *AND* EXEC *FUNCTIONS*

Just as COMMAND.COM creates a child process and runs your program, the program can, in turn, execute a child of its own and run any other executable. The library routines in the process control category provide you with two choices: the *exec* routines or the *spawn* routines. Both sets of routines rely on the MS-DOS EXEC function to create a process, although they have slightly differing capabilities. The *exec* routines load the child into memory in the space previously used by the parent. Thus, the parent is "overlaid" by the child and destroyed. When the child ends, it returns to DOS. The *spawn* routines are more general. They offer you the choice of either overlaying the parent, in which case they behave exactly like their *exec* counterparts, or loading the child into a different place in memory. While the child executes, the parent waits and when the child terminates, the parent process resumes.

Versions of *spawn* and *exec*

The *exec* and *spawn* routines have eight versions each. This large assortment gives you control over how you pass the command-line arguments and the environment to the child process. It is easy enough to decide which routine to use once you know the naming scheme (see Figure 4-4).

The first part of a routine name is *exec* or *spawn*. The next character must be present. It can be either an "l" or a "v" to indicate how command-line arguments and environment (if a new one is provided) are passed. An "l" indicates that the command-line arguments (each a C string) are listed one after another with a NULL ending the list. This list appears in the call to the *spawn* or the *exec* function. You should use this form when the number of command-line arguments and entries in the environment table are fixed and known in advance. A "v" indicates that the strings that make up the command-line arguments and environment are placed in an array, and a pointer to this array is passed to the function. The last element in the array is a NULL pointer. Since this array can be constructed at run-time, this form of the routines is suitable when there is a variable number of command-line arguments to be passed to the child process.

The next letters, "p" or "e" or the pair "pe," are optional. Whenever a p is included in the name, the PATH environment variable of the parent process is used as the list of directories that will be searched when trying to locate the executable file that will be excuted as a child process. The e signifies that instead of inheriting the parent's environment, a new environment is being specified. The format used to specify the environment is the same as that for the command-line arguments and is determined by which of the letters "l" or "v" is present in the function's name.

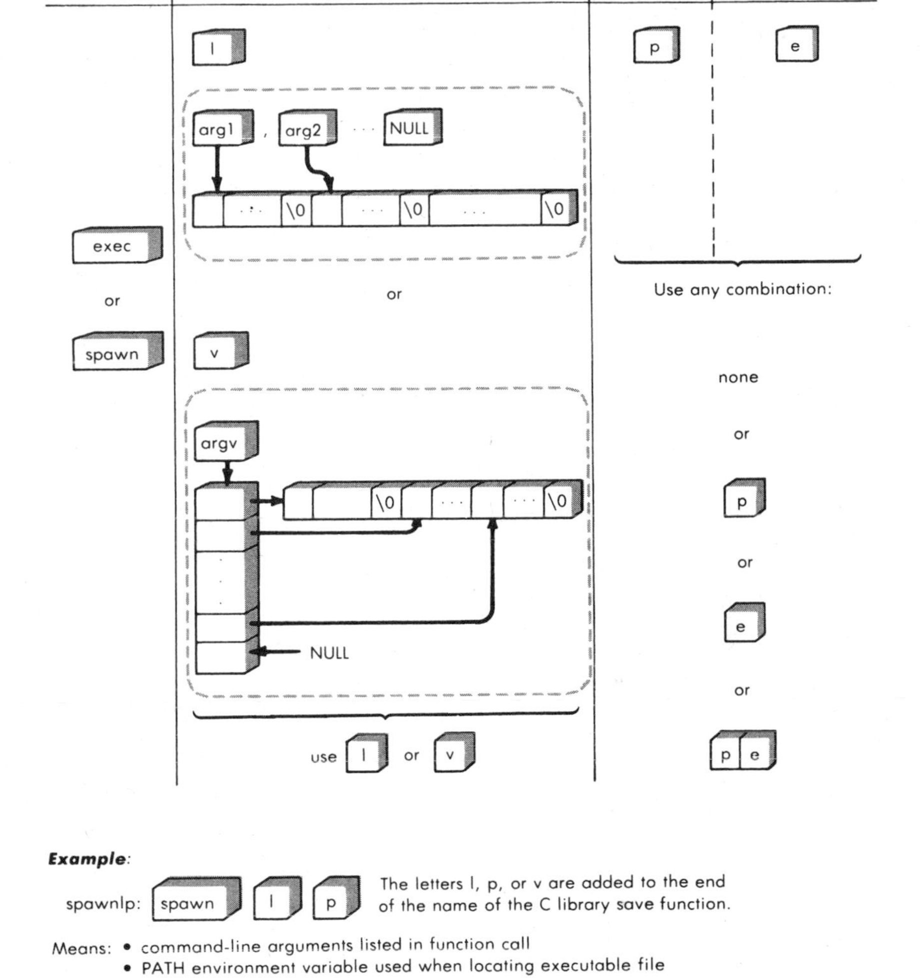

Sample invocation: spawnlp(P_WAIT,"TEST.EXE","C:\TEST\TEST.EXE","One","Two","Three",NULL);

Figure 4-4. ***Naming conventions and use of* exec *and* spawn *functions***

spawn or *exec*: Which One to Use

The *spawn* and *exec* functions allow you to start a child process and execute another program. The choice of one over the other depends on your application. If you want to use a tool like an editor and return to your program, then one of the *spawn* functions will meet your needs. There are situations in which *exec* is more suitable. Suppose your application can be broken up into three programs, MODULE1.EXE, MODULE2.EXE, and MODULE3.EXE, each independent of the other. You can run your application by first executing MODULE1.EXE in which you use *exec* to launch a child process, MODULE2.EXE. When MODULE2.EXE ends, you can switch to MODULE3.EXE by another *exec* call. Thus you can chain from one program to another by using the *exec* functions. Despite this, you may decide to use *spawn* exclusively because the functionality of *exec* can be obtained by invoking the *spawn* functions with the execution mode P_OVERLAY.

EXECUTING DOS COMMANDS

What if you want to use an MS-DOS command, like DIR, from your C program? Since DOS commands are only understood by COMMAND.COM, the *exec* or *spawn* functions have to spawn a copy of COMMAND.COM to execute any DOS command. This task is made simple by the Microsoft C library routine *system*, which can accept and execute any MS-DOS command. The *system* function actually looks at the COMSPEC environment variable to locate a copy of COMMAND.COM to run as a child while your program waits. The PATH environment variable is used when executing the command that you provide to *system*.

TERMINATING A PROCESS

Three functions can terminate a process: *abort*, *_exit*, and *exit*. Of course any process terminates automatically when its body of code ends. When a C process terminates normally via a call to *exit* or when its execution is complete, several things happen. First a set of up to 32 routines (installed earlier by calls to *atexit*) will be called one after another in a last-in first-out (LIFO) manner. Then, all buffers associated with files open for buffered I/O will be "flushed," which involves writing out the contents of a buffer to its associated file. Finally, the process ends and returns to its parent.

The *abort* and *_exit* functions terminate a process without going through the niceties of normal termination. The buffers are not flushed (desirable when you know that the data in the buffers may be corrupted), nor do they call the routines that are supposed to be called upon program termination. The *abort* function even prints a message indicating that the program terminated abnormally.

Cautions

- The child process does not inherit the signal handlers you may have installed in the parent. All signal handlers revert to the default settings.
- The combined length of all the strings that form the command-line arguments to the child cannot exceed 128 bytes.
- You should be aware of some limits on the size of the environment table. The total length of the entire environment cannot exceed 32 K and the size of individual definitions is limited to 128 bytes.

Further Reading

The use of the *exec* and the *spawn* functions as well as the handling of signals has been covered in Prata's text[1] and in Hansen's book[2].

1. Stephen Prata, The Waite Group, *Advanced C Primer++*, Howard W. Sams & Company, Indianapolis, IN, 1986, 502 pages.
2. Augie Hansen, *Proficient C*, Microsoft Press, Redmond, WA, 1987, 492 pages.

abort

COMPATIBILITY

TC1	TC1.5	TC2	TC++	MSC3	MSC4	MSC5	MSC6	QC1	QC2	QC2.5	ANSI	UNIX V	XNX
▲	▲	▲	▲	▲	▲	▲	▲	▲	▲	▲	▲	▲	▲

PURPOSE Use *abort* to exit your program abnormally.

SYNTAX

```
void abort(void);
```

EXAMPLE CALL

```
abort();
```

INCLUDES

```
#include <process.h>
```

For function declaration

or

```
#include <stdlib.h>
```

DESCRIPTION The *abort* function first prints the message *Abnormal program termination* to *stderr* and then calls *_exit* with exit code 3 to terminate the calling process and return to the parent process or MS-DOS. Note that *abort*, unlike *exit*, will not flush the file buffers or call the routines set up by *atexit*.

SEE ALSO

`exit, _exit` *To terminate a process*

`raise, signal` *To generate and handle exceptions*

EXAMPLE Write a program that uses *abort* to exit when it is invoked without any command-line arguments. Otherwise, the program simply prints out the arguments.

```
#include <stdio.h>
#include <stdlib.h>
main(int argc, char **argv)
{
    int i;
    if(argc < 2)
    {
        printf("Not enough arguments!\n");
        abort();
    }
    for (i=0; i<argc; i++)
    {
        printf("Argument %d = %s\n", i+1, argv[i]);
    }
```

```
    return 0;
}
```

COMPATIBILITY

assert

TC1	TC1.5	TC2	TC++	MSC3	MSC4	MSC5	MSC6	QC1	QC2	QC2.5	ANSI	UNIX V	XNX
▲	▲	▲	▲	▲	▲	▲	▲	▲	▲	▲	▲	▲	▲

PURPOSE Use *assert* to print an error message and abort the program if a specific assertion is false.

SYNTAX

```
void assert(<expression>);
```

`<expression>` *C statements specifying assertion being tested*

EXAMPLE CALL

```
assert(arg_value >= 0);
```

INCLUDES

`#include <stdio.h>` *For definition of stderr, used in definition of* assert

`#include <assert.h>` *For definition of* assert

DESCRIPTION The *assert* macro is defined in such a way that if the expression is false (i.e., evaluates to zero), it prints a diagnostic message of the form

```
Assertion failed: expression, file (filename), line (linenumber)
```

and calls *abort.* In the diagnostic message, *filename* is the name of the source file and *linenumber* is the line number where the *assert* macro appears in the source file.

COMMON USES The *assert* macro identifies program errors during the debugging phase. After the program is debugged, you can disable all occurrences of the *assert* macro either by using the option –DNDEBUG=1 in the compiler's command line or by inserting a *#define NDEBUG 1* in the source file.

SEE ALSO `abort` *To abort a program*

EXAMPLE This program considers it a fatal error if it is invoked without any argument on the command line. This test is implemented by *assert.* When invoked with one or more arguments, the program simply prints the arguments.

```
#include <stdio.h>
#include <assert.h>
```

```
main(int argc, char **argv)
{
    int i;
/* Make sure that there is more than one argument */
    assert(argc > 1);
/* Just print out the arguments */
    printf("Thanks for these \"arguments\"\n");
    for (i=0; i<argc; i++)
    {
        printf("Argument %d = %s\n", i+1, argv[i]);
    }
    return 0;
}
```

atexit

COMPATIBILITY

TC1	TC1.5	TC2	TC++	MSC3	MSC4	MSC5	MSC6	QC1	QC2	QC2.5	ANSI	UNIX V	XNX
▲	▲	▲	▲			▲	▲	▲	▲	▲	▲		

PURPOSE Use *atexit* to set up a stack of up to 32 functions that the system will call in a LIFO manner when your program terminates normally.

SYNTAX

```
int atexit(atexit_t func);
```

`atexit_t func;` *Pointer to function to be called*

EXAMPLE CALL

```
atexit (cleanup);
```

INCLUDES `#include <stdlib.h>` *For function declaration and definition of* atexit_t

DESCRIPTION The *atexit* function places the function pointer *func* on a stack of functions to be called when the program terminates. (Note that the name of a function denotes a pointer to it.) The called function is of type *atexit_t*, which is defined by a *typedef* statement in *stdlib.h*. Up to 32 functions can be specified with *atexit*. These are invoked in a LIFO manner when the calling program exits. (The function whose address you provide in the first call to *atexit* is called last.) Note that the functions passed to *atexit* cannot take any arguments.

COMMON USES The *atexit* function allows you to set up "house cleaning" functions that should be performed when exiting your application program. These might include making sure all files are updated and saving the last setting of internal parameters to a disk file.

RETURNS The *atexit* function returns a zero if successful. If you have already called *atexit* more than 32 times, the return value will be nonzero.

SEE ALSO `exit` *To terminate process (after calling functions installed by* atexit)

EXAMPLE Demonstrate the use of *atexit* by calling it with three functions. Let each function print out an identifying message. Notice that the functions are called in the reverse order. Thus the first function "registered" with *atexit* gets called last.

```
#include <stdio.h>
#include <stdlib.h>
main(int argc, char **argv)
{
    atexit_t first, second, third;
    atexit(first);
    atexit(second);
    atexit(third);
    printf("Now exiting...\n");
    return 0;
}

/*-------------------------------------------------*/
atexit_t first(void)
{
    printf("Function number 1: called last\n");
}
/*-------------------------------------------------*/
atexit_t second(void)
{
    printf("Function number 2:\n");
}
/*-------------------------------------------------*/
atexit_t third(void)
{
    printf("Function number 3: called first\n");
}
/*-------------------------------------------------*/
```

exec functions

COMPATIBILITY

TC1	TC1.5	TC2	TC++	MSC3	MSC4	MSC5	MSC6	QC1	QC2	QC2.5	ANSI	UNIX V	XNX
▲	▲	▲	▲		▲	▲	▲	▲	▲	▲		▲	▲

PURPOSE Use one of the *exec* functions to load and execute a child process in the memory currently occupied by your program's code.

SYNTAX

```
int execl(char *path, char *arg0, char *arg1,..., NULL);

int execle(char *path, char *arg0, char *arg1,..., NULL,
           char *envp[]);

int execlp(char *path, char *arg0, char *arg1,..., NULL);

int execlpe(char *path, char *arg0, char *arg1,..., NULL,
            char *envp[]);

int execv(char *path, char *argv[]);

int execve(char *path, char *argv[], char *envp[]);

int execvp(char *path, char *argv[]);

int execvpe(char *path, char *argv[], char *envp[]);
```

`char *path;` *Pathname of file to be executed as a child process*

`char *arg0, *arg1, ..., NULL;` *Command-line arguments for the child process (ends with a NULL)*

`char *argv[];` *Array of command-line arguments for the child process*

`char *envp[];` *The environment parameter table*

EXAMPLE CALL `execv ("child.exe", argv);`

INCLUDES `#include <process.h>` *For function declaration*

DESCRIPTION The *exec* functions create a child process to load and execute the program specified by the argument *path*. In doing so, they destroy the calling process. The variations among the different forms of the *exec* functions are due to the way in which arguments and environment variables are passed to the child process. Table 4-5 uses the name of each function as a key to tabulate its action.

Table 4-5. exec *Functions*

Fifth Letter of Name	Meaning
l	Command-line arguments to the child process are listed on the statement that invokes the *exec* function. These forms are useful when the number of arguments is known in advance. The arguments, *arg0, arg1* . . . , are listed one after another with NULL marking the end.
v	Command-line arguments are passed in the form of a pointer to an array of argument strings. This is useful when the number of arguments is not known in advance. In this case, you prepare an array of NULL-terminated strings, each representing one command-line argument for the child program, put NULL to mark the end of the list, and pass the pointer to this array, *argv*, to the child process via the *exec* function.

Next Two Letters	How Environment Variables Are Handled
none	Child process inherits parent's environment variables.
p	PATH environment variable is used to locate the executable file. In this case, the *path* argument may specify a program name without any directory information and COMMAND.COM will locate the program if it is present in one of the directories included in your PATH environment variable.
e	Child process receives a pointer *envp* to an array of environment strings. Each environment variable definition is of the form *NAME=value of variable*, and the end of the array is marked by NULL.
pe	This is a combination of letters described above. The PATH environment variable is used and the child process gets a pointer to a table of environment variables that you prepare.

As you can see, the fifth letter of the name, "l" or "v," determines how command-line arguments are received by the child process. The next one or two letters indicate how environment variables are passed to the child process.

If the sixth letter of the name is a "p," then the PATH environment variable is used by COMMAND.COM to locate the executable program whose name you specify in the argument *path*. Otherwise, you must specify the full pathname of the file to be executed or specify a path beginning at the current working directory. If the *path* argument does not have an extension, the *exec* function first searches for a file without an extension. If none is found and *path* does not end with a period, it tries the extensions .COM and .EXE, in that order.

Note that the combined length of all the command-line argument strings, including a separating space between each adjoining argument, must not exceed 128 bytes. Although a different string will not produce any error, it is customary to provide the full pathname of the executable file as the first command-line argument to the child process.

The last two points to note are about files and signal handlers. In the child process, all signal handlers are reset to the default ones. Files that were open in the parent remain open in the child.

COMMON USES The *exec* functions may be used to chain the execution from one program to another.

RETURNS If successful, the *exec* functions do not return to the parent. If an error occurs, the return value is −1 and the global variable *errno* is set to one of the constants shown in Table 4-6, indicating the cause of the error.

Table 4-6. *Error Codes Returned by* exec *Functions*

Error	Cause of Error
E2BIG	Either the total length of the command-line arguments exceeds 128 bytes, or the memory required for the environment variables exceeds 32 K.
EACCES	You are running MS-DOS 3.0 or higher with file-sharing enabled and the file specified in *path* is either locked or not set up for sharing.
EMFILE	COMMAND.COM has to open the specified file first to determine if it is executable. This error means there were already too many files open (20) to prevent COMMAND.COM from doing this.
ENOENT	Either the path or the file specified in the argument *path* was not found.
ENOEXEC	The specified file is not executable because its format does not match the DOS specification for an executable file.
ENOMEM	Either there is not enough memory to load and execute the child process or available memory is corrupted or an invalid block of memory was located, indicating that the parent process was incorrectly loaded.

COMMENTS Since the *exec* functions overwrite the parent in memory, they are good only for chaining one program to another. Use the *spawn* functions if you want to launch a program and return to the original program.

SEE ALSO `spawn functions` *To launch a program and return when it terminates*

EXAMPLE Demonstrate the use of the *exec* functions in a program that allows a child process to run using any one of the eight *exec* functions. Prepare data in a structure allocated in the parent program and pass the data to the child by encoding the address as a character string and using that string as a command-line argument. In the child program, print the command-line arguments and the environment passed to it. Then access the data structure using the address passed in the command line and display the various

fields. *Note:* Remember to compile and link the child program first and save it in a file named *child.exe.*

```
/*====================== PARENT =====================*/
#include <stdio.h>
#include <process.h>
#include <alloc.h>
#include <string.h>
typedef struct TEST_DATA
{
    char name[20];
    int n;
    double x;
} TEST_DATA;
/* PARENT: Test the "exec" functions. Pass address of
 *         data in command-line arguments as well as
 *         environment variables when appropriate.
 */
char *envp[] =
{
    "PARENT=EXEC FUNCTIONS",
    NULL
};
main()
{
    char *argv[4], buf[20], rname[40];
    TEST_DATA *pdata;
/* Set up a data structure and initialize it */
    if((pdata=(TEST_DATA *)
        alloc(sizeof(TEST_DATA))) == NULL) abort();
    strcpy(pdata->name, "PARENT");
    pdata->n = 100;
    pdata->x = 1000.99;
/* Set up the arguments for the child process */
    argv[0] = "child.exe",
    argv[1] = rname;
    sprintf(buf, "%Fp", (void far *)pdata);
    argv[2] = buf;
    argv[3] = NULL;
/* Ask user which "exec" routine to call */
    printf("Enter name of \"exec\" function to call:");
    gets(rname);
    strlwr(rname);
/* Call the "exec" function requested by the user */
    if(strcmp(rname, "execl") == 0)
```

```
        {
            execl("child.exe",
                   "child.exe", "execl", buf, NULL);
        }
        if(strcmp(rname, "execle") == 0)
        {
            execle("child.exe",
            "child.exe", "execle", buf, NULL, envp);
        }
        if(strcmp(rname, "execlp") == 0)
        {
            execlp("child.exe",
                   "child.exe", "execlp", buf, NULL);
        }
        if(strcmp(rname, "execlpe") == 0)
        {
            execlpe("child.exe",
            "child.exe", "execlpe", buf, NULL, envp);
        }
        if(strcmp(rname, "execv") == 0)
        {
            execv("child.exe", argv);
        }
        if(strcmp(rname, "execve") == 0)
        {
            execve("child.exe", argv, envp);
        }
        if(strcmp(rname, "execvp") == 0)
        {
            execvp("child.exe", argv);
        }
        if(strcmp(rname, "execvpe") == 0)
        {
            execvpe("child.exe", argv, envp);
        }
/* Check if we could call child or not */
        if(strcmp(pdata->name, "CHILD") == 0)
        {
            printf("Back from child: name = %s, n = %d, \
x= %f\n", pdata->name, pdata->n, pdata->x);
        }
        else
        {
             printf("Don't know: %s\n", rname);
        }
```

Process Control

```
    return 0;
}

/*====================== CHILD ======================*/
/*      Must be in a file named:  CHILD.EXE          */
#include <stdio.h>
#include <dos.h>
#include <string.h>
typedef struct TEST_DATA
{
    char name[20];
    int n;
    double x;
} TEST_DATA;
/* Child: First argument is program name,
 *        Second one tells us how child was invoked
 *        Third argument is an address in the form
 *        SSSS:OOOO (segment:offset). This is the
 *        address of a data structure allocated in
 *        the parent.
 */
static char far *cname = "CHILD";
void main(int argc, char **argv, char **envp)
{
    char  **p_table;
    TEST_DATA far *pdata;
    void far *p_s1;
    void far *p_s2;
    printf("CHILD: received %d arguments\n", argc);
    if(argc < 3){
        printf("not enough arguments\n");
        exit(1);
    }
    printf("CHILD invoked by a %s call.\n", argv[1]);

/* Now print the environment passed to CHILD     */
    printf("==== CHILD: Environment contains ====\n");
    for(p_table = envp;
        *p_table != NULL;
        p_table++) printf("%s\n", *p_table);

/* Read in address of parent's data from argv[2] */
    sscanf(argv[2], "%Fp", (void far *)&pdata);
    printf("In child: name = %Fs, n = %d, x= %f\n",
           pdata->name, pdata->n, pdata->x);
```

```
/* Put new values in the data structure. If CHILD was
 * created by a "spawn" function call, this data will
 * be available to the parent when child exits.
 * Notice that we have to use "movedata" to copy
 * "far" data in small or medium model.
 */
    p_s1 = (void far *)cname;
    p_s2 = (void far *)pdata->name;
    movedata(FP_SEG(p_s1), FP_OFF(p_s1),
             FP_SEG(p_s2), FP_OFF(p_s2), 6);
    pdata->n = 101;
    pdata->x = 999.99;
    exit(0);
}
```

exit

COMPATIBILITY

TC1	TC1.5	TC2	TC++	MSC3	MSC4	MSC5	MSC6	QC1	QC2	QC2.5	ANSI	UNIX V	XNX
▲	▲	▲	▲	▲	▲	▲	▲	▲	▲	▲	▲	▲	▲

PURPOSE Use *exit* to terminate your program normally by flushing file buffers, closing files, and invoking functions set up with *atexit.*

SYNTAX

```
void exit(int status);

int status;        Exit status code
```

EXAMPLE CALL

```
exit(0);
```

INCLUDES

```
#include <stdlib.h>       For function declaration
```

or

```
#include <process.h>
```

DESCRIPTION The *exit* function flushes all buffers associated with files opened for buffered I/O, closes all files, and then invokes in LIFO order the functions set up by earlier calls to *atexit.* After the calls are complete, *exit* terminates the program and makes available to the parent process or DOS the low-order byte of the argument *status.* Ordinarily, a *status* of zero means normal exit, whereas nonzero values indicate errors. If the program was invoked from an MS-DOS batch file, the value of *status* can be checked from the batch file with the command IF_ERRORLEVEL.

SEE ALSO

`_exit` *To terminate process without performing the normal "housekeeping" chores*

`atexit` *To set up functions called when a process terminates normally*

EXAMPLE Illustrate how file buffers are flushed when a program *exits* by opening a file, writing a line to it, and using *exit* to terminate. The line appears in the file because *exit* flushed the buffer.

```
#include <stdio.h>
void main()
{
    FILE *fp;
    char filename[40];
    printf("Enter name of a file to be opened \
for writing:");
    gets(filename);
    if((fp = fopen(filename, "w+")) == NULL)
    {
        perror("File open error");
        abort();
    }
    fprintf(fp, "If you use \"exit\", this line will \
appear in the file\nbecause it flushes buffers\n");
    printf("TYPE %s to see if buffers were flushed\n",
            filename);
    exit(0);
}
```

COMPATIBILITY

_exit

TC1	TC1.5	TC2	TC++	MSC3	MSC4	MSC5	MSC6	QC1	QC2	QC2.5	ANSI	UNIX V	XNX
▲	▲	▲	▲	▲	▲	▲	▲	▲	▲	▲			

PURPOSE Use *_exit* to terminate your program immediately without flushing file buffers.

SYNTAX `void _exit(int status);`

`int status;` *_exit status code*

EXAMPLE CALL `_exit(0);`

INCLUDES `#include <stdlib.h>` *For function declaration* or

```
#include <process.h>
```

DESCRIPTION The *_exit* function terminates the program immediately, without flushing the buffers associated with files opened for buffered I/O. The files are closed "as-is" and, after terminating the program, *_exit* makes available to the parent process or to DOS the low-order byte of the argument *status*. Ordinarily a *status* of zero means normal exit, whereas nonzero values indicate errors. If the program was invoked from an MS-DOS batch file, the value of *status* can be checked with the command IF_ERRORLEVEL.

SEE ALSO `exit` *To terminate process after performing "housekeeping" chores*

EXAMPLE Illustrate that file buffers are not flushed when a program *_exit*s by opening a file, writing a line to it and using *_exit* to terminate the program. Notice that the line does not appear in the file because *_exit* did not flush the buffer when exiting the program.

```
#include <stdio.h>
void main()
{
    FILE *fp;
    char filename[40];
    printf("Enter name of a file to be opened \
for writing:");
    gets(filename);
    if((fp = fopen(filename, "w+")) == NULL)
    {
        perror("File open error");
        abort();
    }
    fprintf(fp, "If you use \"_exit\", this line will \
not appear in the file\nbecause buffers are not \
flushed\n");
    printf("TYPE %s to see if buffers were flushed\n",
            filename);
    _exit(0);
}
```

COMPATIBILITY

getenv

TC1	TC1.5	TC2	TC++	MSC3	MSC4	MSC5	MSC6	QC1	QC2	QC2.5	ANSI	UNIX V	XNX
▲	▲	▲	▲	▲	▲	▲	▲	▲	▲	▲	▲	▲	▲

PURPOSE Use *getenv* to get the definition of a variable from the environment table of the process.

SYNTAX

```
char *getenv(const char *varname);

const char *varname;       Name of environment variable to look for
```

EXAMPLE CALL

```
current_path = getenv("PATH");
```

INCLUDES

```
#include <stdlib.h>       For function declaration
```

DESCRIPTION The *getenv* function uses the global variable *environ* to locate the list of environment variables and then it searches the list for an entry for the variable named *varname*.

RETURNS If *varname* is found, *getenv* returns a pointer to the string value of *varname*. Thus if the environment variable LIB is defined as LIB=C:\LIB in the environment table, invoking *getenv* with LIB as *varname* returns a pointer to the string C:\LIB. If *varname* is undefined, *getenv* returns a NULL.

COMMENTS Under MS-DOS, the *main* function can get a pointer to the list of environment variables as a third argument, say, *envp*. The library routine *putenv* may alter the location of this list, however, and render *envp* useless. So, it is safer to use the functions *getenv* and *putenv*, respectively, to locate and modify the environment table.

SEE ALSO putenv — *To add the definition of a new variable to the environment table of the process*

EXAMPLE Prepare a small utility program that lets you see the setting of an environment variable. Assume that the name of the environment variable is given on the command line. Use *getenv* to get the value of that variable and print it.

```
#include <stdio.h>
#include <stdlib.h>
main(int argc, char **argv)
{
    char *value;
    if(argc < 2)
```

```
    {
        printf("Usage: %s <env_var_name>\n", argv[0]);
        exit(0);
    }
/* Get the value of the environment variable */
    strupr(argv[1]);
    if ((value = getenv(argv[1])) == NULL)
    {
        printf("%s <-- no such environment variable\n",
                 argv[1]);
    }
    else
    {
        printf("%s=%s\n", argv[1], value);
    }
    return 0;
}
```

localeconv

COMPATIBILITY

TC1	TC1.5	TC2	TC++	MSC3	MSC4	MSC5	MSC6	QC1	QC2	QC2.5	ANSI	UNIX V	XNX
			▲				▲		▲	▲	▲		

PURPOSE Use the *localeconv* function to obtain detailed information on formatting monetary and numeric values.

SYNTAX `struct lconv *localeconv(void);`

EXAMPLE CALL `p_lconv = localeconv();`

INCLUDES `#include <locale.h>` *For function declaration and definition of lconv structure*

DESCRIPTION The *localeconv* function is an ANSI-standard routine that allows you to determine how monetary and numeric values are to be formatted for the current locale (see tutorial). Use *setlocale* to set the current locale.

The information is returned in an *lconv* structure, which is declared in *locale.h* as follows:

```
struct lconv
{
    char *decimal_point;      /* Decimal point character for
                                 nonmonetary quantities */
```

```
char *thousands_sep;      /* Separator for groups of digits
                             to the left of decimal point for
                             nonmonetary quantities */

char *grouping;           /* Size of each group of digits in
                             nonmonetary quantities */

char *int_curr_symbol;    /* International currency symbol
                             for the current locale */

char *currency_symbol;    /* Local currency symbol
                             for the current locale */

char *mon_decimal_point; /* Decimal point character for
                             monetary quantities */

char *mon_thousands_sep; /* Separator for groups of digits
                             to the left of decimal point for
                             monetary quantities */

char *mon_grouping;       /* Size of each group of digits in
                             monetary quantities */

char *positive_sign;      /* String denoting sign for non-
                             negative monetary quantities */

char *negative_sign;      /* String denoting sign for
                             negative monetary quantities */

char int_frac_digits;     /* Number of digits to the right of
                             decimal point in internationally
                             formatted monetary quantities */

char frac_digits;         /* Number of digits to the right of
                             decimal point in formatted
                             monetary quantities */

char p_cs_precedes;       /* 1 = currency_symbol precedes,
                             0 = succeeds positive value */

char p_sep_by_space;      /* 1 = space, 0 = no space between
                             currency_symbol and positive
                             formatted values */

char n_cs_precedes;       /* 1 = currency_symbol precedes,
                             0 = succeeds negative value */
```

```
    char n_sep_by_space;      /* 1 = space, 0 = no space between
                                 currency_symbol and negative
                                 formatted values */

    char p_sign_posn;         /* Position of positive_sign in
                                 positive monetary quantities */

    char n_sign_posn;         /* Position of negative_sign in
                                 negative monetary quantities */

};
```

COMMON USES The *localeconv* function together with its companion *setlocale* are used for *internationalization* of applications. The term refers to the process of ensuring that applications display information according to the customs followed in a country or a locality.

RETURNS The *localeconv* function returns a pointer to a statically allocated *lconv* structure whose fields are filled in with formatting information appropriate for the current locale.

SEE ALSO setlocale

EXAMPLE Display information about the current locale's formatting rules.

```
#include <stdio.h>
#include <locale.h>

main()
{
    struct lconv *p_lc;

/* Get the formatting information for current locale */
    p_lc = localeconv();

/* Display the information */

    printf("decimal_point = %s\n",  p_lc->decimal_point);
    printf("thousands_sep = %s\n", p_lc->thousands_sep);
    printf("grouping = %s\n", p_lc->grouping);
    printf("int_curr_symbol = %s\n", p_lc->int_curr_symbol);
    printf("currency_symbol = %s\n", p_lc->currency_symbol);
    printf("mon_decimal_point = %s\n", p_lc->mon_decimal_point);
    printf("mon_thousands_sep = %s\n", p_lc->mon_thousands_sep);
```

```
    printf("mon_grouping = %s\n", p_lc->mon_grouping);
    printf("positive_sign = %s\n", p_lc->positive_sign);
    printf("negative_sign = %s\n", p_lc->negative_sign);
    printf("int_frac_digits = %d\n", p_lc->int_frac_digits);
    printf("frac_digits = %d\n", p_lc->frac_digits);
    printf("p_cs_precedes = %d\n", p_lc->p_cs_precedes);
    printf("p_sep_by_space = %d\n", p_lc->p_sep_by_space);
    printf("n_cs_precedes = %d\n", p_lc->n_cs_precedes);
    printf("n_sep_by_space = %d\n", p_lc->n_sep_by_space);
    printf("p_sign_posn = %d\n", p_lc->p_sign_posn);
    printf("n_sign_posn = %d\n", p_lc->n_sign_posn);
    return 0;
}
```

longjmp

COMPATIBILITY

TC1	TC1.5	TC2	TC++	MSC3	MSC4	MSC5	MSC6	QC1	QC2	QC2.5	ANSI	UNIX V	XNX
▲	▲	▲	▲	▲	▲	▲	▲	▲	▲	▲	▲	▲	▲

PURPOSE Use *longjmp* to restore a stack environment that was saved by an earlier call to *setjmp*, thus restoring all local variables to their previous states and returning as if from the last call to *setjmp*.

SYNTAX `void longjmp(jmp_buf env, int value);`

`jmp_buf env;` *Data type in which the registers and a return address representing the stack environment are stored*

`int value;` *Value that appears to be returned by the earlier call to* setjmp

EXAMPLE CALL `longjmp(stack_env, 1);`

INCLUDES `#include <setjmp.h>` *For function declaration and definition of the data type* jmp_buf

DESCRIPTION The *longjmp* function restores the registers saved in *env* as part of the stack environment saved earlier by a call to *setjmp*. Then it jumps to the return address for *setjmp* which is also saved in *env*. This restores all stack-based local variables to their state when the *setjmp* function was called, making it appear as if *setjmp* returned again. The argument *value* is used in this "forced" return from *setjmp*. However, this process might not properly restore all register-based variables to the routine where the call to *setjmp* occurred. Since *longjmp* jumps to the return address of the corresponding call to *setjmp*, you must make sure that the call to *longjmp* occurs before the function in which you called *setjmp* has returned.

COMMON USES The *longjmp* function is used in conjunction with its companion *setjmp* to divert the flow of execution to error-recovery code without using the normal function call and return conventions. First a call to *setjmp* is necessary to set up the place to which *longjmp* can return control when called. After that, when the error condition occurs, you can call *longjmp* and jump to the point where the *setjmp* function would have returned.

COMMENTS It is a little difficult to understand the behavior of *setjmp* and *longjmp* but, essentially, they give you the flexibility of jumping to an arbitrary location from within C. This is akin to a "goto" statement which lets you jump from one function to another.

SEE ALSO `setjmp` *To save a stack environment to be used in a subsequent call to* longjmp

EXAMPLE The pair of *setjmp* and *longjmp* is ideal for error-handling or handling special conditions in a program. You call *setjmp* at a place where you have code that you may want to execute later. Then whenever the conditions are met, call *longjmp* with the stack environment variable saved earlier by *setjmp*. This places you where *setjmp* was called originally. It will appear as though the *setjmp* function returned a second time, this time with the value from the second argument to *longjmp*. Here is a small program to illustrate a way to use this versatile duo.

```
#include <stdio.h>
#include <setjmp.h>
static jmp_buf mark_place;
static void call_longjmp(void);
void main()
{
    int rvalue;
    rvalue = setjmp(mark_place);
    if(rvalue != 0)
    {
        printf("Second return from \"setjmp\" induced \
by call to \"longjmp\"\n");
        printf("Return value = %d\n", rvalue);
        exit(rvalue);
    }
    printf("Calling \"longjmp\" next...\n");
    call_longjmp();
}
/*-------------------------------------------------*/
```

```
static void call_longjmp(void)
{
    longjmp(mark_place, 3);
}
```

COMPATIBILITY

perror

TC1	TC1.5	TC2	TC++	MSC3	MSC4	MSC5	MSC6	QC1	QC2	QC2.5	ANSI	UNIX V	XNX
▲	▲	▲	▲	▲	▲	▲	▲	▲	▲	▲	▲	▲	▲

PURPOSE Use *perror* to construct an error message by concatenating your message with that from the system which corresponds to the current value in the global variable *errno*. The message prints to *stderr*.

SYNTAX

```
void perror(const char *string);

const char *string;
```

Your part of the message

EXAMPLE CALL

```
perror("Error closing file");
```

INCLUDES

```
#include <stdio.h>
```

For function declaration

DESCRIPTION The *perror* function takes the message from the argument "string," appends a colon and a space, and concatenates to this the message from the system's error message table corresponding to the value in the global variable *errno*. The value in *errno* is the error number corresponding to the last error that occurred in a C library routine. All error messages are stored in a table of strings called *sys_errlist*. There is no need, however, to declare or to directly access these variables in your program.

COMMON USES When an error occurs in certain C library routines, the variable *errno* is set to a value that reflects the cause of the error. Typically, *perror* is called immediately after an error return from a library routine to print a message detailing the error. This message then prints to *stderr*.

COMMENTS Rather than access *errno* and the system error-message list *sys_errlist* directly, you should always use *perror* to print the error message when a library routine returns with an error. This approach is safer because it does not use error numbers, which very well can change during a later release of the compiler.

SEE ALSO `_strerror, strerror` *Alternate functions to prepare error messages*

EXAMPLE Demonstrate the use of *perror* by creating the error of closing a file with a bad handle and then printing an error message.

```
#include <stdio.h>
#include <io.h>
main()
{
    printf("We'll call \"close\" with an invalid file \
handle\n");
    if (close (100) == -1)
    {
/* Error occurred. Use perror to print error message */
        perror("Error closing file");
    }
    return 0;
}
```

putenv

COMPATIBILITY

TC1	TC1.5	TC2	TC++	MSC3	MSC4	MSC5	MSC6	QC1	QC2	QC2.5	ANSI	UNIX V	XNX
▲		▲	▲	▲	▲	▲	▲	▲	▲	▲		▲	▲

PURPOSE Use *putenv* to enter the definition of a new variable into the environment table of the process.

SYNTAX

```
int putenv(char *envstring);
```

`char *envstring;` *Definition of environment variable to be added*

EXAMPLE CALL

```
putenv("TMP=c:\\mydir\\temp");
```

INCLUDES `#include <stdlib.h>` *For function declaration*

DESCRIPTION The *putenv* function uses the global variable *environ* to locate the copy of the environment table that the process inherits from the parent. To this table it adds the new definition specified in the argument *envstring*, which must be of the form:

```
VARNAME=definition
```

If the environment variable named VARNAME already exists, its definition is changed to the new definition. Otherwise, an entirely new definition is added to the environment table. Note that the environment table altered by *putenv* is only a copy. Once the process terminates, the environment definitions revert to the original ones under the parent process. Thus, you cannot use *putenv* in a program to alter the environment variable settings seen at DOS command level. Any process launched by your program via *exec* or *spawn* functions, however, gets a copy of the environment settings with all the alterations you made with *putenv*.

COMMON USES The *putenv* function is useful to add new application-specific definitions to the environment table, which revert to their original meanings once the program exits.

RETURNS The *putenv* function returns a 0 if successful. A return value of −1 indicates failure due to lack of memory in the environment space of the process.

COMMENTS Under MS-DOS, the *main* function can get a pointer to the list of environment variables as a third argument, for instance, *envp*. The library routine *putenv* may alter the location of this list, however, rendering *envp* useless. So it is safer to use the functions *getenv* and *putenv*, respectively, to locate and modify the environment table.

SEE ALSO `getenv` *To get the definition of a variable from the environment table of the process*

EXAMPLE Write a program that enables you to define a new environment variable or redefine an existing one. Accept the definition on the command line and use *putenv* to add the definition to the list of current environment variables. Notice that anything you define is gone when you exit the program.

```
#include <stdio.h>
#include <stdlib.h>
main(int argc, char **argv)
{
    char *value;
    if(argc < 2)
    {
        printf("Usage: %s <env_var_def.>\n", argv[0]);
        exit(0);
    }
/* Add new definition to the environment table */
    strupr(argv[1]);
    if (putenv(argv[1]) == -1)
    {
        printf("Error adding the definition: %s\n",
               argv[1]);
    }
```

```
        else
        {
            printf("Added to environment table: %s\n",
                    argv[1]);
            printf("This definition will be gone once the \
program exits.\n");
        }
        return 0;
}
```

raise

COMPATIBILITY

TC1	TC1.5	TC2	TC++	MSC3	MSC4	MSC5	MSC6	QC1	QC2	QC2.5	ANSI	UNIX V	XNX
▲	▲		▲			▲	▲	▲	▲	▲	▲		

PURPOSE Use *raise* to "raise a signal" that generates an exception, leading to special handling.

SYNTAX

```
int raise(int signum);

int signum;        Signal number to be raised
```

EXAMPLE CALL

```
raise(SIGABRT);
```

INCLUDES

```
#include <signal.h>        For function declaration
```

DESCRIPTION The *raise* function creates an exception condition corresponding to the number *signum*. The exception will be handled by invoking a routine that was set up earlier by calling the function *signal*. If this was not done, certain default actions are performed for that particular exception. Table 4-7 in the reference pages on *signal* shows the default action for each exception condition and the defined constants for signals used as arguments to *raise*.

RETURNS If successful, *raise* returns a zero. Otherwise, it returns a nonzero value.

SEE ALSO `signal` *To install exception handlers for signals*

EXAMPLE Demonstrate the use of *raise* by generating the signal SIGABRT, signifying "abnormal termination" of a process.

```
#include <stdio.h>
#include <signal.h>
```

```
void main()
{
    printf("Raising SIGABRT...\n");
    raise(SIGABRT);
}
```

COMPATIBILITY

setjmp

TC1	TC1.5	TC2	TC++	MSC3	MSC4	MSC5	MSC6	QC1	QC2	QC2.5	ANSI	UNIX V	XNX
▲	▲	▲	▲	▲	▲	▲	▲	▲	▲	▲	▲	▲	▲

PURPOSE Use *setjmp* to save a stack environment before calling another function. This environment can be restored by a call to *longjmp*, achieving the effect of a nonlocal *goto*.

SYNTAX
```
int setjmp(jmp_buf env);
```

`jmp_buf env;` *Data type where the registers and a return address representing the stack environment are stored*

EXAMPLE CALL
```
if (setjmp(env) != 0) printf("Returned from longjmp\n");
```

INCLUDES `#include <setjmp.h>` *For function declaration and definition of the data type* jmp_buf

DESCRIPTION The *setjmp* function saves certain registers and its own return address in the argument *env*, which is of type *jmp_buf* as defined in *setjmp.h*. The saved values represent the stack environment at the statement where the call to *setjmp* occurred. When *longjmp* is later called with the saved stack environment, it restores all stack-based local variables in the routine to the values they had when *setjmp* was called and jumps to the return address that *setjmp* had saved. This will feel like a return, one more time, from the last call to *setjmp*. Note that this process does not guarantee the proper restoration of register-based variables.

COMMON USES The *setjmp* function is used in conjunction with *longjmp* to pass control of execution to error-recovery code without using the normal function call and return conventions.

RETURNS After saving the stack environment, *setjmp* returns a zero. When *longjmp* is called with the environment saved by this particular call to *setjmp*, the effect is the same as returning from *setjmp* again, this time with the second argument of *longjmp* as the return value.

COMMENTS It is a little difficult to understand the behavior of *setjmp* and *longjmp*. Essentially, these routines give you the flexibility of jumping to an arbitrary location from within C. This is akin to a "goto" statement that lets you jump from one function to another.

SEE ALSO `longjmp` *To jump back to where* setjmp *was called earlier*

EXAMPLE Demonstrate the functioning of *setjmp* in a program that sets up the stack environment and then calls a function that in turn calls *longjmp* with the environment saved earlier. Notice how the effect is one of returning twice from the first call to *setjmp*. The second return is with a different return value than the first one, so you can do some extra processing after *longjmp* is called. Note too that you can return from a function without using the normal *return* statement.

```
#include <stdio.h>
#include <setjmp.h>
static jmp_buf this_place;
static void fake_error(void);
void main()
{
    int retval;
    retval = setjmp(this_place);
    if(retval == 0)
    {
        printf("First return from \"setjmp\"\n");
    }
    else
    {
        printf("Second return from \"setjmp\" induced \
by call to \"longjmp\"\n");

/* Do processing that's otherwise skipped. For example,
 * error recovery.
 */
        printf("There may be an error handler here.\n\
We simply exit.\n");
        exit(retval);
    }
/* Somewhere else, in another function call longjmp */
    printf("Everything seemed fine until suddenly...\n");
    fake_error();
}
/*-----------------------------------------------*/
static void fake_error(void)
```

```
{
    printf("Illegal instruction\n");
    printf("--- longjmp called ---\n");
    longjmp(this_place, 1);
}
```

COMPATIBILITY

setlocale

TC1	TC1.5	TC2	TC++	MSC3	MSC4	MSC5	MSC6	QC1	QC2	QC2.5	ANSI	UNIX V	XNX
			▲				▲		▲	▲	▲		

PURPOSE Use *setlocale* to define the current locale.

SYNTAX

```
char *setlocale(int category, const char *locale_name);
```

`int category;` *Indicates the parts of your program's locale-dependent aspects for which you are defining a locale, one of: LC_ALL, LC_COLLATE, LC_CTYPE, LC_MONETARY, LC_NUMERIC, or LC_TIME*

`char *locale_name;` *The name of locale that will control the specified category*

EXAMPLE CALL

```
setlocale(LC_ALL, "C");
```

INCLUDES `#include <locale.h>` *For function declaration and definition of locale names*

DESCRIPTION The *setlocale* function sets the locale to the one named in the string *locale_name* for the locale-dependent aspects of your program specified by the argument *category*. The *category* can take one of the values shown in Table 4.2.

COMMON USES The pair of functions, *setlocale* and *localeconv*, help you internationalize your applications—make them aware of different ways of formatting monetary and numerical information. However, Turbo C++ supports only the default "C" locale, which is not much help for making your application international.

RETURNS If *locale_name* is not NULL and *setlocale* is successful, it returns the string associated with the specified category for the new locale. Otherwise, *setlocale* returns a NULL and the program's locale is not changed.

SEE ALSO `localeconv`

signal

COMPATIBILITY

TC1	TC1.5	TC2	TC++	MSC3	MSC4	MSC5	MSC6	QC1	QC2	QC2.5	ANSI	UNIX V	XNX
		▲	▲	▲	▲	▲	▲	▲	▲	▲	▲	▲	▲

PURPOSE Use *signal* to define a function that handles an exception condition.

SYNTAX

```
void (*signal(int signum,
        void (*func)(int signum[, int subcode])))(int signum);
```

`int signum;` *Signal number for which a handler is being set up*

`void (*func)(int , int);` *Pointer to handler that can accept the signal number and an optional subcode as arguments*

INCLUDES `#include <signal.h>` *For function declaration*

DESCRIPTION The *signal* function sets up the routine *func* as the handler for the exception or signal number (*signum*). The handler is expected to accept the signal number and an optional error code as arguments. The signal number must be one of the constants shown in Table 4-7. These are defined in the include file *signal.h*. The default handling of each exception is also explained in Table 4-7. The argument *func* must be either the address of a C or assembly language routine or one of the constants SIG_DFL or SIG_IGN. Table 4-8 summarizes the action taken by these exception handlers.

Table 4-7. ***Exception Conditions***

Signal	Exception Condition	Default Action
SIGABRT	Abnormal termination of program.	Terminate program with exit code 3.
SIGFPE	Floating-point error, such as overflow, division by zero, etc.	Terminate program.
SIGILL	Illegal instruction. This exception is not generated by MS-DOS, but is included for ANSI compatibility.	Not applicable in MS-DOS.
SIGINT	Generated when user hits Control-C.	Generate software interrupt number 23h.
SIGSEGV	Illegal memory access. This exception is not generated under MS-DOS, but is included for ANSI compatibility.	Not applicable in MS-DOS.
SIGTERM	Termination request sent to the program. This is not generated in MS-DOS, but is included for ANSI compatibility.	Not applicable in MS-DOS.

Table 4-8. *Exception Handlers*

Handler	Action
SIG_DFL	This refers to the default handler. If the program is terminated, files will be closed, but buffers associated with files open for buffered I/O will not be flushed.
SIG_IGN	If you provide this as the handler, the exception condition will be ignored. This should not be used as the handler for the SIGFPE signal because this leaves the floating-point package unusable.
Function Address	The function will be called with the signal and an optional code as the arguments. The SIGINT and SIGFPE exceptions are handled differently. For the SIGINT exception, the handler will be called with SIGINT as the argument. At the same time, SIG_DFL is set up as the handler for subsequent SIGINT signals. Of course, you can reset the handler in the function called as a result of SIGINT. For SIGFPE exceptions, the installed handler will be called with the value SIGFPE and an integer code representing the floating-point error. This second argument is a constant of FPE_<code> where the constants are defined in the include file *float.h*. The handler for SIGFPE should call *_fpreset* to reset the floating-point package and clear the error condition.

RETURNS If successful, *signal* returns the pointer to the previous handler. In case of error, it returns the constant SIG_ERR and sets the global variable *errno* to EINVAL to indicate an invalid signal number.

SEE ALSO `raise` *To generate a signal*

EXAMPLE The SIGINT signal is generated when you hit Control-C. The default handler for this signal terminates the program. Use *signal* in a program to install your own handler for SIGINT. This way, instead of abruptly ending the program, the user has a chance to cancel the signal.

```
#include <stdio.h>
#include <signal.h>
void ctrlc_handler(int);
int back_again = 0;
main()
{
/* Take over the Control-C interrupt */
    if(signal(SIGINT, ctrlc_handler) == SIG_ERR)
    {
        perror("signal failed");
        exit(0);
    }
    printf("Installed SIGINT signal handler\n");
```

```
    printf("Hit Control-C to exit:");
    while(1)
    {
        kbhit();
        if(back_again != 0)
        {
            back_again = 0;
            printf("\nHit Control-C to exit:");
        }
    }
    return 0;
}

/*-----------------------------------------------------*/
void ctrlc_handler(int sig)
{
    int c;
/* First arrange to ignore further SIGINT */
    signal(SIGINT, SIG_IGN);
    printf("\nInterrupted. Quit?");
    c = getche();
    if(c == 'y' || c == 'Y') exit(0);
/* Reenable interrupt handler -- and return */
    back_again = 1;
    signal(SIGINT, ctrlc_handler);
}
```

spawn functions

COMPATIBILITY

TC1	TC1.5	TC2	TC++	MSC3	MSC4	MSC5	MSC6	QC1	QC2	QC2.5	ANSI	UNIX V	XNX
▲	▲	▲	▲		▲	▲	▲	▲	▲	▲			

PURPOSE Use any one of the *spawn* functions to load and execute a child process and to return to your program when the child process terminates.

SYNTAX

```
int spawnl(int modeflag, char *path, char *arg0, char *arg1,...,
           NULL);

int spawnle(int modeflag, char *path, char *arg0, char *arg1,...,
            NULL, char *envp[]);

int spawnlp(int modeflag, char *path, char *arg0, char *arg1,...,
            NULL);
```

```
int spawnlpe(int modeflag, char *path, char *arg0, char *arg1,...,
            NULL, char *envp[]);

int spawnv(int modeflag, char *path, char *argv[]);

int spawnve(int modeflag, char *path, char *argv[], char *envp[]);

int spawnvp(int modeflag, char *path, char *argv[]);

int spawnvpe(int modeflag, char *path, char *argv[], char *envp[]);
```

`int modeflag;` *Execution mode of calling process*

`char *path;` *Pathname of file to be executed as a child process*

`char *arg0, *arg1, . . . , NULL;` *Command-line arguments for the child process (ends with a NULL)*

`char *argv[];` *Array of command-line arguments for the child process*

`char *envp[];` *The environment parameter table*

INCLUDES `#include <process.h>` *For function declaration and definition of the constants P_WAIT, P_OVERLAY, and P_NOWAIT*

DESCRIPTION The *spawn* functions create a child process to load and execute the program specified by the argument *path*. The argument *modeflag* indicates how the parent process should be treated while the child is running. Under MS-DOS, this flag can take either of the values P_WAIT or P_OVERLAY. The P_WAIT flag indicates that the parent process should be suspended until the child finishes, whereas P_OVERLAY means that the child overwrites the parent in memory, destroying the parent. The P_OVERLAY mode has the same effect as the *exec* functions have. A third constant, P_NOWAIT, is defined in *process.h* and is meant for concurrent execution of parent and child, but use of this mode under MS-DOS produces an error. This mode might be useful in a multitasking operating system of the future.

The variations among the *spawn* functions are reflections of the way in which arguments and environment variables are passed to the child process. Table 4-9 describes each function's action. The fifth letter of the name, "1" or "v," determines how command-line arguments are received by the child process. The next one or two letters indicate how environment variables are passed to the child process. If the sixth letter of the name is a "p," the PATH environment variable is used by COMMAND.COM to locate the executable program you specify in the argument *path*. Otherwise, you must specify the full pathname of the file to be executed or specify a path beginning at the current working directory. If the *path* argument does not have an extension, the *spawn* function first searches for a file without an extension. If none is found and *path* does not end with a period, it tries the extensions .COM and .EXE, in that order.

Table 4-9. ***The* spawn *Functions***

Fifth Letter of Name	Meaning
l	Command-line arguments to the child process are listed on the statement that invokes the *spawn* function. These forms are useful when the number of arguments is known in advance. The arguments *arg0, arg1 . . .* are listed one after another with a NULL marking the end.
v	Command-line arguments are passed in the form of a pointer to an array of argument strings. This is useful when the number of arguments is not known in advance. In this case, you prepare an array of NULL-terminated strings, each representing one command-line argument for the child program, put a NULL to mark the end of the list and pass the pointer to this array (*argv*) to the child process via the *spawn* function.

Next Two Letters	How Environment Variables Are Handled
none	Child process inherits parent's environment variables.
p	PATH environment variable is used to locate the executable file. In this case, the *path* argument may specify a program name without any directory information and COMMAND.COM will locate the program, if present, in any one of the directories included in your PATH environment variable.
e	Child process receives a pointer *envp* to an array of environment strings. Each environment variable definition is of the form *NAME=value of variable*, and the end of the array is marked by a NULL.
pe	This is a combination of the letters described above. Thus, in this, the PATH environment variable is used and the child process gets a pointer to a table of environment variables that you prepare.

Note that the combined length of all the command-line argument strings, including a separating space between adjoining arguments, must not exceed 128 bytes. It is customary to provide the full pathname of the executable file as the first command-line argument to the child process, although using a different string will not produce an error.

In the child process, all signal handlers are reset to the default ones. Files that were open in the parent remain open in the child.

Process Control

COMMON USES The *spawn* functions are useful when you want to execute a separately compiled and linked application from your program and return to your main program when that process terminates. The example below illustrates how you can pass pointers to data areas for sharing between the two processes.

RETURNS When used with P_WAIT as *modeflags*, the *spawn* functions return the exit status of the child process to the parent. The P_NOWAIT mode is not currently available. If the child process cannot be started, the return value is −1 and *errno* is set to one of the constants shown in Table 4-10, indicating the cause of the error.

Table 4-10. *Error Codes Returned by* spawn *Functions*

Error	Cause of Error
E2BIG	Either the total length of the command-line arguments exceeds 128 bytes or the memory required for the environment variables exceeds 32 K.
EINVAL	The *modeflag* argument is invalid.
ENOENT	Either the path or the file specified in the argument *path* was not found.
ENOEXEC	The specified file is not executable because its format does not match the DOS specification for an executable file.
ENOMEM	There is not enough memory to load and execute the child process or available memory is corrupted or an invalid block of memory was located, indicating the parent process was incorrectly loaded.

COMMENTS The *spawn* functions provide a powerful mechanism to make your application versatile. Essentially, you can let programs that are "well-behaved" toward your application (in that they do not hinder its performance) run from the application, giving the functionality of terminate-but-stay-resident (TSR) utilities that are so prevalent in the MS-DOS world.

SEE ALSO `exec functions` *To launch a process that overlays its parent in memory*

EXAMPLE Demonstrate their use in a program that allows a child process to run using any one of the eight *spawn* functions. Prepare data in a structure allocated in the parent program and pass this data to the child by encoding the address as a character string and using that string as a command-line argument. In the child program, print the command-line arguments and the environment passed to it. Then, using the address passed in the command-line, access the data structure and display the various fields. Finally, make changes to the data structure and exit. In the parent program, print the values in the data structure to show that the changes made in the child came through. Note: Remember to compile and link the child program first and save it in a file named *child.exe*.

```
/*====================== PARENT ======================*/
#include <stdio.h>
#include <process.h>
#include <alloc.h>
#include <string.h>
typedef struct TEST_DATA
{
    char name[20];
    int n;
    double x;
} TEST_DATA;
/* PARENT: Test the "spawn" functions. Pass address of
 *         data in command-line arguments as well as
 *         environment variables when appropriate.
 */
char *envp[]=
{
    "PARENT=SPAWN FUNCTIONS",
    NULL
};
main()
{
    char *argv[4], buf[20], rname[40];
    TEST_DATA *pdata;
/* Set up a data structure and initialize it */
    if((pdata=(TEST_DATA *)
        alloc(sizeof(TEST_DATA))) == NULL) abort();
    strcpy(pdata->name, "PARENT");
    pdata->n = 100;
    pdata->x = 1000.99;
/* Set up the arguments for the child process */
    argv[0] = "child.exe",
    argv[1] = rname;
    sprintf(buf, "%Fp", (void far *)pdata);
    argv[2] = buf;
    argv[3] = NULL;
/* Ask user which "spawn" routine to call */
    printf("Enter name of \"spawn\" function to call:");
    gets(rname);
    strlwr(rname);
/* Call the "spawn" function requested by the user */
    if(strcmp(rname, "spawnl") == 0)
    {
        spawnl(P_WAIT, "child.exe",
               "child.exe", "spawnl", buf, NULL);
```

```
    }
    if(strcmp(rname, "spawnle") == 0)
    {
        spawnle(P_WAIT, "child.exe",
        "child.exe", "spawnle", buf, NULL, envp);
    }
    if(strcmp(rname, "spawnlp") == 0)
    {
        spawnlp(P_WAIT, "child.exe",
                "child.exe", "spawnlp", buf, NULL);
    }
    if(strcmp(rname, "spawnlpe") == 0)
    {
        spawnlpe(P_WAIT, "child.exe",
        "child.exe", "spawnlpe", buf, NULL, envp);
    }
    if(strcmp(rname, "spawnv") == 0)
    {
        spawnv(P_WAIT, "child.exe", argv);
    }
    if(strcmp(rname, "spawnve") == 0)
    {
        spawnve(P_WAIT, "child.exe", argv, envp);
    }
    if(strcmp(rname, "spawnvp") == 0)
    {
        spawnvp(P_WAIT, "child.exe", argv);
    }
    if(strcmp(rname, "spawnvpe") == 0)
    {
        spawnvpe(P_WAIT, "child.exe", argv, envp);
    }
/* Check if we could call child or not */
    if(strcmp(pdata->name, "CHILD") == 0)
    {
        printf("Back from child: name = %s, n = %d, \
x= %f\n", pdata->name, pdata->n, pdata->x);
    }
    else
    {
        printf("Don't know: %s\n", rname);
    }
    return 0;
}
```

```
/*====================== CHILD ======================*/
/*     Must be in a file named:  CHILD.EXE          */
#include <stdio.h>
#include <dos.h>
#include <string.h>
typedef struct TEST_DATA
{
    char name[20];
    int n;
    double x;
} TEST_DATA;
/* Child: First argument is program name,
 *        Second one tells us how child was invoked
 *        Third argument is an address in the form
 *        SSSS:OOOO (segment:offset). This is the
 *        address of a data structure allocated in
 *        the parent.
 */
static char far *cname = "CHILD";
void main(int argc, char **argv, char **envp)
{
    char  **p_table;
    TEST_DATA far *pdata;
    void far *p_s1;
    void far *p_s2;
    printf("CHILD: received %d arguments\n", argc);
    if(argc < 3){
        printf("not enough arguments\n");
        exit(1);
    }
    printf("CHILD invoked by a %s call.\n", argv[1]);

/* Now print the environment passed to CHILD     */
    printf("==== CHILD: Environment contains ====\n");
    for(p_table = envp;
        *p_table != NULL;
        p_table++) printf("%s\n", *p_table);

/* Read in address of parent's data from argv[2] */
    sscanf(argv[2], "%Fp", (void far *)&pdata);
    printf("In child: name = %Fs, n = %d, x= %f\n",
            pdata->name, pdata->n, pdata->x);
/* Put new values in the data structure. If CHILD was
 * created by a "spawn" function call, this data will
 * be available to the parent when child exits.
```

```
 * Notice that we have to use "movedata" to copy
 * "far" data in small or medium model.
 */
    p_s1 = (void far *)cname;
    p_s2 = (void far *)pdata->name;
    movedata(FP_SEG(p_s1), FP_OFF(p_s1),
             FP_SEG(p_s2), FP_OFF(p_s2), 6);
    pdata->n = 101;
    pdata->x = 999.99;
    exit(0);
}
```

COMPATIBILITY

system

TC1	TC1.5	TC2	TC++	MSC3	MSC4	MSC5	MSC6	QC1	QC2	QC2.5	ANSI	UNIX V	XNX
▲	▲	▲	▲	▲	▲	▲	▲	▲	▲	▲	▲	▲	▲

PURPOSE Use *system* to execute an MS-DOS command from your program.

SYNTAX

```
int system(const char *string);

const char *string;        MS-DOS command to be executed
```

INCLUDES

```
#include <process.h>       For function declaration
```

or

```
#include <stdlib.h>
```

DESCRIPTION The *system* function uses the environment variable COMSPEC to locate a copy of COMMAND.COM and passes to it the argument *string* as a command to be executed. The environment variable PATH is used to locate any program whose execution may be specified in the command *string*. If *string* is NULL, *system* will only check to see if COMMAND.COM is present.

RETURNS If *string* is not NULL, *system* returns 0 if the command was successfully executed. In case of error, *system* returns −1. If *string* is NULL and COMMAND.COM is found, *system* returns a nonzero value. In case COMMAND.COM cannot be located using the environment variable COMSPEC, *system* will return a zero. Note that syntax errors in the specified command are not considered "errors"; only errors resulting in the inability to execute COMMAND.COM are returned.

SEE ALSO `exec functions, spawn functions` *To launch a process*

EXAMPLE Write a program that lets you type a command and have it executed by a copy of COMMAND.COM that is launched by calling *system*.

```
#include <stdio.h>
#include <stdlib.h>
void main()
{
    char command[80];
    while(1)
    {
        printf("Enter command (\"quit\" to exit):");
        gets(command);
        strlwr(command);
/* Exit if user typed "quit" */
        if(strcmp(command, "quit") == 0) exit(0);
/* Otherwise pass command to a copy of COMMAND.COM */
        if(system(command) == -1)
        {
            perror("error in system");
        }
    }
}
```

Chapter 5 Variable-Length Argument List

Introduction

In writing C programs you encounter functions, such as *printf*, that can take a variable number of arguments. Take, for instance, a routine (*findmax*) that picks the largest integer from an array (*a,b,c,d*). If the routine can accept a variable number of arguments, you can use such calls as *findmax(1,2,3)* and *findmax(a,b,c,d)* to find the maximum of any number of arguments. Fortunately this can be done quite easily in C because of its convention of passing arguments on the stack. A set of macros in the Turbo C++ library makes a straightforward task of handling a variable number of arguments. This section explains how this is done.

Concepts

The secret to handling a variable number of arguments in C lies in the way arguments are passed to a function. Figure 5-1 shows the contents of the state at the moment a C and a FORTRAN or a Pascal function are entered. When a function is called, the arguments followed by the return address (the place in the calling program to which the microprocessor will ultimately return) are placed on the stack.

THE STACK: C AND FORTRAN OR PASCAL

As you can see in Figure 5-1, in FORTRAN and Pascal the arguments of the function are placed on the stack in the order they appear in the function call, exactly the opposite of a C function call. The result is that the first argument in C is always at a fixed positive offset (the number of bytes needed to store the return address) from the stack pointer SP, so no matter how many arguments are passed to a C function, the first argument is always easily reachable. This is not true in FORTRAN and Pascal. In fact, in these, if you do not pass the required number of arguments, the addresses computed for each argument will be erroneous.

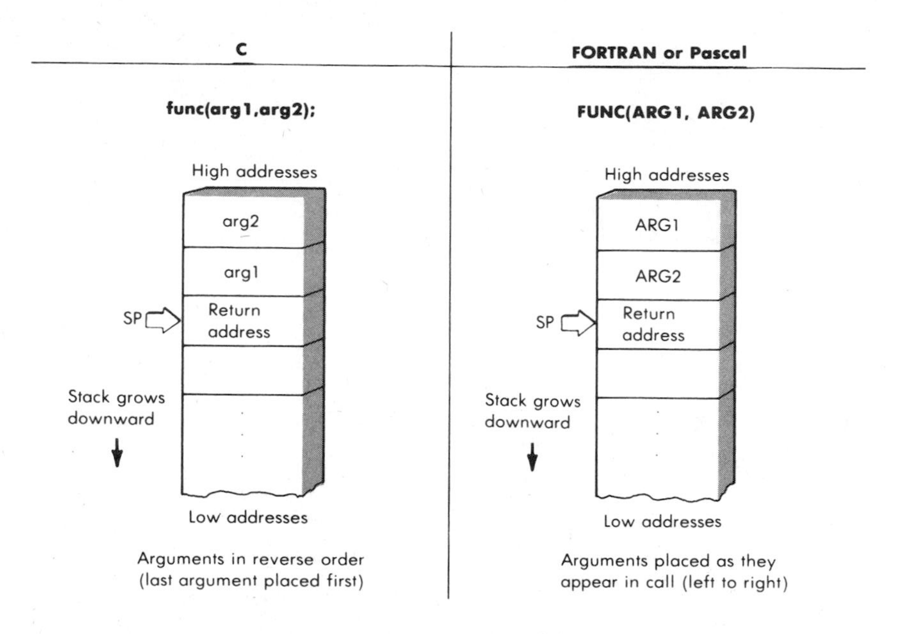

Figure 5-1. ***The stack upon entry to a function***

GETTING TO THE ARGUMENTS IN C

The parameter-passing conventions in C help us access a variable number of arguments. As shown in Figure 5-2, upon entry to the C function the first argument appears on the stack just above the return address (meaning it has the next higher address). Additional arguments have successively higher addresses. If you could get to the first argument on the stack and you knew the size of all other arguments you could retrieve the arguments one by one. This, respectively, is what the *va_start* and the *va_arg* macros do.

While the macros help us access the arguments on the stack, they cannot tell us when the argument list ends. In fact, the only way to find this is by adopting a convention. If each argument were a pointer, for example, you could mark the end of the argument list with a NULL value. To illustrate how the arguments are accessed using these macros, suppose we are writing the *findmax* function to accept a variable number of integers and return the largest of the arguments. Since we want positive numbers only, we assume that a value of –9999 indicates the end of the argument list. Here is one way to implement the *findmax* function:

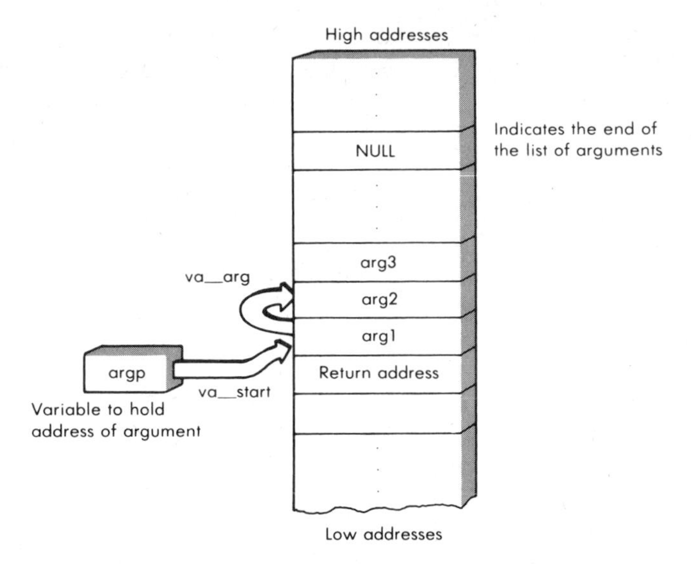

Figure 5-2. ***Accessing a variable number of arguments in C***

```
int findmax(int firstint, ...)
{
    int maxval = -9999, x = 0;
    va_list argp;
/* Get the first optional parameter using "va_start" */
    va_start(argp, firstint);
    x = firstint;
    while(x != -9999)  /* -9999 marks end of arguments */
    {
            if(maxval < x) maxval = x;
            x = va_arg(argp, int);
    }
    return (maxval);
}
```

The variable *argp* of type *va_list* is used to point to arguments. (In Turbo C++, *va_list* is defined to be a void pointer.) The first step in accessing the arguments is to use *va_start* to initialize *argp*. The ANSI standard requires that a function accepting a variable number of arguments must have at least one required argument. The *va_start* macro uses the address of this compulsory first argument to set up *argp*. Once this is done, you can get subsequent arguments by repeatedly using the *va_arg* macro. The approach to accessing the arguments is based on the stack layout shown in Figure 5-2. The function accepting variable-length arguments must declare a pointer to hold the address of the current argument. The macro *va_start* must be used first to initialize this pointer. Each successive use of the macro *va_arg* sets the pointer to the next argument. The type of variables on the stack must be given as an argument to these macros. The macro *va_end* is not needed because it sets the local argument pointer to NULL, which you can do yourself if you want to repeat the process. See Table 5-1 for a description of these macros.

Table 5-1. ***Variable-Length Argument List Macros***

Macro	Description
va_arg	Gets the next argument from the stack.
va_end	Sets the argument pointer to NULL.
va_start	Initializes the argument pointer to the address of the first argument on the stack.

Notes

The macros for handling variable-length argument lists are defined in the header file *stdarg.h*.

COMPATIBILITY

va_start, va_arg, va_end

TC1	TC1.5	TC2	TC++	MSC3	MSC4	MSC5	MSC6	QC1	QC2	QC2.5	ANSI	UNIX V	XNX
▲	▲	▲	▲		▲	▲	▲	▲	▲	▲	▲	1	

PURPOSE Use the *va_start, va_arg,* and *va_end* macros to access arguments in a function that accepts a variable number of arguments.

SYNTAX

```
void va_start(va_list arg_ptr, prev_param);

<type> va_arg(va_list arg_ptr, <type>);

void va_end(va_list arg_ptr);
```

`va_list arg_ptr;`	*Pointer to list of arguments*
`prev_param`	*Name of parameter preceding first optional argument*
`<type>`	*Type of argument to be retrieved*

INCLUDES `#include <stdarg.h>` *For macro declarations and definition of data type* va_list

DESCRIPTION The *va_start, va_arg,* and *va_end* macros provide an ANSI-standard method for accessing the arguments of a function when the function takes a fixed number of required arguments followed by a variable number of optional arguments. The required arguments are in standard style and are accessed by parameter names. The optional arguments are accessed using the macros *va_start, va_arg,* and *va_end.* These, respectively, are used to initialize a pointer to the beginning of the list of optional arguments, to advance the pointer to the next argument of a particular type, and to reset the pointer to NULL when all the arguments are used. The procedure for accessing the optional arguments is outlined below:

1. Access the required arguments by name. These arguments are declared as parameters in the usual manner. Declare a variable *arg_ptr* of type *va_list.*
2. Use the *va_start* macro with *arg_ptr* and the name of the last required argument. This sets *arg_ptr* to the beginning of the list of optional arguments to the function. *Caution:* If the last required argument is declared with the *register* storage class, *va_start* will not work properly.
3. Use the *va_arg* macro to retrieve the next argument. This macro updates *arg_ptr* and returns a pointer to the argument being sought. Repeat this step until you have accessed all the arguments. You have to decide on a value that will mark the end of the list. For example, if

you are accessing integer arguments, you might use a value of −1 to mark the end of the argument list.

4. Use the *va_end* macro to set *arg_ptr* to NULL.

Note that an identical set of macros with slightly different usage exists to access variable-length arguments as specified by the UNIX System V standard.

1. Similar macros exist for UNIX V.

COMMON USES These macros can be used in conjunction with the routines *vfprintf*, *vprintf*, and *vsprintf* to design error-handling routines that accept variable-length arguments.

RETURNS The *va_arg* macro returns a pointer to the next argument of a given type. The *va_start* macro sets a pointer to the beginning of the list of arguments; *va_end* resets this pointer to NULL.

EXAMPLE Demonstrate the use of ANSI-style variable-length argument processing by writing a function that accepts a variable number of integer arguments and returns the largest value. Assume that a value of −999 marks the end of the argument list. Write a main program that shows how the function is used.

```
#include <stdio.h>
#include <stdarg.h>
int findmax(int, ...);
main()
{
    int maxvalue;
/* The end of the list of integers is marked by -9999 */
    maxvalue = findmax(-1, 20, 30, 50, -9999);

    printf("findmax(-1, 20, 30, 50, -9999) returns: \
    %d\n", maxvalue);
    maxvalue = findmax(1, 2, 3, 4, 5, 6, 7, 8, -9999);
    printf("findmax(1, 2, 3, 4, 5, 6, 7, 8, -9999)\
returns: %d\n", maxvalue);
    return 0;
}
/*-------------------------------------------------------*/
/* The "findmax" finds the largest value in a list
 * of integers. It uses the "va...." macros to get
 * the arguments. This is the ANSI version.
 */
int findmax(int firstint, ...)
```

```
{
    int maxval = -9999, x = 0;
    va_list argp;
/* Get the first optional parameter using "va_start" */
    va_start(argp, firstint);
    x = firstint;
    while(x != -9999)
    {
            if(maxval < x) maxval = x;
            x = va_arg(argp, int);
    }
    return (maxval);
}
```

Chapter 6 Memory Allocation and Management

Introduction

Most computer systems, including the PC, operate on a single basic concept. They store instructions and data in memory and use a central processing unit (CPU) such as the 8086 microprocessor to repeatedly retrieve instructions from memory and execute them. The operating system, itself a program residing in memory, takes care of loading other programs and executing them. It has its own scheme of managing the available memory for its data and the memory for other programs as well.

In older programming languages, such as FORTRAN, there is no provision for requesting memory at run-time. All data items and arrays have to be declared before the program is compiled. You have to guess the maximum size of an array beforehand and you cannot exceed the maximum other than by recompiling the program. This is inefficient because you are locking in your program's maximum amount of memory. With the prevalence of terminate-and-stay-resident (TSR) programs, memory is often a scarce resource.

In most modern languages, including C, you can request blocks of memory at run-time and release the blocks when your program no longer needs them. A major advantage of this capability is that you can design your application to exploit all available memory in the system. For example, if your application is a text editor, and your system has a limited amount of memory, using this dynamic memory allocation you can design your application so only a small portion of a file is loaded into memory. The rest is swapped in and out of the disk as needed. On the other hand, when running on a system with more memory, the editor can load more of the file into memory at once, providing increased speed. Such a thoughtful design can also win you the support of your users. Nothing is more annoying than to discover that your investment in additional kilobytes for your system is useless because your favorite application ignores the extra memory.

Like most other capabilities in C, this capability comes in the form of a set of library routines, known as the "memory allocation" routines. We will go through the salient features of this set of routines next.

Concepts: Memory Layout and Addressing

First, we present some concepts and terminology necessary for understanding memory allocation in Turbo C++ under MS-DOS. The questions we answer here include: How is memory addressed in an 8086 microprocessor? What is the layout of memory during the execution of a C program? How does DOS manage the PC's memory, and how does Turbo C++ add another level of management?

MEMORY ADDRESSING IN THE IBM PC

Physically, the 8086 microprocessor uses a 20-bit address to access memory. This usually means that systems based on the 8086 can accommodate a maximum memory size of 1,024 K—one megabyte (note that 1 K = 1,024 bytes). We said "usually" because it is possible to circumvent this limit with the so-called "expanded memory" mechanisms. Also, the newer members of the 8086 family, from the 80286 on, have larger memory address spaces, which can be accessed as extended memory under what is called "protected" mode. When these newer microprocessors run DOS in the "real" mode, however, the limit on memory size still applies.

Segments and Offsets

The 8086 microprocessors have 16-bit internal registers (except the 80386, which has 32-bit registers) and a single register cannot hold the entire 20-bit physical address. Thus a different approach is taken in the implementation of memory addressing in the 8086 microprocessor. Each memory address is constructed of two parts: a segment address and an offset, each a 16-bit value. In this model, as shown in Figure 6-1, we view the physical memory as a collection of segments. The segment address is the address of the first byte of a segment. The offset tells us the location of an arbitrary byte with respect to the beginning of the segment. In hexadecimal (hex) notation, it is customary to denote the segment and offset addresses in the form *SSSS:OOOO* in which the two sets of hexadecimal digits are separated by a colon. With this scheme, two registers, one containing the segment address and the other the offset, can specify the address of any byte in memory.

Since both the segment address and the offset use a 16-bit representation, we can have at most 65,536 segments with each segment at most 64 K in size. Although this implementation of the addressing scheme implies a much larger amount of memory size than we previously claimed, the mapping of segment and offset addresses to a physical address explains the apparent discrepancy: the physical address is 20 bits, so the maximum number of bytes that can be addressed is 2^{20}, which is equal to 1,024 K or 1 megabyte (Mb). The physical address of a memory location is computed by shifting the segment address to the left by four bits and adding the offset to the result.

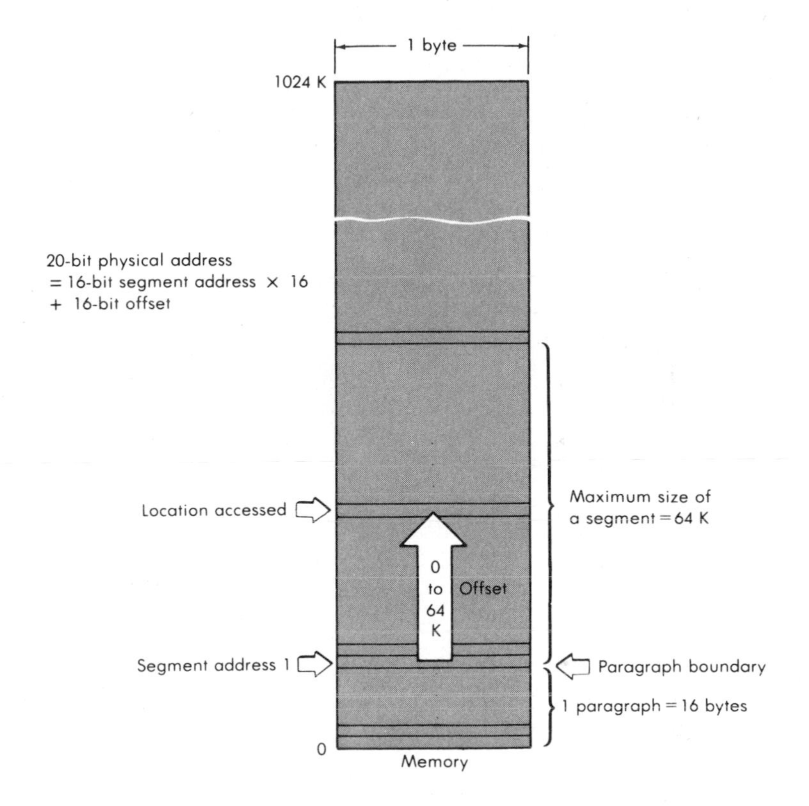

Figure 6-1. *Memory addressing in IBM PC*

Paragraphs

Shifting the segment address to the left by four bits corresponds to multiplying it by 16 (which is the same as 10 hex). In fact, a group of 16 contiguous bytes has a special name in the PC: a "paragraph." This means that in the PC we can have, at most, 65,536 paragraphs. The address of a paragraph is that of the first byte in the paragraph. Since paragraphs are located at 16-byte boundaries, in terms of segment and offset notation each paragraph address has a zero offset. Thus when DOS allocates a certain number of paragraphs, it only returns the segment address.

MEMORY LAYOUT OF A TYPICAL C PROGRAM

Suppose you have written, compiled, and linked a C program into an executable file. Now you begin running the program. How are the different components of the program laid out in memory?

Code Segment

Let's take a snapshot of low memory just as the program begins executing. Starting at a paragraph boundary, you find all the instructions of your program. This is the so-called "code" segment (see Figure 6-2). The segment register CS holds the segment address of the code segment, and the instruction pointer (IP) in the 8086 microprocessor, by holding its offset, keeps track of the current instruction to execute.

Data Segment and the Stack

At the next highest paragraph address after the program's code, you find the data for your program. This is called the "data segment," and its address is stored in the DS register. After the data, a fixed-size block (4 K by default) of memory is used for passing arguments during function calls and

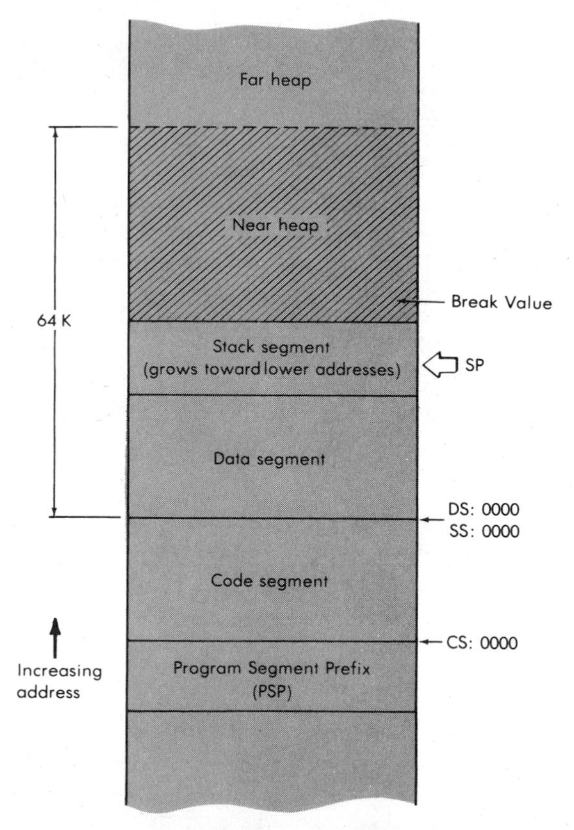

Figure 6-2. ***Memory layout of a Turbo C++ program in IBM PC***

for storing local variables. This block is known as the "stack segment," and it is used as a LIFO buffer. The 8086 microprocessor uses a stack pointer (SP) register to keep track of the current place in the stack. The segment address of the stack is kept in the segment register SS.

In 8086-based computers, the stack always grows downward. This means that when placing an element on the stack, the stack pointer is first decremented and then the element is saved at the address SS:SP.

The Break Value

The first address beyond the data segment of a program is called the "break value" of the process, and it denotes the boundary of the memory allocated to the process (see Figure 6-2). To alter the break value and enlarge the memory currently in use by your process, you can use the *brk* and *sbrk* functions in the library.

MEMORY MODELS IN TURBO C++

Because of the segment:offset addressing scheme in the PC several memory models are available in the Turbo C++ compiler. For each item of code or data, the compiler can either generate explicit segment and offset addresses or can use the offset alone with a default segment address. Each combination of code and data address generation defines a specific memory model.

Near and Far Data

When the compiler uses offsets alone for data addresses, the data items are said to have "near" addresses. Often the items are referred to as "near data." All near data items have the same segment address which is stored in the segment register DS. Analogously, when explicit segment and offset addresses are generated for data items, they are called "far data." Far data items can be located anywhere in memory, and the compiler generates code that explicitly loads an 8086 segment register, such as ES, to access them.

Segment:Offset or Offset Alone: Pros and Cons

The selection of a memory model also has other implications. For example, when offsets alone are used in addressing data or accessing instructions in the code segment, the code executes faster because it does not have to explicitly load a segment register. But the drawback is that at most 64 K of data is available. Instead of forcing a decision like this upon users, the Turbo C++ compiler provides users the option of selecting one out of six different memory models, each trading off execution speed against program size.

Tiny Model

The tiny memory model allows a single segment for both data and code. All four segment registers, CS, DS, SS, and ES, are set to the same segment address. This model is suitable for small programs. Note, however, that Turbo C++ does not allow calls to the graphics functions (see Chapters 18 through 20) from tiny model programs.

Small and Medium Models

The small and medium memory models allow only a single segment of data. The small model also limits code to a single segment, but the medium model allows multiple segments of code. As shown in Figure 6-3, all data addresses for these models use offsets with respect to the segment address in the register DS. These models are most useful when the amount

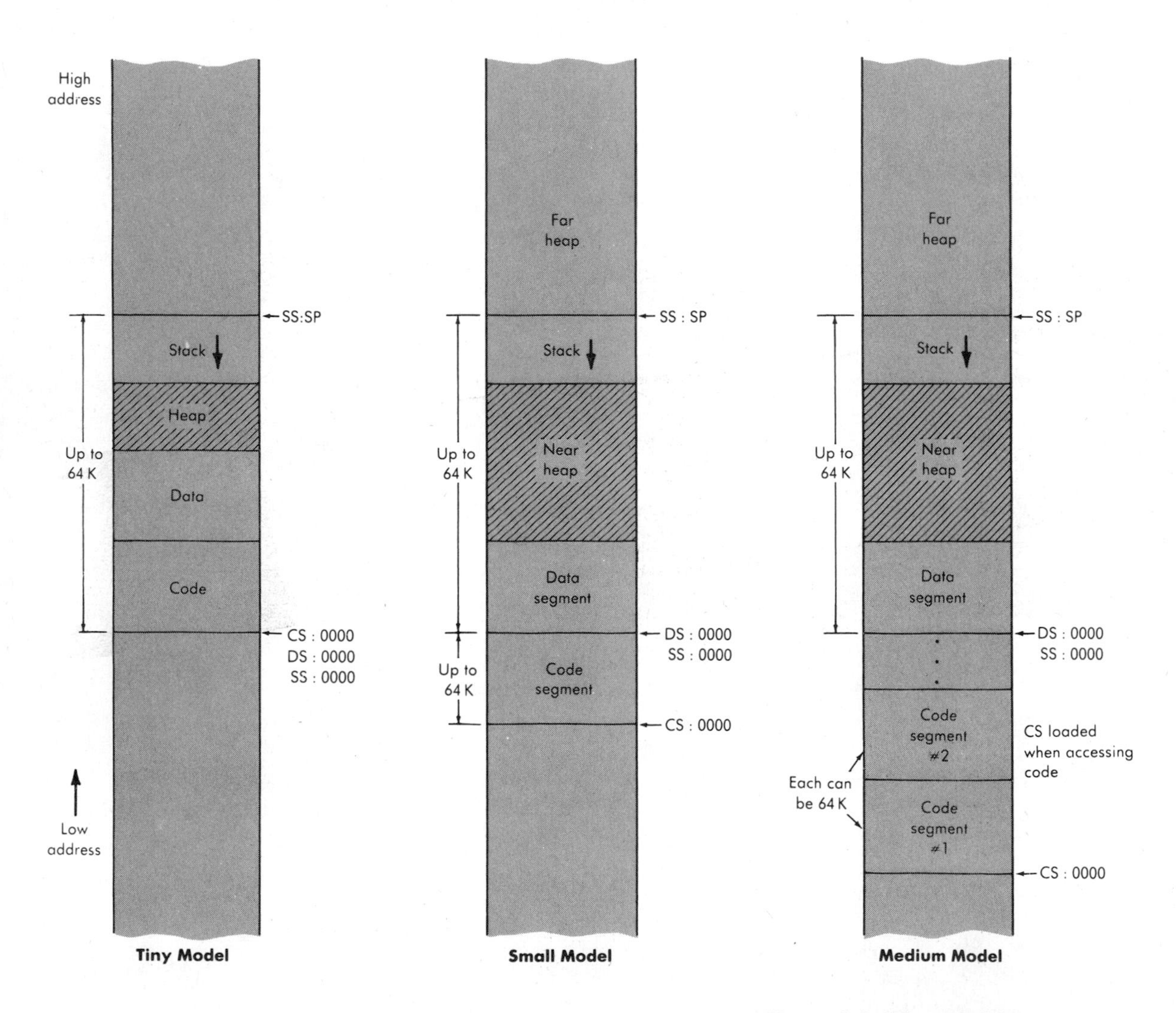

Figure 6-3. *Memory layout*

of data is expected to be limited. When program size is also small, select the small model; for lengthy programs, use the medium model.

Compact and Large Models

In these two models, the compiler generates explicit segment and offset addresses for all data items. Thus these models allow an unlimited amount of data with only one constraint: *no single data item can exceed 64 K.* The compact model allows only a single code segment, whereas the large model allows unlimited code and data, subject only to the condition that each data item fit into a single 64-K segment. Actually, when we say "unlimited" we mean "limited only by available physical memory." Some

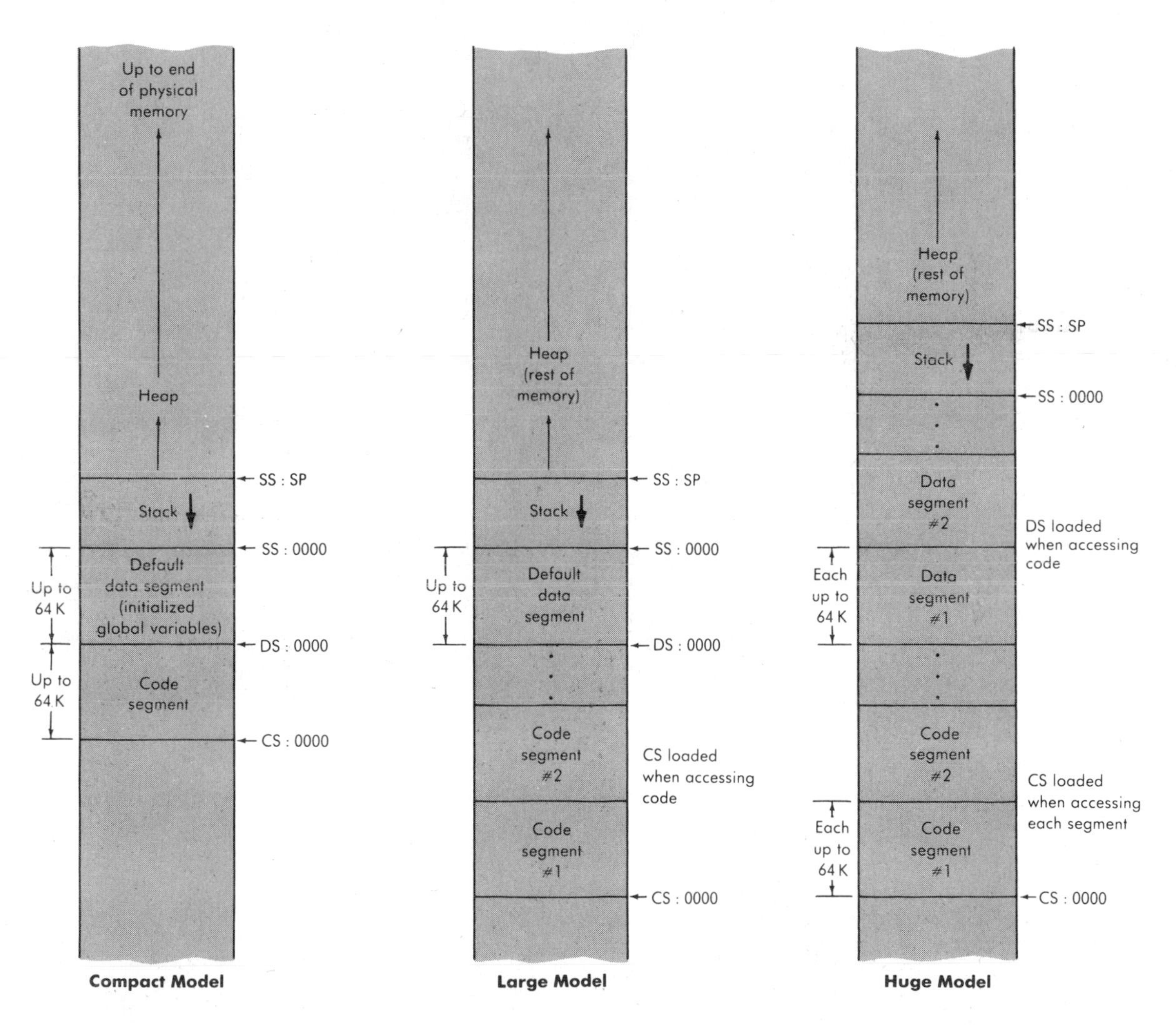

for Turbo C++ memory models

operating systems support "virtual memory," which allows code or data to be swapped out to disk when physical memory is exceeded.

Although these two models allow multiple data segments, all initialized global and static data is still placed in a segment whose address is in DS. Normally, the stack is also located in a separate segment.

Huge Memory Model

The huge memory model removes the single data item's 64-K barrier. A single array can exceed 64 K. The huge model is identical to the large model except that all address calculations are performed by considering each address as a full 32-bit value stored in an unsigned long integer (with the segment address in the high-order bytes). The address is maintained in a "normalized" form by first converting the segment:address pair to the 20-bit physical address and then taking the high-order 16 bits as the segment address and the low-order 4 bits as the offset. Normalization guarantees that each huge pointer refers to a unique location in the physical memory. In the huge model, you pay a penalty because of the overhead involved in normalizing pointers during pointer arithmetic.

Custom Memory Models: *near*, *far*, and *huge* Keywords

The six predefined memory models suffice for most applications, but occasionally you want to address a far data item (for instance, to access video memory directly) in a small model, which lacks such capability. Fortunately, the Turbo C++ compiler allows you to mix and match an occasional data item of a type not available in the selected model. In the compact, large, and huge models, you can use the keyword *near* to signify that certain pieces of data reside in the default data segment (one whose segment address is in the DS register). Similarly, in the small and the medium memory models you can use the *far* keyword to tell the compiler to use explicit segment and offset addresses when generating code that accesses a specific data item (the ES segment register is used to hold the segment addresses of such data items). A third keyword, *huge*, allows you to use a huge data item (size exceeding 64 K) in any memory model.

THE HEAP: NEAR AND FAR

Now we are ready to identify the region of memory from which allocation normally takes place. Of the 64-K "default data segment," 4 K is used as a stack and an indeterminate amount is used by the data and static variables of the program. The rest of the memory in the segment, in the region above the static data and below the stack (see Figures 6-2 and 6-3), is known as the "heap"—or more accurately, the "near heap"—because all locations in this block are reached by an offset from the segment address in DS. When allocation of far data items is requested, an area beyond the default data segment is used and this pool is called the "far heap." Note that there is no near heap in compact, large, and huge models.

The heap is a bit more than simply a block of memory—it is partitioned into smaller blocks, some of which are in use and some free (see Figure 6-4). Also, there are links allowing the memory allocation routines to search for a free block and assign the block to a requesting function. These tasks fall under the category of memory management.

MEMORY MANAGEMENT: A TWO-STEP PROCESS

Memory management is done in two steps in programs compiled and linked with the Turbo C++ memory allocation routines. As an operating system, MS-DOS has to keep track of the memory so that it can load and execute programs. Essentially, it keeps track of the first free paragraph address and provides a service that can dole out a specified number of paragraphs to a requesting process.

The steps involved in accessing the heap depend on the memory model. In the small and medium models, the memory remaining in the

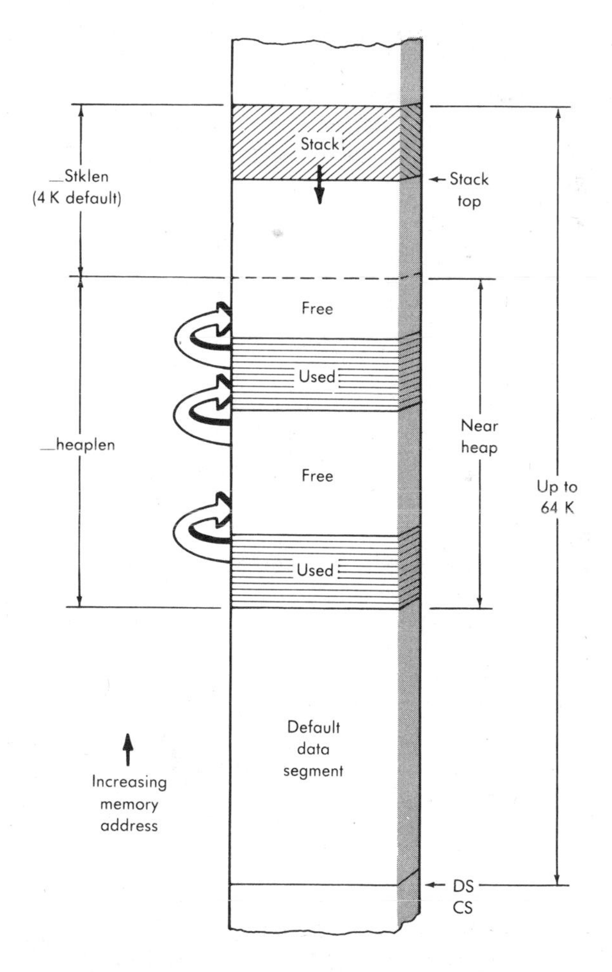

Figure 6-4. ***The heap in memory (the near heap is shown here)***

default data segment (near heap) after allocating the stack is used as a free pool.

You can adjust the size of the stack and the near heap by assigning appropriate values to the *unsigned* global variables *_stklen* and *_heaplen*, respectively.

In the compact and large models, which use far data, the Turbo C++ allocation routines *farcalloc* and *farmalloc* allocate memory from the far heap, which is beyond the stack segment (see Figure 6-3). The allocation of huge data is also handled by *farcalloc* and *farmalloc*.

Notes

The memory allocation routines, cataloged in Table 6-1, give you all the memory management tools necessary for building complex applications that use the available memory intelligently. Note that many of these routines perform similar functions but for different heaps. See Table 6-2 for a breakdown of generic and heap-specific routines.

Table 6-1. ***Memory Allocation Routines***

Routine	Description
brk	Sets a new break value.
calloc	Allocates a number of bytes from the heap (near heap in small and medium models, far heap in large, compact, and huge models) and initializes them to zero.
coreleft	Returns the amount of memory available for allocation.
farcalloc	Allocates an array of elements in the far heap and initializes them to zero.
farcoreleft	Returns the amount of available memory in the far heap.
farfree	Frees a block of memory allocated from the far heap.
farheapcheck	Tests the far heap for consistency.
farheapcheckfree	Tests the free blocks in the far heap.
farheapchecknode	Checks a single node in the linked list of the far heap.
farheapfillfree	Sets all free blocks in the far heap to a specified value.
farheapwalk	Traverses the far heap and returns information on each block of memory.
farmalloc	Allocates a block of memory from the far heap.
farrealloc	Alters the size of a block of memory allocated from the far heap.
free	Frees previously allocated memory (near heap in small and medium models, far heap in large and compact models).
heapcheck	Checks heap for consistency (near heap in small and medium models, far heap in large and compact models).

Table 6-1. *(cont.)*

Routine	Description
heapfillfree	Sets heap elements to specified value (near heap in small and medium models, far heap in large and compact models).
heapwalk	Traverses heap entries and returns information on each entry (near heap in small and medium models, far heap in compact, large and huge models).
malloc	Allocates a number of bytes from the heap (near heap in small and medium models, far heap in large, compact, and huge models).
realloc	Enlarges or shrinks a previously allocated block of memory, moving the block in the heap, if necessary.
sbrk	Sets to a new value the address of the first byte of memory beyond that used by all the data in the program (this is the break value).

THE MEMORY ALLOCATION ROUTINES BY TASK

Table 6-2 lists the memory allocation routines grouped according to the tasks they perform. The most important purpose of these routines is the allocation and the deallocation of memory from the heap, but they can also allocate memory from the stack. Another crucial task is obtaining size information about memory blocks: both allocated and available. Lastly, an entire subcategory of routines provides the capability to *snoop* around in the heap and help us in *debugging* any problems related to the heap. Note that the routines marked *generic* call the routine for the appropriate heap dependent on the selected memory model of the program.

Table 6-2. ***Memory Allocation Routines by Task***

Task	Routines
Allocate memory.	calloc, malloc (generic), farcalloc (far heap), farmalloc (far heap)
Free memory.	free (generic), farfree (far heap)
Alter size of allocated block.	realloc (generic), farrealloc (far heap)
Determine amount available in the heap for allocation.	coreleft (generic), farcoreleft (far heap)
Set the break value (address of first byte beyond all data in the program).	brk, sbrk
Check consistency of heap.	heapcheck (generic), heapcheckfree (generic), heapchecknode (generic), farheapcheck (far heap), farheapcheckfree (far heap), farheapchecknode (far heap)
Fill heap with specified value.	heapfillfree (generic) farheapfillfree (far heap)
Step through elements in heap.	heapwalk (generic), farheapwalk (far heap)

TYPICAL USE OF MEMORY ALLOCATION

You need memory allocation capabilities when you cannot determine in advance the exact amount of space you will need to store the data used or generated in your program. If the data is generated during the course of the program, you may simply want to get space as and when needed. (You may also want to free memory when it is no longer needed.) Typically, the data elements are in the form of a C structure with a field containing pointers to the next element. This enables you to link one element to the next and keep them accessible via a single pointer to the beginning of the linked list. It is also common to want to allocate, at run-time, a number of data elements contiguously. Such a structure, called an "array," provides faster access to arbitrary data elements than linked lists because you do not have to start at the beginning and trace through the links. In either case, the allocation of memory proceeds as described below.

Requesting Memory

You can use either *malloc* or *calloc* to get the needed memory. While *malloc* simply returns a block of memory of specified size, *calloc* allocates room for an array of a specified number of elements, each of a given size, and it also initializes all the allocated bytes to zero. Use the *sizeof* statement to get the size of a data element. For *far* data types, use *farmalloc* or *farcalloc*.

Using the Allocated Block

The allocation routines return the address of the allocated block as a pointer to a *void* data item. You should always cast this pointer into a pointer of the type of data for which you requested space in order to handle data items correctly. This pointer is the only way to access the newly allocated block. By assigning it to a pointer variable, you ensure that it cannot be destroyed. If the request for memory fails, the return value will be NULL. So you must always check for a NULL return value when you call an allocation routine. Otherwise, you will see the error message "Null pointer assignment" when you exit your program.

Releasing Memory

If the data you have stored in a block of memory is no longer needed and you do not plan to store anything in that memory, you should call *free* to release that block to the heap for use by other routines. Use *farfree* to release blocks allocated by *farmalloc* or *farcalloc*.

Altering the Size of a Block

What if you allocated room for an array and later discovered that you need room for more elements? The C library includes routines that can either enlarge or shrink the size of an allocated block. Both the *realloc* and the *farrealloc* routines do the job. Both routines guarantee that the data taking up to the old size of the block will remain intact.

Getting the Size Information

The Turbo C library includes several routines that let you determine the amount of memory available for allocation. The *coreleft* routine returns the size of available memory in bytes. The value depends on the memory model in use. In *near* data models (small and medium) this is the amount available in the near heap. The *farcoreleft* routine returns the number of bytes available in the far heap.

SNOOPING AROUND THE HEAP

Dynamic memory allocation can often be the source of strange errors. For example, you may allocate an array of, say, 100 integers, and by mistake write into array indices above 99 (the last element position). This may overwrite critical information in the heap's data structures and cause the program to fail when a memory allocation routine is called later in your program. Turbo C++ includes several routines that can help you track down such errors.

The *heapcheck* routine is meant to check the consistency of the heap. It will make sure that all the entries in the heap have valid addresses for the blocks of memory used and it will report any bad node entry it finds in the linked list. You can use *heapchecknode* to check a specific block and *heapcheckfree* to verify that the free blocks are consistent.

You can set each byte in all free blocks of memory in the heap to a specified *fill character* by calling *heapfillfree*. Lastly, the *heapwalk* routine will let you examine each entry in the linked list data structure of the heap. Using a combination of these routines, you can isolate problems that are caused by damage to the heap.

In the compact, large, and huge memory models, calls to *heapcheck*, *heapchecknode*, *heapcheckfree*, *heapfillfree*, and *heapwalk* routines map to *farheapcheck*, *farheapchecknode*, *farheapcheckfree*, *farheapfillfree*, and *farheapwalk*, respectively. The *far* routines are also available to check the far heap from small and medium memory models.

Cautions

- Always pass a valid pointer to the deallocation routine *free*. If you pass a pointer that was not returned by the corresponding allocation routine, later calls to the memory allocation functions will produce errors.
- The *brk* and *sbrk* routines that adjust the "break value" should not be used together with other allocation routines. Decreasing the break value using *sbrk* may cause other memory allocation routines to misbehave.

Further Reading

Memory management is covered in most textbooks on operating systems. The book on XINU by Comer[1] and the book on MINIX by Tanenbaum[2] describe memory management from the point of view of an operating system. Each includes samples of C code that implement the memory management algorithms. Knuth's classic text[3] describes the basic algorithms used in deciding how to assign a particular block of memory to satisfy a request. For a more practical and relevant description of the C memory allocation routines and their usage, consult Prata's book[4].

1. Douglas Comer, *Operating System Design, The XINU Approach*, Prentice-Hall, Inc. Englewood Cliffs, NJ, 1984, 486 pages.
2. Andrew S. Tanenbaum, *Operating Systems Design and Implementation*, Prentice-Hall, Inc. Englewood Cliffs, NJ, 1987, 719 pages.
3. Donald E. Knuth, *The Art of Computer Programming, Volume 1: Fundamental Algorithms*, Addison-Wesley, Reading, MA, 1968, 656 pages.
4. Stephen Prata, The Waite Group, *Advanced C Primer++*, Howard W. Sams & Company, Indianapolis, IN, 1986, 502 pages.

COMPATIBILITY

brk

TC1	TC1.5	TC2	TC++	MSC3	MSC4	MSC5	MSC6	QC1	QC2	QC2.5	ANSI	UNIX V	XNX
▲	▲	▲	▲									▲	▲

PURPOSE Use *brk* to alter the "break value" of a program. The break value is the address of the first location beyond the end of a program's data segment.

SYNTAX

```
int  brk (void *endds);

void *endds;
```

New address for the break value (`void *endds;`)

EXAMPLE CALL

```
if(brk(new_break) == -1) perror("brk failed");
```

INCLUDES

```
#include <alloc.h>
```

For function prototype

DESCRIPTION The *brk* function sets the "break value" of the program to the address specified in the argument *endds*. The break value indicates the number of bytes that the process is currently using in the default data segment: it is the address of the last byte in the data segment of the program. By altering this address, you are effectively altering the size of the program in memory.

COMMON USES The *brk* function provides an alternate method of reserving memory.

RETURNS When successful, *brk* returns a zero. Otherwise, it returns −1 and sets the global variable *errno* to the constant ENOMEM to indicate that there was not enough memory.

COMMENTS The *brk* function is provided for compatibility with the UNIX C library. It is impractical to use *brk* because you have to know the address of the end of the data segment before you can alter it intelligently. If you have to reserve or release memory by altering the break value, it is best to do so using *sbrk*.

If possible, avoid altering the break value and use *malloc* for memory allocation because *malloc* is portable, it conforms to the ANSI standard, and it works in all memory models except the huge model. In the huge model, use *farmalloc*.

SEE ALSO

`malloc` *Most general-purpose memory allocation routine*

`farmalloc` *To allocate huge (greater than 64 K) arrays*

`free` *To release memory allocated earlier*

`sbrk` *To increment or decrement the current break value*

EXAMPLE Use *brk* to allocate room for the buffer to hold 80 characters at the end of the default data segment in a small model program. (Hint: Use *sbrk* to get the current break value.) Prompt the user for a string and store it in the buffer you allocated. Call *brk* with the original break value to deallocate this memory.

```
#include <stdio.h>
#include <alloc.h>
char *buffer;
main()
{
/* Call sbrk and get the current break value */
    if((buffer = (char *)sbrk(0)) == (char *)-1)
    {
        printf("sbrk failed.\n");
        exit(0);
    }
/* Allocate a buffer by adding 80 to the break value */
    if (brk(buffer+80) == -1)
    {
        printf("brk failed.\n");
        exit(0);
    }
    printf("Buffer allocated. Enter string to store: ");
    gets(buffer);
    printf("\nYou entered: %s\n",buffer);
    brk(buffer);  /* Deallocate the buffer */
    printf("Buffer deallocated\n");
    return 0;
}
```

calloc

COMPATIBILITY

TC1	TC1.5	TC2	TC++	MSC3	MSC4	MSC5	MSC6	QC1	QC2	QC2.5	ANSI	UNIX V	XNX
▲	▲	▲	▲	▲	▲	▲	▲	▲	▲	▲	▲	▲	▲

PURPOSE Use *calloc* to allocate memory for an array of a given number of elements, each having a specified size. All bytes of the allocated array are initialized to zero.

SYNTAX `void *calloc(size_t num_elems, size_t elem_size);`

`size_t   num_elems;`   *Number of elements*

```
size_t   elem_size;
```
Size of each element in bytes

EXAMPLE CALL

```
p_int = (int *) calloc(100, sizeof(int));
```

INCLUDES

`#include <alloc.h>` *For function declaration and definition of data type* size_t

`#include <stdlib.h>` *For ANSI compatibility*

DESCRIPTION

The *calloc* function computes the number of bytes it must allocate by multiplying the number of elements *num_elems* by the size of each *elem_size*. Then it allocates the memory and sets each byte of the allocated memory to zero.

COMMON USES

The *calloc* function creates and initializes to zero arrays of data objects at run-time. This allows your application to get memory as needed instead of setting aside a fixed amount and running the risk of filling up the space with no way of getting additional room. You can use *calloc*, for example, to set aside memory for 100 elements, each 80 bytes long.

RETURNS

The return value from *calloc* is a pointer to a type *void*, representing the address of the allocated memory. The storage locations are guaranteed to be able to hold data objects of any kind. If the memory allocation is unsuccessful because of insufficient space or bad values of the arguments, a NULL is returned.

SEE ALSO

`malloc` *General-purpose memory allocation routine*

`free` *To release memory allocated earlier*

EXAMPLES

Use *calloc* to allocate room for a buffer to hold 100 lines of text, each 80 characters long. Prompt the user for a string and store it in the buffer.

```
#include <stdio.h>
#include <stdlib.h>
#include <alloc.h>
char *buffer;
main()
{
    buffer = (char *) calloc(100, 80);
    if (buffer == NULL)
    {
        printf("Allocation Failed.\n");
        exit(0);
    }
    printf("Buffer allocated. Enter string to store: ");
```

```
    gets(buffer);
    printf("\nYou entered: %s\n",buffer);
    return 0;
}
```

Suppose you are developing a small data base of your client's vital statistics. You have grouped all information about a single client in a C data structure of type CLIENT_T. Define this data type and use *calloc* to allocate enough memory for 100 clients.

```
#include <stdio.h>
#include <alloc.h>
#include <stdlib.h>
#define MAX_CHR     80
#define MAX_CLIENTS 100
typedef struct CLIENT_T     /* Define a data structure */
{
        char      name[MAX_CHR];
        unsigned  age;
        double    networth;
} CLIENT_T;

main()
{
    CLIENT_T *client_list;  /* Define pointer to data */
    if( (client_list =      /* Cast returned pointer  */
        (CLIENT_T *) calloc(MAX_CLIENTS,
                            sizeof(CLIENT_T))) == NULL)
    {
        fprintf(stderr,"No room for clients!\n");
    }
    else
    {
        printf("Client list allocated successfully.\n");
    }
/* The array of structures can now be accessed by using
 * the pointer "client_list". For example the net worth
 * of client number 10 is --   client_list[10].networth
 */
        return 0;
}
```

Memory Allocation and Management

COMPATIBILITY

coreleft

TC1	TC1.5	TC2	TC++	MSC3	MSC4	MSC5	MSC6	QC1	QC2	QC2.5	ANSI	UNIX V	XNX
▲	▲	▲	▲										

PURPOSE Use *coreleft* to determine the amount of unused memory. The value returned depends upon the memory model.

SYNTAX

```
unsigned long  coreleft (void);  /* HUGE,LARGE, COMPACT models */
unsigned       coreleft (void);  /* SMALL, MEDIUM, TINY models */
```

EXAMPLE CALL

```
mem_avail = coreleft();
```

INCLUDES `#include <alloc.h>` *For function prototype*

DESCRIPTION The *coreleft* function returns the amount of memory available for allocation. In small, medium, and tiny memory models, this is the amount left in the near heap. In compact, large, and huge models, *coreleft* returns the total amount of system memory available for allocation.

COMMON USES You can use *coreleft* to estimate the largest amount of memory you can request from the memory allocation routines.

RETURNS In memory models with near data (tiny, small, and medium) the return value is an unsigned integer containing the number of bytes free in the near heap. In the other memory models, the return value is an unsigned long integer containing the total number of bytes free in the system.

SEE ALSO

`farcoreleft` *To get number of bytes free in the far heap*

`malloc, calloc` *To allocate memory*

EXAMPLE Use *coreleft* in a program that gets the memory available for allocation in the system and displays the information.

```
#include <stdio.h>
#include <alloc.h>

main()
{
    unsigned long mem_avail;
    mem_avail = coreleft();
    printf("%lu bytes available for allocation\n", mem_avail);
    return 0;
}
```

farcalloc

COMPATIBILITY

TC1	TC1.5	TC2	TC++	MSC3	MSC4	MSC5	MSC6	QC1	QC2	QC2.5	ANSI	UNIX V	XNX
▲	▲	▲	▲				1						

PURPOSE Use *farcalloc* to allocate memory from the far heap for an array of elements. The block size can exceed 64-K bytes.

SYNTAX

```
void far  *farcalloc (unsigned long nelem, unsigned long elemsize);
```

`unsigned long nelem;` *Number of elements in array*

`unsigned long elemsize;` *Size of each element in bytes*

EXAMPLE CALL

```
if((bigarray = farcalloc(20000L, sizeof(int))) == NULL)
                printf("Memory allocation failed!\n");
```

INCLUDES `#include <alloc.h>` *For function prototype*

DESCRIPTION The *farcalloc* function allocates *nelem* elements each *elemsize* bytes long from the far heap. The entire amount of unused memory in the system is available for allocation by *farcalloc*. Also, the array size can exceed 64-K bytes. The allocated array is initialized to zeros.

1. The equivalent function for *farcalloc* in Microsoft C 6.0 is *_fcalloc*.

RETURNS If successful, the *farcalloc* function returns a far pointer to the allocated block of memory. If the requested amount of memory could not be allocated, *farcalloc* returns a NULL.

COMMENTS The tiny memory model cannot use this function.

SEE ALSO

`farfree` *To deallocate memory in the far heap*

`farmalloc` *To allocate an uninitialized block of memory from the far heap*

`calloc, malloc` *Standard memory allocation routines*

EXAMPLE Use *farcalloc* to allocate space for an array of 20,000 integers.

```
#include <stdio.h>
#include <alloc.h>

main()
{
    int far *bigarray;
```

```
    if((bigarray = farcalloc(20000L, sizeof(int))) == NULL)
    {
        printf("Memory allocation failed!\n");
        exit(1);
    }
    printf("Array of 20,000 integers allocated at %Fp\n",
            bigarray);
    return 0;
}
```

farcoreleft

COMPATIBILITY

TC1	TC1.5	TC2	TC++	MSC3	MSC4	MSC5	MSC6	QC1	QC2	QC2.5	ANSI	UNIX V	XNX
▲	▲	▲	▲										

PURPOSE Use *farcoreleft* to determine the total number of available bytes in the system.

SYNTAX `unsigned long  farcoreleft (void);`

EXAMPLE CALL `total_mem_avail = farcoreleft();`

INCLUDES `#include <alloc.h>` *For function prototype*

DESCRIPTION The *farcoreleft* function returns the total amount of system memory available for allocation.

COMMON USES The *farcoreleft* function can be used to estimate the largest amount of memory you can request from the far heap.

RETURNS The return value is an unsigned long integer containing the total number of bytes free in the system.

SEE ALSO `coreleft` *To get number of bytes free in the heap (near or far, depending on memory model)*

`farcalloc, farmalloc` *To allocate memory from far heap*

EXAMPLE Use *farcoreleft* to write a utility program that reports the total number of free bytes in the system.

```
#include <stdio.h>
#include <alloc.h>
```

```
main()
{
    unsigned long total_mem_avail;
    total_mem_avail = farcoreleft();
    printf("%lu bytes available for allocation\n",
           total_mem_avail);
    return 0;
}
```

farfree

COMPATIBILITY

TC1	TC1.5	TC2	TC++	MSC3	MSC4	MSC5	MSC6	QC1	QC2	QC2.5	ANSI	UNIX V	XNX
▲	▲	▲	▲		1	1	1						

PURPOSE Use *farfree* to release memory allocated from the far heap by *farcalloc, farmalloc,* or *farrealloc.*

SYNTAX

```
void   farfree (void far *block);
```

`void far *block;` *Far pointer to block of memory to be released*

EXAMPLE CALL `farfree(bigarray);`

INCLUDES `#include <alloc.h>` *For function prototype*

DESCRIPTION The *farfree* function deallocates memory allocated from the far heap by any of the functions *farcalloc, farmalloc,* or *farrealloc.*

1. The equivalent function for *farfree* in Microsoft C 3.0 is *hfree.*

COMMENTS In small and medium models, memory allocated by *calloc* and *malloc* cannot be freed by calling *farfree.* The heaps used by *malloc* and *farmalloc* are distinct in these memory models.

SEE ALSO

`farcalloc, farmalloc, farrealloc` *To allocate memory from the far heap*

`free` *Standard memory deallocation routine*

EXAMPLE Demonstrate the use of *farfree* to release memory allocated from the far heap.

```
#include <stdio.h>
#include <alloc.h>
```

```
main()
{
    int far *bigblock;
    printf("%lu bytes available in the far heap\n",
           farcoreleft());
    if((bigblock = farmalloc(80000L)) == NULL)
    {
        printf("Memory allocation failed!\n");
        exit(1);
    }
    printf("Block of 80,000 bytes allocated at %Fp\n",
           bigblock);
    printf("%lu bytes available in the far heap "
           "after allocation\n", farcoreleft());
/* Now free the block */
    farfree(bigblock);
    printf("%lu bytes available in the far heap "
           "after freeing block\n", farcoreleft());
    return 0;
}
```

COMPATIBILITY

farheapcheck

TC1	TC1.5	TC2	TC++	MSC3	MSC4	MSC5	MSC6	QC1	QC2	QC2.5	ANSI	UNIX V	XNX
			▲			1	1						

PURPOSE Use *farheapcheck* to check the consistency of the far heap.

SYNTAX `int farheapcheck(void);`

EXAMPLE CALL `heapstatus = farheapcheck();`

INCLUDES `#include <alloc.h>` *For function declaration*

DESCRIPTION The *farheapcheck* function checks the linked list of memory blocks, called the far heap, located *outside* the default data segment. This is the pool of memory from which data blocks referenced by far pointers (see Tutorial) are allocated by routines such as *farcalloc* and *farmalloc*.

The check involves ensuring that all entries in the heap data structure make sense; for example, if an entry is the address of a block of memory in use, it must be within the limits of the pool of memory currently assigned to the far heap.

1. The equivalent function for *farheapcheck* in Microsoft C 5.0 and 6.0 is *_fheapchk.*

RETURNS The return values from *farheapcheck* are interpreted according to Table 6-3. Essentially, any negative return value indicates that a problem was found with the heap.

Table 6-3. *Possible Results of a Heap Consistency Check*

Constants	Interpretation of the Constant
_HEAPOK	All entries in the linked list that make up the heap appear to be consistent (all addresses are within the limits of the memory block assigned to the heap).
_HEAPEMPTY	The heap is probably not initialized. This means the "heap checking" utility routine could not find any linked list data structure that would indicate an existing heap. This is the condition before any of the allocation routines are called.
_HEAPCORRUPT	Heap has been corrupted.

COMMENTS The *farheapcheck* function is intended for checking the consistency of the far heap, the free memory pool outside the default data segment from which memory is allocated for data objects that are to be accessed by far pointers (see Tutorial). It is not necessary to call *farheapcheck* directly unless you are mixing memory models, for example, allocating a data array with far addresses in a small or medium model.

SEE ALSO

`farheapcheckfree:`	*To check that the free blocks are not overwritten*
`farheapchecknode:`	*To check a single block of memory*
`farheapwalk`	*To traverse the linked list of nodes in the far heap*
`heapfillfree`	*To fill all unallocated memory in the heap with a specified character*
`heapwalk`	*To navigate through the heap's linked list data structure and check the size and status (free or used) of blocks*
`heapcheck`	*To check the heap in any memory model*

EXAMPLE Use *farmalloc* and *farfree* to allocate and deallocate a few blocks of memory in the far heap. Then call *farheapcheck* to check the heap and display the returned information. Note that you can compile and link this program in any memory model because we are explicitly using far data pointers and calls to the far allocation routine *farmalloc.*

```
#include <stdio.h>
#include <alloc.h>
main()
{
   char far *buffer1, far *buffer2;
   int heapstatus;
/* Perform some allocations and deallocations */
   buffer1 = (char far *) farmalloc(500);
   buffer2 = (char far *) farmalloc(1024);
   farfree(buffer2);

/* Now get the status of the far heap by calling farheapcheck */
   heapstatus = farheapcheck();
   switch (heapstatus)
   {
       case _HEAPOK:       printf("Heap OK\n");
                           break;
       case _HEAPEMPTY:    printf("Heap not initialized\n");
                           break;
       case _HEAPCORRUPT:  printf("Heap is corrupted\n");
                           break;
   }
   return 0;
}
```

COMPATIBILITY

farheapcheckfree

TC1	TC1.5	TC2	TC++	MSC3	MSC4	MSC5	MSC6	QC1	QC2	QC2.5	ANSI	UNIX V	XNX
			▲										

PURPOSE Use *farheapcheckfree* to check the consistency of the free blocks in the far heap. Call *farheapfillfree* beforehand to fill the free blocks with a known character.

SYNTAX `int farheapcheckfree(unsigned int fill_char);`

`unsigned int fill_char;` *Character used to fill the free blocks*

EXAMPLE CALL `heapstatus = farheapcheckfree('F');`

INCLUDES `#include <alloc.h>` *For function declaration*

DESCRIPTION The *farheapcheckfree* function checks the free blocks in the far heap. This is the pool of memory from which data blocks referenced by far pointers (see Tutorial) are allocated by routines such as *farcalloc* and *farmalloc*.

The check involves ensuring that all entries in the heap data structure make sense and all free blocks contain the specified fill character, *fill_char*. You should call *farheapfillfree* to fill all free blocks with that character before calling *farheapcheckfree*.

COMMON USES The *farheapcheckfree* function is used in conjunction with *farheapfillfree*. First, fill the free blocks with a known value by calling *farheapfillfree*. Later on, after working with allocated arrays, you can call *farheapcheckfree* to verify that none of the free locations are overwritten.

RETURNS The *farheapcheckfree* function returns one of the values shown in Table 6-3. Additionally, it returns the _BADVALUE constant if it finds any free location with a value other than *fill_char*.

SEE ALSO

farheapfillfree	*To fill free blocks with a known value*
farheapwalk	*To traverse the linked list of nodes in the far heap*
heapfillfree	*To fill all unallocated memory in the heap with a specified character*
heapcheckfree	*To check the free blocks in the heap in any memory model*
heapwalk	*To navigate through the heap's linked list data structure and check the size and status (free or used) of blocks*

EXAMPLE Allocate two blocks of memory from the far heap. Free the first block to create a free block. Now, use *farheapfillfree* to set each byte in the free block of the far heap to the character 'F'. Set a character in the free block to something other than 'F'. Call *farheapcheckfree* to check the free block. When you run the program, it should report a bad value in the free block.

```
#include <stdio.h>
#include <alloc.h>
main()
{
   char far *buffer1, far *buffer2;
   int      i, heapstatus;
/* Allocate two buffers in the far heap and free the first one */
   buffer1 = (char far *) farmalloc(80);
   buffer2 = (char far *) farmalloc(100);
   farfree(buffer1);

/* Fill the free block with 'F' */
   heapstatus = farheapfillfree('F');
```

```
/* Place a bad value somewhere in the free block */
   buffer1[10] = 'X';

/* Check status of free blocks */
   heapstatus = farheapcheckfree('F');

   switch (heapstatus)
   {
       case _HEAPOK:       printf("Heap OK\n");
                           break;
       case _HEAPEMPTY:    printf("Heap not initialized\n");
                           break;
       case _HEAPCORRUPT:  printf("Heap corrupted\n");
                           break;
       case _BADVALUE:     printf("Bad value in free block\n");
                           break;
   }
   return 0;
}
```

COMPATIBILITY

farheapchecknode

TC1	TC1.5	TC2	TC++	MSC3	MSC4	MSC5	MSC6	QC1	QC2	QC2.5	ANSI	UNIX V	XNX
			▲										

PURPOSE Use *farheapchecknode* to check the consistency of a single block in the far heap.

SYNTAX `int farheapchecknode(void *block);`

`void *block;` *Pointer to block of memory in far heap*

EXAMPLE CALL `heapstatus = farheapchecknode(bigarray);`

INCLUDES `#include <alloc.h>` *For function declaration*

DESCRIPTION The *farheapchecknode* function checks the block of memory identified by the pointer *block*.

RETURNS The *farheapchecknode* function returns one of the values shown in Table 6-4. Any negative return value indicates an error.

Table 6-4. *Possible Results of Checking a Node*

Constants	Interpretation of the Constant
_HEAPEMPTY	The heap is not yet initialized. This is the condition before any of the allocation routines are called.
_HEAPCORRUPT	Heap has been corrupted.
_BADNODE	No node was found for the given address of the block.
_FREEENTRY	This block is free.
_USEDENTRY	This block is in use.

SEE ALSO

`farheapcheck` *To check the entire far heap*

`farheapwalk` *To traverse the linked list of nodes in the far heap*

`heapfillfree` *To fill all unallocated memory in the heap with a specified character*

`heapcheckfree` *To check the free blocks in the heap in any memory model*

`heapwalk` *To navigate through the heap's linked list data structure and check the size and status (free or used) of blocks*

EXAMPLE Allocate two blocks of memory, then free one. Call *farheapchecknode* with the addresses of both blocks. The program should show one block as free and the other as used.

```
#include <stdio.h>
#include <alloc.h>
main()
{
   char far *buffer[2];
   int  i, heapstatus;
/* Allocate two buffers and free the first one */
   buffer[0] = (char far *) farmalloc(200);
   buffer[1] = (char far *) farmalloc(100);
   farfree(buffer[0]);

/* Check the nodes one by one */
    for(i = 0; i < 2; i++)
    {
        heapstatus = farheapchecknode(buffer[i]);
     printf("Checking node at: %Fp\n", buffer[i]);

        switch (heapstatus)
        {
```

```
                    case _BADNODE:    printf("\tBad node\n");
                                      break;
                    case _FREEENTRY: printf("\tFree block\n");
                                      break;
                    case _USEDENTRY: printf("\tUsed block\n");
                                      break;
                    case _HEAPEMPTY: printf("\tHeap not initialized\n");
                                      break;
                    case _HEAPCORRUPT: printf("\tHeap corrupted\n");
                                        break;
                }
            }
            return 0;
        }
```

COMPATIBILITY

farheapfillfree

TC1	TC1.5	TC2	TC++	MSC3	MSC4	MSC5	MSC6	QC1	QC2	QC2.5	ANSI	UNIX V	XNX
			▲			1	1						

PURPOSE Use *farheapfillfree* to set to a specific character each byte in all unused blocks in the far heap.

SYNTAX

```
int farheapfillfree(unsigned int fill_char);

unsigned int fill_char;     Character used to fill all unused
                            memory location in the heap
```

EXAMPLE CALL

```
heapstatus = farheapfillfree('X');
```

INCLUDES

```
#include <alloc.h>        For function declaration
```

DESCRIPTION The *farheapfillfree* function first checks the consistency of the far heap and then fills all unused blocks with the character specified in the argument *fill_char*.

1. The equivalent function for *farheapfillfree* in Microsoft C 5.0 and 6.0 is *_fheapset.*

COMMON USES You use *farheapfillfree* in conjunction with *farheapcheckfree*. First use *farheapfillfree* to fill the free blocks with a known character. Then, after some allocation and deallocation from the far heap, you can call *farheapcheckfree* to verify that you have not inadvertently overwritten anything in the free blocks.

RETURNS The return value from *farheapfillfree* is the result of the consistency check performed on the far heap. The return value must be intrepreted by comparing it with the defined constants shown in Table 6-3.

COMMENTS The *farheapfillfree* function should be called directly only when you are mixing memory models, for example, allocating a data array with far address in a small or medium model. In other cases, you can use *heapfillfree.*

SEE ALSO

`farheapcheckfree:`	*To check that the free blocks are not overwritten*
`farheapchecknode:`	*To check a single block of memory*
`farheapwalk`	*To traverse the linked list of nodes in the far heap*
`heapfillfree:`	*To fill all unallocated memory in the heap with a specified character (for all memory models)*
`heapwalk:`	*To navigate through the heap's linked list data structure and check the size and status (free or used) of blocks*

EXAMPLE See the example of *farheapcheckfree.*

Memory Allocation

farheapwalk

COMPATIBILITY

TC1	TC1.5	TC2	TC++	MSC3	MSC4	MSC5	MSC6	QC1	QC2	QC2.5	ANSI	UNIX V	XNX
			▲			1	1						

PURPOSE Use the *farheapwalk* function to obtain information about the entries in the far heap.

SYNTAX

```
int farheapwalk(struct farheapinfo *heap_entry);
```

`struct farheapinfo *heap_entry;` *Pointer to data structure in which information about next heap entry is returned*

EXAMPLE CALL

```
struct far heapinfo heap_entry;
heapstatus = farheapwalk(&heap_entry);
```

INCLUDES `#include <alloc.h>` *For function declaration and definition of structure* farheapinfo

DESCRIPTION The *farheapwalk* function returns information about the next entry in the far heap in a data structure of type *farheapinfo* which is defined in the header file *alloc.h* as:

```
struct farheapinfo
{
    void huge     *ptr;   /* Address of block     */
    unsigned long size;   /* Bytes used by block  */
    int           in_use; /* 1 = in use, 0 = free */
};
```

You must allocate a structure of type *farheapinfo* and provide its address in the argument *heap_entry*.

When using *farheapwalk*, you should first set the *ptr* field of the *farheapinfo* structure to NULL. Before returning, *farheapwalk* will set this to the address of the first block and return information about it. Each subsequent call to *farheapwalk* returns information about the next block in the heap.

1. The equivalent function for *farheapwalk* in Microsoft C 5.0 and 6.0 is *_fheapwalk*.

RETURNS The return value from *farheapwalk* should be interpreted by comparing it with the constants shown in Table 6-3. The information in the *farheapinfo* structure is valid only if the return value is _HEAPOK.

COMMENTS The *farheapwalk* function should be called to examine blocks of memory in the far heap only when you are mixing memory models in your programs. For example, you may be allocating some data objects to be addressed by far pointers in a small or medium model program. In programs where a single memory model is used throughout, the *heapwalk* function is a better choice because the compiler automatically uses the version appropriate for the memory model being used. This makes it easier to change memory models at a later date.

SEE ALSO

`heapcheck:` *To check the heap's linked list data structure for consistency*

`heapwalk:` *To step through the heap's linked list data structure and check the size and status (free or used) of blocks—for any memory model*

EXAMPLES Use *farmalloc* to allocate several data arrays in the far heap. Then call *farheapwalk* to traverse through all the entries of the heap and print a short report about the entries. Here is what the program shows for a sample run:

```
-------- BEGIN HEAP TRAVERSAL ---------
Address: 8673:0004  Status:  USED  Size:    96
Address: 8679:0004  Status:  FREE  Size:   512
Address: 8699:0004  Status:  FREE  Size:    16
```

```
Address: 869A:0004  Status:   FREE  Size:    16
Address: 869B:0004  Status:   FREE  Size:    32
----------- END HEAP TRAVERSAL --------
```

Notice how, for a block of 4 bytes (the third line), the size is 16 bytes—an overhead of 12 bytes!

```
#include <stdio.h>
#include <alloc.h>
main()
{
    struct farheapinfo heapentry;
    char far *buffer;
/* Allocate a buffer in the far heap */
    buffer = (char far *) farmalloc(80);
    farmalloc(500);     /* Another one  . . .   */
    farmalloc(4);
    farmalloc(8);
    farmalloc(16);
    farfree(buffer);    /* Free the first one */
/* Now check the heap entries. Set the ptr field to
 * NULL to begin at first entry
 */
    heapentry.ptr = NULL;
/* Keep calling farheapwalk as long as return value
 * is _HEAPOK. Print information about entry from the
 * structure 'heapentry'
 */
    printf("-------- BEGIN HEAP TRAVERSAL ---------\n");
    while (  farheapwalk(&heapentry) == _HEAPOK)
    {
        printf("Address: %Fp  Status: %6s  Size: %5lu\n",
               heapentry.ptr,
               (heapentry.in_use ? "FREE" : "USED"),
               heapentry.size);
    }
    printf("----------- END HEAP TRAVERSAL --------\n");
    return 0;
}
```

Memory Allocation and Management

COMPATIBILITY

farmalloc

TC1	TC1.5	TC2	TC++	MSC3	MSC4	MSC5	MSC6	QC1	QC2	QC2.5	ANSI	UNIX V	XNX
▲	▲	▲	▲		1	1	1						

PURPOSE Use *farmalloc* to allocate a block of memory, possibly exceeding 64-K bytes, from the far heap (all of memory beyond the stack).

SYNTAX

```
void far  *farmalloc (unsigned long numbytes);

unsigned long numbytes;     Number of bytes to allocate
```

EXAMPLE CALL

```
if((bigblock = farmalloc(80000L)) == NULL)
                   printf("Memory allocation failed!\n");
```

INCLUDES

```
#include <alloc.h>      For function prototype
```

DESCRIPTION The *farmalloc* function allocates *numbytes* bytes from the far heap. The entire amount of memory above the stack is available for allocation by *farmalloc*. Also, the block size can exceed 64-K bytes.

1. The equivalent function for *farmalloc* in Microsoft C 4.0, 5.0, and 6.0 is *halloc*.

RETURNS If successful, the *farmalloc* function returns a far pointer to the allocated block of memory. If the requested amount of memory could not be allocated, *farmalloc* returns a NULL.

COMMENTS The tiny memory model cannot use this function.

SEE ALSO

`farfree` *To deallocate memory in the far heap*

`farcalloc` *To allocate a large initialized block of memory from the far heap*

`calloc, malloc` *Standard memory allocation routines*

EXAMPLE Use *farmalloc* to allocate space for 80,000 bytes.

```
#include <stdio.h>
#include <alloc.h>

main()
{
     int far *bigblock;
     if((bigblock = farmalloc(80000L)) == NULL)
     {
```

```
        printf("Memory allocation failed!\n");
        exit(1);
    }
    printf("Block of 80,000 bytes allocated at %Fp\n",
            bigblock);
    return 0;
}
```

farrealloc

COMPATIBILITY

TC1	TC1.5	TC2	TC++	MSC3	MSC4	MSC5	MSC6	QC1	QC2	QC2.5	ANSI	UNIX V	XNX
▲	▲	▲	▲				1						

PURPOSE Use *farrealloc* to alter the size of a previously allocated block of memory in the far heap.

SYNTAX

```
void far  *farrealloc (void far *oldblock, unsigned long nbytes);
```

`void far      *oldblock;` *Far pointer to block of memory whose size is to be altered*

`unsigned long nbytes;` *Number of bytes to allocate*

EXAMPLE CALL

```
if((biggerblock = farrealloc(bigblock, 120000L)) == NULL)
                printf("Memory reallocation failed!\n");
```

INCLUDES `#include <alloc.h>` *For function prototype*

DESCRIPTION The *farrealloc* function alters the size of a block of memory in the far heap. The address of the previously allocated block is in the argument *oldblock* and the new size of the block in bytes is specified by *nbytes*. The *farrealloc* function will copy the block to a new location if necessary.

1. The equivalent function for *farrealloc* in Microsoft C 6.0 is *_frealloc*.

COMMON USES The *farrealloc* function allows you to dynamically adjust the size of an allocated block of memory.

RETURNS If successful, the *farrealloc* function returns a far pointer to the adjusted block of memory. If the old block of memory could not be enlarged as requested, *farrealloc* returns a NULL.

COMMENTS The tiny memory model cannot use this function.

SEE ALSO

farfree	*To deallocate memory in the far heap*
farcalloc	*To allocate a large initialized block of memory from the far heap*
calloc, malloc	*Standard memory allocation routines*

EXAMPLE Use *farmalloc* to allocate space for 1,000 bytes in the far heap. Next allocate another smaller sized block in the far heap (this will ensure that the first block cannot be enlarged without moving to a new location). Now enlarge the first block to 80,000 bytes. If you print the address of the block before and after reallocation, you will notice that the block has moved to a new address.

```
#include <stdio.h>
#include <alloc.h>

main()
{
    int far *block1, *block2;
    if((block1 = farmalloc(1000L)) == NULL)
    {
        printf("Block1 allocation failed!\n");
        exit(1);
    }
    printf("First block of 1,000 bytes allocated at %Fp\n",
            block1);
    if((block2 = farmalloc(100L)) == NULL)
    {
        printf("Block2 allocation failed!\n");
        exit(1);
    }
    printf("Second block of 100 bytes allocated at %Fp\n",
            block2);
/* Now enlarge the first block to 80,000 bytes */
    if((block1 = farrealloc(block1, 80000L)) == NULL)
    {
        printf("Block1 reallocation failed!\n");
        exit(1);
    }
    printf("Size of first block adjusted to 80,000 bytes"
            "at %Fp\n", block1);
    return 0;
}
```

free

COMPATIBILITY

TC1	TC1.5	TC2	TC++	MSC3	MSC4	MSC5	MSC6	QC1	QC2	QC2.5	ANSI	UNIX V	XNX
▲	▲	▲	▲	▲	▲	▲	▲	▲	▲	▲	▲	▲	▲

PURPOSE Use the *free* function to release an allocated storage block to the pool of free memory.

SYNTAX

```
void free(void *mem_address);

void *mem_address;        Pointer to block of memory to be released
```

EXAMPLE CALL

```
free(buffer);
```

INCLUDES

```
#include <alloc.h>        For function declaration

#include <stdlib.h>       For ANSI compatibility
```

DESCRIPTION The *free* function returns to the pool of free memory a block of memory that was allocated earlier by *malloc, calloc*, or *realloc*. The address of the block is specified by the argument *mem_address*, which is a pointer to the starting byte of the block. A NULL pointer argument is ignored by *free*.

COMMON USES The *free* function is used with *malloc, calloc*, and *realloc* to free memory used by data objects that are no longer needed.

SEE ALSO

`malloc` *To allocate a block of storage*

`calloc` *To allocate and initialize an array*

`realloc` *To alter size of allocated block of memory*

EXAMPLE Use *malloc* to allocate room for an 80-character string. Prompt the user for a string and store it in the buffer you allocate. Print the string and then deallocate the buffer by calling *free*.

```
#include <stdio.h>
#include <stdlib.h>
#include <alloc.h>
#define MAX_CHR 80
main()
{
    char *buffer;
/* Allocate room for string and check for NULL */
```

```
    if( (buffer = (char *)malloc(MAX_CHR)) == NULL)
    {
            printf("Allocation Failed.\n");
            exit(0);
    }
    printf("Buffer allocated. Enter string to store: ");
    gets(buffer);
    printf("\nYou entered: %s\n",buffer);
    free((void *)buffer);    /* Deallocate the memory */
    printf("Buffer deallocated.\n");
    return 0;
}
```

COMPATIBILITY

heapcheck

TC1	TC1.5	TC2	TC++	MSC3	MSC4	MSC5	MSC6	QC1	QC2	QC2.5	ANSI	UNIX V	XNX
			▲			1	1						

PURPOSE Use *heapcheck* to check the consistency of the heap—the pool of free memory.

SYNTAX `int heapcheck(void);`

EXAMPLE CALL `heapstatus = heapcheck();`

INCLUDES `#include <alloc.h>` *For function declaration*

DESCRIPTION The *heapcheck* function checks the linked list of memory blocks, called "heap," from which memory allocation is done by Turbo C++'s heap management routines. The entries in the linked lists are addresses of free and used blocks of memory. The *heapcheck* function checks to see that the entries are within the first and last addresses of the heap and it returns code signifying the results of the check.

The *heapcheck* function is mapped to *farheapcheck* when in the compact, large, or huge model. In mixed memory models, you can explicitly call *farheapcheck* to check the far heap, which is the available memory outside the default data segment.

1. The equivalent function for *heapcheck* in Microsoft C 5.0 and 6.0 is *_heapchk*.

COMMON USES The *heapcheck* function is used with its companions *heapfillfree* and *heapwalk* to pinpoint problems related to the heap, for example, overwriting allocated memory.

RETURNS The return value from *heapcheck* should be interpreted by comparing it with the constants shown in Table 6-3 and defined in the include file *alloc.h*.

COMMENTS The *heapcheck* function is meant to be used in conjunction with *heapfillfree* and *heapwalk* to locate causes of program failure that are related to the heap. A typical problem is allocating room, for example, for an 80-character string and then storing, perhaps, 100 characters into the string. Such mistakes can overwrite information in the heap's own linked list data structure and cause the program to fail.

SEE ALSO

heapcheckfree	*To check the free blocks in the heap*
heapchecknode	*To check a single block in the heap*
heapfillfree:	*To fill all unallocated memory in the heap with a specified character*
heapwalk:	*To navigate through the heap's linked list data structure and check the size and status (free or used) of blocks*
farheapcheck:	*To check the far heap (ouside the default data segment)*

EXAMPLE Use *malloc* and *free* to allocate and deallocate a few blocks of memory. Then call *heapcheck* to check if the heap is in good shape. Display the information returned by *heapcheck*.

```
#include <stdio.h>
#include <alloc.h>
main()
{
   char  *buffer;
   int heapstatus;
/* Perform some allocations and deallocations */
   buffer = (char  *) malloc(500);
   malloc(800);
   free((void  *)buffer);
/* Now get the status of the  heap by calling heapcheck */
   heapstatus = heapcheck();
   switch (heapstatus)
   {
       case _HEAPOK:      printf("Heap OK\n");
                          break;
       case _HEAPEMPTY:   printf("Heap not initialized\n");
                          break;
       case _HEAPCORRUPT: printf("Heap is corrupted\n");
                          break;
```

```
    }
    return 0;
}
```

COMPATIBILITY

heapcheckfree

TC1	TC1.5	TC2	TC++	MSC3	MSC4	MSC5	MSC6	QC1	QC2	QC2.5	ANSI	UNIX V	XNX
			▲										

PURPOSE Use *heapcheckfree* to check the consistency of the free blocks in the heap. Call *heapfillfree* beforehand to fill the free blocks with a known character.

SYNTAX

```
int heapcheckfree(unsigned int fill_char);

unsigned int fill_char;        Character used to fill the free blocks
```

EXAMPLE CALL

```
heapstatus = heapcheckfree('N');
```

INCLUDES

```
#include <alloc.h>        For function declaration
```

DESCRIPTION The *heapcheckfree* function checks the free blocks in the heap. This is the pool of memory from which data blocks are allocated by routines such as *calloc* and *malloc*.

The check involves ensuring that all entries in the heap data structure make sense and all free blocks contain the specified fill character, *fill_char*. You should call *heapfillfree* to fill all free blocks with that character before calling *heapcheckfree*.

COMMON USES The *heapcheckfree* function is used in conjunction with *heapfillfree*. First, fill the free blocks with a known value by calling *heapfillfree*. Later on, after working with allocated arrays, you can call *heapcheckfree* to verify that none of the free locations are overwritten.

RETURNS The *heapcheckfree* function returns one of the values shown in Table 6-3. Additionally, it returns the _BADVALUE constant if it finds any free location with a value other than *fill_char*.

SEE ALSO

`farheapcheckfree` — *To check the free blocks in the far heap*

`heapfillfree` — *To fill free blocks with a known value*

`heapwalk` — *To navigate through the heap's linked list data structure and check the size and status (free or used) of blocks*

EXAMPLE Allocate two blocks of memory from the heap. Free the first block to create a free block. Now, use *heapfillfree* to set each byte in the free block of the heap to the character 'N'. Set a character in the free block to something other than 'N'. Call *heapcheckfree* to check the free block. When you run the program, it should report a bad value in the free block.

```
#include <stdio.h>
#include <alloc.h>
main()
{
   char  *buffer1,  *buffer2;
   int   i, heapstatus;

/* Allocate two buffers in the  heap and free the first one */
   buffer1 = (char  *) malloc(80);
   buffer2 = (char  *) malloc(100);
   free(buffer1);

/* Fill the free block with 'N' */
   heapstatus = heapfillfree('N');

/* Place a bad value somewhere in the free block */
   buffer1[10] = 'X';

/* Check status of free blocks */
   heapstatus = heapcheckfree('N');

   switch (heapstatus)
   {
       case _HEAPOK:      printf("Heap OK\n");
                          break;
       case _HEAPEMPTY:   printf("Heap not initialized\n");
                          break;
       case _HEAPCORRUPT: printf("Heap corrupted\n");
                          break;
       case _BADVALUE:    printf("Bad value in free block\n");
                          break;
   }
   return 0;
}
```

Memory Allocation and Management

COMPATIBILITY

heapchecknode

TC1	TC1.5	TC2	TC++	MSC3	MSC4	MSC5	MSC6	QC1	QC2	QC2.5	ANSI	UNIX V	XNX
			▲										

PURPOSE Use *heapchecknode* to check the consistency of a single block in the heap.

SYNTAX

```
int heapchecknode(void *block);
```

`void *block;` *Pointer to block of memory in heap*

EXAMPLE CALL

```
heapstatus = heapchecknode(array);
```

INCLUDES `#include <alloc.h>` *For function declaration*

DESCRIPTION The *heapchecknode* function checks the block of memory identified by the pointer *block*.

RETURNS The *heapchecknode* function returns one of the values shown in Table 6-4. Any negative return value indicates an error.

SEE ALSO

farheapchecknode	*To check a node in the far heap*
heapcheck	*To check the entire heap*
heapcheckfree	*To check the free blocks in the heap in any memory model*
heapfillfree	*To fill all unallocated memory in the heap with a specified character*
heapwalk	*To navigate through the heap's linked list data structure and check the size and status (free or used) of blocks*

EXAMPLE Allocate two blocks of memory, then free one. Call *heapchecknode* with the addresses of both blocks. The program should show one block as free and the other as used.

```
#include <stdio.h>
#include <alloc.h>
main()
{
   char *buffer[2];
   int  i, heapstatus;
```

```
/* Allocate two buffers and free the first one */
   buffer[0] = (char *) malloc(200);
   buffer[1] = (char *) malloc(100);
   free(buffer[0]);

/* Check the nodes one by one */
    for(i = 0; i < 2; i++)
    {
        heapstatus = heapchecknode(buffer[i]);
     printf("Checking node at: %p\n", buffer[i]);

        switch (heapstatus)
        {
            case _BADNODE:   printf("\tBad node\n");
                             break;
            case _FREEENTRY: printf("\tFree block\n");
                             break;
            case _USEDENTRY: printf("\tUsed block\n");
                             break;
         case _HEAPEMPTY: printf("\tHeap not initialized\n");
                             break;
            case _HEAPCORRUPT: printf("\tHeap corrupted\n");
                               break;
        }
    }
    return 0;
}
```

Memory Allocation

heapfillfree

COMPATIBILITY

TC1	TC1.5	TC2	TC++	MSC3	MSC4	MSC5	MSC6	QC1	QC2	QC2.5	ANSI	UNIX V	XNX
			▲			1	1						

PURPOSE Use the *heapfillfree* function to fill each byte in all unused blocks of memory in the heap with a specified character value.

SYNTAX

```
int heapfillfree(unsigned fill_char);
```

`unsigned int fill_char;` *Character used to fill all unused memory location in the heap*

EXAMPLE CALL

```
heapstatus = heapfillfree('Z');
```

Memory Allocation and Management

INCLUDES `#include <alloc.h>` *For function declaration*

DESCRIPTION The *heapfillfree* function first checks the consistency of the linked list of memory blocks, called "heap," from which memory is allocated by Turbo C++'s heap management routines. The consistency check is similar to the one performed by *heapcheck*. After the check, *heapfillfree* will fill every byte of each unused block of memory with the character specified in the argument *fill_char*.

The *heapfillfree* function is mapped to *farheapfillfree* when in the compact, large, or huge model. In mixed memory models, you can explicitly call *farheapfillfree* to fill the far heap (the pool of memory used for allocation outside the default data segment).

1. In Microsoft C 5.0 and 6.0, use *_heapset*.

COMMON USES The *heapfillfree* function is used to locate errors in the program that may be overwriting dynamically allocated data in the heap. By first filling the unused memory with a known character, you can determine overwritten locations by examining them with *heapcheckfree*.

RETURNS The return value from *heapfillfree* is the result of the consistency check that is performed before filling the unused memory locations. This value must be interpreted in the same manner as the value returned by *heapcheck*. See Table 6-3 for a list of defined constants that may be returned by *heapfillfree*.

COMMENTS The *heapfillfree* function is meant for use with its companion *heapcheckfree* to locate causes of program failure due to overwriting dynamically created data objects in the heap. While *heapfillfree* lets you fill the unused memory with a known character, *heapcheckfree* allows you to verify that all free blocks are intact.

Call a memory allocation function before using *heapfillfree* so that the heap is initialized; otherwise, there will not be any blocks, free or used, to work with.

SEE ALSO

`heapcheck:` *To check the heap's linked list data structure for consistency*

`heapcheckfree` *To check the free blocks*

`heapwalk:` *To traverse through the heap's linked list data structure and check the size and status (free or used) of blocks*

`farheapfillfree:` *To check the unused memory blocks in the far heap (ouside the default data segment)*

EXAMPLE See example in *heapcheckfree*.

Memory Allocation

heapwalk

COMPATIBILITY

TC1	TC1.5	TC2	TC++	MSC3	MSC4	MSC5	MSC6	QC1	QC2	QC2.5	ANSI	UNIX V	XNX
			▲			1	1						

PURPOSE Use the *heapwalk* function to obtain information about the entries in the heap.

SYNTAX
```
int heapwalk(struct heapinfo *heap_entry);
```

```
struct heapinfo *heap_entry;
```
Pointer to data structure in which information about next heap entry is returned

EXAMPLE CALL
```
struct  heapinfo heap_entry;
heapstatus = heapwalk(&heap_entry);
```

INCLUDES
```
#include <alloc.h>
```
For function declaration and definition of structure heapinfo

DESCRIPTION The *heapwalk* function returns information about the next entry in the heap in a data structure of type *heapinfo*, which is defined in the header file *alloc.h* as:

```
struct heapinfo
{
    void         *ptr;    /* Address of block     */
    unsigned int size;    /* Bytes used by block  */
    int          in_use;  /* 1 = in use, 0 = free */
};
```

You must allocate a structure of type *heapinfo* and provide its address in the argument *heap_entry*.

When using *heapwalk*, you should first set the *ptr* field of the *heapinfo* structure to NULL. Before returning, *heapwalk* will set this to the address of the first block and return information about it. Each subsequent call to *heapwalk* returns information about the next block in the heap.

1. The equivalent function for *heapwalk* in Microsoft C 5.0 and 6.0 is *_heapwalk*.

RETURNS The return value from *heapwalk* should be interpreted by comparing it with the constants shown in Table 6-3. The information in the *heapinfo* structure is valid only if the return value is _HEAPOK.

SEE ALSO heapcheck: *To check the heap's linked list data structure for consistency*

`farheapwalk:` *To step through the far heap's linked list data structure and check the size and status (free or used) of blocks*

EXAMPLES Use *malloc* to allocate several data arrays in the heap. Then call *heapwalk* to traverse through all the entries of the heap and print a short report about the entries. Here is what the program shows for a sample run:

```
-------- BEGIN HEAP TRAVERSAL ---------
Address: 03B2  Status:   FREE  Size:   516
Address: 05B6  Status:   FREE  Size:   516
Address: 07BA  Status:   USED  Size:    84
Address: 080E  Status:   FREE  Size:   504
Address: 0A06  Status:   FREE  Size:     8
Address: 0A0E  Status:   FREE  Size:    12
Address: 0A1A  Status:   FREE  Size:    20
----------- END HEAP TRAVERSAL --------
```

Notice that there are two blocks at the beginning of the heap that are used by *malloc* and not anything allocated by our program. Also note that compared to *farmalloc*, overhead for a 4-byte block allocated by *malloc* is only 4 more bytes. A total of 8 bytes is needed for the 4-byte allocation, whereas the same block would require 16 bytes in the far heap.

```
#include <stdio.h>
#include <alloc.h>
main()
{
    struct heapinfo heapentry;
    char  *buffer;
/* Allocate a buffer in the  heap */
    buffer = (char  *) malloc(80);
    malloc(500);     /* Another one . . .    */
    malloc(4);
    malloc(8);
    malloc(16);
    free(buffer);    /* Free the first one */
/* Now check the heap entries. Set the ptr field to
 * NULL to begin at first entry
 */
    heapentry.ptr = NULL;
/* Keep calling heapwalk as long as return value
 * is _HEAPOK. Print information about entry from the
 * structure 'heapentry'
 */
```

```
    printf("-------- BEGIN HEAP TRAVERSAL ---------\n");
    while (  heapwalk(&heapentry) == _HEAPOK)
    {
        printf("Address: %p  Status: %6s  Size: %5u\n",
               heapentry.ptr,
               (heapentry.in_use ? "FREE" : "USED"),
               heapentry.size);
    }
    printf("----------- END HEAP TRAVERSAL --------\n");
    return 0;
}
```

malloc

COMPATIBILITY

TC1	TC1.5	TC2	TC++	MSC3	MSC4	MSC5	MSC6	QC1	QC2	QC2.5	ANSI	UNIX V	XNX
▲	▲	▲	▲	▲	▲	▲	▲	▲	▲	▲	▲	▲	▲

PURPOSE Use *malloc* to allocate memory for an array of a given number of bytes. Note that *malloc* can only allocate memory for an array whose size is less than 64 K.

SYNTAX

```
void *malloc(size_t num_bytes);

size_t num_bytes;       Number of bytes needed
```

EXAMPLE CALL

```
buffer = (char *)malloc(100*sizeof(char));
```

INCLUDES

```
#include <alloc.h>      For function declaration and definition of data type size_t

#include <stdlib.h>     For ANSI compatibility
```

DESCRIPTION The *malloc* function allocates the number of bytes requested in the argument *num_bytes* by calling internal Turbo C heap management routines. The *malloc* function will work properly for all memory models.

COMMON USES The *malloc* function creates room for arrays of data objects at run-time, allowing you to write programs without having to guess beforehand the amount of storage you will need at run-time.

RETURNS The *malloc* function returns a pointer that is the starting address of the memory allocated. The allocated memory is properly aligned (the address of the first byte meets the requirements for storing any type of C variable). If the memory allocation is unsuccessful because of insufficient space or bad values of the arguments, a NULL is returned.

COMMENTS Note that when using *malloc* to allocate storage for a specific data type, you should cast the returned *void* pointer to that type.

SEE ALSO

`calloc`	*To allocate and initialize an array*
`realloc`	*To alter size of previously allocated block of memory*
`free`	*To release memory allocated earlier*

EXAMPLE Use *malloc* to allocate room for an 80-character string. Prompt the user for a string and store it in the buffer you allocate.

```
#include <stdio.h>
#include <stdlib.h>
#include <alloc.h>
#define MAX_CHR 80
main()
{
    char *buffer;
/* Allocate room for string and check for NULL pointer*/
    if( (buffer = (char *)malloc(MAX_CHR)) == NULL)
    {
        printf("Allocation Failed.\n");
        exit(0);
    }
    printf("Buffer allocated. Enter string to store: ");
    gets(buffer);
    printf("\nYou entered: %s\n",buffer);
    return 0;
}
```

realloc

COMPATIBILITY

TC1	TC1.5	TC2	TC++	MSC3	MSC4	MSC5	MSC6	QC1	QC2	QC2.5	ANSI	UNIX V	XNX
▲	▲	▲	▲	▲	▲	▲	▲	▲	▲	▲	▲	▲	▲

PURPOSE Use *realloc* to adjust the size of a block of memory allocated by *malloc* or *calloc*.

SYNTAX

```
void *realloc(void *mem_address, size_t newsize);
```

`void *mem_address;`	*Pointer to the block of memory whose size is to be altered*
`size_t newsize;`	*New size of the block in bytes*

EXAMPLE CALL

```
new_buffer = realloc(old_buffer, old_size+100);
```

INCLUDES

`#include <alloc.h>` *For function declaration*

`#include <stdlib.h>` *For ANSI compatibility and definition of data type* size_t

DESCRIPTION

The *realloc* function alters the size of an allocated block of memory to a size given in the argument *newsize*. The address of the block is specified by the pointer to a *void* type, *mem_address*. This pointer must be either NULL or a value returned by an earlier call to *malloc, calloc*, or *realloc*. If the argument *mem_address* is a NULL, then *realloc* behaves like *malloc* and allocates a new block of memory of size *newsize*. The memory block of altered size may not be located at the same address, but the contents of the new block (up to its old size) is guaranteed to be unchanged.

COMMON USES

Normally the *realloc* function is used to enlarge a block of memory as the need arises to store more data elements, enabling you to write programs that work with arrays that enlarge or shrink as data is added or removed.

RETURNS

The *realloc* function returns the address of the block of memory cast as a pointer to a *void* data type. The resized block of memory is guaranteed to meet the alignment requirements for any type of data storage. The alignment refers to a requirement often imposed by hardware that the address of the first byte have certain properties, for example, that it be even or a multiple of 16. If the new size is zero or if there is no more room to enlarge the block of memory, *realloc* frees the block and returns a NULL.

SEE ALSO

`calloc` *To allocate and initialize an array*

`malloc` *To allocate a block of memory*

`free` *To release memory allocated earlier*

EXAMPLE

Use *malloc* to allocate room for a string of 10 characters. Read in a short string and store it in the allocated buffer. Then enlarge the buffer to hold an 80-character string. Show the user the contents again to verify that the original string is still there.

```
#include <stdio.h>
#include <stdlib.h>
#include <alloc.h>

main()
{
    unsigned char *buffer;
```

```
/* Allocate room for string and check for NULL */
    if( (buffer = (char *)malloc(10)) == NULL )
    {
            printf("Allocation Failed.\n");
            exit(0);
    }
    printf("Buffer allocated. Enter string to store: ");
    gets(buffer);
    printf("\nYou entered: %s\n",buffer);
/* Now enlarge size of buffer and redisplay string */
    if( (buffer = (char *)realloc((void *)buffer, 80))
         == NULL )
    {
            printf("Reallocation Failed.\n");
            exit(0);
    }
    printf("Buffer still contains: %s\n",buffer);
    return 0;
}
```

COMPATIBILITY

sbrk

TC1	TC1.5	TC2	TC++	MSC3	MSC4	MSC5	MSC6	QC1	QC2	QC2.5	ANSI	UNIX V	XNX
▲	▲	▲	▲	▲	▲	▲	▲	▲	▲	▲		▲	▲

PURPOSE Use *sbrk* to alter the break value of a process. The break value is the address of the first available byte in the default data segment beyond the memory already being used by the data in the process.

SYNTAX `void *sbrk(int change);`

`int change;` *Number of bytes by which the break value is to be changed*

EXAMPLE CALL `buffer = (char *) sbrk(80);`

INCLUDES `#include <alloc.h>` *For function declaration*

DESCRIPTION The *sbrk* function adds the number of bytes specified in the argument *change* to the break value of the process from which *sbrk* is called. The break value indicates the number of bytes that the process is currently using in the default data segment. In fact, it is the offset at which the heap (the chunk of memory from which new blocks may be allocated) begins.

Since *sbrk* adds the argument *change* to the current break value, specifying a negative value in *change* reduces the memory being used by the process.

COMMON USES The *sbrk* function is used as an alternate memory allocation routine.

RETURNS The return value from *sbrk* is a pointer to a type *void*, representing the address of the previous break value. If the break value could not be altered because of insufficient space, a character pointer to a value of −1 is returned and the global variable *errno* is set to ENOMEM. See the example below for a sample error check.

COMMENTS The *sbrk* function provides compatibility with UNIX System V library. It is better to use *malloc* for memory allocation because it is portable, it conforms to the ANSI standard, and it works in all memory models except the huge model.

SEE ALSO

`malloc`	*Most general-purpose memory allocation routine*
`free`	*To release memory allocated earlier*

EXAMPLE Use *sbrk* to allocate room for a buffer to hold 80 characters at the end of the default data segment in a small model program. Prompt the user for a string and store it in the buffer you allocated. Call *sbrk* with a negative argument to deallocate this memory.

```
#include <stdio.h>
#include <alloc.h>
unsigned char *buffer;
main()
{
/* Allocate a buffer by adding 80 to the break value */
     buffer = (char *) sbrk(80);
    if (buffer == (void *) -1)
    {
            printf("sbrk failed.\n");
            exit(0);
    }
    printf("Buffer allocated. Enter string to store: ");
    gets(buffer);
    printf("\nYou entered: %s\n",buffer);
    sbrk(-80);  /* Deallocate the buffer */
    printf("Buffer deallocated\n");
    return 0;
}
```

Memory Allocation and Management

Chapter 7 Buffer Manipulation

Introduction

The buffer manipulation routines manipulate bytes in memory. They allow you to copy data from one area of memory to another, initialize a block of memory, search for the occurrence of a specific character (actually, this can be any value that fits into a byte), and compare the contents of two buffers. These routines are helpful, for example, when you are directly copying a screenful of text (or image) from a buffer to the video memory. Another interesting example of using the buffer manipulation routines is in a file comparison utility. Provided you have enough memory, you could copy two files into memory and use a routine *memcmp* to see if the files match.

Concepts: Buffers, Pointers, and Byte Ordering

To use the buffer manipulation routines effectively, you need to be familiar with the concept of a buffer and its address. The routines are similar to the string manipulation routines we discuss in Chapter 11.

BUFFERS A buffer is a contiguous set of bytes in the computer's memory. The contents of the buffer can be ASCII characters, which most of the routines expect to operate on, or numerical (binary) values. As shown in Figure 7-1, the buffer is accessed by a pointer to the first byte. The figure shows Buffer 2 with the string *Hello.* Strings in C are similar to buffers except they always end with a null character (\0—a byte containing zero) while buffer manipulation routines require an argument to specify the number of bytes to be manipulated. Many buffer routines have corresponding string versions. Although the buffer

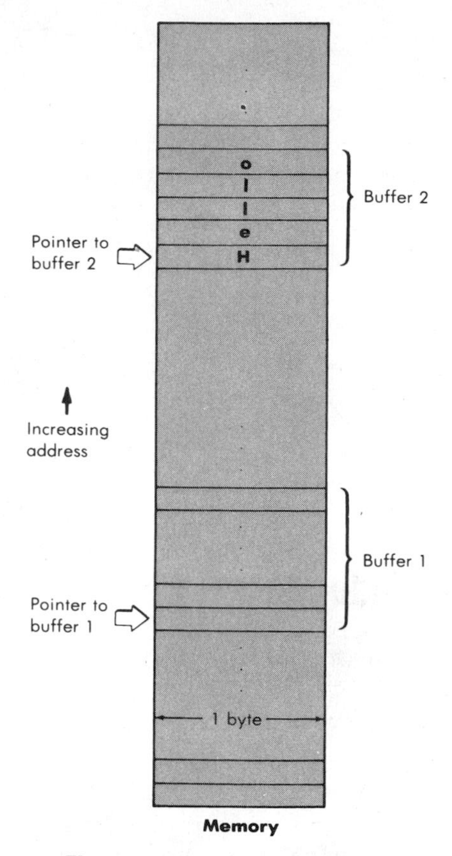

Figure 7-1. ***Buffers in memory***

manipulation routines can handle strings as well, there are many functions that deal specifically with strings and these are usually easier to use.

BUFFER POINTERS: SEGMENTS AND OFFSETS

The pointer to the buffer is an address that consists of two parts, segment and offset, each 16 bits long, as we explained in the tutorial in Chapter 6. The 20-bit physical address used by the 8086 microprocessor is constructed by shifting the segment address 4 bits to the left and adding the offset to the result. The buffer address is specified as the name of an array or as a pointer variable. The segment and offset addresses are implicit in the memory model of the program. For example, in the small and medium memory models all data is assumed to reside within a single 64-K segment of memory whose address is specified in the DS segment register (see Chapter 3). In this case, the pointer to a buffer is the 16-bit offset of the first byte of the buffer within that segment (which can be 64 K at most). Thus in the small and the medium models the buffers being manipulated, like all other data items, are confined to a single segment.

In the compact, large, and huge memory models, all pointers have full segment and offset addresses. In these models, the buffers can be anywhere in memory. The size of a single buffer in the compact and large models is still limited to 64 K; in huge models, the size of a buffer is limited only by available memory.

BYTE ORDERING

One special buffer manipulation routine, *swab*, provides a special service: it swaps adjacent pairs of bytes in a buffer. This routine takes care of the mismatch among different computer systems in "byte ordering," which refers to how the bytes of a 2- or 4-byte integer are arranged in memory. Consider, as an example, a short integer variable *shortvar* that occupies 2 bytes in memory. Suppose we store the hexadecimal value 0x0201 into this variable. What will the byte at the address of *shortvar* contain? What about the byte at the next higher address? In the 8086 family, as illustrated in Figure 7-2, the least significant byte (in this case, 01) is at the address of *shortvar* while the most significant byte is at the next higher address. And

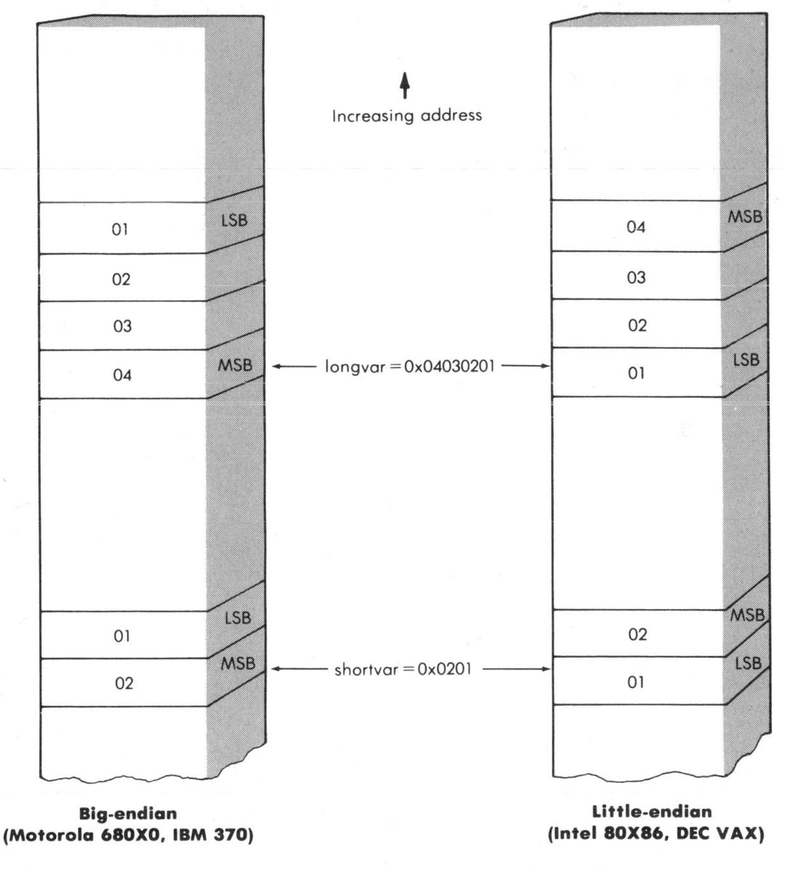

Figure 7-2. ***Byte ordering***

if we load the value 0x04030201 into a long integer variable *longvar*, the ordering in the 8086 family would again start with the least significant byte at the lowest address and the bytes of ever higher significance placed at successive higher addresses (Figure 7-2). Thus, the order of bytes in short and long integers is the same in the 8086 family of computers. This ordering scheme is sometimes called "little-endian" because the least significant byte is at the lowest address. Exactly the reverse order of placing the bytes is used in many other microprocessors—most notably the 680×0 family and the IBM 370. These machines are called "big-endian" systems because the most significant byte is at the lowest address.

Normally you need not worry about the exact ordering of bytes. Today, however, many different computer systems are often connected together in networks. In such an environment, you do have to worry about the byte ordering if you transfer binary data between a little-endian system (IBM PC, for instance) and a big-endian one (Macintosh, for instance). Back where we started, the Turbo C++ library includes the *swab* routine which can swap adjacent bytes. You can use it to convert short integers from one form of ordering to another.

Notes on Using the Buffer Routines

The buffer manipulation routines (see Table 7-1) are a more general form of the string manipulation routines which operate on C strings. The operation of a buffer routine is clarified by comparing it with its string counterpart. The difference between them is that the buffer manipulation routines always need a byte count whereas the string routines determine the end of a string by looking for the null character. For example, *memchr* works like *strchr*, *memcmp* like *strcmp*, *memcpy* and *memmove* like *strcpy*, *memicmp* like *stricmp*, and *memset* like *strset*. The *memccpy* function works like *memcpy* except that it takes an additional argument: a character that it uses as a marker. It copies the source buffer to the destination until either a specified number of bytes has been used or until *memccpy* encounters that character in the source buffer. The call

```
char title[81], this_book[] = "Turbo C Bible";
memccpy(title, this_book, '\0', 81);
```

copies 81 characters or up to (and including) the null character, from *this_book* into *title*. In this case, since the string *this_book* has a null character before the 81st position, the entire string is copied to *title*.

The *movedata* is a special-purpose routine to move data from two buffers anywhere in memory. In the small and medium memory models, the buffers are constrained to be in the same segment because all addresses are offsets from the segment address specified in the DS register.

Table 7-1. *Buffer Manipulation Routines*

Routine	Description
memccpy	Copies bytes from one buffer to another until a specific character is encountered or until a specified number of bytes have been copied.
memchr	Searches for a specific character in a given number of bytes of the buffer.
memcmp	Compares a specified number of bytes of two buffers.
memcpy	Copies a specified number of bytes from one buffer to another (*not for overlapping source and destination*).
memicmp	Compares a specified number of bytes of two buffers without regard to the case of the letters.
memmove	Copies a specified number of bytes from one buffer to another (*handles overlapping source and destination*).
memset	Sets specified number of bytes of a buffer to a given value.
movedata	Copies a specified number of bytes from one buffer to another in possibly different segment.
movmem	Copies a block of bytes from one buffer to another (handles overlapping source and destination).
setmem	Sets a specified number of bytes of a buffer to a given value.
swab	Takes an array of bytes and swaps contents of each pair of adjacent bytes.

In this case, you cannot use the buffer copy routines, such as *memcpy*, to copy data from a buffer in your program to the video memory (treated as a buffer at a specified address) because the video memory is outside your program's data segment. The *movedata* routine lets you specify the segment and offset addresses of the source and destination buffers explicitly. Use the function *segread* or the macros *FP_SEG* and *FP_OFF* to get the necessary values for your buffers. For example, in the Color Graphics Adapter and the Enhanced Graphics Adapter in text mode, the video memory begins at the address B800:0000. You can view this as 25 rows by 80 columns of 2-byte values, laid out by row starting at the address B800:0000. Each 2-byte value corresponding to a screen position has 1 byte (the high-order byte) with the attribute (such as normal, reverse video, blinking) and the other byte with the actual character. If we have another buffer in memory with the same organization, we can prepare a screenful of text in this buffer and display it by copying the buffer to the video memory. Here is an example:

```
    void far *address;
    short dispbuf[25][80]; /* Display buffer */
/* Set all locations to zero */
    memset(dispbuf, '\0', sizeof(dispbuf));
/* Get segment, offset of dispbuf */
```

```
    address = (void far *)dispbuf;
    bufseg = FP_SEG(address);
    bufoff = FP_OFF(address);
/* Copy buffer into video memory -- clears screen */
    movedata(bufseg, bufoff, 0xb800, 0x0000,
             sizeof(dispbuf));
```

We set up a buffer, *dispbuf*, which is set to all zeroes by calling *memset*. The segment and offset of the buffer are obtained using FP_SEG and FP_OFF, respectively. We had to copy the address of *dispbuf* into a far pointer variable *address* because the FP_SEG and FP_OFF macros work properly with far addresses only. In the last statement, we call *movedata* to copy *dispbuf* to the video memory. The result is a cleared screen.

Table 7-2 summarizes the buffer manipulation routines by task. As you can see, the routines are primarily intended for copying, comparing, and initializing regions of memory.

Table 7-2. ***Buffer Manipulation Routines by Task***

Task	Routines
Copies one buffer into another.	memccpy, memcpy, memmove, movedata, movmem
Compares two buffers.	memcmp, memicmp
Initializes all bytes of a buffer.	memset, setmem
Locates a specific character in buffer.	memchr
Swaps the contents of the high-order byte with that of the low-order one in a 2-byte word.	swab

Cautions

There are a few pitfalls you must be wary of when using the buffer manipulation routines.

- The *memcpy* function does not properly handle copying between overlapping source and destination buffers. Only *memmove* is guaranteed to handle overlapping buffers.
- In the small and the medium memory models, the source and destination buffers are both in the same segment (because addresses are offsets from the segment address in the DS register). If you have to copy bytes between buffers in different segments, use *movedata* because it accepts explicit segment:offset addresses of the buffers being manipulated.

COMPATIBILITY

memccpy

TC1	TC1.5	TC2	TC++	MSC3	MSC4	MSC5	MSC6	QC1	QC2	QC2.5	ANSI	UNIX V	XNX
▲	▲	▲	▲	▲	▲	▲	▲	▲	▲	▲		▲	▲

PURPOSE Use *memccpy* to copy bytes from one memory buffer to another. Copying continues until *memccpy* encounters a specified character or until a specified number of bytes have been copied, whichever happens first.

SYNTAX

```
void *memccpy(void *dest, void *source, int c, unsigned count);
```

`void *dest;` *Pointer to buffer to which data will be copied*

`void *source;` *Pointer to buffer from which data will be copied*

`int c` *Last character to be copied*

`unsigned count;` *Maximum number of bytes to be copied*

EXAMPLE CALL

```
memccpy(dest_buf, inbuf, '\0', 81);
```

INCLUDES `#include <mem.h>` *For function declaration*

or

`#include <string.h>`

DESCRIPTION The *memccpy* function copies bytes from the buffer at the *source* address to another buffer at *dest*. The copying starts at the first byte of the source and continues until one of two events occur: *memccpy* encounters a byte containing the character *c* in the source buffer or the total number of bytes copied from the source to *dest* equals the count specified in the argument *count*. When *memccpy* stops because of the first event, it copies the character *c* before returning.

Note that you are responsible for allocating enough space for the destination buffer. If you copy more bytes than the size allocated, *memccpy* may destroy other data and cause the program to fail in mysterious ways.

COMMON USES The *memccpy* function and its counterparts *memcpy*, *memmove*, and *movedata*, are efficient tools for copying large blocks of data from one array to another.

RETURNS If *memccpy* stops after encountering the character *c* in *source*, it returns a pointer to the character following *c* in the *dest* buffer. Otherwise, *memccpy* returns a NULL.

COMMENTS Be sure that there is enough room in the destination buffer before calling any string or memory copy functions. This is a major source of error in C programs.

SEE ALSO

memcpy, memmove, movmem	*To copy one buffer to another*
movedata	*To copy buffers even if the source and destination are in different segments*

EXAMPLE Use *memccpy* to copy a string typed in by the user from an input buffer to an internal buffer. Copy until the null character (\0) is encountered or until 81 bytes are copied.

```
#include <stdio.h>
#include <mem.h>
static char dest[81];   /* Destination buffer */
main()
{
    char inbuf[81];
    printf("Enter a string: ");
    gets(inbuf);
    memccpy(dest, inbuf, '\0', 81);
    printf("Destination buffer has: %s\n", dest);
    return 0;
}
```

memchr

COMPATIBILITY

TC1	TC1.5	TC2	TC++	MSC3	MSC4	MSC5	MSC6	QC1	QC2	QC2.5	ANSI	UNIX V	XNX
▲	▲	▲	▲	▲	▲	▲	▲	▲	▲	▲	▲	▲	▲

PURPOSE Use the *memchr* function to search a memory buffer for a specific character.

SYNTAX

```
void *memchr(const void *buffer, int c, size_t count);
```

const void *buffer;	*Pointer to buffer in which search takes place*
int c;	*Character to look for*
size_t count;	*Maximum number of bytes to be examined*

EXAMPLE CALL

```
/* Look for the first occurrence of 'I' in a 100 byte buffer */
    first_i = memchr(start_address, 'I', 100);
```

INCLUDES `#include <mem.h>` *For function declaration and definition of* size_t

or

`#include <string.h>`

DESCRIPTION The *memchr* function looks through the first *count* bytes in the buffer at the address buffer and stops when it finds the character *c*. The search terminates if *memchr* does not find *c* after examining all the *count* bytes.

RETURNS If *memchr* finds the character *c*, it returns a pointer to it. Otherwise, *memchr* returns a NULL.

SEE ALSO `memcmp, memicmp` *To compare characters in two buffers*

EXAMPLE The listing of the ROM BIOS in the *IBM PC Technical Reference Manual* shows that IBM's copyright notice appears at offset E000h in the BIOS segment F000h. Use *memchr* in a large memory model program to look for the I in IBM's copyright notice. If you do not have an IBM, substitute an appropriate character and address. On successful return, copy the next eight characters into a local buffer and print them out.

```
/* Use the the large memory model (-ml flag)        */
#include <stdio.h>
#include <dos.h>
#include <mem.h>
/* Copyright notice begins at segment F000 and offset
 * E000
 */
#define  COPYRIGHT_NOTICE  MK_FP(0xf000,0xe000)
static char dest[81];           /* Destination buffer */
main()
{
    void *copr_address, *first_i;
    copr_address = COPYRIGHT_NOTICE;
/* Look for the 'I' of IBM in the copyright notice   */
    if((first_i = memchr(copr_address, 'I', 24))
        == NULL)
    {
        printf("Search failed!\n");
    }
    else
    {
        printf("Found an 'I'at %p\n", first_i);
/* Copy next 8 characters into buffer 'dest' for
```

```
 * printing
 */
        memcpy(dest, first_i, 8);
        dest[8] = '\0';
        printf("The next 8 characters are: %s\n", dest);
  }
  return 0;
}
```

memcmp

COMPATIBILITY

TC1	TC1.5	TC2	TC++	MSC3	MSC4	MSC5	MSC6	QC1	QC2	QC2.5	ANSI	UNIX V	XNX
▲	▲	▲	▲	▲	▲	▲	▲	▲	▲				

PURPOSE Use *memcmp* to compare a number of bytes from one buffer with those in another.

SYNTAX

```
int memcmp(const void *buffer1, const void *buffer2,
                size_t count);

const void *buffer1;        Pointer to first buffer
const void *buffer2;        Pointer to second buffer

size_t count;               Number of bytes to be compared
```

EXAMPLE CALL

```
if (memcmp(buffer1, buffer2, sizeof(buffer1)) == 0)
                printf("The buffers are identical\n");
```

INCLUDES

```
#include <mem.h>        For function declaration and definition of size_t
```

or

```
#include <string.h>
```

DESCRIPTION The *memcmp* function compares the first *count* bytes of *buffer1* and *buffer2* and returns an integer value indicating the order in which these two sets of characters would have appeared in a dictionary.

COMMON USES Because the other string-comparison routine, *strcmp*, can be used only with null-terminated strings, the *memcmp* function is preferable for comparing portions of two strings.

RETURNS The integer values returned by *memcmp* have the following meanings:

Value	Interpretation
Less than 0	The first *count* characters in *buffer1* are less than those of *buffer2*, meaning *buffer1* would have appeared before *buffer2* if they were in a dictionary.
Equal to 0	The two buffers are equal up to the first *count* characters.
Greater than 0	*buffer1* is greater than *buffer2*.

SEE ALSO memicmp — *To compare one buffer to another without regard to case of the characters*

EXAMPLE Use *memcmp* to compare two buffers. Let one be in uppercase and the other in lowercase. Notice that unlike *memicmp*, *memcmp* considers *buffer1* greater than *buffer2*.

```
#include <stdio.h>
#include <mem.h>
static char buffer1[81] = "Buffer 1",
            buffer2[81] = "BUFFER 1";
main()
{
    int result;
    printf("First buffer = %s\nSecond buffer = %s\n",
            buffer1, buffer2);
    result = memcmp(buffer1, buffer2, sizeof(buffer1));
    if(result == 0) printf("The buffers are equal.\n");
    if(result < 0) printf("%s less than %s\n", buffer1,
                           buffer2);
    if(result > 0) printf("%s greater than %s\n",
                           buffer1, buffer2);
    return 0;
}
```

COMPATIBILITY

memcpy

TC1	TC1.5	TC2	TC++	MSC3	MSC4	MSC5	MSC6	QC1	QC2	QC2.5	ANSI	UNIX V	XNX
▲	▲	▲	▲	▲	▲	▲	▲	▲	▲	▲	▲	▲	▲

PURPOSE Use *memcpy* to copy bytes from one memory buffer to another.

SYNTAX

```
void *memcpy(void *dest, const void *source, size_t count);
```

void *dest; — *Pointer to buffer to which data will be copied*

```
const void *source;      Pointer to buffer from which data will be copied

size_t count;            Maximum number of bytes to be copied
```

EXAMPLE CALL

```
memcpy(dest, src, 80); /* Copy 80 bytes from src to dest */
```

INCLUDES

`#include <mem.h>` *For function declaration and definition of* size_t

or

`#include <string.h>`

DESCRIPTION The *memcpy* function copies *count* bytes from the buffer at address *source* to another buffer at *dest*. This function can be used to copy a screen image from an offscreen buffer to the video memory. (This is true only in large data models; use *movedata* in small and medium models.)

RETURNS The *memcpy* function returns a pointer to the destination buffer *dest*.

COMMENTS If some parts of the source and destination buffers overlap, *memcpy* does not ensure that the bytes in *source* are copied before being overwritten. Only the *memmove* function handles copying between overlapping buffers properly so you should use *memmove* when you copy to and from overlapping buffers.

SEE ALSO

memccpy, memmove *To copy one buffer to another*

movedata *To copy buffers even if the source and destination are in different segments*

EXAMPLE Use *memcpy* to copy 80 bytes from one buffer to another. Print both buffers before and after the move to verify the results.

```
#include <stdio.h>
#include <mem.h>
static char src[80]="This is the SOURCE buffer\n";
static char dest[80]="Destination\n";
main()
{
    printf("Before memcpy: Source = %s Destination \
= %s", src, dest);
/* Copy from source to destination */
    memcpy(dest, src, 80);
    printf("After  memcpy: Source = %s Destination \
```

```
= %s", src, dest);
    return 0;
}
```

COMPATIBILITY

memicmp

TC1	TC1.5	TC2	TC++	MSC3	MSC4	MSC5	MSC6	QC1	QC2	QC2.5	ANSI	UNIX V	XNX
▲	▲	▲	▲	▲	▲	▲	▲					▲	

PURPOSE Use *memicmp* to compare a number of bytes from one buffer with those in another without regard to the case of the letters in the two buffers.

SYNTAX

```
int memicmp(const void *buffer1, const void *buffer2, size_t count);
```

`const void *buffer1;`	*Pointer to first buffer*
`const void *buffer2;`	*Pointer to second buffer*
`size_t count;`	*Number of bytes to be compared*

EXAMPLE CALL

```
if(memicmp(buffer1, buffer2, 10) == 0)
    puts("The buffers are equal up to the first 10 bytes\n");
```

INCLUDES `#include <mem.h>` *For function declaration*

or

`#include <string.h>`

DESCRIPTION The *memicmp* function converts the first *count* characters in *buffer1* and *buffer2* into lowercase letters. Then it compares the first *count* bytes of the two buffers and returns an integer value indicating the order in which these two sets of characters would have appeared in a dictionary.

RETURNS The integer values returned by *memicmp* have the following meanings:

Value	Interpretation
Less than 0	The first *count* characters in *buffer1* are less than those of *buffer2*, meaning *buffer1* would have appeared before *buffer2* if they were in a dictionary.
Equal to 0	The two buffers are equal up to the first *count* characters.
Greater than 0	*buffer1* is greater than *buffer2*.

SEE ALSO `memcmp` *To compare one buffer to another (the case of letters matters)*

EXAMPLE Use *memicmp* to compare two buffers. Let one be in uppercase and the other in lowercase. Note that unlike *memcmp*, *memicmp* considers the buffers equal regardless of the case of the letters.

```
#include <stdio.h>
#include <mem.h>
static char buffer1[81] = "Buffer 1",
            buffer2[81] = "BUFFER 1";
main()
{
    int result;
    printf("First buffer = %s\nSecond buffer = %s\n",
            buffer1, buffer2);
    result = memicmp(buffer1, buffer2, sizeof(buffer1));
    if(result == 0) printf("The buffers are equal.\n");
    if(result < 0) printf("%s less than %s\n", buffer1,
                          buffer2);
    if(result > 0) printf("%s greater than %s\n",
                          buffer1, buffer2);
    return 0;
}
```

memmove

COMPATIBILITY

TC1	TC1.5	TC2	TC++	MSC3	MSC4	MSC5	MSC6	QC1	QC2	QC2.5	ANSI	UNIX V	XNX
▲	▲	▲	▲	▲	▲	▲	▲	▲	▲	▲	▲		

PURPOSE Use *memmove* to copy bytes from one memory buffer to another. The *memmove* function can correctly copy to and from overlapping buffers.

SYNTAX `void *memmove(void *dest, const void *source, size_t count);`

`void *dest;` *Pointer to buffer to which data will be copied*

`const void *source;` *Pointer to buffer from which data will be copied*

`size_t count;` *Maximum number of bytes to be copied*

EXAMPLE CALL `memmove(dest, src, sizeof(src));`

INCLUDES `#include <string.h>` *For function declaration and definition of* `size_t`

DESCRIPTION The *memmove* function copies *count* bytes from the buffer at address *source* to another buffer at *dest*. The source and destination buffers may overlap.

RETURNS The *memmove* function returns a pointer to *dest*.

SEE ALSO

`memccpy, memcpy`	*To copy one buffer to another*
`movedata`	*To copy buffers even if the source and destination are in different segments*

EXAMPLE Use *memmove* to copy 80 bytes from one part of a buffer to another. Print the buffer before and after the move to verify that *memmove* can handle overlapping source and destination buffers properly.

```
#include <stdio.h>
#include <string.h>
static char src[80]="FirstSecond";
main()
{
    printf("Before memmove:Source = %s\n", src);
/* Copy from source to itself */
    memmove(&src[5], src, sizeof(src));
    printf("After  memmove:Source = %s\n", src);
    return 0;
}
```

COMPATIBILITY

memset

TC1	TC1.5	TC2	TC++	MSC3	MSC4	MSC5	MSC6	QC1	QC2	QC2.5	ANSI	UNIX V	XNX
▲	▲	▲	▲	▲	▲	▲	▲	▲	▲	▲	▲	▲	▲

PURPOSE Use *memset* to set a specified number of bytes in memory to a specific character.

SYNTAX `void *memset(void *buffer, int c, size_t count);`

`void *buffer;`	*Pointer to memory where bytes are to be set*
`int c;`	*Each byte in buffer is set to this character*
`size_t count;`	*Maximum number of bytes to be set*

EXAMPLE CALL `memset(big_buffer, '\0', 2048);`

INCLUDES `#include <mem.h>` *For function declaration and definition of* size_t

or

`#include <string.h>`

DESCRIPTION The *memset* function sets the first *count* bytes in the buffer to the character *c*.

COMMON USES The *memset* function is useful for initializing large chunks of memory. For example, *calloc* calls *memset* to set each byte of the allocated block of memory to zero.

RETURNS The *memset* function returns a pointer *buffer* to the buffer.

COMMENTS There is an intrinsic version of *memset* also, but that version cannot handle huge arrays in compact or large model programs.

SEE ALSO `memccpy, memcpy, memmove, movmem` *To copy one buffer to another*

`setmem` *To set a number of bytes to a specific value*

EXAMPLE Set all bytes in a buffer to the letter Z, append a null character, and print the resulting C string.

```
#include <stdio.h>
#include <mem.h>
static char buffer[41];     /* Destination buffer */
main()
{
    char *result;
    result = memset(buffer, 'Z', 40);
    buffer[40] = '\0';
    printf("The buffer now contains: %s\n", buffer);
    return 0;
}
```

COMPATIBILITY

movedata

TC1	TC1.5	TC2	TC++	MSC3	MSC4	MSC5	MSC6	QC1	QC2	QC2.5	ANSI	UNIX V	XNX
▲	▲	▲	▲	▲	▲	▲	▲	▲	▲	▲			

PURPOSE Use the *movedata* function to copy a specified number of bytes from a source address to a destination address that can be in a different segment.

SYNTAX

```
void movedata(unsigned source_seg, unsigned source_off,
              unsigned dest_seg, unsigned dest_off, size_t count);
```

```
unsigned  source_seg;
```
Segment address of source buffer

```
unsigned  source_off;
```
Offset address of source buffer

```
unsigned  dest_seg;
```
Segment address of destination

```
unsigned  dest_off;
```
Offset address of destination

```
size_t count;
```
Number of bytes to be copied

EXAMPLE CALL

```
movedata(src_seg, src_off, dest_seg, dest_off, 4096);
```

INCLUDES

```
#include <mem.h>
```
For function declaration

or

```
#include <string.h>
```

DESCRIPTION The *movedata* function copies *count* bytes from the source address given by *source_seg:source_off* to the destination address *dest_seg:dest_off*. Since the addresses are in segment and offset format, *movedata* can copy from one segment to another.

COMMON USES The *movedata* function is useful for moving data from one *far* array to another in small and medium memory models. It can also be used to copy data directly into the video memory.

COMMENTS In large and compact models, the *memcpy* and *memmove* functions perform the same as *movedata* because all data objects in these models are addressed using explicit segment and offset values.

SEE ALSO `memcpy, memmove, movmem` *To copy one buffer to another*

segread	*To get current values of the segment registers*
FP_OFF, FP_SEG	*Macros to determine segment and offset addresses of a* far *data item*

EXAMPLES Write a C program that calls *movedata* to copy the first 22 bytes from the address F000:E000 (in ROM BIOS) to a buffer in your program. Append a null character (\0) and print the resulting C string. On an IBM PC-AT this will print the IBM copyright notice.

```
#include <stdio.h>
#include <dos.h>          /* For FP_OFF and FP_SEG    */
#include <mem.h>
static char buffer[41];   /* Destination buffer */
main()
{
    void far *address;
    unsigned bufseg, bufoff;
/* Get segment and offset address of buffer */
    address = (void far *)buffer;
    bufseg = FP_SEG(address);
    bufoff = FP_OFF(address);
    movedata(0xf000, 0xe000, bufseg, bufoff, 22);
    buffer[22] = '\0';
/* Use the 'F' address modifier when printing buffer */
    printf("The buffer now contains: %s\n", buffer);
    return 0;
}
```

In a Color Graphics Adapter (and EGA in text mode), the video memory starts at the address B800:0000. Prepare a buffer with 2,000 (25 rows by 80 columns) short integers. Initialize the entire buffer to zero (use *memset*). Now use *movedata* to copy the contents of the buffer into video memory. The effect of setting the video memory to zeroes is to clear the display screen. This approach is used for preparing text output offscreen and for updating the display very rapidly.

```
#include <stdio.h>
#include <dos.h>
#include <mem.h>
static short dispbuf[25][80]; /* Display buffer */
main()
{
    void far *address;
    unsigned bufseg, bufoff;
```

```
/* Initialize display buffer to zero */
    memset(dispbuf, '\0', sizeof(dispbuf));
/* Get segment and offset address of buffer */
    address = (void far *)dispbuf;
    bufseg = FP_SEG(address);
    bufoff = FP_OFF(address);
/* Copy buffer into video memory -- clears screen */
    movedata( bufseg, bufoff, 0xb800, 0x0000,
              sizeof(dispbuf));
    return 0;
}
```

COMPATIBILITY

movmem

TC1	TC1.5	TC2	TC++	MSC3	MSC4	MSC5	MSC6	QC1	QC2	QC2.5	ANSI	UNIX V	XNX
▲	▲	▲	▲										

PURPOSE Use *movmem* to move a specified number of bytes from a source buffer to a destination buffer (overlapping buffers are handled properly).

SYNTAX

```
void movmem (void *src, void *dest, unsigned nbytes);
```

`void     *src;`	*Address of the source buffer*
`void     *dest;`	*Address of the destination buffer*
`unsigned nbytes;`	*Number of bytes to be copied*

EXAMPLE CALL `movmem(source, destination, numbytes);`

INCLUDES `#include <mem.h>` *For function prototype*

DESCRIPTION The *movmem* function copies *nbytes* bytes from the buffer at address *src* to the buffer at *dest*. The copying is done so that overlapping source and destination buffers are handled properly.

COMMENTS The ANSI-compatible *memmove* routine provides the exact functionality of *movmem*. Therefore, you should use *memmove* in your programs.

SEE ALSO `memmove` *ANSI-compatible function for copying buffers*

EXAMPLE Use *movmem* to copy 80 bytes from one buffer to another part of itself. Print the buffer before and after the move to verify the results. This illustrates that *movmem* can handle overlapping source and destination buffers properly.

```
#include <stdio.h>
#include <string.h>
static char src[80]="FirstSecond";
main()
{
    printf("Before movmem:Source = %s\n", src);
/* Copy from source to itself */
    movmem(&src[5], src, sizeof(src));
    printf("After  movmem:Source = %s\n", src);
    return 0;
}
```

setmem

COMPATIBILITY

TC1	TC1.5	TC2	TC++	MSC3	MSC4	MSC5	MSC6	QC1	QC2	QC2.5	ANSI	UNIX V	XNX
▲	▲	▲	▲										

PURPOSE Use *setmem* to set a specified number of bytes in a buffer to a specific character.

SYNTAX

```
void setmem(void *buffer, int count, char c);
```

`void`	`*buffer;`	*Pointer to memory where bytes are to be set*
`int`	`count;`	*Number of bytes to be set*
`char`	`c;`	*Each byte in buffer will be set to this character*

EXAMPLE CALL

```
setmem(big_buffer, 2048, '\0');
```

INCLUDES `#include <mem.h>` *For function declaration*

DESCRIPTION The *setmem* function will set the first *count* bytes in the *buffer* to the character *c*.

COMMON USES The *setmem* function is useful for initializing buffers.

COMMENTS There is an ANSI version of this routine, *memset*, which performs in the same way as *setmem*, but is more portable.

SEE ALSO `memset` *ANSI-compatible version of* setmem

EXAMPLE Set all bytes in a buffer to the letter Z, append a null character and print the resulting C string.

```
#include <stdio.h>
#include <mem.h>
static char buffer[41];    /* Destination buffer */
main()
{
    setmem(buffer, 40, 'Z');
    buffer[40] = '\0';
    printf("The buffer now contains: %s\n", buffer);
    return 0;
}
```

COMPATIBILITY

swab

TC1	TC1.5	TC2	TC++	MSC3	MSC4	MSC5	MSC6	QC1	QC2	QC2.5	ANSI	UNIX V	XNX
▲	▲	▲	▲	▲	▲	▲	▲	▲	▲	▲		▲	▲

PURPOSE Use *swab* to copy an even number of bytes from one location to another, at the same time swapping each pair of adjacent bytes.

SYNTAX `void swab(char *source, char *destination, int n);`

`char *source;` *Data to be copied after byte swapping*

`char *destination;` *Buffer for byte-swapped data*

`int n;` *Number of bytes to copy (must be even)*

EXAMPLE CALL `swab("badc", result, 4); /* result will be "abcd" */`

INCLUDES `#include <stdlib.h>` *For function definition*

DESCRIPTION The *swab* function copies *n* bytes of data from the buffer *source* to another buffer at *dest*, taking two adjacent bytes at a time and swapping their positions in *dest*. The number *n* should be even to allow *swab* to perform the byte swapping.

COMMON USES The byte-swapping capability afforded by *swab* is useful when preparing binary data to be read by a system in which the ordering of least significant and most significant bytes in a short integer is just the opposite of the order in the current system.

COMMENTS Although most computer systems today use the 8-bit byte as the smallest unit for data storage, there is no such standard for which byte is least significant and which most significant in multibyte data objects. Even in the simplest case of a short integer with 2 bytes in it you have two possibilities: the least significant byte is either the one at the lower address or the one at the higher memory address. The situation is more complicated in a network environment where machines with differing conventions may be connected together. In these situations you have to use such functions as *swab* to convert the byte ordering of one machine to the liking of another.

EXAMPLE Illustrate the use of *swab* in a program that takes a string on the command line (with no blanks embedded) and copies it into another buffer. Print the copy made by *swab*.

```
#include <stdio.h>
#include <stdlib.h>
#include <string.h>
main(int argc, char **argv)
{
    size_t len;
    char src[80], dst[80];
/* Make sure that there are at least 2 arguments */
    if(argc < 2)
    {
        printf("Usage: %s <string for \"swab\">\n",
                argv[0]);
        abort();
    }
/* Take an even no. of characters and feed it to swab */
    len = 2*(strlen(argv[1])/2);
    strncpy(src, argv[1], len);
/* Mark the end of string in both source and dest.    */
    src[len] = '\0';
    dst[len] = '\0';
/* Now copy after swapping adjacent bytes */
    swab(src, dst, len);
    printf("Input string to \"swab\" : %s\n\
Output string to \"swab\": %s\n", src, dst);
    return 0;
}
```

Buffer Manipulation

III Data Processing

- Data Conversion Routines
- Math Routines
- Character Classification and Conversion
- String Comparison and Manipulation
- Searching and Sorting
- Time Routines

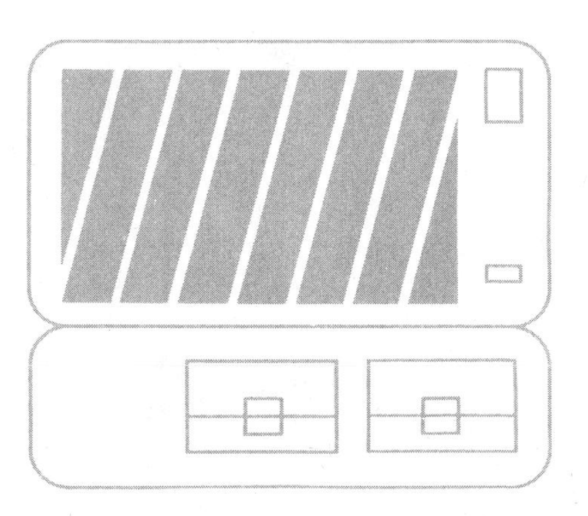

Chapter 8 Data Conversion Routines

Introduction

Information management with microcomputers frequently requires crunching numbers. These numbers are represented internally in several forms depending on the type of C variable in which the value is held. The data conversion routines allow us to convert back and forth between the internal form of a C variable and the character string representations that we can read.

Concepts: Internal Representations of Data

The data conversion routines rely on several internal representations of a number—as a series of bytes in memory containing a binary representation as well as in a character string (with the values expressed in decimal and hexadecimal, among other numbering systems).

NUMBERS IN MANY FORMS

All computers store numbers in binary representation in their memory locations. This is true of all types of numbers, floating-point or integer. As illustrated in Figure 8-1, the character string representation of a value depends on the radix, or the base of the number system in which the value is being expressed. For example, decimal 100 is written as 64 in hexadecimal, 144 in octal, and 1100100 in binary. Figure 8-1 also shows the internal binary representations of the value 100 stored as a short integer and as an Institute of Electrical and Electronics Engineers (IEEE) format double-precision floating-point number. The character string, though, is the form we deal with to obtain numbers from the user or to format and print numbers calculated by the program.

NUMBERS FOR THE MICRO-PROCESSORS

The pattern of bits that represents a value (such as decimal 100) in memory is determined by the type of C variable used to hold that value. If the variable type is *int*, which has a size of two bytes on the IBM PC, the value will be stored in binary in these two bytes (Figure 8-1). On the other hand, if we were to store 100 in a variable of type *double*, eight bytes will be used to hold the value and the bit pattern will depend on a format known as the IEEE format for double-precision numbers. Both the 8086 microprocessor and its "math whiz" companion 8087 store floating-point numbers in the IEEE format. See Chapter 10 of The Waite Group's *MS-DOS Developer's Guide*[1] for a detailed presentation of binary representation of floating-point numbers in the 8087 math coprocessor.

Notes on Using the Data Conversion Routines

The data conversion routines help us create a bridge between the two styles of representing numbers: the human readable text string and the machine readable binary form. Table 8-1 lists the routines at our disposal.

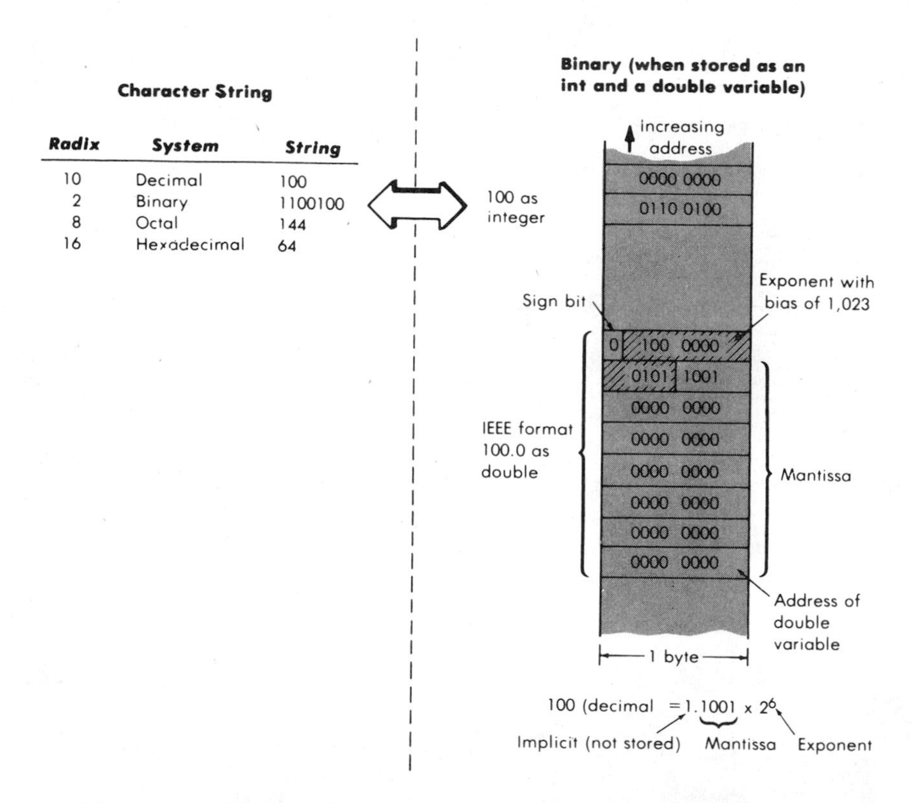

Figure 8-1. ***Decimal 100 as a character string and in internal forms***

Table 8-1. ***Data Conversion Routines***

Routine	Description
atof	Converts a string to a double-precision floating-point value.
atoi	Converts a string to an integer.
atol	Converts a string to a long integer.
ecvt	Converts a double-precision floating-point value into a string without an embedded decimal point (the sign of the value and the position of the decimal point are returned separately).
fcvt	Almost identical to ecvt, but it rounds the value to a specified number of digits.
gcvt	Converts a double-precision floating-point value into a string using a specified number of significant digits and having an embedded decimal point.
itoa	Converts an integer value to a string.
ltoa	Converts a long integer value to a string.
strtod	Converts a string to a double-precision floating-point value.
strtol	Converts a string to a long integer.
strtoul	Converts a string to an unsigned long integer.
ultoa	Converts an unsigned long integer value to a string.

The conversion routines are ideal for converting command-line arguments from their string representation into the internal format. For example, we may want the user to invoke a small calculator utility in the form

```
eval 4.5 + 2.3
```

where *eval* is the name of the program that accepts command-line arguments of the form <*value1*> <*operator*> <*value2*> and prints out the answer to the operation. In the sample invocation above, we get back 6.8 as the answer. When implementing the program *eval*, we can make use of the function *atof* to convert the second and the fourth command-line argument (the first argument is always the name of the program) to *double* variables. The code implementing the addition operator might be

```
:
value1 = atof(argv[1]);
value2 = atof(argv[3]);
switch(argv[2][0])
{
:
    case '+': result = value1 + value2;
              break;
:
```

```
}
printf("%f", result);
```

In this example, we assumed a decimal calculator. If we want a hexadecimal calculator (so that all input and output is in hexadecimal), we can use *strtoul* to convert the input arguments to unsigned long integers. Use *ultoa* and specify a hexadecimal base to convert the result to a string.

Since the conversion routines are mostly used to read numerical values typed in by the user and to convert them to internal formats, you must consider the maximum values that each type of C variable can hold. Table 8-2 summarizes this information. Note that the range of values and the sizes shown in Table 8-2 apply only to Turbo C++ on the IBM PC, XT, AT, and compatibles.

Table 8-2. ***Limits of Values That Can Fit into C Variables***

Type	Bytes	Limits
double	8	15 significant digits, exponent ranging from −306 to 306
int	2	−32,767 to 32,767
long	4	−2,147,483,647 to 2,147,483,647
unsigned int	2	0 to 65,535
unsigned long	4	0 to 4,294,967,295

DATA CONVERSION ROUTINES BY TASK

The twelve data conversion routines perform two basic tasks: converting a C numerical value to a string or converting a string to a specific type of C variable. Table 8-3 shows the routines grouped by task.

Table 8-3. ***Data Conversion Routines by Task***

Task	Routines
Convert character string to floating-point value.	atof, strtod
Convert character string to integer.	atoi
Convert character string to long integer.	atol, strtol
Convert character string to unsigned long integer.	strtoul
Convert floating-point values to character string.	ecvt, fcvt, gcvt
Convert integer values to string.	itoa
Convert long integer to string.	ltoa
Convert unsigned long integer to string.	ultoa

OTHER DATA CONVERSION RESOURCES

A few other routines in the C library provide data conversion facilities. The *sprintf* and the *sscanf* functions in the I/O category convert internal values to strings and strings back to internal representations, respectively. The *sprintf* routine, however, lacks the ability to convert an integer to a string using an arbitrary radix—only decimal and hexadecimal formats are supported. To print a value in binary or octal you have to use such routines as *itoa, ltoa,* or *ultoa.*

Further Reading

Waite Group's *MS-DOS Developer's Guide*[1] devotes Chapter 10 to the subject of writing programs for the 8087 math coprocessor. That chapter also describes the binary representation of floating-point numbers.

1. The Waite Group, *MS-DOS Developer's Guide*, Second Edition, Howard W. Sams & Company, Indianapolis, IN, 1988, 813 pages.

atof

COMPATIBILITY

TC1	TC1.5	TC2	TC++	MSC3	MSC4	MSC5	MSC6	QC1	QC2	QC2.5	ANSI	UNIX V	XNX
▲	▲	▲	▲	▲	▲	▲	▲	▲	▲	▲	▲	▲	▲

PURPOSE Use *atof* to convert a character string to a double-precision floating-point value.

SYNTAX

```
double atof(const char *string);

const char *string;        String to be converted
```

EXAMPLE CALL

```
dbl_value = atof(input_string);
```

INCLUDES

```
#include <math.h>        For function declaration
```

or

```
#include <stdlib.h>
```

DESCRIPTION The *atof* function converts the argument "string" into a double value. The string is expected to be of the form

[whitespace][sign][digits.digits] [exponent_letter][sign][digits]

The "whitespace" characters are optional blanks and tab characters, the "sign" is optional, and the "digits" are decimal digits. The "exponent_letter" is either d, D, e, or E, marking the beginning of the exponent field. (No matter which letter appears in the exponent field, the exponent always denotes a power of 10.) If a decimal point appears without any digits preceding it, at least one digit must appear after the decimal point. The conversion of characters from the string continues until *atof* encounters a character it cannot handle (the null character will suffice).

RETURNS The *atof* function returns the double-precision value after conversion. The return value is plus or minus HUGE_VAL if an overflow occurred during conversion.

SEE ALSO

`atoi, atol` *To convert strings to integers and long integer values*

`ecvt, fcvt, gcvt` *To convert floating-point values to strings*

EXAMPLE Write a program that accepts a floating-point number, uses *atof* to convert it to internal representation, and then prints that value.

```
#include <stdio.h>
#include <math.h>
main(int argc, char **argv)
{
    double value;
    if(argc < 2)
    {
        printf("Usage: %s <value>\n", argv[0]);
    }
    else
    {
        value = atof(argv[1]);
        printf("Value entered = %g\n", value);
    }
    return 0;
}
```

atoi

COMPATIBILITY

TC1	TC1.5	TC2	TC++	MSC3	MSC4	MSC5	MSC6	QC1	QC2	QC2.5	ANSI	UNIX V	XNX
▲	▲	▲	▲	▲	▲	▲	▲	▲	▲	▲	▲	▲	▲

PURPOSE Use *atoi* to convert a character string to an *int* value.

SYNTAX

```
int atoi(const char *string);

const char *string;     String to be converted
```

EXAMPLE CALL

```
int_value = atoi(input_string);
```

INCLUDES

```
#include stdlib.h>     For function declaration
```

DESCRIPTION The *atoi* function converts the argument *string* into an *int* value. The string is expected to be of the form

[whitespace][sign][digits]

The "whitespace" characters are optional blanks and tab characters, the "sign" is optional, and the "digits" are decimal digits. The conversion of characters from the string continues until *atoi* encounters a character it cannot handle (for example, a terminating null character, a decimal point, or a letter).

RETURNS The *atoi* function returns the integer value as an *int* variable. The return value is undefined if it is too large to fit an *int* variable.

SEE ALSO

atof	*To convert strings to floating-point values*
atol	*To convert strings to long integers*
itoa, ltoa, ultoa	*To convert integers to strings*

EXAMPLE Write a program that accepts a sequence of decimal integers, uses *atoi* to convert it to an integer, and then prints that integer.

```
#include <stdio.h>
#include <stdlib.h>
main(int argc, char **argv)
{
    int value;
    if(argc < 2)
    {
        printf("Usage: %s <value>\n", argv[0]);
    }
    else
    {
        value = atoi(argv[1]);
        printf("Value entered = %d\n", value);
    }
    return 0;
}
```

atol

COMPATIBILITY

TC1	TC1.5	TC2	TC++	MSC3	MSC4	MSC5	MSC6	QC1	QC2	QC2.5	ANSI	UNIX V	XNX
▲	▲	▲	▲	▲	▲	▲	▲	▲	▲	▲	▲	▲	▲

PURPOSE Use *atol* to convert a character string to a *long* integer value.

SYNTAX `int atol(const char *string);`

`const char *string;` *String to be converted*

EXAMPLE CALL `long_value = atol(input_string);`

INCLUDES `#include <stdlib.h>` *For function declaration*

DESCRIPTION The *atol* function converts the argument *string* into a *long* integer value. The string is expected to be of the form

[whitespace][sign][digits]

The "whitespace" characters are optional blanks and tab characters, the "sign" is optional, and the "digits" are decimal digits. The conversion of characters from the string continues until *atol* encounters a character it cannot handle (for example, a terminating null character, a decimal point, or a letter).

RETURNS The *atol* function returns the integer value as a *long* variable. The return value is undefined if it is too large to fit a *long* integer.

SEE ALSO

`atof`	*To convert strings to floating-point values*
`atoi`	*To convert strings to integers*
`itoa, ltoa, ultoa`	*To convert integers to strings*

EXAMPLE Write a program that accepts a sequence of decimal integers, uses *atol* to convert it to a long integer, and then prints that long integer.

```
#include <stdio.h>
#include <stdlib.h>
main(int argc, char **argv)
{
    long value;
    if(argc < 2)
    {
        printf("Usage: %s <value>\n", argv[0]);
    }
    else
    {
        value = atol(argv[1]);
        printf("Value entered = %ld\n", value);
    }
    return 0;
}
```

ecvt

COMPATIBILITY

TC1	TC1.5	TC2	TC++	MSC3	MSC4	MSC5	MSC6	QC1	QC2	QC2.5	ANSI	UNIX V	XNX
▲	▲	▲	▲	▲	▲	▲	▲	▲	▲	▲		▲	▲

PURPOSE Use *ecvt* to convert a floating-point value to a character string.

SYNTAX

```
char *ecvt(double value, int count, int *dec, int *sign);
```

`double value;`	*Floating-point value to be converted to string*
`int count;`	*Number of digits to be stored*
`int *dec;`	*Pointer to integer where position of decimal point is returned*
`int *sign;`	*Pointer to integer where sign of the number is returned*

EXAMPLE CALL

```
string = ecvt(value, precision, &d_position, &sign);
```

INCLUDES `#include <stdlib.h>` *For function declaration*

DESCRIPTION The *ecvt* function converts the *double* argument *value* into a null-terminated character string with *count* digits. If the number of digits in *value* exceeds *count*, the last digit is rounded. On the other hand, if there are fewer than *count* digits, the string is padded with zeroes.

You must specify the addresses of integer variables *dec* and *sign*, which are used by *ecvt* to return the location of the decimal point from the beginning of the string and from the sign of the number, respectively. If *ecvt* returns a zero or a negative number in *dec*, the decimal point lies at the beginning of the string or to the left of the first digit. If the value in *sign* is zero, the number is positive. Otherwise, it is negative.

RETURNS The *ecvt* function returns a pointer to an internal string where the string of digits is stored. The next call to either *ecvt* or *fcvt* destroys the result.

SEE ALSO

`atof`	*To convert strings to floating-point values*
`fcvt, gcvt`	*To convert floating-point numbers to strings*
`itoa, ltoa, ultoa`	*To convert integers to strings*

EXAMPLE Write a program that accepts a floating-point number, uses *atof* to convert it to internal form, and prepares a character string representing the value of that number by calling *ecvt* with a precision of 10 digits. Print the buffer prepared by *ecvt*, the location of the decimal point, and the value of the sign indicator.

```
#include <stdio.h>
#include <math.h>
#include <stdlib.h>
main(int argc, char **argv)
{
    int dec, sign, precision = 10;
    double value;
    char  *p_buffer;
    if(argc < 2)
    {
        printf("Usage: %s <value>\n", argv[0]);
    }
    else
    {
/* Convert the number to internal form. Then call ecvt */
        value = atof(argv[1]);
        p_buffer = ecvt(value, precision, &dec, &sign);
        printf("Buffer from ecvt contains: %s\n\
Location of decimal point: %d\n\
Sign (0 = pos, 1 = neg)  : %d\n", p_buffer, dec, sign);
    }
    return 0;
}
```

COMPATIBILITY

fcvt

TC1	TC1.5	TC2	TC++	MSC3	MSC4	MSC5	MSC6	QC1	QC2	QC2.5	ANSI	UNIX V	XNX
▲	▲	▲	▲	▲	▲	▲	▲	▲	▲	▲		▲	▲

PURPOSE Use *fcvt* to convert a floating-point value to a character string. The function of *fcvt* is similar to that of *ecvt* but *fcvt* rounds the number to a specified number of digits.

SYNTAX

```
char *fcvt(double value, int count, int *dec, int *sign);
```

`double value;` *Floating-point value to be converted to string*

`int count;` *Number of digits to be stored*

`int *dec;` *Pointer to integer where position of decimal point is returned*

`int *sign;` *Pointer to integer where sign of the number is returned*

EXAMPLE CALL

```
string = fcvt(value, precision, &d_position, &sign);
```

INCLUDES

`#include <stdlib.h>` *For function declaration*

DESCRIPTION

Like *ecvt*, the *fcvt* function converts the *double* argument *value* into a character string with *count* digits. If the number of digits in *value* exceeds *count*, the excess digits are rounded off to *count* places. On the other hand, if there are fewer than *count* digits, the string is padded with zeroes. You must specify the addresses of integer variables *dec* and *sign*, which are used by *fcvt* to return the location of the decimal point from the beginning of the string and from the sign of the number, respectively. If *fcvt* returns a zero or a negative number in *dec*, the decimal point lies at the beginning of the string or to the left of the first digit. If the value in *sign* is zero, the number is positive. Otherwise, it is negative.

RETURNS

The *fcvt* function returns a pointer to an internal string where the string of digits is stored. The next call to either *fcvt* or *ecvt* destroys the result.

SEE ALSO

`atof`	*To convert strings to floating-point values*
`ecvt, gcvt`	*To convert floating-point numbers to strings*
`itoa, ltoa, ultoa`	*To convert integers to strings*

EXAMPLE

Write a program that accepts a floating-point number, uses *atof* to convert it to internal form, and prepares a character string representing the value of that number by calling *ecvt* with a precision of 10 digits. Print the buffer prepared by *fcvt*, the location of the decimal point, and the value of the sign indicator.

```
#include <stdio.h>
#include <math.h>
#include <stdlib.h>
main(int argc, char **argv)
{
    int dec, sign, precision = 10;
    double value;
    char  *p_buffer;

    if(argc < 2)
    {
        printf("Usage: %s <value>\n", argv[0]);
    }
    else
    {
```

```
/* Convert the number to internal form. Then call fcvt */
        value = atof(argv[1]);
        p_buffer = fcvt(value, precision, &dec, &sign);
        printf("Buffer from fcvt contains: %s\n\
Location of decimal point: %d\n\
Sign (0 = pos, 1 = neg)  : %d\n", p_buffer, dec, sign);
    }
    return 0;
}
```

COMPATIBILITY

gcvt

TC1	TC1.5	TC2	TC++	MSC3	MSC4	MSC5	MSC6	QC1	QC2	QC2.5	ANSI	UNIX V	XNX
▲	▲	▲	▲	▲	▲	▲	▲	▲	▲	▲		▲	▲

PURPOSE Use *gcvt* to convert a floating-point value to a character string. Unlike *ecvt* and *fcvt*, *gcvt* returns the results in a character buffer supplied by you.

SYNTAX `char *gcvt(double value, int digits, char *buffer);`

`double value;` *Floating-point value to be converted to string*

`int digits;` *Number of significant digits to be stored*

`char *buffer;` *Pointer to character array where result is returned*

EXAMPLE CALL `gcvt(value, significant_digits, resulting_string);`

INCLUDES `#include <stdlib.h>` *For function declaration*

DESCRIPTION The *gcvt* function converts the *double* argument *value* into a character string that it saves in the buffer whose address is given in the argument *buffer*. You must allocate enough room in the buffer to hold all digits of the converted string and the terminating null character (\0).

The argument *digits* specifies the number of significant digits that *gcvt* should produce in the character string. If *gcvt* cannot meet this requirement in normal decimal format, it generates a string in scientific notation using mantissa and exponent (e.g., 1.234e−7 as opposed to 0.0000001234).

RETURNS The *gcvt* function returns a pointer to the string of digits, i.e., it returns the argument *buffer*.

COMMENTS Unlike *ecvt* and *fcvt*, *gcvt* uses a string supplied by you and it includes the decimal point and the sign in the result.

SEE ALSO

`atof`	*To convert strings to floating-point values*
`ecvt, fcvt`	*To convert floating-point numbers to strings*
`itoa, ltoa, ultoa`	*To convert integers to strings*

EXAMPLE Write a program that accepts a floating-point number, uses *atof* to convert it to internal form, and prepares a formatted representation of that number (with six significant digits) by calling *gcvt*. Print the resulting string.

```
#include <stdio.h>
#include <math.h>
#include <stdlib.h>
main(int argc, char **argv)
{
    int significant_digits = 6;
    double value;
    char  buffer[80];              /* Buffer for gcvt */
    if(argc < 2)
    {
        printf("Usage: %s <value>\n", argv[0]);
    }
    else
    {
/* Convert the number to internal form. Then call gcvt */
        value = atof(argv[1]);
        gcvt(value, significant_digits, buffer);
        printf("Buffer from gcvt contains: %s\n",
                buffer);
    }
    return 0;
}
```

itoa

COMPATIBILITY

TC1	TC1.5	TC2	TC++	MSC3	MSC4	MSC5	MSC6	QC1	QC2	QC2.5	ANSI	UNIX V	XNX
▲	▲	▲	▲	▲	▲	▲	▲	▲	▲	▲			

PURPOSE Use *itoa* to convert an integer value to a null-terminated character string.

SYNTAX

```
char *itoa(int value, char *string, int radix);
```

`int value;` *Integer value to be converted to string*

`char *string;` *Pointer to character array where result is returned*

`int radix;` *Radix in which the result is expressed (in the range 2–36)*

EXAMPLE CALL

```
itoa(32, buffer, 16); /* buffer will contain "20" */
```

INCLUDES `#include <stdlib.h>` *For function declaration*

DESCRIPTION The *itoa* function converts the *int* argument *value* into a null-terminated character string using the argument *radix* as the base of the number system. The resulting string with a length of up to 17 bytes is saved in the buffer whose address is given in the argument *string*. You must allocate enough room in the buffer to hold all digits of the converted string plus the terminating null character (\0). For radixes other than 10, the sign bit is not interpreted; instead, the bit pattern of *value* is simply expressed in the requested *radix*.

The argument *radix* specifies the base (between 2 and 36) of the number system in which the string representation of *value* is expressed. For example, using either 2, 8, 10, or 16 as *radix*, you can convert *value* into its binary, octal, decimal, or hexadecimal representation, respectively. When *radix* is 10 and the *value* is negative, the converted string will start with a minus sign.

RETURNS The *itoa* function returns the pointer to the string of digits (i.e., it returns the argument *string*).

SEE ALSO

`ecvt, fcvt, gcvt` *To convert floating-point numbers to strings*

`ltoa, ultoa` *To convert long and unsigned long integers to strings*

EXAMPLE Write a program to print an integer value using a specified radix. Assume the program will be invoked with the decimal value and the radix on the command line. Use *itoa* to generate the formatted string.

```
#include <stdio.h>
#include <stdlib.h>
main(int argc, char **argv)
{
    char buffer[17];              /* Buffer for itoa  */
    int value, radix;
    if(argc < 3)
    {
        printf("Usage: %s <value> <radix>\n", argv[0]);
    }
    else
    {
        value = atoi(argv[1]);
        radix = atoi(argv[2]);
        itoa(value, buffer, radix);
        printf("%s in radix %s = %s\n", argv[1], argv[2],
               buffer);
    }
    return 0;
}
```

ltoa

COMPATIBILITY

TC1	TC1.5	TC2	TC++	MSC3	MSC4	MSC5	MSC6	QC1	QC2	QC2.5	ANSI	UNIX V	XNX
▲	▲	▲	▲	▲	▲	▲	▲	▲	▲	▲			

PURPOSE Use *ltoa* to convert a *long* integer value to a null-terminated character string.

SYNTAX

```
char *ltoa(long value, char *string, int radix);
```

`long value;` *Long integer value to be converted to string*

`char *string;` *Pointer to character array where result is returned*

`int radix;` *Radix in which the result is expressed (in the range 2–36)*

EXAMPLE CALL

```
ltoa(0x10000, string, 10); /* string = "65536"  */
```

INCLUDES `#include <stdlib.h>` *For function declaration*

DESCRIPTION The *ltoa* function converts the *long* argument *value* into a character string using the argument *radix* as the base of the number system. A *long* integer

has 32 bits when expressed in radix 2, so the string can occupy a maximum of 33 bytes with the terminating null character. The resulting string is returned in the buffer whose address is given in the argument *string*.

The argument *radix* specifies the base (between 2 and 36) of the number system in which the string representation of *value* is expressed. For example, using either 2, 8, 10, or 16 as *radix*, you can convert *value* into its binary, octal, decimal, or hexadecimal representation, respectively. When *radix* is 10 and the *value* is negative, the converted string will start with a minus sign.

RETURNS The *ltoa* function returns the pointer to the converted string (i.e., it returns the argument *string*).

SEE ALSO

`ecvt, fcvt, gcvt`	*To convert floating-point numbers to strings*
`itoa, ultoa`	*To convert* int *and* unsigned long *integers to strings*

EXAMPLE Write a program that accepts a long integer value and a radix on the command line and then calls *ltoa* to prepare a character representation of that number in the specified radix and prints the string.

```
#include <stdio.h>
#include <stdlib.h>
main(int argc, char **argv)
{
    char buffer[33];              /* Buffer for ltoa  */
    int  radix;
    long value;
    if(argc < 3)
    {
        printf("Usage: %s <value> <radix>\n", argv[0]);
    }
    else
    {
        value = atol(argv[1]);
        radix = atoi(argv[2]);
        ltoa(value, buffer, radix);
        printf("%s in radix %s = %s\n", argv[1], argv[2],
               buffer);
    }
    return 0;
}
```

strtod

COMPATIBILITY

TC1	TC1.5	TC2	TC++	MSC3	MSC4	MSC5	MSC6	QC1	QC2	QC2.5	ANSI	UNIX V	XNX
▲	▲	▲	▲		▲	▲	▲	▲	▲	▲	▲	▲	▲

PURPOSE Use *strtod* to convert a character string to a double-precision value.

SYNTAX

```
double strtod(const char *string, char **endptr);
```

`const char  *string;` *Pointer to character array from which double-precision value is extracted*

`char **endptr;` *On return, points to character in* string *where conversion stopped*

EXAMPLE CALL

```
dbl_value = strtod(input_string, &endptr);
```

INCLUDES

`#include <stdlib.h>` *For function declaration*

`#include <float.h>` *For the definition of the constant HUGE_VAL*

`#include <math.h>` *For the definition of ERANGE*

DESCRIPTION The *strtod* function converts the *string* to a double-precision value. The string is expected to be of the form

[whitespace][sign][digits.digits][exponent_letter][sign][digits]

where "whitespace" refers to (optional) blanks and tab characters, "sign" is a + or a −, and the "digits" are decimal digits. The "exponent_letter" can be either d, D, e, or E. (No matter which exponent letter is used, the exponent always denotes a power of 10.) If there is a decimal point without a preceding digit, there must be at least one digit following it.

The *strtod* function begins the conversion process with the first character of *string* and continues until it finds a character that does not fit the above form. Then it sets *endptr* to point to the leftover string. In compact and large model programs *strtod* can only handle strings with a maximum length of 100 characters.

RETURNS The *strtod* function returns the double-precision value as long as it is not too large. If it is too large, an overflow occurs and the return value is the constant HUGE_VAL with the same sign as the number represented in *string*. Additionally, the global variable *errno* is set to the constant ERANGE.

COMMENTS The advantage of using *strtod* over *atof* is that *strtod* returns a pointer to the character where the conversion stopped, enabling you to handle the rest of the string any way you wish.

SEE ALSO

`atof`	*To convert strings to double-precision values*
`strtol, strtoul`	*To convert strings to long and unsigned long integers*

EXAMPLE Prompt the user for a floating-point number followed by arbitrary characters. Then call *strtod* to convert the floating-point number to internal form. Print the number and the rest of the string, which in a more realistic program would be processed further.

```
#include <stdio.h>
#include <stdlib.h>
main()
{
    char input[80], *stop_at;
    double value;
    printf(
   "Enter a number followed by other characters:\n");
   gets(input);
/* Now convert the number to internal value */
    value = strtod(input, &stop_at);
    printf("Value = %g\n\
Stopped at: %s\n", value, stop_at);
    return 0;
}
```

COMPATIBILITY

strtol

TC1	TC1.5	TC2	TC++	MSC3	MSC4	MSC5	MSC6	QC1	QC2	QC2.5	ANSI	UNIX V	XNX
▲	▲	▲	▲		▲	▲	▲	▲	▲	▲	▲	▲	▲

PURPOSE Use *strtol* to convert a character string to a long integer value.

SYNTAX `long strtol(const char *string, char **endptr, int radix);`

`const char *string;`	*Pointer to character array from which the long integer value is extracted*
`char **endptr;`	*On return, points to character in* string *where conversion stopped*

```
int radix;
```
Radix in which the value is expressed in the string (radix must be in the range 2–36)

EXAMPLE CALL

```
value = strtol(input, &endptr, radix);
```

INCLUDES

```
#include <stdlib.h>
```
For function declaration

```
#include <limits.h>
```
For the definition of the constants LONG_MIN and LONG_MAX

```
#include <math.h>
```
For the definition of ERANGE

DESCRIPTION The *strtol* function converts the *string* to a long integer value. The string is expected to be of the form

[whitespace][sign][0][x or X][digits]

where "whitespace" refers to optional blanks and tab characters, "sign" is a + or a −, and the "digits" are decimal digits. The string is expected to contain a representation of the long integer using the argument *radix* as the base of the number system. If *radix* is given as zero, though, *strtol* will use the first character in *string* to determine the radix of the value. The rules are given in the table.

First Character	Next Character	Radix Selected
0	0–7	Radix 8 is used (octal digits expected).
0	x or X	Radix 16 (hexadecimal digits expected).
1–9	—	Radix 10 (decimal digits expected).

Of course, other radixes may be specified via the argument *radix*. The letters a through z (or A through Z) are assigned values of 10 through 35. For a specified radix, *strtol* expects only those letters whose assigned values are less than the *radix*.

The *strtol* function begins the conversion process with the first character of *string* and continues until it finds a character that meets the above requirements. Then, before returning, *strtol* sets *endptr* to point to that character.

RETURNS The *strtol* function returns the long integer value except when it would cause an overflow. In which case, *strtol* sets *errno* to ERANGE and returns either LONG_MIN or LONG_MAX depending on whether the value was negative or positive.

COMMENTS The advantage of using *strtol* over *atol* is that *strtol* allows radix values other than 10 and it can determine the radix automatically based on the

first two characters of the string. Unlike *atol*, *strtol* returns a pointer to the character where the conversion stopped, enabling you to handle the rest of the string any way you wish.

SEE ALSO

atol	*To convert strings to long integer values*
ltoa	*To convert long integers to strings*
strtoul	*To convert strings to unsigned long integers*

EXAMPLE Write a program that accepts on the command line a long integer value followed by the radix in which the value is represented. Use *strtol* with the radix to convert the representation of that number to an internal value. Print this value.

```
#include <stdio.h>
#include <stdlib.h>
main(int argc, char **argv)
{
    char *stop_at;    /* Marks where strtol stopped  */
    int  radix;
    long value;
    if(argc < 3)
    {
        printf("Usage: %s <value> <radix>\n", argv[0]);
    }
    else
    {
        radix = atoi(argv[2]);
        value = strtol(argv[1], &stop_at, radix);
        printf("Value read in radix %d = %ld\n\
Stopped at: %s\n", radix, value, stop_at);

    }
    return 0;
}
```

strtoul

COMPATIBILITY

TC1	TC1.5	TC2	TC++	MSC3	MSC4	MSC5	MSC6	QC1	QC2	QC2.5	ANSI	UNIX V	XNX
	▲	▲	▲			▲	▲	▲	▲	▲	▲		

PURPOSE Use *strtoul* to convert a character string to an unsigned long integer.

SYNTAX

```
unsigned long strtoul(const char *string, char **endptr, int radix);
```

`const char *string;` *Pointer to character array from which the unsigned long value is extracted*

`char **endptr;` *On return, points to character in* string *where conversion stopped*

`int radix;` *Radix in which the value is expressed in the string (radix must be in the range 2–36)*

EXAMPLE CALL

```
value = strtoul(input_string, &stop_at, radix);
```

INCLUDES

`#include stdlib.h>` *For function declaration*

`#include <limits.h>` *For the definition of the constant ULONG_MAX*

`#include <math.h>` *For the definition of ERANGE*

DESCRIPTION The *strtoul* function converts the *string* to an unsigned long integer value. The string is expected to be of the form

[whitespace][0][x or X][digits]

where "whitespace" refers to optional blanks and tab characters, "sign" is a + or a –, and the "digits" are decimal digits. The string is expected to contain a representation of the unsigned long integer with the argument *radix* as the base of the number system. If *radix* is given as zero, however, *strtoul* uses the first character in *string* to determine the radix of the value. The rules are shown in the table.

First Character	Next Character	Radix Selected
0	0–7	Radix 8 is used (octal digits expected).
0	x or X	Radix 16 (hexadecimal digits expected).
1–9	—	Radix 10 (decimal digits expected).

Of course, another radix may be specified via the argument *radix*. The letters a through z (or A through Z) are assigned values 10 through 35. For a specified radix, *strtoul* expects only those letters whose assigned values are less than the *radix*.

The *strtoul* function begins the conversion process with the first character of *string* and continues until it finds a character that meets the above requirements. Then before returning, *strtoul* sets *endptr* to point to that character.

RETURNS The *strtoul* function returns the unsigned long integer value except when it will cause an overflow. In which case, *strtoul* sets *errno* to ERANGE and returns the value ULONG_MAX.

SEE ALSO

`atol`	*To convert strings to long integer values*
`ultoa`	*To convert unsigned long integers to strings*
`strtol`	*To convert strings to long integers*

EXAMPLE Write a program that accepts on the command line an unsigned long integer value followed by the radix in which the value is represented. Use *strtoul* with the radix to convert the representation of that number to an internal value. Print this value.

```
#include <stdio.h>
#include <stdlib.h>
main(int argc, char **argv)
{
    char *stop_at;    /* Marks where strtoul stopped */
    int  radix;
    unsigned long value;
    if(argc < 3)
    {
        printf("Usage: %s <value> <radix>\n", argv[0]);
    }
    else
    {
        radix = atoi(argv[2]);
        value = strtoul(argv[1], &stop_at, radix);
        printf("Value read in radix %d = %lu\n\
Stopped at: %s\n", radix, value, stop_at);

    }
    return 0;
}
```

ultoa

COMPATIBILITY

TC1	TC1.5	TC2	TC++	MSC3	MSC4	MSC5	MSC6	QC1	QC2	QC2.5	ANSI	UNIX V	XNX
▲	▲	▲	▲	▲	▲	▲	▲	▲	▲	▲			

PURPOSE Use *ultoa* to convert an *unsigned long* integer value to a character string.

SYNTAX

```
char *ultoa(unsigned long value, char *string, int radix);
```

`unsigned long value;` *Unsigned long integer value to be converted to string*

`char *string;` *Pointer to character array where result is returned*

`int radix;` *Radix in which the result is expressed (in the range 2–36)*

EXAMPLE CALL

```
ultoa(0x20000, string, 10); /* string = "131072"  */
```

INCLUDES `#include <stdlib.h>` *For function declaration*

DESCRIPTION The *ultoa* function converts the *unsigned long* argument *value* into a null-terminated character string using the argument *radix* as the base of the number system. A *long* integer has 32 bits when expressed in radix 2, so the string can occupy a maximum of 33 bytes with the terminating null character. The resulting string is returned by *ultoa* in the buffer whose address is given in the argument *string*.

The argument *radix* specifies the base (between 2 and 36) of the number system in which the string representation of *value* is expressed. For example, using either 2, 8, 10, or 16 as *radix*, you can convert *value* into its binary, octal, decimal, or hexadecimal representation, respectively.

RETURNS The *ultoa* function returns the pointer to the converted string (i.e., it returns the argument *string*).

SEE ALSO

`ecvt, fcvt, gcvt` *To convert floating-point numbers to strings*

`itoa, ltoa` *To convert* int *and* long *integers to strings*

EXAMPLE Write a program to print an unsigned long integer value in a specific radix. Assume that the program accepts the value followed by the radix on the command line. Use *ultoa* to prepare the character representation of the number in the radix.

```
#include <stdio.h>
#include <stdlib.h>
```

```
main(int argc, char **argv)
{
    char buffer[33];            /* Buffer for ultoa */
    int  radix;
    unsigned long value;
    if(argc < 3)
    {
        printf("Usage: %s <value> <radix>\n", argv[0]);
    }
    else
    {
        value = atol(argv[1]);
        radix = atoi(argv[2]);
        ultoa(value, buffer, radix);
        printf("%s in radix %s = %s\n", argv[1], argv[2],
                buffer);
    }
    return 0;
}
```

Chapter 9 Math Routines

Introduction

You often need computational capabilities beyond basic arithmetic operations. The 8086 microprocessor does not have machine instructions to perform such arithmetic operations as addition or multiplication of real or floating-point numbers directly. It needs support from an 8087 math coprocessor (or a software library) to do these computations. In C the support for all floating-point operations is provided by a floating-point package. Using compiler options, you can ask the compiler to generate code for an 8087 coprocessor or to use its software library that implements similar capabilities using 8086 instructions. In addition to the support for basic floating-point operations, the Turbo C++ library also includes a set of functions, the *math functions*, to control the operational characteristics of the underlying floating-point package and to compute common mathematical functions such as the sine and the cosine. This tutorial provides a summary of the capabilities of the math library in Turbo C++.

Concepts: Floating-Point Operations

Most of the math functions operate on floating-point variables, so we begin by explaining how floating-point numbers are stored and manipulated in the PC.

FLOATING-POINT FORMATS

Floating-point variables hold floating-point numbers—numbers with fractional parts. When writing such numbers, we usually use a decimal point, for example, 1.2345×10^5. This way of writing floating-point numbers is known as scientific or engineering notation. In fact, any floating-point number can be represented in this form: a "mantissa" (the number's significant digits) multiplied by 10 raised to the power of an integer "exponent." The mantissa and exponent form is how floating-point numbers are represented in the PC, except that instead of the exponent representing a power of 10, it represents a power of 2, since base 2 is a computer's natural format.

Precision: Single and Double

The number of bytes used to represent a floating-point number depends on the precision of the variable. The C variable type *float* is used to declare *single-precision* floating-point variables. The type *double* denotes *double-precision* values. As shown in Figure 9-1, the single-precision *float* variables require 4 bytes of storage while *double* variables use 8 bytes. The representation of the mantissa and the exponent in the variables is in accordance with the IEEE floating-point standards and is used in Turbo C++ and understood by the 8087 math coprocessor.

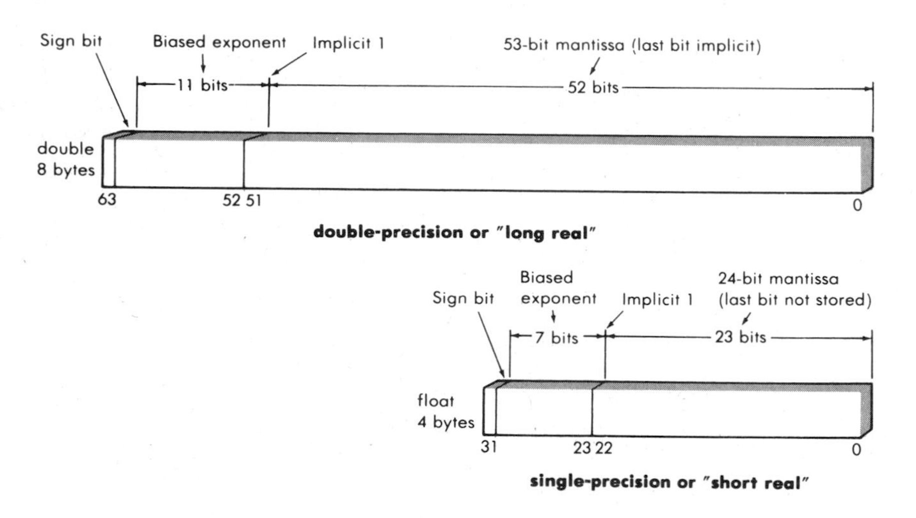

Figure 9-1. ***IEEE format for binary representation of floating-point numbers***

IEEE Format for Floating-Point Numbers

The IEEE format expresses a floating-point number in binary form known as "normalized." Normalization involves adjusting the exponent so that the "binary point" (the binary analog of the decimal point) in the mantissa always lies to the right of the most significant nonzero digit. In binary representation, this means that the most significant digit of the mantissa is always a 1. This property of the normalized representation is exploited by the IEEE format when storing the mantissa.

Consider an example of generating the normalized form of a floating-point number. Suppose, we want to represent the decimal number 5.375. Since this can be written as

$4 + 1 + \frac{1}{4} + \frac{1}{8}$

the binary form will be

101.011

The normalized form is obtained by adjusting the exponent until the decimal point is to the right of the 1 in the most significant position. In this case, the result is

1.01011×2^2

The IEEE format for floating-point storage uses a sign bit, a mantissa, and an exponent representing the power of 2. The "sign bit" denotes the sign of the number: a 0 represents a positive value and a 1 denotes a negative value. The mantissa is represented in binary. Constraining the floating-point number to be in normalized form results in a mantissa whose most significant binary digit is always 1. The IEEE format takes advantage of this by not storing this bit at all. The exponent is an integer stored in unsigned binary format after adding a positive integer "bias" to ensure that the stored exponent is always positive. The value of the bias depends upon the precision of the floating-point representation.

The single-precision *float* variable uses 4 bytes (32 bits) comprising 1 sign bit and 7 bits for the exponent and allows a 24-bit mantissa that can be stored in the rest of the 23 bits because the most significant bit is always 1 (Figure 9-1). The exponent is stored with a bias of 127. Thus, the smallest positive value you can store in a *float* variable is 2^{-126}, which is approximately 1.175×10^{-38}. The largest positive value is 2^{128}, which is about 3.4×10^{38}. About seven significant decimal digits can be handled in a *float* variable.

The double-precision *double* variable uses 8 bytes providing 64 bits of storage. As shown in Figure 9-1, the first bit is used for the sign bit and the next 11 bits hold the exponent, which has a bias of 1,023 added to it. The rest of the 52 bits contain the 53-bit mantissa. This representation allows about 15 significant decimal digits and the smallest positive value is 2^{-1022}, which is approximately 2.23×10^{-308}. The largest positive value that can be held in a *double* variable is 2^{1024}, which is approximately 1.8×10^{308}.

The IEEE format also specifies certain bit-patterns that represent such special conditions as infinite values or NANs (for "not a number"), but we will not go into the details here.

COMPILER OPTIONS FOR THE FLOATING-POINT LIBRARY

If an 8087 math coprocessor is not present in your system, the Turbo C++ library is equipped with alternatives to handle all floating-point calculations. Table 9-1 lists the compiler options for floating-point libraries. The –f87 option requires a math coprocessor at run-time and should not be used for applications that will be distributed widely. For such applications, the option *–f* generates code that uses the 8087 if the PC has one, but uses a software emulator if no 8087 is found. The –f287 option is meant for generating code for an 80287 coprocessor.

Table 9-1. *Compiler Options for Floating-Point Libraries*

Option	8087 or 80287 Required?	Description
–ff	No	"Fast-floating-point" option that generates optimized code for floating-point computations (may not be ANSI standard compliant).
–f	No	Generates in-line 8087 instructions that will use the 8087 if found. Otherwise, these instructions will be fielded by the emulator library. This is the default.
–f87	Yes	Generates in-line 8087 instructions that require the coprocessor at run-time.
–f287	Yes	Generates in-line 80287 instructions.

THE FLOATING-POINT PACKAGE

The IEEE standard for binary floating-point arithmetic is used in the 8087 family of math coprocessors. The software implementation that emulates the 8087 when no coprocessor is present in the system also uses the IEEE standard. The routines that handle floating-point calculations are collectively called the "floating-point package."

You can control certain parameters of the floating-point package, such as precision of the calculations and method of rounding the numbers, with the library routines *_clear87*, *_control87*, and *_status87*. The floating-point package maintains two 16-bit registers, the control word and the status word, for this purpose. There are similarly named registers in the 8087 processors. As their names imply, the "status word" maintains the current status of the floating-point package and the "control word" lets you control the precision of the computations and decide how a floating-point result should be truncated to fit in the number of bits available for that precision.

FLOATING-POINT EXCEPTIONS

When certain errors occur in the floating-point package, it raises the signal SIGFPE (see the tutorial in Chapter 4 for details on signals). The exceptional conditions, "exceptions" for short, that raise the signal can be controlled by setting bits in the control word with the function *_control87*. The floating-point package has six exceptions (as does the 8087): invalid operation, unnormalized operand, divide by zero, overflow, underflow, and loss of precision (inexact result).

Error Handling in the Floating-Point Package

When an error occurs in a math function, the *_matherr* function is called. The *_matherr* function, in turn, calls *matherr* which is supposed to resolve the error condition. A default, *matherr* is supplied in the Turbo C++ library, but you can write your own version of *matherr* to handle errors differently.

Notes

Table 9-2 catalogs the math functions available in the Turbo C++ library. While most routines are for computing specific functions, a few are meant for other chores, such as error handling, format conversion, and controlling the floating-point package.

Table 9-2. ***Library Math Functions***

Routine	Description
abs	Returns the absolute value of an integer argument.
acos	Computes the arc cosine of a value between -1 and 1 and returns an angle between 0 and π radian.
asin	Computes the arc sine of a value between -1 and 1 and returns an angle between $-\pi/2$ and $\pi/2$ radians.
atan	Computes the arc tangent of a value and returns an angle between $-\pi/2$ and $\pi/2$ radians.
atan2	Computes the arc tangent of one argument divided by the other and returns an angle between $-\pi$ and π radians.
cabs	Computes the magnitude of a complex number.
ceil	Finds the smallest integer larger than or equal to the function's floating-point argument.
_clear87	Clears the status word of the floating-point package.
_control87	Gets and sets the control word of the floating-point package.
cos	Evaluates the cosine of an angle in radians.
cosh	Evaluates the hyperbolic cosine of its argument.
div	Divides one integer by another and returns an integer quotient and an integer remainder.
exp	Computes the exponential of a floating-point argument.
fabs	Returns the absolute value of a floating-point argument.
floor	Finds the largest integer smaller than or equal to the function's floating-point argument.
fmod	Computes the floating-point remainder after dividing one floating-point value by another so that the quotient is the largest possible integer for that division.
_fpreset	Reinitializes the floating-point math package.
frexp	Breaks down a floating-point value into a mantissa between 0.5 and 1 and an integer exponent so that the value is equal to the mantissa $\times$ 2 raised to the power of the exponent.

Table 9-2. ***(cont.)***

Routine	Description
hypot	Computes the length of the hypotenuse of a right-angled triangle.
labs	Returns the absolute value of a long integer argument.
ldexp	Computes a floating-point value equal to a mantissa $\times$ 2 raised to power of an integer exponent.
ldiv	Divides one long integer by another and returns a long integer quotient and a long integer remainder.
log	Evaluates the natural logarithm of its floating-point argument.
log10	Evaluates the logarithm to the base 10 of its floating-point argument.
_lrotl	Rotates an unsigned long integer left by a given number of bits.
_lrotr	Rotates an unsigned long integer right by a given number of bits.
_matherr	Calls *matherr* to handle floating-point errors (internal routine called by other math functions when errors occur).
matherr	Handles error conditions occurring in the functions of the math library package.
max	Returns the maximum of two numeric arguments.
min	Returns the minimum of two numeric arguments.
modf	Breaks down a floating-point value into its integer part and its fractional part.
poly	Evaluates a polynomial for a given argument.
pow	Computes the value of one argument raised to the power of a second one.
pow10	Computes the value of 10 raised to the power of an argument.
rand	Returns a random integer between 0 and 32,767.
random	Returns a random integer between 0 and a specified maximum value.
randomize	Initializes the random number generator with a seed derived from the current time.
_rotl	Rotates an unsigned integer left by a given number of bits.
_rotr	Rotates an unsigned integer right by a given number of bits.
sin	Evaluates the sine of an angle in radians.
sinh	Evaluates the hyperbolic sine of its argument.
sqrt	Computes the square root of a positive floating-point number.
srand	Sets the starting point for the sequence of random numbers generated by *rand*.
_status87	Gets the status word of the floating-point package.
tan	Evaluates the tangent of an angle in radians.
tanh	Evaluates the hyperbolic tangent of its argument.

THE MATH FUNCTIONS BY TASK

When we categorize the math functions in terms of the tasks (Table 9-3), we find that several important types of computation are supported in the library.

Table 9-3. ***Math Functions by Task***

Task	Routines
Evaluate trigonometric functions.	acos, asin, atan, atan2, cos, sin, tan
Evaluate powers and logarithms.	exp, frexp, ldexp, log, log10, pow, pow10
Compute square root.	sqrt
Compute magnitudes and absolute values.	abs, cabs, fabs, hypot
Find integer limits (lower and upper) for floating-point numbers.	ceil, floor
Evaluate hyperbolic functions.	cosh, sinh, tanh
Break down floating-point number into integer and fraction.	modf
Find floating-point remainder.	fmod
Integer arithmetic.	abs, div, labs, ldiv
Rotate bits.	_lrotl, _lrotr, _rotl, _rotr
Generate random numbers.	rand, random, randomize, srand
Handle errors.	matherr, _matherr
Manipulate floating-point package (status and control information).	_clear87, _control87, _fpreset, _status87
Find maximum or minimum.	max, min
Evaluate a polynomial.	poly

Basic Math Functions

The trigonometric functions *cos, sin, tan, acos, asin, atan*, and *atan2* respectively evaluate the cosines, sines, and tangents of any angle in radians and compute their respective inverses. You will find these routines useful for tasks such as changing from rectangular to polar coordinates, which often occurs in graphics programs. The hyperbolic functions *cosh, sinh*, and *tanh* are uncommon, but they are available if you need them.

Unlike FORTRAN, which has built-in support for complex variables and has an exponentiation operator, you have to use library routines in C for these tasks. The *pow* routine lets you raise one number to the power of another. The *cabs* and the *hypot* functions can compute the magnitude of a complex number. Other commonly needed functions include *sqrt* to compute square roots. The *log* and *log10* return the logarithm, natural and to the base 10, respectively, of an argument. Exponentials (for example, $e^{1.5}$) can be computed by *exp*. The *abs* and *fabs* functions return the absolute value of an argument. The *ceil* and *floor* routines find the nearest integer larger or smaller than a given floating-point number.

INTEGER ARITHMETIC

There are four routines that use integer arguments to handle arithmetic. The routines *abs* and *labs* return the absolute value of an integer and a long integer, respectively. The *div* function divides one integer by another and returns the integer quotient and an integer remainder. The *ldiv* function operates similarly, but with long integer arguments.

ROTATING BITS

The bit shift operators are ideal for extracting a specified number of bits from an integer variable. Sometimes, however, you may want to *rotate* the bits rather than shift. For example, you can implement the byte-swapping capability of *swab* by rotating the bits of each 2-byte integer to the right by 8 bits.

At each step in the shift operation, one bit is discarded at one end while a zero bit is inserted at the other end, as shown in Figure 9-2. Rotation is similar to shift *except* that the bit being shifted out is brought into the other end. The routines *_rotl* and *_lrotl* rotate an unsigned integer and an unsigned long integer, respectively, to the left by a specified number of bits. The corresponding routines for rotating right are *_rotr* and *_lrotr*.

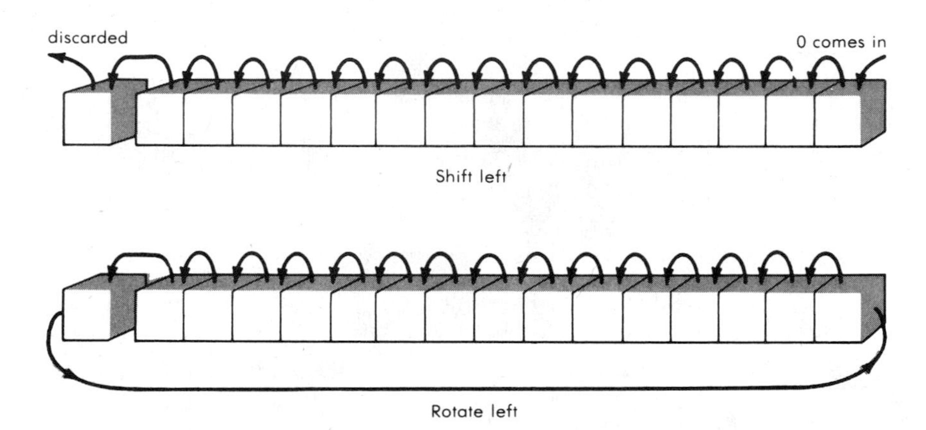

Figure 9-2. *Shift vs rotate*

GENERATING RANDOM NUMBERS

If you need to generate random numbers for a random screen pattern, a game, or a statistical analysis problem, for instance, the Turbo C++ library includes a routine *rand* that can generate a random positive integer in the range 0–32,767. Using it is like throwing a die with 32,768 faces. The numbers are generated by an algorithm that, given a starting number, always generates the same sequence of numbers. So instead of being truly random, the sequence generated by *rand* is a pseudorandom sequence. If the algorithm used to generate the numbers is good, the sequence will have such good properties as not repeating itself too soon and any of the numbers between 0 and 32,767 will appear with equal probability. (A poor algorithm is analogous to a loaded die.) The function *srand* sets the starting point of the random sequence. Turbo C++ also provides the *randomize* macro, which uses the system time as the argument to *srand* to set a new random seed for *rand.*

The *complex* Class in C++

The *math.h* header file in the ANSI-standard Turbo C++ library includes a *complex* structure defined as follows:

```
struct complex
{
    double x;  /* Real part of the complex number      */
    double y;  /* Imaginary part of the complex number */
}
```

Using this definition, you can declare and initialize a complex number like this:

```
#include <math.h>

struct complex z = {0.5, 0.5};  /* z = 0.5 + i 0.5 */
```

You can also use the C library routine, *cabs*, to compute the magnitude of the complex number:

```
zmag = cabs(z);
```

Any other manipulation of the *complex* structure is rather cumbersome. For example, if you want to add two complex numbers *a* and *b*, you have to explicitly add the real and imaginary parts as follows:

```
#include <math.h>
struct complex a, b, c;

c.x = a.x + b.x;
c.y = a.y + b.y;
```

Because C++ allows programmers to define new data types together with operations on the type, the complex numbers seem an ideal candidate for a new type of data. Indeed, Turbo C++ comes with a *complex* class, defined in the header file *complex.h* that implements the *complex* data type.

USING THE COMPLEX CLASS

To use the *complex* class in a C++ program, you have to include the header file *complex.h*. As expected, the *complex* class has a real part and an imaginary part, but these variables are not available outside the class. You can declare and use complex data items as follows:

```
#include <iostream.h>
#include <complex.h>

void main(void)
{
    complex current = 2,      // Real part = 2
            voltage(4,2),     // Another way of initializing
            impedance;
    impedance = voltage / current;
    cout << "Impedance = " << impedance << "\n";
}
```

The example shows several ways of initializing complex as the division (/) are done in a natural manner without worrying about the real and imaginary parts of a complex number. Also, printing the value is straightforward with the << operator. The ease of use is possible because the *complex* class has defined operators such as / and >> to suit its needs. You can look in the header file, *complex.h* to see how this is done.

OPERATIONS ON COMPLEX CLASS

The *complex* class defines the operators: +, −, *, /, +=, −=, *=, /=, ==, and !=. A large number of math functions are also defined to work with complex data types. These include: *abs, acos, asin, atan, atan2, cos, cosh, log, log10, pow, sin, sinh, sqrt, tan,* and *tanh*. Additionally, there are several functions that make sense to complex data only: *real* and *imag* to get the real and imaginary parts, *conj* to return the conjugate, *norm* and *arg* to get the magnitude and angle in the polar representation.

The *bcd* Class in Turbo C++

In addition to the *complex* class, Turbo C++ also includes a *bcd* class that allows you to manipulate numbers stored in the binary-coded decimal (BCD) representation. Many business-related applications of the computer require processing monetary data that consists of decimal integers. The BCD format is suitable for representing and manipulating currency values because you can minimize the effects of round-off errors associated with arithmetic operations on values stored in C *float* or *double* variables.

BCD NUMBERS

To understand the BCD representation, consider the decimal digits 0 through 9. Each of these digits can be represented by a 4-bit binary value. Thus, you can express each digit in a decimal number by a byte which contains the binary representation of the digit. So, 2,495 in decimal becomes

00000010 00000100 00001001 00000101
(2) (4) (9) (5)

in BCD. Since each decimal digit takes only 4 bits, a byte can hold up to 2 BCD values. This results in the packed BCD format which stores 2 BCD values in each byte. In the packed format, we can represent 2,495 as

00100100 10010101
(2) (4) (9) (5)

in just 2 bytes instead of 4. The BCD representation does not make as efficient use of storage space as does the plain binary form. For example, a single byte can only represent the values from 0 to 99 in BCD, but it can hold 0 through 255 in binary.

You can represent a floating-point number in BCD format by first representing the value in a mantissa and exponent format and then storing both the mantissa and the exponent.

BCD ARITHMETIC

You can use the *bcd* class in C++ programs only. You also have to include the header file *bcd.h*. There are several ways to declare and initialize BCD variables:

```
#include <iostream.h>
#include <bcd.h>

void main(void)
{
    bcd price = bcd(24.95, 2); // Price accurate to a penny
    bcd units = bcd(3);        // Store an integer

// Report total price
    cout << "Total cost = $" << units*price << "\n";
}
```

Note that the second argument in *bcd(24.95, 2)* specifies the number of decimal digits after the decimal point that are to be carried over when the *bcd* value is converted to C's floating-point types.

If you load this program in the Turbo C++ environment and run it, you get the following result:

```
Totalcost = $74.85
```

Note from the example that the *bcd* class overloads the multiplication operator (*) to work with BCD values. In fact, the *bcd* class overloads all arithmetic and logical operators, as well as several math functions such as *sqrt* and *log*, to work with BCD arguments. You should look at the prototypes of the member functions in the header file *bcd.h* to learn more about the operations that you can perform on *bcd* variables.

Converting from BCD to Floating-Point Format

The *bcd* class includes a member function named *real* with the following prototype:

```
friend long double _Cdecl real(bcd&); // Return the real part
```

This function takes a *bcd* variable and returns the value as a *long double*. You can convert the *long double* into *float* and *double* by simple assignments. For instance, the results of the computations performed in the earlier example can be converted to *float* and *double* variables as follows:

```
// Convert to float
float x = real(units*price);
cout << "x = " << x <<"\n";
// Convert to double
double y = real(units*price);
cout << "y = " << y << "\n";
```

Incidentally, this code prints the following results:

```
x = 74.849998
y = 74.85
```

Because of the limited precision of the *float* data type, the value of *x* prints as *74.849998* instead of the actual *74.85*. This is the type of problem that you can avoid by using the *bcd* class.

ACCURACY OF BCD NUMBERS Because a byte is needed to store 2 BCD digits, the number of significant digits in a BCD representation depends on the number of bytes available for storage. The *bcd* class in Turbo C++ provides up to 17 decimal digits of precision. This class stores the exponent in such a way that you can represent floating-point numbers in the range 10^{-125} to 10^{125}.

Cautions

- If you install your own handler for the floating-point exception SIGFPE, your handler should call *_fpreset* to reset the floating-point package before returning.
- The basic math function capabilities exist in all C libraries, but the functions that deal with the floating-point package are specific to MS-DOS.

Further Reading

Consult the book by Morgan and Waite[1] for further details on the floating-point data types supported by the 8087 math coprocessor (or, Numeric Data Processor). If you need to use the trigonometric and the Bessel functions often, the handbook by Abramowitz and Stegun[2] is a good reference. If you are interested in programming the 8087 math coprocessor in assembly language, the developer's guide by The Waite Group[3] devotes a chapter to this topic.

1. Christopher L. Morgan and Mitchell Waite, *8086/8088 16-bit Microprocessor Primer*, BYTE/McGraw-Hill, Peterborough, NH, 1982, 355 pages.
2. Milton Abramowitz and Irene A. Stegun, Eds., *Handbook of Mathematical Functions with Formulas, Graphs and Mathematical Tables*, Dover Publications, New York, NY, 1972, 1046 pages.
3. The Waite Group, *MS-DOS Developer's Guide*, Second Edition, Howard W. Sams & Company, Indianapolis, IN, 1988, 813 pages.

abs

COMPATIBILITY

TC1	TC1.5	TC2	TC++	MSC3	MSC4	MSC5	MSC6	QC1	QC2	QC2.5	ANSI	UNIX V	XNX
▲	▲	▲	▲	▲	▲	▲	▲	▲	▲	▲	▲	▲	▲

PURPOSE Use *abs* to get the absolute value of an integer.

SYNTAX

```
int abs(int n);
```

`int n;` *Integer whose absolute value is returned*

EXAMPLE CALL

```
x = abs(-5); /* x will be 5 now */
```

INCLUDES `#include <stdlib.h>` *For function declaration*

DESCRIPTION The *abs* function returns the absolute value of the integer argument *n*. Thus *abs (−10)* returns +10.

RETURNS The integer returned by *abs* is the absolute value of *n*.

COMMENTS In C++ programs, you can use *abs* to get the magnitude of a complex variable. The header file *complex.h* defines the *complex* class.

SEE ALSO

`cabs` *To obtain the magnitude (or absolute value) of a complex number*

`fabs` *To get the absolute values of a floating-point number*

`labs` *To get the absolute values of a long integer*

EXAMPLE Write a program that reads an integer value as a command-line argument and prints its absolute value.

```
#include <stdio.h>
#include <stdlib.h>
main(int argc, char **argv)
{
    int value, result;
    if(argc < 2)
    {
        printf("Usage: %s <integer_value>\n", argv[0]);
    }
    else
    {
        value = atoi(argv[1]);
        result = abs(value);
```

```
        printf("Absolute value of %d = %d\n",
                value, result);
    }
    return 0;
}
```

COMPATIBILITY

acos

TC1	TC1.5	TC2	TC++	MSC3	MSC4	MSC5	MSC6	QC1	QC2	QC2.5	ANSI	UNIX V	XNX
▲	▲	▲	▲	▲	▲	▲	▲	▲	▲	▲	▲	▲	▲

PURPOSE Use *acos* to compute the arc cosine of a *double* variable whose value lies between −1 and 1.

SYNTAX `double acos(double x);`

`double x;` *Argument whose arc cosine is to be computed*

EXAMPLE CALL `angle = acos(0.5); /* angle is "pi"/3 */`

INCLUDES `#include <math.h>` *For function declaration and definition of constants EDOM and DOMAIN*

DESCRIPTION The *acos* function accepts an argument *x* whose value lies in the range −1 to 1 and computes its arc cosine. The result is an angle with value between 0 and π radians.

RETURNS When the value of the argument *x* is in the valid range of −1 to 1, *acos* returns the result. If the argument's value is outside the acceptable range, *acos* sets the global variable *errno* to the constant EDOM which is defined in *math.h*, prints a DOMAIN error message to *stderr*, and returns a value of NAN. You can write your own error-handling routine with the name *matherr* to perform differently when an error occurs.

SEE ALSO `matherr` *To handle math errors (you can add your own)*

`cos` *To compute a cosine of an angle*

EXAMPLE Write a program that accepts a floating-point number on the command line and computes the arc cosine of that number if it lies between −1 and 1.

```
#include <stdio.h>
#include <math.h>
```

```
#include <stdlib.h>          /* errno is defined here */
#define  R_TO_D   57.29578 /* radians to degrees   */
main(int argc, char **argv)
{
    double result;
    if(argc < 2)
    {
        printf("Usage: %s <value>\n", argv[0]);
    }
    else
    {
        result = acos(atof(argv[1])) * R_TO_D;
        if(errno != EDOM)
        {
            printf("Arc cosine (%s) = %f deg.\n",
                    argv[1], result);
        }
    }
    return 0;
}
```

asin

COMPATIBILITY

TC1	TC1.5	TC2	TC++	MSC3	MSC4	MSC5	MSC6	QC1	QC2	QC2.5	ANSI	UNIX V	XNX
▲	▲	▲	▲	▲	▲	▲	▲	▲	▲	▲	▲	▲	▲

PURPOSE Use *asin* to compute the arc sine of a *double* variable whose value lies between −1 and 1.

SYNTAX `double asin(double x);`

`double x;` *Argument whose arc sine is to be computed*

EXAMPLE CALL `angle = asin(0.707)  /* angle is roughly "pi"/4  */`

INCLUDES `#include <math.h>` *For function declaration and definition of constants EDOM and DOMAIN*

DESCRIPTION The *asin* function computes the arc sine of the argument *x* provided its value lies in the range −1 to 1. The result is an angle with value between $-\pi/2$ and $\pi/2$ radians.

RETURNS For a valid argument *x* with values between −1 and 1, *asin* returns an angle whose sine is equal to *x*. If the argument's value lies outside the acceptable range, however, *asin* sets the global variable *errno* to the constant EDOM which is defined in *math.h*, prints a DOMAIN error message to *stderr*, and returns a value of NAN. You can write your own error-handling routine with the name *matherr* to perform differently when an error occurs.

SEE ALSO

`matherr`	*To handle math errors (you can add your own)*
`sin`	*To compute a sine of an angle*

EXAMPLE Write a program that computes and prints the arc sine of 10 numbers between −1 and 1, starting with −1 and advancing to 1 with a stepsize of 0.2.

```
#include <stdio.h>
#include <math.h>
#include <stdlib.h>        /* errno is defined here */
#define  R_TO_D   57.29578 /* radians to degrees  */
main()
{
    double value, result;
    for (value = -1.0; value <= 1.0; value += 0.2)
    {
        result = asin(value) * R_TO_D;
        if(errno != EDOM)
        {
            printf("Arc sine (%f) = %f deg.\n",
                    value, result);
        }
    }
    return 0;
}
```

COMPATIBILITY

atan

TC1	TC1.5	TC2	TC++	MSC3	MSC4	MSC5	MSC6	QC1	QC2	QC2.5	ANSI	UNIX V	XNX
▲	▲	▲	▲	▲	▲	▲	▲	▲	▲	▲	▲	▲	▲

PURPOSE Use *atan* to compute the arc tangent of a variable.

SYNTAX `double atan(double x);`

`double x;` *Argument whose arc tangent is to be computed*

EXAMPLE CALL `angle = atan(1.0)  /* angle is "pi"/4  */`

INCLUDES `#include <math.h>` *For function declaration*

DESCRIPTION The *atan* function computes the arc tangent of the argument *x*. The result is an angle with value between $-\pi/2$ and $\pi/2$ radians.

RETURNS The *atan* function returns the angle in the range $-\pi/2$ and $\pi/2$ whose tangent is equal to *x*.

SEE ALSO `atan2` *To compute arc tangent of the ratio of two arguments*

EXAMPLE Write a program that prompts for a floating-point number and then computes the arc tangent of that number.

```
#include <stdio.h>
#include <math.h>
#include <stdlib.h>        /* errno is defined here */
#define  R_TO_D   57.29578 /* radians to degrees   */
main()
{
    double tanvalue, result;
    printf("Enter value whose arctangent you want \
to evaluate: ");
    scanf(" %le", &tanvalue);
    result = atan(tanvalue) * R_TO_D;
    if(errno != EDOM)
    {
        printf("Arc tangent (%f) = %f deg.\n",
                tanvalue, result);
    }
    return 0;
}
```

atan2

COMPATIBILITY

TC1	TC1.5	TC2	TC++	MSC3	MSC4	MSC5	MSC6	QC1	QC2	QC2.5	ANSI	UNIX V	XNX
▲	▲	▲	▲	▲	▲	▲	▲	▲	▲	▲	▲	▲	▲

PURPOSE Use *atan2* to compute the arc tangent of the ratio of two nonzero variables.

SYNTAX `double atan2(double y, double x);`

`double x, y;` *Arc tangent of y/x will be computed*

EXAMPLE CALL `angle = atan2(y, x);`

INCLUDES `#include <math.h>` *For function declaration and definition of constants EDOM and DOMAIN*

DESCRIPTION The *atan2* function computes the arc tangent of the ratio of the arguments *y/x*. The result is an angle with value between $-\pi$ and π radians. In contrast to *atan*, which takes a single argument, *atan2* can use the sign of its two arguments to determine the quadrant (a 90° sector in cartesian coordinates) in which the angle should lie.

RETURNS Provided both arguments *x* and *y* are nonzero, *atan2* returns an angle whose tangent is equal to *x*. If both arguments are zero, however, *atan2* sets the global variable *errno* to the constant EDOM, prints a DOMAIN error message to *stderr*, and returns a value of NAN. You can write your own error-handling routine to perform differently when an error occurs with the name *matherr*.

SEE ALSO

`atan` *To compute arc tangent of an argument*

`matherr` *To handle math errors (you can add your own)*

`tan` *To compute a tangent of an angle*

EXAMPLE Write a program that accepts two floating-point numbers *y* and *x* on the command line and computes the arc tangent of *y/x*.

```
#include <stdio.h>
#include <math.h>
#include <stdlib.h>        /* errno is defined here */
#define  R_TO_D   57.29578 /* radians to degrees  */
main(int argc, char **argv)
{
    double result;
    if(argc < 3)
    {
        printf("Usage: %s <y> <x>\n", argv[0]);
    }
    else
    {

        result = atan2(atof(argv[1]),
                       atof(argv[2])) * R_TO_D;
        if(errno != EDOM)
        {
            printf("Arc tangent (%s/%s) = %f deg.\n",
                    argv[1], argv[2], result);
        }
```

```
    }
    return 0;
}
```

cabs

COMPATIBILITY

TC1	TC1.5	TC2	TC++	MSC3	MSC4	MSC5	MSC6	QC1	QC2	QC2.5	ANSI	UNIX V	XNX
▲	▲	▲	▲	▲	▲	▲	▲	▲	▲	▲		▲	▲

PURPOSE Use *cabs* to compute the magnitude of a complex number stored in a structure of type *complex.*

SYNTAX

```
double cabs(struct complex z);
```

struct complex z; *Structure containing the complex number whose magnitude is computed*

EXAMPLE CALL

```
magnitude = cabs(z);
```

INCLUDES #include <math.h> *For function declaration and definition of the structure complex*

DESCRIPTION The *cabs* function computes the magnitude of a complex number *z* stored in a structure of type *complex* which is defined in *math.h* as follows:

```
struct complex
{
    double x;     /* Real part of the complex number      */
    double y;     /* Imaginary part of the complex number */
};
```

The magnitude of *z* is computed with the expression

```
magnitude = sqrt(z.x*z.x + z.y*z.y);
```

RETURNS If the magnitude of *z* is too large, *cabs* calls the routine *matherr* to handle the error. In this case, it returns a value HUGE_VAL defined in *math.h* and sets the variable *errno* to the constant ERANGE. If all goes well, *cabs* returns the magnitude of the complex number.

COMMENTS If you are writing a C++ program, you can use the *complex* class defined in the header file *complex.h.* This class defines an overloaded version of the *abs* function that returns the magnitude of a complex number.

SEE ALSO

`matherr` — *To handle math errors (you can add your own)*

`hypot` — *To compute the length of the hypotenuse of a right triangle*

`fabs` — *To compute the absolute value of a* double *variable*

EXAMPLE Write a program that accepts the real and the imaginary part of a complex number on the command line and computes the magnitude of the complex number by using *cabs*.

```
#include <stdio.h>
#include <math.h>
#include <stdlib.h>      /* errno is defined here */
main()
{
    struct complex z;
    double result;
    printf("Enter complex number in the form \
\"(real, imaginary)\":");
    scanf(" (%le , %le )", &z.x, &z.y);
    result = cabs(z);
    if(errno != ERANGE)
    {
        printf("Magnitude of (%f, %f) = %f\n",
                z.x, z.y, result);
    }
    return 0;
}
```

COMPATIBILITY

ceil

TC1	TC1.5	TC2	TC++	MSC3	MSC4	MSC5	MSC6	QC1	QC2	QC2.5	ANSI	UNIX V	XNX
▲	▲	▲	▲	▲	▲	▲	▲	▲	▲	▲	▲	▲	▲

PURPOSE Use *ceil* to compute the *ceiling*, the smallest integer value that is greater than or equal to a *double* variable.

SYNTAX `double ceil(double x);`

`double x;` — *Variable whose "ceiling" is to be returned*

EXAMPLE CALL `x_ceiling = ceil(4.1);  /* x_ceiling is 5.0 */`

INCLUDES `#include <math.h>` — *For function declaration*

DESCRIPTION The *ceil* function finds the ceiling of a *double* argument *x*. The ceiling is the smallest integral value that is equal to or that just exceeds *x*. This can be used in rounding a *double* value *up* to the next integer.

RETURNS The return value is the ceiling of *x* expressed as a *double*.

SEE ALSO `floor` *To determine the largest integer that is just less than a variable*

EXAMPLE Write a program that accepts a floating-point number on the command line and prints the ceiling of that number.

```
#include <stdio.h>
#include <math.h>
main(int argc, char **argv)
{
    double result;
    if(argc < 2)
    {
        printf("Usage: %s <value>\n", argv[0]);
    }
    else
    {
        result = ceil(atof(argv[1]));
        printf("ceil of %s = %f\n", argv[1], result);
    }
    return 0;
}
```

_clear87

COMPATIBILITY

TC1	TC1.5	TC2	TC++	MSC3	MSC4	MSC5	MSC6	QC1	QC2	QC2.5	ANSI	UNIX V	XNX
▲	▲	▲	▲		▲	▲	▲	▲	▲	▲			

PURPOSE Use *_clear87* to retrieve the current contents of the floating-point status word and reset all bits to zero.

SYNTAX `unsigned int _clear87(void);`

EXAMPLE CALL `status = _clear87();`

INCLUDES `#include <float.h>` *For function declaration and definition of constants denoting status-word bit settings*

INCLUDES `#include <float.h>` *For function declaration and definition of constants denoting status-word bit settings*

DESCRIPTION The *_clear87* function retrieves the status word of the floating-point package of the C library and clears all its bits before returning. This status word is a composite of the status word of the 8087 math coprocessor and other conditions detected by the 8087 exception handler. (See the reference page on *_status87* for details on the bit settings of the status word.)

RETURNS The *_clear87* function returns the prior contents of the floating-point status word.

SEE ALSO `_status87` *To get the floating-point status word*

`_control87` *To alter bits in the floating-point control word*

EXAMPLE Copy a small *double* variable into a *float* variable and generate an underflow and an inexact result. Now call *_clear87* to clear the status word. The return value reflects the error that occurred, but if you read the status again with *_status87*, it will show a cleared status word.

```
#include <stdio.h>
#include <float.h>
main()
{
    float a;
    double b = 1.e-40;
    unsigned fpstatus;
/* Perform operation that produces underflow and
 * an inexact result
 */
    a = b;   /* This will produce inexact result */
    printf("After undeflow/inexact ");
 /* Clear status word. It'll return prior status */
    fpstatus = _clear87();
    printf("status word was: %X\n", fpstatus);
    fpstatus = _status87();
    printf("After _clear87, status word is: %X\n",
                                        fpstatus);
    return 0;
}
```

_control87

COMPATIBILITY

TC1	TC1.5	TC2	TC++	MSC3	MSC4	MSC5	MSC6	QC1	QC2	QC2.5	ANSI	UNIX V	XNX
▲	▲	▲	▲		▲	▲	▲	▲	▲	▲			

PURPOSE Use *_control87* to get and set the floating-point control word. When an 8087 math coprocessor is being used, *_control87* sets its control word.

SYNTAX

```
unsigned int _control87(unsigned new, unsigned mask);
```

```
unsigned int new;
```
New control-word bit values

```
unsigned int mask;
```
Mask to indicate which bits of control word to set

EXAMPLE CALL

```
status = _control87(PC_24, MCW_PC); /* 24-bit precision */
```

INCLUDES

```
#include <float.h>
```
For function declaration and definition of constants denoting control-word bit settings

DESCRIPTION The *_control87* function gets and sets the floating-point control word. The settings control the precision, the rounding, the infinity mode, and the exceptions that will be generated. The value of the argument *mask* determines which of these four categories is being changed. The possible values are shown in Table 9-4 in terms of constants defined in *float.h*. If the *mask* is zero, *_control87* simply returns the value of the status word. For any other mask setting from Table 9-4, you must specify the new value, given in the argument *new*, for that option from the list under that mask value. Thus, to set the precision to 24 bits, you need the call *_control87(PC_24, MCW_PC);*.

Table 9-4. ***Floating-Point Control Word***

Mask Constant	Mask Meaning	Value	Meaning of Value
MCW_EM	Controls the conditions under which interrupts will be generated by the floating-point package. Choose from these values:	EM_INVALID	Exception on invalid operation.
		EM_DENORMAL	Exception if denormalized argument.
		EM_ZERODIVIDE	Exception on divide by zero.
		EM_OVERFLOW	Exception on overflow.
		EM_UNDERFLOW	Exception on underflow.

Table 9-4. *(cont.)*

Mask Constant	Mask Meaning	Value	Meaning of Value
		EM_INEXACT	Exception on loss of precision.
MCW_IC	Controls the interpretation of "infinity" by the package.	IC_AFFINE	Use "affine" infinity (affine infinity distinguishes between positive and negative infinity, projective infinity does not).
		IC_PROJECTIVE	Use "projective" infinity.
MCW_RC	Controls the rounding options.	RC_CHOP	Round off results by chopping.
		RC_UP	Round to next higher number.
		RC_DOWN	Round to next lower number.
		RC_NEAR	Round to nearest number.
MCW_PC	Controls the level of precision of the results.	PC_24	24-bit precision.
		PC_53	53-bit precision.
		PC_64	64-bit precision.

RETURNS The *_control87* function returns the floating-point control word.

SEE ALSO `_status87` *To get the floating-point status word*

`_clear87` *To get and clear the floating-point status word*

EXAMPLE Get and display the current contents of the floating-point control word. Now set the precision to 24 bits and compute the product of 0.1 with itself. Display the result and note the difference from 0.01. Use the constant CW_DEFAULT to set the control word back to its default. The precision will now be 64 bits. Repeat the previous computation and note the improvement in the accuracy of the results.

```
#include <stdio.h>
#include <float.h>
main()
{
    double a = 0.1;
/* Read current floating-point control word        */
```

```
    printf("Current control word = %.4X\n",
                _control87(0,0));
/* Now lower the precision to 24 bits              */
    _control87(PC_24, MCW_PC);
/* Perform a math operation and see the result     */
    printf("0.1 x 0.1 = 0.01 in 24-bit precision\
 = %.15e\n", a*a);
/* Restore precision to default 64 bits and redo */
    _control87(CW_DEFAULT, 0xffff);
    printf("0.1 x 0.1 = 0.01 in 64-bit precision\
 = %.15e\n", a*a);
    return 0;
}
```

cos

COMPATIBILITY

TC1	TC1.5	TC2	TC++	MSC3	MSC4	MSC5	MSC6	QC1	QC2	QC2.5	ANSI	UNIX V	XNX
▲	▲	▲	▲	▲	▲	▲	▲	▲	▲	▲	▲	▲	▲

PURPOSE Use *cos* to compute the cosine of an angle whose value is given in radians.

SYNTAX `double cos(double x);`

`double x;` *Angle in radians whose cosine is to be computed*

EXAMPLE CALL `cos_angle = cos(ang_radian);`

INCLUDES `#include <math.h>` *For function declaration and definition of error constants*

DESCRIPTION The *cos* function computes the cosine of *double* argument *x*.

RETURNS The *cos* function returns the cosine of *x*.

SEE ALSO `acos` *To compute the arc cosine of a variable*

`sin` *To compute the sine of an angle*

EXAMPLE Write a program that prints a table showing the cosine of the angles between 0 and 180° in steps of 10°

```
#include <stdio.h>
#include <math.h>
#include <stdlib.h>      /* errno is defined here */
```

```
#define  R_TO_D   57.29578 /* radians to degrees  */
main()
{
    double angle, result;
    printf("------- Table of Cosines --------\n");
    printf("Angle\t\tCosine\n");
    for(angle = 0.0; angle <= 180.0; angle += 10.0)
    {
        result = cos(angle / R_TO_D);
        printf("%f deg.\t%f\n", angle, result);
    }
    return 0;
}
```

COMPATIBILITY

cosh

TC1	TC1.5	TC2	TC++	MSC3	MSC4	MSC5	MSC6	QC1	QC2	QC2.5	ANSI	UNIX V	XNX
▲	▲	▲	▲	▲	▲	▲	▲	▲	▲	▲	▲	▲	▲

PURPOSE Use *cosh* to compute the hyperbolic cosine of a *double* variable.

SYNTAX `double cosh(double x);`

`double x;` *Variable whose hyperbolic cosine is to be computed*

EXAMPLE CALL `result = cosh(x);`

INCLUDES `#include <math.h>` *For function declaration and definition of error constants*

DESCRIPTION The *cosh* function computes the hyperbolic cosine of the *double* variable *x*.

RETURNS Normally, *cosh* returns the hyperbolic cosine of *x*. If the value of the result is too large (a *double* variable can be as large as 10^{308}), *cosh* returns the value HUGE_VAL and, at the same time, sets *errno* to the constant ERANGE.

SEE ALSO `sinh` *To compute the hyperbolic sine of a variable*

EXAMPLE Write a program that accepts a floating-point number on the command line and computes its hyperbolic cosine.

```
#include <stdio.h>
#include <math.h>
```

```
#include <stdlib.h>      /* errno is defined here */
main(int argc, char **argv)
{
    double result;
    if(argc < 2)
    {
        printf("Usage: %s <value>\n", argv[0]);
    }
    else
    {
        result = cosh(atof(argv[1]));
        if(errno != ERANGE)
        {
            printf("Hyperbolic cosine of %s = %f\n",
                    argv[1], result);
        }
    }
    return 0;
}
```

div

COMPATIBILITY

TC1	TC1.5	TC2	TC++	MSC3	MSC4	MSC5	MSC6	QC1	QC2	QC2.5	ANSI	UNIX V	XNX
▲	▲	▲	▲			▲	▲	▲	▲	▲	▲		

PURPOSE Use *div* to divide one integer value by another and get the quotient and remainder in a structure of type *div_t*.

SYNTAX

```
div_t div(int numer, int denom);
```

`int numer;` *Numerator*

`int denom;` *Denominator*

EXAMPLE CALL

```
result = div(32, 5);
/* result.quot = 6 and result.rem = 2 */
```

INCLUDES `#include <stdlib.h>` *For function declaration and definition of structure* div_t

DESCRIPTION The *div* function divides the first integer *numer* by the second one *denom* and returns the resulting quotient and remainder packed in a structure of type *div_t*. The structure of type *div_t* is defined in *stdlib.h* as

```
typedef struct
{
    int quot;    /* The quotient  */
    int rem;     /* The remainder */
} div_t;
```

RETURNS The *div* function returns a structure of type *div_t* containing the quotient and remainder of the division.

SEE ALSO ldiv *To divide one long integer by another*

EXAMPLE Write a program that accepts a numerator and a denominator on the command line and uses *div* to compute the quotient and the remainder of the division.

```
#include <stdio.h>
#include <stdlib.h>
main(int argc, char **argv)
{
    int x, y;
    div_t result;
/* Make sure that there are at least 3 arguments */
    if(argc < 3)
    {
        printf("Usage: %s <int numerator> <int denom>\n",
                argv[0]);
        exit(0);
    }
/* Divide first integer by second and display
 * quotient and remainder
 */
    x = atoi(argv[1]);
    y = atoi(argv[2]);
    result = div(x,y);
    printf("Dividing %d by %d. Quotient = %d and \
remainder = %d\n", x, y, result.quot, result.rem);
    return 0;
}
```

exp

COMPATIBILITY

TC1	TC1.5	TC2	TC++	MSC3	MSC4	MSC5	MSC6	QC1	QC2	QC2.5	ANSI	UNIX V	XNX
▲	▲	▲	▲	▲	▲	▲	▲	▲	▲	▲	▲	▲	▲

PURPOSE Use *exp* to compute the exponential of a *double* variable.

SYNTAX

```
double exp(double x);
```

`double x;` *Variable whose exponential is to be computed*

EXAMPLE CALL

```
y = exp(x);
```

INCLUDES `#include <math.h>` *For function declaration and definition of error constants*

DESCRIPTION The *exp* function computes the exponential of the *double* variable *x*. The exponential of a variable *x* is e^x where *e* is the base of natural logarithm ($e = 2.7182818$).

RETURNS Normally, *exp* returns the exponential of *x*. In case of overflow (the value of the result is too large), *exp* returns the value HUGE_VAL and sets *errno* to the constant ERANGE. On underflow, the return value will be zero, but *errno* is not set.

SEE ALSO

`log` *To compute the natural logarithm (the inverse of the exponential) of a variable*

`pow` *To raise* x *to the power* y

EXAMPLE Write a program that accepts a floating-point number on the command line and computes its exponential.

```
#include <stdio.h>
#include <math.h>
#include <stdlib.h>  /* errno is declared here */
main(int argc, char **argv)
{
    double result;
    if(argc < 2)
    {
        printf("Usage: %s <value>\n", argv[0]);
    }
    else
    {
        result = exp(atof(argv[1]));
        printf("exp (%s) = %f\n", argv[1], result);
```

```
    }
    return 0;
}
```

fabs

COMPATIBILITY

TC1	TC1.5	TC2	TC++	MSC3	MSC4	MSC5	MSC6	QC1	QC2	QC2.5	ANSI	UNIX V	XNX
▲	▲	▲	▲	▲	▲	▲	▲	▲	▲	▲	▲	▲	▲

PURPOSE Use *fabs* to compute the absolute value of a *double* variable.

SYNTAX `double fabs(double x);`

`double x;` *Variable whose absolute value is to be returned*

EXAMPLE CALL `y = fabs(-5.15); /* y will be 5.15 */`

INCLUDES `#include <math.h>` *For function declaration*

DESCRIPTION The *fabs* function returns the absolute value of its argument *x*.

RETURNS The return value is of type *double* with a positive value that is the absolute value of *x*.

SEE ALSO `cabs` *To compute the magnitude of a complex variable*

EXAMPLE Write a program that accepts a floating-point number on the command line and computes the absolute value of the number by using *fabs*.

```
#include <stdio.h>
#include <math.h>
main(int argc, char **argv)

{
    double result;
    if(argc < 2)
    {
        printf("Usage: %s <value>\n", argv[0]);
    }
    else
    {
        result = fabs(atof(argv[1]));
        printf("Absolute value of %s = %f\n", argv[1], result);
```

```
    }
    return 0;
}
```

floor

COMPATIBILITY

TC1	TC1.5	TC2	TC++	MSC3	MSC4	MSC5	MSC6	QC1	QC2	QC2.5	ANSI	UNIX V	XNX
▲	▲	▲	▲	▲	▲	▲	▲	▲	▲	▲	▲	▲	▲

PURPOSE Use *floor* to compute the "floor," the largest integer value that is less than or equal to a *double* variable.

SYNTAX

```
double floor(double x);
```

`double x;` *Variable whose floor is to be returned*

EXAMPLE CALL

```
x = floor(4.15);  /* x will be 4.0 */
```

INCLUDES `#include <math.h>` *For function declaration*

DESCRIPTION The *floor* function finds the floor of a *double* argument *x*. The floor is the largest integral value that is less than or equal to *x*. This can be used in rounding a *double* value *down* to the preceding integer.

RETURNS The return value is the floor of *x* expressed as a *double*.

SEE ALSO `ceil` *To determine the smallest integer that just exceeds a variable*

EXAMPLE Write a program that accepts a floating-point number on the command line and prints the floor of that number.

```
#include <stdio.h>
#include <math.h>
main(int argc, char **argv)
{
    double result;
    if(argc < 2)
    {
        printf("Usage: %s <value>\n", argv[0]);
    }
    else
    {
        result = floor(atof(argv[1]));
        printf("floor of %s = %f\n", argv[1], result);
```

```
    }
    return 0;
}
```

COMPATIBILITY

fmod

TC1	TC1.5	TC2	TC++	MSC3	MSC4	MSC5	MSC6	QC1	QC2	QC2.5	ANSI	UNIX V	XNX
▲	▲	▲	▲	▲	▲	▲	▲	▲	▲	▲	▲	▲	▲

PURPOSE Use *fmod* to compute the floating-point remainder after dividing one floating-point number by another and ensuring that the quotient is the largest possible integer.

SYNTAX

```
double fmod(double x, double y);
```

`double x, y;` *The remainder after the division x/y is returned*

EXAMPLE CALL

```
rem = fmod(24.95, 5.5); /* rem will be 2.95 */
```

INCLUDES `#include <math.h>` *For function declaration*

DESCRIPTION The *fmod* function divides x by y and finds the integral floor of the quotient, the largest integer that is less than or equal to the quotient. If this result is n, *fmod* returns the value r computed from the expression $r = x - n*y$. The entire operation is equivalent to

```
double n, r;
:
:
n = floor(x/y);
r = x - n*y;
```

RETURNS When y is zero, *fmod* returns a zero. Otherwise, it returns the remainder computed as described above.

SEE ALSO `floor` *To find the largest integer that is less than or equal to a floating-point value*

EXAMPLE Write a program that takes two real numbers and computes the floating-point remainder after dividing the first number by the second and ensuring that the quotient is the largest integer possible.

```
#include <stdio.h>
#include <math.h>
#include <stdlib.h>      /* errno is defined here */
```

```
main(int argc, char **argv)
{
    double x, y, result;
    if(argc < 3)
    {
        printf("Usage: %s <x> <y>\n", argv[0]);
    }
    else
    {
        x = atof(argv[1]);

        y = atof(argv[2]);
        result = fmod(x,y);
        printf("fmod(%s, %s) = %f\n",
                        argv[1], argv[2], result);
    }
    return 0;
}
```

_fpreset

COMPATIBILITY

TC1	TC1.5	TC2	TC++	MSC3	MSC4	MSC5	MSC6	QC1	QC2	QC2.5	ANSI	UNIX V	XNX
▲	▲	▲	▲		▲	▲	▲	▲	▲	▲			

PURPOSE Use *_fpreset* to reinitialize the floating-point math package.

SYNTAX `void _fpreset(void);`

EXAMPLE CALL `_fpreset();`

INCLUDES `#include <float.h>` *For function declaration*

DESCRIPTION The *_fpreset* function reinitializes the floating-point math package. This function is provided so that you can begin with a clean floating-point system after using functions from the *system, signal* and *spawn, exec* families, which should not be used within floating-point calculations. As an example, if you trap floating-point errors using *signal* with the constant SIGFPE, the exception handler can safely recover from floating-point errors by calling *_fpreset* followed by a *longjmp.*

SEE ALSO `signal` *This can be used to trap floating-point exceptions*

EXAMPLE The *signal* function of the C library allows you to set up SIGFPE signals to handle floating-point errors. When a floating-point error occurs, the handler is invoked. As suggested above, inside the handler you should initialize the floating-point package before returning. Test the program by using *setjmp* and *longjmp* and a deliberate divide-by-zero error.

```
#include <stdio.h>
#include <float.h>
#include <setjmp.h>
#include <signal.h>
void myfphandler(int);
jmp_buf this_point;
main()
{
    double a = 1.0, b = 0.0, c;
/* Set up floating-point error handler           */
    if(signal(SIGFPE, myfphandler) == SIG_ERR)
    {
        abort();
    }
/* Mark the place where we jump back after error */
    if(setjmp(this_point) == 0)
    {
/* Create a math error, divide by zero           */
        c = a/b;
    }
/* "longjmp" will get up here from "myfphandler" */
    printf("Recovered from floating-point error\n");
    return 0;
}
/*-----------------------------------------------------*/
void myfphandler(int sig)
{
    printf("In handler: signal = %d\n", sig);
/* As recommended, initialize floating-point package */
    _fpreset();
/* Use "longjmp" to return                           */
    longjmp(this_point, -1);
    return 0;
}
```

frexp

COMPATIBILITY

TC1	TC1.5	TC2	TC++	MSC3	MSC4	MSC5	MSC6	QC1	QC2	QC2.5	ANSI	UNIX V	XNX
▲	▲	▲	▲	▲	▲	▲	▲	▲	▲	▲	▲	▲	▲

PURPOSE Use *frexp* to compute a mantissa with an absolute value between 0.5 and 1.0 and an integer exponent such that the floating-point argument to *frexp* is equal to the mantissa $\times 2^n$.

SYNTAX

```
double frexp(double x, int *expptr);
```

`double x;` *Floating-point argument to be decomposed*

`int *expptr;` *Pointer to an integer where the exponent is returned*

EXAMPLE CALL

```
mantissa = frexp(5.1, &exponent);
```

INCLUDES `#include <math.h>` *For function declaration*

DESCRIPTION The *frexp* function breaks down the floating-point number *x* into a mantissa *m*, whose absolute value lies between 0.5 and 1.0, and an integer exponent *n*, so that $x = m \times 2^n$.

The exponent *n* is stored by *frexp* in the location whose address is given in the argument *expptr*. If *x* is zero, the exponent will also be zero.

COMMON USES You can use *frexp* to generate the binary representation of a floating-point number. (The tutorial section explains how floating-point numbers are represented in binary form in computers.)

RETURNS Normally *frexp* returns the mantissa *m* computed as described above. When *x* is zero, *frexp* returns a zero as the mantissa.

SEE ALSO

`ldexp` *To reconstruct a floating-point number from mantissa and exponent, as computed by* frexp

`modf` *To decompose a floating-point number into its fractional and integral parts*

EXAMPLE Use *frexp* in a program to decompose a real value into a mantissa (between 0.5 and 1) and an exponent of 2.

```
#include <stdio.h>
#include <math.h>
#include <stdlib.h>      /* errno is defined here */
main(int argc, char **argv)
{
    int exponent;
```

```
    double x, mantissa;
    if(argc < 2)
    {
        printf("Usage: %s <x>\n", argv[0]);
    }
    else
    {
        x = atof(argv[1]);
        mantissa = frexp(x, &exponent);
        printf("%s = %f times 2 raised to %d\n",
                        argv[1], mantissa, exponent);
    }
    return 0;
}
```

hypot

COMPATIBILITY

TC1	TC1.5	TC2	TC++	MSC3	MSC4	MSC5	MSC6	QC1	QC2	QC2.5	ANSI	UNIX V	XNX
▲	▲	▲	▲	▲	▲	▲	▲	▲	▲	▲		▲	▲

PURPOSE Use *hypot* to compute the length of the hypotenuse of a right triangle, given the length of the other two sides.

SYNTAX

```
double hypot(double x, double y);

double x, y;
```

*sqrt(x*x + y*y) will be returned*

EXAMPLE CALL

```
length = hypot(3.0, 4.0); /* length = 5.0 */
```

INCLUDES

```
#include <math.h>
```

For function declaration and definition of constants ERANGE and HUGE_VAL

DESCRIPTION The *hypot* function computes the square root of the sum of the squares of the arguments *x* and *y*, giving the return value

```
return_value = sqrt(x*x + y*y);
```

If *x* and *y* are the sides of a right triangle (i.e., these two sides met at a right angle), by the Pythagorean theorem the value returned by *hypot* corresponds to the length of the hypotenuse of the right triangle. If *x* and *y* represented the real and the imaginary parts of a complex number, respectively, the value returned by *hypot* is the magnitude (i.e., the absolute value) of the complex number represented by *x* and *y*. Thus *hypot* can be used to achieve the functionality of *cabs* as well.

RETURNS The normal return value is the length of the hypotenuse as described above. If the result is too large, however, *hypot* returns the value HUGE_VAL and sets *errno* to the constant ERANGE.

SEE ALSO cabs *To compute magnitude of a complex number*

EXAMPLE Write a program that computes the length of the hypotenuse of a right triangle whose sides are entered on the command line.

```
#include <stdio.h>
#include <math.h>
#include <stdlib.h>        /* errno is defined here */
main(int argc, char **argv)
{
    double x, y, result;
    if(argc < 3)
    {
        printf("Usage: %s <x> <y>\n", argv[0]);
    }
    else
    {
        x = atof(argv[1]);
        y = atof(argv[2]);
        result = hypot(x,y);
        if(errno != ERANGE)
        {
            printf("hypot(%s, %s) = %f\n",
                    argv[1], argv[2], result);
        }
    }
    return 0;
}
```

COMPATIBILITY

labs

TC1	TC1.5	TC2	TC++	MSC3	MSC4	MSC5	MSC6	QC1	QC2	QC2.5	ANSI	UNIX V	XNX
▲	▲	▲	▲	▲	▲	▲	▲	▲	▲	▲	▲		

PURPOSE Use *labs* to get the absolute value of a long integer value.

SYNTAX

```
long labs(long n);
```

`long n;` *Long integer whose absolute value is returned*

EXAMPLE CALL

```
lresult = labs(-65540L); /* result will be 65540 */
```

INCLUDES `#include <stdlib.h>` *For function declaration*

DESCRIPTION The *labs* function returns the absolute value of the long integer argument *n*. For example, *labs(-999999L)* returns 999999.

RETURNS The long integer returned by *labs* is the absolute value of *n*.

SEE ALSO

`abs` *To get the absolute value of an integer*

`cabs` *To obtain the magnitude (or absolute value) of a complex number*

`fabs` *To get the absolute value of a floating-point number*

EXAMPLE Use *labs* to obtain the absolute value of a long integer entered as a command-line argument to a program.

```
#include <stdio.h>
#include <stdlib.h>
main(int argc, char **argv)
{
    long value, result;
    if(argc < 2)
    {
        printf("Usage: %s <long_integer_value>\n",
               argv[0]);
    }
    else
    {
        value = atol(argv[1]);
        result = labs(value);
        printf("Absolute value of %ld = %ld\n",
               value, result);
```

```
    }
    return 0;
}
```

ldexp

COMPATIBILITY

TC1	TC1.5	TC2	TC++	MSC3	MSC4	MSC5	MSC6	QC1	QC2	QC2.5	ANSI	UNIX V	XNX
▲	▲	▲	▲	▲	▲	▲	▲	▲	▲	▲	▲	▲	▲

PURPOSE Use *ldexp* to compute a floating-point number from a mantissa and an integer exponent such that the floating-point number is equal to the mantissa × 2^{exp}.

SYNTAX

```
double ldexp(double x, int exp);
```

`double x;` *Floating-point value of the mantissa*

`int exp;` *Integer exponent*

EXAMPLE CALL

```
value = ldexp(mantissa, binary_exponent);
```

INCLUDES `#include <math.h>` *For function declaration*

DESCRIPTION The *ldexp* function computes and returns the floating-point number equal to $x \times 2^{exp}$.

COMMON USES The *ldexp* complements *frexp* by enabling you to determine the floating-point value corresponding to a binary representation in the mantissa-exponent form. (See the tutorial section for an explanation.)

RETURNS Normally *ldexp* returns the value computed as described above. When the result is too large, *ldexp* returns the value HUGE_VAL (with the sign of *x*) and sets *errno* to ERANGE.

SEE ALSO

`frexp` *To decompose a floating-point number into a mantissa and an exponent as required by* ldexp

`modf` *To decompose a floating-point number into its fractional and integral parts*

EXAMPLE Write a program to accept a mantissa and an exponent of 2 and compute the number they represent.

```
#include <stdio.h>
#include <math.h>
```

```
#include <stdlib.h>        /* errno is defined here */
main(int argc, char **argv)
{
    double mantissa, result;
    int    exponent;
    if(argc < 3)
    {
        printf("Usage: %s <mantissa> <exponent>\n",
                argv[0]);
    }
    else
    {
        mantissa = atof(argv[1]);
        exponent = atoi(argv[2]);
        result = ldexp(mantissa, exponent);
        if(errno != ERANGE)
        {
            printf("%s times 2 raised to %s = %f\n",
                    argv[1], argv[2], result);
        }
    }
    return 0;
}
```

ldiv

COMPATIBILITY

TC1	TC1.5	TC2	TC++	MSC3	MSC4	MSC5	MSC6	QC1	QC2	QC2.5	ANSI	UNIX V	XNX
▲	▲	▲	▲			▲	▲	▲	▲	▲	▲		

PURPOSE Use *ldiv* to divide one long integer value by another and get the quotient and remainder in a structure of type *ldiv_t*.

SYNTAX

```
ldiv_t ldiv(long numer, long denom);
```

`long numer;` *Numerator*

`long denom;` *Denominator*

EXAMPLE CALL

```
lresult = ldiv(65540L, 65536L);
/* lresult.quot = 1, lresult.rem = 4 */
```

INCLUDES `#include <stdlib.h>` *For function declaration and definition of structure* ldiv_t

DESCRIPTION The *ldiv* function divides the long integer *numer* by another long integer, *denom*, and returns the resulting quotient and remainder packed in a structure of type *ldiv_t*. The structure type *ldiv_t* is defined in *stdlib.h* as

```
typedef struct
{
    long quot;   /* The quotient  */
    long rem;    /* The remainder */
} ldiv_t;
```

RETURNS The *ldiv* function returns a structure of type *ldiv_t* containing the quotient and remainder of the division.

SEE ALSO div *To divide one integer by another*

EXAMPLE Write a program that accepts two long integers, a numerator and a denominator, on the command line and uses *ldiv* to compute the quotient and remainder of the division.

```
#include <stdio.h>
#include <stdlib.h>
main(int argc, char **argv)
{
    long int x, y;
    ldiv_t result;
/* Make sure that there are at least 3 arguments */
    if(argc < 3)
    {
        printf("Usage: %s <long numerator> <long denom>\n",
                argv[0]);
        exit(0);

    }
/* Divide first long integer by second and display
 * quotient and remainder
 */
    x = atol(argv[1]);
    y = atol(argv[2]);
    result = ldiv(x,y);
    printf("Dividing %ld by %ld. Quotient = %ld and \
remainder = %ld\n", x, y, result.quot, result.rem);
    return 0;
}
```

log, log10

COMPATIBILITY

TC1	TC1.5	TC2	TC++	MSC3	MSC4	MSC5	MSC6	QC1	QC2	QC2.5	ANSI	UNIX V	XNX
▲	▲	▲	▲	▲	▲	▲	▲	▲	▲	▲	▲	▲	▲

PURPOSE Use *log* and *log10* respectively to compute the natural logarithm and logarithm to the base 10 of a positive *double* variable.

SYNTAX

```
double log(double x);

double log10(double x);

double x;        Variable whose logarithm is to be computed
```

EXAMPLE CALL

```
y = log(x);
a = log10(b);
```

INCLUDES `#include <math.h>` *For function declaration and definition of error constants*

DESCRIPTION The *log* function computes the natural logarithm (base *e*) of the *double* variable *x* (i.e., the exponential of the result should be equal to *x*).

The *log10* function computes the logarithm of *x* with respect to base 10. Thus 10 raised to the power of the result should be *x*.

RETURNS Normally, *log* and *log10* return the logarithm of *x*. If *x* is negative, both functions return the value HUGE_VAL, print a DOMAIN error on *stderr*, and set *errno* to the constant EDOM. If *x* is zero, both functions will print a SING error message to indicate a singularity (a point where the function's value is infinity), return the value HUGE_VAL, and set *errno* to ERANGE.

SEE ALSO

`exp` *To compute the exponential (the inverse of the natural logarithm) of a variable*

`pow` *To compute the value of one variable raised to the power of another*

EXAMPLE Write a small program that accepts a number and computes its natural logarithm as well as its logarithm to the base 10.

```
#include <stdio.h>
#include <math.h>
#include <stdlib.h>  /* errno is declared here */
main(int argc, char **argv)
{
    double result;
    if(argc < 2)
    {
```

```
            printf("Usage: %s <value>\n", argv[0]);
        }
        else
        {
/* Compute the natural logarithm                          */
            result = log(atof(argv[1]));
            if (errno != EDOM && errno != ERANGE)
                printf("log (%s) = %f\n", argv[1], result);

/* Now compute the logarithm to the base 10               */
            result = log10(atof(argv[1]));
            if (errno != EDOM && errno != ERANGE)
                printf("log10 (%s) = %f\n", argv[1], result);
        }
        return 0;
}
```

_lrotl

COMPATIBILITY

TC1	TC1.5	TC2	TC++	MSC3	MSC4	MSC5	MSC6	QC1	QC2	QC2.5	ANSI	UNIX V	XNX
	▲	▲	▲			▲	▲	▲	▲	▲			

PURPOSE Use *_lrotl* to rotate to the left the bits in an unsigned long integer variable.

SYNTAX

```
unsigned long int _lrotl(unsigned long value, int shift);
```

`unsigned long value;` *Value to be rotated left*

`int shift;` *Number of bits to shift*

EXAMPLE CALL

```
result = _lrotl(0x01234567L, 4) /* result is 0x12345670 */
```

INCLUDES `#include <stdlib.h>` *For function declaration*

DESCRIPTION The *_lrotl* function rotates to the left the bits in the unsigned long variable *value* by shifting bit positions. Bit rotation to the left by one position means that the leftmost bit is shifted out and inserted into the rightmost bit and all the other bits shift one step to the left.

RETURNS The unsigned long integer returned by *_lrotl* is the *value* rotated left.

SEE ALSO `_lrotr` *To rotate an unsigned long integer to the right*

`_rotl, _rotr` *To rotate unsigned integers*

EXAMPLE Write a program to illustrate the effect of rotating a long integer to the left. Ask the user for a value (up to eight digits) in hexadecimal. Use *_lrotl* to rotate the number to the left 32 times, printing the result in hexadecimal after each rotation.

```
#include <stdio.h>
#include <stdlib.h>
main()
{
    char input[80];
    int bits;
    unsigned long value;
    char **eptr;
    printf("Enter long integer to rotate (in hex): ");
    gets(input);
/* Convert string to unsigned long integer */
    value = strtoul(input, eptr, 16);
    for (bits = 1; bits < 33; bits++)
        printf(
        "%#8.8lx rotated left by %d bits = %#8.8lx\n",
        value, bits, _lrotl(value,bits));
    return 0;
}
```

_lrotr

COMPATIBILITY

TC1	TC1.5	TC2	TC++	MSC3	MSC4	MSC5	MSC6	QC1	QC2	QC2.5	ANSI	UNIX V	XNX
	▲	▲	▲			▲	▲	▲	▲	▲			

PURPOSE Use *_lrotr* to rotate to the right the bits in an unsigned long integer variable.

SYNTAX `unsigned long int _lrotr(unsigned long value, int shift);`

`unsigned long value;` *Value to be rotated right*

`int shift;` *Number of bits to shift*

EXAMPLE CALL `result = _lrotr(0x01234567L, 16) /* result is 0x45670123 */`

INCLUDES `#include <stdlib.h>` *For function declaration*

DESCRIPTION The *_lrotr* function rotates to the right the bits in the unsigned long variable *value* by shifting bit positions. Bit rotation to the right by one position means that the rightmost bit is shifted out and inserted into the leftmost bit and all the other bits shift one step to the right.

RETURNS The unsigned long integer returned by *_lrotr* is the *value* rotated right.

SEE ALSO `_lrotl` *To rotate an unsigned long integer to the left*

`_rotl, _rotr` *To rotate unsigned integers*

EXAMPLE Write a program to illustrate the effect of rotating a long integer to the right. Assume that the value (up to eight digits) in hexadecimal and the number of bits to rotate are entered on the command line. Use *_lrotr* to perform the rotation and then print the result. You can see the effect of rotation best if the number of bits to rotate is a multiple of 4.

```
#include <stdio.h>
#include <stdlib.h>
main(int argc, char **argv)
{
    int bits;
    unsigned long value;
    char **eptr;
    if(argc < 3)

    {
        printf("Usage: %s <hex value (max 8 digits)>\
<no. bits to rotate right>\n",
                argv[0]);
        exit(0);
    }
/* Convert argument to unsigned long integer */
    value = strtoul(argv[1], eptr, 16);
    bits = atoi(argv[2]);
    printf("%#8.8lx rotated right by %d bits = %#8.8lx\n",
            value, bits, _lrotr(value,bits));
    return 0;
}
```

COMPATIBILITY

_matherr

TC1	TC1.5	TC2	TC++	MSC3	MSC4	MSC5	MSC6	QC1	QC2	QC2.5	ANSI	UNIX V	XNX
▲	▲	▲	▲				▲		▲	▲			

PURPOSE This is an internal routine that calls and processes the value returned by the user-defined math error handler *matherr*.

SYNTAX

```
double _matherr (_mexcep why, char *func, double  *arg1p,
                 double  *arg2p, double  retval);
```

`_mexcep why;`	*Type of math error*
`char    *func;`	*Name of math function where error occurred*
`double  *arg1p;`	*First argument to the function where error occurred*
`double  *arg2p;`	*Second argument, if any*
`double  retval;`	*Value to be returned by the function*

EXAMPLE CALL Not to be called directly.

INCLUDES `#include <math.h>` *For function prototype and definition of enumerated type* _mexcep

DESCRIPTION The *_matherr* is an internal routine that gets called whenever any error occurs in a math library function. This routine in turn calls the *matherr* function. The arguments to *_matherr* are passed on to *matherr* via the fields of an *exception* structure (see *matherr* for more details). If the value returned by *matherr* is 0 (meaning that the error could not be handled in that routine), *_matherr* prints a message and sets the global variable *errno* to one of the defined constants EDOM or ERANGE. If *matherr* returns a nonzero value, *_matherr* skips this step.

RETURNS The *_matherr* function returns the argument *retval* to the calling function. Remember that you can alter this value in the user-defined math error handler *matherr* which is called by *_matherr*.

SEE ALSO `matherr` *User-defined math error handler*

matherr

COMPATIBILITY

TC1	TC1.5	TC2	TC++	MSC3	MSC4	MSC5	MSC6	QC1	QC2	QC2.5	ANSI	UNIX V	XNX
▲	▲	▲	▲	▲	▲	▲	▲	▲	▲	▲		▲	▲

PURPOSE The default *matherr* function is called by a math function when an error occurs. You can develop your own version of *matherr* to customize error handling.

SYNTAX

```
int matherr(struct exception *error_info);

struct exception *error_info;
```

Pointer to a structure that contains information about the error that just occurred

INCLUDES

```
#include <math.h>
```

For function declaration

DESCRIPTION The *matherr* function is called with a pointer to a structure of type *exception*, which is defined in *math.h* as follows:

```
struct exception
{
    int type;           /* exception type - see below          */
    char *name;         /* name of function where error occurred */
    double arg1;        /* first argument to function          */
    double arg2;        /* second argument (if any) to function */
    double retval;      /* value to be returned by function    */
} ;
```

The value put into *retval* by *matherr* is returned by the math function to its calling process.

A *matherr* is present in the library, but you can supply your own version as long as it conforms to the description provided here.

RETURNS The *matherr* function returns a zero to indicate an error and a nonzero to indicate successful corrective action. If *matherr* returns a zero the math function that called *matherr* displays an error message and sets *errno* to an appropriate value. Keep this in mind when writing your own *matherr* function.

SEE ALSO

```
acos, asin, atan, atan2, cabs,
cos, cosh, exp, hypot, log, log10,
pow, sin, sinh, sqrt, tan
```

How the math functions behave with the default matherr

EXAMPLE As described above, you can write your own version of *matherr* to handle mathematical errors your way. As an example, write a *matherr* function that handles the DOMAIN error by returning the square root of the absolute value of a number when *sqrt* is called with a negative argument.

```
/*  Use /NOE option with linker to use our copy of
 *  matherr error handler without complaining.
 */
#include <stdio.h>
#include <math.h>
#include <string.h>
main(int argc, char **argv)
{
    double result;
    if(argc < 2)
    {
        printf("Usage: %s <value>\n", argv[0]);
    }
    else
    {
        result = sqrt(atof(argv[1]));
        printf("sqrt (%s) = %f\n", argv[1], result);
    }
    return 0;
}
/*----------------------------------------------------*/
/*  Our own custom error handler. We will check if
 *  the function is "sqrt". If yes, and the error type
 *  is DOMAIN, we will return square root of the
 *  absolute value. Otherwise, our matherr will return
 *  zero to force the default actions.
 */
int matherr(struct exception *errorinfo)
{
    if(errorinfo->type == DOMAIN)
    {
        if(strcmp(errorinfo->name, "sqrt") == 0)

        {
          errorinfo->retval = sqrt(-(errorinfo->arg1));
          return(1);    /* return 1 == no more error  */
        }
    }
    return(0);  /* return 0 to indicate error        */
}
```

max

COMPATIBILITY

TC1	TC1.5	TC2	TC++	MSC3	MSC4	MSC5	MSC6	QC1	QC2	QC2.5	ANSI	UNIX V	XNX
▲	▲	▲	▲			▲	▲	▲	▲	▲			

PURPOSE Use the *max* macro to obtain the larger of two values of any numerical data type, signed or unsigned.

SYNTAX

```
<type> max(<type> a, <type> b);

<type> a, b;
```

`<type> a, b;` *Values to be compared, <type> denotes any numerical data type*

EXAMPLE CALL

```
double dbl1, dbl2, dblmax;
int i1, i2, intmax;
dblmax = max(dbl1, dbl2);
intmax = max(i1, i2);
```

INCLUDES `#include <stdlib.h>` *For definition of the macro*

DESCRIPTION The *max* macro is defined in *stdlib.h*:

```
#define max(a,b)    (((a) > (b)) ? (a) : (b))
```

It accepts two values (constants or variables) of any numerical data type and returns the value of the larger of the two. For example, if a = 9 and b = 11, max(a,b) returns b.

RETURNS The *max* macro evaluates to the larger value of the two arguments *a* and *b*.

SEE ALSO `min` *Macro to get the smaller of two values*

EXAMPLE Write a utility program that accepts a single character to indicate the variable type (*i* for integer, *l* for long, and *d* for floating-point), followed by two values, and prints the maximum of the two values. Use *max* to obtain the larger of the two values.

```
#include <stdio.h>
#include <stdlib.h>
main(int argc, char **argv)
{
    int    i1, i2, ir;
    long   l1, l2, lr;
    double d1, d2, dr;
    if(argc < 4)
```

```
    {
        printf("Usage: %s <type> <value1> <value2>\n",
                argv[0]);
    }
    else
    {
        switch(argv[1][0])
        {
            case 'i':
            case 'I':
                i1 = atoi(argv[2]);
                i2 = atoi(argv[3]);
                ir = max(i1, i2);
                printf("Larger of %d and %d = %d\n",
                        i1, i2, ir);
                break;
            case 'l':
            case 'L':
                l1 = atol(argv[2]);
                l2 = atol(argv[3]);
                lr = max(l1, l2);
                printf("Larger of %ld and %ld = %ld\n",
                        l1, l2, lr);
                break;
            case 'd':
            case 'D':
                d1 = atof(argv[2]);
                d2 = atof(argv[3]);
                dr = max(d1, d2);
                printf("Larger of %g and %g = %g\n",
                        d1, d2, dr);
                break;


            default:  printf("Don't know type: %c\n",
                              argv[1][0]);
        }
    }
    return 0;
}
```

min

COMPATIBILITY

TC1	TC1.5	TC2	TC++	MSC3	MSC4	MSC5	MSC6	QC1	QC2	QC2.5	ANSI	UNIX V	XNX
▲	▲	▲	▲			▲	▲	▲	▲	▲			

PURPOSE Use the *min* macro to obtain the smaller of two values of any numerical data type, signed or unsigned.

SYNTAX

```
<type> min(<type> a, <type> b);

<type> a, b;
```

Values to be compared, <type> denotes any numerical data type

EXAMPLE CALL

```
double dbl1, dbl2, dblmin;
int i1, i2, intmin;
dblmin = min(dbl1, dbl2);
intmin = min(i1, i2);
```

INCLUDES

```
#include <stdlib.h>
```

For definition of the macro

DESCRIPTION The *min* macro is defined in *stdlib.h*:

```
#define min(a,b)    (((a) < (b)) ? (a) : (b))
```

It accepts two values (constants or variables) of any numerical data type and returns the smaller of the two. For example, if a = 9 and b = 11, min(a,b) returns a.

RETURNS The *min* macro evaluates to the smaller of the two arguments *a* and *b*.

SEE ALSO `max` *Macro to get the larger of two values*

EXAMPLE Write a program that accepts a single character to indicate the variable type (*i* for integer, *l* for long and *d* for floating-point), followed by two values, and prints the smaller of the two values. Use *min* to obtain the minimum of the two values.

```
#include <stdio.h>
#include <stdlib.h>
main(int argc, char **argv)
{
    int    i1, i2, ir;
    long   l1, l2, lr;
    double d1, d2, dr;
    if(argc < 4)
```

```
    {
        printf("Usage: %s <type> <value1> <value2>\n",
                argv[0]);
    }
    else
    {
        switch(argv[1][0])
        {
            case 'i':
            case 'I':
                i1 = atoi(argv[2]);
                i2 = atoi(argv[3]);
                ir = min(i1, i2);
                printf("Smaller of %d and %d = %d\n",
                        i1, i2, ir);
                break;
            case 'l':
            case 'L':
                l1 = atol(argv[2]);
                l2 = atol(argv[3]);
                lr = min(l1, l2);
                printf("Smaller of %ld and %ld = %ld\n",
                        l1, l2, lr);
                break;
            case 'd':
            case 'D':
                d1 = atof(argv[2]);
                d2 = atof(argv[3]);
                dr = min(d1, d2);
                printf("Smaller of %g and %g = %g\n",
                        d1, d2, dr);
                break;


            default:  printf("Don't know type: %c\n",
                              argv[1][0]);
        }
    }
    return 0;
}
```

modf

COMPATIBILITY

TC1	TC1.5	TC2	TC++	MSC3	MSC4	MSC5	MSC6	QC1	QC2	QC2.5	ANSI	UNIX V	XNX
▲	▲	▲	▲	▲	▲	▲	▲	▲	▲	▲	▲	▲	▲

PURPOSE Use *modf* to decompose a floating-point number into its fractional and integral parts.

SYNTAX

```
double modf(double x, double *intptr);
```

`double x;` *Floating-point value to be decomposed*

`double *intptr;` *Integral part of* x *is returned here*

EXAMPLE CALL

```
fraction = modf(24.95, &int_part); /* fraction is .95 */
```

INCLUDES `#include <math.h>` *For function declaration*

DESCRIPTION The *modf* function separates the floating-point number *x* into its fractional part and its integral part. The integer part is returned as a floating-point value in the location whose address is given in the argument *intptr*.

RETURNS The *modf* function returns the signed fractional part of *x*.

SEE ALSO `frexp` *To decompose a floating-point number into a mantissa and an exponent*

`ldexp` *To construct a floating-point number from its mantissa and exponent*

EXAMPLE Write a program that accepts a real number and decomposes it into its integral part and its fractional part.

```
#include <stdio.h>
#include <math.h>
#include <stdlib.h>      /* errno is defined here */
main(int argc, char **argv)
{
    double x, intpart, fract;
    if(argc < 2)
    {
        printf("Usage: %s <x>\n", argv[0]);
    }
    else
    {
        x = atof(argv[1]);
        fract = modf(x, &intpart);
```

```
        printf("Integer part of %s    = %\f\n
Fractional part of %s = %f\n", argv[1], intpart,
        argv[1], fract);
    }
    return 0;
}
```

COMPATIBILITY

poly

TC1	TC1.5	TC2	TC++	MSC3	MSC4	MSC5	MSC6	QC1	QC2	QC2.5	ANSI	UNIX V	XNX
▲	▲	▲	▲										

PURPOSE Use *poly* to evaluate a polynomial for a given argument.

SYNTAX

```
double poly (double x, int n, double c[]);
```

`double x` *Value of variable for which polynomial is to be evaluated*

`int n` *Degree of the polynomial*

`double c[];` *Array of coefficients (degree+ 1 element)*

EXAMPLE CALL

```
/* Polynomial is: 3x**2 + 2x -1 */
double c[] = {-1.0, 2.0, 3.0};
value_at_10 = poly(10.0, 2, c);
```

INCLUDES `#include <math.h>` *For function prototype*

DESCRIPTION The *poly* function evaluates a polynomial of degree *n* whose coefficients are given in the array *c* containing *n+ 1* coefficients. The expression used to evaluate the polynomial is given by: $c[n]x^{n}+c[n-1]x^{(n-1)}+ \ldots +c[2]x^{2}+ c[1]x+c[0]$.

RETURNS The *poly* function returns the value of the polynomial when the value of the variable is *x*.

SEE ALSO `pow` *To raise a variable to a given power*

EXAMPLE Use *poly* to evaluate the polynomial $3x^2+2x-1$ when x=10. The result should be 319.

```
#include <stdio.h>
#include <math.h>
```

```
/* Polynomial is: 3x**2 + 2x -1 */
double c[] = {-1.0, 2.0, 3.0};

main()
{
    double value_at_10;
    value_at_10 = poly(10.0, 2, c);
    printf("3x**2+2x-1 evaluated at 10.0 = %f\n",
           value_at_10);
    return 0;
}
```

pow

COMPATIBILITY

TC1	TC1.5	TC2	TC++	MSC3	MSC4	MSC5	MSC6	QC1	QC2	QC2.5	ANSI	UNIX V	XNX
▲	▲	▲	▲	▲	▲	▲	▲	▲	▲	▲	▲	▲	▲

PURPOSE Use *pow* to compute the value of one argument raised to the power of another.

SYNTAX

```
double pow(double x, double y);

double x, y;        x raised to the power y is computed
```

EXAMPLE CALL

```
x = pow(2.0, 3.0); /* x will be 8.0 */
```

INCLUDES `#include <math.h>` *For function declaration and definition of constants EDOM, ERANGE, DOMAIN, and HUGE_VAL*

DESCRIPTION The *pow* function computes the value of *x* raised to the power *y*. When *x* is negative, *y* can only take integral values less than 2^{64}.

RETURNS When both *x* and *y* are nonzero positive numbers, *pow* returns the value *x* raised to the power *y*. If *x* is nonzero and *y* is zero, the return value is unity (one). When *x* is zero and *y* is negative, *pow* returns the value HUGE_VAL and sets *errno* to EDOM. If both *x* and *y* are zero or if *x* is negative and *y* is not an integral value, *pow* returns a one, sets *errno* to EDOM, and prints a DOMAIN error message to *stderr*. If the result is too large, *pow* prints no message but returns the value HUGE_VAL.

SEE ALSO

`exp` *To compute exponential*

`matherr` *To handle math errors (you can add your own)*

`log, log10`	*To compute logarithms*
`pow10`	*To compute 10 raised to an integer power*
`sqrt`	*To compute square root*

EXAMPLE Write a program to accept floating-point numbers *x* and *y* on the command line and compute the value of *x* raised to the power *y*.

```
#include <stdio.h>
#include <math.h>
#include <stdlib.h>        /* errno is defined here */
main(int argc, char **argv)
{
    double x, y, result;
    if(argc < 3)
    {
        printf("Usage: %s <x> <y>\n", argv[0]);
    }
    else
    {
        x = atof(argv[1]);
        y = atof(argv[2]);
        result = pow(x,y);
        if(errno != ERANGE)
        {
            printf("%s raised to the power %s = %f\n",
                    argv[1], argv[2], result);
        }
    }
    return 0;
}
```

COMPATIBILITY

pow10

TC1	TC1.5	TC2	TC++	MSC3	MSC4	MSC5	MSC6	QC1	QC2	QC2.5	ANSI	UNIX V	XNX
▲	▲	▲	▲										

PURPOSE Use *pow10* to compute 10 raised to a given integer power.

SYNTAX `double pow10 (int p);`

`int p;` *Desired power of 10*

EXAMPLE CALL `ten_raised_to_5 = pow10(5);`

INCLUDES `#include <math.h>` *For function prototype*

DESCRIPTION The *pow10* function computes 10 raised to the power *p* where *p* is an integer.

RETURNS The *pow10* function returns 10 raised to the power *p*.

SEE ALSO `pow` *To raise one argument to the power of another*

EXAMPLE Use *pow10* to write a program that accepts an integer and returns 10 raised to the power of that integer.

```
#include <stdio.h>
#include <math.h>
#include <stdlib.h>
main(int argc, char **argv)
{
    int p;
    if (argc < 2)
    {
        printf("Usage: %s <integer_power>\n",
                argv[0]);
        exit(1);
    }
    p = atoi(argv[1]);
    printf("10 to the power %d = %f\n", p, pow10(p));
    return 0;
}
```

rand

COMPATIBILITY

TC1	TC1.5	TC2	TC++	MSC3	MSC4	MSC5	MSC6	QC1	QC2	QC2.5	ANSI	UNIX V	XNX
▲	▲	▲	▲	▲	▲	▲	▲	▲	▲	▲	▲	▲	▲

PURPOSE Use *rand* to generate a pseudorandom integer with a value in the range 0–32,767.

SYNTAX `int rand(void);`

EXAMPLE CALL `random_value = rand();`

INCLUDES `#include <stdlib.h>` *For function definition*

DESCRIPTION The *rand* function generates a pseudorandom integer with a value between 0 and 32,767. The starting point of the pseudorandom integers (the "seed") is set by calling *srand*.

RETURNS The *rand* function returns the pseudorandom integer it generates.

COMMENTS We say the integer returned by *rand* is pseudorandom, instead of random, because, given the seed, the sequence of numbers to be generated is predictable. After all, they are generated by a fixed algorithm. If the algorithm is well designed, though, the numbers within the sequence appear to be random.

Select a random seed each time you call *srand* to get a new sequence of numbers each time.

SEE ALSO

`random`	*To get a random number between 0 and a specified positive value*
`randomize`	*To set a new random seed*
`srand`	*To set a new seed for the random number generator*

EXAMPLE Call *rand* and generate 20 pseudorandom integers. Print the integers and note that the same sequence is generated every time the program is run. A different sequence can be obtained by changing the starting seed.

```
#include <stdio.h>
#include <stdlib.h>
main()
{
    int i;
/* Generate and display 20 pseudorandom integers */
    printf("20 pseudorandom integers from \"rand\"\n");
    for(i=0; i<20; i++)
    {
        printf("%d\n", rand());
    }
    return 0;
}
```

random

COMPATIBILITY

TC1	TC1.5	TC2	TC++	MSC3	MSC4	MSC5	MSC6	QC1	QC2	QC2.5	ANSI	UNIX V	XNX
	▲	▲	▲										

PURPOSE Use *random* to generate a random number between 0 and a specified maximum value.

SYNTAX

```
int random(int num);
```

`int num;` *Random numbers will lie between 0 and num−1*

EXAMPLE CALL

```
/* Get a random number between 0 and 20 */
    rnum = random(21);
```

INCLUDES `#include <stdlib.h>` *For macro definition*

DESCRIPTION The *random* macro is defined in terms of the *rand* function as

```
#define random(num)      (rand() % (num))
```

Thus it restricts the random numbers between 0 and *num−1.*

COMMON USES The *random* macro is a convenient way to generate random numbers that lie within a specified range.

RETURNS The *random* macro returns a random number between 0 and *num−1.*

SEE ALSO

`rand` *The random number generator*

`randomize` *To select a random seed for* rand

EXAMPLE Use *random* to generate a random sequence of the numbers between 1 and 20. This means that the sequence must contain only the numbers 1 through 20 in a random order with no number appearing more than once.

```
#include <stdio.h>
#include <stdlib.h>
#include <time.h>     /* randomize() uses time() */
main()
{
    int seq[20], count=0, i, randnum;
/* Initialize the random number generator */
    randomize();
```

```
    while(count < 20)
    {
        randnum = random(20) + 1;
/* Is this number already present in seq[] */
        for(i=0; i<count; i++)
        {
            if(randnum == seq[i]) break;
        }
        if(i>=count)    /* Not in seq[] */
        {
            seq[count] = randnum;
            count++;
        }
    }
/* Print the random sequence */
    printf("Random sequence (1-20) = \n");
    for(i=0; i<count; i++) printf("%d  ", seq[i]);
    printf("\n");
    return 0;
}
```

COMPATIBILITY

randomize

TC1	TC1.5	TC2	TC++	MSC3	MSC4	MSC5	MSC6	QC1	QC2	QC2.5	ANSI	UNIX V	XNX
	▲	▲	▲										

PURPOSE Use *randomize* to initialize the random number generator *rand* with a random seed.

SYNTAX `void randomize(void);`

EXAMPLE CALL `randomize();`

INCLUDES `#include <stdlib.h>` *For function prototype*

`#include <time.h>` *For prototype of* time

DESCRIPTION The *randomize* function uses the *time* function to generate a random seed for *rand*, the random number generator. The *randomize* macro is defined in terms of the *srand* function as follows:

```
#define randomize()     srand((unsigned)time(NULL))
```

COMMON USES The *randomize* function is useful for generating a random starting seed for the random number generator.

SEE ALSO

`rand`	*To generate a random number*
`random`	*To generate random numbers that lie between 0 and a specified maximum value*
`srand`	*To set the starting seed for* rand

EXAMPLE See example for *random*.

_rotl

COMPATIBILITY

TC1	TC1.5	TC2	TC++	MSC3	MSC4	MSC5	MSC6	QC1	QC2	QC2.5	ANSI	UNIX V	XNX
	▲	▲	▲			▲	▲	▲	▲	▲			

PURPOSE Use *_rotl* to rotate to the left the bits in an unsigned integer variable.

SYNTAX

```
unsigned _rotl(unsigned value, int shift);
```

`unsigned int value;`	*Value to be rotated left*
`int shift;`	*Number of bits to shift*

EXAMPLE CALL

```
new_pattern = _rotl(0x1234, 8); /* result is 3412h */
```

INCLUDES `#include <stdlib.h>` *For function declaration*

DESCRIPTION The *_rotl* function rotates to the left the bits in the *value* by shifting bit positions. Bit rotation to the left by one position means that the leftmost bit is shifted out and inserted into the rightmost bit and all the other bits shift one step to the left.

RETURNS The unsigned integer returned by *_rotl* is the *value* rotated left. For example, *_rotl(0x0123, 4)* returns *0x1230*.

SEE ALSO

`_lrotl, _lrotr`	*To rotate unsigned long integers*
`_rotr`	*To rotate an unsigned integer to the right*

EXAMPLE Write a program that accepts an integer value in hexadecimal form and the number of bits to rotate, uses *_rotl* to rotate that number to the left, and

displays the result in hexadecimal. The effect of left rotation is most apparent if you run the program with shifts of 4 and 8.

```
#include <stdio.h>
#include <stdlib.h>
main(int argc, char **argv)
{
    int bits;
    unsigned value;
    if(argc < 3)
    {
        printf("Usage: %s <hex value (max 4 digits)>\
<no. bits to rotate left>\n",
                argv[0]);
        exit(0);
    }
/* Convert argument to unsigned long integer */
    sscanf(argv[1], "%4x", &value);
    bits = atoi(argv[2]);
    printf("%#4.4x rotated left by %d bits = %#4.4x\n",
            value, bits, _rotl(value,bits));
    return 0;
}
```

_rotr

COMPATIBILITY

TC1	TC1.5	TC2	TC++	MSC3	MSC4	MSC5	MSC6	QC1	QC2	QC2.5	ANSI	UNIX V	XNX
	▲	▲	▲			▲	▲	▲	▲	▲			

PURPOSE Use *_rotr* to rotate to the right the bits in an unsigned integer variable.

SYNTAX `unsigned _rotr(unsigned value, int shift);`

`unsigned int value;` *Value to be rotated right*

`int shift;` *Number of bits to shift*

EXAMPLE CALL `rotated_value = _rotr(0x1234, 4); /* result is 4123h */`

INCLUDES `#include stdlib.h>` *For function declaration*

DESCRIPTION The *_rotr* function rotates the bits in the *value* to the right by shifting bit positions. Bit rotation to the right by one position means that the rightmost bit is shifted out and inserted into the leftmost bit and all the other bits shift one step to the right.

RETURNS The unsigned integer returned by *_rotr* is the *value* rotated right. For example, *_rotr(0x0123, 4)* will return *0x3012*.

SEE ALSO

`_lrotl, _lrotr`	*To rotate unsigned long integers*
`_rotl`	*To rotate an unsigned integer to the left*

EXAMPLE Write a program that accepts an integer value in hexadecimal form, uses *_rotr* to rotate that number 16 times to the right, and displays the result in hexadecimal at each step.

```
#include <stdio.h>
#include <stdlib.h>
main()
{
    int bits;
    unsigned value;
    printf("Enter a hexadecimal value to be rotated :");
    scanf("%4x", &value);
    for (bits = 1; bits < 17; bits++)
        printf(
        "%#4.4x rotated right by %d bits = %#4.4x\n",
        value, bits, _rotr(value,bits));
    return 0;
}
```

sin

COMPATIBILITY

TC1	TC1.5	TC2	TC++	MSC3	MSC4	MSC5	MSC6	QC1	QC2	QC2.5	ANSI	UNIX V	XNX
▲	▲	▲	▲	▲	▲	▲	▲	▲	▲	▲	▲	▲	▲

PURPOSE Use *sin* to compute the sine of an angle whose value is expressed in radians.

SYNTAX `double sin(double x);`

`double x;` *Angle in radians whose sine is to be computed*

EXAMPLE CALL `y = sin(x)`

INCLUDES `#include <math.h>` *For function declaration and definition of error constants*

Math Routines

DESCRIPTION The *sin* function computes the sine of *double* argument *x*, which represents an angle in radians.

RETURNS The *sin* function returns the sine of *x*.

SEE ALSO `asin` *To compute the arc sine of a variable*

`cos` *To compute cosine of an angle*

EXAMPLE Write a program that accepts an angle in degrees and prints its sine.

```
#include <stdio.h>
#include <math.h>
#include <stdlib.h>       /* errno is defined here */
#define  R_TO_D   57.29578 /* radians to degrees  */
main(int argc, char **argv)
{
    double result;
    if(argc < 2)
    {
        printf("Usage: %s <degrees>\n", argv[0]);
    }
    else
    {
        result = sin(atof(argv[1]) / R_TO_D);
        printf("Sine (%s deg.) = %f\n",
                     argv[1], result);
    }
    return 0;
}
```

sinh

COMPATIBILITY

TC1	TC1.5	TC2	TC++	MSC3	MSC4	MSC5	MSC6	QC1	QC2	QC2.5	ANSI	UNIX V	XNX
▲	▲	▲	▲	▲	▲	▲	▲	▲	▲	▲	▲	▲	▲

PURPOSE Use *sinh* to compute the hyperbolic sine of a *double* variable.

SYNTAX `double sinh(double x);`

`double x;` *Variable whose hyperbolic sine is to be computed*

EXAMPLE CALL `a = sinh(b);`

INCLUDES `#include <math.h>` *For function declaration and definition of error constants*

DESCRIPTION The *sinh* function computes the hyperbolic sine of the *double* variable *x*.

RETURNS Normally, *sinh* returns the hyperbolic sine of *x*. If the result is too large (a *double* variable can be as large as approximately 10^{308}), *sinh* returns the value HUGE_VAL and sets *errno* to the constant ERANGE.

SEE ALSO `cosh` *To compute the hyperbolic cosine of a variable*

EXAMPLE Write a program that accepts a floating-point number on the command line and computes its hyperbolic sine.

```
#include <stdio.h>
#include <math.h>
#include <stdlib.h>       /* errno is defined here */
main(int argc, char **argv)
{
    double result;
    if(argc < 2)
    {
        printf("Usage: %s <value>\n", argv[0]);
    }
    else
    {
        result = sinh(atof(argv[1]));
        if(errno != ERANGE)
        {
            printf("Hyperbolic sine of %s = %f\n",
                    argv[1], result);
        }
    }
    return 0;
}
```

sqrt

COMPATIBILITY

TC1	TC1.5	TC2	TC++	MSC3	MSC4	MSC5	MSC6	QC1	QC2	QC2.5	ANSI	UNIX V	XNX
▲	▲	▲	▲	▲	▲	▲	▲	▲	▲	▲	▲	▲	▲

PURPOSE Use *sqrt* to compute the square root of a nonnegative *double* variable.

SYNTAX `double sqrt(double x);`

`double x;` *Variable whose square root is to be computed*

EXAMPLE CALL `sqrt_2 = sqrt(2.0); /* sqrt_2 = 1.414 */`

INCLUDES `#include <math.h>` *For function declaration*

DESCRIPTION The *sqrt* function computes the square root of the *double* variable *x*, provided *x* is not negative.

RETURNS The *sqrt* function returns the square root of *x*. If *x* is negative, though, *sqrt* prints a DOMAIN error message to *stderr*, sets the global variable *errno* to EDOM, and returns a zero.

SEE ALSO `pow` *To compute the value of one argument raised to the power of another*

EXAMPLE Write a program that accepts a number and computes its square root.

```
#include <stdio.h>
#include <math.h>
#include <stdlib.h>  /* errno is declared here */
main(int argc, char **argv)
{
    double result;
    if(argc < 2)
    {
        printf("Usage: %s <value>\n", argv[0]);
    }
    else
    {
        result = sqrt(atof(argv[1]));
        if (errno != EDOM)
            printf("sqrt (%s) = %f\n", argv[1], result);
    }
    return 0;
}
```

COMPATIBILITY

srand

TC1	TC1.5	TC2	TC++	MSC3	MSC4	MSC5	MSC6	QC1	QC2	QC2.5	ANSI	UNIX V	XNX
▲	▲	▲	▲	▲	▲	▲	▲	▲	▲	▲	▲	▲	▲

PURPOSE Use *srand* to set the starting value (seed) for generating a sequence of pseudorandom integer values.

SYNTAX `void srand(unsigned seed);`

`unsigned seed;` *Starting point for random number generator*

EXAMPLE CALL `srand(new_seed);`

INCLUDES `#include <stdlib.h>` *For function definition*

DESCRIPTION The *srand* function sets the seed of the random number generation algorithm used by the function *rand*.

If the seed is 1, the random number generator is initialized to its default starting point, generating the sequence that is produced when *rand* is called without prior calls to *srand*. Any other value for the seed sets a random starting point for the pseudorandom sequence to be generated by *rand*.

SEE ALSO `rand` *To obtain a random integer value*

`randomize` *To set a random seed using the system time*

EXAMPLE Write a program that uses *srand* to set the seed for a sequence of pseudorandom integers generated by *rand*. Notice that the same seed always generates the same sequence of numbers (instead of its being purely random). That is why we call the sequence of numbers "pseudorandom" (instead of being purely random).

```
#include <stdio.h>
#include <stdlib.h>
main()
{
    int i;
    unsigned seed;
/* Ask user to enter a new seed */
    printf("Enter a seed: ");
    scanf(" %u", &seed);
/* Set new seed by calling "srand" */
    srand(seed);
/* Generate and display 20 pseudorandom integers */
    printf("20 pseudorandom integers from \"rand\"\n");
    for(i=0; i<20; i++)
    {
        printf("%d\n", rand());
    }
    printf("Try again with the same seed.\n\
You'll get the same sequence.\n");
    return 0;
}
```

Math Routines

COMPATIBILITY

_status87

TC1	TC1.5	TC2	TC++	MSC3	MSC4	MSC5	MSC6	QC1	QC2	QC2.5	ANSI	UNIX V	XNX
▲	▲	▲	▲		▲	▲	▲	▲	▲	▲			

PURPOSE Use *_status87* to get the contents of the floating-point status word, which is a combination of the 8087 math coprocessor status word and other conditions detected by the 8087 exception handler.

SYNTAX

```
unsigned int _status87(void);
```

EXAMPLE CALL

```
if(_status87() & SW_ZERODIVIDE) puts("Zero divide error");
```

INCLUDES #include <float.h> *For function declaration and definition of constants denoting status-word bit settings*

DESCRIPTION The *_status87* function returns the status word of the floating-point package. This status word is a composite of the status word of the 8087 math coprocessor and other conditions detected by the 8087 exception handler. You can use the status word to detect error conditions in your own floating-point exception handler.

You should check the return value by performing a bitwise AND with the constant from Table 9-5 that matches the condition you are verifying and then comparing that result for equality with the constant itself. In other words, if the return value is *status*, checking for a loss of precision is done by the code fragment

```
    status = _status87();
    if ((status & SW_INEXACT) == SW_INEXACT)
    {
/* A loss of precision has occurred */
         :
         :
    }
```

RETURNS The bits in the value returned by *_status87* indicate the status of the floating-point package. Table 9-5 shows the constants defined in *float.h* to indicate specific conditions.

SEE ALSO _clear87 *To reset the floating-point status word*

_control87 *To alter bits in the floating-point control word*

EXAMPLE Read and display the current floating-point status word. Now copy a small double variable into a *float* one and create an underflow and an inexact

Table 9-5. *The Floating-Point Status Word*

Status Constant	Meaning
SW_INVALID	Invalid operation.
SW_DENORMAL	Operands are stored in a "normalized" form in in the 8087 math coprocessor. This bit indicates a denormalized operand.
SW_ZERODIVIDE	Divide-by-zero attempted.
SW_OVERFLOW	Floating-point overflow.
SW_UNDERFLOW	Floating-point underflow.
SW_INEXACT	Loss of precision in result.

result. Read and display the status word again; the new value reflects the error.

```
#include <stdio.h>
#include <float.h>
main()
{
    float a;
    double b = 1.e-40;
    unsigned fpstatus;
    printf("Before any computations ");
    fpstatus = _status87();
    printf("status word is: %X\n", fpstatus);
/* Perform operation that produces underflow and
 * an inexact result
 */
    a = b;   /* This will produce inexact result */
    printf("After undeflow/inexact ");
    fpstatus = _status87();
    printf("status word is: %X\n", fpstatus);
    return 0;
}
```

Math Routines

COMPATIBILITY

tan

TC1	TC1.5	TC2	TC++	MSC3	MSC4	MSC5	MSC6	QC1	QC2	QC2.5	ANSI	UNIX V	XNX
▲	▲	▲	▲	▲	▲	▲	▲	▲	▲	▲	▲	▲	▲

PURPOSE Use *tan* to compute the tangent of an angle whose value is expressed in radians.

SYNTAX `double tan(double x);`

`double x;` *Angle in radians whose tangent is to be computed*

EXAMPLE CALL `y = tan(x);`

INCLUDES `#include <math.h>` *For function declaration and definition of error constants*

DESCRIPTION The *tan* function computes the tangent of *double* argument *x*, which represents an angle in radians.

RETURNS The *tan* function returns the tangent of *x*.

SEE ALSO `atan` *To compute the arc tangent of a variable*

EXAMPLE Write a program that accepts an angle in degrees and prints its tangent.

```
#include <stdio.h>
#include <math.h>
#include <stdlib.h>      /* errno is defined here */
#define  R_TO_D   57.29578 /* radians to degrees   */
main(int argc, char **argv)
{
    double result;
    if(argc < 2)
    {
        printf("Usage: %s <degrees>\n", argv[0]);
    }
    else
    {
        result = tan(atof(argv[1]) / R_TO_D);
        if(errno != ERANGE)
        {
            printf("Tangent (%s deg.) = %f\n",
                    argv[1], result);
        }
```

```
    }
    return 0;
}
```

tanh

COMPATIBILITY

TC1	TC1.5	TC2	TC++	MSC3	MSC4	MSC5	MSC6	QC1	QC2	QC2.5	ANSI	UNIX V	XNX
▲	▲	▲	▲	▲	▲	▲	▲	▲	▲	▲	▲	▲	▲

PURPOSE Use *tanh* to compute the hyperbolic tangent of a *double* variable.

SYNTAX `double tanh(double x);`

`double x;` *Variable whose hyperbolic tangent is to be computed*

EXAMPLE CALL `a = tanh(b);`

INCLUDES `#include <math.h>` *For function declaration*

DESCRIPTION The *tanh* function computes the hyperbolic tangent of the *double* variable *x*.

RETURNS The *tanh* function returns the hyperbolic tangent of *x*.

SEE ALSO `cosh, sinh` *To compute the hyperbolic cosine and hyperbolic sine of a variable*

EXAMPLE Write a program that accepts a floating-point number on the command line and computes its hyperbolic tangent.

```
#include <stdio.h>
#include <math.h>
#include <stdlib.h>      /* errno is defined here */
main(int argc, char **argv)
{
    double result;
    if(argc < 2)
    {
        printf("Usage: %s <value>\n", argv[0]);
    }
    else
    {
        result = tanh(atof(argv[1]));
        if(errno != ERANGE)
```

```
        {
            printf("Hyperbolic tangent of %s = %f\n",
                    argv[1], result);
        }
    }
    return 0;
}
```

Chapter 10 Character Classification and Conversion

Introduction

C uses the American Standard Code for Information Interchange (ASCII) character set, which contains characters that can be printed as well as some that have special meanings and are not printable. Often you need to determine the category of a character or to convert a character from one case to another. The C library includes character classification macros for this purpose. (See Table 10-1.)

THE ASCII CHARACTER SET

The ASCII character set relies on a 7-bit code to represent all letters, numbers, punctuation symbols, and some special (unprintable) control characters. The 128 ASCII characters are shown in Figure 10-1. The single-

Second hexadecimal digit

First digit	0	1	2	3	4	5	6	7	8	9	A	B	C	D	E	F
0	NUL	SOH	STX	ETX	EOT	ENQ	ACK	BEL	BS	HT	LF	VT	FF	CR	SO	SI
1	DLE	DC1	DC2	DC3	DC4	NAK	SYN	ETB	CAN	EM	SUB	ESC	FS	GS	RS	US
2	SP	!	"	#	$	%	&	'	(	)	*	+	,	-	.	/
3	0	1	2	3	4	5	6	7	8	9	:	;	<	=	>	?
4	@	A	B	C	D	E	F	G	H	I	J	K	L	M	N	O
5	P	Q	R	S	T	U	V	W	X	Y	Z	[	\	]	^	_
6	`	a	b	c	d	e	f	g	h	i	j	k	l	m	n	o
7	p	q	r	s	t	u	v	w	x	y	z	{	|	}	~	DEL
	0	1	2	3	4	5	6	7	8	9	A	B	C	D	E	F

Figure 10-1. *The ASCII character set*

character entries are printable. The two- and three-letter codes are unprintable (except SP which denotes a blank space).

Beyond the basic 128, the IBM PC also supports character codes from 128 through 255 that a single unsigned C character variable can represent. Often called the "IBM PC extended ASCII character set," these are a collection of Greek, accented, and graphical characters. In fact, even the nonprinting ASCII characters can be displayed on the IBM PC and some are useful for drawing borders of pop-up menus and windows in PC applications. Most printers meant for the IBM PC also support the extended character set. The C character classification macros, however, work with the ASCII (128) character set only.

Notes on Character Classification and Conversion

Table 10-1 shows catalogs of the available character classification macros. The macros are defined in the header file *ctype.h* where you can examine them. Table 10-2 groups the macros by task.

Table 10-1. *Character Classification Macros*

Macro	Description
isalnum	Tests if a character is alphanumeric.
isalpha	Tests if a character is alphabetic.
isascii	Tests if an integer value is a valid ASCII character.
iscntrl	Tests if a character belongs to the set of control characters.
isdigit	Tests if a character is a numerical digit.
isgraph	Tests if a character is printable (excluding the space character).
islower	Tests if a character is lowercase.
isprint	Tests if a character is printable (including the space character).
ispunct	Tests if a character belongs to the set of punctuation characters.
isspace	Tests if a character belongs to the set of whitespace characters.
isupper	Tests if a character is uppercase.
isxdigit	Tests if a character is a hexadecimal digit.
toascii	Converts an integer value to a valid ASCII character.
tolower	Converts a character to lowercase if that character is an uppercase letter.
_tolower	Converts a character to lowercase without checking if it is a uppercase letter.
toupper	Converts a character to uppercase if that character is a lowercase letter.
_toupper	Converts a character to uppercase without checking if it is a lowercase letter.

Table 10-2. *Character Classification Macros by Task*

Task	Macros
Classify a character.	isalnum, isalpha, isascii, iscntrl, isdigit, isgraph, islower, isprint, ispunct, isspace, isupper, isxdigit
Convert from uppercase to lowercase.	tolower, _tolower
Convert from lowercase to uppercase.	toupper, _toupper

CHARACTER CLASSIFICATION: BEHIND THE SCENES

Turbo C++ maintains an array named *_ctype* containing unsigned characters and information that is used in the macro definitions to classify the characters. If 'c' is an ASCII character, the unsigned character _ctype [c+1] contains the classification information about that character. By testing the contents of _ctype[c+1], the macros determine whether 'c' belongs to a category (for example, uppercase letters). That information is encoded in the bits of the single byte in the array *_ctype* that corresponds to the character 'c'. For example, the uppercase 'c' has bit 2 of _ctype[c+1] set to 1. Thus 'c' is uppercase if

```
(_ctype[c+1] & 4)
```

is true (or 1). We could rewrite the test for uppercase letters to compare the ASCII code of the test character with the ASCII codes 'A' and 'Z' and to conclude that the character is uppercase if it satisfies

```
if(c >= 'A' && c <= 'Z') /* character is uppercase */
```

Both approaches work fine, but the library macros are faster because they use a single test while our method needs two logical tests.

The bit patterns in *_ctype* that determine the classification of characters comprise eight basic categories. These and the range of ASCII characters that belong to each are shown in Table 10-3.

Table 10-3. *Basic Categories of Character Classification*

<table>
<tr><th>Category</th><th>ASCII Characters</th></tr>
<tr><td>Uppercase letter</td><td>'A' through 'Z'</td></tr>
<tr><td>Lowercase letter</td><td>'a' through 'z'</td></tr>
<tr><td>Digit (0 through 9)</td><td>'0' through '9'</td></tr>
<tr><td>Whitespace</td><td>Space, tab, line feed (newline), vertical feed, form feed and carriage return</td></tr>
<tr><td>Punctuation character</td><td>! " # $ % & ' ( ) * + , – . / : ; < = > ? @ [\ ] ^ _ ` { | } ~</td></tr>
<tr><td>Control character</td><td>All characters with codes 0 through 1F and the final character 7F</td></tr>
</table>

Table 10-3. ***(cont.)***

Category	ASCII Characters
Blank space	The blank space character
Hexadecimal digit	'0' through '9', 'A' through 'F', and 'a' through 'f'

All the macros are based on these basic classification categories. Table 10-4 summarizes the categories of characters that satisfy the classification macros.

Table 10-4. ***Tests Performed by Classification Macros***

Macro	Test for Basic Categories
isalpha	Uppercase or lowercase letter
isupper	Uppercase letter
islower	Lowercase letter
isdigit	Digit
isxdigit	Hexadecimal digit
isspace	Whitespace
ispunct	Punctuation character
isalnum	Uppercase or lowercase letter or digit
isprint	Blank space or punctuation character or uppercase letter or lowercase letter or digit
isgraph	Punctuation character or uppercase letter or lowercase letter or digit
iscntrl	Control character
isascii	Value less than 80 hex

Cautions

- ▶ Although the macros *_tolower* and *_toupper* run faster because they do no checking of the characters, do not use them unless the character is known to be of the appropriate case. Otherwise, the character will be mapped to another, possibly invalid, value.
- ▶ Note that the *toascii* macro converts an integer value to ASCII by chopping off all high-order bits above the seventh one.

isalnum

COMPATIBILITY

TC1	TC1.5	TC2	TC++	MSC3	MSC4	MSC5	MSC6	QC1	QC2	QC2.5	ANSI	UNIX V	XNX
▲	▲	▲	▲	▲	▲	▲	▲	▲	▲	▲	▲	▲	▲

PURPOSE Use the *isalnum* macro to check whether an ASCII character is alphanumeric.

SYNTAX

```
int isalnum(int c);

int c;        Integer with ASCII character
```

EXAMPLE CALL

```
if(isalnum(c) != 0) printf("%c is alphanumeric\n", c);
```

INCLUDES

```
#include <ctype.h>        For macro definition
```

DESCRIPTION The *isalnum* macro determines if the value in the integer argument *c* is one of the digits 0 to 9, a lowercase letter from a to z, or an uppercase letter from A to Z. The *isalnum* macro can handle only valid ASCII values (from 0 to 127) and the constant EOF, defined in *stdio.h*.

RETURNS The *isalnum* macro returns a nonzero value if the *c* is an alphanumeric character. Otherwise it returns a zero.

SEE ALSO `isascii` *To test if an arbitrary integer value is a valid ASCII character*

EXAMPLE Write a program that prints out the ASCII table with a special mark next to each character that satisfies *isalnum*.

```
#include <stdio.h>
#include <ctype.h>
main()
{
    int ch, count,
        mark = 0xdb; /* to mark characters */
/* Go over entire ASCII table and display the
 * alphanumeric ones.
 */
    printf(
    "Alphanumeric ones are marked with a %c\n",
          mark);
    for(count = 0, ch = 0; ch <= 0x7f; ch++)
    {
        printf("%#02x ", ch);
/* Print character -- if printable           */
```

```
            if(isprint(ch))
            {
                printf(" %c", ch);
            }
            else
            {
                printf("  ");
            }
/* Perform test and put a mark if test succeeds */
            if(isalnum(ch) != 0)
            {
                printf(" %c", mark);
            }
            else
            {
                printf("  ", ch);
            }
            count++;
            if(count == 8)
            {
                printf(" \n");
                count = 0;
            }
        }
        return 0;
}
```

isalpha

COMPATIBILITY

TC1	TC1.5	TC2	TC++	MSC3	MSC4	MSC5	MSC6	QC1	QC2	QC2.5	ANSI	UNIX V	XNX
▲	▲	▲	▲	▲	▲	▲	▲	▲	▲	▲	▲	▲	▲

PURPOSE Use the *isalpha* macro to check whether an ASCII character is alphabetic.

SYNTAX `int isalpha(int c);`

`int c;` *Integer with ASCII character*

EXAMPLE CALL `if(isalpha(c) != 0) printf("%c is letter\n", c);`

INCLUDES `#include <ctype.h>` *For macro definition*

DESCRIPTION The *isalpha* macro determines if the value in the integer argument *c* is a lowercase letter from a to z or an uppercase letter from A to Z. The *isalpha* macro can handle only valid ASCII values (from 0 to 127) and the constant EOF, defined in *stdio.h*.

RETURNS The *isalpha* macro returns a nonzero value if the *c* is indeed a letter. Otherwise it returns a zero.

SEE ALSO `isascii` *To test whether an arbitrary integer value is a valid ASCII character*

EXAMPLE Write a program that prints out the ASCII table with a special mark next to each character that satisfies *isalpha*.

```
#include <stdio.h>
#include <ctype.h>
main()
{
    int ch, count,
        mark = 0xdb; /* to mark characters */
/* Go over entire ASCII table and display the
 * alphabetic ones.
 */
    printf(
    "Letters are marked with a %c\n", mark);
    for(count = 0, ch = 0; ch <= 0x7f; ch++)
    {
        printf("%#02x ", ch);
/* Print character -- if printable              */
        if(isprint(ch))
        {
            printf(" %c", ch);
        }
        else
        {
            printf("  ");
        }
/* Perform test and put a mark if test succeeds */
        if(isalpha(ch) != 0)
        {
            printf(" %c", mark);
        }
        else
        {
            printf("  ", ch);
        }
        count++;
```

```
            if(count == 8)
            {
                printf(" \n");
                count = 0;
            }
        }
        return 0;
    }
```

isascii

COMPATIBILITY

TC1	TC1.5	TC2	TC++	MSC3	MSC4	MSC5	MSC6	QC1	QC2	QC2.5	ANSI	UNIX V	XNX
▲	▲	▲	▲	▲	▲	▲	▲	▲	▲	▲		▲	▲

PURPOSE Use the *isascii* macro to check whether an arbitrary integer value is a valid ASCII character.

SYNTAX `int isascii(int c);`

`int c;` *Integer value being checked*

EXAMPLE CALL `if(isascii(c) == 0) printf("%d - not ASCII value\n", c);`

INCLUDES `#include ctype.h>` *For macro definition*

DESCRIPTION The *isascii* macro determines if the value of the integer argument *c* is in the range 0–127 (the range of values that the ASCII character set occupies).

RETURNS The *isascii* macro returns a nonzero value if the *c* is a valid ASCII character. Otherwise it returns a zero.

COMMENTS The IBM PC supports extended ASCII characters (those with codes from 128 to 255). The *isascii* macro treats these as non-ASCII.

SEE ALSO `toascii` *To convert an arbitrary integer value to a valid ASCII character*

EXAMPLE Write a program that accepts an integer value on the command line and prints out a message indicating whether that value is an ASCII character. (This is true if the value is between 0 and 127.)

```
#include <stdio.h>
#include <ctype.h>
```

```
main(int argc, char **argv)
{
    int ch;
    if(argc < 2)
    {
        printf("Usage: %s <integer_value>\n",
                argv[0]);
    }
    else
    {
        if (isascii(ch = atoi(argv[1])) != 0)
        {
            printf("%s is an ASCII character\n\
It prints as %c on the IBM PC\n", argv[1],  ch);
        }
        else
        {
            printf("%s is not an ASCII char.\n",
                    argv[1]);
        }
    }
    return 0:
}
```

iscntrl, isdigit, isgraph, islower, isprint, ispunct, isspace, isupper, isxdigit

COMPATIBILITY

TC1	TC1.5	TC2	TC++	MSC3	MSC4	MSC5	MSC6	QC1	QC2	QC2.5	ANSI	UNIX V	XNX
▲	▲	▲	▲	▲	▲	▲	▲	▲	▲	▲	▲	▲	▲

PURPOSE Use this group of macros to determine specific properties of an ASCII character: whether it is a control character, a digit, a lowercase letter, printable, and so on.

SYNTAX

```
int iscntrl(int c);

int isdigit(int c);

int isgraph(int c);

int islower(int c);

int isprint(int c);
```

```
int ispunct(int c);

int isspace(int c);

int isupper(int c);

int isxdigit(int c);

int c;          Integer with ASCII character
```

EXAMPLE CALL

```
if(isprint(c) != 0) printf("%c is printable\n", c);
if(isdigit(c) != 0) printf("%c is a digit\n", c);
if(iscntrl(c) != 0) printf("%d is a control char\n", c);
```

INCLUDES

```
#include <ctype.h>        For macro definitions
```

DESCRIPTION This group of macros determines if the value in the integer argument *c* satisfies a specific condition. The macros can handle only valid ASCII values (from 0 to 127) and the constant EOF, defined in *stdio.h*. Table 10-5 shows the test performed by each of the macros.

Table 10-5. *Character Classification Tests*

Macro	Tests For	Acceptable Values
iscntrl	Control character	7Fh or in the range 0 to 1Fh
isdigit	Decimal digit	'0' to '9'
isgraph	Printable character excluding the space	21h to 7Eh
islower	Lowercase character	'a' to 'z'
isprint	Printable character	'a' to 'z'
ispunct	Punctuation character	21h to 2Fh or 3Ah to 40h or 5Bh to 60h or 7Bh to 7Eh
isspace	Whitespace character	9h to Dh or 20h (space)
isupper	Uppercase character	'A' to 'Z'
isxdigit	Hexadecimal digit	'0' to '9' or 'A' to 'F' or 'a' to 'f'

RETURNS Each macro returns a nonzero value if the *c* satisfies the criteria for that macro. Otherwise it returns a zero.

COMMENTS You should use *isascii* first to verify that the integer value is indeed a valid ASCII character. Only then should you use any one of these macros to test for specific properties of that ASCII value.

The Turbo C++ library maintains a list of characters classified according to these tests, allowing the macros to perform the tests swiftly. You can determine how these tests work by studying the file *ctype.h*. In particular, try printing out the external array *(_ctype+1)* for index 0 through 127. For example, each character code for which a 64 (which is equal to the defined constant _IS_PUN in *ctype.h*) appears in the array is a punctuation character.

SEE ALSO

`isascii` *To test whether an arbitrary integer value is a valid ASCII character*

EXAMPLE

Write a program that accepts the name of one of the macros *iscntrl, isdigit, isgraph, islower, isprint, ispunct, isspace, isupper,* or *isxdigit* and prints the ASCII table with a mark next to each character that satisfies the test. This is a convenient tool. Figure 10-2 shows the output for the macro *ispunct*. See if your understanding of punctuation characters matches those of the C library.

```
Those marked with a ■ satisfy ispunct

00          0×01        0×02        0×03        0×04        0×05        0×06        0×07
0×08        0×09        0×0a        0×0b        0×0c        0×0d        0×0e        0×0f
0×10        0×11        0×12        0×13        0×14        0×15        0×16        0×17
0×18        0×19        0×1a        0×1b        0×1c        0×1d        0×1e        0×1f
0×20        0×21 ! ■    0×22 " ■    0×23 # ■    0×24 $ ■    0×25 % ■    0×26 & ■    0×27   ■
0×28 ( ■    0×29 ) ■    0×2a * ■    0×2b + ■    0×2c , ■    0×2d - ■    0×2e . ■    0×2f / ■
0×30 0      0×31 1      0×32 2      0×33 3      0×34 4      0×35 5      0×36 6      0×37 7
0×38 8      0×39 9      0×3a : ■    0×3b ; ■    0×3c < ■    0×3d = ■    0×3e > ■    0×3f ? ■
0×40 @ ■    0×41 A      0×42 B      0×43 C      0×44 D      0×45 E      0×46 F      0×47 G
0×48 H      0×49 I      0×4a J      0×4b K      0×4c L      0×4d M      0×4e N      0×4f O
0×50 P      0×51 Q      0×52 R      0×53 S      0×54 T      0×55 U      0×56 V      0×57 W
0×58 X      0×59 Y      0×5a Z      0×5b [ ■    0×5c \ ■    0×5d ] ■    0×5e ^ ■    0×5f _ ■
0×60 ` ■    0×61 a      0×62 b      0×63 c      0×64 d      0×65 e      0×66 f      0×67 g
0×68 h      0×69 i      0×6a j      0×6b k      0×6c l      0×6d m      0×6e n      0×6f o
0×70 p      0×71 q      0×72 r      0×73 s      0×74 t      0×75 u      0×76 v      0×77 w
0×78 x      0×79 y      0×7a z      0×7b { ■    0×7c | ■    0×7d } ■    0×7e ~ ■    0×7f
```

Figure 10-2. ***ASCII characters that satisfy the macro*** **ispunct**

```
#include <stdio.h>
#include <string.h>
#include <ctype.h>
/* Define a table of function names and numbers */
typedef struct FUNC_TABLE
{
    char name[16];
    int  funcnum;
} FUNC_TABLE;
#define CNTRL  0
#define DIGIT  1
#define GRAPH  2
#define LOWER  3
#define PRINT  4
```

```
#define PUNCT  5
#define SPACE  6
#define UPPER  7
#define XDIGIT 8
/* Now declare the table and initialize it      */
static FUNC_TABLE isfuncs[9] =
{
    "iscntrl", CNTRL, "isdigit", DIGIT,
    "isgraph", GRAPH, "islower", LOWER,
    "isprint", PRINT, "ispunct", PUNCT,
    "isspace", SPACE, "isupper", UPPER,
    "isxdigit", XDIGIT
};
static int numfunc = sizeof(isfuncs)/sizeof(FUNC_TABLE);
main(int argc, char **argv)
{
    int ch, count, i, test_result,
        mark = 0xdb; /* to mark characters */
    if (argc < 2)
    {
        printf("Usage: %s <function_name>\n", argv[0]);
        exit(0);
    }
/* Search table for function name and pointer */
    for(i=0; i<numfunc; i++)
    {
        if (strcmp(argv[1], isfuncs[i].name) == 0)
            break;
    }
    if (i >= numfunc)
    {
        printf("Unknown function: %s\n", argv[1]);
        exit(0);
    }
/* Now go over entire ASCII table and mark the
 * characters that satisfy requested test.     */
    printf(
    "Those marked with a %c satisfy %s\n",
            mark, argv[1]);
    for(count = 0, ch = 0; ch <= 0x7f; ch++)
    {
        printf("%#02x ", ch);
/* Print character -- if printable              */
        if(isprint(ch))
        {
```

```
                printf(" %c", ch);
            }
            else
            {
                printf("  ");
            }
/* Perform the test and put a mark if test succeeds */
            switch(isfuncs[i].funcnum)
            {
                case CNTRL: test_result = iscntrl(ch);
                            break;
                case DIGIT: test_result = isdigit(ch);
                            break;
                case GRAPH: test_result = isgraph(ch);
                            break;
                case LOWER: test_result = islower(ch);
                            break;
                case PRINT: test_result = isprint(ch);
                            break;
                case PUNCT: test_result = ispunct(ch);
                            break;
                case SPACE: test_result = isspace(ch);
                            break;
                case UPPER: test_result = isupper(ch);
                            break;
                case XDIGIT: test_result = isxdigit(ch);
                            break;
            }
            if(test_result != 0)
            {
                printf("%c ", mark);
            }
            else
            {
                printf("  ", ch);
            }
            count++;
            if(count == 8)
            {
                printf(" \n");
                count = 0;
            }
        }
        return 0;
}
```

iscntrl, isdigit, isgraph, islower, isprint, ispunct, isspace, isupper, isxdigit

toascii

COMPATIBILITY

TC1	TC1.5	TC2	TC++	MSC3	MSC4	MSC5	MSC6	QC1	QC2	QC2.5	ANSI	UNIX V	XNX
▲	▲	▲	▲	▲	▲	▲	▲	▲	▲	▲		▲	▲

PURPOSE Use the *toascii* macro to convert an arbitrary integer value to a valid ASCII character.

SYNTAX `int toascii(int c);`

`int c;` *Integer to be converted*

EXAMPLE CALL `c = toascii(int_value);`

INCLUDES #include <ctype.h> *For macro definition*

DESCRIPTION The *toascii* macro sets all but the low-order seven bits of the integer *c* to zero so that the converted value represents a valid ASCII character. If *c* is already an ASCII character, it remains unchanged. As an example, this macro could be used to remove the high bit (the most significant bit) from characters in a WordStar document file. (WordStar uses the high bit to store formatting information.)

RETURNS The *toascii* macro returns the converted character.

SEE ALSO `isascii` *To test whether an arbitrary integer value is a valid ASCII character*

EXAMPLE Write a program to convert an integer value to an ASCII character.

```
#include <stdio.h>
#include <stdlib.h>
#include <ctype.h>
main(int argc, char **argv)
{
    int ch;
    if(argc < 2)
    {
        printf("Usage: %s <integer_value>\n",
                argv[0]);
    }
    else
    {
        ch = toascii(atoi(argv[1]));
        printf("%s converted to ASCII character = %#x\n\
It prints as %c on the IBM PC\n", argv[1], ch, ch);
```

```
                argv[0]);
    }
    else
    {
        ch = toascii(atoi(argv[1]));
        printf("%s converted to ASCII character = %#x\n\
It prints as %c on the IBM PC\n", argv[1], ch, ch);
    }
    return 0;
}
```

COMPATIBILITY

_tolower, tolower

TC1	TC1.5	TC2	TC++	MSC3	MSC4	MSC5	MSC6	QC1	QC2	QC2.5	ANSI	UNIX V	XNX
▲	▲	▲	▲	▲	▲	▲	▲	▲	▲	▲	1	▲	▲

PURPOSE Use the *_tolower* and *tolower* to convert an uppercase ASCII character to lowercase. Use *_tolower* only when you are sure that the character being converted is an uppercase letter.

SYNTAX

```
int _tolower(int c);

int tolower(int c);

int c;        ASCII character to be converted
```

EXAMPLE CALL

```
c = tolower('Q'); /* c will become 'q' */
```

INCLUDES

```
#include <ctype.h>        For macro definition
```

DESCRIPTION Both *_tolower* and *tolower* apply a formula to the ASCII character *c* that will convert it to lowercase if *c* is indeed an uppercase letter. Since *tolower* checks to see if *c* is actually an uppercase letter before making the conversion it is safer to use it than to take the risk with *_tolower*.

1. The *_tolower* function is not available in ANSI C.

RETURNS The *_tolower* and *tolower* return a lowercase character.

SEE ALSO

`isascii`	*To test whether an arbitrary integer value is a valid ASCII character*
`_toupper, toupper`	*To convert lowercase letters to uppercase*

```
main()
{
    int i, ch;
    char input[81];
    printf("Enter a string: ");
    gets(input);
    for(i=0; (input[i] != ' ') && (input[i] != '\0');
        i++)
    {
        input[i] = tolower(input[i]);
    }
    printf("Result: %s\n", input);
    return 0;
}
```

_toupper, toupper

COMPATIBILITY

TC1	TC1.5	TC2	TC++	MSC3	MSC4	MSC5	MSC6	QC1	QC2	QC2.5	ANSI	UNIX V	XNX
▲	▲	▲	▲	▲	▲	▲	▲	▲	▲	▲	1	▲	▲

PURPOSE Use the *_toupper* and *toupper* to convert a lowercase ASCII character to uppercase. Use the *_toupper* macro only when you are sure that the character being converted is a lowercase letter.

SYNTAX

```
int _toupper(int c);

int toupper(int c);

int c;        ASCII character to be converted
```

EXAMPLE CALL

```
c = toupper('q'); /* c will become 'Q' */
```

INCLUDES

```
#include <ctype.h>     For macro definition
```

DESCRIPTION Both *_toupper* and *toupper* apply a formula to the ASCII character *c* that will convert it to uppercase if *c* is indeed a lowercase letter. Since *toupper* first checks to see if *c* is actually a lowercase letter before making the conversion it is safer to use it than *_toupper*.

1. The *_toupper* function is not available in ANSI C.

RETURNS Both *_toupper* and *toupper* return an uppercase character.

first checks to see if *c* is actually a lowercase letter before making the conversion it is safer to use it than *_toupper*.

1. The *_toupper* function is not available in ANSI C.

RETURNS Both *_toupper* and *toupper* return an uppercase character.

SEE ALSO

`isascii` *To test whether an arbitrary integer value is a valid ASCII character*

`_tolower, tolower` *To convert uppercase letters to lowercase*

EXAMPLE Write a program that accepts a string from the user and calls *toupper* to convert the characters to uppercase until a blank is encountered or the string ends. Print the results of the conversion.

```
#include <stdio.h>
#include <ctype.h>
main()
{
    int i, ch;
    char input[81];
    printf("Enter a string: ");
    gets(input);
    for(i=0; (input[i] != ' ') && (input[i] != '\0');
        i++)
    {
        input[i] = toupper(input[i]);
    }
    printf("Result: %s\n", input);
    return 0;
}
```

Chapter 11 String Comparison and Manipulation

Introduction

Manipulating text is a major part of many computer applications. The manipulation might involve text editing, word processing, or that part of your application that reads commands typed by the user and interprets them. Typically you read a single line of command into a C string and interpret it. Depending on the syntax of your application's command set, the interpretation might involve such chores as extracting the command and parameters from the string, comparing the command against entries in a stored table, or copying the parameters to separate strings for later use. Although C has no built-in operators for handling strings, the Turbo C++ library has a set of string manipulation routines that provides all the capabilities needed to process strings.

Concepts: Strings in C

C has no basic data type for strings. Instead, strings are treated as arrays of characters, each of which occupies a byte. By convention, the end of a string in C is marked by a byte containing a null character (\0). Because of this, C strings are known as null-terminated strings or ASCIIZ (ASCII characters with a zero marking the end) strings.

DECLARING STRINGS IN C

Since strings are treated as an array of characters, they can be declared in your programs by such a statement as

```
char str1[81], str2[]="A string";
```

Here, *str1* will be a string with room for 81 characters, but because one position is always used by the terminating null (\0), *str1* can hold 80 characters at most. The second string, *str2*, does not show a size, but the compiler can guess its size since it is being initialized. In this case, *str2* takes 9 bytes including the terminating null (see Figure 11-1).

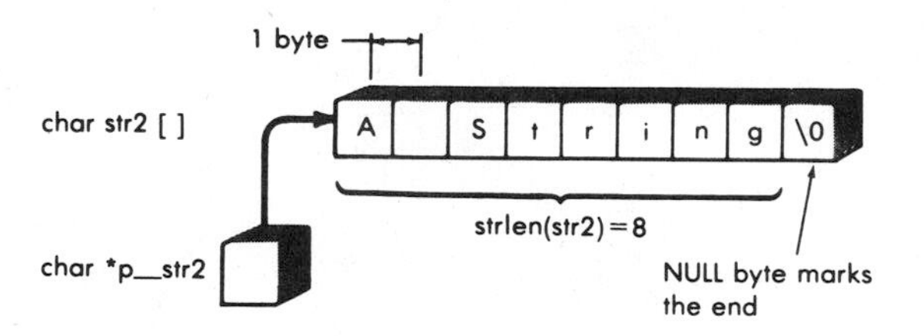

Figure 11-1. *Strings in C*

Another way of accessing a string is through a "pointer," which can hold the address of a variable (see Chapter 1). If you wanted to access the string *str2* using a pointer named *p_str2*, you could use the C code fragment

```
char  str2[] = "A string";
char *p_str2;
p_str2 = str2;
```

Once *p_str2* is initialized, it can be used to access the string in the same manner *str2* is used (see Figure 11-1). Of course, the pointer requires some additional storage space.

You can also declare and initialize a string at the same time with

```
char *p_str = "A string";
```

in which the character pointer *p_str* is initialized to the address of a string constant "A string".

LEXICOGRAPHIC ORDERING

The string comparison routines compare and order strings as they would appear in a dictionary. The comparison is based on the ASCII value of the characters in corresponding bytes of the two strings, but the order of the ASCII codes is such that the collating sequence of the letters correspond to their place in the lexicon. Thus the ordering is known as "lexicographic" ordering.

Notes on String Manipulation

The string manipulation routines provide a host of capabilities. (See Table 11-1 for a catalog.) If you group the capabilities into categories, you will find that most routines are for comparing two strings, copying one string into another, and searching for the occurrence of a character in a string. (See Table 11-2 for a list by task.)

Table 11-1. *String Manipulation Routines*

Routine	Description
stpcpy	Copies one string to another.
strcat	Appends one string to another.
strchr	Locates the first occurrence of a character in a string.
strcmp	Compares one string to another and differentiates between lowercase and uppercase letters.
strcmpi	Compares one string to another without regard to case of the letters.
strcoll	Compares two strings using a collating sequence specified by the LC_COLLATE category of current locale.
strcpy	Copies one string to another.
strcspn	Returns the position in the string of the first character that belongs to a given set of characters.
strdup	Allocates memory and makes a duplicate copy of a string.
strerror	Returns a string containing the system error message corresponding to an error number.
_strerror	Returns a string constructed out of a user-supplied message concatenated to the system error message for the last error that occurred in a library routine.
stricmp	Identical to strcmpi.
strlen	Returns the length of a string as the number of bytes in the string, excluding the terminating null (\0).
strlwr	Converts all characters in a string to lowercase.
strncat	Appends a specified number of characters of one string to another.
strncmp	Compares a specified number of characters of two strings while maintaining the distinction between lowercase and uppercase letters.
strncpy	Copies a specified number of characters from one string to another. (Note that the resulting string will not automatically have a null character appended.)
strnicmp	Compares a specified number of characters of two strings without regard to the case of the letters.
strnset	Copies the same character into a specified number of positions in a string.
strpbrk	Locates the first occurrence of any character from one string in another.
strrchr	Locates the last occurrence of a character in a string.
strrev	Reverses a string.
strset	Copies the same character to every position in a string.
strspn	Returns the position in the string of the first character that does not belong to a given set of characters.
strstr	Locates the first occurrence of one string in another.
strtok	Returns the next token in a string with the token delimiters specified in a string.

Table 11-1. ***(cont.)***

Routine	Description
strupr	Converts all characters in a string to uppercase.
strxfrm	Transforms a string to a new form so that if *strcmp* is applied to two transformed strings the returned result is the same as that returned when *strcoll* is applied to the original strings.

LENGTH OF A STRING

The length of a C string is determined by the number of bytes in the string, not counting the terminating null byte. For example, the string *str2* in Figure 11-1 is 8 bytes long, although 9 bytes are needed to store the entire string.

Table 11-2. ***String Manipulation Routines by Task***

Task	Routines
Find length of a string.	strlen
Compare two strings lexicographically.	strcmp, strcmpi, stricmp, strncmp, strnicmp, strcoll, strxfrm
Copy, append, and duplicate.	stpcpy, strcat, strcpy, strdup, strncat, strncpy
Convert a string from uppercase to lowercase and back.	strlwr, strupr
Search for a character or a substring.	strchr, strcspn, strpbrk, strrchr, strspn, strstr
Extract tokens from a string.	strtok
Load the same character into every position in a string.	strnset, strset
Reverse a string.	strrev
Prepare error message in a string.	strerror, _strerror

COMPARING C STRINGS

Five functions in the library, *strcmp, strcmpi, stricmp, strncmp*, and *strnicmp*, can compare two strings. Each function returns a zero when the strings match. A value less than zero indicates that the first string argument is lexicographically less than the second, which means that it appears before the second one in a dictionary. Similarly, a positive return value indicates that the first string is lexicographically greater than the second.

The routine *strcmp* compares the entire length of two strings, and it differentiates between lowercase and uppercase letters. The *strncmp* function is like *strcmp*, but it only compares a specified number of characters from the beginning of each string.

Identical in function, *strcmpi* and *stricmp* perform like *strcmp* except that they ignore the case of letters when comparing the strings. The *strncmpi* function is a case-insensitive version of *strncmp*. Thus, if we compare the two strings *Turbo* and *TURBO* with *strcmp* it would conclude that *TURBO* is less than *Turbo* (because capital letters come before lowercase in the ASCII code sequence), but *strcmpi* or *stricmp* would find the strings identical and return a zero.

The *strcoll* function is meant for comparing strings using a collating sequence determined by the LC_COLLATE category of the locale (see Chapter 4 for more on locales). The *strxfrm* function is a utility routine that will transform a string into a new form such that if *strcmp* were used to compare two transformed strings the result would be identical to that returned by *strcoll* applied to the original strings.

COPYING, APPENDING, AND DUPLICATING

The *stpcpy, strcat, strcpy, strdup, strncat,* and *strncpy* are for copying, concatenating, and duplicating strings.

The *strcat* function appends the second string argument to the first one, producing a null-terminated string as the result. The *strncat* function is a version of *strcat* that copies only a specified number of characters from the second string to the first.

The *strcpy* function copies the whole second string argument to the first one while *strncpy* only copies a specified number of bytes. When *strncpy* does not copy the entire string, it does not automatically append a null to the result. You must ensure that there is enough room in the first string to hold the second one by declaring an array of characters or by allocating memory at run-time. Because it will perform both steps for you, the *strdup* function is handy. It allocates memory to hold a string and then copies the string into the newly allocated memory. The *stpcpy* works like *strcpy* but returns a pointer to the end of the copied string.

PARSING A COMMAND LINE: EXTRACTING TOKENS

Earlier we alluded to the need for interpretation of application commands. To enable interpretation, you need to separate the command string into its component parts. For example, if you chose a command syntax of the form

```
<COMMAND> <PARAMETER_1> <PARAMETER_2>
```

your command strings will consist of a command word followed by two parameters with blank spaces or tabs as the characters that separate the parts of the command. Now you read a command line of the form

```
copy x y
```

which to your application means copy the value of x into y. In this case, the parts are

```
<COMMAND> = copy
<PARAMETER_1> = x
<PARAMETER_2> = y
```

The process of separating the command line into parts is known as "parsing." Each part is a token.

Extracting Tokens

The C library has routines that help parse a string. The *strtok* function can get the tokens one by one. If you prefer, you can use the routines *strcspn* and *strspn* to construct your own parser, especially if your command language is much more complicated than the one in our example. The *strcspn* function returns the index of the first character (its location in the array) that matches one of the characters in a second string, and *strspn* does just the opposite, returning the first character that does not belong to the second string.

The *strpbrk* routine functions the same as *strcspn*, but it returns a pointer to the matched character rather than the index. The *strstr* function searches for the occurrence of one string in another, and *strchr* and *strrchr* locate a single character in a string. The *strchr* function searches for a character from the beginning, and *strrchr* searches from the end of the string.

Converting Case

Once you parse the command line in our example and get the token <COMMAND>, you can compare that with entries in an internal array of strings to identify the task to be performed. If you decide to store commands in either lowercase or uppercase, you can use either *strlwr* or *strupr* to get the entire command string into lowercase or uppercase, respectively. Following this, you can use *strcmp* to see if the command matches any in your stored table. To avoid the case-conversion step, you would use one of the routines *strcmpi* or *stricmp* that ignore case when performing the string comparison.

MISCELLANEOUS UTILITIES

A few functions in the string manipulation group are hard to categorize. The *strnset* and *strset* functions let you set all positions in a string to the same character; *strnset* sets only a specified number of characters while *strset* works on the whole string. The *strrev* function reverses the characters in a string, and *strerror* and *_strerror* returns a string containing an error message corresponding to an error number.

THE BUFFER MANIPULATION CATEGORY

Since a string is a special kind of buffer, the buffer manipulation routines (see Chapter 7) can also be used to manipulate strings. The reverse is not possible, however, because the string manipulation category always looks for a null byte as the marker indicating the end of a buffer (except for the functions with the *strn* prefix, which take a character count as argument).

Cautions

- When allocating memory for a string, remember to count the null character. If you are allocating memory to hold another copy of a specific string named, say, *str*, you compute the number of bytes you need by adding 1 to the value returned from the call *strlen(str)*.
- When copying a string to another, you must ensure that the destination string has enough room to hold the incoming characters. You will see no error messages if the copy operation continues beyond the last character of the destination string, but the program is likely to fail in a strange way.
- If you use *strncpy* to copy a specific number of bytes—less than the length of the source string—to another one, the resulting string will not have a null character automatically appended to it. So, you have to append a \0 yourself to convert the result to a valid C string.

stpcpy

COMPATIBILITY

TC1	TC1.5	TC2	TC++	MSC3	MSC4	MSC5	MSC6	QC1	QC2	QC2.5	ANSI	UNIX V	XNX
▲	▲	▲	▲										

PURPOSE Use *stpcpy* to copy one string to another. It behaves just like *strcpy*, but the return values are different.

SYNTAX

```
char *stpcpy(char *string1, const char *string2);
```

`char       *string1;` *Destination string*

`const char *string2;` *String to be copied to the first one*

EXAMPLE CALL

```
stpcpy(dos_command, "DIR");
```

INCLUDES `#include <string.h>` *For function prototype*

DESCRIPTION The *stpcpy* function copies the null-terminated C string *string2* to the buffer whose address is given by *string1*. The terminating null character (\0) of the second string is also copied so that *string1* becomes a copy of *string2*.

RETURNS The *stpcpy* function returns a pointer to the end of the copied string, i.e., it returns *string1* + *strlen(string2)*.

COMMENTS The string manipulation routine *stpcpy* is identical to *strcpy* except for the return value.

SEE ALSO

`strcat, strncat` *To concatenate one string to another*

`strcpy` *To copy one string to another*

`strncpy` *To copy a specified number of characters of one string into another*

`strdup` *To allocate storage and create a duplicate copy of a string*

EXAMPLE Write a program to accept a string and copy it into another internal buffer. Use *stpcpy* to do the copying.

```
#include <stdio.h>
#include <string.h>
main()
{
    char str1[80], str2[80];
```

```
    printf("Enter a string: ");
    gets(str2);
    stpcpy(str1, str2);
    printf("String copied. Result is: %s\n", str1);
    return 0;
}
```

COMPATIBILITY

strcat

TC1	TC1.5	TC2	TC++	MSC3	MSC4	MSC5	MSC6	QC1	QC2	QC2.5	ANSI	UNIX V	XNX
▲	▲	▲	▲	▲	▲	▲	▲	▲	▲	▲	▲	▲	▲

PURPOSE Use *strcat* to concatenate (append) one string to another.

SYNTAX

```
char *strcat(char *string1, const char *string2);
```

`char *string1;` *Destination string*

`const char *string2;` *String to be appended to the first one*

EXAMPLE CALL

```
char metoo[7] = "Me ";
strcat(metoo, "too"); /* Result is "Me too" */
```

INCLUDES `#include <string.h>` *For function declaration*

DESCRIPTION The *strcat* function accepts the C strings *string1* and *string2* as arguments. It appends the second string to the first one, terminating the resulting string with a null character (\0). The terminating NULL of the first string is removed and *string1* becomes the concatenation of the old *string1* and *string2*. Note that you are responsible for allocating enough space for the destination string *string1*. If, after appending *string2* to *string1*, the length of the resulting string exceeds the allocated size of *string1*, *strcat* may destroy other data and cause the program to fail.

RETURNS The *strcat* function returns a pointer to the concatenated string (i.e., it returns *string1*).

SEE ALSO

`strncat` *To concatenate a specified number of characters of one string to another*

`strcpy, strncpy` *To copy one string into another*

`strdup` *To allocate storage and create a duplicate of a string*

EXAMPLE Write a program that prompts the user for first name, last name, and middle initial. Then use *strcat* to construct the full name.

```
#include <stdio.h>
#include <string.h>
main()
{
    char fullname[80], last[40], middle[10];
    printf("Enter your first name: ");
    gets(fullname);
    printf("Last name: ");
    gets(last);
    printf("Middle initial: ");
    gets(middle);
/* Append the parts together to get full name */
    strcat(fullname," ");
    strcat(fullname, middle);
    strcat(fullname," ");
    strcat(fullname, last);
    printf("Greetings! %s\n", fullname);
    return 0;
}
```

strchr

COMPATIBILITY

TC1	TC1.5	TC2	TC++	MSC3	MSC4	MSC5	MSC6	QC1	QC2	QC2.5	ANSI	UNIX V	XNX
▲	▲	▲	▲	▲	▲	▲	▲	▲	▲	▲	▲	▲	▲

PURPOSE Use *strchr* to find the first occurrence of a particular character in a given string.

SYNTAX
```
char *strchr(const char *string, int c);
```

`const char *string;` *String to be searched*

`int c;` *Character to be located*

EXAMPLE CALL
```
cost_is = strchr("Estimated cost = $120", '$');
/* Now cost_is will be the C string "$120"  */
```

INCLUDES `#include <string.h>` *For function declaration*

DESCRIPTION The *strchr* function searches for the first occurrence of the character *c* in the C string *string*. The terminating null character is included in the search; it can also be the character to be located.

RETURNS If the character *c* is found, *strchr* returns a pointer to the first occurrence of *c* in *string1*. For example,

```
printf("%s", strchr("Annual salary = $35,750", '$'));
```

will print *$35,750*. If the search fails, *strchr* returns a NULL.

SEE ALSO

`strrchr`	*To locate the last occurrence of a character in a string*
`strcspn, strpbrk`	*To locate the first character in a string that matches one of the characters in another*
`strstr`	*To locate the occurrence of one string in another*

EXAMPLE Prompt the user for a string and a character whose first occurrence in the string will be found by using *strchr*. Display the result of the search.

```
#include <stdio.h>
#include <conio.h>
#include <string.h>
main()
{
    int c;
    char buf[80], *result;
    printf("Enter a string: ");
    gets(buf);
    printf(
"Enter character to be located (first occurrence):");
    c = getche();
    if ((result = strchr(buf, c)) == NULL)
    {
        printf("\n'%c' <-- not in \"%s\"\n", c, buf);
    }
    else
    {
        printf("\n'%c' first occurs at: %s\n",
                                  c, result);
    }
    return 0;
}
```

strcmp

COMPATIBILITY

TC1	TC1.5	TC2	TC++	MSC3	MSC4	MSC5	MSC6	QC1	QC2	QC2.5	ANSI	UNIX V	XNX
▲	▲	▲	▲	▲	▲	▲	▲	▲	▲	▲	▲	▲	▲

PURPOSE Use *strcmp* to compare one string to another. The comparison is case-sensitive.

SYNTAX

```
int strcmp(const char *string1, const char *string2);
```

`const char *string1;` *First string*

`const char *string2;` *Second string*

EXAMPLE CALL

```
if( strcmp(username, "sysmgr") != 0 ) exit(0);
```

INCLUDES `#include <string.h>` *For function declaration*

DESCRIPTION The *strcmp* function accepts the C strings *string1* and *string2* as arguments. It compares the two strings lexicographically and returns an integer value indicating the lexicographic order of *string1* with respect to *string2*. Note that unlike *strcmpi* and *stricmp*, *strcmp* is case-sensitive.

RETURNS The *strcmp* function returns an integer indicating the lexicographic ordering of *string1* with respect to *string2*. The return value is zero if the two strings are identical. If *string1* is less than *string2*, the return value is less than zero. When *string1* is greater than *string2*, *strcmp* returns an integer greater than zero. For example,

```
result = strcmp("ABC", "abc"); /* result less than 0    */
result = strcmp("abc", "abc"); /* result equal to  0    */
result = strcmp("xy",  "abc"); /* result greater than 0 */
```

SEE ALSO

`strncmp` *To compare a specified number of characters of two strings*

`strcmpi, stricmp, strnicmp` *To compare two strings regardless of the case of the characters*

EXAMPLE Write a program that uses *strcmp* to compare two strings typed by the user and display the result.

```
#include <stdio.h>
#include <string.h>
```

```
main()
{
    int result;
    char str1[80], str2[80];
    printf("Enter a string: ");
    gets(str1);
    printf("Enter string to compare with first: ");
    gets(str2);
    printf("Case-sensitive comparison shows that\n");
    result = strcmp(str1, str2);
    if(result == 0)
    {
        printf("\"%s\" == \"%s\"\n", str1, str2);
    }
    if(result < 0)
    {
        printf("\"%s\" < \"%s\"\n", str1, str2);
    }
    if(result > 0)
    {
        printf("\"%s\" > \"%s\"\n", str1, str2);
    }
    return 0;
}
```

strcmpi

COMPATIBILITY

TC1	TC1.5	TC2	TC++	MSC3	MSC4	MSC5	MSC6	QC1	QC2	QC2.5	ANSI	UNIX V	XNX
▲	▲	▲	▲	▲	▲	▲	▲	▲	▲	▲			

PURPOSE Use *strcmpi* to compare one string to another without regard to case.

SYNTAX `int strcmpi(const char *string1, const char *string2);`

`const char *string1;` *First string*

`const char *string2;` *Second string*

EXAMPLE CALL `if( strcmpi(command, "delete") == 0 ) do_delete();`

INCLUDES `#include <string.h>` *For function declaration*

DESCRIPTION The *strcmpi* function first converts all alphabetic characters in strings *string1* and *string2* to lowercase. Then it compares the two strings and returns an integer value indicating the lexicographic order of *string1* with respect to *string2*.

RETURNS The *strcmpi* function returns a zero if the two strings are identical. If *string1* is less than *string2*, the return value is less than zero. When *string1* is greater than *string2*, *strcmpi* returns an integer greater than zero. Thus *strcmpi("XYZ", "xyz");* returns zero.

SEE ALSO

`strnicmp`	*Same as* strcmpi, *but compares only a specified number of characters of the two strings*
`strcmp, strncmp`	*To compare two strings (case-sensitive)*
`stricmp`	*Identical to* strcmpi

EXAMPLE Demonstrate the use of *strcmpi* by comparing two strings entered by user.

```
#include <stdio.h>
#include <string.h>
main()
{
    int result;
    char str1[80], str2[80];
    printf("Enter a string: ");
    gets(str1);
    printf("Enter string to compare with first: ");
    gets(str2);
    printf("Case-insensitive comparison shows that\n");
    result = strcmpi(str1, str2);
    if(result == 0)
    {
        printf("\"%s\" == \"%s\"\n", str1, str2);
    }
    if(result < 0)
    {
        printf("\"%s\" < \"%s\"\n", str1, str2);
    }
    if(result > 0)
    {
        printf("\"%s\" > \"%s\"\n", str1, str2);
    }
    return 0;
}
```

String Comparison and Manipulation

COMPATIBILITY

strcoll

TC1	TC1.5	TC2	TC++	MSC3	MSC4	MSC5	MSC6	QC1	QC2	QC2.5	ANSI	UNIX V	XNX
			▲				▲		▲	▲			

PURPOSE Use the *strcoll* function to compare two strings after interpreting both according to the character collating sequence selected by the LC_COLLATE category of the current locale.

SYNTAX

```
int strcoll(const char *string1, const char *string2);
```

`const char *string1;`	*First null-terminated string*
`const char *string2;`	*Second null-terminated string*

EXAMPLE CALL

```
if( strcoll(username, rootname) != 0 ) exit(EXIT_FAILURE);
```

INCLUDES #include <string.h> *For function declaration*

DESCRIPTION The *strcoll* function is for comparing strings that may not follow the collating sequence implied by the ASCII format. It compares the strings *string1* and *string2* according to the collating sequence specified by the current locale (see Chapter 4). Use *setlocale* to set the current locale.

COMMON USES You can use *strcoll* to compare strings of non-English characters. This helps *internationalize* your programs, so that string comparisons work in languages other than English.

RETURNS The *strcoll* function returns an integer greater than, equal to, or less than 0 according to whether *string1* is greater than, equal to, or less than *string2* when both are interpreted as appropriate to the current locale.

SEE ALSO

`setlocale`	*To set the current locale*
`strcmp, strcmpi, strncmp`	*To compare ASCII strings*
`strxfrm`	*To transform a string so that* strcmp *gives the same results for two transformed strings as does* strcoll *applied to the untransformed ones*

EXAMPLE Here is a program that accepts two strings and compares them using *strcoll.* Note that in the "C" locale (see Chapter 4), there is no difference between using *strcoll* and *strcmp.*

```
#include <stdio.h>
#include <string.h>
main()
{
    int result;
    char str1[80], str2[80];
    printf("Enter a string: ");
    gets(str1);
    printf("Enter string to compare with first: ");
    gets(str2);
    printf("Case-sensitive comparison shows that\n");
    result = strcoll(str1, str2);
    if(result == 0)
    {
        printf("\"%s\" == \"%s\"\n", str1, str2);
    }
    if(result < 0)
    {
        printf("\"%s\" < \"%s\"\n", str1, str2);
    }
    if(result > 0)
    {
        printf("\"%s\" > \"%s\"\n", str1, str2);
    }
    return 0;
}
```

strcpy

COMPATIBILITY

TC1	TC1.5	TC2	TC++	MSC3	MSC4	MSC5	MSC6	QC1	QC2	QC2.5	ANSI	UNIX V	XNX
▲	▲	▲	▲	▲	▲	▲	▲	▲	▲	▲	▲	▲	▲

PURPOSE Use *strcpy* to copy one string to another.

SYNTAX `char *strcpy(char *string1, const char *string2);`

`char *string1;` *Destination string*

`const char *string2;` *String to be copied to the first one*

EXAMPLE CALL `strcpy(dos_command, "DIR");`

INCLUDES `#include <string.h>` *For function declaration*

DESCRIPTION The *strcpy* function copies the string *string2* to the buffer whose address is given by *string1*. The terminating null character of the second string is also copied so *string1* becomes an exact copy of *string2*.

RETURNS The *strcpy* function returns a pointer to the copied string (i.e., it returns *string1*).

COMMENTS The string manipulation routines *strcpy* and *strncpy* can be harmful to your program if you forget to allocate enough room in the buffer *string1* for the entire destination string, including the terminating null character. If, after appending *string2* to *string1*, the length of the resulting string exceeds the allocated size of *string1*, *strcpy* may destroy other data and cause the program to fail.

SEE ALSO

`stpcpy`	*To copy one string to another and return a pointer to the end of the string*
`strcat, strncat`	*To concatenate one string to another*
`strncpy`	*To copy a specified number of characters of one string into another*
`strdup`	*To allocate storage and create a duplicate copy of a string*

EXAMPLE Write a program to accept a string and use *strcpy* to copy it into another internal buffer.

```
#include <stdio.h>
#include <string.h>
main()
{
    char str1[80], str2[80];
    printf("Enter a string: ");
    gets(str2);
    strcpy(str1, str2);
    printf("String copied. Result is: %s\n", str1);
    return 0;
}
```

strcspn

COMPATIBILITY

TC1	TC1.5	TC2	TC++	MSC3	MSC4	MSC5	MSC6	QC1	QC2	QC2.5	ANSI	UNIX V	XNX
▲	▲	▲	▲	▲	▲	▲	▲	▲	▲	▲	▲	▲	▲

PURPOSE Use *strcspn* to locate the position of the first occurrence in a string of any character from another.

SYNTAX

```
size_t strcspn(const char *string1, const char *string2);
```

`const char *string1;` *String to be searched*

`const char *string2;` *String describing set of characters to be located*

EXAMPLE CALL

```
first_q = strcspn("soliloquy", "q"); /* first_q = 6 */
```

INCLUDES `#include <string.h>` *For function declaration*

DESCRIPTION The *strcspn* function locates the first occurrence in *string1* of any character other than the terminating null in *string2*.

RETURNS If successful, the *strcspn* function returns the index of the first character in *string1* that belongs to the set of characters *string2*. Thus this value is the length of the initial substring of *string1* that consists of characters *not* in *string2* (i.e., the substring that does not "span" the character set *string2*).

If *string1* begins with a character from *string2*, the return value is zero. If *string1* is devoid of characters from *string2*, *strcspn* returns the length of *string1*.

SEE ALSO

`strpbrk` *To search for the first occurrence of any character from one string in another*

`strspn` *To find the length of the initial substring made up entirely of characters in another string*

EXAMPLE Prompt the user for a string with some embedded blank spaces. Then use *strcspn* to locate the first occurrence of a space or tab character in the string. This can be used to identify tokens in a string.

```
#include <stdio.h>
#include <string.h>
char *whitespace = " \t\n";
main()
{
    int loc;
    char str1[80];
```

```
    printf("Enter a string with embedded blanks: ");
    gets(str1);
    loc = strcspn(str1, whitespace);
    printf("First whitespace (blank, tab or newline) in"
           "\n%s\n is at location %d\n", str1, loc);
    return 0;
}
```

COMPATIBILITY

strdup

TC1	TC1.5	TC2	TC++	MSC3	MSC4	MSC5	MSC6	QC1	QC2	QC2.5	ANSI	UNIX V	XNX
▲	▲	▲	▲	▲	▲	▲	▲	▲	▲	▲			

PURPOSE Use *strdup* to allocate memory and copy a given string into that space.

SYNTAX `char *strdup(const char *string);`

`const char *string;` *String to be duplicated*

EXAMPLE CALL `saved_command = strdup(command);`

INCLUDES `#include <string.h>` *For function declaration*

DESCRIPTION The *strdup* function first calls *malloc* to allocate enough memory to hold *string*. It then copies the string into the newly allocated buffer.

RETURNS If the *strdup* function succeeds, it returns a pointer to the new copy of the string. If memory allocation fails, *strdup* returns a NULL.

SEE ALSO `strcat, strncat` *To concatenate one string to another*

`strcpy, strncpy` *To copy one string into another*

EXAMPLE Read in a string and make a duplicate by calling the function *strdup*.

```
#include <stdio.h>
#include <string.h>
main()
{
    char str1[80], *str1_copy;
    printf("Enter a string: ");
    gets(str1);
    str1_copy = strdup(str1);
```

```
    printf("String duplicated. Result is: %s\n",
            str1_copy);
    return 0;
}
```

strerror

COMPATIBILITY

TC1	TC1.5	TC2	TC++	MSC3	MSC4	MSC5	MSC6	QC1	QC2	QC2.5	ANSI	UNIX V	XNX
	▲	▲	▲		▲	▲	▲	▲	▲	▲	▲		

PURPOSE Use *strerror* to retrieve an error message corresponding to an error number.

SYNTAX

```
char *strerror(int errnum);

int errnum;        Error number
```

EXAMPLE CALL

```
error_message = strerror(errno);
```

INCLUDES

```
#include <string.h>        For function declaration
```

DESCRIPTION The *strerror* function finds the system error message corresponding to the error number given in the argument *errnum*. The *strerror* function gets the system error message by using the value in the global variable *errno* as the index of a table of error messages called *sys_errlist*, which is declared in the header file *stdlib.h*. In a typical use, you should call *strerror* immediately after an error return from a library routine and provide the value of *errno* as the argument. Note that *strerror* only returns the error message; printing the message is up to you.

RETURNS The *strerror* function returns a pointer to the error message from the table *sys_errlist*.

SEE ALSO

`_strerror` *To construct an error message by appending the system message to one supplied by you*

`perror` *To print an error message*

EXAMPLE Write a program in which you create an error by attempting to close a nonexistent file handle (say, 100). Once the error occurs, call *strerror* with *errno* as argument and print the error message returned by *strerror*. Note that *stdlib.h* is included to provide the appropriate declaration of *errno*.

```
#include <stdio.h>
#include <stdlib.h>
#include <io.h>
#include <string.h>
main()
{
    int handle=100;
    char *errmsg;
/* Generate an error condition by closing a
 * file with nonexistent handle 100
 */
    if(close(handle) == -1)
    {
        errmsg = strerror(errno);
        printf("Error closing file: %s", errmsg);
    }
    return 0;
}
```

COMPATIBILITY

_strerror

TC1	TC1.5	TC2	TC++	MSC3	MSC4	MSC5	MSC6	QC1	QC2	QC2.5	ANSI	UNIX V	XNX
	▲	▲	▲			▲	▲	▲	▲	▲			

PURPOSE Use *_strerror* to construct an error message consisting of your message concatenated with a system message corresponding to the last error that occurred in a library routine.

SYNTAX

```
char *_strerror(const char *string);
```

`char *string;` *String containing user-supplied error message*

EXAMPLE CALL

```
error_message = _strerror("Error opening file");
```

INCLUDES `#include <string.h>` *For function declaration*

DESCRIPTION The *_strerror* function constructs an error message by appending a colon to the contents of *string* and appending a system message that corresponds to the last error occurring in a library routine. The length of *string* can be at most 94 bytes. If *string* is NULL, the message constructed by *_strerror* only contains the system message. The message always has a newline character (\n) at the end.

The _strerror function gets the system error message by using the value in the global variable *errno* as the index of a table of error messages called *sys_errlist*. You should call _strerror immediately after a library routine returns with an error. Otherwise, subsequent calls to other routines may overwrite the value of *errno*. Note that _strerror only prepares the error message; printing the message is up to you.

RETURNS The _strerror function returns a pointer to the error message it constructed.

SEE ALSO

`strerror` *To get system message corresponding to error number (ANSI version)*

`perror` *To print an error message*

EXAMPLE Write a program that illustrates the use of _strerror to construct error messages. Generate an error by attempting to duplicate the file handle 100 (a file not yet open). Display the error message returned by _strerror.

```
#include <stdio.h>
#include <io.h>
#include <string.h>
main()
{
    int handle=100;
    char *errmsg;
/* Generate an error condition by attempting to
 * duplicate a unused file handle (100)
 */
    if(dup(handle) == -1)
    {
        errmsg = _strerror("Error duplicating handle");
        printf(errmsg);
    }
    return 0;
}
```

COMPATIBILITY

stricmp

TC1	TC1.5	TC2	TC++	MSC3	MSC4	MSC5	MSC6	QC1	QC2	QC2.5	ANSI	UNIX V	XNX
▲	▲	▲	▲		▲	▲	▲	▲	▲	▲			

PURPOSE Use *stricmp* to compare one string to another without regard to the case of the letters.

SYNTAX

```
int stricmp(const char *string1, const char *string2);
```

`const char *string1;` *First string*

`const char *string2;` *Second string*

EXAMPLE CALL

```
if( stricmp(answer, "yes") == 0 ) delete_file(fname);
```

INCLUDES `#include <string.h>` *For function declaration*

DESCRIPTION The *stricmp* function converts all alphabetic characters in *string1* and *string2* to lowercase. Then it compares the two strings and returns an integer value indicating the lexicographic order of *string1* with respect to *string2*.

RETURNS The *stricmp* function returns an integer indicating the lexicographic ordering of *string1* with respect to *string2* after all alphabetic characters have been converted to lowercase. The return value is zero if the two strings are identical. If *string1* is less than *string2*, the return value is less than zero. When *string1* is greater than *string2*, *stricmp* returns an integer greater than zero.

SEE ALSO

`strnicmp` *Same as* stricmp, *but compares only a specified number of characters of the two strings*

`strcmp, strncmp` *To compare two strings (case-sensitive)*

`strcmpi` *Identical to* stricmp

EXAMPLE Write a program that uses *stricmp* to perform a comparison of two strings, regardless of cases.

```
#include <stdio.h>
#include <string.h>
main()
{
```

```
        int result;
        char str1[80], str2[80];
        printf("Enter a string: ");
        gets(str1);
        printf("Enter string to compare with first: ");
        gets(str2);
        printf("Case-insensitive comparison shows that\n");
        result = stricmp(str1, str2);
        if(result == 0)
        {
            printf("\"%s\" == \"%s\"\n", str1, str2);
        }
        if(result < 0)
        {
            printf("\"%s\" < \"%s\"\n", str1, str2);
        }
        if(result > 0)
        {
            printf("\"%s\" > \"%s\"\n", str1, str2);
        }
        return 0;
}
```

strlen

COMPATIBILITY

TC1	TC1.5	TC2	TC++	MSC3	MSC4	MSC5	MSC6	QC1	QC2	QC2.5	ANSI	UNIX V	XNX
▲	▲	▲	▲	▲	▲	▲	▲	▲	▲	▲	▲	▲	▲

PURPOSE Use *strlen* to find the length of a string in bytes, not counting the terminating null character.

SYNTAX

```
size_t strlen(const char *string);

const char *string;        String whose length is to be returned
```

EXAMPLE CALL

```
length = strlen(name);
```

INCLUDES

```
#include <string.h>        For function declaration
```

DESCRIPTION The *strlen* function counts the number of bytes in *string*, not including the terminating null character.

RETURNS The *strlen* function returns the length in bytes of *string*.

EXAMPLE Use *strlen* to determine and print the length of a string.

```
#include <stdio.h>
#include <string.h>
main()
{
    size_t len;
    char buf[80];
    printf("Enter a string: ");
    gets(buf);
    len = strlen(buf);
    printf("The length of the string is: %u\n", len);
    return 0;
}
```

COMPATIBILITY

strlwr

TC1	TC1.5	TC2	TC++	MSC3	MSC4	MSC5	MSC6	QC1	QC2	QC2.5	ANSI	UNIX V	XNX
▲	▲	▲	▲	▲	▲	▲	▲	▲	▲	▲			

PURPOSE Use *strlwr* to convert any uppercase letters in a string to lowercase.

SYNTAX

```
char *strlwr(char *string);
```

`char *string;` *String to be converted to lowercase*

EXAMPLE CALL

```
char command[]= "QUIT";
strlwr(command); /* Now command = "quit" */
```

INCLUDES `#include <string.h>` *For function declaration*

DESCRIPTION The *strlwr* function converts any uppercase letters in the *string* to lowercase. Other characters in the string are unaffected.

RETURNS The *strlwr* function returns a pointer to the converted string, (i.e., it returns *string*).

COMMENTS The *strlwr* routine and its companion *strupr* are not part of the ANSI standard C library. You can implement your own versions of these using the macros *tolower* and *toupper*, respectively.

SEE ALSO `strupr` *To convert a string to uppercase*

`tolower` *To convert a single uppercase letter to lowercase*

EXAMPLE Use *strlwr* to convert a string to lowercase.

```
#include <stdio.h>
#include <string.h>
main()
{
    char buf[80];
    printf("Enter a string with uppercase letters: ");
    gets(buf);
    strlwr(buf);
    printf("The string in lowercase is:\n%s\n", buf);
    return 0;
}
```

strncat

COMPATIBILITY

TC1	TC1.5	TC2	TC++	MSC3	MSC4	MSC5	MSC6	QC1	QC2	QC2.5	ANSI	UNIX V	XNX
▲	▲	▲	▲	▲	▲	▲	▲	▲	▲	▲	▲	▲	▲

PURPOSE Use *strncat* to concatenate a specified number of characters of one string to another.

SYNTAX

```
char *strncat(char *string1, const char *string2, size_t n);
```

`char *string1;` *Destination string*

`const char *string2;` *String whose first* n *characters are to be appended to the destination string*

`size_t n;` *Number of characters of* string2 *to be appended to* string1

EXAMPLE CALL

```
char id[16] = "ID = ";
strncat(id, name, 10); /* id is first 10 char of name */
```

INCLUDES `#include <string.h>` *For function declaration*

DESCRIPTION The *strncat* function appends the first *n* characters of *string2* to *string1* and terminates the resulting string with a null character. The terminating null of the first string is removed and *string1* becomes the resulting concatenation. If *n* is larger than the length of *string2*, the entire second string is appended to *string1*.

RETURNS The *strncat* function returns a pointer to the concatenated string (i.e., it returns *string1*).

SEE ALSO

strcat	*To concatenate one string to another*
strcpy, strncpy	*To copy one string into another*
strdup	*To allocate storage and create a duplicate string*

EXAMPLE Use *strncat* to generate and print the sequence of strings:

```
a
ab
abc
abcd
...
...
abcdefghijklmnopqrstuvwxyz

#include <stdio.h>
#include <string.h>
char result[40] = "a";
char rest[]= "bcdefghijklmnopqrstuvwxyz";
unsigned length = sizeof(rest)/sizeof(char);
main()
{
    unsigned i;
    for(i = 0; i<length; i++, result[1]='\0')
    {
        strncat(result, rest, i);
/* Show the current result */
        printf("%s\n", result);
    }
    return 0;
}
```

strncmp

COMPATIBILITY

TC1	TC1.5	TC2	TC++	MSC3	MSC4	MSC5	MSC6	QC1	QC2	QC2.5	ANSI	UNIX V	XNX
▲	▲	▲	▲	▲	▲	▲	▲	▲	▲	▲	▲	▲	▲

PURPOSE Use *strncmp* to compare a specified number of characters of two strings to one another. The comparison is case-sensitive.

SYNTAX

```
int strncmp(const char *string1, const char *string2, size_t n);
```

`const char *string1;`	*First string*
`const char *string2;`	*Second string*
`size_t n;`	*Number of characters of strings to be compared*

EXAMPLE CALL

```
if(strncmp(command, "quit", 2) == 0) quit_program();
```

INCLUDES `#include <string.h>` *For function declaration*

DESCRIPTION The *strncmp* function compares the first *n* characters of *string1* and *string2*. The result of the case-sensitive comparison is returned as an integer value indicating the lexicographic order of the first *n* characters of *string1* with respect to the same part of *string2*.

RETURNS The *strncmp* function returns an integer indicating the lexicographic ordering of the first *n* characters of *string1* with respect to the same part of *string2*. The return value will be zero if the two substrings are identical. If *substring1* is less than *substring2*, the return value is less than zero. When *substring1* is greater than *substring2*, *strncmp* returns an integer greater than zero.

SEE ALSO

`strcmp`	*To compare two strings*
`strncmpi, stricmp, strnicmp`	*To compare two strings disregarding the case of the characters*

EXAMPLE Write a program that accepts two strings and specifies the number of characters that are to be compared. Use *strncmp* to perform the comparison and then display the result.

```
#include <stdio.h>
#include <string.h>
main()
```

```
{
    int len, result;
    char str1[80], str2[80];
    printf("Enter a string: ");
    gets(str1);
    printf("Enter string to compare with first: ");
    gets(str2);
    printf("How many characters to compare:");
    scanf(" %d", &len);
    printf("Based on case-sensitive comparison of \
the first %d characters\n", len);
    result = strncmp(str1, str2, len);
    if(result == 0)
    {
        printf("\"%s\" == \"%s\"\n", str1, str2);
    }
    if(result < 0)
    {
        printf("\"%s\" < \"%s\"\n", str1, str2);
    }
    if(result > 0)
    {
        printf("\"%s\" > \"%s\"\n", str1, str2);
    }
    return 0;
}
```

COMPATIBILITY

strncpy

TC1	TC1.5	TC2	TC++	MSC3	MSC4	MSC5	MSC6	QC1	QC2	QC2.5	ANSI	UNIX V	XNX
▲	▲	▲	▲	▲	▲	▲	▲	▲	▲	▲	▲	▲	▲

PURPOSE Use *strncpy* to copy a specified number of characters of one string to another.

SYNTAX

```
char *strncpy(char *string1, const char *string2, size_t n);
```

`char *string1;` *Destination string*

`const char *string2;` *String whose first* n *characters are to be copied to the destination string*

`size_t n;` *Number of characters to be copied*

EXAMPLE CALL
```
strncpy(fname, "tmp12345678", 8); /* fname = "tmp12345" */
```

INCLUDES `#include <string.h>` *For function declaration*

DESCRIPTION The *strncpy* function copies the first *n* characters of *string2* to the buffer whose address is given by *string1*. The copy is placed starting at the first character position of *string1*. If *n* is less than the length of *string2*, no terminating null character is appended to *string1*. If *n* exceeds the length of *string2*, however, *string1* is padded with null characters until it is *n* bytes long.

You should avoid situations where the *n* bytes following *string1* overlap *string2* because the behavior of *strcpy* with such arguments is not guaranteed to be correct.

RETURNS The *strncpy* function returns a pointer to the copied string (i.e., it returns *string1*).

SEE ALSO

`strcat, strncat` *To concatenate one string to another*

`strcpy` *To copy one string into another*

`strdup` *To allocate storage and create a duplicate of a string*

EXAMPLE Read in a string and copy the first half into another buffer using *strncat*. Note that no null character is appended to the copied string so you have to add one if you want to use it as a C string (for example, when you print it using *printf*).

```
#include <stdio.h>
#include <string.h>
main()
{
    size_t len;
    char str1[80], str2[80];
    printf("Enter a string: ");
    gets(str2);
    len = strlen(str2)/2;
    strncpy(str1, str2, len);
/* Since '\0' is not appended automatically, we have
 * to do so before printing string
 */
    str1[len] = '\0';
    printf("Half the length of string copied. Result:\
 %s\n", str1);
    return 0;
}
```

String Comparison and Manipulation

COMPATIBILITY

strnicmp

TC1	TC1.5	TC2	TC++	MSC3	MSC4	MSC5	MSC6	QC1	QC2	QC2.5	ANSI	UNIX V	XNX
▲	▲	▲	▲		▲	▲	▲	▲	▲	▲			

PURPOSE Use *strnicmp* to compare a specified number of characters of two strings without regard to case.

SYNTAX

```
int strnicmp(const char *string1, const char *string2, size_t n);
```

`const char *string1;` *First string*

`const char *string2;` *Second string*

`size_t n;` *Number of characters of strings to be compared*

EXAMPLE CALL

```
if (strnicmp(command, "exit", 2) == 0) exit_program();
```

INCLUDES `#include <string.h>` *For function declaration*

DESCRIPTION The *strnicmp* function compares the first *n* characters of *string1* with the corresponding ones in *string2*, but the comparison is case-insensitive. The result of this comparison is returned as an integer value indicating the lexicographic ordering of the first *n* characters of *string1* with respect to *string2*.

RETURNS The *strnicmp* function returns zero if the two substrings are identical. If *substring1* is less than *substring2*, the return value is less than zero. When *substring1* is greater than *substring2*, *strnicmp* returns an integer greater than zero.

SEE ALSO `strcmpi, stricmp` *To compare two strings (case-sensitive)*

`strcmp, strncmp` *To compare two strings (case-sensitive)*

EXAMPLE Use *strnicmp* in a program that compares two strings without regard to case. Let the program accept two strings and the number of characters to compare and then display the result of the comparison.

```
#include <stdio.h>
#include <string.h>
main()
{
    int len, result;
    char str1[80], str2[80];
```

```
    printf("Enter a string: ");
    gets(str1);
    printf("Enter string to compare with first: ");
    gets(str2);
    printf("How many characters to compare:");
    scanf(" %d", &len);
    printf("Based on case-insensitive comparison of
the first %d characters\n", len);
    result = strnicmp(str1, str2, len);
    if(result == 0)
    {
        printf("\"%s\" == \"%s\"\n", str1, str2);
    }
    if(result < 0)
    {
        printf("\"%s\" < \"%s\"\n", str1, str2);
    }
    if(result > 0)
    {
        printf("\"%s\" > \"%s\"\n", str1, str2);
    }
    return 0;
}
```

strnset

COMPATIBILITY

TC1	TC1.5	TC2	TC++	MSC3	MSC4	MSC5	MSC6	QC1	QC2	QC2.5	ANSI	UNIX V	XNX
▲	▲	▲	▲	▲	▲	▲	▲	▲	▲	▲			

PURPOSE Use *strnset* to set a specified number of characters in a string, excluding the terminating null, to a specific character value.

SYNTAX
```
char *strnset(char *string, int c, size_t n);
```

`char *string;` *String whose first* n *characters are to be set to* c

`int c;` *Value to be copied into first* n *character positions of* string

`size_t n;` *Number of characters to be set*

EXAMPLE CALL
```
strnset(all_zzz, 'z', 40);
```

INCLUDES `#include <string.h>` *For function declaration*

DESCRIPTION The *strnset* function copies the character in the integer *c* to the first *n* character positions in *string*. If *n* exceeds the length of the string, all character positions, except the last one (the terminating null character), are set.

RETURNS The *strnset* function returns a pointer to the altered string (i.e., it returns *string*).

SEE ALSO `strset` *To set all characters of a string to a specific character value*

EXAMPLE Use *strnset* to fill the first half of a string entered by the user with a character also entered by the user.

```
#include <stdio.h>
#include <conio.h>
#include <string.h>
main()
{
    int c;
    size_t len;
    char buf[80];

    printf("Enter a string: ");
    gets(buf);
    printf(
"Enter character you want half the string set to:");
    c = getche();
    len = strlen(buf)/2;
/* Set first half of string to character in c */
    strnset(buf, c, len);
    printf("\nString is now: %s\n", buf);
    return 0;
}
```

strpbrk

COMPATIBILITY

TC1	TC1.5	TC2	TC++	MSC3	MSC4	MSC5	MSC6	QC1	QC2	QC2.5	ANSI	UNIX V	XNX
▲	▲	▲	▲	▲	▲	▲	▲	▲	▲	▲	▲	▲	▲

PURPOSE Use *strpbrk* to locate the first occurrence of any of the characters from one string in another string.

SYNTAX `char *strpbrk(const char *string1, const char *string2);`

```
const char *string1;
```
String to be searched

```
const char *string2;
```
String describing set of characters to be located

EXAMPLE CALL
```
first_vowel = strpbrk(word, "aeiou");
```

INCLUDES
```
#include <string.h>
```
For function declaration

DESCRIPTION The *strpbrk* function searches for the first occurrence in *string1* of any of the characters from *string2*. The terminating null is not included in the search.

RETURNS If successful, the *strpbrk* function returns a pointer to the first occurrence of any character from *string2* in *string1*. If the search fails, *strpbrk* returns a NULL. Failure implies that *string1* and *string2* have no characters in common.

SEE ALSO

`strchr` *To search for the first occurrence of a character in a string*

`strcspn` *To locate the first character in a string that matches one of the characters in another*

EXAMPLE Use *strpbrk* to locate the first occurrence of a vowel in a word and print the word up to and including the vowel (this will tend to extract the first syllable from the word).

```
#include <stdio.h>
#include <string.h>
char *vowels = "aeiou";
main()
{
    char str1[80], *result;
    printf("Enter a word: ");
    gets(str1);
    if ((result = strpbrk(str1, vowels)) == NULL)
    {
        printf("No vowels in word\n");
    }
    else
    {
        printf("First syllable in %s ", str1);
/* Put a null character just after the first vowel */
        result++;
        *result = '\0';
```

```
        printf("is: %s\n", str1);
    }
    return 0;
}
```

COMPATIBILITY

strrchr

TC1	TC1.5	TC2	TC++	MSC3	MSC4	MSC5	MSC6	QC1	QC2	QC2.5	ANSI	UNIX V	XNX
▲	▲	▲	▲	▲	▲	▲	▲	▲	▲	▲	▲	▲	▲

PURPOSE Use *strrchr* to find the last occurrence of a particular character in a given string.

SYNTAX
```
char *strrchr(const char *string, int c);

const char *string;      String to be searched

int c;                   Character to be located
```

EXAMPLE CALL
```
char line_cost[]= "10 units at $1.20 ea. = $12.00";
total_cost = strrchr(line_cost, '$');
/* Now total_cost will be the string "$12.00" */
```

INCLUDES `#include <string.h>` *For function declaration*

DESCRIPTION The *strrchr* function searches for the last occurrence of the character *c* in *string*. The terminating null character is included in the search and can be the character to be located.

RETURNS If the character *c* is found, *strrchr* returns a pointer to the last occurrence of *c* in *string*. If the search fails, *strrchr* returns a NULL.

SEE ALSO `strchr` *To locate the first occurrence of a character in a string*

EXAMPLE Write a program that accepts a date in the form "MM/DD/YY" and uses *strrchr* to locate the last occurrence of the / character and print the returned string as a year.

```
#include <stdio.h>
#include <string.h>
main()
{
    char buf[80], *result;
```

```
    printf("Enter date: ");
    gets(buf);
    if ((result = strrchr(buf, '/')) == NULL)
    {
        printf("%s <-- not a date!\n", buf);
    }
    else
    {
        result++;    /* Skip the '/' */
        printf("The year is: 19%s\n", result);
    }
    return 0;
}
```

strrev

COMPATIBILITY

TC1	TC1.5	TC2	TC++	MSC3	MSC4	MSC5	MSC6	QC1	QC2	QC2.5	ANSI	UNIX V	XNX
▲	▲	▲	▲	▲	▲	▲	▲	▲	▲	▲			

PURPOSE Use *strrev* to reverse the order of characters in a string.

SYNTAX

```
char *strrev(char *string);

char *string;      String to be reversed
```

EXAMPLE CALL

```
strrev(input_string);
```

INCLUDES

```
#include <string.h>      For function declaration
```

DESCRIPTION The *strrev* function reverses the order of the characters in *string*. The terminating null character remains at the same place.

RETURNS The *strrev* function returns a pointer to the reversed string (it returns the argument *string*).

SEE ALSO `strcpy, strncpy`   *To copy one string to another*

EXAMPLE Use *strrev* to reverse a string typed at the keyboard and print the result. One use of this program is to check whether a string is a "palindrome," that is, whether it reads the same backward and forward.

```
#include <stdio.h>
#include <string.h>
```

```
main()
{
    char buf[80];
    printf("Enter a string: ");
    gets(buf);
    strrev(buf);
    printf("Reversed string is:\n%s\n", buf);
    return 0;
}
```

COMPATIBILITY

strset

TC1	TC1.5	TC2	TC++	MSC3	MSC4	MSC5	MSC6	QC1	QC2	QC2.5	ANSI	UNIX V	XNX
▲	▲	▲	▲	▲	▲	▲	▲	▲	▲	▲	▲	▲	▲

PURPOSE Use *strset* to set all characters in a string, excluding the terminating null, to a specific character value.

SYNTAX

```
char *strset(char *string, int c);
```

`char *string;` *String to be set to* c

`int c;` *Value to be copied into each character position of* string

EXAMPLE CALL

```
char password[16];
strset(password, 'x'); /* Set password to all 'x' */
```

INCLUDES `#include <string.h>` *For function declaration*

DESCRIPTION The *strset* function copies the character in the integer *c* to every character position in *string*, except the terminating null character. This is useful for setting a string to blanks or other default values.

RETURNS The *strset* function returns a pointer to the altered string (i.e, it returns *string*).

SEE ALSO `strnset` *To set a specified number of characters of a string to a specific character value*

EXAMPLE Write a C program that reads in a string from the keyboard, prompts for a fill character, and uses *strset* to set the entire string to that character. Then the program displays the result.

```
#include <stdio.h>
#include <conio.h>
#include <string.h>
main()
{
    int c;
    char buf[80];
    printf("Enter a string: ");
    gets(buf);
    printf(
"Enter character you want entire string set to:");
    c = getche();
    strset(buf, c);
    printf("\nString is now: %s\n", buf);
    return 0;
}
```

strspn

COMPATIBILITY

TC1	TC1.5	TC2	TC++	MSC3	MSC4	MSC5	MSC6	QC1	QC2	QC2.5	ANSI	UNIX V	XNX
▲	▲	▲	▲	▲	▲	▲	▲	▲	▲	▲	▲	▲	▲

PURPOSE Use *strspn* to locate the position of the first character in a string that does not belong to the set of characters in another.

SYNTAX

```
size_t strspn(const char *string1, const char *string2);
```

`const char *string1;` *String to be searched*

`const char *string2;` *String describing set of characters*

EXAMPLE CALL

```
    char *input = "280ZX";
    first_nondigit_at = strspn(input, "1234567890");
/* first_nondigit_at will be  3 */
```

INCLUDES `#include <string.h>` *For function declaration*

DESCRIPTION The *strspn* function locates the first character in *string1* that is not present in *string2*. The terminating null is not included in the search.

RETURNS If successful, the *strspn* function returns the index of the first character in *string1* that does not belong to the set of characters in *string2*. Thus, this value is the length of the initial substring of *string1* that consists entirely of

characters in *string2*, i.e., the substring that spans the character set in *string2*.

If *string1* begins with a character that does not appear in *string2*, the return value is zero. On the other hand, if *string1* only contains characters from *string2*, *strspn* returns the length of *string1*.

SEE ALSO

`strpbrk`	*To search for the first occurrence of any of the characters from one string in another string*
`strcspn`	*To find the length of the initial substring that is made up entirely of characters not in another string*

EXAMPLE Read in a string and use *strspn* to locate the first nonwhitespace character in the string.

```
#include <stdio.h>
#include <string.h>
/*space, tab and newline are the whitespace characters */
char *whitespace = " \t\n";
main()
{
    int loc;
    char str1[80];
    printf("Enter a string with preceding blanks: ");
    gets(str1);
    loc = strspn(str1, whitespace);
    printf("First non-whitespace character in\
\n%s\n is at location %d\n", str1, loc);
    return 0;
}
```

strstr

COMPATIBILITY

TC1	TC1.5	TC2	TC++	MSC3	MSC4	MSC5	MSC6	QC1	QC2	QC2.5	ANSI	UNIX V	XNX
▲	▲	▲	▲	▲	▲	▲	▲	▲	▲	▲	▲		

PURPOSE Use *strstr* to locate the first occurrence of one string in another.

SYNTAX `char *strstr(const char *string1, const char *string2);`

`const char *string1;`	*String to be searched*
`const char *string2;`	*String to be located*

EXAMPLE CALL

```
    char input[]="The account number is MSCB-87-08-01";
    acc_no = strstr(input, "MSCB");
/* Now the string acc_no will be "MSCB-87-08-01" */
```

INCLUDES `#include <string.h>` *For function declaration*

DESCRIPTION The *strstr* function searches for the first occurrence of *string2* in *string1.*

RETURNS If successful, the *strstr* function returns a pointer to the first occurrence of *string2* as a substring in *string1.* If the search fails, *strstr* returns a NULL.

SEE ALSO

`strchr`	*To search for the first occurrence of a character in a string*
`strcspn, strpbrk`	*To locate the first character in a string that matches one of the characters in another string*

EXAMPLE Read in a string and then a substring that you want to find in the first string. Use *strstr* to perform the search. Display the results of the search.

```
#include <stdio.h>
#include <string.h>
main()
{
    char str1[80], str2[80], *result;
    printf("Enter a string: ");
    gets(str1);
    printf("Enter string to locate in the first: ");
    gets(str2);
    if((result = strstr(str1, str2)) == NULL)
    {
        printf("\"%s\" NOT IN \"%s\"\n", str2, str1);
    }
    else
    {
        printf("\"%s\" FOUND.\n\Rest of string: %s\n",
               str2, result);
    }
    return 0;
}
```

COMPATIBILITY **strtok**

TC1	TC1.5	TC2	TC++	MSC3	MSC4	MSC5	MSC6	QC1	QC2	QC2.5	ANSI	UNIX V	XNX
▲	▲	▲	▲	▲	▲	▲	▲	▲	▲	▲	▲	▲	▲

PURPOSE Use *strtok* to get the next token, or substring, in a string delimited by any character from a second string.

SYNTAX

```
char *strtok(char *string1, const char *string2);
```

`char *string1;` *String from which tokens are returned*

`const char *string2;` *String describing set of characters that delimit tokens*

EXAMPLE CALL

```
next_token = strtok(input, "\t, ");
```

INCLUDES `#include <string.h>` *For function declaration*

DESCRIPTION The *strtok* function isolates a token, or substring, from *string1*. The token is marked by delimiting characters given in the second string argument *string2*. All tokens in a particular string *string1* can be extracted through successive calls to *strtok* in the following way. Make the first call to *strtok* with the string to be "tokenized" as the first argument. Provide as the second argument a C string composed from the delimiting characters. After that, call *strtok* with a NULL as the first argument and the delimiting characters appropriate for that token in the second string. This tells *strtok* to continue returning tokens from the old *string1*. The example below illustrates how this is done.

Note that the set of delimiters can change in each call to *strtok*. In the process of separating tokens, *strtok* modifies the string *string1*. It inserts null characters in place of delimiters to convert tokens to C strings.

COMMON USES The *strtok* function is handy when you are developing an application in which the user enters commands using a specified syntax. The routine that parses the command lines can use *strtok* to isolate the tokens. Quite complex syntax can be accommodated by using a different set of delimiters for each token.

RETURNS The first call to *strtok* with the argument *string1* returns a pointer to the first token. Subsequent calls with a NULL as the first argument will return the next tokens. When there are no tokens left, *strtok* returns a NULL.

SEE ALSO `strpbrk, strcspn` *To search for the first occurrence of any character from one string in another*

`strspn`	*To find the first occurrence of a character in a string that does not belong to another string*

EXAMPLE Write a C program that reads a string and separates it into tokens. The tokens are separated by blank spaces, tabs, or commas. This process of converting input strings to tokens is known as "parsing" and is one of the first things any command interpreter or compiler has to do.

```
#include <stdio.h>
#include <string.h>
char tokensep[]= " \t,";
main()
{
    int i = 0;
    char buf[80], *token;
    printf("Enter a string of tokens separated by comma\
 or blank:");
    gets(buf);
/* Call strtok once to get first token and initialize it */
    token = strtok(buf, tokensep);
/* Keep calling strtok to get all tokens                 */
    while(token != NULL)
    {
        i++;
        printf("Token %d = %s\n", i, token);
        token = strtok(NULL, tokensep);
    }
    return 0;
}
```

strupr

COMPATIBILITY

TC1	TC1.5	TC2	TC++	MSC3	MSC4	MSC5	MSC6	QC1	QC2	QC2.5	ANSI	UNIX V	XNX
▲	▲	▲	▲	▲	▲	▲	▲	▲	▲	▲			

PURPOSE Use *strupr* to convert any lowercase letters in a string to uppercase.

SYNTAX `char *strupr(char *string);`

`char *string;` *String to be converted to uppercase*

EXAMPLE CALL `strupr("help"); /* converts it to "HELP" */`

INCLUDES `#include <string.h>` *For function declaration*

DESCRIPTION The *strupr* function converts any lowercase letters in the *string* to uppercase. Other characters in the string are unaffected.

RETURNS The *strupr* function returns a pointer to the converted string (i.e., it returns "string").

COMMENTS The *strupr* routine and its companion *strlwr* are not part of the ANSI C library. Using the macros *toupper* and *tolower*, respectively, you can implement your own versions.

SEE ALSO `strlwr` *To convert a string to lowercase*

`toupper` *To convert a single lowercase letter to uppercase*

EXAMPLE Write a program that reads a string from the keyboard and converts the entire screen to uppercase by calling the function *strupr*.

```
#include <stdio.h>
#include <string.h>
main()
{
    char buf[80];
    printf("Enter a string with lowercase letters: ");
    gets(buf);
    strupr(buf);
    printf("The string in uppercase is:\n%s\n", buf);
    return 0;
}
```

COMPATIBILITY

strxfrm

TC1	TC1.5	TC2	TC++	MSC3	MSC4	MSC5	MSC6	QC1	QC2	QC2.5	ANSI	UNIX V	XNX
			▲				▲		▲	▲			

PURPOSE Use the *strxfrm* function to transform a string to a new form *string1* so that if *strcmp* is applied to two transformed strings, the returned result is the same as that returned when *strcoll* is applied to the original strings.

SYNTAX `size_t strxfrm(char *string1, char *string2, size_t maxchr);`

`char *string1;` *String where transformed version of* string2 *is returned*

```
char       *string2;
```
String to be transformed

```
size_t     maxchr;
```
Maximum number of characters to be placed in string1

EXAMPLE CALL `strxfrm(s_xfrm, s_original);`

INCLUDES `#include <string.h>` *For function declaration*

DESCRIPTION The *strxfrm* function transforms the string *string2* into an ASCII string *string1* so that the result of comparing two transformed strings using *strcmp* is the same as that obtained by applying *strcoll* to the untransformed strings.

No more than *maxchr* characters will be placed in *string1*. If *maxchr* is 0, *string1* can be a NULL. In this case, the return value will be the length of the transformed version of *string2*.

COMMON USES If your programs use string comparison functions such as *strcmp* and if you want your program to work with non-English strings, you should use *strxfrm* prior to calling *strcmp*. You can also call *strcoll* directly.

RETURNS The *strxfrm* function returns the length of the transformed string, not counting the terminating null character. If the return value is *maxchr*, the contents of *string1* may be unusable.

SEE ALSO `strcmp` *To compare strings according to ASCII collating sequence*

`strcoll` *To compare strings according to the collating sequence specified by the current locale*

EXAMPLE The following program accepts two strings, transforms them using *strxfrm*, and compares them with *strcmp*.

```
#include <stdio.h>
#include <string.h>
main()
{
    int result;
    char str1[81], str2[81], str1c[81], str2c[81];
    printf("Enter a string: ");
    gets(str1);
    printf("Enter string to compare with first: ");
    gets(str2);
/* Transform the strings */
    if((strxfrm(str1c, str1, 80) > 80) ||
```

```
        (strxfrm(str2c, str2, 80) > 80))
    {
        printf("Transformed string too long!\n");
        exit(1);
    }
/* Now compare strings using 'strcmp' */
    printf("Case-sensitive comparison shows that\n");
    result = strcmp(str1, str2);
    if(result == 0)
    {
        printf("\"%s\" == \"%s\"\n", str1, str2);
    }
    if(result < 0)
    {
        printf("\"%s\" < \"%s\"\n", str1, str2);
    }
    if(result > 0)
    {
        printf("\"%s\" > \"%s\"\n", str1, str2);
    }
    return 0;
}
```

Chapter 12 Searching and Sorting

Introduction

Searching and *sorting* are commonplace in business applications of the PC. All commercial data base programs have these capabilities. If you implement your own data base program tailored to your specific requirements, you invariably need search and sort capabilities. For example, if your data base contains the names and addresses of the customers of your company, you may want to search the list for information about a certain customer. And for mailings, you might want to print labels for all entries in your data base, sorted by zip code.

If you are developing your data base in C, Turbo C++ makes your job easier by providing four library routines for sorting and searching lists in memory. We describe these routines in this section.

Concepts

Many algorithms are used for searching and sorting, some meant for arrays that fit into memory and others that can handle files much too large to fit into the memory of the PC. The sort and search functions in the Turbo C++ library are for in-memory operations only.

SORTING The typical sort operation involves a data layout like that shown in Figure 12-1. You have an array of pointers each of which contains the address of a data structure (for example, a structure with fields that contain the name, address, and zip code for a customer). Sorting is done not by rearranging the data records themselves, which would be inefficient, but by rearranging the pointers to cause a particular field in the data structure (the "key" for the sort) to appear in ascendant or descendant position. In Figure 12-1 we show the original list and the list after it was sorted with the ZIP code (the key field) ascendant. Notice that only the pointers were rearranged; the data structures stayed put. This improves sorting speed because the pointers are much smaller than the structures themselves, but the pointers require extra storage space.

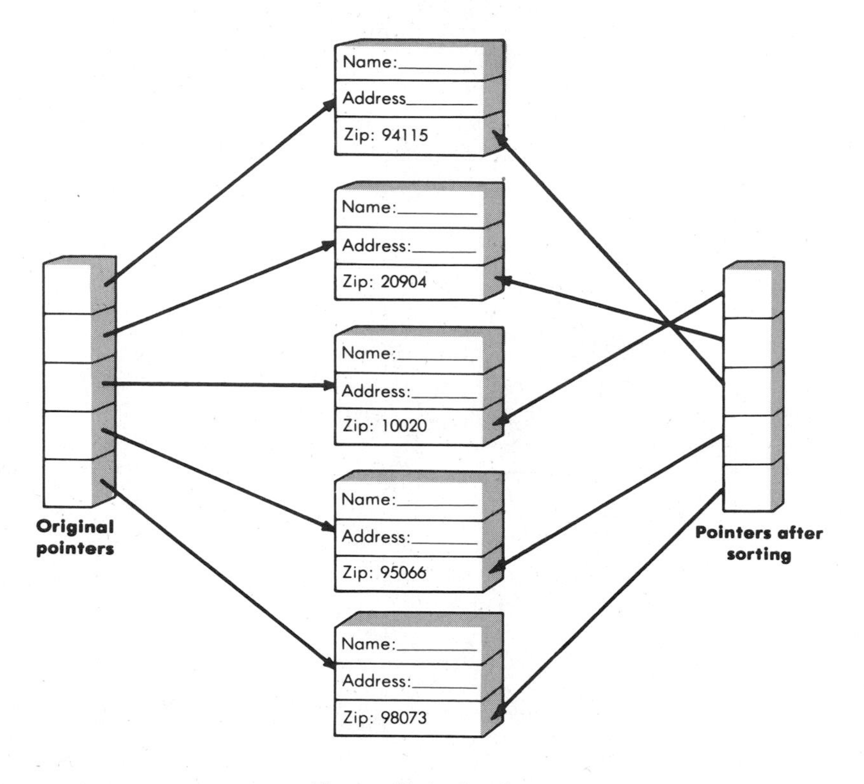

Figure 12-1. ***Sorting***

In its sort and search routines the Turbo C++ library supplies the basic algorithms but you supply the starting address of the array, the number of elements in it, the size (in bytes) of each element, and a pointer to a function that performs the comparison of two elements.

You write the function that compares two elements from the array. The function receives the pointers to the two elements and returns an integer value. A positive return value signifies that the first element is "greater than" the second one. A zero signifies equality, and a negative number means that the first element is "less than" the second one. You define what less than and greater than mean. In the name and address data base example, you could compare the zip code field of the two structures and return a value based on which zip is higher. If you wanted to sort by the name field, you could compare the names alphabetically. With your definition, the *qsort* function sorts the array in ascending order. You can change the order by reversing the less than and greater than definitions in the function performing the comparison.

The Quicksort Algorithm

The only sort routine in the library, *qsort,* is based on the well-known "quicksort" algorithm. This popular, general-purpose sort algorithm was invented by C. A. R. Hoare in 1962. The quicksort algorithm is based on the principle of divide and conquer. The array being sorted is partitioned into two parts and the algorithm is applied to each part. The algorithm can be implemented with the following recursive program:

```
quicksort(lower_bound, upper_bound)
int lower_bound, upper_bound;
{
    int i;
    if (upper_bound > lower_bound)
    {
        i = partition_array(upper_bound, lower_bound);
        quicksort(lower_bound, i);
        quicksort(i+1, upper_bound);
    }
}
```

The *upper_bound* and *lower_bound* are the array indices describing a particular partition. As you can see from the code, the *partitioning of the array* is at the heart of the quicksort algorithm. The partitioning algorithm must satisfy three conditions. First, after the partitioning is complete, one element we'll call X must move to its final position in the sorted array. Second, all elements in the lower half of the new partition must be less than X. Third, all elements in the upper half must be greater than X.

One way to implement the partitioning is to arbitrarily select the element X, at the *upper_bound,* as the one to move into its final place in the sorted array. Then we scan the array from bottom to top until we find an element greater than X, and we also scan it from top to bottom until we find an element less than X. Next we exchange these two elements with one another. This step is repeated until the partitioning is complete, which is indicated by the condition that the scan from top down crosses the one from bottom up. The C code fragment below illustrates this partitioning algorithm (for simplicity, we assume that the array is named *array* and that it contains integer values only).

```
int partition_array(lower_bound, upper_bound)
int lower_bound, upper_bound;
{
    int i, j, X, temp;

    X = array[upper_bound];
    i = lower_bound - 1;
    j = upper_bound;
    while(j <= i)          /* Till partitioning is done */
    {
        while(a[i] >= X) i++;          /* Scan array */
        while(a[j] <= X) j--;          /* Scan array */
/* Exchange elements */
        temp = a[i];
        a[i] = a[j];
        a[j] = temp;
    }
    return(i); /* Return index to indicate partition */
}
```

SEARCHING

The Turbo C++ library includes two searching algorithms: the linear search and the binary search.

The Linear Search Algorithm

The linear search is the simpler method of searching: we look through the array sequentially until the specific element is found or, if the array ends before the element is found, the search fails. The *lfind* routine implements this search.

The Binary Search Algorithm

The binary search algorithm is implemented by the function *bsearch*. Like quicksort, binary search uses a divide and conquer approach to find an element in an array. This approach is analogous to searching for a word in the dictionary. You flip to a page around the middle of the dictionary and if the words on that page occur later in alphabetic order than the word you are looking for, you repeat the search in the first half of the dictionary. This method works because the dictionary is already sorted in a particular order.

The array also must be sorted in ascending order. On such a sorted array, the binary search proceeds as follows. The value of the key field in the middle entry of the array is compared with the value being sought. If the entry has a value either too high or too low, this search step is repeated on the upper half or lower half of the array, respectively. Thus at every step of the search you reduce the length of the array to be searched by half, allowing even a large array to be searched very quickly.

General Usage

Turbo C++ provides four sort and search routines (see Table 12-1). One, *qsort*, is meant for sorting an array of elements. The others, *bsearch, lfind*, and *lsearch* are for searching an array of elements for a given value. These routines are designed to be used in a standard way. Figure 12-2 shows the arguments that you pass to the routines. These include the starting address of the array; the number of elements in it; the size (in bytes) of each element, and a pointer to a function, *compare( )*, that performs the comparison of two elements. Figure 12-2 shows sorting or searching the command-line arguments that are passed to the *main* function in your program. For a declaration of the form *main(int argc, char **argv)*, the number of arguments is in *argc* (the standard way a program accesses its command-line arguments) and the starting address of the array is *argv*. Each element is a pointer to a C string, so the size of each element is given by *sizeof(char *)*. The comparison function is called as *compare(char **elem1, char **elem2)* with two arguments, each a pointer to a variable that points to a string. We can use a string comparison routine such as *strcmp* to perform the comparison inside *compare( )*.

Table 12-1. *Search and Sort Routines*

Routine	Description
bsearch	Performs binary search for an element in a sorted array.
lfind	Performs linear search for an element in an array. The array need not be sorted.
lsearch	Performs linear search like *lfind*, but appends the value being searched to the array if the value is not found.
qsort	Sorts an array of elements using the "quicksort" algorithm.

The Routines

The sorting routine is named *qsort* and it uses the quicksort algorithm. The other three routines, *bsearch, lfind*, and *lsearch*, are for searching. The *bsearch* function performs binary search on a sorted array. You can use *qsort* to perform the sorting before calling *bsearch*. The *lfind* and *lsearch* routines implement a linear search technique, but *lsearch* also provides the additional service of inserting the element into the array if it is not found during the search.

Further Reading

Search and sort algorithms are covered in every computer science text on data structures and algorithms. An entire volume by Knuth[1] deals with sort and search algorithms alone. For a shorter introduction to these algo-

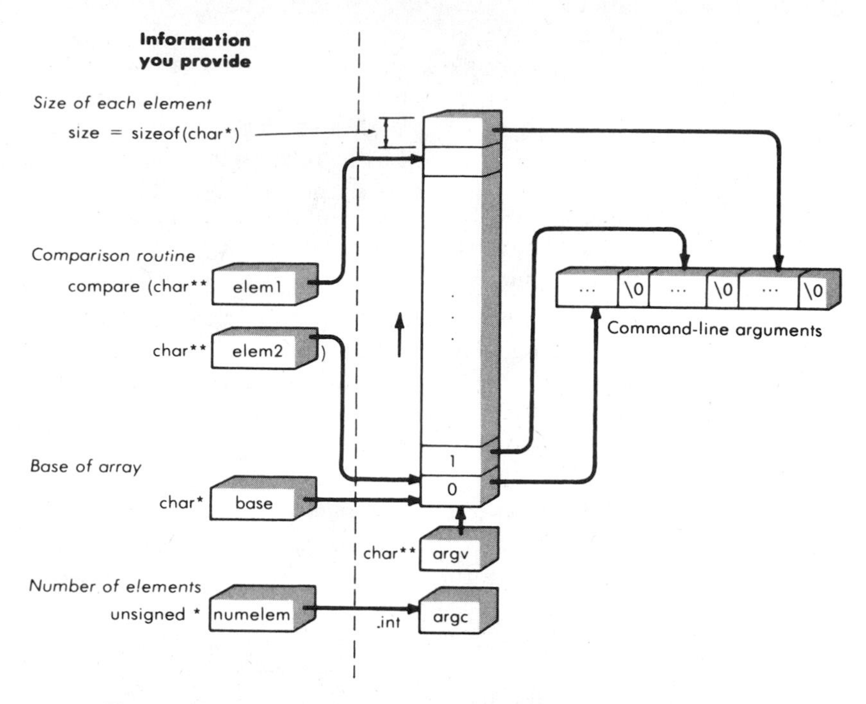

Figure 12-2. *Sorting and searching command-line arguments*

rithms, you can consult the books by Sedgewick[2] and Tremblay and Sorenson[3].

1. Donald E. Knuth, *The Art of Computer Programming, Volume 3: Sorting and Searching*, Addison-Wesley, Reading, MA, 1973.
2. Robert Sedgewick, *Algorithms*, Addison-Wesley, Reading, MA, 1983, 551 pages.
3. Jean-Paul Tremblay and Paul G. Sorenson, *An Introduction to Data Structures with Applications*, Second Edition, McGraw-Hill, Inc., New York, NY, 1984, 861 pages.

COMPATIBILITY

bsearch

TC1	TC1.5	TC2	TC++	MSC3	MSC4	MSC5	MSC6	QC1	QC2	QC2.5	ANSI	UNIX V	XNX
▲	▲	▲	▲	▲	▲	▲	▲	▲	▲	▲	▲	▲	▲

PURPOSE Use *bsearch* to perform a binary search of a sorted array with a specific number of elements, each a fixed number of bytes long.

SYNTAX

```
void *bsearch(const void *key, const void *base, size_t num,
              size_t width,
              int (*compare)(const void *elem1, const void *elem2));
```

`const void *key;` *Pointer to element value being searched for*

`const void *base;` *Pointer to beginning of array being searched*

`size_t num;` *Number of elements in array*

`size_t width;` *Size of each element in bytes*

`int (*compare)(const void *elem1, const void *elem2);` *Pointer to a function that compares two elements,* elem1 *and* elem2, *each of type* const void *

EXAMPLE CALL

```
int mycompare(const void *, const void *);
result = (char **) bsearch((const void *)keyword,
                           (const void *)envp,
                           (size_t)count,
                           (size_t)sizeof(char *),
                           mycompare);
```

INCLUDES `#include <stdlib.h>` *For function declaration and definition of* size_t

DESCRIPTION The *bsearch* function performs a binary search (see the tutorial section) of a sorted array, beginning at the address *base* and comprising *num* elements, each of size *width* bytes. The argument *key* points to the value being sought.

In the argument *compare*, you supply the address of a routine which should accept two arguments *elem1* and *elem2*, each a pointer to an element in the array. The *bsearch* function calls your routine when it has to compare two elements of the array, passing the address of the array elements as arguments. Your routine should compare the two elements and return one of the values shown in the table (for strings, "greater than" and "less than" usually refer to alphabetic order).

Return Value	To Indicate
Negative	First element is less than the second one.
Zero	The two elements are identical to each other.
Positive	First element is greater than the second one.

Note that you can use the *qsort* routine to sort the array before calling *bsearch*.

RETURNS The *bsearch* function returns a pointer to the first occurrence of the value *key* in the array. If the value is not found, *bsearch* returns a NULL.

SEE ALSO lfind, lsearch *To perform a linear search*

qsort *To sort an array using the "quick sort" algorithm*

EXAMPLE In Turbo C++ under MS-DOS, the *main* function is invoked with three arguments: the number of strings in the command line, the command line itself, and the MS-DOS environment table, which is also an array of strings. Write a program that accepts a keyword on the command line and uses *bsearch* to search the environment table for the string beginning with this keyword. First it sorts the environment table using *qsort*, prints it, and then calls *bsearch* to perform the search. Count the number of entries in the table, noting that the end of the environment table is marked by a NULL.

```
#include <stdio.h>
#include <string.h>
#include <stdlib.h>
int mycompare(const void *, const void *);
main(int argc, char **argv, char **envp)
{
    unsigned int i, count;
    char **p_table, **result;
    if(argc < 2)
    {
        printf("Usage: %s <KEYWORD>\n", argv[0]);
        exit(0);
    }
/* Find length of environment table                    */
    for(count = 0, p_table = envp;
        *p_table != NULL;
        p_table++, count++);        /* a null loop     */
/* Sort the environment table using "qsort"            */
    qsort((void *) envp, (size_t)count,
```

```
            (size_t)sizeof(char *), mycompare);
/* Print sorted environment table                          */
    printf("===== Sorted environment table =====\n");
    for(i = 0, p_table = envp; i < count; i++)
    {
        printf("%s\n", *p_table);
        p_table++;
    }
/* Search for the KEY variable in the environment     */
    result = (char **) bsearch((const void *)&argv[1],
                               (const void *)envp,
                               (size_t)count,
                               (size_t)sizeof(char *),
                               mycompare);
    if(result != NULL)
    {
        printf("\nFound %s in\n%s\n", argv[1], *result);
    }
    else
    {
        printf("\n%s not found.\
Try with uppercase keyword\n", argv[1]);
    }
    return 0;
}
/*---------------------------------------------------*/
int mycompare(const void *arg1, const void *arg2)
{
/* Compare two strings up to the length of the key    */
   return(strncmp(*(char**)arg1,
        *(char**)arg2, strlen(*(char**)arg1)));
}
```

COMPATIBILITY

lfind

TC1	TC1.5	TC2	TC++	MSC3	MSC4	MSC5	MSC6	QC1	QC2	QC2.5	ANSI	UNIX V	XNX
▲	▲	▲	▲		▲	▲	▲	▲	▲	▲		▲	▲

PURPOSE Use *lfind* to make a linear search through an array with a specific number of elements, each a fixed number of bytes long.

SYNTAX

```
char *lfind(const void *key, const void *base, size_t *num,
size_t width,
```

```
int (*compare)(const void *elem1, const void *elem2));
```

`const void *key;` *Pointer to element value being searched for*

`const void *base;` *Pointer to beginning of array being searched*

`size_t *num;` *Number of elements in array*

`size_t width;` *Size of each element in bytes*

`int (*compare)(const void *elem1, const void *elem2);`
Pointer to a function that compares two elements, elem1 *and* elem2, *each of type* const void *

EXAMPLE CALL

```
int mycompare(const void *, const void *);
result = (char **)lfind(keyword,
                        envp,
                        &count,
                        sizeof(char *),
                        mycompare);
```

INCLUDES `#include <stdlib.h>` *For function declaration*

DESCRIPTION The *lfind* function makes a linear search through an array that begins at the address *base* and consists of *num* elements, each of size *width* bytes. The argument *key* points to the value being sought.

In the argument *compare*, *lfind* expects the address of a routine to compare a pair of elements from the array. This routine should accept arguments *elem1* and *elem2*, each a pointer to an element in the array. The *lfind* function calls this routine with the address of two array elements as arguments. The routine compares the two elements and returns a zero if the elements are identical. Otherwise, it returns a nonzero value.

RETURNS If the value *key* is found, *lfind* returns a pointer to its first occurrence in the array. If it is not found, *lfind* returns a NULL.

SEE ALSO `lsearch` *To perform a linear search of an array*

`bsearch` *To perform a binary search of a sorted array*

EXAMPLE Write a program that accepts a keyword on the command line and uses *lfind* to find the first occurrence in the process environment table of a string that begins with the keyword. Note that the environment table is automatically the third parameter in the *main* function with Turbo C++ on an MS-DOS system.

```
#include <stdio.h>
#include <stdlib.h>
#include <string.h>
int mycompare(const void *, const void *);
main(int argc, char **argv, char **envp)
{
    unsigned int count;
    char **p_table, **result;
    if(argc < 2)
    {
        printf("Usage: %s <KEYWORD>\n", argv[0]);
        exit(0);
    }
/* Find length of environment table and print it    */
    printf("==== Environment table contains ====\n");
    for(count = 0, p_table = envp;
        *p_table != NULL;
        p_table++, count++) printf("%s\n", *p_table);
/* Search for the KEY variable in the environment   */
    result = (char **)lfind(&argv[1],
                            envp,
                            &count,
                            sizeof(char *),
                            mycompare);
    if(result != NULL)
    {
        printf("\nFound %s in\n%s\n", argv[1], *result);
    }
    else
    {
        printf("\n%s not found.\
Try with uppercase keyword\n", argv[1]);
    }
    return 0;
}
/*--------------------------------------------------*/
int mycompare(const void *arg1, const void *arg2)
{
    return(strncmp(*(char**)arg1, *(char**)arg2,
strlen(*(char**)arg1)));
}
```

lsearch

COMPATIBILITY

TC1	TC1.5	TC2	TC++	MSC3	MSC4	MSC5	MSC6	QC1	QC2	QC2.5	ANSI	UNIX V	XNX
▲	▲	▲	▲		▲	▲	▲	▲	▲	▲		▲	▲

PURPOSE Use *lsearch* to perform a linear search of an array with a specified number of elements, each a fixed number of bytes long. The value being sought is added to the array if it is not found.

SYNTAX

```
char *lsearch(const void *key, const void *base, size_t *num,
size_t width,
            int (*compare)(const void *elem1, const void *elem2));
```

`const void *key;` *Pointer to element value being searched for*

`const void *base;` *Pointer to beginning of array being searched*

`size_t *num;` *Pointer to number of elements in array*

`size_t width;` *Size of each element in bytes*

`int (*compare)(const void *elem1, const void *elem2);`
Pointer to a function that compares two elements, elem1 *and* elem2, *each of type* const void *

EXAMPLE CALL

```
int client_compare(const void *, const void *);
result = (char **) lsearch(client_name,
                           client_table,
                           &count,
                           sizeof(char *),
                           client_compare);
```

INCLUDES `#include <stdlib.h>` *For function declaration*

DESCRIPTION The *lsearch* function performs a linear search (see the tutorial section) of an array beginning at the address *base* and comprising *num* elements, each of size *width* bytes. The argument *key* points to the value being sought.

The *lsearch* function needs a routine that it can call or compare a pair of elements from the array. It should find the address of such a routine in the argument *compare*. You should write this routine to accept arguments *elem1* and *elem2*, each a pointer to an element in the array. The *lsearch* function calls this routine with the address of two array elements as arguments. The routine compares the elements and returns a zero if the elements are identical. Otherwise, the routine returns a nonzero value.

RETURNS The *lsearch* function returns a pointer to the first occurrence of the value *key* in the array. If the value is not found, *lsearch* adds the element at the end of the array, updates the value in *num*, and returns a pointer to the newly added item. If you don't want to add missing items to the array, use *lfind* instead.

SEE ALSO

`lfind` *To perform a linear search without adding element to array*

`bsearch` *To perform a binary search of a sorted array*

EXAMPLE Write a program using *lsearch* to search in a small table of C strings for an entry beginning with a keyword entered on the command line. When the entry is not found, *lsearch* adds the entry into the array and updates the element count. You can verify this by providing a keyword you know is not in the table.

```
#include <stdio.h>
#include <string.h>
#include <stdlib.h>
int mycompare(const void *, const void *);
char *our_table[20] =
{
        "Microsoft C 5.1",
        "Quick C 1.0",
        "Turbo C 2.0",
        NULL
};
main(int argc, char **argv)
{
    unsigned int i, count, oldcount;
    char **p_table, **result;
    if(argc < 2)
    {
        printf("Usage: %s <KEYWORD>\n", argv[0]);
        exit(0);
    }
/* Find length of our table  and print it   */
    printf("==== Our table contains ====\n");
    for(count = 0, p_table = our_table;
        *p_table != NULL;
        p_table++, count++) printf("%s\n", *p_table);
    oldcount = count;
/* Search for the PATH variable in the environment   */
    result = (char **) lsearch(&argv[1],
                               our_table,
```

```
                                          &count,
                                          sizeof(char *),
                                          mycompare);
    if(count == oldcount)
    {
        printf("\nFound %s in\n%s\n", argv[1], *result);
    }
    else
    {
        printf("\n%s was added to table\n", argv[1]);
/* Print table again */

        printf("==== Now table contains ====\n");
        for(i=0; i<count; i++)
            printf("%s\n", our_table[i]);
    }
    return 0;
}
/*--------------------------------------------------*/
int mycompare(const void *arg1, const void *arg2)
{
/* Compare two strings up to the length of the key    */
    return(strncmp(*(char**)arg1, *(char**)arg2,
strlen(*(char**)arg1)));
}
```

qsort

COMPATIBILITY

TC1	TC1.5	TC2	TC++	MSC3	MSC4	MSC5	MSC6	QC1	QC2	QC2.5	ANSI	UNIX V	XNX
▲	▲	▲	▲	▲	▲	▲	▲	▲	▲	▲	▲	▲	▲

PURPOSE Use *qsort* to sort an array having a given number of elements, each a fixed number of bytes long.

SYNTAX

```
void qsort(void *base, size_t num, size_t width,
           int (*compare)(const void *elem1, const void *elem2));
```

`const void *base;` *Pointer to beginning of array being sorted*

`size_t num;` *Number of elements in array*

`size_t width;` *Size of each element in bytes*

```
int (*compare)(const void *elem1, const void *elem2);
```

Pointer to a function that compares two elements, elem1 *and* elem2, *each of type* const void *

EXAMPLE CALL

```
int compare(const void *, const void *);
qsort((void *) envp, (size_t)count,
      (size_t)sizeof(char *), compare);
```

INCLUDES

`#include <stdlib.h>` *For function declaration and definition of* size_t

DESCRIPTION The *qsort* function uses the quick sort algorithm (see the tutorial section) to sort an array beginning at the address *base* and comprised of *num* elements, each of size *width* bytes.

During the sort, *qsort* compares pairs of elements from the array by calling a routine whose address you provide in the argument *compare*. This function should accept arguments *elem1* and *elem2*, each a pointer to an element in the array. The *qsort* function calls this routine using the address of two array elements as arguments. Your routine should compare the two elements and return one of the values shown in the table (for strings, "greater than" and "less than" usually refer to alphabetic order):

Return Value	To Indicate
Negative	First element is less than the second one.
Zero	The two elements are identical to each other.
Positive	First element is greater than the second one.

On the basis of these values, the array is sorted in ascending order of element values, but you can reverse the order by changing the return value of the greater than and less than tests in the function that compares elements from the array.

SEE ALSO

`lfind, lsearch` *To perform a linear search*

`bsearch` *To perform a binary search on a sorted array*

EXAMPLE Illustrate the use of *qsort* by sorting the environment table (an array of strings with a NULL string at the end) that is the third argument in the *main* function with Turbo C++ under MS-DOS.

```
#include <stdio.h>
#include <string.h>
#include <stdlib.h>
int mycompare(const void *, const void *);
```

```
main(int argc, char **argv, char **envp)
{
    unsigned int i, count;
    char **p_table, **result;
/* Find length of environment table and print it    */
    printf("==== Unsorted environment table ====\n");
    for(count = 0, p_table = envp;
        *p_table != NULL;
        p_table++, count++) printf("%s\n", *p_table);
/* Sort the environment table using "qsort"         */
    qsort((void *) envp, (size_t)count,
          (size_t)sizeof(char *), mycompare);
/* Print sorted environment table                   */
    printf("===== Sorted environment table =====\n");
    for(i = 0, p_table = envp; i < count; i++)
    {
        printf("%s\n", *p_table);
        p_table++;
    }
    return 0;
}
/*-----------------------------------------------------*/
int mycompare(const void *arg1, const void *arg2)
{
/* Compare two strings up to the length of the key    */
    return(strncmp(*(char**)arg1, *(char**)arg2,
strlen(*(char**)arg1)));
}
```

Chapter 13 Time Routines

Introduction

Time is of the essence in a computer. The computer executes instructions at a steady rate, once every clock tick—and the clock ticks very fast indeed. You may have noticed advertisements proclaiming 8-, 10- or 12-MHz machines. Each MHz translates to one million clock ticks per second. This is the fast-moving time kept by the system's clock. Time, in hours, minutes, and seconds is also important and is used by the operating system, MS-DOS, for a variety of tasks. An example is the date and time *stamp* on each file in the system, used to record when a file was created and when it was last modified. You see this information when you list the directory with a DIR command at the DOS prompt.

Your C programs may use the date and time information as well. If, for example, you develop a graphical user interface and you wish to display current date and time in a corner of the screen, the Turbo C++ library includes routines for just this kind of task. In fact, it contains many different routines, giving you a choice of getting the date and time information in a variety of formats, each suitable for a specific job.

Concepts: Time in MS-DOS Systems

The 8086 microprocessor uses a *system clock* which ticks several million times a second to execute its instructions. The hardware requires this fast clock, but humans prefer a slower pace. So the PC provides circuitry to generate an interrupt at the rate of 18.2 times a second and includes code in the ROM BIOS (see the tutorial in Chapter 17) to handle these interrupts. The interrupt handler updates a count of such interrupts since the PC was last turned on. In the early days of the IBM PC, if you knew the time when the PC was turned on, these tick counts could be used to compute the current time. This is why MS-DOS always asks for the date and time when you power up your PC. Now, however, most PCs have a "clock/calendar" card or, in the case of the PC-AT and PS/2, a built-in "real-time clock." These are similar to digital clocks and they can keep running even when your PC is off because they use a battery as a backup power supply. The PC-AT and PS/2 get the system date and time at power-up from the real-time clock, so the user is not asked for it by MS-DOS.

THE CLOCK DRIVER

MS-DOS uses device drivers to communicate with peripheral devices and it uses a special driver, identified by a particular bit in the attribute word in the driver's header, to get or set the date and the time. As shown in Figure 13-1, this CLOCK driver maintains the current time and date as a 6-byte sequence. The time is expressed in hours, minutes, seconds, and hundredths of seconds and the date is expressed as the number of days elapsed since January 1, 1980. In fact, none of the time routines understands any date prior to January 1, 1980, since that's when time began for MS-DOS. The CLOCK driver marks directory entries with date and time stamps and provides date and time services to application programs (via DOS functions numbered 2Ah through 2Dh). The fact that MS-DOS uses a driver for those functions made it easy to add a clock/calendar board to the original PC. You just popped the board into your system and loaded the CLOCK driver by placing a statement like *DEVICE=<path name of driver>* in your CONFIG.SYS file.

TIME IN UNIX AND IN TURBO C++

You need not worry about the CLOCK driver when using the time functions in the Turbo C++ library, but you do need to know how time is maintained in UNIX systems. This is because Turbo C++ has maintained a high degree of compatibility with UNIX, helping to ensure portability.

In UNIX, and in Turbo C++, the date and the time are expressed jointly by the number of seconds elapsed since 00:00:00 hours Greenwich

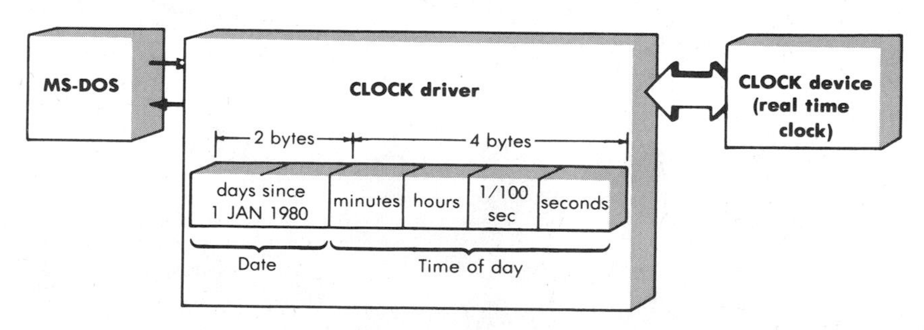

Figure 13-1. ***Time in MS-DOS***

Mean Time (GMT) on January 1, 1970. This is a more universal representation than in MS-DOS because it uses the same reference (GMT) at any location in the world. How is this universal time derived from the local time kept by MS-DOS? Here is the scheme used by Turbo C++.

The TZ Environment Variable

An environment variable (see Chapter 4) named TZ defines the time zone (for example, PST, MST, EST), the difference between the local time and GMT in hours, and whether daylight saving time is honored. You can use the DOS command SET to define the environment variable TZ. For a PC in the Eastern Standard Time with daylight saving honored, for example, the definition of TZ will be *TZ=EST5EDT* because there is a difference of 5 hours between EST and GMT. If TZ is not defined, a default of *TZ=PST8PDT* is assumed.

Global Variables: *daylight, timezone,* and *tzname*

Three global variables store time zone information that is used by several time functions for their operation. The library function *tzset* sets these variables from the setting of the environment variable TZ.

The variable *daylight* is an integer that contains either a 1 or a 0 depending on whether the daylight saving is honored in this time zone. The long integer variable *timezone* contains the number of seconds to be added to the local time to get GMT when both are expressed as seconds elapsed since 00:00:00 hour, January 1, 1970. The *tzname* variable is an array of two strings, the first containing the name of the time zone and the second, the corresponding daylight saving time zone (for example, EST and EDT).

Conversion from Local Time to GMT

Figure 13-2 illustrates the conversion of local time from MS-DOS to the format used in Turbo C++. The date and time from MS-DOS are converted to seconds elapsed since the 00:00:00 hour, January 1, 1970, and the value of *timezone* is added to this number. If daylight savings is honored and on at that time, the value is further modified. The result is what the function *time* returns: the current date and time expressed as seconds elapsed since 00:00:00 hours GMT, 1970.

TIME IN MANY FORMS

The main function of the time routines is to get the current date and time in various formats and to convert from one format to another. A list of the functions is given in Table 13-1 and the functions are classified by task in Table 13-2.

Figure 13-3 depicts the different formats of date and time and conversion among them. The basic function *time* returns a value of type *time_t*, which is defined to be a long integer in the *time.h* header file. This long integer value is converted to a structure named *tm* (defined in the *time.h*

Table 13-1. *Time Routines*

Routine	Description
asctime	Converts time from a structure of type *tm* to a string.
clock	Returns the elapsed processor time in number of ticks.
ctime	Converts time from a value of type *time_t* to a string.
difftime	Computes the difference of two values of type *time_t*.
ftime	Returns the current time in a structure of type *timeb*.
gmtime	Converts time from a value of type *time_t* to a structure of type *tm* that corresponds to GMT.
localtime	Converts time from a value of type *time_t* to a structure of type *tm* that corresponds to the local time.
strftime	Prepares a string with date and time values from a *tm* structure, formatted according to a specified format.
stime	Sets the system time and date.
time	Returns the seconds elapsed since 00:00:00 hour, GMT, January 1, 1970, as a value of type *time_t*.
tzset	Assigns values to the global variables *timezone, daylight,* and *tzname* based on the time zone specified in the environment variable TZ.

header file) by the *gmtime* and *localtime* routines. The *gmtime* function sets all fields in the *tm* structure to correspond to GMT while *localtime* sets them to the local time.

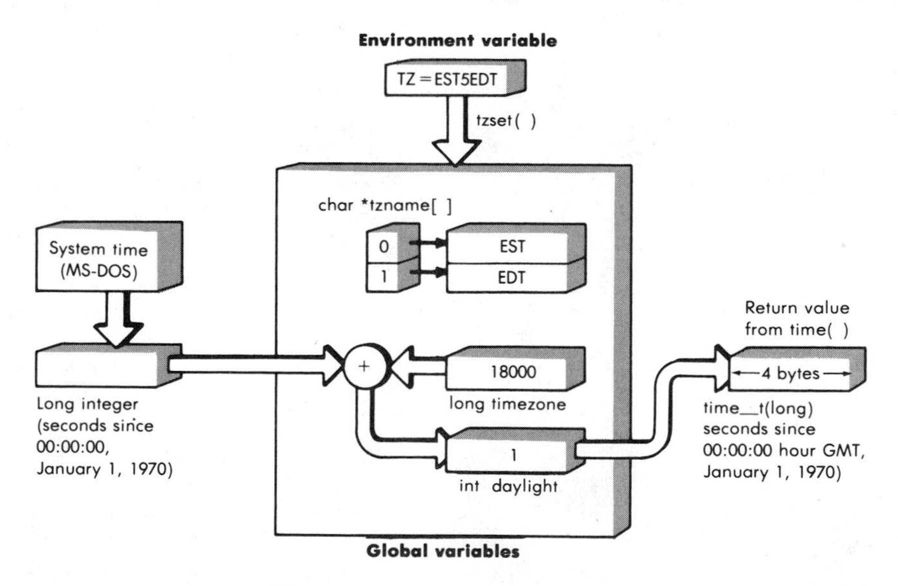

Figure 13-2. *Time in Turbo C++*

Table 13-2. *Time Routines by Task*

Task	Routines
Get current date and time.	ftime, time
Convert time from one form to another.	asctime, ctime, gmtime, localtime
Compute elapsed time.	clock, difftime
Set system time and date.	stime
Load environment variable setting into internal variables.	tzset
Prepare a formatted string with date and time values.	strftime

A different structure, *timeb*, defined in the file *sys\timeb.h*, is used by the *ftime* function to return the current date and time. The field *time* in the *timeb* structure is identical to the value returned by the *time* function.

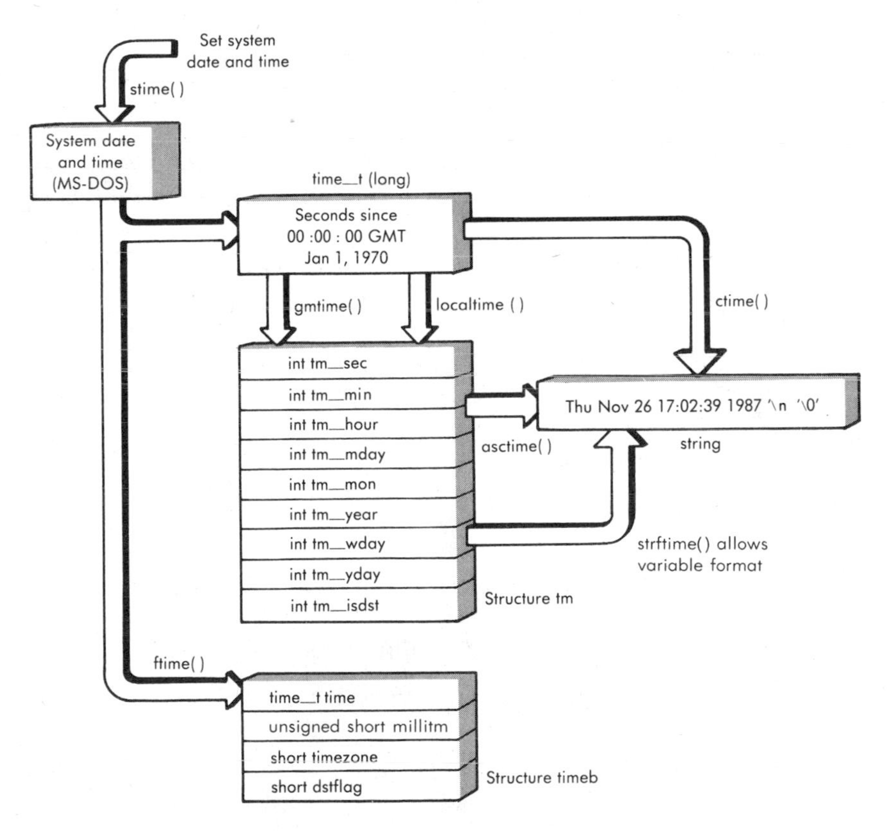

Figure 13-3. *Conversion among different forms of date and time*

Printing Date and Time

The *asctime* function converts the value in a structure of type *tm* to a C string that you can print. The *ctime* function converts the output of *time* directly to a string. The *strftime* function works the same way *asctime* does but allows elaborate formatting options.

ELAPSED TIME

Sometimes you have to compute the time elapsed between two events. The *difftime* function returns the difference of two values of type *time_t* in seconds. The *clock* function returns the number of *clock ticks* used by the process so far. The number of ticks per second is defined in the constant CLK_TCK (in file *time.h*) to be 18.2 (see the example program in the *clock* reference page) which is how often the system time is updated in a PC.

Cautions

- If the TZ environment variable is not set on your system, the computed GMT will be wrong. Since everything in MS-DOS is done in local time, this is important only if you need an accurate universal time. The default settings of TZ imply that local time is Pacific Standard Time.
- The functions *gmtime* and *localtime* use a single structure of type *tm* to store the time. Each call to either function overwrites the result of the previous call.
- The *ctime* and *asctime* functions also use a single character string to store results. Thus any call to one overwrites the result of the previous call.

Further Reading

The time functions have not received much attention in books about C programming on the PC. One exception is Hansen's book[1], which includes a detailed discussion of the time routines in the Microsoft C 4.0 library. Consult Duncan's book[2] on MS-DOS for further information on the CLOCK driver, and on drivers in general, in MS-DOS.

1. Augie Hansen, *Proficient C*, Microsoft Press, Redmond, WA, 1987, 492 pages.
2. Ray Duncan, *Advanced MS-DOS*, Microsoft Press, Redmond, WA, 1986, 468 pages.

COMPATIBILITY

asctime

TC1	TC1.5	TC2	TC++	MSC3	MSC4	MSC5	MSC6	QC1	QC2	QC2.5	ANSI	UNIX V	XNX
▲	▲	▲	▲	▲	▲	▲	▲	▲	▲	▲	▲	▲	▲

PURPOSE Use *asctime* to convert a time stored in a structure of type *tm* to a character string.

SYNTAX

```
char *asctime(const struct tm *time);
```

`const struct tm *time;` *Pointer to a structure containing time to be converted to a string*

EXAMPLE CALL

```
printf("The time is %s\n", asctime(&timedata));
```

INCLUDES `#include <time.h>` *For function declaration and definition of structure* tm

DESCRIPTION The *asctime* function converts to a character string the value of a time stored in the structure of type *tm* at the address *time*. The value is set up by an earlier call to *gmtime* or *localtime*, both of which accept a long integer value for the time, prepare the fields of a structure of type *tm*, and return a pointer to that structure. The structure *tm* is defined in *time.h* as follows:

```
struct tm
{
    int tm_sec;       /* seconds after the minute - [0,59] */
    int tm_min;       /* minutes after the hour - [0,59]   */
    int tm_hour;      /* hours since midnight - [0,23]     */
    int tm_mday;      /* day of the month - [1,31]         */
    int tm_mon;       /* months since January - [0,11]     */
    int tm_year;      /* years since 1900                  */
    int tm_wday;      /* days since Sunday - [0,6]         */
    int tm_yday;      /* days since January 1 - [0,365]    */
    int tm_isdst;     /* daylight savings time flag        */
};
```

The string prepared by *asctime* is 26 characters long, counting the null character at the end, and has the form

```
Thu Nov 26 17:02:39 1987\n\0
```

As the definition shows, a 24-hour clock is used for the time.

RETURNS The *asctime* function returns a pointer to the data area where the string is stored.

COMMENTS To prepare the time for printing, the *asctime* and *ctime* functions use a single static string so it will be destroyed by subsequent calls to these routines.

SEE ALSO `ctime, gmtime, localtime, strftime, time`

EXAMPLE Use *asctime* to get and display the local time.

```
#include <stdio.h>
#include <time.h>
main()
{
    struct tm *curtime;
    time_t bintime;
/* Get time in seconds since 00:00:00 GMT, 1/1/70 */
    time(&bintime);
/* Convert time to local time (default is PST)    */
    curtime = localtime(&bintime);
/* Use asctime to print the date and time         */
    printf("Current time: %s\n", asctime(curtime));
    return 0;
}
```

clock

COMPATIBILITY

TC1	TC1.5	TC2	TC++	MSC3	MSC4	MSC5	MSC6	QC1	QC2	QC2.5	ANSI	UNIX V	XNX
		▲	▲			▲	▲	▲	▲	▲	▲		

PURPOSE Use *clock* to obtain in number of ticks the amount of processor time used by the current process.

SYNTAX `clock_t clock(void);`

EXAMPLE CALL `ticks_now = clock();`

INCLUDES `#include <time.h>` *For function declaration and definition of type* clock_t

DESCRIPTION The *clock* function tells how much processor time has been used by the calling process. The value is expressed as the number of ticks. The constant CLK_TCK, defined in *time.h*, is the number of ticks per second, so the value returned by *clock* should be divided by CLK_TCK to get the elapsed processor time in seconds.

RETURNS If processor time is available to *clock*, it returns the current time in ticks, cast as a value of type *clock_t* which is defined in *time.h*. Otherwise, it returns the value −1, cast as *clock_t*.

SEE ALSO `difftime` *To get the difference of two time values*

`time` *To get the current time as a long integer*

EXAMPLE Use *clock* to determine and display the processor time used in a program that performs a computational loop 10,000 times.

```
#include <stdio.h>
#include <time.h>
main()
{
    unsigned i, tused, count=10000;
    double a, b, c, d;
    clock_t ticksnow;
    for(i=0; i<count; i++)
    {
        a = (double)(i-1);
        b = (double)(i+1);
        c = (double)(i*i);
        d = a*b - c;
    }
/* Get current clock ticks by calling "clock"     */
    if((ticksnow = clock()) == (clock_t)-1)
    {
        printf("Processor time not available!\n");
        abort();
    }
/* Convert processor time to seconds. Use CLK_TCK  */
    tused = (unsigned)ticksnow/CLK_TCK;
    printf("10,000 loops ran for %u seconds\n", tused);
    return 0;
}
```

ctime

COMPATIBILITY

TC1	TC1.5	TC2	TC++	MSC3	MSC4	MSC5	MSC6	QC1	QC2	QC2.5	ANSI	UNIX V	XNX
▲	▲	▲	▲	▲	▲	▲	▲	▲	▲	▲	▲	▲	▲

PURPOSE Use *ctime* to convert to a character string a time stored as a value of type *time_t*.

SYNTAX

```
char *ctime(const time_t *time);
```

`const time_t *time;` *Pointer to variable containing time to be converted to a string*

EXAMPLE CALL

```
printf("Current time = %s\n", ctime(&bintime));
```

INCLUDES `#include <time.h>` *For function declaration and definition of* time_t

DESCRIPTION The *ctime* function converts to a character string the value of time stored in the variable of type *time_t* at the address *time*. This value is obtained by an earlier call to the function *time*, which returns the number of seconds elapsed since 00:00:00 hours GMT, January 1, 1970. The string prepared by *ctime* is 26 characters long, counting the null character at the end, and has the form:

```
Thu Nov 26 17:02:39 1987\n\0
```

As the preceding example shows, a 24-hour clock is used for the time.

RETURNS The *ctime* function returns a pointer to the data area where the character string containing the date and time is stored.

COMMENTS To prepare the time for printing, the *ctime* and *asctime* functions use a single static string so it will be destroyed by subsequent calls to these routines.

SEE ALSO

`asctime` *To convert time from a* tm *structure into a character string*

`strtime` *To convert time from a* tm *structure to a string with detailed formatting*

`time` *To get the current time as a long integer value*

EXAMPLE Use *ctime* to prepare a string version of the value returned by a call to *time* and print this string.

```
#include <stdio.h>
#include <time.h>
main()
{
    time_t bintime;
/* Get time in seconds since 00:00:00 GMT, 1/1/70 */
    time(&bintime);
/* Use ctime to print the date and time            */
    printf("Current time: %s\n", ctime(&bintime));
    return 0;
}
```

COMPATIBILITY

difftime

TC1	TC1.5	TC2	TC++	MSC3	MSC4	MSC5	MSC6	QC1	QC2	QC2.5	ANSI	UNIX V	XNX
▲	▲	▲	▲	▲	▲	▲	▲	▲	▲	▲	▲	▲	▲

PURPOSE Use *difftime* to obtain the difference of two time values, each of type *time_t*.

SYNTAX

```
double difftime(time_t time2, time_t time1);
```

`time_t time2;` *Value of time from which* time1 *will be subtracted*

`time_t time1;` *Value of time to be subtracted from* time2

EXAMPLE CALL

```
seconds_used = difftime(oldtime, newtime);
```

INCLUDES `#include <time.h>` *For function declaration definition of* time_t

DESCRIPTION The *difftime* function computes the difference between time values *time2* and *time1*. These times are obtained by calling *time*, which returns the current time in seconds since 00:00:00 hours GMT, January 1, 1970. This function is useful for computing elapsed time between arbitrary events. Use *clock* for determining how long the current program has been running.

RETURNS The *difftime* function returns the elapsed time, *time2* – *time1*, in seconds as a double-precision number.

SEE ALSO `time` *To get current time in seconds since 00:00:00 hours GMT, January 1, 1970*

EXAMPLE Use *difftime* to determine the time it takes to perform a computational loop a specified number of times.

```
#include <stdio.h>
#include <time.h>
main()
{
    unsigned long i, count;
    double a, b, c, d, tused, tperstep;
    time_t tstart, tstop;
/* Ask user number of times "multiply" to be done */
    printf("Enter number of times loop is run:");
    scanf(" %lu", &count);
/* Get current time by calling "time"            */
    time(&tstart);
    for(i=0; i<count; i++)
    {
        a = (double)(i-1);
        b = (double)(i+1);
        c = (double)(i*i);
        d = a*b - c;
    }
/* Get time again and print time used.           */
    time(&tstop);
    tused = difftime(tstop, tstart);  /* in sec  */
    tperstep = tused/(double)count;
    printf("Total time = %f seconds\n\
Time per iteration: %f milliseconds\n", tused,
           tperstep*1000.0);
    return 0;
}
```

ftime

COMPATIBILITY

TC1	TC1.5	TC2	TC++	MSC3	MSC4	MSC5	MSC6	QC1	QC2	QC2.5	ANSI	UNIX V	XNX
		▲	▲	▲	▲	▲	▲	▲	▲	▲		▲	▲

PURPOSE Use *ftime* to get the current time and store it in a structure of type *timeb.*

SYNTAX

```
void ftime(struct timeb *timeptr);
```

`struct timeb *timeptr;` *Pointer to structure of type* timeb *to which time is returned*

EXAMPLE CALL

```
ftime(&time_buffer);
```

INCLUDES `#include <sys\timeb.h>` *For function declaration and definition of structure* timeb

DESCRIPTION The *ftime* function gets the current time and stores it in a structure of type *timeb* that you allocate and whose address you provide in the argument *timeptr*. The fields in the structure at *timeptr* are set to appropriate values by *ftime*. The *timeb* structure is defined in the include file *sys\timeb.h* as:

```
struct timeb
{
    long          time;     /* Time in seconds since 00:00:00
                               GMT, January 1, 1970          */
    short millitm;          /* Fraction of a second in milli-
                               seconds                        */
    short         timezone; /* Difference in minutes moving
                               westward, between GMT and local
                               time                           */
    short         dstflag;  /* Nonzero if daylight saving is
                               in effect in the local time zone*/
};
```

The *ftime* function uses the settings of the global variables *timezone* and *daylight* in setting the values of the fields *timezone* and *dstflag* in the *timeb* structure. These variables are set by calling *tzset* and using the environment variable TZ. (See the reference page on *tzset* for more details.)

SEE ALSO `time` *To get current time as a long integer value*

`tzset` *To set environment variables that indicate time zones and enable daylight saving hours*

EXAMPLE Use *ftime* to get the current time. Use *ctime* to display the *time* field of the *timeb* structure.

```
#include <stdio.h>
#include <sys\types.h>
#include <sys\timeb.h>
#include <time.h>
main()
{
    struct timeb time_buffer;
    char *date_time;
/* Use "ftime" to get current time into time_buffer */
    ftime(&time_buffer);
/* Convert "time" field to a string and print it    */
```

```
    printf("Time = %s", ctime(&time_buffer.time));
    return 0;
}
```

gmtime

COMPATIBILITY

TC1	TC1.5	TC2	TC++	MSC3	MSC4	MSC5	MSC6	QC1	QC2	QC2.5	ANSI	UNIX V	XNX
▲	▲	▲	▲	▲	▲	▲	▲	▲	▲	▲	▲	▲	▲

PURPOSE Use *gmtime* to separate a time value of type *time_t* into fields of a structure of type *tm*. This results in values that represent the GMT relative to the time zone specified in the environment variable TZ.

SYNTAX

```
struct tm *gmtime(const time_t *time);
```

`const time_t *time;` *Pointer to stored time in seconds elapsed since 00:00:00 GMT, January 1, 1970*

EXAMPLE CALL

```
t_gmt = gmtime(&bintime);
```

INCLUDES `#include <time.h>` *For function declaration and definition of structure* tm *and data type* time_t

DESCRIPTION The *gmtime* function breaks down a time value, stored at the location *time*, to year, month, day, hour, minutes, seconds, and several other fields that it saves in a structure of type *tm*. The value at *time* is the number of seconds elapsed from 00:00:00 hours GMT, January 1, 1970, to a time obtained by calling the function *time*. The structure *tm* is defined in *time.h* as follows:

```
struct tm
{
    int tm_sec;      /* seconds after the minute - [0,59] */
    int tm_min;      /* minutes after the hour - [0,59]   */
    int tm_hour;     /* hours since midnight - [0,23]     */
    int tm_mday;     /* day of the month - [1,31]         */
    int tm_mon;      /* months since January - [0,11]     */
    int tm_year;     /* years since 1900                  */
    int tm_wday;     /* days since Sunday - [0,6]         */
    int tm_yday;     /* days since January 1 - [0,365]    */
    int tm_isdst;    /* daylight savings time flag, nonzero
                        if enabled                        */
};
```

The fields set up by *gmtime* correspond to GMT as dictated by the environment variable TZ, which indicates the time zone and the daylight saving zone for use in converting from local time to GMT. TZ must be set to a three-letter time zone name (such as PST, EST, etc.), followed by a signed number giving the difference between GMT and the local time zone (a positive sign can be omitted). An optional three-letter daylight saving zone name can be added to the setting. The *gmtime* function uses this information to convert the local time to GMT based on the time zone and the daylight saving season. If TZ is not defined, a default setting of PST8PDT is used. Note that TZ is not a part of the ANSI standard; it is a Turbo C++ extension.

RETURNS The *gmtime* function returns a pointer to the structure where the converted time is stored.

COMMENTS MS-DOS does not understand dates prior to 1980, so time values provided to the library routines *gmtime* and *localtime* must be later than 1980. Note that *gmtime* uses the static structure of type *tm* to return the result so each call to this routine destroys the result of the preceding call.

SEE ALSO

`asctime`	*To convert time from a structure of type* tm *into a character string*
`localtime`	*To convert from GMT to local time*
`time`	*To get current time in seconds elapsed since 00:00:00 hours GMT, January 1, 1970*

EXAMPLE Get the current time using *time*, convert it to GMT using *gmtime*, and display this latter time.

```
#include <stdio.h>
#include <time.h>
main()
{
    time_t tnow;
    struct tm *tmnow;
/* Get the time in seconds since 0 hrs GMT, 1/1/70  */
    time(&tnow);
/* Convert it to string showing Greenwich Mean Time */
    tmnow = gmtime(&tnow);
    printf("Greenwich Mean Time = %s\n",
            asctime(tmnow));
    return 0;
}
```

localtime

COMPATIBILITY

TC1	TC1.5	TC2	TC++	MSC3	MSC4	MSC5	MSC6	QC1	QC2	QC2.5	ANSI	UNIX V	XNX
▲	▲	▲	▲	▲	▲	▲	▲	▲	▲	▲	▲	▲	▲

PURPOSE Use *localtime* to separate a time value of type *time_t* into various fields of a structure of type *tm*.

SYNTAX

```
struct tm *localtime(const time_t *time);
```

`const time_t *time;` *Pointer to stored time in seconds elapsed since 00:00:00 hours GMT, January 1, 1970*

EXAMPLE CALL

```
t_local = localtime(&bintime);
```

INCLUDES `#include <time.h>` *For function declaration and definition of structure* tm *and data type* time_t

DESCRIPTION The *localtime* function breaks down the time value, stored at the location *time*, to year, month, day, hour, minutes, seconds, and several other fields that it saves in a structure of type *tm*. The fields set up by *localtime* correspond to local time. The value at *time* is the number of seconds elapsed from 00:00:00 hours GMT, January 1, 1970, to a time obtained by calling the function *time*. The structure *tm* is defined in *time.h* as shown in the reference pages on *gmtime*.

RETURNS The *localtime* function returns a pointer to the structure where the converted time is stored.

COMMENTS MS-DOS does not understand dates prior to 1980, so time values provided to the library routines *localtime* and *gmtime* must be later than 1980. Note that *localtime* uses the static structure of type *tm* to return the result so each call to this routine destroys the result of the preceding call.

SEE ALSO

`asctime` *To convert time from a structure of type* tm *into a character string*

`gmtime` *To convert from local time to GMT*

`time` *To get current time in seconds elapsed since 00:00:00 hours GMT, January 1, 1970*

EXAMPLE Use *time* to get the current time. Convert it to a detailed representation of the local date and time by using *localtime*. Use *asctime* to print the date and time.

```
#include <stdio.h>
#include <time.h>
main()
{
    time_t tnow;
    struct tm *tmnow;
/* Get the time in seconds since 0 hrs GMT, 1/1/70  */
    time(&tnow);
/* Convert it to string showing local time. Use the
 * environment variable TZ and the function "tzset"
 * to set the timezone appropriately.
 * Default time is PST.
 */
    tmnow = localtime(&tnow);
    printf("Local Time = %s\n", asctime(tmnow));
    return 0;
}
```

COMPATIBILITY

strftime

TC1	TC1.5	TC2	TC++	MSC3	MSC4	MSC5	MSC6	QC1	QC2	QC2.5	ANSI	UNIX V	XNX
			▲				▲		▲	▲			

PURPOSE Use the *strftime* function to format a broken-down time in a *tm* structure into a string.

SYNTAX

```
size_t strftime(char *str, size_t maxsize, const char *format_string,
                const struct tm *timeptr);
```

`char        *str;`	*Pointer to array of characters where result is placed*
`size_t      maxsize;`	*Maximum number of characters in* str
`const char *format_string;`	*Formatting codes for converting the time to a string*
`const struct tm *timeptr;`	*Pointer to structure containing broken-down time*

EXAMPLE CALL

```
/* Produce the standard output: Thu Apr 26 19:02:39 1990 */
strftime(s, 80, "%a %b %c\n", &tptr);
```

INCLUDES `#include <time.h>` *For function declaration*

DESCRIPTION The *strftime* function formats a broken-down time in the *tm* structure whose address is in *timeptr* into a string whose address you provide in *str*. At most, *maxsize* characters will be placed in the string. The formatting is done according to the formatting codes given in the string *format_string*. Like *sprintf*, the formatting codes begin with a '%' and are explained in Table 13.3. The argument *format_string* is expected to be in multibyte characters. Characters that do not begin with a '%' are copied unchanged to *str*. The LC_TIME category of the program's locale affects the behavior of *strftime*.

Table 13-3. *Formatting Codes for* strftime

Format	Replaced By
%a	Current locale's abbreviated name for the weekday.
%A	Current locale's full name for the weekday.
%b	Current locale's abbreviated name for the month.
%B	Current locale's full name for the month.
%c	Date and time representation appropriate for the locale.
%d	Day of the month as a decimal number (01-31).
%H	Hour in a 24-hour clock as a decimal number (00-23).
%I	Hour in a 12-hour clock as a decimal number (01-12).
%j	Day of the year as a decimal number (001-366).
%m	Month as a decimal number (01-12).
%M	Minute as a decimal number (00-59).
%P	Current locale's AM/PM indicator.
%S	Second as a decimal number (00-60).
%U	Week of the year as a decimal number (Sunday is taken as the first day of a week) (00-53).
%w	Weekday as a decimal number (Sunday is 0, 0-6).
%W	Week of the year as a decimal number (Monday is taken as the first day of a week) (00-53).
%x	Date representation for current locale.
%X	Time representation for current locale.
%y	Year without the century as a decimal number (00-99).
%Y	Year with the century as a decimal number.
%Z	Name of time zone (or nothing if time zone is unknown).
%%	A percent sign (%).

RETURNS The *strftime* function returns the total number of characters it placed in *str* including the terminating null character. If the number of characters exceeds *maxsize*, *strftime* returns 0 and the contents of the array *str* are indeterminate.

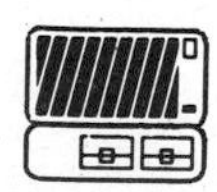

Time Routines

SEE ALSO

`asctime, ctime`	*To convert time into string in a standard fixed format*
`gmtime, localtime`	*To convert from binary time to* tm *structure*
`time`	*To get the number of seconds elapsed since January 1, 1970*

EXAMPLE Get the current time, convert it to a *tm* structure using *localtime*, and print it using *strftime*.

```
#include <stdio.h>
#include <time.h>
main()
{
    struct tm *curtime;
    time_t    bintime;
    char      time_str[80];
/* Get time in seconds since 00:00:00 GMT, 1/1/70 */
    time(&bintime);
/* Convert time to local time (default is PST)    */
    curtime = localtime(&bintime);
/* Use strftime to convert time to a string       */
    strftime(time_str, 80, "Current time: %I:%M:%S %p %Z",
          curtime);
    printf("%s\n", time_str);

    return 0;
}
```

stime

COMPATIBILITY

TC1	TC1.5	TC2	TC++	MSC3	MSC4	MSC5	MSC6	QC1	QC2	QC2.5	ANSI	UNIX V	XNX
▲	▲	▲	▲										

PURPOSE Use *stime* to set the system time and date.

SYNTAX `int  stime(time_t *tp);`

`time_t *tp;` *Address of location containing date and time in UNIX format*

EXAMPLE CALL `stime(&new_time);`

INCLUDES `#include <time.h>` *For function prototype and definition of* time_t

DESCRIPTION The *stime* function sets the system date and time to the value contained in the location whose address is in the argument *tp*. The new date and time must be in the UNIX format—seconds elapsed since 00:00 hour GMT, January 1, 1970.

RETURNS The *stime* function always returns 0. If the specified value of time is invalid (for example a negative value), the system date and time are not changed.

COMMENTS If you have the date and time available in DOS format (the usual MM-DD-YY, HH:MM:SS format), you can use the function *dostounix* to get the UNIX form of the time.

SEE ALSO `dostounix` *To convert time from DOS to UNIX format*

EXAMPLE Use *stime* to set the system date and time. Get the new date and time from the user, and use *dostounix* to convert these values into a UNIX format time.

```
#include <stdio.h>
#include <dos.h>
#include <time.h>
main()
{
    int d, m, y, h, min, sec;
    long uxtime;
    struct date date;
    struct time time;
/* Get current date and time and prompt for new values */
    getdate(&date);
    printf("The date is %d-%d-%d\nEnter new date: ",
           date.da_mon, date.da_day, date.da_year);
    scanf(" %d-%d-%d", &m, &d, &y);
    gettime(&time);
    printf("Current time is %02d:%02d:%02d\nEnter new time:",
          time.ti_hour, time.ti_min, time.ti_sec);
    scanf(" %d:%d:%d", &h, &min, &sec);
/* Copy date and time into the date and time structures */
    date.da_year = y;
    date.da_mon = m;
    date.da_day = d;
    time.ti_hour = h;
    time.ti_min = min;
    time.ti_sec = sec;
/* Convert date and time to UNIX format */
    uxtime = dostounix(&date, &time);
```

```
/* Set date and time using stime */
    stime(&uxtime);
    printf("Date and time set. Verify using DOS"
           " commands DATE and TIME\n");
    return 0;
}
```

time

COMPATIBILITY

TC1	TC1.5	TC2	TC++	MSC3	MSC4	MSC5	MSC6	QC1	QC2	QC2.5	ANSI	UNIX V	XNX
▲	▲	▲	▲	▲	▲	▲	▲	▲	▲	▲	▲	▲	▲

PURPOSE Use *time* to obtain the number of seconds elapsed since 00:00:00 hours, GMT, January 1, 1970.

SYNTAX

```
time_t time(time_t *timeptr);

time_t *timeptr;      Pointer to variable where result is returned
```

EXAMPLE CALL `time(&bintime);`

INCLUDES `#include <time.h>` *For function declaration and definition of* `time_t`

DESCRIPTION The *time* function gets the current time and adjusts it according to the value in the global variable *_timezone* which is set by the function *tzset*. Then it computes the number of seconds elapsed since 00:00:00 hour GMT, January 1, 1970, till the adjusted current time. The result is stored as a variable of type *time_t* at the location *timeptr*. If *timeptr* is NULL, the result is not stored.

RETURNS The *time* function returns the number of elapsed seconds.

COMMENTS The value obtained from *time* can be converted to a string by calling *ctime* and the fields of the date and time can be separated by calling *gmtime* or *localtime*.

SEE ALSO

`ctime` *To convert time into a string*

`gmtime, localtime` *To convert time into a* tm *structure*

`tzset` *To set environment variables that indicate the local time zone*

EXAMPLE Get and display the current time.

```
#include <stdio.h>
#include <time.h>
main()
{
    time_t tnow;
/* Get the time in seconds since 0 hrs GMT, 1/1/70 */
    time(&tnow);
/* Convert the time to a string and print it. This
 * will be your local time provided you have set the
 * environment variable TZ to your time zone. The
 * default is PST with daylight saving enabled.
 * See "tzset" for details.
 */
    printf("Current time = %s\n", ctime(&tnow));
    return 0;
}
```

tzset

COMPATIBILITY

TC1	TC1.5	TC2	TC++	MSC3	MSC4	MSC5	MSC6	QC1	QC2	QC2.5	ANSI	UNIX V	XNX
▲	▲	▲	▲	▲	▲	▲	▲	▲	▲	▲		▲	▲

PURPOSE Use *tzset* to assign values to the global variables *timezone, daylight* and *tzname* based on the time zone specified in the environment variable TZ.

SYNTAX `void tzset(void);`

EXAMPLE CALL `tzet();`

INCLUDES `#include <time.h>` *For function declaration and declaration of the global variables*

DESCRIPTION The *tzset* function uses the current setting of the environment variable TZ to assign appropriate values to the global variables shown in Table 13-4. TZ indicates the time zone and the daylight saving zone for use in converting from GMT to local time. TZ must be set to a three-letter time zone name (PST, EST, etc.), followed by a signed number giving the difference between GMT and the local time zone (a positive sign can be omitted). An optional three-letter daylight saving zone name can be added to the setting. The *tzset* function uses this information to compute and save the values of the global variables shown in Table 13-4. If TZ is not defined, a default setting of PST8PDT is used. TZ and *tzset* are not part of the ANSI standard C; they are Turbo C extensions.

COMMENTS The *gmtime* function uses the global variables as set by *tzset.*

Table 13-4. *Global Variables for Time Zone and Daylight Saving*

Variable	Type and Value
timezone	Long integer. The difference in seconds between GMT and local time. Default value is 28800 (this means that the local time is Pacific Standard Time which is 28,800 seconds or 8 hours later than GMT).
daylight	Integer. Nonzero if a daylight saving time zone is specified TZ. Otherwise it is zero. Default value is 1.
tzname[0]	Character string. Three-letter time zone name from TZ. Default is PST.
tzname[1]	Character string. Three-letter daylight saving time zone name from TZ, or an empty string if omitted from TZ. Default is PDT.

SEE ALSO `localtime, time` *Functions that use the environment variables set up by* tzset

EXAMPLE Use *putenv* to set the environment variable TZ to the value EST5EDT. Then call *tzset* and print the values of the global variables *timezone* and *daylight* and the strings in the array *tz*.

```
#include <stdio.h>
#include <stdlib.h>
#include <time.h>
extern char *tzname[2];
main()
{
    time_t tnow;
/* Set the environment variable TZ to Eastern Standard
 * Time with daylight saving enabled. See text for
 * information on defining TZ.
 */
    if(putenv("TZ=EST5EDT") == -1)
    {
        printf("Error defining TZ\n");
        exit(1);
    }
/* Now call "tzset" to set up internal global variables */
    tzset();
/* Print the current values of the global variables     */
    printf("timezone = %ld, daylight = %d,\n\
tzname[0] = %s\ntzname[1] = %s\n", timezone, daylight,
           tzname[0], tzname[1]);
/* Get and display current local time -- should be EDT   */
    time(&tnow);
    printf("Local time = %s", ctime(&tnow));
    return 0;
}
```

IV Files and I/O

- ▶ File Manipulation
- ▶ Directory Manipulation
- ▶ Input and Output Routines
- ▶ System Calls

Chapter 14 File Manipulation

Introduction

The file system is a key system component of the PC. All applications and data reside in files. If you develop an application, it is likely to use files for temporary storage of its data and results so that they can be reused at a later date. We cover reading from and writing to files in the I/O discussion in Chapter 16. File manipulation covers routines that enable us to determine the status of a file and to perform certain housekeeping chores to keep the files in order.

Concepts

The concepts of file system and of mechanisms used to access files are central to file manipulation.

HIERARCHICAL FILE SYSTEM IN MS-DOS

The file system describes the way files are organized under an operating system. MS-DOS uses a hierarchical file system, which refers to its tree-like structure. As illustrated in Figure 14-1, that file system has a root directory under which there are directories and files. Each directory can have more files and directories under it.

PATHNAMES TO ACCESS FILES

Files under MS-DOS can be specified by their pathnames. This is a string (see Figure 14-2) with four major components: the drive letter, the directory names, the file name, and the extension. The drive letter is a single letter followed by a colon specifying the disk drive in which the file resides. Each directory name starts with the root directory (indicated by a \)

followed by all its subdirectories, each separated from the previous one by a \. The last directory name is followed by a \ and then a file name with up to eight characters and, optionally, a three-letter extension. A period separates the extension from the file name. Files can be renamed with the Turbo C++ routine *rename*. The *fnmerge* and *fnsplit* routines, respectively, let you combine and take apart a pathname by its component parts.

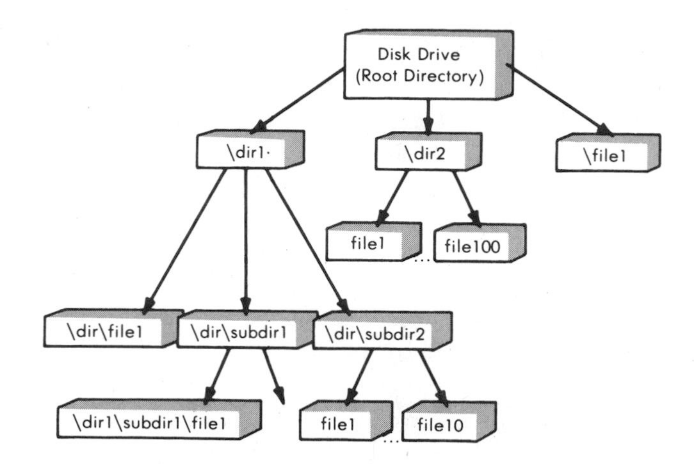

Figure 14-1. *MS-DOS hierarchical file system*

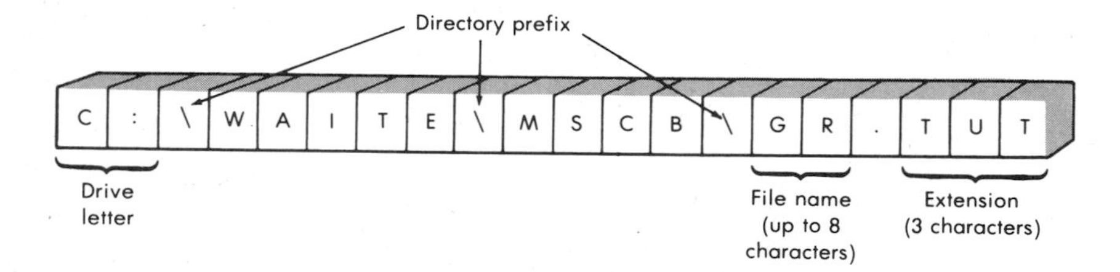

Figure 14-2. *Pathname of a file in MS-DOS*

FILE HANDLES

The pathname of a file is one way of identifying it, but there is another way to reach a file. When you create or open a file using the functions *open*, *sopen* or *creat*, an integer identifier, called the "handle" of the file, is returned. The handle is used by the system to access a structure where certain pertinent information about the open file is stored. When you query the system about an open file, its handle suffices as an identifier.

PERTINENT FILE INFORMATION

To manipulate files, certain pieces of information are crucial to your application, among them "permission" and "permission mask" settings, file size and status, and translation mode.

Permission Settings

Normally, you can read from and write to a file. You may not want to allow others to read from a file, however, if the data is confidential. You may also want certain files to be "read only" because you don't want others to overwrite the data in these files inadvertently. Each operating system provides a means to control access to a file. In MS-DOS certain permission settings are associated with a file. If you think of the read and write access to a file as one-way doors, the permission settings indicate which of these doors are open. As shown in Figure 14-3, for example, in a read-only file, only the read door is open and the write door is locked.

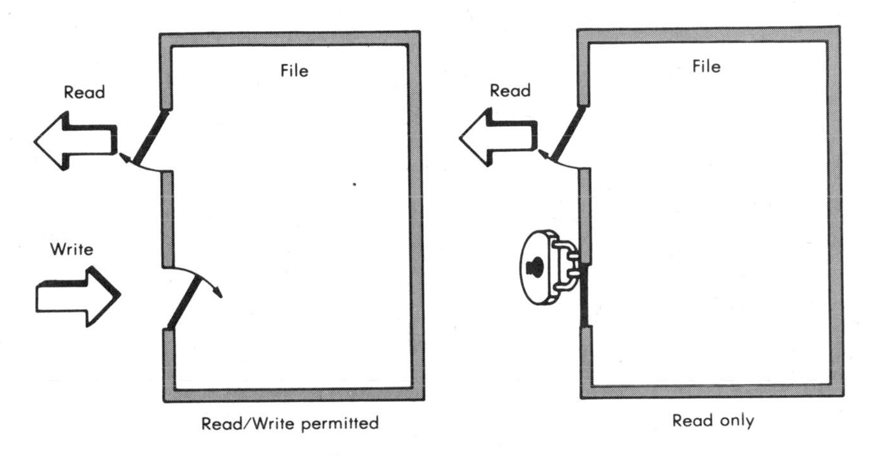

Figure 14-3. ***Permission settings of a file***

There are three types of permission settings. In Turbo C++ the include file *sys\stat.h* contains the constants S_IREAD and S_IWRITE which denote read and write permissions, respectively. When both reading and writing are permitted, permission is set to the bitwise OR of the two, S_IREAD | S_IWRITE. Under MS-DOS, reading and writing are allowed on all directories. Also, all files are always readable under MS-DOS. Thus a file's permission setting to S_IWRITE is equivalent to the setting S_IREAD | S_IWRITE.

The *access* function lets you check the permission settings of a file while *chmod* lets you alter the permission setting of an open file.

Permission Mask

The permission mask is not associated with individual files, but is a bit pattern used by the file creation routines to determine the permission settings of a newly created file. You specify the permission mask with the same permission constants, S_IREAD and S_IWRITE, but their interpretation is different. If the permission mask is S_IREAD, reading from the file is not allowed, so the file will be write only. (This is ignored in MS-DOS, but included for compatibility with UNIX System V.) On the other hand, a permission mask of S_IWRITE implies the file will be read only. You use the routine *umask* to specify the default permission mask.

The permission mask is applied in the following manner. When you create a file by a call to *creat, open,* or *sopen,* you specify the desired permission setting for the new file. If necessary, the file creation routines use the current value of the permission mask to override the requested permission setting. For example, if the mask says that all files should be read only (remember, you cannot have a write only file in MS-DOS), a request for a permission setting of S_IREAD | S_IWRITE is changed to S_IREAD.

File Size and Status

The size or length of a file refers to the number of bytes in the file. For example, the length of the file shown in Figure 14-4 is 8 bytes. You can use the routine *filelength* to determine the length of a file that is already open. The size of an open file can be altered by the routine *chsize.* If the file is not open, you can find its length from its status. The status includes when the file was last modified, its size, and the disk drive where it is located. The information is provided in a structure of type *stat* defined in the header file *sys\stat.h.* Several other fields are included for compatibility with System V UNIX, but they are not used in MS-DOS. For an open file, use *fstat* to get the status. The *stat* provides the same information for a file specified by its pathname.

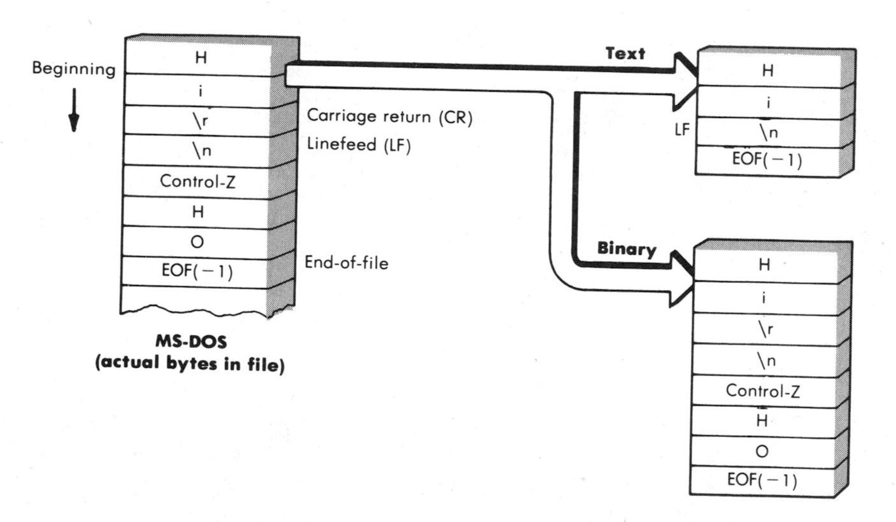

Figure 14-4. ***Text and binary translation modes***

Translation Mode

In Chapter 16 we discuss the way the contents of a file can be interpreted when reading from or writing to the file under MS-DOS. The interpretation depends on which of the two "translation modes" is associated with the open file: text or binary. "Text mode" is useful for reading to and writing from ASCII text files. "Binary mode" is used to read data files.

In binary mode each byte in the file is treated as a value with no special significance, as shown in Figure 14-4. Since the number of bytes in the file is known, the end-of-file is encountered when all the bytes have been read; there is no specific end-of-file value in the binary mode.

In text mode, a carriage return (\r) followed by a linefeed, or newline \n, is translated to a single newline. Also, as soon as a Control-Z is encountered, the file is considered to have ended. Thus anything after a Control-Z cannot be read in this mode.

Figure 14-4 illustrates how the contents of a file are treated when opened in both modes. In text mode, the contents of the file are checked to see if a Control-Z or a carriage return is encountered, but in binary mode, the file's contents are taken literally, without any translation. Use the function *setmode* if you want to change the translation mode of a file that is already open.

Table 14-1 details the routines for file manipulation. Next we explain some of the capabilities described.

Table 14-1. ***File Manipulation Routines***

Routine	Description
access	Checks for existence as well as read/write permission settings of a file.
chmod	Changes the read/write permission settings of a file.
chsize	Extends or truncates a file.
filelength	Returns length of a file in bytes.
fnmerge	Constructs a DOS pathname out of component parts.
fnsplit	Separates a DOS pathname into its component parts.
fstat	Returns information about an open file specified by handle.
isatty	Checks if a file handle refers to a character device.
lock	When file-sharing is enabled (MS-DOS 3.0 and higher), locks a specified number of bytes in an open file.
mktemp	Generates a unique file name by use of a template.
remove	Deletes a file specified by its pathname.
rename	Changes the pathname of a file to a new value (can be used to move file to new directory).
setmode	Changes the translation mode of an open file specified by its handle.
stat	Returns information about a file specified by its pathname.
umask	Sets the default read/write permission mask for the current process.

Table 14-1. *(cont.)*

Routine	Description
unlink	Deletes a file specified by its pathname.
unlock	When file-sharing is enabled (MS-DOS 3.0 and higher), unlocks a specified number of bytes in an open file.

FILE MANIPULATION BY TASK

The file manipulation routines let you modify and obtain certain information about MS-DOS files. They also allow you to delete files (using *remove*, and *unlink*) and perform certain utility functions such as generating temporary file names (with *mktemp*) and locking certain parts of a file that has been opened for sharing. Table 14-2 shows the routines grouped by task.

Table 14-2. *File Manipulation Routines by Task*

Task	Routines
Delete a file.	remove, unlink
Alter and set permission setting.	access, chmod, umask
Get status information of a file.	fstat, stat
Name file.	mktemp, rename
Change or check file size.	chsize, filelength
Check if file is a character device.	isatty
Set translation mode (text or binary).	setmode
Lock/unlock portions of file.	lock, unlock
Assemble and disassemble MS-DOS pathnames.	fnmerge, fnsplit

File or Device

In MS-DOS, devices are opened like files and I/O with devices can be done using a common set of routines. For each open file, the system maintains information to tell devices apart from disk files. The *isatty* function lets you determine if a file handle refers to a device or to a disk file. For example, the preopened files *stdin* and *stdout* are initially connected to the keyboard and the monitor, which are *devices*. If either of these are redirected to a disk file, MS-DOS will mark the handles as such. You can use the *isatty* function to determine whether a handle refers to a disk file or a device.

File-Sharing

Under MS-DOS 3.0 and higher, the command SHARE installs the file-sharing option that allows multiple processes to open and access a file.

After opening a file for sharing (with *sopen*), the actual sharing is achieved by a mechanism (the *lock* and *unlock* functions) that enables you to lock and unlock specific portions of the file.

Cautions

- File-sharing is not available in MS-DOS versions below 3.0 because the *locking* function does not work in those versions.
- Note that several functions require the file handle as an input parameter. If you open the file using a higher-level stream I/O routine (see Chapter 16), use *fileno* to get the handle.
- Remember that MS-DOS imposes a limit of 20 open files per process.

Further Reading

Consult Prata's book[1] for a detailed exposition of the file manipulation routines. Permission settings and translation modes are also explained.

1. Stephen Prata, The Waite Group, *Advanced C Primer++*, Howard W. Sams & Company, Indianapolis, IN, 1986, 502 pages.

access

COMPATIBILITY

TC1	TC1.5	TC2	TC++	MSC3	MSC4	MSC5	MSC6	QC1	QC2	QC2.5	ANSI	UNIX V	XNX
▲	▲	▲	▲	▲	▲	▲	▲	▲	▲	▲		▲	▲

PURPOSE Use *access* to check whether a file exists and if so, whether read and/or write operations are permitted.

SYNTAX

```
int access(const char *path, int mode);

const char *path;      Pathname of file being checked

int mode;              Integer denoting permission setting being checked
```

EXAMPLE CALL

```
if(access("temp.dat", 4) == 0) puts("Data file exists");
```

INCLUDES `#include <io.h>` *For function declaration*

DESCRIPTION The *access* function determines whether the file specified by the pathname *path* exists and whether the permission setting of the file allows the operation indicated by the argument *mode*. Use one of the values shown in the table for the argument *mode*. If the pathname *path* specifies a directory, *access* only verifies whether the directory exists. Under MS-DOS all directories have both read and write permissions, and all files have read permission.

Value of *mode*	Interpretation
00	Only existence of file will be checked.
02	Check if file has write permission.
04	Check if file has read permission.
06	Check if file has read and write permission.

RETURNS If *access* finds that the file or directory specified by *path* exists and allows the access specified by *mode*, it returns a 0. If the pathname does not exist or is not accessible in the specified *mode*, the return value is −1 and the global variable *errno* is set to ENOENT to indicate that the specified pathname is invalid or to EACCES to denote that the requested type of access is not allowed.

SEE ALSO

`chmod` *To alter the permission setting of a file*

`fstat, stat` *To find information about an open file, including permission settings*

EXAMPLE Using *access*, write a program that checks the existence of the file CONFIG.SYS in the root directory of drive C. If the file exists and has read permission, open it with *fopen* and display its contents.

```
#include <io.h>
#include <io.h>
char filename[] = "c:\\config.sys";
main()
{
        FILE *infile;
        char buffer[80];
/* Check if the file exists. Note that we need two '\'*/
        if(access(filename, 4) == -1)
        {
            perror("access failed");
            exit(1);
        }
        if ( (infile = fopen(filename, "r")) == NULL)
        {
            perror("fopen failed");
            exit(1);
        }
        printf("Contents of %s\n", filename);
        while ( fgets(buffer, 80, infile) != NULL)
        {
            printf(buffer);
        }
        return 0;
}
```

COMPATIBILITY

chmod

TC1	TC1.5	TC2	TC++	MSC3	MSC4	MSC5	MSC6	QC1	QC2	QC2.5	ANSI	UNIX V	XNX
▲	▲	▲	▲	▲	▲	▲	▲	▲	▲	▲		▲	▲

PURPOSE Use *chmod* to alter the read/write permission settings of a file.

SYNTAX

```
int chmod(const char *path, int pmode);
```

`const char *path;` *Pathname of file whose permission is being changed*

`int pmode;` *Integer denoting new permission setting for the file*

EXAMPLE CALL `chmod("inventory.lis", S_IWRITE);`

INCLUDES

`#include <stdio.h>`	*For function declaration*
`#include <sys\types.h>`	*Required by* <sys\stat.h>
`#include <sys\stat.h>`	*For definition of constants denoting permission settings*

DESCRIPTION The *chmod* function sets the read/write permission setting of the file whose pathname is given in the argument *path* to the new setting specified in the integer *pmode*. The permission settings are specified in terms of constants defined in the include file *sys\stat.h*. The table below shows the possible combinations of the permission settings and their meanings. Under MS-DOS all files are readable, so it is not possible to give write only permission to a file.

Constant	Interpretation
S_IWRITE	Both reading and writing permitted.
S_IREAD	Only reading permitted.
S_IREAD | S_IWRITE	Both reading and writing permitted.

RETURNS If *chmod* successfully changes the permission setting to *pmode*, it returns a 0. In case of error, the return value is −1 and the global variable *errno* is set to ENOENT to indicate that the specified pathname is invalid.

SEE ALSO

access	*To check if read/write operations are permitted on a file*
fstat, stat	*To find information about an open file, including permission settings*

EXAMPLE Write a small utility program using *chmod* to enable the user to change the read/write permission of a file. Assume that the command-line syntax is: "CHMOD <pathname> <permission>" in which "permission" is a single character R (for read only) or W (both read and write).

```
#include <stdio.h>
#include <sys\types.h>

#include <sys\stat.h>
#include <io.h>
main(int argc, char **argv)
{
    int pmode=-999;
    if(argc < 3)
```

```
    {
        printf(
          "Usage: %s <pathname> <R|W>\n", argv[0]);
    }
    else
    {
/* Convert last argument to permission code          */
        if(argv[2][0]=='R') pmode = S_IREAD;
        if(argv[2][0]=='W') pmode = S_IREAD|S_IWRITE;
        if(pmode==-999)
        {
                printf("Unknown permission: %s\n",
                        argv[2]);
                exit(1);
        }
        if(chmod(argv[1], pmode) == -1)
        {
            perror("Error in \"chmod\"");
        }
    }
    return 0;
}
```

COMPATIBILITY

chsize

TC1	TC1.5	TC2	TC++	MSC3	MSC4	MSC5	MSC6	QC1	QC2	QC2.5	ANSI	UNIX V	XNX
▲	▲	▲	▲	▲	▲	▲	▲	▲	▲	▲		▲	▲

PURPOSE Use *chsize* to extend or truncate a file open for unbuffered, unformatted write operations.

SYNTAX

```
int chsize(int handle, long size);
```

`int handle;` *Handle of file whose size is being changed*

`long size;` *New length of file in bytes*

EXAMPLE CALL

```
chsize(filehandle, 0L);  /* Truncate file to zero length */
```

INCLUDES `#include <io.h>` *For function declaration*

DESCRIPTION The *chsize* function truncates or extends the file specified by the argument *handle* to match the new length in bytes given in the argument *size*. When the file is extended, null characters are appended to the file. When the file is truncated, all data beyond the new *size* is lost.

RETURNS The *chsize* returns a 0 to indicate success. In case of error, the return value is −1 and the global variable *errno* is set to one of the constants shown in Table 14-3.

Table 14-3. *Values of* errno *on Return from* chsize

Error Constant	Interpretation of Error Code
EACCES	Access to file was denied. For DOS 3.0 and above this means the file is locked against writing.
EBADF	File is read only or the handle does not refer to an open file.
ENOSPC	No more space left on the device where the file is stored. This can occur when trying to extend a file on a nearly full disk.

SEE ALSO

`access` *To check if read/write operations are permitted on a file*

`chmod` *To change read/write permissions of a file*

`fstat, stat` *To find information about an open file, including permission settings*

EXAMPLE Prompt the user for the name of an existing file to open and truncate to size zero.

```
#include <stdio.h>
#include <fcntl.h>
#include <io.h>
main()
{
    int  filehandle, answer = 0;
    char filename[80];
    printf("Enter name of file to truncate: ");
    gets(filename);
    if((filehandle = open(filename, O_RDWR)) == -1)
    {
        perror("open failed");
        exit(1);
    }
/* Now give user a warning and a chance to abort      */
    while(answer != 'N' && answer != 'Y')

    {
```

```
            printf("Truncate %s to size zero? (Y or N)",
                    filename);
            scanf(" %1s", &answer);
            answer = toupper(answer);
        }
        if(answer == 'Y')
        {
            if(chsize(filehandle, 0L) == -1)
            {
                perror("chsize failed");
            }
            else
            {
                printf("%s successfully truncated.\n",
                        filename);
            }
        }
        return 0;
    }
```

COMPATIBILITY

filelength

TC1	TC1.5	TC2	TC++	MSC3	MSC4	MSC5	MSC6	QC1	QC2	QC2.5	ANSI	UNIX V	XNX
▲	▲	▲	▲		▲	▲	▲	▲	▲	▲			

PURPOSE Use the *filelength* function to determine the length of a file in bytes. To use this function, you have to specify the file handle (see the tutorial).

SYNTAX

```
long filelength(int file_handle);

int file_handle;        Handle of file whose length is to be returned
```

EXAMPLE CALL

```
filesize = filelength(filehandle);
```

INCLUDES

```
#include <io.h>        For function declaration
```

DESCRIPTION The *filelength* function returns the size in number of bytes of the file whose handle is specified in the argument *file_handle*. To get the handle of a file opened by *fopen*, you use *fileno* and then use *filelength* to get its length.

RETURNS The long integer value returned by *filelength* is the size of the file in number of bytes. If an error occurs, the return value is −1L. If the error is due to an invalid handle, the global variable *errno* is set to constant EBADF.

SEE ALSO `fileno` *To obtain the handle of a file whose pointer to the associated FILE data structure is known*

EXAMPLE Ask the user for a file name. Open the file with *fopen* for read only. Now call *filelength* to determine the size of the file. Use *fileno* to get the handle for the file.

```
#include <io.h>
#include <stdio.h>
main()
{
        char filename[80];
        FILE *infile;
        long filesize;
        printf("Enter the name of an existing file: ");
        gets(filename);
/* Open the file */
        if ( (infile = fopen(filename, "r")) == NULL)
        {
            printf("fopen failed to open: %s\n", filename);
            exit(0);
        }
  /* Get file size and display it. Use fileno to get the handle. */
        if( (filesize = filelength(fileno(infile))) != -1L)
        {
            printf("Size of %s = %ld bytes\n", filename, filesize);
        }
        else
        {
            printf("Error getting file size\n");
        }
        return 0;
}
```

COMPATIBILITY

fnmerge

TC1	TC1.5	TC2	TC++	MSC3	MSC4	MSC5	MSC6	QC1	QC2	QC2.5	ANSI	UNIX V	XNX
▲	▲	▲	▲			1	1	1	1	1			

PURPOSE Use *fnmerge* to create a full pathname composed of a drive letter, directory path, file name, and file extension.

SYNTAX

```
void fnmerge(char *path, const char *drive, const char *dir,
             const char *fname, const char *ext);
```

`char *path;` *Pointer to buffer where full pathname will be returned*

`const char *drive;` *Drive letter*

`const char *dir;` *Directory path*

`const char *fname;` *File name*

`const char *ext;` *File extension*

EXAMPLE CALL

```
    fnmerge(pathname, "c", "\\temp\\", "result", ".dat");
/* pathname will be "c:\temp\result.dat"  */
```

INCLUDES `#include <dir.h>` *For function declaration and definition of the constant MAXPATH*

DESCRIPTION The *fnmerge* function combines the strings *drive, dir, fname,* and *ext* to construct a full pathname and store it in the buffer *path*. You must allocate enough room in the buffer to hold the complete pathname, but the individual strings may be of any length. The constant MAXPATH, defined in *dir.h*, describes the maximum-length pathname that MS-DOS can handle so a size of MAXPATH for *path* is a safe choice, assuming that the combined length of the strings does not exceed MAXPATH. The arguments *drive, dir, fname,* and *ext* are described in Table 14-4.

Table 14-4. *Components of Pathname*

Argument	Description
drive	Contains the drive letter (A, B, C, etc.) followed by an optional colon. If the colon is missing, *fnmerge* inserts it automatically in the pathname. If this string is empty, no drive letter and colon appear in the pathname.
dir	Contains the path of directories, excluding the drive letter and the actual file name. Backward slashes (\) must be used as separators in directory names including the trailing slash. If *dir* is an empty string, nothing is inserted in this

Table 14-4. *(cont.)*

Argument	Description
	position in the complete pathname. Remember that to get a single backslash character, you must have two backslashes in an initialized string.
fname	Contains the file name without the extension.
ext	This is the file's extension with a leading period (.). If this string is empty, no extension appears in the pathname.

1. The equivalent function in Microsoft C versions 4, 5, and 6, and QuickC versions 1, 2, and 2.5, is *_makepath*.

SEE ALSO fnsplit *To separate a pathname into its components*

EXAMPLE Illustrate the use of *fnmerge* by constructing a complete pathname out of component strings entered by the user.

```
#include <stdio.h>
#include <dir.h>
main()
{
    char pathname[MAXPATH], drive[MAXDRIVE],
         dir[MAXDIR], filename[MAXFILE],
         ext[MAXEXT];
/* Prompt user for various components                  */
    printf("Enter drive letter:");
    gets(drive);
    printf("      directory path (%d characters max):",
            MAXDIR-1);
    gets(dir);
    printf("      filename (%d characters max):",
            MAXFILE-1);
    gets(filename);
    printf("      extension (up to 4 letters):");
    gets(ext);
/*  Construct the complete pathname and display it  */
    fnmerge(pathname, drive, dir, filename, ext);
    printf("Pathname is:  %s\n", pathname);
    return 0;
}
```

COMPATIBILITY

fnsplit

TC1	TC1.5	TC2	TC++	MSC3	MSC4	MSC5	MSC6	QC1	QC2	QC2.5	ANSI	UNIX V	XNX
▲	▲	▲	▲			1	1	1	1	1			

PURPOSE Use *fnsplit* to separate a full pathname into its components: drive letter, directory path, file name, and file extension.

SYNTAX

```
void _fnsplit(const char *path, char *drive, char *dir,
              char *fname, char *ext);
```

`const char *path;`	*Pointer to buffer where full pathname is stored*
`char *drive;`	*Drive letter*
`char *dir;`	*Directory path*
`char *fname;`	*File name*
`char *ext;`	*File extension*

EXAMPLE CALL

```
fnsplit(pathname, drive, dir, filename, extension);
```

INCLUDES `#include <dir.h>` *For function declaration and definition of the constants MAXDRIVE, MAXDIR, MAXFILE, and MAXEXT*

DESCRIPTION The *fnsplit* function splits the full pathname given in the argument *path* into its component substrings, which are returned in the strings *drive, dir, fname*, and *ext*. You must allocate enough room for each of these strings. The constants MAXDRIVE, MAXDIR, MAXFILE, and MAXEXT, defined in *dir.h*, denote the maximum lengths of the strings *drive, dir, fname*, and *ext*, respectively, and should be used to declare the strings.

When *fnsplit* returns, *drive* contains the drive letter followed by a colon; *dir* has the directory path with either forward or backward slashes as separators; *fname* is the file name; and *ext* is the extension with a leading period. If a component is absent in the argument *path*, the corresponding string will be empty (it contains a single null character (\0).

1. The equivalent function in Microsoft C versions 5 and 6, and QuickC versions 1, 2, and 2.5, is *_splitpath*.

SEE ALSO `fnmerge` *To construct a pathname from its components*

EXAMPLE Write a program that uses *fnsplit* to parse a complete pathname entered by the user.

```
#include <stdio.h>
#include <stdlib.h>
main()
{
    char pathname[MAXPATH], drive[MAXDRIVE],
         dir[MAXDIR], filename[MAXFILE],
         ext[MAXEXT];
/* Prompt user for a complete pathname               */
    printf("Enter complete pathname to parse:\n");
    gets(pathname);
/*  Decompose complete pathname and display result  */
   fnsplit(pathname, drive, dir, filename, ext);
   printf("Drive          : %s\n", drive);
   printf("Directory path: %s\n", dir);
   printf("Filename       : %s\n", filename);
   printf("Extension      : %s\n", ext);
   return 0;
}
```

fstat

COMPATIBILITY

TC1	TC1.5	TC2	TC++	MSC3	MSC4	MSC5	MSC6	QC1	QC2	QC2.5	ANSI	UNIX V	XNX
▲	▲	▲	▲	▲	▲	▲	▲	▲	▲	▲		▲	▲

PURPOSE Use the *fstat* function to retrieve information about a file that has been opened for unbuffered, unformatted I/O.

SYNTAX `int fstat(int handle, struct stat *buffer);`

`int handle;` *Handle of file whose "vital statistics" will be returned*

`struct stat *buffer;` *Pointer to structure where result will be returned*

EXAMPLE CALL `fstat(filehandle, &stat_buffer);`

INCLUDES `#include <sys\types.h>` *Required by* <sys\stat.h>

`#include <sys\stat.h>` *For function declaration and definition of structure* stat

DESCRIPTION The *fstat* function returns information about the file specified by the argument *handle*. You must allocate a structure of type *stat* and provide a pointer to this structure in the argument *buffer*. After *fstat* returns successfully, this structure contains the information about the file. The structure *stat* is defined in <sys\stat.h> and a commented version of its declaration is shown below. Several fields in the *stat* structure are used in UNIX but not in MS-DOS and are included here for compatibility.

```
struct stat
{
    short       st_dev;   /* Drive number of disk or handle of
                             device containing the file      */
    short       st_ino;   /* Unused in MS-DOS. The "i-node"
                             number of file in UNIX          */
    short       st_mode;  /* Bit mask of file's mode         */
    short       st_nlink; /* Always set to 1 under MS-DOS    */
    int         st_uid;   /* Unused in MS-DOS. For "user-id"
                             under UNIX                      */
    int         st_gid;   /* Unused in MS-DOS. For "group-id"
                             under UNIX                      */
    short       st_rdev;  /* Same as the field st_dev        */
    long        st_size;  /* Size of file in bytes           */
    long        st_atime; /* Time of last modification       */
    long        st_mtime; /* Same as st_atime                */
    long        st_ctime; /* Same as st_atime                */
};
```

RETURNS If *fstat* is successful in obtaining the information about the file, it returns a 0. In case of error, the return value is −1 and the global variable *errno* is set to the constant EBADF to indicate that the specified handle is invalid.

SEE ALSO

`access` *To check if read/write operations are permitted on a file*

`chmod` *To change read/write permissions for a file*

`stat` *To find information about a file specified by a pathname*

EXAMPLE Use *fstat* to display information about the standard output file *stdout* (you can get its handle by using *fileno*).

```
#include <stdio.h>
#include <sys\types.h>
#include <sys\stat.h>
#include <io.h>
main()
{
    struct stat info;
    if (fstat(fileno(stdout), &info) != 0)
    {
```

```
            perror("fstat failed");
            exit(1);
        }
        if ((info.st_mode & S_IFCHR) == S_IFCHR)
        {
            printf("stdout is a device\n");
        }
        if ((info.st_mode & S_IFREG) == S_IFREG)
        {
/* This means stdout has been redirected to a file */
            printf("stdout is a regular file on drive %c\n",
                info.st_dev+65);
        }
        return 0;
}
```

isatty

COMPATIBILITY

TC1	TC1.5	TC2	TC++	MSC3	MSC4	MSC5	MSC6	QC1	QC2	QC2.5	ANSI	UNIX V	XNX
▲	▲	▲	▲	▲	▲	▲	▲	▲	▲	▲		▲	▲

PURPOSE Use the *isatty* function to determine whether a particular file handle refers to a "character device" which, under MS-DOS, means the console, printer, or a serial port.

SYNTAX

```
int isatty(int handle);
```

`int handle;` *Handle about which this query is being made*

EXAMPLE CALL

```
if(isatty(fileno(stdout)) != 0) puts("stdout is console");
```

INCLUDES `#include <io.h>` *For function declaration*

DESCRIPTION The *isatty* function determines whether a specified handle refers to a character device.

COMMON USES The *isatty* function provides a way to determine if I/O redirection is in effect (the return value is zero when the I/O stream is redirected to a file). Knowing that it is might cause you to do things differently in your program. For example, when your application, XYZ, is executed with a command like XYZ>OUTFILE (meaning output from the program XYZ goes to the file OUTFILE), you might not want to make any calls to graphics functions because the user would not be expecting any output on the screen.

RETURNS The *isatty* function returns a nonzero value if the handle refers to a character device. If not, it returns a zero.

EXAMPLE Write a program using *isatty* that determines whether *stdout* is a character device or not. If it is a device, the program must run in interactive mode, in which characters are sent to the display rather than a file.

```
#include <stdio.h>
#include <io.h>
main()
{
   if(!isatty(fileno(stdout)))
   {
        printf("stdout redirected to a file\n");
   }
   else
   {
        printf("Executing in interactive mode\n");
   }
   return 0;
}
```

COMPATIBILITY

lock

TC1	TC1.5	TC2	TC++	MSC3	MSC4	MSC5	MSC6	QC1	QC2	QC2.5	ANSI	UNIX V	XNX
▲	▲	▲	▲			1	1	1	1	1			

PURPOSE Use the *lock* function, under MS-DOS version 3.0 and higher, to lock a number of bytes in a file. This feature is of use when file-sharing.

SYNTAX

```
int lock(int handle, long offset, long nbytes);
```

`int handle;` *Handle of file where data is being locked*

`long offset;` *Offset of byte where locking starts*

`long nbytes;` *Number of bytes to be locked*

EXAMPLE CALL

```
lock(handle, 0L, 256); /* Lock 256 bytes */
```

INCLUDES `#include <io.h>` *For function declaration*

DESCRIPTION The *lock* function is for use when file-sharing is enabled by executing the MS-DOS command SHARE. Because earlier versions of DOS do not have the SHARE command the *lock* function should be used only under MS-DOS versions 3.0 and later.

When called, *lock* performs the lock action on the file specified by the handle. The locking action affects *nbytes* bytes starting with one at the specified *offset* from the beinning of the file.

Locking a number of bytes (a region) prevents further reading and writing of those bytes by any process. Unlocking removes this restriction, but each region that is locked must be unlocked individually, even if two locked regions are adjacent to each other. Many separate regions in a file can be locked simultaneously, but no two regions can overlap. Finally, all locked regions must be unlocked before closing the file or exiting the program. Note: under MS-DOS 3.0 and 3.1 locked files may become unlocked when a child process exits.

1. In Microsoft C versions 5 and 6, and QuickC versions 1, 2, and 2.5 we use the *locking* function.

RETURNS If *lock* succeeds, it returns a 0. Otherwise, it returns a −1.

COMMENTS Under MS-DOS versions earlier than 3.0, the *lock* function does not operate.

SEE ALSO

`sopen` *To open with various file-sharing options*

`unlock` *To unlock a previously locked section of the file*

EXAMPLE Assuming that you are writing an application to be used in a networked environment with file-sharing under DOS, write a sample program that locks a part of the file using *lock* (presumably it updates that portion of the file) and then unlocks it with *unlock* for use by other processes. Remember to run SHARE before executing the program.

```
#include <stdio.h>
#include <io.h>
main()
{
    long curpos;
    int filehandle;

    char filename[80], buffer[80];
    printf("Enter name of file to test with:");
    gets(filename);
    if ((filehandle = open(filename, O_RDONLY)) == -1)
    {
        perror("open failed");
        exit(1);
    }
```

```
/* Read 80 characters from the file                    */
    if (read(filehandle, buffer, 80) == -1)
    {
        perror("read error");
        exit(1);
    }
/* Get and save current position                       */
    curpos = tell(filehandle);
/* Now lock 80 bytes from the beginning of the file */
    if (lock(filehandle, 0L, curpos) == -1)
    {
        perror("locking failed");
    }
    else
    {
        printf("First %ld bytes of file %s locked\n",
                curpos, filename);
/* In an actual program, you would make changes and
 * write these bytes back to the file before unlocking
 */
        if (unlock(filehandle, 0L, curpos)
             == -1)
        {
            perror("unlocking failed");
        }
        else
        {
            printf("File unlocked\n");
        }
    }
    return 0;
}
```

COMPATIBILITY

mktemp

TC1	TC1.5	TC2	TC++	MSC3	MSC4	MSC5	MSC6	QC1	QC2	QC2.5	ANSI	UNIX V	XNX
▲	▲	▲	▲	▲	▲	▲	▲	▲	▲	▲		▲	▲

PURPOSE Use the *mktemp* function to generate unique file names by modifying a given template for the names.

SYNTAX

```
char *mktemp(char *template);
```

`char *template;` *Pattern string to be used in constructing file names*

EXAMPLE CALL

```
char tfilename = "tcbXXXXXX";
mktemp(tfilename);
```

INCLUDES

`#include <dir.h>` *For function declaration*

DESCRIPTION The *mktemp* function uses the string *template* and modifies a portion of it to generate unique file names. The *template* string must be of the form: baseXXXXXX. The "base" of the template consists of one or more characters that appear in every file name. The Xs are treated as place holders to be replaced by two characters followed by a period and a three letter suffix. For the characters, *mktemp* starts with AA.AAA and goes on with AB.AAA, AC.AAA, and so on. Before returning a file name, *mktemp* checks that no file with that name exists in the working directory. Note that *mktemp* is not creating or opening a file, only creating a file name.

COMMON USES If your program creates many temporary files, *mktemp* relieves you of the responsibility of coming up with unique file names.

RETURNS The *mktemp* function returns a pointer to the modified template. In case of an error, for example, when no more unique file names can be created out of a given template, the return value will be NULL.

SEE ALSO

`tmpnam` *Another routine to create temporary file names*

`tmpfile` *To open an unnamed temporary file that is deleted when closed*

EXAMPLE Use *mktemp* to get a unique file name with the prefix "naba" and open the file.

```
#include <stdio.h>
#include <io.h>
static char *our_template = "nabaXXXXXX";
main()
{

    char unique_name[9];
/* First copy template into placeholder for name     */
    strcpy(unique_name, our_template);
    if(mktemp(unique_name) == NULL)
    {
        printf("Could not create unique file name!\n");
    }
    else
    {
        fopen(unique_name, "w");
```

```
        printf("File %s opened\n", unique_name);
    }
    return 0;
}
```

COMPATIBILITY

remove

TC1	TC1.5	TC2	TC++	MSC3	MSC4	MSC5	MSC6	QC1	QC2	QC2.5	ANSI	UNIX V	XNX
▲	▲	▲	▲	▲	▲	▲	▲	▲	▲	▲	▲		

PURPOSE Use *remove* to delete a file specified by its pathname.

SYNTAX

```
int remove(const char *path);

const char *path;      Pathname of file to be deleted
```

EXAMPLE CALL

```
remove("c:\\tmp\\tmp01234"); /* Delete temporary file */
```

INCLUDES `#include <stdio.h>` *For function declaration*

DESCRIPTION The *remove* function deletes the file specified by *path*.

RETURNS If *remove* successfully deletes the specified file, it returns a 0. Otherwise, the return value is −1 and the global variable *errno* is set to either ENOENT if the pathname is not found or to EACCES if the pathname is that of a directory or a read only file.

SEE ALSO `unlink` *Also deletes a file*

EXAMPLE Write a utility program that uses *remove* to delete a file. Assume that the program will be invoked with a command of the form "rm <filename>" where "rm.exe" is the program name.

```
#include <stdio.h>
#include <io.h>
main(int argc, char **argv)
{
    if(argc < 2)
    {
        printf("Usage: %s <pathname>\n", argv[0]);
    }
    else
    {
        printf("File %s ", argv[1]);
```

```
            if(remove(argv[1]) != 0)
            {
                perror("remove failed");
            }
            else
            {
                printf("deleted\n");
            }
        }
        return 0;
    }
```

rename

COMPATIBILITY

TC1	TC1.5	TC2	TC++	MSC3	MSC4	MSC5	MSC6	QC1	QC2	QC2.5	ANSI	UNIX V	XNX
▲	▲	▲	▲	▲	▲	▲	▲	▲	▲	▲	▲		

PURPOSE Use *rename* to change the name of a file or directory specified by its pathname. For example, you can use *rename* to write a program that provides the function of the UNIX command *mv* (to move a file from one directory to another).

SYNTAX

```
int rename(const char *oldname, const char *newname);
```

`const char *oldname;` *Current pathname of file or directory*

`const char *newname;` *New pathname*

EXAMPLE CALL

```
/* Copy "text.exe" from c:\tmp to c:\bin and give it a new name */
    rename("c:\\tmp\\test.exe", "c:\\bin\\grview.exe");
```

INCLUDES `#include <stdio.h>` *For function declaration*

DESCRIPTION The *rename* function changes the name of a file or directory from *oldname* to *newname*. Use *rename* to move a file from one directory to another, but only in the same device. Directories cannot be moved and wildcards are not allowed.

RETURNS If *rename* is successful, it returns a zero. In case of an error, it returns a −1 and the global variable *errno* contains further information. This variable equals the constant EACCES if a file or directory called *newname* exists, if a file with *newname* could not be created, or if *oldname* is a directory and *newname* specifies a different directory path. Attempting to specify a dif-

ferent drive letter results in *errno* set to ENOTSAM or to ENOENT if the pathname *oldname* does not refer to an existing file or directory.

SEE ALSO `creat, fopen, open` *To create and open a file*

EXAMPLE Write a program using *rename* that mimics the UNIX command *mv*.

```
#include <stdio.h>
#include <io.h>
main(int argc, char **argv)
{
    if(argc < 3)
    {
        printf("Usage: %s <oldname> <newname>\n",
                argv[0]);
    }
    else
    {
        printf("File %s ", argv[1]);
        if(rename(argv[1], argv[2]) != 0)
        {
            perror("rename failed");
        }
        else
        {
            printf("renamed to %s\n", argv[2]);
        }
    }
    return 0;
}
```

COMPATIBILITY

setmode

TC1	TC1.5	TC2	TC++	MSC3	MSC4	MSC5	MSC6	QC1	QC2	QC2.5	ANSI	UNIX V	XNX
▲	▲	▲	▲	▲	▲	▲	▲	▲	▲	▲			

PURPOSE Use the *setmode* function to set the translation mode (see the tutorial section) of a file opened for unbuffered, unformatted I/O.

SYNTAX `int setmode(int handle, int mode);`

`int handle;` *Handle of open file*

`int mode;` *Integer denoting new translation mode*

EXAMPLE CALL `setmode(filehandle, O_BINARY); /* Set file mode to binary */`

INCLUDES `#include <io.h>` *For function declaration*

`#include <fcntl.h>` *For definition of constants that are used to specify translation modes*

DESCRIPTION The *setmode* function changes to *mode* the translation mode of the file specified by *handle*. The translation mode specifies how carriage return-linefeed pairs are treated during file I/O. The value of the argument *mode* is either the constant O_TEXT to open in text, or translated, mode or O_BINARY to open in binary, or untranslated, mode. These are both defined in *fcntl.h*.

COMMON USES Typically, the *setmode* function is used to change the default translation modes associated with the files *stdin, stdout, stderr, stdaux*, and *stdprn*. For other files, you can specify the translation mode when opening the file with *open* or *fopen*.

RETURNS When there are no errors, *setmode* returns 0. Otherwise, it returns a −1 and sets the global variable *errno* to EBADF if the file handle is invalid or to EINVAL if the value given for the argument *mode* is not equal to one of the constants O_TEXT or O_BINARY.

SEE ALSO `fopen, open` *To open a file and specify a translation mode*

EXAMPLE Open a file in text mode, write a string, then write some more after changing the mode to O_BINARY. Provided you flush the stream after the first write, the latter output should appear with linefeeds only (without any carriage returns).

```
#include <stdio.h>
#include <io.h>
#include <fcntl.h>
main()
{
    FILE *f;
    if((f = fopen("junk", "wt")) == NULL)
    {
        fprintf(stderr, "Error opening file\n");
        exit(1);
    }
/* Write a string to the file and flush the stream */
    fprintf(f, "Testing setmode\n");
    fflush(f);
```

```
/* Set mode of file to O_BINARY */
    if(setmode(fileno(f), O_BINARY) == -1)
    {
     perror("setmode failed");
    }
    else
    {
     fprintf(f, "f is in binary mode now.\n");
     fprintf(f, "Strings should end with linefeeds only\n");
    }
    fclose(f);
    printf("To see the results, enter the command: TYPE JUNK\n");
    return 0;
}
```

COMPATIBILITY

stat

TC1	TC1.5	TC2	TC++	MSC3	MSC4	MSC5	MSC6	QC1	QC2	QC2.5	ANSI	UNIX V	XNX
▲	▲	▲	▲	▲	▲	▲	▲	▲	▲	▲		▲	▲

PURPOSE Use the *stat* function to obtain information about an existing file specified by its pathname.

SYNTAX

```
int stat(char *path, struct stat *buffer);
```

`char *path;` *Pathname of file whose "vital statistics" will be returned*

`struct stat *buffer;` *Pointer to structure where result will be returned*

EXAMPLE CALL

```
stat("result.dat", &stat_buffer);
```

INCLUDES

`#include <sys\types.h>` *Required by* <sys\stat.h>

`#include <sys\stat.h>` *For function declaration and definition of structure* stat

DESCRIPTION The *stat* function returns certain information about the file or directory specified by the pathname in the argument *path*. The information is stored by *stat* in a structure of type *stat*. A pointer to an allocated structure of this type must be provided in the argument *buffer*. The structure *stat* is defined in <sys\stat.h> and its declaration is of the form

```
struct stat
{
    short        st_dev;   /* Drive number of disk or handle of
                              device containing the file      */
    short        st_ino;   /* Unused in MS-DOS. The "i-node"
                              number of file in UNIX          */
    short        st_mode;  /* Bit mask of file's mode         */
    short        st_nlink; /* Always set to 1 under MS-DOS    */
    int          st_uid;   /* Unused in MS-DOS. For "user-id"
                              under UNIX                      */
    int          st_gid;   /* Unused in MS-DOS. For "group-id"
                              under UNIX                      */
    short        st_rdev;  /* Same as the field st_dev        */
    long         st_size;  /* Size of file in bytes           */
    long         st_atime; /* Time of last modification       */
    long         st_mtime; /* Same as st_atime                */
    long         st_ctime; /* Same as st_atime                */
};
```

If the pathname refers to a directory, the field *st_mode* has the bit corresponding to the constant S_IFDIR set. For a file, on the other hand, the bit corresponding to the value S_IFREG is set. Other bits in this field indicate read/write permissions and whether the *path* refers to a device. When it refers to a device, the values in the time and size fields are meaningless.

RETURNS The *stat* function returns 0 to indicate its success in obtaining the information about the file. Otherwise, the return value is −1 and the global variable *errno* is set to the constant ENOENT, indicating that no file, directory, or device exists by the specified pathname.

SEE ALSO

access — *To check if read/write operations are permitted on a file*

chmod — *To change read/write permissions of a file*

fstat — *To find information about a file specified by a valid handle*

EXAMPLE Use *stat* to write a utility program that prints useful information about a file.

```
#include <stdio.h>
#include <sys\types.h>
#include <sys\stat.h>
#include <time.h>
main(int argc, char **argv)
{
```

```
    struct stat info;
    if(argc < 2)
    {
        printf("Usage: %s <pathname>\n", argv[0]);
    }
    else
    {
        if(stat(argv[1], &info) != 0)
        {
            perror("Error in \"stat\"");
            exit(1);
        }
/* Print out information about the file               */
        printf("File: %s\n\
Drive        :  %c\n\
Size         :  %ld bytes,\n\
Last modified:  %s\n",  argv[1], info.st_dev+65,
                info.st_size, ctime(&info.st_atime));
    }
    return 0;
}
```

umask

COMPATIBILITY

TC1	TC1.5	TC2	TC++	MSC3	MSC4	MSC5	MSC6	QC1	QC2	QC2.5	ANSI	UNIX V	XNX
▲	▲	▲	▲	▲	▲	▲	▲	▲	▲	▲		▲	▲

PURPOSE Use the *umask* function to set the read/write permission mask that modifies the read/write permission settings of subsequent files created by this process.

SYNTAX

```
unsigned umask(unsigned pmode);
```

`unsigned pmode;` *Permission mask to be used in all subsequent new files*

EXAMPLE CALL

```
/* Make all future files read-only */
    oldmask = umask(S_IWRITE);
```

INCLUDES

`#include <io.h>` *For function declaration*

`#include <sys\types.h>` *For definition of data types used in* <sys\stat.h>

`#include <sys\stat.h>` *For definition of constants to specify permission settings of a file*

DESCRIPTION The *umask* function accepts a read/write permission setting mask (see the tutorial) in the integer argument *pmode*. The mask modifies the permission settings for new files created by calls to *creat*, *open*, or *sopen*.

The mask *pmode* is interpreted as follows. If a particular bit is set to 1, the corresponding bit in the file's permission setting is 0 (which means that operation will not be allowed). On the other hand, a 0 in a particular bit of *pmode* implies that the corresponding bit in the permission setting is left unchanged.

The *pmode* argument can take one of the values shown in Table 14-5 expressed in terms of constants that are defined in the include file *sys\stat.h*.

Because MS-DOS always allows reading from a file, only the S_IWRITE setting has use in an MS-DOS system.

Table 14-5. *Possible Values of Permission Mask in* umask

Constant	Interpretation
S_IWRITE	Writing is not allowed.
S_IREAD	Reading is not allowed (that is ignored in MS-DOS).
S_IREAD | S_IWRITE	Both reading and writing disallowed (reading is always allowed in MS-DOS).

RETURNS The *umask* function returns the previous value of the permission mask.

SEE ALSO `creat, open, sopen` *To create and open new files for unformatted I/O*

EXAMPLE Write a program to set the permission mask so that future files are read only. Display the previous value of the mask.

```
#include <stdio.h>
#include <sys\types.h>
#include <sys\stat.h>
#include <io.h>

main()
{
    int oldmask;
/* Make all future files read-only */
    oldmask = umask(S_IWRITE);
    printf("Previous value of permission mask was %X\n",
            oldmask);
    return 0;
}
```

COMPATIBILITY

unlink

TC1	TC1.5	TC2	TC++	MSC3	MSC4	MSC5	MSC6	QC1	QC2	QC2.5	ANSI	UNIX V	XNX
▲	▲	▲	▲	▲	▲	▲	▲	▲	▲	▲		▲	▲

PURPOSE Use *unlink* to delete a file specified by its pathname.

SYNTAX

```
int unlink(const char *path);
```

`const char *path;` *Pathname of file to be deleted*

EXAMPLE CALL

```
unlink("old.dat");
```

INCLUDES `#include <io.h>` *For function declaration*

or

`#include <stdio.h>`

DESCRIPTION The *unlink* function deletes the file specified by the pathname *path*. (This function is more useful under UNIX, in which a file can be linked to multiple directories.)

RETURNS If *unlink* successfully deletes the specified file, it returns a 0. A return value of −1 indicates error. If *unlink* cannot find the file specified by the pathname, the global variable *errno* is set to ENOENT. If the file is read only or if it is a directory, *errno* is set to EACCES.

SEE ALSO `remove` *Also deletes a file*

EXAMPLE Use *unlink* in a program that deletes a file chosen by the user.

```
#include <stdio.h>
#include <io.h>
main(int argc, char **argv)
{
    if(argc < 2)
    {
        printf("Usage: %s <pathname>\n", argv[0]);
    }
    else
    {
        printf("File %s ", argv[1]);
        if(unlink(argv[1]) != 0)
```

```
            {
                perror("unlink failed");
            }
            else
            {
                printf("deleted\n");
            }
        }
        return 0;
    }
```

unlock

COMPATIBILITY

TC1	TC1.5	TC2	TC++	MSC3	MSC4	MSC5	MSC6	QC1	QC2	QC2.5	ANSI	UNIX V	XNX
▲	▲	▲	▲			1	1	1	1	1			

PURPOSE Use the *unlock* function, under MS-DOS versions 3.0 and higher, to unlock a number of previously locked bytes in a file. This feature is useful when file-sharing.

SYNTAX

```
int unlock(int handle, long offset, long nbytes);
```

`int handle;` *Handle of file where data is being unlocked*

`long offset;` *Offset of first byte of block being unlocked*

`long nbytes;` *Number of bytes to be unlocked*

EXAMPLE CALL

```
unlock (handle, 0L, 256); /*Unlock 256 bytes*/
```

INCLUDES `#include <io.h>` *For function declaration*

DESCRIPTION The *unlock* function is used to unlock regions locked by earlier calls to *lock*. The *lock/unlock* functions are useful when file-sharing is enabled by executing the MS-DOS command SHARE, which is available under MS-DOS versions 3.0 and later.

The region being unlocked is identified by the argument *offset* indicating the offset of the first byte from the beginning of the file, and by *nbytes*, which is the number of bytes being unlocked.

Note that every locked region of a file must be unlocked before the file is closed.

1. Use the *locking* function in Microsoft C versions 5, and 6, and in QuickC versions 1, 2, and 2.5.

RETURNS If *unlock* succeeds, it returns a 0. Otherwise, it returns a −1.

SEE ALSO

`lock`	*To lock a number of bytes*
`sopen`	*To open a file with file-sharing options*

EXAMPLE The example in the reference entry on *lock* also illustrates the use of *unlock*.

Chapter 15 Directory Manipulation

Introduction

The MS-DOS operating system comes with a file system that takes care of the physical storage of data and presents a clean model of the filing system.

MS-DOS, like UNIX, uses a hierarchical file system enabling you to organize your files in directories and subdirectories. The "directory manipulation" routines in Turbo C++ provide the basic tools necessary to create, modify, and remove directories from your C program. There is also a host of routines that manipulate the files, which we describe in Chapter 14.

Concepts

Proper use of the directory manipulation routines in Turbo C++ requires an understanding of the MS-DOS file system and where directories fit in that model.

DOS FILE SYSTEM

As we saw in Figure 14-1, the hierarchical file system used by DOS (and many other operating systems) consists of a root directory (on a certain disk drive) under which there are more directories and files. Each directory, in turn, can have additional directories and files under it. In this model of the hierarchical file system, a directory is just a file capable of storing other files inside it. Although the conceptual model is the same for all such file systems, the naming conventions and the way data is stored on the physical medium (the hard disk or the floppy) varies from one operating system to another.

DOS Pathnames

"Pathname" refers to the complete specification necessary to locate a file—the drive (a letter followed by a colon), then the hierarchy of directories leading to the file being located. The pathname of a file is constructed by concatenating the drive name to a list of directory names ending with the name of the file, as we illustrated in Figure 14-2. The topmost directory, known as the "root directory," is represented by a single backslash (\). The individual directory names are separated by backslashes.

Another backslash follows the last directory name. The file name, which can be eight characters followed by an optional three-character extension separated by a period, concludes the pathname. Since a directory is also a file, this naming convention also applies to directories.

Notes

MS-DOS includes such commands as MD, RD, and CD that enable you to create or delete a directory and change the current working directory, respectively. With the directory manipulation routines you can perform these tasks from a C program. The four C routines in this category are summarized in Table 15-1. The fifth routine, named *searchpath*, is useful when you want to find a particular file in a list of directories, including the current working directory, defined in the PATH environment variable. For example, you can use *searchpath* to locate the file AUTOEXEC.BAT in the directories defined in the PATH environment variable by the call

```
buffer = searchpath("autoexec.bat");
```

where *buffer* will point to the full pathname of the file being sought. In this example, if *autoexec.bat* is found in the root directory of drive C, after returning from *searchpath*, *buffer* will point to the string "C:\AUTOEXEC.BAT".

Table 15-1. ***Directory Manipulation Routines***

Routine	Description
chdir	Changes the current working directory.
getcwd	Returns the current working directory.
mkdir	Creates a new directory.
rmdir	Deletes a directory, provided it is empty.
searchpath	Searches for a file in directories listed in the PATH environment variable.

Cautions

- The directory manipulation routines do not allow you to switch to a different drive. To do so, use a call to *setdisk* or a call such as *system("c:")*.
- Watch out for a small detail when initializing C strings with DOS pathnames. The problem stems from the embedded backslashes in DOS pathnames and the special meaning C attaches to backslashes in strings. For example, a newline character is represented by \n and a backspace character is denoted by \b. To avoid misinterpretation, use *two* backslashes to embed a single backslash in a string being initialized to contain a pathname.
- The root directory in the MS-DOS file system is assigned limited space on the storage medium. This limits the number of files you can have at the root level. On a double-sided double-density disk with 9 tracks, the number of files is 112; the PC-AT high-density disk has room for 224 files; the hard disk can hold 512 files at the root level. Since a directory is just a file, the number of files you can have in other directories is limited only by the storage space on that drive.

Further Reading

One aspect of the DOS file system we did not discuss is the physical storage of files. The developer's guide by The Waite Group[1] devotes a chapter to the physical layout files on disks in MS-DOS. Duncan's book[2] is another source for such information.

1. The Waite Group, *MS-DOS Developer's Guide*, Second Edition, Howard W. Sams & Company, Indianapolis, IN, 1989, 813 pages.
2. Ray Duncan, *Advanced MS-DOS*, Microsoft Press, Redmond, WA, 1986, 468 pages.

chdir

COMPATIBILITY

TC1	TC1.5	TC2	TC++	MSC3	MSC4	MSC5	MSC6	QC1	QC2	QC2.5	ANSI	UNIX V	XNX
▲	▲	▲	▲	▲	▲	▲	▲	▲	▲	▲		▲	▲

PURPOSE Use *chdir* to change the current working directory. The *chdir* function works exactly like the MS-DOS command CD.

SYNTAX
```
int chdir(const char *path);
```

`const char *path;` *Pathname of new working directory*

EXAMPLE CALL
```
chdir("c:\\bin\\sample");
```

INCLUDES `#include <dir.h>` *For function declaration*

DESCRIPTION The *chdir* function changes the current working directory to the one specified by the argument *path*. As with the MS-DOS command, CD, you cannot change the default drive. Use the *setdisk* function to change the drive.

COMMON USES The *chdir* function allows you to change working directories while in your application program.

RETURNS When *chdir* succeeds in changing the current directory, it returns a 0. In case of error, it returns a −1 and sets the global variable *errno* to ENOENT to indicate that the specified pathname is invalid.

COMMENTS A call to *chdir* with a pathname that includes a drive specification sets the current working directory to the one on that drive, but the drive name remains unchanged. To use that directory, set the default drive with a call to the DOS function *setdisk* or with the use of *system*.

SEE ALSO

`mkdir, rmdir` *Other functions to manipulate directories*

`setdisk` *To change the default drive*

`system` *To execute an MS-DOS command from a program*

EXAMPLE Write a program using *chdir* that provides the functionality of the MS-DOS command CD.

```
#include <stdio.h>
#include <dir.h>
main(int argc, char **argv)
```

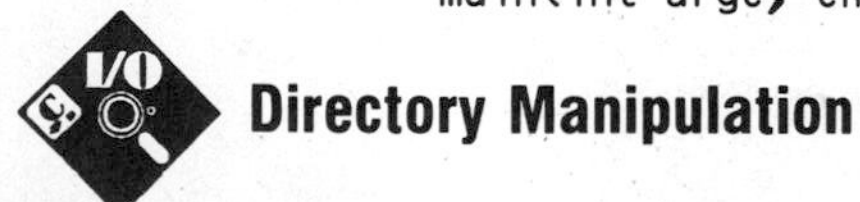

```
{
    if(argc < 2)
    {
        printf("Usage: %s <pathname>\n", argv[0]);
    }
    else
    {
        if(chdir(argv[1]) != 0)
        {
            perror("Error in \"chdir\"");
        }
    }
    return 0;
}
```

COMPATIBILITY

getcwd

TC1	TC1.5	TC2	TC++	MSC3	MSC4	MSC5	MSC6	QC1	QC2	QC2.5	ANSI	UNIX V	XNX
▲	▲	▲	▲	▲	▲	▲	▲	▲	▲	▲		▲	▲

PURPOSE Use *getcwd* to get the full pathname of the current working directory, including the drive name.

SYNTAX

```
char *getcwd(char *path, int numchars);
```

`char *path;` *Buffer where pathname of current working directory is returned*

`int numchars;` *Number of bytes available in the buffer for pathname*

EXAMPLE CALL

```
getcwd(path_buffer, 80);
```

INCLUDES `#include <dir.h>` *For function declaration*

DESCRIPTION The *getcwd* function gets the pathname of the current working directory, including the drive specification, and stores it in the buffer specified by the argument *path*. The integer argument *numchars* tells *getcwd* the maximum number of characters the buffer *path* can hold. If the *path* argument is NULL, *getcwd* allocates *numchars* bytes using *malloc* and stores the pathname in this space. When you no longer need the space, you can free it by calling *free* with the pointer returned by *getcwd* as argument.

COMMON USES The *getcwd* function is useful for getting the current directory name and saving it. If your program changes working directories during its execution, it can use the saved name to restore the original working directory before exiting.

RETURNS The *getcwd* function returns a pointer to the buffer in which the pathname is stored. If *path* is not NULL, the return value is equal to *path* or a pointer to the buffer allocated to hold the pathname. A return value of NULL indicates an error. The global variable *errno* is set to ENOMEM if the *path* argument is NULL and *getcwd* fails when allocating a buffer. If the pathname has more characters than *numchars*, *errno* is set to ERANGE.

SEE ALSO `chdir` *To change current working directory*

EXAMPLE Use *getcwd* to get the pathname of the current working directory and display it.

```
#include <stdio.h>
#include <dir.h>
main()
{
    char pathname[81];
    if (getcwd(pathname, 80) == NULL)
    {
        perror("Error in getcwd");
    }
    else
    {
        printf("Current directory: %s\n", pathname);
    }
    return 0;
}
```

mkdir

COMPATIBILITY

TC1	TC1.5	TC2	TC++	MSC3	MSC4	MSC5	MSC6	QC1	QC2	QC2.5	ANSI	UNIX V	XNX
▲	▲	▲	▲	▲	▲	▲	▲	▲	▲	▲			

PURPOSE Use *mkdir* to create a new directory with a specified pathname.

SYNTAX `int mkdir(const char *path);`

`const char *path;` *Pathname of new directory*

EXAMPLE CALL `mkdir("c:\\waite\\tcb"); /* c:\waite must already exist */`

INCLUDES `#include <dir.h>` *For function declaration*

DESCRIPTION The *mkdir* function creates a new directory with the pathname *path*. The pathname can include drive specification and directory/subdirectory names, but because *mkdir* can only create one directory at a time all but the last subdirectory must already exist. For example, if you have an existing directory named TEMP in the root directory of drive C, you can create a new directory with the pathname *C:\TEMP\NEW_1*, but *C:\TEMP\NEW_1\NEW_2* is illegal because it requires the creation of two directories.

COMMON USES The *mkdir* function is convenient in "setup" programs that you might distribute with your application. It can be used to implement, for example, the setup program provided with Turbo C++ for installing the compiler. Essentially, *mkdir* lets you create new directories from your program.

RETURNS When *mkdir* succeeds in creating the directory, it returns a 0. In case of error, it returns a −1 and sets the global variable *errno* to ENOENT, indicating that the specified pathname is invalid, or to EACCES, indicating that that pathname is that of a drive or an existing file or directory.

SEE ALSO `rmdir` *To delete a directory*

`chdir` *To change the current working directory*

EXAMPLE Write a program using *mkdir* that provides the functionality of the MS-DOS command *md*.

```
#include <stdio.h>
#include <dir.h>
main(int argc, char **argv)
{
    if(argc < 2)
    {
        printf("Usage: %s <pathname>\n", argv[0]);
    }

    else
    {
        if(mkdir(argv[1]) != 0)
        {
            perror("Error in \"mkdir\"");
        }
    }
    return 0;
}
```

rmdir

COMPATIBILITY

TC1	TC1.5	TC2	TC++	MSC3	MSC4	MSC5	MSC6	QC1	QC2	QC2.5	ANSI	UNIX V	XNX
▲	▲	▲	▲	▲	▲	▲	▲	▲	▲	▲			

PURPOSE Use *rmdir* to delete an existing directory with a specified pathname.

SYNTAX

```
int rmdir(const char *path);
```

`const char *path;` *Pathname of directory to delete*

EXAMPLE CALL

```
rmdir("c:\\temp\\last"); /* c:\temp\last must be empty */
```

INCLUDES `#include <dir.h>` *For function declaration*

DESCRIPTION The *rmdir* function deletes an existing directory with the pathname *path*. The pathname can include drive specification, directory, and subdirectory names. As with the MS-DOS command RD, the directory must be empty before it can be deleted. For example, if you have an existing directory named TEMP in the root directory of drive C, you can use *rmdir("c:\\temp")* to delete it, provided it is empty.

RETURNS If *rmdir* successfully deletes the directory, it returns a 0. In case of error, it returns a −1 and sets the global variable *errno* to ENOENT if the specified pathname is invalid or to EACCES if the pathname is that of a drive or an existing file, if the directory is not empty, or if the specified directory is the root directory or the current working directory.

SEE ALSO `mkdir` *To create a new directory*

`chdir` *To change the current working directory*

EXAMPLE Write a program using *rmdir* that provides the functionality of the MS-DOS command *rd*.

```
#include <stdio.h>
#include <dir.h>
main(int argc, char **argv)
{
    if(argc < 2)
    {
        printf("Usage: %s <pathname>\n", argv[0]);
    }
    else
    {
```

```
            if(rmdir(argv[1]) != 0)
            {
                perror("Error in \"rmdir\"");
            }
        }
        return 0;
    }
```

COMPATIBILITY

searchpath

TC1	TC1.5	TC2	TC++	MSC3	MSC4	MSC5	MSC6	QC1	QC2	QC2.5	ANSI	UNIX V	XNX
▲	▲	▲	▲			1	1	1	1	1			

PURPOSE Use *searchpath* to search for a particular file in a list of directories, including the current working directory and those defined in the PATH environment variable.

SYNTAX

```
char *searchpath(const char *name);

const char *name;        Name of file to find
```

EXAMPLE CALL `buffer = searchpath("TC.EXE");`

INCLUDES `#include <dir.h>` *For function declaration*

DESCRIPTION The *searchpath* function first searches in the current working directory for the file whose name is given in the argument *name*. If the file is not found in the current directory, *searchpath* continues the search in each directory path specified in the definition of the DOS environment variable PATH.

1. The equivalent function in Microsoft C versions 5 and 6, and QuickC versions 1, 2, and 2.5, is *_searchenv*.

RETURNS If the file is found, *searchpath* returns a pointer to the file's pathname. If *searchpath* fails to locate the file, it returns NULL.

SEE ALSO `getenv, putenv` *To access and alter the environment table*

EXAMPLE Write a utility that accepts a file name and searches for that file in all directories listed in the PATH environment variable. If found, print the full pathname of the file. Use *searchpath* to locate the file.

```
#include <stdio.h>
#include <dir.h>
```

```
main(int argc, char **argv)
{
    char *path_buffer;
    printf("This program searches for a file in all\n\
the directories specified in the PATH \n\
environment variable\n");
    if(argc < 2)
    {
        printf("Usage: %s <filename>\n", argv[0]);
        exit(0);
    }
/* Use "searchpath" to locate the file */
    path_buffer = searchpath (argv[1]);
    if(path_buffer == NULL)
    {
        printf("File: %s not found\n", argv[1]);
    }
    else
    {
        printf("Found as: %s\n", path_buffer);
    }
    return 0;
}
```

Directory Manipulation

Chapter 16 Input and Output Routines

Introduction

Input and output (I/O) make computers useful as information processing tools. I/O can involve reading from and writing to files in the disk or reading input from the keyboard and sending output to the display screen or sending commands to peripherals. The Turbo C++ library provides a large assortment of I/O routines for each of these tasks. We will discuss the salient features of the Turbo C++ I/O routines here.

The C programming language has no built-in capability to perform any I/O. This is the responsibility of the library accompanying your C compiler. The Turbo C++ library includes the ANSI standard I/O library with a group of I/O routines that provide access to hardware in the PC. Turbo C++ also includes the C++ stream class which you can use in your C++ program.

We will describe the available file types in MS-DOS and the types of I/O necessary to access all IBM PC hardware features. The I/O categories include file I/O and I/O operations with registers in peripheral devices. Then we will describe all Turbo C++ I/O routines, grouping them by common function, and finally we provide some cautions that should help you use these routines properly.

Concepts of File and Other I/O

The concept of a "file" is universal to almost all I/O in MS-DOS and Turbo C++, with the exception of reading or writing to *port* addresses in the peripheral devices attached to the 8086 microprocessor. You can think of a file as a sequence of bytes of data stored on a diskette, a RAM disk, CD ROM, or some external media. A file must be able to receive or impart a stream of bytes; physical storage need not underlie a file, as is shown in Figure 16-1. Thought of in this manner, the keyboard, the serial communications port, and the display screen are all files—precisely the model used by the file I/O routines in Turbo C++.

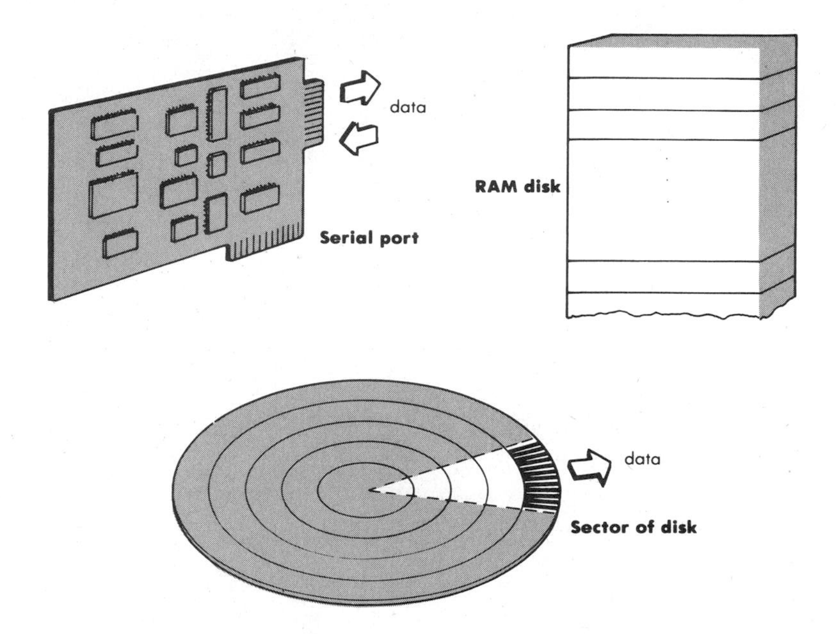

Figure 16-1. ***Files in Turbo C++***

TEXT AND BINARY FILES

In addition to this abstract view of a file as a stream of bytes, C programmers have to remember another distinction among files: how the constituent bytes are interpreted. Under MS-DOS, a file can be either text or binary.

In "text" files, each byte is interpreted as an ASCII character with a Control-Z representing the end of the file. In C (and in UNIX), a newline character (\n) signifies the end of a line (newline is an ASCII 10). In an MS-DOS text file, however, the end of a line of text is marked by a pair of characters: a carriage return (CR) followed by a linefeed (LF). We call this pair the CR-LF. By the way, CR and LF are represented in C by \r and \n respectively. This end-of-line difference between C and MS-DOS can be a problem during file I/O.

Turbo C++ solves this problem by allowing the file I/O routines to perform some translation when interacting with a text file. A Control-Z character in an MS-DOS file opened in text mode signifies the end of that file (even if there is more data after the character). When reading from the file, a CR-LF pair is translated by the C I/O routines to LF (which is the newline character \n in C). When writing to the file using the C I/O routines, a single LF causes a CR-LF pair to be written, allowing proper formatting under MS-DOS. This approach keeps the model of text files fixed in your C program whether it is running under UNIX or MS-DOS. There is little impact on your programming because the translation takes place automatically whenever you open an MS-DOS file in the text mode.

In reading and writing "binary" files using C I/O routines, the bytes are not interpreted in any manner. To understand and use the contents of a binary file you must know what was stored there in the first place. After all, a 4-byte value in the file could be a long integer, a *float* variable, or even two short integers. When you know how the binary file was written, reading from it is straightforward. For example, if you write 1,000 short integer values to a binary file from a 2,000-byte buffer in memory, each two-byte value you later read from the file represents a short integer—a perfect match.

Binary files are ideal for storing numeric data because of the efficient manner of storage. To represent an integer value, say 32,767, in a text file, you would need 5 bytes to store the ASCII representation of the five digits. In binary form, 2 bytes are enough to hold this number. So if you had two files full of such data, the binary one would be 2.5 times smaller than the ASCII counterpart. Note, however, that the binary file would not be readable by a word processor or a text editor.

TYPES OF I/O ROUTINES IN TURBO C++

The Turbo C++ library has three types of I/O routine: the stream routines, followed by the low-level file I/O routines, and finally the console and port I/O routines.

The "stream" routines refer to I/O performed using the model of files as a stream of bytes together with a buffer associated with a file. The "buffer" is a temporary storage area for the stream of bytes being read from or written to the file. The "low-level" routines are similar except that they do not use a buffer. "Console and port I/O" is meant for direct input and output from the keyboard, the monitor, and any peripheral devices (such as the serial adapter) attached to the PC.

Buffered Stream I/O

The stream I/O routines use a buffer to hold data in transit to and from a file. In a buffered read operation from a disk file, as Figure 16-2 illustrates, a fixed chunk of bytes is read from the disk into a buffer of the same size. The routines requesting data from the file actually read from the buffer. When the buffer has no characters left, it is automatically refilled by a disk read operation. A similar sequence occurs when writing to a file.

The use of a buffer leads to efficient I/O on disk files because there are fewer disk accesses which are much slower than reading from a buffer in memory. There is only one drawback of the buffered approach to I/O;

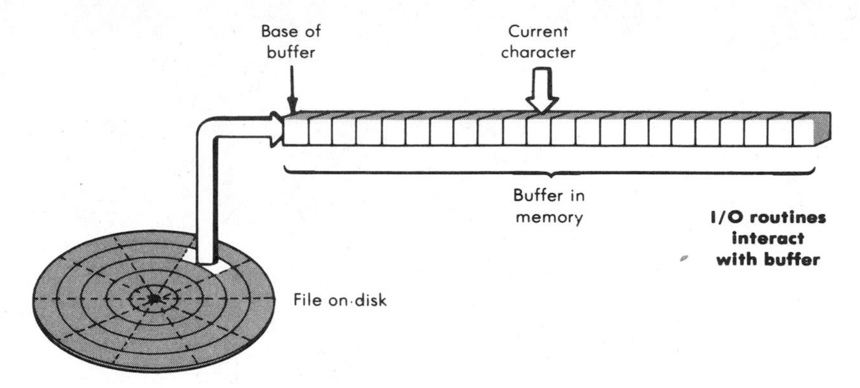

Figure 16-2. ***Buffered file I/O***

data written to a buffer does not actually appear in the disk file until the buffer is written out. This is "flushing" the buffer, a housekeeping chore normally handled automatically in C programs. In certain cases, however, the buffers are not flushed. These include ending the program abnormally because of a fatal error, exiting a C program with a call to the *_exit* function, or the occurrence of a hardware error.

The Turbo C++ stream I/O functions use an internal data structure to maintain information about the file being accessed. The data structure, named FILE, is defined in the include file *stdio.h.* As shown in Figure 16-3, the FILE structure has room for information about the current buffer, including an identifying number for the file (known as the file's "handle") and a single byte flag to indicate such status and control information as whether an end-of-file occurred during a read operation or an error occurred during I/O. When a file is opened by a stream I/O routine such as *fopen*, a pointer to a FILE structure is returned to the calling program. Subsequent stream I/O operations identify the file by the pointer to the associated FILE data structure. In fact, this pointer to the FILE data structure is commonly referred to as the *stream.* Thus, when we say read from the stream *stdin*, we mean read from the file whose associated FILE structure's address is in *stdin.* Incidentally, *stdin* is a stream that refers to the keyboard and it is already open when a C program begins running.

Another important feature of the stream I/O routines is *formatting I/O*, the process of converting internal binary values of variables to character strings that can be written out to a file. For example, suppose a single byte contains the bit pattern: 01100100 (which is a binary representation of the decimal value 100). Converting this binary pattern into three ASCII characters in the string *100* involves formatting. Thus formatting is the step that makes the binary representations printable. Not all stream I/O routines are meant for formatted I/O; the *fread* and *fwrite* routines are for reading and writing unformatted binary data.

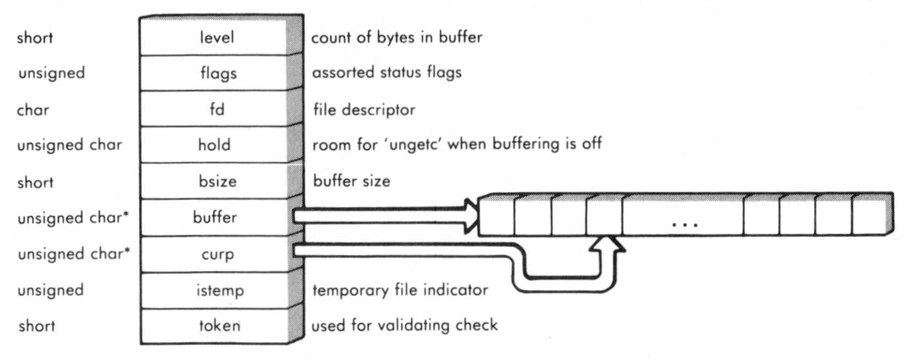

Figure 16-3. *FILE data structure*

Unbuffered Low-Level I/O

Low-level I/O refers to unbuffered I/O, thus no buffer holds data read from the disk. Instead, each read request results in accessing the disk (or the device the file refers to) to fetch a requested number of bytes. Since disk accesses are time-consuming, the low-level routines are meant for reading or writing a significant number of bytes at a time.

The low-level I/O routines include no formatting capability. Since formatting is necessary when reading and writing text files (because we have to convert from character strings to internal representations), the low-level I/O routines are not suitable for performing I/O with text files. Binary files, on the other hand, do not require formatting during read/write operations so the low-level routines are ideal for I/O with binary files.

Like the buffered stream I/O routines, the low-level routines maintain data structures that contain such information as the current read/write position in the file and the permission settings for the file. Instead of the FILE pointer used by the stream routines, the low-level routines use the handle, a unique number, to identify each file. A stream file, with its associated FILE data structure, can also be accessed by a handle, which you can get by using the Turbo C++ library function *fileno*. Similarly, a buffer may be associated with a file opened by a low-level call so that high-level stream I/O routines can be used on that file. This is accomplished by the library routine *fdopen*.

Console and Port I/O

This last category of I/O is not related to file I/O. Instead, these routines are meant for direct access to the keyboard, the screen, and any I/O port in the PC. Note that the keyboard and the monitor together are called the "console." Access to the keyboard and screen using the console I/O routines is similar to using BIOS calls (described in Chapter 17). There is no buffering of any sort and you do not have to formally open the device to perform these I/O operations.

Various hardware subsystems in the IBM PC can be controlled by sending commands to specific registers known as "ports." These registers are similar to memory locations, but they are accessed by an addressing mechanism in the 8086 microprocessor that is separate from the one used to reach conventional memory and video memory. Thus these ports have their own address space—the I/O address space. The port I/O routines allow you to read from and write to the hardware registers using the assembly language instructions IN and OUT, respectively.

Communications and the Serial Port

The *serial port* on the PC is an example of peripheral hardware that can be programmed by reading from and writing to I/O ports. The serial port on the PC is used for communicating with other computers and on-line services such as CompuServe, BIX, Genie, or your local bulletin board system. A plug-in card that fits into a slot in your PC, the serial port has an RS 232C serial adapter for sending data out. In the typical arrangement, shown in Figure 16-4, individual bytes from the computer are converted into an on-off, or digital, signal by a Universal Asynchronous Receiver Transmitter (UART) on the serial adapter. This signal goes out through the serial port into a "modem," which converts the signals into a continuously variable form ("analog" signal) suitable for transmission over telephone lines. At the receiving end, another modem converts the signal back into digital form and finally another UART at the receiving end packs the individual bits from the digital signal into bytes. The UART is controlled by writing to or reading from a set of internal registers which can be accessed via port addresses. Because the port addresses are assigned sequentially, it is enough to know the address of the first port, commonly known as the "base address," of the serial adapter. In the IBM PC, the two serial ports COM1 and COM2 are assigned base port addresses 3F8h and 2F8h, respectively. Thus for the serial adapter COM1, the first register is at 3F8h, the next at 3F9h, and so on.

We will not discuss the function of each register in the UART, except to say that they allow you to control all parameters necessary for communicating data (such as baud rate and word length) and to enable hardware "interrupts" to be generated when certain events occur (such as an incoming byte being ready at the UART or the UART being free to send a byte out). The programming of the registers in the UART can be done by using the Turbo C++ I/O functions *inportb* and *outportb*.

We discuss the concept of interrupts in the section on *System Calls* (Chapter 17). To handle the physical interrupts, you must also program another device—the Intel 8259A Programmable Interrupt Controller in your PC. This device acts as a gatekeeper deciding which device can interrupt the 8086 microprocessor and which ones cannot. The 8259A is also programmed by sending commands to its registers accessible via I/O port addresses (20h and 21h). If your interest is piqued by this summary de-

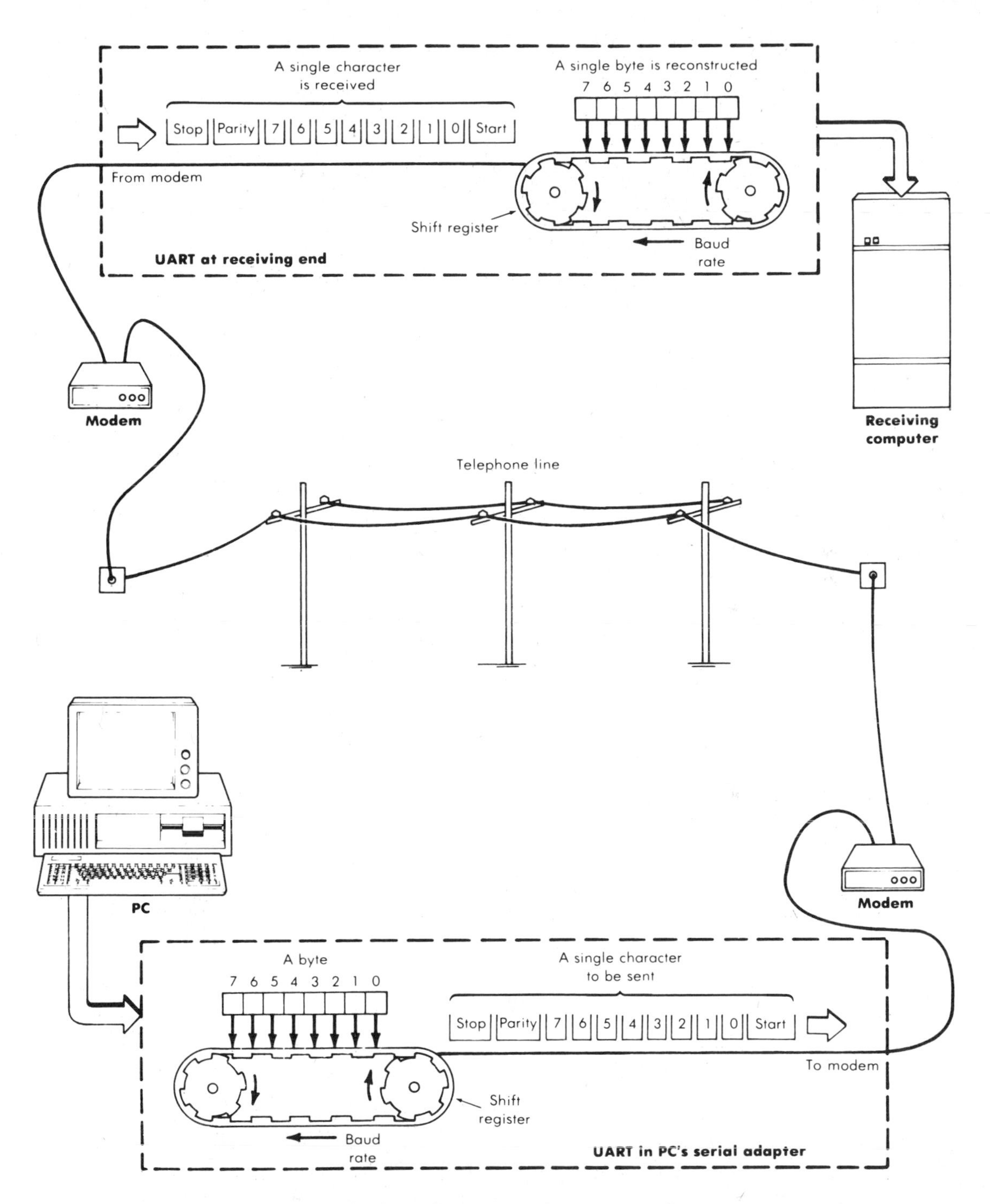

Figure 16-4. ***Communicating via the serial port in the IBM PC***

scription of *communications programming* on the PC, you can get more information in Chapter 13 of the *MS-DOS Papers* (Howard W. Sams & Company, 1988), a compendium on MS-DOS programming by The Waite Group.

FILE-SHARING

The concept of sharing files is important because computers are being increasingly connected in networks so users can reach across and create, open, or modify files in another PC. MS-DOS version 3.0 introduced certain mechanisms to allow multiple processes on different computers in the network to access files at a common node. If you are using MS-DOS version 3.0 or higher, you can enable this file-sharing capability by issuing the DOS command SHARE.

At the programmer's level, file-sharing is achieved by opening the file with a call to the *sopen* library function with the exact mode of sharing specified with flags. Then you use the Turbo C++ function *lock* to lock those parts of the file that you want to work on. When you are finished, use *unlock* to make these portions of the file again available to others. There are several other MS-DOS services that manage shared access to files in MS-NET, Microsoft's network for PCs. Since a detailed discussion of these services is beyond the scope of this tutorial, we refer you to the *MS-DOS Technical Reference Manual* for further details.

In general, the file I/O routines, both stream and low-level, are meant to be used as follows: open the file (where a file can be a device as well), perform the read and write operations, and close the file. In addition to these tasks other routines allow I/O from a specific position in the file, or format a value for printing, or read a single line or a single character, and so on. The console and port I/O routines do not open or close a device; you simply read from or write to the console or the I/O port.

I/O Routines in Turbo C++ Library

In this section we describe the I/O routines included in Turbo C++ library to enable you to use these routines effectively.

DEFAULT MODE: TEXT OR BINARY

In Turbo C++, the default mode of a file is determined by the value of the global integer variable *_fmode*. This is normally set to the constant O_TEXT (a preprocessor constant defined in *fcntl.h*), so all files, by default, are opened as text files. You can change the mode to binary by setting *_fmode* to O_BINARY. You can also select the mode of a file when opening it or you can use the *setmode* library function to change the translation mode of a file that is already open.

FILES ALREADY OPENED FOR YOUR CONVENIENCE

When your C program starts up, the five files shown in Table 16-1 are opened for you by Turbo C++. These may be called as streams or by handles. The first three files, *stdin, stdout,* and *stderr*, get input from the user, display the output, and display error messages, respectively. From DOS, you can redirect *stdin* and *stdout* to other files.

Table 16-1. ***Preopened Files in Turbo C++***

File	Stream Name	Handle Number	Connected to/Mode
Standard input	stdin	0	Console (keyboard)/Text mode
Standard output	stdout	1	Console (display screen)/Text mode
Standard error	stderr	2	Console (display screen)/Text mode
Standard auxiliary	stdaux	3	Cannot be connected/Binary mode
Standard print	stdprn	4	Printer port on PC/Binary mode

OPEN FILE LIMIT IN MS-DOS

MS-DOS imposes a limit of 20 open files per process (processes are defined in Chapter 3). Since 5 files are already opened, your program can open 15 files. Files opened for buffered as well as unbuffered I/O count towards this limit.

GLOBAL VARIABLES AND CONSTANTS THAT MATTER

The I/O routines are affected by certain global variables and preprocessor constants defined by the Turbo C++ library. (We have already mentioned one of the variables, *_fmode*, which determines the default translation mode of a file.) Table 16-2 lists the most important of these as they relate to the I/O routines. Many more predefined constants are significant to individual I/O routines, but these are described in the reference pages for the relevant I/O routines.

Table 16-2. ***Certain Constants and Global Variables Relevant to I/O Routines***

Name	Meaning and Default Value
BUFSIZ	Defines the size of each buffer associated with a stream. Constant is defined in *stdio.h* to be equal to 512.
EOF	Denotes end-of-file. Constant is defined in *stdio.h* as −1.
_fmode	Controls the translation modes (text or binary) of files opened in the program. Global integer's default setting is O_TEXT.
NULL	Signifies error returns defined in *stdio.h* to 0 (or 0L for compact, large, and huge memory models).

THE I/O ROUTINES

Table 16-3 catalogs the I/O routines. Since the number of routines in the entire I/O category is quite large, in addition to listing the routines alphabetically, in Table 16-4 we group them according to the specific tasks they perform. In listing the I/O routines by function, we start with the ones that perform file I/O. This group also includes routines that perform I/O with the preopened streams: *stdin* and *stdout*.

Table 16-3. ***I/O Library Routines***

Routine	Description
	Stream Routines
clearerr	Clears the error indicator of a stream.
fclose	Closes a stream.
fcloseall	Closes all streams that are currently open.
fdopen	Associates a stream with a file already opened by a low-level call.
feof	Returns a nonzero value if current position in a stream is at the end of file.
ferror	Returns a nonzero value if an error had occurred during read/write operations on a stream.
fflush	Writes to the file the contents of the buffer associated with a stream.
fgetc	Reads a character from a stream.
fgetchar	Reads a character from the stream *stdin*.
fgetpos	Returns current position of a stream in an internal format suitable for use by *fsetpos*.
fgets	Reads a line (up to and including the first newline character) from a stream.
fileno	Returns the file handle associated with a stream.
flushall	Flushes all buffers of all open streams to the respective files.
fopen	Opens a named file as a buffered stream (includes options for selecting translation modes and access types).
fprintf	Performs formatted output to a stream.
fputc	Writes a character to a stream.
fputchar	Writes a character to the stream *stdout*.
fputs	Writes a string of characters to a stream.
fread	Reads a specified amount of binary data from a stream.
freopen	Closes a stream and reassigns it to a new file.
fscanf	Performs formatted input from a stream.
fseek	Sets current position to a specific location in the file.
fsetpos	Sets current position of a stream using value returned by an earlier call to *fgetpos*.
ftell	Returns the current position in the file associated with a stream.
fwrite	Writes a specified number of bytes of binary data to a stream.
getc	Reads a character from a stream.
getchar	Reads a character from the stream *stdin*.

Table 16-3. *(cont.)*

Routine	Description
gets	Reads a string up to a newline character from the stream *stdin*.
getw	Reads two bytes of binary data from a stream.
printf	Performs formatted output to the stream *stdout*.
putc	Writes a character to a stream.
putchar	Writes a character to the stream *stdout*.
puts	Writes a C string to the stream *stdout*.
putw	Writes two bytes of binary data to a stream.
rewind	Sets the current position to the beginning of the file associated with a stream.
scanf	Performs formatted input from the stream *stdin*.
setbuf	Assigns a fixed-length user-defined buffer to an open stream.
setvbuf	Assigns a variable-length user-defined buffer to an open stream.
sprintf	Performs formatted output to a buffer.
sscanf	Performs formatted input from a buffer.
tmpfile	Creates a temporary file open for buffered stream I/O.
tmpnam	Generates a temporary file name.
ungetc	Pushes a character back into the buffer associated with a stream.
vfprintf	Version of *fprintf* that accepts a pointer to a list of arguments and performs formatted output to a stream.
vfscanf	Version of *fscanf* that accepts a pointer to a list of arguments and reads formatted input from a stream.
vprintf	Version of *printf* that accepts a pointer to a list of arguments and performs formatted output to the stream *stdout*.
vscanf	Version of *scanf* that accepts a pointer to a list of arguments and reads formatted input from *stdin*.
vsprintf	Version of *sprintf* that accepts a pointer to a list of arguments and performs formatted output to a buffer.
vsscanf	Version of *sscanf* that accepts a pointer to a list of arguments and reads formatted input from a buffer.
	Low-Level Routines
close	Closes a file using its handle.
creat	Creates a new file, opens it, and returns its handle.
creatnew	Creates a new file if none exists (DOS 3.X only).
creattemp	Creates a temporary file (DOS 3.X only).
dup	Creates a second handle given an existing handle associated with an open file.
dup2	Assigns a specified second handle to an existing handle so that both handles refer to the same file.
eof	Checks for end-of-file condition of a file specified by a handle.
lseek	Sets the current position in a file referenced by a handle.
open	Opens a file for low-level I/O and returns a handle.

Table 16-3. ***(cont.)***

Routine	Description
read	Reads a specified number of bytes of binary data from a file open for low-level I/O.
sopen	Opens a file for shared low-level I/O and returns a handle.
tell	Returns the current position in a file referenced by a handle.
write	Writes a specified number of bytes of binary data to a file open for low-level I/O.
	Console and Port Routines
cgets	Reads a string of characters from the console.
cprintf	Performs formatted output to the console.
cputs	Writes a string to the console.
cscanf	Performs formatted input from the console.
getch	Reads (without echoing) a single unbuffered character from the console.
getche	Reads and echoes a single unbuffered character from the console.
getpass	Reads a password without echoing.
inport	Reads two contiguous bytes from a specified I/O port address.
inportb	Reads a single byte from a specified I/O port address.
kbhit	Tests whether there are any keystrokes waiting to be read.
outport	Writes two bytes to a specified I/O port address.
outportb	Writes a single byte to a specified I/O port address.
putch	Writes a single unbuffered character to the console.
ungetch	Pushes a character back to the console.

Table 16-4. ***Library Routines by Task***

I/O Task	Stream I/O	Low-level I/O
Create a file.	fopen	creat, open, sopen
Open a file.	fopen, freopen	open, sopen
Close a File.	fclose, fcloseall	close
Formatted read.	fscanf, scanf, vfscanf, vscanf	—
Formatted write.	fprintf, printf, vfprintf, vprintf	—
Read a character.	fgetc, fgetchar, getc, getchar	—
Write a character.	fputc, fputchar, putc, putchar	—
Read a line.	fgets, gets	—
Write a line.	fputs, puts	—
Set read/write position.	fseek, fsetpos, rewind	lseek
Get read/write position.	fgetpos, ftell	tell
Binary read.	fread, getw	read

Table 16-4. *(cont.)*

I/O Task	Stream I/O	Low-level I/O
Binary write.	fwrite, putw	write
Flush buffer.	fflush, flushall	—
Get handle of a stream.	fileno	—
Assign buffer to a handle.	fdopen	—
Duplicate a handle.	—	dup, dup2
Check error/eof.	clearerr, feof, ferror	eof
Manage temporary files.	tmpfile, tmpnam	—
Control buffering.	setbuf, setvbuf	—
Push character to buffer.	ungetc	—

String I/O

If you think of files as a stream of bytes, the data sources or destinations do not have to be disk files or devices; they can also be buffers in memory. A group of Turbo C++ I/O routines provides the capability to read from and write to arrays of characters ("strings"). These routines allow you to format data and place the result in a string or get characters from a string and convert the characters to internal values. This is often convenient because you can prepare a string that can be output by routines that do not have any formatting capability (for example, the *outtext* routine in the Graphics category). Table 16-5 lists the three string I/O routines according to the task they perform.

Table 16-5. *String I/O Routines by Task*

I/O Task	Routines
Format input from a string.	sscanf, vsscanf
Format output to a string.	sprintf, vsprintf

Console and Port I/O Routines by Task

Table 16-6 shows the console and port I/O routines that interact with the keyboard and the screen, grouped by task. As you can see, the console I/O routines also support formatting. The formatting capabilities are identical to those supported by *printf* and *scanf* which we describe next.

FORMATTED I/O: PRINTF *AND* SCANF

The formatting I/O capabilities of *printf* and *scanf* deserve special attention because they are widely used in C programs and a large number of formatting options are available under each function. Many other functions, such as *cprintf, cscanf, fprintf, fscanf, sprintf,* and *sscanf,* provide identical formatting options. Thus understanding *printf* and *scanf* should help you use all the formatted I/O routines in the Turbo C++ library.

Table 16-6. ***Console and Port I/O Routines Grouped by Task***

I/O Task	Routines
Read from an I/O port address.	inport, inportb
Write to an I/O port address.	outport, outportb
Read character from console.	getch, getche
Write character to console.	putch
Check for waiting keystrokes.	kbhit
Push a character back to console.	ungetch
Read a string from console.	cgets
Write a string to console.	cputs
Format input from the console.	cscanf
Format output to the console.	cprintf

Formatting involves converting internal representation of a variable into a character string that humans can understand. To interpret the contents of a set of memory locations you must know the type of C variable being stored there. For example, a set of four bytes can hold a long integer and it can also hold a single-precision floating-point number. The *printf* and *scanf* functions, responsible for formatting the data, have to be told how the contents of these bytes are to be interpreted. This is done by embedding formatting commands in the arguments passed to *printf* and *scanf.*

Formatted Output with printf

In the simplest case, when printing out values of variables, you can use *printf* with a minimal amount of formatting code:

```
float   floatvar = 24.95;
double  dblvar = 99.95;
int     intvar = 100;
char    string[] = "Turbo C 2.0";
:
:
printf("Float = %f, Double = %f, Integer = %d,\nString = %s\n",
        floatvar, dblvar, intvar, string);
```

In this case, each formatting command consists of a percent sign (%) followed by a single letter that indicates the type of the variable. The format codes are embedded in a string and each command appears exactly where you want the variable to be printed. The string with the formatting codes is followed by the variables that you want printed. Here's what you get if you embed the code fragment above in a C program and execute it.

```
Float = 24.950001, Double = 99.950000, Integer = 100,
String = Turbo C 2.0
```

You may have noticed the discrepancy between the assigned value of the *float* variable and the value shown by *printf*. The single-precision *float* variables are accurate to 7 significant digits. When we used the %f format to print the value, *printf* used more than 7 significant digits (by default it used 6 digits following the decimal point). Since the stored value is only accurate to 7 significant digits, the value prints as *24.950001* instead of the expected *24.950000*. This illustrates an important point about formatted output: you can only print results that can have at best the accuracy present in the stored value. Since a *float* variable is accurate to 7 digits, you cannot expect to get a more accurate value just by asking *printf* to use a formatting option that requires the use of, say, 15 significant digits.

Notice too that both *float* and *double* floating-point values are printed with six digits after the decimal place. The integer value is printed without any leading blanks and the string is printed in its entirety. These are the default settings of the respective formats: %f, %d, and %s. Additional qualifiers can be placed between the percent sign and the type letter to indicate options, such as the number of digits after the decimal point or a fixed size of field within which to print a value.

Other data types can also be printed out, including the *long* and *unsigned* forms of integers as well as single characters and addresses of variables in hexadecimal format. See the reference pages on *printf* for complete coverage of the formatting options and commands. We will not repeat the information here except to note that while *printf* is meant for writing to the stream *stdout*, *fprintf* performs the same operation to a file and *sprintf* writes formatted output to a string. There is even a formatted console output routine named *cprintf*. Each of these accepts the same formatting commands as *printf*.

Formatted Input with scanf

The *scanf* function is meant for formatting input which involves reading characters and converting groups of them into internal representation of C variables. Like *printf*, a string with embedded format codes specifies how the input characters are to be treated during the conversion process. In fact, a call to *scanf* looks like a call to *printf*, except that the argument list has addresses of the variables into which *scanf* loads the values converted from the input string. If we were reading a *float*, a *double*, and an integer, the call might look like this:

```
float   floatvar;
double  dblvar;
int     intvar;
:
:
scanf(" %f %lf %d", &floatvar, &dblvar, &intvar);
```

This formatted read statement reads the three values with any number of blank spaces between them. Note that the format code meant for the *float* variable is different from that for the *double*. The %f code tells *scanf* to convert the string into the internal representation of a *float* variable. The qualifier l between the % and the f tells *scanf* to use the internal representation of a *double* instead of a *float*.

Like *printf*, *scanf* is used with formatted input from the stream *stdin*. The Turbo C++ I/O library also includes *fscanf* for formatted reading from a file and *sscanf* for formatted input from a string. Lastly, there is a formatted input routine for the console called *cscanf*. All of these routines use the same formatting commands as *scanf*. The reference page on *scanf* gives a detailed discussion of the formatting options available to you as a programmer.

Using C++ Stream I/O in Turbo C++

So far you have seen the C stream I/O routines, the prominent ones being the ubiquitous *printf*, *scanf*, and their variants. C++ brings in something new for stream I/O. With its facility for defining objects using the *class* keyword, C++ supports I/O in a simpler manner than using *printf* and *scanf*. Here we give a very brief overview of the C++ stream I/O. For more information, you should consult one of the references on C++ listed at the end of Chapter 2. (Be forewarned, many do not describe the release 2.0 version of the stream library.) The *C++ Primer* by Stanley Lippman covers the new library.

To show how the C++ stream I/O works, let us start with a small example program:

```
#include <iostream.h>       // For Release 2.0 stream I/O

main()
{
    int x = 255;
```

```
    float cost = 26.95;
    cout << "Welcome to Turbo C++\n";
    cout << "The value of x = " << x << "\n";
    cout << "Total cost: $" << cost << "\n";
}
```

If you type this program into a file and run it from Turbo C++, it generates the following output:

```
Welcome to Turbo C++
The value of x = 255
Total cost: $26.950001
```

As you can see, screen output is generated by simply using the << operator with the stream named *cout* (which denotes standard output, analogous to C's *stdout*). The interesting part is that you do not have to specify format strings to print variables. The conversion of a variable's value into a string takes place by the magic of operator overloading. The << operator for a data type takes care of performing the conversion.

C++ STREAMS

Like C's model of a file, the C++ stream I/O classes also consider input and output in terms of a stream of bytes. At this level, there is no distinction made between data types. The iostream library in AT&T's C++ Release 2.0 (which is what Turbo C++ implements) defines the set of operations necessary to perform input and output operations on the built-in data types such as *int*, *double*, and *float*.

There are two classes for I/O: *istream* for input and *ostream* for output. A third class, *iostream*, is derived from both *istream* and *ostream* and it takes care of both input and output. Output operation is performed by the *insertion* operator (<<) and input is handled by the *extraction* operator (>>). If the symbols for the operators seem arbitrary, you can remember them easily by observing that the operator always points to the destination of the data. Thus, when sending a stream of bytes to *cout*, you write

```
cout << "Value = " << x;
```

with the arrows pointing towards the stream *cout*. On the other hand, to read a value from the standard input stream, *cin*, into a variable, you will write

```
cin >> x;      // Read value into x
```

The C++ stream classes are defined in the header file *iostream.h*. Note that prior to Release 2.0 of C++, the header file was called *stream.h*.

You can still use the older style header file in Turbo C++, but this requires that you link your program with the library named *OLDSTRMX.LIB* where the letter *X* is one of S, M, C, L, or H, depending on the memory model (small, medium, compact, large, or huge).

Standard Streams

Like C, C++ also has a number of predefined streams. These are

cin An *istream* object connected to standard input

cout An *ostream* object connected to standard output

cerr An *ostream* object connected to standard error and meant for unbuffered output

clog An *ostream* object connected to standard error and meant for buffered output

Cautions

- Do not mix low-level I/O read and write routines with the buffered stream routines because the two sets are not compatible.
- Remember that the translation mode O_TEXT causes interpretation of the bytes in a file and the number of bytes read or written does not correspond to the number in the file. This means that you cannot rely on absolute byte positions when accessing a file in the text mode.
- Single keystrokes from the console cannot be read by *getchar* (it waits until a carriage return is hit). Use the console routines *getch* or *getche* for this purpose. For example, if you wanted to end a program when the user presses any key, you could use

```
{
    :
    :
    printf("Press any key to exit:");
    getch()  /* Read a keystroke and exit */
}
```

  If you use *getchar*, the function does not return immediately after a key is pressed. It waits until a carriage return to end the read operation.
- When using the buffered I/O routines, the buffers sometimes have to be explicitly written out (flushed) with the library routines *fflush* or *flushall* before output data actually appears in a file. Normally, buffers are flushed during program termination, but not when a program ends with a call to *_exit*.

- The formatting options available in the *printf* and the *scanf* family are quite extensive and several format codes are specific to Turbo C. When portability is a concern, check the appropriate reference pages carefully before using a particular format code.
- Note that file-sharing is supported only under MS-DOS 3.0 and higher.

Further Reading

The standard I/O routines are covered in almost every book on C. Prata's book[1] provides a gentle introduction to these functions, yet includes a detailed exposition of the concepts behind the C I/O library. The basic file I/O routines are also carefully explained in Lafore's text on C[2].

Chapter 13 of the *MS-DOS Papers*[3] covers in detail how you can program the serial port of a PC in Microsoft C, and it includes a complete communications program illustrating the use of the port I/O routines.

For stream I/O in C++, consult the primer by Stanley Lippman.[4] He devotes an Appendix to the topic of the *iostream* library in C++ 2.0.

1. Stephen Prata, The Waite Group, *Advanced C Primer++*, Howard W. Sams & Company, Indianapolis, IN, 1986, 502 pages.
2. Robert Lafore, *The Waite Group's Microsoft C Programming for the PC*, SAMS, Indianapolis, IN, 1990, 742 pages.
3. The Waite Group, *MS-DOS Papers*, Howard W. Sams & Company, Indianapolis, IN, 1988, 608 pages.
4. Stanley B. Lippman, *C++ Primer*, Addison-Wesley, Reading, MA, 1989, 478 pages.

Stream I/O

clearerr

COMPATIBILITY

TC1	TC1.5	TC2	TC++	MSC3	MSC4	MSC5	MSC6	QC1	QC2	QC2.5	ANSI	UNIX V	XNX
▲	▲	▲	▲	▲	▲	▲	▲	▲	▲	▲	▲	▲	▲

PURPOSE Use the *clearerr* function to reset the error and end-of-file indicators of a file specified by a file pointer (i.e., a pointer to the associated FILE data structure).

SYNTAX

```
void clearerr(FILE *file_pointer);
```

`FILE *file_pointer;` *Pointer to FILE data structure associated with the file whose error flag is being cleared*

EXAMPLE CALL

```
clearerr(outfile);
```

INCLUDES `#include <stdio.h>` *For function declaration and definition of the FILE data type*

DESCRIPTION The *clearerr* function sets to zero a flag in the FILE data structure associated with the file specified by the argument *file_pointer*. This flag has a nonzero value after an error or an end-of-file condition occurs. The error indicator for the file remains set until cleared by calling *clearerr*. These conditions may be verified by calling *ferror* and *feof*, respectively.

SEE ALSO

`ferror` *To detect an error condition of a file*

`feof` *To determine an end-of-file condition*

EXAMPLE Write a C program that prompts the user for a file name. Open the file with *fopen* for read operations only. Then create an error condition by trying to write to the file. Call *ferror* to detect the error and call *clearerr* to reset the error flag.

```
#include <stdio.h>
main()
{
    char filename[81];
    FILE *infile;
    long filesize;
    printf("Enter the name of an existing file: ");
    gets(filename);
/* Open the file */
    if ( (infile = fopen(filename, "r")) == NULL)
```

```
    {
        printf("fopen failed to open: %s\n", filename);
        exit(0);
    }
    fprintf(infile, "Test..."); /* Try to write a line*/
    if (ferror(infile) != 0)   /* Check for the error*/
    {
        printf("Error detected\n");
        clearerr(infile);       /* Now clear the error */
        printf("Error cleared\n");
    }
        return 0;
}
```

Stream I/O

fclose

COMPATIBILITY

TC1	TC1.5	TC2	TC++	MSC3	MSC4	MSC5	MSC6	QC1	QC2	QC2.5	ANSI	UNIX V	XNX
▲	▲	▲	▲	▲	▲	▲	▲	▲	▲	▲	▲	▲	▲

PURPOSE Use *fclose* to close a file opened earlier for buffered input and output using *fopen*.

SYNTAX
```
int fclose(FILE *file_pointer);

FILE *file_pointer;        Pointer to file to be closed
```

EXAMPLE CALL
```
fclose(infile);
```

INCLUDES
```
#include <stdio.h>       For function declaration and definition of FILE data type
```

DESCRIPTION The *fclose* function closes the file specified by the argument *file_pointer*. This pointer must have been one returned earlier when the file was opened by *fopen*. If the file is open for writing, the contents of the buffer associated with the file are flushed before the file is closed. The buffer is then released.

COMMON USES To ensure that all buffers get flushed and freed for reuse and that the file is properly closed, use *fclose* for files that you no longer intend to use in your program.

RETURNS If the file is successfully closed, *fclose* returns a zero. In case of an error, the return value is equal to the constant EOF defined in *stdio.h*.

COMMENTS You can use the *fcloseall* function to close all open files at the same time. Since only 20 files opened by *fopen* can be present at the same time, however, for file-intensive applications you may find it necessary to close files with *fclose* when you are done with a file. Note that buffers assigned to a stream with *setbuf* or *setvbuf* will not be automatically freed by *fclose*.

SEE ALSO

`fopen` *To open a file for buffered I/O*

`fcloseall` *To close all open files at the same time*

EXAMPLE Use *fopen* to open a file specified by the user. Read and display the file's contents. Close the file by calling *fclose* and then exit.

```
#include <stdio.h>
char filename[80],     /* Name of file to open        */
     line[81];         /* For lines from the file     */
FILE *inputfile;       /* File pointer to opened file */
main()
{
    printf("Enter name of file to open: ");
    gets(filename);
/* Open the file */
    if ((inputfile = fopen(filename,"r")) == NULL)
    {
        printf("Error opening file: %s\n", filename);
        exit(0);
    }
    printf("==== Contents of input file ====\n");
    while(fgets(line, 80, inputfile) != NULL)
    {
        printf(line);
    }
/* Now close the file and exit */
    fclose(inputfile);
    return 0;
}
```

Stream I/O

fcloseall

COMPATIBILITY

TC1	TC1.5	TC2	TC++	MSC3	MSC4	MSC5	MSC6	QC1	QC2	QC2.5	ANSI	UNIX V	XNX
▲	▲	▲	▲	▲	▲	▲	▲	▲	▲	▲			

PURPOSE Use *fcloseall* to close all files opened for buffered input and output with *fopen* or *tmpfile*, respectively.

SYNTAX

```
int fcloseall(void);
```

EXAMPLE CALL

```
number_closed = fcloseall();
```

INCLUDES `#include <stdio.h>` *For function declaration*

DESCRIPTION The *fcloseall* function closes all files that have been opened by *fopen* or *tmpfile* for buffered I/O. Buffers associated with files opened for writing are written out to the corresponding file before closing.

Note that *fcloseall* does not close the five I/O *streams* (*stdin, stdout, stderr, stdaux,* and *stdprn*) that are preopened by the system (see the tutorial section).

COMMON USES You can use *fcloseall* to close, in a single stroke, all files opened by your program.

RETURNS If files are successfully closed, *fcloseall* returns the number closed. In case of an error, the return value is equal to the constant EOF defined in *stdio.h.*

SEE ALSO `fopen` *To open a file for buffered I/O*

`fclose` *To close a single file*

EXAMPLE We'll illustrate two features of the file I/O routines with this example. The function *tmpfile* enables you to create a temporary file. Write a sample C program in which you attempt to open 20 temporary files. Since MS-DOS allows only 20 files (for buffered I/O) and 5 are already open, the *tmpfile* call will fail after 15 files are open. Now call *fcloseall* to close them all at once. Print the number returned by *fcloseall* to verify that it's 15.

```
#include <stdio.h>
main()
{
    int i;
/* Try opening 20 temporary files -- we'll just throw
```

```
 * away the returned pointers because we are not going
 * to use these files. The file open will fail after 15
 * files are opened. So the number of closed files
 * should be 15.
 */
    for (i=0; i<20; i++)
    {
        if (tmpfile() == NULL)
            printf("Error opening file # %d\n", i);
        else
            printf("Temporary file #%d opened\n", i);
    }
/* Now close all the files and inform user how many were
 * closed
 */
    i = fcloseall();
    printf("%d files were closed -- should be 15\n", i);
    return 0;
}
```

Stream I/O

fdopen

COMPATIBILITY

TC1	TC1.5	TC2	TC++	MSC3	MSC4	MSC5	MSC6	QC1	QC2	QC2.5	ANSI	UNIX V	XNX
▲	▲	▲	▲	▲	▲	▲	▲	▲	▲	▲		▲	▲

PURPOSE Use *fdopen* to associate a buffer with a file that has been opened for unbuffered, unformatted I/O. This allows subsequent buffered, formatted read/write operations with the file.

SYNTAX `FILE *fdopen(int handle, char *access_mode);`

`int handle;` *Handle of open file being upgraded for buffered I/O*

`char *access_mode;` *A character string denoting whether file is being opened for read/write.*

EXAMPLE CALL `p_datafile = fdopen(handle, "rb");`

INCLUDES `#include <stdio.h>` *For function declaration and definition of FILE data type*

DESCRIPTION The *fdopen* function associates a FILE data structure with the file specified by the argument *handle*. The *handle* is an integer returned by low-level

I/O routines such as *open, creat,* and *sopen* that originally opened the file. Once buffered I/O becomes permissible, the type of operations you intend to perform on the file must be indicated by the argument *access_mode*. Table 16-7 lists the possible values of *access_mode* and their meanings.

Table 16-7. *Access Modes When Opening Files for Buffered I/O*

Access Mode String	Interpretation
r	Opens file for read operations only. The *fopen* function fails if the file does not exist.
w	Opens a new file for writing. If the file exists, its contents are destroyed.
a	Opens file for appending. A new file is created if the file does not exist.
r+	Opens an existing file for both read and write operations. Error is returned if file does not exist.
w+	Creates a file and opens it for both reading and writing. If file exists, current contents are destroyed.
a+	Opens file for reading and appending. Creates a new file if one does not exist.

In addition to the basic access modes shown in Table 16-7, one of the characters shown in Table 16-8 can be appended to each of the strings in Table 16-7 to specify how the contents of the file are to be translated. Note that the character denoting the translation mode (see the tutorial section) can come before or after the + in the strings above. For example, *w+b* is considered the same as *wb+* and means "open the file for reading and writing in the binary mode." If no translation mode is specified, the default mode is determined by the global variable *_fmode*, which is declared

Table 16-8. *File Translation Modes for Buffered I/O*

Translation Mode	Interpretation
b	Opens file in untranslated or binary mode. Every character in the file is read as is without the changes described below.
t	Opens file in translated mode. This is a Turbo C++ extension and not an ANSI standard mode. Its purpose is to accommodate MS-DOS file conventions. In this mode, the following interpretations will be in effect: (1) Carriage Return-Line Feed (CR-LF) combinations on input are translated to single linefeeds. During output, single linefeed characters are translated to CR-LF pairs. (2) During input, the Control-Z character is interpreted as the end-of-file character.

in the header file *stdio.h*. When a file is opened for appending with the *a* or *a+* access mode, existing data can never be destroyed because the *file pointer* is moved to the end of the file before writing occurs. This pointer keeps track of the current position where writing occurs. When a file is opened for updating, using the *r+*, *w+*, or *a+* access modes, you must call one of the functions *fsetpos, fseek*, or *rewind* when switching between read and write operations. These calls serve to set the file pointer properly before the operation. You can also call *fsetpos* or *fseek* and set the file pointer to the current position.

COMMON USES The *fdopen* function is used to enable buffered, formatted I/O on a file that was originally opened for unbuffered, unformatted I/O.

RETURNS If successful, *fdopen* returns a pointer to the FILE structure that is associated with the file. In case of an error, *fdopen* returns a NULL. See below for an example of checking for error return from *fdopen*.

COMMENTS The *access-mode* specified in the call to *fdopen* must be compatible with the access and sharing modes used when the file was first opened by *open, creat*, or *sopen*. You should not use *fdopen* with a file that was opened with *sopen* and file-sharing enabled. The buffered operations are inherently incompatible with the concept of file-sharing because the file is not up to date and ready for sharing as long as some of the data resides in the buffer.

SEE ALSO

`fclose`	*To close a file opened by* fdopen
`open`	*To open a file using a handle, a lower-level routine*

EXAMPLE Use *open* to open a file, say, *autoexec.bat* (this is one file every PC has) in the root directory of your current drive, say, drive C. Now call *fdopen* to allow buffered I/O on the file. Read and display all lines in the file.

```
#include <stdio.h>
#include <io.h>
#include <fcntl.h>

main()
{
        int handle;
        FILE *infile;
        char buffer[80];
/* Open the file. Note that we need two '\'  */
        if ( (handle = open("c:\\autoexec.bat",
              O_RDONLY)) == -1)
        {
```

```
                perror("open failed");
                exit(1);
            }
/* Use fdopen to assign a FILE data structure to file */
            if ((infile = fdopen(handle, "r")) == NULL)
            {
                perror("fdopen failed");
                exit(1);
            }
/* All's well. Read and print the contents of the file*/
            printf("Contents of c:autoexec.bat:\n");
            while ( fgets(buffer, 80, infile) != NULL)
            {
                printf(buffer);
            }
            return 0;
}
```

Stream I/O

feof

COMPATIBILITY

TC1	TC1.5	TC2	TC++	MSC3	MSC4	MSC5	MSC6	QC1	QC2	QC2.5	ANSI	UNIX V	XNX
▲	▲	▲	▲	▲	▲	▲	▲	▲	▲	▲	▲	▲	▲

PURPOSE Use the *feof* macro, defined in *stdio.h*, to determine whether the end of a file has been reached.

SYNTAX

```
int feof(FILE *file_pointer);
```

`FILE *file_pointer;` *Pointer to FILE data structure associated with the file whose status is being checked*

EXAMPLE CALL

```
if (feof(infile) != 0) printf("File ended\n");
```

INCLUDES `#include <stdio.h>` *For function declaration and definition of the FILE data type*

DESCRIPTION The *feof* macro returns a value indicating whether the file specified by the argument *file_pointer* has reached its end.

COMMON USES When you get an error return from a read operation, you can call *feof* to determine if the error occurred because you tried to read past the end-of-file.

RETURNS If the end of the file is reached, *feof* returns a nonzero value after the first read operation beyond the end-of-file. Otherwise, it returns a zero.

COMMENTS Since *feof* is implemented as a macro, checking for end-of-file with *feof* does not involve the overhead of calling a function.

SEE ALSO

`clearerr`	*To reset the end-of-file and error indicator of a file*
`rewind`	*To move the file pointer to the beginning of a file*
`fclose`	*To close a single file*

EXAMPLE Use *fopen* to open the file *autoexec.bat* for buffered read operations. Read and display each line until an error is returned by the read routine *fgets*. Then call *feof* to check whether end-of-file is reached. If not, there is another error in reading from the file.

```
#include <stdio.h>
main()
{
        FILE *infile;
        unsigned char buffer[81];
/* Open the file "c:\autoexec.bat". We need two '\'  */
        if ( (infile = fopen("c:\\autoexec.bat", "r"))
             == NULL)
        {
            printf("fopen failed.\n");
            exit(0);
        }
        printf("Contents of c:autoexec.bat:\n");
        while ( fgets(buffer, 80, infile) != NULL)
        {
            printf(buffer);
        }
        if (feof(infile) != 0) /* Check end-of-file */
        {
            printf("*** End-of-file reached ***");
        }
        else
        {
            printf("ERROR: reading from file!\n");
        }
        return 0;
}
```

Stream I/O

ferror

COMPATIBILITY

TC1	TC1.5	TC2	TC++	MSC3	MSC4	MSC5	MSC6	QC1	QC2	QC2.5	ANSI	UNIX V	XNX
▲	▲	▲	▲	▲	▲	▲	▲	▲	▲	▲	▲	▲	▲

PURPOSE Use the *ferror* macro, defined in *stdio.h*, to determine if an error has occurred during a previous read or write operation on a file that had been opened for buffered I/O.

SYNTAX

```
int ferror(FILE *file_pointer);
```

`FILE *file_pointer;` *Pointer to FILE data structure associated with the file whose status is being checked*

EXAMPLE CALL

```
if (ferror(infile) != 0) printf("Error detected\n");
```

INCLUDES `#include <stdio.h>` *For function declaration and definition of the FILE data type*

DESCRIPTION The *ferror* macro returns a value indicating whether there has been an error during a prior read/write operation on the file specified by the argument *file_pointer*. The FILE data structure associated with the file has a flag field that holds the information about the end-of-file and error conditions during read or write operations. The *ferror* macro checks whether the flag equals a predefined constant that indicates an error condition.

COMMON USES If you have not checked for error returns from read/write operations, you can check after the fact by calling *ferror*. If there was an error, you can call *clearerr* to clear the error flag. Rewinding the file also clears the error flag.

RETURNS If an error has occurred during a read or a write operation on the file, *ferror* returns a nonzero value. Otherwise, it returns a zero.

COMMENTS Since *ferror* is implemented as a macro, checking for errors with it does not involve calling a function.

SEE ALSO `clearerr` *To clear the error condition of a file*

EXAMPLE Use *fopen* to open the file *autoexec.bat* for buffered read operations only. Now create an error condition by attempting to write a line to it. Call *ferror* to confirm that there was an error and then call *clearerr* to clear the error condition.

```
#include <stdio.h>
char buffer[81] = "This will not be written";
```

```
main()
{
        FILE *infile;
/* Open the file "c:\autoexec.bat". Note the two '\'  */
        if ( (infile = fopen("c:\\autoexec.bat", "r"))
              == NULL)
        {
           printf("fopen failed.\n");
           exit(0);
        }
        fprintf(infile, "%s\n", buffer);
        if (ferror(infile) != 0)   /* Check for error */
        {
           printf("Error detected\n");
           clearerr(infile);       /* Now clear the error */
           printf("Error cleared\n");
        }
        return 0;
}
```

Stream I/O

fflush

COMPATIBILITY

TC1	TC1.5	TC2	TC++	MSC3	MSC4	MSC5	MSC6	QC1	QC2	QC2.5	ANSI	UNIX V	XNX
▲	▲	▲	▲	▲	▲	▲	▲	▲	▲	▲	▲	▲	▲

PURPOSE Use the *fflush* function to process the current contents of the buffer associated with a file opened for buffered I/O (see the tutorial section).

SYNTAX

```
int fflush(FILE *file_pointer);
```

`FILE *file_pointer;` *Pointer to FILE data structure associated with the file whose buffer is being flushed*

EXAMPLE CALL

```
fflush(stdin);
```

INCLUDES `#include <stdio.h>` *For function declaration and definition of the FILE data type*

DESCRIPTION The *fflush* function flushes the buffer associated with the file specified by the argument *file_pointer*. This pointer to the FILE data structure is the value returned by an earlier call to *fopen*. If the file is open for write operations, the flushing involves writing the contents of the buffer to the file. Otherwise, the buffer is cleared.

COMMON USES You can use *fflush* to ignore and discard data read from a file opened for buffered read operations. For a file opened for write or update operations, you can call *fflush* to ensure that the contents of the buffer are written without waiting for the buffer to get full. This may be necessary when launching a child process (see Chapter 4) to ensure that a file is up to date before the child process uses it.

RETURNS If the buffer is successfully flushed, *fflush* returns a zero. In case of an error, the return value is the constant EOF defined in *stdio.h*.

COMMENTS During buffered I/O from files, the actual read or write operation is performed only when the buffer associated with the file becomes full, the file is closed, or the program exits normally. In most cases, you never have to explicitly call *fflush*. But if you must ensure that when you say "write" you mean write to the file and not hold in a buffer, you can insert a call to *fflush* to accomplish this. This helps ensure data integrity at the cost of some loss in efficiency.

SEE ALSO

`fopen`	*To open a file for buffered I/O*
`fclose`	*To close a single file*

EXAMPLE Use *fopen* to open the file *autoexec.bat* for buffered read operations. Read the first 5 characters with calls to *fgetc* and save them in an array called *line*. Flush the buffer by using *fflush*. Continue reading with *fgetc* until you reach the end of the line or until you have read 80 characters. Now display the array—it should have the first 5 characters of the first line in your *autoexec.bat*, but the rest will be missing because we flushed the buffer after reading those characters.

```
#include <stdio.h>
main()
{

        int i;
        char line[81];
        FILE *infile;
/* Open the file. Note that we need two '\'  */
        if ( (infile = fopen("c:\\autoexec.bat", "r"))
               == NULL)
        {
           printf("fopen failed.\n");
           exit(0);
        }
/* Now read characters using fgetc */
        for (i=0; i<80; i++)
```

```
        {
           line[i] = fgetc(infile);
           if (i==4) fflush(infile); /* Flush buffer */
           if(line[i] == '\n') break;
        }
        line[i+1] = '\0';      /* Mark end of string */
/* Now print the line and see how it looks */
        printf("The line is: %s", line);
        return 0;
}
```

Stream I/O

fgetc

COMPATIBILITY

TC1	TC1.5	TC2	TC++	MSC3	MSC4	MSC5	MSC6	QC1	QC2	QC2.5	ANSI	UNIX V	XNX
▲	▲	▲	▲	▲	▲	▲	▲	▲	▲	▲	▲	▲	▲

PURPOSE Use *fgetc* to read a single character from a file opened for buffered input.

SYNTAX

```
int fgetc(FILE *file_pointer);
```

`FILE *file_pointer;` *Pointer to FILE data structure associated with the file from which a character is to be read*

EXAMPLE CALL

```
char_read = fgetc(infile);
```

INCLUDES `#include <stdio.h>` *For function declaration and definition of FILE data type*

DESCRIPTION The *fgetc* function reads a character from the current position of the file specified by the argument *file_pointer* and then increments this position. The character is returned as an integer. Note that *getc*, defined in *stdio.h* as a macro, also reads a character from a file.

RETURNS If there are no errors, *fgetc* returns the character read. Otherwise, it returns the constant EOF. Call *ferror* and *feof* to determine if there was an error or the file simply reached its end.

SEE ALSO

`getc` *Macro to read a character from a file*

`fgetchar` *Function to read a character from* stdin

`fputc, fputchar, putc, putchar` *To write a character to a file*

EXAMPLE Use *fgetc* to read a line (maximum length of 80 characters or to the newline character \n) from the file *autoexec.bat* and display the line on the screen using *printf*.

```
#include <stdio.h>
main()
{
        FILE *infile;
        char buffer[81];
        int i, c;
/* Open the file. */
        if ( (infile = fopen("c:\\autoexec.bat", "r"))
              == NULL)
        {
            printf("fopen failed.\n");
            exit(0);
        }
        c = fgetc(infile);
        for(i=0; (i<80) && (feof(infile) == 0) &&
                        (c != '\n'); i++)
        {
            buffer[i] = c;
            c = fgetc(infile);
        }
        buffer[i] = '\0';  /* make a C-style string */
        printf("First line of c:autoexec.bat: %s\n",
                buffer);
        return 0;
}
```

Stream I/O

COMPATIBILITY

fgetchar

TC1	TC1.5	TC2	TC++	MSC3	MSC4	MSC5	MSC6	QC1	QC2	QC2.5	ANSI	UNIX V	XNX
▲	▲	▲	▲	▲	▲	▲	▲	▲	▲	▲			

PURPOSE Use *fgetchar* to read a single character from the file *stdin*, normally the keyboard.

SYNTAX `int fgetchar(void);`

EXAMPLE CALL `c = fgetchar();`

INCLUDES `#include <stdio.h>` *For function declaration*

DESCRIPTION The *fgetchar* function reads a character from the file *stdin*. This function is equivalent to *fgetc(stdin)*.

RETURNS If there are no errors, *fgetchar* returns the character read. Otherwise, it returns the constant EOF.

SEE ALSO

`fgetc`	*General function to read a character from a file*
`fputc, fputchar, putc, putchar`	*To write a character to a file*

EXAMPLE Use *fgetchar* to read a line (maximum length of 80 characters or up to the newline character \n) from the keyboard and display the line on the screen using *printf*. Even if you wanted to read only one character, because of the buffered input mechanism, the input does not end until you hit the carriage return key.

```
#include <stdio.h>
main()
{
        char buffer[81];
        int i, c;
        printf("Enter a line (end with a return):\n");
        c = fgetchar();
        for(i=0; (i<80) && (c != '\n'); i++)
        {
            buffer[i] = c;
            c = fgetchar();
        }
        buffer[i] = '\0';  /* make a C-style string */
        printf("You entered: %s\n", buffer);
        return 0;
}
```

Stream I/O

fgetpos

COMPATIBILITY

TC1	TC1.5	TC2	TC++	MSC3	MSC4	MSC5	MSC6	QC1	QC2	QC2.5	ANSI	UNIX V	XNX
▲	▲	▲	▲			▲	▲	▲	▲	▲	▲		

PURPOSE Use *fgetpos* to get and save the current position where reading or writing occurs in a file opened for buffered I/O.

SYNTAX `int fgetpos(FILE *file_pointer, fpos_t *current_pos);`

`FILE *file_pointer;`	*Pointer to FILE data structure associated with file whose current position is requested*
`fpos_t *current_pos;`	*Pointer to location where file's current position is returned*

EXAMPLE CALL `fgetpos(infile, &curpos);`

INCLUDES `#include <stdio.h>` *For function declaration and definition of FILE and* fpos_t *data types*

DESCRIPTION The *fgetpos* function gets the current read or write position of the file specified by the argument *file_pointer*, which is a pointer to the FILE data structure associated with a file that is already open. Next *fgetpos* saves this position in a location specified by the pointer *current_pos*. This location is of type *fpos_t*, which is defined in *stdio.h* to be a *long* integer.

COMMON USES The *fgetpos* function is used with its counterpart *fsetpos* to remember a location in the file and return to it at a later time.

RETURNS The *fgetpos* returns a zero when successful. In case of error, the return value is nonzero.

COMMENTS The value of the current read/write position in the file is meaningful only to the buffered input and output routines. Although you can access this value, you should not interpret it in any way. Thus the retrieved file position should be used only as an input argument to *fsetpos*. Use *ftell* if you want the position expressed in terms of byte offsets from the beginning of the file.

SEE ALSO `fsetpos` *To change the current position indicator of a file*

EXAMPLE Open a file using *fopen* for reading. Read 10 characters into a buffer and save the current position by calling *fgetpos*. Now read in 10 more characters and call *fsetpos* to return to the position saved earlier. Read in another 10 characters. Print the buffer out and note that the last 10 characters are the same as the 10 read earlier.

```
#include <stdio.h>
void read10char(FILE *, char *);
main()
{
        fpos_t curpos;
        FILE *infile;
        char filename[81], buffer[40];
```

```
        printf("Enter name of a text file: ");
        gets(filename);
/* Open the file for reading */
        if ( (infile = fopen(filename, "r")) == NULL)
        {
            printf("fopen failed.\n");
            exit(0);
        }
        read10char(infile, buffer);
/* Save current position */
        if (fgetpos(infile, &curpos) != 0)
            perror("fgetpos failed!");
/* Read another 10 characters */
        read10char(infile, &buffer[11]);
/* Reset to previous position in file */
        if (fsetpos(infile, &curpos) != 0)
            perror("fsetpos failed!");
/* Read another 10 characters -- these should be same
 * as last 10.
 */
        read10char(infile, &buffer[21]);
        buffer[32] = '\0';   /* Convert to C string */
        printf("Buffer now has:\n%s", buffer);
        return 0;
}
/*------------------------------------------------------*/
void read10char(FILE *infile, char *buffer)
{
        int i;
        for(i=0; i<10; i++)

        {
            if((*buffer = fgetc(infile)) == EOF)
            {
                printf("file ended. buffer so far has: \
%s\n", buffer);
                exit(0);
            }
            buffer++;
        }
        *buffer = '\n';
}
```

Stream I/O

COMPATIBILITY

fgets

TC1	TC1.5	TC2	TC++	MSC3	MSC4	MSC5	MSC6	QC1	QC2	QC2.5	ANSI	UNIX V	XNX
▲	▲	▲	▲	▲	▲	▲	▲	▲	▲	▲	▲	▲	▲

PURPOSE Use the *fgets* function to read a line from a file opened for buffered input. The line is read until a newline (\n) character is encountered or until the number of characters reaches a specified maximum.

SYNTAX

```
char *fgets(char *string, int maxchar, FILE *file_pointer);
```

`char *string;` *Pointer to buffer where characters are stored*

`int maxchar;` *Maximum number of characters that can be stored*

`FILE *file_pointer;` *Pointer to FILE data structure associated with file from which a line is read*

EXAMPLE CALL

```
fgets(buffer, 80, infile);
```

INCLUDES `#include <stdio.h>` *For function declaration and definition of FILE data type*

DESCRIPTION The *fgets* function reads a line from the file specified by the argument *file_pointer* and stores the characters in the buffer whose address is given in the argument *string*. Characters are read until a newline (\n) character is encountered or until the total number of characters read is one less than the number specified in *maxchar*. The buffer is converted to a C string by storing a null character (\0) after the last character stored in the buffer. Any newline characters are also included in the string.

Note that *gets* performs similarly but, unlike *fgets*, it reads up to the newline character and then replaces the newline character with a null character (thus the resulting string does not include a newline).

RETURNS If there are no errors, *fgets* returns the argument *string*. Otherwise, it returns a NULL. You can call *ferror* and *feof* to determine whether the error is genuine or if it occurred because the file reached its end.

SEE ALSO

`gets` *To read a line from* stdin

`fputs` *To write a string to a file*

`puts` *To write a string to* stdout

EXAMPLE Use *fgets* to read lines (maximum length, 80 characters) from the file *autoexec.bat* and display the lines on the screen using *fputs* with the file *stdout*.

```
#include <stdio.h>
main()
{
        FILE *infile;
        char string[81];
/* Open the file. Because of the special significance
 * of '\' in C, we need two of them in the pathname for
 * autoexec.bat
 */
        if ( (infile = fopen("c:\\autoexec.bat", "r"))
              == NULL)
        {
            printf("fopen failed.\n");
            exit(0);
        }
        printf("Contents of c:autoexec.bat:\n");
        while ( fgets(string, 80, infile) != NULL)
        {
            fputs(string,stdout);
        }
        return 0;
}
```

Stream I/O

fileno

COMPATIBILITY

TC1	TC1.5	TC2	TC++	MSC3	MSC4	MSC5	MSC6	QC1	QC2	QC2.5	ANSI	UNIX V	XNX
▲	▲	▲	▲	▲	▲	▲	▲	▲	▲	▲		▲	▲

PURPOSE Use the *fileno* macro, defined in *stdio.h*, to obtain the handle of the file currently associated with a specified file pointer. You must have the file handle in order to use some file I/O routines in the run-time library.

SYNTAX

```
int fileno(FILE *file_pointer);
```

`FILE *file_pointer;` *Pointer to FILE data structure associated with the file whose handle is to be returned*

EXAMPLE CALL

```
handle = fileno(file_pointer);
```

INCLUDES `#include <stdio.h>` *For function declaration and definition of the FILE data type*

DESCRIPTION The *fileno* macro returns an integer which constitutes the handle for the file specified by the argument *file_pointer*.

The FILE data structure associated with the file has a field that includes the handle for the file. A call to *fileno* returns this handle. Handles are necessary when performing lower-level, unbuffered I/O using calls to such routines as *read* or *write*.

RETURNS The integer value returned by *fileno* is the handle of the specified file. The return value is undefined if the argument *file_pointer* does not correspond to an open file.

SEE ALSO `fopen` *To open a file for buffered I/O*

EXAMPLE Use *fileno* to get and display the handles for the five files, *stdin, stdout, stderr, stdaux*, and *stdprn*, which are already open in your program.

```
#include <stdio.h>
main()
{
    printf("Handle for stdin: %d\n", fileno(stdin));
    printf("Handle for stdout: %d\n", fileno(stdout));
    printf("Handle for stderr: %d\n", fileno(stderr));
    printf("Handle for stdaux: %d\n", fileno(stdaux));
    printf("Handle for stdprn: %d\n", fileno(stdprn));
    return 0;
}
```

Stream I/O

flushall

COMPATIBILITY

TC1	TC1.5	TC2	TC++	MSC3	MSC4	MSC5	MSC6	QC1	QC2	QC2.5	ANSI	UNIX V	XNX
▲	▲	▲	▲	▲	▲	▲	▲	▲	▲	▲			

PURPOSE Use the *flushall* function to flush all buffers associated with files opened for buffered I/O, including those that are opened as soon as your program begins executing: *stdin, stdout, stderr, stdaux*, and *stdprn*.

SYNTAX `int flushall(void);`

EXAMPLE CALL `flushall();`

INCLUDES `#include <stdio.h>` *For function declaration*

DESCRIPTION The *flushall* function flushes all buffers associated with files opened for buffered I/O. This includes the five files already open when you start up your program: *stdin, stdout, stderr, stdaux*, and *stdprn*. If the file is open for write operations, the flushing involves writing the contents of the buffer to the file. Otherwise, the buffer is cleared.

Note that buffers are automatically flushed when they are full, when a file is closed, or when the program terminates normally.

RETURNS The *flushall* function returns the number of buffers it has flushed, which should match the total number of files currently open for input and output.

SEE ALSO

`fflush` *To flush the buffer of a single file*

`fclose` *To close a single file*

EXAMPLE Call *flushall* in a program and print the number of buffers that were flushed. The number should be 5, corresponding to the preopened files.

```
#include <stdio.h>
main()
{
        int files_open;
/* Flush all buffers */
        files_open = flushall();
/* Now print the total number of buffers flushed */
        printf("%d buffers flushed. So this many files \
are open now.\n", files_open);
        return 0;
}
```

Stream I/O

fopen

COMPATIBILITY

TC1	TC1.5	TC2	TC++	MSC3	MSC4	MSC5	MSC6	QC1	QC2	QC2.5	ANSI	UNIX V	XNX
▲	▲	▲	▲	▲	▲	▲	▲	▲	▲	▲	▲	▲	▲

PURPOSE Use *fopen* to open a file for buffered input and output operations.

SYNTAX `FILE *fopen(const char *filename, const char *access_mode);`

`const char *filename;` *Name of file to be opened including drive and directory specification*

```
const char *access_mode;
```
Character string denoting whether file is being opened for reading or writing, or both

EXAMPLE CALL

```
input_file = fopen("data.in", "rb");
```

INCLUDES

```
#include <stdio.h>
```
For function declaration and definition of FILE data type

DESCRIPTION

The *fopen* function opens the file specified in the argument *filename*. The type of operations you intend to perform on the file must be given in the argument *access_mode*. Table 16-7 explains the values that the *access_mode* string can take.

In addition to the basic access modes shown in Table 16-7, one of the characters from Table 16-8 can be appended to each of the strings in Table 16-7 to specify how the contents of the file are to be translated. Note that the character denoting the translation mode can come before or after the + in the strings above. For example, *w+b* is considered the same as *wb+* and means "create the file and open it for reading and writing in binary mode." If no translation mode is specified, the default mode is determined by the global variable *_fmode*, which is declared in the header file *stdio.h*. When a file is opened for appending with the *a* or *a+* access mode, existing data can never be destroyed because the *file pointer* is moved to the end of the file before writing occurs. This pointer keeps track of the current position where writing occurs.

When a file is opened for updating, using the *r+*, *w+*, or *a+* access modes, you must call one of the functions *fsetpos, fseek*, or *rewind* when switching between read and write operations. These calls serve to set the file pointer properly before the operation. You can also call *fsetpos* or *fseek* and set the file pointer to the current position.

COMMON USES

The *fopen* function is used to open a file before performing buffered I/O operations on it. You must open a file with *fopen* before performing any read or write operations. You can, for example, use *fopen* to open the file *c:\autoexec.bat* and read its contents by calling *fgets*.

RETURNS

If the file is opened successfully, *fopen* returns a pointer to the file. Actually, this is a pointer to a structure of type FILE, which is defined in the header file *stdio.h*. The actual structure is allocated elsewhere and you do not have to allocate it. In case of an error, *fopen* returns a NULL. See below for an example of checking for an error return from *fopen*.

COMMENTS

A maximum of 20 files may be opened by a single process for buffered I/O in MS-DOS. Of these, 5 are already open when the program begins running: *stdin, stdout, stderr, stdprn*, and *stdaux*. This leaves 15 files that your program can simultaneously open with the function *fopen*.

SEE ALSO

`fclose`	*To close a file opened by* fopen
`open`	*To open a file using a handle (a lower-level routine)*
`setmode, fdopen, freopen, fileno, ferror, fcloseall`	*Other functions related to opening files*

EXAMPLES Use *fopen* to open the file *autoexec.bat* for read operations only in the root directory of your current drive, say, drive C. Now read each line and display it on the screen. Use *fclose* to close the file before exiting.

```
#include <stdio.h>
main()
{
        FILE *infile;
        unsigned char buffer[81];
/* Open the file. Note that we need two '\'  because
 * backslash denotes the beginning of a C escape
 * sequence.
 */
        if ( (infile = fopen("c:\\autoexec.bat", "r"))
              == NULL)
        {
            printf("fopen failed.\n");
            exit(0);
        }
        printf("Contents of c:autoexec.bat:\n");
        while ( fgets(buffer, 80, infile) != NULL)
        {
            printf(buffer);
        }
        fclose(infile); /* Close file before exiting */
        return 0;
}
```

Write a C program to save lines typed by the user. Prompt the user for a file name, then open the file for reading and appending in the translation mode (access mode is a+). Next, ask the user to enter lines that you will save in this file. Finally, rewind the file, read it, and display its contents.

```
#include <stdio.h>
char filename[81],      /* Name of file to open         */
     input[80] = "xx"; /* To hold user's input lines  */
FILE *scriptfile;       /* File pointer to opened file */
```

```
main()
{
    printf("Enter name of file to save your input: ");
    gets(filename);
/* Open the file where we will save the user's input */
    if ((scriptfile = fopen(filename,"a+")) == NULL)
    {
        printf("Error opening file: %s\n", filename);
        exit(0);
    }
/* Accept input lines and save them in the file */
    printf("Enter lines. Hit 'q' to stop.\n");
    while(input[0] != 'q' || input[1] !='\0')
    {
        gets(input);                  /* Read a line   */
        fprintf(scriptfile, "%s\n",   /* Write to file */
                input);
    }
/* Now rewind file, read each line and display it */
    rewind(scriptfile);
    printf("==== Contents of script file ====\n");
    while(fgets(input, 80, scriptfile) != NULL)
    {
        printf(input);
    }
/* Now close the file and exit */
    fclose(scriptfile);
    return 0;
}
```

Stream I/O

COMPATIBILITY

fprintf

TC1	TC1.5	TC2	TC++	MSC3	MSC4	MSC5	MSC6	QC1	QC2	QC2.5	ANSI	UNIX V	XNX
▲	▲	▲	▲	▲	▲	▲	▲	▲	▲	▲	▲	▲	▲

PURPOSE Use the *fprintf* function to format and write character strings and values of C variables to a specified file opened for buffered output.

SYNTAX

```
int fprintf(FILE *file_pointer, const char *format_string,...);
```

`FILE *file_pointer;` *Pointer to FILE data structure of the file to which the output goes*

```
const char *format_string;
```
Character string that describes the format to be used

```
...
```
Variable number of arguments depending on the number of items being printed

EXAMPLE CALL

```
fprintf(resultfile, "The result is %f\n", result);
```

INCLUDES

```
#include <stdio.h>
```
For function declaration

DESCRIPTION Like *printf*, *fprintf* accepts a variable number of arguments and prints them out to the file specified in the argument *file_pointer* which must be open for buffered output operations. Although *printf* is more widely used and better known, *fprintf* is more general because it can write formatted output to any file, whereas *printf* can send output to *stdout* only. The values of the arguments are printed in the format specified by *format_string*, an array of characters with embedded formatting commands. The formatting commands begin with a percentage sign (%) and *fprintf* accepts the same formatting commands as *printf* does. By the way, use two percentage signs together to actually print a % to the file. The description of the formats is too long to display here; see Tables 16-9, 16-10, 16-11, and 16-12 in the reference pages on *printf* for more detail.

COMMON USES Although *fprint* can be used in every situation where *printf* is used, one of its common uses is to print error messages to the file *stderr*.

RETURNS The *fprintf* function returns the number of characters it has printed.

SEE ALSO

`printf`	*For printing to* stdout *and for detailed information on formats*
`vfprintf, vprintf`	*For formatted printing to a file using a pointer to a list of arguments*
`sprintf, vsprintf`	*For formatted printing to a string*

EXAMPLE Ask the user for a file to open for writing. After opening the file with *fopen*, use *fprintf* to send output to the file. Later, use the DOS TYPE command to see how *fprintf* worked.

```
#include <stdio.h>
char    str[] = "Testing fprintf...";
char    c     = '\n';
int     i     = 100;
double  x     = 1.23456;
main()
```

```
{
    FILE *outfile;
    char filename[81];
    printf("Enter name of a file to open for WRITING:");
    gets(filename);
/* Open the file for reading */
    if ( (outfile = fopen(filename, "w")) == NULL)
    {
        printf("fopen failed.\n");
        exit(0);
    }
/* Write to this file ... */
    fprintf(outfile, "%s writing to file %s%c", str,
            filename, c);
    fprintf(outfile, "Integer: decimal = %d, \
octal = %o, hex = %X\n", i, i, i);
    fprintf(outfile, "Double: %f(in default f format)\n",
            x);
    fprintf(outfile, "        %.2f(in .2f format)\n",
            x);
    fprintf(outfile, "        %g(in default g format)\n",
            x);
/* Tell user to type file to see results */
    fprintf(stdout,
           "Use the command 'TYPE %s' to see results\n",
            filename);
    return 0;
}
```

Here is how the contents of the file should look:

```
Testing fprintf... writing to file junk1
Integer: decimal = 100, octal = 144, hex = 64
Double: 1.234560(in default f format)
        1.23(in .2f format)
        1.23456(in default g format)
```

Stream I/O

fputc

COMPATIBILITY

TC1	TC1.5	TC2	TC++	MSC3	MSC4	MSC5	MSC6	QC1	QC2	QC2.5	ANSI	UNIX V	XNX
▲	▲	▲	▲	▲	▲	▲	▲	▲	▲	▲	▲	▲	▲

PURPOSE Use *fputc* to write a single character to a file opened for buffered output.

SYNTAX

```
int fputc(int c, FILE *file_pointer);
```

`int c;` *Character to be written*

`FILE *file_pointer;` *Pointer to FILE data structure associated with file to which the character is to be written*

EXAMPLE CALL

```
fputc('X', p_datafile);
```

INCLUDES #include <stdio.h> *For function declaration and definition of FILE data type*

DESCRIPTION The *fputc* function writes a character given in the integer argument *c* to the file specified by the argument *file_pointer*. It writes to the current position of the file and increments this position after writing the character. Note that the *putc* macro, defined in *stdio.h*, also writes a character to a file.

RETURNS If there are no errors, *fputc* returns the character written. Otherwise, it returns the constant EOF. You should call *ferror* to determine whether there was an error or the integer argument *c* just happened to be equal to EOF.

SEE ALSO

`putc` *Macro to write a character to a file*

`fputchar` *Function to write a character to* stdout

`fgetc, fgetchar,`
`getc, getchar` *To read a character from a file*

EXAMPLE Use *fputc* to write a line (maximum length of 80 characters or up to the null character \0) to *stdout.*

```
#include <stdio.h>
char buffer[81] = "Testing fputc on stdout...\n";
main()
{
    int i;
```

```
/* A for loop that uses fputc to print to stdout */
    for(i=0; (i<81) &&
        (fputc(buffer[i], stdout) != EOF);
        i++);
    return 0;
}
```

Stream I/O

fputchar

COMPATIBILITY

TC1	TC1.5	TC2	TC++	MSC3	MSC4	MSC5	MSC6	QC1	QC2	QC2.5	ANSI	UNIX V	XNX
▲	▲	▲	▲	▲	▲	▲	▲	▲	▲	▲			

PURPOSE Use *fputchar* to write a single character to the file *stdout*, which is connected to the display on program startup. The *fputchar* function is equivalent to using *fputc* with *stdout* as the argument.

SYNTAX

```
int fputchar(int c);
```

`int c;` *Character to be written to* stdout

EXAMPLE CALL

```
fputchar('q');
```

INCLUDES `#include <stdio.h>` *For function declaration*

DESCRIPTION The *fputchar* function writes a character to the file *stdout*. This function is equivalent to *fputc(stdout)*.

RETURNS If there are no errors, *fputchar* returns the character written. Otherwise, it returns the constant EOF.

SEE ALSO

`fputc` *General function to write a character to a file*

`fgetc, fgetchar,`
`getc, getchar` *To read a character from a file*

EXAMPLE Use *fputchar* to write a line (maximum length of 80 characters or up to the null character \0) to *stdout*.

```
#include <stdio.h>
char buffer[81] = "Testing fputchar...\n";
main()
{
```

```
    int i;
/* A for loop that uses fputchar to print to stdout */
    for(i=0; (i<81) && (fputchar(buffer[i]) != EOF);
        i++);
    return 0;
}
```

Stream I/O

fputs

COMPATIBILITY

TC1	TC1.5	TC2	TC++	MSC3	MSC4	MSC5	MSC6	QC1	QC2	QC2.5	ANSI	UNIX V	XNX
▲	▲	▲	▲	▲	▲	▲	▲	▲	▲	▲	▲	▲	▲

PURPOSE Use the *fputs* function to write a C string (an array of characters ending with a null character, \0) to a file opened for buffered output.

SYNTAX

```
int fputs(const char *string, FILE *file_pointer);
```

`const char *string;` *Null-terminated character string to be output*

`FILE *file_pointer;` *Pointer to FILE data structure associated with file to which string is output*

EXAMPLE CALL

```
fputs("Sample Input Data", p_datafile);
```

INCLUDES `#include <stdio.h>` *For function declaration and definition of FILE data type*

DESCRIPTION The *fputs* function writes the C string given in the argument "string" to the file specified by the argument *file_pointer*, which is a pointer to the FILE data structure associated with a file that has been opened for write operations.

RETURNS The *fputs* function returns the last character printed when all goes well. In case of error, it returns the constant EOF.

SEE ALSO

`fgets` *To read in a line from a file*

`puts` *To write a string to the display*

`gets` *To read a line from the console*

EXAMPLE Write a program using *fputs* to print a string to the display (which corresponds to the preopened file *stdout*).

```
#include <stdio.h>
char string[81] =
    "Using fputs with stdout is equivalent to puts\n";
main()
{
        fputs(string, stdout);
        return 0;
}
```

Stream I/O

fread

COMPATIBILITY

TC1	TC1.5	TC2	TC++	MSC3	MSC4	MSC5	MSC6	QC1	QC2	QC2.5	ANSI	UNIX V	XNX
▲	▲	▲	▲	▲	▲	▲	▲	▲	▲	▲	▲	▲	▲

PURPOSE Use the *fread* function to read a specified number of data items, each of a given size, from the current position in a file opened for buffered input. The current position is updated after the read.

SYNTAX

```
size_t fread(void *buffer, size_t size, size_t count,
                                   FILE *file_pointer);
```

`void *buffer;` *Pointer to memory where* fread *stores the bytes it reads*

`size_t size;` *Size in bytes of each data item*

`size_t count;` *Maximum number of items to be read*

`FILE *file_pointer;` *Pointer to FILE data structure associated with file from which data items are read*

EXAMPLE CALL `numread = fread(buffer, sizeof(char), 80, infile);`

INCLUDES `#include <stdio.h>` *For function declaration and definition of FILE and* size_t

DESCRIPTION The *fread* function reads *count* data items, each of *size* bytes, starting at the current read position of the file specified by the argument *file_pointer*. After the read is complete, the current position is updated.

You must allocate storage for a buffer to hold the number of bytes that you expect to read. The address of this buffer, in the form of a pointer to a *void* data type, is given in the argument *buffer*. The data items read are saved in this buffer.

COMMON USES The common use of *fread* is to read binary data files. As an example, if you devise a scheme for storing images to a file, you would probably use *fwrite* to write the file and *fread* to read the images back.

RETURNS The *fread* function returns the number of items it successfully read. If the return value is less than you expected, you can call *ferror* and *feof* to determine if a read error has occurred or if end-of-file has been reached.

COMMENTS When *fread* is used on a file opened in the text mode, the CR-LF pairs are translated to single-line feeds.

SEE ALSO `fwrite` *To write data items from a buffer to a file*

`read` *Same function as* fread, *but uses file number or handle*

EXAMPLE Open a file using *fopen* for binary read operations (mode *rb*). Read 80 characters, and then display the buffer and the number of data items that *fread* says it read.

```
#include <stdio.h>
main()
{
    int numread;
    FILE *infile;
    char filename[80], buffer[80];
    printf("Enter name of a text file: ");
    gets(filename);
/* Open the file for reading */
    if ( (infile = fopen(filename, "rb")) == NULL)
    {
        printf("fopen failed.\n");
        exit(0);
    }
/* Read 80 characters and display the buffer */
    numread = fread((void *)buffer, sizeof(char), 80,
                    infile);
    printf("Read these %d characters:\n %s\n",
            numread, buffer);
    return 0;
}
```

Stream I/O

freopen

COMPATIBILITY

TC1	TC1.5	TC2	TC++	MSC3	MSC4	MSC5	MSC6	QC1	QC2	QC2.5	ANSI	UNIX V	XNX
▲	▲	▲	▲	▲	▲	▲	▲	▲	▲	▲	▲	▲	▲

PURPOSE Use *freopen* to close a file and open another file with the same file pointer. For example, you can use *freopen* to redirect I/O from the preopened file *stdout* to a file of your choice.

SYNTAX

```
FILE *freopen(const char *filename, const char *access_mode,
                                          FILE *file_pointer);
```

`const char *filename;` *Name of file to be reopened, including drive and directory specification*

`const char *access_mode;` *Character string denoting whether file is being reopened for read/write*

`FILE *file_pointer;` *Pointer to FILE data structure associated with file being closed*

EXAMPLE CALL `freopen("output.txt", "w", stdout);`

INCLUDES `#include <stdio.h>` *For function declaration and definition of FILE data type*

DESCRIPTION The *freopen* function closes the file specified by the argument *file_pointer*, a pointer to the FILE data structure associated with an open file. Next *freopen* opens a new file with the name specified in the argument *filename* and associates the old file pointer with this new file. Use the argument *access_mode* to indicate the type of operations you intend to perform on the file. Tables 16-6 and 16-7 explain the various values that the *access_mode* string can take.

COMMON USES The *freopen* function is often used to redirect input and output for the preopened files *stdin* and *stdout*.

RETURNS If all goes well, *freopen* returns a pointer to the newly opened file. This pointer is the same as the argument *file_pointer*. In case of error, a NULL is returned. See below for an example of checking for an error return from *freopen*.

SEE ALSO

`fopen` *To open a file*

`fclose` *To close a file opened by* fopen *or* freopen

EXAMPLE Use *freopen* to redirect *stdout* to a file instead of the monitor. Prompt the user for the file name. Use *printf* to print a few lines that go to the file and do not appear on your screen. Exit and observe the contents of the file with the DOS TYPE <filename> command.

```
#include <stdio.h>
main()
{
    char filename[81];
    printf("Enter file name where output should go: ");
    gets(filename);
    printf("If all goes well, use TYPE %s to see \
result.\n", filename);
/* Redirect stdout to this file */
    if ( freopen(filename, "w", stdout) == NULL)
    {
        printf("freopen failed.\n");
        exit(0);
    }
/* Print some lines ... */
    printf("Redirecting stdout to the file %s\n",
            filename);
    printf("All output will be in this file.\n");
    return 0;
}
```

Stream I/O

fscanf

COMPATIBILITY

TC1	TC1.5	TC2	TC++	MSC3	MSC4	MSC5	MSC6	QC1	QC2	QC2.5	ANSI	UNIX V	XNX
▲	▲	▲	▲	▲	▲	▲	▲	▲	▲	▲	▲	▲	▲

PURPOSE Use the *fscanf* function to read characters from a file that has been opened for buffered I/O and to convert the strings to values of C variables according to specified formats.

SYNTAX

```
int fscanf(FILE *file_pointer, const char *format_string,...);
```

`FILE *file_pointer;` *Pointer to the FILE data structure of file from which reading occurs*

`const char *format_string;`	*Character string that describes the format to be used*
`...`	*Variable number of arguments representing addresses of variables whose values are being read*

EXAMPLE CALL

```
fscanf(infile, "Date: %d/%d/%d", &month, &day, &year);
```

INCLUDES

`#include <stdio.h>` *For function declaration and definition of the FILE data structure*

DESCRIPTION

The *fscanf* function reads a stream of characters from the file specified by the argument *file_pointer*, converts the characters to values according to format specifications embedded in the argument *format_string*, and stores the values into C variables whose addresses are provided in the variable length argument list.

Each optional argument indicating a value to be read has a corresponding format specification in the argument *format_string*. The format specification begins with a percentage sign and the formatting commands are identical to the ones used with the function *scanf*. A list of the formats is provided in the reference pages on *scanf*.

RETURNS

The *fscanf* function returns the number of input items that were successfully read, converted, and saved in variables. If an end-of-file is encountered during the read, the return value will be equal to the constant EOF (defined in *stdio.h*).

COMMENTS

The *fscanf* function is used more generally than *scanf*. You can read from any file using *fscanf* and the functions of *scanf* can be duplicated by using the file *stdin* as an argument to *fscanf*. It is customary in C reference books, including ours, however, to describe the format specifications in detail under *scanf*.

SEE ALSO

`scanf`	*Formatted reading from* stdin
`sscanf`	*For formatted reading from a string*
`cscanf`	*Formatted, unbuffered input from console*
`vfscanf`	*Another routine for formatted input from* stdin

EXAMPLE

The %s format reads strings separated by blanks, tabs, or newline characters. Open the file *autoexec.bat* for buffered I/O and then use *fscanf* to read and display the first 10 tokens, character sequences separated by blanks and newlines.

```
#include <stdio.h>
main()
{
    int i;
    FILE *infile;
    char token[80];
/* Open the file. Note that we need two '\'  */
    if ( (infile = fopen("c:\\autoexec.bat", "r"))
           == NULL)
    {
        perror("fopen failed");
        exit(1);
    }
    printf("First 10 blank separated strings in \
c:\\autoexec.bat:\n");
    for(i=0; i<10; i++)
    {
        if( fscanf(infile, " %s", token) == EOF)
        {
            printf("File ended!\n");
            break;
        }
        else
        {
            printf("Token %d = \"%s\"\n", i, token);
        }
    }
    return 0;
}
```

Stream I/O

fseek

COMPATIBILITY

TC1	TC1.5	TC2	TC++	MSC3	MSC4	MSC5	MSC6	QC1	QC2	QC2.5	ANSI	UNIX V	XNX
▲	▲	▲	▲	▲	▲	▲	▲	▲	▲	▲	▲	▲	▲

PURPOSE Use the *fseek* function to move to a new position in a file opened for buffered I/O.

SYNTAX `int fseek(FILE *file_pointer, long offset, int origin);`

`FILE *file_pointer;` *Pointer to FILE data structure associated with file whose current position is to be set*

```
long offset;          Offset of new position (in bytes) from origin

int origin;           Constant indicating the position from which to offset
```

EXAMPLE CALL

```
fseek(infile, 0L, SEEK_SET); /* Go to the beginning */
```

INCLUDES

```
#include <stdio.h>     For function declaration and definition of FILE
```

DESCRIPTION The *fseek* function sets the current read or write position of the file specified by the argument *file_pointer* to a new value indicated by the arguments "offset" and "origin." The "offset" is a long integer indicating how far away the new position is from a specific location given in "origin." One of the constants, defined in *stdio.h* and shown in the table below, *must* be the "origin."

Origin	Interpretation
SEEK_SET	Beginning of file.
SEEK_CUR	Current position in the file.
SEEK_END	End of file.

COMMON USES The *fseek* function is commonly used when reading data from a file in the binary read mode. For example, an application may create a data file with a specific format, say, a header of 512 bytes followed by actual data. When reading from such a file you can use *fseek* to skip over the header and move around in the file to retrieve specific pieces of information with *fread*.

RETURNS When successful, *fseek* returns a zero. In case of error, for example when attempting to set a position before the beginning of the file, *fseek* returns a nonzero value. If the file is associated with a device where setting the current position does not make sense (such as a printer), the return value is meaningless.

COMMENTS You should be aware of a few nuances of *fseek*.

- In text mode (see the tutorial section), you may not be able to give a proper value for offset because of the translation of CR-LF combinations. So only these arguments are guaranteed to work when using *fseek* in the text mode: (1) an offset of 0L from any of the origins, and (2) an offset returned by *ftell* with an origin of SEEK_SET.
- In append mode, the current position is determined solely by the last I/O operation. Even if you move around in the file, the writing always takes place at the end of the file opened for appending.

SEE ALSO `ftell` *To get the offset of the current position in number of bytes from the beginning*

`lseek` *Same function as* fseek, *but works with file handles*

EXAMPLE Open a file using *fopen* for reading. Read and display a line. Now call *fseek* to go back to the beginning and read a line again. The two lines should be identical.

```
#include <stdio.h>
main()
{
    FILE *infile;
    char filename[80], buffer[81];
    printf("Enter name of a text file: ");
    gets(filename);
/* Open the file for reading */
    if ( (infile = fopen(filename, "r")) == NULL)
    {
        printf("fopen failed.\n");
        exit(0);
    }
/* Read and display a line */
    fgets(buffer, 80, infile);
    printf("Line read (before fseek): %s", buffer);
/* Move to beginning using fseek and read a line again */
    if (fseek(infile, 0L, SEEK_SET) != 0)
    {
        perror("fseek failed!");
    }
    else
    {
        fgets(buffer, 80, infile);
        printf("Line read (after fseek) : %s", buffer);
    }
    return 0;
}
```

Stream I/O

fsetpos

COMPATIBILITY

TC1	TC1.5	TC2	TC++	MSC3	MSC4	MSC5	MSC6	QC1	QC2	QC2.5	ANSI	UNIX V	XNX
▲	▲	▲	▲			▲	▲	▲	▲	▲	▲		

PURPOSE Use *fsetpos* to set the position where reading or writing can take place in a file opened for buffered I/O.

SYNTAX

```
int fsetpos(FILE *file_pointer, const fpos_t *current_pos);
```

`FILE *file_pointer;` *Pointer to FILE data structure associated with file whose current position is to be set*

`const fpos_t *current_pos;` *Pointer to location containing new value of file position*

EXAMPLE CALL

```
fgetpos(infile, &curpos);
```

INCLUDES `#include <stdio.h>` *For function declaration and definition of FILE and* fpos_t *data types*

DESCRIPTION The *fsetpos* function sets to a new value the current read or write position of the file specified by the argument *file_pointer*. The new value is given in a location whose address is in the argument *current_pos*. The data type of this variable is *fpos_t*, which is defined in the include file *stdio.h* to be a *long*.

COMMON USES The *fsetpos* function resets the file position to a value obtained by an earlier call to its counterpart *fgetpos*.

RETURNS If successful, *fsetpos* returns a zero. Otherwise, the return value will be nonzero.

COMMENTS Since the value of the current read/write position in the file is meaningful only to the buffered input and output routines, you should always use *fsetpos* with a position obtained by an earlier call to *fgetpos*. You can use *fseek* if you want to set the position to a value expressed in terms of byte offsets from specific locations in the file.

SEE ALSO `fgetpos` *To retrieve the current position indicator of a file*

EXAMPLE Open a file using *fopen* for reading. Call *fgetpos* and remember the current position. Read 10 characters into a buffer and return to the saved position by calling *fsetpos*. Now read in 10 more characters. Display the buffer and note that the first 10 characters are the same as the last 10.

```
#include <stdio.h>
main()
{
    fpos_t curpos;
    FILE *infile;
    char filename[81], buffer1[20], buffer2[20];
    printf("Enter name of a text file: ");
    gets(filename);
/* Open the file for reading */
    if ( (infile = fopen(filename, "r")) == NULL)
    {
        printf("fopen failed.\n");
        exit(0);
    }
/* Save current position */
    if (fgetpos(infile, &curpos) != 0)
                    perror("fgetpos failed!");
/* Read 10 characters */
    if (fgets(buffer1, 10, infile) == NULL)
                   perror("fgets failed");
/* Reset to previous position in file */
    if (fsetpos(infile, &curpos) != 0)
                    perror("fsetpos failed!");
/* Read another 10 characters --
 * these should be same as last 10.
 */
    if (fgets(buffer2, 10, infile) == NULL)
                       perror("fgets failed");
    printf("We read:\n");
    puts(buffer1);
    puts(buffer2);
    return 0;
}
```

Stream I/O

ftell

COMPATIBILITY

TC1	TC1.5	TC2	TC++	MSC3	MSC4	MSC5	MSC6	QC1	QC2	QC2.5	ANSI	UNIX V	XNX
▲	▲	▲	▲	▲	▲	▲	▲	▲	▲	▲	▲	▲	▲

PURPOSE Use *ftell* to obtain the current position in a file opened for buffered I/O. The position is expressed as a byte offset from the beginning of the file.

SYNTAX

```
long ftell(FILE *file_pointer);
```

`FILE *file_pointer;` *Pointer to FILE data structure associated with file whose current position is to be returned*

EXAMPLE CALL

```
curpos = ftell(infile));
```

INCLUDES `#include <stdio.h>` *For function declaration and definition of FILE*

DESCRIPTION The *ftell* function returns the current read or write position of the file specified by the argument *file_pointer*.

RETURNS When successful, *ftell* returns a long integer containing the number of bytes the current position is offset from the beginning of the file. In case of error, *ftell* returns −1L. The return value is undefined if the *file_pointer* is associated with a device (such as the keyboard) because it would not make any sense to move to a new position in the file.

COMMENTS When *ftell* is used on a file opened in the text mode, the physical byte offset in the file may not be the same as the value reported by *ftell*. This is due to the translation of the CR-LF pairs in this mode. Everything works correctly, however, if you use *fseek* in combination with *ftell* to return to a specific position in a file opened in text mode.

SEE ALSO

`fseek` *To set the the current position in a file*

`tell` *Same function as* ftell, *but uses file handles*

EXAMPLE Use *fopen* to open a file for binary read operations (mode *rb*). Read 80 characters and display the buffer. Now call *ftell* and print the value it returns.

```
#include <stdio.h>
main()
{
```

```
    long curpos;
    FILE *infile;
    char filename[80], buffer[80];
    printf("Enter name of a text file: ");
    gets(filename);
/* Open the file for reading */
    if ( (infile = fopen(filename, "rb")) == NULL)
    {
        printf("fopen failed.");
        exit(0);
    }
/* Read 80 characters and display the buffer */
    fread(buffer, sizeof(char), 80, infile);
    printf("Read these 80 characters:\n %s\n", buffer);
/* Get and display current position */
    if ((curpos = ftell(infile)) == -1L)
    {
        perror("ftell failed!");
    }
    else
    {
        printf("Currently at %ld bytes from beginning \
of file\n", curpos);
    }
    return 0;
}
```

Stream I/O

fwrite

COMPATIBILITY

TC1	TC1.5	TC2	TC++	MSC3	MSC4	MSC5	MSC6	QC1	QC2	QC2.5	ANSI	UNIX V	XNX
▲	▲	▲	▲	▲	▲	▲	▲	▲	▲	▲	▲	▲	▲

PURPOSE Use the *fwrite* function to write a specified number of data items, each of a given size, from a buffer to the current position in a file opened for buffered output. The current position is updated after the write.

SYNTAX

```
size_t fwrite(const void *buffer, size_t size, size_t count,
                                        FILE *file_pointer);
```

`const void *buffer;` *Pointer to buffer in memory from which* fwrite *will get the bytes it writes*

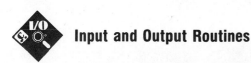

`size_t size;`	*Size in bytes of each data item*
`size_t count;`	*Maximum number of items to be written*
`FILE *file_pointer;`	*Pointer to FILE data structure associated with file to which the data items are to be written*

EXAMPLE CALL `numwrite = fwrite(buffer, sizeof(char), 80, outfile);`

INCLUDES `#include <stdio.h>` *For function declaration and definition of FILE and* size_t

DESCRIPTION The *fwrite* function writes *count* data items, each of *size* bytes, to the file specified by the argument *file_pointer*, starting at the current position. After the write operation is complete, the current position is updated. The data to be written is in the buffer whose address is passed to *fwrite* in the argument *buffer*.

COMMON USES The most common use of *fwrite* is to write binary data files. For example, if you want to save the current status of your application, you can save the values of all the key variables into a file using *fwrite*. Later, you can read these back with the function *fread*.

RETURNS The *fwrite* function returns the number of items it actually wrote. If that value is less than you expected, an error may have occurred.

COMMENTS If *fwrite* is used on a file opened in the text mode, each carriage return is replaced by a CR-LF pair.

SEE ALSO

`fread`	*To read data items from a file to a buffer*
`write`	*Same function as* fwrite, *but uses file number, or handle*

EXAMPLE Open a file using *fopen* for binary write operations (mode *wb*). Write 80 characters and display the number of data items that *fwrite* says it wrote. Type out the file to verify that the write worked.

```
#include <stdio.h>
char buffer[80] = "Testing fwrite\n\
This is the second line.\n";
main()
{
    int numwrite;
    FILE *infile;
    char filename[80];
    printf("Enter name of a file to write to: ");
```

```
    gets(filename);
/* Open the file for writing */
    if ( (infile = fopen(filename, "wb")) == NULL)
    {
        printf("fopen failed.\n");
        exit(0);
    }
/* write 80 characters and display the buffer */
    numwrite = fwrite((void *)buffer, sizeof(char), 80,
                      infile);
    printf("%d characters written to file %s\n",
        numwrite, filename);
    printf("Use 'TYPE %s' to see if it worked\n",
            filename);
    return 0;
}
```

Stream I/O

getc

COMPATIBILITY

TC1	TC1.5	TC2	TC++	MSC3	MSC4	MSC5	MSC6	QC1	QC2	QC2.5	ANSI	UNIX V	XNX
▲	▲	▲	▲	▲	▲	▲	▲	▲	▲	▲	▲	▲	▲

PURPOSE Use the *getc* macro to read a single character from a file opened for buffered input.

SYNTAX

```
int getc(FILE *file_pointer);

FILE *file_pointer;        Pointer to file from which a character is to read
```

EXAMPLE CALL

```
in_char = getc(p_txtfile);
```

INCLUDES

```
#include <stdio.h>        For function declaration definition of FILE data structure
```

DESCRIPTION The *getc* macro reads a character from the file specified by the argument *file_pointer*. The character is read from the current position in the file, and the current position then is advanced to the next character. The *file_pointer* must be a pointer returned earlier by an *fopen* or a *freopen* function call. Note that *fgetc* performs the same as *getc*, but *fgetc* is implemented as a function.

RETURNS The *getc* macro returns the character read as an integer value. A return value of EOF indicates an error. In that case, call the *ferror* and *feof* functions to determine if there was an error or if the file ended.

SEE ALSO

`getchar` *Macro to read a character from* stdin

`fgetc` *Function to read a character from a file*

`fputc, fputchar,`
`putc, putchar` *To write a character to a file*

EXAMPLE Use *getc* to read a line (maximum length of 80 characters or up to the newline character) from the file *config.sys* and display the line on the screen using *printf*.

```
#include <stdio.h>
main()
{
    FILE *infile;
    char buffer[81];
    int i, c;
/* Open the file -- assuming it's at the root directory
 * of drive C:
 */
    if ( (infile = fopen("c:\\config.sys", "r"))
          == NULL)
    {
        printf("fopen failed.\n");
        exit(0);
    }
    c = getc(infile);
    for(i=0; (i<80) && (feof(infile) == 0) &&
                      (c != '\n'); i++)
    {
        buffer[i] = c;
        c = getc(infile);
    }
    buffer[i] = '\0';  /* to make a C-style string */
    printf("First line of c:config.sys: %s\n",
           buffer);
    return 0;
}
```

Stream I/O

getchar

COMPATIBILITY

TC1	TC1.5	TC2	TC++	MSC3	MSC4	MSC5	MSC6	QC1	QC2	QC2.5	ANSI	UNIX V	XNX
▲	▲	▲	▲	▲	▲	▲	▲	▲	▲	▲	▲	▲	▲

PURPOSE Use the *getchar* macro to read a single character from the preopened file *stdin*, which is normally connected to your keyboard input.

SYNTAX

```
int getchar(void);
```

EXAMPLE CALL

```
c = getchar();
```

INCLUDES `#include <stdio.h>` *For function declaration*

DESCRIPTION The *getchar* macro reads a character from *stdin* and is equivalent to the use *getc(stdin)*. Note that *getchar* is the macro equivalent of the *fgetchar* function.

RETURNS The *getchar* macro returns the character read from *stdin* as an integer value. In case of an error, the return value is equal to the constant EOF (defined in *stdio.h*).

COMMENTS You cannot use *getchar* to read a single character from the console because a carriage return must be entered to complete a single buffered read from the keyboard. Use *getch* or *getche* for unbuffered input from the keyboard.

SEE ALSO

`getc` *Macro to read a character from a file*

`fgetc, fgetchar` *To read a character from a file*

`fputc, fputchar, putc, putchar` *To write a character to a file*

EXAMPLE Use *getchar* to read a line (maximum 80 characters) from the standard input. Call *printf* to display the line.

```
#include <stdio.h>
main()
{
    int i, c;
    char buffer[81];
    printf("Enter a line (end with a return):\n");
    c = getchar();
```

```
    for(i=0; (i<80) && (c != '\n'); i++)
    {
        buffer[i] = c;
        c = getchar();
    }
    buffer[i] = '\0';  /* to make a C-style string */
    printf("You entered: %s\n", buffer);
    return 0;
}
```

Stream I/O

COMPATIBILITY

gets

TC1	TC1.5	TC2	TC++	MSC3	MSC4	MSC5	MSC6	QC1	QC2	QC2.5	ANSI	UNIX V	XNX
▲	▲	▲	▲	▲	▲	▲	▲	▲	▲	▲	▲	▲	▲

PURPOSE Use *gets* to read a line from the standard input file *stdin*, which by default, is defined to be the keyboard.

SYNTAX
```
char *gets(char *buffer);
```

`char *buffer;` *Buffer where string will be stored*

EXAMPLE CALL `gets(command_line);`

INCLUDES `#include <stdio.h>` *For function declaration*

DESCRIPTION Until it encounters a newline character, the *gets* function reads and stores characters in the *buffer* from the standard input file *stdin*. When it does, it replaces the newline character with a null character and creates a C string. You must allocate room for the buffer in which the characters will be stored. Note that while *fgets* performs like *gets*, unlike *gets*, it retains the newline character in the final string.

RETURNS If there is no error, *gets* returns its argument. Otherwise, it returns a NULL. Call *ferror* and *feof* to determine whether the error is a read error or if it occurred because the file reached its end.

SEE ALSO `fgets` *To read a line from a file*

`fputs` *To write a string to a file*

`puts` *To write a string to the display*

EXAMPLE Use *gets* to read a line to the standard input. Call *printf* to display the line.

```
#include <stdio.h>
main()
{
    char string[81];
    printf("Enter a line: ");
    gets(string);
    printf("You entered: %s\n", string);
    return 0;
}
```

Stream I/O

getw

COMPATIBILITY

TC1	TC1.5	TC2	TC++	MSC3	MSC4	MSC5	MSC6	QC1	QC2	QC2.5	ANSI	UNIX V	XNX
▲	▲	▲	▲	▲	▲	▲	▲	▲	▲	▲		▲	▲

PURPOSE Use *getw* to read a word (two bytes) from a file that has been opened for buffered binary read operations.

SYNTAX

```
int getw(FILE *file_pointer);
```

`FILE *file_pointer;` *Pointer to FILE data structure associated with file from which a word is read*

EXAMPLE CALL

```
word = getw(infile);
```

INCLUDES `#include <stdio.h>` *For function declaration and definition of FILE*

DESCRIPTION The *getw* function reads a word from the current position of the file specified by the argument *file_pointer*. The current position is incremented by the size of an *int* (2 bytes).

RETURNS If successful, *getw* returns the integer value it read. Otherwise, the return value is the constant EOF (defined in *stdio.h*). Since EOF is also a legitimate integer value, you should call *feof* and *ferror* to determine if the end-of-file was reached or if an error occurred.

SEE ALSO `putw` *To write a word into a file*

EXAMPLE Use *fopen* to open a file for reading in the binary mode. Use *getw* to read the first word and print its value in hexadecimal. To get a feeling for byte ordering, give the name of a text file when running the program. Consult the ASCII code table to see which characters the hexadecimal value printed by the program represents. Use DOS TYPE to print the file out and compare the first two characters with the printed value.

```
#include <stdio.h>
main()
{
    int word1;
    FILE *infile;
    char filename[81];
    printf("Enter name of a file to read from: ");
    gets(filename);
/* Open the file for reading */
    if ( (infile = fopen(filename, "rb")) == NULL)
    {
        printf("fopen failed.\n");
            exit(0);
    }
/* Get first word from file */
    if( (word1 = getw(infile)) == EOF)
    {
/* Check if there was a real error */
        if(feof(infile) != 0)
        {
            printf("File: %s at EOF\n", filename);
            exit(0);
        }
        if(ferror(infile) != 0)
        {
            printf("File: %s Read error\n", filename);
            exit(0);
        }
    }
/* Print out the first word in hexadecimal */
    printf("The first word in file %s is: %X\n",
            filename, word1);

    printf("Use 'TYPE %s' to confirm this.\n", filename);
    return 0;
}
```

Stream I/O

printf

COMPATIBILITY

TC1	TC1.5	TC2	TC++	MSC3	MSC4	MSC5	MSC6	QC1	QC2	QC2.5	ANSI	UNIX V	XNX
▲	▲	▲	▲	▲	▲	▲	▲	▲	▲	▲	▲	▲	▲

PURPOSE Use *printf* to write character strings and values of C variables, formatted in a specified manner, to the standard output file *stdout* (normally the screen).

SYNTAX

```
int printf(const char *format_string,...);
```

`const char *format_string;` *Character string that describes the format to be used*

`...` *Variable number of arguments depending on the number of items being printed*

EXAMPLE CALL

```
printf("The product of %d and %d is %d\n", x, y, x*y);
```

INCLUDES `#include <stdio.h>` *For function declaration*

DESCRIPTION The *printf* function accepts a variable number of arguments and prints them out to the standard output file *stdout*. The value of each argument is formatted according to the codes embedded in the format specification *format_string*. The first argument must be present in a call to *printf*. Calling *printf* is equivalent to using *fprintf* with the file *stdin*.

If the *format_string* does not contain a % character (except for the pair %%, which appears as a single % in the output), no argument is expected and the *format_string* is written out to *stdout*. For example,

```
printf("Hello there!\n");
```

prints "Hello there!" on the screen and skips to the next line because of the newline (\n) in the string. In fact, the *format_string* may contain commonly accepted special characters with a "backslash" as prefix, such as \n (newline), \t (tab), \a (alert or bell), or an ASCII character in octal notation (such as \004, which prints as a diamond in the IBM PC). You can use these characters to align the printed values properly. For example, *printf("Name\t\tPhone Number\n");* will print "Name" and "Phone Number" separated by two tabs.

To print the values of C variables, a format specification must be embedded in the *format_string* for each variable listed in the argument list to *printf*. For most routine printing chores, you can use the formatting commands in their simplest form:

```
int    ivalue = 100;
double dvalue = 95.5;
char   name = "Turbo C";
:
printf("Integer = %d, Double = %f, String = %s\n", ivalue,
               dvalue, name);
```

Here we are printing out the values of an *int*, a *double*, and a character string. The formatting command for each variable consists of a percent sign, followed by a single letter denoting the type of variable being printed.

When you need fine control over the appearance of the printed values, *printf* provides it in the form of optional characters between the % and the character denoting the type of C variable being printed. The complete format specification accepted by the *printf* function in Turbo C has the following form:

Print Format Specification in Turbo C

%[Flags][Width].[Precision][Addressing_mode][Size][Type]

Table 16-9 summarizes the purpose of each field in the format specification. Additional details for each field are given in Tables 16-10, 16-11, and 16-12.

Table 16-9. *Fields in a Format Specification for* printf

Field	Explanation
Flags (Optional)	One or more of the –, +, # characters or a blank space specifies justification, and the appearance of plus/minus signs and the decimal point in the values printed (see Table 16-11).
Width (Optional)	A number that indicates how many characters, at a minimum, must be used to print the value (see Table 16-12).
Precision (Optional)	A number that specifies how many characters, at maximum, can be used to print the value. When printing integer variables, this is the minimum number of digits used (see Table 16-12).
Addressing_mode (Optional)	This field is specific to Turbo C. F (for "far") or N (for "near") can be used to override the default addressing mode of the memory model. Use this field only when the variable being passed to *printf* is a pointer (for example, when printing a string or the value of a pointer). As an example, use F in this field when printing a far string in the small memory model.
Size (Optional)	A character that modifies the *Type* field which comes next. One of the characters h, l, or L appears in this field to differentiate between short and long integers and between float and double. Shown below is a summary of this field:

Table 16-9. ***(cont.)***

Field	Explanation	
	Prefix	**When to Use**
	h	Use when printing integers using *Type* d, i, o, x, or X to indicate that the argument is a short integer. Also, use with *Type* u to indicate that the variable being printed is an unsigned short integer.
	l	Use when printing integers or unsigned integers with a *Type* field of d, i, o, x, X, or u to specify that the variable to be printed is a long integer. Also use with floating-point variables (when the *Type* field is e, E, g, or G) to specify a double, rather than a float.
	L	Use when the floating-point variable being printed is a long double and the *Type* specifier is one of e, E, f, g, or G.
Type (Required)	A letter that indicates the type of variable being printed. Table 16-10 lists the characters and their meanings.	

The most important among these fields is the *Type* field which tells *printf* the type of C variable it has to convert to characters and print. Table 16-10 lists the characters that can appear in this field and the kind of C variable each signifies.

Table 16-10. Type ***Field in Format Specification for*** **printf**

Type	Type in C	Resulting Output Format
c	char	Single character. *printf("%c", 'Z');* prints a *Z*.
d	int	Signed decimal integer as a sequence of digits with or without a sign depending on the flags used. *printf("%d", 95);"* prints *95*.
e	double or float	Signed value in the scientific format. *double* x = −123.4567 printf("%e", x); prints −1.234567e+002.
E	double or float	Signed value in the scientific format; the above example prints −*1.234567E+002* if the %E format is used.
f	double or float	Signed value in the format, (sign)(digits).(digits); the example for *Type* e will print *−123.456700* if the %f format is used. The number of digits before the decimal point depends on the magnitude of the variable, and the number of digits that comes after the decimal point depends on the *Precision* field in the format specification. The default precision is 6. Thus a %f format alone always produces 6 digits after the decimal point, but a %.3f prints the value *−123.457* which is *−123.4567* rounded off to three decimal places.

Table 16-10. *(cont.)*

Type	Type in C	Resulting Output Format
g	double or float	Signed value printed using either the e or f format. The format that generates the most compact output, for the given *Precision* and value, is selected. The e format is used only when the exponent is less than −4 or when it is greater than the value of the *Precision* field. Printing the value *−123.4567* using a %g format results in *−123.457* because the g format rounds off the number.
G	double or float	Signed value printed using the g format, with the letter G in place of e when exponents are printed.
i	int	Signed decimal integer as a sequence of digits with or without a sign depending on the *Flags* field. For example, *printf("%d %+d", x, x);* prints as *123 + 123* when the *int* variable *x* has the value 123.
n	pointer to int	This is not really a printing format. The argument corresponding to this format is a pointer to an integer. Before returning, the *printf* function stores in this integer the total number of characters it has printed to the output file or to the file's buffer. The EXAMPLES section illustrates the use of the %n format.
o	unsigned	Octal digits without any sign.
p	far pointer to void	The address is printed in the form *SSSS:OOOO* where *SSSS* denotes the segment address and *OOOO* is the offset. In small and medium memory models, the argument should be cast as (void far *). If the *Flag* character N is used, as in %Np, only the offset of the address is printed.
s	pointer to char	A character string.
u	unsigned	Unsigned decimal integer as a sequence of digits.
x	unsigned	Hexadecimal digits using lowercase letters, abcdef.
X	unsigned	Hexadecimal digits using uppercase letters, ABCDEF.

Now we'll examine the rest of the components of the format specification and tabulate the choices. First comes the *Flags* field. One or more of the characters shown in Table 16-11 can appear in the *Flags* field. The Default column in Table 16-11 shows what happens when you do not include this optional field in the format specification.

The *Width* field, if present, should be a nonnegative decimal number indicating the minimum number of characters output when printing the value to which the format specification applies. If the value being printed does not occupy the entire *Width*, blanks are added to the left or to the right depending on the justification indicated by the *Flags* field. When the *Width* is prefixed with a zero, all numbers being output are padded with zeroes instead of blanks. Note that specifying a *Width* does not imply that the value being printed will be truncated; this is determined by the *Precision* field.

Table 16-11. Flags *Field in Format Specification for* print

Flag	Meaning	Default
–	Left justify output value within a field wide enough to hold the specified maximum number of characters that can be used for this value.	Right justification.
+	If the output value is a numerical one, print a + or a – according to the sign of the value.	A negative sign is printed for negative numerical values.
blank	Positive numerical values are prefixed with blank spaces. This flag is ignored if the + flag also appears.	No blanks are printed.
#	When used in printing variables of type o, x, or X (i.e., octal or hexadecimal), nonzero output values are prefixed with 0, 0x, or 0X, respectively.	No special prefix appears.
	When the *Type* field in the format specification is e, E, or f, this flag forces the printing of a decimal point.	Decimal point appears only when digits follow it.
	For a g or a G in the *Type* field, the # flag prints a decimal point and all trailing zeroes.	Trailing zeroes are truncated and decimal point appears only when digits follow.

An asterisk in the *Width* field indicates that an integer variable appearing in the argument list contains the value of width to be used for this format. This integer variable has to precede the actual variable to be printed. This is useful because you can compute the width at run-time and generate appropriately tabulated results.

The *Precision* field is separated from the *Width* field by a decimal point that is present only when *Precision* is explicitly specified. This field must be a non-negative decimal number that, as shown in Table 16-12, is interpreted by *printf* differently for each type of variable. The Default column in Table 16-12 indicates what *printf* does when *Precision* is not specified. You can use an asterisk in the *Precision* field to specify the value at run-time just as it is done for the *Width* field.

COMMON USES The *printf* function is one of the most commonly used functions in any C run-time library. It is rare that anyone uses all the possible fields in the format specifications, but when your application needs them the choices are available.

RETURNS The *printf* function returns the number of characters it has printed. In case of error, it returns EOF.

COMMENTS Use two percentage signs when you need to print a percentage sign. In

Table 16-12. *Interpretation of* Precision *for* Type *Fields*

Type	Meaning	Default
c	*Precision* is ignored.	A single character is printed.
d u i o x X	The *Precision* specifies the minimum number of digits to be printed. When the value occupies fewer characters than the *Precision*, the output is padded on the left with zeroes. The value is always expressed fully; even if it requires more characters than the *Precision*, *printf* will not truncate it.	If *Precision* is not specified, or if it is zero or just a decimal point without a number after it, a value of 1 is used for the *Precision*.
e E	The *Precision* tells *printf* the number of digits it should print after the decimal point.	*Precision* is 6. If the decimal point appears with 0 or no number after it, the decimal point is not printed.
f	*Precision* specifies the number of digits to be printed after the decimal point. If a decimal point is printed, at least one digit appears before it.	Default is 6. When *Precision* is explicitly given as 0, no decimal point is printed.
g G	The *Precision* specifies the maximum number of significant digits to be printed.	Default is to print all significant digits.
s	The *Precision* indicates the maximum number of characters to be printed. In this case, *printf* truncates the string and prints only up to *Precision* characters.	The character string is printed until a null character is encountered.

fact, if *printf* finds a character after the % character, it simply prints the character.

Note that several features of *printf* in the Turbo C++ library are nonstandard extensions. In particular, should you want your application program to be portable across multiple systems, avoid the N and F addressing mode modifiers.

SEE ALSO

`vprintf`	*Another routine for printing to* stdout
`fprintf, vfprintf`	*For formatted printing to a file*
`sprintf, vsprintf`	*For formatted printing to a string*
`cprintf`	*Formatted, unbuffered output to console*

EXAMPLES Use *printf* to prompt the user for a string. Print it out, together with a count of characters printed during the first prompt.

```
#include <stdio.h>
main()
{
    int numprint;
    char inbuf[81];
    numprint = printf("Enter a string: ");
    gets(inbuf);
    printf("I printed %d characters and \
You entered:\n%s\n", numprint, inbuf);
    return 0;
}
```

Using the formatting capabilities of *printf*, print a table showing the numbers from 1 to 10 with their squares.

```
#include <stdio.h>
main()
{
    int i;
    printf("Table of squares\n");
    for (i=1; i<=10; i++)
    {
        printf("%4d\t%6d\n", i, i*i);
    }
    return 0;
}
```

Write a small C program to illustrate some of the special features of *printf*. Show the addressing mode modifiers, printing values of pointers, and width and precision fields of a format at run-time.

```
#include <stdio.h>
char far  *strf = "Far string...";
char near *strn = "Near string...";
char *var_name[] = {"long_name_variable",
                    "shorter_var", "short"};
double values[] = { 1.23,  3.4567, 9.87654321};
unsigned int num_vars = sizeof(values)/sizeof(double);
main()
{
    int i, j, numprint, chcount, width, precision=0;
    numprint = printf("Some special features of \
```

```
printf\n%n", &chcount);
    printf("printf returned %d and character count in \
variable is %d\n", numprint, chcount);
/* Use of addressing mode modifiers */
    printf("\nYou can print 'near' and 'far' data \
items properly:\n");
    printf("Example: %Fs (far),\n%Ns (near) will print \
in any model\n", strf, strn);
/* Printing addresses of variables */
    printf("\nYou can even print the addresses:\n");
    printf("Item           Segment:Offset\n");
    printf("'far'  string:    %Fp\n", (void far *)strf);
    printf("'near' string:    %Fp\n", (void far *)strn);

/*  Width and precision can be decided at run-time */
    printf("\nThe format can even be decided \
at run-time\n");
    for(i = 0; i < num_vars; i++)

    {
/* Find maximum length of variable names */
        if( (j = strlen(var_name[i])) > precision)
            precision = j;
    }
/* Make the width 4 characters longer and print names
 * left justified
 */
    width = precision + 4;
    printf("--- Table of Variables ---\n");
    for(i = 0; i < num_vars; i++)
    {
        printf("%-*.*s  %12.8f\n", width, precision,
                                 var_name[i], values[i]);
    }
    return 0;
}
```

This example program produces the following listing (the addresses printed using the p format differ according to machine).

```
Some special features of printf
printf returned 32 and character count in variable is 32

You can print 'near' and 'far' data items properly:
Example: Far string... (far),
```

```
Near string... (near) will print in any model

You can even print the addresses:
Item            Segment:Offset
'far'  string:     1D5B:01B8
'near' string:     1D5B:01C6

The format can even be decided at run-time
--- Table of Variables ---
long_name_variable          1.23000000
shorter_var                 3.45670000
short                       9.87654321
```

Stream I/O

putc

COMPATIBILITY

TC1	TC1.5	TC2	TC++	MSC3	MSC4	MSC5	MSC6	QC1	QC2	QC2.5	ANSI	UNIX V	XNX
▲	▲	▲	▲	▲	▲	▲	▲	▲	▲	▲	▲	▲	▲

PURPOSE Use the *putc* macro to write a single character to a file opened for buffered output.

SYNTAX

```
int putc(int c, FILE *file_pointer);
int c;                     Character to be written

FILE *file_pointer;        Pointer to file to which the character is written
```

EXAMPLE CALL

```
putc('*', outfile);
```

INCLUDES

```
#include <stdio.h>        For function declaration definition of FILE data structure
```

DESCRIPTION The *putc* macro writes the character *c* to the current position of the file specified by the argument *file_pointer*. After writing the character, the current position is advanced to the next character. The *file_pointer* must be a pointer returned earlier by an *fopen* or a *freopen* function call or it can be one of the preopened files such as *stdout* or *stderr* for which writing a character makes sense.

Note that *fputc* performs in the same manner as *putc*, except that *fputc* is implemented as a function.

RETURNS The *putc* macro returns the character it wrote as an integer value. A return value of EOF indicates either an error or end-of-file condition. The *ferror* function should be called to determine if there was an error.

SEE ALSO

`putchar`	*Macro to write a character to* stdout
`fputc`	*Function to write a character to a file*
`fgetc, fgetchar, getc, getchar`	*To read a character from a file*

EXAMPLE Use *putc* to write a line (maximum length of 80 characters or up to the null character) to *stdout.*

```
#include <stdio.h>
char buffer[81] = "Testing putc on stdout...\n";
main()
{
    int i;
/* An empty for loop that uses putc to print to stdout */
    for(i=0; (i<81) && (putc(buffer[i],stdout) != EOF);
        i++);
    return 0;
}
```

Stream I/O

putchar

COMPATIBILITY

TC1	TC1.5	TC2	TC++	MSC3	MSC4	MSC5	MSC6	QC1	QC2	QC2.5	ANSI	UNIX V	XNX
▲	▲	▲	▲	▲	▲	▲	▲	▲	▲	▲	▲	▲	▲

PURPOSE Use the *putchar* macro to write a single character to the preopened file *stdout*, which is initially connected to your display.

SYNTAX

```
int putchar(int c);
```

`int c;` *Character to be written*

EXAMPLE CALL

```
putchar('?');
```

INCLUDES `#include <stdio.h>` *For function declaration*

DESCRIPTION The *putchar* macro writes the character *c* to *stdout* and is equivalent to the use of *putc(stdout)*. Note that *putchar* is the macro equivalent of the *fputchar* function.

RETURNS The *putchar* macro returns the character written to *stdout.* In case of any error, the return value is equal to the constant EOF (defined in *stdio.h*).

COMMENTS Note that you cannot use *putchar* to write a single character to the console because a carriage return must be entered to complete a single buffered write to the keyboard. Use *putch* or *putche* for unbuffered output to the keyboard.

SEE ALSO

putc	*Macro to write a character to a file*
fputc, fputchar	*To write a character to a file*
fputc, fputchar, putc, putchar	*To write a character to a file*

EXAMPLE Use *putchar* to write a line (maximum length of 80 characters) to *stdout*.

```
#include <stdio.h>
char buffer[81] = "Testing putchar...\n";
main()
{
    int i;
/* A for loop that uses putchar to print to stdout */
    for(i=0; (i<81) && (putchar(buffer[i]) != EOF);
        i++);
    return 0;
}
```

Stream I/O

puts

COMPATIBILITY

TC1	TC1.5	TC2	TC++	MSC3	MSC4	MSC5	MSC6	QC1	QC2	QC2.5	ANSI	UNIX V	XNX
▲	▲	▲	▲	▲	▲	▲	▲	▲	▲	▲	▲	▲	▲

PURPOSE Use *puts* to output a string to the standard output file *stdout*.

SYNTAX

```
int puts(const char *string);
```

`const char *string;` *String to be output*

EXAMPLE CALL

```
puts("Do you really want to quit? ");
```

INCLUDES `#include <stdio.h>` *For function declaration*

DESCRIPTION The *puts* function writes the string specified in the argument *string* to the standard output file *stdout*—by default, the screen. The string's terminating null character is replaced by a newline (\n) in the output.

RETURNS When all is well, *puts* returns the last character it wrote. Otherwise, it returns EOF to indicate error.

SEE ALSO

fgets	*To read a line from a file*
fputs	*To write a string to a file*
gets	*To read a line from the standard input,* stdin

EXAMPLE Use *puts* to write a message to the screen, assuming that *stdout* has not been redirected.

```
#include <stdio.h>
char message[81] =
        "Failure reading drive C\nAbort, Retry, Fail?";
main()
{
    puts(message);
    return 0;
}
```

Stream I/O

putw

COMPATIBILITY

TC1	TC1.5	TC2	TC++	MSC3	MSC4	MSC5	MSC6	QC1	QC2	QC2.5	ANSI	UNIX V	XNX
▲	▲	▲	▲	▲	▲	▲	▲	▲	▲	▲		▲	▲

PURPOSE Use *putw* to write word (a binary value of type *int*) into a file opened for buffered binary writing.

SYNTAX

```
int putw(int intval, FILE *file_pointer);
```

int intval;	*Integer value to be written to file*
FILE *file_pointer;	*Pointer to FILE data structure associated with file from which a word is read*

EXAMPLE CALL

```
putw(int_value, outfile);
```

INCLUDES `#include <stdio.h>` *For function declaration and definition of FILE*

DESCRIPTION The *putw* function writes the binary value of the integer argument *intval* at the current position in the file specified by the argument *file_pointer*. As this is a 2-byte value on most MS-DOS machines the file pointer is updated accordingly.

RETURNS The *putw* function returns the integer value it wrote. A return value equal to the constant EOF defined in *stdio.h* may indicate an error. However, since EOF is also a valid integer, you should call *ferror* to determine if an error had actually occurred.

SEE ALSO getw *To read a word from a file*

EXAMPLE Open a file in the binary write (*wb*) mode. Use *putw* to write some words to the file. Since the words are hexadecimal representations of a string, you can use the DOS TYPE command on the file to see how this works.

```
#include <stdio.h>
/* The string "Hi There\n" in hexadecimal. Because of
 * byte-ordering conventions they may not look obvious.
 * By the way, here are the ASCII codes:
 *  H = 48, i = 69, blank = 20, T = 54, h = 68, e = 65,
 *    and r = 72
 */
int words[] = {0x6948, 0x5420, 0x6568, 0x6572, 0x0A0D};
int numw = sizeof(words)/sizeof(int);
main()
{
    int i;
    FILE *infile;
    char filename[81];
    printf("Enter name of a file to write to: ");
    gets(filename);
/* Open the file for reading */
    if ( (infile = fopen(filename, "wb")) == NULL)
    {
        printf("fopen failed.\n");
        exit(0);
    }
/* Write the words to the file */
    for (i=0; i<numw; i++)
    {
        if( putw(words[i], infile) == EOF)
        {
/* Check if there was a real error */
            if(ferror(infile) != 0)
            {
                printf("File: %s write error\n",
```

```
                        filename);
                    exit(0);
                }
            }
        }
/* Ask user to type file out and check */
    printf("To see results use 'TYPE %s'\n", filename);
    return 0;
}
```

Stream I/O

rewind

COMPATIBILITY

TC1	TC1.5	TC2	TC++	MSC3	MSC4	MSC5	MSC6	QC1	QC2	QC2.5	ANSI	UNIX V	XNX
▲	▲	▲	▲	▲	▲	▲	▲	▲	▲	▲	▲	▲	▲

PURPOSE Use the *rewind* function to set the current read or write position associated with a file opened for buffered I/O to the beginning of the file.

SYNTAX `void rewind(FILE *file_pointer);`

`FILE *file_pointer;` *Pointer to FILE data structure associated with file whose current position is to be set to the beginning of the file*

EXAMPLE CALL `rewind(input_file);`

INCLUDES `#include <stdio.h>` *For function declaration and definition of FILE*

DESCRIPTION The *rewind* function sets the current read or write position of the file specified by the argument *file_pointer* to the beginning of the file and clears the end-of-file or error indicator.

COMMON USES The *rewind* function is used to go to the beginning of a file which can also be achieved by calling *fseek* with the proper arguments. However, *fseek* will not clear the error indicator.

SEE ALSO `fseek` *To set the current position indicator of a file*

EXAMPLE Open a file using *fopen* for reading. Read and display a line. Now call *rewind* to go back to the beginning and read a line again. The two lines should be identical.

```
#include <stdio.h>
main()
```

```
{
    FILE *infile;
    char filename[80], buffer[81];
    printf("Enter name of a text file: ");
    gets(filename);
/* Open the file for reading */
    if ( (infile = fopen(filename, "r")) == NULL)
    {
        printf("fopen failed.\n");
        exit(0);
    }
/* Read and display a line */
    fgets(buffer, 80, infile);
    printf("Line read (before rewind): %s", buffer);
/* Rewind and read a line again */
    rewind(infile);
    fgets(buffer, 80, infile);
    printf("Line read (after rewind) : %s", buffer);
    return 0;
}
```

Stream I/O

scanf

COMPATIBILITY

TC1	TC1.5	TC2	TC++	MSC3	MSC4	MSC5	MSC6	QC1	QC2	QC2.5	ANSI	UNIX V	XNX
▲	▲	▲	▲	▲	▲	▲	▲	▲	▲	▲	▲	▲	▲

PURPOSE Use *scanf* to read character strings from the standard input file *stdin* and convert the strings to values of C variables according to specified formats. As an example, you can use *scanf* to read a value into a short integer from the standard input.

SYNTAX

```
int scanf(const char *format_string,...);
```

`const char *format_string;` *Character string that describes the format to be used*

`...` *Variable number of arguments representing addresses of variables whose values are being read*

EXAMPLE CALL

```
scanf(" %d:%d:%d", &hour, &minute, &second);
```

INCLUDES `#include <stdio.h>` *For function declaration*

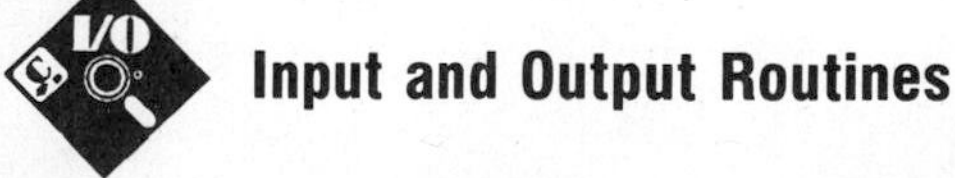

DESCRIPTION The *scanf* function accepts a variable number of arguments, which it interprets as addresses of C variables, and reads character strings from *stdin*, representing their values. It converts them to their internal representations using formatting commands embedded in the argument *format_string* which must be present in a call to *scanf*.

The interpretation of the variables depends on the *format_string*. The formatting command for each variable begins with a percentage sign and can contain other characters as well. A whitespace character (a blank space, a tab, or a newline) may cause *scanf* to ignore whitespace characters from *stdin*. Other nonwhitespace characters, excluding the percentage sign, cause *scanf* to ignore each matching character from the input. It begins to interpret the first nonmatching character as the value of a variable that is being read.

For each C variable whose address is included in the argument list to *scanf*, there must be a format specification embedded in the *format_string*. The format specification for each variable has the following form:

Format Specification for *scanf*

%[*][Width][Addressing_mode][Size][Type]

Table 16-13 summarizes the purpose of each field in the format specification used by *scanf*. Further details are provided in Table 16-14.

Table 16-13. *Fields in a Format Specification for* scanf

Field	Explanation
% (Required)	Indicates the beginning of a format specification. Use %% to read a percentage sign from the input.
* (Optional)	The characters representing the value are read according to the format specification, but the value is not stored. It is not necessary to give an argument corresponding to this format specification.
Width (Optional)	A positive value specifying the maximum number of characters to be read for the value of this variable.
Addressing_mode (Optional)	This field is specific to Turbo C++. Either F (for "far") or N (for "near") can be used here to override the default addressing mode of the memory model being used. As an example, use F in this field when reading the value of a far integer in a small memory model program.
Size (Optional)	A character that modifies the *Type* field which comes next. One of the characters h, l, or L appears in this field to differentiate between short and long integers and between float and double. Shown below is a summary of this field:

Table 16-13. *(cont.)*

Field	Explanation
	Prefix / **When to Use**
	h — Use when reading integers using *Type* d, i, o, x, or X to indicate that the argument is a short integer. Also, use with *Type* u to indicate that the variable being read is an unsigned short integer.
	l — Use when reading integers or unsigned integers with a *Type* field of d, i, o, x, X, or u to specify that the variable to be read is a long integer. Also use with floating-point variables (when the *Type* field is e, E, g, or G) to specify a double, rather than a float.
Type (Required)	A letter that indicates the type of variable being read. Table 16-14 lists the characters and their meanings.

The most important among these fields is the *Type* field which tells *scanf* the type of C variable into which it must convert the input characters. Table 16-14 lists the characters that can appear in the *Type* field and the kind of C variable each one signifies.

Table 16-14. Type *Field in Format Specification for* scanf

Type	Expected Input	Type of Argument
c	Single character. Whitespace characters (space, tab, or newline) will be read in this format.	Pointer to char
d	Decimal integer.	Pointer to int
D	Decimal integer.	Pointer to long
e E f g G	Signed value in the scientific format, for example, −1.234567e+002 and 9.876543e−002 or in the format (sign)(digits).(digits), for example, −1.234567 and 9.876543.	Pointer to float
i	Decimal, hexadecimal, or octal integer.	Pointer to int
I	Decimal, hexadecimal, or octal integer.	Pointer to long
n	This is not really a reading format. The argument corresponding to this format is a pointer to an integer. Before returning, the *scanf* function stores in this integer the total number of characters it has read from the input file or the input file's buffer in this integer.	
o	Octal digits without any sign.	Pointer to int

Table 16-14. *(cont.)*

Type	Expected Input	Type of Argument
O	Octal digits without any sign.	Pointer to long
p	Hexadecimal digits in the form *SSSS:OOOO* using uppercase letters.	Pointer to a far or near pointer
s	Character string.	Pointer to an array of characters large enough to hold input string plus a terminating null
u	Unsigned decimal integer.	Pointer to unsigned int
U	Unsigned decimal integer.	Pointer to unsigned long
x	Hexadecimal digits.	Pointer to int
X	Hexadecimal digits.	Pointer to long

Normally, strings read using the %s format are assumed to be delimited by blank spaces. When you want to read a string delimited by any character other than those in a specific set, you can specify the set of characters within brackets and use this in place of the s in the format specification. If the first character inside the brackets is a caret (^), the set shows the characters that terminate the string. Thus, for example, %[^'\"] reads a string delimited by single or double quote characters.

Strings can be read and stored without the terminating null character by using the %[decimal number]c format in which the *decimal number* denotes the number of characters being read into the character string.

RETURNS The *scanf* function returns the number of input items that were successfully read, converted, and saved in variables. A return value equal to the constant EOF (defined in *stdio.h*) means that an end-of-file was encountered during the read operation.

COMMENTS Use two signs when you need to read a percentage sign. Note that several features of *scanf* in the Turbo C++ library are nonstandard extensions. In particular, should you want your application program to be portable across multiple systems, avoid the N and F addressing mode modifiers.

SEE ALSO

`fscanf`	*Formatted read from any buffered file*
`sscanf`	*For formatted reading from a string*
`cscanf`	*Formatted, unbuffered input from console*
`vscanf`	*Another routine for formatted input from* stdin

EXAMPLE Write a C program that reads the amount of principal, the interest rate, and the number of months to maturity of a certificate of deposit. Use *scanf* to read in the values. Now compute the amount at maturity and print it out.

```
#include <stdio.h>
#include <math.h>
main()
{
    int num_months;
    double interest_rate, principal, final_amount;
/* Ask user to enter all necessary amounts */
    printf("Enter amount of principal, annual interest \
rate:");
    scanf(" %lf %lf", &principal, &interest_rate);
    printf("Enter number of months before deposit \
matures:");
    scanf(" %d", &num_months);
/* Compute amount at maturity and print value */
    final_amount = principal *
                   pow((1.0 + interest_rate/12.0/100.0),
                       (double)num_months);
        printf("$%.2f @%.2f%% annual rate yields $%.2f \
after %d months\n", principal, interest_rate,
               final_amount, num_months);
        return 0;
}
```

Stream I/O

setbuf

COMPATIBILITY

TC1	TC1.5	TC2	TC++	MSC3	MSC4	MSC5	MSC6	QC1	QC2	QC2.5	ANSI	UNIX V	XNX
▲	▲	▲	▲	▲	▲	▲	▲	▲	▲	▲	▲	▲	▲

PURPOSE Use the *setbuf* function to assign your own buffer instead of the system-allocated one for use by a file that has been opened for buffered I/O.

SYNTAX `void setbuf(FILE *file_pointer, char *buffer);`

`FILE *file_pointer;` *Pointer to FILE data structure associated with file whose buffer is being set*

`char *buffer;` *Pointer to buffer (or NULL if no buffering is to be done)*

EXAMPLE CALL `setbuf(infile, mybuffer);`

INCLUDES `#include <stdio.h>` *For function declaration and definition of FILE*

DESCRIPTION The *setbuf* function sets the buffer to be used during I/O involving the file specified by the argument *file_pointer* which must have been returned earlier by *fopen*. If the pointer to buffer given in the argument *buffer* is NULL, *setbuf* turns off buffering for that file. If the pointer is not NULL, it should point to an allocated array of characters BUFSIZ bytes long, where BUFSIZ is a constant defined in *stdio.h* (the declared value is 512). This buffer is used for all subsequent I/O operations with the file specified by the argument *file_pointer*.

COMMENTS While *setbuf* merely lets you switch the buffer used for file I/O to one allocated by you, the companion function *setvbuf* enables you to control the size of the buffer and the level of buffering as well. For example, you would use *setvbuf* if you wanted to read data in chunks larger than the default 512-byte size of the buffer normally used by Turbo C++.

SEE ALSO `setvbuf` *To assign your own buffer with specific size and to control level of buffering during I/O to a file*

EXAMPLE Use *setbuf* to assign your own buffer, at least BUFSIZ characters long, to a file that you have opened with *fopen* for read operations. Now read a character using *fgetc* to initiate a read operation and fill the buffer. Print the buffer to see the effect.

```
#include <stdio.h>
main()
{
    FILE *infile;
    char filename[81], buffer[BUFSIZ+1];
    printf("Enter name of a text file: ");
    gets(filename);
/* Open the file for reading */
    if ( (infile = fopen(filename, "r")) == NULL)
    {
        printf("fopen failed.\n");
        exit(0);
    }
/* Set up a new buffer for the file */
    setbuf(infile, buffer);
/* Now read in a single character -- this should fill
 * up the buffer
 */
    fgetc(infile);
```

```
    buffer[BUFSIZ] = '\0';    /* Make it a C string */
    printf("After reading one character from file \
buffer has:\n%s\n", buffer);
    return 0;
}
```

Stream I/O

setvbuf

COMPATIBILITY

TC1	TC1.5	TC2	TC++	MSC3	MSC4	MSC5	MSC6	QC1	QC2	QC2.5	ANSI	UNIX V	XNX
▲	▲	▲	▲	▲	▲	▲	▲	▲	▲	▲	▲	▲	▲

PURPOSE Use the *setvbuf* function to assign a buffer of a specific size to a file open for buffered I/O. You can also control the type of buffering to be used or turn off buffering for the specified file.

SYNTAX

```
int setvbuf(FILE *file_pointer, char *buffer, int buf_type,
                                          size_t buf_size);
```

`FILE *file_pointer;` *Pointer to FILE data structure associated with file whose buffer is being set*

`char *buffer;` *Pointer to buffer (or NULL if no buffering requested)*

`int buf_type;` *Type of buffering desired (see table below for values)*

`size_t buf_size;` *Size of buffer in bytes, if any assigned*

EXAMPLE CALL `setvbuf(infile, buffer, _IOFBF, 120);`

INCLUDES `#include <stdio.h>` *For function declaration and definition of FILE and* size_t *data types*

DESCRIPTION The *setvbuf* function sets the buffer and the level of buffering for the file specified by the argument *file_pointer* which must have been returned earlier by *fopen*.

First *setvbuf* checks the argument *buf_type* to see the type of buffering requested. This argument can have one of the values shown in the table, each of which indicates a level of buffering.

If the argument *buf_type* is _IONBF, the other arguments are ignored and the internal flags are set so that no buffering is done for the file indicated by *file_pointer*. If the argument *buf_type* is either _IOFBF or _IOLBF, the buffering option is first saved internally. Then *setvbuf* checks if the pointer to the buffer specified in the argument *buffer* is a NULL. If it

Type	Interpretation
_IOFBF	Bytes will be read until buffer is completely filled. This is called "full buffering."
_IOLBF	Each line read from the input stream is buffered. In this "line buffering" mode the reading stops when a whole line has been read.
_IONBF	No buffering is done.

is, *setvbuf* allocates a buffer using the size specified in the argument *buf_size*. If the argument *buffer* is not NULL, it should be a buffer of size *buf_size* bytes allocated by you. This is set by *setvbuf* as the buffer for the specified file.

COMMON USES The *setvbuf* function gives you control over the amount of buffering and the actual buffer to be used by a file.

RETURNS If successful, *setvbuf* returns 0. In case of any error, it returns a nonzero value.

COMMENTS If you only want to switch to a buffer of your own and not to change any other features of buffered I/O, *setbuf* is a much simpler function to use.

SEE ALSO `setbuf` *To assign your own buffer of fixed size to a file*

EXAMPLE Open a file using *fopen* for reading. Use *setvbuf* to assign a 120-byte buffer for the file and to specify buffer type _IOFBF. Now read a character from the file using *fgetc*, and print the buffer out using *putchar*. You will notice that because of buffering during read, the first 120 characters of the file are now in the buffer, even though you only read a single character.

```
#include <stdio.h>
main()
{
    FILE *infile;
    char filename[81], buffer[121];
    printf("Enter name of a text file: ");
    gets(filename);
/* Open the file for reading */
    if ( (infile = fopen(filename, "r")) == NULL)
    {
        printf("fopen failed.\n");
        exit(0);
    }
/* Set up a new buffer for the file */
    if (setvbuf(infile, buffer, _IOFBF, 120) != 0)
```

```
        {
            perror("setvbuf failed");
        }
        else
        {
            fgetc(infile);
            buffer[120] = '\0';
            printf("After reading one character buffer \
has:\n%s\n", buffer);
        }
        return 0;
}
```

Stream I/O

sprintf

COMPATIBILITY

TC1	TC1.5	TC2	TC++	MSC3	MSC4	MSC5	MSC6	QC1	QC2	QC2.5	ANSI	UNIX V	XNX
▲	▲	▲	▲	▲	▲	▲	▲	▲	▲	▲	▲	▲	▲

PURPOSE Use the *sprintf* function to format and write the values of C variables to a string.

SYNTAX

```
int sprintf(char *p_string, const char *format_string,...);
```

`char *p_string;` *Pointer to an array of characters where* sprintf *sends its formatted output*

`const char *format_string;` *Character string that describes the format to be used*

`...` *Variable number of arguments depending on the number of items being printed*

EXAMPLE CALL

```
sprintf(buffer, "FY 88 Profit = %.2f\n", profit);
```

INCLUDES `#include <stdio.h>` *For function declaration*

DESCRIPTION The *sprintf* function accepts a variable number of arguments, converts their values to characters, and stores these characters in the buffer whose address is specified in the argument *p_string*. The performance of *sprintf* is identical to that of *fprintf* and *printf* except that *sprintf* sends its output to a character buffer instead of a file. After formatting and storing the characters in the buffer *p_string*, *sprintf* appends a null character to make the buffer a C string.

As in *printf*, the conversion of values of variables to character strings is done according to formatting commands given in a character string *format_string*. The available formatting commands and options are described in detail in the reference pages on *printf*. In particular, Tables 16-9, 16-10, 16-11, and 16-12 tabulate the characters that appear in the format commands (which always begin with the character %). By the way, to actually print a percent sign (instead of having it interpreted as a formatting command), use two percent signs in a row.

COMMON USES A common use of *sprintf* is to prepare formatted strings for use by such other output routines as *outtext* in the graphics library that do not have any formatting capabilities.

RETURNS The *sprintf* function returns the number of characters it has stored in the buffer, excluding the terminating null character.

SEE ALSO

`printf`	*For printing to* stdout *and for detailed information on formats*
`vprintf`	*Printing to* stdout *using a pointer to a list of arguments*
`fprintf, vfprintf`	*For formatted printing to a file*
`vsprintf`	*Another routine for formatted output to a string*

EXAMPLE Use *fprintf* to prepare a formatted string showing the value of a C variable. Display the string with *printf*.

```
#include <stdio.h>
int     i     = 100;
double  x     = 1.23456;
main()
{
    int numout;
    char outbuf[81];
    numout = sprintf(outbuf, "The value of i = %d and \
the value of x = %g\n", i, x);
    printf("sprintf wrote %d characters and the buffer \
contains:\n%s", numout, outbuf);
    return 0;
}
```

Stream I/O

sscanf

COMPATIBILITY

TC1	TC1.5	TC2	TC++	MSC3	MSC4	MSC5	MSC6	QC1	QC2	QC2.5	ANSI	UNIX V	XNX
▲	▲	▲	▲	▲	▲	▲	▲	▲	▲	▲	▲	▲	▲

PURPOSE Use *sscanf* to read characters from a buffer and to convert and store them in C variables according to specified formats.

SYNTAX

```
int sscanf(const char *buffer, const char *format_string,...);
```

`const char *buffer;` *Pointer to buffer from which characters will be read and converted to values of variables*

`const char *format_string;` *Character string that describes the format to be used*

`...` *Variable number of arguments representing addresses of variables whose values are being read*

EXAMPLE CALL

```
sscanf(buffer, "Name: %s Age: %d", name, &age);
```

INCLUDES `#include <stdio.h>` *For function declaration*

DESCRIPTION The *sscanf* function reads a stream of characters from the buffer specified in the argument *buffer* and converts them to values according to format specifications embedded in the argument *format_string*. It then stores the values in C variables whose addresses are provided in the variable length argument list.

The optional arguments following the *format_string* are addresses of C variables whose values are being read. Each address has a corresponding format specification in the argument *format_string*. The format specification always begins with a percent sign, and the formatting commands are identical to the ones used with the function *scanf*. A detailed list of the formats is provided in the reference pages on *scanf*.

COMMON USES The *sscanf* function is handy for in-memory conversion of characters to values. You may often find it convenient to read in strings using either *gets* or *fgets* and then extract values from the string by using *sscanf*.

RETURNS The *sscanf* function returns the number of fields that were successfully read, converted, and assigned to variables. If the string ends before completing the read operation, the return value is the constant EOF, defined in the include file *stdio.h*.

SEE ALSO `scanf` *Formatted reading from* stdin

`fscanf`	*For formatted, buffered reading from a file*
`cscanf`	*Formatted, unbuffered input from console*
`vsscanf`	*Another routine for formatted input from* stdin

EXAMPLE Suppose you have a program that lets the user set the value of a variable by a command of the form "name = value" (i.e., the name is separated from the value by one or more blanks surrounding an equal sign). One way to implement this is to read the entire line into an internal buffer using *gets*. You can then use *sscanf* to separate the variable name and its value. As you can see from the example below, the features of *sscanf* provide easy ways of implementing such user-friendly features as this.

```
#include <stdio.h>
main()
{
    double value;
    char buffer[81], name[81];
    printf("Enter value of variable as \
\"name=<value>\":");
    gets(buffer);
/* Now use sscanf to separate name and value */
    sscanf(buffer, " %[^=] = %lf", name, &value);
/* Display result to user */
    printf("Value of variable named %s is set to %f\n",
            name, value);
    return 0;
}
```

Stream I/O

tmpfile

COMPATIBILITY

TC1	TC1.5	TC2	TC++	MSC3	MSC4	MSC5	MSC6	QC1	QC2	QC2.5	ANSI	UNIX V	XNX
	▲	▲	▲		▲	▲	▲	▲	▲	▲	▲	▲	▲

PURPOSE Use *tmpfile* to open a temporary file in the current directory for buffered binary read/write operations.

SYNTAX `FILE *tmpfile(void);`

EXAMPLE CALL `p_tfile = tmpfile();`

INCLUDES `#include <stdio.h>` *For function declaration and definition of FILE data type*

DESCRIPTION The *tmpfile* function opens a temporary file in the current working directory. The file is opened in the mode *w+b* which means binary read and write operations can be performed on this file. You have no access to the name of the file that is created nor is the file available to you after a normal exit from the program. The file is automatically deleted when your program terminates normally or when you close the file.

COMMON USES The *tmpfile* function is a convenient way of opening temporary work files in an application.

RETURNS The *tmpfile* function returns a pointer to the FILE data structure of the temporary file it opens. In case of error, the return pointer will be NULL.

COMMENTS Unlike *tmpnam,* which simply generates the file name, a file is opened by *tmpfile* and the file is truly temporary because it is deleted when the program ends.

SEE ALSO `tmpnam` *To generate a unique temporary file name*

EXAMPLE Call *tmpfile* to open a temporary file and write the contents of a buffer to the file. Unfortunately, the file will be gone when you exit the program, so there will be no evidence of the temporary file. Nor is the file name available for printing.

```
#include <stdio.h>
char   message[80] = "Testing tmpfile.... ";
main()
{
    FILE *tfile;
    if ((tfile = tmpfile()) == NULL)
    {
        perror("tmpfile failed");
    }
    else
    {
        printf("Temporary file successfully opened.\n");
        printf("Wrote %d characters to file\n",
              fwrite((void *)message, sizeof(char), 80,
              tfile));
        printf("File will be gone when you exit.\n");
    }
    return 0;
}
```

Stream I/O

tmpnam

COMPATIBILITY

TC1	TC1.5	TC2	TC++	MSC3	MSC4	MSC5	MSC6	QC1	QC2	QC2.5	ANSI	UNIX V	XNX
	▲	▲	▲		▲	▲	▲	▲	▲	▲	▲	▲	▲

PURPOSE Use the *tmpnam* function to generate a temporary file name for your application.

SYNTAX

```
char *tmpnam(char *file_name);
```

`char *file_name;` *Pointer to string where file name will be returned*

EXAMPLE CALL

```
tmpnam(tfilename);
```

INCLUDES `#include <stdio.h>` *For function declaration*

DESCRIPTION The *tmpnam* function generates a file name and returns it in the buffer *file_name*, which must be allocated by you. The size of the buffer that holds the file name must be at least equal to the constant *L_tmpnam*, which is defined in *stdio.h* to be 13. You can generate up to *TMP_MAX* (defined in *stdio.h* to be 32,767) unique file names with *tmpnam*.

If the argument *file_name* is NULL, the generated file name is stored internally by *tmpnam* and a pointer to this name is returned by *tmpnam*. This name is preserved until another call is made to this function. So you can get by with a NULL argument to *tmpnam* and simply use the pointer returned by it as long as you use this name before the next call to *tmpnam*.

COMMON USES The *tmpnam* function is a handy tool if your application generates temporary files.

RETURNS The *tmpnam* function returns a pointer to the name generated. If the generated name is not unique, it returns a NULL.

COMMENTS You are responsible for opening the file using the file name generated by *tmpnam*. You can use *tmpfile* to directly open a temporary file.

SEE ALSO `tmpfile` *To open a temporary file in the current working directory*

EXAMPLE Call *tmpnam* to generate a temporary file name and print this name. Note that we do not allocate any storage for the string itself; we use the pointer returned by *tmpnam*.

```
#include <stdio.h>
main()
```

```
{
    char *tfilename;
    tfilename = tmpnam(NULL);
    if (tfilename == NULL)
    {
        perror("tmpnam failed");
    }
    else
    {
        printf("Temporary file name: %s\n", tfilename);
    }
    return 0;
}
```

Stream I/O

ungetc

COMPATIBILITY

TC1	TC1.5	TC2	TC++	MSC3	MSC4	MSC5	MSC6	QC1	QC2	QC2.5	ANSI	UNIX V	XNX
▲	▲	▲	▲	▲	▲	▲	▲	▲	▲	▲	▲	▲	▲

PURPOSE Use *ungetc* to place any character, except the constant EOF, in the buffer associated with a file opened for buffered input.

SYNTAX `int ungetc(int c, FILE *file_pointer);`

`int c;` *Character to be placed in the file's buffer*

`FILE *file_pointer;` *Pointer to FILE data structure associated with file in whose buffer the character is placed*

EXAMPLE CALL `ungetc(last_char, infile);`

INCLUDES `#include <stdio.h>` *For function declaration and definition of FILE data type*

DESCRIPTION The *ungetc* function places the character given in the integer argument *c* in the buffer associated with the file specified by the argument *file_pointer* so that the next read operation on that file starts with that character. You must read at least once before attempting to place a character in a file's buffer; otherwise, the buffer is not in a usable state. Also, *ungetc* ignores any attempt to push the constant EOF.

Since *ungetc* places the character in the file's buffer, any operation that tampers with the buffer or the file's current position (for example, *fflush, fseek, fsetpos* or *rewind*) may erase the character.

The *ungetc* function affects the file's current position differently for different translation modes. In the text mode the current position remains as it was before the call to *ungetc*. Thus the file's position is undefined until the pushed character is read back or discarded. In the binary mode the file's position is decremented after each call to *ungetc*. Once the file's position reaches zero, however, the value becomes undefined after calls to *ungetc*.

COMMON USES The *ungetc* function is used to reject an invalid character that has just been read. The character can be placed back in the input buffer and then displayed by an error reporting routine.

RETURNS If there are no errors, *ungetc* returns the character it pushed back. Otherwise, it returns the constant EOF to indicate an error.

SEE ALSO

`getc`	*Macro to read a character from a file*
`getchar`	*Function to read a character from* stdin
`fputc, fputchar, putc, putchar`	*To write a character to a file*

EXAMPLE Write a program that asks the user to enter an integer. Use *getchar* to read the digits and accumulate them into an integer. Once a nondigit is reached (use the macro *isdigit* to check), put that character back in the buffer by calling *ungetc*. Now print a message showing the integer value and indicating the first noninteger character that the user typed. This is a classic use of *ungetc*.

```
#include <stdio.h>
#include <ctype.h>     /* For the macro isdigit() */
main()
{
    int intval = 0, c;
    char buff[81];
/* Ask user to type in an integer */
    printf("Enter an integer followed by some other \
characters:");
    while ( (c = getchar()) != EOF && isdigit(c) )
    {
        intval = 10*intval + c - 48; /* 0 is ASCII 48 */
    }
/* Push back the first nondigit read from stdin */
    if (c != EOF) ungetc(c, stdin);
/* Print message to user */
```

```
    printf("Integer you entered = %d.\n\
Rest of the string beginning at the first noninteger \
in buffer: %s\n", intval, gets(buff));
    return 0;
}
```

Stream I/O

vfprintf

COMPATIBILITY

TC1	TC1.5	TC2	TC++	MSC3	MSC4	MSC5	MSC6	QC1	QC2	QC2.5	ANSI	UNIX V	XNX
▲	▲	▲	▲		▲	▲	▲	▲	▲	▲	▲	▲	▲

PURPOSE Use *vfprintf* to write formatted output to a file, just as *fprintf* does, except that *vfprintf* accepts a pointer to the list of variables rather than the variables themselves, allowing a number of items to be printed.

SYNTAX

```
int vfprintf(FILE *file_pointer, const char *format_string,
                                  va_list arg_pointer);
```

`FILE *file_pointer;` *Pointer to FILE data structure of the file to which the output goes*

`const char *format_string;` *Character string that describes the format to be used*

`va_list arg_pointer;` *Pointer to a list containing a variable number of arguments being printed*

EXAMPLE CALL

```
vfprintf(stderr, p_format, p_arg);
```

INCLUDES

`#include <stdio.h>` *For function declaration*

`#include <stdarg.h>` *For definition of va_list*

DESCRIPTION The *vfprintf* function accepts a pointer to a list of a number of arguments in *arg_pointer*, converts their values to characters, and writes them to the file specified by the argument *file_pointer*.

The only difference between *fprintf* and *vfprintf* is that *fprintf* accepts its arguments directly, whereas *vfprintf* accepts a pointer to a list of a variable number of arguments. The format used to print the variables is given in the argument *format_string*, a character string with embedded format commands that begin with a percent sign. Detailed information on the format specification appears in the reference pages on *printf* (see Tables 16-9, 16-10, 16-11, and 16-12).

COMMON USES The *vfprintf* is useful for printing values of arguments in routines that accept arguments of varying length. An example would be a customized error handler that accepts a list of arguments and prints them out.

RETURNS The *vfprintf* function returns the number of characters it has printed, excluding the terminating null character.

SEE ALSO

`printf`	*For printing to* stdout *and for detailed information on formats*
`vprintf`	*Printing to* stdout *using a pointer to a list of arguments*
`fprintf`	*For formatted printing to a file*
`sprintf, vsprintf`	*For formatted output to a string*
`va_start, va_arg, va_end`	*Macros for accessing variable-length argument lists*

EXAMPLE Write a routine to send error messages to *stderr*. The routine should accept a variable number of arguments, the first of which is a format string followed by one or more arguments, just like *fprintf* accepts. The routine, which in this example conforms to the ANSI standard of handling variable arguments, prints the arguments using the given format. Test the routine using a simple main program.

```
#include <stdio.h>
#include <stdarg.h>
void my_errmsg (char*);
char filename[80] = "EXAMPLE.EXE";
main()
{
        int line_no = 131;
/* Call the error handler to print an error message.
 * First just a single line. Then a more detailed
 * message with more arguments.
 */
        my_errmsg("Syntax error\n");

        my_errmsg("File: %s at line_no %d\n", filename,
                  line_no);
        return 0;
}
/*-------------------------------------------------*/
/*  my_errmsg: accepts variable number of arguments
 *             and prints their values to stderr
```

```
 */
void my_errmsg(char *p_format)
{
    va_list p_arg;
/* Use va_start followed by va_arg macros to get to the
 * start of the variable number of arguments. This will
 * alter the pointer p_arg to point to the list of
 * variables to be printed.
 */
    va_start(p_arg, p_format);
    vfprintf(stderr, p_format, p_arg);
/* Use the va_end macro to reset the p_arg to NULL */
    va_end(p_arg);
}
```

Stream I/O

vfscanf

COMPATIBILITY

TC1	TC1.5	TC2	TC++	MSC3	MSC4	MSC5	MSC6	QC1	QC2	QC2.5	ANSI	UNIX V	XNX
▲	▲	▲	▲										

PURPOSE Use *vfscanf* to read formatted input from a file, just like *fscanf,* except that *vfscanf* accepts a pointer to the list of arguments rather than the arguments themselves, allowing a variable number of items to be read.

SYNTAX

```
int vfscanf(FILE *file_pointer, const char *format_string,
                                va_list arg_pointer);
```

`FILE        *file_pointer;` *Pointer to FILE data structure of the file from which to read*

`const char *format_string;` *A character string which describes the format to be used*

`va_list     arg_pointer;` *Pointer to a list containing a variable number of arguments that are being read*

EXAMPLE CALL

```
vfscanf(infile, p_format, p_arg);
```

INCLUDES

`#include <stdio.h>` *For function prototype*

`#include <stdarg.h>` *For definition of macros such as va_list*

DESCRIPTION The *vfscanf* function accepts a pointer to a list of a variable numbers of arguments in *arg_pointer*, reads in their values from the file specified by the argument *file_pointer*.

The only difference between *fscanf* and *vfscanf* is that *fscanf* accepts its arguments directly, whereas *vfscanf* accepts a pointer to a list of variable number of arguments. The format used to print the variables is given in the argument *format_string*. This is a character string with embedded format commands that begin with a percent sign (%). Detailed information on the format specification appears in the reference pages on *scanf*.

RETURNS The *vfscanf* function returns the number of input fields it successfully scanned, converted and stored. If end-of-file is reached before all specified arguments are read, *vfscanf* returns the constant EOF.

SEE ALSO

`scanf`	*For reading from* stdin *and for detailed information on formats*
`vscanf`	*Reading from* stdin *using a pointer to a list of arguments*
`fscanf`	*For formatted input from a file*
`sscanf, vsscanf`	*For formatted input from a string*
`va_start, va_arg, va_end`	*Macros for accessing variable-length argument lists*

EXAMPLES Write a routine to read a variable number of items from a file. The routine should accept a variable number of arguments, the first one of which is a format string followed by one or more arguments, just like the ones to *fscanf*. The routine will simply read in the values of the arguments using the given format. Test the routine with a simple main program. If you save the lines

```
DATABASE:      LIST OF CLONES
Product Name: CloneMaster 286XL
Manufacturer: Cyclone, Inc.
Part #:       286-007          Unit Price:   $995.95
```

in a file named TEST.DAT and use that file as the input to this program, the output is as follows (user input is in italics):

```
Enter name of data file: TEST.DAT
The first record in LIST OF CLONES contains:
Product Name: CloneMaster 286XL
Manufacturer: Cyclone, Inc.
Part #:       286-007
```

```
Unit Price:   $995.95

#include <stdio.h>
#include <stdarg.h>
void getfromfile(FILE *, char *,...);
main()
{
    char filename[80], dbname[80], pname[80],
 mname[80], partno[40];
    FILE *datafile;
    double uprice;
/* Get file name and open it for reading */
    printf("Enter name of data file:");
    gets(filename);
    if((datafile = fopen(filename, "r")) == NULL)
    {
        printf("Error opening file: %s\n", filename);
        exit(1);
    }
/* Call the input routine to read values of variables.
 * First just a single number. Then more than one
 * value.
 */
    getfromfile(datafile, "DATABASE: %[^\n] ", &dbname);
    getfromfile(datafile,
           "Product Name: %[^\n] Manufacturer: %[^\n] "
   "Part #: %s Unit Price: $%lf",
           &pname, &mname, &partno, &uprice);
    printf("The first record in %s contains:\n"
           "Product Name: %s\n"
           "Manufacturer: %s\n"
           "Part #:       %s\n"
           "Unit Price:   $%.2lf\n", dbname, pname,
           mname, partno, uprice);
    return 0;
}


/*-------------------------------------------------------*/
/*  getfromfile: accepts variable number of arguments
 *               and reads formatted values from a file
 */
void getfromfile(FILE *stream, char *my_format,...)
{
    va_list arg_pointer;
/* Use va_start macro to get to the start of the
```

```
 * variable number of arguments. This will alter the
 * pointer arg_pointer to point to the list of
 * variables to be read.
 */
    va_start(arg_pointer, my_format);
    vfscanf(stream, my_format, arg_pointer);
/* Use the va_end macro to reset the arg_pointer */
    va_end(arg_pointer);
}
```

Stream I/O

COMPATIBILITY

vprintf

TC1	TC1.5	TC2	TC++	MSC3	MSC4	MSC5	MSC6	QC1	QC2	QC2.5	ANSI	UNIX V	XNX
▲	▲	▲	▲		▲	▲	▲	▲	▲	▲	▲	▲	▲

PURPOSE Use *vprintf* to write formatted output to *stdout* (that is, perform the same functions as *printf*) when you have only a pointer to the list of variables to be printed, rather than the variables themselves. This allows a variable number of arguments to be printed.

SYNTAX

```
int vprintf(const char *format_string, va_list arg_pointer);
```

`const char *format_string;` *Character string that describes the format to be used*

`va_list arg_pointer;` *Pointer to a list containing a variable number of arguments that are being printed*

EXAMPLE CALL

```
vprintf(p_format, p_arg);
```

INCLUDES

`#include <stdio.h>` *For function declaration*

`#include <stdarg.h>` *For definition of va_list*

DESCRIPTION The *vprintf* function accepts a pointer to a list of a variable number of arguments in *arg_pointer*, converts their values to characters, and writes them to the preopened file *stdout*. Except for accepting a pointer to a list of arguments rather than using the arguments themselves, *vprintf* works as *fprintf* and *printf* do. The argument *format_string* is a character string with embedded format commands that begin with a percent sign. Their meaning is explained in the reference pages on *printf* (see Tables 16-9, 16-10, 16-11, and 16-12).

COMMON USES The *vprintf* is necessary when you have a list of arguments available and want to print them out. A common example is a customized error handler that accepts a list of arguments.

RETURNS The *vprintf* function returns the number of characters it has printed, excluding the terminating null character.

SEE ALSO

`printf`	*For printing to* stdout *and for detailed information on formats*
`fprintf, vfprintf`	*For formatted printing to a file*
`sprintf, vsprintf`	*For formatted output to a string*
`va_start, va_arg, va_end`	*Macros for accessing variable-length argument lists*

EXAMPLE Write an error-handling routine, conforming to the proposed ANSI C standards, that takes a variable number of arguments and prints an error message that includes the values of the passed parameters. Use *vprintf* to do the printing in the error handler. Write a sample main program to demonstrate the use of the error handler.

```
#include <stdio.h>
#include <stdarg.h>      /* ANSI C compatible */
void error_handler(char *,...);
char filename[80] = "COMMAND.COM";
main()
{
    int offset = 0x232A;
/* Call the error handler to print an error message.
 * First just a single line. Then a more detailed
 * message with more arguments.
 */
    error_handler("System error\n");
    error_handler("File %s at offset %X\n",
                  filename, offset);
    return 0;
}

/*----------------------------------------------------*/
/*  error_handler: accepts variable number of arguments
 *                 and prints messages
 */
void error_handler(char *my_format,...)
{
```

```
    va_list arg_pointer;
/* Use va_start macro to get to the start of the
 * variable number of arguments. This will alter the
 * pointer arg_pointer to point to the list of
 * variables to be printed.
 */
    va_start(arg_pointer, my_format);
    vprintf(my_format, arg_pointer);
/* Use the va_end macro to reset the arg_pointer */
    va_end(arg_pointer);
}
```

Stream I/O

vscanf

COMPATIBILITY

TC1	TC1.5	TC2	TC++	MSC3	MSC4	MSC5	MSC6	QC1	QC2	QC2.5	ANSI	UNIX V	XNX
▲	▲	▲	▲										

PURPOSE Use *vscanf* to perform the same functions as *scanf*, that is, read formatted input from *stdin*, when you have only a pointer to a list of addresses of the variables to be read rather than the variables themselves. This allows a variable number of arguments to be read.

SYNTAX

```
int vscanf(const char *format_string, va_list arg_pointer);
```

`const char *format_string;` *A character string which describes the format to be used*

`va_list    arg_pointer;` *Pointer to a list containing a variable number of arguments that are to be read*

EXAMPLE CALL

```
vscanf(p_format, p_arg);
```

INCLUDES

`#include <stdio.h>` *For function prototype*

`#include <stdarg.h>` *For definition of macros such as* va_list

DESCRIPTION The *vscanf* function accepts a pointer to a list of a variable number of arguments in *arg_pointer*, reads their values from the preopened file *stdin*.

Except for accepting a pointer to a list of arguments rather than using the arguments themselves, *vscanf* works in the same manner as *fscanf* and *scanf*. The argument *format_string* is a character string with embedded format commands that begin with a percent sign (%) and their meaning is explained in the reference pages on *scanf.*

COMMON USES The *vscanf* is necessary when you have a list of variables to be read (the number of variables is not known beforehand).

RETURNS The *vscanf* function returns the number of input fields it successfully scanned, converted, and stored.

SEE ALSO

`scanf`	*For reading from* stdin *and for detailed information on formats*
`fscanf, vfscanf`	*For formatted reading from a file*
`sscanf, vsscanf`	*For formatted input from a string*
`va_start, va_arg, va_end`	*Macros for accessing variable-length argument lists*

EXAMPLE Write a routine that will take a variable number of arguments and read in values for the passed parameters. Use *vscanf* to do the reading. Write a sample main program to demonstrate the use of the routine.

```
#include <stdio.h>
#include <stdarg.h>
void getinput(char *,...);
main()
{
    int accno;
    double price, discount;
/* Call the input routine to read values of variables.
 * First just a single number. Then more than one
 * value.
 */
    printf("Enter account number:");
    getinput(" %d", &accno);
    printf("\nEnter price and discount(\%) "
           "separated by a space:");
    getinput(" %lf %lf", &price, &discount);
    printf("$%.2f @%.2f%% discount = $%.2f\n", price,
    discount, price*(1.0-discount/100.));
    return 0;
}

/*-----------------------------------------------------*/
/*  getinput: accepts variable number of arguments
```

```
 *                   and reads formatted values
 */
void getinput(char *my_format,...)
{
    va_list arg_pointer;
/* Use va_start macro to get to the start of the
 * variable number of arguments. This will alter the
 * pointer arg_pointer to point to the list of
 * variables to be read.
 */
    va_start(arg_pointer, my_format);
    vscanf(my_format, arg_pointer);
/* Use the va_end macro to reset the arg_pointer */
    va_end(arg_pointer);
}
```

Stream I/O

vsprintf

COMPATIBILITY

TC1	TC1.5	TC2	TC++	MSC3	MSC4	MSC5	MSC6	QC1	QC2	QC2.5	ANSI	UNIX V	XNX
▲	▲	▲	▲	▲	▲	▲	▲	▲	▲	▲	▲	▲	▲

PURPOSE Use *vsprintf* to write formatted output to a string (that is, perform the same function as *sprintf*), except that *vsprintf* uses a pointer to a list of variables rather than the variables themselves. Thus a variable number of arguments can be formatted.

SYNTAX

```
int vsprintf(char *p_string, const char *format_string,
                                    va_list arg_pointer);
```

`char *p_string;` *Pointer to an array of characters where* vsprintf *sends its formatted output*

`const char *format_string;` *Character string that describes the format to be used*

`va_list arg_pointer;` *Pointer to a list containing a variable number of arguments that are being printed*

EXAMPLE CALL

```
vsprintf(err_msg, p_format, p_arg);
```

INCLUDES

`#include <stdio.h>` *For function declaration*

`#include <stdarg.h>` *For definition of va_list*

DESCRIPTION The *vsprintf* function accepts a pointer to a list of a variable number of arguments in *arg_pointer*, prepares a formatted character string, and saves the string in the area of memory whose address is given in the argument *p_string*. In so doing, it functions exactly as *sprintf* does, except that *vsprintf* accepts a pointer. The conversion of a variable's value to a character string is done according to the format string in the argument *format_string*, which is an ordinary text string containing embedded format commands beginning with a percent sign. Detailed information on format specification appears in the reference pages on *printf* (see Tables 16-9, 16-10, 16-11, and 16-12). On return from *vsprintf*, the *p_string* will be a standard C string.

COMMON USES The *vsprintf* function is useful in preparing a string with the values of the arguments in routines that accept variable-length arguments. This string may be used by other output routines (such as *outtext* in the graphics library, which does not have any formatting capability). An example of such a routine would be an error handler that accepts a list of arguments and prints them out in the graphics mode using *outtext*.

RETURNS The *vsprintf* function returns the number of characters it has printed, excluding the terminating null character.

SEE ALSO

`printf`	*For printing to* stdout *and for detailed information on formats*
`vprintf`	*For printing to* stdout *using a pointer to a list of arguments*
`fprintf, vfprintf`	*For formatted printing to a file*
`sprintf`	*For formatted output to a string*
`va_start, va_arg, va_end`	*Macros for accessing variable-length argument lists*

EXAMPLE Write an error handler, conforming to the ANSI C standard, to display error messages using *cputs*. The routine should accept a variable number of arguments, the first of which is a format string followed by one or more arguments, as would be used with *printf*. The routine should then use *vsprintf* to prepare a string with the values of the arguments in the given format. Test the routine with a simple main program.

```
#include <stdio.h>
#include <stdarg.h>              /* ANSI C compatible  */
#include <conio.h>
void error_handler(char *,...);
char filename[80] = "COMMAND.COM";
```

```
main()
{
    int offset = 0x232A;
/* Assume we are already in text mode                          */
    clrscr();                                /* Clear  screen */
    window (10, 10, 70, 15); /*             Define text window*/
    textattr (YELLOW+(RED <<4)); /* Set background to red    */
    clrscr();                      /* clear out text window   */


/* Once a text window is defined all text positions are
 * relative to upper left corner of the window. Notice
 * that this can be used for pop-up menus.
 */
    gotoxy(1,1);                   /* Set text position    */
/* Call the error handler to print an error message.
 * First just a single line. Then a more detailed
 * message with more arguments.
 */
    error_handler("System error\n");
    error_handler("File %s at offset %X\n", filename,
                  offset);
    return 0;
}

/*--------------------------------------------------*/
/*  error_handler: accepts variable number of arguments
 *                 and prints messages
 */
void error_handler(char *my_format,...)
{
    va_list arg_pointer;
    char buffer[80];    /* Buffer for text string */
/* Use va_start macro to get to the start of the
 * variable number of arguments. This will alter the
 * pointer arg_pointer to point to the list of
 * variables to be printed.
 */
    va_start(arg_pointer, my_format);
    vsprintf(buffer, my_format, arg_pointer);
/* Now display the message by calling cputs     */
   cputs (buffer);
   cputs("\r");
/* Use the va_end macro to reset the arg_pointer */
    va_end(arg_pointer);
}
```

Stream I/O

vsscanf

COMPATIBILITY

TC1	TC1.5	TC2	TC++	MSC3	MSC4	MSC5	MSC6	QC1	QC2	QC2.5	ANSI	UNIX V	XNX
▲	▲	▲	▲										

PURPOSE Use *vsscanf* to perform the same function as *sscanf*, i.e., write formatted input from a string, except that *vsscanf* uses a pointer to a list of variables rather than the variables themselves. Thus a variable number of arguments can be read.

SYNTAX

```
int vsscanf(char *p_string, const char *format_string,
                                va_list arg_pointer);
```

`char        *p_string;`	*Pointer to an array of characters from which* vsscanf *gets its formatted input*
`const char *format_string;`	*A character string which describes the format to be used*
`va_list     arg_pointer;`	*Pointer to a list containing a variable number of arguments that are to be read*

EXAMPLE CALL

```
vsscanf(in_buffer, p_format, p_arg);
```

INCLUDES

`#include <stdio.h>`	*For function prototype*
`#include <stdarg.h>`	*For definition of macros such as va_list*

DESCRIPTION The *vsscanf* function accepts a pointer to a list of a variable number of arguments in *arg_pointer* and reads in the values of these arguments from the string whose address is given in the argument *p_string*.

The *vsscanf* function performs the same way as *sscanf* does, except that *vsscanf* accepts a pointer to a list with a variable number of arguments. The conversion of a variable's value from the character string is done according to the format string in the argument *format_string*. The format string is an ordinary text string containing embedded format commands that begin with a percent sign (%). Detailed information on the format specification appears in the reference pages on *scanf*.

RETURNS The *vsscanf* function returns the number of input fields it successfully scanned, converted, and stored. If the terminating null character in the string is reached before all values are read, *vsscanf* returns the constant EOF.

SEE ALSO

`scanf`	*For reading from* stdin *and for detailed information on formats*
`vscanf`	*Reading from* stdin *using a pointer to a list of arguments*
`fscanf, vfscanf`	*For formatted input from a file*
`sscanf`	*For formatted input from a string*
`va_start, va_arg, va_end`	*Macros for accessing variable-length argument lists*

EXAMPLE The *vsscanf* function may be used to read from a string just as *vfscanf* reads from a file. See the example in *vfscanf* for guidance.

Low-level I/O

close

COMPATIBILITY

TC1	TC1.5	TC2	TC++	MSC3	MSC4	MSC5	MSC6	QC1	QC2	QC2.5	ANSI	UNIX V	XNX
▲	▲	▲	▲	▲	▲	▲	▲	▲	▲	▲		▲	▲

PURPOSE Use *close* to close a file specified by a valid handle, an integer returned by a prior call to *open*.

SYNTAX

```
int close(int handle);
```

`int handle;` *Handle of an open file*

EXAMPLE CALL

```
close(handle);
```

INCLUDES `#include <io.h>` *For function declaration*

DESCRIPTION The *close* function closes the file specified by the argument *handle*. The *handle* must be the integer returned by a previous call to the function *open* or *creat*.

RETURNS If the file is successfully closed, *close* returns a 0. Otherwise, it returns a value of −1 to indicate error and sets the global variable *errno* to the constant EBADF, indicating an invalid file handle.

SEE ALSO

`open`	*To open a file for unformatted, unbuffered I/O*
`fopen, fclose`	*File opening and closing for buffered I/O*

EXAMPLE Illustrate the use of *close* by attempting to close a file that is not open. Use *perror* to print the error message returned by the system.

```
#include <stdio.h>
#include <io.h>
main()
{
/* Call close with an invalid file handle. Handles 0
 * thru 4 are in use by stdin, stdout, stderr, stdaux
 * and stdprn. So, let's use handle 5.
 */
    printf("Attempting to close file handle 5...\n");
    if ( close(5) != 0)
    {
        perror("Close failed");
    }
    return 0;
}
```

Low-level I/O

creat

COMPATIBILITY

TC1	TC1.5	TC2	TC++	MSC3	MSC4	MSC5	MSC6	QC1	QC2	QC2.5	ANSI	UNIX V	XNX
▲	▲	▲	▲	▲	▲	▲	▲	▲	▲	▲		▲	▲

PURPOSE Use *creat* to make a new file or truncate an existing file. The file is specified by its name which may include a path specification.

SYNTAX

```
int creat(const char *filename, int pmode);
```

`const char *filename;` *File name and path specification*

`int pmode;` *Permission settings for the file, indicating whether reading, writing, or both are permitted*

EXAMPLE CALL

```
handle = creat("temp.dat", S_IREAD|S_IWRITE);
```

INCLUDES

`#include <io.h>` *For function declaration*

`#include <sys\types.h>` *For definition of data types used in <sys\stat.h>*

`#include <sys\stat.h>` *For definition of constants to specify permission settings of a file*

DESCRIPTION The *creat* function first checks whether the file named *filename* exists. If it does, the file is truncated, opened for writing and the previous contents of the file are destroyed. If the file does not exist, a new one is created. The argument *filename* includes the directory specification as well as the name of the file. If no directory specification is present, the file is created in the current working directory. Thus if the *filename* is *"c:\\temp\\test.dat"* the file is created in directory \TEMP of drive C, even if the current directory is something else.

The integer argument *pmode* specifies the newly created file's permission setting, which is applied to the file when it is closed. The permission setting is given in terms of predefined constants. The permission settings given in *pmode* are validated against the current default settings defined by *umask*. Consult the reference pages on *umask* for this validation process. The possible values of *pmode* are given in Table 16-16.

RETURNS If the file is successfully created (or truncated), *creat* returns a valid handle to the file. In case of error, it returns a −1 and sets the global variable *errno* to one of the constants defined in the file *errno.h*. These are defined in the table below.

Error Constant	Meaning
EACCES	Cannot access file. This means the given file name refers to a directory, or the file is read only, or file-sharing is enabled and sharing mode does not allow the operation being attempted.
EMFILE	No more file handles available. This means you have hit the MS-DOS enforced limit of 20 files that a single process can open simultaneously.
ENOENT	File was not found or a directory corresponding to the path specification in the file name is nonexistent.

COMMENTS The function of *creat* is provided by *open* with the flags O_CREAT and O_TRUNC.

SEE ALSO

`open` *To open a file for unformatted, unbuffered I/O*

`umask` *To specify default permission setting*

EXAMPLE Write a C program that prompts the user for a file name and then uses *creat* to open that file with both read and write permission settings. Use *perror* to inform the user of errors.

```
#include <stdio.h>
#include <sys\types.h>
#include <sys\stat.h>
```

```
#include <io.h>

main()
{
    int handle;
    unsigned char filename[81];

/* Ask user for file name */
    printf("Enter name of file to be created: ");
    gets(filename);
    if ( (handle = creat(filename, S_IREAD|S_IWRITE))
          == -1)
    {
        perror("Error creating file!");
    }
    else
    {
        printf("\nFile %s created\n", filename);
    }
    return 0;
}
```

Low-level I/O

creatnew

COMPATIBILITY

TC1	TC1.5	TC2	TC++	MSC3	MSC4	MSC5	MSC6	QC1	QC2	QC2.5	ANSI	UNIX V	XNX
▲	▲	▲	▲										

PURPOSE Use the *creatnew* function, in MS-DOS versions 3.0 or later, to create a new file with specified attributes.

SYNTAX

```
int creatnew(const char *path, int attribute);
```

`const char *path;` *The pathname of the file to be created*

`int attribute;` *The MS-DOS file attributes for the new file*

EXAMPLE CALL

```
if((handle = creatnew("temp.dat", 0)) == -1)
     perror("Error in creatnew");
```

INCLUDES

`#include <io.h>` *For function prototype*

`#include <dos.h>` *For names of MS-DOS file attributes*

DESCRIPTION The *creatnew* function creates a new file with the pathname provided in the argument *path* provided that a file with the same pathname does not already exist. The new file will have the file attributes specified in the argument *attribute*. The attribute indicates whether a file is read only, whether it is hidden, and so on. You can specify the attribute by using the bitwise OR of attribute names picked from Table 17-21. The attribute constants are defined in *dos.h*. Note that specifying 0 as the *attribute* creates a normal file.

COMMON USES You can use *creatnew* to create new files, but *open* or *fopen* are more portable ways of doing this.

RETURNS Once the file is successfully created, an identifying number or "handle" is returned. You should save this handle because you will need it for future references to this file. In case of error, it returns a −1 and sets the global variable *errno* to one of the constants shown in the Table 17-22. The meaning of the error code is explained in the table.

COMMENTS The *creatnew* function is identical to *_creat* except that unlike *_creat*, *creatnew* returns an error if a file with the same name already exists.

SEE ALSO

`_creat` *To create a file (destroys existing file)*

`fopen` *ANSI function to open or create a file*

`open` *Also opens and creates files*

EXAMPLE Illustrate the use of *creatnew* in a program. Notice that we use the global variable *_osmajor* to determine whether the program is running under the appropriate version of DOS.

```
#include <stdio.h>
#include <dos.h>
#include <io.h>
extern unsigned char _osmajor;
main()
{
    int handle;
    char filename[60];
    if(_osmajor < 3)
    {
        printf("'creatnew' needs DOS version 3.0"
               " or higher\n");
        exit(0);
    }
```

```
    printf("Enter name of file to be created: ");
    gets(filename);
/* Call 'creatnew' to create the file. Mode 0 means
 * a normal file.
 */
    if((handle = creatnew(filename, 0)) == -1)
          perror("Error in creatnew");
    else  printf("File %s created\n", filename);
    return 0;
}
```

Low-level I/O

creattemp

COMPATIBILITY

TC1	TC1.5	TC2	TC++	MSC3	MSC4	MSC5	MSC6	QC1	QC2	QC2.5	ANSI	UNIX V	XNX
▲	▲	▲	▲										

PURPOSE Use the *creattemp* function, in MS-DOS versions 3.0 or later, to create a temporary file in a given directory with specified attributes.

SYNTAX

```
int creattemp(char *path, int attribute);
```

`char *path;` *The pathname of the directory where the temporary file will be created*

`int attribute;` *The MS-DOS file attributes for the new file*

EXAMPLE CALL

```
if((handle = creattemp("c:\\tmp", 0)) == -1)
        perror("Error in creattemp");
```

INCLUDES

`#include <io.h>` *For function prototype*

`#include <dos.h>` *For names of MS-DOS file attributes*

DESCRIPTION The *creattemp* function prepares a unique file name and creates a file with that name in the directory given in the argument *path*. The new file will be created with the file attributes given in the argument *attribute* and opened in the translation mode (see tutorial section) specified by the global variable *_fmode*. The attribute indicates whether a file is read only, whether it is hidden, and so on. You can specify the attribute by using the bitwise OR of attribute names picked from Table 17-21. The attribute constants are defined in *dos.h*. Note that specifying 0 as the *attribute* creates a normal file.

The name of the file is copied by *creattemp* into the buffer *path*. You can use this information to delete the file when you no longer need it.

COMMON USES You can use *creattemp* to create temporary files, but *tmpfile* is the ANSI standard method of doing this.

RETURNS Once the file is successfully created, an identifying number or "handle" is returned. You should save this handle because you will need it for future references to this file. In case of error, it returns a −1 and sets the global variable *errno* to one of the constants shown in the Table 17-22. The meaning of the error code is explained in the table.

SEE ALSO `tmpfile` *To open a temporary file (ANSI standard)*

EXAMPLE Illustrate the use of *creattemp* in a program. Use the global variable *_osmajor* to make sure that the program is running under DOS versions 3.0 or higher. Note that the temporary file is not automatically deleted when the program ends. You have to delete it yourself.

```
#include <stdio.h>
#include <dos.h>
#include <io.h>
extern unsigned char _osmajor;
main()
{
    int handle;
    char dirname[60];
    if(_osmajor < 3)
    {
        printf("'creattemp' needs DOS version 3.0"
               " or higher\n");
        exit(0);
    }
    printf("Enter name of directory where the "
           "temporary file will be created: ");
    gets(dirname);
/* Call 'creattemp' to create the file. Mode 0 means
 * a normal file.
 */
    if((handle = creattemp(dirname, 0)) == -1)
          perror("Error in creattemp");
    else  printf("Temporary file %s created.\nRemember "
                 "to delete it.\n", dirname);
    return 0;
}
```

Low-level I/O

dup

COMPATIBILITY

TC1	TC1.5	TC2	TC++	MSC3	MSC4	MSC5	MSC6	QC1	QC2	QC2.5	ANSI	UNIX V	XNX
▲	▲	▲	▲	▲	▲	▲	▲	▲	▲	▲		▲	▲

PURPOSE Use *dup* to create a second handle for a file that is already open and has a valid handle.

SYNTAX

```
int dup(int handle);

int handle;        Handle of an open file
```

EXAMPLE CALL

```
new_handle = dup(old_handle);
```

INCLUDES

```
#include <io.h>        For function declaration
```

DESCRIPTION The *dup* function assigns another handle to a file that is already open and has a valid handle. The current handle must be given in the argument *handle*. The creation of a duplicate handle counts as a new open file and is subject to the 20-file limit imposed by MS-DOS.

COMMON USES In UNIX systems, *dup* is used to perform I/O with an interprocess communication mechanism called "pipes."

RETURNS If a new handle is successfully created, *dup* returns the duplicate handle. Otherwise, it returns a value of −1 to indicate error and sets the global variable *errno* to either EMFILE, if no more file handles are possible, or to EBADF, indicating that the argument *handle* is not a valid file handle.

SEE ALSO

`open` *To open a file for unformatted, unbuffered I/O*

`creat` *To create a new file and open it for unformatted, unbuffered I/O*

EXAMPLE Create a new handle for *stdout* that is assigned the handle 1 when the program starts running. Write a string to the new handle to show that indeed the new handle refers to stdout.

```
#include <stdio.h>
#include <io.h>
char message[] =
"Testing dup. This should appear on stdout\n";
main()
{
```

```
    int newhandle;
/* By default, stdout has handle 1.
 * create another handle for stdout
 */
    if((newhandle = dup(1)) == -1)
    {
            perror("dup on handle 1 failed!");
    }
    else
    {
            printf("New handle for stdout is %d\n", newhandle);
            write(newhandle, message, sizeof(message));
    }
    return 0;
}
```

Low-level I/O

dup2

COMPATIBILITY

TC1	TC1.5	TC2	TC++	MSC3	MSC4	MSC5	MSC6	QC1	QC2	QC2.5	ANSI	UNIX V	XNX
▲	▲	▲	▲	▲	▲	▲	▲	▲	▲	▲		▲	▲

PURPOSE Use *dup2* to force a second file handle to refer to the same file as a first one. The first handle must be a valid one, associated with a file that is already open.

SYNTAX

```
int dup2(int handle1, int handle2);
```

`int handle1;` *Handle of an open file*

`int handle2;` *Another handle that will become associated with the same file as* handle1

EXAMPLE CALL

```
dup2(oldhandle, newhandle);
```

INCLUDES `#include <io.h>` *For function declaration*

DESCRIPTION The *dup2* function forces *handle2* to refer to the same file as *handle1*, a valid handle to a file that is currently open. If *handle2* also refers to an open file, that file is closed and *handle2* is then assigned to the file associated with *handle1*. After successful return from *dup2*, either handle may be used to refer to the file.

COMMON USES The *dup2* function is used to redirect the standard input and output streams, *stdin* and *stdout.*

RETURNS If *handle2* is successfully assigned to the file associated with *handle1, dup2* returns a 0. Otherwise, it returns a −1 to indicate error and sets the global variable *errno* to either EMFILE if no more file handles are possible or to the constant EBADF, indicating that *handle1* is not a valid file handle.

SEE ALSO

`open` *To open a file for unformatted, unbuffered I/O*

`creat` *To create a new file and open it for unformatted, unbuffered I/O*

EXAMPLE Use *dup2* to write a program that redirects *stdout* to a file of your choice. Open a file and use *dup2* to assign *handle1* (the usual handle for *stdout*) to the newly opened file (use the macro *fileno* to find this). Now write some messages to *stdout* and they should go to the file. Remember to flush the buffers, close the file, and reassign handle 1 to *stdout.*

```
#include <stdio.h>
#include <io.h>
main()
{
    int saved_handle;
    char filename[81];
    FILE *new_stdout;
/* Ask for filename to which stdout will be assigned */
    printf("Enter filename to which stdout will be \
assigned:");

    gets(filename);
    if((new_stdout = fopen(filename, "w")) == NULL)
    {
            perror("fopen failed");
            exit(1);
    }
/* First duplicate the handle for stdout so that we can
 * reset things at the end
 */
    if((saved_handle = dup(1)) == -1)
    {
            perror("dup failed on handle 1!");
            exit(1);
    }
/* Get the handle of the new file using 'fileno' and
 * assign handle 1 (stdout) to it by calling dup2
```

```
*/
    if(dup2(fileno(new_stdout), 1) == -1)
    {
            perror("dup2 failed to assign handle 1!");
    }
    else
    {
            printf("New handle for stdout is %d\n",
                fileno(new_stdout));
        printf("Testing dup2. \
This should be in file: %s\n", filename);
/* Flush to send output to open file */
        fflush(stdout);
/* Reassign stdout to handle 1 before exiting */
        fclose(new_stdout);
        dup2(saved_handle, 1);
        printf("Enter 'TYPE %s' to see result\n",
                filename);
    }
    return 0;
}
```

Low-level I/O

eof

COMPATIBILITY

TC1	TC1.5	TC2	TC++	MSC3	MSC4	MSC5	MSC6	QC1	QC2	QC2.5	ANSI	UNIX V	XNX
▲	▲	▲	▲	▲	▲	▲	▲	▲	▲	▲			

PURPOSE Use the *eof* function to determine whether end-of-file has been reached in a file specified by its handle.

SYNTAX `int eof(int handle);`

`int handle;` *Handle of an open file*

EXAMPLE CALL `if(eof(handle) != 0) printf("File ended!\n");`

INCLUDES `#include <io.h>` *For function declaration*

DESCRIPTION The *eof* function checks whether the file specified by the argument *handle* is at the end-of-file. The analogous function for stream I/O is *feof*. Many low-level I/O routines return a −1 to indicate an error. Since low-level I/O routines are used primarily to read binary data and a data byte could very well contain a −1 (FF in hexadecimal), a function such as *eof* is necessary to determine if the file actually ended or you simply read a byte containing the value −1.

RETURNS For a valid file handle, *eof* returns a 1 to indicate an end-of-file and a 0 when not. If the specified file handle is invalid, it returns a −1 and sets the global variable *errno* to the constant EBADF.

SEE ALSO `feof, ferror` *To determine end-of-file and error conditions for files opened for buffered I/O*

EXAMPLE Write a program that opens up the file *autoexec.bat* in the root directory of drive C and reads it, 80 bytes at a time, until end-of-file is reached. Use the *eof* function to test for end-of-file. Display the data read.

```
#include <stdio.h>
#include <io.h>
#include <fcntl.h>
main()
{
    int fhandle, total=0, count;
    unsigned char buffer[80];
/* Open the file "autoexec.bat." Note the two '\'  */
    if ( (fhandle = open("c:\\autoexec.bat",
                         O_RDONLY)) == -1)
    {
           printf("open failed");
                  exit(1);
    }
    printf("Contents of c:autoexec.bat:\n");
    while ( !eof(fhandle))          /* Read until EOF */
    {
           if ((count = read(fhandle, buffer, 80)) == -1)
           {
               perror("read error");
               break;   /* exit from while loop */
           }
           total += count;
           write(1, buffer, count);
    }
    printf("=== %d bytes read ===\n", total);
    return 0;
}
```

Low-level I/O

COMPATIBILITY

lseek

TC1	TC1.5	TC2	TC++	MSC3	MSC4	MSC5	MSC6	QC1	QC2	QC2.5	ANSI	UNIX V	XNX
▲	▲	▲	▲	▲	▲	▲	▲	▲	▲	▲		▲	▲

PURPOSE Use the *lseek* function to move to a new position in a file opened for unbuffered and unformatted I/O.

SYNTAX

```
long lseek(int handle, long offset, int origin);
```

`int handle;`	*Handle associated with file whose current position is to be set*
`long offset;`	*Offset of new position (in bytes) from origin*
`int origin;`	*Constant indicating the position from which to offset*

EXAMPLE CALL

```
lseek(fhandle, 512L, SEEK_SET); /* Skip 512 bytes */
```

INCLUDES

`#include <stdio.h>`	*For definition of constants used to specify "origin"*
`#include <io.h>`	*For function declaration*

DESCRIPTION The *lseek* function sets the current read or write position of the file specified by the argument *handle* to a new value indicated by the arguments *offset* and *origin.* The *offset* is a long integer indicating how far away the new position is from a specific location given in *origin.* The *origin,* defined in *stdio.h*, must be one of the constants shown in the following table.

The file position may be set anywhere in the file except before the beginning of the file.

Origin	Interpretation
SEEK_SET	Beginning of file
SEEK_CUR	Current position in the file
SEEK_END	End of file

COMMON USES The *lseek* function is used when reading unformatted data from files in a random manner. For example, an application may create a data file with a specific format, say, a header of 512 bytes followed by actual data. When reading from such a file, you can use *lseek* to jump over the header and retrieve specific pieces of information with *read.*

RETURNS When successful, *lseek* returns the offset of the current position from the beginning of the file. In case of error, the return value is −1 and the global variable *errno* is set to either EBADF, indicating that the file handle is invalid, or to EINVAL if an attempt is made to set position before the beginning of the file. If the handle is associated with a device for which setting the current position does not make sense, the return value is meaningless.

SEE ALSO

`tell` *To get the offset of the current position in a file in number of bytes from the beginning*

`fseek` *Counterpart of* lseek *for files opened for buffered I/O*

EXAMPLE Open a file, *autoexec.bat*, in your system and go to the end of the file using *lseek* with SEEK_END as origin. Report the value returned by *lseek*. This is the size of the file in bytes. Now move back 20 bytes and read the last 20 bytes in the file. Display the characters read.

```
#include <stdio.h>
#include <io.h>
#include <fcntl.h>
main()
{
    int fhandle, count;
    long curpos;
    unsigned char buffer[20];
/* Open the file "autoexec.bat." */
    if ( (fhandle = open("c:\\autoexec.bat",
                    O_RDONLY)) == -1)
    {
           printf("open failed");
                      exit(1);
    }
/* Go to end of file using "lseek" and SEEK_END */
    curpos = lseek(fhandle, 0L, SEEK_END);
    printf("End of file in 'autoexec.bat' is %ld bytes \
from beginning\n", curpos);
/* Move back 20 bytes, read the last 20 bytes
 * and print the characters that were read in.
 */
    lseek(fhandle, -20L, SEEK_CUR);
    if ((count = read(fhandle, buffer, 20)) == -1)
    {
           perror("read error");
           exit(1);
```

```
    }
    printf("The last 20 characters in 'autoexec.bat' are:\n");
    write(1, buffer, count);
    return 0;
}
```

Low-level I/O

open

COMPATIBILITY

TC1	TC1.5	TC2	TC++	MSC3	MSC4	MSC5	MSC6	QC1	QC2	QC2.5	ANSI	UNIX V	XNX
▲	▲	▲	▲	▲	▲	▲	▲	▲	▲	▲		▲	▲

PURPOSE Before performing any read or write operations, use *open* to open a file for unbuffered and unformatted I/O operations.

SYNTAX

```
int open(const char *filename, int oflag [, unsigned pmode]);
```

`const char *filename;`	*Name of file to be opened, including drive and directory specification*
`int oflag;`	*Integer formed by bitwise OR of predefined constants that indicate the types of operations allowed on that file*
`unsigned;`	*Optional argument to specify whether reading, writing, or both are permitted*

EXAMPLE CALL

```
filehandle = open("temp.dat", O_WRONLY|O_CREAT, S_IWRITE);
```

INCLUDES

`#include <io.h>`	*For function declaration*
`#include <fcntl.h>`	*For definition of constants to indicate valid operations*
`#include <sys\types.h>`	*For definition of data types used in <sys\stat.h>*
`#include <sys\stat.h>`	*For definition of constants to specify permission settings of a file*

DESCRIPTION The *open* function opens the file specified in the argument *filename*. The type of operations you intend to perform on the file once it is opened must be indicated by the argument *oflag*. This is an integer formed by the bitwise OR of the constants shown in Table 16-15. The constants are defined in the include file *fcntl.h*.

Table 16-15. *Constants Indicating Type of Operations Allowed on File*

Constant	Interpretation
O_APPEND	Writing always occurs at the end of the file.
O_BINARY	File is opened in the binary, or untranslated, mode. This is the same binary mode used with *fopen*; see its reference pages for more explanation.
O_CREAT	Creates and opens a file for writing if the named file does not exist.
O_EXCL	Returns an error value if file already exists and O_CREAT was specified.
O_RDONLY	File is opened for reading only. When O_RDONLY is given, O_WRONLY and O_RDWR are disallowed.
O_RDWR	File is opened for both reading and writing. When O_RDWR is given, O_RDONLY and O_WRONLY are disallowed.
O_TEXT	File is opened in text, or translated, mode. This is the same text mode used with *fopen*; see its reference pages for elaboration.
O_TRUNC	Opens an existing file and truncates it to zero length, destroying its current contents. The file must have write permission for this to succeed.
O_WRONLY	File is opened for writing only. When O_WRONLY is used, O_RDONLY and O_RDWR are not allowed.

The third argument to *open*, *pmode*, you need only when requesting the creation of a new file by using the flag O_CREAT. If the file does not exist, the value of *pmode* is used to set the permission of the newly created file. Table 16-16 shows the possible values of the argument *pmode*. These constants are defined in the header file *sys\stat.h*. As you can see in the table, a file in MS-DOS always has read permission. The permission setting indicated by the *pmode* argument is modified by the permission mask that you can set with *umask*. Consult its reference pages to see how this is done.

Table 16-16. *Permission Settings for Newly Created Files*

Constant	Interpretation
S_IWRITE	Both reading and writing permitted.
S_IREAD	Only reading permitted.
S_IREAD ¦ S_IWRITE	Both reading and writing permitted.

Microsoft warns users of a bug under MS-DOS versions 3.0 and above that can occur when file-sharing is enabled. The sharing is enabled by executing SHARE.EXE, which comes with these versions of MS-DOS. Once this is done and a file is opened with *oflag* set to O_CREAT¦O_READONLY or O_CREAT¦O_WRONLY, DOS prematurely

closes the file during any system calls made within *open*. The suggested remedy is to open the file with *pmode* equal to S_IWRITE. Then, after closing the file you can call *chmod* to change the permission back to *S_IREAD*. Another remedy is to open the file with *pmode* set to S_IREAD and *oflag* equal to O_CREAT¦O_RDWR.

COMMON USES The *open* function is used to open a file before performing any unbuffered and unformatted I/O (see the tutorial section) operations on it.

RETURNS If the file is successfully opened, *open* returns the file handle, an integer to be used in subsequent I/O operations on the file using the functions *read* and *write*. In case of an error, *open* returns a −1. At the same time, the global variable *errno* is set to one of the constants shown in Table 16-17 and defined in *errno.h*.

Table 16-17. *Error Codes Returned by* open

Error Constant	Meaning of Error Value
EACCES	Cannot access file. This means the file name refers to a directory, or an attempt was made to open a read-only file for write operations, or file-sharing is enabled and sharing mode does not allow the operation being attempted.
EEXIST	This error is returned when the flags O_CREAT and O_EXCL are specified but the file already exists.
EMFILE	No more file handles available. This means you have hit the MS-DOS 20-file limit that a single process can open simultaneously.
ENOENT	File was not found or a directory corresponding to the path specification in the file name is nonexistent.

SEE ALSO `close` *To close a file opened by* open

`fopen` *To open a file for buffered I/O*

EXAMPLE Write a program that prompts for a file name and opens that file for write operations. Use the O_CREAT and the O_EXCL operation flags to ensure that an existing file is not destroyed.

```
#include <stdio.h>
#include <io.h>
#include <fcntl.h>
#include <sys\types.h>
#include <sys\stat.h>

main()
```

```
{
    int handle;
    char filename[81];
    printf("Enter name of a file to open: ");
    gets(filename);
/* Open the file for write operations.
 * Don't overwrite existing file.
 */
    if ((handle = open(filename, O_WRONLY¦O_CREAT¦O_EXCL,
                  S_IREAD¦S_IWRITE))  == -1)
    {
/* Use perror to print the message so that we also see
 * the error message corresponding to the value of
 * 'errno'
 */
            perror("Open failed! ");
    }
    else
    {
            printf("File %s opened successfully\n",filename);
/* In an actual program we will use the file for I/O.
 * Here we simply exit.
 */
    }
    return 0;
}
```

Low-level I/O

read

COMPATIBILITY

TC1	TC1.5	TC2	TC++	MSC3	MSC4	MSC5	MSC6	QC1	QC2	QC2.5	ANSI	UNIX V	XNX
▲	▲	▲	▲	▲	▲	▲	▲	▲	▲	▲		▲	▲

PURPOSE Use *read* to retrieve a specified number of bytes of data, without any formatting, from the current position in a file that has been opened for unformatted I/O.

SYNTAX `int read(int handle, char *buffer, unsigned count);`

`int handle;` *Handle of file from which data will be read*

`char *buffer;` *Pointer to buffer into which data will be copied*

`unsigned count;` *Number of bytes to be read*

EXAMPLE CALL

```
if ((bytes_read = read(fhandle, bigbuffer, 60000)) == -1)
                    perror("read error");
```

INCLUDES

```
#include <io.h>        For function declaration
```

DESCRIPTION The *read* function copies the number of bytes specified in the argument *count* from the file whose handle is in the integer argument *handle* to the array of characters, *buffer*. Reading starts at the current position, which is incremented when the operation is completed. If the file is opened in the text mode, each CR-LF pair read from the file is replaced by a newline character in the *buffer*, and a Control-Z is character interpreted as end-of-file.

RETURNS The *read* function returns the number of bytes actually read from the file. In case of an error, *read* returns −1 and sets *errno* to EBADF to indicate an invalid file handle or that the file was not opened for writing. In MS-DOS 3.0 and higher, read errors may occur due to a locked file.

COMMENTS Since *read* returns a signed integer, the return value should be converted to *unsigned int* when reading more than 32 K of data from a file or the return value will be negative. Because the number of bytes to be read is specified in an unsigned integer argument, you could theoretically read 65,535 bytes at a time. But, 65,535 (or FFFFh) also means −1 in signed representation so when reading 65,535 bytes the return value indicates an error. The practical maximum then is 65,534.

SEE ALSO

`creat, open, sopen` *To create and open new files for unformatted I/O*

`write` *To write a specified number of bytes to a file*

EXAMPLE Write a program that opens a file, say, "autoexec.bat," in the root directory of drive C, reads 60,000 bytes from it, and displays the number of bytes read. Compile the program using the large model (-ml option).

```
#include <stdio.h>
#include <io.h>
#include <fcntl.h>
static char bigbuffer[60000];
main()
{
        int fhandle;
        int bytes_read;

/* Open the file "autoexec.bat." Note that we need two '\'  */
        if ( (fhandle = open("c:autoexec.bat",
```

```
                                            O_RDONLY)) == -1)
        {
            printf("open failed");
            exit(1);
        }
        printf(
        "Attempting to read 60000 bytes from c:autoexec.bat:\n");
        if ((bytes_read = read(fhandle, bigbuffer, 60000)) == -1)
        {
            perror("read error");
            exit(1);
        }
        printf("Only %u bytes read. Here's what was read:\n",
                bytes_read);
        write(1, bigbuffer, bytes_read);
        return 0;
}
```

Low-level I/O

sopen

COMPATIBILITY

TC1	TC1.5	TC2	TC++	MSC3	MSC4	MSC5	MSC6	QC1	QC2	QC2.5	ANSI	UNIX V	XNX
▲	▲	▲	▲	▲	▲	▲	▲	▲	▲	▲			

PURPOSE Use *sopen* to open a file for shared, unbuffered, and unformatted I/O operations. File-sharing is ignored if SHARE.EXE has not been run. Note that SHARE.EXE (or SHARE.COM), commands that facilitate use of MS-DOS systems in local area networks, is present only in MS-DOS versions 3.0 and higher.

SYNTAX

```
int sopen(char *filename, int oflag, int shflag, unsigned pmode);
```

`char *filename;` *Name of file to be opened, including drive and directory specification*

`int oflag;` *Integer formed by bitwise OR of predefined constants that indicate the types of operations allowed on file being opened*

`int shflag;` *Integer formed by bitwise OR of predefined constants that indicate the modes of sharing to be enabled*

`unsigned pmode;` *Argument to specify whether reading, writing, or both are permitted*

EXAMPLE CALL

```
fhandle = sopen("c:\\autoexec.bat", O_RDONLY, SH_DENYRW);
```

INCLUDES

`#include <io.h>`	*For function declaration*
`#include <share.h>`	*For definition of constants to indicate modes of sharing*
`#include <fcntl.h>`	*For definition of constants to indicate valid operations*
`#include <sys\types.h>`	*For definition of data types used in <sys\stat.h>*
`#include <sys\stat.h>`	*For definition of constants to specify permission settings of a file*

DESCRIPTION

The *sopen* function opens the file specified in the argument *filename*. The type of operations you intend to perform on the file once it is opened must be indicated by the argument *oflag*, an integer formed by the bitwise OR of constants shown in Table 16-15. The constants are defined in the include file *fcntl.h*.

The argument *shflag* is used to specify the level of sharing enabled. It is specified by bitwise OR of an appropriate combination of constants defined in the file *share.h* and shown in Table 16-18. The argument is ignored if you have not enabled file-sharing by running SHARE.EXE (or SHARE.COM).

Table 16-18. ***Constants That Indicate Level of File-Sharing***

Constant	Interpretation
SH_COMPAT	No other process is allowed to access the file. This is called the "compatibility mode" and the same process can open the file any number of times in this mode. This is how DOS normally operates, hence the name.
SH_DENYRW	A single process has exclusive read and write access to the file. The process must close the file before opening it again.
SH_DENYWR	No other process can access the file for writing.
SH_DENYRD	No other process can access the file for reading.
SH_DENYNO	Any process may access the file for both reading and for writing.

The last argument to *sopen*, *pmode*, is necessary only when requesting the creation of a new file by the flag O_CREAT. If the file does not already exist, the value of *pmode* is used to set the permission of the newly created file. Table 16-16 shows the various values of the argument *pmode*. As you can see in Table 16-16, an MS-DOS file always has read permission. The permission setting indicated by the *pmode* argument is modified by the permission mask set by calling *umask*. Consult the reference pages on *umask* to see how this is done. These *pmode* constants are defined in the header file *sys\stat.h*.

Microsoft warns users of a bug under MS-DOS versions 3.0 and above that can occur when opening a file with *sopen* with file-sharing enabled. File-sharing is enabled by executing SHARE.EXE which comes with these versions of MS-DOS. Once this is done and a file is opened with *oflag* set to O_CREAT¦O_READONLY or O_CREAT¦O_WRONLY and *sh_flag* set to SH_COMPAT, DOS prematurely closes the file during any system calls made within *sopen* or it will generate a "sharing violation" interrupt (number 24h). The suggested remedy is to sopen the file with *pmode* set to S_IWRITE. Then, after closing the file you can call *chmod* to change the permission back to S_IREAD. Another remedy is to sopen the file with *pmode* set to S_IREAD and *oflag* equal to O_CREAT¦O_RDWR and *shflag* set to SH_COMPAT.

COMMON USES The *sopen* function is used to open files for sharing in networks. It works in the same way as *open* except that it can also specify the level of file-sharing allowed.

RETURNS If the file is successfully opened, *sopen* returns the file handle, an integer to be used in subsequent I/O operations on the file using the functions *read* and *write*. In case of an error, *sopen* returns a −1. At the same time, the global variable *errno* is set to one of the constants shown in Table 16-17 and defined in *errno.h*.

COMMENTS File-sharing modes work properly only with unbuffered files. So you should not call *fdopen* to associate a FILE data structure and enable buffering for a file opened by *sopen*.

SEE ALSO

`close` *To close a file opened by* sopen

`fopen` *To open a file for buffered I/O*

EXAMPLE If you are running MS-DOS version 3.0 or higher, install file-sharing by typing SHARE to run the program SHARE.EXE distributed with DOS. Now open a file, *autoexec.bat*, by calling *sopen* with the "share flag" equal to SH_DENYRW. Try to open the file once more. If it fails, you have not installed file-sharing. On the other hand, if SHARE has been run, this second call will fail because the file is already open and no one has permission to read or write (not even the same process!).

```
#include <stdio.h>
#include <io.h>
#include <fcntl.h>
```

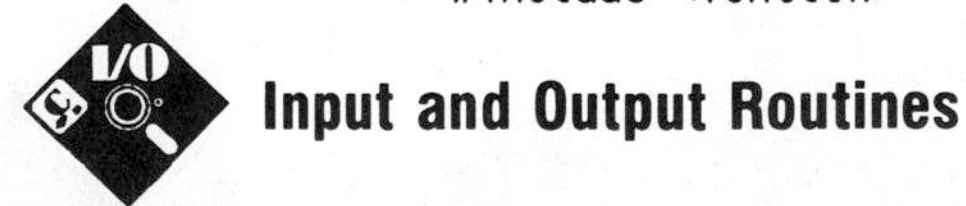

```
#include <share.h>
#include <sys\stat.h>
main()
{
    int fhandle1, fhandle2;

/* Open the file "autoexec.bat." */
    if ( (fhandle1 = sopen("c:\\autoexec.bat",
                      O_RDONLY, SH_DENYRW, S_IREAD)) == -1)
    {
           perror("open failed");
           exit(1);
    }
    printf("AUTOEXEC.BAT opened once. Handle = %d\n",
             fhandle1);
/* Now open again */
    if ( (fhandle2 = sopen("c:autoexec.bat",
                      O_RDONLY, SH_DENYRW, S_IREAD)) == -1)
    {
           perror("open failed");
           printf("SHARE installed\n");
           exit(1);
    }
    printf("AUTOEXEC.BAT opened again. Handle = %d\n",
             fhandle2);

    printf("SHARE has not been installed\n");
    return 0;
}
```

Low-level I/O

COMPATIBILITY

tell

TC1	TC1.5	TC2	TC++	MSC3	MSC4	MSC5	MSC6	QC1	QC2	QC2.5	ANSI	UNIX V	XNX
▲	▲	▲	▲	▲	▲	▲	▲	▲	▲	▲			

PURPOSE Use *tell* to determine the current position in a file specified by its handle.

SYNTAX

```
long tell(int handle);
```

`int handle;` *Handle of an open file*

EXAMPLE CALL

```
curpos = tell(filehandle);
```

INCLUDES `#include <io.h>` *For function declaration*

DESCRIPTION The *tell* function returns the current position in the file specified by the argument *handle*. The position is returned as the number of bytes from the beginning of the file.

RETURNS For a valid file handle, *tell* returns the current position as a long integer value containing the byte offset of the current location in the file from its beginning. If the specified file handle is invalid, it returns a −1 and sets the global variable *errno* to the constant EBADF. If the handle refers to a device for which the file position cannot be set arbitrarily, the value returned by *tell* is meaningless.

SEE ALSO `lseek` *To set the current position in a file opened for unformatted I/O*

`ftell` *Counterpart of* tell *for files opened for buffered I/O*

EXAMPLE Write a program that opens a file and uses *tell* to report the current position in the file. Now read 80 bytes from the file using *read*. Check and report the position again after the read.

```
#include <stdio.h>
#include <io.h>
#include <fcntl.h>
main()
{
    int fhandle, count;
    long curpos;
    unsigned char buffer[80];
/* Open the file "autoexec.bat." */
    if ( (fhandle = open("c:\\autoexec.bat",
                               O_RDONLY)) == -1)
    {
           printf("open failed");
           exit(1);
    }
/* Display current position using "tell" */
    curpos = tell(fhandle);
    printf("Currently at position %ld \
in 'autoexec.bat'\n", curpos);
/* Now read 80 bytes and check position again */
    if ((count = read(fhandle, buffer, 80)) == -1)
    {
           perror("read error");
           exit(1);
```

```
    }
    printf("Read following 80 characters:\n");
    write(1, buffer, count);
    curpos = tell(fhandle);
    printf("\nNow at position: %ld bytes from beginning\n",
               curpos);
    return 0;
}
```

Low-level I/O

write

COMPATIBILITY

TC1	TC1.5	TC2	TC++	MSC3	MSC4	MSC5	MSC6	QC1	QC2	QC2.5	ANSI	UNIX V	XNX
▲	▲	▲	▲	▲	▲	▲	▲	▲	▲	▲		▲	▲

PURPOSE Use *write* to save a specified number of bytes of data, without any formatting, at the current position in a file opened for unformatted I/O.

SYNTAX

```
int write(int handle, char *buffer, unsigned count);
```

`int handle;`	*Handle of file to which data will be written*
`char *buffer;`	*Pointer to array of characters representing data to be written*
`unsigned count;`	*Number of bytes to be written*

EXAMPLE CALL

```
write(handle, data_buffer, 1024);
```

INCLUDES

```
#include <io.h>
```

For function declaration

DESCRIPTION In a file opened by a call to *open* for writing or appending, the *write* function copies the number of bytes specified in the argument *count* from the array at *buffer* to the file whose handle is in the integer argument *handle*. The writing of the data begins at the current position in the file and the current position is appropriately incremented after writing out the data. If the file is opened for appending, the writing will always take place at the end of the file.

If the file is opened in text mode, each newline character in the data is replaced by a CR-LF pair in the file. Note that *write* treats a Control-Z character as the logical end-of-file.

RETURNS The *write* function returns the number of bytes actually written to the file. If, for example, the disk space runs out before all the data is written, the return value may be something less than *count.* A return value of −1 indicates an error. The value in the global variable *errno* will contain an error code; if it is equal to the constant EBADF, the error was caused by giving an invalid file handle. If the file is not opened for writing, *errno* is set to the constant EACCES.

COMMENTS When writing more than 32 K of data to a file, you receive the value returned by *write* in an *unsigned int* variable; otherwise an *int* shows a negative value. A consequence of returning a −1 to indicate error is that you can write no more than 65,534 bytes to a file at a time and still be able to tell if an error has occurred because 65,535 (or FFFF in hexadecimal) is also the representation of −1 in the microprocessor.

SEE ALSO

`creat, open, sopen`	*To create and open new files for unformatted I/O*
`read`	*To read a specified number of bytes from a file*

EXAMPLE Open a file for write operations and write a large number of bytes to the file. Report the value returned by *write.* Initialize the buffer to be written with a test message that ends with a Control-Z (\032) so you can type the file with the TYPE command and have the printing stop after that because it interprets Control-Z as the end-of-file. Compile the program using the large memory model (−ml option)

```
#include <stdio.h>
#include <sys\types.h>
#include <sys\stat.h>
#include <fcntl.h>
#include <io.h>
/* Initialize array with a string plus Control-Z to
 * mark end of file.
 */
static char bigbuffer[60000]="Testing write\n\032";
main()
{
    int bytes_written;
    int filehandle;
    char filename[81];
    printf("Enter name of file to be opened for \
writing:");
    gets(filename);
/* Open the file for write operations.
 * Don't overwrite existing file.
 */
    if ((filehandle = open(filename,
```

```
        O_WRONLY|O_CREAT|O_EXCL, S_IREAD|S_IWRITE))  == -1)
        {
            perror("Open failed! ");
            exit(1);
        }
/* Now write out 60,000 bytes of data.
 * Most of it'll be junk.
 */
        if((bytes_written = write(filehandle, bigbuffer,
                                  60000)) == -1)
        {
            perror("write failed");
        }
        else
        {
            printf("%u bytes written to file: %s\n",
                    bytes_written,  filename);
            printf("Use 'TYPE %s' to see result\n",
                    filename);
        }
        return 0;
}
```

Console and Port I/O

cgets

COMPATIBILITY

TC1	TC1.5	TC2	TC++	MSC3	MSC4	MSC5	MSC6	QC1	QC2	QC2.5	ANSI	UNIX V	XNX
▲	▲	▲	▲	▲	▲	▲	▲	▲	▲	▲			

PURPOSE Use *cgets* to read a string of characters from the keyboard. The line is read until a newline character is reached and replaced by a null character, which generates a C string. You must allocate the buffer in which the string is stored. Store as the first byte the maximum number of characters to be read.

SYNTAX `char *cgets(char *buffer);`

`char *buffer;` *Buffer where string will be stored*

EXAMPLE CALL `cgets(user_input);`

INCLUDES `#include <conio.h>` *For function declaration*

DESCRIPTION The *cgets* function begins by reading the value in the first character of the buffer whose address is given in the argument *buffer*. The function uses that as the maximum number of characters to be read. It accepts keystrokes and stores them in *buffer* starting at the third location (i.e., *buffer2*). The reading from the keyboard continues until a newline character is encountered or until the specified maximum number of characters has been read. Then *cgets* replaces the newline character with a null character and returns after storing in *buffer1* the number of characters it read. Note that the buffer whose address is given in the argument *buffer* must have enough room to hold all the characters, including the null character and the additional two bytes used to store the two lengths.

RETURNS The *cgets* function returns a pointer to the beginning of the string (i.e., the location *buffer2*).

SEE ALSO `cputs` *To write a string to the console*

EXAMPLE Use *cgets* to read a line from the console. Display the line using *cprintf*.

```
#include <conio.h>
main()
{
    int numread;
    char string[82], *input;
    string[0] = 80;      /* Max no. of characters */
    cprintf("Enter a line: ");
    input = cgets(string);
    numread = string[1];    /* Number of chars read*/
    cprintf("\nYou entered: %d characters. \
The string is \r\n%s\r\n",  numread, input);
    return 0;
}
```

Console and Port I/O

cprintf

COMPATIBILITY

TC1	TC1.5	TC2	TC++	MSC3	MSC4	MSC5	MSC6	QC1	QC2	QC2.5	ANSI	UNIX V	XNX
▲	▲	▲	▲	▲	▲	▲	▲	▲	▲	▲			

PURPOSE Use *cprintf* to convert the values of C variables into a character string according to specified formats and print the string on the display. This function provides the function of *printf* for console output operations.

SYNTAX `int cprintf(const char *format_string, ...);`

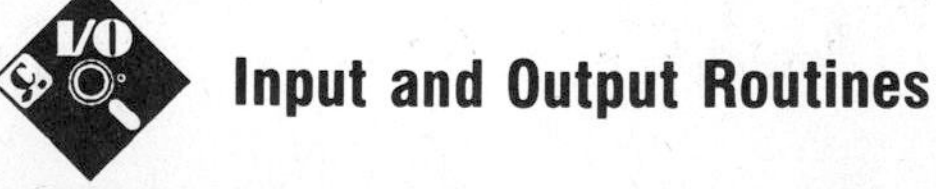

`const char *format_string;` *Character string that describes the format to be used*

`...` *Variable number of arguments depending on the number of items being printed*

EXAMPLE CALL `cprintf("File %s has %d bytes of data\n", fname, size);`

INCLUDES `#include <conio.h>` *For function declaration*

DESCRIPTION The *cprintf* function accepts a variable number of arguments and formats and prints them to the console. The format to be used for each variable is specified in *format_string*, an array of characters with embedded formatting commands that start with a percentage sign. The reference pages on *printf* describe in detail the formatting options available.

Note that *cprintf* does not translate the newline character (\n) to a CR-LF combination, instead \n is interpreted as a linefeed and \r should be used to indicate a carriage return.

RETURNS The *cprintf* function returns the number of characters it has printed on the console.

SEE ALSO `printf` *For printing to* stdout *and for detailed information on formats*

EXAMPLE Use *cprintf* to display a formatted table of the cubes of the numbers from 1 to 10 on the screen.

```
#include <conio.h>
main()
{
    int i;
    cprintf("Table of cubes\r\n");
    for(i=1; i<11; i++)
    {
        cprintf("The cube of %2d is %4d\r\n", i, i*i*i);
    }
    return 0;
}
```

Console and Port I/O

cputs

COMPATIBILITY

TC1	TC1.5	TC2	TC++	MSC3	MSC4	MSC5	MSC6	QC1	QC2	QC2.5	ANSI	UNIX V	XNX
▲	▲	▲	▲	▲	▲	▲	▲	▲	▲	▲			

PURPOSE Use *cputs* to write a string to the display. No newline character is sent after the string.

SYNTAX

```
int cputs(const char *string);

const char *string;        String to be output
```

EXAMPLE CALL

```
cputs("Are you sure (Y/N)? ");
```

INCLUDES

```
#include <conio.h>        For function declaration
```

DESCRIPTION The *cputs* function writes the string specified in the argument *string* to the display. Unlike *puts*, *cputs* does not automatically send a newline character after writing the string to the display.

RETURNS The *cputs* function returns the last character it printed.

SEE ALSO `cgets` *To read a line from the console*

EXAMPLE Use *cputs* to write a message to the screen.

```
#include <stdio.h>
char message[81] =
        "Insert the 'Upgrade 1.1' disk into drive A:\n";
main()
{
    cputs(message);
    return 0;
}
```

Console and Port I/O

COMPATIBILITY

cscanf

TC1	TC1.5	TC2	TC++	MSC3	MSC4	MSC5	MSC6	QC1	QC2	QC2.5	ANSI	UNIX V	XNX
▲	▲	▲	▲	▲	▲	▲	▲	▲	▲	▲			

PURPOSE Use *cscanf* to read characters directly from the keyboard, convert them into values using specified formats, and store the values in C variables.

SYNTAX

```
int cscanf(const char *format_string,...);
```

`const char *format_string;` *Character string that describes the format to be used*

`...` *Variable number of arguments representing addresses of variables whose values are being read*

EXAMPLE CALL

```
cscanf(" %d/%d/%d", &month, &day, &year);
```

INCLUDES `#include <conio.h>` *For function declaration*

DESCRIPTION The *cscanf* function reads an unbuffered stream of characters directly from the keyboard and converts them to values according to the format specifications embedded in the argument *format_string*. It then stores the values in C variables whose addresses are provided in the rest of the variable-length argument list. Each variable must have a corresponding formatting command in *format_string*. The format specification for a variable always begins with a percentage sign and the formatting options are the same as the ones available with the function *scanf*. (See its reference pages for a detailed list of the specifications.)

RETURNS The *cscanf* function returns the number of fields that were successfully read, converted, and assigned to variables. The count excludes items that were read but not assigned to any variable. The constant EOF is returned in case of an end-of-file during the read.

SEE ALSO

`scanf` *Formatted reading from* stdin

`fscanf` *For formatted, buffered reading from a file*

`sscanf` *Formatted reading from a string*

EXAMPLE Use *cscanf* with the %p format to read a memory address from the keyboard. The address is of the form *SSSS:OOOO* in which the S and O are uppercase hexadecimal digits. Now dump out, as ASCII characters, the values in the 25 bytes following that memory address. Try the address *F000:E000* for an interesting result. (How about extending this to a small tool to examine memory in various formats—say, hexadecimal digits or integers?)

```
/* Compile this program with the -ml option */
#include <conio.h>
main()
{
    int i;
    char far *far_ptr;
    cprintf("Enter memory address to dump in the form \
SSSS:OOOO\r\n(Try F0000:E0000)    ");
    cscanf(" %p", &far_ptr);
    cprintf("Dump of 25 bytes at %p\r\n", far_ptr);
    for(i=0; i<25; i++)
    {
            cprintf("%Fc", *(far_ptr+i));
    }
    return 0;
}
```

Console and Port I/O

getch

COMPATIBILITY

TC1	TC1.5	TC2	TC++	MSC3	MSC4	MSC5	MSC6	QC1	QC2	QC2.5	ANSI	UNIX V	XNX
▲	▲	▲	▲	▲	▲	▲	▲	▲	▲	▲			

PURPOSE Use the *getch* function to read a character from the keyboard without echoing it to the display.

SYNTAX `int getch(void);`

EXAMPLE CALL `in_char = getch();`

INCLUDES `#include <conio.h>` *For function declaration*

DESCRIPTION The *getch* function reads a character from the console without any buffering and the character is not echoed to the screen. Typing CONTROL-C during a call to *getch* generates the 8086 software interrupt number 23h.

COMMON USES The *getch* function is useful in implementing user interfaces in which the user hits a single key to indicate a choice and the choice is acted on as soon as the key is pressed.

RETURNS The *getch* function returns the character read from the keyboard.

SEE ALSO

getche — *To read a keystroke and echo it to the display*

getchar — *For buffered read from* stdin

EXAMPLE Write a small C program enabling the user to hit any key to exit. Use *getch* to read the keystroke and exit as soon as it's done.

```
#include <stdio.h>
#include <conio.h>

main()
{
    printf("Hit any character to exit:");
    getch();  /* Ignore character being read */
    return 0;
}
```

Console and Port I/O

getche

COMPATIBILITY

TC1	TC1.5	TC2	TC++	MSC3	MSC4	MSC5	MSC6	QC1	QC2	QC2.5	ANSI	UNIX V	XNX
▲	▲	▲	▲	▲	▲	▲	▲	▲	▲	▲			

PURPOSE Use the *getche* function to read a character from the keyboard and echo it to the display.

SYNTAX

```
int getche(void);
```

EXAMPLE CALL

```
in_char = getche();
```

INCLUDES `#include <conio.h>` *For function declaration*

DESCRIPTION The *getche* function reads a character from the keyboard without any buffering and echoes the character to the screen. Typing CONTROL-C during a call to *getche* generates software interrupt number 23h.

RETURNS The *getche* function returns the character read from the keyboard.

SEE ALSO

`getch` *To read a keystroke without echoing it to the display*

`getchar` *For buffered read from* stdin

EXAMPLE Write a program to read characters from the keyboard until a carriage return or until 80 characters have been read. Convert uppercase letters to lowercase and print the string entered. Note that you have to compare the value returned by *getche* with \r to confirm that it is a carriage return (comparing it with \n will not work).

```
#include <conio.h>

main()
{
    int i, c;
    char buffer[81];
    cprintf("Enter a line:");
    for(i=0; i<80; i++)
    {
        if((buffer[i] = tolower(getche())) == '\r')
            break;
    }
    buffer[i] = '\0';
    cprintf("\nYou entered: %s", buffer);
    return 0;
}
```

Console and Port I/O

getpass

COMPATIBILITY

TC1	TC1.5	TC2	TC++	MSC3	MSC4	MSC5	MSC6	QC1	QC2	QC2.5	ANSI	UNIX V	XNX
▲	▲	▲	▲										

PURPOSE Use *getpass* to prompt for a string on the display screen and read it from the keyboard without echoing it back. The string to be read must be less than eight characters long.

SYNTAX `char *getpass  (const char *prompt);`

`const char *prompt;` *The prompt string printed before reading the input string*

EXAMPLE CALL `passwd = getpass("Enter password: ");`

INCLUDES `#include <conio.h>` *For function prototype*

DESCRIPTION The *getpass* function prints the string *prompt* on the console, and then reads up to eight characters from the keyboard without echoing the characters back. These characters are saved in an internal string whose address is later returned.

COMMON USES You can use *getpass* to read passwords.

RETURNS The *getpass* function returns a pointer to the null-terminated string read from the keyboard. This string is a static string that gets overwritten after each call to *getpass*.

SEE ALSO `getch` *To read a character from the console without echoing*

EXAMPLES Illustrate the use of *getpass* in a program.

```
#include <conio.h>
main()
{
    printf("You entered: %s\n", getpass("Password: "));
    return 0;
}
```

Console and Port I/O

inport

COMPATIBILITY

TC1	TC1.5	TC2	TC++	MSC3	MSC4	MSC5	MSC6	QC1	QC2	QC2.5	ANSI	UNIX V	XNX
▲	▲	▲	▲			1	1	1	1	1			

PURPOSE Use *inport* to read a 16-bit word from a specific I/O port. For example, you can use *inport* to read two adjacent ports at once.

SYNTAX `int inport(int port);`

`int port;` *Address of the port from which a word is to be read*

EXAMPLE CALL `word_8259 = inport(0x20);`

INCLUDES `#include <dos.h>` *For function declaration*

DESCRIPTION The *inport* function uses the assembly language instruction IN to read a word (2 bytes) of data from the port address specified in the argument *port*.

1. The equivalent function for Microsoft C 5.0 and 6.0, and QuickC 1.0, 2.0, and 2.5, is *inpw*.

COMMON USES The *inport* function is useful in reading two adjacent ports at once.

RETURNS The *inport* function returns an unsigned integer containing the 16-bit word it read from the port address.

SEE ALSO

`inportb`	*To read a byte from a port address*
`outport, outportb`	*To write to an I/O port*

EXAMPLE The Intel 8259A programmable interrupt controller schedules and sometimes blocks interrupt signals generated by peripheral devices and meant for the microprocessor. The 8259A is programmed through two registers at port addresses 20h and 21h. Use *inportb* to read the contents of each register and display them. Then, using the *inport* function, read both registers simultaneously and display the contents in hexadecimal format. Compare these with the values you read individually.

```
#include <stdio.h>
#include <conio.h>
#define PORT_8259_20   0x20
#define PORT_8259_21   0x21

main()
{
    unsigned int word_8259;
    int p20, p21;
/* Read both ports of the 8259A */
    word_8259 = inport(PORT_8259_20);
/* Now read them individually */
    p20 = inportb(PORT_8259_20);
    p21 = inportb(PORT_8259_21);
    printf("Current contents of register \
at port 20h: %X\n", p20);
    printf("Current contents of register \
at port 21h: %X\n", p21);
    printf("Result of reading with inpw at \
port 20h:  %X\n", word_8259);
    return 0;
}
```

inportb

COMPATIBILITY

TC1	TC1.5	TC2	TC++	MSC3	MSC4	MSC5	MSC6	QC1	QC2	QC2.5	ANSI	UNIX V	XNX
▲	▲	▲	▲	1	1	1	1	1	1	1			

PURPOSE Use *inportb* to read a byte from a specific I/O port whose address you provide as an argument. For example, you can use *inportb* read from port 21h to determine which interrupt numbers are currently acknowledged by the 8259A programmable interrupt controller.

SYNTAX

```
unsigned char inportb (int port);
```

`int port;` *Address of the port from which a byte is to be read*

EXAMPLE CALL

```
byte_read = inportb(0x3f8);
```

INCLUDES `#include <dos.h>` *For function declaration*

DESCRIPTION The *inportb* function uses the assembly language instruction IN to read a byte of data from the port address specified in the argument *port*.

1. In Microsoft C 3.0 through 6.0, and QuickC 1.0 through 2.5, use *inp*.

COMMON USES The *inportb* function is used to control input/output devices. The control circuitry of these devices has registers which are accessible through the IN and OUT instructions of the 8086 microprocessor family. The *inportb* function is a C language interface to the IN instruction.

RETURNS The *inportb* function returns the byte read from the port.

COMMENTS Everyone knows that in the IBM PC world, we are supposed to use DOS or BIOS to talk to the I/O devices (keyboard, video display, etc.). DOS and BIOS lack adequate support, however, for several important peripherals including the serial port and the speaker. In these cases you must access the device's registers using appropriate port addresses and the functions *inportb* and *outportb* come in handy.

SEE ALSO

`inport` *To read a word from a port address*

`outportb, outport` *To write to an I/O port*

EXAMPLE The PC's peripheral devices get the microprocessor's attention by generating interrupts that are fielded by an integrated circuit (the Intel 8259A programmable interrupt controller). The 8259A looks at the bits in a register, reached via port number 21h, to decide which interrupts go on to the

CPU. Read the contents of this register using the *inportb* function and display the contents in hexadecimal format.

```
#include <stdio.h>
#include <dos.h>
#define PORT_8259   0x21

main()
{
    int int_ack_status;
/* Read 8259's status */
    int_ack_status = inportb(PORT_8259);
    printf("Current contents of register at \
port 21h: %X\n", int_ack_status);
    return 0;
}
```

Console and Port I/O

kbhit

COMPATIBILITY

TC1	TC1.5	TC2	TC++	MSC3	MSC4	MSC5	MSC6	QC1	QC2	QC2.5	ANSI	UNIX V	XNX
▲	▲	▲	▲	▲	▲	▲	▲	▲	▲	▲			

PURPOSE Use the console I/O function *kbhit* to check whether any keystrokes are waiting to be read. Since *kbhit* does not wait for a key to be pressed, it is ideal for applications in which you can continue with your normal processing until the user interrupts by hitting a key.

SYNTAX

```
int kbhit(void);
```

EXAMPLE CALL

```
/* Do your thing until user presses a key */
    while( !kbhit() ) do_your_thing();
```

INCLUDES `#include <conio.h>` *For function declaration*

DESCRIPTION The *kbhit* function checks if any keystrokes are in the keyboard buffer waiting to be read.

COMMON USES The *kbhit* function is useful in writing applications where you can continue doing whatever your program is meant to do until the user actually hits a key. All you have to do is keep checking for any keystroke using *kbhit* every so often (such as at the beginning of an outer loop) and perform a read only when a keystroke is waiting.

RETURNS If a key was pressed, *kbhit* returns a nonzero value. Otherwise, it returns a zero.

COMMENTS The *kbhit* function is one function in the Turbo C++ library that you cannot do without if you want to develop an event-driven application. Consider for example, an application such as a "terminal emulator." This will have a main loop where you must respond to two types of events (at least): characters arriving from the serial port and characters being entered from the keyboard. If you attempted to handle the keyboard events by using a function such as *getch*, you would soon discover that the program will keep waiting in that function until a character is actually entered and other events, such as serial input, would be lost. With *kbhit*, however, you are able to check and move on if nothing was hit on the keyboard.

EXAMPLE The graphics function *putimage* can be used to perform rudimentary animation. Modify the example shown in the reference pages on *putimage* to move the small stick figure on the screen continuously until the user hits a key. Use *kbhit* in an endless loop to achieve this.

```
#include <stdio.h>
#include <alloc.h>
#include <graphics.h>
main()
{
    char far *image;            /* Storage for image */
    char buffer[80];
    int x=0, y=0, xmax, ymax, gerror;
    unsigned numbytes;
    int gdriver=DETECT, gmode;
    initgraph (&gdriver, &gmode, "c:\\turboc");
    if (gerror=graphresult()) !=grOk
    {
/* Error setting mode */
        printf("Error: %s\n",grapherrormsg(gerror));
        exit(0);
    }
    xmax=getmaxx();
    ymax=getmaxy();
/* Draw a small stick figure to save */
    setcolor(YELLOW);
    fillellipse(5,5,5,5);
    moveto(5,10);
    lineto(5,20);
    lineto(0,30);
    moveto(10,30);
```

```
    lineto(5,20);
    moveto(0,15);
    lineto(0,10);
    lineto(10,15);
/* Determine storage needed for entire screen and
 * display result.
 */
    numbytes = imagesize(0,0,10,30);
/* Allocate buffer for image */
    if ((image = (char far *) malloc(numbytes))
        == (char far *)NULL)
    {
        closegraph();
        printf("Not enough memory for image storage\n");
        exit(0);
    }
    getimage(x,y,10,30,image); /* Save the image */
/* Now clear screen and draw saved image at several
 * screen locations.
 */
    clearviewport();
    outtextxy(10,10,"Demonstrating animation with putimage");
    outtextxy(10, ymax-50,"Hit any key to exit:");
    x = xmax/2;
    y = ymax/2;
    putimage(x,y,image,XOR_PUT);
/* Using kbhit and putimage, perform animation
 * until user hits a key.
 */
    while( !kbhit() )
    {
/* Erase at last position */
        putimage(x,y,image,XOR_PUT);
         y += 2;
         x += 2;
         if(x> xmax-50) x = 50;
         if(y> ymax-50) y = 50;
/* Redraw at new position */
        putimage(x,y,image,XOR_PUT);
    }
/* Restore original mode  */
    closegraph();
    return 0;
}
```

Console and Port I/O

COMPATIBILITY

outport

TC1	TC1.5	TC2	TC++	MSC3	MSC4	MSC5	MSC6	QC1	QC2	QC2.5	ANSI	UNIX V	XNX
▲	▲	▲	▲			1	1	1	1	1			

PURPOSE Use the *outport* function to write a 16-bit word to a specified I/O port address. For example, you can use *outport* to send 2 bytes simultaneously to the control registers in your enhanced graphics adapter when programming it directly for graphics.

SYNTAX

```
void outport(int port, int word);
```

`int port;` *Address of the port to which the word is sent*

`int word;` *Word to be written to the port*

EXAMPLE CALL

```
outport(0x3ce, (2<<8) | 0x5);  /* Put EGA in write mode 2 */
```

INCLUDES `#include <dos.h>` *For function declaration*

DESCRIPTION The *outport* function uses the assembly language instruction OUT to send a 16-bit word given in the argument *word* to the port address specified by the argument *port*.

1. The equivalent function in Microsoft C 5.0 and 6.0, and QuickC 1.0, 2.0, and 2.5, is *outpw*.

COMMON USES The *outport* function allows you to send 2 bytes of data to two adjacent I/O ports by a single function call. As shown in the example, this comes in handy when programming the EGA.

COMMENTS Each I/O address on the IBM PC provides access to an 8-bit register. If you use *outport* to send 2 bytes to, say, I/O address 3CEh, the first byte goes to the register at 3CEh and the second byte goes to the adjoining register at 3CFh. Thus when programming a peripheral such as the EGA, to which you often send specific data to two registers with addresses next to each other, it's advantageous to use *outport*.

SEE ALSO `outportb` *To write a byte to a port address*

`inport, inportb` *To read from an I/O port*

EXAMPLE The EGA can be programmed in its 640×350 high-resolution mode by manipulating the registers directly and sending data to its video memory. The programming involves sending a "register select" command to an I/O port followed by the register number to the next port. This can be achieved by a single call to *outport.* The example below, meant to draw a rectangle filled with color, illustrates this.

```
#include <stdio.h>
#include <dos.h>

#define EGA_RAM ((unsigned char far *)0xA0000000)
#define MAX_GR_COLS  640
#define MAX_GR_ROWS  350
#define MAX_COL_BYTES (MAX_GR_COLS/8)

#define BIOS_VIDEO 0x10
#define SETMODE    0    /* BIOS Service: set video mode*/
#define EGAMODE    16   /* EGA mode for high resolution*/

#define EGA_GR12 0x3ce  /* Port to select register     */
#define EGA_GR_MODE 0x5 /* Register no. for write mode*/

/* The box size and the color */
#define XSTART  120
#define YSTART  120
#define XSIZE   280
#define YSIZE   200
#define COLOR   2

static union REGS xr, yr;
static char far *videoram;

main()
{
    int ynum, bytecount, startadrs, startbyte, stopbyte,
        horbytes, skipbytes;
    unsigned temp, egacommand;

/* Use BIOS to put EGA in high-res graphics mode */
    xr.h.ah = SETMODE;
    xr.h.al = EGAMODE;
    int86 (BIOS_VIDEO, &xr, &yr);

/* Compute starting address */
    startbyte = XSTART/8;
    startadrs = 80*YSTART + startbyte;
    videoram = EGA_RAM + startadrs;
    skipbytes = MAX_COL_BYTES;
```

```
/* Put EGA in write mode 2. Use outpw. The following
 * code is  equivalent to 2 lines:
 *           outportb (EGA_GR12, EGA_GR_MODE);
 *           outportb (EGA_GR_PORT, 2);
 */
    egacommand = (2<<8) | EGA_GR_MODE;
    outport(EGA_GR12, egacommand);

    stopbyte = (XSTART + XSIZE - 1)/8;
    horbytes = stopbyte - startbyte;
    skipbytes = MAX_COL_BYTES - horbytes;

/* We already have the proper graphics mode settings */
        for (ynum = 0; ynum < YSIZE; ynum++)
        {
            for (bytecount = 0; bytecount < horbytes;
                  bytecount++)
            {
/* Fill in 8 bits at a time.
 * First read to latch in bytes.
 */
                temp = *videoram;
/* Now write out pixel value to all 8 bits at once */
                *videoram = COLOR;
                videoram++;
            }
/* Skip to next row */
            videoram += skipbytes;
        }

/* Reset graphics environment back to BIOS standard */
    egacommand = EGA_GR_MODE;
    outport(EGA_GR12, egacommand);
    return 0;
}
```

Console and Port I/O

outportb

COMPATIBILITY

TC1	TC1.5	TC2	TC++	MSC3	MSC4	MSC5	MSC6	QC1	QC2	QC2.5	ANSI	UNIX V	XNX
▲	▲	▲	▲	1	1	1	1	1	1	1			

PURPOSE Use *outportb* to write a byte to a specified I/O port. For example, you can use *outportb* to generate sound on the IBM PC by sending appropriate data to the Intel 8255 programmable peripheral interface chip via port address 61h.

SYNTAX

```
void outportb(int port, unsigned char byte);
```

`int port;` *Address of the port to which the byte is sent*

`unsigned char;` *Byte to be written to the port*

EXAMPLE CALL

```
outportb(0x43, 0xb6);
```

INCLUDES `#include <dos.h>` *For function declaration*

DESCRIPTION The *outportb* function uses the assembly language instruction OUT to send a byte of data from the argument *byte* to the port address specified in the argument *port.*

1. The equivalent function in Microsoft C 3.0 through 6.0, and QuickC 1.0 through 2.5, is *outp*.

COMMON USES Use the *outportb* function in conjunction with *inportb* to access registers in input/output devices. The *outportb* function is a C language interface to the OUT instruction.

COMMENTS Some peripheral devices such as the speaker and the serial ports are not adequately supported in the IBM PC's BIOS. In particular, the speaker is accessible only through the IN and OUT instructions; the Turbo C++ library functions *inportb* and *outportb* are invaluable in such a situation.

SEE ALSO

`outport` *To write a 16-bit word to a port address*

`inport, inportb` *To read from an I/O port*

EXAMPLE The IBM PC's speaker can be used to generate a tone by programming it via the 8255 chip at port address 61h and using the system timer (Intel 8254 chip) to control the speaker. Here is how it works. First you will set up the timer as an oscillator by sending the data byte B6h to the port 43h. Then you compute the ratio of the frequency of sound you want and the frequency of the timer's clock (1.19 MHz). Write this value to port 42h.

Tell the 8255 chip to drive the speaker under the control of the timer by reading the port 61h and writing the value back with the first 2 bits set to 1 (perform a logical OR with 3). This gets the sound going. Let the sound continue as long as you wish. Shut the speaker off by reading port 61h again and setting bits 0 and 1 to 0.

```
#include <dos.h>
#include <conio.h>

#define TIMER_FREQ       1193180L /* Timer freq = 1.19 MHz */
#define TIMER_COUNT      0x42     /* 8253 timer -- count       */
#define TIMER_MODE       0x43     /* 8253 timer control port   */
#define TIMER_OSC        0xb6     /*To use timer as oscillator */
#define OUT_8255         0x61     /* 8255 PPI output port adrs */
#define SPKRON           3        /* Bit 0 = control spkr by timer*/
                                  /* Bit 1 = speaker on/off       */

main()
{
        unsigned freq, status, ratio, part_ratio;
        char input[81];
        cprintf("Enter frequency in Hz \
(between 100 and 15000):");
        cscanf("%hu", &freq);
/* First read and save status of the 8255 chip */
        status = inportb (OUT_8255);
/* Put timer in oscillator mode */
        outportb (TIMER_MODE, TIMER_OSC);
        ratio = (unsigned)(TIMER_FREQ/freq);
        part_ratio = ratio & 0xff; /* low byte of ratio    */
        outportb(TIMER_COUNT, part_ratio);
        part_ratio = (ratio >> 8) & 0xff; /* high byte     */
        outportb(TIMER_COUNT, part_ratio);
/* Finally turn on speaker */
        outportb (OUT_8255, (status | SPKRON));

/* Ask user to indicate when to stop the
 * annoying tone...
 */
        cprintf("\nHit return to exit:");
        cgets(input);

/* Now turn off speaker */
        status = inportb (OUT_8255); /* get current status */
/* Turn speaker off */
```

```
        outportb (OUT_8255, (status & ~SPKRON));
        return 0;
}
```

Console and Port I/O

putch

COMPATIBILITY

TC1	TC1.5	TC2	TC++	MSC3	MSC4	MSC5	MSC6	QC1	QC2	QC2.5	ANSI	UNIX V	XNX
▲	▲	▲	▲	▲	▲	▲	▲	▲	▲	▲			

PURPOSE Use the *putch* function to write a single character to the display without intermediate buffering.

SYNTAX

```
int putch(int c);

int c;          Character to be written
```

EXAMPLE CALL

```
putch('>');
```

INCLUDES

```
#include <conio.h>        For function declaration
```

DESCRIPTION The *putch* function writes the character *c* to the display.

RETURNS The *putch function*, when successful, returns the character it wrote. Otherwise it returns the constant EOF (defined in *stdio.h*).

SEE ALSO `getch, getche` *For unbuffered read from the keyboard*

EXAMPLE Use *putch* to write a line (maximum length of 80 characters) to the standard output.

```
#include <conio.h>
char buffer[81] = "Testing putch...\n";
main()
{
    int i;
/* Write characters to display until we reach the null */
    for(i=0; i<81 && buffer[i] != '\0'; i++)
    {
        putch(buffer[i]);
    }
    return 0;
}
```

Console and Port I/O

COMPATIBILITY

ungetch

TC1	TC1.5	TC2	TC++	MSC3	MSC4	MSC5	MSC6	QC1	QC2	QC2.5	ANSI	UNIX V	XNX
▲	▲	▲	▲	▲	▲	▲	▲	▲	▲	▲			

PURPOSE Use the *ungetch* function to place a single character in the keyboard buffer so that it is the next character read from the console. You cannot place more than one character before the next read.

SYNTAX

```
int ungetch(int c);
```

`int c;` *Character to be placed in the keyboard buffer*

EXAMPLE CALL

```
ungetch(last_char);
```

INCLUDES `#include <conio.h>` *For function declaration*

DESCRIPTION The *ungetch* function places the character given in the integer argument *c* into the keyboard buffer so that the next console read operation returns that character. You can place only one character in the buffer before reading and the character must not be equal to the constant EOF defined in *stdio.h*.

RETURNS If there are no errors, *ungetch* returns the character it pushed back. Otherwise, it returns the constant EOF to indicate an error—which is why you should not try to push back EOF.

SEE ALSO `getch, getche` *To read a character from the console*

EXAMPLE Write a program that asks the user to enter an integer. Use *getche* to read the digits and accumulate them into an integer. Once you reach a nondigit (use the macro *isdigit* to check), put that character back into the console by calling *ungetch*. Now print a message showing the integer value and indicating the first noninteger character typed.

```
#include <stdio.h>
#include <conio.h>
#include <ctype.h>  /* For the macro isdigit() */
main()
{
    int intval = 0, c;
    char buff[81];
/* Ask user to type in an integer */
```

```
    printf("Enter an integer followed by some other \
characters:");
    while ( (c = getche()) != EOF && isdigit(c) )
    {
        intval = 10*intval + c - 48; /* 0 is ASCII 48 */
    }
/* Push back the first nondigit read from stdin */
    if (c != EOF) ungetch(c);
/* Print message to user */
    printf("\nInteger you entered = %d.\n\
First noninteger encountered: %c\n", intval, getch());
    return 0;
}
```

Input and Output Routines

Chapter 17 System Calls

Introduction

All IBM-compatible MS-DOS machines come with a basic input/output system or BIOS built into the read-only memory (ROM). This set of rudimentary I/O routines accesses peripheral devices such as the keyboard, display, printer, serial port, and floppy or hard disk. In addition to the built-in ROM BIOS, MS-DOS itself has a host of standard utility functions that also perform I/O and provide access to the DOS file system. Essentially, you can count on both of these sets of services being present on every IBM PC or compatible that uses MS-DOS as its operating system. The DOS services are more portable than the BIOS ones because the BIOS code in PC-compatibles is only a functional copy of the original IBM BIOS, whereas the MS-DOS routines are part of the operating system software which is consistent across all machines. In general, however, programs that use DOS or BIOS calls to perform various I/O functions are likely to work properly in all IBM-compatible computers. Programs that directly access hardware using I/O port addresses or video memory addresses obtain the greatest processing speed, but may not work on all PC compatibles. Thus it is advantageous to be able to use these portable DOS and BIOS services in your programs whenever there are no overriding performance considerations.

The Turbo C++ library includes a set of functions that provide access to the BIOS and DOS services from your C programs. These functions for making "system calls" enable you to harness the full potential of the PC without having to write, in most cases, even a single line of code in 8086 assembly language.

Although the same BIOS and DOS services are available to users of any PC, each C compiler vendor has a different name for each of these routines. However, the basic set of *int86, int86x, intdos* and *intdosx* appear to be present in most C compilers for the IBM PC. You can check the compatibility sections of the reference entries to find equivalent Microsoft C routines.

We should also point out that many of the services offered by the system calls category are duplicated elsewhere in the Turbo C++ library. Entire categories of portable routines from the standard C library exist for memory allocation, file I/O, and date/time information. For these tasks, you are better off using the standard library routines because they are not dependent on the PC hardware or on DOS. In general, use the most portable routine that provides acceptable performance. Doing so will make porting the program to a new system much easier.

Basics of BIOS and DOS Interface

C programmers are familiar with the concept of compiling groups of functions to generate object code and using the linker to construct an executable file. In such a situation, you normally invoke a given routine's code by a C function call. The parameters you pass to the function are transferred via the stack.

Now consider the case of BIOS and DOS functions. These routines are also in compiled object-code form, but you cannot link your program with them because the addresses of the routines are not known to you (even if they were, it would pose a problem if they changed in future revisions of the BIOS and DOS). A more fundamental access mechanism is needed, a method that can be counted upon to work on every PC irrespective of where the actual object code of the BIOS and DOS functions resides. The assembly language instruction INT that generates a software interrupt on an 8086 microprocessor provides the solution.

INTERRUPTS ON 8086 MICROPROCESSOR

In a PC, a "hardware interrupt" refers to a mechanism that hardware devices use to get the attention of the microprocessor they service. The 8086 microprocessor keeps a table of function addresses called an "interrupt vector table" in the memory. Whenever the microprocessor receives an interrupt signal, it first saves the contents of the internal registers as well as the address of the code it was executing at that moment. Next it determines the interrupt number from the interrupt signal and locates the entry in the "interrupt vector table." Then it jumps to that function address and begins executing the code there, which presumably does everything necessary to satisfy the needs of the device that generated the interrupt signal in the first place. How does the microprocessor return to the code it was executing when it was interrupted? It will return as soon as it executes the assembly language instruction IRET. Thus the function that handles or services the interrupt must end with an IRET (Figure 17-1).

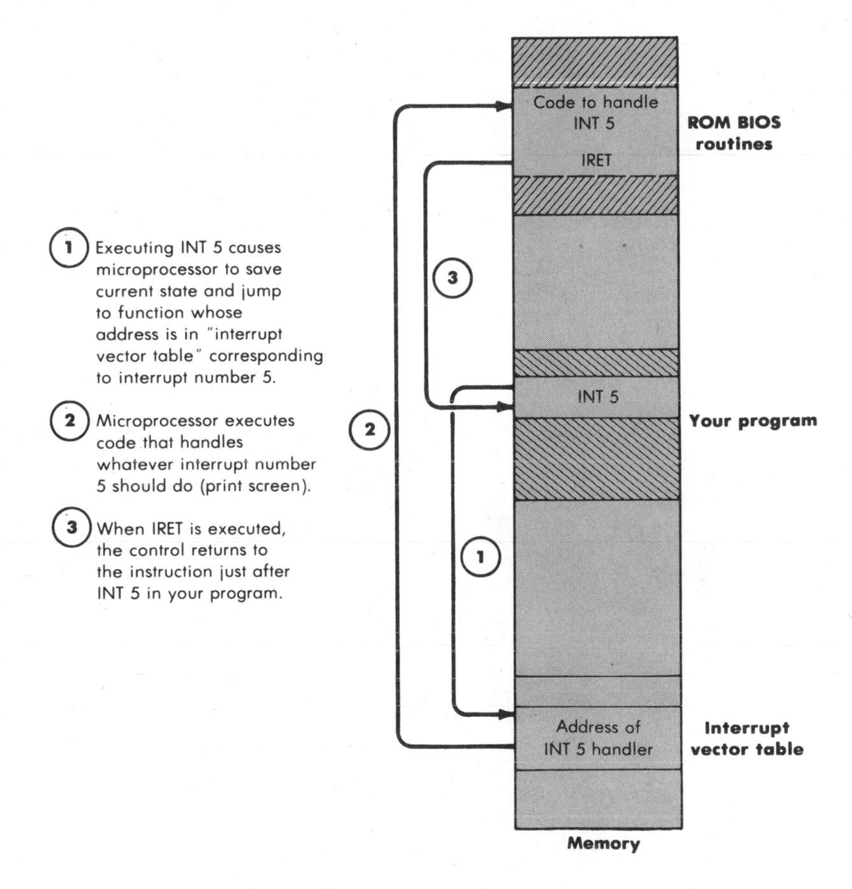

Figure 17-1. ***Accessing BIOS and DOS functions via software interrupts***

SOFTWARE INTERRUPTS

Software interrupts behave in the same way as hardware interrupts, except that they are generated by an assembly language of the form *INT* <*int_number*> where <*int_number*> is the interrupt number we want generated. If we write a routine to perform a task, end it with an IRET instruction, and place its address in the entry corresponding to the interrupt number <*int_number*> in the interrupt vector table, this routine can now be invoked by executing the instruction *INT* <*int_number*>, which is precisely how the BIOS and DOS functions are made available to assembly language programmers. Parameters are passed from C to these routines by placing them in the microprocessor's registers, and results are also returned through the registers. Since the routines in the system calls category allow us to generate software interrupts, they allow access to the BIOS and DOS functions.

Typically, a single interrupt number provides access to an entire category of services, with the specific service selected by a value in a register. For example, interrupt number 21h provides access to almost a hundred functions embedded in MS-DOS. The exact function to be invoked is specified by a function number placed in the AH register.

SOFTWARE INTERRUPTS FROM TURBO C++

Turbo C++ provides the routines *int86* and *int86x* for generating arbitrary software interrupts. These routines accept the register settings in a "union" (see Chapter 1) named REGS which is defined in *dos.h* and is the overlay of two structures, one named *x* of type WORDREGS and the other named *h* of type BYTEREGS (see Figure 17-2). This arrangement means that the member *x* in the "union" REGS provides access to the 16-bit word registers AX, BX, CX, and DX, while the member *h* is used for accessing the corresponding 8-bit halves, AH, AL, BH, BL, CH, CL, DH, and DL. The segment registers ES, CS, SS, and DS are passed via a "structure" named SREGS which is also defined in the include file *dos.h* (Figure 17-2).

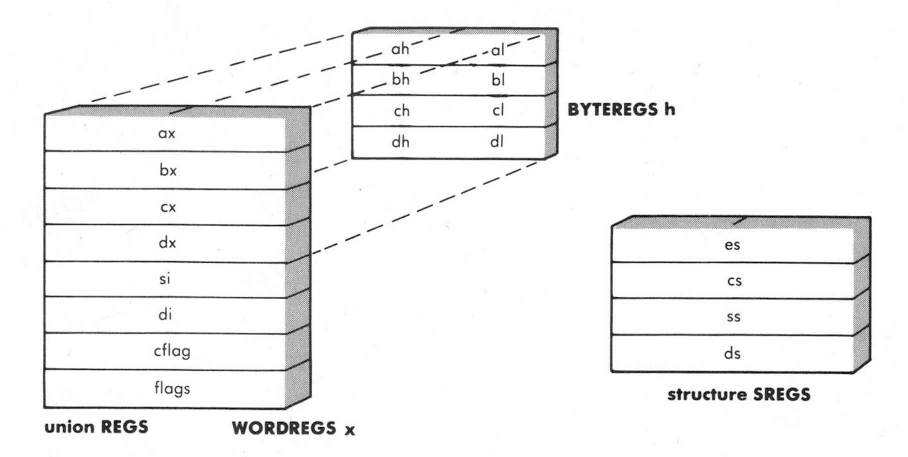

Figure 17-2. ***Union REGS and structure SREGS***

To pass register values you have to declare data items of type REGS and SREGS as appropriate and set the internal fields of these structures to the desired register values. The interface routine in the C library loads the registers from these data structures before generating the software interrupt necessary to access the desired BIOS or DOS service. Upon return from the interrupt, the interface routine copies the register values into another structure which you also allocate and whose address you pass to the routine. This allows the program to obtain the results or error codes returned by the service called.

Table 17-1 shows the interrupt numbers for the BIOS services. The DOS services all use interrupt number 21h, with a function number specified in the AH register. Table 17-2 lists the DOS services according to function number. Each table also shows the name of specific Turbo C++ routines that provide access to a particular service. For more information, consult the appropriate reference pages of the relevant Turbo C++ routines. Where no special purpose Turbo C++ routine exists, you can use the general purpose interrupt routines *int86x* or *intdosx* to access the service. In this case, you can find further details in reference books on MS-DOS (Duncan[3]) and IBM PC (Norton[5], Smith[6]) listed under Further Reading at the end of this chapter.

Table 17-1. *Interrupts to Access ROM BIOS Routines*

Interrupt No. (Hex)	Purpose	Turbo C++ Interface Routine
05	Print screen	N/A
10	Video I/O	N/A
11	Equipment determination	biosequip
12	Memory size determination	biosmemory
13	Diskette I/O (and hard disk I/O on AT, XT, and PS/2)	biosdisk
14	I/O with RS-232C serial communications port	bioscom
15	Cassette I/O (and system services on AT, XT, and PS/2)	N/A
16	Keyboard I/O	bioskey
17	Printer I/O	biosprint
18	Access ROM-resident BASIC	N/A
19	Bootstrap loader to load operating system from disk	N/A
1A	Time of day	biostime
1B	Keyboard break address	N/A
1C	Timer tick	N/A

Table 17-2. *MS-DOS Functions*

Function No. (Hex)	Action	Turbo C++ Interface
00	Terminates program and returns to DOS.	
01	Reads a character from keyboard (AL has character).	
02	Displays character in DL on screen.	
03	Reads character from AUX into AL.	
04	Writes character in DL to AUX.	
05	Sends character in DL to printer port.	

Table 17-2. *(cont.)*

Function No. (Hex)	Action	Turbo C++ Interface
06	Performs direct console I/O (DL=FF means input).	
07	Directly inputs a character from STDIN.	
08	Reads a character from keyboard without echoing it.	
09	Prints a string ending in a $.	
0A	Reads characters from keyboard into a buffer.	
0B	Checks status of STDIN.	
0C	Clears keyboard buffer.	
0D	Resets disk and flushes all disk buffers.	
0E	Sets the default disk drive.	setdisk
0F	Opens a disk file (requires File Control Block, FCB).	
10	Closes a disk file (specified by FCB).	
11	Searches for first occurrence of a file using FCB.	
12	Searches for next occurrence of a file using FCB.	
13	Deletes file specified by an FCB.	
14	Reads a disk file sequentially.	
15	Writes sequentially to a disk file.	
16	Creates a disk file.	
17	Renames a disk file.	
18	Reserved.	
19	Returns default disk drive number in AL.	getdisk
1A	Sets up a Disk Transfer Address (DTA).	setdta
1B	Returns allocation information about default disk drive.	getfatd
1C	Returns allocation information of a specific drive.	getfat
1D	Reserved.	
1E	Reserved.	
1F	Reserved.	
20	Reserved.	
21	Reads a record from disk (random access).	
22	Writes a record to disk (random access).	
23	Returns file size in FCB, if file found.	
24	Sets up record number for random access read/write.	
25	Sets up a new interrupt vector.	setvect
26	Creates a Program Segment Prefix (PSP).	
27	Reads a block of records from disk (random access).	randbrd
28	Writes a block of records to disk (random access).	randbwr
29	Parses a file name.	parsfnm
2A	Returns current date (DL=day, DH=month, CX=year).	getdate
2B	Sets the current date.	setdate

Table 17-2. *(cont.)*

Function No. (Hex)	Action	Turbo C++ Interface
2C	Returns the current time.	gettime
2D	Sets the current time.	settime
2E	Sets verify flag on or off.	getverify, setverify
2F	Returns the DTA.	getdta
30	Returns version of DOS.	
31	Terminates program but leaves it intact in memory.	keep
32	Used internally by DOS to get drive parameter block.	
33	Gets or sets Control-Break flag.	getcbrk, setcbrk
34	Used internally by DOS to get a pointer to a byte that indicates when DOS is in a "critical section." (When flag is set it is not safe to call DOS functions; this feature is used by many TSR utilities.) This is not officially documented by Microsoft.	
35	Returns the interrupt vector for a specific interrupt.	getvect
36	Returns information about total and unused space on a specified disk drive.	getdfree
37	Used internally (switch character and device availability). This is not officially documented by Microsoft.	getswitchar, setswitchar
38	Gets or sets country-dependent information. (See also function 65h.)	country
39	Creates a subdirectory.	
3A	Removes a subdirectory.	
3B	Changes the current directory.	
3C	Creates a named disk file and returns handle in AX.	_creat
3D	Opens a named disk file and returns handle in AX.	_open
3E	Closes a file specified by a handle.	_close
3F	Reads a number of bytes from a disk file specified by a handle.	_read
40	Writes a number of bytes to a disk file specified by a handle.	_write
41	Deletes a named disk file.	
42	Moves the read/write pointer of a file specified by a handle.	
43	Gets or sets the attributes of a file. (Attributes determine if a file is hidden, read only, and so on.)	_chmod
44	Provides device driver control (IOCTL).	ioctl
45	Creates a duplicate file handle.	
46	Forces a new file handle to point to the same file as an existing handle.	
47	Returns current directory name.	getcurdir
48	Allocates a specified number of paragraphs of memory and returns the segment address of the allocated memory.	allocmem

Table 17-2. *(cont.)*

Function No. (Hex)	Action	Turbo C++ Interface
49	Releases a previously allocated block of memory.	freemem
4A	Adjusts the size of a previously allocated block of memory.	setblock
4B	Loads and/or executes a program.	
4C	Terminates a program and returns an exit code.	
4D	Returns exit code of a subprogram.	
4E	Searches for first occurrence of a named file.	findfirst
4F	Searches for next occurrence of a named file.	findnext
50	Used internally to set new PSP segment.	
51	Used internally to get current PSP segment.	
52	Used internally by DOS to get list of disks.	
53	Used internally by DOS to translate the BIOS parameter block.	
54	Returns the verify flag in AH.	
55	Used internally by DOS to create a PSP.	
56	Renames a file.	
57	Gets or sets the modification time and date of a disk file specified by its handle.	getftime
58	Gets or sets the memory allocation strategy to be used by DOS (*DOS 3.X only*).	
59	Returns extended error information (*DOS 3.X only*).	dosexterr
5A	Creates a temporary file (*DOS 3.X only*).	
5B	Creates a new file (*DOS 3.X only*).	
5C	Locks or unlocks a file for shared access (*DOS 3.X only*).	
5D	Used internally by DOS.	
5E	Returns machine name and printer set up (*DOS 3.X only*).	
5F	Gets list of device redirections in Microsoft network (*DOS 3.X only*).	
60	Used internally by DOS.	
61	Reserved.	
62	Returns the PSP (*DOS 3.X only*).	getpsp
63	Returns lead byte table (*DOS 2.25 only*).	
64	Reserved.	
65	Returns extended country information (*DOS 3.3 only*).	country
66	Gets or sets global page table (*DOS 3.3 only*).	
67	Sets the maximum number of file handles (must be less than 255). This breaks the "20 open file per process" limit of DOS 3.2 and less (*DOS 3.3 only*).	
68	Writes all buffered data meant for a file to the disk (*DOS 3.3 only*).	

Notes on BIOS and DOS Services

The functions in the system calls category allow you to use virtually all routines in the IBM PC ROM BIOS as well as all functions in DOS that are accessible via interrupt number 21h. Table 17-3 is a list of the Turbo C++ routines that provide access to the system services, grouped according to the tasks they perform. The BIOS routines (discussed later) are not listed because each one performs a distinct task.

Table 17-3. ***Turbo C++ System Interface Routines by Task***

Task	Routines
Generate 8086 software interrupt.	geninterrupt, int86, int86x, intr
Call any DOS function.	bdos, bdosptr, intdos, intdosx
Manipulate segment and offset addresses.	FP_OFF, FP_SEG, MK_FP, segread
Perform file I/O using DOS (see I/O routines in Chapter 16).	_close, _creat, _open, _read, _write
Find and alter file information.	_chmod, findfirst, findnext, getcurdir, getdfree, getdisk,getfat, getfatd, getftime, setdisk, setftime
Perform file I/O using FCBs.	getdta, parsfnm, randbrd, randbwr, setdta
Handle interrupts and help in developing TSRs.	ctrlbrk, disable, enable, getpsp, getvect, keep, setvect
Allocate and free memory (see Chapter 6 for others).	allocmem, freemem, setblock
Date and time services (see Chapter 13 for Time category).	delay, dostounix, getdate, gettime, setdate, settime, sleep, unixtodos
Generate sound.	nosound, sound
Perform raw disk I/O.	absread, abswrite
Handle hardware and other errors.	dosexterr, harderr, hardresume, hardretn
Get and set DOS flags, and communicate with device drivers.	country, ctrlbrk, getcbrk, getswitchar, getverify, ioctl, setswitchar, setverify
Access memory.	peek, peekb, poke, pokeb
Initialize expanded or extended memory for overlays.	_OvrlnitEms, _OvrlnitExt

TURBO C++ INTERFACE TO DOS AND BIOS SERVICES

Turbo C++ provides three ways to access the DOS services (see Figure 17-3). The first approach is to use the general software interrupts, *int86*, *int86x*, and *intr*, and call DOS directly using interrupt number 21h. The second method uses the generic DOS interrupt routines *bdos*, *bdosptr*, *intdos*, and *intdosx*. The third method is to use the specific DOS system calls.

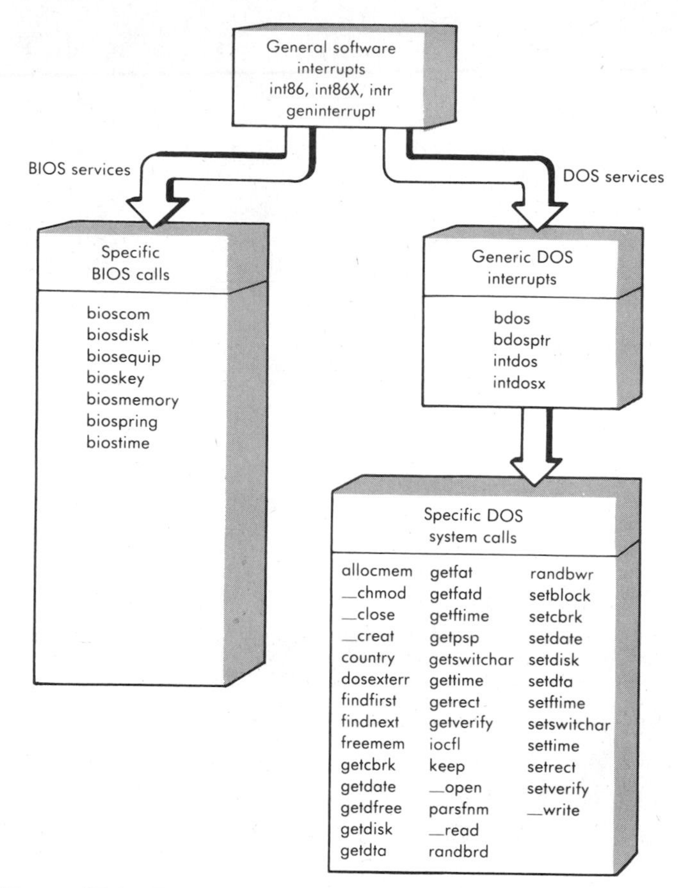

Figure 17-3. ***Turbo C++ Interface for BIOS and DOS services***

BIOS services are accessed by two methods: via the general purpose interrupt routines or by calling a specific BIOS interface routine listed in Table 17-4.

To call a DOS or BIOS service using the general-purpose interrupt routine, you have to set up the registers by using a "union" REGS data type and then provide the interrupt number to *int86* (or *int86x* if the service requires the use of the DS and ES registers). For DOS the interrupt number is always 21h. Different services are accessed by placing the DOS function number in the AH register. Other register values depend on the DOS function's being called. For example, the DOS time function (number 2Ch) may be called as follows:

```
#include <stdio.h>
#include <dos.h>
#define DOS_GETTIME 0x2c
```

```
main()
{
    union REGS xr, yr;
    xr.h.ah = DOS_GETTIME;
    int86(0x21, &xr, &yr);
    printf("Current time is %.2d:%.2d:%.2d\n",
           yr.h.ch, yr.h.cl, yr.h.dh);
    return 0;
}
```

The *dos.h* include file is necessary for the function prototypes and the definition of the union REGS. If we were to use the *intdos* interface (we do not have to use *intdosx* because the service does not need anything in the segment registers), the line containing the call to *int86* in our example will be replaced by

```
intdos(&xr, &yr);
```

Lastly, if we make use of the interface routine *gettime* provided specifically for accessing the system time, the example will become

```
#include <stdio.h>
#include <dos.h>
main()
{
    struct time time;
    gettime(&time);
    printf("Current time: %d:%d:%d.%d\n", time.hour,
           time.minute, time.second, time.hsecond);
    return 0;
}
```

The use of the function is more natural to C programmers because it does not involve the use of the 8086 specific data structures (REGS and SREGS).

The general purpose interrupt routines, *int86* and *int86x*, are important because they enable you to generate any software interrupt on the PC. The difference between them is that plain *int86* allows you to set all registers except the segment registers and *int86x* also lets you specify new values for the segment registers (only the DS and ES segment registers can be set to new values because CS contains the segment address of our code while SS holds the current stack segment address).

Despite their versatility, there is one drawback of using the *int86* and *int86x* functions. To use them effectively, you have to know what each interrupt number accesses and the relevant register settings. The *intdos* and *intdosx* are versions of *int86* and *int86x* that are set to generate interrupt number 21h. Thus these two routines can access any one of the hundred or so DOS functions. Like the *int86* pair, *intdosx* allows you to specify new values for the segment registers DS and ES while *intdos* uses the default settings of DS and ES.

Many DOS and BIOS functions require you to specify both the segment address and the offset of a data item. You can get these values by using the macros FP_SEG and FP_OFF, respectively. The function *segread* lets you get the current values of the segment registers DS, ES, CS, and SS. You can use the MK_FP macro to construct a far pointer out of a segment address and an offset.

ACCESSING THE BIOS SERVICES

The BIOS has a relatively small number of functions that provide access to the following peripherals:

- disk (hard disk and diskette)
- keyboard
- video
- printer
- serial communications port
- system timer

Table 17-1 shows the list of interrupt numbers that are used with the INT instruction to invoke the BIOS services. The Turbo C++ library provides interface routines for most of these interrupts. Where applicable, these routines are also listed in the table. Each routine is described in detail in its reference page and is also summarized in Table 17-4. Note that no explicit interface is included for the video services accessed via interrupt number 10h, because there is an entire category of graphics routines (see Chapters 18, 19, and 20) available in versions 1.5 and higher of Turbo C and Turbo C++. You can still use *int86* to call the BIOS video routines.

Specific Interface Routines for BIOS

Table 17-4 summarizes the routines that are specifically meant for calling BIOS functions. In Table 17-1, we listed the interrupt numbers used to access the ROM BIOS services. Accessing the services through the interrupt number, however, requires you to set up the registers using the REGS and SREGS data structures and then use either *int86* or *int86x* to generate the interrupt. The BIOS interface routines listed in Table 17-4 simplify the task. They are easier to use because they accept normal C arguments and return values normally rather than use the REGS and SREGS structures. They also have descriptive names. Table 17-4 also shows the interrupt number to which the function provides an interface. The interrupt numbers are provided as cross reference to entries in Table 17-1.

Table 17-4. *BIOS Interface Routines in Turbo C++*

Name of Routine	Interrupt No. (Hex)	Purpose of Routine
bioscom	14	Perform I/O with RS-232C serial port (initialize port, send and receive a character).
biosdisk	13	Access physical sectors in floppy and hard disk (hard disk only on XT, AT, and PS/2).
biosequip	11	Obtain a list of peripherals attached to the PC.
bioskey	16	Read character from keyboard and query the status of function, Alt, and Shift keys.
biosmemory	12	Determine amount of memory in the system.
biosprint	17	Send character to parallel printer port and determine status of printer.
biostime	1A	Read and set current clock setting (also, access the real-time clock in AT, XT, and PS/2).

ACCESSING THE DOS SERVICES

Compared to the BIOS, MS-DOS services are far more numerous. They generally affect the file system, memory management, process management, and input and output functions. Unlike the BIOS, all MS-DOS functions are accessible via a single interrupt, the *INT 21h* instruction with the exact function specified in the AH register. In Table 17-2 we list the most common DOS functions. The function number shown in the table has to be put in the AH register before generating interrupt 21h. In certain cases, Turbo C++ provides a special purpose routine for accessing that DOS function. These routines are listed where applicable. Consult the reference pages for specific routines for further information. Table 17-3 summarizes all the DOS interface routines in Turbo C++. Short summaries of some important DOS services follow.

Access to the MS-DOS File System

A large percentage of the DOS interface routines provide access to the MS-DOS file system. You can find substitutes for each of the routines for performing file I/O. These substitutes are portable and are described in Chapter 15. There is, however, no substitute for the routines that allow you to get and set file attributes, and let you search for files in the directory (*findfirst* and *findnext*). For these tasks, the DOS interface is very useful.

Turbo C++ also includes several routines that allow you to perform file I/O using the CP/M-style approach based on File Control Blocks (FCBs) and Disk Transfer Addresses (DTAs). In this method, the file is viewed as a set of records of fixed size. The file name, record size, and other pertinent information is set up in an FCB data structure. During reading and writing, data transfer takes place between a DTA and the disk.

The *parsfnm* routine lets you parse a file name and load the name into an FCB. You have to open the file for FCB-oriented operations by using DOS function number 0Fh, and you have to set up a buffer to hold the data being read (or the data to be written). The address of this buffer is the DTA, and you can use the functions *getdta* and *setdta* to perform the chores of saving the old DTA and setting up the new one. The actual reading and writing are done by calling the functions *randbrd* and *randbwr*, respectively. Curiously, there is no interface routine in Turbo C++ to open or close a file using an FCB.

The FCB approach was included in MS-DOS for compatibility with the older CP/M machines, but by now, this approach is largely replaced by the new DOS file I/O routines that use handles. The handle-based method is compatible with UNIX, and unlike the FCB-based method, it can handle a hierarchical file system. (FCBs cannot handle multiple levels of directories!) If you plan to use the DOS file I/O functions, it is best to confine your choices to the more powerful handle-based routines.

Servicing Interrupts

When we discussed hardware interrupts we mentioned installing a function in the interrupt vector table to process whatever a particular hardware interrupt requires. There are a few hidden treasures in Turbo C++ and its library that can help you write an interrupt handler entirely in C. The first is the newly introduced *interrupt* attribute for functions (see Chapter 3 for details) which causes the compiler to push all registers upon entry to the function and to use an IRET instruction for exiting the function. The other treasures are the library routines *disable* and *enable* which are C equivalents of the assembly language instructions CLI and STI, respectively. Last but not the least are the routines *getvect* and *setvect* for retrieving and setting particular entries in the interrupt vector table. Using these new features you can write routines that, for example, can perform interrupt-driven I/O with the serial port on the PC.

Memory Allocation and Time

You also get to access the DOS functions for memory allocation and for getting or setting the date and the time. These routines are redundant, though, because there is an assortment of memory allocation (Chapter 6) and time (Chapter 13) routines in the Turbo C library.

Error Handling

Hardware errors on the PC cause an interrupt 24h to be generated. There are three routines, *harderr*, *hardresume*, and *hardretn*, to help you set up an appropriate handler for this interrupt. By the way, the normal handler for this interrupt is the originator of the infamous message "Abort, Retry, Ignore?" ("Abort, Retry, Fail?" in DOS 3.3).

Specific Interface Routines for DOS

Table 17-5 lists the Turbo C++ routines that are specifically meant as gateways to a few selected DOS functions. These DOS interface routines make it easier to pass arguments and receive return values. Each routine in Table 17-5 also has an entry showing the DOS function number for which the routine serves as an interface. If you have the need to use one of the DOS functions listed in Table 17-2 for which no simple interface routine exists, you can access the DOS function using the *intdos* and *intdosx* routines. The function number has to be placed in the AH register (of a REGS structure) and you have to consult a *DOS Technical Reference Manual* or a book such as Duncan[3] for details on the input and output parameters for the DOS function you want to call.

Table 17-5. ***MS-DOS Interface Routines in Turbo C++***

Name of Routine	DOS Function No. (Hex)	Purpose of Routine
bdos, bdosptr	—	Access any DOS function that makes use of only AL and DX registers.
allocmem	48	Allocate a specified number of paragraphs of memory.
_chmod	43	Get or set the attribute of a file. This tells us if the file is: read only, hidden, a system file, a volume label, a subdirectory, or changed since last backup.
_close	3E	Close a file specified by a handle.
_creat	3C	Create and truncate a file of given name (null-terminated string) and get a handle back (deletes existing file of same name).
country	38 65	Get country-dependent settings for formats of date, time, and currency.
dosexterr	59	Get detailed error information about the last error that occurred during an "INT 21h" instruction. The information is returned in the registers and you will have to consult a DOS reference guide for exact meaning of the values that are returned.
findfirst	4E	Find the first occurrence of a named file (name is a null-terminated string). Requires a Disk Transfer Address (DTA) which can be set up by function 1Ah.
findnext	4F	For a file name containing wildcard characters (* or ?), finds the next occurrence of a file of that name. Assumes _dos_findfirst was called and it found a file.
freemem	49	Free a block of memory.
getcbrk	33	Get the status of the Control-Break flag (if set, DOS checks key presses for Control-C or Control-Break).
getdate	2A	Get the current date (day, month, and year).
getdfree	36	Get the total number of clusters and the number available for use on a disk drive. The number of bytes per cluster

Table 17-5. *(cont.)*

Name of Routine	DOS Function No. (Hex)	Purpose of Routine
		is also returned. So the total storage capacity of a disk and the amount free can be computed easily.
getdisk	19	Get the current drive (0 means A, 1 means B, and so on).
getdta	2F	Get the address of the current DTA used by certain DOS file I/O routines.
getfat	1C	Get the file allocation table of a specified drive.
getfatd	1B	Get the file allocation table of the default drive.
getftime	57	Get the time and date a file was last modified (file specified by handle).
getpsp	62	Get the Program Segment Prefix (PSP) address.
getswitchar	37	Get the current "switch character" (the character that precedes options in DOS commands).
gettime	2C	Get the current time in hours, minutes, seconds, and hundredths of a second. Note that system time is updated 18.2 times a second.
getvect	35	Get the contents of the interrupt vector table for a specified interrupt number.
getverify	2E	Get the current value of the VERIFY flag (if set, DOS will read after each disk write operation).
intdos	any	Call any DOS function by placing function number in AH (using the REGS union). Not useful for those functions that require the use of DS and ES segment registers.
intdosx	any	Used to call any DOS function including those requiring the use of DS and ES segment registers.
ioctl	44	Communicate with installable DOS device drivers.
keep	31	Terminate current program but leave it intact in memory (used to install the so called "terminate-but-stay-resident" or TSR utilities).
_open	3D	Open a named file for a specific type of access and obtain a 16-bit handle to uniquely identify the open file.
parsfnm	29	Extract drive, file name, and extension from a command line.
_read	3F	Read a specified number of bytes from a file into a buffer in memory.
randbrd	27	Read a number of records from a file starting at a specified random block.
randbwr	28	Write a number of records to a file starting at a specified random block.
setblock	4A	Change the size of a previously allocated block of memory.
setcbrk	33	Set the Control-Break flag. This lets you enable or disable the checking of Control-C and Control-Break keypresses.
setdate	2B	Set the system date.

Table 17-5. *(cont.)*

Name of Routine	DOS Function No. (Hex)	Purpose of Routine
setdisk	0E	Set the default disk drive (specified by a number, 0 means A, 1=B, and so on).
setdta	1A	Set a new DTA.
setftime	57	Set the modification time of a file (file specified by handle).
setswitchar	37	Set a new "switch character" (the character that precedes the options for a DOS command).
settime	2D	Set the current system time.
setvect	25	Set the entry in the interrupt vector table corresponding to a given interrupt number. The new value should be the address of a routine designed to handle that interrupt number.
setverify	2E	Set the VERIFY flag. When enabled, DOS will read after each write operation.
_write	40	Write a specified number of bytes from a buffer to an open file (need handle).

MISCELLANEOUS INTERFACE ROUTINES

In addition to the BIOS and DOS interface routines, the system calls category of the Turbo C++ library also includes routines for obtaining register values of the 8086 microprocessor, handling hardware errors in the MS-DOS system, enabling and disabling interrupts, and installing interrupt handlers. We have already discussed these features in our overview of the system call routines. They are detailed in Table 17-6. Note that *int86* and *int86x* are considered basic system interface routines because their primary purpose is to generate software interrupts in the 8086 microprocessor. Thus, all the ROM BIOS and DOS functions can be accessed using the *int86* and *int86x* routines.

You should note that the availability of the routines *sound* and *nosound* allows you to generate sound using the PC's speaker. These two routines, introduced in Turbo C version 1.5, are handy if you are developing applications that use sound as a means of alerting the user.

Table 17-6. *System Interface Routines in Turbo C++*

Name of Routine	Interrupt No. (Hex)	Purpose of Routine
absread	25	Use interrupt number 25h to read a number of logical sectors from a disk.
abswrite	26	Use interrupt number 26h to write to a number of logical sectors in a disk.

Table 17-6. *(cont.)*

Name of Routine	Interrupt No. (Hex)	Purpose of Routine
ctrlbrk	none	Set up an interrupt handler for interrupt 23h (Control-C interrupt).
delay	none	Wait a specified number of milliseconds before returning.
disable	none	Execute a CLI instruction thus disabling all interrupts.
dostounix	none	Convert date and time in DOS format to UNIX format (seconds elapsed since 00:00 hour GMT, 1 January, 1970).
__emit__	none	Embed bytes of data directly in the object code being generated by the compiler (requires in-depth knowledge of 8086 opcodes and operands to use correctly).
enable	none	Execute an STI instruction to enable interrupts again.
FP_OFF	none	Return the offset address of a far pointer (see Chapter 3).
FP_SEG	none	Return the segment address of a far pointer (see Chapter 3).
geninterrupt	any	Generate a specified software interrupt.
harderr	24	This does not generate the interrupt number 24h, rather this function sets the interrupt vector entry for 24h to a given function address. Since the system generates an interrupt 24h whenever a hardware error occurs, this function is meant to handle fatal hardware errors. Guess what the default function does? (Hint: Type DIR A: without placing a diskette in drive A.)
hardresume	none	Return to MS-DOS after a hardware error (or interrupt 24h).
hardretn	none	Return to application where hardware error (or interrupt 24h) had occurred.
int86	any	Call any function accessible by a software interrupt. Not useful for those functions that require the use of DS and ES segment registers.
int86x	any	Used to call any function including those requiring the use of DS and ES segment registers.
intr	any	Used to call DOS and BIOS functions via software interrupts (functions line *int86x*).
MK_FP	none	Construct a far pointer out of a segment address and an offset.
nosound	none	Turn off the PC's speaker.
_OvrlnitEms		Initialize EMS memory for use by overlay manager.
_OvrlnitExt		Initialize extended memory for use as overlay swap space.
peek, peekb	none	Get a word or a byte from a memory location.
poke, pokeb	none	Place a value in a word or a byte at a specified memory address.
segread	none	Obtain the current contents of the segment registers CS, DS, ES, and SS.
sleep	none	Suspend execution of program for a specified number of seconds.
sound	none	Activate the PC's speaker at a specified frequency.
unixtodos	none	Convert time in UNIX format (seconds elapsed since 00:00 hour GMT, 1 January, 1970) to date and time in DOS format.

Cautions

- The system calls category of the Turbo C++ library contains routines that allow you to perform tasks that are often intimately tied to hardware. It is thus necessary to understand the basic operation of the IBM PC hardware as well as that of MS-DOS before you can use these functions effectively.
- Programs that depend on system calls will run on MS-DOS machines only and will not be portable to other systems.
- If you are not familiar with the interrupt concept, the physical layout of a diskette, and the DOS file system, consult the references suggested at the end of this tutorial.
- Note that the Turbo C++ library has other file I/O routines that use handles to access files. Although they may seem similar, you should not mix the DOS file I/O calls with those from the Input and Output category (see Chapter 16). In fact, there is no reason to use the file I/O routines described in this chapter because the functionality of the regular C library I/O routines surpasses that of the ones in the system calls category. Besides, the I/O routines listed in Chapter 16 are portable because many of them are part of the proposed ANSI standard definition of C.

Further Reading

The number of system features and peripherals that you can access and manipulate using the *system call* set of routines is quite large. Although a detailed discussion of all the things you can do with these interface routines is beyond the scope of this book, there are quite a few resources that can help you.

The recent book by Lafore[1] is excellent for anyone learning C on the IBM PC. In the course of teaching the language, it also goes over the basics of the ROM BIOS routines. Prata's book[2] covers the same ground in a bit more advanced manner. For detailed information on MS-DOS, the book by Duncan[3] is ideal. The developer's guide by The Waite Group[4] has an excellent discussion of the physical layout of diskettes and of the DOS file system.

The ROM BIOS functions are also discussed in considerable detail in the book by Norton[5] and information specific to the IBM PC/AT appears in Smith's book[6].

1. Robert Lafore, *The Waite Group's C Programming Using Turbo C++*, SAMS, Carmel, IN, 1990, 825 pages.

2. Stephen Prata, The Waite Group, *Advanced C Primer++*, Howard W. Sams & Company, Indianapolis, IN, 1986, 502 pages.
3. Ray Duncan, *Advanced MS-DOS*, Microsoft Press, Redmond, WA, 1986, 468 pages.
4. The Waite Group, *MS-DOS Developer's Guide*, Second Edition, Howard W. Sams & Company, Indianapolis, IN, 1989, 813 pages.
5. Peter Norton, *The Peter Norton Programmer's Guide to the IBM PC*, Microsoft Press, Redmond, WA, 1985, 426 pages.
6. James T. Smith, *The IBM PC AT Programmer's Guide*, Prentice-Hall, New York, NY, 1986, 277 pages.

absread

COMPATIBILITY

TC1	TC1.5	TC2	TC++	MSC3	MSC4	MSC5	MSC6	QC1	QC2	QC2.5	ANSI	UNIX V	XNX
▲	▲	▲	▲										

PURPOSE Use *absread* to read data from logical disk sectors into a buffer in memory.

SYNTAX

```
int   absread (int drive, int nsects, int lsect, void *buffer);
```

`int drive;` *Drive number to be read (0 = A, 1 = B, and so on)*

`int nsects;` *Number of sectors to be read*

`int lsect;` *Logical sector number where reading begins*

`void *buffer;` *Address of buffer to which data is transferred*

EXAMPLE CALL

```
absread(0, 1, 0, buff);  /* Read logical sector 0 of drive A */
```

INCLUDES `#include <dos.h>` *For function declaration*

DESCRIPTION The *absread* function uses interrupt 25h to read data from logical disk sectors into a buffer in memory (do not confuse this with DOS function 25h accessible via the routine *setvect* which enables you to install a handler for a specific interrupt number.) The argument *drive* specifies the disk drive from which data is read. A drive number of 0 implies drive A, 1 means drive B, and so on. The reading begins at the logical sector number *lsect*, and *absread* will read data from a total of *nsects* successive logical sectors. You must allocate a buffer to hold the data and provide its address in the argument *buffer*.

The *absread* function provides access to raw logical disk sectors, without regard to the MS-DOS file system. To use this function effectively, you should be familiar with the physical organization of disks (the ideas of "sector," "track," and "head"), as well as how logical sectors are numbered. For example, logical sectors numbered 0 and 1 need not be physically next to each other. For efficient access to consecutive logical sectors, many disk controllers assign logical sector numbers to physical sectors that are a fixed distance apart. This is known as "interleaving."

COMMON USES The *absread* function is useful when you want to develop a disk utility that can display sector-level information to the user.

RETURNS The *absread* function returns a zero if all goes well. In case of any error, *absread* returns −1 and sets the global variable *errno* to the value of AX register returned by the handler in DOS for interrupt 25h. The error code in the lower byte (AL) should be interpreted according to the entries in Table 17-27. The upper byte (AH) will contain one of the error codes shown in Table 17-7.

Table 17-7. *Upper Byte Error Codes*

AH (Hex.)	Meaning
80	Disk drive failed to respond.
40	Seek operation on drive failed.
20	Disk controller failed.
10	Data error detected via cyclic redundancy check (CRC).
08	Failed during direct memory access (DMA).
04	Requested sector was not found.
03	Disk is write protected.
02	Bad address mark (these are marks placed during formatting to identify a sector).
01	Bad command.

COMMENTS The ROM BIOS disk routine invoked by interrupt 13h provides even lower level access (using specific head, track, and physical sector numbers) to disks, which is necessary for tasks such as formatting a disk. You can access these services through the library routine *biosdisk*.

SEE ALSO `abswrite` *To write data to logical disk sectors*

`biosdisk` *To access BIOS disk services*

EXAMPLE On MS-DOS diskettes, logical sector 0 (known as the "bootstrap sector") contains information about the characteristics of the diskette. Starting at the fourth byte in the boot sector, you will find an eight byte OEM (Original Equipment Manufacturer) name and a version number (this is the DOS version number). Write a Turbo C program that uses *absread* to read logical sector 0. Extract the OEM name and version number, and display the information. On an IBM PC running DOS 3.1, the program shown below will print

```
Insert a diskette into drive A and press any key
Read OK.
OEM name and version from boot sector:
IBM  3.1
```

```
#include <stdio.h>
#include <dos.h>
```

```
int main(void)
{
    int i, strt, ch_out, sector;
    char buf[512];

    printf("Insert a diskette into drive A and"
           " press any key\n");
    getch();
 /* Read logical sector 0. This "bootstrap" sector
  * contains information about the disk's
  * characteristics
  */
    sector = 0;
    if(absread(0,1,sector, &buf) != 0)
    {
        printf("Error in 'absread'!\n");
        exit(0);
    }
    printf("Read OK.\n");
    printf("OEM name and version from boot sector:\n");
    strt = 3;
    for (i=0; i<8; i++)
    {
        ch_out = buf[strt+i];
        putchar(ch_out);
    }
        printf("\n");
    return 0;
}
```

abswrite

COMPATIBILITY

TC1	TC1.5	TC2	TC++	MSC3	MSC4	MSC5	MSC6	QC1	QC2	QC2.5	ANSI	UNIX V	XNX
▲	▲	▲	▲										

PURPOSE Use *abswrite* to read data from a specified memory buffer to logical disk sectors.

SYNTAX

```
int abswrite(int drive, int nsects, int lsect, void *buffer);

int  drive;         Drive number (0 = A, 1 = B, and so on)
```

```
int  nsects;
```
Number of sectors to be written

```
int lsect;
```
Logical sector number where writing begins

```
void *buffer;
```
Address of buffer from which data is transferred

EXAMPLE CALL

```
abswrite(2, 1, 3, buff);  /* Write to logical sector 3 of drive C */
```

INCLUDES

```
#include <dos.h>
```
For function declaration

DESCRIPTION The *abswrite* function uses interrupt 26h to write data from a buffer in memory to logical disk sectors. The argument *drive* specifies the disk drive to which data is written. A drive number of 0 implies drive A, 1 means drive B, 2 means drive C, and so on. The writing begins at the logical sector number *lsect,* and *abswrite* will write data from *buffer* to a total of *nsects* successive logical sectors.

The *abswrite* function provides access to raw logical disk sectors, without regard to the MS-DOS file system. To use this function effectively, you should be familiar with the physical organization of disks (the ideas of "sector," "track," and "head"), as well as how logical sectors are numbered.

RETURNS The *abswrite* function returns a zero if all goes well. In case of any error, *abswrite* returns −1 and sets the global variable *errno* to the value of AX register returned by the handler in DOS for interrupt 26h. The error code in the lower byte (AL) should be interpreted according to the entries in Table 17-27. The upper byte (AH) will contain one of the error codes shown in the reference entry for the function *absread.*

COMMENTS The ROM BIOS disk routine invoked by interrupt 13h provides even lower level access (using specific head, track, and physical sector numbers) to disks, which is necessary for tasks such as formatting a disk. You can access these services through the library routine *biosdisk.*

Since the *abswrite* function overwrites disk sectors without regard to the DOS file structure, it is dangerous to experiment with this function.

SEE ALSO

`absread` *To read data from logical disk sectors*

`biosdisk` *To access BIOS disk services*

EXAMPLE The use of *abswrite* is similar to that of its companion function *absread.* Experimenting with *abswrite* can be dangerous because you can easily damage the DOS file structure on a disk by overwriting sectors. Therefore, no example is provided for this function.

System Calls

allocmem

COMPATIBILITY

TC1	TC1.5	TC2	TC++	MSC3	MSC4	MSC5	MSC6	QC1	QC2	QC2.5	ANSI	UNIX V	XNX
▲	▲	▲	▲			1	1	1	1	1			

PURPOSE Use *allocmem* to allocate memory in 16-byte chunks (called "paragraphs") from a pool maintained by DOS. Remember to free the memory using the companion function *freemem* when you no longer need it.

SYNTAX

```
int allocmem (unsigned size, unsigned *segp);
```

`unsigned size;` *Number of 16-byte paragraphs to be allocated*

`unsigned *segp;` *Location where segment address of allocated memory will be returned*

EXAMPLE CALL

```
if(allocmem(size, &segadd) != -1)
                    printf("Error allocating memory\n");
```

INCLUDES `#include <dos.h>` *For function declaration*

DESCRIPTION The *allocmem* function calls the DOS function 48h to allocate the paragraphs of memory requested in the argument *size* and returns the segment address of the block through the unsigned integer whose address is in the argument *segp*. The offset is always zero. The address of the allocated memory should be saved for use in freeing the block later with *freemem*. The example below illustrates one way to use the memory allocated by *allocmem*.

1. The compatible function in Microsoft C 5 and 6, and QuickC 1.0, 2.0, and 2.5, is *_dos_allocmem*.

RETURNS The *allocmem* function returns −1 if memory was successfully allocated. If the requested amount of memory could not be allocated, *allocmem* will return the maximum available memory size (in paragraphs).

COMMENTS The *allocmem* and *freemem* functions are MS-DOS specific. There are other standard memory allocation functions (for example, *malloc*, *calloc*, and *free*) that are more portable (for example, when moving your program to a UNIX system). It is interesting to note that the standard allocation routines use a memory pool that the Turbo C++ startup routine initially gets by requesting a chunk of memory from DOS using the same DOS function that *allocmem* invokes.

SEE ALSO

`freemem` *To free memory allocated by* allocmem

`setblock` *To alter the size of a chunk of memory allocated by* allocmem

`calloc, malloc` *Standard memory allocation routines*

EXAMPLE Use the *allocmem* to allocate as many paragraphs of memory as the user requests. Make sure it is enough to hold 80 characters. Store a sample string in the newly allocated buffer and then print the string out. Finally free the allocated buffer.

```
#include <stdio.h>
#include <dos.h>
#define DOS_PRTSTR 0x09
char str[80]=
"Successfully allocated memory using allocmem...\n$";
main()
{
    union REGS xr;
    struct SREGS sr;
    int retval;
    char far *stradd;
    unsigned int segadd, size;
    stradd = (char far *)(&str[0]);
    printf("Enter number of paragraphs requested:");
    scanf(" %u", &size);
    if(size < 5) size = 5; /* Need at least 5 paras */
    printf("Allocating %u paragraphs of memory\n",
    size);
    if ((retval=allocmem(size, &segadd)) != -1)
    {
        printf("Memory allocation failed!\n");
printf("Only %d paragraphs available!\n",retval);
        exit(0);
    }
/* Copy string into allocated memory using movedata */
    movedata(FP_SEG(stradd),FP_OFF(stradd),
             segadd, 0, 80);
    sr.ds = segadd;
    xr.x.dx = 0;
    xr.h.ah = DOS_PRTSTR;
    intdosx(&xr, &xr, &sr);

/* Free memory before exiting */
    freemem(segadd);
    return 0;
}
```

COMPATIBILITY

bdos

TC1	TC1.5	TC2	TC++	MSC3	MSC4	MSC5	MSC6	QC1	QC2	QC2.5	ANSI	UNIX V	XNX
▲	▲	▲	▲	▲	▲	▲	▲	▲	▲	▲			

PURPOSE Use the *bdos* function to call a subset of the DOS functions that can be invoked by an INT 21h instruction. You can use *bdos* to call only those DOS functions that require no arguments or that take arguments in the *DX* and the *AL* registers only. For example, you can use *bdos* with function number 1 to read a character from the keyboard. The returned character will be in the low-order byte of the return value. In contrast to the more general purpose *intdos* and *intdosx* functions, *bdos* is a simplified way to access a small set of DOS functions.

SYNTAX

```
int   bdos (int dosfun, unsigned dosdx, unsigned dosal);
```

`int dosfun;` *DOS function number*

`unsigned dosdx;` *DX register value*

`unsigned dosal;` *AL register value*

EXAMPLE CALL

```
bdos(2, 'q', 0);  /* Use DOS function 2 to display 'q' */
```

INCLUDES `#include <dos.h>` *For function declaration*

DESCRIPTION The function *bdos* provides simplified access to a subset of the DOS functions accessed by an INT 21h instruction. The *bdos* function can be used to access any DOS function that either requires no arguments or takes arguments in the *DX* and *AL* registers only. This function first copies the values from the unsigned integer arguments *dosdx* and *dosal* into the system's *DX* and *AL* registers, respectively. Then it invokes the DOS function number *dosfun* with an *INT 21h* instruction. At the end of the DOS call, *bdos* returns the contents of the *AX* register. The meaning of this value depends on the DOS service requested in *dosfun*.

COMMON USES The *bdos* function is commonly used to read characters from the keyboard and write characters to the screen using the MS-DOS interface. The advantage of using these services is that your programs will work on all MS-DOS computers.

The *intdos* and *intdosx* functions are more general gateways to the entire collection of DOS functions, but *bdos* has the advantage of being simpler to use. Of course, if the DOS function being called requires you to provide arguments in registers other than DX and AL, then you cannot use *bdos.*

RETURNS The return value is the content of the *AX* register at the end of the DOS call. The meaning of this return value depends on the DOS function that was called. The *bdos* function simply passes back whatever the DOS function puts in the AX register. For example, if the DOS call returns a value in *AL*, you can get this value by ignoring the high-order byte of the return value (see example below).

COMMENTS Note that the *intdosx* function provides the most versatile "gateway" to the DOS functions because it allows you to set up all register values before calling DOS via INT 21h. You should use *bdos* only when the specific conditions described above are met.

SEE ALSO

`bdosptr`	*Use when a pointer argument is required by the DOS function (DS:DX)*
`intdosx, intdos`	*More general mechanism to access DOS functions*
Table 17-5	*Simplified access to several DOS functions*

EXAMPLES Read a character from the keyboard using DOS function 1. The character is returned in the *AL* register. Remember that *bdos* returns the value of the *AX* register.

```
#include <stdio.h>
#include <dos.h>
/* DOS function to read from keyboard */
#define DOS_KBDIN 1
main()
{
    unsigned int ch_read;
/* Nothing needs to be specified for DX and AL. Use 0's
 * Also, zero out the high-order byte by bitwise AND
 * with FFh
 */
    ch_read = bdos(DOS_KBDIN, 0, 0) & 0xff;
    printf("\nCharacter read = %c\n", ch_read);
    return 0;
}
```

Use DOS function 2 to display on your monitor a character placed in the *DL* register (perhaps a character you just read from the keyboard). The return value has no meaning in this case.

```
#include <stdio.h>
#include <dos.h>
#define DOS_KBDIN    1
#define DOS_DISPCHAR 2
main()
{
    unsigned int ch_read;
/* First read a character. (see previous example) */
    ch_read = bdos(DOS_KBDIN, 0, 0) & 0xff;

/* Now display the character. DX is the character.
 * Nothing is needed in AL.
 */
    printf("\nHere's what you typed: ");
    bdos(DOS_DISPCHAR, ch_read, 0);
    return 0;
}
```

bdosptr

COMPATIBILITY

TC1	TC1.5	TC2	TC++	MSC3	MSC4	MSC5	MSC6	QC1	QC2	QC2.5	ANSI	UNIX V	XNX
▲	▲	▲	▲										

PURPOSE Use the *bdosptr* function to call a subset of the DOS functions that can be invoked by an INT 21h instruction. You should use *bdosptr* to call only those DOS functions that expect an address (pointer) in the registers DS and DX, and an argument in AL.

SYNTAX

```
int bdos(int dosfun, void *argument, unsigned dosal);
```

`int dosfun;` *DOS function number*

`void *argument;` *Address of argument to be placed in DS:DX*

`unsigned dosal;` *AX register value*

EXAMPLE CALL

```
char new_directory[] = "\\INCLUDE";
bdosptr(0x3b, new_directory, 0); /* Change current directory */
```

INCLUDES `#include <dos.h>` *For function declaration*

DESCRIPTION Like *bdos*, *bdosptr* provides simplified access to the set of DOS functions by an INT 21h instruction. You should use *bdosptr* to access any DOS function that requires address of an argument in the register pair DS:DX, and another argument in AL. The *bdosptr* function first sets up the DS:DX registers using the address of the argument given in *argument*. Next it copies the value from the unsigned integer argument *dosal* into the system's AL register. Then it invokes the DOS function number *dosfun* with an *INT 21h* instruction. At the end of the DOS call, *bdosptr* returns the contents of the *AX* register. The meaning of this value depends on the DOS service requested in *dosfun*.

COMMON USES The *bdosptr* function is useful in accessing functions such as "print a string (DOS function 9h)," and "change default directory (DOS function 3Bh)" that require a pointer to a buffer in DS:DX.

RETURNS The return value is the content of the *AX* register at the end of the DOS call. The meaning of this return value depends on the DOS function that was called. The *bdosptr* function simply passes back whatever the DOS function puts in the AX register. In case of an error, the return value is −1, and the global variables *errno* and *_doserrno* will contain error codes.

COMMENTS Note that the *intdosx* function provides the most versatile "gateway" to the DOS functions because it allows you to set up all register values before calling DOS via INT 21h. You should use *bdosptr* only when the specific conditions described above are met.

SEE ALSO

`bdos`	*Use when the DOS function requires arguments in DX and AL only*
`intdosx, intdos`	*More general mechanism to access DOS functions*
Table 17-5	*Simplified access to several DOS functions*

EXAMPLE Change the current directory using DOS function 3Bh.

```
#include <stdio.h>
#include <stdlib.h>
#include <dos.h>
/* DOS function to change current directory */
#define DOS_CHDIR  0x3b
main()
{
    char newdir[80];
    printf("Change current directory to: ");
    gets(newdir);
/* Nothing needs to be specified for AL. Use a 0. */
    bdosptr(DOS_CHDIR, newdir, 0);
/* Check current directory with the DOS 'dir' command */
```

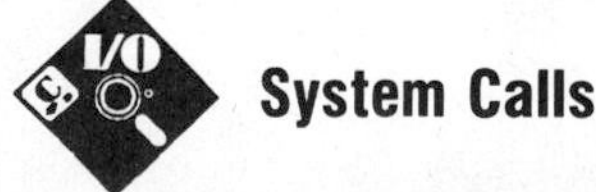

```
    printf("Current directory is: ");
    system("dir/w");
    return 0;
}
```

COMPATIBILITY

bioscom

TC1	TC1.5	TC2	TC++	MSC3	MSC4	MSC5	MSC6	QC1	QC2	QC2.5	ANSI	UNIX V	XNX
▲	▲	▲	▲			1	1	1	1	1			

PURPOSE Use *bioscom* to access the RS-232 serial ports (COM1 and COM2) of the PC. You can use this function to perform "polled" I/O, set communications parameters (for example, baud rate, parity etc.), and to check the status of the port.

SYNTAX

```
int  bioscom(int cmd, char abyte, int port);
```

`int  cmd;` *Service requested*

`char abyte;` *Character to be sent or communications parameters*

`int port;` *Serial port number, 0=COM1 and 1=COM2*

EXAMPLE CALL

```
ch_rcvd = 0xff & bioscom(2, 0, COM1); /* Receive a character */
```

INCLUDES `#include <bios.h>` *For function declaration*

DESCRIPTION The *bioscom* function lets you use the services offered by the BIOS routines normally accessible by interrupt number 14h. Only the ports COM1 and COM2 can be handled by this routine. The argument *port* specifies the port number, a 0 means COM1 and a 1 indicates COM2. The function performs the service requested in the argument *cmd* using the character data *abyte* where necessary. The commands shown in Table 17-8 can be used as the *cmd* argument.

There are several communications parameters that must be initialized before using the serial port. Specifically, these parameters are: the word length, specifying how many bits make up one character; the number of stop bits, indicating the end of a character; the parity to be used; and the baud rate, which indicates how fast the port sends out the bits that make up a single character. It is fairly simple to specify the parameters: pick one value from each of the four categories shown in Table 17-9 and bitwise OR them together to construct the character *abyte* indicating your choice of the communications parameters.

Table 17-8. *Service Codes for* bioscom

Service Code	Service Performed
0	Initialize the serial port using the communications parameters given in *data*. (See Table 17-9 for information on the parameters.)
1	Send the character in the low-order byte of *data* over the serial port *port*.
2	Receive a character from *port* and return it in the low-order byte of the return value.
3	Return the current status of the port. (See explanation of return value for more details.)

Table 17-9. *Communications Parameters*

Category Name	Acceptable Values	Communications Parameter Setting
word length	0x02	7 bits per character
	0x03	8 bits per character
stop bits	0x00	1 stop bit
	0x04	2 stop bits
Parity	0x00	No parity bit
	0x08	Odd parity, parity bit is such that total number of 1s is odd.
	0x18	Even parity, parity bit is such that total number of 1s is even
Baud rate	0x00	110 baud
	0x20	150 baud
	0x40	300 baud
	0x60	600 baud
	0x80	1200 baud
	0xA0	2400 baud
	0xC0	4800 baud
	0xE0	9600 baud

For example, if you select 8-bit word length, 1 stop bit, no parity and a baud rate of 300 baud, use (0x03 ¦ 0x00 ¦ 0x00 ¦ 0x40) (the bar separating the values is the bitwise OR operator in C) as the *abyte* argument with the service code 0 (initialize port).

1. The compatible function in Microsoft C 5 and 6, and QuickC 1.0, 2.0, and 2.5, is *_bios_serialcom.*

COMMON USES The *bioscom* function is useful for simple polled I/O from the serial port at baud rates of up to 300 baud. Beyond this rate, the characters arrive so fast that your program will not be able to keep up if it reads from the port in this manner.

For higher performance, it is necessary to use an interrupt-driven approach where the serial port invokes an interrupt handler whenever it needs attention. (See Chapter 13 of *MS-DOS Papers* by The Waite Group for an example of an interrupt-driven serial I/O package.)

RETURNS The high-order byte of the return value always represents the status of the communications port. The meaning of the specific bits is shown in Table 17-10.

Table 17-10. *Interpreting the Status of the Serial Port*

Bit	Interpretation When Bit is 1
8	Received data is ready.
9	A data overrun error occurred (a character was received before the last one was read).
10	A parity error occurred.
11	A framing error occurred (the end of a character was not recognized properly).
12	A "break" signal was detected (this means that the signal on the receive line went dead for a while).
13	Register that holds a character to be transmitted is empty.
14	Shift register that moves the character out for transmission is empty.
15	The serial port has timed out.

For the "send character" service, the low-order byte of the return value should contain the character just sent out. As shown in Table 17-10, if bit 15 is set then the character was not sent because the port was not ready within a specified period of time.

When reading a character from the serial port using the "receive character" service, the low-order byte of the return value is the character just read, provided that none of the bits in the high-order byte is set. If any bit in the high-order byte is set, an error had occurred and the cause of the error is indicated by the bit that is set (consult Table 17-10 for interpretation).

For the "initialize port" and "get port status" services, the low-order byte contains the status of the modem. The meanings of the bits in this case are as shown in Table 17-11.

Table 17-11. *Meaning of Modem Status*

Bit	Interpretation When Bit is 1
0	Change in "Clear To Send" signal (see bit 4).
1	Change in "Data Set Ready" signal (see bit 5).
2	Trailing edge ring indicator.

Table 17-11. *(cont.)*

Bit	Interpretation When Bit is 1
3	Change detected in quality of signal in the receive line.
4	Clear To Send (means modem is ready to receive data from the serial port).
5	Data Set Ready (means modem is connected to phone line).
6	Modem is receiving a "ring" voltage (means an incoming telephone call is detected).
7	Signal detected in the receive line.

SEE ALSO `int86` *For access to the BIOS serial I/O services through 80x86 software interrupt number 14h*

EXAMPLE Use *bioscom* to set up the serial port at 300 baud, 8-bit word length, 1 stop bit, and no parity. Once you have set the port, if you have a Hayes-compatible modem connected there, you can try conversing with it. For example, if you type "AT," the modem should answer back with an "OK" (if there is no response try typing "ATE1V1" to set up the modem properly). Assume that you are using the COM1 port.

```
#include <stdio.h>
#include <bios.h>
#define COM1        0  /* Change this to 1 for COM2 */
#define COM_INIT    0
#define COM_SEND    1
#define COM_RECEIVE 2
#define COM_STATUS  3
#define KEYBRD_READ  0
#define KEYBRD_READY 1
main()
{
    int c;
    unsigned service, data, status;
    data = (0x03 | 0x00 | 0x00 | 0x40);
    bioscom(COM_INIT, data, COM1);
    printf("Connecting to serial port 1. \
Type 'q' to exit\n");

    while(1)
    {
/* First see if "DATA READY" flag is set. If yes read
 * character from serial port.
 */
        status = 0x100 &
```

```
                bioscom(COM_STATUS, 0, COM1);
        if (status == 0x100)
        {
/* If there is a character, get it and display it */
            c = 0xff &
                bioscom(COM_RECEIVE, 0, COM1);
            printf("%c", c);
        }

/* Now check if any key has been pressed */
        if(bioskey(KEYBRD_READY))
        {
/* If yes, read the keyboard buffer */
            c = bioskey(KEYBRD_READ) & 0xff;
            if((c == 'q') || (c == 'Q'))
            {
/* Exit if it's a 'q' or a 'Q' */
                printf("Exiting...\n");
                exit(0);
            }

/* Else, wait until "transmit holding register empty"
 * flag is set. Once it's set, send out character to
 * serial port.
 */
            status = 0x2000 &
                bioscom(COM_STATUS, 0, COM1);
            while (status != 0x2000)
            {
                status = 0x2000 &
                bioscom(COM_STATUS, 0, COM1);
            }
            bioscom(COM_SEND, c, COM1);
            if ((status & 0x8000) == 0x8000)
            {
                printf("Error sending: %c\n", c);
            }
        }
    }
    return 0;
}
```

biosdisk

COMPATIBILITY

TC1	TC1.5	TC2	TC++	MSC3	MSC4	MSC5	MSC6	QC1	QC2	QC2.5	ANSI	UNIX V	XNX
▲	▲	▲	▲			1	1	1	1	1			

PURPOSE Use the *biosdisk* function to perform raw disk I/O operations on the PC's disk drives by using the BIOS. For example, you can use *biosdisk* to read and write physical sectors from a diskette, to determine the status of the floppy disk drive, and even format a diskette (as an alternative to the DOS FORMAT command).

Since this function allows you to perform low-level disk I/O directly, you should use it with caution because it can destroy data and damage the MS-DOS file system that may already exist on your disk.

SYNTAX

```
int  biosdisk(int cmd, int drive, int head, int track, int sector,
              int nsects, void *buffer);
```

`int cmd;`	*Operation to be performed*
`int drive;`	*Drive number (0 = first floppy disk, 1 = second floppy, and so on, 80 = first hard disk, 81 = second one, and so on)*
`int head;`	*Head number*
`int track;`	*Track number*
`int sector;`	*Start sector number*
`int nsectors;`	*Number of sectors for which requested service is to be performed*
`void *buffer;`	*Pointer to buffer in memory for use during requested service*

EXAMPLE CALL

```
/* Read sector 6 from drive A */
biosdisk(2, 0, 0, 0, 6, 1, dir_buf);
```

INCLUDES `#include <bios.h>` *For function declaration*

DESCRIPTION The *biosdisk* function is a gateway to a set of ROM BIOS routines that provide access to the PC's disk drive via software interrupt number 13h. It provides a cleaner calling convention than generating an INT 13h using the *int86x* function. The *biosdisk* function performs the task requested in the argument *cmd*. It expects information about the disk drive (for example, the head number, track number, etc.) in the arguments *drive*, *head*, *track*, *sector*, and *nsects*.

As shown in Table 17-12, the valid range of values for number of sectors and tracks depends on the type of diskette.

Table 17-12. ***Tracks and Sectors of Various Diskettes***

Diskette Capacity	Drive Capacity	Valid Track No.	Valid Sector No.
	5.25-inch diskettes		
320 K	320/360 K	0 through 39	1 through 8
360 K	320/360 K	0 through 39	1 through 9
320 K	1.2 M (AT)	0 through 39	1 through 8
360 K	1.2 M (AT)	0 through 39	1 through 9
1.2 M	1.2 M (AT)	0 through 79	1 through 15
	3.5-inch diskettes (AT and PS/2)		
Diskette Capacity	**Drive Capacity**	**Valid Track No.**	**Valid Sector No.**
720 K	720 K	0 through 79	1 through 9
1.44 M	1.44 M	0 through 79	1 through 18

Enough memory must be allocated for the buffer used by *biosdisk*. For example, since a single sector in an IBM PC diskette can hold 512 bytes, to read n sectors the buffer size must be at least $n \times 512$ bytes.

The service requested from *biosdisk* can be specified by using the values for the six services shown in Table 17-13. This list shows the services that are available on any IBM PC or compatible. On PC XT and PC AT, there are several other services available. Consult a reference guide such as the pocket reference *IBM ROM BIOS* by Ray Duncan (Microsoft Press, 1988) for further details.

Table 17-13. ***Service Codes Accepted by*** **biosdisk**

Service Code	Function Performed	Arguments Used
0	Resets the disk controller so that status is set to zero to indicate that no error has occurred. Useful for resetting after an error.	drive
1	Gets status of last disk operation. See description of "return value" below for details of the status code.	drive
2	Reads specifed number of sectors into buffer in memory. Return value indicates error, if any.	drive, head, track, sector, nsectors, buffer
3	Writes data from the memory buffer to specified number of sectors on the diskette. This is the reverse of service code 2.	drive, head, track, sector, nsectors, buffer
4	First verifies that specified sectors exist and can be read. Then a cyclic redundancy check (CRC) is performed to verify that data in these sectors is correct. Since the stored data includes a CRC value it is possible to tell if any data has been corrupted.	drive, head, track, sector, nsectors

Table 17-13. *(cont.)*

Service Code	Function Performed	Arguments Used
	This service is similar to code 2 except that the memory buffer is not used. Return value indicates error, if any.	
5	Formats one track on one head of the diskette. This is similar to "disk write" except that the sector information is not used. For proper formatting, the buffer pointer must point to a data area that contains a set of four byte codes that describe the layout and the size of the sectors in that track.	drive, head, track, buffer

1. In Microsoft C 5 and 6, and QuickC 1.0, 2.0, and 2.5, use *_bios_disk*.

COMMON USES This function is useful for developing disk utilities that allow the user to read and examine individual sectors, and format diskettes, perhaps providing an alternative to the DOS FORMAT command with a nicer user interface. There are several commercial utility packages that allow you to "unerase" files and change file attributes—for example, to let you mark a file "hidden" so that it does not show up on directory listings. You can develop similar functionality on your own by using the *biosdisk* function.

RETURNS The *biosdisk* function always returns the contents of the *AX* register at the end of the call. Since it uses an INT 13h call, after a read, write, or verify operation *AL* contains the total number of sectors for which the operation was to have been performed, while an 8-bit status code indicating success or cause of failure of the operation is returned in *AH*. When the operation is completed successfully, *AH* will be zero. Thus, a good way to tell whether there has been an error is to compare the value returned by *biosdisk* with the *nsectors* field of the *info* data structure (see example below). If they are equal then the operation went well, otherwise the high-order byte of the return value contains the error code. The error codes are summarized in Table 17-14 (these error codes are also defined in the BIOS listings in the *IBM PC Technical Reference Manual).*

COMMENTS You need a good understanding of how the MS-DOS file system is related to the physical tracks and sectors to make effective use of this function. Its use also calls for some care since the capability to format and to write data directly to sectors of a diskette also means that it is possible to inadvertently damage existing files and, worse, destroy crucial sectors with information about how the sectors are allocated to files (e.g., the File Allocation Table or FAT). Consult a book such as *MS-DOS Developer's Guide* by The Waite Group[4] for detailed information on these topics.

Table 17-14. ***Error Codes Returned by*** **biosdisk**

High-Order Byte of Return Value (Hexadecimal)	Meaning
01	Command not known to Diskette I/O system.
02	Could not find address marks that identify the side, the track, the sector, and the sector size on soft-sectored diskettes.
03	Could not write because diskette is "write-protected."
04	Could not find specified sector.
05	Reset failed.
08	Data transfers can occur directly between the diskette and the PC's memory in an interrupt-driven approach. This is known as DMA or "direct memory access" and there are "DMA controller Chips" on the PC to perform this task. This error code means that some data was lost during a DMA transfer.
09	DMA transfers (see error code 8) are not allowed to write to memory across a 64-K boundary. This error indicates that there was an attempt to do this.
10	The diskette controller stores a cyclic redundancy check (CRC) value for each sector of data. During a read operation it can compute the CRC value again and conclude whether the data has been corrupted. This error code tells us that CRC check indicates an error.
20	Diskette controller failed.
40	Could not move to requested track.
80	Disk drive timed out or failed to respond because either the door is open or the drive motor has not come up to speed yet. A retry is recommended.

EXAMPLE Under MS-DOS, on double-sided, double-density (9-track, 40-sector, 360-K) diskettes the directory entries begin at Track 0, Sector 6. A 512-byte sector has 16 directory entries, each 32-bytes long. The first 11 bytes of a directory entry is the name of the file (8-character name followed by 3-character extensions). Use *biosdisk* to directly read the first directory sector from this DSDD diskette and display the first 10 names found in it. If you have erased files or the diskette is newly formatted, you may see some strange filenames—this is perfectly normal. Also, if your diskette has a volume name, that will be the first filename displayed.

```
#include <stdio.h>
#include <dos.h>
#include <bios.h>
#define DOS_DISPCHAR 2
#define DISK_READ    2
```

```
main()
{
    int i, j, retry, strt;
    unsigned ch_out, status = 0;
    char buf[512];
    int drive, head, track, sector, nsectors;

/* Set up diskette information */
    drive = 0;  /* Drive A, use 1 for drive B */
    head = 0;
    track = 0;
    sector = 6; /* Location of first directory
                   entry for DSDD diskettes   */
    nsectors = 1;

/* Read sector making up to 3 retries. Retries are
 * necessary to make sure that any error is not due to
 * motor start-up delay. See explanation for error code
 * 80h above.
 */
    for (retry = 0; retry <= 3; retry++)
    {
        if ((status = biosdisk(DISK_READ, drive, head,
                        track, sector, nsectors, buf))
            == 0)
        {
            printf("Read OK.\n");
            printf("First 10 directory entries are:\n");
            for (i=0; i<10; i++)
            {
            strt = 32*i; /* Each entry is 32 bytes */
                /* Each name is 11 bytes */
                for (j=0; j<11; j++)
                {
                    ch_out = buf[strt+j];
                    bdos(DOS_DISPCHAR, ch_out, 0);
                }
                printf("\n");
            }
            exit(0);
        }
    }

/* Read failed despite 3 retries. Report error */
    printf("Error reading from diskette! status=%x\n",
```

```
                status);
        return 0;
}
```

COMPATIBILITY

biosequip

TC1	TC1.5	TC2	TC++	MSC3	MSC4	MSC5	MSC6	QC1	QC2	QC2.5	ANSI	UNIX V	XNX
▲	▲	▲	▲			1	1	1	1	1			

PURPOSE Use *biosequip* to get information about the hardware and peripherals in the user's PC. The list of equipment is returned in coded form in a single unsigned integer, whose bit values are shown in Table 17-15.

SYNTAX `int biosequip (void);`

EXAMPLE CALL `equip_flag = biosequip();`

INCLUDES `#include <bios.h>` *For function declaration*

DESCRIPTION The *biosequip* function uses the BIOS interrupt 11h to get a list of hardware and peripherals currently installed in the PC. The combination of bits in the return value indicates the presence or absence of specific hardware and peripherals (see Table 17-15).

Table 17-15. ***Meaning of Bits in Value Returned by*** **biosequip**

Bits	Meaning
0	1 = one or more disk drives attached, 0 means no disk drives.
1	1 = a math coprocessor is present.
2-3	Size of system memory in units of 4 K.
4-5	Initial video mode (00 = unused, 01 = 40×25 black and white text with color card, 10 = 80×25 black and white text with color card, 11 = 80×25 text on monochrome card.
6-7	Number of disk drives installed (00 = 1, 01 = 2). Only floppy disk drives are reported.
8	Set to 0 only if a DMA (direct memory access) chip is present.
9-11	Number of RS 232C serial ports in the system.
12	1 = a game adapter is installed.
13	1 = a serial printer is attached.
14-15	Number of printers attached to system.

1. Use *_bios_equiplist* in Microsoft C 5 and 6, and QuickC 1.0, 2.0, and 2.5.

RETURNS This function returns the contents of the *AX* register of BIOS interrupt 11h. The bits of the return value must be interpreted as shown in Table 17-11. Note that bit 0 is the least significant bit.

COMMENTS This function is of limited usefulness. For example, bits 4 and 5 indicate the initial video mode, but not the current mode. This function does, however, provide some basic information such as the number of RS232 serial ports, the number of diskette drives, and the number of printers attached to the PC.

SEE ALSO `int86` *For another way of generating BIOS interrupt 11h*

EXAMPLE Use the *biosequip* to obtain the number of diskette drives, the number of serial ports, and the number of printers on the user's system, and to determine if a math coprocessor is available. This approach can be used to ensure that the user's system has the minimal configuration necessary to run a program, as well as to allow a program to use optional hardware.

```
#include <stdio.h>
#include <bios.h>
main()
{
    unsigned elist, d_drives=0, s_ports=0, printers=0;
    elist = biosequip();
/* Extract each item from the return value */
    if(elist & 0x0001)
    {
        d_drives = ((elist & 0x00c0) >> 6) + 1;
    }
    s_ports = (elist & 0x0e00) >> 9;
    printers = (elist & 0xc000) >> 14;
    printf("This system ");
    if((elist & 0x0002)>>1)
    {
        printf("has a math coprocessor, ");
    }
    printf("%d diskette drives,\n", d_drives);
    printf("%d serial ports and %d printers\n",
           s_ports, printers);
    return 0;
}
```

COMPATIBILITY

bioskey

TC1	TC1.5	TC2	TC++	MSC3	MSC4	MSC5	MSC6	QC1	QC2	QC2.5	ANSI	UNIX V	XNX
▲	▲	▲	▲			1	1	1	1	1			

PURPOSE Use *bioskey* to access the BIOS routines for keyboard I/O. You can use it to read the next available character, to check if a character is waiting to be read, and to check if the special keys such as ALT, CTRL, and SHIFT are being pressed.

SYNTAX

```
int bioskey (int cmd);

int cmd;        Keyboard function requested
```

EXAMPLE CALL

```
ch_read = bioskey(0) & 0xff; /* Read from keyboard */
```

INCLUDES

```
#include <bios.h>        For function declaration
```

DESCRIPTION The *bioskey* routine accesses the BIOS keyboard services by generating 80x86 interrupt number 16h. The service to be performed is specified by the value of the argument *cmd*. The acceptable values and the tasks they perform are summarized in Table 17-16.

Table 17-16. *Services Offered by* bioskey

Service Name	Service Performed
0	Reads next available character from the keyboard buffer. Waits for a character if necessary. (See returns for more information.)
1	Checks the keyboard buffer for characters waiting to be read. (See returns for explanation.)
2	Returns current status of the SHIFT, CTRL, and ALT keys, and whether the SCROLL LOCK, NUM LOCK, and CAPS LOCK indicators are on.

1. In Microsoft C 5 and 6, and QuickC 1.0 through 2.5, use *_bios_keybrd*.

RETURNS After the call *bioskey(0)*, the low-order byte of the return value contains the ASCII code of the character just read and the high-order byte has the *scan code*—a unique byte generated by the keyboard whenever a key is either pressed or released. (See the *IBM PC Technical Reference Manual* for a list of the scan codes for the IBM PC keyboard.) The character read is removed from the buffer.

The service code 1 returns a 0 if the keyboard buffer is empty; otherwise it returns the character in the same way that "keyboard read" (code 0) does, but does not remove the character from the buffer.

The service code 2 provides in the low-order byte of the return value the current settings of the three LED indicators (CAPS LOCK, NUM LOCK, and SCROLL LOCK) and whether any of the keys Right SHIFT, Left SHIFT, ALT, or CTRL are being pressed. As shown in Table 17-17, one bit is used to represent each status.

Table 17-17. *Interpreting the SHIFT Status Byte Returned by* bioskey

Bit	Interpretation When Bit Is 1
0	Rightmost SHIFT key pressed.
1	Leftmost SHIFT key pressed.
2	CTRL key pressed.
3	ALT key pressed.
4	Scroll Lock indicator is ON.
5	Num Lock indicator is ON.
6	Caps Lock indicator is ON.
7	In insert mode.

COMMENTS The "keyboard ready" service (code 1) is very helpful when you want to continue doing something until the user presses a key. You can do your work in a loop using this service to see if a key has been pressed. Since this service does not wait for a character to be typed, you can actually continue the work and yet respond quickly to the user's keystrokes. The *kbhit* function also provides this service and is easier to use.

SEE ALSO `int86` *Alternate ways to access BIOS keyboard functions using interrupt 16h*

`kbhit` *Another way to check for a keypress*

EXAMPLE Use the "keyboard ready" service (code 1) to check if a key has been pressed. If not, keep updating a count until a key is pressed or the count is 50000.

```
#include <stdio.h>
#include <bios.h>
#define KEYBRD_READY 1
#define KEYBRD_READ  0
main()
{
    unsigned count=0, c=0;
    while(count<50000)
    {
```

```
            if(bioskey(KEYBRD_READY))
            {
/* Read the keystroke and mask out the high byte */
                c = bioskey(KEYBRD_READ) & 0xff;
                printf("You entered: %c\n", c);
                break;
            }
            count++;
        }
        printf("Count is %u\n", count);
        return 0;
}
```

COMPATIBILITY

biosmemory

TC1	TC1.5	TC2	TC++	MSC3	MSC4	MSC5	MSC6	QC1	QC2	QC2.5	ANSI	UNIX V	XNX
▲	▲	▲	▲			1	1	1	1	1			

PURPOSE Use *biosmemory* to determine the amount of memory in the PC. A program can use this to check if there is enough memory for it to run.

SYNTAX `unsigned biosmemory (void);`

EXAMPLE CALL `total_kilobytes = biosmemory();`

INCLUDES `#include <bios.h>` *For function declaration*

DESCRIPTION This function gets the amount of memory in the system by using BIOS interrupt 12h.

1. The compatible function in Microsoft C 5 and 6, and QuickC 1.0 through 2.5, is *_bios_memsize*.

RETURNS The return value is the total memory in the system in 1-K (1,024 bytes) blocks.

EXAMPLE Check the amount of memory on the system using *biosmemory*.

```
#include <bios.h>
main()
{
    unsigned memsize;
    memsize = biosmemory();
    printf("This system has %dK memory.\n", memsize);
    return 0;
}
```

biosprint

COMPATIBILITY

TC1	TC1.5	TC2	TC++	MSC3	MSC4	MSC5	MSC6	QC1	QC2	QC2.5	ANSI	UNIX V	XNX
▲	▲	▲	▲			1	1	1	1	1			

PURPOSE Use *biosprint* to communicate with the printer. You can initialize the printer, determine its status, and send characters to the printer using this function.

SYNTAX

```
int  biosprint(int cmd, int abyte, int port);
```

`int cmd;` *Printer function requested*

`int abyte;` *Character being sent to printer*

`int port;` *Printer port, 0=LPT1:, 1=LPT2:*

EXAMPLE CALL

```
biosprint(0, 'x', LPT1); /* Print an 'x' */
```

INCLUDES `#include <bios.h>` *For function declaration*

DESCRIPTION The *biosprint* function is an interface to the BIOS printer routines accessible through software interrupt number 17h. The routine performs the service indicated by the argument *cmd* on the printer port selected by the argument *port*, using the data *abyte* where needed. Table 17-18 shows the service codes with their meanings.

Table 17-18. *Service Codes for* biosprint

Service Name	Service Performed
0	Sends the low-order byte of *data* to the printer and returns the status after the operation.
1	Initializes printer connected to specified port. Note that *printer* = 0 means LPT1, 1 means LPT2 and so on. The value of *data* is ignored. The status is returned.
2	Returns status of the printer (see explanation in returns for meaning).

1. In Microsoft C 5 and 6, and QuickC 1.0, 2.0, and 2.5, use *_bios_printer*.

RETURNS The low-order byte of the return value represents the status of the printer. The meaning of the bits is shown in Table 17-19.

SEE ALSO `int86` *For another way to access the BIOS printer services*

Table 17-19. *Interpreting the Status Byte of the Printer*

Bit	Interpretation When Bit Is 1
0	Printer has timed out.
1	Not used.
2	Not used.
3	I/O error has occurred.
4	Printer is selected for output.
5	Printer is out of paper.
6	Acknowledgment from printer.
7	Printer not busy (if bit is 0, printer is busy).

EXAMPLE Use *biosprint* to initialize a printer at port LPT1 and print out a line if the printer is ready.

```
#include <stdio.h>
#include <bios.h>
#define LPT1 0
#define PRINTER_WRITE   0
#define PRINTER_INIT    1
char str[] = "\rTesting BIOS printing routine\n\r";
main()
{
    int i, status, data;
    status = biosprint(PRINTER_INIT, data, LPT1);
    for (i=0; str[i] != '\0'; i++)
    {
        data = str[i];
        biosprint(PRINTER_WRITE, data, LPT1);
    }
    return 0;
}
```

biostime

COMPATIBILITY

TC1	TC1.5	TC2	TC++	MSC3	MSC4	MSC5	MSC6	QC1	QC2	QC2.5	ANSI	UNIX V	XNX
▲	▲	▲	▲			1	1	1	1	1			

PURPOSE Use the *biostime* function to retrieve or set the current system clock count on the PC. Knowing that the clock count is incremented 18.2 times a second, you can use this function to wait for a specified number of seconds, albeit with a resolution of 1/18.2 sec (or about 55 milliseconds) only.

SYNTAX

```
long  biostime(int cmd, long newtime);

int       cmd;          Service code

long      newtime;      New value for timer clock count (used when setting timer)
```

EXAMPLE CALL

```
clock_count = biostime(0, 0L); /* Get current clock count */
```

INCLUDES

```
#include <bios.h>       For function declaration
```

DESCRIPTION The *biostime* function invokes the ROM BIOS time-of-day interrupt (number 1Ah) to get the current clock count or to reset the clock count to a new value. This count is incremented 18.2 times a second. Thus the count can serve as a timer with a resolution of 1/18.2 second (or 55 milliseconds).

The exact service requested is specified by using a service code specified in the argument *cmd*. Table 17-20 explains the use of the service codes.

Table 17-20. ***Service Codes for* biostime**

Service Name	Service Performed
0	Returns the current value of the clock count as a long integer.
1	Sets the current system clock count to the value specified in the long integer argument *newtime*. The return value is unspecified.

1. The compatible function in Microsoft C 5 and 6, and QuickC 1.0 through 2.5, is *_bios_timeofday*.

COMMON USES This function is useful in writing "delay" routines that wait for a specified number of seconds before returning.

RETURNS The return value is defined only when *service* is 0. In this case the long integer return value is the current time count.

COMMENTS One drawback of using *biostime* as a timer is the "coarseness" of the clock counts which are updated once every 55 milliseconds only.

SEE ALSO `int86` *For general purpose access to BIOS INT 1Ah services*

EXAMPLE Write a routine that uses *biostime* to wait for a specified number of seconds before exiting.

```
#include <stdio.h>
#include <bios.h>
#define TIME_GETCLOCK 0
main()
```

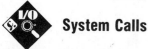

```
{
    long oldcount, newcount;
    int ticks;
    printf("How many seconds to wait? ");
    scanf("%d", &ticks);
    ticks *= 18.2;
    oldcount = biostime(TIME_GETCLOCK, 0L);
    newcount =oldcount;
    while ((newcount-oldcount) < ticks)
    {
        newcount = biostime(TIME_GETCLOCK, 0L);
    }
    printf("\nWaited for %d clock ticks\n", ticks);
    return 0;
}
```

_chmod

COMPATIBILITY

TC1	TC1.5	TC2	TC++	MSC3	MSC4	MSC5	MSC6	QC1	QC2	QC2.5	ANSI	UNIX V	XNX
▲	▲	▲	▲			1	1	1	1	1			

PURPOSE Use *_chmod* to obtain or to change the current attributes of an MS-DOS file. For example, you can determine if a file is a normal file or a subdirectory by using this function. Also, you can make a file "hidden" so that it does not show up on an MS-DOS DIR command.

SYNTAX

```
int _chmod (const char *pathname, int func, .../* int attr */);
```

`const char *pathname;` *Pathname of file whose attributes will be returned or set*

`int func;` *Service being requested (0 = get attribute, 1 = set attribute)*

`int attr;` *New file attribute (needed only when setting attribute)*

EXAMPLE CALL

```
_chmod("secret.dat", 1, FA_HIDDEN); /* Hide file */
```

INCLUDES #include <io.h> *For function declaration*

#include <dos.h> *For definition of attribute names*

DESCRIPTION The *_chmod* function calls DOS function 43h to get or to alter the attributes of the file whose name is in the character string *pathname*. The attribute of an MS-DOS file indicates whether the file is read-only, whether it is a subdirectory, and so on.

You have to specify the service to be performed by *_chmod* in the argument *func*. A function code equal to 0 means you want to get the current file attributes. A value of 1 in *func* requests alteration of the attributes in which case the new attributes for the file are specified in the optional argument *attr*.

When specifying a new attribute, you can select a combination of attributes by specifying a value created by the bitwise OR of attribute names picked from Table 17-21. These attribute constants are defined in *dos.h*.

1. In Microsoft C 5 and 6, and QuickC 1.0 through 2.5, use *_dos_getfileattr* to get the current attributes of a file or directory and *_dos_setfileattr* to set the current attributes of a file or directory.

RETURNS Upon successful completion, *_chmod* returns the current attributes of the file. Otherwise, it returns a −1.

You can test for an exact combination of attributes by comparing the returned attribute with the bitwise OR of attribute names picked from Table 17-21.

Sometimes it is necessary to check only if the file has a certain attribute set. For example, if you simply want to determine whether a file has the archive attribute (FA_ARCH) set, you can do so by first performing a bitwise AND of the returned attribute value with FA_ARCH and then comparing the result for equality with FA_ARCH. The attribute is set if the test succeeds.

In case of an error, the global variable *errno* is set either to ENOENT to indicate that the file could not be located, or to EACCES if permission for the specified operation was denied.

SEE ALSO chmod *To alter the read/write access permissions of a file*

EXAMPLES Use *_chmod* to "hide" a file whose name is provided by the user. (You can write a similar program to make the file normal again.)

```
#include <stdio.h>
#include <io.h>
#include <dos.h>
main()
{
    char filename[80], *p_fname;
    printf("Enter name of file to hide: ");
    p_fname = gets(filename);
/* If you want to make a hidden file visible again,
 * simply change the last argument in the call to
 * _chmod to 0
 */
    if (_chmod(p_fname, 1, FA_HIDDEN) == -1)
    {
        printf("Error in _chmod call!\n");
        exit(0);
    }
```

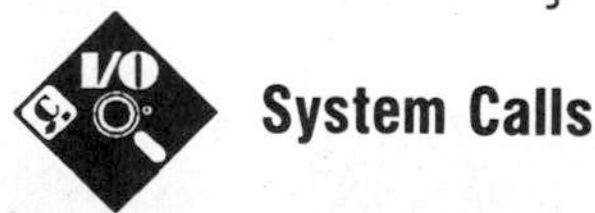

```
    printf("%s is now hidden. Try DIR to verify.\n",
           filename);
    return 0;
}
```

Use *_chmod* to check if a file whose name is provided by the user is a subdirectory.

```
#include <stdio.h>
#include <dos.h>
main()
{
    int attribute;
    char filename[80], *p_fname;
    printf("Enter filename: ");
    p_fname = gets(filename);
    if ( (attribute = _chmod(p_fname, 0)) == -1 )
    {
        printf("Error in _chmod call!\n");
        exit(0);
    }
    if ( (attribute & FA_DIREC) == FA_DIREC )
    {
        printf("%s is a subdirectory.\n", filename);
    }
    else
    {
        printf("%s is NOT a subdirectory.\n", filename);
    }
    return 0;
}
```

_close

COMPATIBILITY

TC1	TC1.5	TC2	TC++	MSC3	MSC4	MSC5	MSC6	QC1	QC2	QC2.5	ANSI	UNIX V	XNX
▲	▲	▲	▲			1	1	1	1	1			

PURPOSE Use *_close* to close a file that you had opened earlier by calling *_open* or that you had created by using *_creat*.

SYNTAX

```
int  _close (int handle);

int handle;
```

The file "handle" or identifier

EXAMPLE CALL

```
_close(handle);
```

INCLUDES

`#include <io.h>` *For function declaration*

DESCRIPTION

The *_close* function calls DOS function 3Eh to close the file specified by the identifying number or "handle" in the argument *handle*. This operation involves flushing (writing) all internal MS-DOS buffers associated with that file to the disk, closing the file, and releasing the handle for reuse. The date stamp, the time stamp, and the file size are also updated.

The file handle must be one that had been returned when the file was opened by *_open* or perhaps created by *_creat*.

1. The compatible function in Microsoft C 5 and 6, and QuickC 1.0 through 2.5, is *_dos_close*.

RETURNS

This function returns zero if successful; otherwise, it returns a −1 and sets the global variable *errno* to the constant EBADF, indicating that the file handle is invalid.

COMMENTS

The functions *open* and *close* offer a more portable means of achieving the same result as these DOS specific functions.

SEE ALSO

`_open` *To open an existing file using a DOS call*

`_creat` *To create a new file*

`open, close` *Portable versions of similar file opening and closing functions*

EXAMPLE

Use *_close* to close a file that was opened by *_open*.

```
#include <stdio.h>
#include <fcntl.h>
#include <io.h>
main()
{
    char fname[40], *p_fname;
    int filehandle;

    printf("Enter name of file to open using _open: ");
    p_fname = gets(fname);

/* Open the file using _open */
    if ( (filehandle = _open(p_fname, O_RDONLY)) == -1)
    {
        printf("Error opening file: %s\n", fname);
```

```
        exit(0);
    }
    printf("File %s opened.\n", fname);

/* Now close file */
    if (_close(filehandle) != 0)
    {
        perror("Error closing file with _close");
        exit(0);
    }
    printf("File %s closed.\n", fname);
    return 0;
}
```

COMPATIBILITY

_creat

TC1	TC1.5	TC2	TC++	MSC3	MSC4	MSC5	MSC6	QC1	QC2	QC2.5	ANSI	UNIX V	XNX
▲	▲	▲	▲			1	1	1	1	1			

PURPOSE Use *_creat* to create a new file or to truncate an existing file to zero length.

SYNTAX

```
int   _creat  (const char *path, int attribute);

char      *path;          Filename including path

int       attribute;      Attributes of the file
```

EXAMPLE CALL

```
filehandle = _creat("c:\\tmp\\tmp001", 0);
```

INCLUDES

```
#include <io.h>        For function declaration

#include <dos.h>       For definition of attribute names
```

DESCRIPTION The *_creat* function calls the DOS function 3Ch to create the file whose name (including the full DOS pathname) is specified by the argument *path* and whose attributes are in the argument *attribute*. If the file already exists, it is truncated to zero length and its old attributes are retained.

The attribute indicates whether a file is read only, whether it is hidden, and so on. You can specify the attribute by using the bitwise OR of attribute names picked from Table 17-21. The attribute constants are defined in *dos.h*.

Table 17-21. *Interpretation of File Attribute Constants*

Attribute Name	Interpretation
FA_RDONLY	File cannot be opened for write operations.
FA_HIDDEN	File will not show up on directory search.
FA_SYSTEM	File is marked as a system file; it will be excluded from normal directory searches.
FA_LABEL	Volume name, can exist only in root directory.
FA_DIREC	Subdirectory name (means the file is a subdirectory).
FA_ARCH	If set, file will be archived by MS-DOS *BACKUP* command. This attribute is set after any changes to the file.

1. In Microsoft C 5 and 6, and QuickC 1.0, 2.0, and 2.5, use *_dos_creat.*

RETURNS Once the file is successfully opened, an identifying number or "handle" is returned. You should save this handle because you will need it for future references to this file. In case of error, it returns a −1 and sets the global variable *errno* to one of the constants shown in the Table 17-22. The meaning of the error code is explained in the table.

Table 17-22. *Error Codes Returned by* _creat

Error Code	Interpretation
ENOENT	Path not found.
EMFILE	Too many files open (limit is 20 for a process).
EACCES	Access was denied (for example, the file exists and cannot be overwritten, or the root directory is full).

COMMENTS The *creat* function provides a more portable means of achieving the same result as does this DOS-specific function.

Under MS-DOS, the maximum number of concurrently open files for a single process is 20.

SEE ALSO

`_close`	*To close a file*
`creatnew`	*To create a new file but not overwrite existing ones*
`creat`	*Portable versions of similar file creation function*

EXAMPLE Use *_creat* to create a file. Close the file by calling *_close.*

```
#include <stdio.h>
#include <io.h>
main()
{
```

```
    int filehandle;

    printf("Enter name of file to create using"
           "_creat:");
    p_fname = gets(fname);

/* Create the file using _creat */
    if ( (filehandle = _creat(p_fname, 0)) == -1)
    {
        perror("Error creating file");
        exit(0);
    }
    printf("File %s created.\n", fname);

/* Now close file */
    if (_close(filehandle) != 0)
    {
        perror("Error closing file with _close");
        exit(0);
    }
    printf("File %s closed.\n", fname);
    return 0;
}
```

COMPATIBILITY

country

TC1	TC1.5	TC2	TC++	MSC3	MSC4	MSC5	MSC6	QC1	QC2	QC2.5	ANSI	UNIX V	XNX
▲	▲	▲	▲										

PURPOSE Use *country* to get (DOS 2.0 and above) or set (only in DOS 3.0 and above) country-dependent date, time, and currency formatting information used in MS-DOS.

SYNTAX `struct country *country (int xcode, struct country *cp);`

`int xcode;` *Country code*

`struct country *cp;` *Pointer to structure where country-dependent information is returned*

EXAMPLE CALL `country(0, &country_info); /* Get info for current country */`

INCLUDES `#include <dos.h>` *For function declaration*

DESCRIPTION The *country* function uses DOS function 38h to return country-dependent formatting information used in MS-DOS (versions 2.0 and above). In DOS 3.0 and above, you can also set a new country code.

When requesting information, you must allocate a *country* structure and provide a pointer to this structure in the argument *cp*. The *country* structure is defined in *dos.h* as follows:

```
struct  country
{
  int  co_date;          /* Date format:
                               0  = USA       month  day   year
                               1  = Europe    day   month  year
                               2  = Japan     year  month  day  */
  char  co_curr[5];      /* Currency symbol                    */
  char  co_thsep[2];     /* Thousands separator character      */
  char  co_desep[2];     /* Decimal separator character        */
  char  co_dtsep[2];     /* Date separator character           */
  char  co_tmsep[2];     /* Time separator character           */
  char  co_currstyle;    /* Currency style:
                               0 = Currency symbol precedes value
                                   with no gap between the symbol
                                   and the number
                               1 = Currency symbol follows value
                                   with no gap between the symbol
                                   and the number
                               2 = Currency symbol precedes value
                                   with a space between the symbol
                                   and the number
                               3 = Currency symbol follows value
                                   with a space between the symbol
                                   and the number              */
  char  co_digits;       /* Number of significant digits in
                               currency                        */
  char  co_time;         /* Time format:
                               0 = 12 hour clock
                               1 = 24 hour clock               */
  long  co_case;         /* Address of case map routine        */
  char  co_dasep[2];     /* Data separator character           */
  char  co_fill[10];     /* Reserved for future use            */
};
```

If the argument *cp* is −1, the current country is set to the code specified in the argument *xcode*. Otherwise, *country* fills the structure whose address is in *cp* with information about the country specified by *xcode*. A zero in *xcode* means you want information about the current country. Other values of *xcode* indicate specific countries. The international telephone prefix code is usually the country code.

COMMON USES The *country* function allows you to write a program that can easily adapt to the time, date, and currency formats of different countries.

RETURNS The *country* function returns the argument *cp*.

COMMENTS You should use this function only in DOS versions 3.0 or higher because all the capabilities are not present in earlier versions (2.x).

EXAMPLE Get the date, time, and currency formatting information for the current country. Display the retrieved information. Here's what the following program prints when the country is U.S.A.

```
======== For this country ========
Date is of the form: MM-DD-YY
Time is of the form: HH:MM:SS
Currency style: $9,999.99

#include <stdio.h>
#include <dos.h>

main()
{
    struct country c_info;
/* Get date, time and currency format for
 * current country
 */
    country(0, &c_info);
/* Display the information */
    printf("======== For this country ========\n");
    printf("Date is of the form: ");
    switch(c_info.co_date)
    {
        case 0:
            printf("MM%sDD%sYY\n", c_info.co_dtsep,
                   c_info.co_dtsep);
            break;
        case 1:
            printf("DD%sMM%sYY\n", c_info.co_dtsep,
                   c_info.co_dtsep);
            break;
        case 2:
            printf("YY%sMM%sDD\n", c_info.co_dtsep,
```

```
                        c_info.co_dtsep);
                break;
        }
        printf("Time is of the form: HH%sMM%sSS\n",
                c_info.co_tmsep, c_info.co_tmsep);
        printf("Currency style: ");
        switch(c_info.co_currstyle)
        {
            case 0:
                printf("%s9%s999%s99\n", c_info.co_curr,
                        c_info.co_thsep, c_info.co_desep);
                break;
            case 1:
                printf("9%s999%s99%s\n", c_info.co_thsep,
                        c_info.co_desep, c_info.co_curr);
                break;
            case 3:
                printf("%s 9%s999%s99\n", c_info.co_curr,
                        c_info.co_thsep, c_info.co_desep);
                break;
            case 4:
                printf("9%s999%s99 %s\n", c_info.co_thsep,
                        c_info.co_desep, c_info.co_curr);
                break;
        }
        return 0;
}
```

ctrlbrk

COMPATIBILITY

TC1	TC1.5	TC2	TC++	MSC3	MSC4	MSC5	MSC6	QC1	QC2	QC2.5	ANSI	UNIX V	XNX
▲	▲	▲	▲										

PURPOSE Use *ctrlbrk* to set a function that will be called whenever the Control-Break key is pressed.

SYNTAX

```
void   ctrlbrk (int  (*fptr)(void));
```

`int (*fptr)(void);` *Pointer to the function that you want called when Control-Break (or Control-C) is pressed*

EXAMPLE CALL `ctrlbrk(our_cbrk_handler);`

INCLUDES `#include <dos.h>` *For function declaration*

DESCRIPTION The *ctrlbrk* function accepts a pointer to a function in the argument *fptr* and arranges it so that that function is called whenever Control-Break or Control-C is hit. The function name that you supply does not have to be an interrupt handler. The *ctrlbrk* function establishes an interrupt handler for interrupt 23h (which occurs when you press Control-Break or Control-C on the keyboard) that calls the function indicated by the argument *fptr*.

The handler function can either exit the program or use *longjmp* to return back to a desired place in your program (for example, return to the top-level command interpreter of your application).

COMMON USES A well-designed application should be able to handle exceptions and errors properly. The *ctrlbrk* function provides you with the means to install a handler for the exceptional condition that occurs when a user presses Control-Break (or, Control-C) on the keyboard.

RETURNS The *ctrlbrk* function returns nothing, but the installed handler should return 0 if it wants to abort the program. If it returns a nonzero value, the program will resume execution after return from the Control-Break interrupt (interrupt number 23h).

COMMENTS Another way to handle the Control-Break interrupt is to use the more general (and standard) *signal* mechanism. Turbo C 2.0 and Turbo C++ include the *signal* function which can handle Control-Break interrupts via a signal named SIGINT. In Turbo C versions 1.0 and 1.5 the *ctrlbrk* function is the only way to intercept the Control-Break interrupt.

SEE ALSO

`getcbrk`	*To determine the current status of the Control-Break checking flag*
`longjmp, setjmp`	*A mechanism for nonlocal jumps from one function to another*
`setcbrk`	*To turn Control-Break checking on or off*
`signal`	*To handle other exceptions (Turbo C 2.0 and Turbo C++)*

EXAMPLE Install a Control-Break handler using *ctrlbrk*. Show how the handler can be used to exit from an infinite loop. The example also shows a typical use of the Turbo C++ functions *setjmp* and *longjmp*.

```
#include <stdio.h>
#include <dos.h>
#include <setjmp.h>
```

```
int cbrk_handler(void);
/* Buffer used by setjmp and longjmp */
jmp_buf main_menu;

main()
{
    char input[80];
    int choice=0;

/* Install the Control-Break handler */
    ctrlbrk(cbrk_handler);

/* Call 'setjmp' to set up for returning to this
 * point after user presses Control-C
 */
    if(setjmp(main_menu) != 0)
    {
/* Returning from a 'longjmp' -- print message */
        printf("Interrupted...\n");
    }

/* This is the main menu of the program */
    printf("1  Loop endlessly...\n"
            "anything else to exit\n\n"
            "Enter Choice: ");
    gets(input);
    choice = atoi(input);
    switch(choice)
    {
        case 1: for(;;) printf("Looping...\n");

        default: exit(0);
    }
    return 0;
}
/*--------------------------------------------------*/
int cbrk_handler(void)
{
/* Return to the main menu */
    longjmp(main_menu, 1);
    return 0;
}
```

COMPATIBILITY

delay

TC1	TC1.5	TC2	TC++	MSC3	MSC4	MSC5	MSC6	QC1	QC2	QC2.5	ANSI	UNIX V	XNX
	▲	▲	▲										

PURPOSE Use *delay* to suspend program execution for a specified number of milliseconds.

SYNTAX

```
void   delay (unsigned milliseconds);

unsigned milliseconds;        Number of milliseconds to wait
```

EXAMPLE CALL

```
delay(500);  /* Wait for half a second */
```

INCLUDES

```
#include <dos.h>        For function declaration
```

DESCRIPTION The *delay* function waits the number of milliseconds specified in the argument *milliseconds* before proceeding with further execution of the program. The resolution of the delay is limited by the system timer interrupts (see *biostime*) which occur approximately once every 55 milliseconds. In other words, don't expect to use this function for accurately delaying execution for any time interval less than about 55 milliseconds.

COMMON USES You can use *delay* with the function *sound* to generate a tone for a specified duration of time.

SEE ALSO

biostime *BIOS time-of-the-day function*

sound *To generate a continuous tone*

EXAMPLE Use *delay* in a program that generates a 440-Hz tone for a specified number of milliseconds.

```
#include <dos.h>
main()
{
    unsigned duration;
    printf("Enter duration of 440-Hz tone "
           "(in milliseconds): ");
    scanf(" %u", &duration);
    sound(440);
    delay(duration);
    nosound();
    return 0;
}
```

disable

COMPATIBILITY

TC1	TC1.5	TC2	TC++	MSC3	MSC4	MSC5	MSC6	QC1	QC2	QC2.5	ANSI	UNIX V	XNX
▲	▲	▲	▲			1	1	1	1	1			

PURPOSE Use the *disable* function to turn off interrupts on the 80x86 microprocessor by a CLI instruction. You may, for example, want to turn off interrupts when installing a new "handler" for an interrupt. Remember to call *enable* to turn interrupts back on as soon as possible.

SYNTAX

```
void disable(void);
```

EXAMPLE CALL

```
disable();
```

INCLUDES `#include <dos.h>` *For function declaration*

DESCRIPTION The *disable* function executes an 80x86 *CLI* instruction.

1. Use *_disable* in Microsoft C 5 and 6, and QuickC 1.0 through 2.5.

COMMON USES The *disable* function is useful when interrupts have to be turned off in critical sections of a program. Such cases typically arise in programs that install or remove interrupt handlers (see the Tutorial section).

COMMENTS The availability of the *disable* function greatly enhances your capability to write software such as interrupt handlers almost entirely in C, but you must use this function with care because of its intimate ties to the hardware. You should understand the interrupt mechanism of the 80x86 microprocessor before using this function. In particular, the system clock is updated by interrupts. So, disabling interrupts for long periods of time will interfere with the time-keeping. This function is a good example of the low-level access to hardware afforded by Turbo C++ on the IBM PC.

SEE ALSO `enable` *To enable 80x86 interrupts*

EXAMPLE See the example in the reference page on *setvect* for sample usage of *disable* and *enable*.

COMPATIBILITY

dosexterr

TC1	TC1.5	TC2	TC++	MSC3	MSC4	MSC5	MSC6	QC1	QC2	QC2.5	ANSI	UNIX V	XNX
▲	▲	▲	▲	▲	▲	▲	▲	▲	▲	▲			

PURPOSE On MS-DOS 3.0 or higher, use *dosexterr* after an error return from a DOS function call to obtain detailed information on the exact cause of the error and possible remedial action.

SYNTAX

```
int dosexterr (struct DOSERROR *errbuf);
```

`struct DOSERROR *errbuf;` *Pointer to structure that will contain information on return*

EXAMPLE CALL

```
dosexterr(&errbuf);
```

INCLUDES `#include <dos.h>` *For function declaration and declaration of the DOSERROR structure*

DESCRIPTION The *dosexterr* function calls DOS function 59h to get detailed information on the cause of a previous unsuccessful call to a DOS function (INT 21h). This function is available only under MS-DOS 3.0 or higher.

The information about the error is returned in a structure of type DOSERROR, and a pointer to one such structure must be passed in the argument *errbuf*. The DOSERROR structure is defined in *dos.h* and its C declaration is shown below.

```
struct DOSERROR
{
    int  de_exterror;  /* Extended error code */
    char de_class;     /* Error class         */
    char de_action;    /* Recommended action  */
    char de_locus;     /* Error locus -- device
                          where it occurred   */
};
```

The *exterror* field in this structure can be interpreted using Table 17-23. For more detailed information on this and the other fields consult the *MS-DOS Technical Reference Manual.*

Table 17-23. *Extended Error Codes from* dosexterr

Value of *exterror* (Hexadecimal)	Interpretation
0	No error in previous DOS function call.
1	Invalid function number.
2	File not found.

Table 17-23. ***(cont.)***

Value of ***exterror*** (Hexadecimal)	Interpretation
3	Path not found (bad drive or directory name).
4	Too many open files.
5	Access was denied.
6	Invalid file handle.
7	Memory control blocks destroyed.
8	Insufficient memory.
9	Invalid memory block address.
A	Invalid environment.
B	Invalid format.
C	Invalid access code.
D	Invalid data.
E	– Reserved –
F	Invalid disk drive.
10	Attempt to remove current directory.
11	Not the same device.
12	No more files.
13	Disk write-protected.
14	Unknown unit.
15	Drive not ready.
16	Unknown command.
17	CRC error in data.
18	Bad request structure length.
19	Seek error.
1A	Unknown medium.
1B	Sector not found.
1C	Printer out of paper.
1D	Write fault.
1E	Read fault.
1F	General failure.
20	Sharing violation.
21	Lock violation.
22	Invalid disk change.
23	File Control Block (FCB) unavailable.
24-4F	– Reserved –
50	File already exists.
51	– Reserved –
52	Cannot make directory.
53	Failed during critical error interrupt (INT 24h).

RETURNS The return value is identical to the field *exterror* which is actually the value of the *AX* register.

SEE ALSO `perror` *To print an error message*

EXAMPLE Try to close a nonexistent file using a DOS function call. Then call *dosexterr* to get the error code. You should get a report that *exterror* is 6, which means the file handle is invalid.

```
#include <stdio.h>
#include <dos.h>

main()
{
    struct DOSERROR errbuf;
/* Try closing a nonexistent file */
    if (_close(1000) != 0)
    {
        printf("Error closing file.\n");
        dosexterr(&errbuf);
        printf("exterror=%x, class=%x, action=%x, \
locus=%x\n", errbuf.de_exterror, errbuf.de_class,
        errbuf.de_action, errbuf.de_locus);
    }
    return 0;
}
```

dostounix

COMPATIBILITY

TC1	TC1.5	TC2	TC++	MSC3	MSC4	MSC5	MSC6	QC1	QC2	QC2.5	ANSI	UNIX V	XNX
▲	▲	▲	▲										

PURPOSE Use *dostounix* to convert to UNIX format the date and time returned by the DOS functions *getdate* and *gettime*, respectively.

SYNTAX `long   dostounix (struct date *d, struct time *t);`

`struct date *d;` *Pointer to structure holding date in DOS format*

`struct time *t;` *Pointer to structure holding time in DOS format*

EXAMPLE CALL

```
getdate(&d_dos);
gettime(&t_dos);
```

```
/* Convert to seconds elapsed since 00:00:00 GMT, Jan 1, 1970 */
t_unix = dostounix(&d_dos, &t_dos);
```

INCLUDES `#include <dos.h>` *For function declaration*

DESCRIPTION The time in UNIX systems is expressed as the number of seconds elapsed since 00:00:00 hours GMT (Greenwich Mean Time), January 1, 1970. The *dostounix* function accepts date and time in DOS formats and returns a long integer representing the UNIX time.

The DOS time and date are stored in *date* and *time* structures whose addresses are provided in the arguments *d* and *t* respectively. The functions *getdate* and *gettime* may be used to get the date and the time in DOS format.

COMMON USES The *dostounix* function allows you to print DOS date and time information using the formatting routines *ctime* which accepts UNIX-style time.

RETURNS The *dostounix* function returns the UNIX form of the date and time specified by the structures *d* and *t* respectively.

COMMENTS The library routine *time* returns the time in UNIX format. Rather than using *dostounix* to convert date and time from DOS format, you should use the *time* function directly.

SEE ALSO

`ctime` *To format a UNIX-style time into a string*

`getdate` *To get the current date from DOS*

`gettime` *To get the current time from DOS*

EXAMPLE Get the DOS date and time using the routines *getdate* and *gettime*. Then call *dostounix* to convert the date and time into UNIX format. Print the result by converting it to a string with *ctime*.

```
#include <dos.h>
#include <time.h>
main()
{
    struct date date;
    struct time time;
    time_t tunix;

/* Get date and time from DOS */
    getdate(&date);
    gettime(&time);
/* Convert to UNIX format */
```

```
    tunix = dostounix(&date, &time);
/* Print the date and time using 'ctime' */
    printf("%s\n", ctime(&tunix));
    return 0;
}
```

__emit__

COMPATIBILITY

TC1	TC1.5	TC2	TC++	MSC3	MSC4	MSC5	MSC6	QC1	QC2	QC2.5	ANSI	UNIX V	XNX
		▲	▲										

PURPOSE Use *__emit__* to embed bytes of 8086 machine instructions directly into the object code being generated by the Turbo C++ compiler.

SYNTAX

```
void __emit__(arguments,...);
```

`arguments` *Literal values or data that can be used to initialize static variables in a C program*

EXAMPLE CALL

```
/* Embed a PUSHF instruction in the code */
__emit__((unsigned char)0x9c);
```

INCLUDES `#include <dos.h>` *For function declaration*

DESCRIPTION The *__emit__* function, introduced in Turbo C 2.0, copies the literal values given in the *arguments* into the object code being generated by the Turbo C++ compiler. The arguments can also be expressions that can be evaluated at compile time. You can use any expression that is allowed as an initializer for a static variable.

You can control the number of bytes sent to the output code by casting the literal values to appropriate types. For example, a cast of *(unsigned char)* ensures that a value between 0 and 255 is stored in a single byte (with a DB assembly language statement). Similarly, a cast of *(unsigned)* will generate a word. You can also use local variables in the *arguments*—the offset of the variable from the BP register will be emitted in this case. See the example below for a sample use of the *__emit__* function.

COMMON USES The *__emit__* function is useful if you are knowledgeable about the 8086 machine instruction and want to embed 8086 opcodes and operands directly in the program. If you are more comfortable with assembly language, you can use Turbo C's *asm* keyword, and compile the program with the –B compiler option.

EXAMPLE Illustrate the use *__emit__* in a routine that allows you to call an interrupt handler from a function. When calling an interrupt handler, we must first push the flags on the stack with a PUSHF instruction, then use CALL DWORD PTR [BP+4], where the argument to the function is a pointer to the interrupt handler. The function *chain_int* in the following listing illustrates this. A sample use of such a routine is shown by setting up an interrupt handler for the BIOS video interrupts (number 10h). In our interrupt handler, we simply chain to the old handler by using the *chain_int* function. Try something with the video interrupt to see if this scheme works. For example, you can use the function that allows you to change the cursor shape and see if everything works. Before exiting, reset the interrupt vector to its original state. (Notice the use of the *disable* and *enable* pair to ensure that nothing goes wrong while we are taking over an interrupt vector).

```
#include <stdio.h>
#include <conio.h>
#include <dos.h>
#define BIOS_VIDEO 0x10
void interrupt vio_handler(void);
void interrupt (*old_handler)(void);
void chain_int(void interrupt (*p_func)());
main()
{
    union REGS xr, yr;
    int c;
/* Install the new handler named vio_handler
 * Disable interrupts when changing handler
 */
    disable();
    old_handler = getvect(BIOS_VIDEO);
    setvect(BIOS_VIDEO, vio_handler);
    enable();
/* Print out address of old handler using %p format */
    printf("\nThe address of the old handler is : "
           "%Fp\n", old_handler);
    printf("Installed new handler: %Fp\n", vio_handler);
/* Do some video I/O -- change cursor to a solid block*/
    xr.h.ah = 1;
    xr.h.ch = 0;
    xr.h.cl = 8;
    int86(BIOS_VIDEO, &xr, &yr);
/* Quit when user says so */
    printf("Hit q to quit: ");
    while ((c=getch()) != 'q'); /* Keep looping till 'q'*/
```

```
/* Reset vector. Disable interrupts when doing this     */
    disable();
    setvect(BIOS_VIDEO, old_handler);
    enable();
   return 0;
}
/*--------------------------------------------------*/
void interrupt vio_handler(void)
{
/* Our handler simply chains to the old_handler using
 * chain_int (see below)
 */
    chain_int(old_handler);
}
/*--------------------------------------------------*/
void chain_int(void (interrupt *p_func)())
{
/* Embed machine code to properly call an interrupt
 * handler by using the library routine __emit__.
 * Note that Turbo C would have generated
 * correct code (push flags, then call handler) even
 * if we had invoked the old handler with the usual
 * (*old_handler)(), but we wanted to show how
 * __emit__ works.
 */
/*  PUSHF  */
    __emit__((unsigned char)0x9c);
/* CALL FAR [BP+4] */
     __emit__((unsigned char)0xff, 0x5e, &p_func);
}
```

enable

COMPATIBILITY

TC1	TC1.5	TC2	TC++	MSC3	MSC4	MSC5	MSC6	QC1	QC2	QC2.5	ANSI	UNIX V	XNX
▲	▲	▲	▲			1	1	1	1	1			

PURPOSE Use *enable* to allow the 80x86 microprocessor to acknowledge interrupts. You should call *enable* after you had turned off interrupts by calling *disable*.

SYNTAX

```
void enable(void);
```

EXAMPLE CALL

```
enable();
```

INCLUDES `#include <dos.h>` *For function declaration*

DESCRIPTION The *enable* function executes an 80x86 *STI* instruction.

1. In Microsoft C 5 and 6, and QuickC 1.0 through 2.5, the compatible function is *_enable*.

COMMON USES The *enable* function is used in conjunction with *disable* to protect a section of code from being interrupted. You will not need the *enable* function for routine programming chores, but its availability allows you to write system programs such as "interrupt handlers" in Turbo C++ (see the tutorial section for a description of interrupt handlers).

SEE ALSO `disable` *To disable 80x86 interrupts*

EXAMPLE See the example in the reference page on *_dos_setvect* for sample usage of *disable* and *enable*.

findfirst

COMPATIBILITY

TC1	TC1.5	TC2	TC++	MSC3	MSC4	MSC5	MSC6	QC1	QC2	QC2.5	ANSI	UNIX V	XNX
▲	▲	▲	▲			1	1	1	1	1			

PURPOSE Use *findfirst* to find the first file whose name and attributes match the specified values. Since the specified name can have wildcard characters (* and ?), you can use this function to find, for example, the first file with a *.C* extension by searching for all **.C* files.

SYNTAX

```
int findfirst(const char *pathname, struct ffblk *fileinfo
                                    int attribute);
```

`const char *pathname;` *Filename to search for including path*

`struct ffblk *fileinfo;` *Structure to hold results of search*

`int attribute;` *File attributes to match*

EXAMPLE CALL

```
/* Search for volume name */
findfirst("\*.*", &fileinfo, FA_LABEL);
```

INCLUDES

```
#include <dir.h>          For function declaration

#include <dos.h>          For definition of attribute names
```

DESCRIPTION

The *findfirst* function calls the DOS function 4Eh to get the information about the first file whose name matches the one in the character string *pathname* and whose attributes are identical to that given in the argument *attribute*. The file name can have the wildcard characters * and ?.

The attribute to be matched can be specified by using a value created by the bitwise OR of attribute names picked from Table 17-22. These attribute constants are defined in *dos.h*.

The results of the search are returned in a structure of type *ffblk*. A pointer to one structure must be provided in the argument *fileinfo*. The structure *ffblk* is defined in *dir.h*. Its layout and its C declaration are shown below.

```
struct ffblk
{
    char     ff_reserved[21]; /* Reserved for use by MS-DOS */
    char     ff_attrib;       /* Attribute byte of file     */
    unsigned ff_ftime;        /* Time of last file update   */
    unsigned ff_fdate;        /* Date of last file update   */
    long     ff_fsize;        /* File's length in bytes     */
    char     ff_name[13];     /* Null-terminated file name  */
};
```

After this function returns successfully, the field *ff_name* contains the null-terminated name (not the entire path, just the file name and extension) of the first file that met all the search criteria. The attribute of this file is copied into the field *ff_attrib*. The date and time of the last write to this file will be in *ff_fdate* and *ff_ftime* respectively. Finally, the long integer field *ff_fsize* will contain the length of the file in bytes.

Note that *findfirst* sets the MS-DOS Disk Transfer Address (DTA) to *fileinfo*. If you need to preserve this address in your program, you should call *getdta* before calling *findfirst* and restore the saved DTA using *setdta* after the return from *findfirst*.

1. In Microsoft C 5 and 6, and QuickC 1.0, 2.0, and 2.5, use *_dos_findfirst*.

COMMON USES

This function is commonly used with its companion *findnext* to find all occurrences of a file name with a wildcard specification such as all **.C* files.

RETURNS

The *findfirst* function returns zero if successful; otherwise, it returns a −1 and sets the global variable *errno* either to the constant ENOENT indicating that the file could not be found, or to ENMFILE to indicate that there are no more files.

SEE ALSO findnext *To get the next file that also meets the search criteria.*

EXAMPLE Use *findfirst* to find the volume name. You will have to specify a search name *.* and an attribute of FA_LABEL to do this.

```
#include <stdio.h>
#include <dos.h>
#include <dir.h>
main()
{
    struct ffblk fileinfo;

    if (findfirst("\*.*", &fileinfo, FA_LABEL) != 0)
    {
        printf("Unsuccessful findfirst call!\n");
        exit(0);
    }
    printf("The volume name is: %s\n",
            fileinfo.ff_name);
    return 0;
}
```

findnext

COMPATIBILITY

TC1	TC1.5	TC2	TC++	MSC3	MSC4	MSC5	MSC6	QC1	QC2	QC2.5	ANSI	UNIX V	XNX
▲	▲	▲	▲			1	1	1	1	1			

PURPOSE Use *findnext* right after *findfirst* to find the remaining instances of files whose names and attributes match the values used during the *findfirst* call. You will call *findnext* only if the file name specified in the call to *findfirst* contained one or more wildcard characters (* and ?). You can use this function to find, for example, all the files with a *.C* extension by searching for all **.C* files, first with a call to *findfirst*, and then repeated calls to *findnext*.

SYNTAX `void findnext(struct ffblk *fileinfo);`

`struct ffblk *fileinfo;` *Structure to hold results of search*

EXAMPLE CALL `findnext(&fileinfo);`

INCLUDES `#include <dir.h>` *For function declaration*

`#include <dos.h>` *For definition of attribute names*

DESCRIPTION The *findnext* function calls the DOS function 4Fh to find the next file whose name and attributes are identical to that given in the call to the *findfirst* function.

The results of the search by *findnext* are returned in a structure of type *ffblk*. A pointer to a structure of this type must be provided in the argument *fileinfo* when you call *findnext*. The structure *ffblk* is defined in *dos.h*. Its layout and its C declaration are shown in the description of the companion function *findfirst*.

After this function returns successfully, the field *ff_name* contains the null-terminated name (not the entire path, just the file name and extension) of the next file that met the search criteria. The attribute of this file is copied into the field *ff_attrib* of the *ffblk* structure. The date and time of the last write operation on this file will be in *ff_fdate* and *ff_ftime*, respectively. Finally, the long integer field *ff_fsize* will contain the length of the file in bytes.

Note that *findnext* sets the MS-DOS Disk Transfer Address (DTA) to *fileinfo*. If you need to preserve this address in your program, you should call *getdta* before calling *findfirst* and restore the saved DTA using *setdta* after returning from *findnext*.

1. In Microsoft C 5 and 6, and QuickC 1.0 through 2.5, the compatible function is *_dos_findnext*.

COMMON USES This function is called in a loop right after *findfirst* to find the remaining occurrences of a file with a wildcard specification such as all **.C* files.

RETURNS The function returns zero if successful, otherwise, it returns −1 and sets the global variable *errno* either to the constant ENOENT indicating that the search failed, or to ENMFILE signifying that there are no more files to be searched.

SEE ALSO `findfirst` *To begin the search and find the first file that meets the search criteria.*

EXAMPLE Use *findnext* to find all files with a *.C* extension. You will have to call *findfirst* to set up the search and get the first file that matches the specified name and attribute.

```
#include <stdio.h>
#include <dos.h>
#include <dir.h>
main()
{
    int count;
    long totalsize;
    struct ffblk fileinfo;
    if (findfirst("*.c", &fileinfo, 0) == -1)
```

```
    {
        printf("Unsuccessful findfirst call!\n");
        exit(0);
    }
    printf("Listing of *.c files:\n");
    printf("%12s  %8ld bytes\n", fileinfo.ff_name,
                                 fileinfo.ff_fsize);
    count = 1;
    totalsize = fileinfo.ff_fsize;
    while (findnext(&fileinfo) == 0)
    {
        count++;
        totalsize += fileinfo.ff_fsize;
/* Now print the name and size of each matching file */
        printf("%12s  %8ld bytes\n",
                fileinfo.ff_name, fileinfo.ff_fsize);
    }
    printf("\n%d files %ld bytes.\n", count, totalsize);
    return 0;
}
```

FP_OFF

COMPATIBILITY

TC1	TC1.5	TC2	TC++	MSC3	MSC4	MSC5	MSC6	QC1	QC2	QC2.5	ANSI	UNIX V	XNX
▲	▲	▲	▲	▲	▲	▲	▲	▲	▲	▲			

PURPOSE *FP_OFF* is a C macro to get the 16-bit offset portion of the address of any data element. The macro expects as a parameter a far (32-bit) pointer to a memory location, such as the beginning of an array or a C structure. For example, you can use *FP_OFF* to get the offset of a string that you want to display using the DOS function 9h. The *FP_OFF* macro is the only way to get the offset of a data element in a C program.

SYNTAX

```
unsigned FP_OFF(void far *address);
```

`void far *address;` *Far pointer to memory location*

EXAMPLE CALL

```
offset_buf = FP_OFF(p_buf); /* p_buf is a far pointer */

FP_OFF(p_buf)=0x10; /* Initialize the offset */
```

INCLUDES `#include <dos.h>` *For definition of the macro*

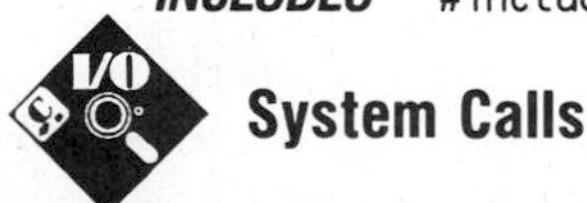

DESCRIPTION The *FP_OFF* function, implemented as a macro, accepts a 32-bit far pointer as an argument and returns the 16-bit offset portion of the pointer. When using *FP_OFF*, the argument *address* should be cast to be of type *(void far *)*.

COMMON USES *FP_OFF* is commonly used with its counterpart *FP_SEG* to generate 16-bit offset and "segment" addresses of strings and functions for use in DOS function calls. You can also use *FP_OFF* to initialize the offset portion of a far pointer.

RETURNS *FP_OFF* returns the offset as an unsigned 16-bit integer.

SEE ALSO FP_SEG *For segment address*

EXAMPLE Use *FP_OFF* to obtain the offset of a string. You'll need this, for example, when printing a string using DOS function number 9h so that you can pass the offset address to the print function.

```
#include <stdio.h>
#include <dos.h>
char sample[] = "Test string";
main()
{
    void far *ps;
    unsigned off_sample;
/* Cast the address of the first character as a far
 * pointer
 */
    ps = (void far *)sample;
    off_sample = FP_OFF(ps);
    printf("The offset of the string is: %x\n",
           off_sample);
    return 0;
}
```

COMPATIBILITY

FP_SEG

TC1	TC1.5	TC2	TC++	MSC3	MSC4	MSC5	MSC6	QC1	QC2	QC2.5	ANSI	UNIX V	XNX
▲	▲	▲	▲	▲	▲	▲	▲	▲	▲	▲			

PURPOSE Use the *FP_SEG* macro to get the "segment" address of a memory location. The macro expects as parameter a far (32-bit) pointer to a memory location. For example, you can use *FP_SEG* to get the segment address of a string that you want to display using the DOS function 9h. You will have to use *FP_SEG* whenever a BIOS or DOS call requires the segment address of a data element explicitly.

SYNTAX

```
unsigned FP_SEG(void far *address);

void far *address;        Far pointer to memory location
```

EXAMPLE CALL

```
segadd_buf = FP_SEG(p_buf); /* p_buf is a far pointer */
FP_SEG(p_buf) = 0x40; /*Initialize the segment */
```

INCLUDES

```
#include <dos.h>        For definition of the macro
```

DESCRIPTION The *FP_SEG* function, implemented as a macro, accepts a 32-bit far pointer as an argument and returns the segment address of the pointer. When using *FP_OFF*, the argument *address* should be cast to be of type *(void far *)*.

COMMON USES *FP_SEG* is commonly used with its counterpart *FP_OFF* to generate segment and offset addresses of strings and functions for use in DOS function calls. You can also use *FP_SEG* to initialize the segment address in a far pointer.

RETURNS *FP_SEG* returns the offset as an unsigned 16-bit integer.

SEE ALSO FP_OFF *For the offset address*

EXAMPLE Use *FP_SEG* to obtain the segment address of a string. For example, if you were trying to print the string using DOS function 9h, you will need to specify the offset and the segment address of the string. You can use the *FP_SEG* macro in this case.

```
#include <stdio.h>
#include <dos.h>
char sample[] = "Test string";
main()
{
    void far *ps;
    unsigned seg_sample;
/* Cast the address of the first character as a far
 * pointer
 */
    ps = (void far *)sample;
    seg_sample = FP_SEG(ps);
    printf("The segment address of the string is: %x\n",
                                             seg_sample);
    return 0;
}
```

System Calls

COMPATIBILITY

freemem

TC1	TC1.5	TC2	TC++	MSC3	MSC4	MSC5	MSC6	QC1	QC2	QC2.5	ANSI	UNIX V	XNX
▲	▲	▲	▲			1	1	1	1	1			

PURPOSE Use *freemem* to free memory allocated earlier by calling the *allocmem* function. Use the segment address returned by *allocmem* to indicate which chunk of memory you are freeing up.

SYNTAX

```
int   freemem (unsigned segadd);
```

`unsigned segadd;` *Segment address of allocated memory*

EXAMPLE CALL

```
freemem(segment);
```

INCLUDES `#include <dos.h>` *For function declaration*

DESCRIPTION The *freemem* function calls DOS function 49h to free a block of memory previously allocated using the *allocmem* function. The segment address of the block freed is specified through the unsigned integer *segadd.* The offset is always zero. This should be the same segment address that was returned by *allocmem* when the memory was allocated.

1. The equivalent function in Microsoft C 5 and 6, and QuickC 1.0 through 2.5, is *_dos_freemem.*

RETURNS This function returns 0 if memory was successfully released. Otherwise, the return value is −1 and the global variable *errno* is set to the constant ENOMEM indicating a bad segment value.

SEE ALSO

`allocmem` *The corresponding routine to allocate memory; also shows how to use* freemem

`setblock` *To alter the size of the chunk allocated by* allocmem

`farfree, free` *Other routines that release memory*

EXAMPLE Use *allocmem* to allocate 10 paragraphs of memory. Next call *freemem* to free this block of memory.

```
#include <stdio.h>
#include <dos.h>
main()
{
```

```
    unsigned segadd;
    if (allocmem(10, &segadd) != -1)
    {
        perror("Memory allocation failed");
        exit(0);
    }
    printf("10 paragraphs of memory allocated\n"
              "at segment address: %x\n", segadd);
/* Free memory before exiting */
    if(freemem(segadd) != 0)
    {
        perror("freemem failed");
    }
    else
    {
        printf("The memory is released now.\n");
    }
    return 0;
}
```

geninterrupt

COMPATIBILITY

TC1	TC1.5	TC2	TC++	MSC3	MSC4	MSC5	MSC6	QC1	QC2	QC2.5	ANSI	UNIX V	XNX
▲	▲	▲	▲										

PURPOSE Use *geninterrupt* to initiate a software interrupt with a specified interrupt number.

SYNTAX

```
void  geninterrupt (int interruptnum);

int interruptnum;        Interrupt number to be initiated
```

EXAMPLE CALL

```
geninterrupt(5);  /* Print the screen using INT 5 */
```

INCLUDES

```
#include <dos.h>        For function declaration
```

DESCRIPTION The *geninterrupt* macro invokes an assembly language function that initiates the software interrupt number specified in the argument *interruptnum* using the 80x86 assembly language instruction INT.

COMMON USES The *geninterrupt* macro can be used to access BIOS and DOS functions which are accessible via software interrupts.

RETURNS The return value is the content of the AX register upon return from the interrupt.

COMMENTS There are more general routines, such as *int86x* and *intdosx*, for accessing DOS and BIOS functions through interrupts. You may want to use these routines instead of *geninterrupt* when you need to generate an interrupt.

SEE ALSO

`disable, enable`	*To disable and enable software interrupts*
`int86x, intdosx`	*Other routines to generate interrupt*

EXAMPLE The software interrupt 5 invokes the Print Screen facility in a PC. Use the *geninterrupt* macro to dump the contents of the screen to the printer.

```
#include <stdio.h>
#include <dos.h>
#define BIOS_PRNTSCR  5

union REGS xr;
main()
{
    printf("Printing screen via 'geninterrupt'\n");
    geninterrupt(BIOS_PRNTSCR);
    return 0;
}
```

COMPATIBILITY

getcbrk

TC1	TC1.5	TC2	TC++	MSC3	MSC4	MSC5	MSC6	QC1	QC2	QC2.5	ANSI	UNIX V	XNX
▲	▲	▲	▲										

PURPOSE Use *getcbrk* to determine whether Control-Break (or Control-C) checking is currently enabled or disabled.

SYNTAX `int getcbrk(void);`

EXAMPLE CALL `if(getcbrk()) printf("Control-Break checking is enabled!\n");`

INCLUDES `#include <dos.h>` *For function declaration*

DESCRIPTION MS-DOS maintains a flag that indicates whether DOS will ignore or respond to a Control-Break or Control-C keypress. When this flag is enabled (1), DOS will check if a keypress is Control-Break or Control-C. If it is, control will be transferred to the Control-Break handler (interrupt 23h). Note that you can use the Turbo C++ routine *ctrlbrk* to designate a function that will get called when this happens.

The *getcbrk* function calls the DOS function 33h to determine the current status of this checking flag.

COMMON USES You can use *getcbrk* to retrieve and save the current Control-Break checking flag and then turn off checking by calling the routine *setbrk* so that some crucial operation, such as disk I/O, is not interrupted by a Control-C keypress. After the critical operation is complete, you can restore the Control-Break checking flag from the saved value. It is very important that you save and restore this flag because once you turn the flag off, it remains off even after your program terminates.

RETURNS The *getcbrk* function returns the current value of the Control-Break checking flag. The return value is 0 if Control-Break checking is off and the value is 1 when checking is on.

SEE ALSO

`ctrlbrk` *To set up a function which will be called when a Control-C is entered (provided checking is on)*

`setcbrk` *To turn Control-Break checking on or off*

EXAMPLE Get and print the current status of Control-Break checking flag.

```
#include <dos.h>
main()
{
    printf("Control-Break checking flag = %d\n",
            getcbrk());
    return 0;
}
```

getcurdir

COMPATIBILITY

TC1	TC1.5	TC2	TC++	MSC3	MSC4	MSC5	MSC6	QC1	QC2	QC2.5	ANSI	UNIX V	XNX
▲	▲	▲	▲										

PURPOSE Use *getcurdir* to determine the current directory in a specified drive.

SYNTAX

```
int   getcurdir (int drive, char *directory);
```

`int drive;` *Drive number whose current directory is being requested (0=default, 1=A, 2=B, and so on)*

```
char *directory;        Buffer where name of current directory will be returned
```

EXAMPLE CALL

```
/* Get current directory of the default drive */
getcurdir(0, dirname);
```

INCLUDES

```
#include <dir.h>        For function declaration
```

DESCRIPTION The *getcurdir* function returns the name of the current directory for the drive specified by the argument *drive*. The drive number 0 indicates the current default drive, 1 means drive A, 2 is drive B, and so on.

You must allocate a buffer of size MAXDIR (a constant defined in *dir.h*) to hold the name of the directory and provide its address in the argument *directory*. Note that the directory name will not contain the drive specification and it does not begin with a backslash.

RETURNS The *getcurdir* function returns a zero on success, otherwise it returns −1 to indicate an error.

SEE ALSO

getcwd — *To get the current working directory (full pathname including drive specification)*

getdisk — *To get the current default drive number*

EXAMPLE Use *getdisk* and *getcurdir* to get the full pathname of the current directory on the default device.

```
#include <stdio.h>
#include <dir.h>
main()
{
    int cur_drive;
    char path[MAXPATH]; /* MAXPATH is defined in dir.h */
/* First get the current drive */
    cur_drive = getdisk();
/* Convert drive number to a letter */
    path[0] = cur_drive + 'A';
    path[1] = ':';
    path[2] = '\\';
/* Now get the directory name to complete the pathname*/
    getcurdir(0, path+3);
    printf("Current pathname is: %s\n", path);
    return 0;
}
```

getdate

COMPATIBILITY

TC1	TC1.5	TC2	TC++	MSC3	MSC4	MSC5	MSC6	QC1	QC2	QC2.5	ANSI	UNIX V	XNX
▲	▲	▲	▲			1	1	1	1	1			

PURPOSE Use *getdate* to get the current system date, as maintained by DOS.

SYNTAX

```
void   getdate (struct date *datep);

struct  date *datep;
```

Pointer to a structure that will hold the components of date

EXAMPLE CALL

```
getdate(&date);
```

INCLUDES

```
#include <dos.h>
```

For function declaration and definition of the date *structure*

DESCRIPTION The *getdate* function calls DOS function 2Ah to get the current system date. The components of the date—the day, the month, and the year—are stored in fields of the *date* structure which is defined in *dos.h.* The layout of this structure along with the C declaration of the internal fields is shown below.

```
struct date
{
    int da_year;        /* Current year (range 1980-2099) */
    char da_day;        /* Day of the month (range 1-31)  */
    char da_mon;        /* Month (range 1-12), 1= January */
};
```

You have to declare one such structure and provide its address in the argument *datep*.

1. Use *_dos_getdate* in Microsoft C 5 and 6, and QuickC 1.0 through 2.5.

SEE ALSO

setdate — *The corresponding routine that sets the system date*

gettime, settime — *To get and set the system time*

dostounix — *To convert DOS date and time to UNIX format*

EXAMPLE Use the *getdate* to get and display the current system date.

```
#include <stdio.h>
#include <dos.h>
char *months[] ={"JAN", "FEB", "MAR", "APR", "MAY", "JUN",
                 "JUL", "AUG", "SEP", "OCT", "NOV", "DEC"};
```

```
main()
{
    struct date date;
    getdate(&date);
    printf("Date: %d %s %d\n", date.da_day,
            months[date.da_mon-1],
            date.da_year);
    return 0;
}
```

COMPATIBILITY

getdfree

TC1	TC1.5	TC2	TC++	MSC3	MSC4	MSC5	MSC6	QC1	QC2	QC2.5	ANSI	UNIX V	XNX
▲	▲	▲	▲			1	1	1	1	1			

PURPOSE Use *getdfree* to determine the total capacity of a particular disk as well as the amount of free space.

SYNTAX

```
unsigned getdfree(unsigned drive, struct dfree *dfinfo);
```

`unsigned char drive;` *Drive number, 0=default, 1=A, 2=B, and so on*

`struct dfree *dfinfo;` *Pointer to structure that will hold information on disk space*

EXAMPLE CALL

```
getdfree (0, &dfinfo); /* Get disk space info for current drive */
```

INCLUDES `#include <dos.h>` *For function declaration and declaration of structure dfree*

DESCRIPTION The *getdfree* function calls the DOS function 36h to retrieve information on the total and free disk space available on the drive specified by the argument *drive*. If this argument is a zero then information about the current default drive is returned. A value of 1 means drive A, 2 means B, and so on.

The requested information is returned in a structure of type *dfree* whose address is specified in the argument *dfinfo*. The data structure is declared in *dos.h*. Its C declaration is shown below.

```
struct dfree
{
    unsigned df_avail;  /* Number of available clusters */
    unsigned df_total;  /* Number of total clusters     */
    unsigned df_bsec;   /* Bytes per sector             */
```

```
    unsigned df_sclus;  /* Sectors per cluster          */
};
```

The information about disk space is returned in terms of the total number of clusters on the disk and the number of them not in use. These values are in the fields *df_total* and *df_avail* respectively. Since a cluster is a collection of sectors, by using the value of sectors per cluster given in *df_sclus* and the number of bytes per sector from the field *df_bsec*, we can compute the total disk space as well as the unused amount in bytes.

In case of error, the *getdfree* function sets the field *df_sclus* to −1.

1. The compatible function in Microsoft C 5 and 6, and QuickC 1.0 through 2.5, is *_dos_getdiskfree*.

COMMON USES This function can be used to verify that there is enough free space on the current disk before attempting a critical operation such as saving a file.

SEE ALSO getdisk, setdisk — *To get information about or to change the current default drive*

EXAMPLE Use *getdfree* to get and display the total capacity of your drive in bytes and the amount not in use.

```
#include <stdio.h>
#include <dos.h>
main()
{
    unsigned long total_space, free_space,
                  bytes_per_cluster;
    struct dfree dfinfo;
    getdfree (0, &dfinfo);
    if( dfinfo.df_sclus == -1)
    {
        printf("Error in getdfree\n");
        exit(0);
    }
    bytes_per_cluster = dfinfo.df_sclus * dfinfo.df_bsec;
    total_space = dfinfo.df_total * bytes_per_cluster;
    free_space = dfinfo.df_avail * bytes_per_cluster;
    printf ("%ld bytes free out of %ld bytes of total "
            "space.\n", free_space, total_space);
    return 0;
}
```

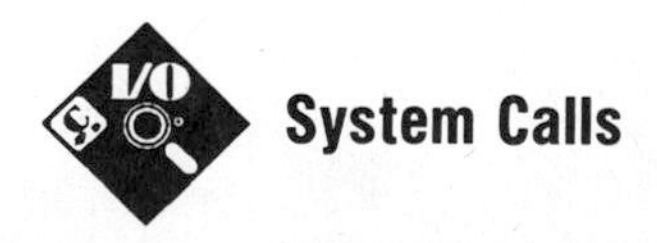

COMPATIBILITY

getdisk

TC1	TC1.5	TC2	TC++	MSC3	MSC4	MSC5	MSC6	QC1	QC2	QC2.5	ANSI	UNIX V	XNX
▲	▲	▲	▲			1	1	1	1	1			

PURPOSE Use *getdisk* to determine the current default drive number.

SYNTAX

```
int getdisk(void);
```

EXAMPLE CALL

```
drive_number = getdisk();
```

INCLUDES `#include <dir.h>` *For function declaration*

DESCRIPTION The *getdisk* function calls the DOS function 19h to get the current default drive number.

1. The compatible function in Microsoft C 5 and 6, and QuickC 1.0 through 2.5, is *_dos_getdrive*.

COMMON USES When creating a file or performing file I/O, if a drive is not explicitly specified, DOS assumes that we are referring to the file on the current default drive. The drive number returned by *getdisk* tells us what this default drive is.

RETURNS The *getdisk* function returns the current drive number which is interpreted as follows: a 0 means drive A, a 1 means drive B, and so on. See example below for clarification.

SEE ALSO `setdisk` *To change the current default drive number*

EXAMPLE Use *getdisk* to show the current default drive name.

```
#include <stdio.h>
#include <dir.h>
main()
{
    int drive;
    drive = getdisk();
    printf ("The current drive is: %c\n", drive+'A');
    return 0;
}
```

getdta

COMPATIBILITY

TC1	TC1.5	TC2	TC++	MSC3	MSC4	MSC5	MSC6	QC1	QC2	QC2.5	ANSI	UNIX V	XNX
▲	▲	▲	▲										

PURPOSE Use *getdta* to retrieve the address of the current Disk Transfer Address (DTA).

SYNTAX

```
char far *getdta(void);
```

EXAMPLE CALL

```
cur_dta = getdta();
```

INCLUDES `#include <dos.h>` *For function declaration*

DESCRIPTION MS-DOS supports two types of file operations. One is the CP/M-compatible service that uses File Control Blocks (FCBs) and Disk Transfer Addresses (DTAs) for its workings. The other one is the UNIX-compatible I/O that is based on file handles. The latter approach is more commonplace nowadays, and it is also more portable. However, the CP/M-style functions may be used by some programs, and are still a part of the DOS file I/O routines. The Turbo C routines *findfirst* and *findnext* alter the DTA. The *getdta* function is provided so that you can retrieve and save the current DTA before changing the DTA either directly with a call to *setdta*, or indirectly via functions such as *findfirst.*

COMMON USES The *getdta* function lets you get and save the DTA before altering it.

RETURNS The *getdta* function returns a far pointer to the current DTA.

SEE ALSO

`randbrd, randbwr` *For sample use of* getdta

`setdta` *To set the DTA to a new value*

EXAMPLE *getdta* is used in FCB-based file I/O routines. The examples for the routines *randbrd* and *randbwr* show how *getdta* is used.

COMPATIBILITY

getfat, getfatd

TC1	TC1.5	TC2	TC++	MSC3	MSC4	MSC5	MSC6	QC1	QC2	QC2.5	ANSI	UNIX V	XNX
▲	▲	▲	▲										

PURPOSE Use *getfat* to obtain information about the File Allocation Table (FAT) of the MS-DOS file system on a specified drive. Use *getfatd* for information on the default drive.

SYNTAX

```
void   getfat (unsigned char drive, struct fatinfo *dtable);
void   getfatd (struct fatinfo *dtable);
```

`unsigned char     drive;` *Drive number (0=default, 1=A, 2=B, and so on)*

`struct   fatinfo  *dtable;` *Pointer to a structure where information from the FAT is returned*

EXAMPLE CALL

```
getfat(1, &fatdata); /* Get FAT info of diskette in A */
```

INCLUDES `#include <dos.h>` *For function declaration*

DESCRIPTION The File Allocation Table (FAT) specifies how clusters (a group of a fixed number of sectors) are allocated to specific files in a DOS file system. The *getfat* function returns information from the FAT for the drive specified by the argument *drive*. A drive number of zero implies the current default drive, 1 means drive A, 2 is drive B, and so on. The *getfatd* function is identical to *getfat* except that it always returns information about the current default drive.

The information about the FAT is returned in an *fatinfo* structure which is declared in *dos.h* as follows:

```
struct  fatinfo
{
  char  fi_sclus;  /* Number of sectors per cluster  */
  char  fi_fatid;  /* FAT identification byte        */
  int   fi_nclus;  /* Number of clusters             */
  int   fi_bysec;  /* Number of bytes per sector     */
};
```

You must allocate an *fatinfo* structure and provide its address in the argument *dtable*.

COMMON USES The information returned by *getfat* can be used to decipher the contents of the FAT which describes the layout of an MS-DOS file on the disk.

EXAMPLE Use *getfat* to get information from the file allocation block of the default drive. Display the retrieved information. Here is what the program displays when running from the hard disk (drive C) of a PC-AT.

```
FAT of drive C
Sectors per cluster 4
FAT ID              F8
Number of clusters  10405
Bytes per sector:   512
TOTAL CAPACITY:      21309440 bytes
```

```
#include <stdio.h>
#include <dos.h>

main()
{
    struct fatinfo fat;
    unsigned char fatid;
    long capacity;
/* Get information from the FAT of current drive */
    getfat(0, &fat);
    printf("FAT of drive %c\n", getdisk()+'A');
    fatid = fat.fi_fatid;
    printf("Sectors per cluster %d\n"
           "FAT ID              %X\n"
           "Number of clusters  %d\n"
           "Bytes per sector:   %d\n",
           fat.fi_sclus, fatid,
           fat.fi_nclus, fat.fi_bysec);
    capacity = (long)fat.fi_sclus *
       (long)fat.fi_nclus *
       (long)fat.fi_bysec;
    printf("TOTAL CAPACITY:     %ld bytes\n",
   capacity);
    return 0;
}
```

COMPATIBILITY

getftime

TC1	TC1.5	TC2	TC++	MSC3	MSC4	MSC5	MSC6	QC1	QC2	QC2.5	ANSI	UNIX V	XNX
▲	▲	▲	▲			1	1	1	1	1			

PURPOSE Use *getftime* to get the date and time when a file was last modified. You will need a handle returned by a function such as *_open* or *_creat* when requesting this information.

SYNTAX

```
int   getftime  (int handle, struct ftime *ftimep);
```

```
int        filehandle;
```
File "handle" or identifier

```
struct ftime *ftimep;
```
Pointer to location to hold date and time information

EXAMPLE CALL

```
getftime(handle, &dt_info);
```

INCLUDES

```
#include <io.h>
```
For function declaration and definition of ftime *structure*

DESCRIPTION For each file, DOS records the time and date when the file was last modified. This is the information you see when you type the DIR command. The date and time information is maintained in coded form. The date is stored in a 16-bit word whose bits are interpreted as follows:

Bits	Contents
0-4	Day of the month (value between 1 and 31).
5-8	Month (value between 1 and 12).
9-15	Years since 1980 (for example, 1988 is stored as 8).

The last update time of the file is also maintained in a 16-bit word. The meaning of the bits in this word is as follows:

Bits	Contents
0-4	Number of 2 second increments (value between 0 and 29).
5-10	Minutes (value between 0 and 59).
11-15	Hours (value between 0 and 23).

The *getftime* function calls the DOS function 57h to return the date and time stamp information of the file specified by the identifying number or handle in the argument *filehandle*. The date and time information is returned in an *ftime* structure whose address is given in the argument *ftimep*. The *ftime* structure is declared in *io.h* as follows:

```
struct  ftime
{
  unsigned  ft_tsec   : 5;  /* Number of 2 second intervals */
  unsigned  ft_min   : 6;   /* Minutes                      */
  unsigned  ft_hour   : 5;  /* Hours                        */
  unsigned  ft_day   : 5;   /* Days                         */
  unsigned  ft_month : 4;   /* Months                       */
  unsigned  ft_year   : 7;  /* Years since 1980             */
};
```

The file handle must be one that had been returned when the file was opened by *_open* or perhaps created by *_creat*.

1. In Microsoft C 5 and 6, and QuickC 1.0 through 2.5, use *_dos_getftime*.

RETURNS This function returns zero if successful; otherwise, it returns −1 and sets the global variable *errno* either to the constant EBADF indicating that the file handle is invalid, or to EINVFNC signifying an invalid function number.

SEE ALSO

setftime	*To change the date and time stamp of a file*
_open	*To open an existing file using a DOS call*
_creat	*To create a new file*

EXAMPLE Use *_open* to open a file and then call *getftime* to display its date and time stamp.

```
#include <stdio.h>
#include <io.h>
#include <fcntl.h>
#include <dos.h>
main()
{
    char fname[40], *p_fname;
    int filehandle;
    struct ftime dtinfo;
    unsigned date, time, day, month, year,
             hour, minute, second;
```

```
    printf("Enter name of an existing file: ");
    p_fname = gets(fname);


/* Open the file using _open */
    if ((filehandle = _open(p_fname, O_RDONLY)) == -1)
    {
        printf("Error opening file: %s\n", fname);
        exit(0);
    }
    printf("File %s opened.\n", fname);


/* Get file's date and time stamp */
    getftime(filehandle, &dtinfo);


/* Now extract the time and date information */
    second = 2 * dtinfo.ft_tsec;
    minute = dtinfo.ft_min;
    hour = dtinfo.ft_hour;
    day = dtinfo.ft_day;
    month = dtinfo.ft_month;
/* NOTE: year is relative to 1980.
 * So we are adding 80.
 */
    year = dtinfo.ft_year + 80;
    printf("File: %s  Date: %d-%d-%d Time: %.2d:%.2d:\
%.2d\n", fname, month, day, year, hour, minute, second);


/* Now close file */
    if (_close(filehandle) != 0)
    {
        printf("Error closing file with _close\n");
        exit(0);
    }
    printf("File %s closed.\n", fname);
    return 0;
}
```

getpsp

COMPATIBILITY

TC1	TC1.5	TC2	TC++	MSC3	MSC4	MSC5	MSC6	QC1	QC2	QC2.5	ANSI	UNIX V	XNX
▲	▲	▲	▲										

PURPOSE Use *getpsp* to get the segment address of your program's Program Segment Prefix (PSP).

SYNTAX

```
unsigned  getpsp (void);
```

EXAMPLE CALL

```
my_psp = getpsp();
```

INCLUDES

```
#include <dos.h>        For function declaration
```

DESCRIPTION In MS-DOS, each executing program has a 256-byte area that is set up by DOS and filled with various information about the program. The *getpsp* routine calls DOS function 62h to get the segment address of the PSP for the program being executed.

Note this function can only be called in MS-DOS 3.0 and above because the function 62h does not exist in earlier versions. If you are using an earlier version of MS-DOS, you can access the PSP by referencing the global variable *_psp* which is also set up to contain the address of the PSP.

COMMON USES The PSP contains the command line which invoked the program as well as the segment address of the environment strings for the program. The *getpsp* function lets you access these items.

RETURNS The *getpsp* function returns the segment address of the PSP.

EXAMPLE Get the Program Segment Prefix (PSP) of the current program and display some information from the PSP.

```
#include <stdio.h>
#include <dos.h>

main()
{
    unsigned int mypsp, last_seg;
    long mem_allocated;
/* If DOS version is at least 3.0, call getpsp */
    if(_osmajor == 3) mypsp = getpsp();
/* else use global variable _psp to access PSP */
    else  mypsp = _psp;
```

```
/* Display some information from the PSP */
    printf("PSP starts at %X:0000\n", mypsp);
/* Address of last allocated memory is at offset 2 */
    last_seg = *((unsigned far *)(MK_FP(mypsp,2)));
    printf("End of allocated memory at %X:0000\n",
            last_seg);
    mem_allocated = 16*(long)(last_seg - mypsp);
    printf("%ld bytes of memory allocated to this "
            "program\n", mem_allocated);
    return 0;
}
```

COMPATIBILITY

getswitchar

TC1	TC1.5	TC2	TC++	MSC3	MSC4	MSC5	MSC6	QC1	QC2	QC2.5	ANSI	UNIX V	XNX
▲	▲	▲	▲										

PURPOSE The undocumented *getswitchar* function returns the current switch character (the character that precedes options in an MS-DOS command).

SYNTAX `int getswitchar (void);`

EXAMPLE CALL `sw_char = getswitchar();`

INCLUDES `#include <dos.h>` *For function declaration*

DESCRIPTION The *getswitchar* function calls an undocumented DOS function (37h) to get the current character used to specify command line options in MS-DOS. This character, known as the switch character, is normally a slash (/). For example, in the DOS command *DIR/W*, the slash (/) is the switch character.

A companion function, *setswitchar*, is available to set a new switch character for DOS commands.

RETURNS The *getswitchar* function returns the current switch character that precedes options in DOS commands.

COMMENTS The *getswitchar* function is *not* documented in the Turbo C++ reference manual perhaps because it uses the undocumented DOS function 37h.

SEE ALSO `setswitchar` *To set a new switch character for DOS commands*

EXAMPLE Get the current switch character by calling *getswitchar*. If you have not altered it using *setswitchar*, it should be a /.

```
#include <stdio.h>
#include <dos.h>
main()
{
    int c;
    c = getswitchar();
    printf("The current switch char is %c\n", c);
    return 0;
}
```

gettime

COMPATIBILITY

TC1	TC1.5	TC2	TC++	MSC3	MSC4	MSC5	MSC6	QC1	QC2	QC2.5	ANSI	UNIX V	XNX
▲	▲	▲	▲			1	1	1	1	1			

PURPOSE Use *gettime* to get the current system time as maintained by DOS.

SYNTAX

```
void   gettime (struct time *timep);
```

`struct  time *timep;` *Pointer to a structure that will hold the components of time*

EXAMPLE CALL

```
gettime(&time_info);
```

INCLUDES `#include <dos.h>` *For function declaration and for definition of the* time *structure*

DESCRIPTION The *gettime* function calls DOS function 2Ch to get the current system time. The components of the time—the hour, the minutes, the seconds, and the hundredths of a second—are stored in fields of the *time* structure which is defined in *dos.h*. The C declaration of the structure *time* is shown below.

```
struct time
{
    unsigned char ti_min;   /* Minutes (range 0-59)             */
    unsigned char ti_hour;  /* Hour (range 0-23)                */
    unsigned char ti_hund;  /* Hundredth of a second (range 0-99) */
    unsigned char ti_sec;   /* Seconds (range 0-59)             */
};
```

You have to declare one such structure and provide its address in the argument *timep*.

1. In Microsoft C 5 and 6, and QuickC 1.0 through 2.5, use *_dos_gettime*.

SEE ALSO

`settime`	*The corresponding routine that sets the system time*
`getdate, setdate`	*To get and set the system date*
`dostounix`	*To convert DOS date and time to UNIX format*

EXAMPLE Use the *gettime* to get and display the current system time.

```
#include <stdio.h>
#include <dos.h>
main()
{
    struct time dtime;
    gettime(&dtime);
    printf("Current time: %d:%d:%d.%d\n", dtime.ti_hour,
            dtime.ti_min, dtime.ti_sec, dtime.ti_hund);
    return 0;
}
```

getvect

COMPATIBILITY

TC1	TC1.5	TC2	TC++	MSC3	MSC4	MSC5	MSC6	QC1	QC2	QC2.5	ANSI	UNIX V	XNX
▲	▲	▲	▲			1	1	1	1	1			

PURPOSE Use *getvect* to get the current value of the interrupt vector for a specific interrupt number. The interrupt vector is the address of the routine that is invoked when the interrupt occurs.

SYNTAX

```
void interrupt  (*getvect(int interruptno)) ();
```

`int interruptno;` *Interrupt number whose handler's address is returned*

EXAMPLE CALL

```
void interrupt (*int_handler)();
int_handler = getvect(int_number);
```

INCLUDES `#include <dos.h>` *For function declaration*

DESCRIPTION The *getvect* function calls the DOS function 35h to retrieve the address of the current interrupt handler for the interrupt whose number is specified in the argument *interruptno.*

1. Use *_dos_getvect* in Microsoft C 5 and 6, and QuickC 1.0 through 2.5.

COMMON USES This function is commonly used to get the current address of the interrupt handler before setting it to a new value by calling the companion function *setvect.* Another use of this function is to get the address of certain tables that BIOS and DOS let you access via interrupt vectors.

RETURNS The return value is a far pointer to the interrupt handler, which is a function of type *interrupt.* This keyword allows you to write interrupt handlers in C (see Chapter 3 for more details).

SEE ALSO `setvect` *To install a new interrupt handler*

EXAMPLE Use the *getvect* function to get and report the current interrupt vector corresponding to an interrupt number entered by the user. Try the interrupt number 18h (the vector to ROM-resident BASIC. On a PC-AT the vector should be F600:0000. On other machines, the technical reference guide may list the vector for resident BASIC.)

```
#include <stdio.h>
#include <dos.h>

main()
{
    void interrupt (*int_handler)();
    int intno;
    printf("Enter interrupt number in hexadecimal"
           " format: ");
    scanf(" %x", &intno);
    int_handler = getvect(intno);
/* Print out address of handler using the %p format.
 * Use the F qualifier to get the segment address also.
 */
    printf("\nThe address of the handler is : %Fp\n",
           int_handler);
    return 0;
}
```

COMPATIBILITY

getverify

TC1	TC1.5	TC2	TC++	MSC3	MSC4	MSC5	MSC6	QC1	QC2	QC2.5	ANSI	UNIX V	XNX
▲	▲	▲	▲										

PURPOSE Use *getverify* to get the current state of the verify flag which indicates whether DOS verifies disk write operations.

SYNTAX

```
int   getverify (void);
```

EXAMPLE CALL

```
vflag = getverify();
```

INCLUDES `#include <dos.h>` *For function declaration*

DESCRIPTION MS-DOS maintains a verify flag which, when turned on, instructs DOS to perform a read after each disk write to ensure that data was written correctly. The *getverify* routine calls the DOS function 54h to get the current value of this flag.

A companion function, *setverify*, can be used to set the verify flag. You can also check the verify flag using the DOS command VERIFY.

RETURNS The *getverify* function returns the current value of the verify flag. The return value can be either 0(off) or 1 (on).

SEE ALSO `setverify` *To set the verify flag on or off*

EXAMPLE Get the current setting of the verify flag by calling *getverify*. If you have not altered it using *setverify* or the DOS command VERIFY, it is usually off (0).

```
#include <stdio.h>
#include <dos.h>
main()
{
    int vflag;
    vflag = getverify();
    printf("Current value of the verify flag = %d\n",
            vflag);
    return 0;
}
```

harderr

COMPATIBILITY

TC1	TC1.5	TC2	TC++	MSC3	MSC4	MSC5	MSC6	QC1	QC2	QC2.5	ANSI	UNIX V	XNX
▲	▲	▲	▲			1	1	1	1	1			

PURPOSE Use *harderr* to install a new handler for interrupt 24h (critical error) that will call a routine whose address you provide to *harderr* as an argument. This interrupt occurs on hardware errors during I/O operations such as trying to read from a diskette with the drive door open.

SYNTAX

```
void   harderr (int  (*funcptr)());
```

`int (*funcptr)();` *Pointer to the function that will be called by the new INT 24h handler*

EXAMPLE CALL

```
int harderror_handler(int errval, int ax, int bp, int si);
harderr(harderror_handler);
```

INCLUDES `#include <dos.h>` *For declaration of function*

DESCRIPTION The *harderr* function installs a new handler for interrupt number 24h to handle a critical error, which usually occurs when hardware malfunctions. The address of the routine to be called is specified in the argument *funcptr*.

The installed handler will call the specified function with four arguments in the following manner:

```
(* funcptr)(int errval, int ax, int bp, int si);
```

where *errval*, *ax*, *bp*, and *si* are integers containing, respectively, the *DI*, *AX*, *BP*, and *SI* register values that MS-DOS passes to the INT 24h handler. The arguments *bp* and *si* together are a far pointer to a "device header" structure that contains descriptive information about the device on which the error occurred. The routine which you want called should not alter anything in this device header.

The value in the low-order byte of the argument *errval* indicates the type of error that occurred. Table 17-24 shows the interpretation of this error code.

If the error had occurred during disk I/O, bit 15 (the most significant bit) of the *ax* argument will be set to 0 and the *ax* will provide more detailed information about the disk error. The bits and their meanings are shown in Table 17-25.

The low-order byte of *ax* will contain the drive number where the error occurred. A 0 indicates drive A, a 1 means drive B, and so on for other drives.

Table 17-24. *Error Codes Indicated by Low Byte of* errval

Error Code (Hexadecimal)	Meaning
0	Attempted to write to a write-protected disk.
1	Unknown unit (source of error not known).
2	Drive not ready.
3	Unknown command.
4	CRC indicates error in data.
5	Length of "drive request structure"is bad.
6	Seek error.
7	Unknown media type.
8	Sector not found.
9	Printer out of paper.
A	Write fault.
B	Read fault.
C	General failure.

Table 17-25. *Disk Error Information in Critical Error Handler*

Bit	Meaning
15	If 0, it's a disk error. IGNORE rest if this bit is 1.
14	— Not used —
13	If 0, "Ignore" response is not allowed.
12	If 0, "Retry" response is not allowed.
11	If 0, "Abort" response is not allowed.
9–10	Indicates area where error occurred:
	00 MS-DOS
	01 File Allocation Table (FAT)
	10 Directory
	11 Data area
8	If 1, it's a write error. 0 means read error.

If bit 15 of *ax* is 1, then the error did not occur during disk I/O, and you have to look elsewhere to find the cause. A word located at offset 4 in the device header contains further information about where the error occurred. Access it as an unsigned integer at the address *devhdr+4* where *devhdr* is the address BP:SI). Table 17-26 tells you how to interpret the source of the error in this case.

In the function, whose pointer you are specifying in the argument *funcptr*, you can also make certain MS-DOS function calls. Specifically, you can issue calls to DOS functions 01 through 0Ch and function 59h. Note, however that many C library routines can not be used within this function because they call MS-DOS functions to do their job.

Table 17-26. *Source of Nondisk I/O Errors*

Bits of the Word at (devhdr+4)	Source of Error
15	0 = bad memory image of FAT. 1 = error in a character device, interpret error source from bits 0 through 3 of word at address *devhdr*. 0001 = error in standard input 0010 = error in standard output 0100 = error in null device 1000 = error in clock device

Note, however, that many C library routines can not be used within this function because they call MS-DOS functions to do their job.

If you want to return to MS-DOS, this function should end with a *return* or a call to *hardresume*. You have the option of returning to the program where the error occurred by issuing a call to *hardretn*.

1. The equivalent function in Microsoft C 5 and 6, and QuickC 1.0 through 2.5, is *_harderr*.

COMMON USES This function is useful in writing robust application programs where user mistakes such as trying to read from a diskette with nothing in the drive do not require aborting from the application.

COMMENTS It is a good idea to install your own critical error handler. The default MS-DOS handler is somewhat crude and often results in aborting the current application. The availability of this function makes it very easy to develop the error handler entirely in Turbo C++.

SEE ALSO

`hardresume`	*To return to DOS from the error handler*
`hardretn`	*To return to the program where the error originally occurred*
`getvect`	*To retrieve an existing interrupt vector*
`setvect`	*To install a new interrupt vector*
`keep`	*To install "terminate-and-stay-resident" programs*

EXAMPLE Write a critical error handler that checks for a "drive not ready" error that occurs, for example, when you try to find the disk space on drive A when the drive is empty. Let the handler print a message asking the user to insert a diskette and continue when the user strikes an appropriate key. Assume that the current default drive is not A. Notice the global flag to indicate when a critical error occurs so that we can tell when the call to *getdfree* fails because of a "drive not ready" error.

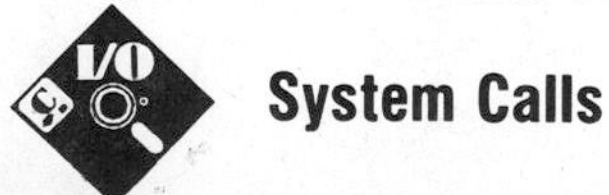

```
#include <stdio.h>
#include <dos.h>
/* Prototype of our critical error handler */
int harderror_handler(int, int, int, int);
unsigned error_flag = 0;
main()
{
    unsigned drivea =1;
    unsigned long total_space, free_space,
              bytes_per_cluster;
    struct dfree dfinfo;
/* Install our critical error handler */
    harderr(harderror_handler);
    printf("We will check our critical error handler.\n\
Make sure drive A: is empty. Hit any key to continue: ");
    getch();
/* Try an operation on drive A: */
    getdfree(drivea, &dfinfo);

/* If error_flag is set, repeat call to getdfree */
    while(error_flag)
    {
        error_flag = 0;
        getdfree(drivea, &dfinfo);
    }

/* Compute space statistics and display result */
    bytes_per_cluster = dfinfo.df_sclus *
                        dfinfo.df_bsec;
    total_space = dfinfo.df_total * bytes_per_cluster;
    free_space = dfinfo.df_avail * bytes_per_cluster;
    printf ("\n%ld bytes free out of %ld bytes of \
total space.\n", free_space, total_space);
    return 0;
}
/*-----------------------------------------------------*/
/* Critical error handler                              */

#define DRIVE_NOT_READY 2
#define HARDERR_ABORT   2

int harderror_handler(int errorcode, int deverror,
                      int bpval, int sival)
{
    unsigned far *devhdr;
```

```
    char dletter;
/* Set up pointer to device header                    */
    devhdr = MK_FP((unsigned)bpval, (unsigned)sival);
/* Set a flag to let our program know about the error */
    error_flag = 1;

/* Check if this is a "drive not ready" error */
    if ((errorcode & 0xff) == DRIVE_NOT_READY)
    {
/* Find out which drive, it's in low byte of deverror */
        dletter = 'A' + (deverror & 0xff);
/* Ask user to insert a diskette into the drive */
        printf("\nDrive %c is not ready.\n\
Please insert a diskette and hit any key to continue:",
               dletter);
        getch();  /* Read key before returning */
/* Use hardretn to go back to your program    */
        hardretn(-1);
    }
    else
    {
/* Unknown error, print message and abort program */
        printf("Unknown critical error. Aborting...\n");
        hardresume(HARDERR_ABORT);
    }
}
```

hardresume

COMPATIBILITY

TC1	TC1.5	TC2	TC++	MSC3	MSC4	MSC5	MSC6	QC1	QC2	QC2.5	ANSI	UNIX V	XNX
▲	▲	▲	▲			1	1	1	1	1			

PURPOSE Use *hardresume* to return to MS-DOS from your own critical error handler, which can be installed by calling the function *harderr*).

SYNTAX `void hardresume (int returncode);`

`int returncode;` *Tells DOS how the handler is returning*

EXAMPLE CALL `hardresume(2); /* Return to DOS and abort program */`

INCLUDES `#include <dos.h>` *For function declaration*

DESCRIPTION The *hardresume* function is used to return to DOS from a routine that you install to process interrupt number 24h, which is triggered by critical hardware errors that might occur during an I/O request. The installation of the handler is done by passing its address to the function *harderr.*

The argument *returncode* tells *hardresume* what to do upon returning to DOS. Use one of the values given in Table 17-27 to specify the action.

Table 17-27. *Error Codes Used by* hardresume

Return Code Value	Action Taken by MS-DOS
0	Ignore the error.
1	Retry the operation that caused the error.
2	Abort the program by invoking INT 23h.
3	Fail the MS-DOS system call in progress (only under MS-DOS 3.0 and higher).

1. The equivalent function in Microsoft C 5 and 6, and QuickC 1.0 through 2.5, is *_hardresume.*

COMMENTS The *hardresume* function is used only in a user-installed critical error handler. This function is not intended for any other use.

SEE ALSO `hardretn` *To return to the application program from the error handler*

EXAMPLE The example on *harderr* also shows how to use *hardresume.*

hardretn

COMPATIBILITY

TC1	TC1.5	TC2	TC++	MSC3	MSC4	MSC5	MSC6	QC1	QC2	QC2.5	ANSI	UNIX V	XNX
▲	▲	▲	▲			1	1	1	1	1			

PURPOSE Use *hardretn* to return to the application program from your own critical error handler, which can be installed by calling the function *harderr.*

SYNTAX

```
void hardretn (int errorcode);

int errorcode;       MS-DOS error code returned to application program
```

EXAMPLE CALL

```
hardretn(-1);
```

INCLUDES

```
#include <dos.h>       For function declaration
```

DESCRIPTION The *hardretn* function is used to return directly to an application program from an error-handling routine designed to process critical hardware errors that might occur during an I/O request. This error-handling routine should be installed as the handler for interrupt 24h by passing its address to the function *harderr*.

A call to *hardretn* will force a return to the application program just past the point where the erroneous I/O request occurred. When invoking *hardretn* the argument *errorcode* should be an MS-DOS error code appropriate for the I/O operation during which the error occurred. The application program should have code to deal with a returned error condition.

If the number of the DOS function during which the error occurred is 38h or greater, the *hardretn* function will load *AX* with the value of *errorcode* before forcing the return. Since integer and unsigned return values from C functions are passed in the *AX* register, this has the effect of fooling the application program into thinking that a DOS error occurred (instead of a hardware error).

If the hardware error occurred during a DOS I/O function 37h or less, then the return value seen by the application program will be FFh. No error code is returned to the application if the error occurs during a DOS function that does not have a way of returning an error condition. In these cases the argument *errorcode* is ignored.

1. In Microsoft C 5 and 6, and QuickC 1.0 through 2.5, use *_hardretn*.

COMMENTS The *hardretn* function is used only in a user-installed critical error handler. This function is not intended for any other use.

SEE ALSO `hardresume` *To return to DOS from the error handler*

EXAMPLE The example on *harderr* also shows how *hardretn* is used to return to the application program.

int86

COMPATIBILITY

TC1	TC1.5	TC2	TC++	MSC3	MSC4	MSC5	MSC6	QC1	QC2	QC2.5	ANSI	UNIX V	XNX
▲	▲	▲	▲	▲	▲	▲	▲	▲	▲	▲			

PURPOSE Use the *int86* function to invoke any BIOS and DOS service routines that can be accessed by generating an 80x86 software interrupt of specified number. You should use *int86* when the function you are calling via interrupt does not require you to pass any argument through the segment registers *DS* and *ES* or when you are using a memory model that does not

require you to explicitly specify the segment registers to access data. For example, you can use *int86* to call the ROM BIOS video function to position the cursor on the screen. The *int86* function uses the REGS data structure to pass register values back and forth (see the tutorial section).

SYNTAX

```
int int86( int intno, union REGS *inregs, union REGS *outregs);

int  intno;                   Interrupt number

union REGS * inregs;          Input registers

union REGS * outregs;         Output registers
```

EXAMPLE CALL

```
int86(0x10, &inregs, &outregs);
```

INCLUDES

`#include <dos.h>` *For function declaration and definition of REGS*

DESCRIPTION

The *int86* function first copies the values for the registers from the C structure *inregs* into the corresponding registers in the microprocessor. Then it generates the software interrupt number *intno* via the INT instruction. After returning from the interrupt, the function copies the contents of the 80x86 registers and the system carry flag into corresponding elements in the C structure *outregs.*

The arguments *inregs* and *outregs* are the union of two structures and are defined in the include file *dos.h* (see the tutorial section). Examples below illustrate how the register values are specified.

COMMON USES

The most common use of the *int86* function is to access the BIOS functions on the PC. The BIOS routines, for example, allow you to move the cursor, read the keyboard, perform screen I/O, and more. Turbo C provides a number of simpler routines specifically set up to access a number of individual BIOS and DOS functions. The *int86* function still has its place, however. Since its underlying function is to generate software interrupts, you can use it to initiate any interrupt you want, and consequently access any function that can be invoked by an interrupt. See Tables 17-1 and 17-2 for a list of all BIOS and DOS functions that can be called by software interrupts.

RETURNS

The *int86* function returns the contents of the *AX* register after the interrupt. An error is indicated by a nonzero value in *outregs.x.cflag*. A global variable named *_doserrno* is set to an appropriate error code. You can use this to determine what caused the error. See Table 17-26 for list of error codes.

COMMENTS

The arguments required by the actual DOS or BIOS function invoked by the interrupt determine whether or not the segment registers *DS* and *ES* need to be loaded before executing the interrupt. For example if a register, say, *DX* is supposed to contain the offset of a data element and you are using the large model, then you may explicitly want to set the data segment register *DS* to point to your data area. In this case, you should use the *int86x* function for the interrupt because it allows you to load the *DS* register with a new value before making the software interrupt.

SEE ALSO

`int86x`	*For software interrupts that require you to set up segment registers DS and ES*
`bdos, intdos, intdosx`	*To make an MS-DOS system call with an INT 21h instruction*
Table 17-4	*Simplified access to several BIOS functions*
Table 17-5	*Simplified access to specific MS-DOS functions*

EXAMPLES Write a routine that uses the BIOS video services to position the cursor at column "col" and row number "row" on the screen. NOTE: (0,0) is the upper left corner of the screen.

```
#include <dos.h>
#define BIOS_VIDEO 0x10

void putcursor(int row, int col)
{
    union REGS xr;

    xr.h.ah = 2;     /* Function number to set cursor */
    xr.h.dh = row;
    xr.h.dl = col;
    xr.h.bh = 0;     /* Assume video page 0           */
                     /* Use xr for both input/output  */
    int86(BIOS_VIDEO, &xr, &xr);
    return 0;
}
```

When you press the SHIFT and the PrtSc keys together on an IBM PC, the keyboard generates interrupt number 5. The BIOS already includes a routine to print the screen when this interrupt occurs. Use *int86* to print the screen by initiating interrupt 5.

```
#include <stdio.h>
#include <dos.h>
#define BIOS_PRNTSCR  5
```

```
union REGS xr;
main()
{
    printf("Test: Printing screen\n");
    int86(BIOS_PRNTSCR, &xr, &xr);
    return 0;
}
```

A large number of DOS functions are available via 80x86 interrupt number 21h. For example, by specifying function 2Ah in AH, you can get the current date with the day in DL, month in DH and year in CX. The program below shows how:

```
#include <stdio.h>
#include <dos.h>

#define DOS_GETDATE 0x2a
#define DOS_INT     0x21

static char *months[] = { "---", "JAN", "FEB", "MAR", "APR",
     "MAY", "JUN", "JUL", "AUG", "SEP", "OCT", "NOV", "DEC"};

main()
{
    union REGS xr, yr;
    xr.h.ah = DOS_GETDATE;
    int86 (DOS_INT, &xr, &yr);
    printf("Today's date is: %.2d-%s-%.4d\n",
           yr.h.dl, months[yr.h.dh], yr.x.cx);
    return 0;
}
```

If you have an Enhanced Graphics Adapter (EGA), the BIOS video interrupt (interrupt number 10h with AH=12h and BL=10h) lets you find out how much physical memory is available on the graphics adapter and which video mode it is in. Write a routine using *int86* to get this information about the EGA.

```
#include <stdio.h>
#include <dos.h>
static union REGS xr, yr;
#define BIOS_VIDEO 0x10
main()
{
/* Set up registers as needed by BIOS video function. */
```

```
        xr.h.ah = 0x12;
        xr.h.bl = 0x10;
        int86 (BIOS_VIDEO, &xr, &yr);

    /* Upon return values are in structure yr */
        if (yr.h.bh == 0) printf("EGA in color mode\n");
        if (yr.h.bh == 1) printf("EGA in mono mode\n");
        printf("Memory size: ");
        switch (yr.h.bl)
        {
            case 0: printf("64K\n");
                    break;
            case 1: printf("128K\n");
                    break;
            case 2: printf("192K\n");
                    break;
            case 3: printf("256K\n");
                    break;
        }
        return 0;
    }
```

int86x

COMPATIBILITY

TC1	TC1.5	TC2	TC++	MSC3	MSC4	MSC5	MSC6	QC1	QC2	QC2.5	ANSI	UNIX V	XNX
▲	▲	▲	▲	▲	▲	▲	▲	▲	▲	▲			

PURPOSE Use the *int86x* function to generate an 80x86 software interrupt of specified number. You should use *int86x* when the function called by the interrupt requires arguments placed in the segment registers DS and ES or when you are using a memory model that requires you to explicitly specify the segment registers to access data. For example, you can use *int86x* with interrupt 21h to access the MS-DOS function 3Bh, which allows you to change the current directory from your program. The *int86x* function uses the REGS and SREGS structures as shown below.

SYNTAX

```
int int86x(int intno, union REGS *inr, union REGS *outr,
               struct SREGS *segr);
```

`int  intno;` *Interrupt number*

`union  REGS  * inr;` *Input registers*

```
union  REGS  * outr;
```
Output registers

```
struct SREGS * segr;
```
Segment registers

EXAMPLE CALL
```
int86x(0x21, &inregs, &outregs, &segregs);
```

INCLUDES
```
#include <dos.h>
```
For function declaration and definition of REGS and SREGS

DESCRIPTION The *int86x* function first copies the values of the registers from the C structure *inr* into the corresponding registers in the microprocessor. It saves the DS register and then copies new values from the *segr* structure into DS and ES. After that, it generates the software interrupt *intno* via the INT instruction. After returning from the interrupt, *int86x* copies the contents of the 80x86 registers and the system carry flag into corresponding elements in the C structure *outr*. It also restores the DS register before returning.

The arguments *inr* and *outr* are the union of two structures. This and the structure SREGS are defined in the include file *dos.h* (see the tutorial section). Examples below illustrate how the register values are specified.

COMMON USES The most common use of the *int86x* function is to access the MS-DOS and BIOS functions on the PC, especially those that either accept arguments or return values via the segment registers DS and ES. The BIOS and DOS functions, for example, allow you to read from the floppy disk, change current directory, and print a string. Since the underlying function of *int86x* is to make software interrupts, you can use it to initiate any interrupt you want and consequently access anything on the PC that is reached by an interrupt. This includes all DOS services as well. See Tables 17-1 and 17-2 for a list of all significant DOS and BIOS functions invoked by software interrupts.

RETURNS The *int86x* function returns the value of the register AX after the interrupt. Error is indicated by a nonzero value in *outr.x.cflag*. A global variable named *_doserrno* is set to an appropriate error code. You can use this to determine what caused the error. See Table 17-26 for a list of error codes.

COMMENTS The arguments required by the actual function invoked by the interrupt determine whether or not the segment registers DS and ES need to be loaded before executing the interrupt. You must use *int86x* whenever arguments have to be passed through DS and ES.

The *int86x* function is the most general interface to the BIOS and MS-DOS services. The Turbo C run-time library includes several special functions designed as gateways to specific DOS and BIOS calls. However, you should note that *every* interrupt service on the PC is accessible via *int86x*.

SEE ALSO

int86	*For software interrupts that do not require you to set up segment registers DS and ES*
bdos, intdos, intdosx	*To make an MS-DOS system call with an INT 21h instruction*
Table 17-4	*Simplified access to several BIOS functions*
Table 17-5	*Simplified access to specific MS-DOS functions*

EXAMPLES Change the current directory by calling DOS function 3Bh with *int86x*. Use the *FP_OFF* and *FP_SEG* macros to find offset and segment addresses of strings that have to be passed to the DOS function 3Bh.

```
#include <stdio.h>
#include <dos.h>
/* Interrupt number for DOS functions */
#define DOS_INT 0x21
/* DOS "change directory" function    */
#define DOS_CHDIR 0x3b
/* Buffer to hold path name           */
static char buff[80];
main()
{
/* Far pointer to directory name string*/
    char far *dirname;
/* Set up the structure for registers  */
    union REGS xr;
    struct SREGS sr;
    printf("Enter pathname: ");
    gets(buff);
 /* Set up far pointer to name*/
    dirname = &buff[0];
    xr.h.ah = DOS_CHDIR;
/* Offset of string to DX    */
    xr.x.dx = FP_OFF(dirname);
/* Segment of string to DS   */
    sr.ds = FP_SEG(dirname);
    int86x(DOS_INT, &xr, &xr, &sr);
    return 0;
}
```

Use *int86x* to access the MS-DOS function 9h, accessible via interrupt number 21h, to print a string terminated with a $. Use the *FP_SEG* and *FP_OFF* macros to get the segment and offset addresses of the string to be printed.

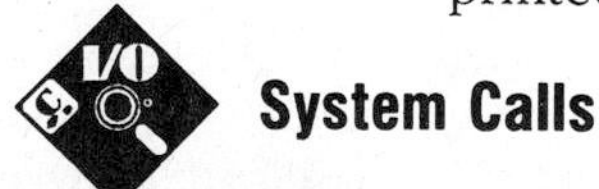

```
#include <dos.h>
#define DOS_INT     0x21
/* DOS "print string" function */
#define DOS_PRTSTR  0x9

char str[]="Testing String Print Function$";
main()
{
    union  REGS  xr;
    struct SREGS sr;

    xr.h.ah = DOS_PRTSTR;
/* Offset string to DX         */
    xr.x.dx = FP_OFF(str);
/* Segment of string to DS     */
    sr.ds = FP_SEG(str);
    int86x(DOS_INT, &xr, &xr, &sr);
   return 0;
}
```

COMPATIBILITY

intdos

TC1	TC1.5	TC2	TC++	MSC3	MSC4	MSC5	MSC6	QC1	QC2	QC2.5	ANSI	UNIX V	XNX
▲	▲	▲	▲	▲	▲	▲	▲	▲	▲	▲			

PURPOSE Use the *intdos* function to access the comprehensive set of MS-DOS system utility routines that are normally called via 80x86 software interrupt 21h. Use *intdos* when the DOS function does not require you to exchange any arguments through the segment registers DS and ES or when you are using a memory model that does not require you to explicitly specify the segment registers to access data. For example, you can use *intdos* with function 19h to get the current disk drive number.

Since the *int86* function can generate any software interrupt, you can duplicate the effect of *intdos* by calling *int86* with interrupt 21h. The only advantage of the *intdos* function is its shorter list of arguments.

SYNTAX

```
int intdos( union REGS *inregs, union REGS *outregs);
```

`union REGS *inregs;` *Input registers*

`union REGS *outregs;` *Output registers*

EXAMPLE CALL

```
intdos(&inregs, &outregs);
```

INCLUDES `#include <dos.h>` *For function declaration and definition of REGS*

DESCRIPTION The *intdos* function first copies the values of the registers from the C structure *inregs* into the corresponding registers in the microprocessor. Then it generates the software interrupt 21h to access the MS-DOS system functions. After returning from the interrupt, *intdos* copies the contents of the 80x86 registers and the system carry flag into corresponding elements in the C structure *outregs*. The task performed by DOS depends on the function number specified in the AH register.

The arguments *inregs* and *outregs* are the union of two structures and are defined in the include file *dos.h* (see the tutorial section). The examples below illustrate how the register values are specified.

COMMON USES The *intdos* function is used to access the MS-DOS system routines that are accessible through an INT 21h instruction. These routines, for example, allow you to read the keyboard, write to the screen, and manipulate DOS directories and files. Table 17-2 shows a complete list of all DOS functions.

RETURNS The *intdos* function returns the value of the register AX after the interrupt. An error is indicated by a nonzero value in the field *outregs.x.cflag*. A global variable named *_doserrno* is set to an appropriate error code. You can use this to determine what caused the error. See Table 17-23 for a list of error codes.

COMMENTS The arguments required by the MS-DOS function invoked by *intdos* determine whether or not the segment registers DS and ES need to be loaded before calling this function. For example if register DX is supposed to contain the offset of a data element and you are using the large model, then you may explicitly want to set data segment register DS to point to your data area. In this case, you should use the *intdosx* function because it allows you to load the DS register with a new value before invoking the DOS function.

SEE ALSO

`int86, int86x` *For other software interrupts*

`intdosx` *To access MS-DOS functions that require arguments in segment registers DS and ES*

`bdos` *To access those MS-DOS routines that take arguments in the DX and AL registers only*

Table 17-5 *These functions provide simplified access to specific MS-DOS services*

EXAMPLES MS-DOS function 19h returns the default drive number in the AL register. Access this function via *intdos* and get the current drive number (0 means A, 1 means B, 2 means C, and so on).

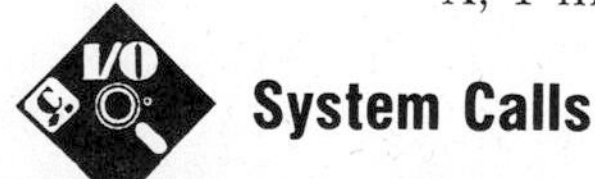

```
#include <stdio.h>
#include <dos.h>
#define DOS_GETDRIVE 0x19
union REGS xr;
main()
{
    xr.h.ah = DOS_GETDRIVE;
    intdos(&xr, &xr);
/* Adding 65 to the value gives us the drive letter */
    printf("Current drive: %c\n", xr.h.al+65);
    return 0;
}
```

DOS function 2Ch returns the current time with the hours in *CH*, minutes in *CL*, and seconds in *DH*. Use *intdos* to get the current time and display it.

```
#include <stdio.h>
#include <dos.h>
#define DOS_GETTIME 0x2c
main()
{
    union REGS xr, yr;
    xr.h.ah = DOS_GETTIME;
    intdos(&xr, &yr);
    printf("Current time is %.2d:%.2d:%.2d\ n",
           yr.h.ch, yr.h.cl, yr.h.dh);
    return 0;
}
```

intdosx

COMPATIBILITY

TC1	TC1.5	TC2	TC++	MSC3	MSC4	MSC5	MSC6	QC1	QC2	QC2.5	ANSI	UNIX V	XNX
▲	▲	▲	▲	▲	▲	▲	▲	▲	▲	▲			

PURPOSE Use the *intdosx* function to access any MS-DOS system function, even those that require arguments in the segment registers DS and ES (*intdos* cannot handle these cases). You must use *intdosx* when the DOS function requires arguments exchanged through segment registers DS and ES or when you are using a memory model that requires you to explicitly specify the segment registers to access data. For example, you can use *intdosx* with function 39h to create a subdirectory.

SYNTAX

```
int intdosx(union  REGS *inr, union  REGS *outr,
                  struct SREGS *segr);
```

`union  REGS  *inr;` *Input registers*

`union  REGS  *outr;` *Output registers*

`struct SREGS *segr;` *Segment registers*

EXAMPLE CALL

```
intdosx(&inregs, &outregs, &segregs);
```

INCLUDES

`#include <dos.h>` *For function declaration and definition of REGS and SREGS*

DESCRIPTION

The *intdosx* function copies the values of the registers from the C structure *inr* into the corresponding registers in the microprocessor. It saves the DS register and then copies new values from segr into DS and ES. After that, it calls DOS by an INT 21h instruction. After returning from DOS, *intdosx* copies the contents of the 80x86 registers and the system carry flag into corresponding elements in the C union *outr*. It also restores the DS register before returning. The actions performed by DOS depend on the function number specified in the AH register.

The arguments *inr* and *outr* are the union of two structures. This and the structure SREGS are defined in the include file *dos.h* (see the tutorial section). The examples below illustrate how the register values are specified.

COMMON USES

The *intdosx* function is used to call MS-DOS functions on the PC, especially those that either accept arguments or return values via the segment registers DS and ES. The DOS functions, for example, allow you to read from the floppy disk, change the current directory, and create a subdirectory. See Table 17-2 for a list of all DOS functions that can be called by software interrupts.

RETURNS

The *intdosx* function returns contents of the AX register after the interrupt return. An error is indicated by a nonzero value in *outr.x.cflag*. A global variable named *_doserrno* is set to an appropriate error code. You can use this to determine what caused the error. See Table 17-23 for a list of error codes.

COMMENTS

The arguments required by the DOS function invoked by *intdosx* determine whether or not the segment registers DS and ES need to be loaded before calling *intdosx*. You must use *intdosx* whenever parameters are exchanged through the segment registers DS and ES.

The *intdosx* function is a general interface to the MS-DOS functions. The Turbo C++ run-time library includes several special functions de-

signed as gateways to specific DOS calls. However, you should note that every DOS function on the PC is accessible via *intdosx*.

SEE ALSO

`int86, int86x`	*To generate any 80x86 software interrupt*
`intdos`	*For MS-DOS calls that do not require you to set up segment registers DS and ES*
`bdos`	*To access those MS-DOS routines that take arguments in the DX and AL registers only*
Table 17-5	*These functions provide simplified access to specific MS-DOS services*

EXAMPLES Use the MS-DOS function 39h to create a subdirectory in the current directory. The segment and offset of the subdirectory name should be specified via the registers DS and DX, respectively.

```
#include <stdio.h>
#include <dos.h>

#define  DOS_MAKEDIR 0x39

union REGS xr;
struct SREGS sr;

main()
{
    char pathname[80];
    printf("Enter name of subdirectory: ");
    gets(pathname);

    xr.h.ah = DOS_MAKEDIR;
    sr.ds = FP_SEG(pathname);
    xr.x.dx = FP_OFF(pathname);
    intdosx(&xr, &xr, &sr);

    if (xr.x.cflag == 1)
    {
        printf("\nError creating subdirectory\n");
    }
    return 0;
}
```

Use DOS function Ah to read a line from the keyboard up to and including a carriage return. The line read is stored in a buffer whose segment address must be in DS and the offset in DX. The first byte of the buffer contains the maximum number of characters to be read. On return the second byte will have the actual number of characters read.

```
#include <stdio.h>
#include <dos.h>
#define DOS_BUFIN 0x0a
static char buffer[82] = {80, 0};
main()
{
    union REGS xr;
    struct SREGS sr;
    int numchars;
    char far *pbuf;
    pbuf = (char far *)(&buffer[0]);
    printf("Enter a line: ");
    sr.ds = FP_SEG(pbuf);
    xr.h.ah = DOS_BUFIN;
    xr.x.dx = FP_OFF(pbuf);
    intdosx(&xr, &xr, &sr);
/* The number of characters not counting the carriage
 * return
 */
    numchars = buffer[1];
/* Make it an ASCIIZ string by adding a 0 at the end*/
    buffer[numchars+2] = '\0';
    printf("\nYou typed %d characters\n", numchars);
    printf("The string is: %s", buffer+2);
    return 0;
}
```

intr

COMPATIBILITY

TC1	TC1.5	TC2	TC++	MSC3	MSC4	MSC5	MSC6	QC1	QC2	QC2.5	ANSI	UNIX V	XNX
▲	▲	▲	▲										

PURPOSE Use *intr* as an alternate way to generate software interrupts on an IBM PC. The *int86x* is a more portable function for generating the interrupts.

SYNTAX

```
void intr(int int_num, struct REGPACK *preg);
```

`int int_num;` *Interrupt number*

`struct REGPACK *preg;` *Pointer to structure containing the registers and flags*

EXAMPLE CALL `intr(0x10, &all_regs);`

INCLUDES `#include <dos.h>` *For function declaration*

DESCRIPTION The *intr* function generates software interrupts on IBM PC and compatibles in the same manner as does *int86x*. The register values are passed in a REGPACK structure which is defined in *dos.h* as follows:

```
struct  REGPACK
{
  unsigned  r_ax,     /* AX register          */
            r_bx,     /* BX register          */
            r_cx,     /* CX register          */
            r_dx;     /* DX register          */
  unsigned  r_bp,     /* BP register          */
            r_si,     /* SI register          */
            r_di,     /* DI register          */
            r_ds,     /* DS segment register */
            r_es,     /* ES segment register */
            r_flags;  /* 8086 Flags           */
};
```

You must allocate one such structure and provide its address in the argument *preg*. The *intr* function copies the values from **preg* into corresponding registers. Then it uses the assembly language instruction INT to initiate the interrupt number specified in the argument *intr_num*.

After return from the interrupt, *intr* copies the registers into the corresponding files in **preg*.

COMMENTS The *int86x* function is more widely supported by compiler vendors that sell C compilers for the IBM PC and compatibles. Therefore, you should use the *int86x* function for generating software interrupts on the PC.

SEE ALSO `int86x` *To generate software interrupts*

EXAMPLE Change the current directory by calling DOS function 3Bh with *intr*. Use the *FP_OFF* and *FP_SEG* macros to find offset and segment addresses of strings that have to be passed to the DOS function 3Bh.

```
#include <stdio.h>
#include <dos.h>
/* Interrupt number for DOS functions */
#define DOS_INT 0x21
/* DOS "change directory" function    */
#define DOS_CHDIR 0x3b
```

```
/* Buffer to hold pathname          */
static char buff[80];
main()
{
/* Far pointer to directory name string*/
    char far *dirname;
/* Set up the structure for registers  */
    regpack regs;

    printf("Enter pathname: ");
    gets(buff);
 /* Set up far pointer to name*/
    dirname = &buff[0];
    regs.r_ax = DOS_CHDIR << 8;
/* Offset of string to DX    */
    regs.r_dx = FP_OFF(dirname);
/* Segment of string to DS   */
    regs.r_ds = FP_SEG(dirname);
    intr(DOS_INT, &regs);
    return 0;
}
```

ioctl

COMPATIBILITY

TC1	TC1.5	TC2	TC++	MSC3	MSC4	MSC5	MSC6	QC1	QC2	QC2.5	ANSI	UNIX V	XNX
▲	▲	▲	▲										

PURPOSE Use *ioctl* for interacting with MS-DOS device drivers and controlling their behavior.

SYNTAX

```
int   ioctl  (int handle, int cmd, ...);
  /* optional 3rd and 4th args are: void * argdx, int argcx */
```

`int  handle;` *Drive number of file handle*

`int  cmd;` *Function to be performed by* ioctl

EXAMPLE CALL `ret = ioctl(0,8); /* Check if the default drive is removable */`

INCLUDES `#include <io.h>` *For function declaration*

DESCRIPTION Device drivers support a mechanism known as IOCTL (I/O Control) that defines a protocol for information exchange between application programs

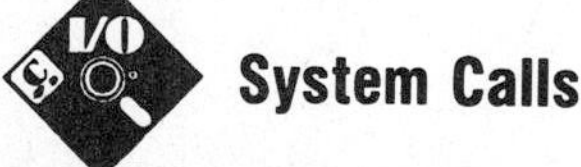

and the driver. The IOCTL exists in device drivers on most operating systems including MS-DOS and UNIX. However, the specifics of the IOCTL mechanism differ from one system to another. The *ioctl* function in Turbo C++ provides a direct hook to the DOS function 44h which is meant for IOCTL for installable device drivers under DOS.

The function performed by *ioctl* depends on the value of the parameter *cmd*. Table 17-28 shows the meaning of *cmd*. The argument handle specifies the drive number or the file handle depending on the device being controlled by the driver. Two optional arguments, **argdx* and *argcx*, may be used to pass values to the DX and CX registers during the IOCTL call.

Table 17-28. *MS-DOS IOCTL Function Operations*

Value of *cmd*	Description
0	Get device information (returned in location whose address is in *argdx*).
1	Set device information (specified by the bits of **argdx* as follows:
	Bit 0 = 1 means device is console input device
	Bit 1 = 1 means device is console output device
	Bit 2 = 1 means device is null device
	Bit 3 = 1 means device is clock device
	Bit 4 = 1 means device is special
	Bit 5 = 1 means device is operating in binary mode
	Bit 6 = 0 means End of File on input
	Bit 7 = 1 means character device, 0 means bits 0 to 5 are block device number
	Bit 12 = 1 means network device
	Bit 14 = 1 means device can process control strings (this bit is read only)
	Other bits are reserved
2	Read the number of bytes specified in *argcx* from the device control channel specified by *handle* to the buffer whose address is in *argdx*.
3	Write the number of bytes specified in *argcx* from the buffer whose address is in *argdx* to the device control channel specified by *handle*.
4	Same as 2, but *handle* is interpreted as a drive number (0=default, 1=A, 2=B, and so on).
5	Same as 3, but *handle* is interpreted as a drive number (0=default, 1=A, 2=B, and so on).
6	Get input status (returns −1 if ready, 0 if not).
7	Get output status (returns −1 if ready, 0 if not).
8	Is block device specified by *handle* removable? (Returns 1 if yes, 0 if no.)
	NOTE: DOS 3.0 and above only.
9	Is logical device specified by *handle* local or remote? (Yes if **argdx* & 1000h = 0.)
	NOTE: DOS 3.0 and above only.

Table 17-28. *(cont.)*

Value of *cmd*	Description
10	Is logical device specified by the *handle* local or remote? (Yes if * *argdx* & 8000h = 0.) NOTE: DOS 3.0 and above only.
11	Set the sharing retry count (the number of times access is attempted when device or file is not accessible because of sharing constraints) to **argdx* and the retry delay (the time between two successive retries) to *argcx*. NOTE: DOS 3.0 and above only.
12	General IOCTL introduced in DOS 3.3 (consult *DOS 3.3 Technical Reference Manual* for details).

COMMON USES The *ioctl* function is useful for controlling a device when its driver offers functions that are available through the DOS IOCTL interface. For example, a serial port driver might allow you to set the communications parameters such as baud rate, word length, parity, and number of stop bits, using IOCTL.

RETURNS The value returned by *ioctl* depends on the function being performed. For *cmd* values 2 through 5, *ioctl* returns the number of bytes actually transferred. When *cmd* is 6 or 7, the return value is the status of the device or file.

In case of any error, *ioctl* returns −1 and sets the global variable *errno* to one of:

EINVAL	*Invalid argument*
EBADF	*Bad file handle*
EINVDAT	*Invalid data*

COMMENTS Although IOCTL exists in UNIX, the mechanism is different from that in DOS. In general, IOCTL calls are very much device-dependent because even in DOS the interpretation of the IOCTL commands could vary from one device driver to another.

Note that the IOCTL commands 8 through 11 are available only in DOS 3.0 and above, and the command 12 is only available in DOS 3.3.

EXAMPLE Use *ioctl* to write a program that can set the mode of the standard output device to either "raw" mode (control characters are not intercepted) or "cooked" mode (this is the normal mode of operation). Using the standard output in raw mode can enhance the speed of output to the screen.

```
#include <stdio.h>
#include <io.h>
#define RAW_BIT 0x20
main(int argc, char **argv)
{
    int raw_mode, handle = 1, /* standard output */
        cmd, argdx;
    if(argc < 2)
    {
        printf("Usage: %s <COOKED or RAW>\n", argv[0]);
        exit(0);
    }
    if((strcmp(argv[1], "COOKED") == 0) ||
       (strcmp(argv[1], "cooked") == 0)) raw_mode = 0;
    else
    {
        if((strcmp(argv[1], "RAW") == 0) ||
           (strcmp(argv[1], "raw") == 0)) raw_mode = 1;
        else
        {
            printf("Unknown mode: %s\n", argv[1]);
            exit(0);
        }
    }
/* Get device information (cmd = 0) using IOCTL */
    cmd = 0;
    ioctl(handle, cmd, &argdx);
/* Set raw/cooked bit on or off depending on value
 * of variable "raw_mode"
 */
     argdx &= 0xff;
     if(raw_mode) argdx |= RAW_BIT;
     else argdx &= (~RAW_BIT);
/* Call ioctl to set the raw/cooked mode bit */
    cmd = 1;
    ioctl(handle, cmd, &argdx);
    printf("Standard output is now in %s mode\n",
            argv[1]);
    printf("(If mode is RAW, remember to reset it to "
           "COOKED when you are done)");
    return 0;
}
```

keep

COMPATIBILITY

TC1	TC1.5	TC2	TC++	MSC3	MSC4	MSC5	MSC6	QC1	QC2	QC2.5	ANSI	UNIX V	XNX
▲	▲	▲	▲			1	1	1	1	1			

PURPOSE Use *keep* to install terminate-and-stay-resident (TSR) programs.

SYNTAX

```
void keep(unsigned char status, unsigned memsize);

unsigned char status;        Status code to be returned to calling process

unsigned memsize;            Size of memory needed by TSR program,
                             in 16-byte paragraphs
```

EXAMPLE CALL

```
keep(0, programsize_in_paragraphs);
```

INCLUDES

```
#include <dos.h>        For declaration of function
```

DESCRIPTION The *keep* function calls DOS function 31h to install the current program in memory, reserving the number of paragraphs specified in the argument *memsize*. Then it exits the program, returning the value specified in *status* to its parent (normally DOS).

The return code is analogous to the code used with the *exit* routine. As in *exit*, a *status* equal to zero means there were no errors. Other values may be used to signify errors.

1. Use *_dos_keep* in Microsoft C 5 and 6, and QuickC 1.0 through 2.5.

COMMON USES This function can be used to install your own memory-resident programs in the system.

COMMENTS It is not clear, however, how you can set the argument *memsize* in the call to *keep*. One approach would be to use our knowledge of the layout of the program in memory. The global variable *_psp* provides the segment address of the Program Segment Prefix, which is where the program starts. The end point of the program is the top of the stack. We can get the stack segment address and the current stack pointer using the pseudo-variables *_SS* and *_SP*, respectively. Then a good estimate of the program's size will be

```
prog_size = _SS + (_SP + safety_margin)/16 - _psp;
```

where *safety_margin* is a small number of bytes (around 100) to account for uncertainties in our estimate. The division by 16 is necessary to convert the stack pointer to paragraphs.

for uncertainties in our estimate. The division by 16 is necessary to convert the stack pointer to paragraphs.

You should gain some familiarity with the concepts of terminate-and-stay-resident programs before using the *keep* function.

SEE ALSO `getvect, setvect` *To retrieve current interrupt vector and to install a new one*

EXAMPLE See the February 1988 issue of *Computer Language* (pp. 37–57) for an article by Al Stevens, "Writing Terminate-and-Stay-Resident Programs, Part I: TSRs in Turbo C," in which he shows how to use *keep* to write a TSR utility entirely in Turbo C.

MK_FP

COMPATIBILITY

TC1	TC1.5	TC2	TC++	MSC3	MSC4	MSC5	MSC6	QC1	QC2	QC2.5	ANSI	UNIX V	XNX
▲	▲	▲	▲										

PURPOSE Use the *MK_FP* macro to construct a far pointer from a segment address and an offset.

SYNTAX

```
void far *MK_FP(unsigned seg, unsigned offset);
```

`unsigned seg;` *Segment address*

`unsigned offset;` *Offset address*

EXAMPLE CALL

```
ega_ram = MK_FP(0xA000, 0); /* Construct pointer to EGA memory */
```

INCLUDES `#include <dos.h>` *For function declaration*

DESCRIPTION The *MK_FP* macro constructs a far pointer using the components *seg* and *offset* which are the segment address and the offset of the pointer, respectively.

COMMON USES The *MK_FP* macro is convenient for creating pointers to video memory and BIOS data areas.

RETURNS The *MK_FP* macro creates a far pointer.

SEE ALSO `FP_OFF, FP_SEG` *To take apart the offset and the segment addresses of a far pointer*

EXAMPLES The examples for *harderr* and *getpsp* show the use of the macro *MK_FP*.

nosound

COMPATIBILITY

TC1	TC1.5	TC2	TC++	MSC3	MSC4	MSC5	MSC6	QC1	QC2	QC2.5	ANSI	UNIX V	XNX
	▲	▲	▲										

PURPOSE Use *nosound* to turn off the speaker in the PC.

SYNTAX

```
void nosound (void);
```

EXAMPLE CALL

```
nosound();
```

INCLUDES `#include <dos.h>` *For function declaration*

DESCRIPTION The PC's speaker can be activated to generate sound at a specified frequency by using the *sound* function introduced in Turbo C 1.5. The companion function *nosound* is provided so that you can turn the speaker off.

COMMON USES The *sound* and *nosound* functions are used to generate sound from the PC's speaker. Sound can be used as a means of alerting the user.

SEE ALSO `sound` *To begin generating sound of a specified frequency*

EXAMPLE See the example for *sound*.

_open

COMPATIBILITY

TC1	TC1.5	TC2	TC++	MSC3	MSC4	MSC5	MSC6	QC1	QC2	QC2.5	ANSI	UNIX V	XNX
▲	▲	▲	▲			1	1	1	1	1			

PURPOSE Use *_open* to open an existing file.

SYNTAX

```
int   _open  (const char *filename, int mode);

const char *filename;      File name including path

int        mode;           Permissions for operations to be performed on the file
```

EXAMPLE CALL

```
/* Open the file  "data" for exclusive read only operations */
_open("data", O_DENYALL|O_RDONLY, &filehandle);
```

INCLUDES `#include <dos.h>` *For function declaration*

`#include <fcntl.h>` *For definition of permission mode names*

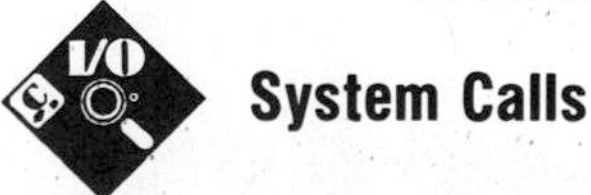

DESCRIPTION The *_open* function calls DOS function 3Dh to open the file whose name (including the full DOS pathname) is specified by the argument *filename*. The operations that are allowed to be performed on the file are indicated by the argument *mode*. The mode indicates how the file can be accessed, how much sharing is allowed, and whether the file can be inherited by a child process. This argument is specified by a value created by the bitwise OR of mode names picked from Table 17-29. You should pick, at most, one name from each category. These names are defined in the include file *fcntl.h*.

Table 17-29. ***Modes in Which Files Can Be Opened***

Category Name	Mode Name	Interpretation
Access	O_RDONLY	Only reading allowed.
	O_WRONLY	Only writing allowed.
	O_RDWR	Both reading and writing allowed.
Sharing	O_DENYALL	No one else can read from or write to this file.
	O_DENYWRITE	No one else can write to this file.
	O_DENYREAD	No one else can read from this file.
	O_DENYNONE	File is completely shareable.
Inheritance	O_NOINHERIT	File will not be inherited by any child process.

In MS-DOS 2.x, you are limited to using only the *Access* category of flags from Table 17-29.

1. In Microsoft C 5 and 6, and QuickC 1.0 through 2.5, use *_dos_open*.

RETURNS Once the file is successfully opened, *_open* returns an identifying number or handle that you should use in future references to this file.

In case of error, *_open* returns −1 and sets the global variable *errno* to one of the constants shown in Table 17-30. The meaning of the error code is explained in the table.

Table 17-30. ***Error Codes Set by*** **_open**

Error Code	Interpretation
EINVACC	Either access mode value is invalid or a sharing mode value is specified when file-sharing routines are not loaded.
ENOENT	File not found.
EMFILE	Too many files open (limit is 20 for a process).
EACCES	Access was denied (for example, trying to open a read only file for writing).

COMMENTS The functions *open* and *close* offer a more portable means of achieving the same result as these DOS specific functions.

Under MS-DOS, the maximum number of concurrently open files for a single process is 20.

SEE ALSO

`_close`	*To close a file opened by* _open
`_creat, creatnew`	*To create a new file*
`open, close`	*Portable versions of similar file opening and closing functions*

EXAMPLE Use *_open* to open a file. Close the file by calling *_close*.

```
#include <stdio.h>
#include <fcntl.h>
#include <dos.h>
#include <io.h>
main()
{
    char fname[40], *p_fname;
    int filehandle;

    printf("Enter name of file to open using \
_open: ");
    p_fname = gets(fname);

/* Open the file in "DENY ALL" mode and for reading
 *  only
 */
    if((filehandle = _open(p_fname, O_DENYALL|O_RDONLY))
        == -1)
    {
        printf("Error opening file: %s\n", fname);
        exit(0);
    }
    printf("File %s opened.\n", fname);

/* Now close file */
    if (_close(filehandle) == -1)
    {
        printf("Error closing file with _close\n");
        exit(0);
    }
    printf("File %s closed.\n", fname);
```

```
    return 0;
}
```

COMPATIBILITY

_OvrInitEms

TC1	TC1.5	TC2	TC++	MSC3	MSC4	MSC5	MSC6	QC1	QC2	QC2.5	ANSI	UNIX V	XNX
			▲										

PURPOSE Use *_OvrInitEms* to set up expanded memory (managed according to the Expanded Memory Specification or EMS) for swapping overlays.

SYNTAX

```
int far _OvrInitEms( unsigned EMSHandle, unsigned EMSFirst, unsigned
EMSPages );
```

`unsigned EMSHandle;`	*A valid EMS handle to a block of memory or zero, if you want the overlay manager to look for EMS memory*
`unsigned EMSFirst;`	*The first page where swapping can occur*
`unsigned EMSPages;`	*How many pages are allotted as swap space*

EXAMPLE CALL

```
if(_OvrInitEms(0, 0, 8) == 0)
    printf("EMS memory to be used for overlay swapping\n");
```

INCLUDES `#include <dos.h>` *For function declaration*

DESCRIPTION The *_OvrInitEms* function sets up expanded memory to be used for swapping overlays by Turbo C++'s overlay manager. If *EMSHandle* is zero, the overlay manager will look for expanded memory conforming to the Lotus-Intel-Microsoft Expanded Memory Specification (EMS) and allocate, for swapping, the number of pages (each page is 16 K bytes) specified by the *EMSPages* argument. The *EMSFirst* argument is ignored if *EMSHandle* is zero.

If *EMSHandle* is nonzero, it must be a valid handle as specified by EMS. In this case, the *EMSFirst* argument is the first page to be used for swap space and *EMSPages* is the size of the swap area in number of 16 K EMS pages.

Note that overlays are supported in medium, large, and huge memory models only. Also, to use *_OvrInitEms*, you must link your program with the OVERLAY.LIB library.

RETURNS *_OvrInitEms* returns a zero if all goes well. Otherwise, it returns a nonzero value.

COMMENTS If you plan to use a nonzero value for *EMSHandle*, you have to understand how to use EMS memory. A good reference for this topic is Chapter 7 of The Waite Group's *MS-DOS Developer's Guide*[1].

SEE ALSO `_OvrInitExt` *To set up extended memory for overlay swapping*

EXAMPLE Assume that you are writing a large program that uses Turbo C++'s overlay facility. At the beginning of your program, look for expanded (EMS) memory for swapping. If none is found, try to use extended memory. If both attempts fail, you can assume that overlays will be swapped to a disk file.

```
#include <stdio.h>
#include <dos.h>

#define  DISK_SWAP 0
#define  EMS_SWAP  1
#define  EXT_SWAP  2

int swap = DISK_SWAP;   /* Default is "swap to disk" */

main()
{
/* First see if expanded memory can be used for swapping */
    if(_OvrInitEms(0, 0, 8))
    {
        printf("Unable to use expanded memory "
               "for swapping\n");

/* Try to use extended memory for overlays */
        if(_OvrInitExt(0x100000, 0))
            printf("Unable to use extended memory "
                   "for swapping\n");
        else
            swap = EXT_SWAP;
    }
    else
    {
        swap = EMS_SWAP;
    }

    printf("Overlays will be swapped to disk\n");
    return 0;
}
```

System Calls

COMPATIBILITY

_OvrInitExt

TC1	TC1.5	TC2	TC++	MSC3	MSC4	MSC5	MSC6	QC1	QC2	QC2.5	ANSI	UNIX V	XNX
			▲										

PURPOSE Use *_OvrInitExt* to set up extended memory (memory in the address space above 1 MB) for swapping overlays.

SYNTAX

```
int far _OvrInitExt( unsigned long EXTStart, unsigned long EXTLength );
```

`unsigned long EXTStart;` *Starting address of swap space in extended memory*

`unsigned long EXTLength;` *Number of bytes to be used as swap space or zero, if you want the overlay manager to pick a value*

EXAMPLE CALL

```
if(_OvrInitExt(0x100000L, 0L) == 0)
    printf("Extended memory to be used for overlay swapping\n");
```

INCLUDES `#include <dos.h>` *For function declaration*

DESCRIPTION The *_OvrInitExt* function sets up extended memory to be used for swapping overlays by Turbo C++'s overlay manager. The *EXTStart* argument specifies the starting address of the memory to be used for swapping while *EXTLength* is the size of the swap space in bytes. If you want the overlay manager to determine the address, use a zero for *EXTLength*. Also, if *EXTStart* is zero, the overlay manager will attempt to determine ths starting location for the swap space.

Note that overlays are supported in medium, large, and huge memory models only. Also, to use *_OvrInitEms*, you must link your program with the OVERLAY.LIB library.

RETURNS *_OvrInitExt* returns a zero if all goes well. Otherwise, it returns a nonzero value.

COMMENTS Methods for accessing extended memory are not as standardized as those for EMS memory. Therefore, you have to use the *_OvrInitExt* function with caution, lest the chunk of memory you select is in use by another program (perhaps a RAM disk).

SEE ALSO *_OvrInitEms* To set up EMS memory for overlay swapping

EXAMPLE See example for *_OvrInitEms*.

parsfnm

COMPATIBILITY

TC1	TC1.5	TC2	TC++	MSC3	MSC4	MSC5	MSC6	QC1	QC2	QC2.5	ANSI	UNIX V	XNX
▲	▲	▲											

PURPOSE Use *parsfnm* to parse a file name from a command line and load the result into various fields of a File Control Block (FCB).

SYNTAX

```
char *parsfnm (const char *cmdline, struct fcb *fcb, int opt);
```

`const char *cmdline;`	*Command line from which file name is to be parsed*
`struct fcb *fcb;`	*Pointer to the File Control Block which will be set up using the parsed information*
`int opt;`	*Options to control the parsing*

EXAMPLE CALL

```
parsfnm(command_line, &my_fcb, 0xff);
```

INCLUDES #include <dos.h> *For function declaration*

DESCRIPTION The *parsfnm* routine uses DOS function 29h to parse a file name from the string *cmdline* and fill the fields in an *fcb* structure. The *fcb* structure is defined in *dos.h* as follows:

```
struct  fcb
{
  char  fcb_drive;      /* Drive 0 = default, 1 = A, 2 = B */
  char  fcb_name[8];    /* File name                       */
  char  fcb_ext[3];     /* File extension                  */
  short fcb_curblk;     /* Current block number            */
  short fcb_recsize;    /* Logical record size in bytes    */
  long  fcb_filsize;    /* File size in bytes              */
  short fcb_date;       /* Date file was last modofied     */
  char  fcb_resv[10];   /* Reserved for DOS                */
  char  fcb_currec;     /* Current record in block         */
  long  fcb_random;     /* Random record number            */
};
```

The *parsfnm* function fills the drive number, file name, and extension fields in the *fcb* structure from the file name appearing in the string *cmdline*. You have to provide the address of an *fcb* structure in the argument *fcb*.

The *opt* argument controls the details of the parsing process. Table

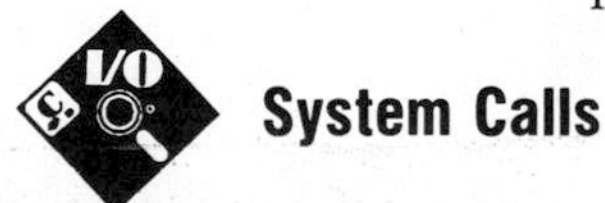

17-31 shows the meanings of the bits of *opt.* During parsing the following characters are regarded as *separator* characters:

```
: . ; , = + tab space
```

and the following are considered to be *terminator* characters

```
: . ; , = + tab space < > | / " [ ]
```

If a * is found in the file name, all characters in the name from that point on are set to ? which matches any character. This is why the DOS command *ERASE *A. ** erases *all* files in that directory instead of deleting only those files whose names end with an A (which is what you would intuitively expect).

Note that *parsfnm* cannot handle a pathname (a file name with multiple levels of directories). This is an inherent limitation of using FCBs for file access.

Table 17-31. opt *Bit Definitions*

Bit Number	Interpretation
3	If this bit is 1, the extension field *fcb_ext* will be modified only if there is a file extension in *cmdline*. Otherwise, *fcb_ext* will be modified even if none appears in the name (in this case, extension will be set to three blanks).
2	Interpretation is same as bit 3, but applies to the file name filed, *fcb_name*.
1	Interpretation is same as bit 3, but applies to the drive number filed, *fcb_drive*.
0	If this bit is 1, all leading *separator* characters will be ignored. Otherwise, leading separators are considered significant.

RETURNS When successful, the *parsfnm* function returns a pointer to the character immediately following the terminator character for the file name. In case of any error, *parsfnm* returns the NULL pointer.

EXAMPLE Illustrate the use of *parsfnm* to parse a file name into its component parts. Note that *parsfnm* cannot handle the hierarchical file system.

```
#include <stdio.h>
#include <dos.h>

main()
{
    char input[80], *rest;
    int option;      /* Options for parsfnm     */
```

```
    struct fcb fcb; /* File Control Block, FCB */

    printf("Enter string containing file name to be "
    "parsed\n(for example, A:MYFILE.DAT):");
    gets(input);

/* Parse file name using 'parsfnm' and  an FCB */
    option = 1; /* means skip leading separators */
    rest = parsfnm(input, &fcb, option);

/* Print results from the fcb structure */
    printf("Drive number: %d\n"
           "File name:    %s\n"
           "Extension:    %s\n", fcb.fcb_drive,
           fcb.fcb_name, fcb.fcb_ext);
    printf("Rest of the input line = %s\n", rest);
    return 0;
}
```

peek, peekb

COMPATIBILITY

TC1	TC1.5	TC2	TC++	MSC3	MSC4	MSC5	MSC6	QC1	QC2	QC2.5	ANSI	UNIX V	XNX
▲	▲	▲	▲										

PURPOSE Use *peek* and *peekb* to obtain the contents of a memory location at a specified address.

SYNTAX

```
int     peek (unsigned segment, unsigned offset);

char    peekb (unsigned segment, unsigned offset);
```

`unsigned segment;` *Segment address of memory location whose contents are being sought*

`unsigned offset;` *Offset address of memory location whose contents are being sought*

EXAMPLE CALL

```
char a_byte;
int an_integer;
a_byte = peekb(0xA000, 0);  /* Get a byte */
an_int = peek(0x40, 0);     /* Get a word */
```

INCLUDES `#include <dos.h>` *For function declaration*

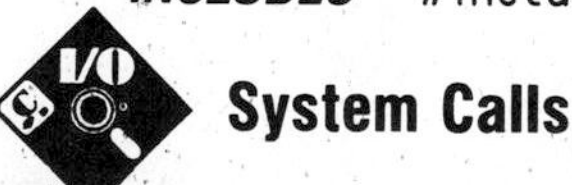

DESCRIPTION The *peek* function returns the 16-bit word at the address *segment:offset*. The *peekb* function returns the byte at this address.

The *peek* and *peekb* routines are available as macros in *dos.h*, and also as callable functions. The function form is used if you do not include *dos.h* or if you *#undef* the macros.

COMMON USES The *peek* and *peekb* functions are useful for accessing video memory and BIOS data areas.

RETURNS The *peek* function returns the 16-bit word at the address *segment:offset*, whereas *peekb* returns the character containing the value of the byte at that location.

SEE ALSO `poke, pokeb` *To write directly to a memory location specified by a segment address and an offset*

EXAMPLE Use *peek* to display the contents of a word at a specified address. (Try the address 40:0. If you have a serial adapter, the content of this word will be 3F8, the base port address of the serial port COM1.)

```
#include <stdio.h>
#include <dos.h>
main()
{
    unsigned seg, off;
    printf("Enter address (SSSS:0000) of memory \n"
           "location whose contents you want to get: ");
    scanf(" %x:%x", &seg, &off);
/* Use 'peek' to get contents of that location */
    printf("The word at %X:%X contains %X\n", seg, off,
           peek(seg, off));
    return 0;
}
```

poke, pokeb

COMPATIBILITY

TC1	TC1.5	TC2	TC++	MSC3	MSC4	MSC5	MSC6	QC1	QC2	QC2.5	ANSI	UNIX V	XNX
▲	▲	▲	▲										

PURPOSE Use *poke* and *pokeb* to write a word or a byte to a memory location at a specified address.

SYNTAX

```
void   poke (unsigned segment, unsigned offset, int value);
```

```
void   pokeb (unsigned segment, unsigned offset, char value);
```

`unsigned segment;` *Segment address of memory location to be written*

`unsigned offset;` *Offset address of memory location to be written*

`int value;` *Integer value to be written out by* poke

`char value;` *Byte to be written out by* pokeb

EXAMPLE CALL

```
char a_byte;
int an_integer;
pokeb(0xA000, 0, a_byte);  /* Write a byte */
poke(0x40, 0, an_integer); /* Write a word */
```

INCLUDES `#include <dos.h>` *For function declaration*

DESCRIPTION The *poke* function deposits the 16-bit value from the argument *value* into the memory location at the address *segment:offset*. The *pokeb* function is similar. It writes *value* to the byte at the address *segment:offset*.

The *poke* and *pokeb* routines are available as macros in *dos.h*, and also as callable functions. The function form is used if you do not include *dos.h* or if you *#undef* the macros.

COMMON USES The *poke* and *pokeb* functions are useful for writing to video memory and to BIOS data areas.

SEE ALSO `peek, peekb` *To read the contents of a memory location specified by a segment address and an offset*

EXAMPLE Write a utility program that lets the user alter the contents of any byte in memory. You can use such a program to directly manipulate the bytes in the display adapter's memory. For example, on a system with a monochrome display adapter, the ASCII code of the character at the upper left hand corner of the screen is located at the address B0000:0000. If you alter it to another ASCII code, you will see the results immediately on the screen.

```
#include <stdio.h>
#include <dos.h>
main()
{
    unsigned seg, off;
    unsigned char c;
```

```
    printf("Enter address (SSSS:0000) of byte\n"
       "location whose contents you want to change:");
    printf("\n(Try B800:0 for CGA or B000:0 for a "
    "monochrome display\n");
    scanf(" %x:%x", &seg, &off);
/* First get the contents using 'peekb' */
    c = peek(seg, off);
    printf("(%X:%X) contains %X(hex) or %c\n"
   "Change to (in hex): ",
          seg, off, c, c);
    scanf(" %x", &c);
/* Use 'pokeb' to load c into that location */
    pokeb(seg, off, c);
    return 0;
}
```

COMPATIBILITY

randbrd

TC1	TC1.5	TC2	TC++	MSC3	MSC4	MSC5	MSC6	QC1	QC2	QC2.5	ANSI	UNIX V	XNX
▲	▲	▲	▲										

PURPOSE Use *randbrd* to read one or more sequential records from a file into the current Disk Transfer Address, starting at a random record number within the file.

SYNTAX

```
int   randbrd (struct fcb *fcb, int numrecs);
```

`struct fcb *fcb;` *Pointer to File Control Block (FCB) structure where you set up the random record number and the record size*

`int numrecs;` *Number of records to read*

EXAMPLE CALL

```
if( randbrd(&my_fcb, 4) != 0) printf("Error reading records!\n");
```

INCLUDES `#include <dos.h>` *For function declaration*

DESCRIPTION The *randbrd* routine uses the DOS function 27h to read a number of records from a file using the FCB-based approach. In this method, the FCB structure contains information about the file name and extension, the drive where the file resides, the record size of data, and the record number where reading will start. The data read by DOS function 27h goes to a Disk Transfer Address or DTA. Therefore, before using *randbrd*, you must set up a DTA by calling the Turbo C++ routine *setdta*. You should retrieve the current DTA (using *getdta*) and save it before altering the DTA. The new DTA should have enough room to hold all the data you plan to read from the file.

The *randbrd* function requires you to specify in the argument *numrecs* the number of records being read. The rest of the information should be set up in the *fcb* structure whose address is in the argument *fcb*. The *fcb* structure is defined in the include file *dos.h* as follows:

```
struct  fcb
{
  char  fcb_drive;      /* Drive 0 = default, 1 = A, 2 = B */
  char  fcb_name[8];    /* File name                       */
  char  fcb_ext[3];     /* File extension                  */
  short fcb_curblk;     /* Current block number            */
  short fcb_recsize;    /* Logical record size in bytes    */
  long  fcb_filsize;    /* File size in bytes              */
  short fcb_date;       /* Date file was last modified     */
  char  fcb_resv[10];   /* Reserved for DOS                */
  char  fcb_currec;     /* Current record in block         */
  long  fcb_random;     /* Random record number            */
};
```

Before calling *randbrd*, you have to fill in the drive number, the file name, the file extension, the record size, and the random record number fields in the *fcb* structure.

COMMON USES The *randbrd* function lets you use CP/M-style read operations using a File Control Block (FCB) and a Data Transfer Address (DTA).

RETURNS The *randbrd* function returns a code to indicate the success or failure of the read operation. The returned value can be interpreted as follows:

0 = all records were successfully read

1 = end of file was reached, last record read is complete

2 = DTA is too small, as many records as possible have been read

3 = end of file reached before the last record being read was complete

COMMENTS The *read* function is a more portable way of reading an arbitrary number of bytes from any position in a file. You may want to use a combination of *read* and *lseek* instead of *randbrd*.

SEE ALSO `lseek` *To position the file pointer in a file*

System Calls

randbwr	*To write a number of records to a file*
read, write	*Portable versions of similar read and write functions*

EXAMPLE Write a program that uses *randbrd* to read a number of blocks from a file into a buffer. Use *parsfnm* to parse the file name into an FCB structure, then use DOS function 0Fh to open the file for I/O using FCBs. Save the current DTA by calling *getdta*, and set up a new DTA with *setdta*. Before calling *randbrd*, initialize the fields *fcb_random* and *fcb_recsize* in the *fcb* structure to appropriate values.

```
#include <stdio.h>
#include <dos.h>
#define FCB_OPEN 0x0f
main()
{
    char input[80], buffer[256], far *old_dta;
    int option;      /* Options for parsfnm     */
    struct fcb fcb; /* File Control Block, FCB */
    int i, result;

    printf("Enter name of file from which we will "
    "read two 128-byte records:\n(only drive and file "
    "name allowed, for example, A:MYFILE.DAT):");
    gets(input);

/* Parse file name using 'parsfnm' and  an FCB */
    option = 1; /* means skip leading separators */
    parsfnm(input, &fcb, option);
    printf("Reading from\nDrive number: %d\n"
           "File name:    %s\n", fcb.fcb_drive,
           fcb.fcb_name);

/* Now open the file using DOS function 0Fh (this
 * is not the same as "_open" which uses handles
 */
    if(bdosptr(FCB_OPEN, &fcb, 0) == -1)
    {
        printf("File open error!\n");
        exit(1);
    }

/* Save current disk transfer address and set up a
 * new one with enough room for data being read.
 */
```

```
    old_dta = getdta();
    setdta(buffer);
/* Now set up the record size and starting block */
    fcb.fcb_recsize = 128;
    fcb.fcb_random = 0L; /* Start at record 0 */
    result = randbrd(&fcb, 2);
    printf("result = %d\n", result);
    if(result == 0) printf("Read ok\n");
    if(result == 1 || result == 3)
        printf("File ended during read\n");
/* Print data read (assume ASCII text data) */
    printf("The first 26 characters are:\n");
    for(i=0; i<256; i++)
        putchar(buffer[i]);

/* Reset DTA to old value */
    setdta(old_dta);
   return 0;
}
```

randbwr

COMPATIBILITY

TC1	TC1.5	TC2	TC++	MSC3	MSC4	MSC5	MSC6	QC1	QC2	QC2.5	ANSI	UNIX V	XNX
▲	▲	▲	▲										

PURPOSE Use *randbwr* to write one or more sequential records from the current Disk Transfer Address to a file, starting at a random record number within the file.

SYNTAX

```
int   randbwr (struct fcb *fcb, int numrecs);
```

`struct fcb *fcb;` *Pointer to File Control Block (FCB) structure where you set up the random record number and the record size*

`int numrecs;` *Number of records to write*

EXAMPLE CALL

```
if( randbwr(&my_fcb, 4) != 0) printf("Error writing records!\n");
```

INCLUDES `#include <dos.h>` *For function declaration*

DESCRIPTION The *randbwr* routine uses the DOS function 28h to write a number of records from memory to a file using the file I/O mechanism based on File Control Blocks (FCBs) and Disk Transfer Addresses (DTAs). In this

method, the FCB structure contains information about the file name and extension, the drive where the file resides, the record size of data, and the record number where reading will start. The data to be written by DOS function 28h must be in the current DTA. Therefore, before using *randbwr*, you must set up a DTA by calling the Turbo C++ routine *setdta*. You should retrieve the current DTA (using *getdta*) and save it before altering the DTA. The new DTA should contain all the data you plan to write to the file.

The *randbwr* function requires you to specify in the argument *numrecs* the number of records to be written. The rest of the information should be set up in the *fcb* structure whose address is in the argument *fcb*. The *fcb* structure is defined in the include file *dos.h* as follows:

```
struct  fcb
{
  char  fcb_drive;     /* Drive 0 = default, 1 = A, 2 = B */
  char  fcb_name[8];   /* File name                       */
  char  fcb_ext[3];    /* File extension                  */
  short fcb_curblk;    /* Current block number            */
  short fcb_recsize;   /* Logical record size in bytes    */
  long  fcb_filsize;   /* File size in bytes              */
  short fcb_date;      /* Date file was last modified     */
  char  fcb_resv[10];  /* Reserved for DOS                */
  char  fcb_currec;    /* Current record in block         */
  long  fcb_random;    /* Random record number            */
};
```

Before calling *randbwr*, you have to fill in the drive number, the file name, the file extension, the record size, and the random record number fields in the *fcb* structure. If you specify a zero for *numrecs*, the file will be truncated at the record number indicated in the *fcb_random* field in the FCB.

COMMON USES The *randbwr* function lets you use CP/M-style write operations using a File Control Block (FCB) and a Data Transfer Address (DTA).

RETURNS The *randbwr* function returns a code to indicate the success or failure of the write operation. The returned value can be interpreted as follows:

0 = all records were successfully written

1 = disk is full

2 = DTA is at such a location that accessing the specified number of records would take us beyond the end of that segment (as many records as possible are written before returning with this error code)

COMMENTS The *write* function is a more portable way of writing an arbitrary number of bytes from any position in a file. You may want to use a combination of *lseek* and *write* instead of *randbwr*.

SEE ALSO

`lseek`	*To position the file pointer in a file*
`randbrd`	*To read a number of records from a file*
`read, write`	*Portable versions of similar read and write functions*

EXAMPLE Write a program that uses *randbwr* to write a number of blocks from a buffer into a file. Use *parsfnm* to parse the file name into an FCB structure, then use DOS function 16h to create the file and open it for I/O using FCBs. Save the current DTA by calling *getdta*, and set up the buffer as the new DTA with *setdta*. Before calling *randbwr*, initialize the fields *fcb_random* and *fcb_recsize* in the *fcb* structure to appropriate values. Finally, close the file using DOS function 10h.

```
#include <stdio.h>
#include <dos.h>
#define FCB_CREAT  0x16
#define FCB_CLOSE  0x10

char buffer[256] = "Testing randbwr...";

main()
{
    char input[80], far *old_dta;
    int option;      /* Options for parsfnm     */
    struct fcb fcb; /* File Control Block, FCB */
    int i, result;

    printf("Enter name of NEW file to which we will "
    "write two 128-byte records:\n(only drive and file "
    "name allowed, for example, A:MYFILE.DAT):");
    gets(input);

/* Parse file name using 'parsfnm' and  an FCB */
    option = 1; /* means skip leading separators */
    parsfnm(input, &fcb, option);
    printf("Writing to\nDrive number: %d\n"
           "File name:    %s\n", fcb.fcb_drive,
           fcb.fcb_name);
/* Now create the file using DOS function 16h (this
 * is not the same as "_creat" which uses handles
```

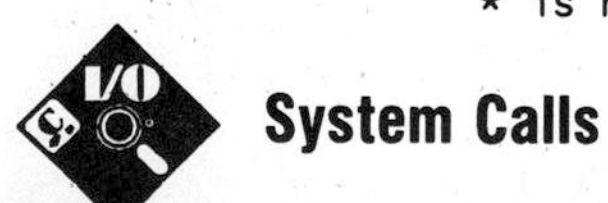

```
 */
    if(bdosptr(FCB_CREAT, &fcb, 0) == -1)
    {
         printf("Error creating file!\n");
         exit(1);
    }
/* Save current disk transfer address and set up
 * the new one as the DTA
 */
    old_dta = getdta();
    setdta(buffer);
/* Now set up the record size and starting block */
    fcb.fcb_recsize = 128;
    fcb.fcb_random = 0L; /* Start at record 0 */
    result = randbwr(&fcb, 2);
    printf("result = %d\n", result);
    if(result == 0) printf("Write ok\n");
    if(result == 1) printf("Disk full!\n");

/* Finally, close the file using DOS function 10h (this
 * is not the same as "_close" which uses handles)
 */
    if(bdosptr(FCB_CLOSE, &fcb, 0) == -1)
    {
         printf("Error closing file!\n");
         exit(1);
    }
/* Reset DTA to old value */
    setdta(old_dta);
   return 0;
}
```

_read

COMPATIBILITY

TC1	TC1.5	TC2	TC++	MSC3	MSC4	MSC5	MSC6	QC1	QC2	QC2.5	ANSI	UNIX V	XNX
▲	▲	▲	▲			1	1	1	1	1			

PURPOSE Use *_read* to read a specified number of bytes from a file into a buffer. You will need a handle returned by a function such as *_open* or *_creat* before calling this function.

SYNTAX

```
int   _read  (int filehandle, void *buffer, unsigned readcount);
```

`int filehandle;`	*The file handle or identifier*
`void *buffer;`	*Pointer to buffer where the data read from the file will be stored*
`unsigned readcount;`	*Number of bytes to be read*

EXAMPLE CALL

```
bytes_read = _read(filehandle, pbuf, 80);
```

INCLUDES `#include <io.h>` *For function declaration*

DESCRIPTION The *_read* function calls DOS function 3Fh to transfer the number of bytes requested in the argument *readcount* from the current position in the file to the locations accessed through the pointer *buffer*.

The file from which you want to read is specified by the identifying number or handle in the argument *filehandle*. This file handle must be one that had been returned when the file was opened by *_open* or perhaps created by *_creat*.

1. Use *_dos_read* in Microsoft C 5 and 6, and QuickC 1.0 through 2.5.

RETURNS If successful, *_read* function returns the actual number of bytes read. Otherwise, it returns −1 and sets the global variable *errno* either to the constant EBADF indicating that the file handle is invalid, or to EACCES to indicate that access was denied (probably the file is not open for read access).

COMMENTS The functions *read* and *write* offer a more portable means of achieving the same result as these DOS specific functions.

SEE ALSO

`_write`	*To write a buffer out to a file*
`read, write`	*Portable versions of similar read and write functions*
`_open`	*To open an existing file using a DOS call*
`_close`	*To close a file*
`_creat`	*To create a new file*

EXAMPLE Use *_open* to open an existing text file and then call *_read* to read the first 80 characters into a buffer. Display the contents of the buffer. Finally close the file using *_close*.

```
#include <stdio.h>
#include <fcntl.h>
#include <io.h>
main()
{
    char fname[40], *p_fname;
    char buffer[80];
    int filehandle, bytes_read;

    printf("Enter name of an existing file: ");
    p_fname = gets(fname);

/* Open the file using _open */
    if ((filehandle = _open(p_fname, O_RDONLY)) == -1)
    {
        printf("Error opening file: %s\n", fname);
        exit(0);
    }
    printf("File %s opened.\n", fname);

/* Now read the first 80 bytes */
    if((bytes_read = _read(filehandle, buffer, 80)) != -1)
    {
        printf("%d bytes read\n", bytes_read);
        printf("The bytes read are:\n%s\n", buffer);
    }
    else
    {
        printf("Error reading from file: %s\n", fname);
    }
/* Now close file */
    if (_close(filehandle) != 0)
    {
        printf("Error closing file with _close\n");
        exit(0);
    }
    printf("File %s closed.\n", fname);
    return 0;
}
```

segread

COMPATIBILITY

TC1	TC1.5	TC2	TC++	MSC3	MSC4	MSC5	MSC6	QC1	QC2	QC2.5	ANSI	UNIX V	XNX
▲	▲	▲	▲	▲	▲	▲	▲	▲	▲	▲			

PURPOSE Use the *segread* function to retrieve the values of the 80x86 segment registers CS, DS, ES, and SS from C programs. For example, you may want to read and save the value of ES before it is altered during a call to *int86x* or *ntdosx* or you may want to check the segment register values to debug your C program.

SYNTAX

```
void segread (struct SREGS *segregs);

struct SREGS *segregs;      C structure to hold segment registers
```

EXAMPLE CALL

```
segread(&segregs);
```

INCLUDES

```
#include <dos.h>      For function declaration and definition of SREGS structure
```

DESCRIPTION The *segread* function copies the current values of the 80x86 segment registers into the C structure *segregs* which has one unsigned integer variable for each segment register. These variables are intuitively named *cs, ds, es,* and *ss*, respectively.

COMMON USES This function is commonly used to save the value of ES before calling *int86x* or *intdosx* since ES is frequently used by BIOS routines.

COMMENTS The segment register values are usually of no concern to C programmers except when accessing system-level functions.

SEE ALSO `int86x, intdosx` *For 80x86 software interrupts that may require you to set up segment registers DS and ES*

EXAMPLE Use the *segread* function to display current values of the 80x86 segment registers.

```
#include <stdio.h>
#include <dos.h>
struct SREGS sr;

main()
{
    segread(&sr);
    printf("Currently cs = %x, ds = %x, es = %x, ss = %x\n",
            sr.cs, sr.ds, sr.es, sr.ss);
```

```
    return 0;
}
```

COMPATIBILITY

setblock

TC1	TC1.5	TC2	TC++	MSC3	MSC4	MSC5	MSC6	QC1	QC2	QC2.5	ANSI	UNIX V	XNX
▲	▲	▲	▲			1	1	1	1	1			

PURPOSE Use *setblock* to adjust the size of a block of memory previously allocated by *allocmem*.

SYNTAX

```
int setblock (unsigned segadd, unsigned newsize);
```

`unsigned segadd;` *Segment address of block*

`unsigned newsize;` *New size of block in units of 16-byte paragraphs*

EXAMPLE CALL

```
setblock (segadd, 5);
```

INCLUDES `#include <dos.h>` *For function declaration*

DESCRIPTION The *setblock* function calls DOS function 4Ah to enlarge the size of a block of memory previously allocated by *allocmem*. The argument *newsize* specifies the desired size of the block in units of paragraphs (16 bytes = 1 paragraph), and *segadd* is the segment address of the block previously returned by *allocmem*.

1. The compatible function in Microsoft C 5 and 6, and QuickC 1.0 through 2.5, is *_dos_setblock*.

RETURNS This function returns −1 if memory is successfully allocated. Otherwise, the return value is the maximum number of paragraphs that is available and the global variable *errno* is set to the constant ENOMEM indicating that there is not enough memory to satisfy the request.

COMMENTS The *setblock* function is analogous to the standard library routine *realloc*. Of course, *setblock* must be used only to enlarge or shrink blocks allocated by its counterpart *allocmem*.

SEE ALSO

`allocmem` *The corresponding routine that allocated the memory in the first place*

`freemem` *To free up memory allocated by* allocmem

`realloc` *Other memory block resizing routines*

EXAMPLE Use the *allocmem* to allocate 1 paragraph of memory. Now use *setblock* to enlarge the block size to 5 paragraphs so that we have enough storage for 80 characters. Store a string in the newly allocated buffer and then print the string out. Finally free the allocated buffer.

```
#include <stdio.h>
#include <dos.h>
#include <mem.h>
#define DOS_PRTSTR  9
char str[80]="Testing allocmem...\n$";
main()
{
    union REGS xr;
    struct SREGS sr;
    char far *stradd;
    unsigned int segadd, maxsize;
    stradd = (char far *)(&str[0]);
    if (allocmem(1, &segadd) != -1)
    {
        printf("Memory allocation failed!\n");
        exit(0);
    }

    if ((maxsize = setblock(segadd, 5)) == -1)
    {
        printf("setblock failed!\n");
        printf("Maximum size possible = %d "
               "paragraphs\n", maxsize);
        exit(0);
    }
/* Use movedata to copy the string to allocated memory*/
    movedata(FP_SEG(stradd),FP_OFF(stradd), segadd,
             0, 80);
    sr.ds = segadd;
    xr.x.dx = 0;
    xr.h.ah = DOS_PRTSTR;
    intdosx(&xr, &xr, &sr);

/* Free memory before exiting */
    freemem(segadd);
    return 0;
}
```

COMPATIBILITY

setcbrk

TC1	TC1.5	TC2	TC++	MSC3	MSC4	MSC5	MSC6	QC1	QC2	QC2.5	ANSI	UNIX V	XNX
▲	▲	▲	▲										

PURPOSE Use *setcbrk* to enable or disable Control-Break (or Control-C) checking by DOS.

SYNTAX

```
int setcbrk(int value);
```

`int value;` *New value of Control-Break checking flag (1 = enable, 0 = disable)*

EXAMPLE CALL

```
if(setcbrk(1)) printf("Control-Break checking is enabled!\n");
```

INCLUDES `#include <dos.h>` *For function declaration*

DESCRIPTION MS-DOS maintains a flag that indicates whether DOS will ignore or respond to a Control-Break or Control-C keypress. When this flag is enabled (1), DOS will check if a keypress is Control-Break or Control-C. If it is, control will be transferred to the Control-Break handler (interrupt 23h). Note that you can use the Turbo C++ routine *ctrlbrk* to designate a function that will get called when this happens.

The *setcbrk* function calls the DOS function 33h to alter this checking flag. The new value of the flag is specified in the argument *value*. The Control-Break checking is enabled or disabled depending on whether *value* is 1 or 0.

COMMON USES You can use *setcbrk* to turn off Control-Break checking so that some crucial operation, such as disk I/O, is not interrupted by a Control-C keypress. You should always call *getcbrk* beforehand to retrieve and save the current Control-Break checking flag. Then, after the critical operation is complete, you can restore the Control-Break checking flag from the saved value. It is very important that you save and restore this flag because once you turn the flag off, it remains off even after your program terminates.

RETURNS The *setcbrk* function returns the argument *value*.

COMMENTS The Control-Break checking flag does not affect I/O operations involving the standard input, output, and auxiliary device. This means that even if you turn the Control-Break checking flag off, a Control-C pressed at the keyboard will still cause interrupt 23h.

SEE ALSO `ctrlbrk` *To set up a function which will be called when a Control-C is entered (provided checking is on)* `getcbrk` *To get the Control-Break checking flag*

EXAMPLE Write a program that uses *setcbrk* to turn the Control-Break checking flag on or off.

```
#include <stdio.h>
#include <dos.h>
#include <string.h>
main(int argc, char **argv)
{
    int cbrk_flag;
    if(argc < 2)
    {
        printf("Usage: %s <ON or OFF>\n", argv[0]);
        exit(0);
    }
    if((strcmp(argv[1], "ON") == 0) ||
       (strcmp(argv[1], "on") == 0)) cbrk_flag = 1;
    else
    {
        if((strcmp(argv[1], "OFF") == 0) ||
           (strcmp(argv[1], "off") == 0)) cbrk_flag = 0;
        else
        {
            printf("Unknown flag: %s\n", argv[1]);
            exit(0);
        }
    }
/* Set the flag and print new value of flag */
    setcbrk(cbrk_flag);
    printf("Current value of the Control-Break checking "
           "flag = %d\n", getcbrk());
    return 0;
}
```

COMPATIBILITY

setdate

TC1	TC1.5	TC2	TC++	MSC3	MSC4	MSC5	MSC6	QC1	QC2	QC2.5	ANSI	UNIX V	XNX
▲	▲	▲	▲			1	1	1	1	1			

PURPOSE Use *setdate* to change the current system date.

SYNTAX

```
void setdate (struct date *datep);
```

`struct date *datep;` *Pointer to a structure that will hold the components of date*

EXAMPLE CALL

```
setdate(&date_info);
```

INCLUDES `#include <dos.h>` *For function declaration and definition of the* date *structure*

DESCRIPTION The *setdate* function calls DOS function 2Bh to set the current system date. The components of the date—the day, the month, the year, and the day of the week—should be specified by placing appropriate values in fields of the *date* structure, which is defined in *dos.h*. The C declaration of the structure is shown below.

```
struct date
{
    int da_year;                    /* Current year (range 1980-2099) */
    char da_day;                    /* Day of the month (range 1-31)  */
    char da_mon;                    /* Month (range 1-12), 1= January */
};
```

You have to declare one such structure and provide its address in the argument *datep*.

1. In Microsoft C 5 and 6, and QuickC 1.0 through 2.5, use *_dos_setdate*.

SEE ALSO

`getdate` *The corresponding routine that returns the system date*

`gettime, settime` *To get and set the system time*

`dostounix` *To convert DOS date and time to UNIX format*

EXAMPLE Use the *setdate* to change the current system date.

```
#include <stdio.h>
#include <dos.h>
main()
{
```

```
    int month, day, year;
    struct date date;
    printf ("Enter new date in the form MM/DD/YY:");
    scanf("%d/%d/%d", &month, &day, &year);
/* Set up the files of the date structure */
    date.da_day = day;
    date.da_mon = month;
    date.da_year = year + 1900;
/* Set the new date */
    setdate(&date);
    printf("New date: %d/%d/%d\n", date.da_mon,
            date.da_day, date.da_year -1900);
    return 0;
}
```

setdisk

COMPATIBILITY

TC1	TC1.5	TC2	TC++	MSC3	MSC4	MSC5	MSC6	QC1	QC2	QC2.5	ANSI	UNIX V	XNX
▲	▲	▲	▲			1	1	1	1	1			

PURPOSE Use *setdisk* to change to a new default drive number. For example, you can use this function to make drive A the default drive after starting your program from drive C.

SYNTAX

```
int   setdisk  (int driveno);

int   driveno;
```
New default drive number (driveno)

EXAMPLE CALL

```
maxdrives = setdisk(0); /* New drive is A: */
```

INCLUDES

```
#include <dos.h>
```
For function declaration

DESCRIPTION The *setdisk* function calls DOS function 0Eh to set the current default drive to that specified by the argument *driveno*. This argument is intrepreted as follows: 0 means drive A, 1 means drive B, and so on.

1. The compatible function in Microsoft C 5 and 6, and QuickC 1.0 through 2.5, is *_dos_setdrive*.

COMMON USES MS-DOS uses the concept of "current default drive" when locating files. If all of your file I/O will be from a particular disk drive, you can use the *setdisk* function to set up the default drive before performing any file I/O.

RETURNS The *setdisk* function returns the total number of logical drives in the system.

SEE ALSO `getdisk` *To get the current default drive number*

EXAMPLE Use *setdisk* to change the default drive number to the one requested by the user. Call *getdisk* to verify that the new default is in effect.

```
#include <stdio.h>
#include <ctype.h>
#include <dos.h>
main()
{
    int ch_in;
    int drive, maxdrives;
    printf("Enter new drive name (A, B etc):");
    scanf("%c", &ch_in);
/* Convert the letter into a number, 0 for A, 1 for B */
    drive = toupper(ch_in) - 'A';
    maxdrives = setdisk(drive);
    drive = getdisk();
    printf ("The current drive is: %c\n", drive+'A');
    printf ("There are %d logical drives on the "
            "system\n", maxdrives);
    returnl 0;
}
```

setdta

COMPATIBILITY

TC1	TC1.5	TC2	TC++	MSC3	MSC4	MSC5	MSC6	QC1	QC2	QC2.5	ANSI	UNIX V	XNX
▲	▲	▲	▲										

PURPOSE Use *setdta* to set up a new Disk Transfer Address (DTA).

SYNTAX `void setdta(char far *dta);`

`char far *dta;` *Pointer to new data*

EXAMPLE CALL

```
char far my_dta[4096];

setdta(my_dta);
```

INCLUDES `#include <dos.h>` *For function declaration*

DESCRIPTION MS-DOS supports two types of file operations. One is the CP/M-compatible service that uses File Control Blocks (FCBs) and Disk Transfer Addresses (DTAs) for its workings. The other one is the UNIX-compatible I/O that is based on file handles. The latter approach is more commonplace nowadays, and it is also more portable. However, the CP/M-style functions may be used by some programs, and are still a part of the DOS file I/O routines. The Turbo C routines *randbrd* and *randbwr* transfer data between a file and a DTA. The *setdta* function is provided so that you can set up a DTA with enough storage to hold the amount of data being read from or written to the disk.

You have to provide the address of the new DTA in the argument *dta*.

COMMON USES The *setdta* function lets you set up the DTA before initiating an FCB-based disk read or write operation (for example, *randbrd* or *randbwr*).

SEE ALSO

`randbrd, randbwr`	*For sample usage of* setdta
`getdta`	*To get the address of the current DTA*

EXAMPLE See examples of *randbrd* and *randbwr* for sample uses of *setdta*.

setftime

COMPATIBILITY

TC1	TC1.5	TC2	TC++	MSC3	MSC4	MSC5	MSC6	QC1	QC2	QC2.5	ANSI	UNIX V	XNX
▲	▲	▲	▲			1	1	1	1	1			

PURPOSE Use *setftime* to change the date and time stamp of a file. You will need a handle returned by a function such as *_open* or *_creat* before calling this function.

SYNTAX

```
int   setftime  (int filehandle, struct ftime *ftimep);
```

`int filehandle;`	*The file handle or identifier*
`struct ftime *ftimep;`	*Pointer to location to hold date and time information*

EXAMPLE CALL

```
setftime(handle, &dt_info);
```

INCLUDES

`#include <io.h>`	*For function declaration and definition of* ftime *structure*

DESCRIPTION The *setftime* function calls DOS function 57h to change the date and time stamp of the file specified by the identifying number, or handle, in the argument *filehandle*. The date and time information is entered in the *ftime* structure whose address is in the argument *ftimep*.

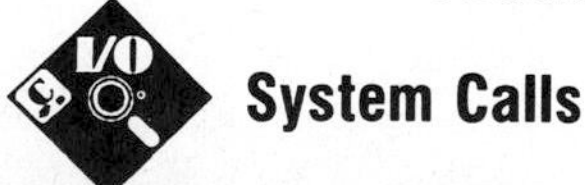

The file handle must be one that had been returned when the file was opened by *_open* or created by *_creat*.

The date and time stamps indicate when the file was last modified. You need to set up this information in an *ftime* structure and provide the address of the structure in the argument *ftimep*. The *ftime* structure is defined in the include file *io.h* as follows:

```
struct  ftime
{
  unsigned  ft_tsec   : 5;  /* Number of 2 second intervals */
  unsigned  ft_min    : 6;  /* Minutes                      */
  unsigned  ft_hour   : 5;  /* Hours                        */
  unsigned  ft_day    : 5;  /* Days                         */
  unsigned  ft_month  : 4;  /* Months                       */
  unsigned  ft_year   : 7;  /* Years since 1980             */
};
```

Note that the value stored in the *ft_year* field should be relative to 1980, i.e., it is the current year minus 1980.

1. Use *_dos_setftime* in Microsoft C 5 and 6, and QuickC 1.0 through 2.5.

RETURNS This function returns zero if successful; otherwise, it returns −1 and sets the global variable *errno* either to the constant EBADF (indicating that the file handle is invalid) or to EINVFNC signifying an invalid function number.

SEE ALSO

getftime	*To get the date and time stamp of a file*
_open	*To open an existing file using a DOS call*
_creat	*To create a new file*

EXAMPLE Use *_open* to open a file and then call *setftime* to store a new date and time stamp. Then use *getftime* to verify that the date and time stamps have indeed changed.

```
#include <stdio.h>
#include <fcntl.h>
#include <io.h>
main()
{
    char fname[40], *p_fname;
    int filehandle;
    unsigned date, time, day, month, year,
             hour, minute, second;
```

```
              hour, minute, second;
    struct ftime dtinfo;

    printf("Enter name of an existing file: ");
    p_fname = gets(fname);

/* Open the file using _open */
    if((filehandle = _open(p_fname, O_RDONLY)) == -1)
    {
        printf("Error opening file: %s\n", fname);
        exit(0);
    }
    printf("File %s opened.\n", fname);

/* Ask for new date and time stamp: */
    printf("Enter new date in the format MM-DD-YY:");
    scanf("%u-%u-%u", &month, &day, &year);
    printf("Enter new time in the format HH:MM:SS ");
    scanf("%u:%u:%u", &hour, &minute, &second);

/* Pack date and time information into single words */
    dtinfo.ft_tsec = second/2;
    dtinfo.ft_min = minute;
    dtinfo.ft_hour = hour;
    dtinfo.ft_day = day;
    dtinfo.ft_month = month;
/* NOTE: year is relative to 1980.
 * So we are subtracting 80.
 */
    dtinfo.ft_year = year - 80;

/* Set the date and time stamp */
    setftime(filehandle, &dtinfo);

/* Get file's date and time stamp to verify the new
 * date and time
 */
    getftime(filehandle, &dtinfo);

/* Now extract the time and date information */
    second = 2 * dtinfo.ft_tsec;
    minute = dtinfo.ft_min;
    hour = dtinfo.ft_hour;
    day = dtinfo.ft_day;
    month = dtinfo.ft_month;
/* NOTE: year is relative to 1980. So we are adding 80*/
```

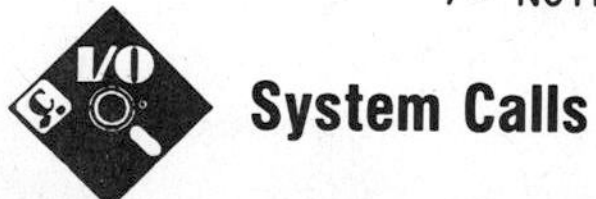

```
    printf("File: %s  Date: %d-%d-%d Time: %.2d:%.2d:\
%.2d\n", fname, month, day, year, hour, minute, second);

/* Now close file */
    if (_close(filehandle) != 0)
    {
        printf("Error closing file with _dos_close\n");
        exit(0);
    }
    printf("File %s closed.\n", fname);
    return 0;
}
```

COMPATIBILITY

setswitchar

TC1	TC1.5	TC2	TC++	MSC3	MSC4	MSC5	MSC6	QC1	QC2	QC2.5	ANSI	UNIX V	XNX
▲	▲	▲	▲										

PURPOSE The undocumented *setswitchar* function sets the "switch character" (the character that precedes options in an MS-DOS command).

SYNTAX

```
void  setswitchar (char schar);

char schar;        New switch character
```

EXAMPLE CALL

```
setswitchar(sw_char);
```

INCLUDES

```
#include <dos.h>        For function declaration
```

DESCRIPTION The *setswitchar* function calls an undocumented DOS function (37h) to set the character used to specify command-line options in MS-DOS. This character, known as the "switch character," is normally a slash (/). For example, in the DOS command *DIR/W*, the slash (/) is the switch character. You could set the switch character to—for greater compatibility with UNIX. This would also allow you to use / for the pathname separator.

A companion function, *getswitchar*, is available to retrieve the current switch character for DOS commands.

COMMENTS The *setswitchar* function is *not* documented in the Turbo C++ reference manual, perhaps because it uses the undocumented DOS function 37h.

SEE ALSO `getswitchar` *To get the current switch character for DOS commands*

EXAMPLE Set a new switch character by calling *setswitchar*. For verification, use *getswitchar* to retrieve the switch character and print it.

```
#include <stdio.h>
#include <dos.h>
main(int argc, char**argv)
{
    char c;
    if (argc < 2)
    {
        printf("Usage: %s <swich_char>\n", argv[0]);
    }
/* Set new switch character */
    c = argv[1][0];
    setswitchar(c);
/* Verify the new switch character */
    printf("The current switch char is %c\n",
            getswitchar());
    return 0;
}
```

COMPATIBILITY

settime

TC1	TC1.5	TC2	TC++	MSC3	MSC4	MSC5	MSC6	QC1	QC2	QC2.5	ANSI	UNIX V	XNX
▲	▲	▲	▲			1	1	1	1	1			

PURPOSE Use *settime* to change the current system time.

SYNTAX

```
void settime (struct  time *timep);
```

`struct  time *timep;` *Pointer to a structure that will hold the components of time*

EXAMPLE CALL

```
settime(&time_info);
```

INCLUDES `#include <dos.h>` *For function declaration and definition of the* time *structure*

DESCRIPTION The *settime* function calls DOS function 2Dh to set the current system time. The components of the time—the hour, the minutes, the seconds, and the hundredth of a second—must be loaded into appropriate fields of the structure type *time* , which is defined in *dos.h*. The layout of this structure along with the C declaration of the internal fields is shown below:

```
struct time
{
    unsigned char ti_min;   /* Minutes (range 0-59)              */
    unsigned char ti_hour;  /* Hour (range 0-23)                 */
    unsigned char ti_hund;  /* Hundredth of a second (range 0-99) */
    unsigned char ti_sec;   /* Seconds (range 0-59)              */
};
```

You must declare one such structure, initialize its fields, and provide its address in the argument *timep*.

1. The equivalent function in Microsoft C 5 and 6, and QuickC 1.0 through 2.5, is *_dos_settime*.

SEE ALSO

gettime	*The corresponding routine that returns the system time*
getdate, setdate	*To get and set the system date*
dostounix	*To convert DOS date and time to UNIX format*

EXAMPLE Use the *settime* to change the current system time.

```
#include <stdio.h>
#include <dos.h>
main()
{
    unsigned hour, minute, second;
    struct time time;
    printf ("Enter new time in the form HH:MM:SS:");
    scanf("%d:%d:%d", &hour, &minute, &second);
    time.ti_hour = hour;
    time.ti_min = minute;
    time.ti_sec = second;
    settime(&time);
/* Verify the time using gettime */
    gettime(&time);
    printf("New time: %d:%d:%d.%d\n", time.ti_hour,
            time.ti_min, time.ti_sec, time.ti_hund);
    return 0;
}
```

setvect

COMPATIBILITY

TC1	TC1.5	TC2	TC++	MSC3	MSC4	MSC5	MSC6	QC1	QC2	QC2.5	ANSI	UNIX V	XNX
▲	▲	▲	▲			1	1	1	1	1			

PURPOSE Use *setvect* to install a new interrupt vector for a specific interrupt number. The interrupt vector is the address of the routine that is invoked when the interrupt occurs.

SYNTAX

```
void   setvect (int intno, void interrupt (*handler) ());
```

`int intno;` *Interrupt number whose vector is being set*

`void interrupt (*handler)();` *Pointer to the new handler, a function of type* interrupt

EXAMPLE CALL

```
void interrupt our_handler(void);

setvect(int_number, our_handler);
```

INCLUDES `#include <dos.h>` *For function declaration*

DESCRIPTION The *setvect* function calls the DOS function 25h to install the address of the interrupt handler specified in the argument *handler* as the new vector for the interrupt number specified in the argument *intno*. The argument *handler* is a pointer to the interrupt handler. The handler is a function of type *interrupt*, which is a Turbo C++ keyword to allow writing interrupt handlers in C (see Chapter 3 for a discussion of the *interrupt* keyword).

1. Use *_dos_setvect* in Microsoft C 5 and 6, and QuickC 1.0 through 2.5.

COMMON USES This function is commonly used to install a new interrupt handler. For example, if you were writing an interrupt-driven I/O routine for the serial port, you would use this routine to install your handler in place of the default one.

COMMENTS It is good practice to get the interrupt vector and save it before installing a new one. That way you can restore the system to its original status when your program exits.

SEE ALSO `getvect` *To get the address of the current interrupt handler*

EXAMPLE In the IBM PC, interrupt 1Ch is generated at every clock tick. These are the clock ticks that occur about 18.2 times a second and that are used to main-

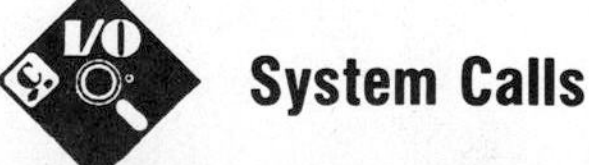

tain the time in the system. You are allowed to hook your routine onto this interrupt and have the routine executed at every clock tick. Write a routine using *getvect* and *setvect* to install your own interrupt handler for interrupt number 1Ch. You can increment a counter in the interrupt handler to show that the program worked.

```
#include <stdio.h>
#include <dos.h>
#define TIMER_TICK 0x1c
unsigned long tickcount = 0;
void interrupt our_handler(void);
main()
{
    unsigned c;
    void interrupt (*old_handler)();
    unsigned intno = TIMER_TICK;
    old_handler = getvect(intno);
/* Print out address of old handler using the %p
 * format
 */
    printf("\nThe address of the old handler is : %Fp\n",
           old_handler);
/* Install the new handler named our_handler
 * Disable interrupts when changing handler
 */
    disable();
    setvect(intno, our_handler);
    enable();
    printf("Installed new handler: %p\n", our_handler);
    printf("Hit q to quit: ");

    while ((c=getch()) != 'q'); /* Keep looping till 'q'*/
/* Reset vector and print the tickcount. Again disable
 * interrupts when doing this.
 */
    disable();
    setvect(intno, old_handler);
    enable();
    printf("The tick counter is now: %ld\n", tickcount);
    return 0;
}
/*-------------------------------------------------*/
void interrupt our_handler()
{
/* Our handler simply increments a counter. But this
```

```
 * will be proof enough that the handler works because
 * we are not calling it explicitly in the main program
 * and the only way it gets called is via INT 1Ch.
 */
    tickcount++;
}
```

setverify

COMPATIBILITY

TC1	TC1.5	TC2	TC++	MSC3	MSC4	MSC5	MSC6	QC1	QC2	QC2.5	ANSI	UNIX V	XNX
▲	▲	▲	▲										

PURPOSE Use *setverify* to set the state of the verify flag which tells DOS whether it should verify disk write operations or not.

SYNTAX `void setverify (int vflag);`

`int vflag;` *New verify flag (1=verify on, 0 = verify off)*

EXAMPLE CALL `vflag = setverify();`

INCLUDES `#include <dos.h>` *For function declaration*

DESCRIPTION MS-DOS maintains a verify flag which, when turned on, instructs DOS to perform a read after each disk write to ensure that data was written correctly. The *setverify* routine calls the DOS function 2Eh to set the current value of this flag. The new value of the flag can be either 0 or 1, respectively, indicating that the verify flag should be turned off (0) or on (1).

A companion function, *getverify*, can be used to retrieve the current status of the verify flag. You can also check the verify flag using the DOS command VERIFY.

SEE ALSO `getverify` *To get the verify flag*

EXAMPLE Write a utility program that allows setting the verify flag on or off by calling *setverify*. Get the setting immediately after this and print it to show the new changed value.

```
#include <stdio.h>
#include <dos.h>
#include <string.h>
main(int argc, char **argv)
{
```

```
    int vflag;
    if(argc < 2)
    {
        printf("Usage: %s <ON or OFF>\n", argv[0]);
        exit(0);
    }
    if((strcmp(argv[1], "ON") == 0) ||
       (strcmp(argv[1], "on") == 0)) vflag = 1;
    else
    {
        if((strcmp(argv[1], "OFF") == 0) ||
           (strcmp(argv[1], "off") == 0)) vflag = 0;
        else
        {
            printf("Unknown flag: %s\n", argv[1]);
            exit(0);
        }
    }
/* Set the flag and print new value of flag */
    setverify(vflag);
    printf("Current value of the verify flag = %d\n",
              getverify());
    return 0;
}
```

sleep

COMPATIBILITY

TC1	TC1.5	TC2	TC++	MSC3	MSC4	MSC5	MSC6	QC1	QC2	QC2.5	ANSI	UNIX V	XNX
▲	▲	▲	▲										

PURPOSE Use *sleep* to suspend execution of your program for a specified number of seconds.

SYNTAX

```
void   sleep (unsigned seconds);

unsigned seconds;        Number of seconds to wait
```

EXAMPLE CALL

```
sleep(5); /* Wait for 5 seconds */
```

INCLUDES

```
#include <dos.h>        For function declaration
```

DESCRIPTION The *sleep* function waits a specified number of seconds before returning. The delay in seconds is given in the argument *seconds*. The accuracy of the delay is limited by the accuracy of the system clock ticks which occur 18.2 times a second.

COMMON USES The *sleep* function is convenient in writing stand-alone "demo" programs where you can set up a sequence of events and have them occur one after another with a fixed amount of delay in between.

SEE ALSO `biostime` *To get the system clock ticks from BIOS*

EXAMPLE Use *sleep* to generate the delay between activation and deactivation of the PC's speaker when generating sound.

```
#include <dos.h>
main()
{
    unsigned duration;
    printf("Enter duration of 440-Hz tone "
           "(in seconds): ");
    scanf(" %u", &duration);
    sound(440);
    sleep(duration);
    nosound();
    return 0;
}
```

sound

COMPATIBILITY

TC1	TC1.5	TC2	TC++	MSC3	MSC4	MSC5	MSC6	QC1	QC2	QC2.5	ANSI	UNIX V	XNX
	▲	▲	▲										

PURPOSE Use *sound* to start generating a tone at a specified frequency from the PC's speaker.

SYNTAX `void sound (unsigned frequency);`

`unsigned frequency;` *Frequency of sound in hertz (Hz)*

EXAMPLE CALL `sound(440);` */* Start generating a 440-Hz tone */*

INCLUDES `#include <dos.h>` *For function declaration*

DESCRIPTION The *sound* function, introduced in Turbo C 1.5, activates the PC's speaker to produce a continuous tone of the frequency specified by the argument

frequency. You have to turn the speaker off by calling the *nosound* function to stop the sound.

If you want to generate a tone for a fixed duration of time, you should use *sound* to initiate the tone, then call either *delay* or *sleep* to wait for the desired number of seconds, and finally stop the sound by calling *nosound*.

COMMON USES The *sound* and *nosound* functions can be used to generate an audible alert to get the user's attention.

SEE ALSO `nosound` *To turn the speaker off*

EXAMPLE Use *sound* and *nosound* to generate a tone lasting a specified number of milliseconds and having a specific frequency. Use the *delay* function to wait between the calls to *sound* and *nosound*.

```
#include <dos.h>
main()
{
    unsigned duration, frequency;
    printf("Enter frequency of sound(in Hz): ");
    scanf(" %u", &frequency);
    printf("Enter duration of 440-Hz tone "
           "(in milliseconds): ");
    scanf(" %u", &duration);
    sound(frequency);
    delay(duration);
    nosound();
    return 0;
}
```

COMPATIBILITY

unixtodos

TC1	TC1.5	TC2	TC++	MSC3	MSC4	MSC5	MSC6	QC1	QC2	QC2.5	ANSI	UNIX V	XNX
▲	▲	▲	▲										

PURPOSE Use *unixtodos* to convert to DOS format a value of time in the UNIX format (expressed as the number of seconds elapsed since 00:00:00 hours GMT, 1 January, 1970).

SYNTAX `void unixtodos (long time, struct date *d, struct time *t);`

`long time;` *Time in UNIX format*

```
struct date *d;
```
Pointer to structure to hold date in DOS format

```
struct time *t;
```
Pointer to structure to hold time in DOS format

EXAMPLE CALL

```
time(&t_unix);
/* Convert to DOS format date and time */
unixtodos(t_unix, &d_dos, &t_dos);
```

INCLUDES

```
#include <dos.h>
```
For function declaration

DESCRIPTION The time in UNIX systems is expressed as the number of seconds elapsed since 00:00:00 hours GMT (Greenwich Mean Time), January 1, 1970. The *unixtodos* function accepts time in the UNIX format in the long integer argument *time* and converts it to date and time in the DOS format.

The DOS time and date are returned in the *date* and *time* structures whose addresses are provided in the arguments *d* and *t* respectively. Consult the reference entries of the functions *getdate* and *gettime* for details on the *date* and *time* structures.

COMMON USES The *unixtodos* function allows you to set the DOS date and time using the UNIX-style time returned by the function *time*.

SEE ALSO

`getdate` *To get the current date from DOS*

`gettime` *To get the current time from DOS*

`time` *To get the current date and time in UNIX format*

`setdate` *To set the date as maintained by DOS*

`settime` *To set the time as maintained by DOS*

EXAMPLE Get the current date and time in UNIX format by calling *time*. Convert this to DOS format using *unixtodos*. Print the DOS format date and time returned by *unixtodos*.

```
#include <dos.h>
#include <time.h>

main()
{
    struct date date;
    struct time timep;
    time_t tunix;

/* Get date and time in UNIX format */
```

```
    time(&tunix);
/* Convert to DOS style date and time */
    unixtodos((long)tunix, &date, &timep);
/* Print date and time */
    printf("Current date: %d-%d-%d\n", date.da_mon,
            date.da_day, date.da_year);
    printf("Current time: %d:%d:%d.%d\n", timep.ti_hour,
            timep.ti_min, timep.ti_sec, timep.ti_hund);
    return 0;
}
```

COMPATIBILITY

_write

TC1	TC1.5	TC2	TC++	MSC3	MSC4	MSC5	MSC6	QC1	QC2	QC2.5	ANSI	UNIX V	XNX
▲	▲	▲	▲			1	1	1	1	1			

PURPOSE Use *_write* to write a specified number of bytes from a buffer into a file at the current location in that file. You will need a handle returned by a function such as *_open* or *_creat* before calling this function. DOS function 42h can be used to move the current location in a file.

SYNTAX

```
int _write(int filehandle, void *buffer, unsigned writecount);
```

`int filehandle;` *File "handle" or identifier*

`void far *buffer;` *Pointer to buffer where the data read from the file will be stored*

`unsigned writecount;` *Number of bytes to be written*

EXAMPLE CALL

```
bytes_written = _write(filehandle, pbuf, 80);
```

INCLUDES `#include <io.h>` *For function declaration*

DESCRIPTION The *_write* function calls DOS function 40h to transfer the number of bytes specified in the argument *writecount* from the memory locations accessed through the pointer *buffer* into the file whose handle, or identifying number, is given in the argument *filehandle*. The data is written at the current position of the file pointer in the file and the file pointer is updated after the writing is complete.

The file handle must be one that had been returned when the file was opened by *_open* or perhaps created by *_creat*.

1. The equivalent function in Microsoft C 5 and 6, and QuickC 1.0 through 2.5, is *_dos_write*.

RETURNS If successful, the *_write* function returns the actual number of bytes written to the file. Otherwise, it returns −1 and sets the global variable *errno* either to the constant EBADF (indicating that the file handle is invalid) or to EACCES to indicate that access was denied (probably the file is not open for write access).

COMMENTS The functions *read* and *write* offer a more portable means of achieving the same result as these DOS specific functions.

SEE ALSO

`_read`	*To read from a file using DOS function 3Fh*
`read, write`	*Portable versions of similar read and write functions*
`_open`	*To open an existing file using a DOS call*
`_close`	*To close a file opened by* _open
`_creat`	*To create a new file*

EXAMPLE Use *_open* to open an existing text file then use *_write* to write an extra line at the beginning of the file. Finally, close the file using *_close*.

```
#include <stdio.h>
#include <fcntl.h>
#include <io.h>
char buffer[80] = "Testing _write ........ ";
main()
{
    char fname[40], *p_fname;
    int filehandle, bytes;

    printf("Enter name of an existing file: ");
    p_fname = gets(fname);

/* Open the file using _open */
    if((filehandle = _open(p_fname, O_RDWR)) == -1)
    {
        printf("Error opening file: %s\n", fname);
        exit(0);
    }
    printf("File %s opened.\n", fname);
```

```
/* Now write out buffer */
    if((bytes = _write(filehandle, buffer, 80)) != -1)
    {
        printf("%d bytes written\n", bytes);
    }

/* Now close file */
    if (_close(filehandle) != 0)
    {
        printf("Error closing file with _close\n");
        exit(0);
    }
    printf("File %s closed.\n", fname);
    return 0;
}
```

V Graphics

- Graphics Modes, Coordinates, and Attributes
- Drawing and Animation
- Combining Graphics and Text
- Text Mode Routines

Chapter 18 Graphics Modes, Coordinates, and Attributes

Introduction

Increasingly, graphics user interfaces are the norm for PC-based applications, as the older text-based DOS makes way for OS/2 with its promise of a bit-mapped window-oriented interface. An application also needs good text output capabilities to be competitive. Even though we recognize the need, the task of programming a user interface with good graphics as well as text capabilities remains a particularly complicated business in the PC world because of the variety of graphics adapters and the various displays that can be used with these adapters. Adding to this complexity is the IBM PC's limited support for video I/O in the ROM BIOS (see Chapter 17). This meant that, until recently, creating an effective screen-oriented program involved writing many parts of the program in assembly language.

All this has changed with Turbo C 1.5 and 2.0—thanks to the addition of over a hundred graphics routines which we will discuss in this part of the book. These new library routines make the task of creating graphics-based programs much simpler by providing the basic tools to anyone who programs in Turbo C. The Turbo C graphics routines perform well and provide all the basic capabilities necessary to develop graphics applications. For example, there are routines to determine what video equipment is installed and set an appropriate video mode. You can select colors, line styles, and fill patterns; draw primitive shapes such as a straight line, rectangle, arc, and ellipse; mix text and graphics on the screen; and even perform animation by saving and restoring screen images.

In the next four chapters we will describe the graphics library routines that you will find in Turbo C 2.0 and Turbo C++. This chapter (Chapter 18) presents the information you need to get started with the Turbo C graphics library. In Chapter 19 we describe the drawing and animation routines, and in Chapter 20, the routines for text output in graphics mode. The last chapter (Chapter 21) is about routines for developing user interfaces with the graphics adapter operating in a text mode.

We will start with a discussion of the options available for graphics programming on the PC, the video modes in which the common graphics adapters operate, and the coordinate systems used in the Turbo C++ graphics library. We will then describe the library routines that let you control the modes and attributes of the graphics programming model used in Turbo C++. Details of the graphics hardware are limited to only those aspects that directly affect graphics programming with the Turbo library routines. Thus, we present information on such things as the number of colors and resolutions, but skip unnecessary details such as the scan rate of monitors and exact screen sizes.

Basics of PC Graphics

In the IBM PC (and compatibles), screen output relies on two components: the display adapter and the display monitor. The "adapter" is a hardware card that you plug into one of the slots inside the PC while the "monitor" is the display screen where the actual characters and graphics appear. In the newer IBM Personal System/2 (PS/2), the display adapter is built into the system board.

Whether we can display graphics on a monitor or not depends entirely on the adapter. Any monitor is capable of displaying an array of dots known as "pixels." For example, when a monitor is displaying characters, each character is built with a pattern of pixels which is sent to the monitor by the adapter. The ability to display graphics, therefore, depends on the type of adapter.

ADAPTERS AND MONITORS FOR THE IBM PC

There are three standard display adapters in the IBM PC marketplace: Monochrome Display Adapter (MDA), Color Graphics Adapter (CGA), and Enhanced Graphics Adapter (EGA). A fourth adapter, Hercules Graphics Card (HGC), is a monochrome graphics adapter capable of displaying graphics on the monochrome monitor. Three monitors are available: the monochrome display, the color display, and the enhanced color display.

The MDA is the display adapter used in the original IBM PC. It can display 80 characters (columns) by 25 lines (rows) of text output (no graphics) on the monochrome display. The HGC can display text too, like the MDA, but it can also display graphics on the monochrome monitor at a resolution of 720 pixels horizontally and 348 pixels vertically. (Another way of saying this is that the HGC has a resolution of 720×348. From now on we will express resolutions this way.)

The CGA can also display text as well as graphics, and it does so in color on a color display monitor. Specifically, the CGA can display text using a combination of any 1 of 16 foreground colors and 1 of 8 background colors. Graphics can be in 4 colors with 320×200 resolution. If you choose 2-color (black and white) graphics, the resolution goes up to 640×200. We will soon explain this trade-off between number of colors and resolution.

The EGA, introduced by IBM in 1984, moves towards higher resolution graphics and more colors. It displays text and graphics in color on an enhanced color display monitor. To retain compatibility with earlier hardware, the EGA supports operational modes in which it can display text on a monochrome monitor and emulate a CGA. In its highest resolution mode, the EGA can generate graphics output in 16 colors with 640×350 resolution.

DISPLAY SYSTEMS IN IBM PS/2

With the new PS/2 systems IBM introduced two new adapters: the Multi Color Graphics Array (MCGA) and the Video Graphics Array (VGA). The VGA is meant to be a successor to the EGA. In one video mode (mode 12h), the VGA offers 640×480 resolution graphics with 16 colors out of a possible 256 simultaneous colors. The VGA can also provide 320×200 resolution graphics with 256 colors (mode 13h). The MCGA resembles the CGA in many ways, but it has a two-color 640×480 mode. It is available on the PS/2 Model 30 which has a PC compatible bus. The VGA is built into all other PS/2 models. These two adapters are designed to drive an "analog monitor" as opposed to the "digital" ones that are used with MDA, CGA, and EGA in the PC. As the name implies, a digital monitor uses a fixed number of on/off signals. For example, the enhanced color display monitor accepts the six on/off signals: red, green, and blue and intensified versions of each, so it is capable of displaying 64 distinct colors ($2^6 = 64$), but it is actually limited to 16 of these because there are only 4 bits of storage for each pixel in the video memory on the display adapter. In an analog monitor, however, the three red, green, and blue signals can vary continuously instead of being simply on or off. This allows continuously varying shades of colors. Inside the MCGA and VGA adapters, the colors are still represented digitally, limiting the number of colors available. For example, in MCGA, red, green, and blue are each represented by 6-bit values. A *Digital-to-Analog Converter* (DAC) converts these digital values to analog signals to be fed to the monitor.

As you can see, in graphics programming on the PC and PS/2 we have to deal with quite a few combinations of adapters and monitors. So any help in the form of library routines that can be called from C is greatly appreciated. As you will see, the graphics library in Turbo C takes much of the work out of dealing with the graphics hardware.

PROGRAMMING THE DISPLAY ADAPTERS

Like most peripheral devices in the IBM PC and PS/2, the display adapters are programmed via 8-bit registers that are accessible by unique input port addresses (see the tutorial in Chapter 16 for a description of port I/O routines in Turbo C++). In addition to these control registers, all PC display adapters share one common property: they are "memory-mapped." Each pixel on the display screen corresponds to 1 or more bits in a memory location (in the video adapter) accessible just like the rest of the memory locations in the system. This memory, called the "video memory" (or video RAM) is physically present on the display adapter but has addresses that map into the normal address space of the microprocessor. The circuitry in the adapter reads values from the video RAM and displays the pixels on the monitor. Thus, you can show text and graphics on the monitor by directly manipulating the video RAM, provided you know how it is organized. The method of storing information in the video memory depends on whether text or graphics is being displayed.

In text display modes, a rectangular grid of pixels is used to display one character. In this case, each character is typically stored using two bytes: one for the 8-bit ASCII code of the character being displayed and the other to store the display attributes for that character. These attributes determine characteristics such as the color of the character and of the background pixels and whether the character is blinking. The exact pattern of pixels necessary to draw each character is stored in a separate table in memory. Sets of such patterns are referred to as "fonts."

In graphics modes, the number of bits necessary to represent a pixel depends on the number of colors to be displayed. For a black and white monitor, each pixel simply has to be either on or off, which means that a single bit is enough to store all the information necessary to display a pixel. By the same token, to display 16 colors we need four bits of storage per pixel. The maximum number of colors that can be displayed is given by 2^n where n is the number of bits per pixel. Since the amount of memory on the adapter is fixed, there is always a trade-off between the number of on-screen pixels and the number of colors.

The physical organization of the video RAM varies quite a bit from one adapter to another, and the details (especially in EGA and VGA) can be overwhelming even for a simple program. The Turbo C graphics routines eliminate the need to learn the detailed organization of the video memory and display adapters.

BIOS VIDEO ROUTINES

The BIOS routines which reside in the read only memory (ROM) of every PC provide a portable way to program the video adapters. Using software interrupt 10h (see the tutorial in Chapter 17), you can invoke a set of functions that allow you to set the video mode, and to read and write pixel values. A number of video modes for text or graphics output is available in the BIOS video routines, each suitable for a specific monitor (if that adapter supports multiple monitor types). In a text mode you can write a character to the screen with an associated attribute to control its appearance. In a graphics mode, you are limited to either writing a pixel or reading the color at a single point on the screen. BIOS is adequate for basic display programming. But for very fast screen drawing or animations, especially in graphics modes, directly writing to the video memory may be preferred, even at the expense of loss of portability of the code.

THE TURBO C++ SOLUTION

Where does the Turbo C++ graphics library fit in this picture? The Turbo C++ graphics routines perform better than the BIOS video routines and they provide many more basic capabilities than does BIOS interrupt 10h. Additionally, the Turbo C++ graphics library routines are much easier to use than the BIOS routines, which must be invoked via software interrupts. To use the Turbo C++ graphics library, you do not have to know the implementation details of the routines, but you do have to understand the graphics "model" used by Turbo C++.

The Turbo C++ Graphics Model

The Turbo C++ graphics model is the collection of such concepts as coordinates, colors, palettes, line-styles, fill-masks, and primitive shapes that the library uses. Many of the ideas have their roots in the hardware, and we will make these connections clear as the concepts are discussed.

THE DISPLAY SCREEN AND THE COORDINATE SYSTEMS

There are two ways to view the display screen in the Turbo C++'s graphics model. As shown in Figure 18-1, in text modes the entire screen is viewed as a grid of cells, usually 25 rows by 80 columns. Each cell can hold a character with certain foreground and background colors if the monitor is capable of displaying colors. In text modes, a location on the screen is expressed in terms of rows and columns with the upper left hand corner corresponding to (1,1), the column numbers increasing from left to right and the row numbers increasing vertically downwards.

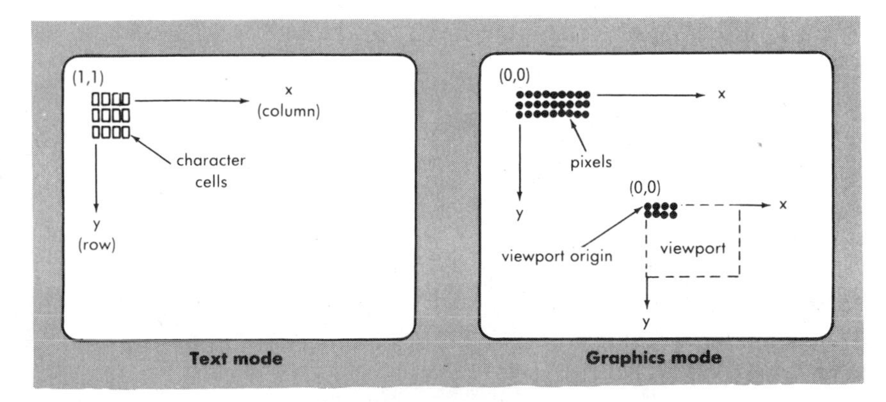

Figure 18-1. *Coordinate frames in text and graphics modes*

In graphics modes, the screen is seen as a matrix of pixels each capable of displaying one or more colors. Depending on the graphics mode and display adapter, the width and height of this matrix, in pixels, can be one of: 320×200 (CGA 4-color mode and VGA 256-color mode), 640×200 (CGA 2-color mode), 640×350 (EGA 16-color mode), or 640×480 (VGA 16-color mode). The Turbo C++ graphics coordinate system has its origin at the upper left hand corner of the physical screen with the x-axis positive to the right and the y-axis positive going downwards.

All graphics functions in the library work with a coordinate frame whose origin is located at the upper left hand corner of the current "viewport," a rectangular region within which all current graphics output appears. Any part of a drawing that falls outside the viewport may be optionally "clipped" or thrown away. Figure 18-1 shows a viewport in the middle of the screen. You can define a viewport using the *setviewport* function.

VIDEO MODES

When using the graphics library in Turbo C++, you must be aware of the various modes (text as well as graphics) and their capabilities before you can make use of all the functions. There are routines in Turbo C++ that make it easy to determine the hardware configuration so your application can work reasonably well in almost all display environments.

The current video mode in the Turbo graphics library determines whether the display adapter should be configured for text output only, or for both graphics and text output. The mode also specifies the number of colors and the graphics resolution of the screen. In Chapter 20, we will describe the text modes supported in the Turbo C++ graphics library. Here we consider the graphics modes only.

Table 18-1 shows the video mode constants known to the Turbo C++ graphics library. The adapter in which this video mode is supported is listed in the last column of the table. The mode constants, shown in the first column, are defined in the header file *graphics.h*, and each one represents a video mode for a particular adapter. You have to use these constants when selecting a video mode with a call to *initgraph*.

Table 18-1. ***Video Modes in Turbo C++ Graphics Library***

Mode Constant	Interpretation	Adapter
CGAC0	320×200 palette 0, 1-page	CGA
CGAC1	320×200 palette 1, 1-page	CGA
CGAC2	320×200 palette 2, 1-page	CGA
CGAC3	320×200 palette 3, 1-page	CGA
CGAHI	640×200 2-color, 1-page	CGA
MCGAC0	320×200 palette 0, 1-page	MCGA

Table 18-1. ***(cont.)***

Mode Constant	Interpretation	Adapter
MCGAC1	320×200 palette 1, 1-page	MCGA
MCGAC2	320×200 palette 2, 1-page	MCGA
MCGAC3	320×200 palette 3, 1-page	MCGA
MCGAMED	640×200 2-color, 1-page	MCGA
MCGAHI	640×480 2-color, 1-page	MCGA
EGALO	640×200 16-color, 4-page	EGA
EGAHI	640×350 16-color, 2-page	EGA
EGA64LO	640×200 16-color, 1-page	EGA
EGA64HI	640×350 4-color, 1-page	EGA
EGAMONOHI	640×350 64-K on card, 1-page, 256-K video memory, 4-page	EGA
HERCMONOHI	720×348 2-page	HERCULES
ATT400C0	320×200 palette 0, 1-page	AT&T
ATT400C1	320×200 palette 1, 1-page	AT&T
ATT400C2	320×200 palette 2, 1-page	AT&T
ATT400C3	320×200 palette 3, 1-page	AT&T
ATT400MED	640×200 1-page	AT&T
ATT400HI	640×400 1-page	AT&T
VGALO	640×200 16-color, 4-page	VGA
VGAMED	640×350 16-color, 2-page	VGA
VGAHI	640×480 16-color, 1-page	VGA
PC3270HI	720×350 1-page	IBM PC 3270
IBM8514LO	640×480 256-color	IBM 8514
IBM8514HI	1024×768 256-color	IBM 8514

BORLAND GRAPHICS INTERFACE: GRAPHICS DEVICE DRIVERS

The output routines in a graphics library depend on the adapter and the monitor being used. The Turbo C++ graphics library is no exception. This usually means that special code has to be built into the library to handle each specific adapter. Adding the support for a new adapter means releasing a new version of the library with the output routines for the new adapter. To avoid this problem, Borland International has used the concept of a "graphics device driver" to isolate the device-dependent output routines. These are not MS-DOS device drivers, but object code in files with Borland's own format. They, however, work like normal MS-DOS device drivers because the selected driver is loaded from the disk during the initialization of the graphics library during the call to *initgraph*. The advantage of this approach is that Borland can support a new display adapter by supplying a driver and instructing users how to load the driver at run-time. This method also reduces the size of programs because the code to support each and every possible adapter is not linked into the executable. In Turbo C 2.0 and Turbo

C++, Borland provides a library routine, *installuserdriver*, to let you add new driver names (.BGI file names) to an internal table that is maintained by the graphics package. The format of the .BGI files is available in the Compuserve on-line service. This information allows you to write a Turbo C-compatible graphics driver for any display adapter.

The graphics device drivers are distributed in files which have names with the extension .BGI (for *Borland Graphics Interface*). If you develop a graphics application that you plan to distribute, you can link the graphics drivers into your program. Use a utility named BGIOBJ, included in the Turbo C++ distribution, to convert the graphics drivers into object files with the .OBJ extension. You can then link these object files with your program as you would any other object module. Later, further information on using these drivers in your programs will be presented. Borland also provides loadable font files (with extension .CHR). We will discuss them in detail in Chapter 20.

SELECTING A VIDEO MODE

As mentioned earlier, one of the problems in developing graphics software for the IBM PC is the diversity of hardware configurations that your software will encounter once it is out of your hands. One common trend among developers seems to be to use what we call the "least common denominator" approach—make use of the lowest resolution video mode, usually a CGA mode that is guaranteed to be emulated on most other adapters. While this works, it is also very disheartening to see the advanced capabilities of the better adapters (EGA and VGA) going to waste for want of software that supports them. The situation is improving gradually, and if you are developing an application using the Turbo C++ graphics library, you can make use of its facilities to settle for the best video mode that the hardware can support, instead of assuming a safe but dull choice.

You can do this using the following steps. Any graphics program in Turbo C++ must start with a call to *initgraph* of the form

```
int graphdriver = EGA, graphmode = EGAHI;
initgraph(&graphdriver, &graphmode, "c:\\tc\\bgi");
```

where *graphdriver* is an integer containing a constant representing a specific graphics driver (see Table 18-8 in the reference page on *initgraph* for a list), *graphmode* is another integer denoting the video mode (as shown in Table 18-1), and the third argument, the name of the directory where the graphics drivers (the .BGI files) are located. In the example, we initialize an EGA for high-resolution 640×350 16-color graphics by setting *graphdriver* to EGA, and *graphmode* to EGAHI.

There is another feature of the *initgraph* routine that makes it very useful for selecting the best video mode. If you call *initgraph* with *graphdriver = DETECT*, it will actually detect the type of graphics hardware you have, load the appropriate driver (.BGI file), and set the adapter to its highest resolution graphics mode. The selected graphics driver and mode are returned in the integers *graphdriver* and *graphmode*.

If you do not want a mode selected automatically, you can call the routine *detectgraph* to find the driver suitable for the hardware as well as the recommended mode. You may use the information about the adapter to select a different mode which is more suitable for your purpose.

Once you decide on a mode, use *initgraph* to put the display adapter in that mode and load the graphics driver. This will also initalize parameters such as line styles, fill patterns, and color palettes to default settings. At this point, your application can display graphics output. You will have to consider the parameters such as graphics position, text position, line style, fill mask, and others that the graphics library uses during its operation. Set these parameters to appropriate values before calling graphics or text output routines. We will discuss these attributes and parameters later.

When your application is ready to exit, call *closegraph*. This will restore the hardware to its initial configuration. Here is how the skeleton of a graphics application written in Turbo C++ looks:

```
#include <graphics.h>   /* Graphics programs always need this */
     :
     :
int graphdriver;    /* Graphics driver     */
int graphmode;      /* Graphics video mode */
int g_errorcode;    /* Graphics error code */
     :
     :
/*  Detect adapter, load driver, and select best mode. Last
 * argument is directory name where .BGI files reside.
 */
graphdriver = DETECT;
initgraph(&graphdriver, &graphmode, "C:\\TC\\BGI");
g_errorcode = graphresult(); /* Get result code     */
if (g_errorcode != grOK)  /* Always check for error */
{
     printf("Graphics error: %s\n", grapherrormsg(g_errorcode));
     exit(1);
}

/* Set color, line style, fill mask and draw the graphics you want */
     :
     :
/* Close graphics system and restore original settings */
closegraph();
     :
     :
```

COLORS AND PALETTES

Any color can be represented by a combination of the primary colors: red (R), green (G), and blue (B). In a digital scheme, a fixed number of bits is used to represent the permissible levels in each component of the RGB signal. If we have two bits for each component, we have a total of 2^6 or 64 colors (each combination of R, G, and B is a color). Even though an analog monitor has an infinite number of possible colors, we do not truly have an infinite number of levels in the RGB signal. In the MCGA and the VGA, for example, each component of RGB is represented by an 8-bit value of which the two high-order bits are always zero. Thus each component has a 6-bit value or 64 levels. This means we can have a total of $64 \times 64 \times 64 = 262{,}144$ (or 256-K) possible colors in the VGA. Although an adapter may be able to "understand" 256-K color values, we will need a lot of video memory to display these colors because, with 6 bits per primary color, the RGB value at each pixel will require at least 18 bits (3×6 bits) of storage.

With 4 bits of storage for each pixel (as in EGA mode 10h and VGA mode 12h), the value stored at each video memory location corresponding to a pixel can be any value from 0 to 15 ($2^4 - 1$). Suppose the monitor is capable of accepting 64 (a 6-bit value) different colors and the display adapter is designed to generate the 6-bit value. How should the 4-bit value in a pixel be mapped into a 6-bit value sent to the monitor? The solution is to use a "palette," which is a table with as many entries as there are possible pixel values (16) and each pixel value having an entry showing one of the possible colors (a number from 0 to 63). The adapter simply uses the pixel value to look up the color it must send to the monitor. Figure 18-2 illustrates the concept of pixel values mapped to colors via the palette. Figure 18-2 also shows the video memory organized as 4 bit-planes.

The pixel value or "color number" refers to the contents of the bits in the video memory corresponding to a pixel. The "color value" is the digital signal (even an analog monitor receives a digital signal that has been converted to analog form using a Digital-to-Analog Converter) that causes a monitor to display a specific color from the current palette. Stated another way, the color number or pixel value is what is stored at a memory location corresponding to a pixel and the color value denotes an RGB signal level that causes the monitor to display a specific color by use of the palette.

The pixel value 0 has a special significance in the display adapters. All display adapters treat pixels containing a zero as part of the background. Thus on adapters like EGA and VGA, where the current palette can be redefined, if you change the entry corresponding to the pixel value 0 in the palette, the background will change color. For example, *setpalette(0, EGA_BLUE);* will change the background to blue (constants for common colors are defined in the file *graphics.h* and listed in Table 18-3).

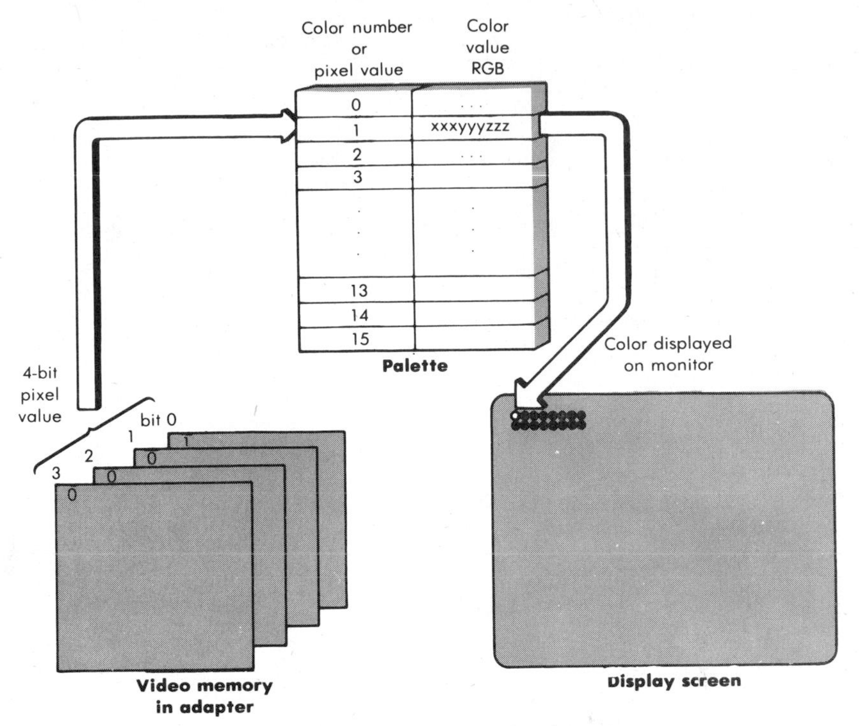

Figure 18-2. *Colors and palettes*

Palettes in CGA

There are four predefined palettes in CGA, each with four colors. Color number 0 in each palette is the background color and can be separately selected as any one of the color constants for CGA from Table 18-3. You can assign a background color with a call to *setbkcolor*. For example,

```
setbkcolor(LIGHTBLUE);
```

sets the CGA background color to light blue.

Colors 1 through 3 of these four palettes are shown in Table 18-2. Each palette is selected by using the mode constant shown in the first column of Table 18-2. These constants are defined in the header file *graphics.h*. You should select these modes only when the graphics adapter is CGA.

Palettes in EGA and VGA

The default definition of the palette in the 16 color modes in the EGA and the VGA is shown in Table 18-3. However, you are free to redefine the palette in EGA and VGA by using the functions *setpalette* and *setallpalette*. For example, *setpalette(1, EGA_RED)* will map pixel value 1 to the color red.

Table 18-2. ***The Four CGA Palettes***

CGA Mode Constant	Palette Number	Pixel Value		
		1	*2*	*3*
CGAC0	0	Light Green	Light Red	Yellow
CGAC1	1	Light Cyan	Light Magenta	White
CGAC2	2	Green	Red	Brown
CGAC3	3	Cyan	Magenta	Light Gray

Table 18-3. ***Color Constants and Their Values***

Adapter	Color Constant	Value	Adapter	Color Constant	Value
EGA/VGA	EGA_BLACK	0	CGA	BLACK	0
	EGA_BLUE	1		BLUE	1
	EGA_GREEN	2		GREEN	2
	EGA_CYAN	3		CYAN	3
	EGA_RED	4		RED	4
	EGA_MAGENTA	5		MAGENTA	5
	EGA_BROWN	20		BROWN	6
	EGA_LIGHTGRAY	7		LIGHTGRAY	7
	EGA_DARKGRAY	56		DARKGRAY	8
	EGA_LIGHTBLUE	57		LIGHTBLUE	9
	EGA_LIGHTGREEN	58		LIGHTGREEN	10
	EGA_LIGHTCYAN	59		LIGHTCYAN	11
	EGA_LIGHTRED	60		LIGHTRED	12
	EGA_LIGHTMAGENTA	61		LIGHTMAGENTA	13
	EGA_YELLOW	62		YELLOW	14
	EGA_WHITE	63		WHITE	15

VIDEO PAGES

Although all PC displays are memory-mapped, the actual amount of video memory necessary for all pixels displayed on the screen depends on the video mode. In some modes, there is enough video memory for all the screen pixels several times over. This allows multiple "video pages." Each area of memory sufficient to hold a full screen is called a "page." Only one page is displayed, but the adapter will allow switching from one page to another. Since this "flipping of the video page" happens very fast, it can be used to your advantage in your programs to provide very fast screen updates. The trick is to prepare the entire screen in a video page that is not being shown and then switch to that video page to display its contents on the screen.

The number of video pages available in an adapter depends on the amount of video memory on the adapter and the mode in which the adapter is being operated. For example, the EGA with 256 K of video RAM supports up to four video pages in the mode EGALO. On the other hand, it can have two video pages even in the high-resolution graphics mode EGAHI (see the reference pages on *setactivepage* for an example program showing page flipping on the EGA in the 640×350 16-color mode).

The video pages are numbered starting at 0. The page where all drawing occurs is called the "active" page and the page being displayed on the monitor is known as the "visual" page. Initially both active and visual pages are 0. You can select a new active page by calling *setactivepage* and perhaps display yet another page with the call *setvisualpage*. For example, *setvisualpage(1)* will begin displaying video page 1 on the screen.

CURRENT POSITIONS, LINE STYLES, AND FILL MASKS

The drawing and text output routines in the Turbo C++ graphics library rely on several internally maintained attributes and parameters. Table 18-4 summarizes these parameters, including the name of the relevant functions in the library. The functions themselves are listed according to subcategories in the next chapter. Each function is described in detail in the reference pages which follow this tutorial.

Table 18-4. ***Parameters Maintained by the Turbo C++ Graphics Library Routines***

Parameter	Meaning
Active Page	When there is enough memory for more than one video page, the active page denotes the portion of video memory where all current graphics and text output goes. TO SET: use *setactivepage*. TO GET: cannot get.
Aspect Ratio	This tells you how the x and y dimensions of a drawing have to be scaled so that it appears geometrically correct when displayed on the screen. When aspect ratio is not 1, a circle will appear as an ellipse, unless you scale the coordinates. TO SET: use *setaspectratio*. TO GET: use *getaspectratio*.
Background Color	This is the color that will appear in the background color. In graphics mode, setting the background color involves redefining color number 0 in the palette. TO SET: use *setbkcolor*. TO GET: use *getbkcolor*.
Current Position	This is a pixel position in (x,y) coordinates representing the location where subsequent graphics output starts. The graphics drawing functions update this position as they generate output to the screen. TO SET: use *moveto* or *moverel*.

Table 18-4. ***(cont.)***

Parameter	Meaning
	TO GET: use *getx* and *gety*.
Drawing Color	This is the color number or pixel value to be used for all subsequent graphics output that uses color (for example, line drawing by *line* or *lineto*). TO SET: use *setcolor*. TO GET: use *getcolor*.
Fill Mask	When filling an area, the fill pattern determines the mask used in the fill operation. As shown in Figure 18-3, the fill pattern is specified by an 8-byte bit pattern. This is viewed as an 8×8 array of bits. The area being filled is also subdivided into 8×8 blocks of pixels. The fill pattern is then applied to each 8×8 block as follows: wherever a 1 appears in the pattern, the corresponding pixel on the screen is set to the current fill color. A 0 in the mask leaves the corresponding screen pixel unchanged. TO SET: use *setfillpattern*. TO GET: use *getfillpattern*.
Fill Style	These are pairs of fill color and fill pattern that are already defined for your convenience in the include file *graphics.h*. They are described further in this chapter. TO SET: use *setfillstyle*. TO GET: use *getfillsettings*.
Font	This is the font used by the text output routines in graphics mode (see Chapter 20). The fonts are stored in files with .CHR extension. You can install a new font in the graphics system by calling the *installuserfont* routine. TO SET: use *settextstyle*. TO GET: use *gettextsettings*.
Graphics Buffer	This is a buffer, with a default size of 4 K, used by routines such as *floodfill* for its operation. You can reset the value to a different size by calling *setgraphbufsize* before you call *initgraph*.
Graphics Driver	This is code that performs I/O with the display adapter. You must specify the driver name when initializing the graphics package by calling *initgraph*. You can install a new driver (.BGI) into the graphics system by calling *installuserdriver*. TO SET: use *initgraph*. TO GET: use *getdrivername*.
Graphics Errorcode	This is the result of the last graphics operation. TO SET: automatically set by graphics operations. TO GET: use *graphresult*.
Graphics Mode	This is the current graphics mode. TO SET: use *setgraphmode*. TO GET: use *getgraphmode*.
Line Drawing Mode	When drawing a line in the graphics mode, the drawing mode determines the color of the pixels that lie on the line. If the mode is COPY_PUT, each pixel on the line is set to the specified color. A

Table 18-4. ***(cont.)***

Parameter	Meaning
	mode of XOR_PUT directs the line drawing routines (see Chapter 19) to determine the color of each pixel by an exclusive-OR of the specified color with the color already present in that pixel. The constants COPY_PUT and XOR_PUT are defined in *graphics.h*. TO SET: use *setwritemode*. TO GET: cannot get.
Line Style	When drawing a line in the graphics mode, the line style determines the appearance of the line on the screen. There is a set of line styles already defined in *graphics.h*, but you can define your own style as well. The line style is specified by a 16-bit unsigned integer. As shown in Figure 18-3, the line style value is viewed as an array of 16 bits. The line being drawn on the screen is also subdivided into 16-pixel chunks. The line style is applied as follows: if a bit is 1, the corresponding screen pixel is set to the current color, if a bit is zero, the corresponding pixel on the screen is left unchanged. TO SET: use *setlinestyle*. TO GET: use *getlinesettings*.
Palette	This is the mapping of pixel values or color numbers to actual colors displayed on the monitor. The palette can be redefined only in EGA and VGA. TO SET: use *setallpalette*, *setpalette*. TO GET: use *getdefaultpalette*, *getpalette*, *getpalettesize*.
Viewport	The viewport is a rectangle on the screen specified by the physical coordinates of its upper left and lower right corners. Optionally, all graphics output falling outside this rectangle may be clipped. TO SET: use *setviewport*. TO GET: use *getviewsettings*.
Visual Page	When there is enough display memory on the adapter for more than one video page, the visual page denotes the portion of video memory that is currently being mapped to the display screen. TO SET: use *setvisualpage*. TO GET: cannot get.

ERROR HANDLING IN TURBO C++ GRAPHICS

Each graphics function in Turbo C++ sets the graphics error code to indicate the success or failure of that function. You can query the current value of the error code by calling the function *graphresult*. There are sixteen error codes, each of which can be referenced in your program using symbolic constants defined in the include file *graphics.h*. A complete list of the error codes appears in Table 18-7 (in the reference entry for *graphresult*). You can also retrieve an error message corresponding to a specific error code by calling *grapherrormsg*.

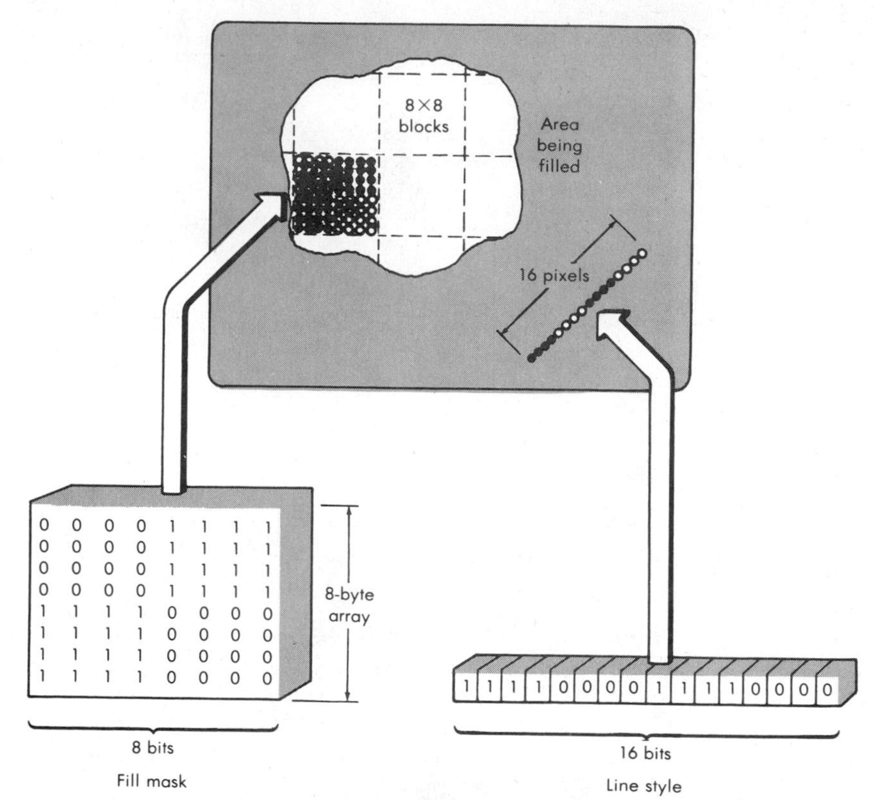

Figure 18-3. ***Fillmask and linestyle***

In order to save space, many examples in this book do not check the results of a graphics operation for error returns, but your application should always explicitly check the result of any library function call for possible errors. The general form of error-checking code is

```
    int g_errorcode;
    :
    :
/* Call graphics routine here, for example, pieslice */
    pieslice(100,100, 0, 30, 50);
    g_errorcode = graphresult(); /* Get result code     */
    if (g_errorcode != grOk)  /* Always check for error */
    {
        printf("Graphics error: %s\n", grapherrormsg(g_errorcode));
        exit(1);
    }
    :
    :
```

where you call *graphresult* immediately after using a specific graphics routine (in this case, *pieslice*), and get the error code. If the error code is *grOk* everything went well. Otherwise, there was an error, and your program can print the error message retrieved by calling *grapherrormsg* with the error code as a parameter. If printing the message will ruin the screen's appearance, you may decide to handle the error in a different manner.

Routines to Control Modes and Attributes

There are 48 routines in the graphics library that are meant for setting modes and attributes as well as for querying their current values. Table 18-5 is a list of these routines organized according to attributes being controlled (an alphabetically arranged list of the routines appears in Table 18-6). In this chapter we will present general information on using some of these routines. Each routine is further described in the alphabetically arranged reference entries that follow the tutorial.

Table 18-5. *Mode and Attribute Control Routines by Task*

Task	Routines
Determine available display hardware, the best video mode, and initialize, close, and reset the graphics system.	closegraph, detectgraph, graphdefaults, initgraph
Check errors.	graphresult, grapherrormsg
Manipulate video modes.	getgraphmode, getmaxmode, getmodename, getmoderange, setgraphmode, restorecrtmode
Set up and get information on viewport.	getviewsettings, setviewport
Manipulate coordinates.	getarccoords, getaspectratio, getmaxx, getmaxy, getx, gety, setaspectratio
Control colors and palettes.	getbkcolor, getcolor, getdefaultpalette, getmaxcolor, getpalette, getpalettesize, setallpalette, setbkcolor, setcolor, setpalette, setrgbpalette (for IBM 8514)
Control fill pattern and line style.	getfillpattern, getfillsettings, getlinesettings, setfillpattern, setfillstyle, setlinestyle, setwritemode
Control video pages.	setactivepage, setvisualpage
Handle graphics drivers.	installuserdriver, getdrivername, registerbgidriver, registerfarbgidriver
Resize graphics buffer, allocate and deallocate memory for graphics routines.	_graphfreemem, _graphgetmem, setgraphbufsize

Table 18-6. ***Mode and Attribute Control Routines***

Routine	Description
closegraph	Closes the Turbo C graphics system.
detectgraph	Detects graphics adapter and returns highest resolution graphics mode.
getarccoords	Returns the start and end points of the last arc drawn (useful for making a line meet the end of an arc).
getaspectratio	Returns the aspect ratio of the screen.
getbkcolor	Returns the current background color.
getcolor	Returns the current drawing color.
getdefaultpalette	Returns a pointer to a *palettetype* structure containing the default palette set up by the current driver when it was initialized.
getdrivername	Returns a string containing the name of the current graphics driver.
getfillpattern	Returns the current fill pattern.
getfillsettings	Returns information about the current fill color and current fill pattern.
getgraphmode	Returns current graphics mode.
getlinesettings	Returns current line style, pattern, and thickness.
getmaxcolor	Returns the highest valid pixel value for current graphics mode.
getmaxmode	Returns the maximum valid mode number for the current graphics driver.
getmaxx	Returns the maximum x coordinate of screen.
getmaxy	Returns the maximum y coordinate of screen.
getmodename	Returns a string containing the mode name corresponding to a valid graphics mode number.
getmoderange	Returns the range of valid graphics mode numbers for a specific graphics adapter.
getpalette	Returns the current palette.
getpalettesize	Returns the number of colors in the current palette.
getviewsettings	Returns information about the current viewport and whether clipping is enabled or not.
getx	Returns the x coordinate of the current point relative to the upper left hand corner of the viewport.
gety	Returns the y coordinate of the current point relative to the upper left hand corner of the viewport.
graphdefaults	Resets all graphics parameters to their settings.
grapherrormsg	Returns a string with the error message corresponding to a given error code.
_graphfreemem	Allocates memory for use by graphics routines (normally calls *malloc*, but may be modified by user).
_graphgetmem	Frees memory allocated by *_graphgetmem* (normally done by calling *free*, but may be modified by user).
graphresult	Returns error code corresponding to the last unsuccessful graphics operation.

Table 18-6. ***(cont.)***

Routine	Description
initgraph	Initializes the graphics system.
installuserdriver	Adds a new graphics device driver to the the device driver table that is maintained by the graphics package.
registerbgidriver	Registers graphics driver linked into an executable.
registerfarbgidriver	Registers graphics driver linked into an executable (this version is used when linked-in driver is in a far segment).
restorecrtmode	Resets the adapter to the mode in use before *initgraph* was called.
setactivepage	Selects the video page where all subsequent graphics output will go.
setallpalette	Changes all palette colors to a specified set.
setaspectratio	Sets the aspect ratio to be used by the graphics routines.
setbkcolor	Sets the current background color.
setcolor	Sets the current drawing color.
setfillpattern	Sets a user-defined pattern used during fill operations.
setfillstyle	Sets the fill color and fill pattern for subsequent fills.
setgraphbufsize	Sets the size of a buffer used by graphics routines such as *floodfill* (must be called before *initgraph*).
setgraphmode	Sets adapter to a specified graphics mode.
setlinestyle	Selects a line pattern and thickness.
setpalette	Redefines a single pixel value in the current palette.
setrgbpalette	Defines a pixel value (color number) in the IBM 8514 adapter.
setviewport	Defines a viewport.
setvisualpage	Selects the video page to be displayed on the screen.
setwritemode	Sets the writing mode for line drawing.

HANDLING GRAPHICS DEVICE DRIVERS

The graphics device drivers encapsulate the output routines specific to the display adapters. The drivers used by the Turbo C++ graphics library reside in files with the .BGI extension, and the selected driver is loaded into memory at run-time. The *initgraph* routine performs this chore.

This approach of loading the driver from a file means that the executable program is not self-contained, you must have both the executable and the .BGI files to use the graphics capabilities. Turbo C++ provides a way to include (or link in) selected drivers into your executable program and create a single file that you can distribute. You have to use a utility named BGIOBJ to convert a driver's .BGI file into an object file with the .OBJ extension. At your option, you can generate an .OBJ file to be loaded in the same segment as other drivers, or a *far* segment for that driver alone. The ability to make each driver's object code into a separate segment is necessary when your program uses several drivers or fonts (loading fonts is described in Chapter 20) because they may not all fit into a single segment.

Once a driver's .BGI file has been converted into an .OBJ file, it can be linked (using TLINK) with other object files that make up your program. Before using such linked-in drivers in your program, you must "register" each driver by a calling *registerbgidriver* (or, *registerfarbgidriver* when a driver is in its own segment). This informs the graphics system that the drivers are already loaded and need not be read from files. Since *initgraph* is responsible for loading drivers, you must register the linked-in drivers before calling *initgraph*. The steps involved are as follows:

Step 1: Use BGIOBJ to convert each driver's .BGI file to .OBJ. For example, *BGIOBJ EGAVGA* will generate the file EGAVGA.OBJ. Use the option /F with BGIOBJ to associate a separate code segment with each driver's code. An example is: *BGIOBJ/F HERC.*

Step 2: You can now add the object modules to the library GRAPHICS.LIB, or specify them explicitly when you use TCC or TLINK to link your program. For example, you can build the executable by the command

```
tcc myprog.c graphics.lib egavga.obj herc.obj
```

Step 3: In your program register the drivers as follows:

```
#include <graphics.h>
/* Register drivers */
    if (registerbgidriver(EGAVGAdriver) <0) exit(1);
    if (registerbgidriver(HERCdriverfar) <0) exit(1);
/* Initalize graphics system */
    initgraph(...);
```

Note that the argument to *registerbgidriver* is the name of the driver routine which is constructed by appending *_driver* to the name of the driver. When the driver's object file is created with "BGIOBJ /F," the name needs an additional *_far* as suffix.

LINKING WITH GRAPHICS.LIB

The Turbo C++ libraries do not include the graphics functions. Thus in the interactive environment (when you run TC), the graphics library will not be automatically searched when a program is being linked. You can force a search by creating a "project" (see Chapter 3 for more details) with your program and GRAPHICS.LIB in it. Another more convenient approach (at the cost of more disk space) is to add the graphics routines to the standard libraries for each memory model. To save disk space, you may want to add the graphics routines only to the libraries corresponding to a few specific memory models. The following steps explain how this is done:

Step 1: Go to the directory where the Turbo C++ library files (.LIB) reside.

Step 2: Decide which memory models you will use most. Then use TLIB to add GRAPHICS.LIB to the standard library for that memory model by the command

```
TLIB Cm +GRAPHICS.LIB
```

where the letter *m* stands for the memory model and can be one of S, M, C, L, and H denoting, respectively, small, medium, compact, large, and huge.

If you always build your programs using the command-line version of Turbo C++ (TCC) only, you can avoid these steps and simply specify GRAPHICS.LIB on the command line, as in TCC MYPROG.C GRAPHICS.LIB.

Further Reading

Although a graphics library, like the one in Turbo C++, hides much of the details of the display hardware, it is often necessary to know about the inner working of the adapter to make the graphics application work right. Here are some references that can help you get familiar with PC graphics.

Norton's guide[1] discusses the basics of video and has details of the CGA and MDA. The EGA and VGA are only recently beginning to be discussed in books. The recent book by Wilton[3] is an excellent reference on PC and PS/2 video programming, complete with sample assembly language routines that can be called from C. Kliewer's book[4], and can also serve as an EGA/VGA programmer's reference, although it does not have the depth and detail of Wilton's text[3]. Also, Lafore[5,6] covers CGA and EGA programming in his books[5].

Hansen's book[7] shows the development of a library of utility functions, including a set for screen display. He also shows several tricks used to determine the display hardware in a system and a way to write to the CGA memory without generating so called "snow" on the screen.

The book by Rochkind[8], the author of the EDIX editor, is devoted solely to the subject of developing a portable text-oriented display package. It has an excellent presentation of the gradual development of a modular display library that can help you manage any types of displays effectively.

On the graphics side, Johnson[9] presents the development of an EGA-based graphics package with complete source listings.

Another good source of information for graphics programming in C is the book by Stevens[10].

1. Peter Norton, *The Peter Norton Programmer's Guide to the IBM PC*, Microsoft Press, Redmond, WA, 1985, 426 pages.

2. Charles Petzold, Exploring the EGA, parts I and II, *PC Magazine*, August 1986, pp. 367-384 and September 1986, pp. 287-313.
3. Richard Wilton, *Programmer's Guide to PC & PS/2 Video Systems*, Microsoft Press, Redmond, WA, 1987, 531 pages.
4. Bradley D. Kliewer, *EGA/VGA A Programmer's Reference Guide*, Intertext Publications, Inc., New York, N.Y., 1988, 269 pages.
5. Robert Lafore, *The Waite Group's Turbo C Programming for the IBM*, Revised Edition, Howard W. Sams & Company, Indianapolis, IN, 1989, 720 pages.
6. ———, *The Waite's Group's C Programming Using Turbo C++*, SAMS, Carmel, IN, 1990, 825 pages.
7. Augie Hansen, *Proficient C*, Microsoft Press, Redmond, WA, 1987, 492 pages.
8. Marc J. Rochkind, *Advanced C Programming for Displays*, Prentice-Hall, Englewood Cliffs, NJ, 1988, 331 pages.
9. Nelson Johnson, *Advanced Graphics in C*, Osborne McGraw-Hill, Berkeley, CA, 1987, 670 pages.
10. Roger T. Stevens, *Graphics Programming in C*, M&T Press, Redwood City, CA, 1988, 650 pages.

COMPATIBILITY

closegraph

TC1	TC1.5	TC2	TC++	MSC3	MSC4	MSC5	MSC6	QC1	QC2	QC2.5	ANSI	UNIX V	XNX
	▲	▲	▲										

PURPOSE Use *closegraph* to release memory allocated by the Turbo C++ graphics system and reset the screen to its mode prior to the initialization of the graphics system.

SYNTAX

```
void far  closegraph(void);
```

EXAMPLE CALL

```
closegraph();
```

INCLUDES `#include <graphics.h>` *For function declaration.*

DESCRIPTION The *closegraph* routine performs housekeeping chores before exiting the graphics system. When the Turbo C++ graphics system is initialized by calling *initgraph*, it allocates memory for loading fonts and graphics drivers. Also a buffer is allocated for use during the flood fill operation. The *closegraph* function deallocates these blocks of memory by calling *_graphfreemem*, and resets the display adapter to its mode prior to the call to *initgraph*.

COMMON USES You should always call *closegraph* to exit the Turbo C++ graphics system.

COMMENTS You can provide your own version of the *_graphfreemem* routine that gets called by *closegraph* to deallocate memory. The default version of *_graphfreemem* simply calls the standard C library routine *free* to do the job.

SEE ALSO

`initgraph` *To initialize the Turbo C++ graphics system*

`restorecrtmode` *To switch to the text mode from which* initgraph *was called*

EXAMPLE Initialize the Turbo C++ graphics system and print a message in graphics text using the Sans Serif font. Use *closegraph* to close the graphics system before exiting.

```
#include <graphics.h>

main()
{
  int errorcode;
  int graphdriver = DETECT;
  int graphmode;
```

```
/* Detect and initialize graphics system */
  initgraph(&graphdriver, &graphmode, "c:\\tc\\bgi");
  errorcode = graphresult();
  if (errorcode != grOk)
  {
    printf("Graphics error: %s\n",
    grapherrormsg(errorcode));
    exit(1);
  };

  settextjustify(CENTER_TEXT, CENTER_TEXT);
  settextstyle(SANS_SERIF_FONT, HORIZ_DIR, 1);
  outtextxy( getmaxx() / 2, getmaxy() / 2,
      "Graphics programs need initgraph() and "
      "closegraph()");
  outtextxy(getmaxx()/2, getmaxy() - 50,
"Press any key to exit:");
  getch();        /* Wait until a key is pressed */

  closegraph();          /* Exit graphics library */
  return 0;
}
```

detectgraph

COMPATIBILITY

TC1	TC1.5	TC2	TC++	MSC3	MSC4	MSC5	MSC6	QC1	QC2	QC2.5	ANSI	UNIX V	XNX
	▲	▲	▲			1	1	1	1	1			

PURPOSE Use *detectgraph* to determine the graphics adapter and obtain the highest resolution mode possible for the adapter and monitor installed in the user's system.

SYNTAX

```
void far  detectgraph(int far *graphdriver, int far *graphmode);
```

`int far *graphdriver;` *Address of integer for driver number*

`int far *graphmode;` *Address of integer for mode number*

EXAMPLE CALL

```
int graphdriver, graphmode;
detectgraph(&graphdriver, &graphmode);
```

INCLUDES `#include <graphics.h>` *For function declaration*

DESCRIPTION The *detectgraph* function determines the display adapter and the currently active monitor in the PC. Then the function determines the graphics driver (see the tutorial section) suitable for that adapter, and the graphics mode that will provide the maximum resolution for that combination of adapter and monitor. This information is returned in two integer variables whose addresses must be provided in the arguments *graphdriver* and *graphmode*.

You can interpret the driver and the mode returned by *detectgraph* by comparing them against the defined constants shown in Table 18-8. See the example for a typical use of the information returned by *detectgraph*.

If the system's display hardware is incapable of operating in any graphics mode, *detectgraph* will set **graphdriver* and the graphics system's internal error code to −2.

The *detectgraph* routine will be automatically called by *initgraph* if you specify the constant DETECT (defined in *graphics.h*) as the graphics driver parameter to *initgraph*.

1. The equivalent function in Microsoft C 5 and 6, and QuickC 1.0 through 2.5, is *_getvideoconfig*.

COMMON USES When *initgraph* calls *detectgraph*, it goes ahead and sets the display to the video mode recommended by *detectgraph*. By calling *detectgraph* directly, you can choose to use a video mode different from the one returned by *detectgraph*. See the example below for further details.

COMMENTS You should always check for erroneous results by calling *graphresult* following the call to *detectgraph*. That way you can find out whether graphics capabilities exist or not, before going ahead with the call to *initgraph*.

SEE ALSO `initgraph` *To initialize the Turbo C graphics system*

EXAMPLE Write a Turbo C++ program that uses *detectgraph* to determine the graphics hardware. Report the findings.

```
/* Example program to detect and report hardware */

  #include <graphics.h>

  main()
  {
    int errorcode;
    int graphdriver;
    int graphmode;
/* Call detectgraph to determine hardware */
    detectgraph(&graphdriver, &graphmode);
    if (graphdriver < 0)
    {
printf("No graphics hardware available!\n");
```

```
exit(1);
    }
 /* Report detected hardware */
    printf("'detectgraph()' reports: ");
    switch (graphdriver)
    {
case CGA:
    printf("Color Graphics Adapter");
    break;
case MCGA:
    printf("Multicolor Graphics Array");
    break;
case EGA:
case EGA64:
case EGAMONO:
    printf("Enhanced Graphics Adapter");
    break;
case HERCMONO:
    printf("Hercules Color Card");
    break;
case ATT400:
    printf("AT&T 640x400 card");
    break;
case VGA:
    printf("Video Graphics Array or IBM 8514");
    break;
case PC3270:
    printf("IBM PC 3270");
    break;
    }
    printf("\n");
    return 0;
 }
```

getarccoords

COMPATIBILITY

TC1	TC1.5	TC2	TC++	MSC3	MSC4	MSC5	MSC6	QC1	QC2	QC2.5	ANSI	UNIX V	XNX
	▲	▲	▲										

PURPOSE Use *getarccoords* to get the coordinates of the end points of the last arc drawn by calling *arc*.

SYNTAX

```
void far  getarccoords(struct arccoordstype far *arccoords);
```

```
struct arccoordstype far *arccoords;
```
Pointer to structure where arc coordinates are returned

EXAMPLE CALL

```
struct arccoordstype arc_ends;
getarccoords(&arc_ends);
```

INCLUDES

```
#include <graphics.h>
```
For function declaration

DESCRIPTION

The *getarccoords* function accepts the pointer, *arccoords*, to an *arccoordstype* structure, and returns in it the coordinates of the end points and the center of the last arc drawn by the *arc* routine.

The *arccoordstype* structure is defined as follows in the include file *graphics.h*:

```
struct arccoordstype
{
int x,      y;        /* Center point of the arc      */
int xstart, ystart;   /* Starting position of the arc */
int xend,   yend;     /* Ending position of the arc   */
};
```

COMMON USES

The *getarccords* function is useful when you have to draw a line that meets an end point of an arc. You can first draw the arc, then draw the line using the coordinates of the end points of the arc obtained by calling *getarccoords*.

SEE ALSO

arc *To draw a circular arc*

EXAMPLE

Draw a 60-degree arc. Use *getarccoords* to get the coordinates of the end points of the arc. Use this information to draw the chord (the line joining the end points of the circular arc).

```
/* Join ends of arc using getarccoords */
  #include <graphics.h>

  main()
  {
    int graphdriver = DETECT, graphmode;
    struct arccoordstype  arc_ends;

/* Initialize the graphics system */
    initgraph(&graphdriver, &graphmode, "c:\\tc\\bgi");

/* Draw a 60-degree arc with radius of 100 */
    arc( 150, 120, 0, 59, 100 );
```

```
/* Get the coordinates of the end points of the
 * arc and connect ends with a line
 */
    getarccoords(&arc_ends);
    line( arc_ends.xstart, arc_ends.ystart,
          arc_ends.xend, arc_ends.yend );

/* Wait until user hits a key, then exit */
    getch();
    closegraph();
    return 0;
  }
```

getaspectratio

COMPATIBILITY

TC1	TC1.5	TC2	TC++	MSC3	MSC4	MSC5	MSC6	QC1	QC2	QC2.5	ANSI	UNIX V	XNX
	▲	▲	▲										

PURPOSE Use *getaspectratio* to get the aspect ratio of the current display screen that can be used to ensure that circles and squares are not distorted when shown on the screen.

SYNTAX

```
void far  getaspectratio(int far *xasp, int far *yasp);
```

`int far *xasp;` *Pointer to integer where the x parameter is returned (normally, the x parameter's value is less than 10,000)*

`int far *yasp;` *Pointer to integer where the y parameter is returned (the y parameter's value is always 10,000)*

EXAMPLE CALL

```
int xasp, yasp;
getaspectratio(&xasp, &yasp);
```

INCLUDES `#include <graphics.h>` *For function declaration*

DESCRIPTION The *aspect ratio* is a measure of the shape of an individual pixel on the display screen. On most monitors, a pixel looks like an ellipse with the longer axis vertical (somewhat like an egg standing on its end). As a consequence of this, if you draw a line 100 pixels long, it looks shorter when the line is horizontal than when it is vertical. Thus, a square looks like a rectangle with its vertical edges longer than the horizontal ones, and a circle becomes an ellipse on the screen. The solution to this problem is to enlarge the horizontal (*x*) dimensions of a figure by an amount that corres-

ponds to the ratio of the height (y-dimension) of a pixel to its width (x-dimension). The height and width may be expressed by the inverse of the number of pixels that will respectively fit into a vertical and a horizontal line of fixed length on the screen.

This is precisely the information provided by *getaspectratio*. It returns the height of a pixel in the integer whose address is in *yasp* and the width of a pixel in the integer whose address is given in the argument *xasp*. Because only the ratio of these dimensions matters, *getaspectratio* always returns the value 10,000 in **yasp*, whereas **xasp* is something less than 10,000 (for most PC displays, the pixels are taller than they are wide). Only the new displays using VGA, have the same pixel density along both axes. Thus, **xasp* is 10,000 on the VGA.

The example below shows how you can use the values returned in **xasp* and **yasp* to get accurate rendering of geometrical figures on the screen.

COMMON USES The *getaspectratio* function is very useful in drawing correctly proportioned figures on the screen.

COMMENTS The graphics routines *arc*, *circle*, and *pieslice* automatically use the aspect ratio (you do not have to call *getaspectratio* to activate) to generate circles properly.

SEE ALSO

`arc, circle, pieslice`	*To draw circular arcs and pie wedges*
`ellipse`	*To draw elliptical arcs*
`rectange`	*To draw rectangles*

EXAMPLE Get the aspect ratio for the current graphics mode and use it to draw a square.

```
#include <graphics.h>

main()
{
  int graphdriver = DETECT, graphmode;
  char    buffer[80];
  int     xasp, yasp;
  long    xnew;

  initgraph(&graphdriver, &graphmode, "c:\\tc\\bgi");

/* Get the "aspect ratio." and use it to draw a square*/
  getaspectratio( &xasp, &yasp );
```

```
    xnew = ( 50L * (long) yasp ) / (long) xasp;
    rectangle( 40, 40, 40+(int) xnew, 40+50 );
    sprintf(buffer,"Aspect ratio: xasp = %d, yasp = %d",
    xasp, yasp);
    outtextxy(10,10, buffer);
    outtextxy(getmaxx()/2, getmaxy() - 50,
"Press any key to exit:");
    getch();         /* Wait until a key is pressed */

    closegraph();         /* Exit graphics library */
    return 0;
  }
```

getbkcolor

COMPATIBILITY

TC1	TC1.5	TC2	TC++	MSC3	MSC4	MSC5	MSC6	QC1	QC2	QC2.5	ANSI	UNIX V	XNX
	▲	▲	▲			1	1	1	1	1			

PURPOSE Use the *getbkcolor* function to get the value of the current background color.

SYNTAX `int far getbkcolor(void);`

EXAMPLE CALL `bcolor = getbkcolor();   /* Retrieve background color */`

INCLUDES `#include <graphics.h>`   *For function declaration*

DESCRIPTION The *getbkcolor* function returns the "pixel value" for those pixels that are part of the background. The return value can be interpreted by comparing the value against the constants shown in Table 18-12.

The current background color can be set by calling *setbkcolor.*

1. Use *_getbkcolor* in Microsoft C 5 and 6, and QuickC 1.0 through 2.5.

COMMON USES The *getbkcolor* function is useful for saving the current background color number before altering it in a program.

RETURNS The *getbkcolor* function returns an integer which is the current background color.

SEE ALSO `setbkcolor`   *To change the current background color*

EXAMPLE Write a program that uses *getbkcolor* to retrieve and save the current background color. Then use *setbkcolor* to repeatedly switch the background color (pick a random color). Reset the background to the saved value once the user presses any key.

```
#include <graphics.h>
#include <stdlib.h>

main()
{
    int graphdriver = DETECT, graphmode;
    int bcolor, maxcolor;

/* Initialize the graphics system */
    initgraph(&graphdriver, &graphmode, "c:\\tc\\bgi");
/* Get current background color and save it */
    bcolor = getbkcolor();
/* Now keep switching background colors randomly */
    maxcolor = getmaxcolor();
    randomize(); /* Initialize random number generator */
    outtextxy(10,20, "Press any key to exit");
    while (!kbhit())
    {
        setbkcolor(random(maxcolor));
        delay(1000);  /* Pause for 1 second */
    }
/* Wait for 1 second, then restore previous color */
    delay(1000);
    setbkcolor(bcolor);
    delay(1000);  /* Let user see the change */
    closegraph();
    return 0;
}
```

getcolor

COMPATIBILITY

TC1	TC1.5	TC2	TC++	MSC3	MSC4	MSC5	MSC6	QC1	QC2	QC2.5	ANSI	UNIX V	XNX
	▲	▲	▲			1	1	1	1	1			

PURPOSE Use the *getcolor* function to obtain the current drawing color.

SYNTAX

```
int far  getcolor(void);
```

EXAMPLE CALL

```
current_color = getcolor();
```

INCLUDES `#include <graphics.h>` *For function declaration*

DESCRIPTION The *getcolor* function is used to get back the current drawing color. This color is used by all line drawing routines. Until a color is set, the default value is the highest numbered color from the current palette (see the tutorial for an explanation of palettes). The current color may be set by calling *setcolor*.

1. In Microsoft C 5 and 6, and QuickC 1.0 through 2.5, use *_getcolor*.

COMMON USES The *getcolor* function is used to get the current color and save it so that if necessary it can be restored to its original value.

RETURNS The *getcolor* function returns the current color number.

SEE ALSO `setcolor` *To change to a new drawing color*

EXAMPLE Get the current color and draw a line to show that color. Then change to a new color, and verify that the change occurred by calling *getcolor*.

```
#include <stdio.h>
#include <graphics.h>

main()
{
    int graphdriver = DETECT, graphmode;
    int oldcolor;
    int y = 60;
    char buffer[80];

/* Initialize the graphics system */
    initgraph(&graphdriver, &graphmode, "c:\\tc\\bgi");
    outtextxy(10, 20, "Demonstrating getcolor");
/* Get current color */
    oldcolor = getcolor();
    sprintf(buffer,"Current color: %d", oldcolor);
    outtextxy(10, 40, buffer);
    moveto(0,y);
    lineto(500,y);
    y += 40;
/* Select a new color and verify by calling getcolor */
    setcolor(RED);
    sprintf(buffer,"New color: %d (should be 4)",
                    getcolor());
    outtextxy(10, y-20, buffer);
```

```
    moveto(0,y);
    lineto(500,y);
/* Restore previous color */
    setcolor(oldcolor);
/* Give user a chance to see the result */
    outtextxy(10, y+60, "Hit any key to exit:");
    getch();
    closegraph();  /* Close graphics system */
    return 0;
}
```

COMPATIBILITY

getdefaultpalette

TC1	TC1.5	TC2	TC++	MSC3	MSC4	MSC5	MSC6	QC1	QC2	QC2.5	ANSI	UNIX V	XNX
		▲	▲										

PURPOSE Use *getdefaultpalette* to obtain the palette set up by the current graphics driver when it was initialized during the call to *initgraph*.

SYNTAX

```
struct palettetype * far getdefaultpalette(void);
```

EXAMPLE CALL

```
struct palettetype *p_pal;
p_pal = getdefaultpalette();
printf("The default palette has %d colors\n",
        p_pal->size);
```

INCLUDES `#include <graphics.h>` *For function declaration*

DESCRIPTION The *getdefaultpalette* function returns a pointer to a *palettetype* structure that will contain information about the default palette set up by the current graphics driver during initialization. The *palettetype* structure is defined in the header file *graphics.h* as

```
struct palettetype
{
    unsigned char size;                /* Number of colors */
    signed   char colors[MAXCOLORS+1]; /* Current entries  */
};
```

where MAXCOLORS is a constant, defined to be 15. The field *size* in the *palettetype* structure will be the number of colors in the palette, and the actual color values will be in the array *colors*, elements zero through *size-1*.

COMMON USES The *getdefaultpalette* allows you to retrieve the default palette which can be used as an input to *setpalette* to revert to the original color settings of a driver.

RETURNS The *getdefaultpalette* function returns a pointer to a *palettetype* structure containing the default palette of the current driver.

SEE ALSO

`initgraph`	*To initialize the graphics system and load a graphics driver*
`getpalette`	*To get the current palette*
`getpalettesize`	*To get the number of colors in the current palette*
`setpalette`	*To set the palette*

EXAMPLE Use *getdefaultpalette* to get and print the number of colors in the default palette of the current driver.

```
#include <stdio.h>
#include <conio.h>
#include <graphics.h>
main()
{
    int graphdriver=DETECT, graphmode, numcolors;;
    struct palettetype *p_pal;
/* Detect and initialize the graphics system */
    initgraph(&graphdriver, &graphmode, "c:\\tc\\bgi");
/* Display the default palette of the current graphics driver */
    p_pal = getdefaultpalette();
    numcolors = p_pal->size;
    printf("The %s driver's default palette in %s mode "
           "has %d colors\n", getdrivername(),
           getmodename(graphmode), numcolors);

/* Wait for a keystroke before exiting */
    getch();
    closegraph();
    return 0;
}
```

Graphics Modes, Coordinates, and Attributes

COMPATIBILITY

getdrivername

TC1	TC1.5	TC2	TC++	MSC3	MSC4	MSC5	MSC6	QC1	QC2	QC2.5	ANSI	UNIX V	XNX
		▲	▲										

PURPOSE Use *getdrivername* to obtain the name of the current graphics driver (this is the name of the file with the .BGI extension that contains the driver code).

SYNTAX

```
char * far getdrivername(void);
```

EXAMPLE CALL

```
printf("Current graphics driver: %s\n", getdrivername());
```

INCLUDES

```
#include <graphics.h>      For function declaration
```

DESCRIPTION The *getdrivername* function allows you to obtain the name of the graphics driver (more specifically, the name of the driver's file with a .BGI extension) that is currently loaded. For example, in an EGA or VGA system, *getdrivername* will return the string EGAVGA.

RETURNS The *getdrivername* function returns a pointer to a string containing the name of the current driver.

COMMENTS When *initgraph* is called with the constant DETECT as the driver parameter, *initgraph* determines the system's graphics hardware and loads an appropriate graphics driver. In Turbo C 1.5, your program had no way of finding the name of the driver that was loaded by *initgraph*. The *getdrivername* function was introduced in Turbo C 2.0 to provide this capability.

SEE ALSO initgraph *To initialize the graphics system and load a graphics driver*

EXAMPLE Display the name of the graphics driver that is currently loaded. Use *getdrivername* to get the name of the driver.

```
#include <stdio.h>
#include <conio.h>
#include <graphics.h>
main()
{
    int graphdriver=DETECT, graphmode;
/* Detect and initialize the graphics system */
    initgraph(&graphdriver, &graphmode, "c:\\tc\\bgi");
/* Display the name of current graphics driver */
    printf("Current graphics driver: %s\n", getdrivername());
```

```
/* Wait for a keystroke before exiting */
    getch();
    closegraph();
    return 0;
}
```

getfillpattern

COMPATIBILITY

TC1	TC1.5	TC2	TC++	MSC3	MSC4	MSC5	MSC6	QC1	QC2	QC2.5	ANSI	UNIX V	XNX
	▲	▲	▲			1	1	1	1	1			

PURPOSE Use *getfillpattern* to retrieve the 8 bytes that define the current 8×8 pattern for use by the routines *bar, bar3d, fillpoly,* and *floodfill* to fill an area with the current fill color. See description of *setfillpattern* for an explanation of how the fill pattern is used.

SYNTAX

```
void far  getfillpattern(char far *pattern);

char far *pattern;
```

8x8 bit pattern that determines how the filled area looks

EXAMPLE CALL

```
char current_pattern[8];
getfillpattern(current_pattern);
```

INCLUDES

```
#include <graphics.h>
```

For function declaration

DESCRIPTION The *getfillpattern* function is used to retrieve the 8×8 pattern of bits that serves as the current pattern to be used by the routines *bar, bar3d, fillpoly,* and *floodfill* to fill an area with the current fill color.

The fill pattern is returned in 8 bytes whose starting address is provided to *getfillpattern* in the argument *pattern.* The reference page on *setfillpattern* explains how to interpret the fill pattern.

1. The compatible function in Microsoft C 5 and 6, and QuickC 1.0 through 2.5, is *_getfillmask.*

COMMON USES This function is used to get and save the current user-defined fill pattern so that the pattern can be restored to its original value before exiting a graphics routine.

COMMENTS The Turbo C++ graphics library provides a set of predefined fill patterns. You can select one of these with the function *setfillstyle.* The corresponding function for getting information on the current fill style is *getfillsettings.*

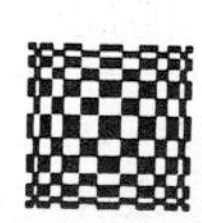

SEE ALSO

`getfillsettings`	*To get information on current fill style*
`setfillpattern`	*To define a new fill pattern*
`setfillstyle`	*To select a predefined fill style*

EXAMPLE Write a Turbo C++ program to define a fill pattern by using *setfillpattern*. Verify that this has indeed happened by calling *getfillpattern*.

```
#include <stdio.h>
#include <graphics.h>
/* Define a fill pattern */
char fillpat[8] =
    {1, 3, 7, 0xf, 0x1f, 0x3f, 0x7f, 0xff},
     oldpat[8];  /* Placeholder for old fill pattern */
main()
{
    int graphdriver = DETECT, graphmode;
    char buffer[80];

/* Initialize the graphics system */
    initgraph(&graphdriver, &graphmode, "c:\\tc\\bgi");
    outtextxy(10, 20, "Demonstrating getfillpattern");

/* Define a new pattern */
    setfillpattern(fillpat, RED);
    getfillpattern(oldpat);
    sprintf(buffer, "Current fill pattern is: %x %x %x \
%x %x %x %x %x", oldpat[0],oldpat[1],oldpat[2],oldpat[3], oldpat
[4],oldpat[5],oldpat[6],oldpat[7]);
    outtextxy(10, 40, buffer);
    outtextxy(10, 60, "Here is how it looks:");
/* Draw a bar with current fill pattern */
    bar(100, 100, 140, 200);
/* Give user a chance to see the result */
    outtextxy(10, 220, "Hit any key to exit:");
    getch();
    closegraph();  /* Close graphics system */
    return 0;
}
```

getfillsettings

COMPATIBILITY

TC1	TC1.5	TC2	TC++	MSC3	MSC4	MSC5	MSC6	QC1	QC2	QC2.5	ANSI	UNIX V	XNX
	▲	▲	▲										

PURPOSE Use *getfillsettings* to determine the current fill pattern and current fill color.

SYNTAX

```
void far  getfillsettings(struct fillsettingstype far *fillinfo);
```

```
struct fillsettingstype far *fillinfo;
```
Pointer to structure where fill pattern and color are returned

EXAMPLE CALL

```
struct fillsettingstype fsettings;
getfillsettings(&fsettings);
```

INCLUDES

```
#include <graphics.h>
```
For function declaration

DESCRIPTION The Turbo C++ graphics library includes twelve predefined fill patterns that can be referenced by the constants shown in Table 18-13. The *getfill-settings* function returns the current pattern number and current fill color in a *fillsettingstype* structure. This structure is defined in *graphics.h* as

```
struct fillsettingstype
{
    int pattern;    /* Pattern number */
    int color;      /* Fill color     */
};
```

You must allocate a *fillsettingstype* structure and provide its address to *getfillsettings* in the argument *fillinfo*. If a user-defined pattern is being used, the *pattern* field in the *fillsettingstype* structure will be equal to the constant USER_FILL.

COMMON USES You can use *getfillsettings* to determine if a user-defined pattern is in use. If you plan to define your own pattern, you can retrieve and save the previous user-defined pattern by calling *getfillpattern* so that later on you can restore the old fill pattern.

SEE ALSO

`getfillpattern` *To get the current fill pattern*

`setfillpattern` *To define a new fill pattern*

`setfillstyle` *To select a predefined fill style*

Graphics Modes, Coordinates, and Attributes

EXAMPLE Use *getfillsettings* to get information on the current fill pattern. Fill an area with this fill style.

```
#include <stdio.h>
#include <graphics.h>
/* Define the pattern names */
char *patname[] =
{ "Empty", "Solid", "Lines", "Thin slashes",
  "Thick slashes", "Thick backslashes",
  "Thin backslashes", "Hatch", "Crosshatch",
  "Interleaving lines", "Widely spaced dots",
  "Closely spaced dots", "User defined pattern"};

main()
{
    int graphdriver = DETECT, graphmode;
    struct fillsettingstype fsettings;
    char buffer[80];

/* Initialize the graphics system */
    initgraph(&graphdriver, &graphmode, "c:\\tc\\bgi");
    outtextxy(10, 20, "Demonstrating getfilsettings");

/* Get current fill settings and describe them */
    getfillsettings(&fsettings);
    sprintf(buffer,
        "Fill pattern is %s, fill color = %d",
         patname[fsettings.pattern], fsettings.color);
    outtextxy(10, 60, buffer);
    outtextxy(10, 80, "Here's how it looks");
    bar(100, 100, 120, 200);
/* Give user a chance to see the result */
    outtextxy(10, 220, "Hit any key to exit:");
    getch();
    closegraph();  /* Close graphics system */
    return 0;
}
```

getgraphmode

COMPATIBILITY

TC1	TC1.5	TC2	TC++	MSC3	MSC4	MSC5	MSC6	QC1	QC2	QC2.5	ANSI	UNIX V	XNX
	▲	▲	▲										

PURPOSE Use *getgraphmode* to determine the current graphics mode set by *initgraph* or *setgraphmode.*

SYNTAX

```
int far  getgraphmode(void);
```

EXAMPLE CALL

```
g_mode = getgraphmode();
```

INCLUDES #include <graphics.h> *For function declaration*

DESCRIPTION The graphics library in Turbo C++ assigns a range of mode numbers to each graphics device driver. For example, the CGA graphics driver has five modes numbered 0 through 4, and identified by the symbolic constants CGAC0, CGAC1, CGAC2, CGAC3, and CGAHI (Table 18-9 shows the mode constants for the other drivers). The *getgraphmode* function returns the mode in which the current driver is operating. For the CGA system, if you had let *initgraph* pick the default mode, the mode will be CGAHI which is the 640×200 two-color mode of the CGA.

COMMON USES If you switch graphics modes using *setgraphmode*, you can use *getgraphmode* to first get and save the old mode. That way, you can restore the old mode when you exit the graphics mode of your choice.

RETURNS The *getgraphmode* function returns the current graphics mode number.

COMMENTS You should be aware that the mode number used in Turbo C++ is not related to the BIOS video modes. In fact, mode 0 will have different meanings on different graphics drivers. For example, in CGA it is the 320×200 mode with palette 0, but in a Hercules driver (identified by the constant HERCMONO) it means the 720×348 two-color mode.

SEE ALSO

getmaxmode	*To get the maximum mode number allowed by the current graphics driver*
getmodename	*To get the name of a graphics mode*
getmoderange	*To determine the range of mode numbers valid for a specific graphics driver*
initgraph	*To set a driver to a specific mode*
setgraphmode	*To switch to a different graphics mode*

Graphics Modes, Coordinates, and Attributes

EXAMPLE Initialize the Turbo C++ graphics system. Then get the current mode using *getgraphmode* and display the mode number.

```
#include <graphics.h>

main()
{
  int errorcode;
  int graphdriver = DETECT;
  int graphmode, gmode;
  char buffer[80];

 /* Detect and initialize graphics system */
  initgraph(&graphdriver, &graphmode, "c:\\tc\\bgi");
  gmode = getgraphmode();
  sprintf(buffer,"Currently in graphics mode %d "
              "on driver %d", gmode, graphdriver);
  outtextxy( 10, getmaxy() / 2, buffer);

  outtextxy(getmaxx()/2, getmaxy() - 50,
"Press any key to exit:");
  getch();        /* Wait until a key is pressed */

  closegraph();          /* Exit graphics library */
  return 0;
}
```

getlinesettings

COMPATIBILITY

TC1	TC1.5	TC2	TC++	MSC3	MSC4	MSC5	MSC6	QC1	QC2	QC2.5	ANSI	UNIX V	XNX
	▲	▲	▲			1	1	1	1	1			

PURPOSE Use *getlinesettings* to retrieve the current line style used by the routines *line*, *lineto*, *rectangle*, *drawpoly*, and *pieslice* when drawing straight lines.

SYNTAX

```
void far  getlinesettings(struct linesettingstype far *lineinfo);
```

`struct linesettingstype far *lineinfo;` *Pointer to structure where line style is returned*

EXAMPLE CALL

```
struct linesettingstype lsetting;
getlinestyle(&lsetting);
```

INCLUDES `#include <graphics.h>` *For function declaration*

DESCRIPTION The *getlinesettings* function returns information about the current line style and width in a *linesettingstype* structure whose address is passed in the argument *lineinfo*. The *linesettingstype* structure is defined in the include file *graphics.h* as follows:

```
struct linesettingstype
{
    int      linestyle; /* Line style number                  */
    unsigned upattern;  /* Pattern, used only when linestyle
                           is USERBIT_LINE (4)                */
    int      thickness; /* Thickness 1 or 3 pixels            */
};
```

The *linestyle* denotes a predefined line style. The valid style numbers are identified by the constants listed in Table 18-14. When *linestyle* is equal to the constant USERBIT_LINE (which is defined in *graphics.h* as 4), the unsigned integer *upattern* in the *linesettingstype* structure represents a 16-bit pattern which determines the appearance of lines drawn by the routines such as *line*, *lineto*, and *rectangle*. The pattern defines whether the line is solid or dashed and, if dashed, the pattern of the dashes. The reference page on *setlinestyle* explains how the pattern is used.

1. In Microsoft C 5 and 6, and QuickC 1.0 through 2.5, use *_getlinestyle*.

COMMON USES The *getlinesettings* function is used to get and save the current line style before changing the style. That way, the line style can be reset to its original value at a later time.

SEE ALSO `setlinestyle` *To change to a new line style*

EXAMPLE Use *getlinesettings* to get the default line style and display the pertinent information. Draw a line to show how the current style looks. You will notice that the default style is a solid line with a width of one pixel.

```
#include <stdio.h>
#include <graphics.h>
/* Define the pattern names */
char *patname[] =
{ "Solid", "Dotted", "Centered", "Dashed",
  "User defined pattern"};

main()
```

```
{
    int graphdriver = DETECT, graphmode;
    struct linesettingstype lsettings;
    char buffer[80];

/* Initialize the graphics system */
    initgraph(&graphdriver, &graphmode, "c:\\tc\\bgi");
    outtextxy(10, 20, "Demonstrating getlinesettings");

/* Get current line settings and describe them */
    getlinesettings(&lsettings);
    sprintf(buffer,
        "Line style is %s, %d pixels wide",
         patname[lsettings.linestyle],
         lsettings.thickness);
    outtextxy(10, 60, buffer);
    sprintf(buffer, "Current line pattern is: %x",
            lsettings.upattern);
    outtextxy(10, 70, buffer);
    outtextxy(10, 90, "Here's how it looks");
    line(10,100,210,100);
/* Give user a chance to see the result */
    outtextxy(10, 220, "Hit any key to exit:");
    getch();
    closegraph();  /* Close graphics system */
    return 0;
}
```

COMPATIBILITY

getmaxcolor

TC1	TC1.5	TC2	TC++	MSC3	MSC4	MSC5	MSC6	QC1	QC2	QC2.5	ANSI	UNIX V	XNX
	▲	▲	▲										

PURPOSE Use *getmaxcolor* to determine the maximum possible pixel value for the current graphics mode.

SYNTAX `int far  getmaxcolor(void);`

EXAMPLE CALL `max_color = getmaxcolor();`

INCLUDES `#include <graphics.h>` *For function declaration*

DESCRIPTION The maximum possible pixel value is one less than the number of colors allowed in a graphics mode. The *getmaxcolor* function returns this number.

COMMON USES The *getmaxcolor* routine allows you to determine the range of valid colors for a particular graphics mode.

RETURNS The *getmaxcolor* function returns the maximum possible color number for the current mode.

SEE ALSO `getbkcolor` *To get the current background color*

`getpalette` *To determine the entire palette*

EXAMPLE Use *getmaxcolor* to get the maximum number of colors for the current mode. Then fill a set of rectangles with each of these colors.

```
#include <stdio.h>
#include <graphics.h>

main()
{
     int graphdriver = DETECT, graphmode;
     int i, maxcol;
     char buffer[80];

/* Initialize the graphics system */
     initgraph(&graphdriver, &graphmode, "c:\\tc\\bgi");
     outtextxy(10, 20, "Demonstrating getmaxcolor");

/* Get maximum color number and show it */
     maxcol = getmaxcolor();
     sprintf(buffer, "Maximum color number is %d",
             maxcol);
     outtextxy(10, 60, buffer);
     outtextxy(10, 80, "Here are all the colors");
     for (i=0; i<=maxcol; i++)
     {
         setfillstyle(SOLID_FILL, i);
         bar(100, 100+(i-1)*10, 120, 100+i*10);
     }
/* Give user a chance to see the result */
     outtextxy(10, 270, "Hit any key to exit:");
     getch();
     closegraph();  /* Close graphics system */
     return 0;
}
```

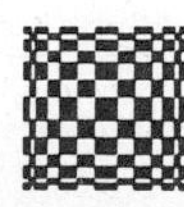

Graphics Modes, Coordinates, and Attributes

COMPATIBILITY

getmaxmode

TC1	TC1.5	TC2	TC++	MSC3	MSC4	MSC5	MSC6	QC1	QC2	QC2.5	ANSI	UNIX V	XNX
		▲	▲										

PURPOSE Use *getmaxmode* to determine the maximum mode number allowed in the current graphics driver. This function will work with any driver, whereas the *getmoderange* function works only with Borland-supplied graphics drivers.

SYNTAX

```
int far getmaxmode(void);
```

EXAMPLE CALL

```
max_mode = getmaxmode();
```

INCLUDES `#include <graphics.h>` *For function declaration*

DESCRIPTION The *getmaxmode* function allows you to query the current graphics driver (see the tutorial section for details) and get the maximum mode number that can be used when setting a graphics mode with *setgraphmode*.

RETURNS The *getmaxmode* function returns the maximum possible mode number in the current graphics driver.

COMMENTS The *getmoderange* function provides a similar capability, but it works with Borland graphics drivers only. The *getmaxmode* function, however, is designed to work with any graphics driver including ones that may have been developed by you (using specifications provided by Borland).

SEE ALSO `getmodename` *To get the name of a graphics mode*

`getmoderange` *To get the range of modes possible in a Borland supplied graphics driver*

EXAMPLE Use *getmaxmode* to get the maximum mode number allowed by the current graphics driver.

```
#include <stdio.h>
#include <conio.h>
#include <graphics.h>
main()
{
    int graphdriver=DETECT, graphmode;
/* Detect and initialize the graphics system */
    initgraph(&graphdriver, &graphmode, "c:\\tc\\bgi");
/* Print value of maximum mode number allowed */
```

```
    printf("Maximum mode number allowed on "
           "current graphics driver: %d\n",
            getmaxmode());
/* Wait for a keystroke before exiting */
    getch();
    closegraph();
    return 0;
}
```

getmaxx

COMPATIBILITY

TC1	TC1.5	TC2	TC++	MSC3	MSC4	MSC5	MSC6	QC1	QC2	QC2.5	ANSI	UNIX V	XNX
	▲	▲	▲										

PURPOSE Use *getmaxx* to obtain the maximum x-coordinate for the current display screen.

SYNTAX

```
int far  getmaxx(void);
```

EXAMPLE CALL

```
xmax = getmaxx();
```

INCLUDES `#include <graphics.h>` *For function declaration*

DESCRIPTION The *getmaxx* function allows you to determine the maximum possible x-coordinate of the display screen for the current driver and mode. For example, in CGA's 640×200 mode, *getmaxx* will return 639.

COMMON USES The *getmaxx* function and its companion *getmaxy* are useful for centering figures on the screen, and for scaling drawings to fit the available screen area.

RETURNS The *getmaxx* function returns the maximum x-coordinate of the screen in the current graphics mode.

SEE ALSO `getmaxy` *To get the maximum y-coordinate of the screen*

`getx, gety` *To get the x- and y-coordinates of the current position*

EXAMPLE Initialize for Turbo C++ graphics and display the maximum possible x-coordinate. Use *getmaxx* to obtain this information.

```
#include <stdio.h>
#include <graphics.h>
```

```
main()
{
    int graphdriver = DETECT, graphmode;
    int i, maxx;
    char buffer[80];

/* Initialize the graphics system */
    initgraph(&graphdriver, &graphmode, "c:\\tc\\bgi");
    outtextxy(10, 20, "Demonstrating getmaxx");

/* Get maximum x-coordinate and show it */
    maxx = getmaxx();
    sprintf(buffer, "Maximum x coordinate is %d",
            maxx);
    outtextxy(10, 60, buffer);
/* Give user a chance to see the result */
    outtextxy(10, 270, "Hit any key to exit:");
    getch();
    closegraph();  /* Close graphics system */
    return 0;
}
```

getmaxy

COMPATIBILITY

TC1	TC1.5	TC2	TC++	MSC3	MSC4	MSC5	MSC6	QC1	QC2	QC2.5	ANSI	UNIX V	XNX
	▲	▲	▲										

PURPOSE Use *getmaxy* to obtain the maximum y-coordinate for the current display screen.

SYNTAX `int far  getmaxy(void);`

EXAMPLE CALL `ymax = getmaxy();`

INCLUDES `#include <graphics.h>` *For function declaration*

DESCRIPTION The *getmaxy* function allows you to determine the maximum y-coordinate of the display screen for the current driver and mode. For example, in CGA's 320×200 mode, *getmaxy* will return 199.

COMMON USES The *getmaxy* function and its companion *getmaxx* are useful for centering figures on the screen, and for scaling drawings to fit the available screen area.

RETURNS The *getmaxy* function returns the maximum y-coordinate of the screen in the current graphics mode.

SEE ALSO `getmaxx` *To get the maximum x-coordinate of the screen*

`getx, gety` *To get the x- and y-coordinates of the current position*

EXAMPLE Show the maximum y-coordinate possible in the default graphics mode. Use *getmaxy* to obtain this information.

```
#include <stdio.h>
#include <graphics.h>

main()
{
    int graphdriver = DETECT, graphmode;
    int i, maxy;
    char buffer[80];

/* Initialize the graphics system */
    initgraph(&graphdriver, &graphmode, "c:\\tc\\bgi");
    outtextxy(10, 20, "Demonstrating getmaxy");

/* Get maximum y-coordinate and show it */
    maxy = getmaxy();
    sprintf(buffer, "Maximum y coordinate is %d",
            maxy);
    outtextxy(10, 60, buffer);
/* Give user a chance to see the result */
    outtextxy(10, 270, "Hit any key to exit:");
    getch();
    closegraph();  /* Close graphics system */
    return 0;
}
```

Graphics Modes, Coordinates, and Attributes

COMPATIBILITY

getmodename

TC1	TC1.5	TC2	TC++	MSC3	MSC4	MSC5	MSC6	QC1	QC2	QC2.5	ANSI	UNIX V	XNX
		▲	▲										

PURPOSE Use *getmodename* to determine the name of a graphics mode in the current graphics driver.

SYNTAX

```
char * far getmodename(int mode_number);
```

```
int mode_number;
```
Mode number whose name is requested

EXAMPLE CALL

```
printf("Current mode is: %s\n", getmodename(graphmode));
```

INCLUDES

```
#include <graphics.h>
```
For function declaration

DESCRIPTION The *getmodename* function allows you to get a string containing the descriptive name of the mode specified in the argument *mode_number*. The *mode_number* must lie within the range of mode numbers allowed by the current graphics driver. You can use the *getmaxmode* function to get the maximum mode number allowed by the current driver.

COMMON USES You can use the mode names to construct a menu of mode numbers available on a graphics driver. The range of mode numbers can be obtained by calling either *getmoderange* (for Borland drivers) or *getmaxmode* (for any driver).

RETURNS The *getmodename* function returns a string that contains the name of the graphics mode corresponding to *mode_number*.

SEE ALSO

getmaxmode — *To get the maximum possible mode number on the current graphics driver*

getmoderange — *To get the range of modes allowed on a Borland graphics driver*

EXAMPLE Get and display the name of the current graphics mode.

```
#include <stdio.h>
#include <conio.h>
#include <graphics.h>
main()
{
    int graphdriver=DETECT, graphmode;
/* Detect and initialize the graphics system */
```

```
    initgraph(&graphdriver, &graphmode, "c:\\tc\\bgi");
/* Display the name of current mode */
    printf("Current mode is: %s\n", getmodename(graphmode));
/* Wait for a keystroke before exiting */
    getch();
    closegraph();
    return 0;
}
```

getmoderange

COMPATIBILITY

TC1	TC1.5	TC2	TC++	MSC3	MSC4	MSC5	MSC6	QC1	QC2	QC2.5	ANSI	UNIX V	XNX
	▲	▲	▲										

PURPOSE Use *getmoderange* to determine the range of valid mode numbers for a specific graphics driver.

SYNTAX

```
void far  getmoderange(int graphdriver, int far *lomode,
                        int far *himode);
```

`int graphdriver;` *Graphics driver*

`int far *lomode;` *Address of integer where lowest permissible mode number is returned*

`int far *himode;` *Address of integer where highest permissible mode number is returned*

EXAMPLE CALL

```
int mode_low, mode_high;
getmoderange(VGA, &mode_low, &mode_high);
```

INCLUDES `#include <graphics.h>` *For function declaration*

DESCRIPTION The *getmoderange* function returns the range of acceptable mode numbers for a specified graphics driver (see the tutorial section). The argument *graphdriver* identifies the graphics adapter about which information is being sought. Table 18-9 lists the constants that may be used to specify the different graphics drivers. The lowest and highest values of the mode numbers are returned, respectively, in the integers whose addresses are in the arguments *lomode* and *himode*.

If *graphdriver* specifies an invalid graphics driver, *getmoderange* will set both **lomode* and **himode* to −1. To get the range of modes for the current graphics driver, call *getmoderange* with the argument *graphdriver* set to −1.

SEE ALSO

detectgraph	*To determine the graphics driver suitable for the graphics hardware on a system*
getgraphmode	*To get the current graphics mode*
getmaxmode	*To get the maximum mode number allowed by the current driver*
getmodename	*To get the descriptive name of a mode specified by a mode number*

EXAMPLE Determine the current display hardware using *detectgraph*. Then use *getmoderange* to obtain the valid Turbo C++ mode numbers for that adapter. Print your findings. Note that these mode numbers are not the same as the ones used by the BIOS routines.

```
  #include <graphics.h>

  main()
  {
    int graphdriver, graphmode, errorcode,
        lomode, himode;

/* Call detectgraph to determine hardware */
    detectgraph(&graphdriver, &graphmode);
    if (graphdriver < 0)
    {
printf("No graphics hardware available!\n");
exit(1);
    }
/* Now call getmoderange to determine the range of
 * modes supported by this adapter and report findings
 */
    getmoderange(graphdriver, &lomode, &himode);
    printf("'detectgraph()' reports: ");
    switch (graphdriver)
    {
case CGA:
    printf("Color Graphics Adapter");
    break;
case MCGA:
    printf("Multicolor Graphics Array");
    break;
case EGA:
```

```
case EGA64:
case EGAMONO:
    printf("Enhanced Graphics Adapter");
    break;
case HERCMONO:
    printf("Hercules Color Card");
    break;
case ATT400:
    printf("AT&T 640x400 card");
    break;
case VGA:
    printf("Video Graphics Array or IBM 8514");
    break;
case PC3270:
    printf("IBM PC 3270");
    break;
    }
    printf("\nwhich supports modes %d through %d\n",
            lomode, himode);
    printf("NOTE: These are not BIOS video modes\n");
    return 0;
  }
```

getpalette

COMPATIBILITY

TC1	TC1.5	TC2	TC++	MSC3	MSC4	MSC5	MSC6	QC1	QC2	QC2.5	ANSI	UNIX V	XNX
	▲	▲	▲										

PURPOSE Use *getpalette* to retrieve the current palette.

SYNTAX

```
void far  getpalette(struct palettetype far *palette);
```

`struct palettetype far *palette;` *Pointer to structure where the current palette is returned*

EXAMPLE CALL

```
struct palettetype cur_palette;
getpalette(&cur_palette);
```

INCLUDES `#include <graphics.h>` *For function declaration*

DESCRIPTION The *getpalette* function returns the current palette in a *palettetype* structure whose address you must provide in the argument *palette*. The *palettetype* structure is defined in the include file *graphics.h* as

```
struct palettetype
{
    unsigned char size;                /* Number of colors */
    signed   char colors[MAXCOLORS+1]; /* Current entries  */
};
```

where MAXCOLORS is a constant, defined to be 15 in *graphics.h*. The field *size* in the *palettetype* structure will be the number of colors in the palette, and the actual color values will be in the array *colors*, elements zero through *size-1*.

The default palettes for the CGA and the EGA/VGA are shown in Table 18-3. You can redefine the palette in EGA or VGA by using *setallpalette* or *setpalette*. On the CGA, only the first entry in the palette (which is pixel value 0 representing the background color) may be redefined.

COMMON USES The *getpalette* function lets you get and save the current palette on an EGA or a VGA before you use *setallpalette* to redefine the palette.

SEE ALSO

getdefaultpalette	*To get the default palette of the current driver*
getmaxcolor	*To get the maximum valid pixel value which is the same as* size-1
getpalettesize	*To get the number of colors in the current palette*
setpalette	*To redefine a single entry in the current palette*
setallpalette	*To redefine the entire palette*

EXAMPLE Write a Turbo C++ program to get and display the colors in the current palette.

```
#include <stdio.h>
#include <graphics.h>

main()
{
    int graphdriver = DETECT, graphmode, i;
    struct palettetype cur_palette;
    char buffer[80];

/* Initialize the graphics system */
    initgraph(&graphdriver, &graphmode, "c:\\tc\\bgi");
    outtextxy(10, 20, "Demonstrating getpalette");
```

```
/* Get current palette and print it out */
    getpalette(&cur_palette);
    sprintf(buffer, "Current palette has %d colors",
            cur_palette.size);
    outtextxy(10, 60, buffer);
    outtextxy(10, 70, "The entries are: ");
    moveto(10,80);
    for(i=0; i<cur_palette.size; i++)
    {
        sprintf(buffer, "%2d ", cur_palette.colors[i]);
        outtext(buffer);
    }
/* Give user a chance to see the result */
    outtextxy(10, 270, "Hit any key to exit:");
    getch();
    closegraph();  /* Close graphics system */
    return 0;
}
```

getpalettesize

COMPATIBILITY

TC1	TC1.5	TC2	TC++	MSC3	MSC4	MSC5	MSC6	QC1	QC2	QC2.5	ANSI	UNIX V	XNX
		▲	▲										

PURPOSE Use *getpalettesize* to obtain the number of colors in the current palette.

SYNTAX

```
int far getpalettesize(void);
```

EXAMPLE CALL

```
printf("Current palette has %d colors\n", getpalettesize());
```

INCLUDES

```
#include <graphics.h>
```

For function declaration

DESCRIPTION The *getpalettesize* routine is used to get the number of colors available in the current palette. For example, if your system has an EGA set in the high-resolution color mode, *getpalettesize* will return 16.

RETURNS The *getpalettesize* routine returns the number of colors available in the current palette.

SEE ALSO

`getpalette` *To get the current palette*

`setallpalette, setpalette` *To redefine the palette in EGA/VGA*

Graphics Modes, Coordinates, and Attributes

EXAMPLE Use *getpalettesize* to get the number of colors available in the current palette.

```
#include <stdio.h>
#include <conio.h>
#include <graphics.h>
main()
{
    int graphdriver=DETECT, graphmode;
/* Detect and initialize the graphics system */
    initgraph(&graphdriver, &graphmode, "c:\\tc\\bgi");
/* Get the number of colors in the current palette */
    printf("Current palette has %d colors\n",
            getpalettesize());
/* Wait for a keystroke before exiting */
    getch();
    closegraph();
    return 0;
}
```

COMPATIBILITY

getviewsettings

TC1	TC1.5	TC2	TC++	MSC3	MSC4	MSC5	MSC6	QC1	QC2	QC2.5	ANSI	UNIX V	XNX
	▲	▲	▲										

PURPOSE Use *getviewsettings* to get information about the current viewport.

SYNTAX

```
void far  getviewsettings(struct viewporttype far *viewport);
```

`struct viewporttype far *viewport;` *Pointer to structure where information about viewport is returned*

EXAMPLE CALL

```
struct viewporttype cur_view;
getviewsettings(&cur_view);
```

INCLUDES `#include <graphics.h>` *For function declaration*

DESCRIPTION The *viewport* is a rectangular area on the screen. The upper left hand corner of the viewport is used as the origin of the coordinate system used by all graphics functions, and optionally, graphics output can be clipped at the boundary of the viewport. Initially, the entire screen is used as the viewport.

The *getviewsettings* function returns information about the current viewport in a *viewporttype* structure which is defined in the header file *graphics.h* as

```
struct viewporttype
{
    int left,  top;       /* Coordinates of top left corner     */
    int right, bottom;    /* Coordinates of bottom right corner */
    int clip;             /* Clip flag (1 = ON, 0 = OFF)        */
};
```

You must define a *viewporttype* structure in your program, and pass its address in the argument *viewport*.

COMMON USES The main use of *getviewsettings* is to get and save the settings of the current viewport before defining a new one. This allows you to revert to the original viewport at a later time.

SEE ALSO

`setviewport` *To define a new viewport*

`clearviewport` *To erase the current viewport*

EXAMPLE Use *getviewsettings* to get the current viewport dimensions and display the retrieved information.

```
#include <stdio.h>
#include <graphics.h>

main()
{
    int graphdriver = DETECT, graphmode;
    struct viewporttype cur_view;
    char buffer[80];

/* Initialize the graphics system */
    initgraph(&graphdriver, &graphmode, "c:\\tc\\bgi");
    outtextxy(10, 20, "Demonstrating getviewsettings");

/* Get current viewport and print it out */
    getviewsettings(&cur_view);
    outtextxy(10, 60, "Current viewport settings");
    sprintf(buffer,"Left, top     = %d, %d",
                cur_view.left, cur_view.top);
    outtextxy(10, 70, buffer);
    sprintf(buffer,"Right, bottom = %d, %d",
                cur_view.right, cur_view.bottom);
```

```
    outtextxy(10, 80, buffer);
    if(!cur_view.clip)
        outtextxy(10,90,"Clipping OFF");
    else
        outtextxy(10,90,"Clipping ON");

/* Give user a chance to see the result */
    outtextxy(10, 270, "Hit any key to exit:");
    getch();
    closegraph();  /* Close graphics system */
    return 0;
}
```

COMPATIBILITY

getx

TC1	TC1.5	TC2	TC++	MSC3	MSC4	MSC5	MSC6	QC1	QC2	QC2.5	ANSI	UNIX V	XNX
	▲	▲	▲			1	1	1	1	1			

PURPOSE Use *getx* to obtain the x-coordinate of the current position with respect to the upper left corner of the current viewport.

SYNTAX

```
int far  getx(void);
```

EXAMPLE CALL

```
x_pos = getx();
```

INCLUDES `#include <graphics.h>` *For function declaration*

DESCRIPTION The graphics system in Turbo C++ maintains a current position. The *getx* function returns the x-coordinate of this position. Remember that the origin (0,0) of the coordinate system is at the top left corner of the current viewport.

1. Use *_getcurrentposition* in Microsoft C 5 and 6, and QuickC 1.0 through 2.5.

COMMON USES When drawing a closed polygon, you can use *getx* and *gety* to get and remember the current position so that you can close the figure by drawing a line from the last point to this remembered position.

RETURNS The *getx* function returns the x-coordinate of the current position.

SEE ALSO `getviewsettings` *To get the screen coordinates of the corners of the current viewport*

`gety`	*To get the y-coordinate of the current position*
`moveto`	*To move the current point in the viewport*

EXAMPLE Demonstrate the use of *getx* and *gety* to draw random triangles on the screen. First move to a point whose x and y coordinates are generated randomly. Use *getx* and *gety* to retrieve and save these coordinates. Now draw two more lines (use *lineto*) to random points. Finally join the last point to the first point using the coordinates you saved earlier.

```
#include <stdio.h>
#include <stdlib.h>
#include <graphics.h>

main()
{
    int graphdriver = DETECT, graphmode;
    int oldx, oldy;
    char buffer[80];

/* Initialize the graphics system */
    initgraph(&graphdriver, &graphmode, "c:\\tc\\bgi");
    outtextxy(10, 20, "Demonstrating getx and gety");

/* Draw random polygons with three vertices */
    randomize();
    moveto(random(getmaxx()), random(getmaxy()));
/* Save first point to close the figure */
    oldx = getx();
    oldy = gety();
/* Draw two line segments */
    lineto(random(getmaxx()), random(getmaxy()));
    lineto(random(getmaxx()), random(getmaxy()));
/* Now draw a line to first point to close figure */
    lineto(oldx, oldy);
/* Give user a chance to see the result */
    outtextxy(10, 270, "Hit any key to exit:");
    getch();
    closegraph();  /* Close graphics system */
    return 0;
}
```

Graphics Modes, Coordinates, and Attributes

COMPATIBILITY

gety

TC1	TC1.5	TC2	TC++	MSC3	MSC4	MSC5	MSC6	QC1	QC2	QC2.5	ANSI	UNIX V	XNX
	▲	▲	▲			1	1	1	1	1			

PURPOSE Use *gety* to obtain the y-coordinate of the current position with respect to the upper left corner of the current viewport.

SYNTAX

```
int far  gety(void);
```

EXAMPLE CALL

```
y_pos = gety();
```

INCLUDES `#include <graphics.h>` *For function declaration*

DESCRIPTION The graphics system in Turbo C++ maintains a current position. The *gety* function returns the y-coordinate of this position. Remember that the origin (0,0) of the coordinate system is at the top left corner of the current viewport.

1. The compatible function in Microsoft C 5 and 6, and QuickC 1.0 through 2.5, is *_getcurrentposition.*

COMMON USES When drawing a closed polygon, you can use *getx* and *gety* to get and remember the current position so that you can close the figure by drawing a line from the last point to this remembered posiiton.

RETURNS The *gety* function returns the y-coordinate of the current position.

SEE ALSO

`getviewsettings` *To get the screen coordinates of the corners of the current viewport*

`getx` *To get the x-coordinate of the current position*

`moveto` *To move the current point in the viewport*

EXAMPLE See the example in *getx.*

COMPATIBILITY

graphdefaults

TC1	TC1.5	TC2	TC++	MSC3	MSC4	MSC5	MSC6	QC1	QC2	QC2.5	ANSI	UNIX V	XNX
	▲	▲	▲										

PURPOSE Use *graphdefaults* to reset all settings of the Turbo C++ graphics system to their default values.

SYNTAX

```
void far  graphdefaults(void);
```

EXAMPLE CALL

```
graphdefaults();
```

INCLUDES `#include <graphics.h>` *For function declaration*

DESCRIPTION The Turbo C++ graphics library has default settings for its internal parameters. You can revert to the default settings by calling *graphdefaults*. Specifically, after the call to *graphdefaults*, the following settings take effect

- The entire screen becomes the current viewport with clipping enabled.
- The current position is moved to (0,0).
- The palette reverts to the default (see Table 18-3) with black background and white as the current drawing color.
- The fill style is solid with white as the fill color.
- The line style becomes solid.
- Graphics text is output using the 8×8 bit-mapped font, from left to right, with the lower left corner of text at the current position.

COMMON USES The *graphdefaults* function provides a way to reset the graphics system.

SEE ALSO `initgraph` *To initialize the graphics system*

EXAMPLE Define some graphics parameters such as viewport, line style, and color in a Turbo C++ program and draw a line. Now call *graphdefaults* and illustrate the default settings by redrawing the line.

```
#include <stdio.h>
#include <graphics.h>

main()
{
    int graphdriver = DETECT, graphmode;
    struct viewporttype cur_view;
    char buffer[80];

/* Initialize the graphics system */
    initgraph(&graphdriver, &graphmode, "c:\\tc\\bgi");
    outtextxy(10, 20, "Demonstrating graphdefaults");
/* Define a viewport with clipping ON */
    setviewport(10,100, 300, 300, 1);
/* Select color and line style */
    setcolor(RED);
    setlinestyle(DASHED_LINE, 0, THICK_WIDTH);
/* Draw a line from (10,50) to (getmaxx(),50) to
 * illustrate the viewport
 */
```

```
      line(10,50, getmaxx(),50);
/* Now revert back to default settings */
    outtextxy(10,20,"Press a key to call graphdefaults");
    getch();
    graphdefaults();
/* Repeat previous line drawing command to show result */
      line(10,50, getmaxx(),50);

/* Give user a chance to see the result */
    outtextxy(10, 270, "Press any key to exit:");
    getch();
    closegraph();  /* Close graphics system */
    return 0;
}
```

COMPATIBILITY

grapherrormsg

TC1	TC1.5	TC2	TC++	MSC3	MSC4	MSC5	MSC6	QC1	QC2	QC2.5	ANSI	UNIX V	XNX
	▲	▲	▲										

PURPOSE Use *grapherrormsg* to retrieve an error message using the error number returned by *graphresult.*

SYNTAX

```
char * far grapherrormsg(int errorcode);

int errorcode;        Error code returned by graphresult
```

EXAMPLE CALL

```
g_errorcode = graphresult();
if (g_errorcode != grOk)
    printf("%s\n", grapherrormsg(g_errorcode));
```

INCLUDES

```
#include <graphics.h>       For function declaration
```

DESCRIPTION The Turbo C++ graphics routines set an error code to indicate their completion status. You can obtain this error code by calling *graphresult.* The *grapherrormsg* function returns an error message string corresponding to the error code specified in the argument *errorcode.*

COMMON USES The *grapherrormsg* allows you to display a meaningful message when an error occurs (instead of printing a cryptic error code).

RETURNS The *grapherrormsg* function returns a pointer to a string containing the error message.

COMMENTS Each call to *graphresult* resets the error code to zero (or the constant *grOk* which means "no error"). If you plan to use the error code in several statements, you should get it and save it in a variable. For example,

```
if (graphresult() != grOk)
    printf("%s\n", grapherrormsg(graphresult()));
```

is incorrect because after the first call to *graphresult*, the error code is reset to zero. See the Example Call for a correct use.

SEE ALSO `graphresult` *To get the error code*

EXAMPLE Generate an error by calling *initgraph* with a wrong pathname for the graphics drivers (this is the directory where the .BGI files reside). Use *grapherrormsg* to print the error message corresponding to the resulting error code.

```
#include <stdio.h>
#include <graphics.h>

main()
{
    int graphdriver = DETECT, graphmode, errorcode;

/* Generate an error by calling initgraph with
 * wrong pathname for device drivers
 */
    initgraph(&graphdriver, &graphmode, "c:\\");
/* Display error message */
    printf(grapherrormsg(graphresult()));
    return 0;
}
```

Graphics Modes, Coordinates, and Attributes

COMPATIBILITY

_graphfreemem

TC1	TC1.5	TC2	TC++	MSC3	MSC4	MSC5	MSC6	QC1	QC2	QC2.5	ANSI	UNIX V	XNX
	▲	▲	▲										

PURPOSE The Turbo C++ graphics library calls *_graphfreemem* to free memory allocated by *initgraph* during initialization. Redefine *_graphfreemem* if you are supplying your own memory management routines for the graphics system.

SYNTAX

```
void far  _graphfreemem(void far *ptr, unsigned size);
```

`void far *ptr;` *Pointer to block of memory being released*

`unsigned size;` *Number of bytes in the block being released*

EXAMPLE CALL You do not have to call *_graphfreemem* directly.

INCLUDES `#include <graphics.h>` *For function declaration*

DESCRIPTION The Turbo C++ graphics library uses dynamically allocated memory for loading the graphics driver and the fonts, and for storing intermediate results of the flood fill operation. During initialization, *initgraph* calls the routine *_graphgetmem* to allocate this memory. When you exit the graphics system by calling *closegraph*, these memory blocks are released by calling *_graphfreemem*. The default version of *_graphfreemem* included in the library simply calls the standard library routine *free* to do its job.

Turbo C++ gives you the option of using your own memory management scheme. If you take this approach, you have to provide the routines *_graphfreemem* and *_graphgetmem*, which the graphics system will use to deallocate and allocate memory, respectively.

COMMON USES You may decide to use the far heap for graphics memory while in a small or medium memory model. In this case, you could redefine *_graphfreemem* to *farfree*.

COMMENTS When you replace *_graphfreemem*, make sure you also redefine *_graphgetmem* so that the allocation and deallocation schemes remain compatible with each other.

Note that *_graphfreemem* is called with the pointer as well as the size of the block of memory being deallocated. When a standard routine such as *free* is used to do the actual deallocation, the *size* argument is ignored. This argument is available in case your memory management scheme needs it.

SEE ALSO

`_graphgetmem`	*Corresponding allocation routine*
`closegraph`	*This routine calls* _graphfreemem

EXAMPLE See the example in *_graphgetmem*.

_graphgetmem

COMPATIBILITY

TC1	TC1.5	TC2	TC++	MSC3	MSC4	MSC5	MSC6	QC1	QC2	QC2.5	ANSI	UNIX V	XNX
	▲	▲	▲										

PURPOSE The Turbo C++ graphics library calls *_graphgetmem* during initialization to allocate memory necessary for graphics drivers and fonts. Redefine *_graphgetmem* if you are supplying your own memory management routines for the graphics system.

SYNTAX

```
void far * far  _graphgetmem(unsigned size);

unsigned size;        Number of bytes to be allocated
```

EXAMPLE CALL You do not have to call *_graphgetmem* directly.

INCLUDES `#include <graphics.h>` *For function declaration*

DESCRIPTION During initialization of the Turbo C++ graphics system, *initgraph* calls the routine *_graphgetmem* to allocate memory for loading the graphics driver and the fonts, and for storing the intermediate results of the flood fill operation. The default version of *_graphgetmem* included in the library simply calls the standard library routine *malloc* to do its job.

Turbo C++ gives you the option of using your own memory management scheme. If you take this approach, you have to provide the routines *_graphgetmem* and *_graphfreemem*, which the graphics system will use to allocate and deallocate memory, respectively.

COMMON USES A possible use is to use the far heap for graphics memory while in a small or medium memory model. In this case, you could redefine *_graphgetmem* to *farmalloc*.

COMMENTS When you replace *_graphgetmem*, make sure you also redefine *_graphfreemem* so that the allocation and deallocation schemes remain compatible with each other.

SEE ALSO

`_graphfreemem`	*Corresponding deallocation routine*
`initgraph`	*This routine calls* _graphgetmem

Graphics Modes, Coordinates, and Attributes

EXAMPLE Illustrate the use of your own memory allocation routines by writing *_graphgetmem* and *_graphfreemem*, which use the routines *farmalloc* and *farfree,* respectively, to do the job. Print a diagnostic message in each of these routines. These messages indicate that, in this example, the allocation routine, *_graphgetmem,* will be called twice during *initgraph*: once for the graphics driver and the second time for the 4-K buffer to be used by the fill algorithms. Then *_graphgetmem* is called a third time when you select a font with *settextstyle* . This is the memory used to load the font. Later on, *_graphfreemem* is called from *closegraph* to deallocate each of these blocks.

```
#include <stdio.h>
#include <graphics.h>
#include <alloc.h>

main()
{
  int errorcode;
  int graphdriver = DETECT;
  int graphmode;

/* Detect and initialize graphics system */
  initgraph(&graphdriver, &graphmode, "c:\\tc\\bgi");
  errorcode = graphresult();
  if (errorcode != grOk)
  {
    printf("Graphics error: %s\n",
    grapherrormsg(errorcode));
    exit(1);
  };

  settextjustify(CENTER_TEXT, CENTER_TEXT);
  settextstyle(SANS_SERIF_FONT, HORIZ_DIR, 1);
  outtextxy( getmaxx() / 2, getmaxy() / 2,
  "Illustrating  user-defined memory allocation");

  outtextxy(getmaxx()/2, getmaxy() - 50,
            "Press any key to exit:");
  getch();        /* Wait until a key is pressed */

  closegraph();         /* Exit graphics library */
  return 0;
}
/*-----------------------------------------------------*/
  void far * far _graphgetmem(unsigned size)
```

```
  {
      printf("\nMemory of size %d requested from \
_graphmem\n", size);
      printf("Press any key to continue...");
      getch();
/* Allocate memory from far heap */
      return(farmalloc(size));
  }
/*--------------------------------------------------*/
  void far _graphfreemem(void far *memptr,
                                 unsigned size)
  {
      printf("\nFreeing memory of size %d \
(_graphfreemem)\n", size);
      printf("Press any key to continue...");
      getch();
/* Release far memory */
      farfree(memptr);
  }
```

graphresult

COMPATIBILITY

TC1	TC1.5	TC2	TC++	MSC3	MSC4	MSC5	MSC6	QC1	QC2	QC2.5	ANSI	UNIX V	XNX
	▲	▲	▲										

PURPOSE Use *graphresult* to obtain the error code for the last graphics operation.

SYNTAX `int far  graphresult(void);`

EXAMPLE CALL `g_errorcode = graphresult();`

INCLUDES `#include <graphics.h>` *For function declaration*

DESCRIPTION The Turbo C++ graphics routines set an internal error code to indicate whether the graphics operation was successful or not. The *graphresult* function returns the current error code. It resets the error code to zero before returning. Thus, you should save the retrieved value if you plan to use it in subsequent statements.

COMMON USES The *graphresult* routine should be called after every graphics routine that may produce an error. It is best to use it in conjunction with *grapherrormsg* in the following manner:

```
g_errorcode = graphresult();
if (g_errorcode != grOk)
{
    printf("Graphics error: %s\n", grapherrormsg(g_errorcode));
/* Exit if you cannot go on after the error */
}
```

RETURNS The *graphresult* function returns the graphics error code. You should interpret the error code by comparing with the constants shown in Table 18-7. These error codes are defined in the include file *graphics.h* as the enumeration set of the *graphics_errors* enumeration type. You can retrieve the error message corresponding to an error code by calling *grapherrormsg.*

Table 18-7. *Turbo C Graphics Error Codes*

graphics_errors Constant	Value	Error Message
grOk	0	No error.
grNoInitGraph	−1	(BGI) graphics not installed (use *initgraph*.
grNotDetected	−2	Graphics hardware not detected.
grFileNotFound	−3	Device driver file not found.
grInvalidDriver	−4	Invalid device driver file.
grNoLoadMem	−5	Not enough memory to load driver.
grNoScanMem	−6	Out of memory in scan fill.
grNoFloodMem	−7	Out of memory in flood fill.
grFontNotFound	−8	Font file not found.
grNoFontMem	−9	Not enough memory to load font.
grInvalidMode	−10	Invalid graphics mode for selected driver.
grError	−11	Graphics error.
grIOerror	−12	Graphics I/O error.
grInvalidFont	−13	Invalid font file.
grInvalidFontNum	−14	Invalid font number
grInvalidDeviceNum	−15	Invalid device number.
grInvalidVersion	−18	Invalid version number (the .BGI drivers from Turbo C 1.5 will not work with Turbo C 2.0).

COMMENTS Error handling is one of the crucial aspects of a successful commercial software product. If you are developing graphics applications in Turbo C++, you should make use of *graphresult* and *grapherrormsg* to handle the error conditions and avoid surprises.

SEE ALSO `grapherrormsg` *To get the error message corresponding to an error code returned by* graphresult

EXAMPLE Demonstrate the use of *graphresult* to get the error code after a graphics operation.

```
#include <stdio.h>
#include <graphics.h>

main()
{
    int graphdriver = DETECT, graphmode, errorcode;
/* Generate an error by calling initgraph with
 * wrong pathname for device drivers
 */
    initgraph(&graphdriver, &graphmode, "c:\\");
    errorcode = graphresult();
    if(errorcode != 0)
    {
        printf("Graphics error!");
        printf("Error code is %d\n", errorcode);
    }
    else
        printf("No error detected\n");
    return 0;
}
```

initgraph

COMPATIBILITY

TC1	TC1.5	TC2	TC++	MSC3	MSC4	MSC5	MSC6	QC1	QC2	QC2.5	ANSI	UNIX V	XNX
	▲	▲	▲										

PURPOSE Use *initgraph* to initialize the Turbo C++ graphics system.

SYNTAX

```
void far  initgraph(int  far *graphdriver, int  far *graphmode, char far
*pathtodriver);
```

`int far  *graphdriver;`	*Pointer to integer that holds the graphics driver number*
`int far  *graphmode;`	*Pointer to integer representing the mode*
`char far *pathtodriver;`	*Full pathname of directory where the driver files (the .BGI files) reside*

EXAMPLE CALL

```
int graphdriver = DETECT, graphmode;
/* Automatically detect graphics hardware and initialize */
initgraph(&graphdriver, &graphmode, "c:\\tc\\bgi");
```

INCLUDES `#include <graphics.h>` *For function declaration*

DESCRIPTION The *initgraph* function initializes the Turbo C++ graphics system by loading a device driver (see the tutorial section) and putting the adapter in a graphics mode. The graphics driver and mode are specified in two integers whose addresses you must provide in the arguments *graphdriver* and *graphmode* respectively. You can specify the driver using a constant from Table 18-8. Each driver supports a number of modes. Symbolic constants for the modes are shown in Table 18-9. The driver constants are of enumeration type *graphics_drivers* and the mode constants are of enumeration type *graphics_modes*, both defined in the include file *graphics.h*.

The third argument to *initgraph*, *pathtodriver*, is a string that indicates the drive and the directory where the graphics driver files (the files with the .BGI extension) reside. In the example call above, we have assumed that the drivers are in C:\TURBOC. When specifying this pathname via a string constant, you must remember to use two backslashes as directory separators because the backslash is an escape character in C.

If the driver is not found in the specifed path, *initgraph* will also search the current directory for the .BGI files. Thus, if *pathtodriver* is NULL, the drivers must be in the current directory.

Turboc C++ provides a way to initialize the graphics system even when you do not know the type of graphics adapter present in a system. If you specify the constant DETECT as the driver, *initgraph* will call *detectgraph* to select a driver and the highest resolution mode allowed on that adapter, and go on to initialize the system based on this information.

In addition to putting the adapter in graphics mode, *initgraph* calls *_graphgetmem* to allocate memory necessary for the device driver, and for storing intermediate results of the fill operations. It also resets all graphics settings to their defaults (see *graphdefaults* for details).

The Turbo C++ graphics library gives you the option of linking graphics drivers into your program. In this case, you must call *registerbgidriver* or *registerfarbgidriver* to make the drivers known to the graphics system. This should be done before calling *initgraph*. Then *initgraph* will not attempt to load the drivers from the disk.

If *initgraph* encounters an error condition, it will set the error code, and also copy the error code to the integer **graphdriver*. The four possible errors are:

Enumerated Constant	Value	Description
grNotDetected	−2	Graphics hardware not detected.
grFileNotFound	−3	Device driver file not found.
grInvalidDriver	−4	Invalid device driver file.
grNoLoadMem	−5	Not enough memory to load driver.

You can retrieve the error code by calling *graphresult.*

Table 18-8. ***Graphics Drivers in Turbo C++***

graphics_drivers Enumerated Constant	Value	Description
DETECT	0	Automatic detection requested.
CGA	1	Color Graphics Adapter.
MCGA	2	Multicolor Graphics Array.
EGA	3	Enhanced Graphics Adapter with 128 K or more memory and enhanced color display monitor.
EGA64	4	Enhanced Graphics Adapter with 64 K memory and enhanced color display monitor.
EGAMONO	5	Enhanced Graphics Adapter with a monochrome monitor.
IBM8514	6	IBM 8514 graphics card with 8514 analog monitor.
HERCMONO	7	Hercules Graphics Card with a monochrome monitor.
ATT400	8	AT&T 400-line graphics adapter.
VGA	9	Video Graphics Array and analog monitor.
PC3270	10	IBM 3270 PC graphics adapter.

Table 18-9. ***Graphics Modes for Various Drivers in Turbo C++***

Mode Constant	Interpretation	Graphics Driver
CGAC0	320×200 palette 0, 1 page	CGA
CGAC1	320×200 palette 1, 1-page	CGA
CGAC2	320×200 palette 2, 1-page	CGA
CGAC3	320×200 palette 3, 1-page	CGA
CGAHI	640×200 2-color, 1-page	CGA
MCGAC0	320×200 palette 0, 1-page	MCGA
MCGAC1	320×200 palette 1, 1-page	MCGA
MCGAC2	320×200 palette 2, 1-page	MCGA
MCGAC3	320×200 palette 3, 1-page	MCGA
MCGAMED	640×200 2-color, 1-page	MCGA
MCGAHI	640×480 2-color, 1-page	MCGA
EGALO	640×200 16-color, 4-page	EGA
EGAHI	640×350 16-color, 2-page	EGA
EGA64LO	640×200 16-color, 1-page	EGA64
EGA64HI	640×350 4-color, 1-page	EGA64
EGAMONOHI	640×350 64 K on card, 1-page, 256-K video memory, 4-page	EGAMONO
HERCMONOHI	720×348 2-page	HERCMONO

Graphics Modes, Coordinates, and Attributes

Table 18-9. *(cont.)*

Mode Constant	Interpretation	Graphics Driver
ATT400C0	320×200 palette 0, 1-page	ATT400
ATT400C1	320×200 palette 1, 1-page	ATT400
ATT400C2	320×200 palette 2, 1-page	ATT400
ATT400C3	320×200 palette 3, 1-page	ATT400
ATT400MED	640×200 1-page	ATT400
ATT400HI	640×400 1-page	ATT400
VGALO	640×200 16-color, 4-page	VGA
VGAMED	640×350 16-color, 2-page	VGA
VGAHI	640×480 16 color 1 page	VGA
PC3270HI	720×350 1 page	PC3270
IBM8514LO	640×480 256-color	IBM8514
IBM8514HI	1024×768 256-color	IBM8514

COMMON USES You must use *initgraph* to initialize the Turbo C++ graphics system before any graphics function can be called. The most common approach is to call *initgraph* with the driver set to DETECT so that the hardware is automatically detected and the highest resolution graphics mode selected.

COMMENTS Since initialization is a crucial step in using the Turbo C++ graphics routines, you should always check for error during initialization. The example below shows a typical method of checking for errors during initialization.

SEE ALSO

`closegraph` — *To exit the graphics system*

`detectgraph` — *To determine the driver and mode suitable for existing graphics adapter and monitor*

`getdrivername` — *To get the name of the .BGI file that is currently loaded*

`installuserdriver` — *To install a new graphics driver*

`registerbgidriver, registerfarbgidriver` — *To register linked-in graphics drivers*

`restorecrtmode` — *To switch to text mode*

`setgraphbufsize` — *To specify size of buffer to be used by fill routines*

EXAMPLE The *initgraph* function appears in any Turbo C++ program that uses the graphics system. Here is a small program that shows the steps that should be taken to properly initialize the Turbo C++ graphics library.

```
#include <graphics.h>

main()
{
  int errorcode;
  int graphdriver = DETECT;
  int graphmode;

/* Detect and initialize graphics system */
  initgraph(&graphdriver, &graphmode, "c:\\tc\\bgi");
  errorcode = graphresult();
  if (errorcode != grOk)
  {
    printf("Graphics error: %s\n",
    grapherrormsg(errorcode));
    exit(1);
  };

  settextjustify(CENTER_TEXT, CENTER_TEXT);
  settextstyle(SANS_SERIF_FONT, HORIZ_DIR, 1);
  outtextxy( getmaxx() / 2, getmaxy() / 2,
  "Graphics programs must start with initgraph()");
   outtextxy(getmaxx()/2, getmaxy() - 50,
                  "Press any key to exit:");
  getch();         /* Wait until a key is pressed */
  closegraph();          /* Exit graphics library */
}
```

installuserdriver

COMPATIBILITY

TC1	TC1.5	TC2	TC++	MSC3	MSC4	MSC5	MSC6	QC1	QC2	QC2.5	ANSI	UNIX V	XNX
		▲	▲										

PURPOSE Use *installuserdriver* to add the name of a new graphics driver to the internal table that is maintained by the Turbo C++ graphics system.

SYNTAX

```
int far installuserdriver(char far *name, int huge (*detect)(void));
```

`char far *name;` *The name of the new driver*

```
int huge (*detect)(void);
```
The function that will be called during the automatic detection and selection of a graphics driver

EXAMPLE CALL

```
installuserdriver("MYDRIVER", detect_me);
```

INCLUDES

```
#include <graphics.h>
```
For function declaration

DESCRIPTION The *installuserdriver* function adds to an internal table the name of the graphics driver (see the the tutorial section for more on such drivers) specified in the argument *name*. The driver's code is expected to reside in a disk file with the same name and a .BGI extension. The argument *detect* is the address of a function in the driver that will be called by the graphics system during the initialization process when detecting and selecting a graphics driver appropriate for the graphics hardware present in the system.

COMMON USES This function makes it possible to add new graphics drivers to the Turbo C++ graphics library. Since the format of the .BGI files has been released, the function is useful with user-written drivers that support new graphics displays and adapters.

RETURNS The *installuserdriver* function returns an integer which you should save. You can provide this number to *initgraph* as the driver identifier when you want to explicitly load this driver.

COMMENTS This function is very useful, because Borland has released the specifications for the .BGI graphics driver. With this information you could write your own drivers for specialized graphics devices and use the new drivers with the Turbo C++ graphics library.

SEE ALSO

`initgraph`	*To initialize the graphics system*
`registerbgidriver`	*To inform the graphics system about a linked-in graphics driver*

registerbgidriver, registerfarbgidriver

COMPATIBILITY

TC1	TC1.5	TC2	TC++	MSC3	MSC4	MSC5	MSC6	QC1	QC2	QC2.5	ANSI	UNIX V	XNX
	▲	▲	▲										

PURPOSE Use *registerbgidriver* and *registerfarbgidriver* to inform the graphics system about linked-in graphics driver code (see the tutorial section for details of graphics drivers).

SYNTAX

```
int  registerbgidriver(void (*driver)(void));
int far  registerfarbgidriver(void far *driver);
```

`driver` *Use a name constructed by appending "_driver" or "_driver_far" to the name of the .BGI file of the driver*

EXAMPLE CALL

```
if(registerbgidriver(EGAVGA_driver) < 0)
{
    printf("Error registering driver: EGAVGA\n");
    exit(1);
}
```

INCLUDES

`#include <graphics.h>` *For function declaration*

DESCRIPTION

The Turbo C++ graphics library supports output to specific graphics adapters through an installable graphics driver. These drivers are stored in files with the .BGI extension. When the graphics system is initialized by calling *initgraph*, the appropriate graphics driver is loaded into memory, and certain far function pointers are initialized to point to the driver's code. From then on, the graphics system accesses the driver through this function pointer.

Normally, *initgraph* loads a selected graphics driver from the disk (a file with the .BGI extension), and sets up the function pointer to this driver. Turbo C++ provides a way to link the driver code directly into your program's executable file. This is done by first converting a driver from its .BGI file to an object code file (.OBJ extension) using the BGIOBJ utility, and then linking this object file to the rest of your program in the usual way. The tutorial section contains a detailed discussion of the steps involved in linking with a driver.

The *registerbgidriver* and *registerfarbgidriver* functions are necessary when a program has linked in one or more drivers. These routines essentially tell the graphics system that the drivers are already present, so that *initgraph* does not try to load them from the disk. These *registration* routines must be called before *initgraph*.

BGIOBJ can convert a .BGI file into object code that uses a fixed segment name. In this case, you have to use *registerbgidriver* to register a driver. The use of a fixed segment name can cause a problem when there are several drivers and they cannot all fit into a single 64-K physical segment. When this happens, you can use the /F option flag with BGIOBJ to generate an object file with a unique segment name. For .OBJ files converted using BGIOBJ /F, you must use *registerfarbgidriver* for registration. For example, if you converted and linked two driver files, EGAVGA.BGI and HERC.BGI, the first with BGIOBJ alone, and the second with the /F flag, the registration calls will be

```
if(registerbgidriver(EGAVGA_driver) < 0)
{
    printf("Error registering driver: EGAVGA\n");
    exit(1)
}
if(registerfarbgidriver(Herc_driver_far) < 0)
{
    printf("Error registering driver: HERC\n");
    exit(1)
}
initgraph(&graphdriver, &graphmode, NULL);
```

The name of the driver is constructed by appending *_driver* to the name of the .BGI file. When the /F option is used with BGIOBJ, the name has an extra *_far* appended to it. Table 18-10 lists the drivers by name and shows the driver name you must use when registering the driver.

Table 18-10. *Graphics Drivers (.BGI Files) in Turbo C 2.0 and Turbo C++*

Driver File (.BGI)	Name When Used with *registerbgidriver*	Name When Used with *registerfarbgidriver*
CGA	CGA_driver	CGA_driver_far
EGAVGA	EGAVGA_driver	EGAVGA_driver_far
IBM8514	IBM8514_driver	IBM8514_driver_far
Herc	Herc_driver	Herc_driver_far
ATT	ATT_driver	ATT_driver_far
PC3270	PC3270_driver	PC3270_driver_far

COMMON USES The *registerbgidriver* and *registerfarbgidriver* routines are used when you have to link in graphics drivers with your programs. This will often be the case with software that is being distributed because bundling the driver makes the program self-contained.

RETURNS Both *registerbgidriver* and *registerfarbgidriver* return nonnegative values when they are successful. In case of error, each returns a negative value.

COMMENTS The concept of a graphics driver (explained further in the tutorial section) is useful in isolating device dependencies in Turbo C++ graphics programs. The graphics library can support additional graphics adapters simply by providing a driver for the new hardware. Because the format is known, even you or I could add our own graphics drivers. Turbo C++ uses a similar technique to handle the stroke fonts used in graphics text output.

SEE ALSO

`getdrivername`	*To get the name of the .BGI file that is currently loaded*
`initgraph`	*To initialize the graphics system*
`installuserdriver`	*To add a new graphics driver to the internal tables that are maintained by the Turbo C graphics system*
`registerbgifont, registerfarbgifont`	*To register loadable stroke fonts*

EXAMPLE This example assumes that you are using an EGA/VGA system. For other systems, use the driver name for your graphics hardware. First use *BGIOBJ* to convert the file EGAVGA.BGI to EGAVGA.OBJ. Then prepare a project file with the following contents:

```
rbgi
egavga.obj
```

where we assumed that the example program, shown below, resides in the file named RBGI.C. Now you can use the Turbo C environment, TC, to build and test the program.

```
/* Use a project file with this program and EGAVGA.OBJ
 * in it. Use BGIOBJ to convert EGAVGA.BGI to EGAVGA.OBJ
 * before linking the program.
 */

  #include <stdio.h>
  #include <graphics.h>
  #include <alloc.h>

  main()
  {
    int errorcode;
    int graphdriver = DETECT;
    int graphmode;
  /* Register the linked-in driver EGAVGA */
    if(registerbgidriver(EGAVGA_driver) < 0)
    {
printf("Driver could not be registered!\n");
exit(0);
    }
  /* Detect and initialize graphics system */
    initgraph(&graphdriver, &graphmode, NULL);
    errorcode = graphresult();
    if (errorcode != grOk)
```

```
{
  printf("Graphics error: %s\n",
  grapherrormsg(errorcode));
  exit(1);
};

settextjustify(CENTER_TEXT, CENTER_TEXT);
settextstyle(SANS_SERIF_FONT, HORIZ_DIR, 1);
outtextxy( getmaxx() / 2, getmaxy() / 2,
"This program uses a linked-in driver: EGAVGA");

outtextxy(getmaxx()/2, getmaxy() - 50,
          "Press any key to exit:");
getch();        /* Wait until a key is pressed */
closegraph();         /* Exit graphics library */
return 0;
}
```

restorecrtmode

COMPATIBILITY

TC1	TC1.5	TC2	TC++	MSC3	MSC4	MSC5	MSC6	QC1	QC2	QC2.5	ANSI	UNIX V	XNX
	▲	▲	▲										

PURPOSE Use *restorecrtmode* to reset the screen to the original video mode detected by *initgraph* before it initialized the graphics system.

SYNTAX

```
void far  restorecrtmode(void);
```

EXAMPLE CALL

```
restorecrtmode();
```

INCLUDES `#include <graphics.h>` *For function declaration*

DESCRIPTION When *initgraph* initializes the graphics system, it detects and saves the video mode from which *initgraph* was originally called. Typically, this is a text mode. The *restorecrtmode* function reverts the display to that saved mode.

COMMON USES Normally, *restorecrtmode* is used to go back to the text mode from a graphics mode.

COMMENTS You should retrieve the current graphics mode by using *getgraphmode* before you call *restorecrtmode*. Then you can use *setgraphmode* to return to the graphics mode.

SEE ALSO

getgraphmode — *To obtain the current graphics mode*

setgraphmode — *To go to a graphics mode*

EXAMPLE Illustrate the use of *restorecrtmode* to return to the text mode from a graphics mode. Note that you can use *setgraphmode* to return to the graphics mode.

```
#include <graphics.h>
#include <conio.h>

main()
{
  int errorcode;
  int graphdriver = DETECT;
  int graphmode;

/* Detect and initialize graphics system */
  initgraph(&graphdriver, &graphmode, "c:\\tc\\bgi");

  settextjustify(CENTER_TEXT, CENTER_TEXT);
  settextstyle(SANS_SERIF_FONT, HORIZ_DIR, 1);
  outtextxy( getmaxx() / 2, getmaxy() / 2,
  "You are in graphics mode now...");
   outtextxy(getmaxx()/2, getmaxy() - 50,
      "Press any key to switch to text mode");
  getch();
/* Switch to text mode */
  restorecrtmode();
  gotoxy(20,1);
  cputs(      "Press any key to return to graphics mode...");
  getch();
/* Back to graphics mode again */
  setgraphmode(graphmode);
  outtextxy( 10, getmaxy() / 2,
 "Graphics mode again. Notice everything's reset.");
  outtextxy(getmaxx()/2, getmaxy() - 50,
                 "Press any key to exit:");
  getch();        /* Wait until a key is pressed */
  closegraph();         /* Exit graphics library */
  return 0;
}
```

Graphics Modes, Coordinates, and Attributes

COMPATIBILITY

setactivepage

TC1	TC1.5	TC2	TC++	MSC3	MSC4	MSC5	MSC6	QC1	QC2	QC2.5	ANSI	UNIX V	XNX
	▲	▲	▲			1	1	1	1	1			

PURPOSE Use *setactivepage* to select the current "page" or portion of display memory where graphics operations are performed. This function will work only when the adapter has enough video memory to support multiple pages.

SYNTAX

```
void far  setactivepage(int page);
```

`int page;` *The video page number to be used for all further graphics output*

EXAMPLE CALL

```
setactivepage(1);
```

INCLUDES `#include <graphics.h>` *For function declaration*

DESCRIPTION The *setactivepage* function selects the page specified in the argument *page* as the current "active" page. This determines the section of video memory where graphics output will go.

A page in this context means a chunk of storage in the video memory that can hold the contents of a screen in the current video mode. For example, if the video adapter has enough memory to hold two screenfuls of graphics, then you can have two pages. Only EGA and VGA with 256 K of video memory and the Hercules graphics card support multiple pages in graphics modes.

Just as the current active page determines the portion of video memory where results of graphics operations are stored, the current "visual" page determines the portion of video memory that is actually mapped onto the display screen. Use *setvisualpage* to select the page being displayed. By default, page 0 is used as both "active" and "visual" page.

1. In Microsoft C 5 and 6, and QuickC 1.0 through 2.5, use *_setactivepage*.

COMMON USES Provided you have enough video memory for multiple pages, the *setactivepage* function is useful for preparing a page in display memory while another is being shown to the user. This can speed up the display or allow for smoother animation.

SEE ALSO `setvisualpage` *To select the page being displayed*

EXAMPLE Assuming you have an EGA with 256 K of graphics memory, you can have two graphics pages, each page capable of storing one 640×350, 16-color display screen. Draw a red rectangle on page 0, and while this is being displayed, use *setactivepage* to select page 1 and draw a yellow ellipse on this page. Next let the user flip through the two pages (use the *setvisualpage* function).

```
#include <stdio.h>
#include <graphics.h>

main()
{
    int i;
    short page = 0;
    int graphdriver = DETECT;
    int graphmode;

  /* Detect and initialize graphics system */
    initgraph(&graphdriver, &graphmode, "c:\\tc\\bgi");
    if (graphdriver != EGA || graphmode != EGAHI)
    {
      printf("Need EGA with 256 K in 640x350 mode\n");
      exit(1);
    };
/* Default active page is page 0. Draw a red rectangle
 * in page 0.
 */
    setcolor(RED);
    outtextxy(10, 10, "This is page 0");
    rectangle(20, 50, 120, 100);
/* Now set active page to 1 */
    setactivepage(1);
/* Draw a yellow ellipse on this page */
    setcolor(YELLOW);
    outtextxy(10, 10, "This is page 1");
    ellipse(50,75, 30,25, 0,360);
    setactivepage(0);
/* Let user alternate between the two pages and see the
 * effect
 */
    while(1)
    {
        outtextxy( 10, getmaxy()/2,
    "Hit 'q' to exit, any other key to change page:");
        if(getch() == 'q')
        {
/* Close the graphics system */
            closegraph();
            exit(0);
        }
```

Graphics Modes, Coordinates, and Attributes

```
        page++;
/* Select the other page as the visual page */
/* Page number must be between 0 and 1      */
        setvisualpage(page & 1);
        setactivepage(page & 1);
    }
    return 0;
}
```

COMPATIBILITY

setallpalette

TC1	TC1.5	TC2	TC++	MSC3	MSC4	MSC5	MSC6	QC1	QC2	QC2.5	ANSI	UNIX V	XNX
	▲	▲	▲			1	1	1	1	1			

PURPOSE Use *setallpalette* in an EGA or VGA environment to redefine how the values of a pixel are associated with colors displayed on the screen. Thus, this function redefines the entire EGA or VGA palette.

SYNTAX

```
void far  setallpalette(struct palettetype far *palette);
```

`struct palettetype far *palette;` *Pointer to structure containing the definition of the palette*

EXAMPLE CALL

```
struct palettetype new_palette;
setallpalette(&new_palette);
```

INCLUDES `#include <graphics.h>` *For function declaration and the definition of color constants*

DESCRIPTION The *setallpalette* function, applicable only in EGA and VGA environments, accepts the definition of a new palette in a *palettetype* structure which is defined in *graphics.h* as

```
struct palettetype
{
    unsigned char size;               /* Number of colors */
    signed   char colors[MAXCOLORS+1]; /* Palette entries */
};
```

where MAXCOLORS is a constant, defined in *graphics.h*, representing the maximum pixel value possible in an EGA/VGA environment (15). You must define a *palettetype* structure and pass its address in the parameter *palette*. The field *size* in the *palettetype* structure denotes the number of available colors, with the array *colors* holding the actual color values. For example, a pixel value of 0 represents the background color. Thus if you define a palette with the first entry in *colors* as 1, the background will change to blue (because a color value of 1 represents blue in EGA/VGA).

The *setallpalette* function associates the colors specified in the array of characters *colors* with pixel values. The colors are assigned to the pixel values sequentially, starting with the pixel value 0 and continuing on to the maximum permissible value that a pixel can take in that graphics mode. Thus, the array of long integers must have at least as many elements as the number of colors that can be simultaneously displayed on the hardware in the current graphics mode. For example, on the 16-color graphics mode on the VGA or the EGA, there must be 16 colors in the array specified by the array *colors* in the *palettetype* structure whose address is in the argument *palette*.

You can use the color constants shown in Table 18-11 to define the palette. In fact, Table 18-11 shows the default palette in EGA. You can also use color values between 0 and 63 directly as entries in the *colors* array in the *palettetype* structure (because the EGA high-resolution mode allows you to choose 16 colors out of 64). The redefinition of the EGA's palette is illustrated in the example below.

The existing palette can be had by calling *getpalette*. If any entry in the *colors* array is set to −1, *setallpalette* will not redefine the color for that pixel value. Note that once the pixel values are redefined, all existing text and graphics will change to the new colors immediately.

Table 18-11. ***The Default EGA Palette***

Pixel Value	Color Constant	Color Value
0	EGA_BLACK	0
1	EGA_BLUE	1
2	EGA_GREEN	2
3	EGA_CYAN	3
4	EGA_RED	4
5	EGA_MAGENTA	5
6	EGA_BROWN	20
7	EGA_LIGHTGRAY	7
8	EGA_DARKGRAY	56
9	EGA_LIGHTBLUE	57
10	EGA_LIGHTGREEN	58
11	EGA_LIGHTCYAN	59
12	EGA_LIGHTRED	60
13	EGA_LIGHTMAGENTA	61
14	EGA_YELLOW	62
15	EGA_WHITE	63

1. Use *_remappalette* in Microsoft C 5 and 6, and QuickC 1.0 through 2.5.

Graphics Modes, Coordinates, and Attributes

COMMON USES The *setallpalette* and its companion *setpalette* functions are useful on EGA and VGA systems for designing user interfaces that can take advantage of the ability to quickly swap colors. You can, for example, highlight selected menu items by simply redefining the displayed color from a subdued one to another that really catches the eye.

RETURNS If the input to *setallpalette* is invalid, the graphics error code is set to grError (–11), and a subsequent call to *graphresult* will return this code.

SEE ALSO

`getpalette`	*To get the current palette in all adapters except the IBM 8514*
`getpalettesize`	*To determine the number of colors in the current palette*
`setpalette`	*To redefine a single pixel value*
`setrgbpalette`	*To redefine a pixel value in IBM 8514*

EXAMPLE Assuming you have either EGA or VGA hardware, set the display to a graphics mode. Display 16 rectangles each filled with a color from the current palette. This illustrates the interpretation of each pixel value in the default palette, black for 0, blue for 1, and so on. When the user hits any key, call *setallpalette* to redefine the entire palette. Exchange the positions of cyan and black, and red and blue. You will see that the background will immediately become cyan (because pixel value 0 is always background), and the red rectangle will swap places with the blue one.

```
#include <stdio.h>
#include <graphics.h>
/* Define new color map using defined constants from
 * graphics.h. Notice that we have swapped red with blue
 * and cyan with black. So the background will become
 * cyan now.
 */
struct palettetype newcolormap[] =
    {16,
     EGA_CYAN, EGA_RED, EGA_GREEN, EGA_BLACK, EGA_BLUE,
     EGA_MAGENTA, EGA_BROWN, EGA_LIGHTGRAY,
     EGA_DARKGRAY, EGA_LIGHTBLUE, EGA_LIGHTGREEN,
     EGA_LIGHTCYAN, EGA_LIGHTRED, EGA_LIGHTMAGENTA,
     EGA_YELLOW, EGA_WHITE};

main()
{
    int i;
    short color=0, x1=0, y1=60, x2=100, y2=70;
```

```
    int graphdriver = DETECT;
    int graphmode;


  /* Detect and initialize graphics system */
    initgraph(&graphdriver, &graphmode, "c:\\tc\\bgi");
    if (graphdriver != EGA && graphdriver != VGA)
    {
/* Error setting mode */
        printf("Not EGA/VGA hardware\n");
        exit(0);
    }
/* Display rectangles filled with colors from current
 * palette
 */
    outtextxy(10,10,
"Remapping the color palette using setallpalette");
/* Draw the filled rectangles */
    for (i=1; i<=8; i++)
    {
        color = 2*i-1;
        setfillstyle(SOLID_FILL, color);
        bar(x1, y1, x2, y2);
        setfillstyle(SOLID_FILL, color+1);
        bar(x1+150, y1, x2+150, y2);
        y1 += 20;
        y2 += 20;
    }
/* Now remap entire palette--swap red with blue, cyan
 * with black
 */
    setcolor(EGA_RED);
    outtextxy(10, 30,
      "Hit any key to remap the entire palette:");
    getch();
/* Display changes immediately */
    setallpalette(newcolormap);
/* Restore mode back to where we originally started */
/* Give user a chance to see the result */
    outtextxy(10, getmaxy()-50, "Hit any key to exit:");
    getch();
    closegraph();
    return 0;
}
```

Graphics Modes, Coordinates, and Attributes

COMPATIBILITY

setaspectratio

TC1	TC1.5	TC2	TC++	MSC3	MSC4	MSC5	MSC6	QC1	QC2	QC2.5	ANSI	UNIX V	XNX
		▲	▲										

PURPOSE Use *setaspectratio* to alter the default aspect ratio correction factor used by the Turbo C++ graphics library.

SYNTAX

```
void far setaspectratio(int xasp, int yasp);
```

`int xasp;` *A value proportional to the width of a pixel on the monitor*

`int yasp;` *A value proportional to the height of a pixel on the monitor*

EXAMPLE CALL

```
setaspectratio(75, 100);
```

INCLUDES `#include <graphics.h>` *For function declaration*

DESCRIPTION The *setaspectratio* function allows you to override the default setting of the aspect ratio (see description of *getaspectratio* for more details) that is used by the Turbo C++ graphics routines to draw accurate representations of objects such as circles and rectangles on the monitor's screen.

The new aspect ratio is specified in terms of the height and the width of a pixel on the screen given in the arguments *xasp* and *yasp*, respectively. Since only the ratio of *xasp* and *yasp* is important, you can scale both numbers equally by arbitrary factors. For example, if your monitor displays pixels that are 1.1 times as tall as they are wide, you can set the aspect ratio by the call *setaspectratio(10,11)*.

COMMON USES If you are using a nonstandard monitor that Turbo C++ does not recognize or if your monitor's alignments are incorrect, the default aspect ratio will be inaccurate (circles will look oval). You can use *setaspectratio* to explicitly specify the ratio of pixel height and width. You will also need *setaspectratio* if you decide to allow the user to alter the aspect ratio.

SEE ALSO `getaspectratio` *To get the default aspect ratio for the current mode of the adapter*

EXAMPLE Draw a circle and let the user change its appearance by altering the aspect ratio. Ask the user to enter the x and y parameters to be used in the call to *setaspectratio*.

```
#include <stdio.h>
#include <graphics.h>
```

```
main()
{
   int graphdriver = DETECT, graphmode;
   char    buffer[80];
   int     xasp, yasp, bcolor, width;

   initgraph(&graphdriver, &graphmode, "c:\\tc\\bgi");
   bcolor = getbkcolor();
   setfillstyle(EMPTY_FILL, 0);
   settextjustify(LEFT_TEXT,BOTTOM_TEXT);
/* Get the current "aspect ratio" and display it */
   getaspectratio( &xasp, &yasp );
   sprintf(buffer,"Aspect ratio: xasp = %d, yasp = %d",
   xasp, yasp);
   outtextxy(100,30, buffer);
   width = textwidth(buffer);
   outtextxy(100,10,"Enter xasp, yasp (0,0 to exit): ");
/* Draw a circle */
   setcolor(RED);
   circle(120,120, 80);
/* Now let user alter the aspect ratio */
   while(1)
   {
/* Read new aspect ratio parameters */
      scanf(" %d , %d", &xasp, &yasp);
/* Exit if either xasp or yasp is 0 */
      if(xasp == 0 || yasp == 0) break;
/* Erase the previous circle */
      setcolor(bcolor);
      circle(120,120, 80);
/* Set the aspect ratio and redraw it */
      setaspectratio(xasp,yasp);
      setcolor(RED);
      circle(120,120, 80);
/* Display the new aspect ratio */
bar(100, 30-textheight("H"), 100+width, 30);
      sprintf(buffer,"Aspect ratio: xasp = %d, yasp = %d",
   xasp, yasp);
      outtextxy(100,30, buffer);
   }
   closegraph();         /* Exit graphics library */
   return 0;
}
```

Graphics Modes, Coordinates, and Attributes

COMPATIBILITY **setbkcolor**

TC1	TC1.5	TC2	TC++	MSC3	MSC4	MSC5	MSC6	QC1	QC2	QC2.5	ANSI	UNIX V	XNX
	▲	▲	▲			1	1	1	1	1			

PURPOSE Use the *setbkcolor* function to select a new background color.

SYNTAX

```
void far  setbkcolor(int color);

int color;      New color value
```

EXAMPLE CALL

```
setbkcolor(RED); /* select red background */
```

INCLUDES

```
#include <graphics.h>     For function declaration and definition of color constants
```

DESCRIPTION The *setbkcolor* function is used to set the current background color to the value given in the integer argument *color*. The change becomes visible immediately.

The background color is specified by a color value. In CGA, you can specify any value between 0 and 15, or use the equivalent constants shown in Table 18-12 (and defined in *graphics.h*). In EGA or VGA, the color value can be between 0 and 63, representing the 64 possible colors.

Table 18-12. ***List of Color Names and Their Values***

Color Constant	Color Value
BLACK	0
BLUE	1
GREEN	2
CYAN	3
RED	4
MAGENTA	5
BROWN	6
LIGHTGRAY	7
DARKGRAY	8
LIGHTBLUE	9
LIGHTGREEN	10
LIGHTCYAN	11
LIGHTRED	12
LIGHTMAGENTA	13
YELLOW	14
WHITE	15

As an example, in the CGA as well as in EGA and VGA, color value 4 is red. Thus the call *setbkcolor(4)* will set the screen's background to red. You can reset the background to black by *setbkcolor(0)*.

1. In Microsoft C 5 and 6, and QuickC 1.0 through 2.5, use *_setbkcolor*.

COMMON USES The *setbkcolor* function is used to set a new background color.

COMMENTS In video memory, when the display adapter is in graphics mode, the pixels that have the background color always contain zeros—so the background color number is 0 in graphics mode. This "pixel value" is mapped, however, to a specific color via the current palette. Some hardware, such as EGA and VGA, allow remapping of palettes—meaning that although black is the default color associated with a pixel value of zero, you could set, for example, red to be the color corresponding to a 0 pixel value. So during EGA and VGA graphics, you can change the background color by using the *setpalette* function to redefine the meaning of a zero "pixel value." See the description of *setpalette* for an explanation of "remapping" of palettes. The entire palette can be remapped by *setallpalette*. The CGA allows remapping of pixel value 0 (the background color) only, using *setpalette*.

SEE ALSO

`getbkcolor`	*To retrieve the value of the current background color*
`getpalette`	*To obtain the current palette*
`setpalette`	*To alter background color by redefining pixel value zero*

EXAMPLE Write a Turbo C++ program that uses *setbkcolor* to set the background to a randomly chosen color. Keep changing the background color, pausing for a second between each change, until the user presses any key.

```
#include <graphics.h>
#include <stdlib.h>

main()
{
    int graphdriver = DETECT, graphmode;
    int maxcolor;

/* Initialize the graphics system */
    initgraph(&graphdriver, &graphmode, "c:\\tc\\bgi");
/* Now keep switching background colors randomly */
    maxcolor = getmaxcolor();
/* Initialize random number generator */
    randomize();
    outtextxy(10,20, "Demonstrating setbkcolor");
    outtextxy(10,30, "Press any key to exit");
```

```
    while (!kbhit())
    {
        setbkcolor(random(maxcolor));
        delay(1000);  /* Pause for 1 second */
    }
/* Wait for 1 second, then exit */
    delay(1000);
    closegraph();
    return 0;
}
```

COMPATIBILITY

setcolor

TC1	TC1.5	TC2	TC++	MSC3	MSC4	MSC5	MSC6	QC1	QC2	QC2.5	ANSI	UNIX V	XNX
	▲	▲	▲			1	1	1	1	1			

PURPOSE Use *setcolor* to select the drawing color to be used by all future calls to the drawing functions *arc*, *ellipse*, *line*, *linerel*, *lineto*, *pieslice*, *rectangle*, and *setpixel*.

SYNTAX

```
void far  setcolor(int color);
```

`int color;` *Selected color number*

EXAMPLE CALL `setcolor(4);`

INCLUDES `#include <graphics.h>` *For function declaration*

DESCRIPTION The *setcolor* routine sets the current color to the color number specified in the argument *color*. This color number is used as the drawing color by the routines: *arc*, *ellipse*, *line*, *linerel*, *lineto*, *pieslice*, *rectangle*, and *setpixel*. The actual color displayed depends on the current palette.

Until a color has been set, these routines use the highest color number in the current palette (see *setallpalette* to set the color palette).

There is no return value, but if the color number *color* is out of the range of values allowed by the current palette, *setcolor* will leave the current color unchanged.

1. The compatible function in Microsoft C 5 and 6, and QuickC 1.0 through 2.5, is *_setcolor*.

SEE ALSO

`getcolor` *To obtain the current drawing color*

`getpalette` *To get the colors in the current palette*

`setallpalette` *To define a color palette in EGA/VGA*

EXAMPLE Write a Turbo C++ program that displays the outline of a rectangle drawn using a randomly selected color. Keep changing the color, with a one-second pause between changes, until the user presses a key.

```
#include <graphics.h>
#include <stdlib.h>

main()
{
    int graphdriver = DETECT, graphmode;
    int maxcolor, color;
    char buffer[80];

/* Initialize the graphics system */
    initgraph(&graphdriver, &graphmode, "c:\\tc\\bgi");
/* Now keep switching background colors randomly */
    maxcolor = getmaxcolor();
/* Initialize random number generator */
    randomize();
    outtextxy(10,20, "Demonstrating setcolor");
    outtextxy(10,30, "Press any key to exit");
    while (!kbhit())
    {
        color = random(maxcolor);
        setcolor(color);
        rectangle(50,50, 150,90);
        sprintf(buffer, "Color number %2d", color);
 /* Erase the area where color number will be shown */
        setfillstyle(EMPTY_FILL, color);
bar(50,100, 50+textwidth(buffer),
    100+2*textheight(buffer));
setcolor(WHITE);
        outtextxy(50,100+textheight("H"), buffer);
        delay(1000);  /* Pause for 1 second */
    }
/* Wait for 1 second, then exit */
    delay(1000);
    closegraph();
    return 0;
}
```

Graphics Modes, Coordinates, and Attributes

COMPATIBILITY

setfillpattern

TC1	TC1.5	TC2	TC++	MSC3	MSC4	MSC5	MSC6	QC1	QC2	QC2.5	ANSI	UNIX V	XNX
	▲	▲	▲			1	1	1	1	1			

PURPOSE Use *setfillpattern* to select a fill color and define the pattern to be used by the routines *bar, bar3d, fillpoly, floodfill,* and *pieslice* when filling an area. Until you define a fill pattern, a solid white fill pattern is used.

SYNTAX

```
void far  setfillpattern(char far *fillpattern, int color);

char far *fillpattern;
```

8×8 bit pattern that determines how the filled area looks

```
int       color;
```

Fill color

EXAMPLE CALL

```
char far pattern1[] =  {1, 3, 7, 0xf, 0x1f, 0x3f, 0x7f, 0xff};
setfillpattern(pattern1, RED);
```

INCLUDES

```
#include <graphics.h>
```

For function declaration

DESCRIPTION The *setfillpattern* function allows you to select a fill color and define an 8×8 pattern of bits as the current pattern to be used by the routines *bar, bar3d, fillpoly, floodfill,* and *pieslice* when filling an area.

The fill color is specified by the integer argument *color,* and the pattern is specified by the argument *fillpattern* which is a far pointer to an array of 8 characters. Since each character has 8 bits, you can think of this 8×8 array of bits as a model of an area on the screen, 8 pixels wide and 8 pixels tall, with the first character representing the first row of the area. When filling an 8×8 area using the pattern, those pixels that correspond to 0 bits are left untouched while the rest are filled with the current color. Thus, a solid fill is specified when all 8 characters contain the value FFh. This is the default value of the fill style in the graphics package. For areas larger than 8×8 pixels, the fill operation is done by repeatedly using the pattern on successive 8×8 blocks of the screen until the entire area is covered. The example below shows how to specify other fill patterns using this method.

1. In Microsoft C 5 and 6, and QuickC 1.0 through 2.5, the compatible function is *_setfillmask.*

COMMON USES This function is used to select different fill styles so that objects such as slices of a pie chart can be distinguished from one another.

COMMENTS If you switch fill patterns in a graphics routine, it is a good idea to first retrieve the current pattern using *getfillpattern* so that you can restore the style back to normal before returning from the routine.

In Turbo C++, there are 12 predefined fill patterns that you can choose with the *setfillstyle* function. The *setfillpattern* function is provided so that you can define your own patterns.

SEE ALSO

`getfillpattern`	*To determine the current fill pattern*
`getfillsettings`	*To get information on current fill pattern and fill color*
`setfillstyle`	*To select a predefined fill pattern*

EXAMPLE Write a Turbo C++ program to illustrate some of the fill styles that can be created using the *setfillpattern* function. Since this is a self-contained program, there is no need to save and restore the the old fill pattern.

```
#include <graphics.h>
/* Define the fill style masks */
unsigned char fillpattern[4][8] =
{
/* First mask */
    1, 3, 7, 0xf, 0x1f, 0x3f, 0x7f, 0xff,
/* Mask 2     */
    0xf0, 0xf0, 0xf0, 0xf0, 0xf, 0xf, 0xf, 0xf,
/* Mask 3     */
    0xcc, 0x33, 0xcc, 0x33, 0xcc, 0x33, 0xcc, 0x33,
/* Mask 4     */
    0xc3, 0xc3, 0xc,  0xc,  0x30, 0x30, 0xc3, 0xc3
};
main()
{
    int graphdriver = DETECT;
    int graphmode;
    int i, x1=0, y1=40;

  /* Detect and initialize graphics system */
    initgraph(&graphdriver, &graphmode, "c:\\tc\\bgi");
    outtextxy(10,10,
         "Illustrating different fill styles:");
/* Draw filled rectangle with different fill styles */
    for (i=1; i<=2; i++)
    {
        setfillpattern(fillpattern[2*i-2], RED);
        bar(x1, y1, x1+100, y1+60);
        setfillpattern(fillpattern[2*i-1], YELLOW);
        bar(x1+150, y1, x1+250, y1+60);
        y1 += 100;
    }
```

Graphics Modes, Coordinates, and Attributes

```
/* Give user a chance to see the result */
    outtextxy(getmaxx()/2, getmaxy() - 50,
                         "Press any key to exit:");
    getch();        /* Wait until a key is pressed */
    closegraph();         /* Exit graphics library */
    return 0;
}
```

COMPATIBILITY

setfillstyle

TC1	TC1.5	TC2	TC++	MSC3	MSC4	MSC5	MSC6	QC1	QC2	QC2.5	ANSI	UNIX V	XNX
	▲	▲	▲										

PURPOSE Use *setfillstyle* to select a predefined fill pattern and a fill color to be used in subsequent fill operations.

SYNTAX

```
void far  setfillstyle(int pattern, int color);
```

`int pattern;` *Constant denoting predefined fill pattern*

`int color;` *Fill color*

EXAMPLE CALL

```
setfillstyle(HATCH_FILL, YELLOW);
```

INCLUDES `#include <graphics.h>` *For function declaration and symbolic names of fill patterns*

DESCRIPTION The *setfillstyle* function is used to select a predefined fill pattern and a fill color to be used by the routines *bar*, *bar3d*, *fillpoly*, *floodfill*, and *pieslice* that fill an area.

The fill color is specified by the integer argument *color*. You can use constants defined in *graphics.h* for the colors. Table 18-3 shows the names of colors for the CGA and the EGA.

You must provide the fill pattern in the argument *pattern*. You can use symbolic names of the fill patterns defined in the enumeration *fill_patterns* in the include file *graphics.h*. These constants and their values are shown in Table 18-13.

Note that, to define a new pattern, you must use *setfillpattern*. Simply setting *pattern* to USER_FILL in *setfillstyle* is not enough. The constant USER_FILL is actually for use by *getfillsettings* which, when called after defining your own pattern, will return USER_FILL as the current pattern number.

COMMON USES This function is used to select different fill styles so that objects such as bars in a bar graph can be distinguished from one another.

Table 18-13. *Predefined Fill Patterns in Turbo C++ Graphics Library*

fill_patterns Constant	Value	Description
EMPTY_FILL	0	Fill with background color.
SOLID_FILL	1	Solid fill with current fill color.
LINE_FILL	2	Fill with line (---).
LTSLASH_FILL	3	Fill with /// normal width lines.
SLASH_FILL	4	Fill with /// thick lines.
BKSLASH_FILL	5	Fill with \\\ thick lines.
LTBKSLASH_FILL	6	Fill with \\\ normal width lines.
HATCH_FILL	7	Light hatch fill.
XHATCH_FILL	8	Heavy cross hatch fill.
INTERLEAVE_FILL	9	Interleaving line fill.
WIDE_DOT_FILL	10	Widely spaced dot fill.
CLOSE_DOT_FILL	11	Closely spaced dot fill.
USER_FILL	12	User-defined fill pattern.

COMMENTS If you switch fill styles in a graphics routine, it is a good idea to first retrieve information about the current style using *getfillsettings* so that you can restore the style to normal before returning from the routine. In addition to the predefined patterns, you can also define your own fill pattern by using the *setfillpattern* function.

SEE ALSO

`getfillpattern` *To determine the current fill pattern*

`getfillsettings` *To get information on current fill pattern and fill color*

`setfillpattern` *To define your own fill pattern*

EXAMPLE Write a Turbo C++ program that displays a box filled with a randomly selected fill pattern and a random fill color. Display the fill color and the pattern number underneath the box. Pause for a second between changes in pattern and color, and exit when the user presses a key.

```
#include <graphics.h>
#include <stdlib.h>

main()
{
    int graphdriver = DETECT, graphmode;
    int maxcolor, color, pattern;
    char buffer1[80], buffer2[80];
```

```
/* Initialize the graphics system */
    initgraph(&graphdriver, &graphmode, "c:\\tc\\bgi");
/* Now keep switching background colors randomly */
    maxcolor = getmaxcolor();
/* Initialize random number generator */
    randomize();
    outtextxy(10,20, "Demonstrating setfillstyle");
    outtextxy(10,30, "Press any key to exit");
    while (!kbhit())
    {
        color = random(maxcolor);
        pattern = random(11);
        setfillstyle(pattern, color);
        bar(50,50, 150,100);
        sprintf(buffer1, "Fill color %2d", color);
sprintf(buffer2, "Pattern # %2d", pattern);
 /* Erase the area where color number will be shown */
        setfillstyle(EMPTY_FILL, color);
bar(50,100, 50+textwidth(buffer1),
    100+3*textheight("H"));
        outtextxy(50,100+textheight("H"), buffer1);
outtextxy(50,100+2*textheight("H"), buffer2);
        delay(1000);  /* Pause for 1 second */
    }
/* Wait for 1 second, then exit */
    delay(1000);
    closegraph();
    return 0;
}
```

COMPATIBILITY

setgraphbufsize

TC1	TC1.5	TC2	TC++	MSC3	MSC4	MSC5	MSC6	QC1	QC2	QC2.5	ANSI	UNIX V	XNX
	▲	▲	▲										

PURPOSE Use *setgraphsize* to specify a size, other than the default 4,096 bytes (4 K), for the internal buffer required by Turbo C++'s graphics library.

SYNTAX `unsigned far setgraphbufsize(unsigned bufsize);`

`unsigned bufsize;` *Desired size of graphics buffer in bytes*

EXAMPLE CALL

```
unsigned old_size, new_size = 2048;
old_size = setgraphbufsize(new_size);
```

INCLUDES

```
#include <graphics.h>        For function declaration
```

DESCRIPTION The Turbo C++ graphics library uses a buffer to store intermediate results during fill operations. This buffer is allocated when *initgraph* is called to initialize the graphics system. The memory reserved for the buffer is released when you exit the graphics system by calling *closegraph*. The default size of this buffer is 4,096 bytes.

You can specify a new size for the graphics buffer by calling *setgraphbufsize* before *initgraph*. The new size of the buffer is specified in the argument *bufsize*.

COMMON USES You may want to reduce the size of the internal graphics buffer if your application does not do any fill operations. On the other hand, if you receive a *grNoFloodMem* error code (which means that there was not enough memory for flood fill), you can insert a call to *setgraphbufsize* with a size greater than the default 4,096 bytes.

RETURNS The *setgraphbufsize* function returns the previous size of the internal graphics buffer.

SEE ALSO

`closegraph` *To deallocate internal graphics buffer and close the graphics system*

`initgraph` *To allocate internal graphics buffer and initialize the Turbo C++ graphics system*

EXAMPLE Call *setgraphbufsize* to alter the size of the graphics buffer. Report the default size returned by *setgraphbufsize*. Note that you have to call *setgraphbufsize* before initializing the graphics system with *initgraph*.

```
#include <graphics.h>
#define NEWBUFSIZE 512
main()
{
    int oldbufsize;
/* Set the graphics buffer */
    oldbufsize = setgraphbufsize(NEWBUFSIZE);
    printf("Graphics buffer size is changed from"
" %d bytes to %d bytes\n", oldbufsize, NEWBUFSIZE);
    printf("*** Call setgraphbufsize before calling"
           "initgraph ***\n");
    return 0;
}
```

Graphics Modes, Coordinates, and Attributes

COMPATIBILITY

setgraphmode

TC1	TC1.5	TC2	TC++	MSC3	MSC4	MSC5	MSC6	QC1	QC2	QC2.5	ANSI	UNIX V	XNX
	▲	▲	▲			1	1	1	1	1			

PURPOSE Use *setgraphmode* to switch to a different graphics mode and clear the screen.

SYNTAX

```
void far  setgraphmode(int mode);

int mode;        Selected mode number
```

EXAMPLE CALL

```
setgraphmode(VGAHI); /* VGA: 640x480 16 color 1 page */
```

INCLUDES

```
#include <graphics.h>       For function declaration and definition of mode names
```

DESCRIPTION The *setgraphmode* function sets up the graphics hardware to work in the graphics mode specified in the argument *mode*, and resets all graphics settings to their default values (see *graphdefaults*).

In Turbo C++'s graphics library, a range of mode numbers is assigned to each graphics device driver. For example, the VGA graphics driver has three modes numbered 0 through 2, and identified by the symbolic constants VGALO, VGAMED, and VGAHI (Table 18-9 shows the mode constants for the other drivers). The *setgraphmode* function is used to switch among different possible modes that are permissible on the current driver. For example, with a VGA, if you had let *initgraph* pick the default mode, the mode will be VGAHI which is the 640×480 16-color mode of the VGA. In this case, you could use the call *setgraphmode(VGALO)* to switch to a 16-color mode at CGA's resolution (640×200).

The argument *mode* to *setgraphmode* must be a valid one for the current graphics adapter. In case of an invalid mode, *setgraphmode* will set the error code to −10 (*grInvalidMode*). The Turbo C++ library includes the routine *getmoderange* which can give you the range of mode numbers that are valid for a specified graphics driver.

1. In Microsoft C 5 and 6, and QuickC 1.0 through 2.5, use *_setvideomode*.

COMMON USES The *setgraphmode* function is normally used to get back to graphics mode after you had switched to a text mode with *restorecrtmode*. It can also be used to switch between different graphics modes supported by the current graphics driver.

SEE ALSO

`getgraphmode` *To get the current graphics mode number*

`getmoderange` *To determine the valid range of modes for a specified graphics driver*

`initgraph`	*To initialize the Turbo C++ graphics system and put the adapter in a graphics mode*
`restorecrtmode`	*To switch to the mode that existed before* initgraph *was called (usually a text mode)*

EXAMPLE Write a Turbo C++ program using *setgraphmode* to demonstrate all the graphics modes available in a graphics driver.

```
#include <graphics.h>

main()
{
  int graphdriver = DETECT, graphmode,
      lomode, himode, mode, c;
  char buffer[80];

/* Detect and initialize graphics system */
  initgraph(&graphdriver, &graphmode, "c:\\tc\\bgi");

/* Now call getmoderange to determine the range of
 * modes supported by this adapter. Switch to each
 * mode and draw a filled box in each mode.
 */
  getmoderange(graphdriver, &lomode, &himode);
  for(mode = lomode; mode <= himode; mode++)
  {
      setgraphmode(mode);
      sprintf(buffer,"Now in graphics mode %d",
              mode);
      outtextxy(10,10, buffer);
setfillstyle(SOLID_FILL,RED);
      bar(50,50, 150,100);
      outtextxy(10, getmaxy() - 50, "Press 'q' to \
exit, or any other key to switch mode");
      if((c = getch()) == 'q') break;
  }
  closegraph();
  return 0;
}
```

Graphics Modes, Coordinates, and Attributes

COMPATIBILITY

setlinestyle

TC1	TC1.5	TC2	TC++	MSC3	MSC4	MSC5	MSC6	QC1	QC2	QC2.5	ANSI	UNIX V	XNX
	▲	▲	▲			1	1	1	1	1			

PURPOSE Use *setlinestyle* to set the current line width to one of four predefined patterns or a new 16-bit pattern that controls how lines look.

SYNTAX

```
void far  setlinestyle(int linestyle, unsigned upattern,
                       int thickness);
```

```
int      linestyle;
```
Style number to indicate predefined pattern or enable a user-defined one

```
unsigned upattern;
```
Bit pattern that determines how the line looks (when linestyle=4)

```
int      thickness;
```
Thickness of lines in pixels (either 1 or 3 pixels)

EXAMPLE CALL

```
setlinestyle(USERBIT_LINE, 0x3ff, THICK_WIDTH);
```

INCLUDES

```
#include <graphics.h>
```
For function declaration and enumerated constants for line style and thickness

DESCRIPTION The *setlinestyle* function is used to define the style of lines to be drawn by the routines *line*, *lineto*, *rectangle*, *drawpoly*, and *pieslice*. The style determines the thickness of the line, and whether the line is solid or dashed, and (if dashed) determines the pattern of the dashes.

The *linestyle* argument specifies which one of the predefined patterns should be used for drawing lines. The enumeration type *line_styles* in *graphics.h* defines the names and values for the five available styles. Table 18-14 shows the styles.

Table 18-14. *Line Patterns in Turbo C++ Graphics*

line_styles Constant	Value	Description
SOLID_LINE	0	Solid line.
DOTTED_LINE	1	Dotted line.
CENTER_LINE	2	Centered line (alternating dash and dot).
DASHED_LINE	3	Dashed line.
USERBIT_LINE	4	User-defined line style.

The argument *upattern* is ignored except when *linestyle* is USERBIT_LINE. A *linestyle* of USERBIT_LINE indicates that you are defining your own line style. In this case, the 16-bit argument *upattern* is used to specify the pattern to be repeated when drawing a line. Think of this pattern as representing a line segment 16 pixels long. If a bit in *linemask* is a 1, the corresponding pixel in that line gets painted with the current color (see *setcolor*). If a bit is 0, the corresponding pixel is left untouched. Note that a value of FFh for *linemask* means a solid line. This is the default value of the line style in the graphics package. The example below shows how to specify other line styles using this method.

The third argument, *thickness*, specifies the thickness of lines in pixels. Only two values, 1 and 3, are permitted. Symbolic names for the thickness are defined by the enumeration *line_widths* in *graphics.h*, and are shown in Table 18-15.

Table 18-15. ***Line Widths in Turbo C++ Graphics***

line_widths Constant	Value	Description
NORM_WIDTH	1	Normal lines (1 pixel wide).
THICK_WIDTH	3	Thick lines (3 pixels wide).

If any of the parameters are invalid, *setlinestyle* will set the graphics error code to −11 (*grError*, generic error). You can get this error code by calling *graphresult*.

1. Use *_setlinestyle* in Microsoft C 5 and 6, and QuickC 1.0 through 2.5.

COMMON USES This function is used to select different line styles so that overlapping graphs can be distinguished from one another.

COMMENTS If you switch line styles in a graphics routine, it is a good idea to first retrieve the current style using *getlinesettings* so that you can restore the style to normal before returning from the routine.

SEE ALSO

`getlinesettings` *To determine the current line style*

`setwritemode` *To set the writing mode of pixels during the line drawing operation*

EXAMPLE Write a Turbo C++ program to illustrate some of the line styles that can be created using the *setlinestyle* function. Since this is a self-contained program, there is no need to save and restore the old line style.

```
#include <graphics.h>

/* Define the line styles */
unsigned linestyle[16] =
{1, 3, 7, 0xf, 0x1f, 0x3f, 0x7f, 0xff,
 0x1ff, 0x3ff, 0x7ff, 0xfff, 0x1fff, 0x3fff, 0x7fff,
 0xffff};
main()
{
    int graphdriver = DETECT, graphmode, i, y = 30;

/* Detect and initialize graphics system */
    initgraph(&graphdriver, &graphmode, "c:\\tc\\bgi");
    outtextxy(10,10,
        "Demonstrating different line styles:");
    setcolor(RED);
    for (i=0; i<16; i++)
    {
/* Select a line style from the array of styles */
        setlinestyle(USERBIT_LINE, linestyle[i],
                     NORM_WIDTH);
        moveto(0,y);
        lineto(500,y);
        y += 10;
    }
/* Give user a chance to see the result */
    outtextxy(10, getmaxy() - 50,
                     "Press any key to exit");
    getch();
    closegraph();
    return 0;
}
```

COMPATIBILITY

setpalette

TC1	TC1.5	TC2	TC++	MSC3	MSC4	MSC5	MSC6	QC1	QC2	QC2.5	ANSI	UNIX V	XNX
	▲	▲	▲			1	1	1	1	1			

PURPOSE Use *setpalette* in an EGA or VGA environment to redefine how a specific value contained in a pixel is associated with a color displayed on the screen. Thus, this function redefines a single pixel value in an EGA or VGA palette. For example, since a pixel value of 0 always signifies background, you can change the background color by simply calling *setpalette* to redefine color number 0 (see example below).

SYNTAX

```
void far  setpalette(int pixel_value, int color);
```

`int pixel_value;` *Pixel value to be redefined*

`int color;` *Color to be associated with the pixel value*

EXAMPLE CALL

```
setpalette(0, CYAN);   /* Display pixel value 0 as cyan */
```

INCLUDES

`#include <graphics.h>` *For function declaration and the definition of color constants*

DESCRIPTION The *setpalette* function, available only in EGA and VGA environments (on a CGA you are limited to redefining the pixel value of 0 only), associates the color specified in the integer argument *color* with the pixel value *pixel_value*. The maximum possible value of the argument *pixel_value* depends on the number of colors that can be simultaneously displayed on the hardware in the current graphics mode. For example, on the 16-color graphics mode on the VGA or the EGA, the pixel value can be from 0 to 15. You can obtain this information by calling the function *getpalette*.

You can specify the *color* with symbolic constants or numerical values. A set of predefined constants for specifying colors is given in the header file *graphics.h*. See Table 18-3 for a list of the colors in the CGA and EGA palettes.

Note that when a pixel value is redefined with *setpalette*, any existing text and graphics that are using the pixel value will show the new color immediately. If you call *setpalette* with an invalid parameter (for example, a pixel value outside the range 0 through 15), the graphics error code will be set to −11 (*grError*, generic graphics error code). You can check the error code by using *graphresult*.

1. In Microsoft C 5 and 6, and QuickC 1.0 through 2.5, use *_remappalette*.

COMMON USES The *setpalette* and its companion *setallpalette* are useful on EGA and VGA systems for special effects that are possible because of an application's ability to redefine palettes at will.

SEE ALSO

`getpalette` *To obtain the current mapping of pixel values to colors (except IBM 8514)*

`setallpalette` *To redefine all possible pixel values in the current palette (EGA/VGA)*

`setrgbpalette` *To redefine a pixel value in IBM 8514*

Graphics Modes, Coordinates, and Attributes

EXAMPLE Assuming you have either EGA or VGA hardware, write a Turbo C++ program to illustrate the effect of changing the definition of a pixel value by using *setpalette*. Display some text using color 1, then redefine colors 0 and 1 using *setpalette*. This will change the color of the text as well as the background color.

```
#include <stdio.h>
#include <graphics.h>
/* Define array of colors using defined constants from
 * graphics.h
 */
int colors[] =
   { EGA_BLACK, EGA_BLUE, EGA_GREEN, EGA_CYAN, EGA_RED,
     EGA_MAGENTA, EGA_BROWN, EGA_LIGHTGRAY,
     EGA_DARKGRAY, EGA_LIGHTBLUE, EGA_LIGHTGREEN,
     EGA_LIGHTCYAN, EGA_LIGHTRED, EGA_LIGHTMAGENTA,
     EGA_YELLOW, EGA_WHITE};

main()
{
    int graphdriver = DETECT, graphmode, i=0;

  /* Detect and initialize graphics system */
    initgraph(&graphdriver, &graphmode, "c:\\tc\\bgi");
    if (graphdriver != EGA && graphdriver != VGA)
    {
/* Error setting mode */
       closegraph();
       printf("Not EGA/VGA hardware\n");
        exit(0);
    }
    setcolor(1);
    outtextxy(10,10, "Demonstrating setpalette");
/* Loop through several colors for pixel
 * values 0 and 1
 */
    outtextxy(10,20,
        "Press any key to go on, 'q' to exit");
    while(1)
    {
        if (getch() == 'q')
        {
/* Reset graphics environment */
             closegraph();
             exit(0);
```

```
        }
    /* Alter pixel value 0 and 1 */
            setpalette(0, colors[i%16]);
            setpalette(1, colors[(i+2)%16]);
    /* Select next color from array */
            i++;
        }
        return 0;
}
```

setrgbpalette

COMPATIBILITY

TC1	TC1.5	TC2	TC++	MSC3	MSC4	MSC5	MSC6	QC1	QC2	QC2.5	ANSI	UNIX V	XNX
	▲	▲	▲										

PURPOSE Use *setrgbpalette* to define the 256-color palette for the IBM 8514 display adapter and the VGA.

SYNTAX

```
void far  setrgbpalette(int colornum,
                        int red, int green, int blue);
```

`int colornum;` *Color number or pixel value being defined*

`int red;` *Value of red component of the color*

`int green;` *Value of green component of the color*

`int blue;` *Value of blue component of the color*

EXAMPLE CALL

```
setrgbpalette(1, 0x3f, 0, 0); /* Define color number 1 as red */
```

INCLUDES `#include <graphics.h>` *For function declaration*

DESCRIPTION The IBM 8514 display adapter can provide up to 1024×768 pixel resolution and display any 256 colors out of the 262,144 possible colors that can be displayed. The *setrgbpalette* function allows you to explictly define how a pixel value or color number in the IBM 8514 adapter maps to an actual on-screen color. The argument *colornum* is the color number between 0 and 255 that is being defined. The arguments *red, green,* and *blue,* respectively, are used to specify the level of the red, green, and blue components of the color corresponding to the pixel value *colornum.*

Note that only the lower order 6 bits of each color component, red, green, and blue, are used. Thus, there are 2^6= 64 possible levels of red, green, and blue in each color. That is why there are 64×64×64 = 262,144 possible colors in the IBM 8514 display system.

COMMENTS You should not use the other palette manipulation routines in the Turbo C++ library, *setallpalette*, *setpalette*, and *getpalette*, with the IBM 8514 graphics driver. The IBM 8514 driver initially defines the first 16 colors of its palette identical to the 16 colors of EGA/VGA.

SEE ALSO

getpalette	*To get information on current palette of graphics adapters other than IBM 8514*
setallpalette	*To define palette in EGA/VGA*
setpalette	*To define a single color number in EGA/VGA or to define color number zero in CGA*

setviewport

COMPATIBILITY

TC1	TC1.5	TC2	TC++	MSC3	MSC4	MSC5	MSC6	QC1	QC2	QC2.5	ANSI	UNIX V	XNX
	▲	▲	▲			1	1	1	1	1			

PURPOSE Use *setviewport* to define a rectangular region of the screen as the current window for graphics, optionally clipping anything outside this region.

SYNTAX

```
void far  setviewport(int left, int top, int right, int bottom,
                      int clip);
```

int left, top;	*Screen coordinates of the top left corner of the viewport*
int right, bottom;	*Screen coordinates of the bottom right corner of the viewport*
int clip;	*Clip flag (if nonzero, graphics is clipped at viewport boundary)*

EXAMPLE CALL

```
setviewport(150, 50, 350, 150, 1);
```

INCLUDES #include <graphics.h> *For function declaration*

DESCRIPTION The *setviewport* function defines an area of the screen ("viewport") as the current window for all graphics operations. The area is specified in terms of the screen coordinates of the top left hand corner *(left,top)* and that of the bottom right corner *(right,bottom)*. After defining the current output region for graphics, *setviewport* also moves current position to the top left corner of the viewport. From this point on, all (x,y) coordinates refer to the top left corner of the viewport as the origin.

1. In Microsoft C 5 and 6, and QuickC 1.0 through 2.5, the compatible function is *_setviewport.*

COMMON USES The *setviewport* function can be used to maintain multiple "virtual" graphics screens, each with its own coordinate system.

COMMENTS Note that *initgraph*, *setgraphmode*, and *graphdefaults* reset the viewport to the entire display screen.

SEE ALSO

`clearviewport`	*To clear a viewport*
`getviewsettings`	*To obtain information about the current graphics viewport*
`window`	*To define a window in text mode*

EXAMPLE Write a Turbo C++ program that initializes the graphics system, calls *setviewport* to define a viewport, and draws a filled pie-shaped wedge in it. Then define a second viewport and repeat the same call to *pieslice*. You will notice that each pie slice appears in its own viewport, and each is clipped according to the size of the viewport. This illustrates the idea of using "viewports" to maintain multiple "virtual" graphics screens.

```
#include <graphics.h>

main()
{
    int graphdriver = DETECT, graphmode;

  /* Detect and initialize graphics system */
    initgraph(&graphdriver, &graphmode, "c:\\tc\\bgi");
    outtextxy(10,10,
    "Demonstration of setviewport with 2 viewports");
/* Set current color to red   */
    setcolor(RED);
/* Dashed lines for boundaries */
    setlinestyle(USERBIT_LINE, 0xf0f, NORM_WIDTH);
/* Set a 200 x 200 viewport */
    setviewport(0,100, 200, 300, 1);
/* Show boundary of viewport */
    rectangle(0,0,200,200);
/* Now draw a pieslice, remember the coordinates of
 * the center are specified in viewport coordinates
 * with the origin at upper left corner of viewport.
 */
    setfillstyle(SOLID_FILL, YELLOW);
```

```
    pieslice(150, 150, 0, 360, 100);
/* Now set another viewport, and redraw same slice   */
/* This is a 150 x 150 viewport                      */
    setviewport(240,100,390,250,1);
/* Again show boundary of the viewport */
    rectangle(0,0,150,150);
    setfillstyle(SLASH_FILL, YELLOW);
/* Draw the same ellipse again. */
    pieslice(150, 150, 0, 360, 100);

/* Exit graphics mode when user strikes any key */
    outtextxy(10, getmaxy() - 50,
                        "Press any key to exit");
    getch();  /* A do-nothing read */
    closegraph();
    return 0;
}
```

COMPATIBILITY

setvisualpage

TC1	TC1.5	TC2	TC++	MSC3	MSC4	MSC5	MSC6	QC1	QC2	QC2.5	ANSI	UNIX V	XNX
	▲	▲	▲			1	1	1	1	1			

PURPOSE Use the *setvisualpage* function to select the current "page" or portion of display memory which is actually being mapped onto the screen and displayed. This function will work only when the adapter has enough video memory to support multiple pages.

SYNTAX

```
void far  setvisualpage(int page);

int page;      The page number actually being displayed
```

EXAMPLE CALL

```
setvisualpage(1);
```

INCLUDES

```
#include <graphics.h>     For function declaration
```

DESCRIPTION The *setvisualpage* function selects the page specified in the argument *page* as the current page being displayed on the screen. This is the portion of video memory which is used for the memory-mapped display operation. See the description of the function *setactivepage* for more details on "pages" in video memory and on setting the active page for current graphics output.

Note that the page where graphics output is stored is selected by the *setactivepage* function and that this need not be the same as the page currently being displayed. By default, page 0 is used as both "visual" and "active" page.

1. The equivalent function in Microsoft C 5 and 6, and QuickC 1.0 through 2.5, is *_setvisualpage.*

COMMON USES The *setvisualpage* function is used together with its counterpart *setactivepage* to prepare complex graphics on one page while the user is viewing what was drawn earlier on another page. This provides for fast updating of the display and in graphics modes; this can be used for smoother animation.

SEE ALSO `setactivepage` *To select the page for current graphics output*

EXAMPLE See the example in *setactivepage*

setwritemode

COMPATIBILITY

TC1	TC1.5	TC2	TC++	MSC3	MSC4	MSC5	MSC6	QC1	QC2	QC2.5	ANSI	UNIX V	XNX
		▲	▲										

PURPOSE Use *setwritemode* to change the writing mode in which *line*, *lineto*, and *drawpoly* functions draw lines.

SYNTAX

```
void far setwritemode(int wmode);

int wmode;
```

Write mode for lines (COPY_PUT or XOR_PUT)

EXAMPLE CALL

```
setwritemode(COPY_PUT); /* Lines overwrite existing pixels */
```

INCLUDES

```
#include <graphics.h>
```

For function declaration

DESCRIPTION The *setwritemode* function is used to set the writing mode for the line drawing functions *line*, *lineto*, and *drawpoly*. The writing mode refers to the way in which pixels representing the line are set. The integer argument *wmode* specifies the mode. It can take the values COPY_PUT and XOR_PUT defined in the file *graphics.h*.

If *wmode* is COPY_PUT, the pixels lying on the line overwrite existing values so that a line drawn in color 1 (usually blue) appears exactly in that color. On the other hand, if *wmode* is XOR_PUT, each pixel belonging to the line will be given a value which is the exclusive OR of the new value and the old one. This means that you can erase a line drawn

earlier in COPY_PUT mode by simply changing the writing mode to XOR_PUT and repeating the line drawing operation.

COMMON USES The *setwritemode* function is useful in drawing and erasing lines by alternating the mode between COPY_PUT and XOR_PUT.

SEE ALSO

`line, lineto, drawpoly`	*Line drawing functions that use the writing mode set by* setwritemode
`putimage`	*Further discussion of the COPY_PUT and XOR_PUT operators*

EXAMPLE Demonstrate the use of *setwritemode* by animating a line on the screen. You can do this by drawing the line in COPY_PUT mode and then redrawing it in XOR_PUT mode.

```
#include <stdlib.h>
#include <graphics.h>

main()
{
    int graphdriver = DETECT, graphmode, x1, x2,
        y1, y2, maxx, maxy, maxcolor;
/* Detect adapter type and initialize graphics system */
    initgraph(&graphdriver, &graphmode, "c:\\tc\\bgi");
    outtextxy(10,10, "Animating a line using 'setwritemode'");
    maxx = getmaxx()-100;
    maxy = getmaxy()-60;
    maxcolor = getmaxcolor();
    randomize(); /* Initialize random number generator */
/* Exit when user presses a key */
    outtextxy(10, getmaxy()-30," Press any key to exit");
    while (!kbhit())
    {
/* Generate random end points for the lines */
        x1 = random(maxx) + 50;
        x2 = random(maxx) + 50;
        y1 = random(maxy) + 30;
        y2 = random(maxy) + 30;
        setcolor(random(maxcolor));
/* Now draw the line */
        setwritemode(COPY_PUT);
        line(x1,y1, x2,y2);
/* and erase it by redrawing it in XOR_PUT mode */
        setwritemode(XOR_PUT);
```

```
        line(x1,y1, x2,y2);
    }
    closegraph();
    return 0;
}
```

Graphics Modes, Coordinates, and Attributes

Chapter 19 Drawing and Animation

The Turbo C++ graphics library includes a set of routines to draw basic shapes and manipulate color bit-mapped images. The library currently has provisions for drawing arcs, bars, circles, ellipses, pie slices, polygons, and rectangles. Many of these figures can be optionally filled with the current fill color using the current fill pattern (see the tutorial in Chapter 18). The image manipulation routines are capable of saving a rectangular area of the screen in a buffer and restoring the image from the buffer at a specified screen coordinate. These functions can be used to achieve "animation," which is the process of creating the visual effect of motion of an object on the screen. The drawing routines are the building blocks for your graphics applications. With the basic shapes and the ability to color pixels at arbitrary screen coordinates, you can draw quite complicated images on the screen. This chapter describes the use of the basic drawing routines.

Notes on Drawing and Animation

There are 24 drawing and image manipulation routines in the Turbo C++ graphics library. Table 19-1 lists these routines by task and Table 19-2 is a catalog explaining the purpose of each routine. Note that you must initialize the graphics system using *initgraph* before these drawing routines can be used (see Chapter 18 for details).

Table 19-1. ***Drawing and Animation Routines by Task***

Task	Routines
Clear a selected area of the screen.	cleardevice, clearviewport
Draw a single point.	getpixel, putpixel

Table 19-1. ***(cont.)***

Task	Routines
Draw a straight line.	line, linerel, lineto, moverel, moveto
Draw basic shapes.	arc, bar, bar3d, circle, drawpoly, ellipse, fillellipse, pieslice, rectangle, sector
Fill a region with color.	fillpoly, floodfill
Save and restore images.	getimage, imagesize, putimage

Table 19-2. ***Catalog of Drawing and Animation Routines***

Name	Purpose
arc	Draws a circular arc.
bar	Draws a filled-in rectangular bar.
bar3d	Draws a three-dimensional bar with specifed depth.
circle	Draws a circle of specified radius centered at a given point.
cleardevice	Clears the graphics screen and sets the current position to (0,0).
clearviewport	Clears the current viewport and sets the current position to (0,0), the upper left hand corner of the viewport.
drawpoly	Draws the outline of a polygon with a specified number of points (to close the polygon, use same start and end points).
ellipse	Draws an ellipse or an elliptical arc with given center, and major and minor axes.
fillellipse	Draws and fills an ellipse using current fill color and fill style.
fillpoly	Draws and fills a polygon using current fill color and fill style.
floodfill	Fills an area of screen bounded by a border of specific color.
getimage	Saves the image of a rectangular area of the screen in an off-screen buffer.
getpixel	Gets the color of a specific pixel.
imagesize	Returns the size of memory (in bytes) needed to save a particular rectangular region of screen using *getimage*.
line	Draws a line between two specified points, but does not update the current position.
linerel	Draws a line from the current point to another located at a relative distance from the current point.
lineto	Draws a line from the current point to another specified point.
moverel	Moves the current point by specified distances in the x and y directions.
moveto	Makes a given point the new *current point*.
pieslice	Draws and fills a pie slice.
putimage	Restores an image from off-screen memory and displays it on the screen in a specified manner.
putpixel	Sets a pixel to a specific color.
rectangle	Draws a rectangle in the current line style, line thickness, and drawing color.
sector	Draws and fills an elliptical sector using current fill color and fill style.

PARAMETERS AND ATTRIBUTES THAT AFFECT DRAWING

All the drawing routines generate output in the current *viewport*, which is a rectangular area of the screen. The initial viewport is the entire display screen. You can define new viewports by the command *setviewport*. When defining a viewport, you have to specify whether you want to clip the output outside the viewport. Each graphics drawing routine expects the (x,y) coordinates to lie in a coordinate frame whose origin (0,0) is at the upper left corner of the viewport. The viewport is useful in managing graphics output windows in your application. Since all drawing operations are specified in viewport-relative coordinates, you can display the drawings in a viewing window anywhere on the screen by simply defining a suitable viewport.

The current position, color, line style, and fill style are basic parameters of the Turbo C++ graphics model that affect the drawing routines. The Turbo C++ graphics model and these parameters are described in the tutorial in Chapter 18.

DRAWING A SINGLE POINT

A basic operation in graphics is to set an arbitrary point (pixel) on the screen to a selected color. This involves setting the current color and setting the selected point to the current color. You can do this in Turbo C++ by the code

```
setcolor(BLUE);
putpixel(100,50);   /* Turn pixel to current color */
```

which will set the point at (100,50) in the current viewport to blue.

You can also "clear" a point, which simply means that you set that point to the background color. In the graphics modes, color number 0 is always the background color. Thus the point (100,50) can be reset to background by

```
setcolor(0);
putpixel(100,50);
```

You can use *getpixel* to determine the current contents of a pixel.

DRAWING LINES

Drawing lines is another basic capability of any graphics library. The Turbo C++ routines *moveto*, *moverel*, *line*, *lineto*, and *linerel* all play a part in drawing lines. All except the *line* function use the current position that is maintained internally by the Turbo C++ graphics system. You can use *moveto* to move the current position to any arbitrary point in the viewport, or use *moverel* to shift it by specified *x* and *y* distances. In the following example,

```
moveto(10,10);  /* Make (10,10) the current position */
moverel(5, 10); /* Move x coord by 5 and y by 10 */
```

moveto defines (10,10) as the current position, while *moverel* shifts the x and y coordinates of the current position by specified amounts. Thus, after the call to *moverel*, the current position will be (15,20).

The *lineto* function draws a line from the current position to the specified point and updates the current position after the line is drawn. It uses the current color to set the color of the line and the current line style to determine the appearance of the line. For example,

```
/* Draw a dashed line from (10,10) to (100,100) */
     setcolor(RED);
/* Define pattern and thickness of line */
     setlinestyle(USERBIT_LINE, 0xff00, NORM_WIDTH);
     moveto(10,10);  /* First move to (10,10) */
     lineto(100,100);    /* Then draw        */
```

will draw a red dashed line (using the user-defined line style) from the point (10,10) to the point (100,100). At the end of the drawing, the current point will be (100,100). Thus, a subsequent call such as *lineto(200,100)* will draw a line joining (100,100) to (200,100). The *linerel* function behaves like *lineto* except that it draws a line from the current point to another which is at a specified distance away along the x- and y-coordinate axes.

Finally, you can draw a line between two explicitly specified points with the *line* function. In this case, the current position is not updated.

LINE STYLE

In the line drawing example, we used *setlinestyle* to set up a dashed line style. The first argument to *setlinestyle* is a constant that indicates whether you are choosing a standard line style or defining your own. If this argument is USERBIT_LINE, the second argument is taken as a pattern that describes how a line looks when it is drawn. The pattern is a 16-bit mask which is applied when drawing a line. Think of this mask as representing a line segment 16 pixels long. If a bit in the mask is a 1, the corresponding pixel in that line is painted with the current color (see *setcolor*). If a bit is 0, the corresponding pixel is left untouched. Note that a value of FFh for the pattern means a solid line. This is the default value of the line style in the graphics package.

The third argument to *setlinestyle* specifies the thickness of the lines. It can be either NORM_WIDTH for normal width, or THICK_WIDTH for thicker lines.

WRITING MODES IN LINE DRAWING

In addition to specifying line styles, you can also specify how Turbo C++ should draw each individual pixel lying on a line being drawn. This is referred to as the "writing mode" of lines. The line drawing routines *line* and *lineto* (as well as the polygon drawing routine *drawpoly*) are affected by this writing mode. You can use the *setwritemode* function to specify the writing mode. For example, *setwritemode (COPY_PUT)* tells the line drawing functions to set each pixel on the line to the current color, overwriting the previous contents of the pixel. On the other hand, *setwritemode (XOR_PUT)* means each pixel is set by an exclusive OR operation of the current color with the previous contents of the pixel. You can switch between these two writing modes to draw and erase lines. This is illustrated in example for *setwritemode* in Chapter 18.

BASIC SHAPES The arc, bar, circle, ellipse, pie, polygon, and rectangle are the basic shapes supported in the Turbo C++ graphics library. The circle forms the basis of the arc and the pie because these two shapes are parts of a circle (see Figure 19-1). The ellipse can be used to draw an elliptical arc as well.

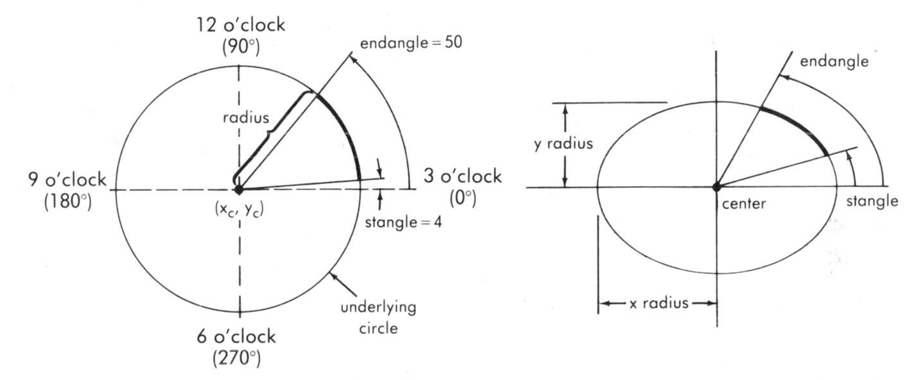

***Result of* arc (x_c, y_c, stangle, endangle radius)** **ellipse (xcenter, ycenter, stangle, endangle, xradius, yradius)**

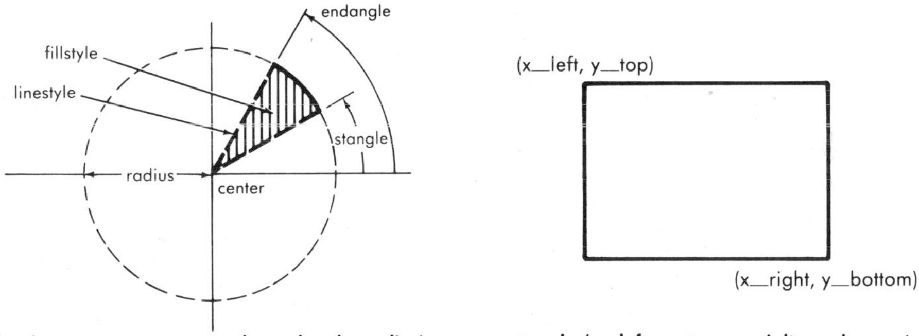

pieslice (xcenter, ycenter, stangle, endangle, radius) **rectangle (x_left, y_top, x_right, y_bottom)**

Figure 19-1. *Drawing basic shapes*

Arc, Circle, and Pie

The routines for drawing the arc, the circle, and the pie are, respectively, called *arc*, *circle*, and *pieslice*. As shown in Figure 19-1, drawing the arc, the circle, and the pie involves specifying the center point and the radius.

In case of the arc and the pie, you also specify the start and end angles to indicate how much of a circle is drawn. As expected, drawing the circle requires only the center and the radius.

For the arc, the circular segment is drawn as follows. The start angle, measured counterclockwise, with 0 degrees at 3 o'clock, defines the point where the arc begins. The end angle, specified similarly, indicates where the arc should end. When drawing the pie, lines are drawn from the center to the start and to the end of the circular segment. Also, the inside of the pie-shaped wedge is filled with the current fill color using the current fill pattern. For example, the following code will draw an arc and a pie slice that complements it.

```
/* Draw an arc: center, start, and end angle, and radius */
    arc(150, 150, 45, 315, 100);
/* A wedge of pie to complete the circle */
    setfillstyle(HATCH_FILL, 1);
    pieslice(150, 150, 316, 44);
```

Ellipse, Elliptical Arc, and Elliptical Sectors

The *ellipse* function can be used to draw a complete ellipse or an elliptical arc. In this case, you have to specify the center of the ellipse and its x and y radii. As with the *arc* function, you can specify a start and an end angle to indicate how much of the ellipse you want drawn. A complete ellipse can be drawn by specifying a start angle of 0 degrees and an end angle of 359 degrees. The following example draws a complete ellipse and a 45-degree segment of a smaller ellipse.

```
    :
/* Specify center, start angle, end angle, x and y radius */
    ellipse(150,150, 0, 359, 50, 100);
    ellipse(150, 150, 0, 45, 20, 40);
    :
```

You can use *fillellipse* to draw a filled ellipse, and *sector* to draw a filled sector of an ellipse. For the sector, the start and end points are specified in terms of angles, just as you do for an elliptical arc. The filling is done in the current color fill and fill style.

Bars and Rectangles

You can draw bars and rectangles with the functions *bar* and *rectangle* respectively. Both the bar and the rectangle require you to specify the (x,y) coordinates of the upper left hand and the lower right hand corners. For example, you can draw a 20×20 rectangle in the current line style and thickness, and with the upper left corner located at (10, 30) by

```
rectangle(10,30,30,50);
```

The bar is meant for "bar graphs" popular in business presentations. You can add a three-dimensional effect to your bar graphs with the *bar3d* function (Figure 19-2). The *bar* function is called just as you would call *rectangle* and works similarly, except that the rectangle drawn by *bar* is always filled with the current fill color and fill pattern. Also, no outline is drawn by *bar*. The *bar3d* function requires a *depth* argument and can draw a three-dimensional bar without the top so that you can stack several of them, one atop the other.

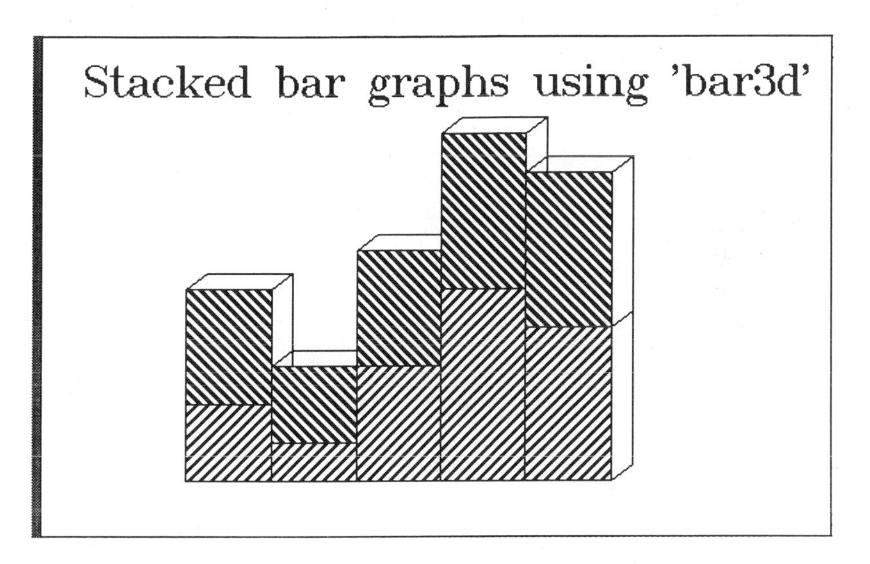

Figure 19-2. ***Three-dimensional bar graphs in Turbo C++***

ASPECT RATIO If your application has to produce an accurate rendition of all geometric figures such as squares and circles, you must take into account the "aspect ratio" of the monitor, which is the ratio of the number of pixels along a horizontal line on the screen to that along a vertical line of the same length (or, equivalently, the ratio of height of a pixel to its width). You must multiply the horizontal (x-axis) dimensions of the objects by the aspect ratio to display a properly proportioned drawing. The Turbo C++ graphics routines *arc*, *circle*, and *ellipse* automatically take into account the aspect ratio to produce correctly proportioned drawings on the screen. You can find out about the aspect ratio being used in Turbo C++ by calling the query routine *getaspectratio* as follows:

```
int xasp, yasp;
getaspectratio(&xasp, &yasp);
```

On return, *yasp* should be 10,000 (because the graphics system normalizes *yasp* to this value), and *xasp*, some value less than 10,000 (except in the VGA where *xasp* will also be 10,000). If you want to draw a square on the screen using the *rectangle* function (which does not automatically use the aspect ratio) use the values in *yasp* and *xasp*:

```
  :
int  xcorner = 10, ycorner = 20, xside, yside, side = 100;
long aspect_ratio;
  :
xside = (int) ((long)side * (long)yasp / (long)xasp);
yside = side;
/* Now the rectangle on the screen should appear "square" */
rectangle(xcorner, ycorner, xcorner+xside, ycorner+yside);
  :
```

By default, Turbo C++ uses an aspect ratio that is based on the current graphics mode and the assumed dimensions of the monitor in the system. If you draw a circle using the *circle* function and it appears as an ellipse on the screen, Turbo C++'s assumption about the aspect ratio of your display is incorrect. In this case, you should use the *setaspectratio* function to specify new values for the parameters *xasp* and *yasp* which, in turn, will force Turbo C++ to use a new aspect ratio.

POLYGONS

The *drawpoly* routine is meant for drawing a number of straight line segments. Thus it is useful for drawing x-y graphs. Figure 19-3 is an example of this application.

You can also use *drawpoly* to draw a polygon by specifying the same start and end point, thus closing the figure. The example below draws a triangle with the vertices (50,100), (100,100), and (75,25).

```
#include <graphics.h>
    :
/* Set up the vertices of the triangle */
    int triangle[] = {50,100, 100,100, 75,25, 50,100};
    int numpoints = sizeof(triangle)/(2*sizeof(int));
    :
    drawpoly(numpoints, triangle);
```

Note, in the example, the same start and end point is used to draw a closed figure, a triangle.

Another function, named *fillpoly*, lets you draw and fill a polygon at

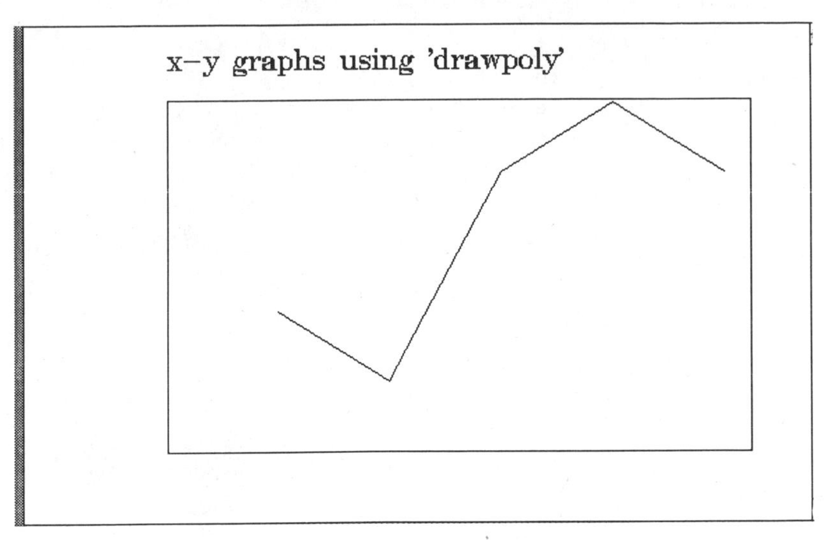

Figure 19-3. ***An x-y graph using*** **_drawpoly**

the same time. This routine behaves exactly like *drawpoly*, except that it automatically connects the first and the last point to generate a closed figure before filling it with color and pattern.

FILLING AN AREA WITH A COLOR AND A PATTERN

There is also a different way to fill an area with the current fill color and fill pattern. You can use *floodfill*. The filling begins at a point inside the area and spreads in all directions until *floodfill* encounters a specified boundary color. Thus it is important to have a solid boundary for *floodfill* to work correctly.

When filling an area, *floodfill* also applies a pattern, which is either defined with the *setfillpattern* routine or selected from a repertoire of predefined patterns by the *setfillstyle* routine. The fill pattern is also used when filling shapes such as bars, polygons (with *fillpoly*), pie slices, and elliptical sectors. Here are some examples of filling figures:

```
#include <graphics.h>
    :
    char far pattern[] =
        {0x0f, 0x0f, 0x0f, 0x0f, 0xf0, 0xf0, 0xf0, 0xf0);
    :
/* First use a predefined style */
    setfillstyle(HATCH_FILL, BLUE);
    bar(100, 100, 120, 200);

/* Now use our own pattern. Set up pattern and color */
    setfillpattern(pattern, BLUE);
```

```
/* Draw the figure with a different border color      */
    setcolor(RED);
    rectangle(10, 10, 110, 110);
/* Use floodfill to fill the rectangle                */
    floodfill(50, 50, RED);         /* Stop at color 4 */
```

We first set up a fill pattern with color BLUE (1), and draw a rectangle with a border in color RED (4). Then call *floodfill* to fill the rectangle with the selected color and pattern.

USER-DEFINED FILL PATTERN

The *setfillpattern* function is used to define an 8×8 pattern of bits as the current pattern to be used by the routines *floodfill*, *bar*, *bar3d*, *fillpoly*, and *pieslice* that fill an area with the current color.

The fill pattern is specified by a far pointer to an array of 8 characters. Since each character has 8 bits, you can think of this 8×8 array of bits as a model of an area on the screen, 8 pixels wide and 8 pixels tall, with the first character representing the first row of the area. When filling an 8×8 area using the pattern, those pixels that correspond to 0 bits are left untouched and the rest are filled with the current color. For areas larger than 8×8 pixels, the fill operation is done by repeatedly using the pattern on successive 8×8 blocks of the screen until the entire area is covered. Thus, a solid fill is specified when all 8 characters contain the value FFh. This is the default value of the fill style in the graphics package. See the pie slice in Figure 19-1 for an illustration of the concept.

IMAGE SAVE AND RESTORE

The graphics library also includes a provision for saving a graphics image (*getimage*) in a memory buffer and restoring the image (*putimage*). Also included is a routine (*imagesize*) to determine the size of memory necessary to store an image of specified size.

Saving an image is straightforward. You call *getimage* with the coordinates of the upper left and lower right corners of a rectangle on the screen and the address of the buffer where you want the image in that area of the screen to be saved. You can use *malloc* to allocate the buffer before saving the image. When doing so, you will need the size of the image. This can be had by calling *imagesize* with the same rectangle as input. For example, you can save a 20×20 rectangular image by

```
void far *buffer;
  :
buffer = (void far *) malloc((size_t)imagesize(0,0,20,20);
getimage(0,0,20,20, buffer);
```

The image can be restored somewhere else on the screen by calling *putimage*. You only need to specify the point on the screen where the upper left hand corner of the saved image will be placed. For example, we can recreate the saved image at (100,100) by

```
putimage(100,100, buffer, COPY_PUT);
```

As you can see, restoring the image involves specifying another option. This option determines how the image will be reconstructed on the screen. In the example above, the constant COPY_PUT specifies that the pixel values in the image should be copied into the pixels in the new area. Other options include logical OR, AND, or exclusive OR with existing pixel values. The reference pages on *putimage* further explain the meaning of this argument.

ANIMATION USING GETIMAGE *AND* PUTIMAGE

The ability to save and restore images can be exploited to make an object appear to move on the display screen. To achieve this effect, you have to first draw the object and save it once into a buffer. After that you must restore it again at the old location with the last argument of *putimage* set to XOR_PUT. This exclusive OR operation will clear out the old image. Now you can use *putimage* at the new location and restore it again with the XOR_PUT option. Repeating this in a loop will make the image appear to move around in the screen. Here is how the loop might look:

```
/* Draw image once */
        putimage(x,y,image,XOR_PUT);
/* Perform some animation */
        while(!kbhit())
        {
/* First erase at last position */
            putimage(x,y,image,XOR_PUT);
            x +=10;
            y += 5;
            if(x >= numxpixels) x = 0;
            if(y >= numxpixels) y = 0;
/* Redraw at new position */
            putimage(x,y,image,XOR_PUT);
        }
```

In this example, the image is drawn and saved in the buffer named *image*. Then the *while* loop animates the figure until the user presses any key. The example in the reference pages on *putimage* shows a complete animation program.

ANIMATION BY FLIPPING VIDEO PAGE

If your graphics adapter has enough memory to support at least two pages in graphics mode, you can use the *setactivepage* and the *setvisualpage* functions (see Chapter 18 for a discussion of video pages) to perform some animation. The *setactivepage* sets up the area of video memory to which all graphics go. The page being displayed is set by *setvisualpage*. The idea is to draw the next stage of an image on the active page while the user is watching the current visual page, and then simply swap the two pages. Now you can clear out the old image and prepare the next frame of animation and repeat the cycle to achieve the effect of movement.

The EGA with 256 K of video memory can support two pages of graphics that can be exploited for animation. See the example in the reference pages on *setactivepage* for an example that shows the swapping of graphics pages on an EGA.

COMPATIBILITY **arc**

TC1	TC1.5	TC2	TC++	MSC3	MSC4	MSC5	MSC6	QC1	QC2	QC2.5	ANSI	UNIX V	XNX
	▲	▲	▲			1	1	1	1	1			

PURPOSE Use *arc* to draw a circular arc of any angular extent using the current drawing color. The method of specifying the arc is described below.

SYNTAX

```
void far  arc(int x, int y, int stangle, int endangle,
              int radius);
```

`int x, y;` *Coordinates of the center of the circle to which the arc belongs*

`int stangle;` *Starting angle of arc*

`int endangle;` *Angle where arc ends*

`int radius;` *Radius of circle to which the arc belongs*

EXAMPLE CALL

```
arc(100, 100, 0, 29, 50); /* A 30-degree arc with radius 50 */
```

INCLUDES `#include <graphics.h>` *For function declaration*

DESCRIPTION The *arc* function draws a segment of a circle of radius *radius*, centered at *(x,y)* in the viewport. As shown in Figure 19-1, the start and the end points of the arc are specified in terms of two angles, *stangle* and *endangle*, measured counterclockwise, with 0 degrees at 3 o'clock, 90 degrees at 12 o'clock, and so on. Thus, a radial line to the 3 o'clock point is the reference line for specifying angles.

The arc starts at the point where the circle is cut by a radial line at an angle of *stangle* degrees counterclockwise from the reference line. Starting at this point, *arc* traces the outline of the underlying circle in a counterclockwise direction using the current drawing color, until it reaches the point where the circle is met by a radial line drawn at *endangle* degrees measured counterclockwise from the reference line. For example, you can draw a complete circle by specifying *stangle* as 0 and *endangle* equal to 359.

Unlike the line drawing functions such as *bar*, *line*, and *lineto*, *arc* uses the solid line style exclusively and it does not update the current position after drawing the arc. The *arc* function uses the aspect ratio of the current graphics mode to ensure that the arc appears circular on the screen (see the tutorial section for more on *aspect ratio*).

1. In Microsoft C 5 and 6, and QuickC 1.0 through 2.5, the equivalent function is *_arc*.

COMMON USES This function is useful in constructing line drawings that include curved sections. Several arcs can be pieced together to form a curved section.

COMMENTS Turbo C++ makes it easy to join straight lines to circular arcs. The *getarccords* function returns the center and the end points of the last arc drawn by *arc*.

SEE ALSO

`circle`	*To draw a circle*
`ellipse`	*To draw an elliptical arc or an ellipse*
`getaspectratio`	*To get the aspect ratio of current graphics mode*
`setcolor`	*To set the current color*

EXAMPLE Write a Turbo C++ program that draws an arc with parameters entered by the user.

```
#include <graphics.h>

main()
{
    int graphdriver = DETECT, graphmode, xc, yc,
        radius, stangle, endangle;
    char buffer[80];

/* Ask user for parameters of the arc */
    printf("Enter coordinates of center (x,y): ");
    scanf(" %d %d", &xc, &yc);
    printf("\nRadius, start angle and end angle: ");
    scanf(" %d %d %d", &radius, &stangle, &endangle);

/* Detect adapter type and initialize graphics system */
    initgraph(&graphdriver, &graphmode, "c:\\tc\\bgi");

    sprintf(buffer,"arc(%d,%d,%d,%d,%d)",
    xc, yc, stangle, endangle, radius);
    outtextxy(10,10, buffer);

/* Now draw the arc */
    arc(xc,yc, stangle, endangle, radius);

/* Wait until user presses a key */
    outtextxy(10, getmaxy()-50," Press any key to exit");
```

```
    getch();
    closegraph();
    return 0;
}
```

COMPATIBILITY

bar

TC1	TC1.5	TC2	TC++	MSC3	MSC4	MSC5	MSC6	QC1	QC2	QC2.5	ANSI	UNIX V	XNX
	▲	▲	▲										

PURPOSE Use *bar* to draw a rectangular bar filled with the current fill color and current fill pattern.

SYNTAX

```
void far  bar(int left, int top, int right, int bottom);
```

`int left, top;` *Coordinates of the upper left corner of the bar*

`int right, bottom;` *Coordinates of the lower right corner of the bar*

EXAMPLE CALL

```
bar(100, 100, 120, 200);  /* A bar of height 100, width 20 */
```

INCLUDES `#include <graphics.h>` *For function declaration*

DESCRIPTION The *bar* function draws a rectangular bar on the screen, and fills it with the current fill color and the current fill pattern. The bar is specified by the viewport-relative coordinates of its upper left and lower right corners, *(left,top)* and *(right,bottom)*, respectively.

COMMON USES The *bar* function is used to draw bar graphs which are a popular way of presenting data and results.

COMMENTS The *bar* function does not draw a border. Use *bar3d* with a depth of zero to get a bar with border.

SEE ALSO

`bar3d` *To draw a three-dimensional bar*

`setfillpattern` *To define a fill pattern and a fill color*

`setfillstyle` *To select a predefined fill pattern*

EXAMPLE Write a Turbo C++ program that uses *bar* to draw a bar graph.

```
#include <graphics.h>
```

```
#include <stdlib.h>

main()
{
   int graphdriver = DETECT, graphmode,  i,
       data[5] = {2,1,3,5,4}, maxdata = 5, numpt = 5,
       maxheight, maxwidth, xstep, ystep, x, y,
       maxcolor;

/* Detect adapter type and initialize graphics system */
    initgraph(&graphdriver, &graphmode, "c:\\tc\\bgi");
    outtextxy(10,10, "Bar graphs using 'bar'");
/* Now draw the bar graph */
    maxheight = getmaxy()-100;
    ystep = maxheight/maxdata;
    maxwidth = getmaxx()-200;
    xstep = maxwidth/numpt;
    x = 100;
    y = maxheight+40;
/* Use random color */
    randomize();
    maxcolor = getmaxcolor();
    for (i = 0; i<numpt; i++, x += xstep)
    {
        setfillstyle((i%11)+1, random(maxcolor));
        bar(x,y-data[i]*ystep, x+xstep,y);
    }
/* Wait until user presses a key */
    outtextxy(10, getmaxy()-30," Press any key to exit");

    getch();
    closegraph();
    return 0;
}
```

Drawing and Animation

bar3d

COMPATIBILITY

TC1	TC1.5	TC2	TC++	MSC3	MSC4	MSC5	MSC6	QC1	QC2	QC2.5	ANSI	UNIX V	XNX
	▲	▲	▲										

PURPOSE Use *bar3d* to draw a three-dimensional rectangular bar filled with the current fill color and current fill pattern.

SYNTAX

```
void far  bar3d(int left, int top, int right, int bottom,
                int depth, int topflag);
```

`int left, top;`	*Coordinates of the upper left corner of the bar*
`int right, bottom;`	*Coordinates of the lower right corner of the bar*
`int depth;`	*Depth of the three-dimensional bar in pixels*
`int topflag;`	*Top surface of bar is not drawn if this is 0*

EXAMPLE CALL

```
/* A 3D bar of height 100, width 20, depth 5, and with a top*/
bar3d(100, 100, 120, 200, 5, 1);
```

INCLUDES `#include <graphics.h>` *For function declaration*

DESCRIPTION The *bar3d* function draws the outline of a three-dimensional (3-D) rectangular bar in the current drawing color, and fills it with the current fill color and pattern. The bar is specified by its front face and the depth. The depth is given in the argument *depth*. The rectangle representing the front face is specified by the viewport-relative coordinates of its upper left and lower right corners, *(left,top)* and *(right,bottom)*, respectively.

You have the option of not drawing a top on the 3-D view of the bar. The top is drawn only if the argument *topflag* is nonzero. This is useful when you want to stack one 3-D bar atop another (see Figure 19-2).

COMMON USES The *bar* function is used to draw bar graphs which are a popular way of presenting data and results.

SEE ALSO

`bar`	*To draw a bar filled with current fill color and current fill pattern*
`setfillpattern`	*To define a fill pattern and a fill color*
`setfillstyle`	*To select a predefined fill pattern*

EXAMPLE Use *bar3d* to draw a bar graph with three-dimensional bars.

```
#include <graphics.h>
#include <stdlib.h>

main()
{
  int graphdriver = DETECT, graphmode,  i,
      data[5] = {2,1,3,5,4}, maxdata = 5, numpt = 5,
      maxheight, maxwidth, xstep, ystep, x, y, depth,
      maxcolor;

/* Detect adapter type and initialize graphics system */
    initgraph(&graphdriver, &graphmode, "c:\\tc\\bgi");
    outtextxy(10,10, "Bar graphs using 'bar3d'");
/* Now draw the bar graph */
    maxheight = getmaxy()-100;
    ystep = maxheight/maxdata;
    maxwidth = getmaxx()-200;
    xstep = maxwidth/numpt;
    depth = xstep/4;
    x = 100;
    y = maxheight+40;
/* Use random color */
    randomize();
    maxcolor = getmaxcolor();
    for (i = 0; i<numpt; i++, x += xstep)
    {
        setfillstyle((i%11)+1, random(maxcolor));
        bar3d(x,y-data[i]*ystep, x+xstep,y,depth,1);
    }
/* Wait until user presses a key */
    outtextxy(10, getmaxy()-30," Press any key to exit");

    getch();
    closegraph();
    return 0;
}
```

Drawing and Animation

COMPATIBILITY

circle

TC1	TC1.5	TC2	TC++	MSC3	MSC4	MSC5	MSC6	QC1	QC2	QC2.5	ANSI	UNIX V	XNX
	▲	▲	▲										

PURPOSE Use *circle* to draw a circle.

SYNTAX

```
void far  circle(int x, int y, int radius);
```

`int x, y;` *Coordinates (viewport-relative) of the center of the circle*

`int radius;` *Radius of the circle*

EXAMPLE CALL

```
circle(100,100,50);  /* A circle of radius 50 at (100,100) */
```

INCLUDES `#include <graphics.h>` *For function declaration*

DESCRIPTION The *circle* function draws a circle with the radius specified by the argument *radius*, and center located at the point *(x,y)* (where the upper left corner of the current viewport is the origin of the coordinate axes). The outline of the circle is drawn using the current drawing color and in a solid line style. You can use *floodfill* to fill the area inside the circle.

COMMENTS Although *arc* can be used to draw a complete circle, *circle* offers a more straightforward way to do it.

SEE ALSO

`arc` *To draw a circular arc*

`ellipse` *To draw an elliptical arc or an ellipse*

`floodfill` *To fill an area with color and pattern*

`getaspectratio` *To get the aspect ratio of current graphics mode*

`setcolor` *To set the current color*

EXAMPLE Write a Turbo C++ program that draws a circle using parameters entered by the user.

```
#include <graphics.h>

main()
{
  int graphdriver = DETECT, graphmode, xc, yc,
      radius;
  char buffer[80];
```

```
/* Ask user for parameters of the arc */
    printf("Enter coordinates of center (x,y): ");
    scanf(" %d %d", &xc, &yc);
    printf("\nRadius: ");
    scanf(" %d", &radius);

/* Detect adapter type and initialize graphics system */
    initgraph(&graphdriver, &graphmode, "c:\\tc\\bgi");

    sprintf(buffer,"circle(%d,%d,%d)",xc, yc, radius);
    outtextxy(10,10, buffer);

/* Now draw the circle */
    circle(xc,yc, radius);

/* Wait until user presses a key */
    outtextxy(10, getmaxy()-50," Press any key to exit");

    getch();
    closegraph();
    return 0;
  }
```

cleardevice

COMPATIBILITY

TC1	TC1.5	TC2	TC++	MSC3	MSC4	MSC5	MSC6	QC1	QC2	QC2.5	ANSI	UNIX V	XNX
	▲	▲	▲			1	1	1	1	1			

PURPOSE Use *cleardevice* to clear the entire screen and move the current position to the upper left corner of the current viewport.

SYNTAX `void far  cleardevice(void);`

EXAMPLE CALL `cleardevice();     /* Clear the entire screen */`

INCLUDES `#include <graphics.h>` *For function declaration*

DESCRIPTION The *cleardevice* function clears the screen and fills it with the background color. The background color may be altered by calling *setbkcolor*. After clearing the screen, *cleardevice* resets the current position to the origin (the upper left corner) of the current viewport. If you want to clear the current viewport only, use *clearviewport*.

1. Use *_clearscreen* in Microsoft C 5 and 6, and QuickC 1.0 through 2.5.

SEE ALSO

`clearviewport`	*To clear the current viewport*
`setbkcolor`	*To change the current background color*
`setviewport`	*To define a limited area of the screen as a viewport*

EXAMPLE The example below shows how *cleardevice* can be used to erase the graphics screen and fill it with the current background color.

```
#include <graphics.h>

main()
{
  int graphdriver = DETECT, graphmode;

/* Detect adapter type and initialize graphics system */
  initgraph(&graphdriver, &graphmode, "c:\\tc\\bgi");
/* Draw some object on the screen */
  bar(100,100,150,150);
  outtextxy(10,10, "Press any key to clear screen");
  getch();
  cleardevice();
  outtextxy(10,10, "Screen cleared...");

/* Wait until user presses a key */
  outtextxy(10, getmaxy()-50," Press any key to exit");

  getch();
  closegraph();
  return 0;
}
```

clearviewport

COMPATIBILITY

TC1	TC1.5	TC2	TC++	MSC3	MSC4	MSC5	MSC6	QC1	QC2	QC2.5	ANSI	UNIX V	XNX
	▲	▲	▲			1	1	1	1	1			

PURPOSE Use *clearviewport* to clear the current viewport and move the current position to the upper left corner of the viewport.

SYNTAX `void far  clearviewport(void);`

EXAMPLE CALL `clearviewport();     /* Clear the current viewport */`

INCLUDES `#include <graphics.h>` *For function declaration*

DESCRIPTION The *clearviewport* function clears the current viewport and fills it with the background color. The background color may be altered by calling *setbkcolor*. After clearing the viewport, *clearviewport* resets the current position to the origin (the upper left corner) of the current viewport.

If you want to clear the entire screen, use *cleardevice*.

1. In Microsoft C 5 and 6, and QuickC 1.0 through 2.5, the compatible function is *_clearscreen*.

COMMON USES The ability to selectively erase a viewport can be used to implement pop-up and pull-down menus.

SEE ALSO

`cleardevice` *To clear the entire screen*

`setbkcolor` *To change the current background color*

`setviewport` *To define a limited area of the screen as a viewport*

EXAMPLE Write a program that defines a viewport, draws a graphical object, and finally, uses *clearviewport* to erase the viewport. Notice that anything outside the viewport remains untouched.

```
#include <graphics.h>

main()
{
  int graphdriver = DETECT, graphmode;

/* Detect adapter type and initialize graphics system */
    initgraph(&graphdriver, &graphmode, "c:\\tc\\bgi");
    outtextxy(10,10, "Press any key to clear viewport");

/* Define a viewport and draw something in it */
    setviewport(100,50, getmaxx()-100, getmaxy()-60, 1);
/* Draw outline of the viewport */
    rectangle(0,0,getmaxx()-200,getmaxy()-110);
    bar(50,50,100,100);
    getch();   /* Read the keypress */
    clearviewport();
    outtextxy(10,10,
             "Notice only viewport was cleared");
/* Wait until user presses a key */
    outtextxy(10, getmaxy()-50," Press any key to exit");

    getch();
```

Drawing and Animation

```
    closegraph();
    return 0;
}
```

COMPATIBILITY

drawpoly

TC1	TC1.5	TC2	TC++	MSC3	MSC4	MSC5	MSC6	QC1	QC2	QC2.5	ANSI	UNIX V	XNX
	▲	▲	▲										

PURPOSE Use *drawpoly* to draw the outline of a polygon.

SYNTAX

```
void far  drawpoly(int numpoints, int far *polypoints);
```

`int      numpoints;` *Number of points in the polygon (each x,y pair counts as one point)*

`int far *polypoints;` *Pointer to list of x- and y- coordinates that represent the vertices of the polygon*

EXAMPLE CALL

```
int triangle[] = {100,100, 150,50, 200,100, 100,100},
           npts = sizeof(triangle)/(2*sizeof(int));

drawpoly(npts, triangle);  /* Draw a triangle */
```

INCLUDES `#include <graphics.h>` *For function declaration*

DESCRIPTION The *drawpoly* function draws line segments using the current line style and color, joining the points specified in a list whose address is given in the argument *polypoints*. The argument *numpoints* has the total number of x- and y-coordinate pairs in the list. The *setwritemode* function determines the writing mode for the pixels that lie on the line segments (see description of *setwritemode* for more details).

The *drawpoly* function will not automatically draw a closed figure. You can, however, draw a polygon with *n* sides by specifying *n+1* points, the first and the last point being the same. Use *fillpoly* to draw a polygon filled with the current fill color and fill pattern.

COMMON USES Even though the name implies otherwise, the most common use of *drawpoly* is to draw x-y graphs (for example, see Figure 19-3).

SEE ALSO

`fillpoly` *To draw a filled polygon*

`line, linerel, lineto` *To draw a line between two points*

`setlinestyle`	*To set the appearance of lines*
`setwritemode`	*To set the writing mode of lines*

EXAMPLE Write a Turbo C program that uses *drawpoly* to draw an x-y graph of some data. Note that we use *getmaxx* and *getmaxy* to get the maximum x and y coordinates for the current video mode. We use this information to scale the points on the x-y graph to fit within the bounds of the screen. Figure 19-3 shows the output of this program.

```
#include <graphics.h>
#include <stdlib.h>

main()
{
  int graphdriver = DETECT, graphmode,  i,
      y[5] = {2,1,4,5,4}, maxy = 5,
      x[5] = {10, 20, 30, 40, 50}, maxx = 50,
      numpt = sizeof(y)/sizeof(int),
      maxheight, maxwidth, xscale, yscale,
      plotdata[10];

/* Detect adapter type and initialize graphics system */
    initgraph(&graphdriver, &graphmode, "c:\\tc\\bgi");
    settextstyle(TRIPLEX_FONT, HORIZ_DIR, 2);
    outtextxy(100,10, "x-y graphs using 'drawpoly'");
/* Now draw the x-y graph */
    maxheight = getmaxy()-100;
    yscale = maxheight/maxy;
    maxwidth = getmaxx()-300;
    xscale = maxwidth/maxx;
    setviewport(100,50,100+maxwidth,50+maxheight,1);
    rectangle(0,0,maxwidth,maxheight);
/* Scale the data points to fit in assigned area */
    for (i = 0; i < numpt; i++)
    {
        plotdata[2*i] = x[i]*xscale;
/* Our y-coordinates increase as we go up */
        plotdata[2*i+1] = maxheight-y[i]*yscale;
    }
/* Use drawpoly to display the graph */
    drawpoly(numpt, plotdata);
/* Wait until user presses a key */
/*  outtextxy(10, getmaxy()-30,
```

Drawing and Animation

```
                  " Press any key to exit"); */

   getch();
   closegraph();
   returnk 0;
}
```

COMPATIBILITY

ellipse

TC1	TC1.5	TC2	TC++	MSC3	MSC4	MSC5	MSC6	QC1	QC2	QC2.5	ANSI	UNIX V	XNX
	▲	▲	▲			1	1	1	1	1			

PURPOSE Use *ellipse* to draw an elliptical arc or a complete ellipse in the current drawing color.

SYNTAX

```
void far  ellipse(int x, int y, int stangle, int endangle,
                  int xradius, int yradius);
```

`int x, y;`	*Coordinates of the center of the ellipse*
`int stangle;`	*Starting angle of arc*
`int endangle;`	*Angle where arc ends*
`int xradius;`	*Length of horizontal axis of the ellipse*
`int yradius;`	*Length of vertical axis of the ellipse*

EXAMPLE CALL `ellipse(100, 100, 0, 45, 50, 25);`

INCLUDES `#include <graphics.h>` *For function declaration*

DESCRIPTION The *ellipse* function draws a segment of an ellipse with horizontal and vertical axes specified by *xradius* and *yradius*, respectively, and with the center at the point *(x,y)* relative to the origin (the upper left corner) of the current viewport. The start and end points of the elliptical arc are specified by the angles *stangle* and *endangle* (in degrees). See the reference entry of *arc* for the interpretation of these angles.

You can draw a complete ellipse by specifying *stangle* as zero degrees and *endangle* as 359 degrees. Use *floodfill* to fill the ellipse with a pattern and a color.

Unlike the line drawing functions such as *bar*, *line*, and *lineto*, *ellipse* uses the solid line style exclusively and it does not update the current position after drawing the elliptical arc.

1. Use *_ellipse* in Microsoft C 5 and 6, and QuickC 1.0 through 2.5.

COMMON USES This function can be used as a primitive object for building more complex graphical objects.

SEE ALSO

`arc`	*To draw a circular arc*
`circle`	*To draw a circle*
`floodfill`	*To fill an area with current fill color and fill pattern*
`setcolor`	*To set the current color*

EXAMPLE Draw an egg-shaped curve using half an ellipse atop a circular arc.

```
/* Draw an egg-shaped curve using ellipse and arc */

  #include <graphics.h>

  main()
  {
    int errorcode;
    int graphdriver = DETECT;
    int graphmode;
    int xc, yc, yradius = 65, xradius = 50;

  /* Detect and initialize graphics system */
    initgraph(&graphdriver, &graphmode, "c:\\tc\\bgi");
    errorcode = graphresult();
    if (errorcode != grOk)
    {
      printf("Graphics error: %s\n",
      grapherrormsg(errorcode));
      exit(1);
    };
    xc = getmaxx()/2;
    yc = getmaxy()/2;
/* Draw half an ellipse followed by a semicircle */
    ellipse(xc, yc, 0, 180, xradius, yradius);
    arc(xc, yc, 180, 360, xradius);
/* Explain what we've done */
    settextjustify(CENTER_TEXT, CENTER_TEXT);
    settextstyle(SANS_SERIF_FONT, HORIZ_DIR, 1);
    outtextxy( xc, 50, "An egg using arc, ellipse");
    outtextxy(xc, 2*yc-50, "Press any key to exit:");
    getch();         /* Wait until a key is pressed */
```

Drawing and Animation

```
    closegraph();           /* Exit graphics library */
    return 0;
}
```

COMPATIBILITY

fillellipse

TC1	TC1.5	TC2	TC++	MSC3	MSC4	MSC5	MSC6	QC1	QC2	QC2.5	ANSI	UNIX V	XNX
		▲	▲			1	1	1	1	1			

PURPOSE Use *fillellipse* to draw an ellipse filled with the current fill color, and fill pattern.

SYNTAX

```
void far fillellipse(int x, int y, int xradius, int yradius);
```

int x, y; *Coordinates of the center of the ellipse*

int xradius; *Length of horizontal axis of the ellipse*

int yradius; *Length of vertical axis of the ellipse*

EXAMPLE CALL

```
fillellipse(100,100,50,25);
```

INCLUDES #include <graphics.h> *For function declaration*

DESCRIPTION The *fillellipse* function draws a filled ellipse with its center at the point *(x,y)*, and with *xradius* and *yradius* as the horizontal and vertical axes, respectively. The outline of the ellipse is not drawn and its inside is filled with the current fill color using the current fill pattern. The fill color and fill pattern can be set using the functions *setfillpattern* or *setfillstyle*.

1. In Microsoft C 5 and 6, and QuickC 1.0 through 2.5, use *_ellipse*.

COMMENTS If you want to draw the outline of an ellipse or an elliptical arc, use *ellipse*.

SEE ALSO

ellipse *To draw an elliptical arc or an ellipse*

setfillpattern *To define a fill pattern and a fill color*

setfillstyle *To select a predefined fill pattern and set a fill color*

EXAMPLE Illustrate the use *fillellipse* to draw a filled ellipse.

```
#include <graphics.h>
char fillpattern[8] =
{ 0xf0, 0xf0, 0xf0, 0xf0, 0xf, 0xf, 0xf, 0xf };
```

```
main()
{
    int graphdriver = DETECT, graphmode;
/* Detect adapter type and initialize graphics system */
    initgraph(&graphdriver, &graphmode, "c:\\tc\\bgi");
    outtextxy(10,10, "Demonstrating 'fillellipse'");

/* Draw two filled ellipses */
    setfillstyle(SLASH_FILL, RED);
    fillellipse(100, 100, 100, 25);
    setfillpattern(fillpattern, YELLOW);
    fillellipse(200, 200, 100, 25);

/* Exit when user presses a key */
    outtextxy(10, getmaxy()-30," Press any key to exit");
    getch();
    closegraph();
    return 0;
}
```

fillpoly

COMPATIBILITY

TC1	TC1.5	TC2	TC++	MSC3	MSC4	MSC5	MSC6	QC1	QC2	QC2.5	ANSI	UNIX V	XNX
	▲	▲	▲										

PURPOSE Use *fillpoly* to draw the outline of a closed polygon using the current drawing color and fill its inside with the current fill color and fill pattern.

SYNTAX

```
void far  fillpoly(int numpoints, int far *polypoints);
```

`int      numpoints;` *Number of points in the polygon (each x,y pair counts as one point)*

`int far *polypoints;` *Pointer to list of x- and y-coordinates that represent the vertices of the polygon*

EXAMPLE CALL

```
int triangle[] = {100,100, 150,50, 200,100},
          npts = sizeof(triangle)/(2*sizeof(int));

fillpoly(npts, triangle);  /* Draw a filled triangle */
```

INCLUDES `#include <graphics.h>` *For function declaration*

DESCRIPTION The *fillpoly* function draws line segments using the current line style and color joining the points specified in a list whose address is given in the argument *polypoints*. The argument *numpoints* has the total number of x and y coordinate pairs in the list. Unlike *drawpoly*, *fillpoly* automatically connects the first and the last point to generate a closed figure. It also fills the inside of the polygon using the current fill color and fill pattern. Use *setfillpattern* or *setfillstyle* to select the fill color and pattern before calling *fillpoly*.

The fill operation uses an internal buffer to hold intermediate results. If the buffer size turns out to be insufficient, the error code will be set to −6 (*grNoScanMem*). You should use *graphresult* to check this error code after calling *fillpoly*.

SEE ALSO

drawpoly	*To draw outline of a polygon*
setfillpattern	*To define a fill pattern*
setfillstyle	*To select a predefined fill pattern*
setlinestyle	*To set the appearance of lines*

EXAMPLE Draw a filled triangle using *fillpoly*. Notice that unlike *drawpoly*, *fillpoly* joins the last point with the first to produce a closed figure.

```
#include <graphics.h>
#include <stdlib.h>

main()
{
  int graphdriver = DETECT, graphmode,
      triangle[] = {100,100, 150,50, 200,100},
      numpt = sizeof(triangle)/(2*sizeof(int));

/* Detect adapter type and initialize graphics system */
  initgraph(&graphdriver, &graphmode, "c:\\tc\\bgi");
  outtextxy(10,10, "Demonstrating fillpoly");

/* Use fillpoly to draw the filled figure */
  setfillstyle(SOLID_FILL, RED);
  fillpoly(numpt, triangle);

/* Wait until user presses a key */
  outtextxy(10, getmaxy()-30," Press any key to exit");

  getch();
  closegraph();
  return 0;
}
```

floodfill

COMPATIBILITY

TC1	TC1.5	TC2	TC++	MSC3	MSC4	MSC5	MSC6	QC1	QC2	QC2.5	ANSI	UNIX V	XNX
	▲	▲	▲			1	1	1	1	1			

PURPOSE Use *floodfill* to fill a bordered area of the screen with the current fill color and current fill pattern.

SYNTAX

```
void far  floodfill(int x, int y, int border);
```

`int x, y;` *Coordinates of starting point from which the* floodfill *begins*

`int border;` *Color number of the boundary at which filling should stop*

EXAMPLE CALL

```
/* Flood fill from (50,50) up to boundary color 4 */
floodfill(50, 50, 4);
```

INCLUDES `#include <graphics.h>` *For function declaration*

DESCRIPTION The *floodfill* function uses a well-known graphics algorithm of the same name to fill either the inside or the outside of a solid curve whose color is given in the argument *border*. The fill operation begins at the point whose coordinates are specified provided in the arguments *x* and *y* . The region that gets filled depends on the starting "seed" point. If this point is inside the curve, the inside is filled. If it is outside, the region outside the curve gets filled. If you specify a point exactly on the boundary, the fill is not done.

The filling begins at the specified "seed" point and spreads in all directions until *floodfill* encounters a pixel of the specified border color, which should be different from the fill color to prevent the whole screen from being filled. The pattern used for filling is either a predefined one set with *setfillstyle* or a user-defined one specified with *setfillpattern*.

1. In Microsoft C 5 and 6, and QuickC 1.0 through 2.5, use *_floodfill*.

COMMENTS Since the filling algorithm colors all pixels on each row of pixels until it meets a pixel of color *border*, it is important to have a solid boundary for a proper fill (see the example below for a case where we attempt to fill a rectangle with a boundary drawn in dashed line style).

SEE ALSO `setfillpattern` *To select a predefined fill pattern*

`setfillstyle` *To define your own fill pattern*

EXAMPLES Draw a rectangle with a solid white border, and fill it with solid red color using *floodfill*.

```
#include <graphics.h>

main()
{
    int graphdriver = DETECT, graphmode;

/* Detect adapter type and initialize graphics system */
    initgraph(&graphdriver, &graphmode, "c:\\tc\\bgi");
    outtextxy(10,10, "Demonstrating floodfill");

/* First draw a rectangle with a white border and
 * a solid line style
 */
    setlinestyle(USERBIT_LINE,0xffff,THICK_WIDTH);
    setcolor(WHITE);
    rectangle(0, 50, 100, 100);
/* Now use floodfill to fill the interior with red */
    setfillstyle(SOLID_FILL, RED);
    floodfill(25, 75, WHITE);
    outtextxy(10, 20, grapherrormsg(graphresult()));
/* Give user a chance to see the result */
    outtextxy(10, getmaxy()-30," Press any key to exit");

    getch();
    closegraph();
    return 0;
}
```

If the boundary of the region being filled is not solid, the *floodfill* function will leak colors through the holes in the boundary. Demonstrate this effect by drawing a rectangle with a boundary in dashed line style and attempting to fill its inside.

```
#include <graphics.h>

main()
{
    int graphdriver = DETECT, graphmode;

/* Detect adapter type and initialize graphics system */
    initgraph(&graphdriver, &graphmode, "c:\\tc\\bgi");
    outtextxy(10,10, "floodfill needs solid boundary");
```

```
/* First draw a rectangle with a blue border and
 * a dashed line style
 */
    setlinestyle(USERBIT_LINE,0xf0f0,THICK_WIDTH);
    setcolor(BLUE);
    rectangle(0, 50, 100, 100);
/* Now use floodfill to fill the interior with red */
    setfillstyle(SOLID_FILL, RED);
    floodfill(25, 75, BLUE);

/* Give user a chance to see the result */
    outtextxy(10, getmaxy()-30," Press any key to exit");

    getch();
    closegraph();
    return 0;
}
```

getimage

COMPATIBILITY

TC1	TC1.5	TC2	TC++	MSC3	MSC4	MSC5	MSC6	QC1	QC2	QC2.5	ANSI	UNIX V	XNX
	▲	▲	▲			1	1	1	1	1			

PURPOSE Use the *getimage* function to save a rectangular screen image in a buffer. You must allocate a sufficient amount of storage for the buffer and provide the buffer's address to *getimage.*

SYNTAX

```
void far  getimage(int left, int top, int right, int bottom,
                   void far *image_buffer);

void far _getimage(short x1, short y1, short x2, short y2,
                   char far *image_buffer);
```

`int left, top;` *Upper left corner of rectangular boundary of screen image to be saved*

`int right, bottom;` *Lower right corner of rectangular boundary of screen image to be saved*

`void far *image_buffer;` *Buffer where image is to be stored*

EXAMPLE CALL `getimage(50,50,100,100,image); /* Save the image */`

INCLUDES `#include <graphics.h>` *For function declaration*

DESCRIPTION The *getimage* function saves the pixels corresponding to a rectangular region of the screen into the buffer whose address is provided in the argument *image_buffer*. The screen image to be saved is specified by the rectangle whose upper left corner is *(left,top)* and lower right corner is *(right,bottom)*.

Enough storage must be allocated to hold the image. Before using *getimage*, you should call the function *imagesize* to determine the minimum number of bytes necessary to save the specified image. The example shows the necessary steps.

1. The compatible function in Microsoft C 5 and 6, and QuickC 1.0 through 2.5, is *_getimage*.

COMMON USES The *getimage* function is used in conjunction with *putimage* to save and restore screen images. You can, for example, use the *getimage* function to draw an object once, save it, and then reproduce it at several locations on the screen by calling *putimage*. Additionally, erasing the old image before putting the new one enables you to make an image appear to move on the screen (animation).

SEE ALSO

`imagesize` *To determine number of bytes necessary to save a screen image*

`putimage` *To display a stored image*

EXAMPLE In a graphics mode, draw some graphical objects and save them in memory by calling *getimage*. Now clear the screen and use *putimage* to reproduce the objects several times on the screen.

```
#include <alloc.h>
#include <graphics.h>

main()
{
    char far *image;
    char buffer[80];
    unsigned numbytes;
    int graphdriver = DETECT, graphmode;

/* Detect adapter type and initialize graphics system */
    initgraph(&graphdriver, &graphmode, "c:\\tc\\bgi");
/* Draw some graphical objects to save */
    setfillstyle(SOLID_FILL, RED);
    bar(50,50,90,90);
    setcolor(YELLOW);
    ellipse(80,80,0,360,40,40);
/* Determine storage needed for image */
```

```
    numbytes = (unsigned int)imagesize(0,0,50,50);
    sprintf(buffer, "To save 51 x 51 image using \
getimage, we need %u bytes of memory.", numbytes);
    outtextxy(10,10, buffer);

/* Allocate buffer for image */
    if ((image = (char far *) malloc(numbytes)) ==
        (char far *)NULL)
    {
        closegraph();
        printf("Not enough memory for image storage\n");
        exit(0);
    }
    getimage(50,50,100,100,image); /* Save the image */
    outtextxy(10,getmaxy()-50,
              "Image saved. Hit any key to continue");
    getch();
/* Now clear screen and draw saved image at several
 * screen locations
 */
    cleardevice();
    setbkcolor(CYAN); /* Change the background color*/
    outtextxy(10,10,
              "Demonstrating getimage and putimage");
    putimage(80,80,image,OR_PUT);
    putimage(150,20,image,COPY_PUT);
    putimage(300,200,image,NOT_PUT);
/* Once user presses any key, reset mode and exit */
    outtextxy(10, getmaxy()-30," Press any key to exit");
    getch();
    closegraph();
    return 0;
}
```

getpixel

COMPATIBILITY

TC1	TC1.5	TC2	TC++	MSC3	MSC4	MSC5	MSC6	QC1	QC2	QC2.5	ANSI	UNIX V	XNX
	▲	▲	▲			1	1	1	1	1			

PURPOSE Use *getpixel* to retrieve the color of a specific pixel.

SYNTAX `unsigned far getpixel(int x, int y);`

`int x, y;` *Viewport-relative x- and y-coordinates of the pixel whose value is returned*

EXAMPLE CALL `pix_value = getpixel(100, 150);`

INCLUDES `#include <graphics.h>` *For function declaration*

DESCRIPTION The *getpixel* function first checks to see if the pixel specified by the coordinates *(x,y)* lies within the current viewport. If it does, *getpixel* returns the color of that pixel which is the value contained in the video memory location corresponding to the pixel coordinate *(x,y)*.

1. In Microsoft C 5 and 6, and QuickC 1.0 through 2.5, use *_getpixel*.

COMMON USES The *getpixel* function is used to perform operations such as to turn all red pixels to blue. You can use *getpixel* with *setcolor* and *putpixel* to go through the pixels, checking the value of each and changing those containing red to blue. (See the example below.)

RETURNS If the pixel is inside the current viewport, *getpixel* returns the current pixel value. Otherwise, it returns a zero.

SEE ALSO

`setviewport` *To define a limited area of the screen as a viewport for graphics output*

`putpixel` *To set a pixel to current color*

EXAMPLE In a graphics mode, draw a small red rectangle. Then go over a larger rectangular area and use *getpixel* to find all the red pixels. Use *putpixel* to turn each red pixel to blue. Since a zero value indicates a background pixel, you can also turn each pixel containing a 0 to, for example, red.

```
#include <graphics.h>

main()
{
    int graphdriver = DETECT, graphmode,
        x, y, color;
/* Detect adapter type and initialize graphics system */
    initgraph(&graphdriver, &graphmode, "c:\\tc\\bgi");
    outtextxy(10,10, "Changing colors using getpixel \
with putpixel");

/* Draw a red bordered rectangle */
    setcolor(RED);
    rectangle(70,50,130,80);
    outtextxy(10,20,"Press any key to turn red into \
blue:");
    getch();
```

```
/* Go over a rectangular region and change red to blue */
    for(x=50; x<150; x++)
    {
        for(y=40; y<90; y++)
        {
            if(getpixel(x,y) == 0)
            {                           /* it's  background */
                putpixel(x,y,RED); /* turn pixel red */
                continue;          /* skip next check..*/
            }
            if(getpixel(x,y) == RED)
            {                           /* it's  a red pixel */
                putpixel(x,y,BLUE); /* turn pixel blue*/
            }
        }
    }
/* Wait for user to press a key, then reset everything */
    outtextxy(10, getmaxy()-30," Press any key to exit");

    getch();
    closegraph();
    return 0;
}
```

imagesize

COMPATIBILITY

TC1	TC1.5	TC2	TC++	MSC3	MSC4	MSC5	MSC6	QC1	QC2	QC2.5	ANSI	UNIX V	XNX
	▲	▲	▲			1	1	1	1	1			

PURPOSE Use the *imagesize* function to determine the number of bytes necessary to store a rectangular region of the screen in a memory buffer. Call *imagesize* before allocating memory to store an image with *getimage*.

SYNTAX

```
unsigned far imagesize(int left, int top, int right, int bottom);
```

`int left, top;` *Upper left corner of rectangular boundary of image*

`int right, bottom;` *Lower right corner of rectangular boundary of image*

EXAMPLE CALL

```
bytes_needed = imagesize(min_x, min_y, max_x, max_y);
```

INCLUDES `#include <graphics.h>` *For function declaration*

Drawing and Animation

DESCRIPTION The *imagesize* function computes the number of bytes necessary to store the screen image within the rectangular region specified by the upper left corner by *(left,top)* and the lower right corner *(right,bottom)*. This is the minimum amount of storage that the function *getimage* needs to save that rectangular region of screen.

The number of bytes necessary to store the image depends on the number of bits each pixel needs, which depends on the graphics mode in use (see Chapter 18). The pixel values are stored in a packed format. The first two words (16-bit values) are used to store the width and the height of the screen image being saved.

1. The equivalent function in Microsoft C 5 and 6, and QuickC 1.0 through 2.5, is *_imagesize*.

COMMON USES The *getimage* and *putimage* function provide the capability to save and restore screen images in graphics modes. This is useful for moving or animating images on the screen.

When saving an image, you must provide a buffer of adequate size. The *imagesize* function allows you to determine the buffer size, taking into account the number of bits of storage needed in the current video mode.

RETURNS The *imagesize* function returns an unsigned integer containing the number of bytes needed to store the specified rectangular screen image. Since the return value is a 16-bit unsigned integer, only buffer sizes less than 64 K can be computed and returned by *getimage*. If the buffer size required for a selected image size equals or exceeds 64 K, *imagesize* returns the value 0xffff (65,535).

SEE ALSO

`getimage` *To save an image in memory, needs storage buffer*

`putimage` *To display a stored image*

EXAMPLE Write a Turbo C++ program that calls *imagesize* to determine the amount of storage *getimage* will need to save an image of specified size in memory.

```
#include <graphics.h>
main()
{
    int graphdriver = DETECT, graphmode, xsize, ysize;
    unsigned bytesneeded;
    char buffer[80];

    printf("Enter x and y dimensions of image to be \
saved:");
    scanf(" %d %d", &xsize, &ysize);
```

```
   /* Detect and initialize graphics system */
    initgraph(&graphdriver, &graphmode, "c:\\tc\\bgi");

/* Determine memory needed to save image */
    bytesneeded = imagesize(0,0,xsize-1,ysize-1);
    if(bytesneeded != 0xffff)
        sprintf(buffer, "To save a %dx%d image, we need \
%u bytes", xsize, ysize, bytesneeded);
    else
        sprintf(buffer, "To save a %dx%d image, we need \
more than 64 K of storage", xsize, ysize);
    outtextxy(10,10,buffer);

/* Wait until user presses a key */
    outtextxy(10, getmaxy()-30," Press any key to exit");

    getch();
    closegraph();
    return 0;
}
```

line

COMPATIBILITY

TC1	TC1.5	TC2	TC++	MSC3	MSC4	MSC5	MSC6	QC1	QC2	QC2.5	ANSI	UNIX V	XNX
	▲	▲	▲										

PURPOSE Use *line* to draw a line between two explicitly specified points using the current color and the current line style.

SYNTAX

```
void far  line(int x1, int y1, int x2, int y2);
```

`int x1, y1;` *Coordinates of point from which line is drawn*

`int x2, y2;` *Coordinates of point to which line is drawn*

EXAMPLE CALL

```
line(100,100, 120, 200);
```

INCLUDES `#include <graphics.h>` *For function declaration*

DESCRIPTION The *line* function draws a line between the two specified points, *(x1,y1)* and *(x2,y2)*. The line is drawn in the current drawing color, using the current line style and thickness. The *setwritemode* function determines the writing mode for the pixels that lie on the line (see the description of *setwritemode* for more details).

The *line* function does not change the current position.

COMMON USES The *line* function is useful when you want to draw a line without altering the current position.

SEE ALSO

`linerel`	*To draw a line from current position to a point at a specified displacement from it*
`lineto`	*To draw a line from the current position to another point*
`setcolor`	*To set the current drawing color*
`setlinestyle`	*To select line pattern and thickness*
`setwritemode`	*To set the writing mode of lines*

EXAMPLE Write a program that uses *line* to draw lines between two random points using a random color.

```
#include <stdlib.h>
#include <graphics.h>

main()
{
    int graphdriver = DETECT, graphmode, x1, x2,
        y1, y2, maxx, maxy, maxcolor;
/* Detect adapter type and initialize graphics system */
    initgraph(&graphdriver, &graphmode, "c:\\tc\\bgi");
    outtextxy(10,10, "Random lines with 'line'");
    maxx = getmaxx()-100;
    maxy = getmaxy()-60;
    maxcolor = getmaxcolor();
    randomize(); /* Initialize random number generator */
/* Exit when user presses a key */
    outtextxy(10, getmaxy()-30," Press any key to exit");
    while (!kbhit())
    {
/* Generate random end points for the lines */
        x1 = random(maxx) + 50;
        x2 = random(maxx) + 50;
        y1 = random(maxy) + 30;
        y2 = random(maxy) + 30;
        setcolor(random(maxcolor));
```

```
/* Now draw the line */
        line(x1,y1, x2,y2);
    }
    closegraph();
    return 0;
}
```

linerel

COMPATIBILITY

TC1	TC1.5	TC2	TC++	MSC3	MSC4	MSC5	MSC6	QC1	QC2	QC2.5	ANSI	UNIX V	XNX
	▲	▲	▲										

PURPOSE Use *linerel* to draw a line from the current position to a point at a specified offset from it, using the current color and the current line style.

SYNTAX

```
void far  linerel(int dx, int dy);
```

`int dx;` *x-offset of point to which line is drawn*

`int dy;` *y-offset of point to which line is drawn*

EXAMPLE CALL

```
/* Join the current position to a point 10 pixels away horizontally */
linerel(10,0);
```

INCLUDES `#include <graphics.h>` *For function declaration*

DESCRIPTION The *linerel* function draws a line from the current position to a point which is at offsets *dx* horizontally and *dy* vertically from the current position. The line is drawn in the current drawing color, using the current line style and thickness. After drawing the line, the current position is moved to the end point of the line.

You can move the current position, without drawing anything, by using the function *moveto.*

COMMON USES The *linerel* function is useful when the displacements of a point from the current position are more readily available than the absolute coordinates themselves.

SEE ALSO

`line` *To draw line between two specified points*

`lineto` *To draw a line from the current position to another point*

`moveto` *To move the current position without drawing*

`setcolor`	*To set the current drawing color*
`setlinestyle`	*To select line pattern and thickness*

EXAMPLE Write a program that generates random steps along x and y directions, and uses *linerel* to meander around in the screen.

```
#include <stdlib.h>
#include <graphics.h>

main()
{
    int graphdriver = DETECT, graphmode, xstep, ystep,
        maxx, maxy, maxcolor, stepsize, i, numsteps=20;
/* Detect adapter type and initialize graphics system */
    initgraph(&graphdriver, &graphmode, "c:\\tc\\bgi");
    outtextxy(10,10, "Random motion with 'linerel'");
    maxx = getmaxx()-100;
    maxy = getmaxy()-60;
    stepsize = maxy/numsteps;
    maxcolor = getmaxcolor();
    randomize(); /* Initialize random number generator */
/* Exit when user presses a key */
    outtextxy(10, getmaxy()-30," Press any key to exit");
/* Set up initial position */
    moveto(maxx/2+50, maxy/2+30);
    while (!kbhit())
    {
        for(i = 0; i < numsteps; i++)
        {
/* Generate random steps along x and y directions */
            xstep = stepsize/2 - random(stepsize);
            ystep = stepsize/2 - random(stepsize);
            setcolor(random(maxcolor));
/* Draw a line to a point at this relative distance */
            linerel(xstep, ystep);
        }
/* Move current point back to midpoint of screen */
        moveto(maxx/2+50, maxy/2+30);
    }
    closegraph();
    return 0;
}
```

lineto

COMPATIBILITY

TC1	TC1.5	TC2	TC++	MSC3	MSC4	MSC5	MSC6	QC1	QC2	QC2.5	ANSI	UNIX V	XNX
	▲	▲	▲			1	1	1	1	1			

PURPOSE Use *lineto* to draw a line from the current position to another point in the current color, and using the current line style and thickness.

SYNTAX

```
void far  lineto(int x, int y);

int x, y;        Coordinates of the point to which line is drawn
```

EXAMPLE CALL

```
lineto(next_x, next_y);
```

INCLUDES

```
#include <graphics.h>        For function declaration
```

DESCRIPTION The *lineto* function joins the current position to the point whose coordinates are specified by the integer arguments *x* and *y*. The coordinates of the point are relative to the origin (0,0) at the upper left corner of the current viewport.

The line is drawn using the current color (set by *setcolor*) and the current line style (defined by *setlinestyle*). The end point of the line becomes the new current position. You can also change the current position, without drawing anything, by calling *moveto*.

The *setwritemode* function determines the writing mode for the pixels that lie on the line (see the description of *setwritemode* for more details).

1. Use *_lineto* in Microsoft C 5 and 6, and QuickC 1.0 through 2.5.

COMMON USES The *lineto* function provides a basic capability, present in any graphics package, of drawing a line between two points. The *lineto* function together with *moveto*, allows you to draw the most complex of line drawings.

SEE ALSO

`line`	*To draw line between two specified points*
`linerel`	*To draw line from current position to a point at a specified displacement from it*
`moveto`	*To move to a new point without drawing*
`setcolor`	*To set the current drawing color*
`setlinestyle`	*To select line pattern and thickness*
`setwritemode`	*To set the writing mode of lines*

Drawing and Animation

EXAMPLE Use *lineto* with *moveto* to draw a graph showing the sin(x) function against x.

```
#include <math.h>
#include <graphics.h>

#define TWOPI  6.283        /* Approximate value of 2 Pi  */
#define MAXPNT 100          /* Points on the sinusoid     */

main()
{
    int graphdriver = DETECT, graphmode;
    int i, x, y, oldx, oldy, midpoint, maxy, maxx;
    double xd, yd, ampl;
/* Detect adapter type and initialize graphics system */
    initgraph(&graphdriver, &graphmode, "c:\\tc\\bgi");
    outtextxy(10,10, "Demonstrating lineto with a plot \
of sin(x) vs x");
    maxx = getmaxx();
    maxy = getmaxy();
    midpoint = maxy/2 - 1;
    ampl = (double)midpoint - 30.;
    moveto(0,midpoint);
    setcolor(RED);

    for (i=0; i<=MAXPNT; i++)
    {
        yd = ampl *
             sin(TWOPI * ((double)i)/((double)MAXPNT));
        xd = ((double)maxx/2.0 - 1.)* (double)i /
                                      (double)MAXPNT;
        x  = (int)xd;
/* Our y axis is positive upwards */
        y  = midpoint - (int)yd;
/* Now draw a line to the new point by calling lineto */
       lineto(x,y);
    }
/* Wait until user presses a key */
    outtextxy(10, getmaxy()-30," Press any key to exit");
    getch();
    closegraph();
    return 0;
}
```

moverel

COMPATIBILITY

TC1	TC1.5	TC2	TC++	MSC3	MSC4	MSC5	MSC6	QC1	QC2	QC2.5	ANSI	UNIX V	XNX
	▲	▲	▲										

PURPOSE Use *moverel* to move the current position to a new point which is at a specified x and y displacement from the old position.

SYNTAX

```
void far  moverel(int dx, int dy);
```

`int dx;` *x-displacement of the new "current position" from the old one*

`int dy;` *y-displacement of the new "current position" from the old one*

EXAMPLE CALL

```
/* Move to a new point 10 pixels to the right and 5 down */
moverel(10,5);
```

INCLUDES `#include <graphics.h>` *For function declaration*

DESCRIPTION The *moverel* function changes the current position to a new point which is displaced *dx* pixels to the right and *dy* pixels down. You can move it to the left or up by specifying negative displacements.

The current position is used by the routines *linerel* and *lineto* as the starting point of any line they draw.

COMMON USES The *moverel* function is useful for relocating the current position when the displacements of the new position are more readily available than its absolute, viewport-relative coordinates.

SEE ALSO

`linerel` *To draw line from current position to a point at a specified displacement from it*

`moveto` *To set a new current position specified in absolute, viewport-relative coordinates*

EXAMPLE Generate random steps along the x and y directions. Use *moverel* to move to these points and mark the point with an *x*.

```
#include <stdlib.h>
#include <graphics.h>

main()
{
    int graphdriver = DETECT, graphmode, xstep, ystep,
        maxx, maxy, maxcolor, stepsize, i, numsteps=20;
```

```
/* Detect adapter type and initialize graphics system */
    initgraph(&graphdriver, &graphmode, "c:\\tc\\bgi");
    outtextxy(10,10, "Random motion with 'moverel'");
    maxx = getmaxx()-100;
    maxy = getmaxy()-60;
    stepsize = maxy/numsteps;
    maxcolor = getmaxcolor();
    randomize(); /* Initialize random number generator */
/* Exit when user presses a key */
    outtextxy(10, getmaxy()-30," Press any key to exit");
    settextjustify(CENTER_TEXT, CENTER_TEXT);
/* Set up initial position */
    moveto(maxx/2+50, maxy/2+30);
    while (!kbhit())
    {
        for(i = 0; i < numsteps; i++)
        {
/* Generate random steps along x and y directions */
            xstep = stepsize/2 - random(stepsize);
            ystep = stepsize/2 - random(stepsize);
            setcolor(random(maxcolor));
            moverel(xstep, ystep);
/* Draw an 'x' at the new point */
            outtext("x");
        }
/* Move current point back to midpoint of screen */
        moveto(maxx/2+50, maxy/2+30);
    }
    closegraph();
    return 0;
}
```

moveto

COMPATIBILITY

TC1	TC1.5	TC2	TC++	MSC3	MSC4	MSC5	MSC6	QC1	QC2	QC2.5	ANSI	UNIX V	XNX
	▲	▲	▲			1	1	1	1	1			

PURPOSE Use *moveto* to change the current position that is maintained internally by the graphics routines.

SYNTAX

```
void far  moveto(int x, int y);

short x, y;
```

Viewport-relative coordinates of the new position

EXAMPLE CALL `moveto(10, 20);`

INCLUDES `#include <graphics.h>` *For function declaration*

DESCRIPTION The *moveto* function changes the current position that is maintained internally by the graphics routines. The viewport-relative coordinates of this point are specified by the integer arguments *x* and *y*.

The current position is used by the *linerel* and *lineto* routines as the starting point of any line they draw.

1. In Microsoft C 5 and 6, and QuickC 1.0 through 2.5, the equivalent function is *_moveto*.

COMMON USES This function is one of the basic capabilities present in the repertoire of any graphics package. If you think in terms of drawing on a piece of paper with a pen, calling *moveto* is analogous to lifting the pen and moving to a new point on the paper.

SEE ALSO

`linerel` *To draw line from current position to a point at a specified displacement from it*

`lineto` *To draw a line to another point*

`moverel` *To move the current position to a new point at a specified displacement from the current one*

EXAMPLE Use *moveto* to draw a scatter graph of some data.

```
#include <graphics.h>
#include <stdlib.h>

main()
{
   int graphdriver = DETECT, graphmode,  i,
       y[] = {1, 3, 5, 4, 6, 8, 5, 6, 8, 9},
       maxy = 9, x[] = {1, 2, 3, 4, 5, 6, 7,
       8, 9, 10}, maxx = 10,
       numpt = sizeof(y)/sizeof(int),
       maxheight, maxwidth, xscale, yscale;

/* Detect adapter type and initialize graphics system */
   initgraph(&graphdriver, &graphmode, "c:\\tc\\bgi");
   outtextxy(10,10, "Use of 'moveto' in scatter graph");
/* Now draw the x-y graph */
   maxheight = getmaxy()-100;
```

```
    yscale = maxheight/maxy;
    maxwidth = getmaxx()-200;
    xscale = maxwidth/maxx;
    setviewport(100,50,100+maxwidth,50+maxheight,1);
    rectangle(0,0,maxwidth,maxheight);
    setcolor(YELLOW);
    settextjustify(CENTER_TEXT, CENTER_TEXT);
/* Scale the data and draw an 'x' at each point */
    for (i = 0; i < numpt; i++)
    {
/* Our y-coordinates increase as we go up */
        moveto(x[i]*xscale, maxheight-y[i]*yscale);
        outtext("X");
    }

/* Wait until user presses a key */
    outtextxy(10, getmaxy()-30," Press any key to exit");

    getch();
    closegraph();
    return 0;
  }
```

pieslice

COMPATIBILITY

TC1	TC1.5	TC2	TC++	MSC3	MSC4	MSC5	MSC6	QC1	QC2	QC2.5	ANSI	UNIX V	XNX
	▲	▲	▲			1	1	1	1	1			

PURPOSE Use *pieslice* to draw a bordered and filled pie-shaped wedge whose boundary consists of a circular arc and lines joining the center of the circle to the beginning and the end points of the segment.

SYNTAX

```
void far  pieslice(int x, int y, int stangle, int endangle,
                   int radius);
```

`int x, y;` *Coordinates of the center of the circle to which the curved edge of the pie belongs*

`int stangle;` *Starting angle of the circular arc*

`int endangle;` *Angle where circular arc ends*

`int radius;` *Radius of circle to which the arc belongs*

EXAMPLE CALL
```
pieslice(100, 100, 0, 29, 50); /* A 30 degree pie with radius 50 */
```

INCLUDES
```
#include <graphics.h>
```
For function declaration

DESCRIPTION The *pieslice* function draws a segment of a circular arc defined in terms of the center point with coordinates *(x,y)* relative to the origin of the viewport, radius given by the argument *radius*, and the start and end points defined by the angles *stangle* and *endangle*, respectively. Then it constructs a pie-shaped wedge by joining the end points of the arc to the center of the circle. The pie is filled with the current fill color using the current fill pattern. The curved boundary is drawn in the current color using a solid line style. The straight edges of the boundary are drawn in the current color, using the current line style and thickness (see Figure 19-1).

The end points of the curved edge of the pie slice are specified by angles measured counterclockwise from a horizontal reference line extending to the right from the center of the underlying circle. If you superimpose the face of a clock on the circle, the reference line, representing 0 degrees, will be at 3 o'clock. Angles are measured counterclockwise from this reference. Starting from 0 and counting in 1-degree steps, 89 degrees is 12 o'clock and 179 degrees is 9 o'clock. When you think of the circle in this manner, any point on the circumference can be specified by an angle. The start and end points of the curved portion of the pie are, therefore, uniquely identified by the angles *stangle* and *endangle* (in degrees), respectively.

1. The equivalent function in Microsoft C 5 and 6, and QuickC 1.0 through 2.5, is *_pie*.

COMMON USES This function is useful in programs that prepare "pie charts" for business graphics.

SEE ALSO

`arc`	*To draw a circular arc*
`sector`	*To draw an elliptical pie slice*
`setcolor`	*To set the current color*
`setfillpattern`	*To define a new fill pattern*
`setfillstyle`	*To select a predefined fill pattern*

EXAMPLE Write a program to illustrate how *pieslice* can be used to draw filled wedges of a pie that can be used in pie charts.

```
#include <graphics.h>
char fillpattern[8] =
```

```
{ 0xf0, 0xf0, 0xf0, 0xf0, 0xf, 0xf, 0xf, 0xf };

main()
{
    int graphdriver = DETECT, graphmode;
/* Detect adapter type and initialize graphics system */
    initgraph(&graphdriver, &graphmode, "c:\\tc\\bgi");
    outtextxy(10,10, "Demonstrating 'pieslice'");

/* Draw two slices of pie */
    setfillstyle(SLASH_FILL, RED);
    pieslice(100, 100, 0, 45, 50);
    setfillpattern(fillpattern, YELLOW);
    pieslice(100, 100, 46, 360, 50);

/* Exit when user presses a key */
    outtextxy(10, getmaxy()-30," Press any key to exit");
    getch();
    closegraph();
    return 0;
}
```

COMPATIBILITY

putimage

TC1	TC1.5	TC2	TC++	MSC3	MSC4	MSC5	MSC6	QC1	QC2	QC2.5	ANSI	UNIX V	XNX
	▲	▲	▲			1	1	1	1	1			

PURPOSE Use the *putimage* function to display a rectangular screen image saved in a buffer by *getimage*.

SYNTAX

```
void far  putimage(int left, int top, void far *image_buffer,
                   int action);
```

`int left, top;` *Viewport-relative coordinates of point on screen where the upper left corner of the rectangular image will be placed*

`void far *image_buffer;` *Buffer where image has been saved*

`int action;` *Command to* putimage *instructing it to redraw the saved image in a particular manner*

EXAMPLE CALL

```
putimage(100, 200, image, XOR_PUT);
```

INCLUDES `#include <graphics.h>` *For function declaration and definition of action constants*

DESCRIPTION The *putimage* function redraws the image of a rectangular region of the screen saved earlier by *getimage* in the buffer whose address is specified in the argument *image_buffer*. The saved image is drawn with the upper left corner at the point whose coordinates relative to the origin of the current viewport are *(left,top)*. You need not specify the size of the rectangular region because this information is saved with the image.

The manner in which the image is redrawn depends on the value of the integer argument *action*. This argument should be one of the constants defined in the file *graphics.h* as the enumerated type *putimage_ops*. These constants are shown, along with their meanings, in Table 19-3.

Table 19-3. *Interpreting the Action Constants for* putimage

Constant	Interpretation
COPY_PUT	The saved image is drawn at the specified area, completely overwriting any existing image.
XOR_PUT	Each pixel from the saved image is exclusive-ORed with the current pixels in the area where the image is being drawn. Very useful in animation because exclusive-OR of an image with itself erases the image. Thus, the background can be restored easily with this action command.
OR_PUT	The pixel values from the saved image are logically ORed with the existing pixel values in the area where the image is being drawn.
AND_PUT	The image is drawn by performing a logical AND of the existing pixel value with the one from the saved image.
NOT_PUT	Each bit in each pixel of the saved image is logically inverted, then these values are transferred to the screen, overwriting the existing image. Thus, for example, the areas of a saved EGA screen which were yellow (pixel value 14 = 1110 in binary) will become blue (pixel value 1 = 0001 in binary).

1. In Microsoft C 5 and 6, and QuickC 1.0 through 2.5, use *_putimage*.

COMMON USES The *putimage* function is used to redraw screen images saved by *getimage*. For example, you can draw an object, save it by calling *getimage*, and then move it around the screen—in effect perform an animation by using *putimage* with appropriate action commands.

SEE ALSO `imagesize` *To determine number of bytes necessary to save a screen image*

`getimage` *To save a screen image*

EXAMPLE In a graphics mode, draw some graphical object and save in memory by calling *getimage*. Now clear the screen and use *putimage* to animate the object on the screen.

Drawing and Animation

```
#include <stdio.h>
#include <alloc.h>
#include <graphics.h>

main()
{
    int graphdriver = DETECT, graphmode;
    char far *image;
    char buffer[80];
    short x, y;
    unsigned numbytes, c = 0;
/* Detect adapter type and initialize graphics system */
    initgraph(&graphdriver, &graphmode, "c:\\tc\\bgi");

/* Draw a stick figure to animate */
    ellipse(5,5,0,360,5,5);
    setcolor(YELLOW);
    setfillstyle(SOLID_FILL, YELLOW);
    floodfill(5,5,WHITE);
    moveto(5,10);
    lineto(5,20);
    lineto(0,30);
    moveto(10,30);
    lineto(5,20);
    moveto(0,15);
    lineto(0,10);
    lineto(10,15);
/* Determine storage needed for the image */
    numbytes = (unsigned int)imagesize(0,0,10,30);
/* Allocate buffer for image */
    if ((image = (char far *) malloc(numbytes)) ==
         (char far *)NULL)
    {
        closegraph();
        printf(          "Not enough memory for image storage\n");
        exit(0);
    }
    getimage(0,0,10,30,image); /* Save the image */
/* Now clear screen and draw saved image at several
 * screen locations
 */
    cleardevice();
    setcolor(WHITE);
    outtextxy(10,10,
           "Demonstrating animation with putimage");
```

```
    x = getmaxx()/2;
    y = getmaxy()/2;
    putimage(x,y,image,XOR_PUT);
    outtextxy(10, getmaxy()-50,
          "q = exit, h=left, j=down, k=up, l=right");
/* Perform some animation */
    while(c != 'q')
    {
        c = getch();
/* First erase at last position */
        putimage(x,y,image,XOR_PUT);
        switch(c)
        {
            case 'h': x -= 2; /* 2 pixels left */
                      break;
            case 'l': x += 2; /* 2 pixels right */
                      break;
            case 'j': y += 2; /* 2 pixels down */
                      break;
            case 'k': y -= 2; /* 2 pixels up   */
                      break;
        }
/* Redraw at new position */
        putimage(x,y,image,XOR_PUT);
    }
/* Close graphics system when done */
    closegraph();
    return 0;
}
```

putpixel

COMPATIBILITY

TC1	TC1.5	TC2	TC++	MSC3	MSC4	MSC5	MSC6	QC1	QC2	QC2.5	ANSI	UNIX V	XNX
	▲	▲	▲			1	1	1	1	1			

PURPOSE Use *putpixel* to set a pixel to a specified color.

SYNTAX

```
void far  putpixel(int x, int y, int color);
```

`int x, y;` *Viewport-relative x- and y-coordinates of the pixel to be set to the specified color*

`int color;` *Color to which pixel is set*

EXAMPLE CALL

```
putpixel(120, 90, RED); /* Turn pixel (120,90) red */
```

INCLUDES

`#include <graphics.h>` *For function declaration*

DESCRIPTION

The *putpixel* function first checks to see if the pixel specified by the coordinates *(x,y)* lies within the current viewport. If it does, *putpixel* fills the pixel with the color specified in the argument *color*. If the specified pixel lies outside the viewport, the pixel remains unchanged.

1. In Microsoft C 5 and 6, and QuickC 1.0 through 2.5, use *_setpixel.*

COMMON USES

The *putpixel* function can be used for drawing complicated graphics images with multiple colors.

SEE ALSO

`setviewport` *To define a limited area of the screen as the viewport for graphics output*

`getpixel` *To determine the current value of a pixel*

EXAMPLE

Use *putpixel* to draw rectangular strips, each filled with pixels of a selected color.

```
#include <graphics.h>

main()
{
    int graphdriver = DETECT, graphmode, x, y, color,
xstep;

/* Detect adapter type and initialize graphics system */
    initgraph(&graphdriver, &graphmode, "c:\\tc\\bgi");
    outtextxy(10,10,
        "Multicolored rectangle using putpixel");
/* Go over a rectangular region and fill pixels with
 * color
 */
    xstep = (getmaxx()-100)/(getmaxcolor()+1);
    color = 0; /* Initialize to first color in palette*/
    for(x=50; x<getmaxx()-50; x++)
    {
        for(y=40; y<getmaxy()-40; y++)
        {
            putpixel(x,y,color); /* Set pixel to color*/
        }
        if((x%xstep) == 0) color++;/* Go to next color*/
        if(color > getmaxcolor())
```

```
                color=0;
        }
    /* Wait until user presses a key */
        outtextxy(10, getmaxy()-30," Press any key to exit");
        getch();
        closegraph();
        return 0;
    }
```

rectangle

COMPATIBILITY

TC1	TC1.5	TC2	TC++	MSC3	MSC4	MSC5	MSC6	QC1	QC2	QC2.5	ANSI	UNIX V	XNX
	▲	▲	▲			1	1	1	1	1			

PURPOSE Use *rectangle* to draw a rectangle in the current drawing color, line style, and thickness.

SYNTAX

```
void far  rectangle(int left, int top, int right, int bottom);

int left, top;          Coordinates of upper left corner

int right, bottom;      Coordinates of lower right corner
```

EXAMPLE CALL

```
rectangle(100, 140, 250, 200);
```

INCLUDES

```
#include <graphics.h>      For function declaration
```

DESCRIPTION The *rectangle* function draws a rectangle specified by its upper left corner (*left,top*) and its lower right corner (*right,bottom*). The x coordinates go from left to right, and the y coordinates go from top to bottom with (0,0) being at the upper left corner of the current viewport (see *setviewport*).

The border of the rectangle is drawn in the current drawing color, using the current line style and thickness. You can set the drawing color with *setcolor*, and the line style with *setlinestyle*.

1. The compatible function in Microsoft C 5 and 6, and QuickC 1.0 through 2.5, is *_rectangle*.

COMMON USES The *rectangle* function provides a basic shape for constructing complex graphics objects.

COMMENTS If you want to draw a filled rectangle, you can use the *bar* function. Bordered, filled rectangles can be drawn with *bar3d* (specify a zero width).

SEE ALSO

bar	*To draw a filled rectangle*
bar3d	*To draw a bordered, filled rectangle*
setcolor	*To set the current color*
setlinestyle	*To set the current line style*

EXAMPLE Write a program to draw rectangles with random vertices, each drawn in a randomly chosen color.

```
#include <stdlib.h>
#include <graphics.h>
main()
{
    int graphdriver = DETECT, graphmode, x1, x2,
        y1, y2, maxx, maxy, maxcolor;
/* Detect adapter type and initialize graphics system */
    initgraph(&graphdriver, &graphmode, "c:\\tc\\bgi");
    outtextxy(10,10,
        "Random rectangles with 'rectangle'");
    maxx = getmaxx()-100;
    maxy = getmaxy()-60;
    maxcolor = getmaxcolor();
    randomize(); /* Initialize random number generator */
/* Exit when user presses a key */
    outtextxy(10, getmaxy()-30," Press any key to exit");
    while (!kbhit())
    {
/* Generate random points for the corners */
        x1 = random(maxx) + 50;
        x2 = random(maxx) + 50;
        y1 = random(maxy) + 30;
        y2 = random(maxy) + 30;
        setcolor(random(maxcolor));
/* Now draw the rectangle */
        rectangle(min(x1,x2), min(y1,y2),
                  max(x1,x2), max(y1,y2));
    }
    closegraph();
    return 0;
}
```

sector

COMPATIBILITY

TC1	TC1.5	TC2	TC++	MSC3	MSC4	MSC5	MSC6	QC1	QC2	QC2.5	ANSI	UNIX V	XNX
		▲	▲			1	1	1	1	1			

PURPOSE Use *sector* to draw a bordered and filled pie-shaped wedge whose boundary consists of an elliptical arc and lines joining the center of the ellipse to the beginning and the end points of the arc.

SYNTAX

```
void far  sector(int x, int y, int stangle, int endangle,
                          int xradius, int yradius);
```

`int x, y;` *Coordinates of the center of the ellipse on which the curved edge of the pie lies*

`int stangle;` *Starting angle of the elliptical arc*

`int endangle;` *Angle where elliptical arc ends*

`int xradius;` *Length of horizontal axis of ellipse to which the arc belongs*

`int yradius;` *Length of vertical axis of ellipse to which the arc belongs*

EXAMPLE CALL

```
sector(100, 100, 0, 29, 50, 25); /* A 30 degree pie */
```

INCLUDES

```
#include <graphics.h>
```

For function declaration

DESCRIPTION The *sector* function draws a segment of an elliptical arc defined in terms of the center point with coordinates *(x,y)* relative to the origin of the viewport. The horizontal and vertical axes are given by the arguments *xradius* and *yradius* and the start and end points are defined by the angles *stangle* and *endangle*, respectively. Then a pie-shaped wedge is constructed by joining the end points of the arc to the center of the ellipse. The pie-shaped wedge is filled with the current fill color using the current fill pattern. The curved boundary is drawn in the current color using a solid line style. The straight edges of the boundary are drawn in the current color, using the current line style and thickness.

The end points of the curved edge of the pie slice are specified by angles measured counterclockwise from a horizontal reference line extending to the right from the center of the underlying ellipse. If you superimpose the face of a clock on the ellipse, the reference line, representing 0 degrees, will be at 3 o'clock. Angles are measured counterclockwise from this reference. Thus, 89 degrees is 12 o'clock and 179 degrees is 9 o'clock. When you think of the ellipse in this manner, any point on the perimeter of the ellipse can be specified by an angle. The start and end points of the

curved portion of the pie are, therefore, uniquely identified by the angles *stangle* and *endangle* (in degrees), respectively.

1. Use *_pie* in Microsoft C 5 and 6, and QuickC 1.0 through 2.5.

COMMON USES This function is useful in programs that prepare "pie charts" for business graphics.

SEE ALSO

ellipse	*To draw an elliptical arc*
setcolor	*To set the current color*
setfillpattern	*To define a new fill pattern*
setfillstyle	*To select a predefined fill pattern*

EXAMPLE Write a program to illustrate how *sector* can be used to draw the filled wedges of a pie in a pie chart.

```
#include <graphics.h>
char fillpattern[8] =
{ 0xf0, 0xf0, 0xf0, 0xf0, 0xf, 0xf, 0xf, 0xf };

main()
{
    int graphdriver = DETECT, graphmode;
/* Detect adapter type and initialize graphics system */
    initgraph(&graphdriver, &graphmode, "c:\\tc\\bgi");
    outtextxy(10,10, "Demonstrating 'sector'");

/* Draw two slices of pie */
    setfillstyle(SLASH_FILL, RED);
    sector(100, 100, 0, 45, 100, 25);
    setfillpattern(fillpattern, YELLOW);
    sector(100, 100, 46, 360, 100, 25);

/* Exit when user presses a key */
    outtextxy(10, getmaxy()-30," Press any key to exit");
    getch();
    closegraph();
    return 0;
}
```

Chapter 20 Combining Graphics and Text

Introduction

Text is an essential part of graphics. For example, if you prepare a bar graph or a pie chart, you have to annotate the graph so that the user can understand the meaning of the plots. The Turbo C++ graphics library includes eleven routines to control text output in the graphics mode. You can use these routines to load one of several fonts that come with Turbo C++, and position text in a variety of fonts anywhere in the screen.

Notes on Mixing Graphics and Text

Table 20-1 lists the routines available for text output and for controlling the appearance of text on the screen. Table 20-2 categorizes these routines by task. The text output routines are meant specifically for drawing text in the graphics modes. Chapter 21 describes the routines for text mode only.

Table 20-1. ***Text Output Routines***

Routine	Description
gettextsettings	Returns information about current text font, direction, size, and justification.
installuserfont	Loads a new stroke font definition from a .CHR file containing the font's definition.
outtext	Writes a given string using the current font at the current position.
outtextxy	Writes a given string using the current font at a specified point.

Table 20-1. ***(cont.)***

Routine	Description
registerbgifont	Registers a font that has been linked into the executable file of the program.
registerfarbgifont	Registers a font that has been linked into the executable file of the program (applies to font data residing in a far data segment).
settextjustify	Sets the justification of text.
settextstyle	Sets the font, the direction in which text is displayed, and the size of the characters.
setusercharsize	Sets a user-defined magnification factor for the current text fonts.
textheight	Returns the height of a text string in pixels when displayed in the current font.
textwidth	Returns the width of a text string in pixels when displayed in the current font.

Table 20-2. ***Text Output Routines by Task***

Task	Routines
Output text.	outtext, outtextxy
Control appearance of text.	gettextsettings, settextjustify, settextstyle, setusercharsize
Determine character size.	textheight, textwidth
Install new fonts and inform graphics package about fonts linked into the executable program.	installuserfont, registerbgifont, registerfarbgifont

FONTS IN TURBO C++ GRAPHICS

Fonts refer to sets of shapes or outlines of characters. A complete character set with a particular shape and size is a font. There are two types of fonts in Turbo C++: *bit-mapped*, and *stroke*. In a bit-mapped font each character is defined by a fixed size matrix of pixels. On the other hand, a stroke font describes each character as a series of *strokes* or line segments.

A bit-mapped font is easy to draw on the screen because the pixel matrix is already prepared, but the characters cannot be easily scaled (reduced or enlarged). Since a stroke font contains the information on how to draw the outline of each character, it is very easy to generate characters of arbitrary size, at the expense of slightly slower speed during display.

The Turbo C++ graphics library comes with an 8×8 bit-mapped font which is the default, and a selection of stroke fonts which are kept in disk files with the extension .CHR. The stroke fonts are loaded into memory when you select a specific font with the *settextstyle* routine.

There are four stroke fonts available in Turbo C++: Triplex, Small,

Sans-Serif, and Gothic. You can use any of these fonts by specifying the choice with a constant in *settextstyle*. For example, *settextstyle (SANS_SERIF_FONT, HORIZ_DIR, 4)* specifies the use of the sans-serif font in a size four times the standard 8×8 grid, and asks that the text be drawn in a horizontal line. You can optionally draw the characters in a vertical line, one atop another. This is handy for putting titles on the vertical axis of graphs.

The characters in a stroke font can also be scaled by different amounts in width and height by specifying a character size of 0 in *settextstyle* and defining the scale factors using the routine *setusercharsize* (see its reference entry for an explanation of its operation). For example, you can make the characters twice as tall and 50% as wide as the default size by

```
settextstyle(TRIPLEX_FONT, HORIZ_DIR, 0);
setusercharsize(3, 2, 2, 1);
```

The ability to scale fonts in this manner is handy when you have to squeeze labels or other text into a rectangular box of specified size.

OTHER WAYS OF HANDLING STROKE FONTS

The normal method of loading a font from a file means that the executable program is not self-contained, you must have both the executable and the .CHR files (which contain the fonts) to use the graphics text capabilities. Turbo C++ provides a way to include (or link in) selected fonts into your executable program. You can use a utility named BGIOBJ to convert a font's .CHR file into an object file with the .OBJ extension. At your option, you can generate an .OBJ file to be loaded into the same segment as other fonts, or a *far* segment for that font alone. The ability to store the data for each in a separate segment is necessary when your program uses several fonts because they may not all fit into a single segment.

Once a font's .CHR file has been converted into an .OBJ file, it can be linked (using TLINK) with the other object files that make up your program. Before using the fonts in your program, you must "register" each font by calling *registerbgifont* (or, *registerfarbgifont* when a font is in its own separate segment). This informs the graphics system that the fonts are already loaded and need not be read from files. You must register the linked-in fonts before calling *initgraph*. The steps, to be performed at the DOS level, are as follows:

Step 1: Use BGIOBJ to convert each font's .CHR file to .OBJ. For example, *BGIOBJ SANS* will generate the file SANS.OBJ. Use the option /F with BGIOBJ to associate a separate code segment with each font's code. An example is: *BGIOBJ/F TRIP*.

Step 2: You can add the object modules to the library GRAPHICS.LIB, or specify them explicitly when you use TCC or TLINK to link your program. For example, you can build the executable by the command

```
tcc myprog.c graphics.lib sans.obj trip.obj
```

Step 3: Register the fonts as follows:

```
#include <graphics.h>
/* Register fonts */
    if (registerbgifont(sansseriffont) <0) exit(1);
    if (registerbgifont(triplexfontfar) <0) exit(1);
/* Initialize graphics system */
    initgraph(...);
```

Note that the argument to *registerbgifont* is the name of the font routine, which is constructed by appending *_font* to the name of the font. When the font's object file is created with "BGIOBJ /F," the name needs an additional *_far* as suffix.

In Turbo C 2.0, Borland provides a new function, *installuserfont*, that lets you load new stroke fonts from a .CHR file containing the font's data into the graphics package.

GRAPHICS TEXT OUTPUT ROUTINES

The graphics library provides two routines, *outtext* and *outtextxy*, which are designed to output text using the current font and color in graphics modes. The *outtext* routine starts output at the current position (which can be set by calling *moveto* or *moverel*), whereas *outtextxy* requires you to explicitly specify the position where text will be output.

The *outtext* and *outtextxy* routines cannot be formatted. You can still print formatted text, with the help of the string printing routine *sprintf*. You can first prepare the formatted string and then pass that string to *outtext* (or, *outtextxy*) for printing. Here is an example:

```
char string[80];
double result;
 :
sprintf(string, "The result is: %.2f", result);
outtext(string);
```

This will print the string using the current color and font, and at the current position. The current position is updated as each character is output.

JUSTIFICATION AND DIRECTION OF GRAPHICS TEXT

Turbo C++ graphics text routines can draw a character string either horizontally or vertically. This is called the "direction" of graphics text. You specify the direction during font selection with *settextstyle*.

Text justification refers to the actual placement of the string with respect to the current position. In other words, the horizontal and vertical justification options tell the Turbo C++ graphics system where the current position will be within the body of the text string. In the following example:

```
settextstyle(SANS_SERIF_FONT, HORIZ_DIR, 4);
settextjustify(LEFT_TEXT, BOTTOM_TEXT);
outtextxy(50,100, "Turbo C 2.0");
```

we request that the string "Turbo C 2.0" be printed with the bottom left corner of the letter T at the point (50,100). Similarly, we could have printed the string centered around (50,100) with the justification set by *settextjustify(CENTER_TEXT,CENTER_TEXT)*. The other possible choices are described in the reference entry for the function *settextjustify* and illustrated in Figure 20-1.

LINE WRAP

When a long line of text is printed using *outtext* or *outtextxy*, the entire line may not fit within the width of the current viewport. If the clipping flag for the viewport is on, the text is truncated at the boundary of the viewport. Otherwise, the text will spill outside the viewport, and clipping will occur only at the boundary of the screen.

DETERMINING HEIGHT AND WIDTH OF GRAPHICS TEXT

When fonts of arbitrary size are used to output text in the graphics mode, the width and the height of the screen space occupied by a text string depends on the font and the scaling factors being used. Turbo C++ provides two routines, *textheight* and *textwidth*, which can be used to determine the height and width (in pixels), respectively, of a text string if it is drawn in the current font with the current scaling factors. You can use these functions to determine the spacing between lines of text, and to determine the dimensions of a box large enough to hold a string in a particular font.

gettextsettings

COMPATIBILITY

TC1	TC1.5	TC2	TC++	MSC3	MSC4	MSC5	MSC6	QC1	QC2	QC2.5	ANSI	UNIX V	XNX
	▲	▲	▲										

PURPOSE Use *gettextsettings* to obtain information about current text settings such as font, character size, justification, and output direction of graphics text.

SYNTAX

```
void far  gettextsettings(struct textsettingstype far *textinfo);

struct textsettingstype far *textinfo;
```

Pointer to structure where current text settings are returned

EXAMPLE CALL

```
struct textsettingstype gt_setting;
gettextsettings(&gt_setting);
```

INCLUDES

```
#include <graphics.h>
```

For function declaration

DESCRIPTION The *gettextsettings* function returns information on the current font, text output direction, character size, and justification, in a structure of type *textsettingstype* which is defined in the include file *graphics.h* as

```
struct textsettingstype
{
int font;        /* Font number from the enumeration "font_names" */
int direction;   /* Direction of text output (horizontal,vertical)*/
int charsize;    /* Character size, as a factor of 8x8 bitmap    */
int horiz;       /* Horizontal justification code                */
int vert;        /* Vertical justification code                  */
};
```

You are responsible for declaring a *textsettingstype* structure and providing its address as the argument *textinfo*.

Consult the reference entry of *settextstyle* for details on how to interpret (and specify) the font, the direction, and the character size. The reference pages of *settextjustify* describe the way text justification is handled in Turbo C++ graphics mode text output routines, *outtext* and *outtextxy*. Tables of horizontal and vertical justification codes are provided in *settextjustify*.

COMMON USES The *gettextsettings* routine allows you to retrieve and save the current settings of graphics text output, before you change these settings with *settextstyle* and *settextjustify*.

Combining Graphics and Text

SEE ALSO

settextjustify	*To specify the justification of subsequent graphics text output*
settextstyle	*To select a font, writing direction and the character size for graphics text*

EXAMPLE Write a program that calls *gettextsettings* to retrieve all information about current settings for graphics text output. Display this information to the user.

```
#include <graphics.h>

char *font_names[] =
{ "Default Font", "Triplex Font", "Small Font",
  "Sans Serif Font", "Gothic Font"};

char *h_justify[] = { "LEFT", "CENTER", "RIGHT"};

char *v_justify[] = { "BOTTOM", "CENTER", "TOP"};

char *text_dir[] = {"Horizontal", "Vertical"};

main()
{
    int graphdriver = DETECT, graphmode;
    struct textsettingstype textinfo;
    char buf[80];

/* Detect and initialize graphics system */
    initgraph(&graphdriver, &graphmode, "c:\\tc\\bgi");

/* Retrieve current text settings and report them */
    gettextsettings(&textinfo);
    outtextxy(10,10, "Current text settings are:");
    sprintf(buf,"Font: %s",font_names[textinfo.font]);
    outtextxy(10,24, buf);
    sprintf(buf,"Character size: %d", textinfo.charsize);
    outtextxy(10,34,buf);
    sprintf(buf, "Direction of text: %s",
                  text_dir[textinfo.direction]);
    outtextxy(10,44, buf);
    sprintf(buf, "Horizontal justification: %s",
                  h_justify[textinfo.horiz]);
    outtextxy(10,54, buf);
    sprintf(buf, "Verticaljustification: %s",
                  v_justify[textinfo.vert]);
```

```
    outtextxy(10,64, buf);

    outtextxy(getmaxx()/2, getmaxy() - 50,
                           "Press any key to exit:");
    getch();        /* Wait until a key is pressed */

    closegraph();          /* Exit graphics library */
    return 0;
}
```

installuserfont

COMPATIBILITY

TC1	TC1.5	TC2	TC++	MSC3	MSC4	MSC5	MSC6	QC1	QC2	QC2.5	ANSI	UNIX V	XNX
		▲	▲										

PURPOSE Use *installuserfont* to load a new font from a .CHR file for use in the Turbo C++ graphics system.

SYNTAX

```
int far installuserfont(char far *name);

char far *name;       The name of the new font
```

EXAMPLE CALL

```
installuserfont("MYFONT");
```

INCLUDES

```
#include <graphics.h>       For function declaration
```

DESCRIPTION The *installuserfont* function loads the font (see the tutorial section for more on fonts) specified in the argument *name*. The font's data is expected to reside in a disk file with the same name and a .CHR extension.

COMMON USES This function makes it possible to add new fonts to the Turbo C++ graphics library. Since the format of the .CHR files has not been released, the function is only useful for loading fonts that may be distributed by Borland in the future.

RETURNS The *installuserfont* function returns an integer which you should save because you have to provide this number to *settextstyle* as the font identifier when you want to use this font.

COMMENTS This function will prove very useful, if Borland releases the specifications for the font files. With this information in hand, you could develop your own fonts and use them with the Turbo C++ graphics library.

Combining Graphics and Text

SEE ALSO

`initgraph` — *To initialize the graphics system*

`registerbgifont` — *To inform the graphics system about a linked-in font*

COMPATIBILITY

outtext

TC1	TC1.5	TC2	TC++	MSC3	MSC4	MSC5	MSC6	QC1	QC2	QC2.5	ANSI	UNIX V	XNX
	▲	▲	▲			1	1	1	1	1			

PURPOSE Use the *outtext* function to display a null-terminated C string (an array of characters that end with a byte containing zero) at the current position in the current color, using the current text settings.

SYNTAX

```
void far  outtext(char far *textstring);
```

`char far *textstring;` — *Pointer to character buffer that holds the null-terminated string to be printed by* outtext

EXAMPLE CALL

```
outtext("This text begins at the current position");
```

INCLUDES

`#include <graphics.h>` — *For function declaration*

DESCRIPTION The *outtext* function displays the null-terminated C string whose address is specified in the argument *textstring* on the screen. The text output begins at the current position and uses the current text settings which include the font, the output direction, and the character size (set by *settextstyle*), as well as the text justification (set by *settextjustify*).

If the horizontal text justification is LEFT_TEXT (see *settextjustify*) and the text output direction is HORIZ_DIR (see *settextstyle*), *outtext* advances the current position along the x coordinate by an amount equal to *textwidth(textstring)*. Otherwise, the current position remains unchanged.

When graphics text is output in a viewport with clipping enabled (see *setviewport*), the text is clipped at the boundaries of the viewport. Clipping occurs accurately for all stroke fonts (see *settextstyle*), but when the default bit-mapped font is used, the clipping seems to occur on one side of the viewport only. Also, for the bit-mapped font, partial rendering of a single character is not possible.

1. The equivalent function in Microsoft C 5 and 6, and QuickC 1.0 through 2.5, is *_outtext*.

COMMON USES The *outtext* function is extensively used for displaying text during graphics output. Its ability to display text in various fonts, sizes, and colors is especially handy in developing word processing software.

COMMENTS Often you will need to display formatted text, for example, text that includes the ASCII representation of an integer value. Note that *outtext* is not capable of any formatting. Thus, in these cases, you should first prepare the formatted string by calling *sprintf* and then display the resulting string using *outtext*.

SEE ALSO

`gettextsettings`	*To get the settings used by text output routines,* outtext *and* outtextxy
`outtextxy`	*To output graphics text at a specified location*
`settextjustify`	*To specify justification of graphics text*
`settextstyle`	*To set the text font, direction, and character size*

EXAMPLE Use *outtext* to display the title in a Turbo C++ graphics viewport.

```
#include <graphics.h>

char title[] = "Turbo C Graphics Window";

main()
{
    int graphdriver = DETECT, graphmode, xmax, ymax,
        xsize, ysize;

/* Detect and initialize graphics system */
    initgraph(&graphdriver, &graphmode, "c:\\tc\\bgi");

/* Display a graphics window with a title */
    xmax = getmaxx();
    ymax = getmaxy();
    xsize = xmax - 100;
    ysize = ymax - 60;
    setviewport(50, 30, xsize+50, ysize+30,1);
    setfillstyle(SOLID_FILL, RED);
    setcolor(YELLOW);
    bar3d(0,0,xsize,ysize,0,1);
/* Draw title bar and print title with outtext */
    settextstyle(SANS_SERIF_FONT, HORIZ_DIR, 1);
    settextjustify(LEFT_TEXT, BOTTOM_TEXT);
    rectangle(0,0,xsize,textheight("H")+4);
    moveto((xsize-textwidth(title))/2, textheight("H"));
    outtext(title);
 /* Wait until a key is pressed */
```

```
    moveto(10, ysize-10);
    outtext("Press any key to exit:");
    getch();
    closegraph();          /* Exit graphics library */
    return 0;
}
```

COMPATIBILITY

outtextxy

TC1	TC1.5	TC2	TC++	MSC3	MSC4	MSC5	MSC6	QC1	QC2	QC2.5	ANSI	UNIX V	XNX
	▲	▲	▲										

PURPOSE Use the *outtextxy* function to display a null-terminated C string (an array of characters that end with a byte containing zero) at a specified position in the current color, using the current text settings.

SYNTAX

```
void far  outtextxy(int x, int y, char far *textstring);
```

`int x, y;` *Viewport-relative coordinates of point where text output begins*

`char far *textstring;` *Pointer to character buffer that holds the null-terminated string to be printed by* outtext

EXAMPLE CALL

```
outtextxy(10, 20, "This text begins at the point (10,20)");
```

INCLUDES `#include <graphics.h>` *For function declaration*

DESCRIPTION The *outtextxy* function displays the null-terminated C string whose address is specified in the argument *textstring* on the screen. The text output begins at the point whose coordinates are relative to the origin of the current viewport (its upper left corner) is *(x,y)*. The text is rendered on the screen using the current text settings which include the font, the output direction, and the character size (set by *settextstyle*), as well as the text justification (set by *settextjustify*).

If the horizontal text justification is LEFT_TEXT (see *settextjustify*) and the text output direction is HORIZ_DIR (see *settextstyle*), *outtextxy* advances the x-coordinate of the current position by an amount equal to the value returned by the call *textwidth(textstring)*. Otherwise, the current position remains unchanged.

When graphics text is output in a viewport with clipping enabled (see *setviewport*), the text is clipped at the boundaries of the viewport. Clipping occurs accurately for all stroke fonts (see *settextstyle*), but when the default bit-mapped font is used, the clipping seems to occur on one side of the viewport only. Also, for the bit-mapped font, partial rendering of a single character is not possible.

COMMON USES The *outtextxy* function is used to place titles and labels on graphics output. It can even be used to develop a "what-you-see-is-what-you-get" word processor.

COMMENTS Often you will need to display formatted text, for example, text that includes the ASCII representation of an integer value. Note that *outtextxy* is not capable of any formatting. In these cases, you should first prepare the formatted string by calling *sprintf* and then display the resulting string using *outtextxy*.

SEE ALSO

`gettextsettings`	*To get the settings used by the text output routines,* outtext *and* outtextxy
`outtext`	*To output graphics text at the current position*
`settextjustify`	*To specify justification of graphics text*
`settextstyle`	*To set the text font, direction, and character size*

EXAMPLE Write a program that allows the user to move a marker on the screen, and place some text at a selected point by pressing a command key. This approach could be used in an interactive graphics program to place labels on the plots.

```
#include <alloc.h>
#include <graphics.h>

char label[] = "This is a label";

main()
{
    int graphdriver = DETECT, graphmode, xmax, ymax,
        xsize, ysize, x, y, c;
    void *i_buf;

/* Detect and initialize graphics system */
    initgraph(&graphdriver, &graphmode, "c:\\tc\\bgi");

/* Draw a small marker and save it in a buffer */
    lineto(5,0);
    moveto(0,0);
```

```
    lineto(0,5);
/* Allocate buffer -- we skip error checking, but you
 * shouldn't
 */
    i_buf = malloc(imagesize(0,0,5,5));
    getimage(0,0,5,5, i_buf);
    cleardevice();
/* Display instructions for user */
    outtextxy(10, getmaxy()-20,"q = exit, p = place \
label, h=left, j=down, k=up, l=right");
/* Define a viewport */
    xmax = getmaxx();
    ymax = getmaxy();
    xsize = xmax - 100;
    ysize = ymax - 60;
    setviewport(50, 30, xsize+50, ysize+30, 1);
    setfillstyle(SOLID_FILL, RED);
    bar3d(0,0,xsize,ysize,0,1);
    setcolor(YELLOW);
    settextstyle(SANS_SERIF_FONT, HORIZ_DIR, 4);
    settextjustify(LEFT_TEXT, BOTTOM_TEXT);
/* Ask user to position marker and press
 * 'p' to place a label or 'q' to quit.
 */
    x = xsize/2;
    y = ysize/2;
    putimage(x,y,i_buf,XOR_PUT);


    while((c = getch()) != 'q')
    {
/* First erase at last position */
        putimage(x,y,i_buf,XOR_PUT);
        switch(c)
        {
            case 'h': x -= 2; /* 2 pixels left */
                      break;
            case 'l': x += 2; /* 2 pixels right */
                      break;
            case 'j': y += 2; /* 2 pixels down */
                      break;
            case 'k': y -= 2; /* 2 pixels up   */
                      break;
/* If it's 'p' place label using outtextxy */
            case 'p': outtextxy(x,y,label);
                      break;
```

```
        }
/* Redraw at new position */
        putimage(x,y,i_buf,XOR_PUT);
    }
/* Close graphics system when done */
    closegraph();
    return 0;
  }
```

registerbgifont, registerfarbgifont

COMPATIBILITY

TC1	TC1.5	TC2	TC++	MSC3	MSC4	MSC5	MSC6	QC1	QC2	QC2.5	ANSI	UNIX V	XNX
	▲	▲	▲										

PURPOSE Use *registerbgifont* and *registerfarbgifont* to inform the Turbo C++ graphics system about fonts that have already been linked into your executable program. (See the tutorial section for details on how to link fonts with your program.)

SYNTAX

```
int  registerbgifont(void (*font)(void));
int far  registerfarbgifont(void far *font);
```

`font` *Use a name constructed by appending "_font" or "_font_far" to the name of the font*

EXAMPLE CALL

```
if(registerbgifont(sansserif_font) < 0)
{
    printf("Error registering font: SANS_SERIF_FONT\n");
    exit(1);
}
```

INCLUDES `#include <graphics.h>` *For function declaration*

DESCRIPTION The Turbo C++ graphics library supports multiple fonts that are loaded into memory as needed. These fonts are stored in files with the .CHR extension. After the graphics system is initialized by calling *initgraph*, and a font is selected with the *settextstyle* function, the selected font is loaded into memory, and certain far function pointers are initialized to point to the font. From then on, the graphics system uses the font through this function pointer.

Normally, *settextstyle* loads a selected font from the disk (a file with

the .CHR extension), and sets up an internal pointer to this font. Turbo C++ provides an alternate way to link one or more fonts directly into your program's executable file. This is done by first converting a font from its .CHR file to an object code file (.OBJ extension) using the BGIOBJ utility, and then linking this object file to the rest of your program in the usual way. The tutorial section contains a detailed discussion of the steps involved in linking a font.

The *registerbgifont* and *registerfarbgifont* functions are necessary when a program has linked in one or more fonts. These routines essentially tell the graphics system that the fonts are already present, so that *settextstyle* does not try to load them from the disk. Note that you should call these "registration" routines before initializing the graphics system by calling *initgraph*.

The BGIOBJ utility can convert a .CHR file into object code that uses a fixed segment name. In this case, you have to use *registerbgifont* to register a font. The use of a fixed segment name can cause a problem when there are several fonts (and possibly graphics drivers) to be linked, and they cannot all fit into a single 64-K physical segment. When this happens, you can use the /F option flag with BGIOBJ to generate an object file with a unique segment name. For .OBJ files converted using BGIOBJ /F, you must use *registerfarbgifont* for registration. For example, if you converted and linked two driver files, TRIP.CHR and SANS.CHR, the first with BGIOBJ alone, and the second with the /F flag, the registration calls will be

```
if(registerbgifont(triplex_font) < 0)
{
    printf("Error registering font: TRIPLEX_FONT\n");
    exit(1)
}
if(registerfarbgifont(sansserif_font_far) < 0)
{
    printf("Error registering driver: SANS_SERIF_FONT\n");
    exit(1)
}
initgraph(&graphdriver, &graphmode, NULL);
```

The name of the font is constructed by appending *_font* to the symbolic name of the font. When the /F option is used with BGIOBJ, the name has an extra *_far* appended to it. Table 20-3 lists the fonts by name and shows the font name you must use when registering the driver.

COMMON USES The *registerbgifont* and *registerfarbgifont* routines are used when you have to link in fonts with your programs. This will often be the case with software that is to be distributed because bundling the font makes the program self-contained.

Table 20-3. *Fonts (.CHR files) in Turbo C++*

Font File (.CHR)	Name When Used with *registerbgifont*	Name When Used with *registerfarbgifont*
TRIP	triplex_font	triplex_font_far
LITT	small_font	small_font_far
SANS	sansserif_font	sansserif_font_far
GOTH	gothic_font	gothic_font_far

RETURNS Both *registerbgifont* and *registerfarbgifont* return nonnegative values when they are successful. In case of error, each returns a negative value.

COMMENTS The concept of loadable fonts (explained further in the tutorial section) is useful in creating versatile graphics-oriented text processing programs in Turbo C++. The graphics library can support additional fonts simply by providing a .CHR file for the new font. Turbo C++ uses a similar technique to handle the graphics drivers used to generate the screen output of any graphics program written in Turbo C++.

SEE ALSO

`initgraph` — *To initialize the graphics system*

`registerbgidriver, registerfarbgidriver` — *To register loadable graphics drivers*

EXAMPLE Demonstrate how *registerfarbgifont* may be used to register a font that has been read directly from its .CHR file. Use the font to display some sample text. Note this approach is different from actually linking in the font into your executable program.

```
/* Example that loads a font file into memory and uses
 * registerfarbgifont to register and use it.
 */

#include <graphics.h>
#include <io.h>
#include <fcntl.h>
#include <alloc.h>

main()
{
  void *    sserif_fontp;  /* Pointer to font buffer   */
  int       fhandle, graphdriver = DETECT, graphmode,
            errorcode;
  unsigned fontsize;
```

```
 /* Open the font file */
    if((fhandle = open("c:\\tc\\bgi\\SANS.CHR",
                   O_RDONLY|O_BINARY)) == -1)
    {
      printf("unable to open font file 'SANS.CHR'\n");
      exit(1);
    };
    fontsize = filelength(fhandle); /* find out size  */
    if((sserif_fontp =              /* allocate buffer*/
                      malloc(fontsize)) == NULL)
    {
      printf("Failed to allocate memory for font file \
'SANS.CHR'\n");
      exit(1);
    };
/* Read the font data into memory */
    if (read(fhandle, sserif_fontp, fontsize) != fontsize)
    {
      printf("Error reading font file 'SANS.CHR'\n");
      exit(1);
    };
    close(fhandle);              /* close font file */
/* Register the font -- must be done before initgraph */
    if (registerfarbgifont(sserif_fontp) != SANS_SERIF_FONT)
    {
      printf("Error registering font file 'SANS.CHR'\n");
      exit(1);
    };

/* Detect adapter and initialize graphics system */
    initgraph(&graphdriver, &graphmode, "c:\\tc\\bgi");
    errorcode = graphresult();
    if (errorcode != grOk)
    {
      printf(grapherrormsg(errorcode));
      exit(1);
    };

/* Now use the font as usual */
    settextstyle(SANS_SERIF_FONT, HORIZ_DIR, 4);
    settextjustify(CENTER_TEXT, CENTER_TEXT);
    outtextxy( getmaxx() / 2, getmaxy() / 2,
        "Turbo C 2.0 Graphics: Sans Serif Font");
    settextstyle(SANS_SERIF_FONT, HORIZ_DIR, 1);
```

```
/* Wait until a key is pressed */
    outtextxy(getmaxx()/2, getmaxy() - 50,
                            "Press any key to exit:");
    getch();
    closegraph();         /* Exit graphics library */
    return 0
}
```

settextjustify

COMPATIBILITY

TC1	TC1.5	TC2	TC++	MSC3	MSC4	MSC5	MSC6	QC1	QC2	QC2.5	ANSI	UNIX V	XNX
	▲	▲	▲										

PURPOSE Use *settextjustify* to specify the justification of graphics text displayed by the routines *outtext* and *outtextxy*.

SYNTAX

```
void far  settextjustify(int horiz, int vert);
```

`int horiz;` *Horizontal justification code*

`int vert;` *Vertical justification code*

EXAMPLE CALL

```
settextjustify(LEFT_TEXT, BOTTOM_TEXT);
```

INCLUDES `#include <graphics.h>` *For function declaration and justification codes*

DESCRIPTION The justification of graphics text refers to the relative position of a text string with respect to a horizontal and a vertical reference line drawn through the current position. The *settextjustify* function accepts two arguments *horiz* and *vert* which, respectively, specify the horizontal and vertical justification of all subsequent graphics text. You should indicate your choice of justification by using the constants shown in Table 20-4. These justification codes are defined in the include file *graphics.h* under the enumeration *text_just*.

As you can see from the table, and from the sample text in Figure 20-1, usually you would use the option LEFT_TEXT for horizontal and BOTTOM_TEXT for vertical justification. You can use *settextjustify (CENTER_TEXT,BOTTOM_TEXT)* to produce centered titles.

If you pass invalid input to *settextjustify*, it will set the internal error code to −11 (grError). You can check the error code by calling *graphresult*.

COMMON USES The *settextjustify* function allows arbitrary placement of text strings in graphics mode to suit several layout styles.

Combining Graphics and Text

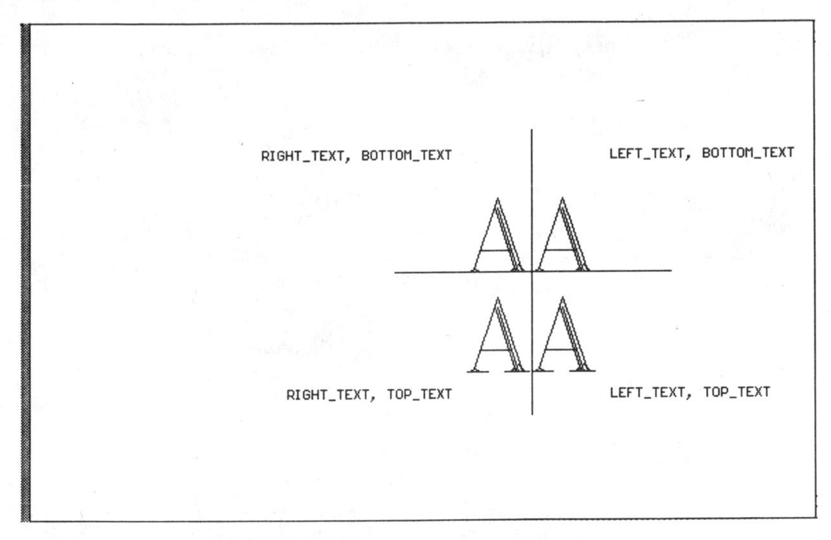

Figure 20-1. ***Text justification for graphics text***

Table 20-4. ***Justification Codes for Graphics Text Output***

Direction of Justification	Symbolic Constant	Description
Horizontal	LEFT_TEXT	Left edge of string is flush against a vertical line drawn through the current position ("vertical reference line").
	CENTER_TEXT	The midpoint of the string is aligned with the vertical reference line.
	RIGHT_TEXT	The rightmost character of the string is flush against the vertical reference line.
Vertical	BOTTOM_TEXT	The bottom of the characters lie on a horizontal line drawn through the current position ("horizontal reference line").
	CENTER_TEXT	The horizontal reference line passes through the middle of the characters in the text string.
	TOP_TEXT	The top of the characters are aligned with the horizontal reference line.

SEE ALSO

`gettextsettings` — *To get the current settings for graphics text output*

`outtext, outtextxy` — *To display graphics text*

`settextstyle` — *To set the font, direction, and character size of graphics text*

EXAMPLE Write a program that shows how several combinations of horizontal and vertical justification look. Mark the current position with a cross hair to clearly illustrate the effect of each type of justification. Figure 20-1 shows the output of this example.

```
#include <graphics.h>
main()
{
    int graphdriver=DETECT, graphmode;
    int x, y, th, tw;

    initgraph(&graphdriver, &graphmode, "C:\\TC\\BGI");
    x = getmaxx()/2;
    y = getmaxy()/2;
/* Mark the point around which text is justified */
    line(x-100, y, x+100, y);
    line(x, y-100, x, y+100);
/* Try all justification choices */
    settextstyle(TRIPLEX_FONT, HORIZ_DIR, 8);
    tw = textwidth("A");
    th = textheight("A");
    settextjustify(LEFT_TEXT, TOP_TEXT);
    outtextxy(x,y,"A");
    settextjustify(LEFT_TEXT, BOTTOM_TEXT);
    outtextxy(x,y,"A");
    settextjustify(RIGHT_TEXT, TOP_TEXT);
    outtextxy(x,y,"A");
    settextjustify(RIGHT_TEXT, BOTTOM_TEXT);
    outtextxy(x,y,"A");
/* Label the choices */
    settextstyle(SMALL_FONT, HORIZ_DIR, 4);
    settextjustify(LEFT_TEXT, BOTTOM_TEXT);
#define XS (tw+10)
#define YS (th+10)
    moveto(x+XS, y-YS);
    outtext("LEFT_TEXT, BOTTOM_TEXT");
    moveto(x+XS, y+YS);
    settextjustify(LEFT_TEXT, TOP_TEXT);
    outtext("LEFT_TEXT, TOP_TEXT");
    moveto(x-XS, y+YS);
    settextjustify(RIGHT_TEXT, TOP_TEXT);
    outtext("RIGHT_TEXT, TOP_TEXT");
    settextjustify(RIGHT_TEXT, BOTTOM_TEXT);
    moveto(x-XS, y-YS);
    outtext("RIGHT_TEXT, BOTTOM_TEXT");
/* Wait until user hits a key */
    getch();
```

Combining Graphics and Text

```
    closegraph();
    return 0;
}
```

COMPATIBILITY

settextstyle

TC1	TC1.5	TC2	TC++	MSC3	MSC4	MSC5	MSC6	QC1	QC2	QC2.5	ANSI	UNIX V	XNX
	▲	▲	▲										

PURPOSE Use *settextstyle* to pick a font, output direction, and character size for subsequent graphics text output by *outtext* and *outtextxy*.

SYNTAX

```
void far  settextstyle(int font, int direction, int charsize);
```

`int font;` *Font to be used (loaded from disk file)*

`int direction;` *Direction of text output (horizontal or vertical)*

`int charsize;` *Size of characters relative to 8×8 bit-mapped font*

EXAMPLE CALL

```
settextstyle(SANS_SERIF_FONT, HORIZ_DIR, 4);
```

INCLUDES `#include <graphics.h>` *For function declaration, font names, and output direction*

DESCRIPTION Turbo C++ provides a default 8×8 bit-mapped font for text output in graphics mode. In addition to this, Turbo C++ has the provision for loading stroke fonts from disk files (the files with the .CHR extension that comes with the Turbo C++ distribution). The *settextstyle* routine loads the font specified in the argument *font* from the disk file, provided it has not already been linked in and registered (see *registerbgifont*). The *font* is specified by one of the symbolic constants shown in Table 20-5. These font names are defined in the enumeration type *font_names* in the include file *graphics.h*.

The *settextstyle* also sets up the text output direction according to the input argument *direction*, and the character size as specified by *charsize*. The direction can be one of the constants HORIZ_DIR or VERT_DIR. HORIZ_DIR specifies that text be displayed horizontally from left to right, whereas VERT_DIR means that the characters will be rotated counterclockwise 90 degrees and printed from bottom to top.

The *charsize* parameter is a scaling factor by which each character is magnified from the default 8×8 size. Thus, a *charsize* of 4 implies that the character cell is a 32×32 pixel. If you set *charsize* to zero, the default bit-mapped font will not be affected, but the stroke fonts will be magnified by

Table 20-5. ***Fonts in Turbo C++***

Font Name	Value	Description	File Name
DEFAULT_FONT	0	8×8 bit-mapped font (DEFAULT)	—
TRIPLEX_FONT	1	Stroked triplex font	TRIP.CHR
SMALL_FONT	2	Stroked small font	LITT.CHR
SANS_SERIF_FONT	3	Sansserif font	SANS.CHR
GOTHIC_FONT	4	Gothic font	GOTH.CHR

the amounts specified by the function *setusercharsize* (if you have not yet called *setusercharsize*, the default is equivalent to a magnification factor of 4). This allows for different magnifications along the horizontal and vertical dimensions.

When *settextstyle* has to load a font from a disk file, it will search for the file in the same path that you specified when initializing the graphics system by calling *initgraph*. In case of error, *settextstyle* may set the error code to any one of the following:

Error Code	Value	Error Message
grOk	0	No error
grFontNotFound	−8	Font file not found
grNoFontMem	−9	Not enough memory to load font
grError	−11	Graphics error
grIOerror	−12	Graphics I/O error
grInvalidFont	−13	Invalid font file
grInvalidFontNum	−14	Invalid font number

You should call *graphresult* to check for any error.

COMMON USES The *settextstyle* function is useful for controlling text style and layout in graphics output.

COMMENTS The availability of a choice of fonts, and the distribution of the fonts in separate .CHR files, make Turbo C++ a good choice for applications such as "what-you-see-is-what-you-get" word processors. Although the current font selection is somewhat meager, it's only a matter of time before the situation changes.

SEE ALSO `gettextsettings` *To obtain the current settings for graphics text output*

Combining Graphics and Text

`initgraph`	*To specify pathname where font files may be found*
`settextjustify`	*To specify the justification of graphics text*
`outtext, outtextxy`	*To output graphics text*

EXAMPLE Write a program that displays horizontal and vertical text directions using the sans-serif font.

```
#include <graphics.h>

main()
{
    int graphdriver = DETECT, graphmode, xmax, ymax,
        xsize, ysize, x, y, c;
    void *i_buf;

/* Detect and initialize graphics system */
    initgraph(&graphdriver, &graphmode, "c:\\tc\\bgi");

/* Define a viewport */
    xmax = getmaxx();
    ymax = getmaxy();
    xsize = xmax - 100;
    ysize = ymax - 60;
    setviewport(50, 30, xsize+50, ysize+30, 1);
    setfillstyle(SOLID_FILL, RED);
    bar3d(0,0,xsize,ysize,0,1);
/* Mark the center of the viewport and show how vertical
 * and horizontal text looks
 */
    x = xsize/2;
    y = ysize/2;
    setlinestyle(DASHED_LINE,0,NORM_WIDTH);
    moveto(0,y);
    lineto(xsize,y);
    moveto(x,0);
    lineto(x,ysize);
    setcolor(YELLOW);
/* Use (left, bottom) justification */
    settextjustify(LEFT_TEXT, BOTTOM_TEXT);
    settextstyle(SANS_SERIF_FONT, HORIZ_DIR, 1);
    outtextxy(x,y,"H o r i z o n t a l");
    settextstyle(SANS_SERIF_FONT, VERT_DIR, 1);
    outtextxy(x,y,"V e r t i c a l");
```

```
/* Print a message in default font */
    settextstyle(DEFAULT_FONT, HORIZ_DIR, 1);
    outtextxy(10,ysize-10, "Press any key to exit");
    getch();
/* Close graphics system when done */
    closegraph();
    return 0;
  }
```

setusercharsize

COMPATIBILITY

TC1	TC1.5	TC2	TC++	MSC3	MSC4	MSC5	MSC6	QC1	QC2	QC2.5	ANSI	UNIX V	XNX
	▲	▲	▲										

PURPOSE Use *setusercharsize* to specify a horizontal and vertical scaling factor for stroke fonts.

SYNTAX

```
void far  setusercharsize(int multx, int divx,
                          int multy, int divy);
```

`int multx, divx;` *Horizontal scaling factor (multx/divx)*

`int multy, divy;` *Vertical scaling factor (multy/divy)*

EXAMPLE CALL

```
setusercharsize(2,1, 3,2); /* Twice as wide, 1.5 times as high */
```

INCLUDES `#include <graphics.h>` *For function declaration*

DESCRIPTION While you can specify a uniform magnification factor with *settextstyle*, *setusercharsize* allows you to selectively scale along x and y axes. However, the factors set by *setusercharsize* are active only when you select the character size as zero in *settextstyle*.

The horizontal scaling factor is specified by the arguments *multx* and *divx*. This means that the width of the characters will be *(multx/divx)* times the default width. Similarly, the vertical scaling factor will be *(multy/divy)*. For example, to get characters that are twice as wide, and one and a half times as tall as the default size, you will use *setusercharsize(2,1,3,2)*.

COMMON USES The *setusercharsize* function is useful for scaling a text string so that it fits into a fixed area on the screen.

SEE ALSO `gettextsettings` *To get current settings for graphics text output*

Combining Graphics and Text

`outtext, outtextxy`	*To display graphics text*
`settextstyle`	*To set the character size to zero so that the settings of* setusercharsize *can take effect*

EXAMPLE Write a program that scales the characters of a selected font by calling *setusercharsize* so that a rather long title string fits inside a rectangular box of predefined dimensions. Note that the multiplication and division factors given as input to *setusercharsize* cannot be too large. The example below illustrates a way of meeting this constraint.

```
#include <graphics.h>
char long_title[] =
{"This title has been scaled to fit inside this box"};
main()
{
    int graphdriver = DETECT, graphmode, xmax, ymax,
        xsize, ysize, textx, texty, multx, multy,
        divx, divy;
    double ratio;

/* Detect and initialize graphics system */
    initgraph(&graphdriver, &graphmode, "c:\\tc\\bgi");

/* Define a viewport */
    xmax = getmaxx();
    ymax = getmaxy();
    xsize = xmax - 100;
    ysize = ymax/5;
    setviewport(50, 30, xsize+50, ysize+30, 1);
    setfillstyle(SOLID_FILL, RED);
    bar3d(0,0,xsize,ysize,0,1);
    setcolor(YELLOW);
    settextjustify(CENTER_TEXT,CENTER_TEXT);
/* Define the scaling necessary to fit title in box.
 * The integers fed to setusercharsize must not be
 * be large. For example,
 *   setusercharsize(500,750,1,1) fails to scale.
 */
    settextstyle(TRIPLEX_FONT,HORIZ_DIR,0);
    setusercharsize(1,1,1,1);
    textx = textwidth(long_title);
    texty = textheight(long_title);
/* If title fits, leave it untouched */
    if(textx < xsize)
```

```
    {
        multx = 1;
        divx = 1;
    }
    else
    {
ratio = 10.*(double)xsize/(double)textx;
        multx = (int)ratio;
        divx = 10;
    }
    if(texty < ysize)
    {
        multy = 1;
        divy = 1;
    }
    else
    {
ratio = 10.*(double)ysize/(double)texty;
        multy = (int)ratio;
        divy = 10;
    }
/* Now set scale and print title */
    setusercharsize(multx,divx,multy,divy);
    settextstyle(TRIPLEX_FONT, HORIZ_DIR, 0);
    outtextxy(xsize/2,ysize/2, long_title);

/* Wait for a key press */
    getch();
/* Close graphics system when done */
    closegraph();
    return 0;
  }
```

textheight

COMPATIBILITY

TC1	TC1.5	TC2	TC++	MSC3	MSC4	MSC5	MSC6	QC1	QC2	QC2.5	ANSI	UNIX V	XNX
	▲	▲	▲										

PURPOSE Use *textheight* to determine the height of a text string (in pixels) when displayed using current font and character size settings.

SYNTAX `int far  textheight(char far *textstring);`

`char far *textstring;`	*Pointer to string whose height (when displayed) is being sought*

EXAMPLE CALL `v_space = textheight("Turbo C");`

INCLUDES `#include <graphics.h>` *For function declaration*

DESCRIPTION The *textheight* function uses information such as the current font, character size, and direction to determine the height (in pixels) of the on-screen rendering of the text string specified by the character pointer *textstring*. The string is not output by *textheight*. You have to call *outtext* or *outtextxy* to perform the actual output.

COMMON USES The *textheight* function and its companion *textwidth* are useful for adjusting the spacing between lines and for computing scaling factors (see *setusercharsize*) that will allow text to fit within a fixed size area on the screen.

RETURNS The *textheight* function returns the heights of a text string in pixels.

COMMENTS You should always use *textheight* and *textwidth* to compute the on-screen dimensions of a text string. This approach will allow the code to work, regardless of the font selected for the actual text output.

SEE ALSO

`gettextsettings`	*To get the current settings for graphics text output*
`outtext, outtextxy`	*To display the text string*
`settextstyle`	*To select a font, direction, and character size*
`setusercharsize`	*To specify x and y scaling for characters*
`textwidth`	*To get the on-screen width of a text string*

EXAMPLE Write a simple word processing program that allows users to type in text. Use *textheight* to determine how far down you must move when going from one line of text to the next. Of course, for a full-fledged word processor, you must add the capability to scroll, and you have to save the typed text in a buffer for later editing.

```
#include <graphics.h>
#define ESC '\033'   /* The ASCII code for Escape */

main()
{
    int graphdriver = DETECT, graphmode, xmax, ymax,
```

```
        xsize, ysize, c, x, y;
    char outstr[2] = " ";

/* Detect and initialize graphics system */
    initgraph(&graphdriver, &graphmode, "c:\\tc\\bgi");

/* Define a viewport */
    xmax = getmaxx();
    ymax = getmaxy();
    xsize = xmax - 100;
    ysize = ymax - 60;
    outtextxy(10,10, "Press Esc followed by any other \
key to exit");
    setviewport(50, 30, xsize+50, ysize+30, 1);
    setfillstyle(SOLID_FILL, RED);
    bar3d(0,0,xsize,ysize,0,1);
    setcolor(YELLOW);
    settextjustify(LEFT_TEXT, BOTTOM_TEXT);
/* Read characters and print them in the viewport.
 * When the edge of the viewport is reached, move
 * down by the height of a character plus 4 pixels.
 * Exit the loop when user presses the Escape key.
 */
    settextstyle(TRIPLEX_FONT,HORIZ_DIR,0);
    x = 4;
    y = textheight("H") + 4;
    moveto(x, y);
    while((c = getch()) != ESC)
    {
        outstr[0] = c;
    if((c == '\r') ||
       (x+textwidth(outstr)) > xsize)
    {
/* Advance to the next line in the viewport */
    x = 4;
        y += textheight("H");
        moveto(x, y);
    }
/* Print text. Don't print carriage return */
        if (c != '\r') outtext(outstr);
        x += textwidth(outstr);
    }
/* Wait for a final key press before exiting*/
    getch();
/* Close graphics system when done */
```

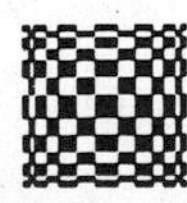

Combining Graphics and Text

```
    closegraph();
    return 0;
}
```

COMPATIBILITY

textwidth

TC1	TC1.5	TC2	TC++	MSC3	MSC4	MSC5	MSC6	QC1	QC2	QC2.5	ANSI	UNIX V	XNX
	▲	▲	▲										

PURPOSE Use *textwidth* to determine the widthof a string in pixels when displayed using the current font and character size selection.

SYNTAX

```
int far  textwidth(char far *textstring);
```

```
char far *textstring;
```
Pointer to string whose width (when displayed) is being sought

EXAMPLE CALL

```
h_space = textwidth("Turbo C");
```

INCLUDES

```
#include <graphics.h>
```
For function declaration

DESCRIPTION The *textwidth* function uses information such as the current font, character size, and direction to determine the width (in pixels) of the on-screen rendering of the text string specified by the character pointer *textstring*. The string is not output by *textwidth*. You have to call *outtext* or *outtextxy* to perform the actual output.

COMMON USES The *textwidth* function and its companion *textheight* are useful for adjusting the spacing between lines and for computing scaling factors (see *setusercharsize*) that will allow text to fit within a fixed size area on the screen.

RETURNS The *textwidth* function returns the width of a text string in pixels.

COMMENTS You should always use *textheight* and *textwidth* to compute the on-screen dimensions of a text string. This approach will let the code work, no matter which font is selected for the actual text output.

SEE ALSO

`gettextsettings` *To get the current settings for graphics text output*

`outtext, outtextxy` *To display the text string*

`settextstyle` *To select a font, direction, and character size*

`setusercharsize`	*To specify x and y scaling for characters*
`textheight`	*To get the on-screen height of a text string*

EXAMPLE Write a program that prints a line of text and underlines it by drawing a line underneath. Use *textwidth* to determine the length of the "underline."

```
#include <graphics.h>

char text[] = "Text to be underlined";

main()
{
    int graphdriver = DETECT, graphmode, xmax, ymax,
        xsize, ysize;

/* Detect and initialize graphics system */
    initgraph(&graphdriver, &graphmode, "c:\\tc\\bgi");

/* Display a graphics window with a text */
    xmax = getmaxx();
    ymax = getmaxy();
    xsize = xmax - 100;
    ysize = ymax - 60;
    setviewport(50, 30, xsize+50, ysize+30,1);
    setfillstyle(SOLID_FILL, RED);
    setcolor(YELLOW);
    bar3d(0,0,xsize,ysize,0,1);
/* Print text, then underline by drawing a line
 * underneath
 */
    settextstyle(SANS_SERIF_FONT, HORIZ_DIR, 1);
    settextjustify(LEFT_TEXT, BOTTOM_TEXT);
    outtextxy(10, ysize/2, text);
    moveto(10, ysize/2+1);
/* Draw the underline */
    linerel(textwidth(text), 0);
 /* Wait until a key is pressed */
    moveto(10, ysize-10);
    outtext("Press any key to exit:");
    getch();
    closegraph();          /* Exit graphics library */
    return 0;
  }
```

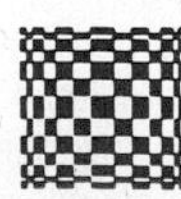

Combining Graphics and Text

Chapter 21 Text Mode Routines

Introduction

Although many modern PC applications use graphics effectively, some PC users do not have graphics output capabilities. Therefore, you may decide to design your application to work entirely in the text mode (or provide a text-only option). You may also opt for a text mode program when the application does not need a graphics interface (for example, a desk-top publishing program or a word processor definitely needs graphics capability, but a programmer's editor does not). Market considerations aside, text mode interfaces have the advantage of operating faster than ones with graphics because display adapters do not have to manipulate individual pixels when operating in the text mode; the screen is treated as an array of character cells, each of fixed size, and the hardware in the display adapter manipulates each cell as a whole.

The Turbo C++ graphics library includes twenty routines that can help you develop text mode interfaces for your applications. With these routines you can position text anywhere in the screen, select text attributes (such as underline, reverse video, blink, and foreground and background colors). You can even have the text confined within a window. You will also find routines to copy one region of screen to another quickly, and save an area of the screen in off-screen memory for later use. With these tools you can build full-screen text editors and user interfaces that work like the one in Turbo C++ itself.

In this chapter, we will summarize the text mode operation of various display adapters, and present the Turbo C++ routines that work in text mode.

Notes on Text Mode Operation

All IBM PC and PS/2 display adapters can operate in text modes where the screen is viewed as a two-dimensional grid of character cells, each of a fixed width and height. Turbo C++ supports a set of text modes common to all existing adapters. Table 21-1 lists the constants used to refer to these text modes in Turbo C++. The symbolic names for the text modes are defined in the include file *conio.h*. You must include *conio.h* to use the text mode constants. You can select a particular text mode with the function *textmode*. For example, *textmode(MONO)* selects the 80-column monochrome mode.

Table 21-1. ***Turbo C++ Text Modes***

Name	Numeric Value	Description
LASTMODE	−1	Previous text mode.
BW40	0	Black and white, 40 columns.
C40	1	16-color, 40 columns.
BW80	2	Black and white, 80 columns.
C80	3	16-color, 80 columns.
MONO	7	Monochrome, 80 columns.

Table 21-2 lists the routines available for text output and for controlling the appearance of text on the screen. In Table 21-3 the routines are categorized by task. These text output routines work in text modes only. Turbo C++ also provides routines capable of generating text output in graphics mode with a choice of fonts. These routines are discussed in Chapter 20.

Table 21-2. ***Text Mode Routines***

Name of Routine	Description
clreol	Clears from the cursor to the end of the line.
clrscr	Clears the current text window.
delline	Deletes the line indicated by the cursor closing up the existing lines.
gettext	Copies a rectangular area of the text screen to an off-screen buffer.
gettextinfo	Returns information regarding the current text mode, window location, and cursor location.
gotoxy	Positions cursor on the character cell at a specified (column, row) coordinate in the current text window.
highvideo	Selects high-intensity (bold) characters.

Table 21-2. *(cont.)*

Name of Routine	Description
insline	Inserts a blank line in the current text window at the cursor position, pushing down the lines below.
lowvideo	Selects low-intensity characters.
movetext	Copies text from one part of screen to another.
normvideo	Selects normal-intensity characters.
puttext	Copies text from a buffer in memory to the screen.
_setcursortype	Sets the cursor shape.
textattr	Sets the attribute (foreground and background colors) for subsequent text display.
textbackground	Selects a new background color for text display.
textcolor	Selects a new foreground color for text display.
textmode	Puts display adapter in a selected text mode.
wherex	Returns the horizontal position of the cursor in the current window.
wherey	Returns the vertical position of the cursor in the current window.
window	Defines a text window, a rectangular area within which all text output is confined.

Table 21-3. *Text Mode Routines by Task*

Task	Routine
Manipulate the cursor and edit text being displayed on the screen.	clreol, clrscr, delline, gotoxy, insline, movetext
Control appearance of characters.	highvideo, lowvideo, normvideo, textattr, textbackground, textcolor
Save and restore areas of screen.	gettext, puttext
Get information about current text mode and set a text mode.	gettextinfo, textmode
Get the current cursor position within a text window.	wherex, wherey
Set up a text window.	window
Set cursor shape.	_setcursortype

FAST SCREEN UPDATES—THE DIRECTVIDEO *VARIABLE*

Turbo C++'s text mode output routines, *cprintf* and *cputs*, check the setting of a global integer variable named *directvideo* to determine how to produce the screen output. If *directvideo* is set to 1, these routines write directly to the video memory. If *directvideo* is 0, the output is through the BIOS video functions (see Chapter 17).

If you know that the user's computer is fully compatible with the IBM PC, you can go ahead and set *directvideo* to 1. This will produce much faster screen updates than that possible with the BIOS functions. On the other hand, when the BIOS routines are used (*directvideo = 0*), your program is guaranteed to work on any PC that has an IBM-compatible ROM BIOS.

TEXT OUTPUT

The console output routines, *cprintf* and *cputs*, are designed to output text using foreground and background colors in text modes. The *cprintf* and *cputs* functions are similar to *printf* and *puts*, respectively, except that they use the current text attributes and they confine the text output within the current text window.

TEXT ATTRIBUTES

When operating in text mode, all IBM PC and PS/2 adapters use a 2-byte word to store each character in video memory. As shown in Figure 21-1, the low-order byte of the word holds the ASCII code for the character, while the high-order byte contains the attribute. The attribute determines the appearance of that character on the display screen. The exact interpretation of the attribute byte depends on the text mode in effect. In color modes, it determines the foreground and background color of the character; in the monochrome mode, the attribute controls features such as reverse video, underlining, high intensity, and blinking.

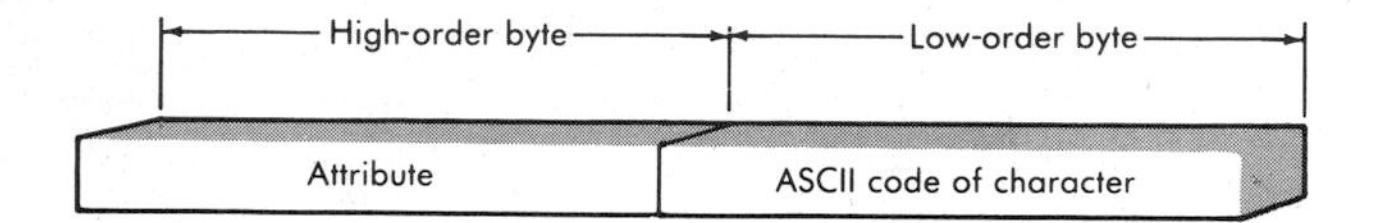

Figure 21-1. *A character and its attributes in text mode*

Figure 21-2 shows the interpretation of the attribute in a color mode. The low-order nibble (bits 0 through 3) contain the foreground color, which can be any one of the colors 0 through 15. The next three bits (4, 5, and 6) hold the background color, a value between 0 and 7. The most significant bit (bit 7) is the blink enable bit. If bit 7 is set, the character will blink.

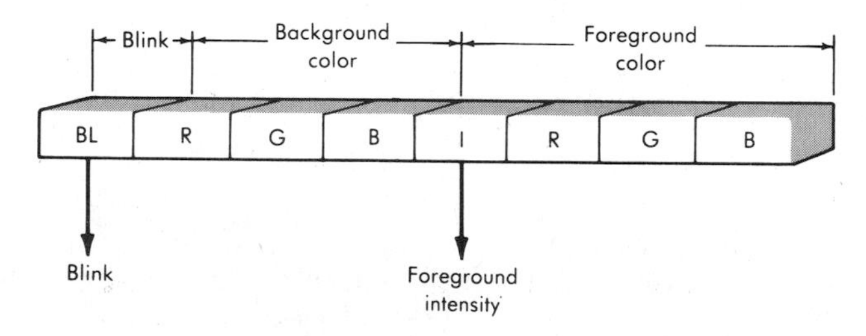

Figure 21-2. *Text attribute byte*

You can set the foreground and background colors for all future text by calling *textcolor* and *textbackground* separately. You can use one of the constants from Table 18-3 (from the CGA column) to indicate the foreground and background colors of your choice. The blink enable bit may be selected by adding the constant BLINK to the foreground color. Thus,

```
textcolor(RED+BLINK);
textbackground(CYAN);
```

selects blinking red characters with a cyan background for future text output. These two steps can be performed in one step by calling the function *textattr* to set the attribute byte in a single step. When using *textattr*, you must construct the complete byte, which means that you must remember to shift the background color to the left by 4 bits before adding it to the foreground color. Thus, the example above will translate to

```
/* Select blinking red characters on a cyan background */
   textattr((CYAN << 4) + RED + BLINK);
```

When interpreting the attribute byte, all video adapters consider bit 3 of the attribute to be the intensity bit. When set to 1, this bit generates lighter colors in color text modes, and high-intensity characters in the monochrome mode. You can manipulate this bit directly with the routines *highvideo*, *lowvideo*, and *normvideo*. You turn the intensity bit on and off, respectively, by calling *highvideo* and *lowvideo*, while *normvideo* sets the bit to the value it had when the program started.

A companion function, *gettextinfo* lets you query the Turbo C graphics package for the current text attribute, mode, and other information such as the coordinates of the text window and the cursor position in the window.

You can take advantage of the *gettextinfo* function to select text colors and backgrounds that are appropriate for the current text mode. This is important because a color combination that works well on a color display may become invisible on a monochrome display. (There is no color on the monochrome adapter; the specified values map to text attributes such as underline, blink, and reverse video.)

TEXT WINDOW AND CURSOR POSITION

The cursor position is where text output occurs. The cursor position is always specified in the (x,y) format with the x- and y-coordinates respectively corresponding to column and row positions of a character cell. Use *gotoxy* to move the cursor to a location within the current window, and, *wherex* and *wherey* to, respectively, find the column and the row coordinate of the cursor.

All cursor positions are relative to the origin (1,1) (the upper left corner) of a rectangular area known as the current text window. The default window is the entire screen, but you can define a smaller window by calling *window*. For example, the code fragment

```
window(10,10,69,14);    /* Define a text window*/
gotoxy(30,2);
cputs("Hello!");
```

will define a rectangular text window, 5 rows by 60 columns, with the upper left corner at column and row coordinates (10,10). Then *gotoxy* moves the cursor to the second row and the thirtieth column in the text window (this translates to the twelfth row and fortieth column on the display screen), and *cputs* prints the message using the current text attributes. Text windows can be used to implement pop-up menus or message windows.

POP-UP MENUS IN TEXT MODE

Pop-up menus overwrite an area of screen, prompting the user for a selection from a menu. Once the choice is made, the menu disappears and the old screen image reappears. Dialog boxes are similar to pop-up menus, except that they are used to present a message to the user and often to ask for some input. Such pop-up menus and dialog boxes are easy to implement with the *window* function which lets you define the box in which the menu or the message will appear. Two more routines, *gettext* and *puttext*, help you save and restore the area of screen where the menu will appear. Before displaying the menu on the screen, you can call *gettext* to save the contents of that rectangular area of screen to a buffer in memory. Then after the user enters the menu choice or indicates that the dialog box is no longer needed, you can restore the screen to its previous state by copying the contents of the buffer back to the screen with a call to *puttext*.

As an example, consider the problem of displaying a message in a dialog box. The following code shows how this might be done:

```
#include <conio.h>
static char txtbuf[2*30*8];  /* Buffer for 30x8 rectangle */
    :
    :
/* Save contents of screen rectangle in buffer */
    if(!gettext(25,8, 54,15, txtbuf))
    {
/* Error saving screen. Handle error here. */
    :
    }

/* Display message */
    window(25,8, 54,15);
    textattr(YELLOW+(RED<<4));
```

```
    clrscr();
    gotoxy(7,4);
    cputs("System Error: -11");
    gotoxy(1,7);
    cputs("Press any key to exit");

/* Wait for user to press a key */
    getch();

/* Restore the screen rectangle from buffer */
    if(!puttext(25,8, 54,15, txtbuf))
    {
/* Error restoring screen. Handle error here. */
    :
    }
```

TEXT EDITING

The text mode routines include a few that are useful for editing the text that is being displayed on the screen. You will find these functions useful if you design applications such as a text editor or a forms entry program. These routines all work within the current text window.

The *clrscr* function clears the entire text window and fills it with the current background color (or background attribute, when the system is monochrome). You can erase from the current cursor position to the end of that line with the *clreol* function. You can use *delline* to erase the entire line on which the cursor rests and close up the existing lines. On the other hand, the *insline* inserts a blank line at the row with the cursor, pushing down the existing lines. Note that all of these operations work within the confines of the current text window.

If you should need to copy a rectangular area of text from one on-screen location to another, you can use the *movetext* function. For copying back and forth between a memory buffer and the screen, you can use the previously discussed *gettext* and *puttext* functions.

clreol

COMPATIBILITY

TC1	TC1.5	TC2	TC++	MSC3	MSC4	MSC5	MSC6	QC1	QC2	QC2.5	ANSI	UNIX V	XNX
	▲	▲	▲										

PURPOSE Use *clreol* to clear from the cursor position to the end of the line.

SYNTAX
```
void clreol(void);
```

EXAMPLE CALL
```
clreol();
```

INCLUDES `#include <conio.h>` *For function declaration*

DESCRIPTION The *clreol* function erases all characters from the cursor position to the end of the line in the current text window. The cursor is not moved. The erased character cells are filled with the current text background color. If you want to remove an entire line without leaving a blank space, you can use *delline.*

COMMON USES The *clreol* function is useful in filling forms and in applications that require text editing.

SEE ALSO

`clrscr` *To clear the entire text window*

`delline` *To delete a line*

`textbackground` *To set the background color for text mode*

`window` *To define a text window*

EXAMPLE Write a small program to illustrate the effect of the *clreol* function.

```
#include <conio.h>
char textstr[] = "Testing clreol. Press any key to "
                 "erase this sentence.";

main()
{
/* Display a line on the screen. When
 * user presses any key position cursor
 * within the line and erase to end of line. */
   gotoxy(10,5);
   cputs(textstr);
   getch();
```

```
    gotoxy(10+16, 5);
    clreol();
    return 0;
}
```

COMPATIBILITY

clrscr

TC1	TC1.5	TC2	TC++	MSC3	MSC4	MSC5	MSC6	QC1	QC2	QC2.5	ANSI	UNIX V	XNX
	▲	▲	▲			1	1	1	1	1			

PURPOSE Use *clrscr* to clear and fill the current text window with the current text background color.

SYNTAX `void clrscr(void);`

EXAMPLE CALL `clrscr();`

INCLUDES `#include <conio.h>` *For function declaration*

DESCRIPTION The *clrscr* function fills all character cells in the current text window with the current text background color. After the text window is cleared, the cursor is placed at the upper left hand corner of the window (position 1,1).

1. The equivalent function in Microsoft C 5 and 6, and QuickC 1.0 through 2.5, is *_clearscreen.*

COMMON USES The *clrscr* function is useful for displaying pop-up menus and dialog boxes for interaction with the user.

SEE ALSO

`clreol`	*To erase from the cursor to the end of the line in the current text window*
`textbackground`	*To set the background color for text mode*
`window`	*To define a text window*

EXAMPLE Write a program that defines a text window and uses *clrscr* to erase the window, fill it with the current text background color, and then display a message. This can be used in pop-up windows used for dialogs and menus.

```
#include <conio.h>

main()
{
/* Define a text window. Set the background
 * color. Call clrscr to clear window and fill
 * it with the background color.
 */
```

```
    window(20,10,60,20);
    textbackground(RED);
    clrscr();
    textcolor(YELLOW);
    gotoxy(10,2);
    cputs("Welcome to Turbo C++\r\n");
    return 0;
}
```

delline

COMPATIBILITY

TC1	TC1.5	TC2	TC++	MSC3	MSC4	MSC5	MSC6	QC1	QC2	QC2.5	ANSI	UNIX V	XNX
	▲	▲	▲										

PURPOSE Use *delline* to delete the entire line containing the cursor. The lines below it are moved up to close up the gap.

SYNTAX `void delline(void);`

EXAMPLE CALL `delline();`

INCLUDES `#include <conio.h>` *For function declaration*

DESCRIPTION The *delline* function deletes the line containing the cursor from the current text window, and moves the lines underneath one row up. If you want to erase an entire line but do not want the space removed, you should place the cursor at the beginning of the line with a call to *gotoxy* and then use *clreol.*

COMMON USES The *delline* routine is useful for performing text editing.

SEE ALSO `clreol` *To erase from cursor to end of line in the current window*

`clrscr` *To clear the entire current text window*

EXAMPLE Write a program that illustrates the effect of *delline.*

```
#include <conio.h>
char text[] =
    "Testing delline. Press any key to go on.";
main()
{
    int i, nlines=11;
```

```
/* Define a text window and fill it with
 * several lines of text.
 */
     window(20,10,60,10+nlines-1);
    textbackground(RED);
    clrscr();
    textcolor(YELLOW);
    for(i = 1; i <= nlines; i++)
    {
        gotoxy(1,i);
        cputs(text);
    }
    gotoxy(1, nlines/2);
    for(i = 0; i < nlines/2; i++)
    {
/* Delete a line everytime the user presses a key */
        getch();
        delline();
    }
    return 0;
}
```

gettext

COMPATIBILITY

TC1	TC1.5	TC2	TC++	MSC3	MSC4	MSC5	MSC6	QC1	QC2	QC2.5	ANSI	UNIX V	XNX
	▲	▲	▲										

PURPOSE Use *gettext* to save the contents of a rectangular region of a text screen in a buffer.

SYNTAX

```
int   gettext  (int left, int top, int right, int bottom,
                void *textbuf);
```

`int left, top;` *Column and row coordinates of the upper left corner of the region being saved*

`int right, bottom;` *Column and row coordinates of the lower right corner of the region being saved*

`void *textbuf;` *Pointer to buffer to which screen contents are copied*

EXAMPLE CALL

```
char saved_screen[20*10*2];
if (!gettext(1,1, 20,10, saved_screen)) puts("gettext failed!");
```

INCLUDES `#include <conio.h>` *For function declaration*

DESCRIPTION The *gettext* function copies the contents of a rectangular area of the screen (in text mode) to the buffer whose address is given in the argument *textbuf.* The arguments *(left,top)* and *(right,bottom)*, respectively, are the absolute column and row coordinates of the upper left and lower right corners of the rectangular area to be saved.

Since each on-screen character needs 2 bytes of storage, one for the character's ASCII code and one for its attribute, the size of the buffer must be at least *2*(right-left+1)*(bottom-top+1)* bytes.

When copying the characters from the screen, *gettext* starts at the upper left corner of the area and sequentially copies them to the buffer from left to right and top to bottom.

COMMON USES When you implement a pop-up menu, the area underneath the menu must be saved. You can use *gettext* for this purpose. The screen can be restored later by *puttext.*

RETURNS The *gettext* function returns a 1 if all goes well. Otherwise, it returns a 0. The *gettext* function will fail if you give it coordinates beyond the limits of the screen for the current text mode.

COMMENTS Although most text mode routines expect coordinates relative to the origin of the current text window, *gettext* and *puttext* require absolute column and row coordinates, *not* window-relative coordinates.

SEE ALSO `movetext` *To copy one on-screen rectangle to another on-screen rectangle*

`puttext` *To restore text screen saved earlier by* gettext

EXAMPLE Use *gettext* with *puttext* to implement a pop-up menu in Turbo C++.

```
#include <alloc.h>
#include <conio.h>
char text[] =
    "Testing gettext/puttext. Press any key to go on.";
main()
{
    int i, left = 20, right = 60, top = 10, bottom = 20,
bufsize;
    char *tbuffer;
/* Fill the screen with several lines of text. */
    for(i = 1; i <= 25; i++)
    {
        gotoxy(1,i);
```

```
        cputs(text);
    }
/* Now use gettext/puttext to implement a pop-up
 * menu.
 */
    bufsize = 2*(bottom-top+1)*(right-left+1);
    if((tbuffer = (char *) malloc(bufsize))
        == NULL)
    {
        cputs("Error allocating buffer!");
        exit(1);
    }
    if(!gettext(left,top,right,bottom,tbuffer))
    {
        cputs("Error saving text!");
        exit(1);
    }
    getch(); /* wait for a keypress */

/* Now define window for menu and display menu */
    window(left,top,right,bottom);
    textbackground(RED);
    clrscr();
    textcolor(YELLOW);
    gotoxy(2,4);
    cputs("Pop-up Menu is easy in Turbo C");
    gotoxy(2,10);
    cputs("Press a key to exit menu:");
    getch();
/* Restore screen using puttext */
    if(!puttext(left,top,right,bottom,tbuffer))
    {
cputs("Error restoring text!");
    }
    return 0;
}
```

gettextinfo

COMPATIBILITY

TC1	TC1.5	TC2	TC++	MSC3	MSC4	MSC5	MSC6	QC1	QC2	QC2.5	ANSI	UNIX V	XNX
	▲	▲	▲										

PURPOSE Use *gettextinfo* to obtain information about the current text window, the text mode, the text attribute, and the cursor position within the window.

SYNTAX

```
void   gettextinfo (struct text_info *p_tinfo);
```

`struct text_info *p_tinfo;` *Pointer to structure where information about current text mode is returned*

EXAMPLE CALL

```
struct text_info info_tmode;
gettextinfo(&info_tmode);
```

INCLUDES `#include <conio.h>` *For function declaration*

DESCRIPTION The *gettextinfo* function returns information such as the coordinates of the current text window, the cursor position within the window, the text attribute, the screen dimensions, and the current text mode. The information is returned in a *text_info* structure. You must allocate such a structure and provide its address in the argument *p_tinfo*. The *text_info* structure is defined in *conio.h* as

```
struct text_info
{
    unsigned char winleft;        /* x- and y-coordinate of  */
    unsigned char wintop;         /* lower right corner of
                                     current text window    */
    unsigned char winright;       /* x- and y-coordinate of  */
    unsigned char winbottom;      /* lower right corner of
                                     current text window    */
    unsigned char attribute;      /* Current text attribute */
    unsigned char normattr;       /* Normal text attribute  */
    unsigned char currmode;       /* Current text mode      */
    unsigned char screenheight;   /* Height of the screen   */
    unsigned char screenwidth;    /* Width of the screen    */
    unsigned char curx;           /* x-coordinate of cursor */
    unsigned char cury;           /* y-coordinate of cursor */
};
```

The meanings of the different fields of the *text_info* structure are shown in the comments within the C declaration of the structure.

COMMON USES The *gettextinfo* function can be used to get and save current window and mode information before changing them in your program. The saved values can be used to restore the old settings later.

SEE ALSO

`textattr, textbackground, textcolor`	*To set text attribute*
`textmode`	*To switch to another text mode*
`wherex, wherey`	*To determine current cursor position*
`window`	*To define a text window*

EXAMPLE Use *gettextinfo* to get the information about text mode output. Display this information in an organized form.

```
#include <conio.h>

main()
{
    struct text_info t_info;
/* Define a text window */
    window(20,10,60,20);
    textbackground(RED);
    textcolor(YELLOW);
    clrscr();
    gotoxy(10,2);
/* Get text mode information and display it */
    gettextinfo(&t_info);
    cprintf("Text Information\r\n");
    cprintf("Window = (%d,%d), (%d,%d)\r\n",
            t_info.winleft,  t_info.wintop,
            t_info.winright, t_info.winbottom);
    cprintf("Mode = %d\r\n", t_info.currmode);
    cprintf("Attribute now = %d, Normal Attribute = %d\r\n",
            t_info.attribute, t_info.normattr);
    cprintf("Screen height = %d, screen width = %d\r\n",
            t_info.screenheight, t_info.screenwidth);
    cprintf("We started at (%d,%d)\r\n",
            t_info.curx, t_info.cury);
    return 0;
}
```

gotoxy

COMPATIBILITY

TC1	TC1.5	TC2	TC++	MSC3	MSC4	MSC5	MSC6	QC1	QC2	QC2.5	ANSI	UNIX V	XNX
	▲	▲	▲			1	1	1	1	1			

PURPOSE Use *gotoxy* to move the cursor to a specified position (column, row) within the current text window.

SYNTAX

```
void gotoxy  (int x, int y);
```

`int x, y;` *The column and row number relative to the upper left corner of the current text window where the cursor is to be positioned*

EXAMPLE CALL

```
gotoxy(20,5);
```

INCLUDES `#include <conio.h>` *For function declaration*

DESCRIPTION The *gotoxy* function places the cursor at the column *x* and row *y* in the current text window. The row and column coordinates are with respect to the upper left corner (1,1) of the text window. If the desired cursor position is beyond the bounds of the current text window, *gotoxy* will ignore the request.

1. In Microsoft C 5 and 6, and QuickC 1.0 through 2.5, use *_settextposition.*

COMMON USES The *gotoxy* function is used to position text in a window.

SEE ALSO

`wherex, wherey` *To get the current cursor position*

`window` *To define a text window*

EXAMPLE Write a form entry program in Turbo C++. Use *gotoxy* to position the cursor at the beginning of a field before accepting input for that field. You can implement data entry applications using this approach.

```
#include <conio.h>
#define ESC '\033'  /* ASCII code for the Esc key */
static char *fieldlabel[4] =
{ "Name:", "Street:", "City/State/ZIP:", "Phone:"};
main()
{
    int left=20, top=10, right=60, bottom=20,
        fieldxy[4][2] = {16,3,16,4,16,5,16,6},
        fieldnum = 0, maxfields = 4,
```

```
        numchar = 0, c, i;
/* Define a text window to be used as a form */
    window(left,top,right,bottom);
    textbackground(RED);
    textcolor(YELLOW);
    clrscr();
/* Let user fields in the form. */
    gotoxy(10,1);
    cputs("C L I E N T   D A T A");
    gotoxy(1,bottom-top);
    cputs("<Enter> for next field. <Esc> to exit");
/* Mark the fields */
    for (i = 0; i < maxfields; i++)
    {
        gotoxy(1, fieldxy[i][1]);
        cputs(fieldlabel[i]);
    }
    gotoxy(fieldxy[fieldnum][0], fieldxy[fieldnum][1]);
    while((c = getch()) != ESC)
    {
        if(c == '\r')
        {
/* Go to next field */
            fieldnum = (fieldnum+1) % maxfields;
            gotoxy(fieldxy[fieldnum][0],
                   fieldxy[fieldnum][1]);
            numchar = 0;
        }
        numchar++;
        if(numchar < (right - left
       - fieldxy[fieldnum][0]))


        {
            if(c != '\r')putch(c);
        }
        else  putch('\007');
    }
    return 0;
}
```

highvideo

COMPATIBILITY

TC1	TC1.5	TC2	TC++	MSC3	MSC4	MSC5	MSC6	QC1	QC2	QC2.5	ANSI	UNIX V	XNX
	▲	▲	▲										

PURPOSE Use *highvideo* to turn on the high-intensity bit (bit 3) of the current text attribute.

SYNTAX

```
void highvideo(void);
```

EXAMPLE CALL

```
textcolor(RED);

highvideo();        /* Make it light red */
```

INCLUDES

```
#include <conio.h>        For function declaration
```

DESCRIPTION As shown in Figure 21-2, bits 0 through 3 of the attribute byte are used to store the foreground color of the text. Bits 0, 1, and 2 correspond to the red, green, and blue signals in color text modes, respectively, and bit 3 corresponds to the intensity signal in color as well as monochrome modes. The *highvideo* function turns this intensity bit on.

Once *highvideo* is called in monochrome mode, all subsequent text becomes intensified; in color mode, the foreground color becomes lighter than usual.

You can use *lowvideo* to reset the intensity bit to zero.

COMMON USES The *highvideo* function is used to control how the text looks on the screen.

COMMENTS Text already on screen is not affected by the call to *highvideo*. Only subsequent text printed by *cprintf* and *cputs* is affected.

SEE ALSO

`lowvideo` *To turn the intensity bit off*

`normvideo` *To revert back to text attribute as it was when the program started*

`textcolor` *To set the foreground of the text attribute*

EXAMPLE Write a program to show how *highvideo* may be used to intensify the text being displayed.

```
#include <conio.h>

main()
{
/* Display a line with current attributes. Then
```

```
 * show a line in high intensity
 */
    gotoxy(10,2);
    cputs("This is in current attribute\r\n");
    highvideo();
    cputs("This is after calling 'highvideo'\r\n");
/* Turn high intensity off before exiting */
    lowvideo();
    return 0;
}
```

insline

COMPATIBILITY

TC1	TC1.5	TC2	TC++	MSC3	MSC4	MSC5	MSC6	QC1	QC2	QC2.5	ANSI	UNIX V	XNX
	▲	▲	▲										

PURPOSE Use *insline* to insert a blank line in the text window at the cursor position.

SYNTAX

```
void insline(void);
```

EXAMPLE CALL

```
insline();
```

INCLUDES `#include <conio.h>` *For function declaration*

DESCRIPTION The *insline* function inserts one blank line into the current text window at the cursor position. The line is filled with the current text background color. All lines below the inserted line are moved down by one row, and the line at the bottom scrolls out of the window.

COMMON USES The *insline* function is useful for text editing applications.

SEE ALSO

`clreol` *To erase from cursor to end of line in current text window*

`delline` *To delete a line from the current text window*

`window` *To define a new text window*

EXAMPLE Write a program that illustrates the effect of calling *insline*.

```
#include <conio.h>
char text[] =
    "Testing insline. Press any key to go on.";
main()
```

```
{
    int i, nlines=11;
/* Define a text window and fill it with
 * several lines of text.
 */
     window(20,10,60,10+nlines-1);
    textbackground(RED);
    clrscr();
    textcolor(YELLOW);
    for(i = 1; i <= nlines; i++)
    {
        gotoxy(1,i);
        cputs(text);
    }
    gotoxy(1, nlines/2);
    for(i = 0; i <= nlines/2; i++)
    {
/* Insert a line everytime the user presses a key */
        getch();
        insline();
    }
    return 0;
}
```

lowvideo

COMPATIBILITY

TC1	TC1.5	TC2	TC++	MSC3	MSC4	MSC5	MSC6	QC1	QC2	QC2.5	ANSI	UNIX V	XNX
	▲	▲	▲										

PURPOSE Use *lowvideo* to turn off the high-intensity bit (bit 3) of the current text attribute.

SYNTAX `void lowvideo(void);`

EXAMPLE CALL

```
textcolor(LIGHTRED);

lowvideo();        /* Make it normal red */
```

INCLUDES `#include <conio.h>` *For function declaration*

DESCRIPTION As shown in Figure 21-2, bits 0 through 3 of the attribute byte are used to store the foreground color of the text. Bits 0, 1, and 2 correspond to the red, green, and blue signals in color text modes, respectively, and bit 3 corresponds to the intensity signal in color as well as monochrome modes. The *lowvideo* function turns this intensity bit off.

You can use *highvideo* to turn the intensity bit back on.

COMMON USES The *lowvideo* function is used to control how the text looks on the screen.

COMMENTS Text already on screen is not affected by the call to *lowvideo*. Only subsequent text printed by *cprintf* and *cputs* is affected.

SEE ALSO

`highvideo` *To turn the intensity bit on*

`normvideo` *To revert back to text attribute as it was when the program started*

`textcolor` *To set the foreground of the text attribute*

EXAMPLE You can call *lowvideo* to undo the effect of calling *highvideo*. Write a program to show how *lowvideo* is used.

```
#include <conio.h>

main()
{
/* Display a line with current attributes. Then
 * show a line in low intensity
 */
    gotoxy(10,2);
    cputs("This is in current attribute\r\n");
    highvideo();
    cputs("This is after calling 'highvideo'\r\n");
    lowvideo();
    cputs("Here is how it looks after 'lowvideo'\r\n");
    return 0;
}
```

movetext

COMPATIBILITY

TC1	TC1.5	TC2	TC++	MSC3	MSC4	MSC5	MSC6	QC1	QC2	QC2.5	ANSI	UNIX V	XNX
	▲	▲	▲										

PURPOSE Use *movetext* to copy the contents of one on-screen rectangle to another on-screen rectangle of the same dimensions.

SYNTAX

```
int   movetext  (int left, int top, int right, int bottom,
                 int newleft, int newtop);
```

`int left, top;` *Column and row coordinates of the upper left corner of the source rectangle*

`int right, bottom;` *Column and row coordinates of the lower right corner of the source rectangle*

`int newleft, newtop;` *Column and row coordinates of the upper left corner of the destination rectangle*

EXAMPLE CALL

```
if (!movetext(1,1, 20,10, 30,30)) puts("movetext failed!");
```

INCLUDES `#include <conio.h>` *For function declaration*

DESCRIPTION The *movetext* function copies the contents of a rectangular area of the screen (in text mode) to another on-screen rectangle of the same dimensions. The arguments *(left,top)* and *(right,bottom)*, respectively, are the absolute column and row coordinates of the upper left and lower right corners of the rectangular area to be copied. Since the destination rectangle is of the same size as the source, only the coordinates of its upper left corner, *(newleft,newtop)*, are necessary.

RETURNS The *movetext* function returns a 1 if all goes well. Otherwise, it returns a 0. The *movetext* function will fail if you give it coordinates beyond the limits of the screen for the current text mode.

COMMENTS Although most text mode routines expect coordinates relative to the origin of the current text window, *movetext* requires absolute column and row coordinates, not window-relative coordinates.

SEE ALSO `gettext` *To copy one on-screen rectangle to a buffer*

`puttext` *To restore text screen saved earlier by* gettext

EXAMPLE Write a Turbo C++ program that uses *movetext* to copy a portion of the text screen to another area of the screen.

```
#include <conio.h>
main()
{
    int i;
    gotoxy(1,1);
    for (i=0; i<5; i++)
        cprintf("T h i s   i s   l i n e #%d\r\n", i);
    cputs("Press any key to copy above text:");
    getch();
```

```
    if(!movetext(1,1,28,5, 30,1))
    {
cputs("\r\nFailed during 'movetext'\r\n");
exit(1);
    }
    gotoxy(1,15);
    highvideo();
    cputs("The copying was done by calling 'movetext'\r\n");
    return 0;
}
```

COMPATIBILITY

normvideo

TC1	TC1.5	TC2	TC++	MSC3	MSC4	MSC5	MSC6	QC1	QC2	QC2.5	ANSI	UNIX V	XNX
	▲	▲	▲										

PURPOSE Use *normvideo* to reset the text attribute to the value it had before the program started.

SYNTAX `void normvideo(void);`

EXAMPLE CALL `normvideo();`

INCLUDES `#include <conio.h>` *For function declaration*

DESCRIPTION The *normvideo* function sets the text attribute (the foreground and background colors of characters) back to the value it had when the program started. This *normal* text attribute is reported in the *normattr* field of the *text_info* structure when you call *gettextinfo*.

SEE ALSO

`highvideo` *To turn on the intensity bit in the current text attribute*

`lowvideo` *To turn off the intensity bit in the current text attribute*

`textattr` *To set both foreground and background of the text attribute*

`textcolor` *To set the foreground of the text attribute*

EXAMPLE Write a program that uses *normvideo* to restore the text attribute back to its original state at the start of the program.

```
#include <conio.h>
```

```
main()
{
/* Define a text window and text attributes */
    window(20,10,60,20);
    textbackground(RED);
    textcolor(YELLOW);
    clrscr();
    gotoxy(10,2);
    cputs("This is the current attribute\r\n");
    normvideo();
    cputs("This is after calling 'normvideo'\r\n");
    return 0;
}
```

puttext

COMPATIBILITY

TC1	TC1.5	TC2	TC++	MSC3	MSC4	MSC5	MSC6	QC1	QC2	QC2.5	ANSI	UNIX V	XNX
	▲	▲	▲										

PURPOSE Use *puttext* to copy the contents of a buffer into a rectangular area of the screen in text mode.

SYNTAX

```
int   puttext  (int left, int top, int right, int bottom,
                void *textbuf);
```

`int left, top;` *Column and row coordinates of the upper left corner of the rectangle where text is put*

`int right, bottom;` *Column and row coordinates of the lower right corner of the rectangle where text is put*

`void *textbuf;` *Pointer to buffer whose contents are copied into the rectangle on the screen*

EXAMPLE CALL

```
char saved_screen[20*10*2];
if (!puttext(5,5, 25,15, saved_screen)) puts("puttext failed!");
```

INCLUDES `#include <conio.h>` *For function declaration*

DESCRIPTION The *puttext* function copies the contents of the buffer whose address is given in the argument *textbuf* to a rectangular area on the screen (in text mode). The arguments *(left,top)* and *(right,bottom)*, respectively, are the absolute screen coordinates of the upper left and lower right corners of the rectangular area to which the buffer is copied.

Since each on-screen character uses two bytes of storage, one for the character's ASCII code and the other byte for its attribute, the size of the buffer whose address is in *textbuf* must be at at least *2*(right-left+1) *(bottom-top+1)* bytes. When copying from the buffer to the screen, *puttext* starts at the upper left corner of the area and sequentially copies bytes to the screen from left to right and top to bottom.

COMMON USES When you implement a pop-up menu, you can save the area underneath the menu using *gettext*. Later on, you can restore that area of the screen by calling *puttext*.

RETURNS The *puttext* function returns a 1 if all goes well. Otherwise, it returns a 0. The *puttext* function will fail if you give it coordinates beyond the limits of the screen for the current text mode.

COMMENTS Although most text mode routines expect coordinates relative to the origin of the current text window, *puttext* and *getttext* require absolute column and row coordinates, not window-relative coordinates.

SEE ALSO

`gettext` *To save a rectangular area of the text screen in a buffer*

`movetext` *To copy one on-screen rectangle to another on-screen rectangle*

EXAMPLE When using *puttext* to restore text saved earlier by *gettext*, you can specify a rectangle with height and width different from that of the original (as long as the total number of characters remains the same). You can essentially "reformat" text using this feature. Write a Turbo C++ program to illustrate this effect.

```
#include <alloc.h>
#include <conio.h>
main()
{
    int i, bufsize,
top=1, left=1, right=80, bottom=5;
    char *tbuffer;

    gotoxy(1,1);
    for (i=1; i<=bottom; i++)
        cprintf("Press any key to save and restore \
these long lines of text in a narrow column\r\n");

/* Now use gettext to save this text in a buffer */
```

```
        bufsize = 2*(bottom-top+1)*(right-left+1);
        if((tbuffer = (char *) malloc(bufsize))
            == NULL)
        {
            cputs("Error allocating buffer!\r\n");
            exit(1);
        }
        if(!gettext(left,top,right,bottom,tbuffer))
        {
            cputs("Error saving text!\r\n");
            exit(1);
        }
        getch(); /* wait for a keypress */

    /* Restore buffer using puttext in a narrower box */
        if(!puttext(left,top+11, right/2, bottom*2+11,
                    tbuffer))
        {
    cputs("Error restoring text!\r\n");
        }
        return 0;
    }
```

_setcursortype

COMPATIBILITY

TC1	TC1.5	TC2	TC++	MSC3	MSC4	MSC5	MSC6	QC1	QC2	QC2.5	ANSI	UNIX V	XNX
			▲			1	1	1	1	1			

PURPOSE Use *_setcursortype* to change the shape of the cursor in text mode.

SYNTAX

```
void _setcursortype(int cursor_style);
```

`int cursor_style;` *_NORMALCURSOR, _NOCURSOR, or _SOLIDCURSOR (constants representing cursor shape)*

EXAMPLE CALL

```
_setcursortype(_SOLIDCURSOR);    /* Use a block cursor */
```

INCLUDES `#include <conio.h>` *For function declaration and definition of constants for cursor shape*

DESCRIPTION The *_setcursortype* function sets the cursor shape in text mode to the style specified by the integer argument *cursor_style*. This argument has to be one of the following constants defined in *conio.h*:

_NOCURSOR	*Turns off the cursor*
_SOLIDCURSOR	*A solid block character is used as cursor*
_NORMALCURSOR	*A blinking underline is used as cursor*

1. Use *_settextcursor* in Microsoft C 5 and 6, and QuickC 1.0 through 2.5.

SEE ALSO cprintf, cputs *To display output in a text-mode screen*

EXAMPLE Write a program, *cursor.exe*, that can be used to change the cursor shape in text mode. It should accept an argument that specifies the desired cursor. For example, *cursor none* should turn the cursor off and *cursor solid* should set a block cursor. When invoked without any argument, the program should set the cursor to the normal blinking underline.

```
/* File: cursor.c  */

#include <string.h>
#include <conio.h>

main(int argc, char **argv)
{
    char normal[] = "normal";
    int cursor_style = _NORMALCURSOR;
    char *style = normal;

    if(argc > 1)
    {
     if(strcmpi("solid", argv[1]) == 0)
         cursor_style = _SOLIDCURSOR;
     if(strcmpi("none", argv[1]) == 0)
         cursor_style = _NOCURSOR;
     if(strcmpi("normal", argv[1]) == 0)
         cursor_style = _NORMALCURSOR;
     style = argv[1];
    }
/* Now set the cursor appearance */
    _setcursortype(cursor_style);
    cprintf("Current cursor style is: %s\r\n", style);
    cprintf("Type 'cursor' to change back to normal\r\n");
}
```

textattr

COMPATIBILITY

TC1	TC1.5	TC2	TC++	MSC3	MSC4	MSC5	MSC6	QC1	QC2	QC2.5	ANSI	UNIX V	XNX
	▲	▲	▲										

PURPOSE Use *textattr* to set the text attribute—both foreground and background—to be used for all subsequent text output by *cprintf* and *cputs*.

SYNTAX

```
void textattr(int newattr);

int newattr;        New text attribute
```

EXAMPLE CALL

```
/* Yellow characters on a red background */
textattr(YELLOW + (RED<<4));
```

INCLUDES

```
#include <conio.h>      For function declaration and symbolic constants for colors
```

DESCRIPTION The *textattr* function sets the text attribute to *newattr*. The routines *cprintf* and *cputs* will use this attribute for all subsequent text output.

When you set the foreground and the background attributes at once by using *textattr* (as opposed to setting them separately by calling *textcolor* and *textbackground*, respectively), you have to pack the foreground and background colors into a single byte according to the format shown in Table 21-4.

Table 21-4. ***Text Attribute Byte***

Bits	Interpretation
0–3	Foreground color. Bit 3 is the intensity bit.
4–6	Background color.
7	When this bit is 1, text will blink.

You can construct the attribute *newattr* with symbolic names for the colors as shown in Table 21-5 (included on the reference page for *textcolor*). For example, to get yellow characters on a red background, you will use

```
textattr(YELLOW + (RED << 4));
```

Notice that you must shift the background color left by 4 bits and add it to the foreground color. If you want to enable blinking, you should add the constant BLINK (defined to be 128 in *conio.h*) to the attribute. Thus, *textattr(YELLOW+(RED<<4)+BLINK)* will produce blinking yellow characters on a red background.

Text Mode Routines

COMMON USES The *textattr* routine is used to control the appearance of text on the screen.

COMMENTS You can use the *textcolor* and *textbackground* functions if you want to control the foreground and the background colors independently.

SEE ALSO

`textbackground`	*To set the background color for text*
`textcolor`	*To set the foreground color for text*

EXAMPLE Write a small utility program in Turbo C++ to help the user select a text attribute. The utility should display the foreground and background colors in columns, and let the user indicate a selection by pressing specific keys. For each selection, you should activate that attribute with a call to *textattr* and display a line of text to show how that attribute will look. You can use this approach in text-oriented user interfaces to let the user customize the looks of the on-screen text.

```
/* A program that lets the user select different
 * components of text attribute and see how each
 * combination looks.
 */
#include <conio.h>
#define ESC '\033'

char *fgnd[] = {"BLACK", "BLUE", "GREEN", "CYAN", "RED",
       "MAGENTA", "BROWN", "LIGHTGRAY", "DARKGRAY",
       "LIGHTBLUE", "LIGHTGREEN", "LIGHTCYAN", "LIGHTRED",
       "LIGHTMAGENTA", "YELLOW", "WHITE"};

char *bgnd[] = {"BLACK", "BLUE", "GREEN", "CYAN", "RED",
                "MAGENTA", "BROWN", "LIGHTGRAY"};

char *blink[] = {"NOBLINK", "BLINK"};
static int column=0, row=0, xypos[3][2]={3,4,23,4,43,4},
           numattrs[3]={16,8,2}, selection[3] = {7,0,0};
static char **colorlist[3] = {fgnd, bgnd, blink};

main()
{
    int i, j, c, attr;
/* Define a text window and display selection for
 * text attributes.
 */
    window(10,1,70,24);
```

```
    clrscr();
    textattr(LIGHTGRAY<<4 + BLACK);
    gotoxy(10,1);
    cputs("Use Tab and Enter to move among columns");
    gotoxy(20,2);
    cputs("Press Esc to exit");
    textattr(LIGHTGRAY);
/* Display foreground, background color list */
    for(i=0; i<3; i++)
    {
        for(j=0; j<numattrs[i]; j++)
        {
            gotoxy(xypos[i][0], xypos[i][1]+j);
            cputs((colorlist[i])[j]);
        }
    }
/* Let user select attributes and display the result */
    while((c = getch()) != ESC)
    {
        textattr(WHITE + (BLACK<<4));
        if(c == '\t')
        {
/* Go to next column */
            column = (column+1) % 3;
        }
        if(c == '\r')
        {
/* Clear the mark on previous selection */
            gotoxy(xypos[column][0]-1,
                   xypos[column][1]+selection[column]);
            putch(' ');
/* Go to next row */
            selection[column] = (selection[column]+1)
                                    % numattrs[column];
        }
/* Mark the current selections */
        for(i=0; i<3; i++)
        {
            gotoxy(xypos[i][0]-1,
                   xypos[i][1]+selection[i]);
            putch('*');
        }
/* Set the selected attribute and print a line */
        attr = (selection[1]<<4) + selection[0];
        if(selection[2] != 0) attr += BLINK;
```

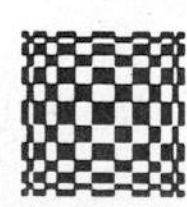

```
        textattr(attr);
        gotoxy(1,20);
        cputs("This is how the current text attribute \
looks");
    }
    return 0;
}
```

COMPATIBILITY

textbackground

TC1	TC1.5	TC2	TC++	MSC3	MSC4	MSC5	MSC6	QC1	QC2	QC2.5	ANSI	UNIX V	XNX
	▲	▲	▲										

PURPOSE Use *textbackground* to set the background color for all subsequent text output by *cprintf* and *cputs*.

SYNTAX

```
void textbackground(int bgcolor);
```

`int bgcolor;` *New background color for text*

EXAMPLE CALL

```
textbackground(RED);
```

INCLUDES `#include <conio.h>` *For function declaration and symbolic constants for colors*

DESCRIPTION The *textbackground* function sets the background color for all subsequent text printed by the console output routines *cprintf* and *cputs*. The argument *bgcolor* specifies the desired background color.

As shown in Table 21-4, only three bits (bits 4, 5, and 6) are used to store the background color in the text attribute byte. Thus, the *bgcolor* can only take the values between zero and seven. You can specify the background color using one of the first eight constant names from Table 21-5. These constants are defined in the include file *conio.h*.

COMMON USES The *textbackground* function is used to control the appearance of text on the screen.

COMMENTS If you want to specify the entire text attribute at once, you can use *textattr*.

SEE ALSO

`textattr` *To set the foreground and background colors at once*

`textcolor` *To set the foreground color for text*

EXAMPLE Write a program that uses *textbackground* to display white text in all available background colors.

```
#include <conio.h>

main()
{
    int i, numbgnd = 8;
/* Select WHITE as foreground. Display white characters
 * in all eight background colors.
 */
     textcolor(WHITE);
     for(i=0; i<numbgnd; i++)
     {
         textbackground(i);
         gotoxy(1,i+1);
         cprintf("Background = %d", i);
     }
    return 0;
}
```

textcolor

COMPATIBILITY

TC1	TC1.5	TC2	TC++	MSC3	MSC4	MSC5	MSC6	QC1	QC2	QC2.5	ANSI	UNIX V	XNX
	▲	▲	▲			1	1	1	1	1			

PURPOSE Use *textcolor* to set the foreground color for all subsequent text output by *cprintf* and *cputs.*

SYNTAX

```
void textcolor(int fgcolor);
```

`int fgcolor;` *New foreground color for text*

EXAMPLE CALL

```
textcolor(YELLOW);
```

INCLUDES `#include <conio.h>` *For function declaration and symbolic constants for colors*

DESCRIPTION The *textcolor* function sets the foreground color for all subsequent text printed by the console output routines *cprintf* and *cputs.* The argument *fgcolor* specifies the desired foreground color.

As shown in Table 21-4, the least significant four bits (bits 0 through 3) are used to store the foreground color in the text attribute byte. Thus, the *fgcolor* can only take a value between 0 and 15. You can specify the

foreground color using one of the constant names from Table 21-5. These constants are defined in the include file *conio.h*.

Table 21-5. *Color Constants for Text Mode Routines*

Color Constant	Value	Foreground or Background
BLACK	0	Both
BLUE	1	Both
GREEN	2	Both
CYAN	3	Both
RED	4	Both
MAGENTA	5	Both
BROWN	6	Both
LIGHTGRAY	7	Both
DARKGRAY	8	Foreground only
LIGHTBLUE	9	Foreground only
LIGHTGREEN	10	Foreground only
LIGHTCYAN	11	Foreground only
LIGHTRED	12	Foreground only
LIGHTMAGENTA	13	Foreground only
YELLOW	14	Foreground only
WHITE	15	Foreground only

1. In Microsoft C 5 and 6, and QuickC 1.0 through 2.5, the equivalent function is *_settextcolor*.

COMMON USES The *textcolor* function is used to control the appearance of text on the screen.

COMMENTS If you want to specify the entire text attribute at once, you can use *textattr*.

On monochrome systems, the foreground and background colors will translate to other text attributes such as bold, underline, and reverse video. See the tutorial section for further discussion of text attributes in monochrome displays.

SEE ALSO

`textattr` *To set the foreground and background colors at once*

`textbackground` *To set the background color for text*

EXAMPLE Write a program that uses *textcolor* to display text in all available colors on a black background.

```
#include <conio.h>

main()
```

```
{
    int i, numcolors = 16;
/* Select BLACK as background. Display characters
 * in all sixteen foreground colors.
 */
     textbackground(BLACK);
     for(i=0; i<numcolors; i++)
     {
         textcolor(i);
         gotoxy(1,i+1);
         cprintf("Text color = %d", i);
     }
    return 0;
}
```

textmode

COMPATIBILITY

TC1	TC1.5	TC2	TC++	MSC3	MSC4	MSC5	MSC6	QC1	QC2	QC2.5	ANSI	UNIX V	XNX
	▲	▲	▲										

PURPOSE Use *textmode* to switch from one text mode to another.

SYNTAX `void textmode(int newmode);`

`int newmode;` *New text mode number*

EXAMPLE CALL `textmode(C40); /* Switch to 40-column color text */`

INCLUDES `#include <conio.h>` *For function declaration and mode names*

DESCRIPTION The *textmode* function switches to the text mode specified by the argument *newmode*. It also resets the text window to the entire screen and sets the text attribute back to normal (the attribute at the time of program startup).

The mode should be specified using the constants of the enumeration type *text_modes* defined in *conio.h* and shown in Table 21-1. Note that you can use the mode name LASTMODE to switch back to the previous text mode.

COMMON USES The *textmode* function is used to switch from one text mode to another.

COMMENTS You should use *restorecrtmode* when switching to a text mode from a graphics mode. The *textmode* function is meant from switching between text modes, not for going from graphics mode to text mode.

SEE ALSO `gettextinfo` *To obtain information on current text mode*

`restorecrtmode` *To switch to a text mode from a graphics mode*

EXAMPLE Use *textmode* in a Turbo C++ program to switch among the available text modes.

```
#include <conio.h>

main()
{
    int oldmode;
    struct text_info t_info;
/* Get text mode information */
    gettextinfo(&t_info);
    oldmode = t_info.currmode;
/* Monochrome mode -- cannot switch mode */
    if(oldmode == MONO)
    {
        cputs("Monochrome mode: Cannot switch to any \
other mode\r\n");
    }
/* Color modes */
    if(oldmode == C40 || oldmode == C80)
    {
        cputs("Color mode\r\n");
        cputs("Press a key to switch mode\n");
        getch();
        if(oldmode == C40) textmode(C80);
        if(oldmode == C80) textmode(C40);
        cputs("Press any key to return to previous mode\r\n");
        getch();
        textmode(oldmode);
    }
/* Black and white modes */
    if(oldmode == BW40 || oldmode == BW80)
    {
        cputs("Black & White mode\r\n");
        cputs("Press a key to switch mode\r\n");
        getch();
        if(oldmode == BW40) textmode(BW80);
        if(oldmode == BW80) textmode(BW40);
```

```
            cputs("Press any key to return to previous mode\r\n");
            getch();
textmode(oldmode);
    }
    Return 0;
}
```

wherex

COMPATIBILITY

TC1	TC1.5	TC2	TC++	MSC3	MSC4	MSC5	MSC6	QC1	QC2	QC2.5	ANSI	UNIX V	XNX
	▲	▲	▲			1	1	1	1	1			

PURPOSE Use *wherex* to determine the x-coordinate (column number) of the cursor location in the current text window.

SYNTAX `int wherex(void);`

EXAMPLE CALL `current_column = wherex();`

INCLUDES `#include <conio.h>` *For function declaration*

DESCRIPTION The *wherex* function returns the x-coordinate of the current cursor position with respect to the origin (the upper left corner) of the current text window. The x-coordinate corresponds to the column number of the cursor location, with the convention that the origin of the window is (1,1)—column 1 and row 1.

1. Use *_gettextposition* in Microsoft C 5 and 6, and QuickC 1.0 through 2.5.

COMMON USES The *wherex* function is useful in determining the current cursor position during text editing operations.

RETURNS The *wherex* function returns the x-coordinate of the cursor position.

SEE ALSO `wherey` *To get the y-coordinate of the cursor position*

`window` *To define a text window*

EXAMPLE Write a Turbo C++ program that prints an X at a position with a random x-coordinate. Use *wherex* to get this x-coordinate and report it.

```
#include <conio.h>
#include <stdlib.h>
#define ESC '\033'  /* ASCII code for the Esc key */
```

```
main()
{
    int xpos, ypos = 5, c = 0;
/* Clear the screen and print an 'X' at a random
 * position
 */
     cprintf("Press Esc to exit\r\n");
     while (c != ESC)
     {
         clrscr();
         gotoxy(1,1);
         cprintf("Press Esc to exit");
         randomize();
         gotoxy(random(40),ypos);
/* Retrieve the x position using wherex() */
         xpos = wherex();
         putch('X');
         gotoxy(1,12);
         cprintf("The 'X' is at x position %d", xpos);
         c = getch();
    }
    return 0;
}
```

wherey

COMPATIBILITY

TC1	TC1.5	TC2	TC++	MSC3	MSC4	MSC5	MSC6	QC1	QC2	QC2.5	ANSI	UNIX V	XNX
	▲	▲	▲			1	1	1	1	1			

PURPOSE Use *wherey* to determine the y-coordinate (row number) of the cursor location in the current text window.

SYNTAX `int wherey(void);`

EXAMPLE CALL `current_row = wherey();`

INCLUDES `#include <conio.h>` *For function declaration*

DESCRIPTION The *wherey* function returns the y-coordinate of the current cursor position with respect to the origin (the upper left corner) of the current text window. The y-coordinate corresponds to the row number of the cursor location, with the convention that the origin of the window is (1,1)—column 1 and row 1.

1. In Microsoft C 5 and 6, and QuickC 1.0 through 2.5, the compatible function is *_gettextposition.*

COMMON USES The *wherey* function is useful in determining the current cursor position during text editing operations.

RETURNS The *wherey* function returns the y-coordinate of the cursor position.

SEE ALSO

`wherex` *To get the x-coordinate of the cursor position*

`window` *To define a text window*

EXAMPLE Write a Turbo C++ program that prints a Y at a position with a random y-coordinate. Use *wherey* to get this y-coordinate and report it.

```
#include <conio.h>
#include <stdlib.h>
#define ESC '\033'  /* ASCII code for the Esc key */
main()
{
    int xpos = 30, ypos, c = 0;
/* Clear the screen and print a 'Y' at a random  position */
     cprintf("Press Esc to exit\r\n");
     while (c != ESC)
     {
         clrscr();
         gotoxy(1,1);
         cprintf("Press Esc to exit");
         randomize();
         gotoxy(xpos, random(25)+1);
/* Retrieve the y position using wherey() */
         ypos = wherey();
         putch('Y');
         gotoxy(1,12);
         cprintf("The 'Y' is at y position %d", ypos);
         c = getch();
    }
    return 0;
}
```

window

COMPATIBILITY

TC1	TC1.5	TC2	TC++	MSC3	MSC4	MSC5	MSC6	QC1	QC2	QC2.5	ANSI	UNIX V	XNX
	▲	▲	▲			1	1	1	1	1			

PURPOSE Use *window* to define a rectangular region of the screen as the current text window.

SYNTAX

```
void window(int left, int top, int right, int bottom);
```

`int left, top;` *Absolute screen coordinates of the upper left corner of the text window being defined*

`int right, bottom;` *Absolute screen coordinates of the lower right corner of the text window being defined*

EXAMPLE CALL

```
window(20,10, 59,19);  /* A 40x10 window with origin at (20,10) */
```

INCLUDES `#include <conio.h>` *For function declaration*

DESCRIPTION The *window* function defines a rectangular region of the screen as the current text window. All subsequent text output by the routines *cprintf* and *cputs* will be confined to this window. The window is defined by the coordinates *(left,top)* and *(right,bottom)* which, respectively, denote its upper left and lower right corners.

The *window* function will do nothing if the specified coordinates are outside the range of valid coordinates for the current text mode, or if either *left=right* or *top=bottom*. Note that the x-coordinate (column number) can be between 1 and 80 in 80-column modes, and between 1 and 40 for 40-column modes. The y-coordinate (row number) must lie between 1 and 25 in any text mode.

1. In Microsoft C 5 and 6, and QuickC 1.0 through 2.5, use *_settextwindow*.

COMMON USES The *window* function is very useful in designing text-based user interfaces. Menus and message or dialog boxes can be built using text windows.

SEE ALSO

`gettextinfo` *To determine the current window coordinates*

`textmode` *To switch from one text mode to another*

EXAMPLE Write a Turbo C++ program that demonstrates multiple text windows on the screen.

```
#include <conio.h>

main()
{
    int xsize = 15, ysize = 7, xorg=0, yorg=0,
        i;
/* Display four windows on the screen */
    for(i=0; i<4; i++)
    {
    xorg += 5;
    yorg += 3;
        textattr(WHITE + ((i+1)<<4));
        window(xorg, yorg, xorg+xsize-1, yorg+ysize-1);
        clrscr();
        gotoxy(1,1);
        cprintf("This is window number %d", i);
    }
}
```

Text Mode Routines

INDEX

C

D

E

G

N

O

P

T

U

V

W

The Waite Group

100 Shoreline Highway, Suite 285 | Mill Valley, CA 94941 | (415) 331-0575
Compuserve: 75146,3515 | usenet: hplabs!well!mitch | AppleLink: D2097

Dear Reader:

Thank you for considering the purchase of our book. Readers have come to know products from **The Waite Group** for the care and quality we put into them. Let me tell you a little about our group and how we make our books.

It started in 1976 when I could not find a computer book that really taught me anything. The books that were available talked down to people, lacked illustrations and examples, were poorly laid out, and were written as if you already understood all the terminology. So I set out to write a good book about microcomputers. This was to be a special book—very graphic, with a friendly and casual style, and filled with examples. The result was an instant best-seller.

Over the years, I developed this approach into a "formula" (nothing really secret here, just a lot of hard work—I am a crazy man about technical accuracy and high-quality illustrations). I began to find writers who wanted to write books in this way. This led to co-authoring and then to multiple-author books and many more titles (over seventy titles currently on the market). As The Waite Group author base grew, I trained a group of editors to manage our products. We now have a team devoted to putting together the best possible book package and maintaining the high standard of our existing books.

We greatly appreciate and use any advice our readers send us (and you send us a lot). We have discovered that our readers are detail nuts: you want indexes that really work, tables of contents that dig deeply into the subject, illustrations, tons of examples, reference cards, and more.

The Waite Group's Turbo C++ Bible is an example of how even a reference book can be made fun to read and use. You'll find compatibility boxes that show how a function works in all popular operating systems and compiler versions, friendly easy-to-follow examples, and much more. Borland's introduction of C++ into their Turbo C compiler is an innovative step that makes object oriented programming accessible to every C programmer. This book provides full coverage of Turbo C++'s library of C functions, as well as its new C++ stream classes and math functions.

If you'd like to extend your knowledge of C and C++ programming, you'll want to take a look at some of our other titles, including *The Waite Group's C Programming Using Turbo C++*, a best-selling tutorial book, and *The Waite Group's C++ Programming*. If you are interested in learning C using the computer as a teacher, you'll want to order our new software product *Master C*, explained in the back of this book. For details on generic, UNIX-based C, take a look at our best-selling title *The Waite Group's New C Primer Plus*. All of these books are available directly from Howard W. Sams & Company and your local bookstore.

Sincerely,

Mitchell Waite
The Waite Group

Turbo C++ Functions by Subject

The Waite Group's Turbo C++ Bible

Waite Group Reader Feedback Card

Help Us Make A Better Book

To better serve our readers, we would like your opinion on the contents and quality of this book. Please fill out this card and return it to *The Waite Group*, 100 Shoreline Hwy., Suite A-285, Mill Valley, CA, 94941 (415) 331-0575.

Name ______________________

Company ______________________

Address ______________________

City ______________________

State ______ ZIP ____________ Phone ______________

1. How would you rate the content of this book?

- ☐ Excellent
- ☐ Very Good
- ☐ Good
- ☐ Fair
- ☐ Below Average
- ☐ Poor

2. What were the things you liked *most* about this book?

- ☐ Content
- ☐ Pace
- ☐ Writing Style
- ☐ Accuracy
- ☐ Compat. Boxes
- ☐ Listings
- ☐ Reference
- ☐ Format
- ☐ Examples
- ☐ Index
- ☐ Jump Table
- ☐ Cover
- ☐ Price
- ☐ Illustrations
- ☐ Construction

3. Please explain the one thing you liked *most* about this book. ______________________

4. What were the things you liked *least* about this book?

- ☐ Content
- ☐ Pace
- ☐ Writing Style
- ☐ Accuracy
- ☐ Compat. Boxes
- ☐ Listings
- ☐ Reference
- ☐ Format
- ☐ Examples
- ☐ Index
- ☐ Jump Table
- ☐ Cover
- ☐ Price
- ☐ Illustrations
- ☐ Construction

5. Please explain the one thing you liked *least* about this book. ______________________

6. How do you use this book? For work, recreation, look-up, self-training, classroom, etc? ______________________

7. Would you be interested in receiving a Pop-Up utility program containing the contents of this book? What would you pay for this? ______________________

8. Where did you purchase this particular book?

- ☐ Book Chain
- ☐ Small Book Store
- ☐ Computer Store
- ☐ Other: ______________________
- ☐ Direct Mail
- ☐ Book Club
- ☐ School Book Store

9. Can you name another similar book you like better than this one, or one that is as good, and tell us why? ______________________

10. How many Waite Group books do you own? ______

11. What are your favorite Waite Group books? ______________________

12. What topics or specific titles would you like to see The Waite Group develop? ______________________

13. What version of Turbo C/Turbo C++ are you using? ______________________

14. What other programming languages do you know? ______________________

15. Any other comments you have about this book or other Waite Group titles? ______________________

16. ☐ Check here to receive a free Waite Group catalog.

Fold Here

From:

Place Stamp Here

The Waite Group, Inc.
100 Shoreline Highway, Suite A–285
Mill Valley, CA 94941

Staple or tape here

22742